REPRINT OF
OFFICIAL REGISTER
OF LAND LOTTERY OF
GEORGIA
1827

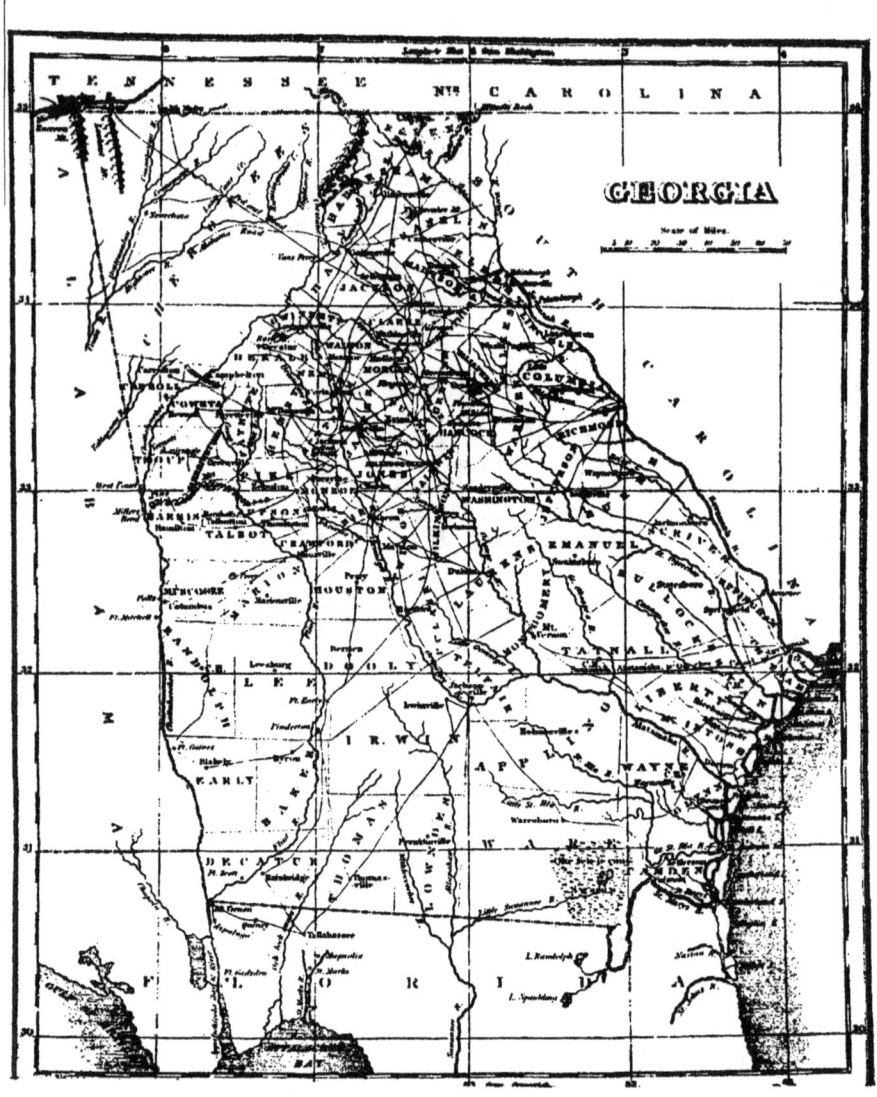

From Sherwood's Gazetteer; Map of Georgia, 1929. The land allotted in 1827 was bounded by the northern boundary of Carroll, the eastern boundary of Coweta thence to and along the Flint River to and and along the southern boundary of Lee and Randolph. There were five counties or sections: 1, Lee; 2, Muscogee; 3, Troup; 4, Coweta; 5, Carroll. The other counties are subdivisions of the original five.

REPRINT
of
OFFICIAL REGISTER
of
LAND LOTTERY OF GEORGIA 1827

Compiled by
MISS MARTHA LOU HOUSTON

CLEARFIELD COMPANY

Originally Published
1827

Reprinted
Columbus, 1929

Reprinted
Genealogical Publishing Company
Baltimore, 1967

Library of Congress Catalog Card Number 67-26475

Reprinted for Clearfield Company, Inc.
by Genealogical Publishing Company Inc.
Baltimore, Maryland 1992

FOREWORD

In offering the reprint of the Official Register of the Land Lottery of 1827 (Grantland & Orme, Milledgeville, 1827) Miss Houston is making generally available information at present obtainable only from the MS. records of Georgia or from a very limited number of copies of the original edition, none of which is to be found in the public libraries of Atlanta or, as far as I can learn, in the public libraries of the state.

The law providing for this lottery names white males above 18, who had been residents of the state for three years, Revolutionary soldiers, widows of Revolutionary soldiers, orphans, and others, who had not drawn land in previous lotteries, as eligible for participation. With the exception of the first class—citizens above 18—the ground of qualification is shown. More than 15,000 names are listed, including approximately 1,500 Revolutionary soldiers and 1,500 soldiers of other wars.

Since there are no census reports of Georgia except the Federal which are still in MS. and on file in Washington, D. C., and since the tax digests, none of which has been published with the exception of a volume of ten counties prior to 1818, are so incomplete, the value of this record from both the historical and the genealogical standpoints is readily discernible.

Georgians are deeply indebted to Miss Houston for this valuable piece of work.

          RUTH BLAIR,
            State Historian.

Atlanta, October 12, 1928.

From PETER A. BRANNON, Curator
Alabama Department Archives and History.
MONTGOMERY, ALA.

The republication of LOTTERY LISTS, 1827—there having been only a few copies originally issued for official use—will make available to students data of great value.

This newly accessible material will mean much both to the historian and the genealogist. Population movements through Georgia form a most fascinating study of subsequent development in other more western states, and this list of land allotments in west Georgia shows many families early settled in Virginia and the Carolinas, who later made marked contributions to the history of the Mississippi Valley.

The section of the state including these lands was ceded by the Indian Springs Treaty of February 12, 1825, which was not ratified, and on account of which Gen. McIntosh was put to death by a delegtaion of his own nation, at his home in the present Carroll county, May 1, 1825. The transfer of this territory to the state was officially consummated by the treaty made at Washington City, January 24, 1826, when an agreement was made that the Creek Indians should vacate on or before January 1, 1827. This treaty was not recognized by Gov. Troup, and he ordered the survey into districts by the terms of the Indian Springs agreement. The Federal government and the state became involved in a serious controversy which was not amicably adjusted until the holding of the conference at Fort Mitchell, (Alabama) November 15, 1827, when the United States agreed to pay the Creek Indians $28,000 for the territory.

Muscogee, Troup, Coweta, Lee, and Carroll counties were then created to embody the newly acquired territory. They were named to honor the Muscogee people, from whom it was acquired; Gov. George McIntosh Troup; the birthplace in the Indian nation, of Gen. William McIntosh; Gen. R. H. Lee, of Virginia; and Charles Carroll, signer of the Declaration of Independence.

Examination of the lists will show many who first settled in the lands acquired by the Cherokee cession of 1817, the Creek cession of 1818, and many of the settlers who came in just after the last war with Great Britain. It is very evident that this eastern country saw a large influx of population during the period from 1815 to 1819.

The student of economic development in Georgia, Alabama and Mississippi, and the territory west, will find names of those who came later to the front in the annals of the Nation. The large number of Revolutionary service notations indicate men of families and affairs, and not mere adventurers in the new fields.

This volume will, without doubt, prove of useful service.

Peter A. Brannon, Curator,
Alabama Department Archives and History,
Montgomery.

GEORGIA LAWS 1825 page 119.
AN ACT

Amendatory of an act passed the ninth June, eighteen hundred and twenty-five to dispose of and distribute the lands lately acquired by the United States for the use of Georgia, of the Creek nation of Indians by a treaty [made] and concluded at the Indian Springs on the twelfth day of February, eighteen hundred and twenty-five.

Be it enacted by the Senate and House of Representatives of the State of Georgia in General Assembly met, and it is hereby enacted by the authority of the same, That the words "Immediately preceding the passage of this act" in the act passed the ninth day of June, eighteen hundred and twenty-five, be and the same are hereby repealed, and the first day of September one thousand eight hundred and twenty-six be adopted in lieu thereof.

Sec. 2. And be it further enacted, by the authority aforesaid, That it shall be the duty of the justices of the inferior court of the respective counties of this state, or majority of the same to cause the above section to be carried into effect.

Sec. 3. And be it further enacted, That the persons appointed by the inferior courts to carry into effect the provisions of this amendatory act, shall insert in the oaths laid down in the before recited act, the words the first day of September, eighteen hundred and twenty-six, instead of the words "the passing of this act" wherever the latter occurs.

Sec. 4. And be it further enacted, That all men of like residence who have been wounded and disabled in the late wars with Great Britain or the Indians, shall be entitled to one additional draw other than they are allowed by the provisions of the before recited act, in consequence of said wound and disability and the persons appointed to carry this act into effect shall administer the following oath to said persons, to wit: I do solemnly swear (or affirm) that I was wounded in the late wars with Great Britain and the Indians, by which wound I am disabled—instead of the oath prescribed in said section.

Sec. 5. Be it further enacted, That all illegitimate children shall be considered and placed on the same footing with orphan children under the provisions of this act, and shall be entitled to a draw or draws in like manner.

Sec. 6. Be it further enacted, That nothing herein contained shall be so construed as to interfere with the rights of persons who have given in their names for chances in the contemplated land lottery, and that so much of the before recited act as militates against this act, be and the same hereby repealed.

DUNCAN G. CAMPBELL,
Speaker pro. tem. of the House of Representatives.
ALLEN B. OWELL,
President of the Senate.

Assented to, Dec. 24, 1825.
G. M. TROUP, Governor.

STATE OF GEORGIA.

By His Excellency George R. Gilmer, Governor and Commander in Chief of the Army and Navy of this State, and of the Militia thereof.
TO ALL TO WHOM THESE PRESENTS SHALL COME, GREETING.
KNOW YE, That in pursuance of the several acts of the General Assembly of this State, passed the 9th of June, and 24th December, 1825, and the 14th and 27th of December, 1826, to make distribution of the land acquired of the Creek Nation of Indians, by a Treaty concluded at the Indian Springs, on the 12th day of February, 1825, and forming the Counties of Lee, Muscogee, Troup, Coweta and Carroll, in this State I HAVE GIVEN AND GRANTED, and by these presents, DO GIVE AND GRANT unto *John Floyd of Burford's* district, Oglethorpe county, his heirs and assigns forever, all that tract or lot of land containing two hundred and a half acres, situate, lying, and being in the *Twenty-second* District, of the Second Section, in the County of Muscogee in said State, which said tract or lot of land is known and distinguished in the plan of said District by the number *One hundred and Sixty Seven* having such shape, form and marks as appear by a plat of the same hereunto annexed: To have and to hold the said tract or lot of land, together with all and singular the rights, members and appurtenances thereof whatsoever, unto the said *John Floyd*, his heirs and assigns, to his and their proper use, benefit and behoof forever in fee simple.

GIVEN under my hand and the Great Seal of the said State this seventeenth day of December, in the year one thousand eight hundred and thirty, and of the Independence of the United States of America the fifty fifth.

Signed by his Excellency the Governor,
   17th day of Dec., 1830.
           GEORGE R. GILMER, Governor
           E. H. PIERCE, S. E. D.
   Registered the 17th day of Dec., 1830.

STATE OF GEORGIA.

By His Excellency George M. Troup, Governor and Commander in Chief of the Army and Navy of this State, and of the Militia thereof.
TO ALL TO WHOM THESE PRESENTS SHALL COME, GREETING.
KNOW YE, That in pursuance of the several acts of the General Assembly of this State, passed the 9th of June, and 24th December, 1825, and the 14th and 27 of December, 1826, to make distribution of the land acquired of the Creek Nation of Indians, by a Treaty concluded at the Indian Springs, on the 12th day of February, 1825, and forming the Counties of Lee, Muscogee, Troup, Coweta and Carroll, in this State I HAVE GIVEN AND GRANTED, and by these presents, DO GIVE AND GRANT unto *Enoch Garrett of Currey's District, Wilkinson County*, his heirs and assigns forever, all that tract or lot of land containing two hundred two and a half acres, situate, lying, and being in the *FIRST* District of the Fourth Section, in the County of *COWETA* in said State, which said tract or lot of land is known and distinguished in the plan of said District by the number *Two Hundred and seventy four* having such shape, form and marks as appear by a plat of the same hereunto annexed: To have and to hold the said tract or lot of land, together with all and singular the rights, members and appurtenances thereof whatsoever, except all valuable ores, mines and minerals, which have been reserved to the State by an act, passed the 24th of December, 1825, unto the said *Enoch Garrett*, his heirs and assigns, to his and their proper use, benefit and behoof forever in fee simple.

GIVEN under my hand and the Great Seal of the said State this Ninth day of May, in the year one thousand eight hundred and twenty seven and of the Independence of the United State of America the fifty first.

Signed by his Excellency the Governor,
   9th day of May, 1827
           G. M. TROUP,
           Fr. JETER S. E. D.
   Registered the *ninth* day of May, 1827.

From THE PUBLISHER

The matter of presenting the Official Register of 1827 has been an expensive luxury, but a joy nevertheless. The book itself is made of extracts from the "draws," the original of which is filed in the office of the Secretary of State of the State of Georgia. The "draws" were listed by counties and by days, beginning the 6th of March, 1827, and continuing through the 25th of May. They were then grouped into numbers, 31 in all, and printed by the State Printers Grantland & Orme, the *first* Official Register of Land Lottery of Georgia of 1827.

Of the small number printed one was purchased by Benjamin Born. So much did he prize his copy that he dressed the pig skin for the cover which safely guards the valuable record to the present day. The book was made ready for republication by supplying the index and explanations. A list of the names of Revolutionary soldiers, widows of Rev. Sol., soldiers of other wars (1785-1827), and widows of these soldiers have been listed and may be published later as a separate volume. All indications of service and eligibility are given in the original.

In order to prove that I held the *only* complete copy, I published pictures of various pages from my copy, inquiring for duplicates. I found a fragment of a copy in the possession of Mr. Louis A. Moore. This he kindly entrusted to me for checking up on my copy. I have included in this introduction a copy of the law for this lottery, Georgia Laws of 1825 page 119; also, a copy of two of the certificates. The map of Georgia nearest the date of the lottery was that of 1829 found in Sherwood's Gazetteer. This was furnished by the courtesy of the Library of Congress.

I hereby certify that exclusive of the preceding pages and the pages of the index—that is to say, the book proper, is a true and correct reprint of the original Official Register of the Land Lottery of Georgia of 1827.

MARTHA LOU HOUSTON.

Columbus, Georgia,
February, 1929.

OFFICIAL

REGISTER

OF THE

LAND LOTTERY

DRAWN IN 1827.

MILLEDGEVILLE:
PRINTED BY GRANTLAND & ORME

LAND LOTTERY REGISTER—No. 1
[RECORDER OFFICE—PUBLISHED BY GRANTLAND & ORME—PRICE $3.]

NOTE.—Section 1 is Lee County—2 Muscogee—3 Troup—4 Coweta—5 Carroll.

First and Second days Drawing—6th & 7th March

Fortunate Drawers Capts. Dist.	No.Dt.Sec.
APPLING.	
George Eaton, Morgans	1 14 2
Silpha Purvis, wid. McDonalds	11 5 2
Lydia Thomas, widow Dyers	230 1 2
Phebe McClelland, wid. Collins	62 10 1
John Alford, Collins	319 15 1
BULLOCH.	
Sarah Therill, widow ,McCalls	210 12 2
R. T. Standland, sol. Standlands	115 8 3
Anna Gray, widow, Lockharts	132 8 5
BUTTS.	
John W. Williams, Robinsons	49 7 4
John Tillery, Johnsons	240 4 2
William Knight, sol. Thaxtons	273 7 5
BRYAN.	
Joshua Beasley, Stephens	139 24 2
Edward Davis, Harveys	90 8 5
BIBB.	
John Chain, Bates	71 15 1
Christopher B. Strong, Carrs	13 19 2
Permelia Pearson, fa. ab. Rutlands	48 7 2
William Pickard, Pickards	235 3 4
John Purkins, R. S., Loyds	124 11 5
John B. Ross, Flanders	239 14 1
BALDWIN.	
Esther Torrance, wid. Buchanans	253 11 3
John Hodge, Bivins	165 6 4
Jacob Keister, Ginns	152 11 2
Shadrack Bivins, Bivins	126 33 1
BURKE.	
James Daniel, Brooms	91 12 2
Jacob Johnson, R. S., Corkers	145 20 1
Thomas Davis, Fountains	104 3 5
Seaborn J. Bell, Bayleys	167 12 1
Sarah Skinner, widow, Wests	254 16 2
Joshua Gray, Bayleys	204 3 1
Jeremiah Burke, Wests	220 3 3
Greenville Spencer, sol. Dukes	172 31 1
Robbin Davis, Thompsons	134 7 4
Jacob Reddick, Wests	41 15 2
Reuben Tepton's orps. Andersons	182 11 1
Josiah Hatcher's orphans, Brooms	100 12 3
CLARK.	
Isaac Hightower, McDonalds	155 17 1
Jacob Bosworth, sr. Vinsons	56 23 2
Martin Crow, McDonalds	192 6 2
James Willer, Gahagans	3 6 2
John Hunton, soldier, Greers	147 31 1
Archibald S. Bryant, Gahagans	160 21 1
Millison, Kersey, Jordan & Sophia Whitton, ors. } Greenes	205 9 3
James Tinsley, Gahagans	90 4 4
James Haynie, soldier, Greers	233 17 2
Daniel Dodson, Frosts	210 22 2
CRAWFORD	
Hughy Gilmore's orphans, Dukes	220 31 1

Fortunate Drawers Capts. Dist.	No.Dt.Sec.
Marshall Ligon, Rhodes	47 3 3
Elijah Kelly, Hicks	253 31 1
Thomas B. Rees, Rhodes	240 11 2
CAMDEN.	
Jane Loftin, widow, Baileys	186 18 2
COLUMBIA.	
Susan Daniel, orphan, Adams	88 1 3
Sylvester Hoof, illegit. Dranes	246 23 2
George Flinn, Adams	78 10 3
Samuel Cone, Stallings	218 14 2
Joseph Lantern, Coles	211 19 2
Elizabeth Stapler, wid. Talberts	49 24 2
Elvy Langston, Ramseys	200 1 1
John C. Tolbert, Tolberts	121 9 5
John Gray's orphans, Carrolls	249 9 2
Richard W. Jones, do	64 26 1
C. L. C. Roberts, orps. Clarks	151 2 2
Nancy A. Langston, wid. Adams	125 6 4
Jas. Blackstone's orps. Ramseys	174 3 1
CHATHAM.	
Henry L. Brasch, Haydens	234 5 4
Margaret Sims, wid. McDonnells	252 10 5
Benjamin Rinchour, Geredons	183 10 1
Eliza Ann Ram, wid. Gaddys	27 12 2
John G. Butler, Gaddys	337 20 2
Dorothy Salfner, wid. Nungazers	91 2 1
DEKALB.	
Henry F. Hendon, Bollings	124 17 1
Elisha Hendon, Lokeys	108 12 2
Delila Davis, illegitimate, Scaifs	239 7 5
James Hill, Edwards	90 8 1
Henry Carlton, Smiths	220 25 1
Joshua Durham, Stephens	158 3 5
Mary Tull's illegit. Bakers	159 10 5
Dennis Cogan, Browns	158 1 3
DECATUR.	
William Kelly, Hawthorns	307 20 2
Samuel Cherry, Douglass	32 32 1
DOOLY.	
Jordan D. Bradshaw, Andersons	180 17 1
J. M. Hilliard's orphans, do	133 18 1
ELBERT.	
Horatio Brewen's orps. Tuckers	14 3 4
Charles Blailock, Dobbs	112 3 2
Moses Haynes, do	214 4 2
James O. Clark, Bells	97 29 1
Thomas Watson, Carpenters	60 5 2
James Alexander, Hortons	105 17 1
Jesse W. Thompson, Carpenters	40 12 1
James N. Brawn, Butlers	10 14 1
James Clark, Merits	147 5 3
George Cox, Hortons	184 26 1
And'w C.Chislumn's orps.Boltons	109 11 1
EMANUEL.	
Daniel Kent, Moores	189 5 4

Fortunate Drawers	Capts. Dist.	No.	Dt.	Sec.
Archibald Culbreth, R. S., Chasons		9	7	4
Gedeon Hay's orphans, McGars		108	7	2
John Griffith's orphans, do		162	18	2
William Kennedy, do.		90	8	4
Berrien Daughtry, Fountains		18	16	5
James Lamb, McGars		324	7	1

EFFINGHAM.

Geo. Powledge, R. S., Waldhaners		62	1	3

EARLY.

Daniel E. Phillips, R. S., Speers		182	23	1
Mark Snellgrove, do		135	1	1
Cavan Freeman, Wilson's		92	3	5
Jesse Williams, do		106	17	2

FRANKLIN.

Obediah Echols, Caudells		15	4	5
John Walker, McDonald's		242	10	2
James Terrell, R. S., Boznells		258	28	1
Daniel Camp, Stephens		120	2	2
Edw'd Chandler's orps. Chandlers		113	25	1
Joshua Horton, Sanders		55	3	3
Marshal Wilbanks, Tabors		59	3	2
George K. Williams, Sanders		109	15	1
Robert Sayre's orphans, Stranges		74	12	1
Nehemiah Norton, Andrews		115	6	4
Vinson Harrison, McDonalds		228	3	2
John W. Payne, Caudells		39	3	1
Ann J. Sims, w. R. S., Bennetts		127	7	4
Wm. Tweedwell, R. S., Chandlers		164	7	4

FAYETTE.

Thomas Chappel, Craigs		55	9	1
Aaron Strother, Dodsons		59	16	1
Nan.Filghman, w. R.S., Whartons		183	23	1
Samuel P. Parsons do		92	13	1
Henry Watts, Craigs		96	32	1
John R. Greene, Dodsons		131	9	2

GWINNETT.

Caroline Norman, widow, Bakers		16	31	1
John C. Chandler, Madduxs		233	11	1
Obadiah Glasgow, Bakers		254	7	1
Thomas Hill, Hills		209	30	1
Ambrose Niles, Madduxs		141	12	2
Elizabeth Thomas, wid. Moores		48	6	2
Joseph Bankston, Caruthers		168	4	4
Joseph Downey, R. S., Moores		21	13	1
David Appling, orphan, Greens		250	23	1
Joseph Bankston, Caruthers		163	4	4
Richard Berry, Hills		102	24	2
William Johnson, Greens		102	15	5
Lewis Wiggins, Moors		266	23	2
James Mayfield, Bakers		59	15	1
Lewis Parham, Robertsons		19	26	1
Aaron Allred, Hills		128	11	3
Edward D. Lowery, Greens		54	4	1

GREENE.

Silas M. Durham, Newsoms		246	28	1
John Mallery, Astins		5	6	3
William A. Mercer, Elys		47	2	4
John Patillo, soldier, Bruces		184	18	2

Fortunate Drawers	Capts. Dist.	No.	Dt.	Sec.
Mel. Emeline Sanford, orp. Dawsons		4	11	1
Math. S. Hightower, orp. Knowles		13	31	1
James Knowles, do.		85	1	5
Aziel Bruce, soldier, Bruces		58	26	1
Nancy Moore, w. R. S., Webbs		126	13	5

GLYNN.

Rigdon Tooton, McLeods		50	17	1

HALL.

Mathew Wilson, Wilsons		196	27	1
George Thornton, Yagers		247	16	2
James Boyd, Harrisons		195	5	4
Rose Rees, Roberts		203	4	3
Enoch Swim, do		208	17	2
Raleigh Harp, Harrisons		8	13	5
Stephen Dye, do		153	6	3

HANCOCK.

T. L. Edwards' orps. 101st dist.		242	13	1
Jesse Minton's orps. 113th dist.		218	4	2
Isaiah Parker, 103rd dist.		191	11	1
Randolph Murphy, 101st dist.		135	15	2
John Hitchcock, 113th dist.		100	16	2
R. B. Binion, soldier, Bishops		13	4	5
John Palemore, 103rd dist.		103	24	1
Bryan Griggs, 102nd dist.		127	22	2

HABERSHAM.

William Hunt, Vickreys		64	23	1
Charles Blythe, Suttons		53	30	1
Joel Baker, Bakers		354	7	1
William Burt, Bryans		117	26	1
Jephthah Taylor, Langstons		144	10	2
John Vaugh, Kenzies		139	4	2
James Rice, Jones		183	14	1
Obadiah Worley, Bryans		188	2	4
Robert Turner, R. S., Bakers		128	8	3
Jeremiah McDaniel, sol. Bryans		2	9	3
James Mince, Fains		115	26	1
Jesse Dooley, Langstons		51	5	5

HENRY.

Uriah Williams, Allens		74	7	5
John Edwards, R. S., Kites		58	23	2
Turner Evans, Grays		93	13	1
William McCauley, Gosdens		77	6	3

HOUSTON.

Rice Henderson, sr. Batemans		220	26	1
Moses Rawls, Farnalls		205	8	5
Morgan Harrall, Hancocks		133	3	5
Thomas Barrow, Farnells		7	11	5
Robert M. Thompson, Pitts		172	6	3

JASPER.

Putnam Adams, Johnsons		256	21	2
James Hays' orphans, Dardens		16	31	1
Pleasant P. Coleman, Wilders		32	16	1
Henry Jocey, Jr. Hands		103	7	5
JamesM.Dawkins, idiot, Johnsons		96	20	2
Floyd Enochs, illegit. Owens		49	5	2
Joseph Wilson's orps. Wilders		28	2	2
Catharine Hill, w. R. S., Baynes		151	11	5

(3)

Fortunate Drawers Capts. Dist.	No.	Dt.	Sec.
Edmond Lloyd's orphans, Hines	358	8	1
Martin M. Crews, Butts	334	14	1
Joseph Phillips, Reeves	303	7	5
Frederick Dukes, Hines	185	13	1
Willis Holifield, do	204	5	3
Morgan Coats, Dardins	96	5	4
Jud. Hardwick, w. R. S., Wilson	197	22	1
Drucilla Knight, widow, Hands	105	15	2
William Simpson, Sparks	231	4	3
Reuben Jones, R. S., Baynes	237	18	1
Thomas Lloyd, R. S., Wilsons	159	29	1
Warten Pierce, Barnetts	201	26	1
Henry Ledbetter, Butts	217	24	1
Mary A. Smith, illegit. Wilsons	256	10	3
Richmond Brown, Holmes	86	9	3
John Ashmore, R. S., Keys	212	11	2
Church. Rispiss' orphans, Hines	122	9	1
John Porter, R. S., do	92	11	2
Wesley Leak, Camerons	153	11	3
Moses Perkins' orps. Shropshires	98	13	1
William Briars, Holmes	232	9	1
Simeon Brantley, Keys	82	1	1

JACKSON.

Sarah Pharr, widow, Wynns	10	1	5
William Stigler, orphan, do	124	3	3
George Burnes, Georges	72	24	2
William Porter, Storys	250	8	5
Moses Widner, 246th dist.	248	6	5
Mary Morgan, w. R. S., Staplers	7	6	4
Lewis S. Harris, Rogers	70	32	1
Archibald McLawrin, Gathrights	21	11	5
John Wafford, Allens	199	21	1
John&Cynthia Miller, ills. Storys	251	18.	2

JEFFERSON.

George Mock's orphans, Beatys	99	18	2
Simon Caldwell's orps. Marshalls	105	17	2
Caleb Welsh, R. S., Waldens	123	10	3
Mathew Londa, Elliotts	135	30	1
Dennis Williams, Ross	92	2	3

IRWIN.

Falian Adams, 5th dist.	3	5	4
Elijah Hunter, Dixons	238	1	2

JONES.

Amos Johnson, Spinks	185	1	1
John Toles, Newbys	70	30	1
Hardy McKenzie, Lows	253	8	5
Walker Herndon, jr. Mullins	75	16	2
Jesse Watson, Bowens	246	7	3
Elizabeth Bennett, hus. ab. Woods	153	11	1
William L. Sanders, do.	203	10	1
Absalom Cawsey, Dosters	184	5	3
Samuel Winfrey, Blounts	55	23	2
JemimaHasty, w.R.S.,Breedloves	167	24	2
James Cox, Hammacks	30	13	1
Frederick Wimberly, Robertsons	211	27	4
Britton Brassell, R. S., Dosters	362	8	1
Moses Simmons, Robertsons	4	4	3

LAURENS.

Fortunate Drawers Capts. Dist.	No.	Dt.	Sec.
William Bohannon, Deans	86	4	2
Martha J. Calhoun, ill. Hodges	99	8	5
Lewis Stuckey's orphans, Mizells	105	2	3
William Forrist, Whiteheads	97	28	1
James Wright, Beachams	78	9	3
Eliz. Montford, w. R.S., Plummers	39	5	4

LINCOLN.

John Suddoth, Prathers	57	4	3
William Davidson, Leveritts	49	8	5
John J. Botts, Graves	184	1	1

LIBERTY.

William L. Patrick, 15th dist.	84	31	1
James S. Wilkins, 14th dist.	261	3	1
William J. Baker's orps. 17th dist.	241	24	1

MONTGOMERY.

Daniel Spikes, Wynns	45	22	1
James Carter, do	16	14	5

MORGAN.

John W. McCowen, Beasleys	32	18	2
Mary Staar, w. R. S., Gains	33	10	3
James Mulkey, do	93	14	2
Edward R. Walton, Dawsons	69	30	1
William Akins, R. S., Jennings	14	13	5
Samuel Parker, R. S., Canifexs	4	12	3
William McCowen's orps. Hills	20	28	1
Elisha Jarvis, sr. R. S., Jennings	200	10	3
Robert B. Wynn, do	103	5	3
Thomas Green, Gains	198	25	1
Robert B. Wynn, Jennings	199	5	3
Elizabeth Mulkey, wid. Brooks	233	6	2
Ernest C. Wittich's orps. Youngs	12	4	5
Aug. C. Fears, orphans, Gains	281	10	2
Burrell Jordan, Beazeleys	67	14	2
Priscilla Terry, w. R. S., do	75	18	1
Zachariah Butt, Gaines	38	9	2
Newett Foster, Boznells	47	29	1

MADISON.

William Edwards, R. S., Hannas	38	17	2
William Reed, Caldwells	32	12	5
Margaret Hopkins, wid. Hanas	18	17	2

MONROE.

Michael Runnymore, Turners	45	32	1
William Stuvail, R. S., Millers	101	9	3
Aug. C. Hawkins, Doctor, do	253	9	1
John McCraw, Woodwards	209	23	1
Lodwick R. Cashan, Wrights	33	12	2
Joseph W. George, Pattersons	203	3	5
John Cooper, Houses	103	10	1
Archibald Davis, sol. Millers	356	3	4
Yancy Thornton, Houses	134	9	3
Lewis Crary, Finches	12	12	2
John Joice, Stallings	97	12	1
Stephen Veazey, sol., Higgins	212	33	1
Alexander Goodson, Pattersons	26	19	2
Joel Mathews, Turners	76	4	1
John Marshall, Douglass	60	18	1
George T. Jarvis, Houses	196	7	3
Thos. Hathorn, R. S., Pattersons	140	7	6

(4)

McINTOSH.

Fortunate Drawers Capts. Dist.	No.	Dt.	Sec.
David, Jane, William & Edward Delegal, orps. Thorps	74	20	1
Emeline, Edward W., Thomas & Henry Delegal, orps. Thorps	136	25	1
Bayard E. Hand, Terrells	198	4	1

NEWTON.

Joel Burgess, soldier, Newnans	206	23	2
Rachel Downs, widow, Pullens	179	18	2
Asap Dotson, Hays	112	28	1
Denson C. Melton, Dyers	248	8	3
Terrell Robinson, ill., Newnans	138	13	2
John Burk, jr. soldier, do	57	21	1

OGLETHORPE.

James Sorrow, sol. Devenports	120	14	2
Ezekiel Giham, Rousseaus	192	7	3
James C. Johnson, Hardemans	177	28	1
Daniel Rainey, soldier, Hills	312	20	2
James Blackwell, Billups	113	29	1
Margaret Murry, wid. Holloways	21	8	2
Adam Simmons, orp. Hardmans	59	24	1
Coleman Tarpley, Arnolds	344	20	2
Urb. B. Oglesby, Rousseaus	9	20	2

PULASKI.

Wm. Horn, R. S., Gilstraps	187	3	5
Edward Banker, Kellums	32	15	5
Moses Right, Hendleys	14	18	1
William Gays, orps. Powells	207	16	1

PUTNAM.

Eli E. Gaither, Bledsoes	144	7	2
Martin Hopson, Brooks	216	9	1
William R. Adams, Marcus	13	1	1
John Stubbs, Kendricks	208	31	1
Asa Read, Duprees	175	10	3
Han. Donnon's orps. Allums	3	20	2
Henry Cooper, R. S., Barnetts	208	11	1
J. Pulaski, (min. of con.) Marcus	190	11	1
Francis Miller, Kendricks	96	2	3
Benj. Jordan's orps. Sanders	58	19	2
Robert Little, Stinsons	189	31	1

PIKE.

John Benson, Suiters	251	5	5
William Sims, Orrs	116	1	4
Augus. F. Jordan, illeg. Hicks	167	11	3

RICHMOND.

Jerh. Bateman, orp. Huntingtons	58	4	3
Elizabeth R. & Susannah M. McDowell, orphans, Ferns	121	5	2
Christopher Fletcher, Blacks	168	10	2
Lewis Ryan, Huntingtons	46	7	5
Mary Murren, widow, do	106	13	2
John Ward, Wilcoxs	176	15	5
John Eagan, R. S., 119th	147	29	1
Samuel Appleton, Blacks	87	22	2

RABUN.

Dread Massingale, jr. Mercers	78	12	3
William Price, Godfreys	163	20	2
Anthony Fowler, Becks	117	24	2

SCRIVEN.

Fortunate Drawers Capts. Dist.	No.	Dt.	Sec.
Wm. D. Camble, Lovets	26	3	3
Sarah Ann Howell, orps. Poythess	43	3	2
Dicey Mercer's orps. McCalls	256	20	1
Josiah T. Scruggs, Hunters	99	16	1
John Brannen's orps. Reaves	196	3	5
John Oliver, Lovetts	30	21	1
Wm. Taylor's orps. Poythess	252	33	1

TALIAFERRO.

John Wynne, Gunns	218	3	5
Jesse Johnson's orps. Guises	190	4	1

TATTNALL.

David Vestal, McCalls	168	4	5
Ephraim Deloach, Deloaches	71	32	1

TWIGGS.

Wright Sanders, Kelleys	179	9	5
T. W. Anderson, Chamberlains	182	5	3
D. J. Griffin, orphan, Graggs	81	9	5
James Bryan's orps. Holidays	32	15	1
Alex. Meriwether, Blackshears	111	20	1
Daniel Ard, Pearsons	240	15	1
Wil. S. Hill's orps. Bosticks	72	23	1
Benjamin Lane, Kellys	178	30	1

TELFAIR.

Daniel Laslie, jr. Lampkins	256	33	1
Nathan Grantham, Wilsons	154	20	1

UPSON.

John Wetherby, sol. Dukes	187	30	1
James D. Smith, sol. Ezells	97	9	1
James Garrat, Haralds	91	5	3
Bent. Lawrence, soldier, Dukes	51	3	3

WILKES.

William Hopkins' orps. Lukers	202	6	5
Russell Bell, Greshams	211	32	1
Hen. B. Gibson, R. S., Greens	243	9	2
Eliz. Bruce, w. R.S., Washingtons	57	29	1

WARREN.

Elbert P. Andrews, Bulls	173	20	1
James White, Sanders	110	2	2
Mary Uptegroves, f. a. Downs	171	7	3
Lucy Fagle, widow, Adkins	275	22	1
Miles Cary, Hills	35	5	5
Drury Pate, soldier, Sanders	155	12	3
Lewis Todd, Kinseys	248	2	2
Wm. Cothern, Hills	85	16	1
S. Yarborough, orps. Brinkleys	207	15	1
Spencer Wooten, Kinseys	113	4	2
John Ansley, Sanders	9	13	2
Jesse Farr, do	310	8	1
Peg. McCrary's illegs. Jones	40	11	3
Thomas Reddick's orps. Parhams	39	20	1

WAYNE.

David Burney's orps. Mannings	87	10	3
T. S. & M. Taylor, f.a. McKinneys	80	17	1

WALTON

Daniel Walker, sr. sol. Rays	92	21	2
Daniel Mack, 503rd dist.	26	8	5
Hugh Edgar, 249th do	162	29	1
Thomas Beard, Hendersons	20	17	1

(5)

Fortunate Drawers Capts. Dist.	No.	Dt.	Sec.
Wm. A. Neely, 503rd dist.	113	6	5
Jacob Pike, Bexleys	233	12	3
Frederick Reaves, do	218	18	1
WASHINGTON.			
Ambrose Whittle, Wimberlys	56	12	2
Hiram Pearson, illeg. Woods	63	7	2
Reuben Whitfield, Whitfields	59	32	1
Wm. Williamson, Woods	143	11	5
Joseph Edwards, Mannings	217	29	1
John Darbey, Avans	182	10	3
Alfred Hodges, do	153	22	2
Britain Pope, Floyds	83	14	2
George Brown, O'Quins	230	11	1
WILKINSON.			
Henry Lezenby, Shows	197	2	3
Edy Jamerson, hus.ab. Mathews	143	11	2
Thomas Norwood, Halls	246	16	1
Brice Pawl's orphs. do	175	24	1
Joseph Riley, Mathews	201	20	1
Barden Acock, Shows	111	1	2
WARE.			
David Sutton, R. S., Motes	106	7	4
Winny R. Henderson, w. Bryans	139	5	4

THIRD DAY'S DRAWING—March 8.

APPLING.			
Wm. Overstreet, McDonalds	16	9	4
BALDWIN.			
Henry Gray, Pitts	184	3	4
John H. Smith's orps. Lesters	80	12	5
BIBB.			
Wm. S. Wilson, Flanders	108	6	2
Jesse Moreran, sol. Swearingins	34	1	4
Amasa Bennett, Bates	90	20	2
Josiah James, Loyds	70	3	3
Lev. F. Chain, Rutlands	206	29	1
BURKE.			
D. J. Evans, soldier, Brooms	9	5	3
Benj. Lightfoot, Roberts	91	3	1
Abi. Bargeron, wid. Thompsons	218	20	1
James Caruthers, Segars	202	12	5
James Galaway, Dugas	317	8	1
Marth. Metcalf, w. R. S., Lesters	79	8	5
Wm. Kemball, Thompsons	154	9	5
CAMDEN.			
Joseph Howell, Coxs	24	15	5
CHATHAM.			
Robert Raiford, Haydens	155	17	2
James Rogerson, McDonnells	116	3	4
James Cleghorn, Tenbrooks	235	6	5
Asa Clark, McDonnells	163	9	5
R. W. Wright, Haydens	271	28	1
Catharine Connerat, wid. Bains	160	8	3
Cos. P. Richardson, Haydens	195	13	1
CLARK.			
Elizabeth Hester, Lumpkins	101	18	2
Robert Perkins' orps. Herndens	124	5	2
Abram Doolittle, Vinsens	33	17	1
George Earnest, R. S., Dickersons	138	24	2

Fortunate Drawers Capts. Dist.	No.	Dt.	Sec.
Wm. Brown, Gahagans	180	2	2
R. L. Rounsaville, do	80	8	2
COLUMBIA.			
James Gay, sr. Dranes	124	22	2
Augustus Dozier, Clarks	208	3	2
John Griffin, jr. Coles	157	26	1
Wm. Stark's orphan, Clarks	19	6	2
Augustus Clay, Coles	65	32	1
CRAWFORD.			
Thomas, Elizabeth, William, Nancy & J. Grant, ors. Rhodes	170	19	2
Anderson Strinbridge, Tillers	43	20	2
John Sealy, Rhodes	175	8	1
DEKALB.			
James Curlee, Lokeys	5	6	2
John Centre, soldier, Harris	249	2	1
DOOLY.			
Benj. Posey's orps. 582nd dist.	123	5	5
EARLY.			
Jesse Morgan, Wilsons	222	7	5
Thomas Clark, soldier, Spiers	21	7	4
George Landrum, Wilsons	159	32	1
James C. Lewis, orps. Spiers	93	12	2
ELBERT.			
William Pulliam, sol. Hortons	152	3	2
Howard Paton, Merits	151	2	3
Wm. W. Ragan, Boltons	98	32	1
James, W. & Th. W. King, illegitimates, Hortons	13	16	1
Elizabeth Hudson, wid. Tuckers	349	7	1
Moses McCurdy, Carpenters	232	3	3
EMANUEL			
Mary Lindsey, illeg. Nabbs	198	22	1
FAYETTE.			
Irwin B. Haines, Wests	220	2	1
John McInnish, Whortons	48	10	5
FRANKLIIN.			
Samuel B. Crow, Cokers	145	3	1
Fields Rumsey, Stephens	116	2	2
Francis Clark, Caudells	215	16	1
William Ash, Hudsons	203	2	3
Jane Pulliam, w. Blankenships	148	13	1
William Sitian, soldier, Jones	340	28	1
Thomas Bush, sol. Sanders	238	18	2
Wiley Mitchell, Chandlers	273	19	2
GREENE.			
Isaac Jones, Astins	158	33	1
Daniel Greer, Sutherlands	213	10	1
Thos. Holland, R. S., Elys	222	2	3
Newel Stoutamires' orps. Robins	15	1	5
Wm. C. Stewart, Halls	304	22	1
Thos. J. Tanner, Robins	36	20	1
Moses Jackson, R. S., Winkfields	22	28	1
GWINNETT.			
Wm. A. Hooper, Hunicuts	116	11	2
Seaborn Thorne, Caruthers	87	14	2
James Taunt, Robertsons	7	17	2
Jeffrey Pitman, Bakers	76	3	3
Edw. Hayes, R. S., Moors	132	15	1

Fortunate Drawers Capts. Dist.	No.	Dt.	Sec.
John Taylor, Robertsons	115	2	4
David G. Ballard, do	142	14	5
John Mills, Rollins	206	28	1
HABERSHAM.			
David K. Beaty, Bryans	95	20	2
HALL.			
Philip C. Liles, Hardens	60	10	5
Abel Kendrick, R. S., Floyds	62	16	2
John Brown, Roberts	136	1	3
HANCOCK.			
Jesse Champion, 108th dist.	83	8	1
William Richardson, 103rd do	228	3	5
Elizabeth Presley, 112th do	64	9	1
Jacob Stephens, 118th do	115	28	1
HENRY.			
Wiley Strickland, Millers	52	7	2
John Treadwell, jr. Shaws	110	17	1
James Hannigan, R. S., Millers	227	18	2
James Turner, Gosdens	95	22	2
Eli Capps, Kites	51	3	2
Aaron Pates, Bryants	207	31	1
Bowling's orphans, Grays	5	10	1
HOUSTON.			
Isaac Vinson, Prices	183	4	4
IRWIN.			
John Bennifield, Bradfords	97	18	2
JACKSON.			
James Ramsey, soldier, Moors	40	28	1
Henry Buchanan, Venables	90	18	1
Joseph Yarbrough, orps. Bowens	111	15	5
Andrew Armor, soldier, Storeys	36	8	5
Sarah Johnson, widow do	65	30	1
JASPER.			
Mary Henderson, w. R. S., Parkers	62	5	5
William Williamson, Comptons	11	3	4
Wm. McCoy, Owens	29	1	1
Ransom Huff, do	127	1	2
John Huston, sr. R. S., Hines	63	15	1
Char. W. C. Wright, Dardens	44	6	3
David Pruitt, Wilders	35	23	2
Sarah Strickland, wid. Keys	91	1	5
Thomas Morris, R. S. Barnetts	98	11	1
Francis Moreland, R. S. Reeves	198	32	1
Wilson H. Coy, Holmes	122	8	1
JEFFERSON.			
Mills Watkins, Elliots	148	23	1
Reason Linsey, Marshalls	156	2	4
Wm. Stedman's orps. Beatys	6	22	2
Sarah Fleming, wid. Jones	129	7	3
Elias Brassell, Waldens	235	4	1
Seth McDowell, Beatys	13	30	1
Daniel Connell, R. S. Beatys	209	18	1
JONES.			
Jesse Johnson, Blounts	244	2	1
Thomas W. Davis, Davis's	136	10	5
Richard Adams, Hammacks	86	4	5
Lewis Alsabrooks, Stewarts	47	14	2
Lucy Onsley's ille. Hendersons	179	4	3

Fortunate Drawers Capts. Dist.	No.	Dt.	Sec.
Wm. B. Roquemore, Gibsons	122	21	2
Joseph Williamson, Popes	89	6	2
Buel Mather, Woods	176	8	3
Wm. Blount, R. S. Blounts	222	17	1
Joshua Kolb's orps. Taylors	195	13	2
LAURENS.			
Wilson Slaughter, Spivys	338	20	2
Joseph Dixon, Mizells	24	27	1
LIBERTY.			
Wm. Barber, 17th dist.	248	13	2
Mary Bailey, lunatic, do	125	33	1
LINCOLN.			
Charles Huguley, Frasers	137	5	5
MADISON.			
James Sanders, R. S. Adairs	176	2	2
Mary Gailey, w. R. S. Caldwells	204	24	1
MONROE.			
John Stuart, Douglass	22	3	1
Arch. Reddin's orps. Pattersons	238	17	2
John Johnson, Rays	220	11	3
Peter S. Reynolds, sol. Higgins	192	6	3
Amos Jones, Browns	55	20	2
John Horn, R. S. Douglass	144	6	3
Fielding McMullen, Greshams	221	7	5
Seth G. Waton, Browns	36	21	1
Samuel Wilkinson, Johnsons	101	5	4
Jer. Thompson's orps. Houses	246	18	2
Thomas B. Watts, Millers	31	13	1
MORGAN.			
James Loyd, Hitchcocks	152	16	1
Nicholas Smith, sen. Canifaxs	144	18	1
Edward Harris' orps. Gains	4	15	1
Edward Gatlin, sol. Boswells	123	11	1
John Hanson, Christians	91	5	4
Wm. H. Amberson, Jennings	63	28	1
Daniel Whitaker, Watsons	302	8	5
Elisha Bearding, Hitchcocks	68	14	2
Alvan Myhand, Gains	199	11	3
NEWTON.			
Th. Cockerel, sr. R. S. Hays	31	1	1
John Farr, do	22	3	5
John King, Newnans	170	22	2
Levin Sparks, Graces	50	12	3
John McLane, Snows	237	23	2
OGLETHORPE.			
Jesse Martin, R. S. Seals	280	1	4
Jno. Richardson, R.S. Holloways	172	5	4
Mary Harrison, w. R. S. Rhodes	201	8	5
Eliz. Pryor's illeg. Devenports	266	3	3
Thomas Edwards, Rousseaus	60	1	1
Wm. R. Brooks, sol. Smith's	129	15	5
Mary Bragg, w. R. S. Rhodes	34	4	4
Dunston Traylor, Lacys	16	10	5
Wm. Christopher, Williamson's	248	10	2
Joseph Embry, R. S. Holloways	48	7	4
Alfred G. Perry, Bells	80	3	1
PIKE.			
Leonard Burns, Mays	1	23	2

(7)

Fortunate Drawers Capts. Dist.	No.	Dt.	Sec.
Stephen H. King, Orrs	103	1	1
PULASKI.			
Moses Wright, Hendleys	148	18	1
Bartlett Barker, Bracewells	52	4	1
PUTNAM.			
John W. Thomas, Sparks	12	33	1
James Mullens, Kendricks	314	7	1
George G. Wheeler, Clarks	149	13	1
William Wheeler, Barnetts	330	20	2
Peter T. Richardson, Bledsoes	57	1	4
James H. Hines, Blacks	16	4	1
John Butt's orphans, Barnetts	219	3	4
David Perryman, soldier, Goods	226	27	1
William Glover, Bledsoes	59	33	1
John B. Pound, Allums	204	6	2
Th. Barrow's orps., Kirkpatricks	14	5	2
Adolphus Underwood, Sparks	248	17	1
RABUN.			
Mabry Carnes, Godfreys	76	1	5
Dread Wall, do	199	8	1
RICHMOND.			
Robert D. Jones, Raifords	10	32	1
William Germond, Huntingtons	1 98	20	2
Majers Watson, James	17	31	1
Steele White's orphans, Mantz	329	28	1
Mary Greene, widow, Blacks	106	4	5
Peter Cone, 600th dist.	46	8	1
George Murrah, Huntingtons	78	11	2
SCRIVEN.			
Wiley Roberts, Kemps	26	12	2
TATTNALL.			
Simeon A. Smith, Graces	138	31	1
Peter Brown, McDuffies	6	24	1
Seaborn Hall, Graces	73	12	1
TELFAIR.			
James W. Rollins, Clements	243	12	3
Alexander Powell, Wilsons	191	18	2
James Burnes, Williams	226	3	1
Hugh McIntyre, Barentines	187	6	5
TWIGGS.			
Joseph Blount, Hollidays	44	14	2
N. Womble, wid. Chamberlains	160	2	3
Hiram Colwell, Pearsons	76	5	2
John R. Pitman, Hollidays	107	4	4
Jno. Domina's orps. Blackshears	138	1	5
UPSON.			
Lewis Holloman, Harrils	71	2	1
James P. Portis, soldier, Ellis	87	6	2
John Hammell, soldier, Ezells	136	5	4
Silvanus Moody, Hattoxs	72	8	1
WALTON.			
William J. Cowen, 249th	170	12	3
James Roberts, 418th	48	31	1
Daniel D. Judd, Hendersons	91	8	4
Eliz. Davis, w. R. S., McQuirters	205	21	1
James John, 503d	144	18	2
John Dicken, soldier, 250th	181	14	2

WARE.			
Fortunate Drawers Capts. Dist.	No.	Dt.	Sec.
Jabez L. Dowling, Dowlings	165	19	2
Wiley Osteen, illegit. Bryans	1	6	3
WARREN.			
Sophronia Kitchens, ill. Downs	147	4	4
Churchwell Gibson, jr. Parhams	31	3	4
Valentine Simmons, Jones	30	3	3
Ambrose Linzy's orps. Downs	256	8	3
WASHINGTON.			
Claiborn Bateman, Rushings	184	8	3
Benjamin Ferguson, sol. Avnas	231	3	5
William Northington, Currys	111	1	1
Iredell Eason, Gilberts	224	18	2
William Osburn, Worthins	103	4	5
Lydia Kelly, wid. Wimberlys	127	20	1
Archibald C. Duggan, Worthins	106	9	1
Richard Childers, R. S., Gilberts	27	24	1
Nancy Wise, widow Wimberlys	247	28	1
Samuel Allen, Whitfields	82	12	3
Jonathan Watson, Tysons	164	6	3
WILKINSON.			
Thomas Frasure, Halls	176	9	5
Samuel Bragg, Shows	130	9	1
Richard T. Porter, jr. Smiths	256	23	2
James Moore, Mayos	160	3	3
Duncan Graham, Fairchilds	141	18	2
Manderson & Martha Todd, illegitimates, Halls	122	1	5
WILKES.			
John W. Willis's orps. Carters	183	20	2
James M. C. Lukers, Lukers	76	18	2
Nathaniel McCoy, Carters	8	15	2

4TH DAY'S DRAWING—9th March

APPLING.

Richard Bennett, jr. Morgans	126	12	3
Jesse Aldredge's orps. Mathis	135	2	2
BALDWIN.			
Nathaniel Ennis' orps. Lingos	225	9	5
John Skinner, Pitts	28	16	1
Bishop Clements, Doles	229	4	1
Moses Wright, Wicks	178	12	2
Eliz. Eli Pickett, ill. Perry's bat.	8	33	1
BIBB.			
Linson E. Jackson, Carrs	101	1	1
John Haswell, Pickards	149	14	5
BULLOCH.			
William Brown, jr. Richardsons	146	12	1
BURKE.			
Anna Bryan, Lynchs	196	1	1
Arthur Royal, Thompsons	308	28	1
Peter Mathis, Brooms	75	26	1
John A. Triggs, Baileys	81	6	2
Amos Attaway, Rogers	166	11	5
Robert McCoy, Andersons	43	3	5
CAMDEN.			
David Mizell, jr. Baileys	107	12	5

(8)

CHATHAM.

Fortunate Drawers Capts. Dist.	No.	Dt.	Sec.
B. B. Rutland, Nungazers	144	12	1
Joseph Brantley's orps. Reeds	4	26	1
John C. Bell, Geredons	214	14	2
James B. Joudon, Haydens	139	11	5
Leonidas Wylly, McDonnells	279	10	2
Robert Scott, Baines	96	12	3
Su. Cunningham, orp. M'Daniels	312	28	1
Maj. P. Deveaux, R. S., Haydens	106	3	3

CLARK.

Rich. A. Meriwether, Gahagans	22	10	3
Harris Hodges, Vinsons	132	20	2
Edward R. Ware, Gahagans	211	9	2
William M. Bethune, Lumpkins	127	5	3
Benj. Elsberry, sr. R. S., Davis	74	11	2

COLUMBIA.

Samuel Marshall, Baileys	134	6	4
John Fuller, Dranes	172	8	4
John Ray's orphans, Boltons	65	21	1
Irey & Elizab. Bird, mins. Coles	67	3	4
Samuel Cone, Stallings	166	21	1
Dicy Rhodes, orphans, Boltons	64	20	2

CRAWFORD.

Stanley Hall, Rhodes	319	28	1

DEKALB.

David Pope, Merritts	6	11	5
Isaac Howell, Howells	122	2	1
Highley Cureton, Smiths	118	5	3
Jesse Harris, Howells	73	4	2
William Williams, Merritts	198	11	5

EARLY.

John Carter, Porters	13	5	2

ELBERT.

Sarah Beck, w. R. S., Alstons	55	23	1
Barsheba Owens, w. R. S., Tuckers	53	5	3
Wm. Rucker, R. S., Carpenters	223	13	1
Mary Burton, widow, Bells	138	8	4
Thomas Hall, Butlers	104	1	5
Joseph Griffin's orps. Boltons	81	12	5

EMANUEL.

William Hall, soldier, 57th dist.	239	20	2

FAYETTE.

Wm. Westmoreland, Roziers	304	20	2
Wilson Chappell, Craigs	156	2	2
Vincent Faulkner, Roziers	244	3	1
John Treadwell, Craigs	160	19	2
John Leopard, Roziers	277	8	1

FRANKLIN.

Joshua Baker, R. S., Jones	20	8	5
John Whittaker, Boswells	29	11	3
Hillary Stone, do	151	9	2
J. McDonald, R. S., McDonalds	250	18	2
Lewis Tucker, Jones	117	4	3
Tarlton Walker, McDonalds	197	10	1
Wm. Flanorigan, R. S., Stephens	79	7	5
John Minnish, Hudsons	38	14	1

GLYNN.

Fortunate Drawers Capts. Dist.	No.	Dt.	Sec.
Alex. Higginbotham, McLeods	184	1	4

GREENE.

Wm. Jordan, Vincents	129	7	4
Ann Anderson, w. R. S. Robins	42	16	1
Isaac Ray, Newsoms	277	1	2
Wm. F. Lumpkins, Sutherlands	112	12	5
James F. Foster, Dawsons	270	22	2
John Kirk, Webbs	220	17	1
Robert Peek, sr. Woodhams	139	7	1

GWINNETT.

Sarah Wooten, wid. Bakers	219	32	1
John M. Dabbs, Bakers	109	2	2
Charity McMichael, w. Hunicuts	143	1	2
James Coggin, Rawlings	102	4	1
Thomas Head, Rollins	72	17	1
Little B. Wright, Hunicuts	49	9	1
Solomon H. Jackson, Davis	19	9	4
Thos. W. Wood, Woodruffs	141	20	1
Isaac Pritchard, Davis	208	11	5
John Greenwood, Dunbars	125	6	5
James Wells, Canthuls	61	21	1

HANCOCK.

Daniel Garrett, 18th dist.	202	10	3
John Denton, R. S., 111th dist.	23	4	1
Sterling Lewis' orps. 103rd do	33	7	5
Peter Conner's orphs. 112th dist.	88	33	1
Catharine Skinner, w. 111th do	128	9	3
Thomas Blount, 113th dist.	111	12	3
James Wilkins, Swints	76	15	2
James Powell's orps. 113th dist.	185	21	2
T. W. Edward's chil. f.a. Mahons	69	18	2
Burwell Brown, soldier, Bishops	121	30	1

HENRY.

Samuel Wyatt, sol. Grays	303	8	1
Sarah Maloins, wid. Bryants	38	6	4
Thos. Crofford, do	56	5	5
John B. Fuller, Kites	218	10	1
Hiram Lovelady, Harris	194	7	1
Andrew B. Baggit, Bryants	226	4	1
John Downs, R. S. Shaws	41	23	1
Joseph Hand, R. S. Bryants	140	5	3

HABERSHAM.

Thomas Moore, Fains	162	13	1
Levin Keel, Suttins	114	2	2
Thomas Turner, Bryans	146	28	1
John Evans, soldier, do	88	23	2
P. C. Thibrand, Martins	48	13	1
Eliz. & R. Stower's orphs. Fains	68	3	1
J. A. & Cora Jones, mins. Jones	124	7	2
John Thompson, Kenzies	119	12	2
Sarah Ledbetter, wid. Martins	345	8	1
Elias Keller, Suttons	291	10	2
James Adams, Vickreys	247	7	1
Thomas Rice, Bakers	162	14	5
Joseph Hansard, Vickreys	127	13	5

LAND LOTTERY REGISTER—No. 2
[RECORDER OFFICE—PUBLISHED BY GRANTLAND & ORME—PRICE $3.]

NOTE.—Section 1 is Lee County—2 Muscogee—3 Troup—4 Coweta—5 Carroll.
Fourth Day's Drawing—Continued.

Fortunate Drawers Capts. Dist.	No.Dt.Sec.
HALL.	
Mary Whistenant w. Floyds	247 10 2
Memory Walker, Roberts	94 5 4
Thos. Whitehead sr. Hardens	19 17 2
Andrew Chalmers, Alreds	91 28 1
Jacob Cochran, Roberts	238 28 1
HOUSTON.	
John Bynum, Yarbroughs	116 2 3
Charly Tanton, Ins, Pattens	40 7 2
Nathan Tanton, Sol., do.	104 13 2
Robert Brooks, Calhouns	88 8 5
IRWIN.	
Thomas Lealman, Dixons	41 3 1
Willis King, 5th	79 27 1
Hamon Crum's orps. Bradfords	176 23 1
JACKSON.	
John J. Scoggin, Bowens	250 22 1
James McNeese, R. S. Allens	196 13 1
Pleasant Turner, R. S. Millers	147 26 1
William Dunston, Staplers	207 3 3
Isaac Burson, R. S. Landrums	280 23 2
Daniel McCowen's orps. Winns	104 22 2
Robert Hancock's orps. Venables	111 13 5
Charles McKinney, R. S. Bowens	133 8 3
JASPER.	
Isaac O. Holland orp. Wilders	240 26 1
Riley Wise, Dardens	218 3 3
Villet Greene, Sparks	166 33 1
Isaac Bailey, Holmes	124 12 1
David Harris, Barnes	63 24 2
Henry Pennington, Hines	134 2 4
Jefferson Mashburn Ill. Sparks	131 7 3
Welcome D. Carroll Ill. Baynes	129 16 1
William A. Reid, Wilders	277 14 1
Judith Steward w. R. S. Baynes	108 31 1
William Fears R. S. Holmes	152 16 2
Peter W. Gautier jr. Do	208 30 1
Dorcas Campbells Ills. Hines	140 20 2
Seaborn Abbot, Barnetts	163 28 1
Ludwell Foster, Keys	72 7 4
Jonathan Fincher, Do	10 2 4
JEFFERSON.	
Richard Jones, Ross'	80 8 3
Alex.&JaneManning,Ills. Causeys	166 11 1
Zachariah Noles, Boyds	188 11 3
Asa Alford, Elliotts	50 12 2
Isaac Merchant, Beatys	270 1 2
Henry Spann, Cunninghams	48 24 1
John S. Berryhill, Beatys	21 12 3
Winney Hyslip, wid. Boyds	135 23 1
Ebenezer J. Cottle, Marshalls	17 1 4
JONES.	
Jem Hasty, w. R. S. Breedloves	86 1 4
William Rollo, Taylors	90 5 5
Nath'l Turbaville, Gibsons	232 11 3
John Thomas, Dosters	154 20 2

Fortunate Drawers Capts. Dist.	No.Dt.Sec.
Samuel McDaniel, Stewarts	170 33 1
Diana Jones, wid. Mullins	159 22 1
Thos. W. Davis, sol., Davis	228 12 1
James R. Edwards, Hamacks	109 20 2
James W. Braswell, Popes	113 8 1
Henry Barron, Newbys	82 4 2
James Stallings, do	185 29 1
John Garland, sen. Stewards	203 20 1
Attis Vinson, Burkes	127 31 1
William C. Ellis, Newbys	105 19 2
Lucy Blount, wid. Blounts	44 4 1
Joseph Lester, Breedloves	149 15 2
LAURENS.	
William Ry's orps. Hodges	47 7 4
James Hay, Barlows	58 15 2
Patrick Tennill, do	132 7 1
Eason Tyson, do.	17 7 2
Clofton Smith, Powers	160 8 5
LIBERTY.	
Ann Powell, w. R. S., 15th	233 2 4
Elizabeth Shumath, wid. 17th	91 14 2
LINCOLN.	
William Fleming, jr. Parks	154 2 2
James S. Loflin, Gideons	116 15 5
F. Barksdale, w. R. S. Wiggintons	134 7 1
Frances Bussey, wid. Graves	27 5 4
John Calhoun, Lonorgans	280 11 2
Allen Fraser, Ross's	32 12 1
Th. Florence, sr. R. S. Frasers	75 20 2
MADISON.	
Andrew Scott, Stephens	120 14 1
James Ware, sol., Hancocks	224 12 1
Reuben Simmons, Christians	129 12 2
Joseph McDerman, R. S., Bones	374 20 2
MONROE.	
James H. Miller, Browns	301 28 1
William Booth, Houses	33 15 5
Alexander McLeod, Wrights	147 18 1
Sol. Beckham, R. S., Pattersons	47 13 1
Jane Scott, wid. Browns	161 2 3
Britain Rogers, R. S., do.	156 12 5
Joel Faulkner, Wrights	192 2 3
Alexander McLeod, do.	37 2 1
Jno. Howard, sol., Stallings	137 11 3
Wm. L. Funderburk, Millers	4 6 3
Ann Long, wid. Browns	136 19 2
Catharine Watson, wid. Houses	25 7 3
Wm. Payne's orps. Greshams	28 3 4
Thomas Freeman, Wrights	151 18 1
John R. Maddux, Finch's	25 3 3
Greene Horseley, Browns	247 23 1
MORGAN.	
Nat. W. Powell's orp. Dawsons	231 16 1
Jacob Leavins, Sparks	199 3 4
Ro. Thompson's orps. Jennings	251 11 2
Benj. Williams' orps. Watsons	66 8 2
M. A. Thompson, orp. Adairs	116 12 1

Fortunate Drawers Capts. Dist.	No.	Dt.	Sec.
M. A. Haslet, hus. ab. Canifaxs	104	10	1
NEWTON.			
John Eastwood, jr. Moss's	172	5	5
Nicholas Welch, R. S. Sumners	211	12	1
Peter H. Stanfield, Zacherys	118	14	2
OGLETHORPE.			
Jesse Bell, Williamsons	29	29	1
George Varner, R. S. Rhodes	28	3	3
Mary Bowden, wid. Dix's	329	8	1
John Carter, Bufords	248	28	1
Sarah Wright, wid. Floyds	119	9	1
Paschal Traylor, Lacys	66	9	1
Albert T. Wallis, Bufords	66	15	1
Robert M. Goodwin, Rousseaus	4	6	2
Thomas J. Stephens, Seals	134	8	5
Lee Walker, Hills	205	27	1
William Spratlin, Burfords	170	14	2
James Williams, orp. Dix's	74	12	5
PIKE.			
William Caldwell, Hartsfields	92	20	2
Adam Hardage, Mays	144	7	5
Gabriel B. Strone, S., Shehee's	226	26	1
PUTNAM.			
John H. Crafton, Blunts	213	5	2
Jesse Custard, Bledsoes	70	4	4
John W. Evans, Chambers	163	6	5
William Womack, Stinsons	249	8	1
Curran Rogers, Barnetts	179	15	1
Josiah Barrow, Allums	133	11	5
George Lambert, R. S., Sawyers	236	22	1
Jos. L. Moultrie, maniac, Barnetts	41	9	5
Sally Wright, wid. Goods	135	4	1
RABUN.			
John Dunn, Milligans	106	1	4
RICHMOND.			
Pierce Stoy, Huntingtons	138	11	1
Mary Fox, wid. (at W. J.) Treadwells	110	18	1
John B. Horn, Augusta	89	13	1
Mary Ann McIntosh, orp. Blacks	194	11	3
Roswell Cook, Treadwells	79	8	1
James Fraughtenberry, James	146	13	1
David Lyner, 120th	51	6	2
William Inglett, James	222	3	1
Chauncey Bradley, Hands	30	31	1
John Bryant, Wilcox	11	14	5
William Bell, idiot, Blacks	76	4	2
Samuel Clark, Huntingtons	54	8	4
SCRIVEN.			
James Rynalder Nix, Reaves	195	10	1
Mary Dampier, wid. Stricklings	110	6	4
TATTNALL.			
Benager Smith, Graces	79	10	2
Piercey Branch, wid. Dees	76	13	2
TELFAIR.			
William Smith, Lampkins	154	23	2
TALIAFERRO.			
James Shorter, Hamacks	83	20	1
Thomas H. Luckett, Townes	38	11	1
TWIGGS.			
Samuel Stanford, Pearsons	80	6	2
William Joyner's orps. Holidays	321	3	4
Elizabeth Brown, ill. Streetmans	205	3	5
dward's orps. Blackshears	166	8	3

Fortunate Drawers Capts. Dist.	No.	Dt.	Sec.
Charlies Railey, R.S. Chamberlains	103	22	1
Dempsey Brown, R. S. Streetmans	134	16	2
Henry Farrell, Holidays	66	23	1
Eanos Davis, do	127	8	1
UPSON.			
Lucy Trayler, W. R. S., Hattoxs	143	1	1
Maxey Parker's orps. Pashells	241	29	1
Dolphin Davis, sol., Duprees	288	3	4
WALTON.			
Ezekiel Pike, Hudsons	150	32	1
David S. Smith, Snows	132	30	1
Jacob Carpenter, Bexleys	61	1	2
William Lewallen, S., 249th dist.	47	8	4
WARREN.			
Benjamin Matthews, Kinseys	135	4	3
Hardy Hopson, Parhams	265	2	4
Willis Rhymes, R. S., Brinkleys	109	7	1
Aaron Jackson, sol. Hills	13	1	3
William Stewart, Adkins	232	20	1
Henry Raley, R. S., Jones	185	7	3
Hansel Beckworth, Downs	328	20	2
James G. Smith, Brinkleys	192	25	1
Thomas P. Harris, orp. Hills	188	18	1
WASHINGTON.			
John Middleton, R. S., Currys	144	19	2
William Twilley, O'Quins	182	5	4
Abram Elton, McLendons	35	3	4
Edwin C. Pridgen, Mannings	161	3	3
Alfred Renfroe, Floyds	104	23	1
James Martin, Gilberts	154	4	5
WILKINSON.			
Mallachi Butler, Halls	94	2	4
Mary Nobles, hus. ab. Smiths	159	9	1
George Dickson, Fairchilds	91	4	1
Neal E. A. Harvill, ill. Shores	217	8	3
Mary Shaw, widow, Mandersons	71	1	4
Jonathan Tipton, sol., Barrys	32	15	2
WILKES.			
John Warthan, Reeves	60	1	2
Dudley Stinson's orps. Chunns	110	11	2
Polly Lockhart, W. R. S., Lukers	46	2	3
John Snelson, Washingtons	116	18	1

5TH DAY'S DRAWING—12th March

	No.	Dt.	Sec.
APPLING.			
John Peterson, Dedges	75	6	4
Henry Boyd orph. Stricklins	134	15	1
BALDWIN.			
Keziah Todd wid. Rowes	123	11	3
Julius A. Wicker, Doles	80	4	5
John Simpson, Lingos	98	15	2
Eliz. Dismukes w. R. S. Weeks	113	1	1
John Sturges orps. Lesters	188	13	2
Ezra B. Jones, Buchanans	48	16	2
Rispy Jowell wid. Buchanans	226	3	5
Seaton Grantland, Do.	180	8	1
Levin J. Smith, Doles	59	4	4
Wm. Quinn, soldier, Pitts	186	32	1
Edm. Brantley, sol. Wicks	235	2	4
BIBB.			
Clement Clements sr. Lloyds	38	6	3
Luanzie Shartles, ill. Swearingins	84	15	1
James Thompson jr. Carrs	22	29	1
BRYAN.			
Stouten Hayman, jr. Harveys	216	4	3

BULLOCK.

Fortunate Drawers	Capts.	Dist.	No.	Dt.	Sec.
John Grover, jr.	Richardsons		189	23	1
John H. Shuffield,	do.		83	12	5
John Holsey,	do.		33	20	2
Phar. Haymes, blind,	Stanlands		241	16	1
And. Kicklighter sr.	Deloachs		187	7	5
Aaron Everitt,	Richardsons		161	6	3

BURKE.

A. S. R. Milton,	Bayleys		12	21	1
Wm. Holland,	Dugas		80	33	1
Nancy Caruthers jr. w.	Segars		235	5	4
Ezekiel Byrd,	Fountains		182	8	5
Nancy Brown, hus. abs.	McHays		36	4	4
Samuel Heath's orps.	Dugas		33	14	5
William Douglas, ill.	Dukes		181	11	2
FrankyD.Rackly, ill.,	Thompsons		352	7	1
John Tenerson's orps.	Lesters		118	16	2
Jesse Grant sr.	Wests		183	8	5
John Stephens,	Lynchs		283	7	5
Sarah Ann Royal wid.	Dugas		63	6	5
Thos. H. Blount,	Bayleys		97	3	5

BUTTS.

David Andrews sol.	Robinsons		80	31	1

CAMDEN.

Joseph Desclaux,	Wards		59	23	1
Isham Peoples,	Hopkins		224	9	5
Theofilus Weeks, R. S.	Coxes		393	28	1
Labourn Taylor,	Browns		56	3	3

CHATHAM.

Claudi P. Leset,	Chatham		147	2	5
Wm. Davis,	Gaddys		148	19	2
Charles Lockhart,			152	4	5
Josiah R. Fisher.	Nungazers		20	6	5
James A. Barney,	McDonnells		238	30	1
George Jones,			18	10	5
Ezekileach East,	Reeds		171	2	2
John Scriven,	Hayden		168	31	1
Naphtali H. Hart,	Geredons		27	15	5

CLARK.

Young Jacks,	Coxs		6	6	4
John H. Borders,	Davenports		253	3	2
Hinchey Winn,	Herndons		227	33	1
John Dalton,	Alreds		120	31	1
Caty Holder wid.	Dickens		127	7	5
Milley Moss, wid.	Andersons		60	11	3
Wm. W. Waddel,	Gahagans		95	12	2
John Briscoes orps.	Andersons		156	18	2
Samuel Minor,	Gahagans		267	8	5
Joseph Elder,	Deans		62	6	3
Louisa Burch, alias Humphries illegitimate,	Frosts		144	15	1

COLUMBIA.

Silas Mote,	Boltons		234	11	2
Jesse H. Morris,	Magruders		101	3	3
Polly Thomsons, Ill.	Culbreaths		196	3	3
Sarah Collier wid.	Livermans		49	14	1
Thos. Garnett,	Culbreaths		233	15	2

CRAWFORD.

Robert Brooks, R. S.	Hicks		142	12	3
Jesse Adams,	Rays		240	25	1
Jesse Harper,	Moores		68	4	2

Fortunate Drawers	Capts.	Dist.	No.	Dt.	Sec.
Sarah McCants wid.	Hamiltons		42	15	2
Josiah Goodin, soldier,	Moors		76	6	4

DECATUR.

Wm. Hawthorn R. S.	Hawthorns		136	3	5
Isaac P. Brooks,	Manns		37	5	3
Joel Cook,	Hawthorns		151	16	1
Eliz. Kelly w. R. S.	Hawthorns		105	1	1

DEKALB.

Wm. James,	Smiths		177	29	1
Wm. M. Maloney,	Browns		37	8	4
Robert Smith,	Howells		133	10	2
Wm. Gilbert, R. S.	Edwards		266	16	2
Joshua Gay, R. S.	Howells		200	19	2
Henry Patrick,	Smiths		19	12	5
Thos. Wooten, R. S.,	Bowlings		253	23	1
Jesse Cantrell,	Meritts		158	10	5

DOOLY.

Sampson Lampkin, R. S.	Hogans		129	8	4
Nathan Grantham,	Harris		215	8	5
Willis Cason, jr. 582nd dist.			227	12	2

EARLY.

Israel Johnson,	Speers		79	9	1
Sarah Jackson wid.	Hairs		250	5	4

EFFINGHAM.

James Watson, sol.	Waldhaners		71	28	1

ELBERT.

Francis Gaines, R. S.	Dunns		199	13	1
Isham G. Rogers,	Butlers		18	7	3
Britton B. Barron,	Tates		12	3	2
Rich Rumsey,	Carpenters		109	6	2
Wm. B. Sadler,	Dobbs		215	23	1
Rowland Cheek,	Merits		89	2	1
H. Wooton w. R. S.	Deadwilders		270	6	5
Nancy Murry w. R. S.	Hortons		225	3	5
Josiah Goolsby,	Butlers		111	11	1
George Upshaw,	Harmons		60	8	1
Anna King hus. absent,	Do.		25	25	1

EMANUEL.

Jonas B. Spivey,	Arlines		33	6	5
Allen White jr.	Swains		230	9	1

FAYETTE.

Gilbert Gay, sol.	Browns		158	7	1

FRANKLIN.

Braddock Harris,	Sanders		103	11	3
Wm. H. Kitchens,	McDonalds		29	27	1
Fielding T. Willis,	Chandlers		135	21	2
Charles J. Hooper,	Boswells		235	10	3
Joshua Hutcherson,	Walters		238	9	4
John Crips,	Walters		115	15	1
Wm. F. Neal,	Stranges		16	27	1
Baker Ayres,	Walters		104	8	1
Geo. W. Borums orps.	Candells		88	19	2

GLYNN.

James Gowen,	McLeods		142	4	4

GREENE.

John Armor, R. S.	Dawsons		84	6	5
Robert F. Griffin,	Woodhams		105	4	1
Daniel Wagnon, R. S.	Bruces		228	6	3
Wm. Burford,	Southerlands		216	12	1
Lucretia Martin wid.	Dawsons		277	1	4
Rachel Haynes,	Winkfields		77	1	4

(12)

Fortunate Drawers Capts. Dist.	No.Dt.Sec.	Fortunate Drawers Capts. Dist.	No.Dt.Sec.
Alanson E. Veazey, Vincents	235 30 1	Francis M. Potts, *ill.* Robinsons	105 11 5
GWINNETT.		Green Culbertson, Baynes	121 1 1
John Horm. Davis'	85 17 2	Riley Garrett, *ill.* Sparks	165 9 2
Thomas Ballard sr. Robertsons	184 2 3	Wm. Kelbys orps. Baynes	274 1 2
Benj. Baker sol. Caruthers	172 10 2	Benj. Buchanan, Trussels	106 31 1
Daniel P. Clower, Do.	120 20 1	Henry Ivey sr. R. S. Hands	29 23 1
Jonathan Barnett, Greens	122 7 1	Wm. Kindal R. S. Robersons	160 22 2
George Allen, Hunicuts	28 16 2	Stephen D. Crane, Holmes	329 7 1
George Faris, Woodroughs	233 2 2	James Sharp, Dardens	62 12 3
Abner Phillips, Moors	4 22 2	Abel Dinion, Holmes	224 6 2
HANCOCK.		John Doresite, Shropshires	15 8 1
Robert Porters orps. 113th dist.	18 18 1	Zachariah Wise, Dardens	71 9 5
Moore Mapp, 109th dist.	11 5 5	George Clark R. S. Sparks	293 1 2
Ryel Black, 102nd, do.	52 6 5	Thos. Hester sol. Robinsons	241 4 3
Zachariah Brantley, 117th dist.	93 7 1	Cullen Lockett, Shropshires	268 2 3
James J. Butts, 101st dist.	133 1 1	James Osborne, Keys	195 12 3
Sarah Vickers wid. 118th dist.	75 9 5	Barnes Pittman, Robersons	20 5 3
Jeffrey Barksdale R.S. 113th dis.	110 5 5	Nathan Davis, Barnes	129 24 2
Greenville Simmons, 101st dist.	185 15 1	Jane Blackwood w. R.S. Barnetts	180 17 2
Daniel Dennies orps. 112th dist.	3 29 1	**JEFFERSON.**	
HENRY.		Willis Walker, Elliotts	19 5 3
Wiley Bradford, Wards	20 9 5	Jacob Farmer fa absent Ross'	192 5 3
William Adams, Gordens	46 8 2	James McJones, Ross'	26 4 4
Henry Young, McVickers	124 24 1	**JONES.**	
Thos. D. Johnson, Grays	275 10 2	Jourdain Pate, Spinks	209 9 2
Samuel M. Wilkins, Morgans	68 17 1	Nancy Slatter wid. Woods	124 9 3
Peter Lewis, R. S. Grays	172 9 3	Elizabeth Driver wid. Mullins	3 14 1
Sarah Heard wid. Morgans	80 12 1	John Herrington, Gibsons	164 14 1
John Todd, Bryans	140 1 1	John J. Slatter, Woods	117 19 2
Henry Night, Harris'	94 3 1	Henry C. Harris, Stewarts	223 20 1
HABERSHAM.		Elias Jordan, Popes	244 17 2
Clement Dooly, minor, Suttons	54 10 1	John Hasty, Breedloves	234 12 3
John Blythe, Tates	80 9 2	Agsa Mizell, Davis	124 15 5
Wm. Bolinger, sr. Martins	146 22 2	Hiram McClusky, Newbys	178 11 3
Abraham Tate, Tates	38 15 2	Benj. Gachet, Breedloves	66 14 1
Joseph Jackson, Kenzies	197 16 2	Griffin Morgans orps. Newbys	236 3 3
Levi Male, Bryans	160 30 1	**LAURENS.**	
Wm. S. Meeks, Bakers	327 1 4	Samuel Perkins minors, Deans	193 26 1
Benj. Crumley, Fains	190 28 1	Job E. W. Smith, Plummers	35 17 1
Humphrey Lindsey, Vickrys	104 4 2	Wm. Brantley, Mizells	169 27 1
Daniel A. Bruce, Suttons	216 2 2	Jehu Smith, Deans	119 3 1
John Dyches, R. S. Langstons	112 7 2	John Tucker, sol. Newmans	34 22 2
HALL.		Walleton Oliver, Whiteheads	236 26 1
Simeon Putman, Garrards	283 10 2	Richard Ricks, Powers	159 12 5
Micajah Landrum, Roberts	264 4 1	Thos. Pullin, jr. Hodges	135 8 5
Joseph W. Cane, Floyds	176 8 5	Micajah Varsar, R. S .Spiveys	195 8 1
Wm. Thurmon, Harrisons	233 5 3	Thomas G. Bell, Plummers	125 3 2
James Morgan, Garrards	47 23 1	**LIBERTY.**	
John Byrd, jr. Walkers	59 13 5	Elizabeth Phelps wid. 15th dist.	152 10 3
HOUSTON.		John Moody 17th dist.	249 4 3
Tekal Taylor, Calhouns	217 3 5	Richard F. Baker, 15th dist.	279 20 2
Lewis Hunt, Hancocks	107 21 1	Newman Bradley, 17th dis.	20 11 1
IRWIN.		Anney C. Surrency & John	
James Rutherford R. S. Dixons	195 10 5	W. Surrency, orps. 16th dist.	197 19 2
JACKSON.		**LINCOLN.**	
Joseph J. Pollard, Storys	170 9 2	Henry Jennings, Leverettes	80 4 2
Abraham Williams sr. R.S. Rogers	150 9 2	John York, R. S. Prathers	36 27 1
Ira L. Martin, Venables	47 30 1	Garland Bostick, Prathers	31 24 1
Nathan C. Williamson, Lindseys	109 18 2	**LOWNDES.**	
JASPER.			
George Moores orps. Owens	196 19 2	Wm. P. Roberts, 11th dist.	216 3 4

(13)

MADISON.
Fortunate Drawers Capts. Dist.	No.	Dt.	Sec.
Richmond Mason, Caldwells	172	8	3
Peter Smiths orps. Do.	236	3	2
Isaac Simmons jr. Hannas	72	1	4
Nathaniel Herelson, Hannahs	192	4	1
Sus. A. Depriest, ill. Culbertsons	188	11	5

M'INTOSH.
John Hutson, Demeries	116	3	2

MONROE.
Tilmon Niblet, R.S., Woodwards	187	11	5
Dolphin Floyd, do	195	20	2
Benjamin Chapman, sol., Millers	84	2	3
George Bennett, Houses	84	17	1
Jonathan Davis' orphans, Turners	56	6	2
Lemuel Parker, Greshams	254	18	2
Leroy H. Tomlinson, do	46	4	3
Hugh Lockett, Browns	58	3	4
Abner Bankston, R.S., Greshams	164	9	1
Jonathan Davis' orphans, Turners	270	15	1

MORGAN.
Agnes Stewart, widow, Jennings	52	31	1
Thomas Long, soldier, Watsons	172	8	1
Marg. Bledsoe, w. R. S. Christians	18	4	5
Samuel Tindale, sen., Sparks	206	12	1
Levi Gatlin, Boswells	214	9	2
John Applewhite, Canifaxs	24	6	4
James Bonner, do	223	15	1
George W. Nelson, Griggs	126	4	4
Hillery Stocks, Whatleys	152	20	1
John Liggon, soldier, Griggs	335	7	1
Benjamin W. Milligan, Boswells	205	20	1
Lewis Wheeless, sr., Shearmans	190	21	1
William Wilson, Christians	190	28	1
John S. Means, Gains	165	3	1

MONTGOMERY.
Neal McRea, McMillons	202	7	3
Granberry Dawster, Penningtons	145	4	4

NEWTON.
James Jones, Allreds	96	1	2
John Downs orps. Pullins	208	3	1
Isaac Hamby, Snows	156	8	3
Elizabeth Whatley, wid. Webbs	286	16	2
Thomas Hudson, sol., Orrs	173	23	2
Thomas Wellborn, Trammells	60	13	5
Jane Roberson, R. S., Orrs	12	1	3
James J. Hanson, Moss's	62	23	2
John N. Williamson, Pullins	78	8	3
Lewis Zachry, S. Zachrys	353	28	1
William Swan, R. S., do	42	24	1
John Dawster, Penningtons	148	4	4

OGLETHORPE.
James B. Patman, soldier, Billups	139	31	1
John Gresham, jun. Dix's	5	13	1
Hezekiah Martin, Seals	7	32	1
Mary Sorrow, w. R. S. Hardmans	255	11	3
George Hixon, Rhodes	69	8	3
Alfred G. Perry, Bells	98	20	1
Stephen Arnold, jun., Arnolds	187	4	4

PIKE.
Thomas B. Daniel, Daniels	199	27	1

PULASKI.
Reamond B. Mason's orps. Kellums	17	13	1

PUTNAM.
Fortunate Drawers Capts. Dist.	No.	Dt.	Sec.
Thomas Stubbs, Kendricks	45	21	1
James Singleton, Bledsoes	66	8	4
Lunsford Heath, Barnetts	165	3	3
Patrick Dickey, R. S., Allums	208	1	2
James D. Bagley, Barnetts	25	12	1
James Z. Dismukes, Dismukes	101	3	5
Eliz. Lunsford, w. R. S. Stinsons	151	3	1
Samuel Cooper, R. S., Choices	5	8	2

RABUN.
Edmond Beloot, Godfreys	2	18	1
Josiah H. Carter, Mercers	116	30	1

RICHMOND.
Christopher Hickle, Wilcoxs	171	5	4
George Dunbar, Treadwells	77	6	4
Edmond Murphy, R. S., Kellys	102	24	1
Reading Wood, Huntingtons	7	2	3
William Inglett, soldier, James	127	11	2
Joshua Pharoah, R. S., do	231	9	1

SCRIVEN.
John Waters, Humphreys	37	10	2
John W. Hodges, do	270	1	4
Maryann Zeagler, ill. Poythress	101	2	2

TATTNALL.
John Sharp, R. S., McCalls	216	10	1

TELFAIR.
Labun Baines, Wilkersons	265	2	3
William Mixon, Barentines	91	7	3
Kaziah Davis, illegitimate, do	150	4	5

TALIAFERRO.
Nathaniel Acree, Moors	35	32	1
William Ogletree, Cobbs	270	4	2

TWIGGS.
S. Coffield, w. R. S. Blackshears	52	22	1
Jonathan Dowden, Solomons	53	18	1
John Lane, Graggs	109	5	4
Samuel Streetman, Pearsons	122	26	1
Jacob Griffess, do	164	19	2

UPSON.
Daniel Walker, Coopers	60	6	3
Ezekiel Wall, soldier, Harralds	166	20	2
John F. Myrick, Hattoxs	150	14	2
Frances Evans, widow, 589th	116	15	2
William Moody, Myricks	65	11	5

WALTON.
James Baird, 418th	231	9	2
James H. Holt, 559th	146	8	3
Simon Holt, soldier, 559th	327	3	4
Wilie Nelson, 249th	263	3	3
Benjamin Strange, 503d	40	10	2
John Baxley, Baxleys	406	2	2
Polly Rasberry, widow, Davis	5	10	5
Batly H. Mitchell, Rays	70	18	1

WILKINSON.
Benjamin Hall, Smiths	159	12	3
Edward Hickman, soldier, Shows	17	17	2
Alpheus Martin, ill., Fairchilds	234	5	3
Elizabeth Hawthorn, wid Smiths	23	15	2
James Justice's orphans, Fairchilds	18	23	2

WILKES.
David Evans, Rices	249	3	2
Joshua Morgan, Moors	166	6	5
Christopher Orr, Amasons	130	27	3

Fortunate Drawers	Capts. Dist.	No.	Dt.	Sec.
Clayburn Tuck, Reeves		86	16	1
Earley Jackson, Amasons		104	27	1
William Thornton, Hopkins		235	24	1
Andrew B. Jones, Greens		106	15	5
David Ogletree's orphans, Rices		195	18	2
Benj. Branham's orps., Charltons		12	15	5
Sarah Colly, widow,	do	106	6	3
Joseph Harley, R. S.	do	83	6	4
Willis Jarrell, Amasons		92	4	4
Henry Pitmon, Rices		94	23	2
Micajah A. Lane, soldier, Chunns		88	11	2
Jane Macklin, w. R.S., Hamocks		103	8	4
WASHINGTON.				
Joseph Rhodes, Tysons		75	16	1
Job Smith, .	do	51	15	2
William Cook, Jordans		200	1	2
John M. Oliver, Gilberts		322	7	5
Jesse Croom's heirs, O'Quinns		63	4	4
Elizabeth Odam, wid., Wimberlys		14	18	1
WARRENS.				
William Jackson's orps., Hills		238	11	1
James Moon, Adkins		219	26	1
Mark Hill, Latimers		105	11	1
Mary Harbuck, wid. R. S., Hales		40	8	2
Aisley Jackson, widow Jones		80	21	2
William Davis, R. S., Parhams		58	4	4
6TH DAY'S DRAWING—March 13				
APPLINIG.				
Enoch Halls orphs. Collins		60	23	1
BALDWIN.				
Sarah H. Jones orph. Buchanans		101	6	4
Wm. Christian, Lesters		101	1	5
Adam Tapley, R. S. Bivins		1	7	1
Isaac W. Burton, Bivins		68	19	2
BIBB.				
Harman Willis, Pickards		1	5	3
John M. Fuller, Bates		180	2	3
James Curley, Do.		29	3	4
Elizabeth Smith wid. Pickards		116	1	1
Charles L. Holmes, Flanders		114	2	4
Wm. Owens, Bates		120	12	1
Patrick Broom, Pickards		182	2	2
Moses Pettis, R. S. Carrs		206	11	3
BULLOCH.				
General Mikell, McCalls		131	6	4
BURKE.				
Jonas Skinner jr. Segars		160	12	1
Elizabeth Hall, ill., Dukes		168	8	5
Wm. Conner, McRays		248	8	1
John G. Baduly, Baleys		252	5	2
Eliz. Mills w. R. S. Thompsons		179	5	3
Charles Sapp, Thompsons		246	7	1
CAMDEN.				
Samuel H. Thomas, Coxs		35	6	2
Sillicea M. Atkinson orp. Wards		49	18	1
Abraham Mott, Coxs		227	16	1
CHATHAM.				
John D. Boilings orps. Williams		144	25	1
John Phillips, Tenbrooks		51	13	2
Rebecca Holmes orp. Haydens		36	6	4

Fortunate Drawers	Capts. Dist.	No.	Dt.	Sec.
Pierce Howard, Haydens		219	6	3
John Fryers orps. Gaddys		176	12	3
Joseph H. Burrough, Haydens		55	12	1
Thomas West		47	6	3
John J. Forsyth, Haydens		4	1	5
CLARK.				
John M. Edwards sol. Andersons		8	2	4
Samuel Collins, Wrights		249	16	1
John Reid, Herndons		36	11	1
Robert H. Patterson, Davis		126	22	1
Jesse Mobbs, R. S. Wrights		261	21	2
Alexander Holmes, Ransoms		125	12	1
Wm. B. Moreland, Lumpkins		20	4	4
Francis M. McKee, McCrees		61	9	5
John Briscoes orps. Andersons		178	6	5
Eleel Melton, soldier, Dickens		112	1	14
COLUMBIA.				
Ralph Briscoe, Baileys		77	5	4
George W. O'Nail, Coles		64	11	1
Ezekiel Reed, do.		84	14	2
Martha S. Huchinson, w. Bealls		101	1	4
James & Wm. Hogan, ill. Dranes		192	11	2
David Harris, Carrolls		267	7	5
Nancy Brown, hus. absent, Coles		207	11	3
CRAWFORD.				
Abel Rooks, Wilsons		135	11	5
DECATUR.				
Needham Norris, Hawthorns		63	12	2
Jacob Miller, Douglass		147	2	4
DEKALB.				
Parham P. Mabry, sol. Andersons		101	12	2
Seaborn J. Kidd, Howells		125	8	1
John Cook, R. S. Conns		135	24	1
John Swinney, Stephens		78	8	5
Obadiah Sisson, Conns		245	9	2
Mary Davis wid. R. S. Browns		172	12	2
John Dabbs, R. S. Hays		188	20	1
James Hunt, Stephens		172	11	1
Wm. A. McKay, Meritts		244	11	3
DOOLY.				
Nixon Lester orp. 582nd dist.		247	2	4
Wm. Slade, Mannings		254	22	1
EARLY.				
James Sheffield, Speers		40	31	1
John Griffiths orphans, Wilsons		58	16	2
ELBERT.				
El. Wiley Jones, Meritts		37	21	1
Joseph A. Lesueur, Boltons		74	20	2
John H. Shackelford, Hortons		253	22	-
George W. Heard, sol. Boltons		38	8	4
EMANUEL				
Wm. Nuton, McGars		27	8	5
Hugh Davis, Moores		102	1	5
Wm. Purvis, soldier, 49th dist.		5	11	5
FAYETTE.				
John R. Greene, soldier, Morgans		63	9	3
Anna Ryle, widow, Craigs		132	10	5
Matilda Barnes, ill. Whartons		101	11	5
FRANKLIN.				
Martha M.&W.J.Beall, ill. Jones		100	4	3
John S. Clements, McDonalds		152	29	1

Fortunate Drawers Capts. Dist.	No.	Dt.	Sec.	Fortunate Drawers Capts. Dist.	No.	Dt.	Sec.
Dor. & Sultana Ayres,*ill.*,Walters	121	19	2	Thomas Davis, Rogers	56	1	4
Jonathan Presley, Cokers	49	1	4	John A. Long, Storys	20	9	3
Wm. Coyler, Tabors	249	11	1	JASPER.			
Ann P. Chapplear, *idiot*, Walters	217	5	5	Samuel Strahan, Dardens	30	7	2
Ambrose Chandler, Bennetts	84	25	1	David Duck, Trussells	108	9	2
Archibald Cook, R. S., Boswells	88	27	1	James C. Henderson, Wilders	186	17	2
GLYNN.				Wm. M. Sample, Butts	121	14	5
James Burney, McLeods	183	11	3	Winnifred Watson w. Camerons	146	8	1
GREENE.				Henry Ivey jr. Hands	128	7	4
Thos. Greenwoods orps. Dawsons	50	10	2	Thomas Jenkins, Sparks	255	3	2
Littleberry Broach, Southerlands	212	15	2	Robert Sanson, Butts	7	5	5
Ezekiel S. Stanley, Winkfields	52	23	1	JEFFERSON.			
John Thompson, Southerlands	216	24	1	Henry Lindseys orps. Marshalls	322	15	1
George A. Dawson, Dawsons	231	21	1	George Eubanks jr. do.	200	11	2
Samuel Hubbards orps. do	87	11	3	John Beasley, Beaties	187	9	2
GWINNETT.				Elizabeth Fort wid. Elliotts	18	5	2
Mary C. Butler, widow, Finches	142	12	1	JONES.			
Martha Moore, widow, Greens	26	15	5	John Porter, soldier, Gibsons	250	10	3
Wm. Nesbitt, soldier, Whortens	35	9	4	Readin Bourden, Robertsons	131	26	1
Thos. Cox, R. S. Bakers	261	9	5	Wm. Poe, Dosters	152	12	3
Thomas Rice, Wallis	110	1	1	James George, Bowens	163	1	1
Polly Martin, *ill.* Moores	76	9	1	Benj. H. Reynolds, Breedloves	112	22	2
Enoch Benson, R. S. Finches	119	33	1	Sterling Lanier, Davis	112	10	3
Wm. Woodall, Shippys	198	1	2	Moses Trawick, Hammacks	24	17	2
James Wells, Caruthers	199	4	2	Benjamin Herndon, Mullins	221	9	2
Sarah Henley, w. R. S. Wallis	198	11	3	Clayton Pippin, Dosters	337	7	1
HANCOCK.				Lovic P. Jordan, Hammacks	40	6	3
John Ellet, 111th district	72	14	1	LAURENS.			
Ellison Worthy, 113th district	94	26	1	Sus. Young w. R. S. Whiteheads	46	11	1
Jacob Hampton, 117th district	56	9	5	William Walbolt, Thomas'	70	24	1
G. Bledsoes, orps. 106th dist.	177	6	3	James Hawood, Newmans	30	17	2
Fred. Freemans orps. 103rd dist.	99	17	2	Thos. Pullin sr. R. S. Plummers	230	17	2
James Hilsman, 107th dist.	65	9	2	Ira Stanley, Deans	52	11	3
John Holloman, 111th district	255	22	2	LIBERTY.			
HENRY.				John Benton, R. S. 16th district	96	27	1
Ephraim W. Mobley, Wards	41	10	1	George Harnage, do.	133	23	1
Alonzo P. Morris, do.	61	1	5	Andrew F. Fraser, sol. 17th dist.	184	12	1
Turner Evans, Grays	144	12	2	LINCOLN.			
Benj. Sanding, Gosdens	15	7	3	Milton E. Aycock, Wiggintons	189	22	1
HABERSHAM.				MADISON.			
John L. Richardson, Fanes	44	15	2	Thos. Lawrence, Christians	74	12	3
Enoch Williams, Vickarys	201	3	4	Daniel Taylor jr. Bones	145	33	1
Wm. Lee, Cross'	187	3	4	R. S. & L. Smith, illegit's, Hannas	12	9	2
Jerh. Cleveland R. S. Langstons	108	3	4	McINTOSH.			
John Downs, Suttons	82	2	4	Daniel Wing, Terrells	273	6	5
Amos Hollingsworth, Suttons	23	21	2	Archibald J. Baggs, McIntoshs	102	6	3
John McMillon sr. Tates	91	5	2	Eliza U. Wing wid. Terrells	164	10	2
HALL.				MONROE.			
Robert Wilson, Wilsons	174	15	1	Wm. Pettis, Millers	15	2	4
John Harris R. S. Dorseys	36	12	3	Val Horseley R. S. Pattersons	90	29	1
Isaac N. Fleming, Roberts	166	4	4	MORGAN.			
Berry Watkins, Alreds	161	2	2	Asa McSwain, Watsons	38	24	2
HOUSTON.				Thos. Duke sr. R. S. Canifaxs	204	4	2
Benj. Bateman, Prices	122	9	5	Wm. P. Melson, Harweils	33	14	1
Lawson J. Keener, Calhouns	18	8	2	John D. Timmons, Beasleys	228	23	2
Loam Brown, Wimberlys	180	19	2	MONTGOMERY.			
IRWIN.				Hartwell R. Mitchell, Popes	93	2	4
Thomas Young, Underwoods	31	8	5	Farquahard McRae, Popes	103	17	1
JACKSON.				NEWTON.			
Michael Wright, Storys	194	20	2	Bennett K. Stansell, Snows	82	4	5
Ann Smith wid. R. S. Duprees	231	20	1	James Spears, Pullens	71	12	5
				John Kelleys orphans, Orrs	253	5	4
				Josiah M. Freeman, Hays	207	23	1

(16)

Fortunate Drawers Capts. Dist.	No.	Dt.	Sec.
Ransom Reeves, Snows	169	6	3
David S. Simms, Newnans	87	6	3
James Parker, Penningtons	152	25	1
Charles Miller, Orrs	54	4	2
OGLETHORPE.			
John W. Moody, soldier, Bells	49	9	4
Thomas Meadows, 235th district	168	10	1
Hiram Wilson, Rousseaus	z250	1	2
John Mealor, Mays	256	24	1
John Birdsong sr. R. S. Rousseaus	265	19	2
Wm. Booth, Rhodes	22	6	5
PIKE.			
Susan Aslin, widow, Mays	175	9	3
Wm. O. Wagon, soldier, Daniels	205	12	3
Lucy R. Hogg, Hicks	165	13	1
PULASKI.			
Frederick Mills, Sparrows	110	24	2
John Caruthers, do.	7	10	1
Sarah Tazhery, Barnetts	21	15	5
PUTNAM.			
Thomas Black, Bledsoes	120	9	1
Elisha Grier, soldier, Slaughters	79	12	3
Joseph Kimball, Clarks	79	25	1
Robert A. Patrick, Mezes	150	1	3
John Morton, Mezes	78	1	1
RABUN.			
William Kelly, Becks	118	15	1
Thomas Houston, Milliagans	59	14	5
Humphrey Gains, Godfreys	48	3	3
John Porks, Mercers	223	14	1
RICHMOND.			
Emily Neighbors, orphan	200	32	1
Lewis Bryant, Blacks	136	1	2
Mary, Dan & J. Lanier ors. Blacks	58	2	1
Leon Brux, Huntingtons	55	15	2
Walton Knight, Treadwells	49	9	5
Thos. Martin, Blacks	222	28	1
Green B. Marshall, Wilcoxs	111	11	3
SCRIVEN.			
Littleton H. Lovett, Poythess	186	2	4
Eliz. Nicholson w. R. S. Reaves	95	8	1
Stephen Allens orps. Lovetts	22	32	1
TATTNALL.			
Thomas F. Anderson, Dees	415	20	2
Wm. Branchs orps. do.	123	22	2
Thos. Starling, Conners	169	9	1
TALIAFERRO.			
E.B.&D.M.Andrews, orps.Alfords	200	5	3
TWIGGS,			
Rhoda Burten w. R.S. Wimberlys	237	26	1
Joseph Will, soldier, Blackshears	76	24	1
Frederick Outlaws orps. Graggs	148	20	1
Crumptons orphans, Solomons	176	18	2
John Dunn, Graggs	33	11	5
Thos. Westbrooks orps. Holidays	29	7	5
Wm. Allens orphans, do.	86	12	5
Orrin H. Dapree, do.	144	15	5
Benj. F. Willis, Pearsons	245	17	2
Joseph Collins, R. S. Bosticks	247	9	2
UPSON.			
Wm. Marshall, Myricks	195	7	3
Williamson Terrell, sol. Hattocks	115	31	1

Fortunate Drawers Capts. Dist.	No.	Dt.	Sec.
Reddick Acock, sol. 503rd dist.	7	7	3
John Edgar, Rays	17	8	4
John Rusk, 559th district	211	25	1
WILKINSON.			
Samuel Mathews, Mathews	305	7	5
Nathaniel Harper, Barrys	194	16	2
John Gilberts orphans, Halls	146	21	1
David Mizell, Halls	220	6	5
John Hatcher, Mathews	74	18	1
Enoch Garrett, Currys	274	1	4
Robert White, Smiths	112	23	2
John Adams, Shows	243	23	2
WILKES.			
Benj. Powell, McDermorts	179	18	1
Leonard Wood, idiot, Lukers	117	1	3
WARREN.			
Wylie Hight, Parhams	180	28	1
Thomas Norris, Kinseys	216	11	1
Sterling J. Pate, soldier, Stewarts	32	22	2
Wingfield Cosby, Parhams	19	16	1
John Kent, father absent, Downs	129	12	5
Thos. Grizzles orps. Brinkleys	248	18	1
Priscilla Holliday, ill. Sanders	195	16	1
WASHINGTON.			
Samuel Whitaker, sol. Gilberts	166	30	1
Alcey Vincen, O'Quinns	4	18	1
James Blairs orphans, Worthens	303	22	1
Charity White, ill. Whitefields	76	17	2

7TH DAY'S DRAWING—14th March.

	No.	Dt.	Sec.
BALDWIN.			
S. B. Clark, w. R. S. Buchanans	149	2	3
William McDaniel, Lesters	12	15	1
William Harriss, Jones	6	16	5
William Triplett, Buchanans	218	19	2
Fanny Lewis, widow, Pitts	31	28	1
Elisha Wood's orps. Buchanans	95	33	1
Richard A. Batson, Bivins	87	2	4
BIBB.			
Leroy Lloyd, Lloyds	109	3	3
Elbert Calhoun, soldier, Beards	148	1	3
James T. Wafford, Bates	135	9	1
Stephen Atkinson, Pickards	50	1	4
James Dorman, Beards	16	8	5
James Woods, Rutlands	170	4	1
BULLOCH.			
John Royalston, R. S., Lockharts	267	22	1
David Snell's orphans, do.	86	14	2
BURKE.			
James Bell, Wests	420	20	2
Rebecca Ivins, widow, Segars	110	8	3
Samuel T. Oats, Forths	107	5	4
Richard Johnson, orp. Lynchs	16	5	1
Bersheba Jenkins orp. Bayleys	52	17	2
William Nichols's orps. McKays	106	6	1
Henry Turner, R. S. do.	240	32	1
Charles W. Waters, Gordons	10	2	2
Archibald Bonnell, Dugas	57	20	1
BUTTS.			
Jas. Bentley, soldier, Hendricks	137	23	1

LAND LOTTERY REGISTER—No. 3
[RECORDER OFFICE—PUBLISHED BY GRANTLAND & ORME—PRICE $3.]

NOTE.—Section 1 is Lee County—2 Muscogee—3 Troup—4 Coweta—5 Carroll.

7TH DAY'S DRAWING—Continued.

Fortunate Drawers Capts. Dist.	No.	Dt.	Sec.

BUTTS.
John V. Dunn, soldier, Thaxtons 10 12 3

CAMDEN.
Amos Latham, Beckwiths 67 2 2
John Gorman, Baileys 131 15 5
William W. Seals, sol., Wards 46 24 1
John Boog's orphans, do. 107 11 1
Wm. G. Tompkins, Beckwiths 209 17 2

CHATHAM.
Joseph Kingsley 136 7 3
Seaborn Harris, Williams 70 10 2
Nathaniel H. Nowlan, Geredons 7 29 1
Benedict Bourquin, Gaddys 163 10 3

CLARK.
Joseph B. Baldwin, Gahagans 289 14 1
Edward Wills's orps. Espys 25 7 4
Jemima Puryear, wid. Frosts 74 28 1
Noah Prince, do. 184 10 5
Reuben Ransom, R. S., Ransoms 6 15 2
David Patterson, soldier, Espys 89 12 3

COLUMBIA.
James Langston, Magruders 44 21 2
Seaborn Harrissons orps. Bealls 156 29 1
Susan. Megahee, w. R. S., Dranes 26 10 3

CRAWFORD.
Henry King, Rhodes 43 5 3
Reuben E. Adams, Tillers 106 6 4

DECATUR.
Bridg. Collins w.R.S. Hawthorns 135 21 1

DEKALB.
Thomas Smith, Bakers 203 21 2
John Bowling, Bowlings 258 7 1
John W. Gober, soldier, Hays's 90 7 2
Wm. Barnett, Meritts 189 8 5
Thos. Walley, Howells 80 6 4
Reuben Holcomb, Bakers 230 20 1
Absalom Gray, soldier, do. 19 18 1
Nancy Adams, illegit. Stephens 161 15 1
Levi Betterton, do. 82 27 1
Gardner Carters orphans, Hays 93 10 1
Ephraim Carson, Howells 7 25 1
Philip Woodall, Conns 29 9 1
John N. Ballinger, Meritts 108 11 2
Mary Howard, wid. Bowlings 187 18 2

DOOLY.
Isaac Foreman, Andersons 132 9 2

EARLY.
John Gilley, Wilsons 362 28 1
Alford West, Grimslys 165 5 3
Alex. Hayes, Hairs 183 3 3

EFFINGHAM.
Rosetta Cope, wid. Waldhaners 7 3 4

ELBERT.
Wm. Taylor jr. Dunns 132 17 1
Edward Brown, R. S. Boltons 251 22 2
Richmond Rich, Tates 164 6 2

EMANUEL.

Fortunate Drawers Capts. Dist.	No.	Dt.	Sec.

Edward S. Thornton, Moores 112 6 4

FAYETTE.
Wiley Davis, Wests 84 10 2
Patrick Duvaine, Roziers 120 11 3
Martha Vaughn, widow, Wests 78 18 2
George P. Parker, sol. Browns 246 5 4
Henrietta Clayton, Roziers 6 10 5
Benj. S. Zachry, sol. Whortons 255 2 2
Burrell Ware, Craigs 174 8 3
Hiram F. Morgan, Roziers 234 13 2
Jorden Gay, Whortons 88 3 5
Wm. Clements, Roziers 132 14 5
John M. White, R. S. Whortons 237 8 5
Lemuel Green, soldier, Morgans 106 22 2

FRANKLIN.
John Williams, Stranges 248 7 1
Robert G. Little, Jones 130 15 5
Robert Carter, McDonalds 235 20 2
Rob. Laughridge, sol., Chandlers 154 24 2
John Morgan, McDonalds 219 6 5
Ann Purcell, deaf & dumb, Tabors 256 6 5
Thos. Hollingsworth, Candells 114 9 2
Francis A. Tabor, Tabors 62 18 2
William Smith, illegit. Candells 64 8 2
John Robertson, Sanders 202 15 1

GLYNN.
Mary Boyd, widow, EcLeods 18 10 3

GREEN.
Stephen Gatlin, Rankins 361 28 1
John Jorden, Vincents 105 23 1
John Wallaces orps. Astins 47 27 1
Thomas Hicks, Greenes 108 17 2
Jane Davis, wid. R. S. Bruces 154 2 1
Isham Tooke, Greenes 194 17 2
Henry Sandford, jr. Dawsons 87 8 4

GWINNETT.
George Hopkins, Shippys 93 8 1
William Kilgore, Rollins 187 3 3
James Wardlaw, sol. Hunnicuts 66 31 1
Martha Culpepper, wid. Wallis 89 11 5
Thos. Baty, jr. Hunnicuts 151 12 3
Wm. Pinder, Moors 124 3 1
Sarah Powell, wid. Hunnicuts 129 7 2
George James, R. S. Greens 185 10 2
M.A.&N.C.Price, orps. Bennetts 301 1 2
Marshal, Wiley, John, Nancy &
   Caroline Ferguson, Caruthers 153 2 3
Stephen Kemp, Moors 58 2 3

HABERSHAM.
Dozier Sutton, Cross 155 7 5
John Hefner, Fains 97 5 5
Jane Brown, widow, Suttons 31 13 5
Amos Ladd, 38 11 2
Rainey Chastain, Kenzies 156 6 2
Thos. Helton, minor, do. 183 8 1
Richard Corbin, Tates 134 14 5
John Stephens, Bryans 206 5 5
Isaac Heath, Fains 174 14 2

(18)

HALL.

Fortunate Drawers Capts. Dist.	No.	Dt.	Sec.
John Jones, Ingrahams	130	3	3
Alex. Boyd, Hendricks	61	12	2
Oburn Buffington sr. Hardages	19	8	2
William Blake, soldier, Smiths	47	2	1
John Ingram, R. S. Roberts	14	13	2
John E. Rives, Hardens	140	30	1
Fanny Bennett, father ab. Walkers	140	12	2
John Savage, Harrisons	106	16	2
Mahala A. Davis, illegit., Floyds	48	6	5
John Evans, Dorseys	124	14	1
Isaac A. Lockhart, Smiths	59	22	2

HANCOCK.

John S. L'Acee, 108th dist.	217	6	3
Isaiah Wafford, 114th district	386	20	2
Matthew Humphrey, 112th dist.	100	18	2
John Roe, jr. Mahons	353	20	2
Jesse Stowers, 102nd district	186	10	2
Robert B. Simms, 107th district	170	16	2
John Brimberry, 106th district	178	2	2

HENRY.

Orrin Jones, Gosdens	111	9	3
Zachariah Deason, R. S. Harris's	85	4	5
William Pressley, do.	78	7	1
Reuben Kelly, Shaws	98	6	1
Ephraim Strickland, Risons	266	3	4
Ransom Catchens, soldier, Wards	322	3	4

HOUSTON.

John Fredricks, orps. Hancocks	172	5	3
John Campbell, soldier, Smiths	41	29	1
Wm. Haddock, Batemans	156	5	4

IRWIN.

James Magee, McCalls	25	10	1
Thos. Young, Underwoods	142	16	1
John S. Whitfield, 5th district	105	5	2

JACKSON.

John Kenly, Winns	30	3	2
Joseph Boyce, Landrums	171	2	4
Jesse Franklin, do.	213	17	1
Malessa Griggs, illegit. Bowens	128	3	1
Williams Burnes, jr. sol. Duncans	148	31	1
Warren Morris, sol. Watersons	108	14	2
Henry Walston, jr. Bowens	96	11	3
David Sailors, soldier, Staplers	312	7	1
John Kenly, Winns	164	2	1
John Stovall, soldier, Rogers	59	17	1

JASPER.

James Cowan, Shropshires	377	20	2
Elizabeth Brown, widow, Baynes	210	13	2
Solomon Gross, Wilsons	32	16	2
David Peavey, Owens	229	8	3
John Cargiles orphans, Holmes	64	31	1
John Dubois, Holmes	136	10	1
James Brannon, Butts	137	1	4
John Webb, R. S. Parkers	84	21	2
Caleb C. Dibble, Holmes	386	7	1
Wm. Whitfield, Baynes	92	23	2
George Vance, Shropshires	70	14	1
Lindsey Deadwilder, Barnetts	139	12	1
John W. Steward, illegit. Owens	218	12	2
Nathan Johnston, Owens	76	2	1
David Adams, R. S. Sparks	5	14	2

JEFFERSON.

Fortunate Drawers Capts. Dist.	No.	Dt.	Sec.
Wm. Jones, orphans, Ross	52	2	3
Sarah S. Smith orp. do.	131	16	2
Jefferson Williams, Cunninghams	164	23	2
Wm. Rountree, Marshalls	65	4	2
Hardy Haral, R. S. Cunninghams	118	7	4
John Milton, Jones	218	23	2
John H. Newton, Waldens	148	17	1

JONES.

Jonathan Poe, Dosters	148	5	2
John B. Dame, Newbys	227	6	1
Warren Herrin, Robertsons	61	3	1
Thos. Brown, Gibsons	15	1	3
James Bardin, Bowens	57	13	5
Joseph Lester, Breedloves	268	23	2
Wilie Barlows orphans, Newbys	255	20	1
Delina Farlie, widow, Hendersons	100	10	2
Nelson C. White, Gibsons	20	4	2
J. D. Weathers, sol. Sullivans	242	19	2
Ann M. Carroll, widow, Bowens	208	5	5
Reason Ethridge, Robertsons	9	6	5
Robert Harrison, Taylors	185	14	1
James Hill, Breedloves	224	3	3
John Arent, soldier, Burks	31	11	2

LAURENS.

John H. Mathews, Davis	120	22	2
Jesse Prices orphans, Powers	40	7	5

LINCOLN.

Elbert Phipps, Lonorgans	363	14	1
Samuel Frasers minors, Frasers	326	7	1
Joseph Phipps minors, Lonorgans	212	18	2
Adam Harnesberger, Frasers	226	11	5
Maddox Wall, Graves	271	3	3

MADISON.

Stephen B. Stephens, Caldwells	83	27	1
James N. Sorrells, Adairs	241	2	2
John B. Adair, do	295	1	2

McINTOSH.

Mary A. Zilpha Ennis orp. McCranies	240	6	3
John Morrison Caulder, Demeries	52	14	1
Joseph Allen, Terrells	186	11	1

MONROE.

John Phinisee, R. S., Houses	139	20	2
John Chappell, R. S., Pattersons	112	15	5
Joseph Grant, Greshams	232	3	1
John C. Anderson, do.	22	4	5
Thomas Hathorn, R. S., Pattersons	16	3	2
Adam Alexander, Wrights	30	29	1
Charles L. Kennon, soldier, Millers	42	18	2
Moses Faver, Millers	16	1	2
Samuel Wilkinson, Johnsons	68	2	2
Mannin Harp, R. S., Millers	279	14	1

MORGAN.

Aaron S. Overton, Brooks	132	20	1
John H. Ponder, soldier, Watsons	313	8	1
Pleasant A. Formby, Adairs	218	3	4
Peter Perry's orphans, Shearmans	228	22	2
James Russell's orphans, Sparks	217	15	1
Leavin Smith, R. S., Harwells	256	30	1
Simon Reeves's orphans, Walkers	203	4	2
Isham Whitechar, Jennings	223	1	2
James Gorden, Watsons	153	7	3
Robert Pearman, soldier, Brooks	226	13	2
Eliza Heard, illegitimate, Watsons	36	8	4
Joseph Morrow, Boswells	18	29	1
William Hayes, Shearmans	33	22	1
Duncan McCowan's orps., Beasleys	142	15	1

(19)

Fortunate Drawers	Capts.	Dist.	No.	Dt.	Sec.
James McGhen,	Dawsons		7	8	2
Malekiah Culpepper, R. S.,	Adairs	79	5	4
NEWTON.					
David Maquoirk, soldier,	Newnans	11	1	3
Joshua Rowe, R. S.	Hays		295	8	1
Larkin Turner,	Clarks		7	16	1
Joseph Hand,	Snows		84	23	2
Jesse Peters, soldier,	Bakers		137	24	1
Silas Brooks,	Snows		120	33	1
John Endsly,	Tallys		83	9	1
Edmund Snow,	Snows		55	10	1
OGLETHORPE.					
David Young,	Billups		220	6	1
Charley Sims,	Hardmans		121	1	5
Samuel McCanless,	Williamsons	85	8	2
Stephen Ham, soldier,	Wilsons	140	18	2
William C. Bradberry,	Floyds		30	17	1
Anderson McLeroy,	Hardmans	271	6	1
Charles Strong, sr. R. S.	Burfords	116	20	2
PIKE.					
Abner Sims,	Mays		229	30	1
Thomas Burnett,	do.		105	8	1
PULASKI.					
Jincy Smith, widow,	Sparrows	183	17	1
John Smith, R. S.,	Scarboroughs	174	2	4
William B. Crofford,	Thomas		23	2	3
Wm. J. Pennington, ill.,	Kellums	196	6	1
PUTNAM.					
Abner Wells,	Stinsons		63	1	2
Dennis McLendon's orps.	Sawyers	85	15	5
Lurania Mason's orphans,	Sparks	244	3	4
Sandlin Hardin,	Blacks		191	3	5
Chloe Williams, widow,	Bledsoes	246	16	2
Jeremiah Godwin,	Vinings		17	15	2
James Ferrill,	Barnetts		144	6	2
Josias Boswell,	Goods		223	31	1
Carlile P. Beman,	Bledsoes		192	18	1
CatharineTurknett,hus.ab.	Vinings	292	28	1
Thomas Ferrell,	Kendricks		240	4	1
RABUN.					
Robert Woods,	Mercers		119	5	5
RICHMOND.					
Wiley Wood,	James		174	10	2
Ezekiel Aulder,	600th		120	3	4
Robert Jones, Colonel,	Kellys	216	16	2
Green B. Holland,	Ferris		78	2	4
Daniel Meigs,	Hands		80	9	3
Cesaire Blome,	Mantz		58	7	4
Emily S. Powers, orp.,	Treadwells	124	31	1
Benjamin Hickey's orphan,	Kellys	15	12	5
Seth Bishop,	Huntingtons		36	3	1
Nancy Henry, widow,	Blacks		1	23	1
Sarah Jones, widow,	Augusta		18	6	1
SCRIVEN.					
William Farmer's orp.,	Stricklings	32	9	1
John H. Mercer's orp.,	Poytress	228	18	1
TATTNALL.					
William Newmans,	Corseys		105	21	2
John T. Sharpe,	McCalls		197	26	1
William Durrence, jr.,	Deloachs	34	13	5
TELFAIR.					
William Fletcher, R. S.,	Barentines	262	2	3
William Hargroves,	Wilkinsons	273	9	3

Fortunate Drawers	Capts.	Dist.	No.	Dt.	Sec.
Holden Matchet,	Lamkins		91	13	2
Jeremiah Davis,	Barentines		227	10	5
TALIAFERRO.					
George Tilley,	Hammacks		187	12	1
John Rhodes,	Justices		218	6	5
TWIGGS.					
Peter Sutton,	Chamberlains		191	9	5
Isham G. Anderson,	Pearsons		16	9	1
Jacob Tison's orps.,	Chamberlains	252	16	2
Robert Reyne's orphans,	Graggs	216	11	3
Mary Leith, widow,	Bosticks		142	1	3
MaryMathews,widow,	Blackshears	248	20	1
UPSON.					
Shadrach Ellis, sen.,	Ellis		224	22	1
Henry C. McCoy,	Saunders		15	5	4
Green A. Alison,	Paschals		94	7	3
Thomas Bailey, soldier,	Hattoxs	214	11	1
Milton Wilder,	do.		73	10	1
WALTON.					
ReubenGregory, illegitimate,	Pools	145	11	5
Martin T. Sentell,	250th		303	1	4
Elizabeth Rainey, widow,	Snows	112	26	1
William Vines,	Bexleys		25	11	2
Alexander Dyer's orphans,	Rays	19	4	2
Mathew Hosch,	249th		43	9	1
James M. Brantley,	250th		72	5	5
WARE.					
Juniper Griffice,	Motes		157	21	2
John Branham's minors,	Dowlings	31	19	2
WAYNE.					
Reuben Turner, R. S.,	Mannings	179	2	4
Allen Roberson,	McKinneys		176	4	2
Cornelius Johnson,	Mannings		17	16	5
Nimrod Ranberson, sol.,	McKinneys	265	15	1
WARREN.					
Joseph Grizzle, orphan,	Bulls		241	7	5
Miles Bryan,	Downs		42	1	5
Edward Taylor, R. S.,	Kinseys		80	11	2
William W. Johnson,	do		62	12	2
Mary McCarty, w. R. S.,	Saunders		60	11	2
John Simmons,	Jones		99	11	2
Benjamin B. Langham,	Brinkleys		7	13	2
Elijah Parham,	Parhams		34	27	1
M., N., & M. McDonald, ills.	Adkins	117	9	3
Rebecca Pate, orphan,	Parhams		207	17	1
Hardy Williford,	Jones		13	12	3
Betsy, M. A. & J. Smith, ills.	Sanders	184	27	1
J., M., M., & E. Newsom ills.	Adkins	116	13	1
Benjamin Bledsoe,	Bulls		161	5	5
WASHINGTON.					
Anna Tindall, widow,	Wimberlys		312	8	1
Elizabeth Shirey, widow,	Woods		11	6	3
Burwell & A. Dawson, orps.,	Avans	147	16	2
John G. Rutherford,	do.		247	16	2
John Martin,	Woods		218	16	1
John Blackburn's orphans,	Gilberts	203	5	4
Daniel Harris,	Jordans		137	9	3
Avey Wright, illegitimate,	McLendons	216	16	1
Daniel New,	Whitfields		213	16	1
Randol Atkins,	Gilberts		38	26	1
Joseph Rachels, ill.	Warthens		188	5	5
WILKINSON.					
James Davis, illegitimate,	Mathews	30	1	4
Henry Thomas, orphans,	Halls		127	13	2
William Hatcher, R. S.,	do.		146	6	1
Wiley Miller,	Curreys		31	10	2
Thaddeus Bairfield,	Smiths		291	20	2
Elizabeth Tatom, orphans,	Mathews	101	6	3
Vinson Tharp, orphan,	Smiths		227	28	1
John H. Wales,	Mandersons		34	11	2
WILKES.					
Willis Hyde,	Lukers		255	10	5
Benjamin Norman,	Richersons		35	29	2

Fortunate Drawers Capts. Dist.	No.	Dt.	Sec.	Fortunate Drawers Capts. Dist.	No.	Dt.	Sec.
John Eldson, soldier, Greshams	215	15	1	Hardy Powell's orphans, Dranes	52	4	5
Geo. Lee Woodward, ill., Ragsdales	281	1	4	Payne Lovell, Culbreaths	171	9	5
Samuel Gardner, soldier, Charltons	152	31	1	Polly Lovell, illegitimate, do.	163	22	2
George Hughes, orphan, Woottens	171	20	1	William T. McDonald, Dranes	81	1	1
				Hensley Sanders, Baileys	323	15	1
				Cassandra Watson, widow, Dranes	208	22	2

8TH DAY'S DRAWING—March 15.

APPLING.

Jean Sykes, orphan, Stricklins	170	6	2
William Way, Collins	69	10	1
Major Hurst, do.	228	9	3
Elizabeth Aldredge, w. R. S., Mathis	263	5	1

BALDWIN.

William B. Ball, Buchanans	160	9	5
John Cone, sen., R. S. Thomas	168	8	3
James Porter, Lingos	20	23	2
Gideons Mims, Bivins	206	16	1
Patience Raiford, w. R. S., Buchanans	378	3	4
Jonathan Thomas's orphans, Thomas	58	10	1
William Hand, R. S., Lesters	172	20	1

BIBB.

Sarah & Eliza Smith, fa. absent, Carrs	96	10	3
James Patton, Flanders	103	4	1
James Brown, soldier, Bates	75	22	2
Samuel H. Powell, Flanders	259	15	1
John Harris' orphans, Bates	172	23	1
John M. Shelman, Swearingins	196	11	1

BULLOCH.

Elander Neasmith, Deloachs	234	16	1
Lucrecy Rogers, w. R. S., Lockharts	101	6	1
Seborn Lastinger, Deloachs	123	12	1
Elizabeth Pridgen, widow, Burnetts	257	3	1
James Newman, do.	48	14	1

BURKE.

Brinson Perkins, Wards	172	1	4
John Thompson's orphans, Gordons	96	16	2
James Lambert, sr. R. S., Thompsons	163	1	2
John U. Wise, orphan, Wards	70	3	3
Henry S. Neyland's orphans, Dukes	11	6	2
David Ward's orphans, Brooms	152	1	1
Middleton Thorn, soldier, Andersons	4	12	2
James Hickey, soldier, Brooms	86	24	1

BUTTS.

Hugh Morrison, soldier, Thaxtons	164	13	1
Bridges Par, jun. do.	75	10	2
Marg. Y. Speaks, illegitimate, Knights	116	16	2

CAMDEN.

Joseph Lockaler Coxs	160	7	2
Hannah McGillis, widow, Wards	128	23	2
Lewis Bachlott, do.	153	10	5
Joseph Tolker, do.	191	3	4

CHATHAM.

Allen A. Denslow, Geredons	123	16	1
Mark Hoag Wakeman, Haydens	63	11	3
William B. Brownjohn, do.	242	9	5
Hugh Cassidy, Geredons	2	4	1
Thomas Pitt, do.	279	17	2

CLARK.

Isaac Hill, R. S., Herndons	55	6	2
James A. Meriwether, Gahagans	4	17	1
Joshua Greer, Herndons	259	2	3
Cicero Holt, Gahagans	320	3	4
Richard Downs, Lumpkins	80	19	2
William H. Kent, Ransoms	204	21	1

COLUMBIA.

William Newman, Carrolls	15	2	3
Thomas Burnsides, soldier, Bynums	255	33	1

CRAWFORD.

Richard C. Ethridge, Rhodes	278	9	3
Ephraim Johnston, do.	197	31	1
David Adams, Dukes	112	18	2

DEKALB.

William Holly, Smiths	155	4	5
James Allcorn, Howells	175	7	3

DECATUR.

John Cook, R. S., Hawthorns	73	11	2
Johnson Cook, do.	132	10	2

EARLY.

Nan., Sar., & J. Long, ills. Grimsleys	151	5	3

EFFINGHAM.

Frederick Ballard, R. S., Edwards	10	6	2

ELBERT.

Thomas Scales, Dobbs	201	22	1
Joel Stodghill, Boltons	102	15	1
Reuben Allen, Dunns	231	25	1
Samuel D. Holt, Boltons	181	6	1
Elizabeth Brewer, widow, Bells	125	31	1
Willis Therlkild, Butlers	44	15	5
Thomas Wallis, Meritts	184	4	4
John Taylor's orphans, Dunns	53	12	1
Nicholas M. Adams, Hortons	202	4	3

EMANUEL.

Hiram M. Jackson, Swains	204	6	1

FAYETTE.

John D. Gittens, Whartons	79	9	3
William Cockrell, do.	286	3	4
Eli Edmonson, Roziers	49	5	1
Edwin Reeves, Browns	198	13	2
Reuben Richards, Wests	72	9	1

FRANKLIN.

Nathaniel Harbin, McDonalds	117	5	4
William Edwards's orps., Chandlers	332	8	1
John Selman, soldier, do.	339	20	2

GLYNN.

Urbanus Dart, Burnetts	164	6	1

GREENE.

Daniel E. Jackson, Webbs	138	9	2
Almira Ann Bennett, ill. Newsoms	94	14	1
John Wilkins, orphan, Southerlands	18	28	1
William Mallory, Woodhams	54	6	3
Sarah Horn, w. R. S., Southerlands	101	5	2
James Akins, sen., R. S., do.	127	1	5
Redic P. Wright, Woodhams	93	32	1
Archibald Lewis's orps. Southerlands	232	10	2

GWINNETT.

David Griffith, soldier, Mattoxs	224	9	3
Samuel Kite, Greens	10	10	3
Elizabeth Langston, wid. Rollins	222	9	2
Wells Thompson, Hunicuts	31	21	1
William M. Greene, Bakers	247	3	4
Little B. Wright, Hunicuts	125	2	1
Ann D. & E. W. Rucks, orps. Greens	77	8	4
Owen Andrews, Woodroughs	96	17	1
Edmond B. Thompson, Hunicuts	39	5	3

HANCOCK.

Jesse H. Everett, 118th	254	2	3
Thomas J. Little, 103rd	46	6	5
John Sturdivant, R. S., 101st	222	5	4
Charles Grant, Bishops	138	10	5

Fortunate Drawers Capts. Dist.	No.Dt.Sec.
Nathaniel Bradford, 118th	152 5 4

HENRY.

John McKnight, Shaws	11 5 4
Henry R. Marchman, Millers	154 16 1
Richard Simmons, Harris	232 10 5
John Gayden, Grays	175 3 5
William H. Pass, do.	87 15 2
John Bateman, Harris	208 12 1
Josiah Grisham, soldier, Shaws	19 15 2
Thomas Yarborough, soldier, do.	62 7 3
Elisha Vinson, R. S., Millers	120 5 2
Abraham McKinny, Bryants	264 4 3

HABERSHAM.

Henry Anderson, Bryans	170 23 1
William Dooly, soldier, do.	141 28 1
Wiley Warwick, sen. do.	207 3 4
Thomas Powers, Langstons	259 8 5
Simeon Lain, illegitimate, Bryans	59 3 1
Elliott Clardy, Fains	215 20 1
David Ritchie, minor, Martins	14 15 2
John T. Carter, Bakers	28 21 2
Levicy Williams, minor, Tates	32 16 5
James Cronan, R. S., Kenzies	194 5 2

HALL.

William Neel, Hardens	93 18 1
Granville Thompson, Garrards	13 2 1
Edward Harrison, R. S., Smiths	112 33 1
Jesse Martin, Roberts	335 28 1
John Tuggle, Smtihs	91 23 2
Isham P. Pool, Roberts	78 11 3
Henry F. Cochran, do.	239 4 2
Adam Elrod, Hendricks	168 9 1

HOUSTON.

William Coll, Becks	261 2 3
Duncan Nicklison, Moores	7 12 3

IRWIN.

Martha Ann Barentine, ill. McCalls	172 3 2
David Gornto, Dixons	195 10 2

JACKSON.

Elizabeth Braziel, widow, Allens	188 23 1
Joshua Wimberly, do.	246 5 3
Peter H. Strickland, Staplers	186 10 3
Samuel A. Wilson, Millers	155 9 3
Mary Green, wid. R. S. Allens	99 5 4
Benjamin Freeman, Lindseys	83 6 5
Joseph T. Cunningham, sol. Storys	58 23 1
Frederick McGuire, soldier, Bowens	243 5 5
Eliz. Ann Ridon, illegitimate, Rogers	44 8 3

JASPER.

Isaac Falkner, orphan, Holmes	148 29 1
Augustin L. Potter, R. S. Reeves	162 10 5
Matthew H. Glenn, Hines	24 7 3
John Hand, soldier, Hands	81 4 5
James Brown, Baynes	134 1 5
Robert Higginbotham's orphans, do.	292 4 1
Sarah Williamson, w. R. S., Wilders	36 15 1
Obadiah Echols, soldier, Farleys	196 3 1
Hardaman Owens, Owens	164 3 3
John G. Smith, Farleys	108 2 3
Ann Anthony, widow, Owens	34 24 2

JEFFERSON.

John Broughton, Ross's	180 5 5
Shadrach Stephens, Beatys	40 1 2
Robert Lowrie's orphans, Ross's	142 8 1
Margaret Jones, wid. R. S., Jones	165 29 1
Dorcas Lanier, orphan, Waldens	157 6 4
William Ferrell, Cunninghams	87 25 1

JONES.

Fortunate Drawers Capts. Dist.	No.Dt.Sec.
Samuel Holliday, Hammacks	8 31 1
Levin S. Vance, Spinks	37 2 2
John Thompson, Taylors	152 3 4
Charles L. Ridley, Duncans	109 18 1
Amasa R. Moore, Spinks	167 1 1
Zachariah Robison, Duncans	193 1 3
Green Davidson, Hammacks	84 11 5
Rigdon Hutchins, Gibsons	72 3 3
Elizabeth Jones, wid. R. S., Newbys	240 11 3
Jesse Rawson, Stewarts	238 5 5
Peyton Ward, Taylors	78 12 2
William F. Phillips, Gibsons	88 3 4
John Dawkins, Taylors	234 1 4

LAURENS.

Elizabeth Clinch, widow, Whiteheads	283 3 4
William W. Tison, Barlows	180 13 2
Eliza Campbell, widow, Deans	170 17 1
John L. Calhoun, Spiveys	160 21 2
Edwin Holmes, Powers	138 23 2
Edward Snegrove, Mizells	42 4 2

LIBERTY.

William Parker, jun., 17th	120 27 1

LINCOLN.

Milly Phipps, wid. Lonorgans	189 11 3

LOWNDES.

John S. Whitfield, soldier, 12th	176 1 4

MADISON.

Mildred Sorrells, w. R. S., Caldwells	71 20 1
Meredith Blake, Hannas	127 14 1
Levi Millican, Caldwells	297 20 2
James R. Chandler, Christians	150 12 2
Meredith Drake, Hannas	127 14 5

MONROE.

John Wilder, Millers	156 27 1
James S. Bonner, Pattersons	162 1 2
William Black, Wrights	233 13 2
Elijah Runnels, Pattersons	179 13 1
Little. Gresham, R. S., Wrights	158 5 3
Wm. Ezell, Finches	89 3 5
A. McKinzie, h. ab. Woodwards	295 6 1
Wm. McKinney, Pattersons	227 25 1
James A. Huey, Woodwards	276 6 1

MORGAN.

Jesse Woodyards orps. Beaslys	16 1 3
John Walker, Walkers	102 4 2
Warren Oneal, Dawsons	252 7 3
Austin Clements orps. Jennings	60 4 2
Capt. Creed M. Jennings, do.	163 7 1
S. Fitzpatrick, w. R. S. Beaslys	249 30 1

MONTGOMERY.

Asa Whitehurst, Pridgeons	93 30 1

NEWTON.

Mark Thompson, soldier, Alreds	128 10 2
Joseph Livingston, Hays	215 3 3
David McMurrian, soldier, Orrs	134 29 1
Littleton A. Godfrey, Pullins	213 10 3
Henry D. Teat, soldier, Bakers	230 10 1
Lamina Wyatt, illegit. Askews	253 5 3
Othiel Pullins, Pullins	23 4 5
John Easterwood, R. S., Moss'	2 9 5
David Harris, Graves	8 17 1
Wm. Lummers, Alreds	122 1 1
Wm. Posey, Clarks	208 23 1
Jas. Moors orphans, Pullins	216 22 2

OGLETHORPE.
Fortunate Drawers	Capts. Dist.	No.	Dt.	Sec.
Peter Goolsbys orphans,	Lacys	196	12	2
Ranford E. Hitchcock,	Holloways	28	3	1
Wm. Winfrey,	do.	247	7	5
Robert M. Kidd,	do.	263	3	3
T. W. Goldings orps.	Burfords	238	1	4
John C. Dansby,	Seals	274	15	1
Gatewood Dunn, R. S.,	Rhodes	238	8	3

PIKE.
Moses Taylor,	Mays	39	24	1
Thos. Scoggin, R. S.	Orrs	173	6	2
Wm. C. Jones,	Mays	57	5	2

PULASKI.
Mary Bryan, w.R.S.	Scarbroughs	104	9	5
Sylvanus Hoskins,	Sparrows	157	1	1
Josiah Wimburn,	Thomas'	244	1	4
Susan Mayo, w. R. S.	Gilstraps	178	6	3
Martin Wallden,	Scarbroughs	207	3	2

PUTNAM.
Elander B. Carter,	Clarks	175	8	5
Eleanor Rees, wid.	Bledsoes	132	6	2
John Ellsworth,	Chambers	167	26	1
Hamton Stephens,	Allums	94	2	3
Riley Rockwell,	Bledsoes	78	10	2

RABUN.
James Kell,	Milligans	33	1	1
Edward Craig, sr.	Mercers	250	5	1
Betsy, S.&G Wilkinson,	Godfreys	150	9	5
Wm. Slewder,	Mercers	99	12	3
James Reed,	Becks	116	32	1
Jas. C. Gains,	Godfreys	61	26	1

RICHMOND.
James Madison Borum,	Wilcoxs	37	16	2
Ann & P. Riddle, orps.	Augusta	51	12	2
Mary Roberts, widow,	Murphys	266	7	1
V. L. McKeen,	Mantzs	187	5	3
Abiel C. Beach,	Huntingtons	64	3	4
Walter Harris,	Kelleys	47	26	1
Jas. C. Philpot,	Mantzs	160	10	1
Alexander Hannah,	Blacks	224	21	2
Sarah Fowler, widow,	do.	22	14	2

SCRIVEN.
Abraham Hunter,	Hunters,	290	6	1
Louiza Rountree, wid.	Poytress	194	20	1
Allen Faircloth,	Kemps	218	9	2
John Sowell,	Reaves	155	22	1
Paul B. Colson,	Stricklings	198	11	1

TATTNALL.
Wm. A. Corsey,	Corseys	218	2	4

TELFAIR.
Isaac Hargroves,	Wilkinsons	102	27	1
Noah Paramore,	Clemons	189	3	5
Hugh McCanne,	Lampkins	63	17	1
Margaret Smith, wid.	Wilsons	163	5	3

TALIAFERRO.
Jehial Watson,	Gunns	95	21	2
Moses Hubert,	Cobbs	64	28	1

TWIGGS.
Kelly Glover,	Blackshears	159	3	1
Garner Mercer,	Graggs	385	7	1

UPSON.
Jane Lundy's, illegits.	Paschalls	194	1	1

Fortunate Drawers	Capts. Dist.	No.	Dt.	Sec.
James Crawford, soldier,	Haralds	65	23	2
Shadrach Pugh, R. S.		90	23	2
Conneil Groom,	Ezells	72	29	1

WALTON.
Elisha Hood, 249th district		141	5	1
Daniel Lake,	Snows	99	29	1
Wm. Watson,	Rays	286	1	2

WARE.
John W. Smith,	Lees	211	17	2

WAYNE.
James Herren,	McKinneys	34	14	2

WARREN.
Solomon Lockett, R. S.	Hills	122	6	3
Nicholas Harbuck, R. S.	Bulls	107	31	1
Pierce Bailey,	Hills	216	21	2
James B. Phillips,	Downs	127	13	1
Hardy Hopson,	Parhams	139	6	3
Mary Fuller, widow,	Kinseys	260	4	3
Charles M. Allen,	Adkins	371	3	4
Joshua Newsom,	do.	143	14	5
Robert Bealls orphans,	Bulls	67	1	4
Allen Parris,	Jones	10	11	1
M.,N.,&M.McDonald ills.	Adkins	19	17	1
Misora King, illegitimate,	Hales	171	13	1
Jacob Gerrard, soldier,	Fords	85	6	3

WASHINGTON.
Sally Taunton, illegit.	Warthens	144	2	4
Zachariah Brown,	Woods	207	5	5
Elijah Watson,	Tysons	265	28	1
Green Hood,	O'Quinns	88	5	1
Harris Brantley, sol.	McLendons	83	5	5
Levi Bright,	Floyds	237	5	1
John Jordan, jr.	Jordans	68	1	1
L. M. Hall, wid. R. S.	Rushings	88	13	2
Isham Nowell,	Mannings	183	2	3

WILKES.
William Triplett, R. S.	Greshams	59	12	1
Wm. Johnsons minors,	Amasons	15	29	1
Benj. Murphy,	Lukers	115	8	5
Hannah Irwin, h. ab.	Washingtons	77	29	1
M. Thompson, h.ab.	Richardsons	173	21	1
Edmund H. Borum,	Carters	45	2	1

WILKINSON.
Permelia Edwards, ill.	Mayos	272	15	1
Mar. Montgomery, w. R. S.	Shows	26	4	2
Nancy Cobb, illegitimate,	do.	204	10	5
Eleazer Brack, sr. R. S	.Fairchilds	88	15	2
Mary Barber, w. R. S.	Curreys	99	14	2
Job McLendon,	Mayos	330	3	4
Thos. Reeves' orphans,	Curreys	77	26	1

9TH DAY'S DRAWING—16th March.

APPLING.
John Griffin,	Morgans	222	6	1

BALDWIN.
Iverson L. Harris,	Ginns	32	21	1
John Bryan,	do.	242	6	3
Major West,	Lesters	226	11	3
S. M. Crenshaw, wid.	Buchanans	64	18	1
Robert Reynolds, Esq.	Thomas'	23	7	4
S. A. Kinley, Reddings	Battalion	222	22	1
Henry L. Densler,	Doles	207	12	2

Fortunate Drawers Capts. Dist.	No.	Dt.	Sec.
Winnifred King, widow, Wicks	100	6	3
BIBB.			
Daniel Hysler, Lloyds	10	9	4
Robert B. Washington, sol. Bates	9	20	1
Ralph King, Bates	58	1	5
BULLOCH.			
Silas Corbin, Richardsons	22	18	2
Sarah Jones, widow, Lockharts	90	28	1
Sarah Hall, wid. McCalls	382	20	2
BURKE.			
George E. Henderson, Dugas	156	14	2
David J. Carsey, Lynchs	259	5	1
Alex. J. Lynn, orphan, Wests	299	22	1
Wm. W. Leverett, Dugas	309	7	1
Simeon Bell, Wests	112	9	2
BUTTS.			
Peter Mitchell, Chapmans	79	3	3
Neil Strahan, Hendricks	77	9	1
CHATHAM.			
H.H.Hines,orp.of Jno.,McDonnells	201	2	3
John Gowan, orphan, Tenbrooks	211	14	2
Charles Cannon, Haydens	5	23	2
Mar. Drummond, or. of Walter,	23	7	1
Joseph Oliver Davis, Haydens	56	10	2
CLARK.			
James Allen, Vinsons	44	17	2
Stephen Crow, R. S. Dickins	123	3	4
Abraham Silvy, soldier, Greers	225	6	1
Lemuel Crawford, R.S. Lumpkins	68	4	1
COLUMBIA.			
Elbert B. Ramsay, Coles	21	10	1
Rosan. Richardson, w. Stallings	203	6	5
James Wood, sr. R. S. Baileys	210	3	4
Hampton Wade, Clarks	99	21	1
John Hobbs, Dranes	146	7	2
James Culbreath, Ramseys	185	7	5
Robert McKorkle, Talberts	135	2	3
DEKALB.			
David Smith, Bakers	187	2	4
Andrew Boyd, Stephens	298	28	1
Williford Grogan, Merritts	226	10	2
Henry Johnson, Bakers	207	5	2
David Franklin, R. S., Stephens	148	6	1
Thos. Ford, Merritts	176	7	3
DOOLY.			
Humphrey Posey, Andersons	84	9	5
Martha Godwins ills. 582nd dist.	122	5	4
EARLY.			
Wylie Jones, Wilsons	62	2	1
Barwell Evans, R. S. Hairs	102	5	1
Alsey Harris, do.	17	8	2
EFFINGHAM.			
Wm. P. Ulmer, Waldhaners	166	28	1
Wm. Black, sr. R. S., Hunters	88	5	3
ELBERT.			
Founten Jourden, R. S., Dunns	211	13	1
Robert S. Barr, Bells	268	1	2
Margaret McDonald, wid. Dobbs	103	1	2
James Vickery, do.	101	23	2
Thos. S. Teasly illegit. Hortons	11	20	1
Frances E. Williams, wid. Bells	64	15	1
John T. Dudley, Meritts	176	13	1

Fortunate Drawers Capts. Dist.	No.	Dt.	Sec.
Thos. Tates orphans, Tates	148	11	2
Wm. Kelley, R. S. Dobbs	82	4	3
EMANUEL.			
Elijah Beasley, Chasons	202	12	3
Josiah Whitney, McGars	222	18	2
FAYETTE.			
R. Williams,w.R.S. McClendons	255	12	3
FRANKLIN.			
John Walters orphans, Walters	193	10	1
Wm. Glover, R. S. Blankinships	240	2	3
Charles Bailey, Walters	135	3	4
Robert Bruce, Chandlers	270	21	1
Hezekiah Bush, Candells	106	10	1
Alex Gaddess, Walters	74	14	1
Wm. Smith, soldier, Chandlers	120	21	2
Francis Clark, Candells	176	6	5
Daniel Bryson, Strange's	93	31	1
Edeth Langston, illegit. Hudsons	49	3	5
Sturdy Garner, Chandlers	37	6	1
Sampson Walls, R. S. Tabors	193	4	2
Joseph D. Reid, Blankinships	74	10	2
John Fowler, Jones	39	3	2
GLYNN.			
Samuel Wrights, Dubignons	57	15	5
Robert Hazlehurst, Burnetts	104	14	1
GREENE.			
Wm. Gillums orphans, Halls	44	5	3
Vincent Meadows, Colcloughs	41	12	3
Wooten O'Neals orphans, do.	71	9	1
Wm. A. Morris, Rankins	39	17	1
Isaac M. Rall, Dawsons	226	3	3
John Ray, Halls	2	12	2
GWINNETT.			
Reuben Sams, Moores	133	5	5
John Whorton, Finchers	99	2	1
John Rutledge, R. S. Wallis	150	26	1
Taprell Landers, R. S. Caruthers	151	8	3
Ittai Pruitt, Moores	247	20	2
Nathan Franklin, Davis	20	22	2
Joseph B. Gordon, Rollins	38	8	3
Jacob Delk soldier, Dunbars	148	11	1
Richard B. Robinson, Evans	120	8	4
Abner Phillips, Moores	54	3	4
Samuel Paschal, Wallis	184	3	3
Robert Harkness, Moores	36	2	4
Roderick R. Taylor, Evans	54	9	5
Wm. Jackson, Hunicuts	73	11	1
Mary Gross, orphan, Madduxs	172	13	2
Martha Thomas illegit. Moores	279	5	4
Robert S. Foster, Greens	107	2	4
Agnes McConnell, wid. Moores	76	2	4
Robert Bradford, Robertsons	7	1	4
HABERSHAM.			
George Dickerson, sol., Martins	43	21	1
George H. Palmer, Suttons	206	1	2
Amos Jackson, Bryans	148	5	3
William Tate, jr., Tates	119	12	1
Abel Taylor, Langstons	121	3	1
George Blare, Worshams	155	4	3
Reuben G. Anderson, Cross's	40	19	2
William Stephens, Jones	158	12	5

HALL.

Fortunate Drawers Capts. Dist.	No.	Dt.	Sec.
Abraham Howard, R. S. Walkers	112	5	2
Aaron Maddox, Hendricks	268	20	2
James Ross, Garrards	4	14	5
Vincent White, R. S., do.	93	3	2
William Wingo, Wilsons	160	12	3
John P. Champion, orp. Floyds	108	7	5

HANCOCK.

Singleton S. Buckner, 113th	216	2	1
James Johnson, 112th	99	5	1
Martha Henderson, orp., 106th	135	3	5
James J. Butts, 101st	29	17	1
John T. Broadnax, sol. Brooks	200	10	5

HENRY.

John Harp, Harris	171	4	3
Reps Asborn, Bryants	17	9	1
John Hambrick, Shaws	276	7	1
Sanford R. Norriss, Harriss	76	13	5
Burrell Nail, do.	140	6	5
Wade H. Turner, soldier, 7th	28	6	5
Thomas Young, Grays	243	12	2
Mary Hartsfield, wid., Kites	220	7	3
Mary Lipham, w. R. S., Shaws	154	3	3
Polly Soxon, widow, Allens	255	9	5

HOUSTON.

William H. Jordan, Bozemans	274	6	1
Ezekiel Wright, Prices	94	13	1
Joseph Calhoun, Smiths	28	13	5
C. Richardson, h. a. Wimberlys	156	12	3

IRWIN.

Jiles Easters, 5th	88	4	3
James Rutherford, Dixons	148	3	5

JACKSON.

Minerva Park, ill., Staplers	39	6	4
William Thompson, do.	74	7	3
Eldridge Fuller, Landrums	104	7	3
Sally Mayo, widow, Allens	89	11	2
Solomon Wilbanks, Rogers	19	10	2
John Cash, R. S., Duprees	23	11	1
William Massee, Bowens	255	5	1
John Hampton, sr. R.S. Lindsays	125	13	5
Agness Britts, ills., Pairs	284	4	1
Elizabeth Joy, w. R. S., Millers	147	3	3
Joseph Banks, Landrums	50	26	1

JASPER.

Lewis Dowdell, Reeves	111	10	2
Elizabeth Phillips, wid. Wilsons	311	8	5
James Knight, orphan, Hands	54	15	1
Anderson Dabney's orps. Baynes	77	3	4
Moses Daniel, do.	111	11	5
Shilldrake Brown, Shropshires	153	14	5
John Houston, Owens	300	5	1
Isaac R. Jackson, Dardens	95	18	1
Daniel Akron, soldier, Hands	159	28	1
Susan Thurmond, wid., Hines	111	1	5
Robert Moreland, R. S., Reeves	151	3	5
John W. Buchanan, Trussells	149	12	3
Arthur Simmons's orps. Wilsons	267	2	3
B. Portwood, sr. R. S., Parkers	133	16	2

JEFFERSON.

Calvin Fokes, Marshalls	188	16	1

JONES.

Fortunate Drawers Capts. Dist.	No.	Dt.	Sec.
M. Cowar, wid. R. S., Marshalls	40	26	1
Ezekiel Causey, sen., Boyds	170	8	1
Eli Walden, sol., Cunninghams	103	16	2
Mary M. Fleming, orp., Jones	118	8	5
Elijah Young's orphans, Ross's	20	29	1

JONES.

Benjamin Todd, Taylors	216	1	1
Daniel C. Davis, Duncans	48	3	2
Howell Alsabrooks, Stewarts	136	2	3
Levi Manning's orps., Hamacks	42	5	5
Mansell W. Hamack, Willings	36	14	1
John M. Williams's orps. Woods	161	9	5
Joseph Smith, Popes	70	14	2
Jno. Garland, sr. R.S., Stewarts	113	5	1
Edward Bowin, Bowins	35	7	4
Jacob Lamb, Mullins	179	12	3
David Daniel, Blounts	80	5	3
M. Prince, min. of Pen. Conv. Blounts	323	7	5
Henry Mitchell, R. S., Mullins	67	8	5
Fanny Whatley, w. R. S., Spinks	15	27	1
Passyrias Roberson, Taylors	105	7	1

LAURENS.

Thomas H. Wilkinson, Mizells	150	7	5
Owen Thomas, Coats	33	10	1
David Register, Thomas	88	4	1
Mary Brackin, orp., Plummers	64	29	1
Nancy Varnadore's ills., Barlows	222	29	1
David Highsmith, Mizells	130	12	1
John Degraffenreed, Barlows	118	7	3

LIBERTY.

John Shepard, sen., 15th	71	31	1

LINCOLN.

Thomas Phipps, Hardys	123	32	1
John Peek's minors, Graves	258	11	2
Lawrence Suddoth, Prathers	164	20	1
Nathan Bussey's minors, Graves	178	5	2

MADISON.

Madison Culbertson, Culbertsons	48	9	3
John Hall, Caldwells	268	22	2
Willis H. Strickland, Phipps	195	2	2
W,E,J,&M.Williford,ills,Hancocks	122	7	4
Stephen B. Stephens, Caldwells	156	12	1
John Shoemaker, Christians	260	3	3
John Angling, R. S., Adairs	65	14	2
Jesse M. Sorrow, Hannas	179	12	5

MONROE.

Wiley Finny, Finchs	35	18	1
Joel J. Johnson, Millers	114	7	3
Larkin Ross, Douglass	182	33	1
Sanford Britton, Greshams	145	4	1
Joel Gammon, Douglass	83	22	2
Gideon Tanner, soldier, Wrights	49	11	2
William Powell, Turners	125	10	5

MORGAN.

Francis Guttery, R. S., Stokes	64	21	1
Charles Allen, Christians	197	5	2
David Allen, R. S., do.	68	4	5
Joseph Thompson, Whatleys	12	6	2
John Akens, R. S., Stokes	96	11	5

NEWTON.

Joseph Tommey, Graves	169	3	3
John Martin, Graces	16	7	5

LAND LOTTERY REGISTER—No. 4
[RECORDER OFFICE—PUBLISHED BY GRANTLAND & ORME—PRICE $3.]

NOTE.—Section 1 is Lee County—2 Muscogee—3 Troup—4 Coweta—5 Carroll.
9TH DAY'S DRAWING—Continued.

Fortunate Drawers Capts. Dist.	No.	Dt.	Sec.
Richrad Loyall, Pullens	24	11	1
William Rhodes's orps. Clarks	168	5	1
OGLETHORPE.			
Charleton C. Thornton, Seals	180	12	2
William Finch, R. S., Bells	102	29	1
James Colquett, sr., R.S., Laceys	203	16	2
Thos. W. Goldin's orps. Burfords	4	6	5
Larkin Hardman, Hardmans	147	17	2
Benier Pye, Floyds	191	5	2
Norris Lyon, Rousseaus	122	4	1
Walton P. Hill, do.	257	2	4
Wm. Christopher, Williamsons	251	33	1
John Davis, soldier, Devenports	69	32	1
PULASKI.			
Edward Smith, Bracewells	21	1	4
William Smith, Powells	88	17	2
Frances Pugh, orphan, Sparrows	32	1	1
William B. Reeves, Gilstraps	16	21	1
PUTNAM.			
Philip Johnson's orphans, Mizes	60	6	5
Rix Wilhight, Allums	178	13	1
Thos. R. Right, Duprees	170	31	1
Robert A. Walton, Brooks	27	9	4
Lucinda Cutliff, widow, Duprees	185	5	4
John Stubbs, Hendricks	178	18	2
Benj. Buckner, R. S. do.	186	22	2
Henry Hunter, Allums	138	23	1
Mary Smith, widow, Vinings	248	29	1
Alfred B. Hill, Allums	45	33	1
David Holliman, jr. Stinsons	16	10	1
Elizabeth Garrard, w. Hendricks	94	18	2
RABUN.			
Elrood Denny, Becks	8	4	5
RICHMOND.			
Nealy Knight, Kellys	157	20	1
Basil Lamar, jr. Wilcoxs	228	5	5
Edward Praters orphans, do.	63	12	5
J. W. Hunter, R.S., 119th dist.	175	17	1
Thos. W. McCoy, Treadwells	235	19	2
Hardy Jones, Augusta	53	11	2
Wm. Harper, Hands	103	15	2
Hugh M. Inglett, James	113	3	5
Wm. Sims, Huntingtons	174	25	1
Eugenia Hain, wid. Treadwells	24	6	5
Patrick H. Smead, Huntingtons	111	3	1
David Dalmeyda, Treadwells	77	33	1
Henry E. May, Hands	251	2	1
Thos. Stewart, Palmers	114	5	2
Joseph James, sr. Blacks	24	4	2
Elizabeth Dismeuk. w. James	220	6	3
Lu.,Ro.&Isa.Latigue orps. Hands	69	5	3
Wm. Mackil, Treadwells	234	17	2
SCRIVEN.			
James C. Dixon, Humphreys	19	9	3
Hardy Hodges, Hunters	64	12	2
Joshua Lee, Humphreys	27	2	4

Fortunate Drawers Capts. Dist.	No.	Dt.	Sec.
Daniel Zorn, Dees	32	18	2
James Duncan, do.	51	20	1
Henry Andersons orps. Dees	163	24	2
Shadrack Sapp, sr., R.S. Corseys	248	12	3
Richard Thompson, Dees	99	6	2
TELFAIR.			
John Ashley, jr., Robisons	28	8	5
Angus Morrison, Lampkins	112	9	5
TALIAFERRO.			
James Runnels, Alfords	230	12	3
Wm. Porter, Echols	39	8	1
Nathaniel Day, Towns	105	32	1
TWIGGS.			
Lewis J. Tippitt, Graggs	317	20	2
Hiram J. Hambrick, Bosticks	87	16	2
Wm. Flowers, Blackshears	44	4	4
Rebecca Perritt, wid. Bosticks	103	6	3
UPSON.			
Joseph Vann, Harrells	16	6	4
James Gorley, Coopers	34	18	2
Robert Duke, Harrells	139	9	2
Samuel Moore, soldier, Hattocks	14	23	2
Julius C. Alford, Myricks	167	1	5
WALTON.			
Robert S. Bullard, Davis	43	8	1
Egbert B. Beall, Rays	198	26	1
Jesse Vandiford, do.	187	18	1
Anderson Baker, do.	162	9	5
Frances Cotneys orps. Hudsons	21	6	5
James W. Dorithy, Rays	154	9	1
Henry Sumiror, Bexleys	232	8	1
WARREN.			
Joshua Howell, soldier, Sanders	146	3	5
Hugh Armstrongs orps. Parhams	261	16	2
Samuel Chawker, Adkins	44	10	2
Gray A. Chandler orp. Bulls	69	18	1
Wm. Powell, Bulls	56	1	1
Frederick B. Heath, Latimers	47	18	1
Wm. B. Hunley, Sanders	74	8	2
James B. Marler, Rogers	75	1	2
WASHINGTON.			
Odin Oliver, Gilberts	143	10	2
James R. Miller, do.	78	3	2
Martin Oliver, Currys	61	14	1
Wm. Cason, Woods	176	14	1
F. Williams, sol., McClendons	162	10	1
Willis Rhodes, Tysons	177	6	2
Stephen Perkins, Mannings	253	13	2
Wm. A. Skrine, Floyds	7	9	5
John Bland, Avans	32	1	5
Joshua Parker, Mannings	38	5	2
Burwell Moore, Whitfields	57	4	5
Eliza C. Howard, illegit. Currys	210	6	5
Margaret Floyd, wid. Warthens	6	23	1
Robert Colemans heirs, Floyds	161	9	1
Allen White, Whitfields	48	22	1
Wm. Griffin, Warthens	210	9	5
Elizabeth Sanders, w. Warthens	111	4	4

Fortunate Drawers Capts. Dist.	No.	Dt.	Sec.
John Page, Whitfields	84	4	3
Henry Taunton, R. S., Warthens	138	14	1
Morgan Brown, soldier, Floyds	258	19	2
Daniel R. Tucker, Avants	15	1	2
WILKES.			
Neson Powells orps. Lukers	184	5	5
Wm. Robertsons orps. Chunns	77	8	3
Chris. W. Bolton, w. R.S. Lukers	50	16	2
Charles Mattox, R. S., Greens	16	30	1
WILKINSON.			
Mariah Rials, illegitimate, Mayos	26	21	2
Solomon Gamage, do.	246	10	5
Jonathan Ridley, Mathews	103	6	5
Richard Garrett, illegit. Currys	107	7	5
Henry Adkerson, R. S. Mathews	18	9	5
Wm. S. Dudley, Smiths	49	19	2
John Gilberts orphans, Halls	65	22	1
Isham Paynes orphs. Fairchilds	274	3	4
Archibald Smith, Mathews	81	23	2
Wm. Simpson, Shows	253	14	1

10TH DAY'S DRAWING—17th March.

Fortunate Drawers Capts. Dist.	No.	Dt.	Sec.
BALDWIN.			
Uriah Brown, R. S., Bivins	104	5	5
Drucilla Brown, widow, Ginns	70	1	5
James Bivins, Bivins	35	9	5
Fielding Lewis, Pitts	136	7	2
William B. Pryor, Wicks	190	6	5
Ro. G. Crittenden, sol. Wheelers	50	8	1
BIBB.			
Benjamin Williams, Rutlands	13	4	1
Thomas Hart, Pickards	122	2	3
George Wright, do.	128	15	2
BRYAN.			
Rebecca Michal, wid. Harveys	66	5	4
BULLOCH.			
James Dickson, Burnetts	169	29	1
BURKE.			
Jeremiah Vinson, Baileys	1	4	1
Alcy Kirsey, widow, Baleys	31	1	2
BUTTS.			
Samuel Burke's orps., Robinsons	131	3	4
CAMDEN.			
William H. Williams, Wards	12	11	2
CHATHAM.			
Frances Dent, widow, Baines	248	9	5
Elijah Broughton, do.	252	22	1
H. J. G. Williams, McDonnells	216	12	2
John D. Parmer, Geredons	135	10	2
Bartholomew Masters, Baines	33	23	1
Lazarus Petty, Geredons	66	7	5
Frederick Rahfus, Haydens	93	21	2
Michael Rose, U. S. sol., Baines	231	6	3
Orps. of Peter Neville, Geredons	252	4	3
Mary Reid, widow, Gaddys	128	32	1
James C. Pierce, Baines	32	9	1
R.T.Gibson,orp.ofRo.S., Haydens	171	4	4
Josiah Tattnall, Tenbrooks	68	3	5
CLARK.			
John G. Richardson, McCrees	141	4	5
David Meriwether, Echols	210	11	3
Thomas A. Wright, Wrights	58	21	1

Fortunate Drawers Capts. Dist.	No.	Dt.	Sec.
James Greer, R. S., Davenports	279	8	5
Charles Garner, R. S., Andersons	101	1	3
William H. Hunt, Gahagans	85	14	5
Pernal Cook, Davenports	238	11	3
Orps. of J. F. Stephens, Vinsons	148	6	5
Stinson S. Carrell, sol., Davenports	6	2	3
Lemuel Brown, soldier, Greers	224	10	1
COLUMBIA.			
David Phillips,s orps. Carrolls	68	10	3
Zadock McGruder's orps. Dranes	223	11	1
Winneford Dunre, w. R.S. Baleys	220	20	1
Jeremiah Dutch, Tolberts	149	12	1
John Gray, Culbreths	18	15	2
Wilder Philips, Carrolls	58	2	5
Henry Burnley, R. S., Dranes	338	7	5
Joseph P. Reynolds, Carrolls	32	11	5
John Langston, Magruders	24	30	1
Robert G. Cleghorn, Ramseys	194	2	1
Robert Randolph, R.S. Talbots	230	6	5
CRAWFORD.			
Henry C. Hutcheson, Lovetts	88	26	1
Samuel Calhoun, soldier, Hicks	172	7	5
Wm.Gorman, illegitimate,Lovetts	161	14	2
George W. Mattocks, Ellis	82	11	2
DECATUR.			
Daniel McDaniel, Douglass	49	21	2
DEKALB			
William Beasley, R. S., Merritts	134	3	1
Thomas S. Robinson, Stephens	40	8	3
John Hamrick, Bowlings	168	4	2
Cyrus Choice, Spencers	87	4	5
John Reid, Browns	246	15	1
Thomas Donaldson, Conns	258	2	1
Young T. Standifer, Stephens	285	6	1
John Butler, Harris	142	1	1
Benjamin Harris, R. S., Edwards	176	11	2
Amos Johnson, Lokeys	212	10	1
EARLY.			
Green L. Dennard, Porters	220	5	3
EFFINGHAM.			
James McCardell, Stricklands	36	7	1
Moore Blitch, do.	6	7	3
Charles Waldhour, Waldhours	38	8	2
John London, Stricklands	22	28	1
John Pitman, Elkins	89	16	1
ELBERT.			
John McDonald's orps., Dobbs	194	10	5
Jonathan Thornton, Blackwells	249	5	4
John S. Hunt, Dunns	114	26	1
Middleton Blair, Merits	132	29	1
Robert Hall's orps. Blackwells	104	2	3
Rowland Brown, Carpenters	207	20	1
EMANUEL.			
Riley Mercer, Nabbs	95	3	1
EFFINGHAM.			
James McCardell, Stricklands	36	7	1
Moore Blitch, Stricklands	6	7	3
Charles Waldhour, Waldhours	38	8	2
John London, Stricklands	22	28	1
John Pitman, Elkins	89	16	1
ELBERT.			
John McDonalds, orps. Dobbs	194	10	5
Jonathan Thornton, Blackwells	249	5	4

(27)

Fortunate Drawers	Capts.	Dist.	No.	Dt.	Sec.
John S. Hunt,	Dunns		114	26	1
Middleton Blair,	Merits		132	29	1
Robert Halls orps.	Blackwells		104	2	3
Rowland Brown,	Carpenters		207	20	1
FAYETTE.					
James Gray,	Wests		271	2	4
Eli Edmonson,	Roziers		51	12	5
Elisha Gentry, soldier,	Morgans		99	10	3
John Evans, soldier,	Landrums		270	28	1
James H. Ball,	Craigs		148	9	3
John Vowel,	do.		80	4	3
FRANKLIN.					
Marion A. Franks,	Walters		229	4	3
Joel Thomas, soldier,	Hudsons		237	2	1
William Nickson,	McDonalds		136	4	1
Joshua Hooper, sol.	Stephens		22	22	1
William T. Crow, D.	Chandlers		166	9	2
Keren Smith, wid. D.	Chandlers		219	12	2
Eliz. Morrow, w. R. S.	Hudsons		220	2	2
John Hoyatt,	Jones		48	11	1
David Clark,	Bennetts		81	10	1
GLYNN.					
Alexander C. Scott,	Dubignons		95	5	5
George March,	McLeods		16	6	3
John Davis,	Dubignons		26	23	1
GREENE.					
Wm. C. Talley,	Robins		269	4	1
William Barnett, R. S.	Webbs		228	26	1
Illegit.chil.ofP.Cogbill,	Woodhams		263	8	5
Hugh Moore,	Rankins		91	16	1
Robert Pullin, R. S.	Rankins		24	14	1
Benjamin Cummins,	Akins		134	5	3
John Cunningham, sol.	Dawsons		121	2	2
Moody Jackson,	Winkfields		231	9	3
Charles Baldwin, soldier,	Rankins		2	32	1
Jeremiah Jacksons orps.	Webbs		39	25	5
James Smiths, orphans,	Bruces		143	14	1
F. Cummings, R. S.	Dawsons		199	31	1
GWINNETT.					
Jonn James,	Greens		214	19	1
John Hughs,	Davis		38	18	1
Thos. Watson, R. S.	Robertsons		65	5	1
Frederick Thompson, jr.	Madduxs		118	9	1
Robert Still,	Woodruffs		21	14	1
Simon Berry,	Hills		346	20	2
Wiley Baker,	Wallers		76	28	1
John S. Wilson,	Hunicuts		74	25	1
James Lowrey,	Greens		278	5	3
John Austin,	Hunnicuts		159	15	1
Patrick L. Dunlap,	do.		207	14	1
Ephram McClane, R.S.,	Caruthers		64	5	3
Alexander Miller,	Greens		84	16	2
John M. Venable,	Moors		252	11	2
Richard Bass,	Robertsons		97	30	1
Philo Hall,	Hunnicutts		197	23	1
HABERSHAM.					
Isom Shuffield,	Kenzies		224	10	3
Eldridge Davis,	Fanes		19	2	4
Philip Oneal,	Tates		132	3	1
Mary Buckner, widow,	Bakers		232	4	3
Orphans of T. Jordan,	Martins		236	16	1
Edmund Smith,	Tates		144	3	2

Fortunate Drawers	Capts.	Dist.	No.	Dt.	Sec.
William Herrin,	Jones		211	3	2
Wm. Cox, jr.	Vickreys		252	15	1
James Puricel,	Cross		130	2	3
Hubbard Barker,	Bryans		61	2	3
Rolen Tankersley,	Jones		216	3	3
John Thomas,	Fains		4	13	2
HALL.					
John Rich, R. S.	Roberts		236	2	4
Benjamin East,	Garrards		162	8	1
John Villard,	Hardens		173	24	1
Memory Walker,	Roberts		135	14	2
John Tallant, R. S.	Hardens		186	2	3
J. S. Griffins orps. 109th district			43	16	1
Jos. Tarbutton, R. S.,	Roberts		67	8	2
Elijah Herrin,	Hendricks		347	20	2
Ezekiel Putman,	Garrards		135	12	2
Rich Y. Otwell,	Yagers		171	10	1
Charles Cochrum,	Alreds		9	23	1
HANCOCK.					
J. McCullochs orphs. 104th dist.			37	15	5
Willard Whitney,	Denisons		170	5	5
Thos. Dickson, jr. 114th district			205	3	2
James S. Griffins, orps. 109th dist.			43	16	1
HENRY.					
Ignacious Russell,	Harriss		232	16	1
William Preston,	Kites		107	19	1
John Barton,	Harriss		136	33	1
Rich. Robertson,	Gosdens		280	22	1
HOUSTON.					
James Hays,	Becks		27	15	2
John Calhouns orphans,	Smiths		16	2	1
JohnHowell.sr.R.S.	Yarboroughgs		100	1	4
Elisha Ashburn,	Prices		194	12	1
Hezekiah Inglet,	Calhouns		232	15	1
Wm. Hollomon, soldier,	Pattens		256	23	1
IRWIN.					
Wm. Gay, R. S.	Underwoods		140	11	1
JACKSON.					
Isaac R. Brooks,	Georges		216	10	3
William H. Bacon, sr.	Allens		193	3	2
Robert A. Watson,	Moons		120	13	5
James Pettyjohn, sol.	Storys		93	1	5
William Miller, R. S.,	Millers		180	20	1
Samuel Bailey,	Millers		245	11	1
John Wheeler,	Duncans		45	12	2
Richard Willbanks,	Rogers		208	13	2
Elijah Calahan,	Duprees		206	33	1
Washington Lambert,	Landrums		29	23	2
John Hobsons orps.	Gathrights		60	21	2
Eldridge Fuller,	Landrums		125	22	2
William Orr,	Lindseys		39	4	2
William Miller, R. S.	Millers		75	9	2
John Thomas, sol.	Storys		117	1	4
JASPER.					
Burwell P. Key,	Wilsons		108	22	1
Rebecca Gray, widow,	Farleys		108	6	3
Newet L. Smith,	Robersons		160	11	5
Dicy Carden, blind,	Prices		73	14	5
Robin Smith,	Prices		25	8	4
David Phelps orphans,	Sparks		162	9	2
Edmund Spearman,	Butts		187	13	2
Christopher Binns,	Dardens		76	6	3
Wade Goolesby,	Hines		128	21	2

(28)

Fortunate Drawers Capts. Dist.	No.	Dt.	Sec.
George Crouch, Parkers	248	10	3
Wm. Foster Smith, Camerons	191	15	1
JEFFERSON.			
James H. Johns, Elliotts	122	23	1
David Thompsons orps. Ross	215	10	3
Wm. W. McNeal, Cunninghams	148	17	2
Henry Wamble, Jones	150	16	1
Robert Umphreys, Boys	109	31	1
JONES.			
Margaret McNeal, wid. Newbys	5	12	2
William W. Key, Taylors	112	13	1
Nathaniel Morris, R. S. Spinks	196	33	1
John G. Worsham, Duncans	10	5	5
Elihu Pitts, Mullins	83	10	3
George Ross, R. S. Blounts	214	7	1
Wm. V. Hoskins, Spinks	69	9	5
James Trices orphs. Popes	140	3	2
John Hammack, sr., Mullins	54	8	5
Nahum Willis, Mullins	148	7	5
Jesse Merrit, Stewarts	72	6	1
John Hoskins, sr., R.S. Hamacks	197	6	5
Isaachar Bates orphan. Woods	284	5	3
Sarah Mills, widow, Robertsons	239	7	3
Jeremiah Reeves, Spinks	17	14	5
Ferdinand Gresham, Blounts	71	1	2
James Kellard, R. S., Dosters	90	25	1
LAURENS.			
Elias Watson, Deans	100	9	5
Levi Glass, R. S. Hodges	89	24	1
James Cox, Barlows	115	23	1
Calip Hollinsworth, Barlows	52	8	4
Redmon Lions, Thomas	77	6	1
H. Albritton, sol. l. w. Bohanans	183	4	5
Richard Glovers orphans, Hodges	27	1	2
Charles H. Higdon, Whiteheads	177	1	1
Daniel Shiver, Coates	28	2	1
Arthoret Collier, wid. Whiteheads	42	3	1
Robert Grinsted, sr. Mizells	10	4	1
Allen Stewart, Hodges	236	18	2
LIBERTY.			
William Johnson, R. S. 17th dist.	69	21	2
Orphan of Wm.Fleming, 14th do.	150	3	2
LINCOLN.			
Richard Prather, Prathers	40	6	1
Thomas C. Curry, jr. Graves	171	8	5
James W. Dunaway, Parks	3	12	5
Josh.Grinages, minors, Lonorgans	178	4	1
MADISON.			
William C. Caruthers, Phipps	154	1	5
William Wright, Adairs	137	11	5
Martin Rowe, Hannas	83	24	1
Bastan Jourdan, Caldwells	129	11	1
Sarah Floyd widow, Hanas	81	3	4
Henry Wheeler, Christians	98	11	3
John Partin, do.	77	21	2
MONROE.			
William Fail, Woodards	222	24	1
James Thweatt, Browns	347	7	5
Howell Cherry, Pattersons	165	26	1
Phileman Lacey, Browns	40	7	3
Elenor Ector, wid. R. S. Wrights	68	11	3
James Herring, Woodwards	67	2	5

Fortunate Drawers Capts. Dist.	No.	Dt.	Sec.
James Phillips, do.	90	24	1
Zach. Chambless, sol. Stallings	140	4	2
Wm. Foster, R. S., Johnsons	112	8	3
Rebecca Crabb, wid. Finches	137	5	3
Obadiah Wright, Wrights	196	9	2
Simeon Clower, Woodwards	158	29	1
MORGAN.			
Joseph Williams orphans, Sparks	287	1	2
John Talley, Sparks	121	27	1
William H. Searsebrook, Boswells	81	8	3
John F. Hearn, Christians	121	9	3
Joshua Butler, Brooks	113	7	4
Lucius L. Wittich, Youngs	2	5	2
James B. Morgan, sol. Osteens	176	5	2
William Mosely, Jennings	42	10	2
William Harris' orphans, Sparks	196	4	2
NEWTON.			
Judith Priddy, w. R. S. Dyers	84	11	2
Edwin Branan, Hays	105	3	4
J., I., M., N., E., & Cynthia Dees orphans, Hays	206	3	3
William Barrow, Hays	183	13	1
Joseph Humphries, Clarks	182	16	1
James M. Smith, Sumners	25	19	2
Thos. Hinesly, Orrs	138	16	2
Louisa Castleberry, wid. Hays	176	2	3
Jane Farley, wid. R. S. Dyers	56	4	3
Thos. Cockerhi, jr. Hays	227	29	1
OGLETHORPE.			
Berry Hartsfield, Hardmans	160	6	5
John Lumpkin, R. S., Arnolds	269	8	5
Jem. Haney, w. R.S. Holloways	43	6	2
Hubbard Williams, Williamsons	113	24	2
David Thomas, 235th district	154	7	2
Robert Zuber, Williams	125	3	5
Elisha Tiller, Floyds	192	14	2
Benj. F. Hardeman, Rousseaus	73	5	5
James Brockman, Dix's	44	16	2
John M. Dowdy, Lacy's	39	22	2
Sarah McLeroy, w. R.S. Hardmans	56	24	2
Armsted Carter, Dicks	114	17	1
James Ray, Dicks	34	24	1
John W. Dickin, Rhodes	59	21	2
James M. Nelson, Rousseaus	194	31	1
PIKE.			
Benj. G. Brown, Daniels	118	20	2
Mary Horn, Pattersons	112	4	1
George Holseys orphans, Orrs	196	5	4
Abner Taylor, Mays	248	8	5
Sarah Philips, w. R. S. Hicks	146	2	4
Martha McDonald, ill. Hicks	167	4	2

Our Lottery Register, when completed, will make a neat octavo volume of near 250 pages, and will be as correct as the strictest care and attention can make it. Subscribers who prefer taking their copies after the drawing is finished, will receive them neatly bound in boards, at our expense. Subscribers who have the sheets sent to them by mail, by returning the whole to us within ten days after the drawing is over, can also have them bound at our expense. The names of Fortunate Drawers are printed by us as they are found on the tickets—many of them were doubtless incorrectly written by the Receivers of names entitled to draws.

LAND LOTTERY REGISTER—No. 5
[RECORDER OFFICE—PUBLISHED BY GRANTLAND & ORME—PRICE $3.]

NOTE.—Section 1 is Lee County—2 Muscogee—3 Troup—4 Coweta—5 Carroll.

10TH DAY'S DRAWING—Continued

PULASKI
Fortunate Drawers	Capts. Dist.	No.	Dt.	Sec.
Edmund Dillard, soldier, Cains		12	8	1
Rutha Bell, w. R. S. Thomas'		343	8	1
Martha Regan, wid. Powells		11	1	4
David Defnal, Sparrows		144	27	1

PUTNAM
Frederick Rainey, Sparks		74	16	1
Geor. R. C. Walton, orp. Bledsoes		145	19	2
David Rees orphans, Chambers		54	1	5
Mathias Gahagan, Bledsoes		238	20	2
Martha Dixon, wid. R. S.	do.	39	11	3
Nancy Shadwick, wid. Allums		209	16	2
Evan Harvey's orphans, Kendricks		168	15	2
Isham Caswell,	do.	220	16	1
Thomas Hogan's orphans, Sparks		166	15	1

RABUN
Hubbard Kerns, Godfreds	38	5	4
Elizabeth Myers, wid. Godfreys	32	26	1
Abraham Nichols, Millicans	126	14	1

RICHMOND
Ann Fulcher, widow, Kellys	248	5	3
Wm. Jackson, Treadwells	66	4	3
John W. Houghton, do.	82	8	2
George R. Rountree, Ferris	179	20	2
John G. Polhill, Blacks	92	4	1
Jacob McCulloch, sr. Kellys	188	3	2
Patsey Radford, w. R. S. Blacks	129	14	2
Wm. Moody, 123rd district	21	26	1

TATTNALL
John Dubberly, R. S., Conners	144	31	1
Hez. Grace, w. R. S., Graces	103	10	2
John Fiveash, R. S., McDuffies	303	5	1
James K. Archer, Conners	112	5	5
Elias Fiveash, Graces	263	28	1
Jacob Blocker, jr., Deloaches	279	15	1
Wm. Rogers, sr., R. S., Conners	40	18	1
John Ruis, jr. Coseys	80	11	1
Caleb Thomas, R. S., McCalls	35	14	1
Elijah Callahan, Duprees	206	33	1

TELFAIR
Normon A. McLeod, Barentines	25	10	5
John Ashleys orps. Wilkinsons	26	10	2

TALIAFERRO
Anderson Maddux, Towns	67	4	5

TWIGGS
John G. Hayes, Blackshears	67	24	1
Fred Towle, Solomans	95	8	5
Jane Eldridge, wid. Pearsons	135	1	5
Kendred Pace, Hollidays	93	1	5
Wiley Lane, Graggs	84	22	2
J. A. Bryan, F. Chamberlains	101	7	2
Liddy Nix, widow, Wimberleys	220	8	1
Griffin Gandy, Pearsons	46	21	1

UPSON
Richard Purnell, sol. Hattocks	62	9	5
Anson Brazell, Coopers	132	6	1

WALTON
William H. Meredith, 503rd dist.	169	2	3

Fortunate Drawers — Capts. Dist. No. Dt. Sec.
Littleberry Eeder, 418th dist.		197	20	2
John H. Sexton, Snows		112	4	3
Woodson Allen, R. S., Pools		248	12	2
Robert Ellison, jr. sol. 250th distfl		79	13	5
George Martin, 559th district		4	2	4
Christian Cobb, wid. 559th dist.		236	9	2

WARE
J.A.,M.&MaryWalker ills. Bogans		200	26	1
Dread Newburn, Greens		41	6	2

WILKINSON
Daniel S. Pierce, Mathews	91	12	1
Ann Brown, w. R. S. Fairchilds	113	2	1
John C. Ursery, illegit. Currys	57	30	1
Hezekiah Williams, Mandersons	247	10	1
Mills Oden, Shows	101	7	3
David Culpepper, do.	135	4	2
Mary A. Castleberry, wid. do.	149	27	1
Abram Laseter, Mayos	217	2	2
Rebecka Stuckey, hus.ab. Currys	137	5	4
Wm. McGanghey, Ragans	45	16	1

WILKES
Micajah Crenshaw, Hamacks	201	6	2
James W. Jack, soldier, Wests	67	4	1
Jonathan Doster, R. S., Greens	166	15	2
Willis Carlisle, Rices	85	26	1
Josiah B. Hudgins, Hopkins	44	24	1
L.,J.,S.&J.D.Hide, ills Ragsdales	201	27	1
Joel Eskles, Reeves	168	9	5
John G. Wellborn, Popes	20	24	2
Jesse Blackburn, Hopkins	269	21	2
John Q. West, Greshams	97	5	1

WAYNE
John Smith, Mannings	51	22	1
S..M.&T.Taylor, fa.ab.McKinneys	195	2	3

WARREN
Elizabeth Finchs illegits. Sanders	15	10	5
John McGlamory, R. S., Adkins	156	10	1
Miles G. Broom, Parhams	205	13	1
Robert Attoway, Adkins	133	2	3
Mary Ann Rivers, w. R.S., Adkins	30	2	2
John Wilson, Kinseys	382	28	1
Benjamin Hurt, Rogers	117	21	2
Nancy Revell orphans, Sanders	116	24	1

WASHINGTON
James Amison, Weathers	113	10	5
George Moye, Gilberts	343	20	2
John Mathis, R. S., Jordans	122	3	5
Alsey Vincen, Oquins	96	7	5
John Bedgood, R. S. Wimberlys	30	2	4
Clem Price, Whitfields	1	9	3
Herod Bowen, soldier, Gilberts	234	12	2
Wm. Forehand, Tysons	116	7	3
Nathan McGehee, Woods	82	17	1

11TH DAY'S DRAWING—19th March

APPLING
Susannah Cook, w. R. S., McDonalds		229	14	2
David Gillet,	do.	161	7	3
William Herren, Morgans		180	9	3

BALDWIN.

Fortunate Drawers	Capts. Dist.	No.	Dt.	Sec.
James Pettigrew's orphans, Bivins		60	27	1
Andrew Du Bourg, Buchanans		77	10	1
Samuel R. Sanders, do.		156	5	1
Jane Birden, orphan		309	1	2
Sarah Smith, w. R. S., Buchanans		284	11	2

BIBB.

	No.	Dt.	Sec.
Henry Land, Flanders	184	3	2
Isabella Clark, widow, do	126	29	1
M. Jackson's children, fa. ab. Lloyds	108	7	4
Elias Williamson, Flanders	178	17	1
Ann M. Dewitt, orphan, Bates	2	6	2

BULLOCH.

	No.	Dt.	Sec.
Nancy Burt, widow, Richardsons	209	11	1
Nancy Benton, widow, do.	188	16	2
John Futch, Deloachs	24	22	1
Dempsey Cannon, do.	71	7	5
William S. Redding, Richardsons	227	5	1
Robert Odum, Deloachs	40	17	1

BURKE.

	No.	Dt.	Sec.
Benjamin Y. Saxon, McKays	70	16	1
Henry D. W. Jones, Dukes	127	8	5
Aaron Barrow, Gordons	209	13	2
William Smith, McKays	46	16	1
Elizabeth Clegg, wid., Thompsons	179	7	2
Wiley Wimberly, Brooms	197	6	2
Thomas Grace's orphans, Seegars	58	14	5
Lucy Linn, widow, Wests	72	32	1
Rigdon Heath, do.	156	9	1
Mary Hutcheons, widow, Lynchs	168	16	1

BUTTS.

	No.	Dt.	Sec.
William Jones, Moors	187	27	1

CHATHAM.

	No.	Dt.	Sec.
Susannah Shly, widow, McDonells	83	3	3
Eli Ajohns, R. S., Baines	164	9	3
Elizabeth Floyd, widow, McDonnells	85	21	2
Mary Demere, widow, Haydens	14	28	1
Mariah McCann, orp. of John Baines	48	15	2
Gardner Tuft's orphans, Haydens	2	27	1
Frederick R. Greene, orp. Nungazers	256	11	3
Benjamin S. Waldson, Gaddys	152	4	2
William Herb, Geredons	148	10	3
H. F. Permenter, orp. of Jno., Baines	47	20	2

CLARK.

	No.	Dt.	Sec.
William E. Strong, Andersons	28	6	3
Howell Elder, soldier, Dickens	91	19	1
William L. Mitchell, Gahagans	48	28	1
William Humphreys, Dickens	52	8	3
Charles M. Sledge, Frosts	92	3	2
Patrick Brown, Ransoms	90	9	1
Martin Vickers, Wrights	35	25	1
Jesse Hinson, Lumpkins	21	5	1
Jas. Carter, illegitimate, Humphreys	348	20	2
Francis Farrar, Wrights	43	9	3
Samuel Simonton, Ransoms	244	11	1
James Hinson, sen., Lumpkins	149	1	5

COLUMBIA.

	No.	Dt.	Sec.
Henry Ball, Bealls	82	6	4
Jesse Steed, Boltons	125	1	4
Elizabeth Reese, w. R. S., Adams	196	8	5
Samuel Ramsey's orphans, Ramseys	278	3	4
Elizabeth Gay, orphan, Dranes	231	5	1
Thomas E. Burnside, Bealls	36	23	1

CRAWFORD.

	No.	Dt.	Sec.
John S. Carley, Ellis	81	20	2
Jonathan Harrison, Rhodes	140	21	1

DEKALB.

Fortunate Drawers	Capts. Dist.	No.	Dt.	Sec.
Hinson Dempsey, Merritts		120	1	1
Alfred Edwards, Hays		29	13	1
Richard Rutledge, Browns		245	24	1
John Ward, jr. Edwards		250	20	2
Benjamin Merritt's orphans, Merritts		120	6	5
Thomas D. Harris, Conns		40	17	2
William Donaldson, do.		141	4	1

DOOLY.

	No.	Dt.	Sec.
Gabriel Parker, Hogans	217	16	1
Samuel P. Bond, do.	262	14	1
Thomas Coleman, Andersons	105	1	4
Asia Joiner, do.	151	30	1

EARLY.

	No.	Dt.	Sec.
Eliz. Branham, illegitimate, Wilsons	212	5	2
William Johnson, Speers	158	4	3
Reuben Wright, sr. R. S., Porters	25	9	5

EFFINGHAM.

	No.	Dt.	Sec.
Felix Hurst, Stricklands	52	29	1

ELBERT.

	No.	Dt.	Sec.
John Merritt, soldier, Hortons	58	14	2
Job Bowers, Merritts	293	8	1
Henry Bramblet, R. S., Hortons	161	20	2
James Lunsford, soldier, do.	189	10	2
James Dudley, R. S. Merritts	53	8	2
William R. Powell, Dunns	159	11	2
Lewis Parker, Merritts	237	7	1
Toren Merritt, R. S., do.	56	6	3
Sarah Couch, widow, Dobbs	127	32	1

EMANUEL.

	No.	Dt.	Sec.
Mary Whiddon, w. R. S., Chasons	4	1	4
Roger Smith, Fountains	25	24	2
Mary Brown, widow, Moors	162	11	5

FAYETTE.

	No.	Dt.	Sec.
John Short, soldier, 9th	26	1	5
Garnett Holmes, Dodsons	139	30	1
Waitus Veal, Whartons	30	12	3

FRANKLIN.

	No.	Dt.	Sec.
Joseph Couch, Cokers	65	18	1
B. Higginbotham, sol., Blankinships	49	16	5
Isaac Gray, Chandlers	267	9	5
Joseph Parsons, McDonalds	253	11	2
Gillam Wilbanks, R. S., Tabors	178	20	2
Milly Jackson, illegitimate, Candells	48	5	3
Thomas G. Edwards, soldier, do.	9	10	5
Hartwell D. Freeman, ill. Hudsons	159	1	3
David Smith, Chandlers	162	18	1

GLYNN.

	No.	Dt.	Sec.
Luke Bandy, McLeods	128	3	2
S., W., J. & T. Tison, orps. McLeods	16	32	1

GREENE.

	No.	Dt.	Sec.
Arthur Foster, R. S., Winkfields	194	5	5
H. P. Mabry, soldier, Woodhams	167	11	5
John H. Veasey, Greens	208	15	1
Robert Langham, Halls	86	14	1
Thomas Holland, R. S., Elys	235	21	2
Liddy Richards, w. R. S. Astins	93	20	1

GWINNETT.

	No.	Dt.	Sec.
Thomas Whorton, Finchers	173	9	5
John D. Kendrick, soldier, Whortons	135	6	5
Susannah Martin, widow, Greens	92	6	4
Joseph Downey, R. S., Moors	26	6	2
Levi Taylor, Greens	248	3	3
Fuldin Maddox, Cupps	292	20	2
Abigail Hamilton, w. R. S., Bakers	36	6	2
John Puckett, Davis	181	9	2
John Pitman, R. S., Bakers	286	6	1
William Clark, Caruthers	27	5	2

Fortunate Drawers	Capts.	Dist.	No.	Dt.	Sec.
Moses Winters	Bakers		288	23	2
Jonathan Blythe	do.		107	4	5
James Lowry	Greens		157	7	5
William Berry	Robertsons		94	2	1

HANCOCK.

Betsy Simmerson, hus. absent, 11th			111	18	2
Joseph Magee, 102d			243	7	3
John Greer, 108th			15	5	5

HENRY.

Thomas B. Johnson	Risons		105	21	1
William Duncan	Wards		210	23	1
Margaret McWalters, w. R. S.	Grays		16	5	4
Jonathan Benton	Millers		53	5	5
Stephen Pace, jr.	Harris		181	11	5
Anthony Crumbley, R. S.	Grays		212	28	1

HABERSHAM.

Hugh Pierce	Langstons		34	15	2
David K. Beaty	Bryans		43	19	1
Clarissa Merrida, widow	Suttons		228	11	2
Cosby Vining	Bryans		190	5	2
Jeremiah Chastain	Tates		148	14	5
Benjamin Forester	Kenzies		51	13	1

HALL.

Samuel McCulloch	Roberts		37	22	2
John Boller, R. S.	Alreds		189	18	1
William Kelly	Floyds		18	19	2
Noah Strong	Smiths		294	3	4

HOUSTON.

David Lewis	Yarboroughs		178	12	3

IRWIN.

Charles McCullers	McCalls		97	17	1

JACKSON

Thomas J. Bowen, soldier	Duncans		229	9	3
Jane Ware, widow	Rogers		371	7	1
John Taylor	Millers		172	29	1
John Justus, R. S.	Lindseys		215	11	5
James A. Baites	Millers		38	29	1
Eldridge Barker	Storys		299	5	3
Amra Edwards, widow	do.		373	3	4

JASPER

Joseph McMichael, sol.	Comptons		46	6	1
Josiah Freeman's orphans	Trussells		95	15	1
Alexander Nelson	Wilsons		14	27	1
Paulina A. Lyons, ill.	Johnsons		9	10	3
Jesse Teal	Wilsons		181	5	5
Jonathan Poulson	Camerons		182	5	5
Thomas Massey	Dardens		98	5	4
Henry Touchstone	Sparks		113	20	1
Robert Sanson	Butts		119	10	1
James Duncan	Wilsons		155	19	1
Jesse Parrot	Butts		273	1	4
Absalom Ramsey	Barnetts		200	15	1
George Guffin	Robersons		157	2	3
James Brooks, R. S.	Barnetts		59	9	4
Alexander Cochran	Dardens		106	2	3
Robert J. McCurdy	Butts		160	12	5
Robert Price	Wilsons		265	5	3
John Lamb	Comptons		50	3	3
George Wayne, R. S.	do.		16	3	1
Christopher C. Frith	Holmes		140	7	2
Nathaniel Bellah	Keys		140	2	4

JEFFERSON.

James Lowe	Causeys		80	2	2
Nancy Gibson, hus. absent	Marshalls		63	3	3

JONES.

Raleigh Spinks	Spinks		239	5	2
Thomas Moon	Dosters		212	9	3
Thomas J. Megee	Mullins		169	7	3

Fortunate Drawers	Capts.	Dist.	No.	Dt.	Sec.
Shadrach Goodwin, R. S.	Blounts		69	13	5
Asa Eiland	Hamacks		72	9	5
Lyman Meacham	Woods		213	19	1
Thomas Stripling	Davis		88	9	1
Robert Baldwin's minors	Blounts		234	3	4
John Smith	Dosters		233	4	1
Felix Lewis	Woods		137	24	2
Anderson Houze	Davis		203	11	1
Henry Mitchell's orphans	Pope's		150	6	5
John Jones, R. S.	Newbys		23	14	2
John Modesett	Duncans		7	20	2
James Stripling	Davis		249	29	1

LAURENS.

Frederick Askew	Plummers		120	8	1
Dennis Hilliard	Deans		186	6	2
John Steptoe	Whiteheads		260	2	3
Martha Martin, widow	Plummers		191	8	5
James Harpe	Whiteheads		104	11	5

LIBERTY.

Henry W. Bacon, orphan, 15th			110	15	5
John Stewart's orphans	do.		163	2	5

LINCOLN.

William Harper	Lonorgans		82	5	2

MADISON.

Wyllie Glover	Christians		208	6	3
Thomas M. Grimes's orps.	Hanas		250	10	1
Noble Clements	Culbertsons		229	6	2
Green Pierce	Caldwells		269	22	1

McINTOSH

James Middleton	McCranies		102	10	1

MONROE.

Isom Alford	Brown		102	2	4
B.,W.&L.R.Mullin, ills.	Greshams		129	17	1
Jordan Lyons	Turners		154	8	3
Sterling Andrews	Millers		248	10	5
Benj. J. Holley	Finches		116	2	4
Benjamin Robison	Houses		123	5	2
Jonathan Rutland	Woodwards		97	9	3
James L. Powell	Turners		86	20	2
Benjamin Robison	Houses		275	5	3
William McGinty	do.		186	16	2
John Teakle	do.		149	9	3
John Wynn orphan	Wrights		171	3	4
Wm. Smiths orphans	Turners		247	2	1
Daniel L. McCurry	Johnsons		118	4	4

MORGAN.

Israel Beckworth	Stokes		88	1	2
Wm. Feagans, sr., R. S.	Jennings		224	33	1
Albert Few	Shermans		19	15	1
Enoch Mathews	Watsons		165	8	3
Levi Lane	Youngs		26	21	1
Creed M. Jennings	Jennings		57	5	3
Nancy Wright, hus. ab.	Christians		165	6	2

MONTGOMERY.

Jas. Brownings orps.	Pridgeons		124	26	1

NEWTON.

Corneluos Jackson	Hays		166	9	5
Sarah Dees, widow	do.		206	14	2
Gabriel Gunn	Dyers		15	7	4
James H. Osborn, orph.	Clarks		136	9	5
Larkin Brown	Clarks		210	3	1
John Truitt	Moss'		237	2	5
David Hudson	Clarks		136	12	1
Frances Thompson, wid.	Snows		151	13	1

Fortunate Drawers	Capts.	Dist.	No.	Dt.	Sec.
Isham Weaver, sol.	Allredds		224	5	2
Warren Bridges, Hays			4	13	1
OGLETHORPE.					
Susannah Patman, wid.	Arnolds		170	29	1
Willie Bush, Lacys			260	6	1
Wm. Simmons orph.	Hardmans		54	3	2
M. & M. Gunnells ills. 235th dist.			54	19	2
Wm. B. Richards, Bells			375	20	2
Wesley Shopsher, Deeks			32	1	2
Nancy Crowder, Burford			141	21	1
John Clements orps.	Holloways		87	3	5
Jesse Gaulding,	do.		137	27	1
Thos. P. Brooks, Blanton Hills			231	11	2
PIKE.					
James Whatley, Mays			195	33	1
PULASKI.					
Allen W. Thomas, Sparrows			60	23	2
John S. Isler, Powells			227	15	1
William Hawl, Bracewells			200	16	1
PUTNAM.					
John Parham, sol., Lamars			129	3	2
John A. Robertsons, Kendricks			136	9	3
Joshua Martins orphs. Duprees			226	10	5
Easter Roberts, wid. Choices			256	13	2
Jas. Ledbetters orphans, Sparks			125	1	5
John Blalock, Allums			198	5	5
L. Tomlinson, Allums			205	30	1
RABUN.					
Joseph Pinson, R. S. Mercers			19	1	1
Henry McCornick, ill., Godfreys			195	1	4
James Smith, Milligans			48	10	3
RICHMOND.					
Mary McTyre, widow, James			249	11	5
George Baulineau, Treadwells			5	31	1
Wm. J. Hobby, jr. Huntingtons			2	8	4
Charles Burch, Kellys			204	6	5
F. B. T. Brown, 600th district			126	9	2
Ann Bulger, widow, Treadwells			200	20	1
Stephen Mullally, Huntingtons			205	22	1
J. A. & W. Panton, ors. Blacks			169	3	4
Wm. McCain, Murphys			61	25	1
James Colley, James			235	10	1
Zach. McGowen, Huntingtons			228	5	4
SCRIVEN.					
Richard Mills, Kemps			221	26	1
TATTNALL.					
Jeremiah Revels, Corseys			79	11	2
Jesse Johnakin, do.			81	5	5
Nathan Brooton, sr. Conners			136	11	1
Brice Andersons orps. do.			61	20	2
James Osteen, Dees			118	29	1
TELFAIR.					
Wm. Morrison's ors. Robertsons			70	3	1
Frederick Brown, Barentines			56	20	1
Wm. Wilkinson, Lampkins			74	12	2
Alex. B. McRae, Robertsons			82	16	1
TWIGGS.					
Milledge Stevens, Kelleys			131	22	1
James F. Wheeler, Streetmans			202	8	1
Laz. Soloman, R. S., Blackshears			41	14	2
Frances Sauls, wid. Wimberlys			223	11	3
Henry Wall, R.S., Solomans			304	3	4

Fortunate Drawers	Capts.	Dist.	No.	Dt.	Sec.
Bartlet Bridger, Hollidays			121	13	1
Lucinda Gilbert, illegit. Graggs			276	15	1
UPSON.					
John S. Traylor, Hattoxs			151	9	1
Stephen Garner, soldire, Ezells			56	2	1
WALTON.					
Stephen Lankford, McQuirters			130	12	5
Thomas Gilbert, Beasleys			53	9	1
Thomas Buse, Hudsons			66	15	5
John Carter, sol., McQuirtors			210	3	5
Bennett Baggett, Hudsons			3	22	1
Nancy Masses, w. R.S., Hudsons			150	1	4
Jesse Black, Snows			154	8	4
WARREN.					
Elizabeth Gunn, widow, Adkins			35	2	1
Gilley Golden, Kinseys			189	25	1
Benjamin Morelands orps. Bulls			73	9	3
Dennis Lindsey, Jones			198	14	2
Rhody Danelly, widow, Jones			104	13	5
James Wilson, Sanders			60	9	2
Sarah Heflin, w. R.S., Rogers			235	15	2
Josiah Mitchell, Sanders			228	7	3
John Mathews, Kinseys			89	6	3
Aug. B. Dunneway, ill. Adkins			274	22	1
John Kitchen,	do.		202	19	2
Randolph Thorp, Kinseys			251	1	4
William Hill, R. S., Brinkleys			200	8	5
William Dickson, Downs			14	15	1
Benjamin Thompson, Sanders			323	28	1
Abner Raley, Jones			222	21	3
WASHINGTON.					
Allen Gilbert, Gilberts			302	10	2
Paton Jackson, Whitfields			163	5	5
Asaph Mills, Mannings			287	15	1
Daniel Williams, sr. sol. Castelows			6	9	1
Sidney Asteen, wid. Currys			238	2	3
Wm. L. Tooke, McLendons			170	9	5
William L. Curry, Jordans			2	11	5
WILKINSON.					
Ester Wilkerson, w. R. S., Mayos			70	13	1
Isaac Stevens, Currys			266	5	3
Hiram Allen, Smiths			218	6	1
Wiley Jones, Curreys			164	5	4
John W. Stephens, R. S., Ragans			153	10	1
Amanda L. Beall orph. Curreys			238	9	3
E. & J. Brown ors. Mandersons			245	5	1
WILKES.					
William Davis, R.S., Wootens			254	2	4
Samuel Willborns orps. Popes			237	10	5
William C. Armor, Reeves			193	19	2
John C. Burdett, Lukers			156	6	4
David Simmons, Greens			179	24	2

12TH DAY'S DRAWING—March 20.

APPLING.					
Harmon Dean, Mathis			28	11	1
BALDWIN.					
James A. Jeter, Ginns			230	24	1
Samuel Beckham, R. S., Bivins			84	3	2
Gideon Flewellen, Wicks			253	4	1
Elizabeth Babb, wid. R. S., Doles			103	20	2
Elijah M. Callaway, Wicks			166	16	1

(33)

BIBB.

Fortunate Drawers Capts. Dist.	No.	Dt.	Sec.
Ebenezer Keeney, Bates	58	3	3
Rice Durritt, Flanders	119	32	1
William Wilson, Rutlands	229	9	2
Ashburn D. Davis, Flanders	43	8	5
M., M., S., & J. Ham, orps. Rutlands	74	8	3
Daniel Monroe, do.	80	77	1
James H. Hardaway, Flanders	95	2	2

BULLOCH.

	No.	Dt.	Sec.
Wiley Bird, Burnetts	292	1	2
Jincy Ponncy, ill. Richardsons	124	7	1
Penelope Bowen, widow, Turners	18	6	4
Dempsey Stunaland, Deloachs	156	17	1
David Lee, R. S., McCalls	286	23	2
George W. Love, orp. do.	239	13	2

BURKE.

	No.	Dt.	Sec.
William Stuart's orphans, Brooms	36	4	1
Gideon M. Coil's orphans, Dugas	257	23	2
Henry Dawson, McKays	130	4	1
Isaac Paris, Thompsons	2	11	2
David Perkins, Wards	77	31	1
Leaston Sneed, Corkers	147	2	3
Elizabeth Coil, widow, Dugas	247	11	2
David Bailey, Thompsons	267	11	2
Benjamin Powell, R. S., Gordons	56	12	2
Seth Tarver, Gaffs	126	12	2
John Nichols, Seegars	63	3	2
Robert Grumbles, Brooms	191	4	1

BUTTS.

	No.	Dt.	Sec.
John Tanner, Kights	12	10	5
John P. McWhorter, Johnsons	200	2	4

CAMDEN.

	No.	Dt.	Sec.
Eliza Fitchett, orphan, Baileys	1	8	5

CHATHAM.

	No.	Dt.	Sec.
John H. Oldershaw,	127	7	3
William H. Baker, Haydens	242	13	2
Elizabeth Remshart, wid. Geredons	174	10	3
Samuel Henry, Gaddys	81	12	2
John Prendergrast,	53	29	1
Lawrence Servoy, Baines	138	10	1
Joseph J. Parks, do.	166	27	1
Victor Hamel's orphans, Geredons	152	6	3
Col. Steele White's orphans, Baines	254	11	3
Robert Harvey, Reeds	122	23	2
Maria Williams, w. R. S., Haydens	135	13	1
Frederick Heinman, Baines	224	14	2
Victor Christie, widow, McDonnells	134	14	2
John Cabos, R. S., Baines	40	5	3

CLARK.

	No.	Dt.	Sec.
Caroline Barnett, widow, Andersons	176	3	3
William Kelly, do.	108	10	3
Wyly A. Jones, McCrees	157	2	5
Henry Mitchell, Andersons	57	8	5
James Beall, Dickins	97	4	5
Nancy Malone, w. R. S., Davenports	188	10	1
William P. Graham, Lumpkins	64	2	2
Montford Strong, McCrees	249	12	1
Virgil M. Akridge, Wrights	301	8	5
John Luke, McDonalds	183	13	1
Charles Prices, Gahagans	19	3	1
William O. Anderson's orps. Wrights	12	5	2

COLUMBIA.

	No.	Dt.	Sec.
George Gray, soldier, Tankersleys	32	13	2
Edward M. Crawford, Ramseys	172	12	3
John Strickland, Adams	116	18	2
Joseph Harley, R. S., Boltons	92	2	4
John Tinsley's orphans, Ramseys	118	7	2
Joseph Davis, soldier, Bealls	71	26	1

Fortunate Drawers Capts. Dist.	No.	Dt.	Sec.
Richard Meriwether, Culbreaths	40	16	2
John Carroll, Drancs	52	5	1
James Taylor, Ramseys	210	33	1
Isaac Stallings, Boltons	172	11	2

DECATUR.

	No.	Dt.	Sec.
Kindred Hall, Ferrells	43	8	4

DEKALB.

	No.	Dt.	Sec.
Francis Ward, Browns	281	17	2
Bienford Caldwell, Merritts	244	16	2
William Sansom, do.	159	7	3
John Trimble, R. S., Conns	234	8	1
Benjamin Plaster, soldier, Merritts	5	16	1
Joseph Simmons, Stephens	324	1	4
John M. Williams, Hays	42	9	1

DOOLY.

	No.	Dt.	Sec.
Harmon Howard, Bowens	60	17	2
Berryan Williams, Harris	133	7	3
Green W. Fountain, Andersons	82	11	3

ELBERT.

	No.	Dt.	Sec.
Gabriel Smether, R. S., Dunns	88	7	2
Wiley Butler, Bells	59	8	4
Thomas Burton, R. S., Tates	217	4	3
Elijah Kelly, lunatic, Paces	16	16	1
Willis Bond, Hortons	31	5	4
Sarah Henry, widow, Paces	105	2	4

EMANUEL.

	No.	Dt.	Sec.
Isaac M. Norman, 57th	139	2	3
Moses Hart, Moors	228	3	3
William W. Heath, illegitimate, 49th	85	22	2
Jeremiah Spence, McGars	94	22	2
Martha Smith's, illegitimate, Daniels	167	17	2

FAYETTE.

	No.	Dt.	Sec.
John Graves, sen., Whortons	218	31	1
William Jackson, Browns	100	14	1
Thomas Cox, Whartons	233	22	1
Tandy Mullican, do.	95	10	2
Anna Hutson, widow, Wests	110	4	4

FRANKLIN.

	No.	Dt.	Sec.
William B. Gillespie, Candells	145	16	2
George W. Humphries, Jones	177	11	5
Rhoda Young, husband ab. Walters	198	5	2
Abner Sheridan, Candells	101	28	1
Christopher Holbrook, Blankinships	98	7	1
Benjamin Holbrook, Blankinships	98	7	1
Benjamin Cleaveland, sol., Bennetts	81	4	4
John Jayroe, Hudsons	87	11	2
Daniel Manley's orphans, Cokers	232	22	1
Levina Howell, deaf, Blankinships	175	16	1

GLYNN.

	No.	Dt.	Sec.
James Russ, Burnetts	144	5	2

GREEN.

	No.	Dt.	Sec.
Henry Joiner, Woodhams	158	24	1
James M. Harris, illegitimate, do.	201	9	1
Nancy Wood, widow, Robins	196	21	2
Jesse Booles, orphan, Newsoms	4	20	2
William W. Coley, Knowles	37	32	1

GWINNETT.

	No.	Dt.	Sec.
W, M, E, I, S & E. Hunt orps. Madduxs	15	13	1
Catharine Ezzell widow, Davis	108	16	2
Mathew Goss, Woodroughs	250	31	1
William Estis, Robertsons	228	7	1
John B. Benson, Greens	238	4	1
William Yancy, Davis	106	4	4
Henry St. J. Sparks, Hunicutts	17	23	2
Solomon Johnson, Hills	107	3	2
William Smith, sen. R. S., Finchers	143	12	1
Th. Stewart, wounded soldier, Hills	238	6	5
Joseph Naler, Greens	70	16	2

(34)

Fortunate Drawers Capts. Dist.	No.	Dt.	Sec.
Henry Sparks, Evans	103	12	1
John Stapp, Moors	272	8	1
William Page, soldier, Dunbars	147	22	1
Britton Osburn, Robertsons	187	26	1
Austin Hide, Madduxs	77	7	1

HANCOCK.

Newell Waller, 108th	228	20	2
Telitha Pullin's illegitimates, 112th	66	6	2
Thos. R. Miller, illegitimate, Coxens	233	23	2
James Jones, 104th	202	6	3
Thomas Little, 108th	31	5	5
Seaborn J. Culver, 111th	25	5	1

HENRY.

Elijah Akin, Allens	72	4	2
James B. A. Crumble, Wards	49	18	2
Micajah Brooks, R. S., Allens	26	24	2
George W. Hill, Gosdens	226	8	1
Alexander McKibbin, Grays	10	3	1

HABERSHAM.

Zachariah Kytle, Suttons	131	8	5
William Perry, Tates	250	23	1
William Callar, minor, Suttons	3	10	3
Elisha Dyer, Kenzies	240	19	2
Abner Center, jr., minor, Langstons	115	9	2
James Ellard, jr. Bryans	57	22	1
Andrew Sperlin, Tates	132	24	1
Henry Woody's orphans, Martins	24	4	1

HALL.

Thomas Savage, sr. R. S., Harrisons	58	28	1
William Wallis, Walkers	61	4	3
Emeline M. Corinton, orp. Dorseys	196	15	1
Hardin Hulsey, illegitimate, Hardens	231	2	2
Robert Little, Alreds	64	14	2
Thomas B. McDow, do.	112	12	3
Elizabeth Fisher, widow, Garrards	152	15	2

HOUSTON.

Isaiah Smith, Smiths	25	9	2
Jacob Johnson, Pattens	67	11	2
Joseph Cutts. R, S., Farnels	125	5	1
Jason Gardner, Becks	199	12	5

IRWIN.

John Sutton, jr., Dixons	5	20	2

JACKSON.

James Bradford, Storys	64	5	5
Hugh Beaty, Doss's	121	12	1
Simeon B. Coffin, Millers	42	6	1
James J. Wilson, soldier, Duncans	173	21	2
Lucy Williams, widow, Rogers	331	20	2
Joseph Tanner, Duncans	248	22	2
Amen Yarbrough, Bowens	138	26	1
James Blanks, sen. R. S., Allens	3	1	3
Josiah C. Wallace, Storys	133	2	5
Mary Smith, illegitimate, Staplers	32	7	1

JASPER.

Joseph Crenshaw, Owens	305	28	1
Benjamin T. Edmonson, Baynes	244	13	2
John Shelar, Wilders	42	8	5
Elizabeth Holland, w. R. S., Owens	21	17	2
Wiley Bullard's orphans, Butts	89	12	1
Robert Chaffin, Trussells	8	10	3
Harriss Samuels, Holmes	28	7	4
Susannah Harper, widow, Camerons	154	2	4
James T. Heath, Robinsons	239	32	1
Celia Jackson, widow, Shropshires	93	11	1

JEFFERSON.

James O. Abbott, soldier, Boyds	303	28	1
William Jones' orphans, Ross's	254	22	2

Fortunate Drawers Capts. Dist.	No.	Dt.	Sec.
Morton N. Burch, soldier, do.	71	7	1
Gideon Thompson's orphans, Beatys	56	5	4
Joshua Watson, R. S., Marshalls	91	10	1
Nathan Bryant, Cunninghams	112	6	5
Elijah Shepherd, Waldens	8	9	3
William Pool, Beatys	102	2	1
James H. Johns, Elliotts	128	11	2

JONES.

John Fails, soldier, Stewarts	158	15	1
John Barnard's orphans, Davis	199	28	1
Rachel Gore, widow, Newbys	131	5	1
John Bentley, Hamacks	68	6	5
James Holliday, do.	60	21	1
Payton Vinson, Gibsons	130	6	3
Joel Riggell, Davis	73	6	4
Elizabeth J. Smith, widow, Popes	150	20	1
Brinkley Hollon, do.	204	7	3
James C. Jordain, Davis	138	22	1
Thomas Clark, orphan, Hendersons	253	17	1
James C. Jordain, Davis	158	11	2
Polly H. Harvey, widow, Sullivans	236	28	1
Wm. Snowden, father absent, Davis	156	16	2
Philip Catchings, Breedloves	142	2	2

LAURENS.

James Stewart, Hodges	75	13	5
Joseph E. Plummer, Plummers	38	10	3
D. Davis's mins. father absent, Deans	28	4	1
Richard Slaughter, ill., Hodges	258	8	1
Josiah Warren's orphans, Plummers	75	8	3
James Hearnden, idiot, Pavers	179	8	5
George Payne, Spiveys	8	23	2

LIBERTY.

Charles E. Cawdee, 15th	116	1	3
Cuyler Parker, 17th	108	11	3

LINCOLN.

William Wethers, Leveritts	145	6	2
John W. Hambrick, Graves	63	5	2
Andrew Lee, sen., Lonorgans	143	17	2
Simeon McKinney, Gideons	230	7	1

MADISON.

John Simmons, Christians	24	1	4
John P. Vaughn, Phipps	190	16	2
John T. Mitchell, do.	76	7	4
John Hopkins, do.	258	22	1

McINTOSH.

P., J., & E. Hornsby, orps. Demeres	197	4	3
Joseph S. Page, Terrells	129	19	2

MONROE.

Julius Sanders, Stallings	79	24	2
Wm. Wills chil. fa. ab. Greshams	28	5	2
J. Baxter, disabled in l.w.Houses	80	18	2
George Bennett, Houses	94	5	5
Mary Tamplin, Pattersons	19	11	2
Samuel Pool, R. S., Douglass	5	12	5
William Sparks, Wrights	45	7	5
George Parker, sol., Houses	218	10	5
David Aislin, Browns	160	9	1
Burrill Morris, R. S., Greshams	67	1	3
Isaac Willingham, Johnsons	41	33	1
Southey Littleton, sen., Houses	111	21	1

MORGAN.

Mary S. Harper, wid. Canifaxs	150	5	4
Carter Tankerlay, Hitchcocks	166	17	2
Seaborn J. Johnson, Youngs	185	12	5
Joseph Parks orphans, Boswells	57	9	3

(35)

Fortunate Drawers	Capts. Dist.	No.	Dt.	Sec.
G. & Mar. Newsom, ills.	Browns	109	1	3
NEWTON.				
Elisha Talley,	Talleys	20	2	5
John Truett,	Orrs	266	20	2
Shadrick Peavy,	Talleys	65	15	1
John Moss' orphans,	Graves	229	25	1
Joseph Watters,	Pullins	252	31	1
M.T.W.&M. Costly, ills.	Summers	74	22	2
James Poitevent,	Pullens	95	3	4
Eliz. B. Hudson, illegit.	Orrs	145	32	1
John Roberson, sen.	Orrs	137	8	4
William M. Morriss,	Webbs	88	7	3
Augustin W. Evans,	Pullens	68	9	1
Thompson Reeves,	Clarks	28	7	2
OGLETHORPE.				
Jesse Gaulding,	Holloways	72	19	2
Cornelius Furcron,	Rousseaus	70	19	2
E.Jones forT.A.Thomas,	Burfords	181	10	5
Mary Drake, blind,	Rhodes	111	8	5
John Lawless, R. S.,	Burfords	2	8	2
Joseph O. Mason,	Arnolds	11	14	2
Valentine Crook, sol.	Devenports	3	4	5
Nathaniel Barnett,	Burfords	228	10	3
William Vaughn, sol.	Devenports	108	2	2
Jemmy Sims, R. S.	Holloways	237	31	1
Nicholas Powers,	Arnolds	34	13	2
PIKE.				
Polly Edenton Pace,	Weavers	187	11	1
PULASKI.				
Nathan King,	Powells	1	24	1
PUTNAM.				
Edmund Pass,	Blacks	192	1	4
George Eastco,	Sawyers	165	20	1
Thos. Moseleys orphans,	Mizes	212	6	5
Warner Sharbutt,	Sparks	67	11	5
Lewis Lynch,		103	8	3
Shadrack Rowe, R. S.	Clarks	146	10	2
John Tinsley,	Sawyers	61	10	5
Thomas Smith,	Brooks	29	8	2
RABUN.				
Ralph Cobb,	Godfreys	156	13	2
John McClain, R. S.	Milligans	258	6	1
Samuel Anderson,	Godfreys	303	15	1
Rutha Carns' 4 illegitimates,	do.	53	16	1
James Suddeth,	Godfreys	288	7	1
Robert Foster,	Mercers	3	23	2
RICHMOND.				
John Stuckeys orphans,	Kellys	161	17	1
John Clarke,	Treadwells	54	10	2
Francis Oconnor,	Augusta	199	18	2
James W. Bogan,	Hands	197	1	4
Samuel Clarke,	Huntingtons	129	16	2
Charles Labuzan,	Ferris'	211	3	5
John S. Lott,	Huntingtons	134	18	1
Phineas Butler,	Ferris'	378	20	2
Samuel C. Delphy,	Bushes	261	4	3
SCRIVEN.				
Sarah Belsher, widow,	Kemps	37	5	2
David B. Newton,	Hunters	28	22	1
TATTNALL.				
Joshua Dasher,	McCalls	196	15	2
Simon P. Smith,	Conners	196	1	2

Fortunate Drawers	Capts. Dist.	No.	Dt.	Sec.
John Lynn,	Conners	15	24	1
John Stanfield,	Dees	293	22	1
TELFAIR.				
Peter Dubose,	Wilkinson	181	11	3
John Pitts, R. S.,	Robertsons	27	10	2
TALIIAFERRO.				
Clemmonthina Allen, ill.	Towns	322	7	1
TWIGGS.				
Ed. Penny, R. S.,	Chamberlains	238	5	3
Wm. Holleys orphans,	Pearsons	68	12	1
Henry Kint, R. S.,	Bosticks	20	26	1
UPSON.				
James Garrott,	Harrells	249	6	1
Nathaniel F. Walker,	Hattoxs	40	7	4
Abel Treblefield,	Myricks	59	7	3
James Roberts, sen.,	Harrells	80	28	1
Asberry Griggs,	Hattoxs	19	24	1
WALTON.				
Joseph Dudley,	Hudsons	26	5	2
Jesse Mitchell,	Rays	48	11	2
Eliz. Davis, w. R.S.	McQuertors	13	12	2
Thos. Childers, R.S., 418th dist.		148	8	4
David Hardwick,	McQuertors	162	31	1
Ripley Moate, 250th district		52	2	4
WAYNE.				
Job Manning,	Staffords	108	9	3
Frances Hogan, wid.	Staffords	236	21	2
WARREN.				
Harrison Beall, R.S.	Kinseys	19	9	5
William Pilcher,	Downs	157	15	1
Elijah Parham, sol.	Latimers	259	11	2
Athellson Andrews,	Brinkleys	225	15	2
Terrell Wynne,	Rogers	259	20	2
William Mays,	Kinseys	13	2	3
Abraham Heeth,	Brinkleys	243	25	1
Cullen L. Brady,	Downs	244	6	3
Winifred Heeth, wid.	Brinkleys	29	11	1
Peter Overbys orps.	Parhams	122	7	5
Winefred Akins, widow,	Rogers	96	5	5
Hackeliah McMath,	Kinseys	18	17	1
William Fagles orps.	Adkins	142	14	2
WASHINGTON.				
Spencer Brantly,	McLendons	30	10	3
Oty Prosser, R. S.	Oquins	81	8	5
Samuel Barwick,	Wimberlys	154	29	1
David Runnels orps.	McLendons	55	8	5
Henry Murphrey orp.	Mannings	211	10	3
Willis Wootan,	Floyds	46	8	5
Moses Robison,	Mannings	53	24	1
John Lawrence, R. S.	Jordans	284	17	2
Sam. Garrotte, R. S.	Wimberlys	108	3	2
John Harris,	Rushings	226	3	4
Soloman Harrell,	Floyds	84	5	4
John Williams,	Mannings	133	8	5
Ranson L. G. Lee,	Currys	55	15	5
David Curry, sol.	do.	256	22	2
WILKINSON.				
Wiley Cannon,	Fairchilds	34	26	1
William Nobles,	Mandersons	57	32	1
Rachel Woodson, wid.	Curreys	118	21	1
Thomas Harding,	Mathews	121	8	1
Martha Lawson, widow,	Halls	115	12	1

Fortunate Drawers Capts. Dist.	No.	Dt.	Sec.
Menry Askews orps. Fairchilds	26	20	1
Mildridge Pace, wid. Curreys	135	32	1
Eliz. Shofner, w.R.S. Mathews	14	8	2
John Ethredge, Mandersons	88	5	5
Clarkey Proctor, illegit. Shows	64	2	5
Peter Bucholts, jr. Smiths	210	19	2
Mathew Ganey, Shows	305	10	2
John Eady, R. S. Mandersons	14	5	1
William Fennel, Halls	54	12	1
John Hatcher, Mathews	81	14	1
Whitmil Criswell, Mandersons	11	5	3
Fanny Johnson, wid. Shows	82	21	2
Wiley Hopsons orps. Smiths	107	21	2
WILKES.			
J. M. Calloway, sol. Wootens	83	2	1
William Proctors orps. Moors	120	6	1
R. Dawsons orps. Washingtons	53	25	1
James Goodwin, R. S. Reeves	102	16	2
William Evans orps. Rices	146	21	2
Mary Lindsey, w.R.S.Richersons	417	20	2
Robert Cadis jr. orphan, do.	186	3	5
James Walker, Chunns	223	4	2
Charles H. Nelson, Charltons	51	4	2
Hannah Cooksey, wid. Lukers	8	24	1
Nancy M. Powell, widow, do.	46	24	2

13th DAY'S DRAWING—March 21

APPLING.			
James Kemps orps. Collins	105	13	1
Frances Hagan, w. R. S. do.	252	2	3
BALDWIN.			
Will. Minor, Turners	75	5	5
Thos. Hill, orph. Buchanans	161	4	1
Charles Malone, Reddings	188	17	1
Benj. Pulley, Turners	166	18	1
Mariah Cook, wid. Buchanans	132	7	3
BIBB.			
Jonathan Wilder, Carrs	62	20	1
Eliz. & B. Harris, ills. Pickards	141	17	2
Thos. Sacrae, Flanders	23	15	5
Thos. Pickard, Pickards	131	4	1
John D. Chapman, sol. Bates	80	22	2
Malcolm G. Wilkerson, do.	141	21	2
BRYAN.			
Wright Alexander, Harveys	282	4	1
BURKE.			
William Tarver, Fountains	179	9	1
Joseph Merit, illegitimate, Baileys	84	10	2
Bradford Colter, Seegars	97	14	1
William W. Hughes, Robinsons	122	10	2
Council B. Ingram, do.	216	12	3
BUTTS			
Richard Hamblet, Johnsons	28	2	5
Simeon Hamil, Chapmans	74	16	2
William Hamlett, do.	14	4	4
CAMDEN.			
William Niblack, R. S. Beckwiths	256	22	1
CHATHAM.			
William Belcher, Tenbrooks	90	1	2
Michael Kenney,	92	22	1
Loami Baldwin, Savannah	219	17	1

Fortunate Drawers Capts. Dist.	No.	Dt.	Sec.
William S. Campbell, Nungazers	104	17	1
Samuel Loper, Williams	360	3	4
Ann Cooper, widow, McDonnells	194	10	2
John J. Keebler, do.	254	28	1
Thomas G. Miller,	3	10	1
L.S.Cannon,orp.ofJas.W., Baines	206	8	3
Henry D. Weed	186	5	5
Sheftall Sheftall, R. S., Haydens	35	2	5
Charles Sauls, Gaddys	84	6	2
CLARK.			
Isabel Durham, w. R. S., Allreds	223	12	3
Anderson Fambrough's orps., do.	260	3	1
William B. Lumpkin, Frosts	98	4	5
John Nesbitt, do.	67	9	1
Charlie Garner, jr., Andersons	243	4	2
Drury Thomas, Herndons	113	17	2
William Hale, Davis	145	3	2
Richard Nail's orps., McDonalds	61	8	2
Alfred Dorman, do.	192	6	1
Elizabeth Kent, widow, Ransoms	41	4	3
John B. Brittain, Andersons	180	23	2
Isaac Matthews, R.S., Herndons	70	4	5
COLUMBIA.			
Orp. of P. Kirkland, ill. Carrolls	77	25	1
Orps. of Sam'l Pullin, Culbreaths	135	4	5
Sarah Magruder, widow, Talbots	100	22	2
Robert Johns, R. S., Clarks	43	1	5
Thomas Cobb, R. S., Talberts	108	6	1
CRAWFORD.			
Joshua Lee, soldier, Hicks	98	4	2
Washington Hatfield, Hamiltons	269	2	1
DECATUR.			
Isaac Shores, Hawthorns	53	4	2
DEKALB.			
John Henry, Smiths	363	20	2
Hambleton Ware, Bowlings	238	5	1
Ferdinand Jett, Bakers	153	2	1
DOOLY.			
John E. Hargroves, Bowens	36	24	1
EARLY.			
Mourning Canaway, ill. Grimslys	136	13	1
EFFIINGHAM.			
Henry L. Grovenstein, Treutlins	142	23	2
Edmond Tison's orphans, Elkins	196	4	1
ELBERT.			
Matthew Quinn, soldier, Paces	186	3	2
Moses Duncan, soldier, Hortons	162	8	4
Robert Adams, Carpenters	96	7	1
Beverly A. Teasley, do.	13	4	2
Robert Smith, Dunns	145	3	4
John Wanslow, R.S., Blackwells	63	10	2
William Maxwell, Tuckers	422	20	2
Lewis Seals, Carpenters	56	10	5
William Trael, Merritts	90	26	1
EMANUEL.			
Claricey Hambleton, ill., Arlines	152	33	1
Robert Green, McGars	204	2	5
William B. Nabb, Nabbs	24	3	3
Nathan Swett, R. S., Fountains	397	20	2
Ashford Jenkins, Chasons	15	6	2
FAYETTE.			
Benjamin Bolt, Browns	261	22	2

LAND LOTTERY REGISTER—No. 6
[RECORDER OFFICE—PUBLISHED BY GRANTLAND & ORME—PRICE $3.]

NOTE.—Section 1 is Lee County—2 Muscogee—3 Troup—4 Coweta—5 Carroll.

13th DAY'S DRAWING—Continued

Fortunate Drawers	Capts.	Dist.	No.	Dt.	Sec.
FAYETTE.					
Geo. B. Davis, sol.,	McClendons	181	4	1	
Seaborn Simmons,	Whartons	126	21	1	
Allen Reeves,	Browns	108	4	3	
Thomas M. King,	Whartons	9	11	3	
Easter Pollard, wid.	Landrums	247	12	1	
Frederick McGuire,	Wests	231	29	1	
FRANKLIIN.					
Chesley Mills,	Andrews	200	6	1	
Samuel Knox,	Stephens	43	2	5	
Parnal Attaway,	Cokers	48	12	1	
Job Dill,	Stephens	227	12	1	
James H. Davis,	Blankinships	255	2	1	
Jedediah Garrison,	Cokers	239	29	1	
Dennis Shay,	Jones	131	30	1	
Fred'k. Stewart's orps.,	Boswells	184	29	1	
GLYNN.					
Robert Montfort,	McLeods	23	12	1	
Elias Rozier,	Burnetts	75	7	5	
Thomas F. Hazzard,	McLeods	47	7	3	
George Pendarvis,	Burnetts	84	11	1	
GREENE.					
Archibald Carlton,	Dawsons	36	11	5	
Joel Newsom, jr.	Newsoms	108	4	4	
John Gilbert Weeb,	Woodhams	94	2	2	
Wm. S. Branch, R. S.,	Robinsons	278	28	1	
GWINNETT.					
ThomasRowlins, for wife,	Cupps	188	8	1	
John McCormack,	Bakers	29	2	2	
Gin. T. Connelly, insane,	Moores	221	18	2	
Edmund Cooper's orphans,	Davis	146	3	1	
Lewis Sims,	Caruthers	201	24	1	
Elisha M. Grimes, ill.,	Shippys	19	2	3	
Richard B. Turner,	Caruthers	54	23	2	
George H. Caspar,	Moores	166	4	5	
William Price,	Woodroughs	130	14	5	
Balaam J. Bridges,	Robertsons	152	9	1	
Barnett Demsey,	Caruthers	100	2	2	
Philip Lamar,	Moores	264	10	2	
Nathan Jeeter,	Rollins	151	7	5	
Sarah Durbin, widow,	Wallis	107	5	1	
HABERSHAM.					
Orphans of William Pierce,	Tates	86	26	1	
William Thompson,	do.	29	25	1	
Ira Ragsdale,	Suttons	107	7	1	
Stephen Poe, R. S.,	do.	284	7	5	
Malinda Burt, minor,	Bryans	223	28	1	
James Gaddes.	Kenzies	252	8	1	
Mercer Fain,	Fains	249	18	1	
HALL.					
George Gordon,	Garrards	52	18	1	
Isaac Greene,	Dorseys	20	10	2	
Samuel Anderson,	Hardages	64	1	3	
Richard Miller, R. S.	Smiths	17	17	1	
Samuel Leathers, R. S.,	Hardens	35	4	1	
HANCOCK.					
Green K. Dennis,	Adams	208	21	2	
Simmons Butts's orphans.	101st	115	16	2	

Fortunate Drawers	Capts.	Dist.	No.	Dt.	Sec.
Isaac Yarbrough,	118th	112	13	5	
Ewell Webb,	116th	173	12	5	
Benjamin T. Chappell,	Adams	77	13	1	
John Radney,	116th	214	5	2	
Susannah Reynolds, w.R.S.,	101st	103	13	5	
Absalom Tarver, R. S.,	117th	79	3	2	
William Cureton,	114th	248	11	1	
HENRY.					
William Green,	Shaws	111	4	1	
William Rose,	Bryants	267	21	1	
Thomas Ingram,	Shaws	56	14	2	
Simon Cardwell,	Risons	185	10	5	
HOUSTON.					
Samuel Calhoun,	Smiths	232	8	5	
Thomas Johnson, soldier,	Pitts	173	32	1	
William Bill,	Blanshards	237	8	1	
JACKSON.					
Mary J. Ashley, fa. ab.,	Staplers	256	9	2	
Thomas Johnson's orps.	Allens	290	23	2	
Henry Strickland, sen.,	Duprees	28	8	2	
James Morris,	Millers	18	6	5	
Henry Sharp,	do.	148	2	1	
Rebecca Maynard's ill.,	Watersons	152	9	3	
JASPER.					
Abner Smith, R. S.,	Sparks	141	5	5	
Judith Huson, widow,	Camerons	13	8	5	
James Hines, sr., sol.,	Johnsons	171	25	1	
Turner Hunt, R. S.	Reeves	99	31	1	
Solomon Johnson,	Butts	31	26	1	
Elizabeth Hollis, w.R.S.	Trussells	121	7	4	
James Crow, orphan,	Hines	24	16	2	
Edmund C. Harvey,	Shropshiers	114	27	1	
Joshua Wilson, sen. R. S.,	Keys	135	15	1	
William Lambert, R. S.,	do.	56	18	2	
JEFFERSON.					
Judy Purdue, widow,	Beatys	63	12	1	
Hinson Quiney,	Boyds	93	20	2	
Wil. Berrien, w. of R.S.,	Causeys	162	10	3	
JONES.					
Hinton Duncan,	Davis	200	4	5	
Brantley McDaniel,	Stewarts	29	20	1	
C. M. McFarling,w.R.S.,	Mullins	125	16	2	
David Asbey,	Spinks	8	12	3	
Hardy Herbert, soldier,	Burkes	152	6	5	
Benjamin Smith,	Bowens	23	18	1	
Samuel Pruett,	Dosters	128	2	2	
Alexander Sa·ders,	Mullins	243	4	2	
Robert Snellings,	Popes	197	3	5	
Daniel Starnes,	Breedloves	183	5	5	
Edward Clark,	Newbys	253	2	2	
Elizabeth Jones, w. R.S.,	Davis	114	7	2	
Mark Cobb,	Duncans	178	1	1	
Samuel Hodges, illegit.	Stewarts	56	7	1	
Wm. H. Tarver,	Gibsons	181	9	3	
Thomas McLeroy,	Spinks	1	20	2	
LAURENS.					
John Hobbs,	Mizells	180	33	1	
Shugar Forest,	Whiteheads	166	9	1	
Thos. Taylor,	Plummers	175	15	1	

(38)

Fortunate Drawers	Capts.	Dist.	No.	Dt.	Sec.
James Hightower,	Plummers		115	2	2
LIBERTY.					
Wm. Dorsey,	17th district		106	16	1
John Way, jr.	14th do.		190	19	2
LINCOLN.					
Minors of John Caver,	Parks		34	6	4
Joseph Bohannon,	Frasers		81	2	4
Richard Brather,	Prathers		178	4	3
Benton Waltons minors,	Prathers		131	10	2
LOWNDES.					
,Sarah Ritcherson, illegits.	Forths		2	2	3
MADISON.					
Thornton Fitzpatrick,	Christians		188	15	1
James Teaver,	Culbertsons		256	12	1
Willis Strickland,	Bones		164	11	3
Berry M. David,	Culbertsons		250	12	2
James Stephens,	Hanas		57	11	3
Valentine Luker, dumb,	Moons		118	12	2
William Bragg, R. S.,	Caldwells		209	10	2
McINTOSH.					
William Day,	Terrells		219	23	1
MONROE.					
A. McKleroys chil. f.a.	Greshams		42	3	2
Thomas Johnston,	Douglass		20	18	2
John Courson,	Browns		149	14	2
William Adkins, R.S.,	Pattersons		8	8	4
Daniel Richardson,	Greshams		225	18	1
Lovet Smith,	Browns		233	26	1
Philip Scogin,	Johnsons		179	31	1
Richard J. Cheshire,	Wrights		14	32	1
Wm. R. Chappell,	Browns		88	22	2
Robert R. Hines,	Finches		292	15	1
Zacheus S. McKleroy,	Greshams		148	4	1
MORGAN.					
William Johnson, R.S.,	Harwells		150	7	4
Penelope Cox, wid.	Christians		143	23	2
William Smiths orps.	Dawsons		41	21	1
Col. W. Harris' orps.	Jennings		21	22	1
Henly H. Fitzpatrick,	Brooks		193	7	5
Daniel Prince,	Christians		159	5	1
Elias C. Downs,	Jennings		44	31	1
MONTGOMERY.					
David Fennell,	Ryals		33	15	1
Thomas W. Howal,	Wynns		213	6	2
Christopher McRae,	Popes		80	7	5
NEWTON.					
Robert C. Craddock,	Askews		55	7	4
James Savage,	Pullens		62	3	5
Elijah Alewine,	Trammells		36	16	1
Joseph Hand,	Snows		100	4	2
Elizabeth Witcher, wid.	Smiths		22	20	1
J. & Rachel Dukes mins.	Clarks		91	19	2
OGLETHORPE.					
Mason Jones, sol.	Holloways		219	23	2
Richard T. Hanson,	Rosseaus		55	18	2
Sarah Wilsons illegit.	Russaws		237	10	1
William Beasleys orphans,	Dixs		12	19	1
Jacob Meadows, sol.	Simmons		32	14	2
Joseph Woodall, R.S.	Burfords		313	1	2
Fanny Davis, widow,	Hills		63	1	4
John B. Harden,	Hills		145	29	1
Charles Ogden,	Mays		326	8	5

Fortunate Drawers	Capts.	Dist.	No.	Dt.	Sec.
Thomas Pass, sr. R. S.	Floyds		216	21	1
Matthew Bell,	Floyds		30	11	5
Stephen Upsons orps.	Rosseaus		27	6	1
Drury Dupree orphan,	Halloways		90	9	2
James Adams,	Williamsons		213	23	1
PIKE.					
William Spradin,	Weavers		335	7	5
Felix McGinnis, sol.,	Pattersons		215	31	1
P. G. Hancock,	Hartsfields		75	8	2
Esther McBurnett, wid.	Hicks		252	3	4
Bartho. Jenkins, sol.	Pattersons		276	19	2
Richard Bassett, jr.	Arlines		237	27	1
Niell Urquhart, sol.	Weavers		219	30	1
PULASKI.					
Sally Christian, w.R.S.	Thomas		104	12	2
Jesse Hines,	Sparrows		192	5	1
PUTNAM.					
John W. Allen,	Barnetts		61	4	1
Benj. Jordans orphans,	Sanders		294	20	2
Eliz. Cabiness minors,	do.		44	22	1
Thomas Dent,	Stinsons		76	17	1
Henry Cooper, R. S.	Barnetts		193	12	3
James R. Harwell,	Bledsoes		39	9	5
John Reynolds,	Blacks		13	8	1
Hamilton Dukes,	Choices		68	14	1
Thomas Grant,	Sparks		116	25	1
RABUN.					
Arthur George,	Godfreys		355	3	4
Alexander Strickland,	Becks		210	8	1
Nancy Coffee, w.R.S.	Godfreys		20	2	3
Robert Rogers,	Becks		79	20	2
David Fowler, sen.	do.		247	6	1
RICHMOND.					
T. M. Hubbell,	Ferris		197	11	1
Wm. B. Oliver,	Treadwells		191	8	3
Martin Crowley,	Augusta		57	23	1
James S. Shaffer, 123rd district			239	26	1
—— Landsell,	Hands		176	27	1
Ann America Hall, ill.	Augusta		122	29	1
James Tinley,	Kelleys		147	4	2
Daniel Hall,	Blacks		253	15	2
Eliza&IrwinHicks, ors.	Wilcoxs		99	1	5
Edward J. Harden,	Treadwells		206	11	2
Henry Howell,	Kellys		294	23	2
Martha Reed, husband absent			318	28	1
B. K. Hill, 600th district			149	24	1
Green B. Butler,	do.		61	30	1
Martin Grannis,	Ferris		148	30	1
Jas. A. & W. Panton, ors.	Blacks		159	30	1
Daniel Hand,	Augusta		98	5	1
SCRIVEN.					
John Gross,	Poythress		258	20	2
Stephen Mills,	Poythress		252	9	2
Joseph Daughtry, R. S.	Kemps		232	12	1
Joseph Rawls, sol.	Poythress		80	14	2
James L. Mobley,	Lovetts		142	15	2
TATTNALL.					
Frank Drace,	Deloachs		162	23	2
James Anderson,	Dees		226	7	5
John Gilford, jr.	Graces		210	18	1
Mial Collins,	Corseys		83	33	1

Fortunate Drawers Capts. Dist.	No.	Dt.	Sec.
John Camron, McDuffies	131	15	1
Joseph Dubberley, Dees	76	10	1
James Stephens, sen. Deloaches	81	32	1
TELFAIR.			
David Allen, Barentines	197	12	5
Philip D. Logan, Wilkersons	168	7	5
William Hatten, Lampkins	6	3	1
TALIAFERRO.			
Nathaniel Acree, Moors	236	29	1
THOMAS.			
Jarard Wild	42	12	2
TWIGGS.			
Wallis Nobles, Wimberlys	128	24	2
E. Hammock, insane, Wimberlys	49	2	2
Nancy Parks, wid. Chamberlains	46	8	3
Calvin Minshaw, Solomans	140	8	5
UPSON.			
Elijah Hattox, Hattoxs	213	30	1
Stith Mitchell, Harrells	2	2	2
John Andleton, Coopers	38	9	5
Jacob Presnal, sol. Duprees	272	2	3
Daniel Callaway, 589th district	154	5	3
M. C. Lavensworth, Hattoxs	150	5	5
David Allin, Hattoxs	191	7	5
WALTON.			
Susan Wheeler, 249th district	191	9	2
Edmond R. Camp, McQuertors	100	29	1
Elias Beall, jr. Rays	86	6	2
John Bullard, Davis'	239	12	2
David Reds illegits. McQuertors	117	13	5
John Neely, 503rd district	143	15	5
Pleasant Vinson, sol. Snows	186	19	2
WARE.			
James Drawdy, sol. Bryans	204	2	3
John Dryden, do.	122	24	1
Nathaniel Permenter, Motes	60	11	5
WARREN.			
John Mathews, Kinseys	4	30	1
Winefred Atchinson,w.R.S.,Hills	239	4	1
Nancy Goyne, wid. Rogers	82	8	5
John Akins' orphans, do.	223	9	2
Robert Monk, Kinseys	146	17	1
F. B. Heith, sol. Latimers	104	20	1
Joel Mathews, R. S., Hills	16	3	3
Edward Allen, Downes	36	11	3
Vincent E. Riviere, Bulls	111	17	1
Linsy Walker, illegit. Adkins	136	26	1
James Ellett, R. S. Hills	30	9	4
John Bales, Downes	242	3	2
Linyear Albritton, do.	69	13	1
William Pilcher, do.	145	6	3
WASHINGTON.			
Archibald Cone, jr. Warthens	21	9	4
Eliz. Burney, w. R. S. Whitfields	60	7	3
Matilda Price, illegit. Curreys	151	3	3
Bryant Whitfield, Whitfields	34	25	1
Thomas Gilmore, Avans	160	2	5
Samuel Bedgood, Whitfields	201	15	2
Fanny Barron, wid. Warthens	21	8	3
James Cook, Currys	105	5	4
Barachias Massey, Floyds	79	12	5
Robert Whitfield, Whitfields	122	10	3

Fortunate Drawers Capts. Dist.	No.	Dt.	Sec.
Simon Rogers, Fairchilds	116	7	4
James H. Johns, Mandersons	122	24	2
Lunice Robinson, illegit. Shows	268	8	1
Wiley G. Weaver, Mathews	202	9	2
Zadock Dykes, Shows	267	21	2
W. & H. Steward, ill., Mayos	20	6	3
Rachel Smiths ills. Mandersons	68	15	2
J. & I. Devenport orps. Smiths	192	9	1
William Etheridge, Mandersons	217	11	3
Elizabeth Devenport, w. Smiths	172	5	2
J.,M.&Eliz. Cook, ills. Fairchilds	185	17	1
John Steward, Mayos	94	8	1
Kindred Jones, Halls	112	5	1
WILKES.			
Elizabeth Evans, w.R.S.Hopkins	92	1	3
John Minton, sol., 164th district	199	19	2
Dudley Poole, Ragsdales	138	9	5
David Updegraft, Popes	100	14	2
Ambrose Downs,R.S.,Wootens	319	8	1

14TH DAY'S DRAWING—March 22.

APPLING.

Washington Knole, McDonalds	181	1	2

BALDWIN.

Jane Kirkpatrick, wid., Lingos	171	13	2
John Cone, sen., Thomas	8	13	2
John R. Brown, R. S., Doles	141	11	1
Thomas Glass' orphans, Rows	247	3	2
Orphans of Henry Brown, Wicks	239	28	1
Jacob Cobb, Reddings	75	2	1

BIBB.

Shurrod Horn, R. S., Beards	67	1	1
John Jones, Flanders	220	9	5
Benjamin J. Philips, do.	84	8	5
Reuben Wilks, do.	280	8	5
James Gamble, soldier, Bates	86	11	3
Leroy Watson, Rutlands	36	15	5
Benjamin Manning, R. S., Carrs	66	20	1

BULLOCH.

William Redding's orps., Richardsons	49	22	2
John Grover, jun. do.	164	6	4
Benjamin Gideons, R. S. Turners	220	18	2
Thomas Futch, Richardsons	211	5	4

BURKE.

John Warnock, Andersons	150	6	3
Mourning Wooten, widow, Corkers	188	2	2
Elias Maulden, Wests	69	6	2
David Hester, R. S., Fountains	28	32	1
Frederick Hill, Brooms	75	1	4
Adam Wallace, Wards	232	7	1
Synthia Wheeler, widow, Roberts	14	4	2
Edward Garlick, Bayleys	12	1	1

CAMDEN.

Langley Bryan, soldier, Wards	173	11	3
E. F., M. S., C. T. & R. E. Cook, ors., Ogden	6	33	1

CHATHAM.

Jane M. Russell, widow, Haydens	152	23	1
William H. Coe, Baines	185	4	5
Anthony Porter, Haydens	107	26	1
Jonathan Cline's orps., McDonnells	135	20	2
John Callaghan, Geredons	95	23	1
Thomas West,	138	12	3
Otis Johnson,	122	3	4
Patrick Reily, McDonnells	269	9	1

(40)

Fortunate Drawers Capts. Dist.	No.	Dt.	Sec.
Fleming Akin's orphans, Baines	102	12	2
Penjamin Burroughs,	277	16	2
Charles Perony Destra, Haydens	111	3	3
John S. Harrison, McDonnells	89	6	1

CLARK.

Peter Edmonson's orps., Lumpkins	19	3	4
Charles Dean, R. S., Ransoms	89	8	3
William B. Moreland, Lumpkins	107	18	2
John Espy, R. S. Espys	227	13	2
Green Evans, Lumpkins	225	28	1
William Ball, Herndons	4	17	2
Henry Niles, Wrights	18	3	3
Tollison Ray, Herndons	15	10	3
Eleanor Hardagree, w. R. S., Cox's	126	4	1
Thomas J. Nall, McDonalds	41	10	3
John C. Wright, Wrights	1	6	4
Eli Bradberry, Herndons	26	32	1

COLUMBIA.

Michael Griffin, soldier, Livermans	229	33	1
Elizabeth Howard, w. R. S., Talberts	81	18	1
John Strickland, Adams	70	21	2
Robert Johns, R. S., Clarks	188	6	3
Martha Harrison, widow, Talberts	85	8	3
James Culbreath, Ramseys	27	1	3
Susannah Wright, w. R. S., Adams	223	22	1
Reuben Sanders, Boltons	183	31	1
Martha C. Shackelford, wid., Bealls	16	12	3

CRAWFORD.

Newsom Taunton, Dukes	249	7	3
Nathaniel Shurley, soldier, Lovetts	28	10	3
Josiah H. T. Abbott, do.	231	26	1

DEKALB.

Bricey M. Owen, Browns	131	8	1
Daniel Ferguson, Scarfes	212	5	5
George Hampton, Conns	100	15	1
Joshua Standifer, Stephens	7	2	2
Beletha Braughton, Lokeys	84	14	1
John Dabbs, Hays	96	18	1

DECATUR.

Philip Pittman, Douglass	225	19	2
William H. Vaughan, do.	184	19	2
Hardy Simpson, Hawthorns	155	4	4
George Laurens, Douglass	239	6	3
Jesse May, do.	217	32	1

DOOLY.

Stephen Vickers, 584th	27	10	3

EFFINGHAM.

Henry Strickland, Stricklands	267	2	1
Hannah Eliz Rhan, wid. Treutlins	172	7	3

ELBERT.

Frances Naish, wid. R. S., Bells	210	18	2
John Highsmith, Carpenters	67	11	1
Pearson Duncan, R. S., Merritts	270	3	1
Barnabas Pace, R. S., do.	100	20	2
Philip Johnson's orphans, Tuckers	135	7	3
Tabitha Skaggs, widow, Dunns	4	25	1
Durret Stodghill, soldier, Boltons	194	13	1

EMANUEL.

Ephraim Runnals, McGars	184	4	3
William Almond, Chasons	228	19	1

FAYETTE.

John M. Walden, Browns	243	33	1
Aaron Dawdy, soldier, 9th	254	10	2
Absalom Strawn, Whartons	284	7	1
John Linville, Roziers	187	1	2
Nimrod Dickens, Whartons	123	23	2
Jeremiah D. Mann, do.	13	5	1
Wiat Heflin, Browns	149	7	6

Fortunate Drawers Capts. Dist.	No.	Dt.	Sec.
Robt. Stringfellow, sol., McLendons	158	20	2

FRANKLIN.

Jeremiah Asworth, Hudsons	145	24	2
William Cox, Stephens	189	33	1
Minors of Joseph Hamilton, Sanders	171	1	1

GREENE.

Josiah Pyron, Halls	248	11	5
Mark Elmore, Astins	38	4	4
Simon Thackston, ill., Newsoms	119	1	2
Nathaniel G. Foster, Winkfields	152	27	1

GWINNETT.

Robert Day, soldier, Dunbars	282	21	1
Hardin Blalach, Moors	96	26	1
James Cook, do.	74	5	4
John Pendley, Jr. do.	286	15	1
John Greenwood, Dunbars	10	27	1
Eliz. & Wash. Allen, orps., Hunicuts	261	2	1
John Butler, Finchers	68	7	5
Jackson Monroe, Madduxs	172	3	1
Henry Cupp, Rollins	297	8	1
James Brown, Davis	301	22	1
Hiram M. Shaw, do.	232	33	1

HANCOCK.

Lewis Boon, 101st	146	31	1
Martha Cureton, wid. R. S., 112th	115	14	2
William Smith, 101st	327	28	1
Anderson Washam, do.	220	2	4
Daniel L. Richardson, sol., Densons	203	17	2
James Evans, R. S., 111th	71	7	3
Jane Ellis, widow, 107th	99	18	1
Jemima Mershon, widow, 113th	176	16	2
David Ingraham, 110th	112	5	4
Sarah Moore, widow, 116th	99	15	2
John Sturdivant, R. S., 101st	58	10	2
Dennis Mercer, 109th	106	21	1

HENRY.

John White, Bryants	24	6	2
Jesse Grice, Risons	296	7	1
John W. Mason, Millers	36	9	2
Lewis Camp, Shaws	12	17	2
Daniel C. Heard, soldier, Grays	254	2	1
Tollison K. Hodge, Millers	7	15	1
Daniel B. McCarty, Allens	91	14	1
Jeremiah Liggett's orphans, Grays	76	6	1

HABERSHAM.

William Thompson, Langstons	85	6	2
Edward Harris, do.	154	7	3
Daniel McDuggle's orphans, Kenzies	112	3	3
Peter Reece's orphans, do.	7	3	3
John Highfill, Jones	273	5	1
John Tate, sen., Cross's	46	21	2
John Langston, Langstons	67	9	3
Thomas Townsend, R. S., Kenzies	38	33	1

HALL.

John Lowrie, orphan, Wilsons	22	1	5
James Grimes, Smiths	28	9	2
Morgan Guthrie, Hardages	251	4	3
John Jones, Ingrahams	215	12	1
George Hawpe, Gerrards	131	10	1
Uriah Posey, Alreds	219	10	3
Makey A. Keith, Hardens	247	5	4

HOUSTON.

Aaron Justice, R. S., Hancocks	17	23	1
James Hobby, Becks	143	4	1

JACKSON.

James Graham, Storys	212	1	4
John Rush, Watersons	106	7	3
Jas., Mos., J.&B.Daily, ills. Bowens	64	2	3

(41)

Fortunate Drawers	Capts. Dist.	No.	Dt.	Sec.
Little Harris, Duncans		222	3	4
Martha Hunter, wid. R. S., Millers		226	8	3
John Ross's orphans, Pairs		321	22	1
Peter Youngblood, Venables		64	10	1
Harvey A. Archer, Millers		297	7	1

JASPER.

Joseph Warren, soldier, Posts		51	25	1
John Davidson, R. S., Robertsons		191	12	3
Claiborn Gibbs, Wilders		10	10	2
Elizabeth Crane, widow, Hines		27	4	4
Wiley F. McLendon's orphans, Dardens		59	11	2
Robert Spearman, Butts		91	5	1
Thomas J. Whatley, Owens		20	21	1
David Winchester, Hines		211	12	3
Jonathan Garrett, Holmes		184	14	2
Benjamin F. Tuggle, Wilders		244	7	5
Jane Featherstone, w. R. S., Keys		81	9	3
Randall P. Wilson, Camerons		133	22	1
George H. Buchanan, R. S., Trussells		96	30	1
James Reddin, Owens		192	2	5
William Dupee's orphans, do.		296	5	1
Jane Stephens, widow, Reeves		136	24	2
Tyre Chaffin, Baynes		250	15	2
Robert O. Beavers, Wilders		114	19	1
William Johnson, Dardens		48	23	1

JEFFERSON.

Etheldred Moore's orps. Causeys		16	20	2
Jesse Pervis, Beatys		234	28	1
Seth Pierce, R. S., Elliotts		84	18	2
Cornelius McCoy's orphans, do.		39	21	2
Dempsey Hall, sen., R. S., Marshalls		62	12	1
Samuel M. Barr, Ross's		127	3	3
Jeremiah Brinson Kings		106	1	1
Elenor McNeely widow Boyds		59	12	3
Sarah Loque, widow, Waldens		203	10	3
Samuel Pool, soldier Kings		58	10	5

JONES.

James Stephenson Robertsons		238	29	1
Charles Davis, Spinks		240	2	5
Sarah Willis, wid. R. S., Mullins		255	20	2
Thomas Braddy, Blounts		252	112	2
William B. Mercer soldier, Stewarts		109	3	4
Solomon S. Simmons, Dosters		153	26	1
John W. Gordon's orphans, Stewarts		35	15	2
George Fulton, Gibsons		152	3	1
Magor Waldroop, Mullins		116	4	3
Peter Kolb, R. S., Bowens		265	7	1
Samuel Chapman, jr. Robertsons		50	8	5

LAURENS.

Calphrey Clarke, Beachams		111	3	4

LINCOLN.

Rebecca Gray, widow, Leveretts		184	16	1
Joshua Age, Graves		89	4	4
James Johnson, Parks		251	20	2

MADISON.

Sarah Brooks, wid. R. S., Christians		63	3	4
Thomas Lester Adairs		31	1	4
William S. Johnson, Culbertsons		91	4	4
James Kelly, Caldwells		244	18	2
Joseph McDannon, Bones		217	11	2
John C. McIver, Caldwells		255	19	1

MONROE.

Parham Buckner, sol. Wrights		228	9	2
Dorcas Bryan, w. R.S. Fergusons		101	12	1
James D. Lester, soldier, do.		224	20	2
James W. Holcomb, Pattersons		163	5	4
William A. Hartsfield, Johnsons		254	25	1

Fortunate Drawers	Capts. Dist.	No.	Dt.	Sec.
Benj. G. Reid, Houses		185	30	1
A. Womack, R. S., Woodwards		69	1	4
George K. Chatham, sol., Millers		27	29	1
James Holloway, Millers		48	21	2
William McKenzie, R. S., Houses		243	2	4
Thomas Hollis, Turners		78	6	2
Mahala A. Winslett, illeg. Millers		240	6	1

MORGAN.

Rachel Benson, wid. Hitchcocks		56	15	1
Barzilla Glover, widow, do.		264	17	2
Isabella Thomson, wid. Adairs		46	7	2
Margaret Shaw, w. R. S., Canifaxs		15	6	5
Loyd Bailey, Butlers		58	9	3
Thomas Swift, Adairs		13	11	3
Zephaniah Templeton, sol. Butlers		50	11	2
John B. Walker, Stokes		138	18	2

NEWTON.

John Pritchet, Talleys		24	12	3
John Thompson, sol., Orrs		170	15	1
James Potts, Summers		85	18	1
David Jester, Graves		238	10	3
Riley Walker, Zachrys		180	4	2

OGLETHORPE.

Josiah Jordan jr.'s orps. Arnolds		221	19	1
Bennett Hubbard, R. S., Lacys		154	19	1
Samuel Thompson, Jr., Hills		189	30	1
Richard P. Bragan, Rosseaus		146	15	2
Samuel Morris' orps. Burfords		150	2	4
Sarah Busbin, w. R. S., Billups		150	23	2
Elijah Butlers orps. Hills		220	10	5
Stephen Gunnels, sol. Simmons		144	8	5

PIKE.

Elisha Palmores minors, Daniels		24	16	5
David Spradlin, Daniels		144	29	1

PULASKI.

Silvy Bynum, w. R. S. Sparrows		66	7	2
Eliz. Frazars chil. Scarbroughs		19	5	4
Lucrecy Saulter, illegit. do.		184	?	?
Sary Armstrong, w.R.S. ,do.		224	9	2
Mary Miller, widow, do.		33	24	1
William Z. Bailey, Gilstraps		176	10	5

PUTNAM

Thomas Davis' orphans, Marcus		229	28	1
Eliz. Tomlinson, wid. Allums		8	20	1
Henry Alford, Kendricks		119	9	2
Richard Carrs orphans, Clarks		256	8	5
John Jacksons orphans, Sawyers		33	5	2
Elizabeth Vial, w. R. S., Goods		104	23	1

RABUN.

Mary Sanders, widow, Becks		166	25	1
Edward Coffee, Godfreys		139	8	4
David Mozley, do.		40	11	2
Juda Crain, w. R. S. Godfreys		44	14	1

RICHMOND.

William Bexley, Bushs		209	1	1
Wm. Savage, (m. d.) Treadwells		67	33	1
Clarissa Coleman, orphan		155	11	1
Henry Dial, Kellys		51	20	2
Patrick McCarty, Huntingtons		188	10	3
Ezekiel Smith, Wilcoxs		201	4	1
Alfred Chichester, Augusta		36	20	2
Robert W. Williams, Ferris		235	2	3

(42)

Fortunate Drawers Capts. Dist.	No.	Dt.	Sec.
William H. Egan, Hands	3	32	1
Francis Wilson, Thomas	73	1	3
Larkin Brown, R. S., 119th dist.	149	19	1
Jourdan James, soldier, James	269	4	3
Ruth Twiggs, w. R. S. Kellys	31	2	5
SCRIVEN.			
John McCleland minor, Roberts	90	13	2
Dor. McCordy, min. Humphreys	32	25	1
John G. Scruggs, Stricklings	198	12	1
Orps of Jno. Williamson, Reaves	60	24	1
John W. Jackson, Hunters	242	25	1
John Boyett, Kemps	168	21	1
Patience Mobley, wid. Lovetts	189	8	3
Ransom Rogers, Humphreys	128	18	2
Bryan Odam, Poythress	210	11	1
Thomas Nicholasson, Reaves	58	11	5
TATTNALL.			
Daniel Kirkland, Graces	132	11	3
Jehu Standfield, Dees	68	4	4
John Grace, jr. Graces	211	31	1
TELFAIR.			
William Lofton, Wilsons	160	4	5
William Matchet, Lampkins	171	8	3
TALIAFERRO.			
Littlebury Sandford, Alfords	268	3	3
TWIGGS.			
Ann Davis, wid. Blackshears	192	13	2
William Summerlin, Solomans	160	14	1
Thomas Glover, Graggs	139	15	5
Calvin Crosby, illegit. Bosticks	120	1	4
Richard Smith, Chamberlains	94	19	1
UPSON.			
Robert Hobbs, 589th district	208	14	1
John Mathews, soldier, Ezells	142	23	1
Joel Moore, R. S., Myricks	179	19	1
Samuel Black, Pettys	293	20	2
WALTON.			
Orps. of Asa Holaway, 418th dis.	204	18	1
James Baird, 418th district	182	6	2
William Potts, Davis'	142	17	2
Jesse Johnson, Bexleys	221	8	1
Edm. J. Randolph, McQuertors	44	28	1
Thomas Inlow, R. S. Hudsons	52	12	1
Mary Pike, widow, do.	28	20	1
WARE.			
Joshua Sharp, R. S. Bryans	84	3	5
WAYNE.			
James Highsmith, McKinneys	218	8	5
James Roberson, R. S., do.	98	18	1
WARREN.			
Jos. Standford, sr. R.S. Sanders	120	10	5
Samuel A. Pardy, Hales	89	21	2
John Newsom, sr., R. S., Adkins	138	4	1
Absalom Joiner, Downs	217	11	1
Soloman Rainwater, Jones	138	21	1
William Cason, Adkins,	265	21	1
James Nobles, illegit. Sanders	144	12	5
Blake Justice, Hills	89	32	1
Ivy Jackson or. of Sam'l, Adkins	140	12	3
James Jackson, Rogers	175	12	5
John Newsom, Adkins	68	8	1

Fortunate Drawers Capts. Dist.	No.	Dt.	Sec.
Daniel Pope, Currys	306	22	1
Sion Hood, soldier, Floyds	9	14	1
Elizabeth Pinson, wid. Floyds	179	5	1
Caroline Siller, illegit. McLendons	72	12	3
Josiah Amison, jr. Warthens	203	8	5
Mary Page, w. R. S., Whitfields	122	12	5
Henry S. Taylor, Mannings	215	5	1
John Martin, Woods	103	32	1
William Winson, Whitfields	89	1	1
Nathan Mott, Warthens	140	28	1
Richard Webster, Floyds	12	2	1
Wiley Cherrys heirs, Mannings	17	32	1
WILKINSON.			
Eleazer Brack, sr. R. S., Fairchilds	27	24	2
James Exum, soldier, do.	34	11	3
Ellis Harvil, Halls	88	16	1
Ralph Smith, Mayos	185	26	1
Henry Easterling orphans, Halls	162	33	1
Hiram Swinny, Halls	40	8	4
Silas Mercer, Mandersons	28	12	1
Edmund Downing, do.	46	30	1
John Kinsawl, Fairchilds	122	28	1
WILKES.			
Mary A. Hackney, illegit. Rices	52	21	1
Marg. Nunnally, w. R. S. Lukers	120	2	5
William A. Calloway, Wootens	194	3	5
Reuben Hudgins, Greshams	220	20	2
Nelson Powells orphans, Lukers	2	17	2
Ann Smith, hus. absent, Chunns	112	2	2
Thomas W. Beck, Amasons	119	8	4
Nancy Fomby, wid. Washingtons	158	16	2

15th DAY'S DRAWING—March 23

BALDWIIN.

Stephen Harvey, Doles	86	1	3
Wiley Jones Tompkins, Lingos	157	6	1
Ezekiel Redding, Wheelers	43	15	5
B. H. Sturges, Buchanans	78	23	1
Polly Ellis, widow, R. S., Wicks	87	33	1
Priscilla Grant, widow, do.	150	3	3
Horatio N. Barksdale, Doles	59	30	1
BIBB.			
William Howard, Rutlands	46	13	5
John McCall, Flanders	59	23	2
Henry Champion, Carrs	91	8	5
Jacob G. & Lurana Braswell, orps. do.	102	8	1
E & M Kennon, fa. absent, Rutlands	225	18	2
Henry Champion, Carrs	103	1	5
Ashbourn D. Davis soldier Bates	76	8	2
BRYAN.			
Raymond P. Demere, Stephens	177	2	4
Stouton Hayman, sr., R. S., Harveys	138	8	1
BULLOCH.			
Charles Lewis, Richardsons	281	20	2
David Blanton, Lockharts	42	23	1
Joseph Hodges, sen. do.	213	2	2
BURKE.			
Sarah Graham, widow, McKays	92	1	2
John Jackson, Dugas	201	10	3
Jacob Watkins, Bayleys	101	22	2
Jincey Shepperson, orphan, Dugas	26	6	3
Sarah Hatcher, wid. R. S., Brooms	81	6	1
Isaac Cross, Lynchs	191	9	1

(43)

Fortunate Drawers Capts. Dist.	No.	Dt.	Sec.	Fortunate Drawers Capts. Dist.	No.	Dt.	Sec.
M. & D. Kite, illegitimates, Gordons	3	9	3	Levi Garrison, Candells	188	26	1
				James Miller, do.	5	1	4
BUTTS.				Thomas Pulliam, sol., Blankinships	227	1	2
Eliza McCurdy, widow, Robinsons	268	8	1	James Sutty, R. S., Cokers	64	16	2
Robert Kilcrease, soldier, Kirksies	106	30	1	Richard C. Bond, R. S., do.	272	11	2
Isham Freeman, Robisons	191	14	2	Randall Gaddess's orphans, Walters	172	27	1
				John Strange, R. S., Stranges	49	12	3
CAMDEN.				Martin Garrison, Candells	8	14	1
Lemuel A. Brockington, Halls	96	7	4				
Genevieve Hon. Ganleer, fa. ab. Wards	129	6	2	**GREEN.**			
Zebulon Rudulph, do.	208	6	1				
James M. Paxton, Browns	151	2	5	Thomas G. Cochran, Webbs	144	32	1
				Claiborn Robinson, do.	163	11	3
CHATHAM.				Sion Parham, Sutherlands	29	14	2
John Pitcher, Savannah	147	2	1	William Anderson, sr. R. S. Dawsons	158	21	2
William J. Spencer's orps. Nungazers	32	12	2	William D. McCaine, Akins	231	6	1
Joseph B. Armstrong, Baines	275	15	1	Thomas Williams, Halls	203	5	1
Dorcas Webber, widow, McDonnells	204	11	2	Bledsoe Brockman, Green s	240	13	1
Sarah Caesar, orp. of Peter, Baines	2	33	1	George G. Morriss, Rankins	269	1	2
John Peter Arnaud, Haydens	68	11	2	Green B. Scoggins, Greens	268	1	4
Miles C. Phillips, Geredons	139	21	2	Martha Atkinson, wid. R. S., Bruces	247	21	1
John Stibb's orphans, Baines	211	4	2				
CLARK.				**GWIINNETT.**			
James W. Harris, Gahagans	1	26	1	Reding Blocker, Woodroughs	54	4	4
				Edward Vann, Robertsons	177	5	2
COLUMBIA.				John Baskin, Hills	198	7	5
John A. Stapler, orphan, Talberts	7	24	1	John S. Head, sen., R. S., Rollins	146	7	3
John Bennefield, Dranes	237	11	5	William Doster soldier, Moors	23	2	2
Sarah & S. R. Boyd, illegitimates, do.	239	9	1	William Morris for wife, Evans	23	2	4
William Redman, Stallings	245	10	1	Job Red, Moors	160	1	1
Orphans of Levi Pearre, Bealls	126	15	5	Joseph Thomas, do.	221	4	1
				Hermon Bagley, R. S., do.	348	7	1
CRAWFORD.				James Harrald, Caruthers	94	5	2
Silas Newsom, Hamiltons	74	8	5	John McDonald, sen., Bakers	102	5	2
DECATUR.				**HANCOCK.**			
Israel Zigler, Douglass	20	2	4				
DEKALB.				Samuel M. Devereux, 116th	220	1	4
Isaac W. Perkerson, Stephens	119	8	3	William Tucker, 102d	192	20	2
Mary James, widow, Smiths	191	11	2	Francis Brooking's orphans, 113th	42	15	1
John McCorquodale, Bakers	5	14	5	John H. Breedlove, 101st	104	1	3
John Woodall, idiot, Conns	35	22	2	Richard Holt, 107th	19	14	2
				Eli Johnston, 108th	73	3	2
DOOLY.				Nimrod S. Childs, 112th	300	8	5
Claborn Alsabrook, R. S., 582d	240	4	3	Levina Murden, w. R. S., 111th	170	10	2
EARLY.				Nancy Ralls, widow, Hunters	180	10	3
Alsey Harris, Hairs	72	10	5	**HENRY.**			
EFFINGHAM.				Benjamin Lewis McVickers	155	15	2
William Shuman, Elkins	230	33	1	John W. McCurdy, orphan, Kites	59	20	2
Thomas D. Porter's orps. Treutlins	34	8	2	Christopher Malone, Allens	10	16	1
Orp. of John W. Fryermuth, Elkins	219	21	2	Margaret Gilkeyson, widow, do.	66	14	2
William Hurt, soldier, Edwards	190	12	3	Demsey Johnson, Shaws	151	12	1
ELBERT.				John Cardwell, soldier, Breeds	202	17	1
Archibald Craft, Blackwells	164	7	3	Reuben Dearing, soldier, Wards	269	28	1
Thomas J. Turman, Harmonds	60	10	3	William Phillips, Millers	121	3	3
Thomas Turner, Dunns	214	11	2	Martin Buckalew, Smiths	92	6	2
John Duncan, sen., R. S. Merritts	53	22	2				
Thomas Pritchett, Carpenters	388	20	2	**HABERSHAM.**			
James V. Richardson, do.	112	14	1				
EMANUEL.				Anderson Dover, Cross's	173	16	1
				Alford Holcombe, Fains	60	17	1
Eliz. Wyche's illegitimates, Normans	112	25	1	William Cox, Vickreys	182	30	1
Henry H. Poacher, Swains	243	11	3	Samuel Woody, Martins	117	22	2
Aaron Bennett, Moors	71	16	1	Asa Tate, Tates	134	31	1
FAYETTE.				Josiah Turner, Jones	243	9	5
Killee Acanes, soldier, Garrisons	60	30	1	Simon Taylor, Bakers	283	28	1
Charles Wakefield, Whartons	254	5	1	**HALL.**			
FRANKLIN.							
Thomas York, Tabors	36	4	2	Eliz. Whitlock, w. R. S., Harrisons	40	9	5
William Holley's orphans, Bennetts	235	1	2	James Gaily, Alreds	221	2	2
Martha Tinsley's ills., Stephens	216	5	2	John S. Porter, Yegers	121	7	5
Orphans of John Sisk, Wallers	131	6	2	Samuel Evans, Hardens	36	1	4
Samuel Moseley, Tabors	246	12	2	Margaret Wilson, w. R. S., Roberts	204	1	4
Gillam Wilbanks, do.	307	7	1	John King, Hardages	22	23	1
David Vaughan, Blankinships	181	11	1	Christian Thomas, widow, Smiths	2	11	3

(44)

Fortunate Drawers	Capts.	Dist.	No.	Dt.	Sec.
Lent Riley,	Roberts		140	7	3
David Craft, soldier,	Alreds		246	6	3

HOUSTON.

John Wimberly,	Batemans		11	16	1
Ire Bradley,	do.		128	1	2

IRWIN.

George Mobley,	Dicksons		102	21	1

JACKSON.

John Smythwick, Moons			332	7	5
Eliz. Hosley, illegitimate child, Pairs			32	10	2
Josiah M. Kennedy, Lindseys			149	29	1
John Goodwin, Storys			118	5	5
Sampson Pugh, Doss's			37	18	2
William Martin's orphans, Pairs			146	2	1
Lewis P. Eaves, Lindseys			214	9	3

JASPER.

Benjamin Milam, R. S., Camerons			171	5	3
Aggy Hogg's illegitimates, Hines			113	1	5
Hartwell Jones, Barnetts			114	12	5
Jeremiah Mapp's orphans, Dardens			109	8	4
Wiley Perry, Camerons			9	12	2
John Houston, Owens			306	10	2
Elias Benham, Posts			49	15	2
Henry Ivy, sen. Hands			112	1	1
Lamach H. Hines, Hines			85	19	1
Francis Malone, soldier, Dales			162	1	5
Burwell Binn's orphans, Dardens			247	30	1
Burwell Greene, R. S., Owens			30	33	1
John B. Robinson, Keys			255	15	1
John Love, Robinsons			202	22	2

JEFFERSON.

Matilda G. Bostick, widow, Beatys			69	10	5
Elijah Sutton, Cunninghams			235	2	5
Benjamin Whitaker's orps. Causeys			175	19	1
Rufus King, Beatys			10	5	1
James Gunn, jr. Cunninghams			168	15	1
David W. Irwin, do.			88	20	1
John S. Holder, R. S., Marshalls			272	20	2

JONES.

William P. Jackson, Mullins			63	6	1
William Alexander, Stewarts			229	8	1
William Moughon, Taylors			108	15	1
Isaac Wadsworth, Davis			141	32	1
Samuel H. Goldsmith, Sullivans			90	19	2
Ezekiel B. Smith, Bowens			23	7	2
Thomas Taylor, Hendersons			103	17	2
Amos Johnson, Spinks			173	19	1
John Pollard, R. S., Dosters			110	3	4
James Taylor, jr. do.			93	5	2
Stewart Boyanton, Stewarts			206	3	1
Jesse Duncan, Davis			160	31	1
Thomas Hunt, Bowens			72	7	1
Lewellen Philips, Gibsons			97	8	2
Julius Driver, Stewarts			137	20	1
George B. Lucas, soldier, Gibsons			14	22	1
Jacob Rogers's minors, Taylors			13	24	2
Benjamin Reynolds, R. S., do.			180	3	3
Cherry Murphy, w. R. S., Bowe ns			278	20	2

LAURENS.

Sarah Glover, widow, Hodges			158	15	2
William Settles, Whiteheads			341	28	1
John Campbell, orphan, Deans			287	14	1
Benjamin Powell, Barlows			76	20	1
Margaret Yarborough, w. R. S., Deans			71	23	1
Thomas Pullin, jr. Hodges			15	23	2

LIBERTY.

William E. W. Quarterman, 15th			138	5	1

LINCOLN.

Fortunate Drawers	Capts.	Dist.	No.	Dt.	Sec.
William Thomas, Graves			206	7	1
Mary Harnsberger, w. R. S., Frasers			232	17	1
Cornelius B. Williams, iggintons,			182	18	1
Joshua Daniel, Hardys			207	10	2
Jabez Garnett, Graves			138	6	2

MADISON.

John R. Streetman, Bones			64	6	2
Gabriel W. Grimes, Hannas			162	21	2
Archelus Moon, soldier, do.			92	8	4
Richardson Hancock, Phipps			149	31	1

McINTOSH.

Abel Usher, Demeries			151	12	3

MONROE.

William Wooten, Browns			1	21	2
Abigail Davis illegit. Finchs			272	7	1
James Trawick, Browns			123	2	2
Edward A. Elder, sol., Wrights			244	15	2
James Gilmore, Millers			55	4	4
William Nelson, Houses			249	20	2
David Stripling, Houses			55	31	1
James Blanton, Millers			211	5	1
Benjamin Fuller, Woodwards			233	18	1
Pitt W. Milner, Millers			146	14	1
David Jones, R. S., Browns			212	12	1
Robert Mitchells orps. Knights			143	5	2

MORGAN.

Green. Templeton, sol., Osteens			188	30	1
Yearby Parties orps. Christians			232	29	1
Elijah Veasey, Beasleys			29	6	3
Orphans of Jos. Wheeler, Adairs			72	2	4
Bradly Haraldson, sol. Griggs			198	16	1
John W. Butler, Gains			28	24	1
Jesse T. S. Warren orp. Baileys			189	18	2
Mary Evans, wid. Shearmans			83	25	1
John Hall, Youngs			51	1	1
Margaret Head, w. R. S. Gains			160	23	1
Nancy Williams, wid. Whatleys			224	23	1
Thomas Hansons orphs. Adairs			159	24	1

MONTGOMERY.

Thomas Clark, Ryals			100	12	5
Fitzgerald Slocum, Pridgeons			147	10	5

NEWTON.

Martin Furlow, illegit. Summers			43	7	4
E.J.,C.D.,P.&P.Smith ors.Pullens			106	11	2
John Reeks, Pullens			298	8	1
William Hambys orphs. Snows			265	9	5
Nancy Morrow, wid. Dyers			110	25	1
Washington Dyer, Graves			170	7	2
Elathan D. Walker, sol. Zachrys			195	24	1
Calvin York, Bakers			192	28	1

OGLETHORPE.

Mathew Mosely, Seals			250	13	1
Chris Allison, w. R.S., Rousseaus			124	11	2
Uriah Bowen. Hills			7	7	4
Joel Hancock, Lacys			53	1	4
Sarah Arnold, widow, Bells			71	6	3
Jesse Starkey, Dixs			136	3	1
John W. A. Beall. Holloways			175	23	2

PIKE.

Daniel Orr, Orrs			70	5	1
William J. Huddleston, Orrs			131	12	1
Stephen Weathers orps. Mays			59	18	1

LAND LOTTERY REGISTER—No. 7
[RECORDER OFFICE—PUBLISHED BY GRANTLAND & ORME—PRICE $3.]

NOTE.—Section 1 is Lee County—2 Muscogee—3 Troup—4 Coweta—5 Carroll.
15th DAY'S DRAWING—Continued.   Fortunate Drawers   Capts. Dist.   No.Dr.Sec.

Fortunate Drawers	No.	Dr.	Sec.
PIKE.			
James Langley, R. S., Longs	31	6	3
PULASKI.			
Wash. Wheeler, ill. Sparrows	160	70	1
Wm. Shuffield, sr. R. S. Hurdleys	212	18	1
Thomas McGriff, Kellams	190	6	3
James Tumlinson, Powells	252	1	4
Robert N. Taylor, Kellams,	179	6·5	
William S. Coleson, Gilstraps	58	15	1
Daniel Williams orph. Hendleys	17	6	3
PUTNAM.			
Clava Harris, widow, Blacks	56	11	2
David Holloman, jr. Stinsons	152	15	1
Elizabeth Purdue, wid. Barnetts	193	20	1
William Barnes, jr. Bledsoes	5	1	5
Josiah Jones, Sawyers	33	16	5
Samuel Bow, Sparks	39	11	1
Henry W. Hall, Dismukes	5	20	1
William Butler, Clarks	107	15	1
John B. Trippe, Bledsoes	103	10	3
Zachariah House, Sawyers	289	23	2
RABUN.			
Soloman Beck, Godfreys	128	7	2
RICHMOND.			
John M. C. Evans, Wilcoxs	133	17	2
William Kibbe, Ferris	47	10	2
Alexander Main, Augusta	23	26	1
George Dunbar, Treadwells	230	14	1
Sid.&Eliza Adeline Wray, deaf,	152	17	2
John Barker orphan, Kellys	113	22	2
Daniel Walker, Wilcoxs	24	5	2
Levi Kent, sol. Bushs	20	3	1
Alexander Bertram, Treadwells	195	20	1
Isaac Owens, James	116	17	2
Daniel Nelms, do.	181	33	1
SCRIVEN.			
Orphs. of Geo. Dudley, Reaves	193	4	4
D.&M.Freeman, mins. Hunters	128	6	5
John Doughtry, Kemps	299	1	2
TATTNALL.			
James Sowell orphan, Corseys	233	11	3
George Lewis, R. S. Conners	298	20	2
Riley S. Glisson, Deloachs	15	9	2
TELFAIR.			
James Jernigan, Lampkins	298	5	3
TALIAFERRO.			
Orphs. of Thos. Swan, Marshalls	183	4	3
THOMAS.			
James J. Blackshear	174	9	3
TWIGGS.			
John M. Thigpen, Graggs	143	8	1
Orph. of L. McMurry, Solomans	256	3	1
Martha Dupree, w. R.S. Blackshears	196	23	2
Martha Hays, w. R.S. Blackshears	97	3	3
Priscilla Jackson, wid.Streetmans	17	11	5
Orps. of Arthur Davis, Holidays	32	4	1
Orps.ofJno.Hollingsworth,Bosticks	180	16	2
John Everett, Solomans	47	10	1
Orps.ofL.P.Desanbleaux,Solomans	114	13	1
John Sanders, Kelleys	223	18	1
Benjamin Sutton. do.	164	24	2
Green Cousins, Blackshears	219	11	3
UPSON.			
Nancy Stewarts illegits. Duprees	14	7	2
Richard Parker, Saunders	134	13	5
Richard Henderson, Ellis'	261	12	3
WALTON.			
Samuel Chappell, Snows	70	25	1
Temple C. Williams, Bexleys	296	15	1
Hardy Harris, Bexleys	283	15	1
Thomas Knight, sr. 503rd dist.	95	6	4
Noah Nelson, 418th district	212	20	1
Rebecca Smith, w.R.S. 250th do.	237	8	3
John Stanford, sol. Hudsons	247	11	3
Oliver Brooks, McQuertors	236	16	2
WAYNE.			
Jacob Highsmith, McKinneys	32	6	1
Ruthy Hall, illegit. Mannings	67	7	3
WARREN.			
Isaac Burson, sol., Sanders	235	3	1
Gideon Newsom, Adkins	4	5	2
John Terry orp. of Wm. Sanders	38	20	2
Sarah Anderson, wid. Brinkleys	25	22	2
Feraby Beall, widow, Bulls	159	6	5
Henry K. Hill, Hills	196	2	4
Sarah Land, widow, Adkins	210	6	1
Charity Green, w. R. S. Hales	46	7	4
Asa Ansley, Sanders	367	8	1
WASHINGTON.			
Harvey Rogers, Currys	220	5	2
Jesse Amison, Warthens	145	4	2
Joseph Page, Whitfields	182	11	2
Hugh McLean, Mannings	81	13	2
Joseph Rhodes, Tysons	56	16	2
Silas Jones, orphan, Gilberts	67	12	5
Martha Ann E. Brady, Tysons	104	17	2
Samuel Robinsons orps. Woods	132	9	5
Samuel Kennedy, Woods	210	5	2
James Kennedy, do.	117	28	1
WILKINSON.			
Hillery Newman, Smiths	82	7	5
Elvy Dickson orphan, Halls	202	14	2
John Crumbly, jr. Currys	222	11	5
George Harrison, Fairchilds	206	3	4
Edmund Culpepper, Shows	164	17	2
Cornelius Bachelor, Shows	87	13	2
Lemuel Burket, R. S. Shows	5	1	1
James Exum, Mathews	37	17	1
WILIKES.			
Zacharah Hendrick, Moors	162	3	1
John J. Sherman orph. Chunns	202	25	1
Edward R. Anderson, Lukers	21	5	5
Elihu Talbot, Greshams	101	4	4
David Bunch, Ragsdales	13	20	1
Jesse Simmons, Greens	127	22	1
Gilbert Hays orps. Charltons	181	12	2

16th DAY'S DRAWING—March 24.
Fortunate Drawers Capts. Dist.   No.Dt.Sec.

BALDWIN.
Wm. D. Evans, R. S. Lingos   124   2 3
John Wilson, Bivins   252   2 4

BIBB.
Stephen C. Hickey, Flanders   213   4 1
Wm. Johnston, R. S. Rutlands   6   4 1
Daniel Matthison, Beards   90   7 5

BRYAN.
Elijah,Eliza,H.&E.Sauls, Harveys 204   8 3

BULLOCH.
Isham Corbetts orps. Lockharts   45 25 1

BURKE.
John Lewis, jr. Wards   90   2 2
Samuel Bush, R. S. Gordons   149   5 4
Mahala Lancaster, w. Fountains   163 14 5

CAMDEN.
Edward Crews, Coxs   87 10 5
Samuel Holder orphan, Baileys   39 13 2
James Loftins orphans, do.   2   6 5
Henry Jones, Beckwiths   9   8 4

CHATHAM.
Wm. A. Pollard, Haydens   32   2 4
Wm. Carter, Gaddys   127   3 4
Anson Haden, Haydens   176   4 1
Shad. Harpers orps. Geredons   79   5 3
Sarah Davies or. of Geo., Gaddys 29   8 5
Patrick Torpy, McDonnells   26 24 1
Johnson Parkman, Haydens   115   5 3

CLARK.
James Carter illegit. Herndons   4   8 4
John Williams, Alreds   264   3 3
Abner Wells, McDonalds   65 15 2
Wm. Clifton, sol. do.   254 18 1
Stephen Hesters orps. Lumpkins   57   4 4
John Mathews, McDonalds   69   3 5
Mary,Sophia,Nancy,Wells,Jas.W.,
&Mar.,A.A.Whiteheadills.Mastins 145   6 1
James Croxton, Gahagans   80   7 4
John Smith, R. S. McCrees   143   1 3

COLUMBIA.
Reuben Blanchards ors. Culbreths 85   3 4
Wm. F. Wilkins, Bealls   199 20 1
Amanda E. Campbell ill. Adams   182   3 3
George Briggs, Culbreths   232 15 2
Benj. Gerrald, lunatic, Talbots 253 10 5
Jesse Albrittons orps. Ramseys   204 14 2
Henry Lynn, Boltons   221 33 1

CRAWFORD.
Standley Hall, Rhodes   226   5 4
Thos. B. Jones, R. S. Wilsons   123 20 2
Wm. Taff, sol. Tillers   271 21 1
Francis M. Wilder ill. Rhodes   17 25 1
George Taff, Tillers   222   4 1
Wm. Greene, Hicks   196   8 3

DECATUR.
Robert Malone, jr. Douglass   144   9 5

DEKALB.
Martha Cavender, wid. Smiths   24 10 2
Rachel Brooks, wid. Bakers   147 19 2
Thos. Henderson, sr. Stephens   116 11 5

EARLY.
Fortunate Drawers Capts. Dist.   No.Dt.Sec.
Green Tinsley, Porters   60   2 5
John Tyner, Wilsons   69 14 1

EFFINGHAM.
Benj. Harveys orps. Elkins   65   8 5
Fred. Ballard, R. S. Edwards   39   6 3
James S. Crum, Elkins   163 32 1

ELBERT.
Washington Craft, Dunns   311   3 4
Wilson McGarity, Dobbs   73   2 1
James Edmonson, Meritts   104 29 1
Lindsey Neal, Dobbs   60   5 3
John Macgee, Carpenters   16   7 3
Samuel Snellings, Bells   51 26 1

FAYETTE.
Job Faulkner, Whortons   221   5 3
Sarah Glass, widow, Craigs   289   8 1
Henry B. Jones, Dodsons   132   3 2
William Duke, Craigs   137 32 1
Elizabeth Echols, wd. Whartons   143   9 3

FRANKLIN.
Stephen Sanders, Sanders'   63 31 1
Wm. Whitworth, Chandlers   124   5 4
John G. White, Boswells   246   9 5
Henry Smith, R. S. Chandlers   235   9 1
Nelson Osborn, Cokers   87 17 1
Jas. Hobson, Blankinships   80   4 4
Daniel Camp, Stephens   135 23 2
Wm. J. Parks, Hudsons   228   1 4
Joel S. Marberry, jr. Tabors   231   8 5
Elcy C. King, illeg. McDonalds   227   2 4
Laban Catlett, Candells   133 29 1
Wm. S. Denman, Chandlers   151   1 3
Mary Hancock, hus.ab. Stephens   146   3 3
Anderson Hill, Candells   132 12 5

GLYNN.
H.,N.,D.&M.Palmer,ors.McLeods   333   3 4

GREENE.
Thos. Hicks, Elys   16 11 3
Jesse Williams, Woodhams   132 13 1
Lovick Meritt, sol. Astins   11   4 4
James Blythes orphans, do.   155 16 1
Patsey Shockley, h. ab. Knowles   10   4 2
Dempsey Jordan, R. S. Vincents   44 32 1

GWINNETT.
Jesse Burrell, Caruthers   30 15 5
John W. Turner, Hunicuts   175   5 1
Orange Smith,   do.   233   4 3
Joseph Howell, Bakers   133   5 4
John Chandler, sr. R. S. Wallis 146   2 3
James Gailer, R. S., Moores   230   4 1
Absalom Duncan, Greens   208   6 2
Luraney Connellys ills. Moores   219 22 1

HANCOCK.
Seth Kennedy, jr. 116th district 128   1 1
Wright Martin, soldier, Lewis   16   3 4
Edward S. Bass, sol. Bishops   69   8 1

HENRY.
Jeremiah Liggetts orps. Grays   21   8 1
Benjamin Wilson, soldier, do.   9 32 1
William Cates, Bryants   180 26 1
Coleman L. Ray, Harris   167 15 5

(47)

Fortunate Drawers Capts. Dist.	No.	Dt.	Sec.
Micajah Ferrill, R. S. Kites	7	12	2
HABERSHAM.			
Jeremiah Ward, Bakers	133	16	1
Thos. Dooly, jr. Cross'	212	23	1
Thos. Edward, Tates	84	7	1
William Dunaway, Suttons	31	25	1
John Hefner, Fains	290	28	1
Melin.&Susan.L.Pence, orps. Cross	1	23	2
John Walker, Langstons	92	32	1
HALL.			
Neely Dobson, Roberts	268	11	2
Uriah Posey, Alreds	41	20	2
Wm. Kelly, R. S. Floyds	211	16	2
Peter Preslar, sr., R. S. Alreds	225	7	3
David Heaton, Floyds	250	25	1
Pinckney Ayres orph. Hardages	70	1	1
HOUSTON.			
Lunsford Pitts, Yarboroughs	15	4	3
Edward A. Burch, do.	250	8	1
IRWIN.			
Bara & Jas. Brown ills. McCalls	206	6	1
JACKSON.			
Adam Todd, Venables	8	3	2
John Wilson, Rogers	146	22	1
JASPER.			
Isaac Jinks, Wilsons	145	1	2
John Cross' orphans, Baynes	280	20	2
Hiram Land, Trussells	19	2	1
Stephen E. Farley, Robersons	208	29	1
John Worsham, sol. Barnes	256	5	1
Thomas Berry, Trussells	160	11	1
Wm. V. Burney, Holmes	101	24	2
Pleasant Evans, Keys	19	4	3
JEFFERSON.			
Ellis Johnson, Waldens	42	13	1
JONES.			
Robert Paul, sr. R. S. Newbys	113	6	2
Lucy Barnard, widow, Davis	31	23	1
Hannah Hambrick, ill. Lows	93	22	2
Reuben H. Lucky, Taylors	268	17	2
Amos G. Right, Mullins	112	7	4
Richard T. Mastin, Dosters	81	7	5
D. B. Worsham, sol. Duncans	256	9	5
Wm. Felton, Duncans	5	6	1
Sarah Mills, w. R. S. Robertsons	231	6	2
Wm. Terrell, soldier, Dosters	246	11	1
Dempsey Butler, sol. Taylors	84	5	2
Larkin Gordon, do.	94	11	3
LAURENS.			
Levy Nobles, Spiveys	207	33	1
Isaac Thomas, do.	156	22	2
Green Lamb, illegit. Millers	349	22	1
LIBERTY.			
Benj.,Rob.&Jno.Bennettorps. 17th	48	12	5
LINCOLN.			
Peter W. Pullin, Wiggintons	197	2	4
Densley Landers, Graves	198	6	5
MADISON.			
Lewis Scarborough, Berrymans	146	1	3
Wilson,Elizabeth,John&Mary Ann Willeford, illegits. Hancocks	302	1	2
Isaac David, R. S. Culbertsons	20	2	2

Fortunate Drawers Capts. Dist.	No.	Dt.	Sec.
Moses Bridwell, do.	215	5	2
Thomas J. Nash, Adairs	222	25	1
MONROE.			
Jones Andress, Wrights	202	23	1
Woody K. Knight, Johnsons	34	2	5
Henry Kindle, R. S., Douglass	20	19	2
John Baxter, soldier, Houses	72	6	2
Reuben Smith, idiot, do.	2	10	1
Sarah Pinckard, widow, Finches	36	10	3
MORGAN.			
Burwell Jordan, Beasleys	114	20	2
Robert R. Billups, Jennings	27	9	2
Aaron Formby, jr. Adairs	148	16	2
MONTGOMERY.			
Elcanor Harrelson, McMillons	93	14	2
NEWTON.			
Sarah Williams, widow, Pullens	205	2	3
Gresham Stewart, sol., Alreds	16	4	2
Ransom Reeves, Snows	19	10	5
John Turner's orphans, Talleys	203	10	3
OGLETHORPE.			
Lewis Taylor, Holloways	220	13	1
Jonathan Norton, Rousseaus	250	11	5
William Center, Hills	15	21	2
Noah Lacy, R. S., Lacys	226	4	2
Micajah Goolsby, Wilsons	180	10	2
PIKE.			
Robert Shaddix, Daniels	262	2	4
PULASKI.			
James J. Word, Kellams	117	15	2
Stephen Kent's orphans, Sparrows	145	8	4
Vincent Yearty, Scarboroughs	198	3	4
Elisha Hodges, Powells	130	29	1
William Flowers's orps. Kellams	108	20	2
PUTNAM.			
James Jernigan's orps. Vinings	221	20	2
John G. Williamson, do.	32	30	1
Asa Crabb, R. S. do.	84	2	2
Bailey Dalton, Clarks	71	6	5
Archibald T. Crafton, Bledsoes	155	12	1
Mary Ann Porch, orphan, Blacks	160	26	1
Nancy Moseley, widow, Mizes	185	33	1
James W. Wright, do.	94	4	1
Richard Porter's orps. Bledsoes	241	33	1
RABUN.			
Elijah Sartain, Milligans	262	21	2
David Elders, Godfreys	200	17	1
Henry Fricks, do.	189	6	1
RICHMOND.			
Elbert A. Holt, Treadwells	199	5	1
M., A., & M. Hill, orps. Hands	206	16	2
John Edwin Miller, orp., Blacks	91	17	2
Joseph B. Stockton, Ferris	252	11	3
SCRIVEN.			
Daniel Husk, Kemps	91	2	2
Mary McKinney, wid. Poytress	116	6	2
John Wilson, Humphreys	52	16	2
John Chisson, Poytress	168	28	1
Henry C. T. McLee, Reaves	221	25	1
TATTNALL.			
Charles F. McCall, McDuffies	2	10	2
Jacob Taylor, Graces	196	6	3
Isham Peacock, R. S., Dees	170	13	1

(48)

TALIAFERRO.

Fortunate Drawers Capts. Dist.	No.	Dt.	Sec.
Seaborn Bridges, Marshalls	29	9	4

TWIGGS.

Orps. of Will'by S. Hill, Bosticks	78	5	2
Benjamin Oglesby, Pearsons	92	16	1
Orps. of Wm. Davis, Blackshears	24	20	1
Powell Hydrick, Pearsons	236	8	5
Cenus Clark, sol. Chamberlains	40	3	1
Nancy Thomas, w. R. S., Bosticks	99	26	1

UPSON.

William Smith, Ellis	63	24	2
Ann & Isaac Stewart ills., Duprees	111	25	1
Lewis C. Depoister, Harrells	61	8	3
Robert Jackson, Hattoxs	17	13	2
Samuel H. Davis, Coopers	152	5	3

WALTON.

Margaret Studdard, wid. 503d	54	13	5
Elizabeth Perry, widow, 249th	84	6	3
Robert Whitten, 503d	68	7	3
Shadrach Jackson, Davis	130	8	4
Mark Williams, 250th	94	6	3
William H. Meredith, 503d	6	25	1

WARE.

John Hawthorn, Motes	72	5	1
Zion Davis, R. S., do.	277	5	3

WAYNE.

Jacob Cherrytree, orp., Staffords	180	2	4
Richard Leverett, do.	23	8	2
Isaac Campbell, McKinneys	115	2	1
Nancy Ammons, illegitimate, do.	177	11	3

WARREN.

Eliz. Wilcher's ill. chil. Mason, Oliver & Fred Downs,	78	8	1

TALIAFERRO. (cont.)

Fortunate Drawers Capts. Dist.	No.	Dt.	Sec.
James McNair, illegitimate, Adkins	199	11	5
Jacob Burkhalter, R. S., Hales	18	11	1
Henry Williams, Sanders	170	10	5
Ann Corum, widow, do.	206	10	1
Edward N. Perry, Parhams	21	12	1
Christian Lockhart, wid. Downs	285	7	1
John Newsom, sr. R. S. Adkins	147	19	1
Pleasant M. Lacy, Stewarts	229	16	1

WASHINGTON.

William Hood, Rushings	103	30	1
Larkin Griffin, do.	6	5	4
Hubbard Horton, Gilberts	163	4	4
Thomas Hardiman, sol., Woods	119	1	3
L. & J. Osburn, ills. Warthens	255	5	2
Elijah Twilly, Oquins	200	24	1
Jonas Turner, Whitfields	100	26	1

WILKINSON.

Aaron Averett, ill., Mandersons	54	15	5
Thomas Davis, Halls	364	8	1
John Freeman, sr. Currys	181	4	4
James Garrett, do.	141	29	1
William Woodson, orp. Fairchilds	67	5	1
John Lunn, Smiths	25	14	1
Wm. H. Cane, illegitimate, Shows	219	22	2
John Polk, R. S. Halls	154	12	2

WILKES.

Wm. McLendon, sol., Ragsdales	112	3	1
Joseph Harrison, R. S. Hamocks	37	5	5
William Smith, sr. Ragsdales	129	12	1

☞ This sheet concludes the drawing up to Monday 26th inst.—nearly a fourth of the prizes have been drawn from the wheel.

LAND LOTTERY REGISTER No. 8
[RECORDER OFFICE—PUBLISHED BY GRANTLAND & ORME—PRICE $3.]

NOTE.—Section 1 is Lee County—2 Muscogee—3 Troup—4 Coweta—5 Carroll.

17th DAY'S DRAWING—March 26.

Fortunate Drawers Capts. Dist. No.Dt.Sec.

APPLING.
Henry J. Hand, Collins	11	13	2
Edward Southwell, orp., McDonalds	185	6	1

BALDWIN.
Catherine Cavenah, widow, Wicks	3	3	1
Hugh Knox, Buchanans	1	15	1
Martin Thomas, Thomas	40	2	2
James Leonard, Lingos	230	9	3
Henry W. Malone, Buchanans	193	6	3
James L. Delaunay, do.	144	14	1
Durham Bowen, Bivins	181	32	1
Zachariah Doles, orphan, Doles	35	6	4
William P. Brown, R. S. Bivins	145	9	1

BIBB.
Zach. Williamson, sr. R. S. Beards	178	7	5
William W. Leonard, Bates	25	16	1
James T. Woffard, do.	6	31	1
Norflect Curl, Lloyds	143	6	2

BRYAN.
Solomon Johnson, Harveys	320	20	2

BULLOCH.
John Hoover, Richardsons	226	4	3
Andrew Golden, R. S. Burnetts	162	27	1
Charles Neasmith, Deloachs	6	10	2

BURKE.
Absalom Kinsey, Andersons	41	12	2
Jane Hughes, wid. R. S. Robinsons	80	15	5
George M. Elliston, Dugas	50	8	4
Stephen Devenport, Seegars	118	10	1
William Hilles, Dugas	203	6	2
Jordan Heath, R. S., do.	233	15	2
Hardy D. McCullars, Corkers	156	10	3
John Bates, R. S., Lewis	233	12	2
Jordan Heath, R. S. Dugas	143	3	1
Moses Heath, do.	232	2	3
Henry M. Wynn, Forths	140	20	1

CHATHAM.
John Caudler, Savannah	48	11	5
John Thompson, Reeds	217	12	1
John M. Sykes, Geredons	168	1	1
William Herb, do.	173	6	5
John Swymer, McDonnells	182	7	5
William B. Bulloch, Haydens	54	26	1
Alonzo Day,	63	24	1
Mary M. Robertson, wid., Haydens	288	16	2
Jennet Gale, widow, McDonnells	5	4	3
Jedediah Barstow, Geredons	4	5	1

CLARK.
George Whitten, Alreds	185	5	1
Peter Puryear, Gahagans	198	15	2
William Wright, R. S., Andersons	178	29	1
Robert Love, Wrights	186	5	2
Orps. of Bev. Purguson, Davenports	139	12	3

COLUMBIA.
Nancy Welch's illegitimate, Carrolls	87	19	2
Seaborn P. Huchingson's orps. Bealls	171	8	1
Nancy Yarborough, wid. Ramseys	280	6	5
John Parish, Dranes	109	5	5
J., E. & J. Crawford, illegits. Dranes	108	16	1
John Luke, Culbreaths	107	18	1
Alfred Tindall, Ramseys	207	7	5
William Jay, sen., Coles	195	1	1
Samuel W. Harris, Talberts	326	20	2

CRAWFORD.
Wm. Jones Jones, R. S., Culbreaths	5	4	2
Hugh Black Smith, Dranes	125	18	2
Johnson Hammock, Ellis	111	6	5

DEKALB.
Samuel Colley, Hayes	112	2	3
William Cannon, Merritts	153	10	3
John Woodall, jr. Conns	2	12	1
Joseph Hubbard, soldier, Andersons	70	9	2
Joshua J. Spears, Bakers	153	20	2
John M. Smith, Howells	178	22	2
Alfred Edwards, Hays	217	7	1
William Sisson, Conns	78	26	1
William Heard, R. S., do.	111	4	2

DOOLY.
Alexander Ramsey, Hogans	207	4	1

EFFINGHAM.
Orps. of Emanuel Rahn, Treutlins	24	7	1
Hezekiah Ambrose, do.	138	7	4

ELBERT.
Elizabeth M. Saxton, w. R. S. Tates	225	25	1
Ansel McGehee, soldier, Carpenters	200	33	1
James Shiflet, do.	78	4	2
William Underwood, soldier, Hortons	18	5	3
Edmund Allen, Dunns	102	4	3

EMANUEL.
Howell McLimore, Chasons	196	20	2
Noah Meek, Whiddons	47	19	1
William Larance, Moors	30	22	1
Thorp Roberts, do.	233	17	1
Geo. Shuffield's chil. fa. ab., Swains	65	19	1
Eph. Herrington, sen., R. S. Chasons	151	28	1

FAYETTE.
Joshua Townsend, Whartons	308	1	4
James Burrough, soldier, 9th	210	19	1
John Williams, Whartons	240	6	2
Robert Priddy, soldier, 9th	418	20	2
William Burks, Dodsons	136	6	3
James Hathorn, soldier, Garrisons	175	1	1

FRANKLIN.
John Cheek, Sanders	35	30	1
William F. Abbott, Chandlers	34	14	5
Thomas Garrison, Caudells	39	16	2
William Brooks, McDonalds	86	3	1
Thomas Carter, T., Chandlers	178	12	5
William Glover, R. S., Blankenships	99	10	2
John Hamby, do.	183	9	2
Martin Williams, Stephens	192	4	2
A. S. & W. J. Bone, fa. ab., Walters	143	11	1

GLYNN.
John McLeod, soldier, McLeods	214	21	2
Samuel Burnett, Burnetts	53	6	3

GREENE.
Robert Astin, R. S., Astins	226	17	1
James G. Gooch, Winkfields	230	23	2
James Mitchell's orps., Colcloughs	222	23	2
Lemuel M. Gatlin, Bruces	140	15	2
Claiborn Robinson, Webbs	58	13	5
Jess Boon, R. S., Greens	227	6	3
James Burford, illegit., Southerlands	75	12	1
William L. Astin, Astins	63	7	4
John Haistin, jr. Vincents	8	11	3
John G. Oliver, Dawsons	218	11	5

(50)

Fortunate Drawers Capts. Dist.	No.	Dt.	Sec.
James Hammest, Elys	201	10	5
John Love, Dawsons	49	4	3
Isaac M. Rall, do.	152	3	5
William Brooks, jr., Rankins	146	10	1

GWINNETT.

Samuel Scott, Caruthers	67	5	3
Robert Harkness, R. S., Moors	125	5	5
Andrew Clements, Hills	326	3	4
Gideon Jarrald, Woodroughs	206	9	1
Reuben Higgins, Finchers	264	6	1
Tapley Camp, Wallis	216	1	4
Stephen Robberds, Moors	127	10	2
Pete Hairstone, Woodroughs	194	22	2
Britton Meeks, R. S. Davis	2	14	2
Abner Wells, Mattoxs	177	22	1
Jesse Brewer, Gholston's	82	20	1
Westley Cochran, ill., Woodroughs	35	19	1
H., J., J., J. J., S. & B. Eves ills. do.	170	1	1

HANCOCK.

Ann Webster, widow, 103d	191	11	5
Samuel Stanley, 118th	14	11	2
James Sasnett, 113th	35	8	4
Henry Jones, 118th	88	6	3
John Brownell, do.	8	10	2

HENRY.

Elizabeth Hearn, widow, Allens	17	9	2
Sarah Yates, widow, Risons	3	5	1
John W. Starr, Allens	30	30	1

HABERSHAM.

Abner Cason, Tates	127	6	5
Peggy Anderson, widow, Kenzies	129	10	3
William Anderson, Taits	262	23	2
Lawson Bowers, Vickreys	72	33	1
Benjamin Allison, sen., do.	41	11	2
Abraham B. Carter, Jones	152	19	2
William Hamrick, sen., Bakers	190	13	2
Jesse Greene, Suttons	256	2	2
Theophilus Taylor, do.	86	3	5
Andrew McLane, do.	20	3	5
Philip McIntire, Fains	94	31	1

HALL.

Harkilles Foster, Roberts	189	14	2
John Smith, Alreds	40	10	3
Milly Woodley, w. R. S., Walkers	119	2	1
S., E., S., M. & N. Reid ills. Wilsons	198	27	1

HOUSTON.

Thomas Simpson, Batemans,	240	9	5
Hugh Carr's orphans, Bozemans	31	9	5
James N. McDuffy, orp., Calhouns	387	7	1

JACKSON.

William Pannell, Allens	204	32	1
John Vandeford, Duprees	168	25	1
Anna Bowden, widow, Pairs	228	8	5
Charles M. Heard, Millers	200	4	2
Jacob Phar's orphans, Watersons	142	18	1
Joseph George, orphan, Landrums	153	8	5
John Duncan, R. S., Bowens	24	26	1
Wm. Barnwell, illegitimate, Duncans	203	11	5
Miles Gathright's orphans, Duprees	226	14	1
William S. Chandler, Lindseys	121	28	1

JASPER.

John L. Barnett, Dardens	5	19	1
Elizabeth Mitchell, widow, Baines	276	11	2
Winston Estes, Owens	55	1	3
John M. Faulkner, Dardens	172	15	5
William W. Gardner, Robersons	156	9	3
Amanda A. Clements, orp. Erwins	209	1	2

Fortunate Drawers Capts. Dist.	No.	Dt.	Sec.
Isaac H. Webb, Shropshiers	36	10	2
Sarah Perkins, widow, do.	170	30	1
Hardaman Owen, Owens	35	9	2
Joseph M. McCorcle, Parkers	237	7	3
Sarah Williamson, widow, Wilders	186	5	1
Owen Roberts, illegitimate, Wilsons	87	3	4
Elisha Crow, Hines,	162	2	3
Andrew Henderson, Parkers	273	22	2
Joseph C. Weeks, Owens	143	14	2
Enoch Knight, Wilsons	21	14	2

JEFFERSON.

Samuel McBride's orphans, Boyds	153	4	5
Isaac G. Jordan, Ross's	10	7	3
Elijah Smith, do.	180	4	5
Jeremiah Welsher, R. S., Waldens	66	12	2
Mathew Jordan, Beatys	74	10	3
Augustus Shelman, Jones	135	6	4

JONES.

James A. Delaunay, Breedloves	301	8	1
Joseph Jolly, Newbys	249	9	5
Thomas A. Middlebrooks, Blounts	98	6	2
John H. Hammack, Hammacks	81	16	2
Ann Comer, wid. R. S., Taylors	168	12	3
Simon W. Nichols, Woods	154	3	4
Samuel W. Wilson, Robertsons	140	26	1
Anderson McNeal, Newbys	64	9	2
John Satterwhite, Dosters	223	2	2
Demsey Toller, Popes	48	30	1

LAURENS.

Presly H. Holley, Deans	128	6	4
Samuel Caldwell, jun. Whiteheads	162	16	1
Mary Stokes, Plummers	8	6	3
Seth Kellum, do.	261	14	1
Thomas Darsey, Whiteheads	73	25	1
James Jackson Nobles, ill., Newmons	208	33	1
Rachel Way, hus. absent, Mizells	120	3	2

LINCOLN.

William Oneal, Gideons	82	2	2
Jacob Winn, Lonorgans	128	21	1
Charles Hardy, Parks	233	20	1
James A. Wallace, do.	183	8	3
Francis Cremer's orphans, Leveretts	49	1	1

MADISON.

Nancy Morris, illegitimate, Bones	91	23	1
Anderson Smith, Caldwells	21	27	1
Charles Millican's orphans, Phipps	166	8	1
Loverd Moore, Culbertsons	68	7	4

MONROE.

John Brown, soldier, Fergasons	72	9	3
Morris Kopman, Millers	144	11	3
William B. Stewart, Millers	70	5	4
Henry Collon, Finchs	254	12	1
Henry Collon, do.	118	4	2
Epsey M. Landrum, ill. Wrights	33	14	2
Josiah Grimes, Fergasons	127	14	2
John S. Ragland, Wrights	111	12	2
Martin Slaughter, Finchs	16	11	1
Burril Morris, Greshams	86	4	4
Jerem. Thompsons orps. Houses	199	7	3
Mary Treadaway, wid. Finchs	160	6	1

MORGAN.

Fanny Caldwells illegit. Greggs	193	16	1
John B. Shields, Brooks	174	12	3
Dredziel Pace, Evans	90	5	3
William Backus, Christians	244	5	4
Benjamin Selmans orps. Baileys	2	19	2

Fortunate Drawers	Capts. Dist.	No.	Dt.	Sec.
Jesse D. McIntosh,	Brooks	269	19	2
Leroy Patillo,	Youngs	193	5	4
WilliamM.J.Chisholm,	Whatleys	232	9	5
William Trainum,	Beasleys	176	9	2
Henry Shaw, soldier,	Sparks	207	12	1
Robert J. D. Barkley,	Jennings	214	3	3
MONTGOMERY.				
Elizabeth Wilford, hus. ab.	Ryals	157	32	1
NEWTON.				
John Loyal,	Pullens	58	17	2
John Winfrey, sol.	Newnans	236	27	1
Wm. D. McCrackin,	Pullens	53	31	1
James Street, soldier,	Talleys	83	19	1
Samuel D. Echols,	Clarks	138	21	2
Coleman Duke, illegit.	Bakers	11	9	2
William Swan,	Zachrys	249	3	1
William Griffith,	Bakers	248	21	1
OGLETHORPE.				
Frances Poss, widow,	Hills	44	10	5
Charles A. Hawkins,	Bells	403	20	2
Cynthia Edwards, widow,	Hills	35	13	1
Wm. S. Wilson,	Seals	60	9	1
Mathew Burfort,	Rhodes	27	4	5
Hugh McWhorters orps.	Bells	80	3	5
Elijah Walker,	Floyds	73	5	1
David Dunn,	Bells	145	9	5
John B. Stewart,	Rousseaus	180	5	3
Joshua Lovett,	Rousseaus	130	18	1
Jesse Brook,	Dixs	10	30	1
Wm. Hatchett, sr. R. S.	Rhodes	169	7	5
John Floyd,	Burfords	167	22	2
James Bridges,	Seals	167	7	2
Armsted Jones,	Smiths	142	5	4
Kezikiah Tabor, R. S.	Seals	86	2	1
PIKE.				
Seaborn Gray,	Hicks	30	11	2
Arthur T. Camp,	Orrs	122	4	2
John McDonald,	Hicks	257	8	5
Allen Brooks,	Mays	69	12	2
Pendleton J. Roberson,	Orrs	128	10	3
Samuel Lane, soldier,	Weavers	140	4	4
PULASKI.				
Sally & John Word, ors.	Kellams	73	5	2
Unity Brinson, w. R. S.	Thomas'	98	3	4
PUTNAM.				
Josiah H. Reed,	Sawyers	110	12	1
Ellender Sanders, wid.	Clarks	25	2	2
John Rousseau,	Kendricks	267	3	1
Asa Marchman,	Duprees	85	4	4
John J. Smith's orphs.	Bledsoes	76	16	2
James Wilson,	Vinings	117	20	2
RABUN.				
Thomas Carver,	Becks	143	18	2
Elisha Coffee,	Godfreys	9	16	1
Amons Williams, do.		272	6	5
James Rogers,	Becks	168	19	1
RICHMOND.				
Alfred Hood, orphan,	Mantzs	159	14	1
William,Alexander,MaryAnn&Eliz-Mathews orphans,	Huntingtons	122	9	2
John James,	Wilcoxs	72	3	2
Eli Mustin,	Treadwells	208	12	5
William Jackson, do.		176	28	1
Greene James,	Wilcoxs	162	8	5
William H. Jones,	Huntingtons	22	17	1
James Holcombe, R. S.	119th	229	9	1
SCRIVEN.				
James Burke,	Kemps	83	30	1
Mourn. Shepherd, w.	Stricklings	118	32	1
Orphs. of D. Brownson,	Poytress	278	16	2
TATTNALL.				
Joseph McLeland,	Dees	14	7	4
Jona. B. Bacons orps.	Deloachs	64	24	1
Martha Powell, widow,	Corseys	117	11	5
TELFAIR.				
John Douglass,	Wilsons	12	18	1
Nancy Hall, w.	R.S.Robertsons	388	7	1
TALIAFERRO.				
Reason D. Bealle,	Gunns	126	11	2
Richard H. Jones, do.		88	13	1
TWIGGS.				
Zelpha Sledge, wid.	Graggs	34	8	5
Dempsey Odam,	Streetmans	87	11	1
Elenor Ham, illegit.	Bosticks	140	4	3
Isaac Hollingsworth, do.		219	5	5
Littleton Barnes,	Pearsons	235	11	1
Jacob W. Cobb,	Bosticks	105	28	1
Gideon A. Wethersby,	Pearsons	61	10	1
UPSON.				
Green Sledge,	Hattoxs	110	7	4
Thomas Batey, do.		311	1	4
Cornelius Jeter,	Coopers	147	3	5
John Stephens,	Myricks	155	2	2
Isabella McCrary,	Paschalls	50	1	1
WALTON.				
Thomas Smith, 503rd dist.		42	6	3
Elisha Watson,	Bixleys	227	6	2
Susannah McMahan, ill.	Hudsons	36	3	5
Benjamin New,	Pools	28	23	2
Joseph Gregory, 250th district		154	5	2
James Brooks orps.	Davis	24	25	1
Joseph Herndon, R. S.	503rd	111	28	1
WARE.				
Bitha Newberns illegit.	Lees	130	24	2
Rachel & Jas. Lee. ills.	Moats	57	6	5
WAYNE.				
James Wainwright,	McKinneys	61	5	4
WARREN.				
John Long,		134	4	4
Richard Rhodes,	Downs	104	10	2
William Story,	Sanders	114	24	1
John Cason,	Adkins	4	32	1
Harris Wood, do.		60	16	1
Reuben McGee, R. S.	Sanders	49	5	5
Gabriel Grimes,	Kinseys	153	12	3
Soloman Granade, sol.	Hills	245	3	4
John Gibson, R. S.	Parhams	69	2	4
Low Jackson,	Jones	86	8	2
Jonathan Dardin, soldier,	Hills	31	17	1
Ishmael McDaniel,	Parhams	168	6	1
John Thompson's orps.	Sanders	162	30	1
William Toler orp. of David, do.		120	16	1

(52)

WASHINGTON.

Fortunate Drawers	Capts. Dist.	No.	Dt.	Sec.
Absalom Wiley,	R. S. Tysons	40	24	1
John W. Pate,	Whitfields	328	3	4
Isaac Taylor, soldier,	Gilberts	175	10	5
Delancy Cox, illegit.	Woods	199	15	1
Richard Childers,	Gilberts	170	12	1
Joshua Robison,	Mannings	108	4	2
Jessy Trawicks heirs,	Oquins	34	6	2
John Brantley,	Wimberlys	58	18	2
Sylvia Coker,	Floyds	86	5	1
James G. Parish,	Oquins	16	12	2
Russell Dorch,	Wimberlys	61	31	1
Cloe Covington, widow,	Tysons	184	17	2

WILKINSON.

William Duncan,	Shows	205	9	5
William Lord,	Mathews	24	12	1
Nathan Gilbert,	Halls	38	11	3
Wyot Meredith,	Mathews	48	10	2
David Mann,	Smiths	156	7	2
Wiley Maridith,	Mathews	161	1	2
Tim. Bloodworth,	Mandersons	127	15	2
William B. Thomas,	Halls	225	5	5
Pool Half,	Mayos	357	3	4

WILKES.

Joseph Victory,	Moors	202	17	2
Jason Watson,	Hamocks	140	2	3
Henry Henderson, sol.,	Wootens	50	9	1
Francis Powell,	R.S.McDermots	91	6	2
John T. Wooten,	Popes	55	22	1
James M. Anderson,	Charltons	232	21	2
Bennett Reeves,	Ragsdales	47	17	2
Humphrey Agees orps.	Hopkins	135	17	1
G.H.Washingtonsol.	Washingtons	161	19	2
Nancy Simons, w. R. S.	Hopkins	229	13	1
Mary Wellborn, sol's. wid.	Popes	164	12	3

18th DAY'S DRAWINIG—March 27.

APPLING.

Moody McLendon,	Collins	208	19	1
Thomas Corson,	McDonalds	85	5	3
David Yawn,	Collins	124	20	1

BALDWIN.

Nicholas Pool's orphans,	Wicks	126	11	1
Betsy Pickett, widow,	Thomas	181	7	3
Martin Hill,	Buchanans	138	15	5
Mary Ann Robertson, widow,	do.	28	14	5
William Mahonn's orphans,	Ginns	15	28	1
Thomas Miles, R. S.,	Lingos	212	27	1
David B. Hill,	Lesters	72	20	1
Munroe's orphans,	Rows	119	5	4
Louisa H. Greene, illegit.,	Thomas	34	16	2

BIBB.

Thomas Red,	Bates	171	23	2
William Wilson,	Beards	99	1	1

BRYAN.

Phillis Manly, widow,	Stephens	312	15	1
David B. Wells,	Harveys	95	4	2
Jacob Simms,	do.	165	5	1
William H. Vanbrackel,	do.	118	33	1

BULLOCH.

Sarah Rawls, widow,	McCalls	155	30	1

BURKE.

Willis Hasty,	Roberts	284	10	2

Fortunate Drawers	Capts. Dist.	No.	Dt.	Sec.
Samuel Heath's orphans,	Dugas	14	2	5
Stephen Chance's orphans,	Wards	41	8	2
Thomas J. Dixon,	Gordons	147	1	5
Feriby Wallace, widow,	Wards	68	30	1
Mary Brinson, wid. R. S.	do.	16	8	1
John Andrews,	Roberts	305	8	1

BUTTS.

John Murray,	Kirkseys	52	8	5
John H. Davis,	Johnsons	109	6	1

CHATHAM.

Abiel Swighoffer,	Baines	54	20	2
Ann Kelly, widow,	Haydens	213	20	2
William Morel soldier,	do.	159	2	2
Mary Baker, orp.ofDaniel,	Savannah	269	7	5
Mary Gordon, orp. of Edward,	Baines	179	4	1
John Williams,	McDonnells	199	3	2
Lucy Cottincan, widow,	Geredons	130	4	3
Mehetabel Kollock, wid.	Haydens	93	2	3

CLARK.

Winniford Rogers, wid.	Gahagans	192	6	5
Thomas G. Hester,	Lumpkins	200	11	3
Wm. Wood's mins. fa. ab.	Andersons	57	20	2
Abraham Durham, R. S.,	McCrees	40	12	5
Thomas A. Wright,	Wrights	175	15	5
Sally Hutson, hus. absent,	Andersons	209	14	2
Isaac Vincent, R. S.,	Davenports	99	12	1
James Young,	Lumpkins	170	21	1

COLUMBIA.

Caroline Lott, lunatic,	Dranes	22	13	2
William Newman,	Carrolls	55	1	2
Isham Pound's orphans,	Bealls	91	31	1
Justin E. Beebee,	Livermans	101	3	1
Elizabeth Flynn,	Adams	129	1	5
David Dubose,	Stallings	227	5	3

CRAWFORD.

Joseph Floyd,	Wilsons	136	14	1
Lemuel D. Slatter,	Ellis	54	7	4
David Barrentine,	Rhodes	222	15	1

DECATUR.

Nathaniel Holton,	Ferrells	164	7	1

DEKALB.

Reuben Stephens, R. S.,	Stephens	282	9	5
William Adcock,	Edwards	180	12	5
John Collins,	Scaifes	56	3	1
William Henry, Jr.,	Smiths	143	15	1
Michael Howell,	Howells	360	20	2
Martin Boon's orphans,	Bowlings	113	15	1
Tyrice Pearce,	Edwards	202	31	1
James Campbell,	Merritts	29	10	1

DOOLY.

Thomas Rhodes's orphans,	Sarrs	34	10	1
John J. Wallace,	Hogans	44	6	5
William A. Tharp,	Andersons	149	9	2

EARLY.

Benjamin Moy,	Wilsons	245	12	2

EFFINGHAM.

John J. Morel,	Treutlins	136	24	1
Wm. J. Spencer's orps.	Waldhaners	86	4	1
Sarah Crane, widow,	do.	118	6	1

ELBERT.

Nathaniel Prothro's orps.	Dobbs	10	1	3
James F. Nunlee, R. S.,	Tuckers	108	29	1
Peter Oliver, R. S.,	Bells	30	3	4
Samuel Shepherd,	Harmonds	83	13	2
William Runnels,	Hortons	117	2	3
Reuben Maxwell,	Blackwells	217	23	2
Wade Speed,	Tates	102	8	5

(53)

Fortunate Drawers	Capts. Dist.	No.	Dt.	Sec.
Joel Hunt, Dunns		174	22	2
Claiborn Webb, Deadwilders		321	7	1
John Baily, Webbs		239	31	1
Bailey White, orphan, Hortons		65	33	1

EMANUEL.

John Larence, Moors		165	11	1
Lyda Taylor's illegitimate, Arlines		133	10	1
Hugh Davis, Moors		188	8	5
Samuel Brown, Chasons		166	7	4

FAYETTE.

Josiah R. Bosworth, Craigs		20	14	2
William Morgan, sen., R. S., Roziers		35	8	3
Henry Watts, Craigs		11	5	5
James Durham, Dodsons		91	20	2
Willis Wood, Browns		200	22	1
Jonathan Mitchell, Whartons		200	2	1
John F. Howell, Browns		216	8	1
William Burks, Dodsons		133	12	1
Nancy Sharp, widow, Browns		385	28	1

FRANKLIN.

Samuel Johnston, McDonalds		33	3	2
Elizabeth Culberson, wid. Hudsons		26	1	3
Vict. Crawford, wid. R. S. Stephens		80	8	5
William Thomas, R. S., Hudsons		145	5	2
John H. McFarran, do.		131	2	1
Wiley Haguewood, D. Chandlers		249	23	1
Edward Bing, Stephens		182	17	1
Charles M. Connelly, Stranges		12	8	2
Labun Catlett, Caudels		73	28	1
John Albritton, R. S. Blankenships		56	8	3
Martha Sayer, widow, Stranges		166	7	2
Pleasant Holly, Boswells		56	8	4

GREENE.

Joseph Fitzpatrick, Winkfields		74	21	2
Drury King, Rankins		31	12	1
Seaborn McMichael Robins		112	20	1
Benjamin Copeland, R. S., Halls		254	14	1
Elizabeth Christopher, w.R.S.Greens		87	2	3
William Brooks, jr. Rankins		112	8	1
Richard Knight, R. S., Astins		226	12	2
Susannah Hammonds, w. R. S. Bruces		256	3	2
Elizabeth Wright, widow, Astins		209	5	2
John Mapp, Bruces		346	8	1
Fielding Wallace, Astins		259	33	1

GWINNETT.

Andrew Covey, Caruthers		159	31	1
Owen Andrews, R. S., Woodroughs		54	5	1
H. A. B. Nunnelly, sol., Whortons		124	32	1
William Griffin, Robertsons		190	5	3
Sterling Callahan, Evans		44	12	2
Mat. Cochran, for wife, Caruthers		210	7	5
James F. Nunn, Wallis		114	6	4
William Warrin, Moors		113	2	3
James Yancy, Rollins		134	20	2
Catharine Nation, widow, Moors		232	6	3
James Smith's orphans, do.		159	6	1
Emanuel Light, Rollins		108	3	3
John Dunn for Marie E. Harrison, illegitimate, Gholstons		95	11	3
Edward Jackson, R. S. Davis		52	14	2
Ambrose Kirkland, Robertsons		144	5	4
Joel Chandler, Wallis		69	6	4

HANCOCK.

Thomas Landreth, 102d		252	13	1
Penelope Bird, lunatic, Reaves		142	19	1
George Barnes, soldier, Bishops		42	18	2
Malone Mullins, 104th		37	12	3
Benjamin M. Collins's orphans, 103d		274	11	2

Fortunate Drawers	Capts. Dist.	No.	Dt.	Sec.
Perry Nelson, 109th		79	3	1
Andrew Danelly, Adams		4	1	1
Burwell Ingram, Bishops		129	29	1

HENRY.

James P. Lowe, Shaw		309	8	1
Henry Nichols, Gosdens		27	20	1
William Adams, do.		231	28	1
Henry McClendon, soldier, Shaws		6	5	5
Robert W. Harkness, Harriss		312	8	5
Charles Ward, soldier, Wards		204	18	2
Jesse Bryant, Kites		211	6	1
William Garner's orphans, Millers		292	7	5
John Jinks, Harriss		219	25	1
John Brannan, Millers		127	4	4

HABERSHAM.

James P. Wade, Bryans		11	9	3
John Owen, Tates		154	10	5
William Eaton Seque, Suttons		18	5	4
John Motes, do.		123	7	2
William Brown, Kenzies		69	3	2
Thomas Watson, Fains		42	14	1
William R. Mulkey, minor, Suttons		106	19	2

HALL.

Joseph Harper, Roberts		38	6	1
John Shaw, Garrards		200	3	4
Peter Preslar, sr. R. S., Alreds		52	22	2
John W. Bates, Hardages		16	6	2
Thomas Lodon, Walkers		179	27	1
Caleb Garrison, Hardens		250	17	2
Aaron Adams, R. S., Harrisons		154	9	2
Martin Pugh, Yagers		232	2	2
Benjamin West, R. S., Hardages		18	23	1

HOUSTON.

William Singleton, Simpsons		107	6	1
Charles M. Jenkins, Becks		190	3	1
William West, soldier, Blanchards		75	8	4
Daniel Pitts, Calhouns		72	2	3

IRWIN.

James Walker, R. S., McCalls		37	5	4

JACKSON.

James Wimberly, Millers		278	1	4
William Vineyard, Lindseys		32	20	1
Clary Pope Camp, illegit. Rogers		87	3	3
Dulcinna Bluster, widow, do.		211	8	1
James W. Espy, Staplers		97	23	2
Wylie Anthony, Rogers		215	2	4
Elisha Bailey, Gathrights		43	20	1

JASPER.

Calvin Fish, Wilders		12	4	3
John Ezell, Butts		255	9	1
Hudson W. Harding, Parkers		220	11	1
Augustus Wise, Dardens		55	5	5
John Bailey's orphans, Wilsons		198	9	1
William A. J. Phillips, Baines		135	6	1
Jane Mathis, widow, Reeves		365	8	1
Wiley Kirk, soldier, Comptons		163	12	1
Charles Patterson, sol., Penningtons		284	1	2
John Turner, Farleys		59	15	5
Thomas P. Webb, Parkers		12	9	3
David Lawson, Robersons		64	15	2
Joseph L. Hill, soldier, Hollands		2	5	5
Henry Butler, Robinsons		77	12	1
Martha Farley, widow, Robersons		279	22	1

JEFFERSON.

Bryant J. Hunter, Waldens		211	1	1
Jacob Gooddown, R. S., Beatys		168	3	2
James Coursey, Jones		252	8	3

(54)

Fortunate Drawers Capts. Dist.	No.	Dt.	Sec.
Susan A. Batty, widow, Jones	221	2	4
Henry Rogers, Kings	285	11	2
JONES.			
Jonathan Poe, Dosters	83	16	2
George Robertson's orphans, Davis	119	9	3
Silas Meacham, Woods	77	19	2
Henry Barron, Newbys	277	22	1
Littleton W. Morris, Popes	154	13	1
Edwin Bowen, Woods	93	5	4
James Sanders, Mullins	224	6	1
Jesse Rawson, Stewarts	342	20	2
William Davison, Davis	253	16	2
Zachariah Hester, Duncans	268	12	3
John McLeroy, Davis	60	15	2
Tapley Booth, Newbys	218	7	3
William V. Hoskins, Spinks	89	11	1
George Miller, R. S., Breedloves	75	5	3
Manusra Barganer, minor, Taylors	131	9	5
Larkin Reynolds, do.	184	13	1
LAURENS.			
Benjamin Skipper, Deans	16	5	2
Eliz. Anderson's ill. chil., Whiteheads	133	25	1
Elizabeth Flowers, w. R. S., Pavers	51	2	1
Eady Newsoms, ill. heirs, Plummers	56	23	1
Catharine Snelgrove, wid. Mizells	28	5	3
LIBERTY.			
Amos Blackman, 15th	174	3	3
Archibald Barber, 17th	12	11	5
LINCOLN.			
Mary Ann Mophit, w. R. S. Lonorgans	236	10	5
Elizabeth Spright, widow, Parks	220	23	2
Jeremiah Thompson, sol., Hardys	202	10	5
Mary Hunter, widow, Parks	202	33	1
Bennington Lamar, Lonorgans	151	1	2
MADISON.			
William Hodge, jr. Adairs	125	1	2
George Clorie, R. S., Phipps	221	12	1
Josiah Hopkins, jun., do.	141	4	3
Gray W. Allen, Higginbothams	137	14	1
McINTOSH.			
James Reid, Demeres	27	5	1
James Popwell, McCranies	172	26	1
MONROE.			
Elijah Currys orps. Pattersons	283	20	2
Cordy D. Stokes, Browns	174	7	2
Thomas Hollis, sol. Fergasons	62	16	1
Alexander Sledge, sol. Pattersons	51	2	4
Erastus W. Jones, Millers	272	4	2
Elizabeth Thompson, w. Houses	179	1	1
Alexander Hall, Johnsons	174	12	1
William Brown, Turners	407	20	2
John Spain, Greshams	241	22	1
Caswell Buias, sol. Pattersons	93	6	4
William Swan, Browns	275	8	5
David Jones, R. S. do.	130	10	3
MORGAN.			
Joseph Baileys orphans, Stokes	80	2	1
Eliza. Whatley, wid. Jennings	142	22	2
William Rileys orphans, Hills	69	12	3
Allen Robertson, Jennings	136	6	4
Eli W. Harrison, Boswells	48	12	3
William Meddows, Canifaxs	35	10	5
Charles Robertson, Jennings	116	4	1
Isham S. Fannins orph. Youngs	91	27	1
Alford Brown, Stokes	82	31	1

Fortunate Drawers Capts. Dist.	No.	Dt.	Sec.
Mastin Clay, Harwells	244	11	5
L. Yarborough, R. S. Christians	80	6	3
James Kelly, do.	47	32	1
Horace T. Shaw, Adairs	235	7	3
MONTGOMERY.			
Samuel Clark, Popes	212	22	1
NEWTON.			
Robert Culberson, Zachrys	268	5	3
Ambrose Brown, R. S. Summers	203	31	1
James Wiggins, Hays	153	6	5
Daniel Hamby, Zachrys	202	11	3
OGLETHORPE.			
Henry S. Yourberry, Decks	96	8	3
George Barber, sol. B. Hills	139	5	2
Erwin Elcans, sol. Billups	46	11	2
Miles W. Collier, Rousseaus	116	13	5
A. Knowlman, R. S., do.	174	26	1
Thomas Farmer, Lacys	60	5	5
Groves Howard, jr., Hills	200	29	1
PIKE.			
Majors Harris, Mays	221	2	3
Sarah Brasel, Mays	144	1	2
Peter Atris, Longs	102	1	1
William Baker, sol. Weavers	59	10	2
PULASKI.			
John Faircloth, Gilstraps	128	14	2
James Robuck, do.	10	7	4
Amos Brown, Bracewells	297	4	1
PUTNAM.			
Riley Shores, Goods	165	5	4
Anderson Harwell, jr. Blacks	217	10	5
Zachariah Hall, Allums	136	23	2
RABUN.			
Martin Keel, Godfreys	132	7	5
Isaac George, do.	146	4	2
Lucinda Myers, orphan, do.	129	9	3
Allan R. Gains, Godfreys	5	9	5
Winneyford Coffee, do.	298	15	1
William Kelley, Becks	8	2	2
RICHMOND.			
Joseph Dausey, James	147	12	2
Jane Barham, wid. Blacks	247	1	4
I.&A.Allen orps. of sol. Blacks	140	16	2
Reddin Atwell, soldier, Kellys	177	23	2
John Sanges, Blacks	57	18	1
Ann F. Polk orphan, Treadwells	270	21	2
Ann Norrell, widow, 123rd	100	8	3
Joseph E. Read, Huntingtons	42	3	4
Joseph S. Carts orphans, Blacks	86	33	1
Charles Lippit, Augusta	155	21	2
J., J., W. & R.Kelly, orphs. 119th	49	2	5
John M. Cooper, Treadwells	143	4	5
Eliz.M.L.&R.W.Bugg ors. do.	168	12	5
SCRIVEN.			
Owin Jinkins, Poytress	88	6	2
Vardaman Rooks	112	24	1
D. & W. Morgan mins. Hunters	79	5	1
TATTNALL.			
John Bowen, McDuffies	139	24	1
Patrick Hardins orps. do.	24	1	5
Littleton Hammock, Dees	206	13	2

Fortunate Drawers Capts. Dist.	No.	Dt.	Sec.	Fortunate Drawers Capts. Dist.	No.	Dt.	Sec.
William Triplet, R. S., Deloachs	12	12	1	Carlton Greer, Shows	124	15	2
TELFAIR.				Richmond Stratham, Halls	123	2	4
William Williams, sr. Lamkins	48	25	1	Daniel McCraney, Mandersons	22	7	1
TWIGGS.				WILKES.			
Mary Sanders, wid., Wimberlys	222	16	1	Solomon Harper, Hamocks	187	8	1
John P. Brown, Bosticks	64	7	1	Fieling Rucker, Chunns	38	2	2
William Ezell, Graggs	227	4	2	Elzy B. Ryenolds, Popes	188	9	1
Orphs. of Collin Sledge, Graggs	104	9	2	James Nolan, sol., Lukers	244	13	1
Uriah Evans, Holidays	5	13	5	Theodo. Robertson, wid. Chunns	308	7	1
William Nobles, sol. Holidays	208	25	1	William Smith, sr. Ragsdales	186	3	4
Stephen Pitts, do.	95	13	2				
UPSON.				19th DAY'S DRAWING—March 28.			
John Passmore, Coopers	36	30	1	APPLING.			
Isaac Horn, Myricks	4	24	2	Thomas Corson, McDonalds	219	16	1
John R. Owens,	314	20	2	Daniel Patterson, Mathis	194	9	5
Priscy Stephens, hus. ab. Pashall	242	5	4	George Overstreet, McDonalds	101	5	3
Edmond Bailey, Coopers	108	1	2	William A. Sturdifant, Mathis	223	31	1
Thomas Ayres, sol. Duprees	218	6	2	BALDWIN.			
WALTON.				Josiah Mathews, Doles	34	5	2
Franklin B. Sansom, 559th	191	10	1	Henry McMullin, Wheelers	154	7	1
William Watson, sol. Hudsons	88	14	1	Solomon Sacicus, orphan, Bivins	112	5	4
Joel Laseter, Davis	3	21	2	William Hand, Lesters	109	3	3
John Smith, 249th	279	5	1	Charles Malone, Reddings	4	5	5
WARE.				Robert E. Wicker, Wicks	109	10	2
Richard Carver, Moats	12	9	1	David Batson, Lingos	133	32	1
Charles Grifface, R. S. Moats	192	31	1	BIBB.			
James Osteen, do.	218	1	2	Henry Smith's orphans, Beards	39	9	1
WARREN.				Marian Vigal's illegit. Swearingins	99	24	2
Robert Barton, Adkins	175	4	2	George Collins, Beards	119	24	1
Charles Raley, Jones	205	6	5	BRYAN.			
James M. Coleman, Bulls	137	3	4	Orps. of T. H. Henden, Stephens	120	1	2
William Tysons orphs. Sanders	34	8	4	Steph.&Matilda Gray, orps. do.	97	7	3
Thomas Holden, orph. Rogers	239	2	4	BULLOCH.			
Robert Black, jr. Kinseys	26	2	5	Mary Gant, wid. R. S., Burnetts	35	8	1
Elisha Roberts, Parhams	188	7	5	BURKE.			
Chapman F. Maddux, Bulls	166	31	1	Betsy T. Harvey, w. R. S. Wards	244	12	3
Josiah Barton, illegit. Adkins	132	4	4	John Lynch's orps. Lynchs	79	6	5
Drury Banks, R. S., Parhams	100	6	5	John Conner, Rogers	245	6	1
Peggy McCrary's illegits. Jones	146	5	5	Henry J. Holliday, Corkers	26	10	5
Wingfield Cosby, Parhams	269	3	4	Elizer Lewis, R. S., do.	24	2	4
Eli. G. Shurmon, Hales	80	8	1	Exum Nelson, Browns	98	13	5
WASHINGTON.				B. M., & K. Roberts, orps. Dukes	228	10	5
David Looper, Tysons	77	9	2	Abraham Roberts, Wards	158	1	4
William S. Shearly, sol. Jordans	199	2	2	Albritton McCuin, Corkers	92	30	1
Alexander Goodgames orps. do.	45	6	5	Josiah H. Hatcher, Gordons	218	19	1
Parmelia Hall, wid. McLendons	272	9	3	CAMDEN.			
Jacob Stephens heirs, Oquins	169	11	2	Orphans of Asa Chancy, Cox's	91	4	5
Temper, Mayo, w.R.S.Jordans	76	7	1	Jaicque Vocille, Wards	41	2	2
Thomas Holt, R.S.Whitfields	151	10	1	Robert Brazell, Browns	104	15	2
Aaron Martin orphan, Floyds	285	12	3	CHATHAM.			
Allen Winhar, Gilberts	211	7	1	Hanford Knapp, Geredons	25	6	1
Martha Marsh, McLendons	136	4	3	Philip K. Wait, Haydens	76	11	3
Moses Sinquefield, jr. Jordans	41	22	2	S.,J.&W.Tucker, ors. McDonnells	56	7	5
WILKINSON.				Samuel Ihly, soldier, Haydens	116	4	2
John McArthur, sol. Currys	36	14	2	Wm. Henry Greene, McDonnells	206	12	2
Rowland Stubbs, Shows	15	3	4	CLARK.			
Shadrack Miller, Smiths	101	9	1	Benjamin M. Grenade,Andersons	242	3	3
Hardy Steward, Mayos	41	1	1	Jesse Jones, Lumpkins	94	9	1
Dennis Lindsy, Halls	100	24	1	Noah T. Prince, Deans	18	32	1
William G. Dudley, Smiths	224	2	2	Gray B. Lasseter, illegit. Wrights	21	2	1
Solomon Williams, Mandersons	89	23	1	David Lynch, Lumpkins	159	25	1

Fortunate Drawers Capts. Dist.	No.	Dt.	Sec.
COLUMBIA.			
John L. B. Lamkin, Culbreaths	9	1	4
Richard Revere's mins. Boltons	171	11	3
Elizabeth Finch, widow, Adams	274	10	2
Hiram Tulley, Ramseys	144	16	2
Sally Stallings, lunatic, Boltons	112	16	1
William P. Jones, Talberts	210	8	3
Phoebe Edwards, wid. Clarks	118	8	3
Philip Tinsley, soldier, Carrolls	243	3	1
CRAWFORD.			
Wyatt Blassingame, Wilsons	73	10	3
Thomas Davis, Lovetts	17	30	1
DECATUR.			
John Browning, Ferrills	176	17	1
DEKALB.			
Thomas Fullar, Conns.	219	20	1
Rachel Broughton, wid. Stephens	61	6	1
John Stephenson, soldier, Harriss	155	1	1
Charles Whitlock, Hays	176	6	2
William Bullard, Scaifs	160	6	2
Jesse Corbit, Bowlings	190	32	1
DOOLY.			
John J. Evans, orphan, Sarrs	104	2	4
Thomas J. Kesterson, Hogans	12	14	1
EARLY.			
Thomas Rosser Ellet, Wilsons	114	9	5
EFFINGHAM.			
Gill Thomas, Stricklands	156	20	1
John Tyner, Edwards	245	15	1
Godlip Snyder, R. S., Stricklands	21	29	1
ELBERT.			
James White, Dunns	166	10	3
Simeon Jones' orp. Carpenters	93	26	1
George Key, Bells	215	17	2
Leroy Burton, soldier, Tates	213	18	1
Jesse Smith, Hortons	124	28	1
Edward Herndon, sr. Blackwells	102	8	4
Milly Rucker, widow, Alstons	109	16	2
EMANUEL.			
Marion Sims, Arlines	16	23	1
Augustus M. Cowart, Fountains	29	22	1
FAYETTE.			
Henry C. Morgan, sol., Morgans	167	8	3
Willis Kilcrease, Roziers	16	21	2
James G. Houston, Browns	234	22	1
FRANKLIN.			
Solomon Holmes, McDonalds	75	3	5
John Towns, Jones	77	3	5
James Bramblet, Tabors	196	25	1
Willis Seales, Blankinships	168	22	2
Andrew Martin, Caudells	88	10	5
Charles Farrell, Blankinships	72	18	2
Jesse Braughner, jr. Stranges	1	31	1
Isham Merritt, Walters	263	15	1
GREENE.			
Gilcrest Overton, Colcloughs	225	5	3
Sam'l Winslet, sr. R. S. Knowles	235	7	1
John Wells, Greenes	166	16	2
Jarril L. Turner, Bruces	48	18	2
J. Harralson, R. S., Southerlands	213	2	4
Isaac G. Stewart, Vincents	109	27	1
Edward B. Bryan, Halls	72	17	2
William S. Branch, Robinsons	134	16	1

Fortunate Drawers Capts. Dist.	No.	Dt.	Sec.
Lucretia Woodruff, wid. Dawsons	158	17	1
ObadiahCopeland's orps.Knowles	164	12	1
Charles D. Stewart, Dawsons	164	1	1
GWINNETT			
Barnett Dempsey, Caruthers	151	17	1
James Phillips, Hills	6	7	2
Jemison Ware, Bakers	162	11	2
William Ezzell's orphans, Davis	233	14	1
Henry Davis, R. S., Mattoxs	279	16	2
John S. Head, sr. R. S. Rollins	66	9	3.
Green B. Turner, Caruthers	204	14	1
Morning Dean, wid. R. S., Bakers	33	31	1
AmbrashHill, wounded, Hunicuts	186	20	1
Thomas L. Tanner, Woodroughs	198	6	3
John Peavy, R. S., Whortons	234	6	5
Nathaniel Austin, Hunicuts	143	32	1
John J. Austin, do.	3	30	1
Ephraim Thompson, Shippys	89	14	1
Jonathan Garrett, Finchers	136	6	2
Washington Osburn, orp. Bakers	63	5	3
William Paton, do. 13	13	2	
HANCOCK.			
Bird W. Brazill, R. S., 114th	187	4	1
ThomasWhitehead's orps.111th	175	4	4
William Horton's orphans, 101st	96	20	1
Jesse F. Pierce, 109th	102	20	1
Mary Ann Blount, widow, 113th	62	3	4
Thomas B. Morgan, 101st	12	13	2
James Brantley, 107th	224	19	2
Joannah Tomerson,w.R.S.,106th	182	9	1
John Giles, soldier, Grantlands	184	7	2
HENRY.			
Aaron Pate, Bryants	266	4	3
Charles Sausing, M. Vickers	92	3	3
William Norriss, R. S., Harriss	350	20	2
William Kilpatrick, Shaws	68	5	5
John Lang, do.	90	15	5
William P. Newell, Bryants	143	9	5
William Deal's orphans, Shaws	220	29	1
HABERSHAM.			
John Butt, sen. Vickreys	209	20	2
Jacob Stover, jr. Kenzies	137	23	2
Robert Beaty, Jones	11	12	1
Moses Rice, soldier, Suttons	43	17	2
HALL.			
Abraham Padget, Hardens	125	11	1
Jeremiah Paterson, Harrisons	137	4	1
Jonathan Pennell, R.S., Garrards	148	16	1
Josiah C. Mattins, Smiths	40	3	4
Carter Evens, Roberts	227	8	5
John Taylor, Hardages	71	22	2
William Gilmon, Smiths	31	29	1
HOUSTON.			
John E. Waters, Becks	195	21	1
Tamar Moree, min. Blanchards	177	11	1
James Kennon, Becks	253	3	3
Jacob Johnson, Pattons	69	17	2
Jane Walker, widow, do.	127	15	1
John Simpson, Batemans	90	24	1
W. Wheeler, son of R.W., Smiths	105	19	1
IRWIN.			
James Griffin, R. S., Dixons	31	3	5
Stephen Townsend, Bradfords	35	14	2

LAND LOTTERY REGISTER—No. 9
[RECORDER OFFICE—PUBLISHED BY GRANTLAND & ORME—PRICE $3.]

NOTE.—Section 1 is Lee County—2 Muscogee—3 Troup—4 Coweta—5 Carroll.

19th *DAY'S DRAWING*—Continued

Fortunate Drawers Capts. Dist.	No.Dt.Sec.
William Brawnin, sr. Underwoods	50 31 1

JACKSON.

Fortunate Drawers Capts. Dist.	No.Dt.Sec.
James Pierce, Venables	5 7 4
John H. Greene, do.	196 24 1
James H. Brack, Duprees	230 17 1
Allen Williams, Rogers	234 11 5
Sarah Nalls, widow, Millers	39 4 1
Thomas Eaves, Lindseys	57 2 1
Philip Rion, Duprees	154 14 5
John Carlile, soldier, Storys	63 21 1
Sarah Bell, w. R. S. Millers	3 14 2
Robert McDowell, R. S., Winns	190 30 1
James S. Bradford, sol., Storys	98 24 2
Wm. G. Morgan, Duprees	121 21 2
John Reiding, do.	209 4 3
Wm. Langford, do.	180 32 1
Pearson Duncan, Storys	120 28 1
John G. Mattox, Lindseys	80 23 1

JASPER.

Joel Gay, Robersons	159 19 2
Nancy Dingler, w.R.S.Trussells	191 20 2
Lewis D. Yancy, sr.R.S.Keys	48 19 2
Orphans of Holifield, Hines	92 9 2
Francis Wisdom, sol. Downeys	268 21 2
John Huston, sr. R.S.Hines	281 6 5
Annis Johnson, illegit. Johnsons	5 9 2
Wm. Tedley, Barnetts	23 22 2
Thos. Phelps, R. S. Farleys	82 26 1
Wallace M. Lemon, Sparks	73 18 1

JEFFERSON.

Kindred Brassel, Waldens	49 10 2
Allen Futral, Elliotts	3 9 1
Ann Hall, w. R. S. Marshalls	78 23 2
J. S. Walker, sol. Cunninghams	184 25 1

JONES.

Jesse A. Goodwin, Blounts	108 14 1
Stephen Bivins, sold. Duncans	153 20 1
George Walkers orps. Spinks	153 3 1
Lee Crittenden, Duncans	5 6 5
William Lott, Stewarts	190 15 1
James S. Newby, Newbys	138 3 4
Polly Radney, wid. Spinks	154 18 2
Wm. G. Maddon, Mullins	220 21 2
Nancy Ruth, illegit. Gibsons	53 6 4
Harry B. Patrick, Blounts	229 5 2
Thos. F. Mitchell, Mullins	39 8 2
Joseph Davie, Duncans	251 10 2
Nancy Wilmouth, w. Robertsons	210 15 2
Wm. A. Wood, Hills	11 24 2
Jesse Fallin, Popes	258 22 2
John Cannon, do.	115 25 1

LAURENS.

Joseph Bohannon, Deans	112 21 1
Benjamin Smith, Mizells	224 23 2
Isaiah Bradford, Whiteheads	30 23 2
Henry Beacham, Beachams	256 5 2

Fortunate Drawers Capts. Dist.	No.Dt.Sec.
William Yates, R.S.Plummers	222 9 5
Lewis Bell, Whiteheads	135 24 2
Susannah Young, widow, do.	236 15 2

LIBERTY.

Mary Ann Simmons orp. 16th	101 4 1
Simeon Moody, 17th	348 28 1
Nancy Griffin, orphan, 17th	90 4 3
William Harn, orphan, 17th	275 1 4
Thomas Shepherd, 14th	220 30 1

LINCOLN.

William House, Wiggintons	214 30 1
Benjamin Remson, Lonorgans	242 12 1
Minors of Jane Bussey, Gideons	168 2 3
David York, Levritts	9 22 2
Jacob Ammons, R. S. Frasers	43 4 5

MADISON.

William Simmons ors. Christians	46 18 1
Robert Griffith, Hanas	172 1 2

McINTOSH.

Thomas E. Barber, Thorps	3 10 2

MONROE.

William Ogletree, R. S. Houses	200 3 2
William E. Nall, sold. Millers	54 14 2
Mar. Barnes, w.R.S., Woodwards	91 21 2
Stephen Foster, Turners	131 18 1
Andrew Zillner, do.	307 22 1
William Lacy, Browns	116 7 1
Fielding McMullen, Greshams	267 7 1
William P. Henry, Finchs	255 13 2

MORGAN.

Alexander Houghton, Stokes	63 2 4
Malaki M. Brand, Canifaxs	308 22 1
Wm. F. Johnston, Harwells	8 3 4
John & W. Laseter, ills. Browns	126 5 2
John Akin, R. S. Harwells	187 8 5
Absalom Castles, sol. Hitchcocks	112 5 3
Robert C. Rankins orps. Stokes	235 .4 2
Elisha Slaton, Adairs	55 24 2
Samuel F. Harriss, Sparks	104 28 1
Josiah Stallings, do.	76 31 1

MONTGOMERY.

S, N, M, T, & E. Simmons, ills. McMillons	347 3 4

NEWTON.

Wm. S. Pryor, min. f. a. Snows	213 22 1
Henry Watson, Hays	18 1 3
Moses Kelly, Graves	86 7 1
John Stanton, R. S. Dyears	175 30 1
Littleton Strawn, Talleys	135 16 2
James Webbs orphans, Allredds	257 5 1

OGLETHORPE.

Eli R. Callaways orphans, Hills	146 25 1
Lewis Taylor, Hardmans	162 6 1
James Hales, soldier, Smiths	238 7 1
Sam'l Ward, sr.R.S.Williamsons	164 18 1
David Roberson, Hills	23 8 3
Jos. D. Patrick, sol. Williamsons	234 15 2
Mary O. Kelly, w. R.S.Hardmans	174 32 1

(58)

Fortunate Drawers Capts. Dist.	No.	Dt.	Sec.
John W. Rabun, Russaws	253	2	3
Robert H. Crawford, Billups	164	13	2
Sherwood Rowling, sol. Mays	103	3	4
Tandy C. Goolsby, Seals	126	32	1
PIKE.			
John Benson, Orrs	37	5	1
Thomas R. Mangham, Hicks	177	24	1
James Spurlin, do.	123	25	1
Wm. M. Amos, sol. Pattersons	159	23	2
John Reed, sr., soldier, Arlines	61	7	5
PULASKI.			
William Singleterry, Gilstraps	110	4	3
Nancy Miller, wid. Scarbroughs	6	16	1
Nontford Taylor, Sparrows	271	21	2
PUTNAM.			
Stoddard Rockwell, Bledsoes	14	26	1
Joseph Bohan, R. S. do.	179	3	1
Freeland Buckner, Allums	111	3	2
William Gray, Clarks	91	1	3
Mathew Hamners orps. Patricks	150	4	2
Elizabeth Lynch, widow, Sparks	57	24	1
RABUN.			
Edward Carter, Mersers	240	31	1
James Strauther, R. S., Becks	36	1	2
Dread Williams, Godfreys	36	26	1
John Foxes orphans, Mersers	244	9	2
RICHMOND.			
Altamount M. Levingston, Kellys	186	2	2
Christopher Bond or. Treadwells	15	9	4
Henry Robertson, Blacks	30	13	5
Obedience Bugg orp. Wilcoxs	80	6	1
Magers Watson, R. S., James	58	7	1
H. J. J. Roberts, Huntingtons	85	12	1
William L. Culbreath, sol. James	63	20	1
Cesaire Blome, Mantzs	208	7	3
John Abbott, orphan, Blacks	60	12	2
SCRIVEN.			
Sarah Dudley, widow, Reaves	173	2	5
Jacob Husk, Kemps	252	13	2
Paul B. Colson, Stricklings	32	22	1
TATTNALL.			
Martha Gause, widow, McCalls	29	18	1
Moses Dees, Dees	21	23	1
William Southwell, McCalls	86	22	1
Barbary Sikes, widow, Conners	67	3	3
Moses Dees, Dees	41	25	1
James P. Daniel, Conners	191	17	2
James Bishop, do.	74	6	4
TELFAIR.			
Thos. Singleterry, jr. Barentines	48	5	2
TWIGGS.			
John C. Averit, Graggs	154	23	1
Josiah Durdin, Pearsons	258	7	5
Am. Sanders, son of Chris. S. do.	169	18	2
Daniel Eldridge, do.	128	29	1
George Jameson, Bosticks	193	29	1
Lucretia Smith, widow, do.	268	9	5
Hiram Waller, Streetmans	192	10	2
UPSON.			
Benjamin Caraway, Petteys	260	8	5
Wilson Simpson, Myricks	216	5	3

WALTON.			
Fortunate Drawers Capts. Dist.	No.	Dt.	Sec.
Eliz. Smithwick w. R. S. Bixleys	64	1	1
William L. Darby, Snows	67	3	1
Henry Harbuck, sol. 250th dist.	97	9	2
Joel Chafin, 418th dist.	236	19	2
William L. Darby, Snows	204	12	3
Priscilla Bakers orps. Hudson	174	4	4
Presley Huff, Pools	47	11	1
Robert Stewart, sol. Hudsons	110	16	2
William Gresham orph. Davis	10	25	1
WARE.			
Joseph Bryan, Bryans	76	30	1
Burwell Jones, Dowlings	184	5	2
Thomas Hillard, Bryans	282	20	2
Joseph Wilkerson, Greens	150	1	1
WAYNE.			
Isham Hatcher, Mannings	203	10	5
WARREN.			
George English, Brinkleys	186	30	1
Robert McNair, Adkins	39	15	5
Shadrack Potts, do.	175	30	1
Miles Joyner, Downs	256	1	2
Elijah Walker, R. S. Sanders	40	1	5
William Aldred, Kinseys	193	5	5
Stewart Thomas, do.	25	31	1
Ephraim McGee, Sanders	32	24	2
Andrew B. Stephens orps. Hills	1	12	2
Wm. J. Monk, Kinseys	265	4	2
Henry Williams, Sanders	206	22	1
Sivel Johnson, w. R.S. Brinkleys	118	28	1
WASHINGTON.			
William Watkins, R. S. Floyds	120	13	1
David Goldstein, do.	283	5	1
Abel Cone, Oquins	232	12	2
Michael Hansome, Floyds	192	32	1
Jeremiah Heardon, Gilberts	80	2	4
John Williams, Warthens	86	10	5
Freeman Johnson, illeg. Jordan	30	4	4
Edwin Brantley, McLendons	211	9	5
James Wood, Tysons	59	8	1
Thomas J. Deyampert, Currys	9	13	5
John Black, Wimberlys	19	6	3
Nimrod Pitman, Rushings	27	9	1
Reuben Osborn, Currys	195	19	1
Samuel Renfroe, Floyds	43	1	4
Sidney Allcock, Tysons	228	11	5
Arthur Manning, Warthens	118	9	5
WILKINSON.			
Andrew Nobles, Smiths	342	7	5
Brice Ragan, sr. R. S. Ragans	162	12	3
Mathew G. Turner, ill. Curreys	232	1	4
John Bowen, sr. R. S. Fairchilds	46	5	1
William Fountain, Curreys	230	19	2
Shadrack Dykes, Shows	220	8	5
Elizabeth Beall, wid. Curreys	120	9	2
John Jones, Mathews	80	10	1
Richard Myrick, Shows	315	1	2
Sereno M. Shoftner orp. Mayos	93	12	5
WILKES.			
Charles Wingfield, Carters	151	6	3
Elizabeth Carter, w. R. S. do.	252	18	2

(59)

Fortunate Drawers Capts. Dist.	No.	Dt.	Sec.
John Hingsons orphs. Popes	183	4	2
James K. Williams, Wottens	175	9	2
Zelotes Adams, Greens	182	31	1
John Levingston, Moors	140	21	2
Fleet Fallan, do.	217	25	1

20th DAY'S DRAWING—March 29

APPLING
John G. Smith, sen., Mathis	186	7	1
William Hand, Collins	175	3	3
Joel McLendon, soldier, do.	68	24	1

BALDWIN.
John D. Young, Buchanans	108	28	1
Orps. of Jeremiah Bridges, Thomas	62	7	1
Elizabeth Green, widow, Doles	179	2	1
William Cooper, Lesters	119	15	5
Joseph L. D. Phelps, Lingos	218	18	2
Myles Greene, jun., Doles	200	15	2

BIBB.
Green Whatley, soldier, Loyds	228	11	3
Hetty Cottrell, hus. ab. Flanders	215	17	1
Richard Bulloch, R. S., Pickards	277	9	3
Mary Brooks, widow, Carrs	113	22	1
Grosvenor Titus, Lloyds	29	7	3
Nathan Parker, do.	158	19	1

BULLOCH.
Jeremiah Hancock, McCalls	122	25	1
Levy Starling, Lockharts	173	3	4
Elizabeth Rowell's illegitimates, do.	187	25	1

BURKE.
William Sills, Fountains	240	13	2
Sarah Ann Moore, orphan, Wests	247	17	1
Jesse Bearfield, Wards	35	27	1
Fielding J. Brown, Gordons	119	6	3
William Dilmon, do..	161	20	1
Lewis Bryant's orps. do..	10	4	4
Rachel Vallaton, wid. Fountains	148	2	2
John Rich, Lynchs	38	14	2
John W. Caswell, Fountains	158	4	5
Dianna Collins, wid. R. S., Brooms	99	22	1
Andrew Carson, Rogers	61	18	1
Stephen Allen's orphans, do.	132	2	3

CAMDEN.
John Lang, Beckwiths	90	6	2

CHATHAM.
John G. Connelly, orp. McDonnells	58	12	3
William Dickerson, Gaddys	99	15	5
Edw'd E. F. Richer, orp., Haydens	252	14	1
Alexander J. Howell, Scotts	256	11	5
Mary Chisler, widow, McDonnells	299	7	5
John W. Barnard's orps. Will. Island	119	7	2
Jacob Waver, McDonnells	106	12	3

CLARK.
Sherwood Strong's orps. Andersons	66	2	1
John R. Hayes, Frosts	88	28	1
William C. Wortham, soldier, Deans	229	3	3
Jesse Hightower, Herndons	181	4	5
Maj. Jas. Meriwether, sol. McDaniels	114	8	4
William Norton, soldier, Greers	206	20	2
Thomas Wood, sen., R. S. McCrees	149	32	1
John C. Grier, soldier, Deans	56	1	3

COLUMBIA.
William Smith, Coles	139	3	4
Major Garnett, Culbreaths	28	11	3
Orph. Betsy Davis, illegit. Carrolls	94	12	3
Jarvis Seale, Culbreaths	275	5	1

Fortunate Drawers Capts. Dist.	No.	Dt.	Sec.
Ennis Guy, Dranes	178	28	1
Robert Shields, Talberts	54	29	1
John Moon, Coles	200	21	1
John H. C. Talbot, orphan Talbots	233	4	2
Thomas Cartledge, Coles	153	7	5
William H. Peavy, illegit., Dranes	215	2	5
Sarah Ross, widow, R. S. Talberts	173	8	1
Edmund Leshley, R. S., Carrolls	226	23	1

CRAWFORD.
William Roberts, Dukes	84	32	1
Thomas Peebles, Tillers	250	2	4

DECATUR.
John Kelly, Hawthorns	134	1	4

DEKALB.
Levi Dempsey, Conns	226	1	1
Benjamin Wadkins, R. S., Bowlings	162	17	1
Zachariah R. Jones, Stephens	13	6	1
William Watson, Howells	234	21	2
William Eades, Scaifs	137	22	2
Thomas Dison, Howells	210	7	3
John Deavenport, Bakers	10	9	1

DOOLY.
Ambrose Powell, Hogans	215	1	4
Mary Posey, widow, 582nd	35	5	4

EARLY.
M. Simon, Grimsleys	282	3	4

EFFINGHAM.
Henry Griffin, Edwards	193	31	1

ELBERT.
Wineford Underwood, wid. Dunns	41	6	3
George J. Gillespie, Alstons	173	2	1
Henry Banks, do.	186	4	1
John W. Therlkild, Butlers	56	10	1
Willis Thirlkild, do.	236	10	1
Wesley Pledger, Harmonds	115	14	1
Jedediah S. Miller, Tates	91	10	2
Leonard Rice, R. S., Merritts	350	28	1
James Oliver, Deadwilders	53	13	1
Andrew B. Moore, illegit., Hortons	203	5	2
Walker Williamson, Dobbs	15	17	2
Joseph Deadwylder, jr., Webbs	57	15	2
James R. Sadler, Carpenters	105	5	1
Orphans of James Edwards, Bells	55	1	4

EMANUEL.
Orphans of John Griffis, Fountains	70	20	1
Daniel Cannady, do.	59	5	4
Alexander Lane, Moors	167	2	5
Jesse Wilkes, Arlines	22	15	2

FAYETTE.
Asa Hulsey, Whartons	191	5	5
Reuben Richards, West	19	25	1
David Dickson, R. S., Whartons	84	12	2
William C. Swain, do.	214	3	2
William Shorts, orphans, do.	86	6	5
Temperance Robinson, ill., Browns	194	5	1
George W. Moore, Landrums	146	23	1
David Austin, Wests	280	14	1

FRANKLIN.
Solomon Barnett, Tabors	168	3	4
William T. Eddins, idiot, Stephens	109	4	5
Nicholas Bellamy, Stranges	99	9	2
Edmund Adcock, Tabors	48	14	2
Augustin D. Carier, Stephens	22	2	4
Joseph Pelfroy, do.	160	25	1
Edward Camp, R. S., do.	260	16	2
Charles W. Bond, Tabors	142	13	2
Samuel Crow, jun., Cokers	28	29	1

(60)

GLYNN.

Fortunate Drawers Capts. Dist.	No.	Dt.	Sec.
James Shearer, Burnetts	106	24	1
Eliz. & Job Carter, orps., McLeods	238	2	1
Harriet, Eliz. & S. Brown, orps. do.	204	16	2
Ann Prichard, Burnetts	263	4	2

GREENE.

Washington Willis, Halls	70	2	2
Cordeal N. Daniel, Greenes	223	12	2
William McGibboney, jr., Vincents	80	15	2
William Vincent, Vincents	237	5	4
Elizabeth Milner, wid. Colcloughs	204	11	1
Isaac Mitchell, Robinsons	138	1	3

GWINNETT.

John M. W. Pearce, Robertsons	231	6	5
Warren Young's orphans, Moores	138	2	4
Rachel Kenney, wid. Hunicutts	135	26	1
Samuel Anthony, Moores	39	9	2
William Rucks, sr. R. S., Greens	51	9	5
Letisha Williamson, wid. R. S., Rollins	148	9	2
Thomas Jones, Finchers	17	15	1
Jehu Cates, Bakers	65	4	4
Posey Maddox, Wallis	247	6	3

HANCOCK.

John Miller, 106th	138	6	3
Newbel Waller, 108th	120	5	3
Mildred McDonald, wid. R. S., 113th	77	28	1
Abraham Howell, 110th	111	27	1
John Layfield, soldier, Brooks	91	10	5
John W. Meredith, 118th	121	32	1

HENRY.

Prucy Richeson, widow, Goshens	120	5	4
James Cook, Shaws	31	3	1
James Smith, Smiths	19	12	3
John Scarborough, Grays	85	5	1
John Crane's orphans, Harriss	143	2	2
John Miller, do.	12	12	5
Zepheniah Estes, Wards	41	24	1
William M. Bathune, Grays	177	18	1

HABERSHAM.

Henry M. Crumley, Suttons	166	6	3
James White, Kenzies	76	4	3
James Edmonds, Suttons	73	2	4
John Mize, Jones	142	18	2

HALL.

George Cook, Dorseys	123	17	1
James Dickson, Hardens	128	2	5
John King, Hardages	42	6	2
John Williams, jun. Walkers	138	20	2
Norman McDuffie's orps., Garrards	54	11	1
Nathaniel Sherley, Hardages	183	21	2
Buckner Walker, Roberts	156	19	1

HOUSTON.

David Adams, Batemans	211	15	1

IRWIN.

John Morrison, 5th	65	2	3
Mikager Oen, McCalls	218	27	1

JACKSON.

Tilman Harrison, Storys	203	27	1
Charles Damron, Millers	168	11	1
Ann Williamson, widow, Lindseys	77	20	1
William Fuller, sr. R. S., Winns	221	21	1
Susannah McCarta, widow, Staplers	52	5	4
Absalom Wafford, R. S., Allens	174	18	2
George Menefee, sr. R. S., Winns	249	23	2
John J. Phipp's orphans, Rogers	260	9	5
Margret Browning, wid. Millers	39	7	2
Jeremiah Skelton, Venables	171	10	3

Fortunate Drawers Capts. Dist.	No.	Dt.	Sec.
Thomas L. Stapler, Duprees	37	8	2

JASPER.

John L. Silman, sol... Penningtons	97	8	5
Sarah Wade, widow, Erwins	25	2	4
Polly A. Jester, wid. Baynes	253	13	1
Caty Goolsby, w. R. S., Hines	12	16	1
John Pryor, R. S., Hardens	128	8	1
William Knight, Camerons	104	9	1
Samuel Stearns, Clemmons	11	2	2
Silas M. Perwrifoy, Reeves	195	30	1
Joshua Wilson, jun. Keys	75	3	2
Wliliam H. Gross, Wilsons	106	5	2
Joseph Evers, Dardens	200	21	2
Richard Jones, Barnetts	91	18	2
Henry Burton, Wilsons	358	28	1
Thomas J. Tuggles, Johnsons	202	3	5
Samuel Edmonson's orps. Baynes	5	32	1
Seaborn Shi, Robinsons	111	33	1

JEFFERSON.

John Clements, jr., Boyds	53	7	3
John Bostick, Marshalls	6	12	3
William Wren, Beatys	21	6	2
William Donaldson, Boyds	158	23	1

JONES.

Thomas Garland, Stewarts	242	20	2
Lewis F. Hicks, Popes	241	11	3
Charles Magnan's orphans, Lows	326	15	1
Stapleton Crutchfield, Stewarts	117	10	1
Balam Stephens, Blounts	87	1	4
Elizabeth Barnes, wid. Duncans	136	7	4
George Lary, soldier, Popes	15	3	1
Walker Hearndon, sen., Mullins	71	3	2
Eliza Ann Hays, illegit. Spinks	48	8	2
Isaac Pippin, Dosters	180	1	2
Nathaniel Turbeville, Gibsons	124	2	1
Laban Chapman's orps. do.	53	20	2
Anderson Honze, Davis	33	12	5
Jno. W. H. Hobson's orps. Newbys	61	12	3
Samuel C. White, Hammacks	69	9	3
Whitmill Eason, Duncans	74	15	2
Vinson P. Roquemire, Gibsons	272	10	2
M. A. Douglass, w. R. S. Blounts	34	32	1
William R.. Sayers. Dosters	203	20	2

LAURENS.

Elizabeth Hines,w.R.S. Plummers	251	6	3
Abigail Smith, wid., Whiteheads	141	11	3
Archibald McDaniel, Spiveys	419	20	2

LIBERTY.

Ruth Anthony, wid. 17th district	247	5	3

LINCOLN.

John Barnett, luna. Wiggindons	88	15	1
Edw'd Carlisles minors, Graves	108	11	1
William Woods, Gideons	60	6	2
Francis Powell, jr. Lonorgans	110	5	2
John R. Winn, Levritts	16	10	2
Henry H. Sealey, Prathers	160	24	2

MADISON.

William Luker, soldier, Moons	58	2	4
John Turner, R. S., Caldwells	60	9	3
Robert J. Hemphill, do.	260	10	2
John Lyon, Culbertsons	185	11	5
John Hayes, Hannas	279	11	2

M'INTOSH.

Fortunate Drawers	Capts.	Dist.	No.	Dt.	Sec.
John Ryalls,	McCranies		130	8	5
William Todd,	Thorps		135	27	1
S.&M.Parnidore	ors. McCranies		231	5	4
Hester Maguire,	wid. Terrells		111	2	4

MONROE.

Martha Haynes, w.R.S.Turners	69	6	4
Mark Rays, R. S. Johnsons	9	2	5
George W. Heard, Wrights	220	4	3
Aairs Gammell, sol. Houses	142	1	2
John Center, Turners	76	12	5
John Horsley, Pattersons	83	31	1
James Nawsworthy, sol. Douglass	73	15	1
Sanford Dorman, J. Millers	234	3	5
Samuel McCorkle, sol. Millers	47	8	5

MORGAN.

John C. Burgess, sol. Hitchcocks	24	13	5
Robert Beasley orphan, Beasleys	63	19	1
Robert T. Hargrove, Youngs	42	15	5
Tilman Hemphill orps. Beasly	25	6	2
John W. Campbell, Youngs	71	6	1
Richard Gainers orps. Griggs	243	9	1
Henry F. Young, Walkers	118	18	1
Greenville Henderson, Sparks	160	20	1
Ellerander Johnston, Ostians	91	11	2

NEWTON.

Charnell Hightower, Graves	215	18	1
John Comes, Trammells	120	6	3
Charlton Ragsdale, Talleys	167	4	4
Jor. Thornton, sol. Penningtons	39	2	1
Jesse Wisdom, Talleys	115	15	5
John Robertson Martin, Graces	17	10	3
Mark M. Ragsdale, Talleys	245	31	1
Nathan Canada, Pullens	296	20	2
Robert G. Harris, Webbs	243	22	2
Joshua Bailey, Pullens	163	6	2

OGLETHORPE.

Nancy H. Garlington, wid. Bells	96	12	1
Miles W. Goolsby, Seals	339	7	5
Jemima Lyon, w. R. S. Smiths	4	31	1
Adam Simmons orps. Hardmans	240	8	3
Nancy Kemble, widow, Hills	106	3	4
William B. Rainey, Bells	142	27	1
Sarah Clement, wid. Holloways	29	4	1
George Davis, sol. B. Hills	193	11	1
John P. Smith, Rousseaus	245	8	5
Robin Hendon, R. S. Holloweys	19	18	2

PIKE.

John M. C. Smith, sol. Daniels	221	6	2
Elijah Bingham, Hartsfields	152	1	4
James Lambert, sol., Weavers	238	10	5
William Stones orps. Daniels	102	3	4
William J. Huddleston, Orrs	117	3	3
Thomas Jones, jr. do.	221	3	3
Ellison Gross, sol. Shehees	118	2	4

PULASKI.

William Shipp, Gilstraps	118	14	5
William T. Snilling, Bracewells	88	21	2
Mary Anderson, wid. Kellams	100	2	3

PUTNAM.

Elijah Wilson, Hailes	106	5	4

Fortunate Drawers	Capts.	Dist.	No.	Dt.	Sec.
Hamilton Carpenter, Marcus			180	9	1
John K. Waller, Barnetts			186	13	1
Thos. C. Singletons ors. Wilks			236	15	1
Sam'l Shadracks orps. Allums			247	10	5
Abner Ragland, soldier, Clarks			251	23	2
Ann Dixon, wid. Choices			92	6	1
James Dowdell, Allums			184	7	1
Wilkins Stevens, do.			100	9	2
William Conners, R.S.Duprees			29	13	2
Thomas Scott orphan, Blacks			404	20	2
Robert Beal, Bledsoes			46	26	1

RABUN.

Robert Rogers, R. S. Becks	259	7	1

RICHMOND.

D. F. Dickinson, Kellys	152	5	2
Chauncey Bradley, Hands	90	15	2
Thomas Robins, James	15	2	2
James Fulcher, R. S. Kellys	82	6	2
Phineas Butler, Ferris	85	23	2
Jane R. Evans, orphan, Bushs	114	14	1
Patrick Kelly, Huntingtons	136	9	1
J., J., & O. Cashin ors. Augusta	254	6	1
John Ward, Blacks	79	7	4
James Davis, Wilcoxs	107	12	1
Hugh Nesbitt, Murphys	51	31	1
Major Daniel, James	36	9	3
E.L.M. Laroche, w. Huntingtons	99	2	5
Eliza. Bogan, w. R.S. Augusta	171	2	3
Jacob Holman, R. S. Blacks	75	18	2
Harbart Stallings, Huntingtons	55	5	1
John Fowler, Wilcoxs	275	9	5

SCRIVEN.

William Burk, Kemps	116	33	1
Dorathy Thompson, wid. Lovetts	194	30	1
William Best, Hunters	169	10	3

TATTNALL.

Ann & Annis Gray, ills. Graces	71	3	4
Nancy Hall, wid. R. S., do.	237	9	2
William Mann, jr., do.	86	30	1

TELFAIR.

James W. Edenfield, Wilsons	326	7	5
Elizabeth Hart, w. Barentines	90	9	3
John Everitts orphans, do.	120	25	1
Nath. T. Sandeford, Wilkinsons	263	10	2

TALIAFERRO.

Sarah R. Watsons illegs. Gunns	148	11	5
Benjamin M. Hill, do.	137	16	2

TWIGGS.

William Johnson, Bosticks	17	26	1
Spencer Bell, do.	110	5	1
J. Streetman w.R.S.Streetmans	168	10	3
John Tomkins orphs. Bosticks	113	3	5
J. Crittenden, R. S. Streetmans	111	26	1
Roger Lawson, sol., Graggs	257	19	2

UPSON.

Chambers Cawan, Ellis'	130	10	5
An., P., F., M. & Jno. Hobbs, ill.	84	6	4
Isaac Self, Ezells	205	12	5

WALTON.

Vincent Haralson, sol. Rays	151	4	4
Meshach Deel, 250th district	107	10	5
Clayborn Sims, 249th do.	67	5	4

Fortunate Drawers Capts. Dist.	No.	Dt.	Sec.
William P. Rude, Hudsons	121	14	1
WARREN.			
Abner Hill, Hills	71	1	3
Joseph Leonard, sol. Sanders	143	6	3
Robert Bealls orphans, Bulls	224	8	5
John Kelly, Adkins	147	5	1
George W. Carter, Kinseys	189	12	5
Ephram Ivey, sr. R. S. Brinkleys	112	10	2
Sampson Wilder, R. S. Parhams	244	20	2
William Battle, Rogers	134	5	4
William Mote, R. S. Adkins	60	7	4
Mary Brooks, wid. Kinseys	34	7	1
WASHINGTON.			
Rolly Boatright, McLendons	67	12	1
John Tompkins, Rushings	270	5	3
Grenn Hood, Oquins	56	29	1
David Bateman, sol., McLendons	7	6	2
James T. Pinkston, Mannings	52	2	1
Wm. Holley, R. S., McLendons	106	8	2
Sarah Stephens, wid. Oquins	202	6	1
Abram A. Ayres, sol. Castelows	140	18	1
Eldridge C. Williamson, Floyds	77	18	1
Reb. Warthen, w. R.S. Warthens	180	10	1
WILKINSON.			
Ann & Mary Steward ills. Mayos	178	7	3
Hansell Lasseter, R. S., Curreys	162	22	1
Solomon Gamage, Mayos	68	13	1
David Steward, Halls	3	11	3
William Bevins, R.S.Mandersons	57	7	5
Ansil Richards, Shows	66	10	2
Polly Cherry, wid. Halls	56	25	1
Richard Graves, Shows	205	7	1
WILKES.			
Edward Waller, Moors	112	23	1
John Burnap, Reeves	155	14	5
Thomas B. Danforth, Ragsdales	50	5	5
John Helmes, Amasons	52	19	2
John Belk, Moors	180	22	2
William J. Gartrell, Charltons	14	22	2
Elmina Bailey illegit. Wests	174	24	2
James Woottens orps. Popes	22	6	2
Keturah C. Grant, w. Charltons	275	11	2
N. McMickens mins. f. a. Lukers	265	23	2
Thos. Lindseys orps. Richersons	227	4	3
John Combs orps. Washingtons	68	6	1
John Slack, sr. R. S. Ragsdales	62	9	1
Sarah Saffold, w. R.S.Richersons	84	12	1

21st DAY'S DRAWING—March 30

BALDWIN.			
Polly Ellis, widow, Wicks	76	14	2
William Brown, Ginns	24	9	2
Appleton Bivins, Pitts	234	9	3
Leroy M. Wiley, Buchanans	213	4	3
John Bryan, Ginns	106	23	1
BIBB.			
Docton Perry, Lloyds	79	1	5
George Herring, R. S. Beards	79	11	1
Joel Chandler, Bates	107	11	5
Allen Buzbee, Rutlands	31	18	1
Magdalena Carrell, illegit. do.	220	24	1

Fortunate Drawers Capts. Dist.	No.	Dt.	Sec.
BULLOCH.			
Joshua Woods, Lockharts	98	2	5
BURKE.			
William Cross, Lynchs	35	7	1
James Brown's orphans, Gordons	95	8	3
Mary Belcher, widow, Wards	96	3	1
Job Griffin's orphans, Dugas	41	17	1
Ann Lepsey, illegitimate, Corkers	46	15	5
George M. Ellison, Dugas	190	23	2
Moses T. Proctor, Fountains	126	5	3
John McCarrell, Dugas	168	14	1
James Glisson's orphans, do.	263	9	5
BUTTS.			
James Reeves, soldier, Robinsons	106	4	1
CHATHAM.			
Thomas Kemp, Nungazers	216	8	5
William Starkey, Haydens	331	3	4
Catherine B. O. Dill, lunatic, Baines	106	11	3
Capt. Thomas Paine, jr., Haydens	26	4	3
Margaret King, widow, do.	71	11	5
Christian Lampe, Nungazers	113	18	1
Daniel Campbell, McDonnells	220	27	1
Henry Timmory, widow, Baines	74	21	1
CLARK.			
A. Hayes, orp. of Edward, Alreds	78	17	2
Orps. of Jeremiah Burnet, Dickins	118	19	1
William Daniell, sen., Vinsons	23	6	2
Margaret Cone, widow, Herndons	225	11	1
Jacke F. Cocke's orps. Gahagans	204	20	2
Harrison W. Elder, Alreds	135	8	1
Hannah Morris, wid. R. S. Herndons	132	21	1
Wyly Edmondson, Wrights	189	21	2
Lucy Connally, widow, Ransoms	75	6	2
Henry J. Pope, Gahagans	27	6	3
Sarah Ann L., John W. & Martha A. E. Roberson, illegits. Coxs	162	4	1
COLUMBIA.			
Sophia Young, lunatic, Magruders	160	7	3
Sarah Winfrey, widow, Carrolls	147	8	5
William Merriwether, Culbreaths	87	4	1
Orphan of Elijah Russell, Ramseys	77	22	1
George Lavender's orphans, Boltons	121	13	2
Edward Prather's orphans, Dranes	202	13	1
CRAWFORD.			
Daniel J. Reese, Rhodes	2	23	2
Francis Evers, orphan, Wilsons	253	4	3
DECATUR.			
Eason Tison, Douglass	196	31	1
Elizabeth French, orphan, do.	223	18	2
DE KALB.			
William Glenn, Bakers	201	12	2
John Jett, do.	162	10	2
William W .White, do.	177	2	5
Keziah Holmes, hus. absent, Conns	82	15	2
William Grant, soldier, Bakers	246	17	2
James A. Carruth, Edwards	169	5	1
Jacob New, R. S., Smiths	203	7	3
Joseph Strickland, Bakers	36	13	2
Jane Akin, wid. R. S., Stephens	98	7	4
Enoch Hooper, Merritts	80	1	4
DOOLY.			
William Roberson's orphans, 582d	86	3	2
William Fowler, soldier, Forrests	112	31	1
EFFINGHAM.			
Zara Powers, Elkins	43	15	1.
Peter Fryermuth, do.	262	19	2
John Futerell, do.	145	7	1

(63)

Fortunate Drawers	Capts.	Dist.	No.	Dt.	Sec.
Jonathan Zipperer, R. S., Waldhaners			66	4	4

ELBERT.

Fortunate Drawers	Capts.	Dist.	No.	Dt.	Sec.
Jeremiah Naish, Alstons			30	14	2
Eli Snoe, Dunns			109	10	3
Wiley W. Barron, Harmons			167	12	2
Rowland Cheek, Merritts			4	9	1

EMANUEL.

John Lawrence, Moors	36	13	5

FAYETTE.

Mitchell J. Roberts, Dodsons	235	11	5
Jacob Mayfield, Wests	172	16	1
Joshua Betterton, Dodsons	207	2	3
Michael Austin, Wests	167	2	3
Green Wood, Craigs	65	12	1
William Morris, soldier, Whartons	158	6	5
Willoughby Hammacks's orps Craigs	19	19	1

FRANKLIN.

Christopher Meadows, Stranges	27	3	1
Mastin Lovern, do	182	8	3
Richard Cockerham's orps Bennetts	135	9	2
Solomon Holcomb, Tabors	70	12	1
Thomas P. Holbrook, Cokers	179	2	5

GLYNN.

Joseph Dubignon, Dubignons	232	13	1

GREENE.

Thomas J G Clark, Bruces	281	4	1
Matthew B. Downing, Astins	299	10	2
Jane Moore, widow, Vincents	240	5	2
Charity Upchurch's ills., Woodhams	124	17	2
Robert Ray, Newsome	146	11	1
Nancy Palmore, widow, Knowles	224	17	1
Isham Tooke, Greenes	262	17	1
Littleton Culwell, Astins	206	10	2
Richard Chrismas, Sutherlands	27	20	2
Israel Nunnely, R. S. Colcloughs	325	22	1
William Evans, R. S. do	215	33	1

GWINNETT.

John M. Venable, Moors	102	6	5
Green Doss,, do	257	1	2
Obadiah Kennemur, Woodroughs	346	28	1
Jesse Collins, Caruthers	69	24	2
Luke Newborn, Wallis	10	22	2
Sarah Wiley's illegitimate, Davis	113	16	2
Federick Knop, Moors	204	15	1
Catherine, Nation, wid., R. S., do	111	7	4
Elijah Foster, Greens	215	20	2

HANCOCK.

William S. Wadsworth, Brantleys	124	11	2
James C. B. Thomas, 108th	131	10	5
James Sharp, 110th	154	6	3

HENRY.

Cannon Chance, Bryants	139	11	2
Elisha Vinson, R. S., Millers	219	9	1
Elijah Cornwell, soldier, Grays	44	7	3
John Cross, sen. Allens	227	10	2
John Presley, R. S., Risons	287	7	1
Moses Mulkey, Harris	194	9	3
Samuel Creighton, Grays	63	8	2
Carter Crew, Harris	160	32	1

HABERSHAM.

David Fain, sen. Vickreys	207	19	1
Elizabeth Okelly, widow,, Kenzies	83	6	2
Charles Slatton, Fains	251	16	1
John Wotten, Kenzes	34	1	2
Richard Cox, jun. Cross	162	1	1
Green H. Obanion, Langstons	256	11	1
Richard Cox, R. S., Cross	222	12	3
Isaac T. Leonard, Vickreys	210	21	2

Fortunate Drawers	Capts.	Dist.	No.	Dt.	Sec.
John Grindall, Kenzies			79	14	2
Eveline & M. McCarter, illegits. Tates			120	4	4
Reuben G. Anderson, Cross,			201	4	3
John Purcel, Kenzies			52	1	4
Jacob Duckett, do			66	2	2
Henry M Crumley, Suttons			105	8	2
Francis J. Dover, Cross			290	20	2

HALL.

Benjamin Jackson, Alreds	208	2	4
William N. Brimer, Hardages	128	12	3
William Parker, Wilsons	134	3	4
Joel Leathers, Roberts	216	29	1
Humphrey Tarbutton, do	84	4	1
Young M Wilson, Harrisons	148	11	3
David Latta, sen. R. S., Hardages	19	23	1
David R. Myers, Garrards	228	4	2
Edmund Harpe, Hardages	288	1	2
Isaac Freeland, Roberts	246	29	1
Ransom Barns, Alreds	52	6	1
Willis Whitehead, Floyds	104	26	1
Nancy West, illegitimate, Hardages	177	25	1

HOUSTON.

William Hathhorn, Batemans	325	7	1
Michael Watson, do	89	7	5
William Bill, Blanshards	227	11	3
Elizabeth D. Boyet, wid Hancocks	36	6	3
Alexander J. Robison, do	215	11	1
William Brunson, Batemans	55	19	2

JACKSON.

Patsey Braziels illegits. Gathrights	79	4	4
Hosea C. Giddeon, Lindseys	43	14	5
Elizabeth Goolsby, widow, Moons	43	10	5
William Pierce, Venables	75	1	1
Sion B Prichard, Staples	112	24	2
Elizabeth Gideon, wid, Venables	184	30	1
James Benton, Dupress	46	1	1
Martin McCan, soldier, Moons	43	12	3
Isaac Flanigan, Landrums	18	18	2

JASPER.

Randal D. Shoulder, Barnes	183	22	2
John M Calvert, Shropshiers	11	15	2
Isa Avary, orphan, Erwins	169	10	2
Thomas Wilson, soldier, Posts	209	12	2
David L. Horn, Holmes	23	11	2
William H. Lovejoy, Robersons	251	15	1
Isaac Berry's orphans, Trussells	77	9	3
Willis Whatley, Barnetts	125	11	3
Drury Long's orphans Keys	191	3	3
John M. Patterson, Holmes	153	21	2
John M. Faulkner, Dardens	118	12	1
James T. Maddux, Wilsons	158	1	2
Obadieh E. Daniel, Baynes	291	23	2
Richard Jones, Barnetts	276	9	5
John S. Lambert, Baynes	237	28	1
Micajah Buchanan, Trussells	86	6	4
Richard S. Adams, Robersons	44	1	3

JEFFERSON.

Sampson G Musgrove Beatys	144	14	5
Stephen Morgan, Elliotts	123	9	3
William Haddin's orphans, Boyds	124	22	1
John S. Holder, R. S., Marshalls	154	12	5

JONES.

Henry H. Low, Blounts	226	21	1
Joshua Hudson, Taylors	268	21	1
James Lucas's orphans, Gibsons	201	3	2
Aaron Pitts, orphan, Dosters	16	8	2
Isaac Pitts, Hendersons	74	15	5
Sarah Moore, widow, Popes	54	16	1

Fortunate Drawers	Capts. Dist.	No.	Dt.	Sec.
Levi Maning,	Hammack	232	26	1
John Henderson's orps	Stewarts	128	5	2
Dorothy Farrow, widow,	Bowens	222	9	3
Mansell W Hammack,	Hammacks	303	6	1
Hope H. Hammack,	Mullins	253	7	1
Lovit Reaves,	Davis.	84	5	1
Thomas H Murphey,	Sullivans	234	9	5
Cogdell Hambleton,	Popes	180	1	4
John Dumas,	Taylors	55	27	1
James A. Hill,	Duncans	1	33	1
Jason Meador, R S	Robertson	30	15	1
Seburn Hilliard,	Popes	34	9	1
Elisha Wright R S,	Bowens	264	22	2

LAURENS.

Fortunate Drawers	Capts. Dist.	No.	Dt.	Sec.
Elizabeth Montford, wid.,	Plummers	203	17	1
Hamilton Nobles,	Whiteheads	234	20	2
Joseph E Plummer,	Plummers	164	10	1

LIBERTY.

Thomas T. Cunningham,	17th	47	11	2
Hester Branch, widow,	17th	125	15	5
Alexander Martins orps.	15th	131	5	2

LINCOLN.

George W. Dallas,	Ross	100	19	1
Francis Powell, sr.	Frasers	204	5	5
J. Simmons, jr. sol.	Wiggintons	106	9	2

MADISON.

John M. Power,	Hannas	220	10	1
John McCurdy,	do.	132	25	1
J. Howington,	Higginbothams	244	29	1
L. W. & C. J. Shinn, orps. do		117	23	1

McINTOSH.

Henry Ryals, sr. R. S.	McCranys	15	8	3

MONROE.

Georg. Downs, dumb,	Gammons	73	18	2
John Watson, sr. R. S.	Finchs	128	7	1
Beverly Robison,	Millers	12	2	5
Robert Baits,	Douglass	207	21	2
Adam Hardin,	Fergasons	60	4	5
William O. Harden,	Pattersons	117	7	4
James S. Bonner,	do	92	7	3
John Edwards, R .S.	Houses	244	10	2
Mordecai Jacobs, sol.	Gammons	216	23	1
Moses More,	Johnsons	160	28	1
William Merit,	Stallings	116	31	1
Thomas T. Napier, sol.	Millers	138	6	1
John Miller,	Douglass	211	16	1

MORGAN.

Lucinda H. Lee, wid.	Jennings	216	6	3
Robert Polly,	Christians	254	17	2
James Boothe,	Youngs	387	20	2
Charles H. Bostwick,	Sparks	148	5	5
William Collier,	Browns	120	5	5
Horrace Mallory,	Sparks	141	13	2
Darcas Johnston, w. R.S.	Ostians	67	2	3
James Thowpson,	Christians	140	14	1
John Hodges orphan,	Gains	235	13	1

MONTGOMERY.

Daniel Davies, R. S.	Wynns	63	2	2

NEWTON

William Brown Swan,	Zachrys	12	21	2
John Fincher,	Webbs	90	20	1
Elizabeth Bass, wid.	Trammells	115	9	1
Purnell Truitt, sol.	Orrs	165	17	2

Fortunate Drawers	Capts. Dist.	No.	Dt.	Sec.
Larkin Ragsdale, R. S.	Talleys	102	13	2
William B. Graves,	Dyers	29	11	2
William Smith, R. S.	Snows	194	32	1
Sally Rhodes, widow,	Clarks	66	33	1
John H. Austin,	Hays	100	8	4
Milly Lowe, widow,,	Graces	85	4	2

OGLETHORPE.

George Crowders orps.	Burfords	167	9	3
Jacob Meadows, R.S.	Hardmans	276	8	5
James Pye, R. S.	Lacys	1	6	2
Robert Smith, sr.	Hollaways	232	11	2
Thomas Albert, sol.	Smiths	208	3	4
D. Gentery, deaf & dumb,	Dixs	206	9	2
Henry Farmer,	Burfords	254	31	1
William S. Wilson,	Seals	59	12	2

PIKE.

William Solley,	Orrs	203	4	1
William B. Horton,	Longs	44	11	2

PULASKI.

Arthur Tookes orps.	Sparrows	236	6	1
David Priel,	Scarbroughs	74	6	2
Uriah Pope, sol.	Bracewells	281	7	1
Epps Wallace,	Thomas'	100	17	1
John W. Carruthers,	Sparrows	166	12	3

PUTNAM.

Allen Hawkins,	Barnetts	196	9	1
Erwin Taunt,	Chambers	192	7	5
Joseph Barker, jr.	Bledsoes	275	28	1
William Williamson,	Chambers	49	1	2
Patterson Veals orphs.	Goods	192	15	1
William Allen,	Barnetts	52	15	1
William Castleberry,	Marcus	116	10	1
Littleton Wynn,	Stinsons	250	11	1
Lewis Legett, illegit.	Kendalls	188	2	3

RABUN.

James B. Neville,	Godfreys	86	23	2
David Page,	do	152	14	1
William Gillespie,	Mercers	25	21	2

RICHMOND.

Mrs. Ellington, widow,	Bushs	175	28	1
Henry Usher,	James	62	13	1
Ruth Sterrett orphan,	Ferris	79	14	5
Rebecca Hamley, w.	Huntingtons	64	6	1
Peter Turbaville,	do	228	16	2
Josua Canter,	do	170	12	2
Polly Wood, lunatic,	James	152	7	2
Henry Mounger,	Huntingtons	194	3	2
M & C. .Walker ors.	Treadwells	217	18	1
Robert Ferris,	Huntingtons	103	18	1
James Holcombe, 119th		70	9	1

SCRIVEN.

Nathaniel Wade, sol.	Pollocks	203	3	5
Charles H. Johnston,	Lovetts	3	2	5

TATTNALL.

General Deloach,	Deloachs	44	7	5
John Joyce, R. .S.	McCalls	88	7	4
Zilphy Hollingsworth, w.	Corseys	192	19	1
Nathan Brooton, sen.	Conners	171	2	5
James Durrence,	do	243	18	1
Jeremiah Revels,	Corseys	393	7	1
Groves Sharpe, jr.	Graces	275	12	3
Thomas Grace,	do	106	23	2

LAND LOTTERY REGISTER—No. 10.
[RECORDER OFFICE—PUBLISHED BY GRANTLAND & ORME—PRICE $3.]

NOTE—Section 1 is Lee County—2 Muscogee—3 Troup—4 Coweta—5 Carroll.

21st DAY'S DRAWING—Continued.

TELFAIR.
Fortunate Drawers	Capts. Dist.	No.	Dt.	Sec.
James Drake, R. S. Wilkinsons		27	2	2
Holden Matchet, Lampkins		233	11	2
Duncan McLeod, Barentines		133	9	5

TWIGGS..
Orps.. of Alex. Turner, Pearsons	123	9	5
Wiat A. Tharp, Bosticks	204	7	5
John Bailey, Graggs	154	9	3
John Ray, soldier, Pearsons	20	10	3
Wright Sanders, Kellys	275	8	1
Sarah Lamb, hus.ab. Wimberlys	253	6	3

UPSON.
Stephen Duke, Myricks	169	13	2
Elizabeth Mims, w|R.S. Coopers	75	2	4
Julious M. Brooks do	211	17	1
John Barron, orphan, 589th	227	17	1
Elijah Pitman, Harralds	44	19	1
Benjamin Jacobs, R.S. Pashalls	1	4	2

WALTON.
Covy Christopher, 503rd	104	19	1
Benjamin Knott, Davis'	181	22	2
Nathan Meredith, McQuertors	213	12	2
Thomas B. Cooksey, Snows	57	9	5
Paul Patrick, soldier, 249th	170	9	1
John B. Bingham, Rays	190	13	1
James Mayn, Bixleys	140	11	3
Nancy Mathews orps.McQpertors	120	24	1

WARE.
William Vinzant, Bryans	214	12	1
John L. Petersons orps. Motes	133	31	1

WAYNE.
James Hatcher, Staffords	242	31	1

WARREN.
John Hancock, Jones	236	24	1
Abuer Sturdevant, R.S. Hills	303	10	2
Henry Lockhart, soldier, Fords	239	9	5
James Allen, Downs	51	12	3
Solomon Rainwater, Stewarts	215	27	1
A. L. Coody orp. ofDavid,Bulls	119	27	1
Chesley Walker, Downs	27	30	1
John McCormick, R.S.Jones	87	30	1
William Hilson, Downs	55	12	2
Washington Huskey,Parhams	62	11	3
William Toller, Downs	116	7	2

WASHINGTON.
William Cokers heirs, Floyds	289	3	4
Benjami nSmiths orps. Jordans	314	1	2
John Rushing, Rushings	77	7	5
Moses Williams, orphan,Floyds	178	9	3
Michael Ikner, Oquins	220	9	3
L.. Sheppard, (farm.) McLendons	367	28	1
Joseph Bridges, sol. Gilberts	139	11	1
Benago Phillips, Woods	246	13	1
William Williams, McLendons	83	13	1
Bennett Massey, Floyds	15	14	2

WILKINSON.
Reloy Fleetwood,f.a.Mandersons	47	9	2

Fortunate Drawers Capts. Dist. No.Dt.Sec.
Elizabeth McDaniel orphan, do	47	14	1
Susannah Daughtry illeg. Halls	31	15	1
Bolin Radford, Mathews	16	2	3
William Hall, Halls	179	30	1
Elizabeth Benson, wid. Curreys	128	13	2

WILKES.
William Slaten, Rices	227	7	1
Drury Cunnnigham, Amasons	104	14	2
Thos. Fombys ors. Washingtons	118	16	1
Anderson Moore, Pope,	155	15	1
Joel Edmunds, Washingtons	118	9	3
Reuben Hudgins, Greshams	230	11	3
Benjamin Herriage, Rices	93	4	1
Green H. Linsey, sol. Gardners	55	30	1
Samuel Danforth, Ragsdales	25	15	1
William Waggoner,R.S.Greens	199	25	1

22nd DAY'S DRAWING—March 31

APPLING.
Neil Campbell, Dodges	220	22	2

BAKER.
Bejamin Smith,sol. Corquadalls	101	14	2

BALDWIN.
M.&M. Leget, illegs. Buchanans	301	4	1
William Lindsey, Pitts	240	15	2
Henry Skinners, orphs. do	96	5	2
Jos. D. Dingly, Buchanans	105	10	1

BIBB.
John W. Mallory, Bates	163	2	1

BRYAN.
Raymond P. Demere, Stephens	26	5	5

BULLOCH.
Synthia Dollar, widow,Turners	130	32	1
James Mathis, Burnetts	31	4	3

BURKE.
Rich. Erwins orphs. Fountains	215	4	2
Wm. Mitchell, senr. Brooms	5	5	1
Alex. F. Harris, Gaffs	84	13	1
Jas. M, Liptrot, illegit. Corkers	215	14	2
Rachael Spain, widow, Lynchs	66	1	4
Wm. Gunn, Brooms	102	7	5
Jos. Hatchers orph., do	13	6	5
Wm. Boyt, Gordens	40	20	2
Jesse Grant, R. S. Wests	1	22	1
Thomas Bell, Bayleys	24	1	3

CAMDEN.
Levy Pearce, Baleys	180	11	1
Jas. C. Dilworths orps. Halls	184	15	2
Tabitha Roberts, w. R.S.Browns	142	3	4
Lewis Nortons orps. Beckwiths	203	18	1

CHATHAM.
Anson Haden, Haydens	90	7	4
Patrick Marlow, do	100	16	1
Wm. F. Leach, Baines	189	27	1
Charles Leseuer, Haydens	245	33	1
Charles W. Rockwell,	246	4	3
Peter Ramondo, Haydens	110	9	2
Allen Beasley, Gaddys	62	9	4

(66)

Fortunate Drawers Capts. Dist.	No.	Dt.	Sec.
Michael Lewis, Baines	195	7	2
CLARK.			
James Brown, R. S. Wrights	132	2	2
Barton Hamilton, R.S.McDonals	202	18	1
Elizabeth Hayles, wid. Davis	279	6	1
Rufus K. Singleton, orp. Deans	2	14	5
John Puryear, Gahagans	278	9	5
John James, Davensports	232	21	1
Moses Beard, Frosts	75	7	1
COLUMBIA.			
W.H.&S.A. Edwards, Clarks	26	2	1
Wm. A. Walsh, Dranes	225	14	2
Thomas Sullivan, Soles	102	18	1
CRAWFORD.			
Wm. J. Hamoc, Wilsons	50	2	2
Jacob Moffit, Rhodes	129	12	3
Verlinda Shinholster orp. Ellis	262	4	1
Wm. H. Braswell, sol. Lovetts	121	20	1
DECATUR.			
George G. Gaines, R.S.Douglass	10	24	2
DEKALB.			
Esther Davis illeg., Andersons	175	13	2
Jonathan Lee, Harris	307	8	5
William Hoopers orps. Meritts	30	14	1
Wm. Barnett, Edwards	122	11	3
George Clifton, Stephens	234	5	1
Uriah Casey, Andersons	22	11	3
W. Rozier,h.k.in the l.w. Howells	62	8	1
EARLY.			
Asa McCulloch, Wilsons	184	3	1
EFFINGHAM.			
Henry Strickland, sol. Edwards	158	9	3
Martha Green, h. a. Stricklands	216	14	1
ELBERT.			
Nancy Gardner, min.f.a.Dobbs	95	29	1
Talton Shoemaker, sol. Harmons	122	5	4
Ealam Alexander, Dunns	20	4	5
John A. Perryman, Boltons	254	19	2
Thos. Knott, Boltons	269	6	1
David Hudson, R. S., Bells	149	21	2
EMANUEL.			
Julian Barnes illegit. 49th	247	18	2
Martha Overstreet, wid. McGars	90	5	4
FAYETTE.			
James W. Smith, R. S. Whortons	31	15	5
Horation H. Strickland, Craigs	71	4	3
Thos. H. Cliate, sol., Landrums	159	5	5
William Maddox, Roziers	67	2	3
Erwin Bagett, Dodsons	143	23	1
FRANKLIN.			
Samuel McKie, R. S., Hudsons	210	11	5
Wm. Cattes, Caudells	158	7	3
Barnett U. Donehoo, Cokers	61	4	2
Zachariah Rice, Sanders	164	28	3
Minyard Sanders, do.	51	8	1
John Bush, soldier, do.	252	19	1
GLYNN.			
Alexander Stapleton, Burnetts	209	5	4
Alexander Thomas, do.	55	13	1
GREENE.			
Parazetta Coleman illegit. Halls	114	6	1
Nicholas M. Lewis, Jr. Dawsons	129	4	5

Fortunate Drawers Capts. Dist.	No.	Dt.	Sec.
Isaac Jones, Astins	91	14	5
Josiah Allens orphans, Halls	103	23	1
Luther Dauchy, Vincents	188	15	2
Thos. W. Kandle, Dawsons	224	21	1
GWINNETT.			
Wm., Matilda, Elijah, Isaac, Sarah & Eliz. Hunt, orps. Madduxs	170	1	4
James J. Jenkins, Gholstons Bat.	168	29	1
John Thompson, Moores	50	5	2
Ephraim Ledbetter, Greens	74	5	3
Wm. A. Cochern, Bakers	82	2	3
Curry Butlers orphans, Finchers	30	2	5
Wm. Mathews, Woodbroughs	121	5	5
Thos. Carrell, do.	43	2	4
Thos. Perry, Evans	77	5	3
Elijah Tuttan, Hills	3	13	1
John Baker, Greens	168	26	1
Lewis Williams, do.	85	7	5
Margaret Minchew wid. Caruthers	14	10	2
Mary Tumlin, w. R. S. Hunicuts	97	21	2
John Butler, R. S. Finchers	77	22	2
Silas Baker, Gholstons	119	22	1
John Thompson, Moors Battalion	4	21	1
Malford Webb, Bakers	76	18	1
Silas Vickers, jr. Hunicuts	78	19	2
HANCOCK.			
James J. Evans, 102nd	160	10	3
John Berrys orphans, 102nd	2	2	4
Abednego A. Wright, 104th	39	29	1
John McDaniels minors,f.a.118th	181	7	2
Nancy Maclellan orph. 110th	35	17	2
Jonathan Roach, sol. Adams	104	32	1
Robert Norris, 118th	33	5	2
John Pullen, R. S., 112th	122	8	3
Jonathan Gladding, 118th	179	8	1
Braddock Camp, 113th	61	32	1
HENRY.			
Jacob Mobley, Grays	28	27	1
Robert W. Hunter, Harriss	90	3	4
Isaac Ledbetter, do.	57	8	1
James A. McCune, do.	26	17	1
Gabriel Bostron, Morgans	108	12	1
S.R.&J.M.Weems ors.M'Vickreys	195	9	3
Ishmael Stuart, Kites	99	23	1
Peter Smith, jr. Morgans	126	17	2
Mary Ann Rutherford, orp. Kites	31	7	1
HABERSHAM.			
Edwin Horton, Bryans	250	14	1
Tab.&Jas.Reece mins. Kunzies	299	1	4
Mathew Ridley, Bakers	6	26	1
Benjamin Allison, sr. Vickreys	146	21	2
Fielding Bowers, do.	132	23	2
James Christwood, Tates	75	21	2
Thos. Ausburn, Martins	192	10	1
Thos. Black, R. S. Bryans	242	19	1
Wm. L. Crow, Suttons	123	20	1
HALL.			
John Garner, Dorsey	239	10	1
John Cannon, do.	77	4	4
Jesse Prickett, Yagers	51	7	4
Robert Freeman, jr. Wilsons	281	22	1
John S. Lusk, Hardens	264	15	1
Bruce Boyd, Hendricks	140	16	1

HOUSTON.			
Fortunate Drawers Capts. Dist.	No.	Dt.	Sec.
Thomas Daniel, Furnals	82	5	3
Benjamin Smith, Hancocks	164	11	1
JACKSON.			
Tandy K. Martin, Venables	128	5	3
James H. Hardin, Rogers	20	3	3
Isaac Borders, soldier, do.	259	4	1
James Hall, Winns	127	11	1
John Boyce, do.	163	23	2
Thos. Phillips, sr. R. S. Winns	76	20	2
JASPER.			
Samuel Post, sol. Posts	96	31	1
Wm. Belcher, Hines	126	19	2
Jacob Slagle, Wilders	50	5	4
Riley Wise, Dardens	201	23	2
Charles Cargile, Holmes	244	2	2
John B. Smith, Robersons	186	12	2
John Gilcoat, Wilsons	253	19	2
C. D. Terhune, Holmes	84	7	4
James E. Wilson, do.	8	11	5
John Williams illegit. Dardens	172	13	1
Isaac Hancock, Butts	89	3	2
Joseph Scotts orphans, Baynes	165	32	1
JEFFERSON.			
Arthur Voss, Cunninghams,	123	15	2
Stephen Durouzeaux, Marshalls	244	25	1
Harris D. Austin, Ross'	218	4	1
Joseph Jackson, sol. Elliotts	187	12	2
Eli Hudson, Waldens	111	18	1
JONES.			
Adam S. Ledlow, Spinks	184	11	3
Wm. F. Williams, Breadloves	196	10	3
Caneth C. Rogers, Davis	42	12	3
George Harrison, Taylors	96	1	4
Hugh Watt, Gibsons	80	15	1
Joseph B. Smith, Duncans	17	10	5
John Whidby, Popes	46	1	2
Elizabeth Bayne, wid. Stewarts	37	4	5
Zadock B. Sanders, Dosters	27	13	5
Wm. Todd, Taylors	189	15	2
Mary Henderson, w.R.S.Gibsons	159	16	2
John J. Beasley, Spinks	148	10	5
Gideon Mason, R. S. Newbys	26	29	1
LAURENS.			
Robert R. Burgiss, Powers	359	20	2
Bennet Joiner, Beachams	66	7	4
Wm. Hopkins, Plummers	287	10	2
LIBERTY.			
Sarah Swilley, wid. R. S. 17th	24	5	3
Simon Fraser, do.	3	22	2
LINCOLN.			
Archibald McCorcle, Gideons	222	26	1
LOWNDES.			
Dixon Bennett, 2d	75	11	2
MADISON.			
Hawkins Bullock, R. S., Adairs	144	4	4
James Polk, Bones	61	5	5
Joseph Oniel, Christians	78	4	4
Joseph McDaman, Bones	22	25	1
Dickerson Lumpkin, fa. absent, do.	137	19	1
McINTOSH.			
Jacob Rockenbaugh, Ferrells	51	7	2
John Bennett, McCranies	216	19	1
John Ryall, do.	46	25	1
John McKee, Woodwards	41	6	5

MONROE.			
Fortunate Drawers Capts. Dist.	No.	Dt.	Sec.
Clement Davis, R. S., Finchs	43	6	1
Mary Davis, widow, Turners	190	6	1
Francis A. Shields, Browns	103	3	5
Joel Hendrick, Houses	221	10	1
John Wells, Knights	244	2	3
Henry Gibson, Turners	73	7	1
MORGAN.			
Joseph Prince, Christians	59	26	1
Levi H. Hussey, Canifaxs	268	7	1
Thomas Summerlin's orps. Jennings	238	17	1
William Tinsley, Whatleys	234	6	2
Abraham Estes, Canifaxs	228	19	2
Seaborn Williams, Sparks	114	7	4
George Herrin, Adairs	170	3	2
Elizabeth Hemphill, w. R. S. Beasleys	14	2	3
Augustus J. Hill, do.	39	2	5
Thomas Thurman, Canifaxs	12	15	2
Joseph B. Huey's orphans, Griggs	54	3	3
John M. Phillips, orphan, Canifaxs	236	20	1
Alexander Beard, Christians	271	15	1
Miles J. Harper, Canifaxs	4	15	5
Henry Nichols, Adairs	21	32	1
Mary Summerlin, widow, Jennings	51	5	1
William Glover, Beasleys	23	1	5
MONTGOMERY.			
Jacob Pope, Popes	40	11	1
NEWTON.			
Tayner Walden, sol. Newnans	42	7	3
William H. Reding, Clarks	62	3	1
William Pace, soldier, Graves	101	21	2
James Jones, Talleys	120	7	4
Ellit Wood, R. S., do.	131	7	4
William Berry, Orrs	155	32	1
Carter Tankersly, do.	22	6	3
William Vicker's orphans, Smiths	163	12	2
OGLETHORPE.			
Joel Gleason, Rousseaus	171	28	1
Thomas P. G. Stephens, Seals	75	4	5
Polly Smith, widow, Hardmans	269	7	1
James Goolsby's orphans, Seals	189	5	5
Frances Penn, w. R. S. Bells	111	8	1
John S. Andrews, Holloways	231	32	1
PIKE.			
John Moore, soldier, Bryans	58	15	5
Elizabeth James, wid. R. S., Daniels	100	23	2
John Simmons, sr. R. S., Orrs	68	23	1
William B. Horton, Longs	199	32	1
PULASKI.			
Wm. Miller's orps. Scarboroughs	202	7	1
Thomas McGriff, Kellams	39	19	1
Elizabeth Yawn, illegit.,Hendleys	201	7	1
PUTNAM.			
Henry Brown, soldier, Dismukes	203	11	3
Jane Young, widow, Vinings	8	32	1
John W. Thomas, Sparks	121	8	3
John Turner, Kendricks	145	30	1
Robert Griggs, Goods	253	7	3
Mary Wilbourn, wid. Sanders	62	21	1
Thomas Bell's orphans, Vinings	218	5	4
Mathew W. Beall, soldier, Clarks	149	33	1
RABUN.			
Edmund Betoot, Godfreys	157	33	1
Elijah Coffee, do.	22	24	1
Anthony Fowler, Becks	94	20	1
John Cason, Mercers	150	22	1
Cleveland Coffee, Milligans	96	19	2

RICHMOND.

Fortunate Drawers	Capts. Dist.	No.	Dt.	Sec.
Alexander H. Fraser,	Treadwells	165	18	2
Allen G. Thorp,	Augusta	240	8	1
Caroline S. McCan, wid.	Wilcoxs	34	4	2
Lewis B. Rhodes,	Kellys	13	5	3
Mary, Louisa, David, Helena & Isaiah Bailey, orps.	Hands	25	4	4
R. B. Duncan,	Huntingdons	124	10	2
James Kirkpatrick,	Kellys	271	10	2
John Newman Philpot,	Blacks	154	3	2
Peter Forman Boisclair,	Blacks	210	14	2

SCRIVEN.

E. Wilder, h.k'ld I.w.	Stricklings	13	10	2
John M. Kelly,	Poytress	303	1	2
John Calton,	Humphreys	6	21	2
William Scruggs,	Stricklings	119	14	5

TATTNALL.

Nancy Anderson, wid.	Conners	58	18	1
Simon Smith, R. S.,	do	82	1	3
James S. Stephens,	Deloachs	126	10	3

TELFAIR.

Samuel Slaughter,	Wilson	107	22	2
Cath. McRae, w.R.S.	Barentines	155	7	4
John Carmichal.	Robertsons	144	4	2

TALIAFERRO.

Mary Johnson, wid.	Guise	60	7	5

TWIGGS.

Orp. of Wm. Deshazo,	Streetmans	34	9	3
Gideon Bedingfield,	Graggs	47	19	2
Henry Anglin, sol.,	Blackshears	59	18	2
D. Thompson, F.	Chamberlains	124	7	4

UPSON.

John Black,	Harrells	72	12	5
Josiah Cooper,	Myricks	175	7	5
Adam S. Caldwell,	Coopers	194	12	3
David Tillman,	Myricks	223	9	5

WALTON.

Fortunate Drawers	Capts. Dist.	No.	Dt.	Sec.
Christopher D. Linor,	Bexleys	196	6	2
Elizabeth Edgar's children,	250th	99	12	5
Alfred Moss,	Snows	361	8	1
William C. Campbell,	Rays	21	28	1
Martin Forister,	250th	8	29	1

WAYNE.

Martha Turner, wid.	Mannings	183	15	1

WARREN.

Henry Raley, R S.,	Jones	49	11	1
George W. Ray,	Sanders	232	9	2
Littleberry Carter,	do	44	3	4
James Todd, jr.	Kinseys	224	5	4
Sarah McCoy, widow,	Downs	108	22	2
Asa Umphlet,	Adkins	44	8	5
Taylor A Walker,	Latimers	147	11	1
John K. Revier,	Bulls	228	21	1

WASHINGTON.

Thomas Barrons orps.	Warthens	211	2	1
James Ivey,	Woods	375	3	4
John Coffield, sol.	Warthens	59	17	2
John Jordan,	Wimberlys	191	8	1
Daniel B McMillan,	Floyds	167	2	4
Jesse Amison, R. S.	Warthens	2	7	3
Jesse B. Drew,	Floyds	23	24	2
Dougald McLean,	Currys	27	4	1
Jefferson Barnes,	do	32	14	1
James Hood,	Rushings	231	33	1
Thomas A. Irwin,	McLendons	72	31	1

WILKINSON.

Charlott T. Patterchal,illeg.	Shows	12	7	5
C., A., Nan. Sumerford,ills.	Halls	232	4	2
James Cooks orphans,	Currys	114	32	1

WILKES.

Reece Bradford,	Wottens	156	9	2
Elem. Sandiford, R. S.	Charltons	140	12	1
Owen O. Bird,	Greshams	198	12	2
Sarah Wellborn, widow,	Popes	159	3	2

LAND LOTTERY REGISTER—No. 11.
[RECORDER OFFICE—PUBLISHED BY GRANTLAND & ORME—PRICE $3.]

NOTE—Section 1 is Lee County—2 Muscogee—3 Troup—4 Coweta—5 Carroll.

Fortunate Drawers Capts. Dist.	No.Dt.Sec.	Fortunate Drawers Capts. Dist.	No.Dt.Sec.
23rd DAY'S DRAWING—April 2nd.		Washington Sanders, Rhodes	109 9 3
		DECATUR.	
APPLING.		David Gray's orphans, Douglass	265 4 1
John Mixon, Collins	176 19 1	Ransom Parham, do.	181 7 5
BALDWIN.		**DEKALB..**	
		David Wilson, for his wife, Bakers	121 8 5
James C. Humphries, Doles	215 2 1	Mark Hudspeth, Howells	158 2 3
Archibald Shaw, Buchanans	80 17 2	Hannah Autery's ill. children, Hays	376 20 2
William G House, Linges	227 12 3	James B. Broughton, Browns	260 20 2
		Reuben Williams, Stephens	210 9 2
BURKE.		Andrew T. Hendon, Bollings	135 7 2
Isaac Cross, Lynchs	69 21 1	Henry Ellison, do	169 6 1
Edmond H. Dyre, Tuttles bat.	38 17 2	Meredith Brown, R. S Stephens	210 13 1
John Scott, Roberts	254 13 1	Charles McMinn, Bakers	232 31 1
James Hines's orphans, Lynchs	107 16 1		
William Almand, Bayleys	140 3 3	**DOOLY.**	
Thomas Ferrow, illegitimate, Forths	203 13 2	Elizabeth Tison, widow, Mannings	83 6 1
Isma Burnett, Lynchs	20 23 1	Joel Pate, Hogans	187 20 2
		Loucreasy Kingsley, wid. Andersons	99 7 1
CAMDEN.			
Charney Garret, Coxs	107 6 3	**EARLY.**	
		Sarah Long, wid. R. S. Hairs	236 8 3
BIBB.			
William Bass, Beards	196 5 5	**EFFINGHAM.**	
Caleb Smith, Rutlands	58 8 4	Anderson Williams, jnn. Stricklands	260 1 4
John F Thompson, Beards	194 13 2	James Bryan, R. S., Waldhaners	195 6 5
Reuben Williams, Pickards	116 5 5	Sarah Gnaun, widow, Stricklands	182 21 2
Benjamin J Phillips, Flanders	48 4 3		
Mary Ann Kimble, widow, Bates	145 11 3	**ELBERT.**	
J, J, & P, Dunaway, fa. ab. Beards	46 28 1	John B. Wilhight, Boltons	254 5 4
		Bedford Harper, Alstons	214 9 1
BULLOCH.		Reuben L. Tiler, Dobbs	27 11 5
Nathan Dixon, Turners	144 9 1	Thomas Ternor, Dunns	48 1 5
John Waters, sen McCalls	100 20 1		
Covington Cribbs, Deloachs	190 22 2	**EMANUEL.**	
Stephen Moore, Burnetts	244 11 2	Martha Miller, widow, Nabbs	15 25 1
John Allen, Lockharts	64 30 1	Edward Brown, Moors	89 1 3
		John S. Raiford, McGars	104 18 2
CHATHAM.		William B. Nabb, Nabbs	125 8 5
Marg. Belinger, W.R.S. McDonnells	22 7 2		
John Nevitt, Haydens	239 3 1	**FAYETTE.**	
John Boyd, McDonnells	144 5 1	Elijah Marshall, Roziers	249 15 2
Benedict Young, do	141 31 1	Larkin Milsaps, do.	37 9 5
Orps of Thomas Burke, Geredons	1 10 3	S. Bailey, wounded sol. McClendons	248 11 3
John H. Watson, do.	83 2 5	Edward Harris, Wests	27 8 5
Louis Craig, Tybee Island	119 15 2	James Richards, 9th	11 32 1
Jacob De Lamotta, Haydens	58 8 2	James Caldwell, soldier, Whartons	144 1 3
Norman Wallace, do	67 11 3		
John Shenk, do	90 10 2	**FRANKLIN.**	
Elisha C. Hopkins, Baines	290 3 4	James Suttey, Cokers	230 22 2
John Atkinson, Haydens	28 15 1	Melessa Cockburn, insane, Bennetts	2 26 1
Catharine Langley, widow. Reeds	50 19 1	Israel P. Davis, T. Chandlers	182 16 2
		James L. Gillespie, Stranges	133 11 1
CLARK..			
William Huff, illegitimate, Greers	139 11 ?	**GLYNN.**	
David Meriwether, R. S.., Alreds	159 2 4	James H. Couper, Dubignons	54 8 3
Joseph Allen, Vinsons	100 1 ?	Francis M. Scarlett, sol., McLeods	292 5 3
Thomas Wade, Herndons	249 2 3	Charles E. Flinn, do.	95 20 1
Adam Cousins, R. S., Andersons	200 30 1		
Isaac Crow, R. S., Dickens	189 4 2	**GREENE.**	
Robert Moore, Davis	93 7 4	Orphans of William White, Astins	118 6 5
		Jane Finley, Winkfields	139 8 1
COLUMBIA.		George W. Sanders, Astins	24 15 1
Elizabeth Chrosbay, w. R. S. Dranes	240 30 1	Samuel Durham's orps. Newsome	143 30 1
Elizabeth Garnett, w. R. S.. Coles	103 20 1	Letitia Greer, widow, Robinsons	114 19 2
Leonard B. Sims, Stallings	119 14 2	Douglass Carrol, R. S. Vincents	156 1 4
John B. Collins, orphan, Coles	118 1 2	Elizabeth Smith, wid. R. S. Bruces	36 28 1
Thos. Howard's mins. fa. ab. Boltons	25 17 1	Travis A. D. Weaver, Dawsons	32 24 1
John Reynolds, soldier, Bynaums	270 2 1	William Anderson, sen R. S., do	142 7 3
George W. Persons, Clark	98 23 1		
		GWINNETT.	
CRAWFORD.		Jesse Watkins, Woodroughs	138 16 1
		John Cupp's orphans, Hunicuts	169 11 1
John B Grace, soldier, Lovetts	187 23 1	David Watson, Caruthers	187 22 1

Fortunate Drawers Capts. Dist.	No.	Dt.	Sec.
Littleton Daniel, Wallis	113	23	1
Pleasant Bake\`, Gholstons Battalion	16	9	5
John Whorton Finchers	153	30	1
Richard Glover Caruthers	44	4	3
David Red Moors	79	11	5
Philip B. Hargis, Whortons	160	6	4
Reuben McLunge, J P, Rollins	171	6	1
G. H. & S. Hamby, ills. Whortons	191	7	1
Martin Bowling, Finchers	33	6	5
Richard J. Watts, soldier, Dunbars	76	10	5
Wilson Goss, Bakers	56	13	1
John Kenny, Hunnicuts	181	13	1
John McGill, Evans	162	7	5
Gabriel Hite, Moors	205	4	2
Edward Wing, Hunicuts	15	3	2
Hardy Burwell, Moors	38	1	3
Jesse Umphreys, do.	178	11	5
William Sudderth do	311	7	5

HANCOCK.

James Butts, R. S., 101st	183	9	1
Benjamin Wallace's orphans, 116th	167	11	2
Richard Holt, 107th	224	30	1
George Ingram, Mahons	360	3	4
John G. Thomas 108th	132	7	4
John Marshall, 116th	263	22	2
Cannon W. Grace, 111th	202	5	4
John G Coleman, 113th	234	7	5
Etheldred Edwards, 108th	210	9	1
Seth Kennedy, R S, 116th	252	30	1

HENRY.

Samuel Gledney, Grays	92	26	1
Elizabeth Gosdin, w R S Gosdins	116	17	1
William Tetchstone, Shaws	104	4	3
Joshua Starrs orphans, Allens	114	15	1
Sampson Barfield, Shaws	140	10	3
Mayfield Beall, Harris	161	10	3

HABERSHAM.

Stephen Sanders, Tates	184	8	5
Jacob Duckett, Kenzies	23	1	4
Jacob Holland, do	196	9	3
Daniel Bennett, R S., Martins	166	23	2
Lawson Dover, Cross	180	18	2
Elisha A. Stanford, illegit. Bryans	106	12	5
Roley Mitchell, Kenzies	60	19	1
William Flake, Suttons	194	18	1

HALL.

Abner Hammond, Wilsons	185	2	3
George W. Lampkins, Garrards	28	25	1
Presley Powell, Roberts	73	27	1
Samuel Sanfer, Smiths	196	10	2
John Wagner, Hendricks	255	4	2
Subel Bolen, Alreds	189	12	2
Benjamin Johnson, Garrards	270	9	3
John Stephens, Roberts	5	4	5

HOUSTON.

James Holt, sen. R S. Farnels	194	4	2
Joseph Barron, R. S., Smiths	165	21	2
Aaron Justice, Hancocks	144	2	2

IRWIN.

Alfred Belote, Underwoods	125	25	1

JACKSON.

John H. Smith, Dupree	41	17	2
Benamin Browning, Millers	18	31	1
William Menifee, Winns	228	13	2

JASPER.

William Porter, sen. R S. Camerons	73	12	2
James L. Martin, Holmes	103	14	1

Fortunate Drawers Capts. Dist.	No.	Dt.	Sec.
George Hadmark, Sparks	189	16	2
Henry Thompson's orphans, do	47	24	2
Samuel Hughes, Camerons	29	12	2
Molly O. Johnson widow, Barnetts	212	15	1
Irwin Lawson, wounded sol. Dales	79	17	1

JEFFERSON.

Richard Howel, sen Elliotts	5	11	3
Wyatt Edwards, illegit Cunninghams	85	29	1
Elijah Hudson, do	70	2	1
Hardy Pool, soldier Kings	230	8	3
Jonas Stephens, jun.. Jones	53	9	2
Thomas Young, jun. Beatys	78	5	1

JONES.

Henry Johnson, Robertsons	212	10	3
Williamson Rose, Gibsons	79	18	2
Rebecca Walker, w R S. Bowens	41	7	3
John P. Turner, Gibsons	40	9	1
David Tidd, R S., Spinks	135	14	1
Larkin Reynolds, Taylors	219	5	1
John C. Slocumb, R. S. Davis	123	3	3

LAURENS.

William Copper, Barlows	133	6	2
John Hammond, do	25	6	4
Joel Hare, Beachams	107	3	1
Abel Ryals, Hodges	74	22	1
Archibald Thomas, R S Spiveys	175	2	2
Thomas Bryant, jr. Whiteheads	257	7	5
James M. Waite, illegi Plummers	38	7	5
Chesley S. Warren, Mizells	255	7	1
James Hawood, Newmons	198	6	1
Reason Whitehead, Whiteheads	88	13	5
Hardy Griffin, do	71	11	3

LIBERTY.

John Tanner dec'd. orph. 16th	133	6	3
Hardy Deloach, R.. S. 15th	52	20	1

LINCOLN.

John Tankisley, Frasers	5	21	1
E. A. Littleton, widow, Parks	92	7	2
John Blackborn, Gideons	156	7	3
James Gray, jr. Leveretts	240	9	1
Johnson L. Dunaway, Parks	22	26	1

MADISON.

Charles McLeroy, Culbertsons	195	32	1
Reuben Simmons, Christians.	126	18	2
Robert Williams. Jr. Bones	54	7	1
John Hall, Caldwells	182	12	1
Wilson Bird, Phipps	281	8	1
Lewis Mannen, Hancocks	272	1	2

McINTOSH.

David Hamilton, Thorps	164	1	4

MONROE.

Evans Myrick soldier, Millers	116	14	5
John J. Culpepper, Turners	230	5	1
James B. Smith, Douglass	219	3	1
Jesse Dewberry, Millers	142	16	2
John Walldriefe, sol. Wrights	200	23	2
Amos Goree, do.	45	1	5
Joseph Stephens, R. S. Millers	86	8	5
Mary Jackson, w. R. S. Fergasons	3	2	4
Cary Fells, Millers	106	1	2
John Trimble, Finchs	97	7	2
Mary Rogers, wid. Woodwards	177	4	2
James D. Beekham, Pattersons	28	1	5
Thomas Watson, Finchs	10	3	4

(71)

Fortunate Drawers	Capts.	Dist.	No.	Dt.	Sec.
Wiley Clemmons,	do		208	9	2
Thomason Fowler,	Wrights		59	13	2
William G. Gains,	Pattersons		136	2	2
Robert McNair,	Turners		86	14	5
MORGAN.					
Allford Brewer,	Stokes		162	8	3
Irbin Mabry,	Dawsons		154	28	1
Winny Barefield, w.	R.S.Youngs		266	19	2
Charles H. Walker,	Sparks		180	19	1
Levi Hadaway,	Christians		234	23	2
MONTGOMERY.					
Nancy Register, wid.	Wynns		208	9	1
William Harrelson,	McMillons		103	7	1
NEWTON.					
Thomas Naron,	Talleys		30	6	4
Moses Brown, R. S.	Clarks		228	6	2
Willis Folkner,	Bakers		140	19	1
John Middlebrook, R. S.	Dyers		179	2	2
Jacob Miller,	Talleys		111	13	2
William Calloway,	Webbs		110	1	5
David Floyd,	Smiths		35	15	1
Michael Houseworth,	Talleys		190	2	3
Sarah Steward, orphan,	Snows		111	23	2
Levey Mercer, soldier,	Orrs		191	22	1
Samuel M. Akin,	Talleys		126	19	1
OGLETHORPE.					
Thomas Hopper, R. S.	Lacys		22	6	1
Elizabeth S. Blake, wid.	Arnolds		87	1	3
Norwell Halloway,	Halloways		126	3	4
Ritter Bridges, wid.	Hardmans		143	19	1
William B. S. Gilmer,	Seals		8	7	3
Marshall Early,	Dixs		17	9	5
John Waltons orphans,	Rousseaus		7	10	2
Martin Dowdy,	Lacys		109	6	5
PIKE.					
William Carter,	Weavers		191	17	1
John Belcher, sol.	Pattersons		18	11	3
Thomas R. Mangham,	Hicks		213	26	1
Turner Crawley,	Suiters		73	6	2
Thomas Jones, sol.	Bryans		164	2	2
PULASKI.					
James R. Butts,	Gilstraps		115	13	5
Cynthia Gardner, w.	Bracewells		182	3	1
James Holland,	Scarbroughs		189	12	3
PUTNAM..					
Al. & P. Wheeler mins.	Barnetts		79	12	2
Nelly Sanders, illegit.	Clarks		40	1	1
Joseph Harralson, sol.	Thomas		106	8	1
Richmond B. Gore,	Kendricks		116	20	1
Mabel Williams, widow,	Bledsoes		76	3	2
Zachariah Bevell,	Vinings		272	16	2
Peter Smith,	Choices		54	30	1
Penelope Mathis, h.. ab.	Dupress		110	1	4
Thomas Coswert,	do		251	20	1
RABUN.					
Thomas Johnson,	Mercers		235	8	1
Josiah H. Carter,	do		144	5	5
George Smith,	Godfreys		60	12	3
RICHMOND.					
John Bones,	Treadwells		8	17	2
Joseph Rivers,	Ferris		149	8	1
J. M. Clarke,	Ferris		227	11	2
Jeremiah Johnson,	Blacks		20	17	2
James Ball,	Treadwells		80	1	1
Joshua Sego,	Kellys		83	2	2
A. & L. Pearson orps.	Wilcoxs		213	5	1
Abraham Neril, idiot,	Blacks		81	26	1
SCRIVEN.					
Thomas H. Burnes,	Poytress		92	15	1
Patience Mootry, w.	Stricklings		188	9	3
Mandass P. Verdery,	Greens		128	22	2
Mathew Faircloth,	Kemps		90	22	1
Christ. G. White,	Stricklings		173	28	1
Thomas H. Usher,	Hunters		317	28	1
TATTNALL.					
Josiah Collins,	Corseys		204	17	2
William Durrence, jr.	Deloaches		88	5	4
TELFAIR.					
Elijah Hubbard, R. S.	Wilsons		241	11	5
Jeptha Durham,	Barentines		24	8	4
Henry Slaughter,	Wilsons		306	28	1
Edward Burke,	Barentines		1	1	2
TWIGGS.					
Orphs. of Jas. Harden,	Solomans		119	3	5
J. Crawford, (w.f.)	Chamberlains		250	4	2
Jonathan Roberts,	Pearsons		44	6	2
Nathan Veal, illegit.	Wimberlys		70	24	2
John Taylor (	Bosticks		158	30	1
John Barker, R. S.	Pearsons		85	3	3
UPSON.					
Cornelius Jeter, sol.	Petties		113	2	2
Benjamin Tilman,	Hattocks		146	16	2
John Flannigan,	Coopers		60	2	1
James Birdsong sol.	Ezells		161	4	2
WALTON.					
Frederick Reeves, sol.	Hudsons		139	27	1
Sarah Mosely, w. R. S.	Bexleys		201	3	1
Elizabeth Hightower, wid.	Pools		180	10	5
Mary Bowen, widow.	249th		51	29	1
Zachariah Harlands orps.	Pools		249	18	2
WARE.					
Richard Godwin,	Lees		162	6	1
Sarah Gatland, wid..	Bryans		61	13	1
WAYNE.					
Charles W. Chonaway,	Mannings		98	2	4
WARREN.					
Mayberry Howell,	Adkins		90	3	5
William Bales,	Downs		155	9	5
Benjamin Johnson, sol.	do		223	7	1
Eliz. Newsom, w. R.	S.Adkins		187	10	1
Willis H. Pass,	Brinkleys		128	8	4
Nath. Brooks orphs.	Parhams		72	6	3
Blake Bakers orphans,	Kinseys		159	10	1
Elizabeth Parris, w.	R.S.Jones		86	10	1
John K. Revier,	Bulls		126	8	5
Washington, Darden,	Hills		107	8	5
Cid. Johnson, for her ills.	Kinseys		70	6	3
Wm. Fagles orphans,	Adkins		122	2	5
Mathew Cox,	Jones		66	5	2
James G. Powers, sol.	Fords		40	12	3
WASHINGTON.					
James Wootan,	Floyds		133	13	2

Fortunate Drawers	Capts. Dist.	No.	Dt.	Sec.
William Hunt, sol. Whitfields		230	23	1
Simon Parkers orps. Warthens		28	21	1
Samuel Gilmore, Floyds		218	5	1
William Suttonfield, sol. Gilberts		227	14	2
Edy Martin, w. R. S. do		184	3	5
John Williams, Warthens		54	11	2
Jos. Brantleys orps. McLendons		129	15	2
WILKINSON.				
Alfred Stapleton, Mandersons		130	30	1
Stephen Lord, Mathews		167	33	1
Stephen Lord, Mathews		167	33	1
Reuben Kelly, Ragans		53	12	5
Samuel Nesbits orps. Mayos		34	6	3
William H. Slappy, Barrys		182	6	1
Henry H. Vincent, Currys		118	1	1
John Smith, Smiths		138	15	1
WILKES.				
John Walmakers orps. Lukers		44	18	2
William Young, Chunns		19	11	3
Charles A. Cox, Hopkins		199	7	5
James Hill, Hamocks		49	14	5
William C. Lyman, Rices		114	6	3
James Dillard Gresham, Greens		100	4	1
Charles F. Sherburn, Charltons		207	19	2
John Burks, do.		248	6	3
Diannah Caid, wid. Richardsons		73	8	3
William Hudspeth, Amasons		32	17	1
William Hancock, soldier, do		281	14	1
M. Barnett, sols. w.. Richardsons		126	25	1
Burwell P. Hill, Wootens		36	23	2
John W. Jones, Popes		60	32	1
24th DAY'S DRAWING—April 3rd.				
BALDWIN.				
James Jones, Llngos		222	2	5
Atchy Worsham's orps. Lesters		186	8	1
Orps. of Theodosius Turk, Wicks		39	20	1
Orphans of Benj. Trice, Reddings		59	2	1
Thomas Miles, R. S., Lingos		34	12	1
John Williams, Rows		23	22	1
BIBB.				
William Jones, Lloyds		131	7	1
Jacob Johnson, Carrs		2	1	4
BULLOCH.				
Charles Neasmith, Deloachs		64	8	3
Henry Hobbs, Richardsons		196	1	4
John Woodrum, Lockharts		121	13	5
John Shuffield, R.S., Richardsons		200	7	3
BURKE.				
John Patterson, soldier, Forths		92	5	3
Joshua S. Treadwell, Wests		186	31	1
Augustus Jenkins, illegit. Lesters		242	15	1
John Dixon's orphans, Gordons		302	15	1
Alexander Sanders, Corkers		124	20	2
Elenor Parker, widow Brooms		220	5	5
John Rich, Lynchs		155	5	2
Luke Sanders, orphans, Corkers		128	6	2
Elijah Walker, Gaffs		171	22	2
S. & M. Whitfield, ills. Gordons		116	14	1
S. L D Scarborough, wid. Dugas		86	7	4
Simeon Finney, Wests		191	14	1
John Tabb, Brooms		132	22	1

Fortunate Drawers	Capts. Dist.	No.	Dt.	Sec.
Alethia Stark, wid McDonnells		122	13	1
Daniel Wilson, U. S. sol. Baines		83	11	3
Horace Blair, do		195	25	1
Abner Bassett		217	27	1
A. B. Fannin, Haydens		130	16	2
Orps. of S. Finninghast, MDonnells		265	15	1
CLARK.				
Elizabeth Sims, wid. Wrights		199	15	2
Mary Watts, widow, Gahagans		225	33	1
George H. Lipham, McCress		205	14	2
James Jackson, Herndons		128	10	5
E. C. Thomas, w.R.S. McDonalds		87	26	1
Polly Thomas, wid R.S. Wrights		68	3	2
Andrew Graham, Gahagans		31	2	2
John Hinton, soldier, Davenports		105	1	5
Clary Newton, widow, Gahagans		167	10	5
David James, Davenports		26	15	1
Lewis Bradberry, R. S., Huntons		137	13	1
COLUMBIA.				
Jane Carlisle, wid. R. S., Coles		94	10	5
Edmund Leshley, R. S,. Carrolls		82	3	3
M A. D. Barnes, wid. Stallings		134	2	2
Elizabeth C Allen, w.RS.Adams		307	7	5
Hensley Sanders, Baileys		68	5	1
Hartwell Felts, Clarks		30	9	3
Ann Lampkin, widow, Culbreaths		210	10	2
Martha S. Bragg, Tolberts		272	8	5
Alexander Steventon, Carrolls		93	15	5
Adam Scott, Magruders		27	23	1
CRAWFORD.				
Vincent Nichols, Tillers		288	28	1
Elijah M. Amos, Lovetts		156	33	1
Irwin Whittington, soldier, Rays		168	1	1
DE KALB.				
Jesse Townsend, Browns		286	5	1
Thomas Dillon, R. S., Conns		155	10	3
William McCurley, Merritts		96	23	2
Thomas Kennedy, Howells		251	7	5
James Marin, Stephens		248	21	2
John Parker, Browns		233	9	3
John Haslet, Bowlings		10	15	5
Thos. P. Wagnon, R.S., Howells		72	5	3
William Hudspeth, do		27	4	3
John Adams, Merritts		360	28	1
EFFINGHAM.				
John C. Griffin, sol Edwards		149	11	1
ELBERT.				
Charles W. Christian. sol. Paces		294	5	1
Orphans of John Rich, Tates		145	6	5
Elizabeth Brewer, w. R.S.Bells		259	1	2
Reuben Wanslow, Blackwells		125	3	1
James Hendrick, Merritts		183	2	5
Lewis McGehee's orphans, do		14	14	5
Harris Tinar, sol., Carpenters		136	4	2
Jinny Fetts widow, Paces		124	15	1
Joseph Smith, Blackwells		197	22	2
Adaline Parrot, illegitimate, Bells		157	21	1
Daniel Dixon, Tates		225	32	1
EMANUEL.				
Allen Sanford, Swains		23	4	4
Margaret Price's illegits., 57th		12	11	1
Starling Swain, Swains		60	3	2

(73)

Fortunate Drawers Capts. Dist.	No.	Dt.	Sec.
Margaret Lindsey's illegits. Arlines	47	5	1
Sarah Thompson's chil Daniels	262	11	2
FAYETTE..			
Henderson Smith, Wests	318	8	1
FRANKLIN.			
James Stone, T. Chandlers	240	28	1
Eliz. Sosebee, w.R S. Andrews	84	19	2
Tavener Rucker, Walters	178	4	2
Minyard Sanders, Sanders	67	6	2
Henry Smith, R.S., T. Chandlers	82	16	2
Capel Tabor, Cokers	359	7	1
Jeremiah Goolsby, sol., Walters	212	7	1
GLYNN.			
Isaac Huston, Burnetts	61	29	1
GREENE.			
Elijah Brockman, Greens	103	2	5
Jesse Woodall, Colcloughs	117	7	2
Edward Mulhorn, Dawsons	168	8	1
Robert Paulin, R S., Rankins	124	6	5
Robert F. Griffin, Woodhams	139	18	2
Rebecca Alford, wid R.S., Webbs	114	25	1
James W. Burran, Knowles	40	32	1
GWINNETT.			
John Carrell, Woodroughs	120	4	2
Joseph Edmondson, Hunicuts	205	1	2
William H. Cole, Woodroughs	154	1	2
Reynolds Harris, Dunbars	150	11	2
Nathan Williams, Hils	283	1	2
Henry Sizemore, sen do	139	4	3
Samuel J. Lowrie, Greens	13	5	4
Isaac York, Hunicuts	209	27	1
Abigail Sizemore, widow, Davis	206	7	5
Reuben Higgins, R.S.,Finchers	122	13	5
James Taunt, Robertsons	228	27	1
Robert Malone, Bakers	165	8	1
HABERSHAM.			
Mary Haigwood, wid Kinzies	103	4	2
Joel Stephens, do	266	1	2
McK., L., &W.Scott,ors.Suttons	29	5	1
Ephraim Clark, Martins	175	7	1
Joseph Hughes, Suttons	188	19	2
Isham Shuffield, Kenzies	219	20	2
Benjamin F. Thompson, Tates	72	13	1
Davison's orphans, Bakers	86	17	1
HALL.			
John Wheeler, Yagers	3	16	1
Nathaniel Smith, sol., Harrisons	120	7	2
John Lancaster, Garrards	75	24	1
Robert Anderson, Hardages	208	4	2
Calvin Barnett, Harrisons	92	12	3
Thomas Shockley, do	10	31	1
Joshua Martin, soldier, Yagers	124	24	2
Joseph Chapman, Hendricks	213	16	2
HANCOCK.			
Robert B. Mabry, 108th	150	16	2
J F. Sherman's orps.Bullingtons	116	14	2
Nancy Dunivant's, illegits., 117th	223	4	8
Ira Allen, 108th	157	5	5
Joseph B. Gonder, Calliers	3	20	1
Elizabeth Murphy, wid. Dixons	203	5	3
Eleanor Grammar, widow. 109th	163	28	1
HENRY.			
Nathan Nall, soldier, Morgane	227	9	3
Josiah M. Bonner, Harriss	161	4	4
John Hunt, soldier, 7th	224	7	3
Thomas McCormack, Millers	194	2	3
John M. Dobbins, Grays	249	28	1
Robert Beard, R. S., Wards	12	5	1
Philip Causey, Kites	181	15	2
Yearly Stroud, soldier, Millers	79	19	2
Patam Parker, Shaws	9	7	3
John Barnwell, Wards	37	30	1
HOUSTON.			
Robert Brooks, Calhouns	242	21	2
Enoch Jordan, Farnals	240	12	1
Scarborough Rambert Wimberlys	59	1	5
Sarah Paine, widow, Farnels	30	20	2
Thomas Gardner, Calhouns	265	8	1
IRWIN.			
Joseph D Thomas, Underwoods	62	6	2
Susannah Jurnigan, orp. Dixons	132	32	1
Neil McNeill, Underwoods	115	20	2
JACKSON.			
Charles Walls, Venables	160	8	1
Jonathan Yarbrough, Bowens	46	13	1
Lewellen Thomas, Georges	1	11	3
JASPER.			
Jesse M. Lumsden, Baynes	39	20	2
John Thornton, Butts	240	24	1
Jonathan Adams, Barnetts	165	9	3
James Cameron,sr RS.,Trussells	150	11	5
William W. Phelps, Sparks	124	16	2
James Donelly, Robinsons	168	12	2
Lamach H. Hines, Hines	182	3	2
Samuel Sistrunk, Botts	44	12	5
John Chatfield, R. S., Barnetts	34	15	1
John P. Okelley, Hines	138	13	1
William Everett's orphans, Dales	75	4	1
Henry T. Smith, sol. Farleys	174	7	1
Henry Steel, R. S. Wilsons	84	2	2
Nancy Dickson, widow, Holmes	260	22	2
Thomas K Reaves, Dardens	102	17	1
John D. Berry,soldier,Hollands	132	5	3
David Allen's orphans, Camerons	146	12	3
JEFFERSON.			
Pet Durouzeaux's orps.Marshalls	146	9	3
W.&H.Harrell,ills..Cunninghams	182	10	5
William Hurd, Elliotts	70	17	2
Asa Holder, Marshalls	153	33	1
Joseph Dillard, Ross	143	32	1
W. C. Smoker,R.S.Cunninghams	27	33	1
JONES.			
George H. Elliot, Popes	208	18	2
Jonathan Barron, Bowers	74	5	1
William Blakey, R.S.,Robertsons	158	8	5
Bud Driver, Mullins	170	11	2
John C. Slocumb, R.S.,Davis	4	2	1
John Perry, Blounts	87	6	1
Appleton W. Melson, Taylors	127	16	1
Chas.&M.Biddel,orps. Popes	84	20	1
Allen Ashburn, Davis	192	17	1
LAURENS.			
J. Spradly's mnis. fa. ab. Spiveys	124	6	4
Drury Maddox, Barlaws	112	11	1
LIBERTY.			
Leonard Dees, soldier, 17th	4	9	4

Fortunate Drawers	Capts. Dist.	No.	Dt.	Sec.
Joseph Hodges, R. S. .16th		122	5	1
LINCOLN.				
Nathan Terry, Parks		6	9	4
John Wright,sr.R.S.Lonograns		149	6	2
Robert Mumfort, Gideons		63	13	5
John Shehee Conner, Parks		135	8	3
MADISON.				
E. L. Christians orps. Higginbothams		245	2	3
Maryann Shinn, widow, do		30	20	1
McINTOSH.				
John Dyall, Terrells		255	17	2
MONROE.				
William Richardson, Millers		226	21	2
Joshua Adams, Houses		199	4	5
Andrew Love, Pattersons		100	7	3
Miles G. Turner, do		296	10	2
Julian Mitchell, illegit. Wrights		65	7	5
Robert M. Stuart, Browns		253	4	2
Drewry Allen's orphs. Douglass		216	28	1
MORGAN.				
John Stephens, Youngs		308	8	5
Edmund Peters, R. S. Adairs		30	23	1
Riley J. Crawford, Christians		298	7	5
Catherine Crawford, w. Ostians		411	7	1
William T. Wortham, Christians		199	4	3
John Farrow, Adairs		181	19	1
NEWTON.				
Leroy Oglesby, sol. Zachrys		5	8	4
Joseph Hobbs, soldier, Orr's		190	5	1
James C. Gathright, Hays		212	4	1
Ann Morrow, widow, do.		166	15	5
Daniel Delany, Smiths		42	11	3
William Willingham, Clarks		136	1	4
OGLETHORPE.				
Jacob Lester, Burfords		68	8	4
Lemuel Blacks orps. Davenports		170	8	5
Eliz. M. Molloy, wid. Rousseaus		156	11	2
David Jennings orps. Arnolds		222	2	2
Thomas Raden, Dixs		110	2	4
W. H., Bankston, Rhodes		252	5	5
R. Hartsfield, R. S. Holloways		77	16	1
John Fielder Harris, idiot, Lacys		83	17	1
PIKE.				
Peter Atris, Longs		16	2	2
Alfred Wiggins, Orrs		58	31	1
PULASKI.				
Aaron Scarbrough, Scarbroughs		14	9	5
Reuben Bynums orps. Sparrows		78	4	1
Elisha Holland, Scarbroughs		30	1	3
John Gregory, sol. Thomas		60	5	4
PUTNAM.				
Jesse Harrisons orps. Clarks		377	28	1
James N. Hall, Blacks		21	10	2
John J. Smiths orps. Bledsoes		372	3	4
Thomas R. Lawson, Sparks		251	7	1
Jones Rivers orphans, do		239	13	1
Polly Frazer, wid. Duprees		124	23	1
William H. Barnett, Barnetts		218	11	3
James K. Stone, Sparks		48	33	1
James Connal Kendricks		224	26	1
RABUN.				
Isham Edwards, Mercers		273	7	1

Fortunate Drawers	Capts. Dist.	No.	Dt.	Sec.
Edward Dudley, Huntingtons		248	18	2
Henry O. Loane, Treadwells		66	26	1
Joseph James James, Blacks		224	16	1
Christopher C. Averett, James		295	8	5
William J. Dudley, Huntingtons		195	14	1
M.,A.,&Mary Hill orps.Hands		161	18	2
Thomas Taunt, Kellys		172	2	3
SCRIVEN.				
John Williams, Hunters		208	6	5
Wm. Hitchcocks mins. Reaves		194	23	2
William Lariscy, R. S. Poytress		264	7	1
TATTNALL.				
Homer Sapp, McDuffies		172	25	1
John Young, R. S. do		133	3	3
Joseph English, Corseys		25	11	3
TELFAIR.				
Arthur Singleterry, Barentines		147	27	1
TALIAFERRO.				
Orrin Wiggins, Marshalls		139	4	4
TWIGGS.				
Peter, Mary, Euphama, Henry &Wm. Newberry ills. Solomons		108	5	5
Jonas Daniel, Chamberlains		412	7	1
William A. Tharp, Bosticks		72	27	1
UPSON.				
Nathan Jones, Coupers		43	12	2
Bevin Brooks, soldier, Pettys		242	12	3
Gilford Couper, Coopers		283	4	1
WALTON.				
Nathan Whitley, jr. Rays		170	26	1
Martin T. Sentell, 250th		129	20	1
William Parks, Rays		6	11	1
Daniel M. Dwight, McQuertors		175	11	2
James Odams orphans, 418th		239	11	2
William Smith, sr. 559th		236	2	5
Elizabeth Radford, w.R.S,250th		216	11	2
James Sturtevant, 249th		39	24	2
John Keadle, McQuertors		145	18	1
Ezekiel Helton, Bexleys		132	22	1
Mathew Knight, 249th		154	10	3
John B. Harvey, 559th		57	11	1
Philip Easten, 418th		237	30	1
WAYNE.				
Warren Moore, McKinneys		6	23	2
WARREN.				
William Carr, R. S. Brinkleys		250	6	1
John Ware, Adkins		34	23	1
Linney Tension, widow, do		52	32	1
John B. Boyd, Brinkleys		140	10	2
Harman Runnells, Rogers		136	9	2
James Sallis, Sanders		32	4	3
Daniel Dennis, Parhams		231	27	1
WASHINGTON.				
Robert Blair, Warthens		170	2	4
John Mathews do		78	22	1
Bryant Allums, Woods		273	23	2
Gabriel Ray, Rushings		246	5	1
Jesse Mills, jr. do.		121	17	1
Malachi Joiner, McLendons		37	22	1
Mary Thomas, w.R.S. Floyds		89	1	2
Ely Brinkley, R. S. do.		60	12	1

(75)

Fortunate Drawers Capts. Dist.	No.	Dt.	Sec.
Daniel Fergason, Gilberts	54	8	2
Samuel Lucas, Warthens	70	12	3

WILKINSON.

James Williams, Curreys	175	8	3
John C. Butler, Fairchilds	45	4	4
Susannah Gainer orph. Smiths	121	14	2
David Mizell, Halls	41	12	5
John Ussery, R. S. Curreys	128	15	1
Sarah Salter, illegit. do	151	27	1
William Bivins R.S. Mandersons	98	11	5
John Eady, R. S. do	7	24	2
Wiley M. Davis do	204	25	1
Isaiah Holmes, Smiths	193	28	1
Lucy Newsom,w.R.S.Fairchilds	366	28	1
Abram Lasseter, Mayos	180	22	1
S. & M. Wm. King orps. Halls	29	7	1

WILKES.

William Maddox, R. S. Moors	189	5	1
William Booker, R. S. Hopkins	277	22	2
Hosea Holtsclaws ors. Greshams	108	8	3
Gideon G. Norman, Ragsdales	216	4	1
John W. Willis' orps. Carters	261	23	2

25th DAY'S DRAWING—April 4th

APPLING.

James Wiley orphan, Collins	143	6	5
William D. Light, Morgans	160	8	4

BALDWIN.

William G. House, Turners	171	2	1
Ann Thornton, widow, Ginns	100	1	1
Christian Jenkins, widow, Thomas	76	3	1
Nathan L. Harriss, Wrights	336	20	2
Christian S. Selby, orphan, Rows	72	19	1
James Scoggin, Thomas	114	1	4

BIBB.

Charles Leith, Bates	96	7	3
Henry B. Hill, do	18	14	1
Patterson Jarratt, soldier, Carrs	159	11	3
M. J. & A. P. Smith, orps., Bates	130	11	1
Charles McGregor, do	101	17	2
Tyre Parrott, Pickards	130	5	2
John Harrison, Bates	240	10	1
William F. Clarke, Rutlands	61	19	1
Jesse Willoughby, do	819	20	2

BRYAN.

William A. Maxwell, do	178	1	4
John Clary, Stephens	128	14	5

BURKE.

John Watts, soldier, Bayleys	198	21	1
Eli Warnock, Wards	234	18	2
Reuben Lively's orphans, Dugas	25	2	5
Izatus Jenkins, Wards	22	19	1
Eliza Bell, orphan, Wests	147	6	3
David D. Travis, soldier, Forths	105	1	3
Solomon Daniel's orphans, Wards	156	15	1

BUTTS.

Avington P. Williams, Hendricks	271	8	5

CHATHAM.

James Dunlap, Haydens	70	23	2
William D Judah	228	2	4
Orphans of Antohony Shaffer, Baines	200	3	1
John D. Street, Tenbrooks	74	13	5
Noble W Jones Bulloch, Geredons	47	15	5
David H. Loper, McDonnells	61	1	4
John Hall,	90	31	1

CLARK.

Fortunate Drawers Capts. Dist.	No.	Dt.	Sec.
Albert Sears, Wrights	71	1	5
William Fuller(McDonalds	182	10	1
Rodman Sisson, Gahagans	84	16	1
Martha Strong, illegitimate, Dickens	239	17	1
John Dawson, Gahagans	257	14	1
Rees Barber, soldier, Davis	44	8	2
William Tolbert, Espys	181	5	1
Falcott G. Smith, Echols	132	2	5
Edward Bowling, R. S., Ransoms	58	22	2
Sherwood Hodges, R. S., Vinsons	127	2	5
William Achin, Gahagans	68	18	1
William Hall, do.	58	6	8

COLUMBIA.

John Durdan's orphans, Adams	88	8	3
John Reeves, R. S., Dranes	243	31	1
Edmund Cartledge, Coles	184	33	1
Nicholas V Prather, Dranes	24	7	2
Stephen Drane, do	117	6	1
Frederick Brown, R.S., Adams	94	22	1
Mary G Pearre, widow, Bealls	176	10	2
Thpomas Morris's orphans, Branes	18	12	5
John Husky, Clarks	83	1	3
Jerusha Wade, widow, Perrys	187	3	1
Elizabeth Harrison,w.R.S.,Talberts	49	11	5
R, S, J, B, E,H.M&M. Hillorps. do.	43	14	2

CRAWFORD.

William Harper, Lovetts	140	15	5
James P. Patterson, Tillers	6	9	3
Samuel Carter, Hamiltons	51	7	1
John Bennett, soldier, Moors	230	7	5
Peter Castleberry, Rhodes	59	20	1
John Kelly, do	101	20	1
Lucus Price, R. S., Hicks	98	24	1

DECATUR.

Nathaniel Pope, Ferrills	235	2	2
Neal Ard's orphans, Douglass	210	17	1
James Coner, do	38	28	1

DE KALB.

Abram Miles, soldier, Harris	182	15	1
William Anderson, Browns	76	15	1
James Nixon, Bakers	244	28	1
Major Waldrope, Conns	73	2	2
Jacob Cobb, soldier, Harris	90	6	3
Brice Ried, Browns	77	12	2
Joseph Minchew, Andersons	2	1	1
Christopher Sewelle, Bakers	19	2	2
Isaac N. Johnson, soldier, Scaifs	139	3	3
Samuel N. Maloney, Bakers	85	14	1
William Bruce, R. S. Merritts	98	1	1
John Patey, for his wife do	7	3	1

EARLY.

Dildatha Odum, Grimsleys	88	16	2
Zachariah Cowart, jr. do	28	24	2

ELBERT.

Nathan Matton, Boltons	42	5	4
John Teasley, Hortons	32	9	2
Simeon Henderson, jr. Blackwells	61	3	2
Robert Smith, Dunns	127	19	1
John Craft, sen. do	203	2	4
Zimry A Tate, Alstons	178	11	1
William Hudson, Tuckers	211	5	5
William Allgood, Butlers	173	17	1
Moses Haynes, Dobbs	241	19	1
Founten Jourden, R. S., Dunne	30	25	1

EMANUEL

Orphans of John Griffis, Fountains	170	15	5
Letis Casey's illegitimate, Swains	45	7	2

(76)

Fortunate Drawers	Capts. Dist.	No.	Dt.	Sec.
Elizzor Cowart, Fountains		114	11	3
Isaac Menshew, Nabbs		110	2	1

FAYETTE.

Wanan C Williams, Roziers		152	2	5
James Hately, Browns		32	13	5
Mat. T Hamilton, sol, McClendons		88	7	1
Sutton H. Haisten, do		100	9	3

FRANKLIN.

Seth Strange, Stranges		89	13	5
Russel J Allen, Jones		151	5	4
George Kitchens, McDonalds		254	11	5
Oswell B. Jones, Boswells		206	13	1
Uriah B. Miller, Jones		278	8	5
Major Neal's orphans, do		164	33	1
George W. White, Boswells		91	24	1
Thomas J Ramsey, Andrews		202	27	1

GLYNN..

Jacob Rumph, Burnetts		280	17	2
William Woodland, do		208	12	3
John Perry, do		121	7	3
Woodford Mabry, do.		168	11	3
Alexander C. Scott, Dubignons		236	2	1

GREENE.

Lewis Wilson, illegit., Southerlands		139	13	1
Thomas G. Jones, Greens		254	10	5
John Park, Webbs		169	25	1
Cullen A. Fretwell, Dawsons		53	11	3

GWINNETT.

Almond Briant, Wallis		68	9	2
Samuel Born, soldier, Moors		132	8	1
Wm. Paton, soldier, Gholstons bat.		82	8	4
Baily Curby, Moors		136	23	1
David Tanner, Davis		274	6	5
Benjamin Rollins, Rollins		165	7	5
Thomas S. Womack, Shippys		143	9	2
James G Williamson, soldier, Moors		35	12	3
Joseph N Plunket, for wife, Whortons		122	1	3
William Thompson, sol., Caruthers		18	3	1
John Hill, Wallis		194	11	2
John Mushborn, R. S., do.		94	7	1
Alexander B. Campbell, Shippys		41	14	1
John Butler, Finchers		181	25	1
John Mcane, Caruthers		247	25	1

HABERSHAM.

William C. Wyley, Langstons		273	8	5
Sarah Hulsey, wid. R. S., Bryans		198	18	2
Edward Harris, Langstons		425	20	2
William Hughes, Suttons		169	5	5
Reuben Perkins, Cross		152	3	3
James C. Hetton, Kenzies		3	7	3
Benjamin Davis's orphans, Suttons		15	15	1
Abel Taylor, Langstons		249	11	3
Henry Martain, Cross		126	30	1
Elijah Chaffin, Kenzies		210	28	1
Minors of Jonathan Coggin, Cross		180	31	1

HALL.

Stephen Clayton, jr Walkers		172	22	1
Harrel Padget, Hardens		184	24	1
Hiram Liles do		43	14	1
I., H E J D., J D Freelan, Roberts		6	18	1
Alexander Smith's orphans, Yagers		157	9	5
David Humphrey, Smiths		221	17	2
Henry Bell, Floyds		255	8	1
Benjamin Rouse, Garrards		252	6	5
William Edwards, Dorseys		240	29	1
Levi L. Mason, illegit., Hardages		120	22	1

HANCOCK.

Fortunate Drawers	Capts. Dist.	No.	Dt.	Sec.
Burwell Brown, 101st		12	14	2
Henry Edwards, 108th		143	5	1
William Terrell, soldier, Adams		133	4	4
Daniel Greene, 116th		236	18	1
Elizabeth Williams widow, 108th		31	16	1
John J. Bass, Mahons		68	18	2
Elijah Brantley, 113th		70	12	2
John K Nelson, Adams		134	11	3
Hamlin L. Wade, 104th		120	10	3
John Lucas, 102d		161	7	5
Benjamin S. Tarver, 117th		207	2	4
Joseph W. Curtis, 102d		244	2	4

HENRY.

Branch Liggan, Shaws		122	3	3
Silas Yarbrough, do		295	10	2
William Drake, Harriss		150	3	1
Edward Britt, R S., Millers		80	3	2
John Lovejoy, Wards		69	19	2
William Taylor, R. S., Shaws		3	2	3
Mary Greene, wid R S do		1	7	2

HOUSTON.

Sarah Frost, widow, Hancocks		97	15	2

IRWIN.

Joshua Platt, Underwoods		43	12	5
John Gibbs, McCalls		29	12	1

JACKSON.

Stephen C Durham, Duprees		221	16	1
Amos Brooks, Landrums		44	12	1
Elias W Dunaway, illegit, Duncans		130	2	5
Charles Gravett, Rogers		62	22	2
John Flanigan, soldier, Georges		3	12	5
Henry Walston, sen. Bowens		18	14	5
Joseph J Pollard, Storys		249	5	2
Francis Hobson, Allens		74	31	
William Thompson, R S., Venables		176	15	1

JASPER.

John C Johnson, Sparks		212	41	1
John Malone, Dardens		130	4	4
Seaborn Jones, Sparks		5	3	4
Alexander Hawkins, Wilders		274	4	3
Henry Howard, Owens		254	28	1
Reuben C Shorter, Holmes		187	5	1
Willis Seats, Robinsons		118	19	2
Elias Osburn, Keys		200	9	5
Sarah Brown, orphan, Camerons		154	4	4
Larkin Newby, Owens		103	12	2
Joseph Beavers, Keys		22	9	1
John Buck, Shropshiers		154	31	1

JEFFERSON.

Anderson Allen, Cunninghams		82	19	2
Samuel Landon, orphan, Ross		167	5	4
Alsa Sinquefield, sol. Cunninghams		214	6	2
Ezekiel Arrington, Ross		74	17	2
Burrel J. Brown's orps. Cunninghams		380	28	1

JONES.

Mark Snipes, Stewart		216	1	2
Wm. Stephens, Dosters		127	4	1
Jeremiah Martin, Robertsons		223	5	5
Mary Stephens, wid. Dosters		177	32	1
Ezekiel Pattersons ors. Duncans		185	9	1
George G.F. Mitchell, Mullins		174	4	2
James J. Carson, Bowens		191	27	1
John Smiths minors, do		190	10	3
John Perry, Robertsons		274	5	1
Josiah Calhouns minors, Bowens		64	7	4

LAND LOTTERY REGISTER—No. 12.
[RECORDER OFFICE—PUBLISHED BY GRANTLAND & ORME—PRICE $3.]

NOTE—Section 1 is Lee County—2 Muscogee—3 Troup—4 Coweta—5 Carroll.
25th *DAY'S DRAWING*—Continued

Fortunate Drawers Capts. Dist.	No.Dt.Sec.		
LAURENS.			
Reason Spell, Plummers	182	5	2
Jefferson Anderson, Whiteheads	141	12	5
Wm. Hester (idiot,) Powers	78	20	1
Abraham Lamb, sol. Hodges	100	23	1
Osborn Beckham, Plummers	151	33	1
LIBERTY.			
Timothy Hubberd, 17th	162	5	4
Samuel Jones, 15th	145	5	5
John F. Sandeford, 17th	26	9	3
Joseph Smith, 16th	92	28	1
Isham Leigh orphan 16th	235	6	3
LINCOLN.			
Daniel Hammock, Graves	55	14	2
Lewis Guice, Lonorgans	89	15	2
John Moss, sr. sol. Wiggintons	161	6	2
Thomas Glaze, Frazers	172	21	2
MADISON.			
Elizabeth Lumpkin, h.ab.Bones	52	10	3
A. Thompsons mins.f.a. Hannas	12	11	3
Willis Stephens illegit. do	138	2	1
Abraham Whitaker, Adairs	163	10	2
Thomas J. Parks, Bones	20	10	1
M'INTOSH.			
Silas Fulton, Demeries	99	3	3
MONROE.			
Joseph T. Robertson, J. Millers	183	1	2
Angus Johnson, R. S. Houses	226	1	2
Allen Congliton, Browns	220	14	1
George Willis' orps. Wrights	169	30	1
David Bivins, Greshams	76	23	1
Blany Griffin, Knights	245	3	3
Solomon Hobbs, Greshams	283	1	4
Thomas B. Aldridge, Houses	208	11	2
James Lathranis' orps. Wrights	42	2	5
Roderick Rutland, Browns	190	10	5
James Cotton orphan, Millers	83	5	1
William Brown, Turners	301	10	2
John D. Chappell, Pattersons	263	17	2
Josiah Hudgins, Stallings	60	22	1
Laban Lawrence, Douglass	76	6	5
Edward Freeman, Pattersons	177	4	1
Mathew Pool, Douglass	222	15	2
James Norriss, Stallings	206	10	5
MORGAN.			
Wm. Claiborn, soldier, Browns	170	24	1
Abraham Whitaker, Watsons	200	4	3
Graves Harris, R. S. Sparks	221	19	2
Malachier Stallings, Adairs	129	18	1
Silas Sanders, Jennings	216	15	1
Charles Weeks, R. S. Adairs	43	17	1
Asa Peal, Harwells	116	7	5
David Shaw, Sparks	118	22	2
Robert Guthrie, Canifaxs	8	2	1
William B. Howard, Baileys	28	12	2
Prudence Perrys illegs. Watsons	226	14	2
Elizabeth Beavers, w.R.S.Stokes	89	22	2

Fortunate Drawers Capts. Dist.	No.Dt.Sec.		
William Finleys, orps. Baileys	48	20	1
MONTGOMERY.			
Jacob Pope, Popes	40	18	2
NEWTON.			
John R. Wester, Pullens	284	20	2
John Carlisle, Snows	156	21	2
Jin.,I.,M.,E.,N., Ed.,&Cynthia Dees orphans, Hays	182	22	1
Timothy Lee, R. S. Clarks	156	4	1
Richard Long, soldier, Bakers	162	13	2
Joel Manns orps. Penningtons	201	6	5
William Stanford, Moss's	203	15	1
William Parish, Webbs	97	32	1
OGLETHORPE.			
Peter Goolsbys orps. Lacys	5	19	2
William Brown, Arnolds	96	4	2
Rachel Talley, widow, Lacys	89	15	1
John C. Short, Rhodes	184	2	4
Adeline F. Williams, Decks	197	10	2
Allen, Pye, Lacys	56	7	4
Sarah Martin, widow, Hills	95	2	3
Obadiah Thomson, B. Hills	174	19	1
Isaac A. Howard, Rousseaus	28	30	1
Harvin Kent, Lacys	46	32	1
PIKE.			
Ginnethon Crawley,, Suiters	118	12	3
PULASKI.			
Caleb Fullington, Thomas'	105	12	2
John Rogers, Bracewells	231	23	2
Elizabeth Haddock, w. Sparrows	90	4	1
PUTNAM.			
Albert Winchil, Brooks	168	20	2
Christopher Parker, Chambers	59	8	3
Mourning Norris, wid. Blounts	208	4	3
David Coalman, soldier, Goods	121	11	3
John Tinsley, Sawyers	102	12	1
Philip J. Eccols, Jones	159	12	1
Peter Blount, Blounts	118	2	5
Green Wiggins, Duprees	230	19	1
Eliza. Smiths, minors, Sanders	70	7	2
Richard Fielders, orps. Stinsons	86	32	1
Vinson Thompson, sol. Lamars	2	20	1
RICHMOND.			
Nathaniel Brown, Treadwells	50	1	3
Nancy Ann Martin orp. Wilcoxs	105	16	2
V. P. Anderson orphan, Mantzs	141	7	2
Bennet Bomans orphs., Wilcoxs	239	24	1
Edmund Stucky, soldier, Seges	21	9	2
Isaac Netherlin, Kellys	43	15	2
John P. Force, Ferris	21	3	1
David P. Hays orps. Roberts	102	2	3
SCRIVEN.			
William T. Gould, Treadwells	120	5	1
Henry Best, Hunters	173	29	1
TATTNALL.			
James Robison, Dees	260	12	3
TELFAIR			
Jonathan Coker, Wilkersons	11	1	2
Charles Numans, Clements	258	6	5

(78)

Fortunate Drawers Capts. Dist.	No.	Dt.	Sec.
William Ashley, sr. Lampkins	219	9	3
TALIAFERRO.			
John P. White, Moores	25	5	5
Wm. B. Johnson, Alfords	189	6	3
THOMAS.			
Dempsey Wood, jr.	107	17	2
TWIGGS.			
Jacob Lewis, (F.) Wimberlys	22	2	5
Daniel Stuckey, Pearsons	56	15	2
James D. Edwards, Blackshears	171	15	5
William Peters, R. S. Wimberlys	44	7	4
Orps.ofT. Westbrook, Holidays	252	3	2
James Lunsford, Blackshears	92	6	3
Silas Clark, (F.) Graggs	123	29	1
UPSON.			
James Tilman, Hattaxs	166	32	1
Jonathan Pray, do	104	6	3
James Culvers orps. Harrells	71	7	2
WALTON.			
William Burks, R. S. 418th	107	6	2
Jesset Goolsby, 559th	24	9	5
James Love, 250th	130	7	2
Elihu Smith, 249th	29	4	3
John F. Tomlinson, Rays	72	4	3
Jesse H. Davis, McQuertors	148	2	3
Bethany Arnold, w. R. S. Rays	188	23	2
James McCarty, McQuertors	158	3	4
James W. Dorithy, Rays	80	20	2
George K. Hamilton, do	39	1	3
Lem.&Em. McCord, ills. 559th	229	2	3
Harington Philips, Pools	115	1	5
Ann Baker, w. R. S. Aays	214	5	4
WARE.			
Josiah Sirmon, Moats	2	19	1
Robert Touchstone, ill. Bryans	197	4	2
John R. Stone, do	322	22	1
WARREN.			
Randolph G. Lacy, Brinkleys	43	23	2
Ed. Hayse, woun.inI.w. Kinseys	55	6	5
Francis A. Martin, do	102	26	1
Robert Atteway, Adkins	120	2	4
Daniel Yates, Kinseys	161	21	2
David Martin, R. S. Adkins	186	3	3
Asa McCrary, Jones	179	6	3
Isaiah Tuckers orps. Parhams	7	2	1
Levid Williford, Bulls	56	2	4
WASHINGTON.			
Benjamin Skrines heirs, Floyds	224	5	5
John Manning, Warthens	189	19	1
Fere. Hartley, w.R.S. McLendons	27	13	2
Barachias Massey, Floyds	52	13	2
Cuthbert Ferrel orph. Rushings	182	7	1
John Holland, do	234	1	1
Arnold Cone, Wimberlys	105	20	1
Joel Albritton, Woods	165	24	1
Federick Tyson,jr.McLendons	115	11	5
Shadrach Carter, Whitfields	27	16	2
James Oliver, Gilberts	71	16	2
John Webb, Floyds	51	19	1
John Pitmans heirs, Rushings	149	7	3
Ada Deen, Gilberts	189	3	4

Fortunate Drawers Capts. Dist.	No.	Dt.	Sec.
Isham Nowell, Mannings	114	8	5
Miles D. Cullens, Floyds	241	9	5
James Singleton, Warthens	188	22	1
Amos Albriton, Woods	172	12	5
WILKINSON.			
Henry Adkerson,R.S. Mathews	153	4	2
Thomas B. Allcut, Halls	144	17	2
William Lord, R. S. Mathews	245	23	2
Dicy Mathews,w.R. S. do	104	5	4
Robert Butler, Halls	38	27	1
Miles Sanders, Curreys	159	18	2
James Boggs, Shows	66	1	3
Larkin Barfield, Smiths	126	3	3
James Ballard,jr.Mandersons	47	11	5
John S. Ard, Smiths	142	26	1
WILKES.			
Camilla Harris illeg. Hopkins	45	12	3
John Psalmons orps. Ragsdales	259	10	2
Fielder Auston, Amasons	170	17	2
David Evans, Rices	104	8	4
Robert Armor, Sol. Amasons	63	5	3
Thomas A. Carter, sol. Charltons	75	14	1
Mary C. Griffin, h. ab. Hopkins	10	5	2
Cary Cotten, Washingtons	141	2	3
Polly Lockhart, widow, Lukers	155	27	1
John Hood, R. S. Reeves	182	29	1

26th DAY'S DRAWING—April 5th.

BALDWIN.

	No.	Dt.	Sec.
Williams Rutherford, Bivins	47	24	1
Thomas Peters, Thomas	76	8	4
Willis Beckwith, soldier, Wrights	52	18	2
John Lawrence, orphan, Lesters	190	9	2
John W. H. Dawson, illegit. Bivins	92	5	4
Orphans of Jonathan Thomas, Thomas	50	14	5
John H. Curry, Pitts	26	17	1

BIBB.

	No.	Dt.	Sec.
Leighton Thompson, Beards	101	12	3
Solomon Williby, Lloyds	164	29	1
William Pace's orphans, Carrs	182	14	1
Joseph Willet, Flanders	71	13	1
Michael Whatley, R. S., Pickards	248	3	2
Thomas Lundy, soldier, Beards	53	2	1
Alexander Scott, Swearingens	71	19	2
Benjamin Cobb, Beards	161	16	2
Patience Smith, orphan, Swearingens	228	9	5
Clement Clements, R. S., Lloyds	91	8	1

BULLOCH.

	No.	Dt.	Sec.
Samuel Cox, Lockharts	374	3	4

BURKE.

	No.	Dt.	Sec.
Sarah Collins, widow, Bayleys	98	28	1
Elizabeth Bargaron, w. R. S., Lewis	89	26	1
Stephen W. Blount,sr.sol. Robinsons	226	22	1
John Knight, Brooms	271	3	1
Mathew E. Slain, orphan, McKays	40	19	1
Mary Ann Lewis widow, Rogers	228	13	1
James McCroan's orphans, do	117	19	1
David Daniel, Brooms	200	12	1
Henry Rutherford, Wests	209	2	1
Evin C. Glisson, Dugas	143	7	5
Drewcilla Hale, widow R.S.Corkers	165	1	1
James Rogers, Fountains	61	15	1
Amelia Wynn, widow, Rogers	230	32	1

(79)

Fortunate Drawers	Capts. Dist.	No.	Dt.	Sec.

BUTTS.

Fortunate Drawers	Capts. Dist.	No.	Dt.	Sec.
Susan Thrash, widow,	Adams	41	9	1
Robert Andrews,	Kirksies	216	3	5
William Bankston,	Johnsons	122	7	2
John Wooten, soldier,	Kirksies	136	21	2
Micajah Andrews,	Robisons	14	33	1
William H. Strahan,	Hendricks	189	12	1

CAMDEN.

John Bailey,	Beckwiths	239	6	5

CHATHAM.

Orphans of D. R. Densler,	Nungazers	188	25	1
Rebecca Mollett, widow,	Baines	204	12	5
Edward Padelford,	Haydens	289	20	2
William Thomas,	Baines	101	21	1
Absalom Burdin,	McDonnells	225	9	2
Miles C. Phillips,	Geredons	192	1	2
James Oliver, soldier,	Scotts	218	13	2
Major Peter Deveaux, R. S.,	Haydens	167	32	1
Michael Dillon,	do	270	2	3

CLARK.

Thomas Epps,	Dickens	5	27	1
Tabitha Salter, widow,	Gahagans	216	22	1
Hiram H. Embry,	Davis	148	22	1
Robert Camron,	Andersons	207	9	5
Elizabeth Harris, idot,	do	278	7	1
Malinda Cagle, widow,	Herndons	123	10	2

COLUMBIA.

Michael H. Megahee,	Dranes	328	7	1
Obadiah S. Morris,	do	44	6	4
Orps. of Westley Lorance,	Stallings	241	11	1
William Beaird,		160	4	3
Frances & Napoleon B. Ryan,	Perrys	208	2	1
Thomas Dooly,	Talbots	294	7	1

CRAWFORD.

E., J., J., & E.Fulsome,illegits.	Tillers	73	4	1
Jacob Presnall,	Wilsons	206	23	1

DECATUR.

John Waters, soldier,	Douglas	225	3	1
Joel Cook,	Hawthorns	63	7	3

DE KALB.

Gardner Carter's orphans,	Hays	176	12	2
William Wodall,	Howells	266	1	4
James Martin, R. S.,	Merritts	294	22	1
Meredith Collier,	do	225	22	1
Samuel Dodson, soldier,	Harris	297	7	5
Thomas Davis,	Bakers	199	23	2
Henry W. M. Daniel,	Stephens	225	28	1
William Akins, soldier,	Andersons	62	30	1

DOOLY.

Thomas Adams,	Andersons	102	23	2
Benjamin Stegall,	do	37	6	2
Joel Williams,	Sarrs	98	19	2
Samuel P. Bond,	Hogans	99	16	2

EARLY.

Michael Lightnor,	Hairs	85	1	4
Julius Weaver,	Grimsleys	159	3	5

EFFINGHAM.

Jane Douglass's illegitimate,	Edwards	10	33	1
Catharine Snyder, wid.,	Waldhaners	156	1	1
Micajah Futrell, soldier,	Elkins	29	2	4
Hannah Thomas, widow,	Stricklands	220	7	5

ELBERT.

Lindscy Smith,	Boltons	134	10	1
Jesse C. Tate,	Tates	211	2	3
Joseph Cunningham,	Blackwells	106	5	3
William Cheek,	Merritts	101	10	3
Joseph Griffin's orphans,	Boltons	136	12	3

Fortunate Drawers	Capts. Dist.	No.	Dt.	Sec.
Elizabeth Carter,w.R.S.,	Blackwells	115	3	2
Isaac Wright,	Dunns	35	24	1

FAYETTE.

James McInvaye,	9th	68	5	4
John C Davis,	Roziers	204	12	1
Henry Carter's orphans,	Craigs	355	28	1
James Stewart,	Wests	87	29	1

FRANKLIN.

Peter Walters, R S,	Blankinships	178	9	2
Robert Fleming, R S	Sanders	92	33	1
Jesse Caudell,	Caudells	138	5	2
Tempy Manly wid. R S,	Cokers	77	1	1
Jacob Groover,	Blankinships	12	20	2
William Glover,	do.	31	24	2
William Pullian, R. S.	do.	315	20	2
Peter J Walters,	do	23	4	3
William Dailey,	Jones	61	4	4
Joel Ford,	do	22	4	2
Mary Bellamy, wid. R. S.,	Stranges	221	9	3
Whitfield Brown,	Sanders	135	3	2
Riley Wilkinson,illegit.	Blonkinships	190	1	2
Absalom Cleveland, R S,	Stephens	110	8	1

GLYNN.

William Summerlin,	Barnetts	122	1	2
Henry Turner,	McLeods	238	19	1

GREENE.

William Hawkins,	Elys,	211	1	2
Nathan Tally,	Mercers	152	11	5
Hannah Sesson,w. R. S.,	Colcloughs	93	18	2
Thomas Greer's orphans,	Robinsons	222	16	2
Elizabeth Stewart,w. R S.,	Rankins	1	3	5
William Clark,jr.	Woodhams	144	4	1
Jane Stoulamire, widow,	Robins	150	21	2
A. K. Craig,	Woodhams	188	9	2
Rhoda Parrish,wid. R. S.,	Robins	101	4	3
Mary E. T. Mounger,orp.	Dawsons	158	21	1
John Thompson's orps	Southerlands	106	15	2

GWINNETT.

Alexander Stephenson,	Caruthers	22	14	1
Nathan Jester,	Rollins	201	30	1
Henry Franklin,	Davis	104	21	2
Balla Pruitt,	Greens	229	32	1
Eph. Thompson,sol.,	Gholstons bat.	4	21	2
Osten Morris,R.S.,	Robertsons	129	5	5
Archibald Leitch,	Woodroughs	114	5	4
Hezekiah Compton's orphans,	Moors	126	9	5
Charles Bradford,	Whartous	47	1	5
Hiram Lott,	Bakers	117	4	1
James Anderson,	Greens	163	15	2
James F Rucks,	do	113	19	2
Seaborn Thorn,	Caruthers	38	23	2
Susanna Brumbalo, illegit.,	Shippys	182	4	1
Eli Massey,	Hunicuts	98	7	3
Thomas Wood,	Bakers	19	10	3

HABERSHAM.

Elijah Pirkins,	Cross	71	13	2
John Sanders,soldier,	Faines	281	22	2
Isaac Anderson,	Tates	237	21	1
Marmsdule Vickery,	Vickerys	78	5	4
George Headrick,	do	158	11	5
Thomas Thomas,	Cross	56	8	5
Benjamin Jones,	do	136	16	2
James R. Peek,	Kenzies	127	18	2
Abraham Littlejohn,	Faines	135	8	4
James Bruce, jun.	Suttons	76	5	5
John Nix, soldier,	Bryans	124	9	5
Celah Jenkins, wid R.S.,	Bakers	17	6	1

(80)

HALL.

Fortunate Drawers	Capts.	Dist.	No.	Dt.	Sec.
Beal Baker, R. S., Hardens			172	32	1
Alexander M. Henderson, Smiths			56	19	2
John Nicholson,jr. Alreds			211	4	3
McNeest Rodgers,Roberts			162	15	2
William Smith's orphans, Yagers			115	12	5
John Shaw, R. S., Garrards			15	16	1
John Rich, Roberts			208	9	3
Mathew Leach, Hardens			64	3	3
George Gordon, Garrards			122	12	2
Lazarus Wood, Hardages			41	21	2
James Smallwood, Harrisons			105	16	1

HANCOCK.

Moreland Lupo, 108th	96	2	5
Lucinda Garrett, illegitimate, 117th	72	1	5
John Palemore, 103d	129	10	2
Pilot H. Edwards, 104th	391	7	1

HENRY.

Min, Ann&Lav.Biffle, ills. T. Hanes	100	18	1
Smith Barron, Harriss	101	5	5
John M Russell, Grays	142	3	1

HOUSTON.

John Boyd, Moores	38	10	2
Aquilla Scott, Calhouns	101	22	1
William Norris, sen. Smiths	49	8	2
William Norris, do	232	9	3
Perry Wimberly, Moores	215	12	3
Martin Johnson, R S.,, Becks	96	22	2

IRWIN.

William Taylor's orphans, Dixens	159	2	5
Lewis Wagner, do	34	31	1

JACKSON.

Alexander Flanegan, Venables	148	12	5
George Cowan, sen R. S., Lindseys	148	13	2
Thomas L Stapler, Staplers	25	13	1
Samuel Chrismess's orps Gathrights	176	5	3
Lloyd W Shackelford, Millers	96	3	2
Sarah Trout, widow, Allens	124	6	1
John B. Carnes, Winns	91	33	1

JASPER.

Sarah Ann R Aikins, fa. ab. Butts	140	8	3
James Scott, Shropshiers	190	26	1
Benjamin H Montgomery, Camerons	285	20	2
Welcome Parks, Holmes	170	14	1
Asa E. Stratten, Shropshiers	76	22	2
Polly Harris, widow, Parkers	103	2	4
Martha Ann Wright, illegit., Hands	13	1	2
Mordecai Hill, R S., Sparks	179	4	2
George Jordan, Dardens	94	10	2
Russel Maxey, do	167	7	4
William Miller, Parkers	8	21	2
William D Delaney, Holmes	64	22	2
Emanuel Teal, R. S., Wilsons	95	21	1
Henry Ellis, Parker	69	6	5
Catharine Findley, hus. absent, Keys	148	3	1
Woody, Dozier, jr. Holmes	128	19	1
William Reedy, Barnetts	32	7	3

JEFFERSON.

Edward Pervis's orphans, Beatys	161	10	5
Orphans of Elias Hodges, Elliotts	236	5	4
John Bostick, Jones	55	4	2
Frederick Fountain, Waldens	117	4	5
Daniel London, Ross	225	29	1
L. Fontain, w. R. S. Cunninghams	331	8	1
Willis Howard, R. S. Beatys	130	22	2
William Jones, Jones	214	7	3
Henry Fontain's orps. Cunninghams	188	29	1

JONES.

Fortunate Drawers	Capts.	Dist.	No.	Dt.	Sec.
John B Dame, Newby's			51	12	5
William Cook, soldier, Burkes			112	4	4
Arthur Finney's orphans, Breedloves			17	15	5
Benjamin H Reynolds, do			170	19	1
William O Banyan's orps. Davis			16	5	3
Moses Stripling, do			233	25	1
James A. Delaunay, R S., Breedloves			21	4	2

LAURENS.

Joseph J Battle, Barlows	252	1	2
Andrew McDaniel, Spivys	210	11	2
Bennet Joiner, Beachams	96	9	2
Martha A Tyson, arphon, Plummers	187	9	5
Mary McDaniel, widow, Spivys	85	8	4
James Kemp, Deans	139	1	3
Charity Harrison, w. R. S., Powers	109	10	1

LIBERTY.

William B. Flemming, 14th	92	17	1

LINCOLN.

Jacob Solly, Parks	125	7	1
Nancy Trammels illegs. Hardys	220	19	2
Mark Shipp, Levritts	186	18	1

MADISON.

John Melicans orps. Hannas	114	17	2
John M. Williford, Christians	46	8	4
William Simmons orphans,do	54	25	1

McINTOSH.

Isaac Snow, Terrells	179	10	5

MONROE.

William Ogletree, R. S. Houses	30	27	1
David Shepperd, sol. Rights	138	5	5
William Stallings, Stallings	180	14	2
William Foster,	57	1	5
James Gates orphs. Douglass	222	3	2
William Davis, Wrights	160	10	2
Wm. M. White, Browns	60	20	2
John Miller, Millers	120	5	3
Enoch Crabbs orps. Finchs	143	20	2
Isaac Furgason, Greshams	212	3	3
Elijah Stephens, Finchs	168	14	2
William A. Adams, Houses	131	10	5
David Crawford,soldier,Houses	179	10	1
Alfred Brooks, Millers	216	7	3

MORGAN.

Seth G. Walton, Browns	172	5	1
Jesse Haralson, Watsons	25	1	2
Milton Akins, Jennings	219	17	2
Math. Mitchells orphs. Hitchcocks	66	25	2
Lancelot Johnston, sol. Walkers	135	15	5
James Parker, Christians	132	9	1
Joseph Parks ors. Boswells	43	31	1
Willie Buke, Christians	64	33	1

MONTGOMERY.

Wm. Clark, Popes	172	33	1

NEWTON.

Reuben Tidwell, Graves	184	13	2
William Belsber, do	7	1	3
Wm. G. Worrell,jr. Snows	36	13	1
Abraham G. Tucker, Pullens	166	4	2
Martha Howard, wid. Graces	192	9	3
Nancy Hamby, wid. Zachrys	44	1	1
William Fannin, sol. Bakers	111	7	1
Mary Costley,h. ab. Summers	62	29	1

(81)

Fortunate Drawers	Capts.	Dist.	No.	Dt.	Sec.
J., L. & J. Wyatt illegs.	Askews		207	21	1
OGLETHORPE.					
Rich. Rhodes, R.S.	Rhodes'		100	8	2
Christopher Bowen,	Hills		24	2	5
Sherwood Wise,	Lacys		71	8	5
James Thomas orph.	Burfords		47	5	5
James Young, sr.	R.S.Bells		128	27	1
Isham Cheatham, sol.	Billups		206	24	1
Samuel Hardman, sol.	Simmons		61	2	5
James Jones,dry fork,	Arnolds		130	18	2
James H. Ravins,	Williamsons		138	27	1
PIKE.					
Hubbar P. Heard,	Daniels		199	20	2
Salley Mitchells illegits.	Hicks		243	1	4
Elizabeth James, wid.	Daniels		178	23	2
Isham Morris,	Longs		94	4	3
Elizabeth Bull, w. R. S.	Hicks		193	10	2
Willis Jinks,	Mays		203	21	1
PULASKI.					
Lovet P. Fan,	Thomas'		241	6	5
John Readon,	Scarbroughs		167	20	1
James Little,	Gilstraps		67	20	1
John Smiths children,	Sparrows		217	10	2
PUTNAM.					
Mahali Barnharts illegits.	Clarks		124	1	5
William Bailey,	Sawyers		196	12	1
James Estes,	Hailes		285	15	1
Rowland B. Cook,	Blacks		184	2	5
John Kendrick,	Wilks		71	5	3
Sarah Purdue, w. R. S.	Goods		202	14	1
James Griggs,	Allums		252	16	1
RABUN.					
James Rogers,	Becks		192	12	2
RICHMOND.					
Sarah Moore, orph.	Treadwells		215	4	1
Frederick Morgan,	do		64	14	1
Gregory O. Green,	Ferris		147	21	1
Ann Power, wid.	Huntingtons		198	1	1
David Bowles,	Wilcoxs		276	5	1
Benner Bomans orps.	Wilcoxs		191	13	1
SCRIVEN.					
William Freeman ill.	Robberts		230	6	2
James Shepherd,	Stricklings		137	7	3
Michael Doughtry,	Kemps		28	1	3
TATTNALL.					
Elizabeth Donold, wid.	Conners		89	12	5
Sarah Conner, w.R.S.	Dees		296	3	4
Joshua Dasher,	McCalls		276	20	2
Charles Arnold,	Graces		29	3	5
Jacob Yerty orphan,	do		100	10	1
TELFAIR.					
David Edinfield,jr.	Wilsons		145	27	1
Joseph Wililams, R. S.	Lamkins		205	3	4
TALIAFERRO.					
James Chivers orphans,	Cobbs		75	5	4
Henry Stamps,	Hammocks		30	24	2
John Sagus,	Echols		215	32	1
TWIGGS.					
Priscilla Jackson,w.Streetmans			72	25	1
Elias Phillips,	Pearsons		50	10	1
Abel Daniel,	Bosticks		323	3	4

Fortunate Drawers	Capts.	Dist.	No.	Dt.	Sec.
R.A.P.McWilliams ill.	Bosticks		244	10	3
UPSON.					
James Duke, sol.	Ezells		186	9	2
John Ellis,	Harrells		178	2	5
Robert Johnson,	Myricks		150	12	3
WALTON.					
Samuel Lackey,	Pools		223	14	2
Lewis J. Rigsby,	Bixleys		143	15	2
William Blair, 250th			87	15	1
Jonathan B Ellis,	Davis'		160	20	2
Henry Jones,	Bixleys		26	19	1
James Love, R. S. 250th			68	2	1
George J. Dodd, soldier,	Snows		182	4	2
WAYNE.					
Gimiah Ammons ill.	Mannings		169	1	1
Duncan Bohanon,	Staffords		18	8	3
WARREN.					
John Moore,	Bulls		92	11	5
Frederick Newsom,	Adkins		85	5	5
Lewis Jackson,	Brinkleys		74	7	1
John Wilson, R. S.	Rogers		195	12	2
William Harbuck,	Bulls		242	4	3
Charles H. Bayne,	Sanders		127	6	3
John Snider,	Downs		30	6	3
Rachel Persons,w.R.S.	Hills		148	10	2
Lucy Silas illegit.	Sanders		142	32	1
Warren Darden,	Hills		20	31	1
WASHINGTON.					
Collins Hardy,	Oquins		244	20	1
James Dickens,	Warthens		37	4	3
John H. Osborne,	Floyds		209	12	5
Sarah Farmer,	Whitfields		175	11	3
Burwell Saunders sol.	Warthens		291	28	1
Sarah Weston,wid.	Mannings		167	3	4
Spencer Brantley,	McLendons		253	11	1
English Smith, sol.	Castelows		88	1	1
Laban Horton,	Oquins		73	3	5
Robert Dickens,	Warthens		161	7	1
William Northington,	Currys		217	17	2
John Hardie,	Mannings		167	8	1
Abraham Bailey,	Warthens		244	21	1
Caroline Parker illegit.	Currys		117	15	1
WILKINSON.					
John Ussery, R. S.	Currys		123	10	5
Hawley Lizenby orph.	Shows		33	4	2
Sarah Morgan, wid.	Fairchilds		184	6	2
Robert Goode,	Halls		174	16	2
Lewis Jones,	Smiths		6	2	2
Alexander Doke,	Mandersons		249	6	5
Phebe Gainor, w.R. S.	Smiths		147	8	1
Rach'l Williams, w.	Mandersons		114	20	1
William Moss illegit.	Currys		301	15	1
William Allday,	Halls		258	10	2
John Waller,	Fairchilds		64	11	2
F. & Jane Shearer orps.	Mayos		101	26	1
Mathew Wicker, sol.	Barrys		28	23	1
WILKES.					
John Smith, R. S.	Hamocks		94	4	1
John L. Flournoy,	Washingtons		38	2	3

Fortunate Drawers Capts. Dist.	No.	Dt.	Sec.
Richard Mattoxs orps. do	206	9	5
James Combs orps. Charltons	3	6	3
Frances Proctor, wid. Moors	168	7	1
Cornelius Slaton, Rices	220	3	1
James O. Burdett, Lukers	56	33	1
William H. White, do	245	3	1
Ann Rutledge, wid Washingtons	55	4	1

27th DAY'S DRAWING—April 6th

BAKER.

Fortunate Drawers Capts. Dist.	No.	Dt.	Sec.
Armager Hall, soldier, Porters	74	23	1

BALDWIN.

Mathew Jourdan, Bivins	108	2	4
Ann Melhado, widow, Doles	194	3	3
Rachel, L. Fair, widow, Rows	100	13	2
James Murry's orphans father died in late war, Bivins	219	9	5

BIBB.

S M. & V A. Minor, orps. Bates	24	10	1
Timothy Dunning, do	3	8	5
C.E.A.&P.Dorrenton,orsPickards	212	8	1
Elizabeth Hixon, window Carrs	32	28	1

BRYAN.

Edward Footman, Stephens	57	17	2

BULLOCH.

Jer. Haymon's orps. Richardsons	356	20	2
Martin T. Miller, Deloachs	22	9	2

BURKE.

Martha Guinn, orphan, Andersons	38	20	1
Leaston Sneed, Corkers	4	14	2
Samuel Foster, Brooms	85	5	4
S.&C. McClainy, orps. Corkers	118	15	5
William West, Seegars	247	18	1
Howell D. Burke, Baileys	211	2	4
Benjamin Ratfief, orphan, Dugas	115	6	1
Andrew B. Lawson, MaKays	56	12	5
C.C.&H.Hubbard, orps. Corkers	127	5	2
William H. Hughes, Robinsons	122	2	4

BUTTS.

James C. Horton. Adams	163	2	4

CAMDEN.

Lewis Lasserre, Wards	168	18	2

CHATHAM.

Ors. of Hugh McLeod, Geredons	188	12	1
John M Warland, Savannah	63	5	5
Orps. of C. Thrower, McDonnells	218	2	5
John Evrighand, jr. Baines	184	2	1
Mary E Allen, widow, Reeds	113	3	3
Eliza A. Mears, orp Geredons	256	7	1
Orphans of Hugh McLeod, do.	42	27	1

CLARK.

Thomas Cawley's orps. Dickens	164	4	1
Fryer Robertson, R. S. Herndons	13	14	2
Mary Wright, widow, Wrights	134	1	3
Abel Fleming, do.	84	9	1
Beverly A. Duke, McDonalds	147	11	3
Tabitha Wilson, widow, Frosts	44	9	1
Miles Jones, Ransoms	4	16	1

COLUMBIA.

Anderson Campbell, Adams	237	2	4
Jesse Morris, sen. R. S., Tolberts	110	5	4
Hardy Hunter's orphans, Coles	159	8	4

CRAWFORD.

Fortunate Drawers Capts. Dist.	No.	Dt.	Sec.
James Shaw, Carrolls	203	1	1
David Brown, Rays	192	23	1

DE KALB.

Henry Mitchell, Baker	72	10	2

EARLY.

Henry F. Mercer, Wilsons	165	12	2
Michael A. Henderson, Porters	32	19	1
James Elliott, Wilsons	152	12	1

EFFINGHAM.

Tabitha Vaughter, illegit. Edwards	57	22	2
Jane Douglas's illegitimates, do	94	10	1

ELBERT.

Whitehead Hendrick, Merritts	59	6	3
ames Coleman, Tates	91	11	1
Francis Hilly, soldier, Hortons	210	12	3
Isaac Alexander's orphans, Dunns	131	17	2
William H. Parker, Merritts	69	7	3
Nathaniel H. Nelms, Hortons	304	10	2
Nancy Murry, widow, do	6	20	2
Thos. D. Wooldridge, Carpenters	192	9	5
Thomas W. Mabury, Dunns	5	23	1
John Fitts" orphans, Paces	19	13	1

EMANUEL.

Jonas B. Spivy, Arlines	29	20	2
Jesse Maulden, Moors	196	8	1
Samuel P. Yowmans, Fountains	107	20	1

FAYETTE.

David Vann, Wests	110	6	1
James Wright, soldier, Whortons	237	15	1

FRANKLIN.

Zachariah Pruitt, Sanders	42	20	2
Minyard Sanders, soldier, do	2	3	5
John Lauridge, T. Chandlers	95	14	5

GLYNN.

Darby Henegan, McLeods	24	6	3

GREENE.

John Paine, R. S., Newsoms	194	2	2
Lawann Tippit, illegit., Rankins	160	3	5
James Curry, Southerlands	151	4	3
Mary Leftwick, widow, Elys	30	9	2
Oshburn S. Furlow, Dawsons	126	5	5
Nancy Swanson, widow, Newsoms	27	22	2
Jeremiah Jackson, R. S., Webbs	17	7	3
George Stovall's orphans, do	144	22	2
James L. Willis, Halls	54	10	5

GWINNETT.

Thomas Cooper, Davis	162	2	1
Absalom Wardlaw, Hunicuts	31	18	2
Patrick L Dunlap, do	176	3	3
Michael Thomas, Moors	40	3	3

HABERSHAM.

Elisha Davidson, Langstons	78	13	2
John B. Chastain, Tates	293	15	1
Franklin Smith, Bryans	147	10	1
Mahala Bullard, minor, Vickreys	145	3	3
Allen Black, Cross	114	5	5
Henry Bramblet, Kenzies	47	6	1
Green H. Obanion Langstons	239	22	1

HALL.

John Williams, jr. Walkers	46	1	3
David Wade, R. S., Dorseys	52	13	1
John Conner, do	26	19	1

(83)

Fortunate Drawers Capts. Dist.	No.	Dt.	Sec.
Alexander Stewart, Hardages	38	21	1
Robert Laurence, Harrisons	127	2	1
Simpson Hamilton, do	66	3	4
Rachel Burton, w. R. S. Roberts	240	18	1
Reuben Harrison, soldier, Alreds	124	29	1
HANCOCK.			
Trimkin J. Richardson, 117th	73	2	3
Zebulon Veazey, R. S., 110th	177	6	5
William R. Battle, 106th	15	23	1
Thomas Mason, jr. 112th	232	23	1
HENRY.			
Alonzo P. Morris, Wards	153	8	4
Burrel Camp, soldier, Shaws	77	3	2
John H. Saxon, Harris	15	10	2
Peter Piles, Bryants	72	8	5
Thomas Pate, do	152	7	5
HOUSTON.			
Arthur Simpson, Batemans	202	13	2
IRWIN.			
Robert McCrochen, Bradsfords	33	1	3
JACKSON.			
Walton Harris, Staplers	250	6	5
James Carr, Duncans	266	4	2
Emilia Roberson, illegit. Georges	211	23	2
Margaret McVay, wid. Venables	204	6	3
Christopher Sailors, R.S. Rogers	18	2	4
Nancy Blanks, idiot, Gathrights	84	6	1
William Pierce, Venables	313	20	2
Alfred Adams, Winns	133	4	2
JASPER.			
Levi Newton, Wilders	32	4	4
William McDowell's orps. Butts	206	13	2
Nathaniel Ramey, Barnetts	198	17	1
Benjamin Clark's orps. Sparks	10	5	4
Amos Edmonds, Holmes	201	22	2
Stephen Stephenson, Reeves	195	6	1
Elijah Kirk, Dardens	8	8	3
Thomas W. Carriel, Owens	216	15	2
Henry Yearby, Holmes	176	26	1
JEFFERSON.			
Penny Cowart, widow, Elliotts	9	10	1
Thomas Brady, Cunninghams	27	31	1
JONES.			
Spencer Brown, Gibsons	33	29	1
Thomas B. Stone, Newbys	8	1	5
George Scroggin, R. S., Mullins	45	13	5
Abner Hill. soldier, Sullivans	12	6	3
Jason Meador, R. S., Robertsons	79	10	3
Dreadsil W. Pace, Davis	286	20	2
Jacob Jordan, Hammacks	51	11	3
Richard M. Manus, do	90	33	1
M. A. Bearfield, illegit., Duncans	356	7	1
Jesse Slocumb, Davis	240	14	1
LAURENS.			
William Burgess. Powers	62	24	2
James Paramore. Mizells	127	17	1
LINCOLN.			
Dennis B. Mahoney, Washingtons	167	3	3
McINTOSH.			
John Gignilliat, Terrells	124	4	4
Hugh W. Proudfoo. Demeries	54	8	1
Jeremiah Cooper, sol. Ferrells	133	19	1

MONROE			
Fortunate Drawers Capts. Dist.	No.	Dt.	Sec.
Richard M. Stuart, Millers	26	1	1
Samuel Winshett, Finchs	53	6	5
A. Hartsfields orps. Johnsons	119	13	1
Josiah Hudgins, Stallings	173	7	1
Barnett R. Powell, sol. Wrights	242	8	3
Sethiel J. McClain, Johnsons	191	16	2
Edmund Powers orps. Houses	140	5	2
John E. Bailey, Millers	7	14	2
Mary Swan, w.R.S. Turners	214	1	4
Alfred Buffington, Johnsons	79	33	1
MORGAN.			
James Douglass, sol. Boswells	78	25	1
John R. Moore, Canifaxs	30	7	5
William Moss, Stokes	107	3	3
Samuel Dover, Boswells	12	22	1
Bennet M. Ware, Canifaxs	104	23	2
W. C. W. Barrett for wife, Hills	137	20	2
Henry Cobb, Jennigs	131	4	3
Tabitha Ligon, w. R. S. Canifaxs	24	3	2
Ewing Morrow, R. S. Boswells	27	17	2
Elizabeth Greer, wid. Whatleys	94	5	1
Amos E. Fuller, Sparks	182	14	2
John Finley, Stokes	122	3	1
MONTGOMERY.			
Hezekiah Hendrix, Popes	80	32	1
Loverd Bryan, Nashs	152	1	2
NEWTON.			
William J. Davis, Pullins	86	5	4
John Chatfield, Webbs	216	2	5
William Harris, Dyers	264	2	1
John Cole, Trammells	83	3	2
Micajah Jones, Dyers	165	21	1
Cicero Heath, Askews	72	21	1
OGLETHORPE.			
Thomas Miller, Rousseaus	265	3	8
A3braham Crowley, Hills	119	20	2
Jasper Haynes, Bells	281	15	1
Bird Parks, soldier, Mays	93	29	1
PIKE.			
Abbey Huckaby, widow, Orrs	9	8	2
PULASKI.			
Han'h Snelling, w.R.S.Sparrows	176	13	1
Hillery Henderson, Gilstraps	235	11	2
William Trull, Kellams	48	9	5
PUTNAM.			
P.,P.&M.Roberson mins. Brooks	224	11	3
Joseph Bohan, R. S. Bledsoes	166	24	1
Mathew Hamners orps. Patricks	149	3	5
RABUN.			
James Nix, sr. Mercers	321	20	3
Noel Hide, Becks	116	6	1
Solomon Lovelady, Godfreys	207	8	3
Joseph Pinson, Mercers	176	10	1
RICHMOND.			
Ezekiel Smith, R. S., Wilcoxs	146	1	1
Jacob J. Hollingsworth. Augusta	29	32	1
Stephen Williamson. James	8	26	1
Edward C. Huntingtons	276	17	2
Richard P. Spelman, do	197	5	1
Carolus Reedy, Hands	183	2	4

(84)

Fortunate Drawers   Capts. Dist.   No.Dt.Sec.

Eliza, Jas. Oliver, Isaac, Lan.
& A. Lawche ors. Huntingtons   182 24 1
Louis Levy, do   10 26 1

SCRIVEN.
John Saucer, Kemps   56 28 1
William Eivy, Stricklings   212 30 1
Delia Bevil, wid. Poytress   239   2 2

TATTNALL.
John Odom, McDuffies   35   5 1

TELFAIR.
Aley Lewis, Wilkinsons   197   7 1
David Allen, Barentines   93 24 2
Frances Walder, h.a. Wilkinsons 180   7 5

TALIAFERRO.
Francis O. Smith, Alfords   151   9 5

TWIGGS.
Benjamin Sanders, Pearsons   31   5 2
John Fort, Blackshears,   191 30 1
Benj. Lane, (F.) Kellys   104   5 1

UPSON.
Eliza Cooper, insane, Petteys   256   4 2
H. J. & L. J. Leverett orps. do   119   4 4
James Kelly, Paschalls   71 14 1

WALTON.
James Brooks orphans, Davis'   174 16 1
Mastin Childers, 418th   250   4 1
Luke Smith, 503rd   252 22 2
Elisha Hood, soldier, 249th   19 28 1
Jeremiah Allen, Bixleys   67   5 5
James Perkins, Rays   165   4 2
Daniel Luke, 249   262   6 1

WARE.
John Coward, Motes   67 27 1
Linza Pitmon, Greens   153 13 1

WARREN.
Fortunate Drawers   Capts. Dist.   No.Dt.Sec.

Ruth Raley, w. R. S. Downs   20 16 2
John Harrell, Sealees   99   3 2
Martha Miller, w.R.S. Parhams   148 21 2
Mary Davis' illegits. Downs   163 33 1
Joseph E. Biggs, Kinseys   111   8 3
Asa Griffin, Downs   65 25 1
Littleton Johnson, Hills   128 29 1
Edmund Hays, sol. Kinseys   218 29 1
Laniel Kinsey, Kinseys   140 14 2
Daniel Kinsey, Kinseys   140 12 2

WASHINGTON.
David Greer, Avans   78 11 5
Seth Barnes, McLendons   255 15 2
Gabriel Ray, Rushings   160 18 1
Benjamin Thomas, R.S. Floyds   215 30 1
John McDaniel, McLendons   253 22 2
Cornelius Herndon, Gilberts   105   9 1

WILKINSON.
Thomas Jones, Mathews   59   9 2
Frederick Frenchs orps. Shows   66   6 3
Hillery Newman, Smiths   88   3 2
Calvin Edson, Curreys   140 25 1

WILKES.
Mary Calloway, wid. Reeves   97 11 2
John Cooper, sr. R. S. Lukers   25 20 2
B. Taliaferros orps. Richardsons 238   5 2
Hannah Weaver, Washingtons   89   2 3
John Gibson, Moors   89   2 3
Samuel Paschall, sol. Hopkins   197 15 2
Joseph Gartrells orps. do   234   9 2
Robert Dawson, Washingtons   156   4 2
James Curray, McDermonts   295   1 4
Willis Whatley, Greens   127   2 4
James H. Hill, Wootens   204 10 2

LAND LOTTERY REGISTER—No. 13.
[RECORDER OFFICE—PUBLISHED BY GRANTLAND & ORME—PRICE $3.]

NOTE—Section 1 is Lee County—2 Muscogee—3 Troup—4 Coweta—5 Carroll.
28th DAY'S DRAWING—April 7th.

APPLING.

Fortunate Drawers Capts. Dist.	No.Dt.Sec.
David McCall, McDonalds	148 19 1

BALDWIN.

Robert Rutherford's orphs. Bivins	11 10 3
William J. Davis, Buchanans	26 12 3
Adaline E. Grizall, widow, Ginns	249 21 2

BIBB.

Docton Perry, Lloyds	20 13 5
Samuel Wade, R S, Rutlands	53 2 5
Elias Jernigan, Carrs	76 6 3
Benjamin Williams, R. S., Rutlands	9 9 5
Sarah Crawford, w. R S, Pickards	32 23 1
James S. Grover, Rutlands	173 8 3

BRYAN.

Mary Hickman, hus. absent, Harveys	112 17 1

BULLOCH.

Francis Devane, Deloachs	189 17 1
James Oneel's orphans, McCalls	154 6 1
Jenjamin Grooms, McCalls	3 14 5
Luke Pridgen's orphans, Burnetts	87 7 1

BURKE.

William Wallace, Wards	213 25 1
Absalom Turner, do	122 11 3
Zachariah Wimberly, Brooms	187 2 2
Benjamin Lynch, Lynchs	17 18 2

CHATHAM.

John C. Kingsmore, Haydens	26 8 2
James J. Tippins, Gaddys	218 5 2
Sarah Carson, widow, Haydens	221 10 5
Orps. of Alexander Irvine, Haydens	244 19 2
David Dotson, Reeds	263 19 2

CLARK.

Thomas Kinney, Gahagans	118 7 1
Marcus A. Sears, Wrights	120 1 3
Fryer Robertson, R S, Herndons	71 6 4
Henry Burt, do	177 7 5
William Daniel, sen., Vinsons	12 14 5
Howell Campbell, Wrights	62 20 2
Alfred W. Wright, Andersons	175 29 1
Wylie Glenn, Gahagans	79 2 4

COLUMBIA.

John Wilson, R. S., Adams	221 28 1
Orphans of Hugh Blair, Bealls	207 6 2
Joseph Larkin, Boltons	17 21 2

CRAWFORD.

John Z. Joiner, Ellis	206 19 1
Wiatt C. Williamson, sol., Lovetts	113 15 5
Riley Bazemoore, idiot, Tillers	236 7 1
Gillam Hicks, do	248 19 2
Enoch Johnson, soldier, Scaifs	236 17 1

DE KALB.

Henry Aldredge, Howells	166 17 1
James H Young, Stephens	91 22 1
John Gunn, Bowlings	139 6 2
James Still, Edwards	269 11 1
Susan Heard's illegitimates, Bakers	238 32 1
Littleton Jackson, Rowlings	11 5 3
Samdel Colly, R. S., Edwards	38 9 1

DOOLY.

William B. Ramsey, Serrs	151 4 1

EARLY.

Fortunate Drawers Capts. Dist.	No.Dt.Sec.
Thomas Bruner, Porters	59 5 1
John Gilley, Wilsons	237 23 1

EFFINGHAM.

Drphans of Philip Jones, Treutlins	171 32 1
John Evers, R. S., Elkins	24 9 3

ELBERT.

William Gaines, R S, Blackwells	48 2 1
Zachariah Dickerson, R S., Alstons	107 1 4
James Holly, illegitimate, Dobbs	115 7 3
Nicholas Pritchet, Carpenters	52 25 1
Lewis Cook, Butlers	154 5 1
Orphan of Nathias Carter, Bells	171 4 5
Edmund Jones, Tuckers	217 3 1
Joel Seales, Carpenters	47 5 2

EMANUEL.

Orphs. of D. Drinkwatters, Whiddons	113 19 1

FAYETTE.

Carlos Stricklin's orphans, Craigs	234 1 2
John T. Davis, do	225 12 2

FRANKLIN.

John Tate, jr. R. S., Andrews	143 1 4
John Waller Kee, R. S., Jones	94 3 3
Allen N. Mays, illegitimate, Sanders	186 9 3
William Wilmoth, R. S., Andrews	85 5 2
Orphans of James Pulliam, Bennetts	78 9 3
William Glove, Blankinships	208 14 2

GLYNN.

Coothes R. Denison, Burnetts	87 2 2

GREENE.

David Davis, Bruces	129 3 3
Gabriel R Shockley, Astins	184 2 2
Elijah Palmore, sr. R. S., Knowles	88 17 1
David Davis, Bruces	63 9 1

GWINNETT.

Nathan Ward, Wallis	118 22 1
Vincent Cox, Greens	213 10 2
William Taunt, Finchers	47 25 1
John Roper, Whortons	74 14 5
Sarah Ann Wimburn,w.R.S.,Moore	114 24 2
John Langley, Greens	86 3 3
J. J. W. & C. Harrell, ills. Caruthers	240 10 5
Claiborn M. Stiles, Bennetts	105 14 5
Judy & F. Wooters, fa. ab. Bakers	88 10 1
William Day, orphan, Greens	249 12 2

HABERSHAM.

John Dooley, Cross	299 6 1
Abner Center, sen. Langstons	56 11 5
Clark Jackson, Bryans	143 12 5
Love Howell, Tates	251 10 5
Silvester Rice, Bakers	76 3 5
Polly W. Washm, orphan, Bryans	174 21 1
James S. Erwin, do	91 9 6

HALL.

E. Henderson, deaf & dumb, Smiths	265 4 3
William Power, Yagers	55 8 4
Robert P. Bond's orphans, Alreds	172 15 2
Thomas Buffington, Haragas	98 16 2
John Pierce, Dorseys	166 3 2

HANCOCK.

Benjamin Henry, soldier, Hunters	238 6 3
Leany Amos, widow R. S., 101st	135 7 4
Milmond M. Petit, 112th	146 10 5

(86)

Fortunate Drawers	Capts.	Dist.	No.	Dt.	Sec.
Joseph Johnson,	101st		163	31	1
Francis P. Crutchfield,	102d		146	15	5
John Jones Sawyer,	R. S.,	106th	142	29	1
John C. Peak,	Hilsmans		56	12	1
Abigail Foster, widow,	103d		175	2	5

HENRY.

Littlebury Camp,	Bryants		11	11	3
Jinnens Hulsey,	R. S.,	Shaws	90	30	1
Robert Grimmett,	Harriss		114	12	1
William Jencks, sen	Risons		81	8	1
Henry Burks,	Wards		20	2	1

HOUSTON.

Michael Watson,	Batemans		206	6	5

JACKSON.

Philip Ryon, soldier,	Staplers		94	28	1

JASPER.

Jarret B. Kelly,	Robersons		165	2	5
John C. Looser,	Clemmons		256	12	3
Elijah Cornwell, sr.	R. S.,	Wilsons	228	5	3
Elijah Phillips,	Camerons		288	4	1
Mose Woodfire,	Johnsons		62	31	1
William Knight,	Keys		203	2	1
Demsey Baker,	Baynes		16	2	1
Abraham Pile,	do		9	11	2
Lewis Gilstrap,	Parkers		181	31	1
John Persons,	Dardens		148	8	3
Barbara Conlson's illegits.	Hines		263	16	2
Thomas Teal,	Wilsons		160	9	2

JEFFERSON.

Moses Brinson, jun.	Beatys		219	4	2
Henry Irby,	Cunninghams		216	33	1
Sarah Bradford, widow,	Jones		214	10	2
D Z. Jones, wounded man,	Beatys		186	12	3
John Bedingfield,	Elliotts		237	13	2
Jacob Young, sr.	R S,	Beatys	11	23	2

JONES.

Christiana McLeroy,w.RS,	Gibsons		277	6	1
Joseph C. White,	Stewarts		117	3	5
Jeremiah Cook,	Breedloves		328	7	5
Henry D. Rose,	Gibsons		129	21	2
Charles Bayne,	Woods		247	31	1
Thomas Gildersleeve,	do		295	28	1
Joshua Harris,	Gibsons		87	12	3
Jesse Braswell, sen	Popes		173	1	5
Bruton Brassell,	R S,	Dosters	45	14	2
Daniel Merkison,	Sullivans		132	3	3

LAURENS.

Mary E. Cary, orphan,	Whiteheads		212	17	2
James Lawson,	Deans		110	7	2
David McDaniel,	Whiteheads		164	11	5

LIBERTY.

John Mathews,	17th		150	17	1

LINCOLN.

John Crosson, R. S.,	Lonorgans		254	11	2
Robert Walton,	Parks		61	10	3
Dempsey Busseys mins.	Graves		95	26	1
Peyton Vincents mins.	Leveretts		177	5	3

LOWNDES.

Henry Parish, sol.	10th		77	30	1

MADISON.

John SeaGroves,	Adairs		193	14	1
Henry L. Bridewell,	Culbertsons		157	12	3
James Cooper, R. S.	Phipps		15	22	1
William Crimes,	Hannas		212	16	2

MONROE.

Fortunate Drawers	Capts.	Dist.	No.	Dt.	Sec.
Terrell Brooks,	Pattersons		267	4	1
Tilman Moore,	Browns		23	12	3
Samuel Holly,	Pattersons		299	28	1
Caroline Caldwell, illeg.	Houses		301	5	1
William Rogers' ors.	Woodwards		36	10	5
Henry Smith,	R. S.	Houses	185	19	2
Wm. Scotts orps.	Browns		17	22	2
Levin Burgay,	Finchs		134	23	2
Thomas Dyess,	Douglass		234	19	1
Robert Humber,	Wrights		105	33	1
Purity J. Tingle,	Finchs		20	12	2
Benjamin Laseter,	Houses		75	10	5
Isabell Modiset,	w.R. S.	Turners	83	8	4

MORGAN.

Willard Bradley,	Stokes		83	13	5
William Johnston, sol.	Walkers		360	7	1
Moses Watson,	Shermons		3	18	1
S. H. Gilmore, sol.	Hitchcocks		164	16	1
S. W. A. Askew,	Walkers		262	28	4
Charles Cozen, orphan,	Millers		18	8	4
Samuel Thomas,	Harwells		44	7	1

NEWTON.

Matilda Williams ill.	Summers		36	12	1
John McLain,	Snows		52	15	2
William Terry,sr.	Clarks		223	30	1
Elijah W. Christian,	Snows		231	24	1

OGLETHORPE.

William S. Dupree,	Billups		197	2	2
Alexander Jones,	Rousseaus		80	5	2
Stokes Allen,	Williamsons		65	1	1
Robert Allison, soldier,	Smiths		153	3	3
Jacob Lawless,	Burfords		156	11	3
Abraham Crowley,	Hills		131	14	5
John Kimble,	do		142	8	3
Joseph Stanfield,	Burfords		50	14	1
Jack A. Johnson,	Holloways		285	1	2
Joel Tribble,	Rousseaus		95	10	3
Jacob Patton,	Seals		12	4	1
Mary Ligon,	wid.	Bells	169	4	3
Rich. Hartsfield,	R.S.	Holloways	148	18	2
——Brooks orps.	Dicks		85	24	2

PIKE.

William Solley,	Orss		60	1	5
Francis L. Mathews,	Mays		48	12	2
Joseph Deson, sol.	Arlines		136	14	2
Fredrick Sessions, soldier,	od		230	21	2

PULASKI.

Mary Tooke, wid.	Sparrows		334	28	1
Robert Lee,	do		22	1	3
William Cunningham,	Gilstraps		215	9	3
Daniel Graham,	Scarbroughs		215	3	2

PUTNAM.

John Pucket,	Bledsoes		44	8	4
Pinkney J. Voss,	Mizes		226	16	1
Albert Marchman,	Clarks		145	11	1
Thomas Hooks,	R. S.	Vinings	89	5	3
John B. Ingram,	do		34	12	3
Hodijah Elam,	do		170	8	4

RABUN.

Eliz. Jones, w.	R. S.	Godfreys	130	14	2

(87)

Fortunate Drawers Capts. Dist.	No.	Dt.	Sec.
Isoh Carnes, do	246	22	2
Luke W. Guinn, Miligans	155	14	1
William Garritt, Mersers	31	22	2
RICHMOND.			
Henry Evans orphans, Wilcoxs	338	22	1
Sarah Garvin, widow, 123rd	263	2	3
Con. Liverman, R.S.Treadwells	208	7	1
Joseph Dawsey, James	162	19	1
John P. Andrews, Augusta	95	6	2
Jas. & Louisa Ricker orps. do	51	9	2
Wm. W. Mann orp. Huntingtons	6	3	3
Leah Greshams illegits, Wilcoxs	47	22	1
Joseph Dailey, do.	125	20	2
TATTNALL.			
William Starling, Conners	52	4	2
David Highsmith, Corseys	209	11	3
Nathaniel T. Bazemore, do	210	22	1
TALIAFERRO.			
Henry P. Bowls, Echols	119	17	2
Harrison Oneal, Moores	6	8	4
TWIGGS.			
Patience Rix, wid. Streetmans	139	20	1
Clar. Coleman, wid. Blackshears	106	2	4
John Dixon, Streetmans	68	15	5
Nicholas L. Loyd, Pearsons	138	10	3
H. H. Harrell, F. Streetmans	137	15	2
Nathan Minshew jr. do	181	20	2
UPSON.			
James Langham, R. S. Ellis	176	24	1
Martin W. Stamper, sol. Pettys	83	23	2
WALTON.			
Allen Baggets orphs. Hudsons	150	4	3
William Norton, Pools	85	15	2
Harrison Camp, 249th	135	18	1
Polly McLendon, 249th	132	18	1
Thomas Bradly, Snows	84	24	2
WARE.			
Wm. G. Henderson, Bryans	114	2	1
WAYNE.			
Edm. Howards ors. Mannings	133	1	3
WARREN.			
Sarah Johnson, wid. Downs	167	27	1
Samuel Pitts, sol. Fords	149	3	3
Adam Jones, jr.sol. Jones	178	5	5
William G. Walden, Downs	73	14	2
Caney R. Berry, wid. Jones	244	10	5
James Hagwood, Bulls	247	8	3
Mary Brooks, w.R.S. Kinseys	187	8	3
Cath. Dennis,w.R.S.Parhams	113	8	3
Calvin J. Ivy, Stewarts	267	22	2
WASHINGTON.			
Sarah Sneed, widow, Floyds	163	3	3
Isaac Hay, R. S. Tysons	240	21	2
John Wises orps. Wimberlys	234	31	1
Cas. Manning, w.s.l.w.Warthens	136	15	5
Wm. Farmers orps. Whitfields	126	1	3
Susan McLendon ill. Warthens	182	6	3
Jonathan Spikes, Woods	60	16	2
Jesse Little, Mannings	178	7	1
Randolph Mitchell, Rushings	192	9	2
WILKINSON.			
Joel Rivers, Shows	5	26	1

Fortunate Drawers Capts. Dist.	No.	Dt.	Sec.
Mark Dees, Currys	26	3	4
N.,E.,G.&P. Searcy, ors. Smiths	39	6	1
Solomon Wright,R.S.Fairchilds	233	7	5
Jemsey N. Chandler, Currys	58	11	2
WILKES.			
Osborn Stone, sol. Gardners	32	9	4
Frances Philips, sol. wid. Reeves	216	17	2
Samuel Darden, Rices	25	8	2
William Murphy's orps. Lukers	73	4	5
Wm. Anderson, sr. R. S. Greens	44	18	1
Thomas Eidson, R. S., Lukers	45	20	1
Thomas Dawson, Washingtons	103	24	2

29th DAY'S DRAWING—April 9th.

APPLING.

	No.	Dt.	Sec.
James Boothe, Morgans	90	2	3
Silas O'Quinn, Collins	207	30	1
BAKER.			
Hillery Hooks, soldier, Corquadalls	12	6	5
William Stafford, soldier, Porters	180	15	1
BALDWIN.			
Wyat Foard, Buchanans	277	17	2
John Myrick, R S., Doles	85	13	2
Whittington Moore, soldier, Pitts	219	18	1
Nancy Edmundson, widow, Reddings	127	4	2
Archer Worsham's orphans, Lesters	84	8	4
BIBB.			
John Sholler, Pickards	3	8	4
Holston Williams, Bates	278	19	2
William Cotton, Lloyds	12	4	4
Nathaniel Barker, Bates	105	2	2
Matthew Jones, Carrs	96	16	1
BULLOCH.			
Peter Strickland, Richardsons	66	21	2
Sarah Griggor, widow, do	216	5	1
BURKE.			
Peter Milton, Jr. Gordons	1	30	1
Buckner Gray, Brooms	228	5	2
Daniel Belcher, Wards	36	24	2
John Thomas, Andersons	191	2	4
Augustin Brown, Gordons	232	19	2
Moses M. Godbee, Lewis	71	20	1
William Godbee's orphans, do	8	19	2
William Cain, Wests	155	9	1
Jesse Carsey, Lynchs	179	12	1
BUTTS.			
Thomas W Ray, soldier, Kirksies	172	3	4
CAMDEN.			
Maryana Fowles, widow, Wards	62	5	1
John Omans, R. S., Hopkins	206	22	2
CHATHAM.			
Ebenezer G. Riggins, lunatic, Gaddys	244	4	3
William Davis, do	183	17	2
William Lavender,jr. Nungazers	188	6	5
M. C. Rily, orp. of Patrick, Haydens	56	18	1
William Hale,	243	2	3
CLARK.			
Martin Crow, McDonalds	157	1	2
Robert Love, Wrights	46	1	5
Charles Conally's orphans, Ransoms	258	4	3
Clarke T. Williams, Lampkins	8	4	1
Robert Stuart, Davenports	190	11	2
Thomas P. Elder, Alreds	235	10	5
Elizabeth Strong, widow, Andersons	21	2	3
Richard Paulett, R S, Vinsons	30	2	8

(88)

Fortunate Drawers Capts. Dist.	No.Dt.Sec.	Fortunate Drawers Capts. Dist.	No.Dt.Sec.
William Houghton's orps. Gahagans	75 32 1	Eliz &J. Chaplings, illegits, Cupps	196 17 2
David Smith, Burchs	32 5 4	John Segers, Finchers	106 4 2
		Isaac Funderburk, Hunicuts	228 8 3
COLUMBIA.		John Gutrie, R. S., Davis	13 9 3
Joseph Ronie, Carrolls	105 4 3	Henry Sizemore, jun Hills	366 8 1
Charles G Gill, Coles	150 30 1	James Bromley, Woodroughs	200 27 1
Philip Steed, Boltons	47 33 1	Richard Plunkett, Whortons	44 15 1
Christian Merchant, widow, Dranes	231 17 1		
Henry Harrison, illegitimate, do	194 15 1	**HANCOCK.**	
CRAWFORD.		Needham Clark, 116th	64 1 4
Joseph Barker, R. S., Hicks	268 5 1	Daniel Murphy's orphans, Dixons	50 2 4
		John Lightfoot, 110th	50 3 4
DECATUR.		William Shuffield, R. S., 104th	197 12 1
Asia Emanuel's orphans, Hawthorne	252 11 1	John Binion, soldier, Adams	72 10 1
Etheldred Pittman, Douglass	27 1 1	Isaac Culver, soldier,, Densons	5 5 3
Lorenzo D. Shepard, do.	244 22 2	Nicholas B. Gary, 117th	148 15 2
DE KALB.		Edward B. Brooking, 113th	138 22 1
Lewis Walker, Conns	110 3 5		
Jesse Roberts, do	156 17 2	**HENRY.**	
Samuel Norwood, Stephens	78 13 5		
Robert Jones, do	24 11 3	William W. Williams, Smiths	187 11 3
Joshua Walston, Bowlings	179 33 1	Robert Cade, Shaws	71 6 2
Thomas G Hudspeth, Howells	64 19 2	Andrew Smith, do	205 2 1
Neil Ferguson, Scaifs	14 3 1	Reuben Edwards, R. S., Grays	189 2 4
Jones Jones, Bowlings	105 12 1	Absalom Autory, Shaws	279 28 1
EARLY.		**HABERSHAM.**	
Garrett T. Freeman, Wilsons	69 7 4		
		Sarah Gibson's chil. fa. ab., Suttons	116 28 1
EFFFINGHAM.		Joseph Henson, jr. Kenzies	52 5 5
John Hurst, Stricklands	33 4 5	Jephthah Freeman, Vickreys	225 7 1
ELBERT.		**HALL.**	
Willis Alexander, Alstons	204 19 1	Absalom Avery, Yagers	47 1 2
Zachariah Rucker, do	141 26 1	Joshua Bridgers, Dorseys	124 6 3
Martha Hickman, wid., Carpenters	144 9 3	Elijah Pinson, Hendricks	100 12 1
Barden Rucker, soldier, Hortons	237 3 3	Fielding Thurmond, Harrisons	79 8 3
Jesse Ginif, Merritts	3 11 5	Dolly Hugins, widow, Yagers	73 9 1
Mildred Banks, widow, Deadwilders	81 3 3	Ches. Calv. Lott.&H.Payne, Roberts	49 10 1
Forster Rowzay, Butlers	52 5 3		
David Bell, Bells	269 14 1	**HOUSTON.**	
EMANUEL.		John Smith, Calhouns	138 8 3
John Proctor, Moors	106 20 2	Green Johnson, do	182 2 5
		Masheck Howel, Wimberlys	44 7 2
FAYETTE.		Henry Summerford, Becks	219 6 1
Thomas Hays, soldier, Morgans	176 22 2	Stephen Royal's orphans, Prices	98 30 1
John Garrett, Wests	89 9 3		
Hardy H Pope, Whortons	246 21 1	**IRWIN.**	
Isaac Smith, soldier, 9th	247 5 1	Thomas Burnett, Dixons	18 7 2
FRANKLIN.		James Wallis, Underwoods	184 19 1
Lucy Pearce, widow, Blankinships,	107 3 5	Hardy Bryant, 5th	40 4 2
Richard Perry,jr McDonalds	378 28 1	**JACKSON.**	
Mary Bellamy, widow, Stranges	134 11 2		
Jesse Thomas, jr. T. Chandlers	87 9 1	Abraham N. Clardy, Doss	236 11 1
Matilda Carter, widow Bennetts	247 21 2	John Owen, Landrums	67 16 2
Aaron Roberts, R S., Walters	192 8 3	Sarah Howard, w. R S., Lindseys	73 6 1
Sarah Chatham,w. R S., Boswells	249 18 1	James Garrard, Storys	151 19 1
		Russell Jones, Duprees	132 19 1
GLYNN.		Robert Smithwick, sol., Gathrights	100 2 4
James Fruin, Dubignons	8 9 2	George W Wilson, Rogers	8 9 1
		William Fuller, sen. Winns	228 15 2
GREENE.		John P. Greenwood, Venables	148 3 2
		Jesse Morgan, Lindseys	191 20 1
Jacob Peeler, Woodhams	97 4 1	Benjamin Freeman, do	178 15 1
Peter B. Brooks, orphans, do	28 9 3		
Daniel E. Jackson, Webbs	161 3 4	**JASPER.**	
Reuben Wright, Dawsons	88 12 2	Elijah Cornwell, sen. Wilsons	104 6 5
Laveing Beman, Newsoms	228 3 1	Benjamin Hill, soldier, Dales	3 10 5
Robert Astin, R. S., Astins	163 1 5	Ann McAlhany, w.R.S., Dales	35 4 3
Elizabeth Brown, wid Woodhams	119 6 2	Benjamin Garrett, jun. Butts	32 2 5
Orps of Thos Greer, son		Thaddeus Pennington, Baynes	180 6 3
of Gilbert, Rankins	168 3 5	Sarah Hill, w. R. S. Dales	212 25 1
		Seaborn Shi, Robinsons	307 1 4
GWINNETT.		William Robinsons's orphans, Keys	249 10 5
Joseph N. Plunket, Rollins	154 6 2	Joseph Twilley, Downies	41 1 2
William Jackson, Hunicuts	61 7 4	Joshua Miles, Holmes	47 22 2
Sarah Wiley's illegitimates, Davis	68 20 1	John Flemister, soldier, Barnes	130 1 1

(89)

Fortunate Drawers	Capts.	Dist.	No.	Dt.	Sec.
Mary George, widow,	Holmes		202	16	1
William L Canant,	Camerons		269	15	1

JEFFERSON.

Elijah Warner's orphans,	Waldens		14	6	2
James Gunn,	Ross		68	17	2
Abel Russell,	Beatys		136	8	4
Rhoda Barber, widow,	Boyds		33	1	4
Reuben Y Burts,	Marshalls		119	5	1
Zerubbabel Hyslip,	Boyds		179	9	2
Elizabeth Causey, w R. S.,	do		234	10	2
Council B. Blount,	Waldens		174	1	4
Evelina Moore, orphan,	Jones		192	29	1

JONES.

John Whitesides,	Robertsons		32	8	1
John McDonald,	Lows		65	10	3
Adam S. Ledlow,	Spinks		93	9	2
Lydia Wheelis, w. R. S.,	Blounts		189	5	3
James Allen,	Dosters		310	3	4
John Hutchison,	Popes		128	7	3
William Childs,	Mullins		13	22	1
Caroline Sturdivant, orphan,	Bowens		196	4	3
Isaac Pippiris, orphans,	Hendersons		41	5	2
William Strong, R. S.,	Dosters		265	17	2
Louisa M Brady, orphan,	Robertsons		353	7	1
John Ivey,	Newbys		144	8	1
John Jefferson, soldier,	Popes		174	24	1
Isaac H. Alford,	Woods		202	28	1

LAURENS.

William Smith,	Whiteheads		13	3	3
James C Hall,	Hodges		130	5	3
John Nobles orphans,	Spivys		76	6	2
Stephen Paramore,	Deans		177	10	1
Margaret Wry, widow,	Hodges		286	22	1
Balaam Palmer,	Mizells		34	28	1

LIBERTY.

John Mathews, 17th			7	4	5
Robert Clark orphan, 17th			105	10	5

LINCOLN.

Robert Hemphill,	Graves		197	27	1
William Agee, miner,	Gideons		49	12	1
William Ansleys minors,	Prathers		103	1	4
John McKinney,	Gideons		164	8	1
William Curry,	Graves		92	12	1
Andrew Lee, sr. R. S.	Lonorgans		202	21	1

MADISON.

John M. Williford,	Christians		190	14	2
Joseph B. Harris,	do		234	4	2
John H. Beasly,	Caldwells		210	31	1
Robt. W. Harris,	Higginbothams		98	3	1

McINTOSH.

William Macmaster,	Terrells		123	4	1
E.,C.&G. Trezevant ors.	Thorps		113	24	1

MONROE.

Ambrose Edwards,	Woodwards		77	2	4
Joel Faulkner,	Wrights		80	14	1
Jeremiah Mickle,	do		163	12	5
John Funderburk, R. S.	Millers		16	29	1
James Carter,	Pattersons		85	3	1
John Adams,	Douglass		233	30	1

MORGAN.

John Maxwell,	Harwells		44	11	1
Burrel Coggin,	Shermons		171	6	3
Jincy Lemons illegits.	Watsons		133	14	2
James Boothe,	Youngs		252	28	1
Henry F. Young, sol.	Walkers		18	21	2
David Irwin,	Dawsons		75	14	2

Fortunate Drawers	Capts.	Dist.	No.	Dt.	Sec.
John Trimble, sol.	Adairs		209	6	1
William Beall, soldier,	Walkers		25	24	1

MONTGOMERY.

Isaac Edwards,	Ryals		102	19	1

NEWTON.

David Huckaby,	Summers		50	1	2
John Allen,	Askews		202	26	1
William Alberson, R. S.	Clarks		230	5	4
Hiram H. Rutherford,	Zachreys		78	3	3
Robert P. Rodgers,	Dyers		107	1	1
Cornelia, Amanda M. & Frances B. Smartt orphans,	Pullens		157	1	3
William McGouirk,	Snows		168	20	1

OGLETHORPE.

Charles G. Hargrove,	Burfords		254	8	3
Jeatham Hopper,	Lacys		215	12	2
Daniel Jenkins,	Rousseaus		97	4	4
Frances M. Barnett,	Holloways		100	11	2
William Rainey,	Rousseaus		52	12	2
William Lawless'sorps.	Holloways		215	10	5
Montfort Carter,	do		52	9	5
Thomas Davis,	Rhodes		175	3	1
John A. Bradley,jr.	Floyds		237	17	1
Sampson Kent, R S.	Lacys		24	19	1

PIKE.

John Harbrook,	Mays		267	28	1
Joseph Scott, jr.	Longs		113	4	1

PULASKI.

R. R. Tarver,	Banchers		132	12	3
John Barkers orphs.	Bledsoes		204	29	1
William Flowers's orps.	Kellams		244	16	1
William Lester, soldier,	Thomas		70	3	5
Margaret Stephens,	Gilstraps		188	21	2
Allen Wheeler,	Sparrows		60	3	3

PUTNAM.

Garrard M. Veal, minor,	Goods		279	1	4
John Barkers orphs.	Bledsoes		204	29	1
Martha Kilpatrick, wid.	Blunts		202	32	1
McCarrell Purifoy,	Allums		123	6	4
John B. Pound,	do		101	2	4
George Ingrams orps.	do		188	5	2
Jesse Harrisons orphans,	Clarks		24	3	1
Jeremiah Clark,	Bledsoes		208	10	5
Daniel W. Bowdin,	Allums		84	17	2
William Wilkerson,	Stinsons		113	14	1
ames Brown, soldier,	Brooks		80	19	1

RICHMOND.

John Shaw,	Kellys		35	13	5
S.&E.S.Jones,orps.	Huntingtons		136	13	2
Thomas Averett orph.	Wilcoxs		240	3	2
Joseph Wheeler,	Augusta		163	6	1
W,E,M,J&C Barry ors.	Mantzs		275	1	2
Robert Delaware Lacy,	Blacks		70	11	1

SCRIVEN.

Vardaman Rooks,woundedinl.w.			194	9	1
Grandville B. Mock illegit.	Ushers		190	16	1
Byons Boykin,	Stricklings		50	29	1

TATTNALL.

Elias Fiveash,	Graces		65	4	5
Erwin Moore,	Deloachs		32	5	5
John Gilford,jr.	Graces		142	20	2
Martha Lord, wid.	Corseys		112	9	1

Fortunate Drawers	Capts.	Dist.	No.	Dt.	Sec.
Jacob Surrency, jr. Dees			4	8	1
TELFAIR.					
Wm. Ashley, jr. Lampkins			198	2	2
Judah Smiths illegits. Wilkinsons			42	11	1
TALIAFERRO.					
Martha Dewberry, wid. Gunns			20	3	4
Larkin R. Gunn, do			143	7	3
TWIGGS.					
Abraham Davis, Pearsons			44	2	4
Wm.H. J. Majors, illegit. Bosticks			30	5	5
Orps. of P. Youngblood, Graggs			144	4	3
Eliz. McMurry, wid. Wimberlys			220	19	1
Wilson Deshazo, Graggs			134	23	1
Everard Hamilton, soldier, do			153	3	5
George Rowland, sol. Wimberlys			83	11	5
UPSON.					
George W. Hamiel, Ellis'			92	11	1
Isaa Cooper, sol. Harralds			1	13	5
Charles Kemp, 589th			184	12	5
John T. Goldsmith, sol. Ezells			223	12	1
Austin Martin, Pashalls			211	11	1
John Mott, Hattoxs			178	26	1
WALTON.					
James Humphries, Hudsons			289	6	1
Anna Barnett, widow, Rays			238	6	2
Josiah B. Scott, McQuertors			161	3	5
James Burton, 250th			206	4	2
William Palmore, Bexleys			175	2	3
William Wilkerson, soldier, Snows			32	8	5
Siah Hendrick, R S. 249th			227	31	1
James Nowel, Snows			192	3	1
John Winkles, McQuertors			188	7	3
Nancy McCord illegit 559th			74	29	1
WARE.					
Moses Prescutt, Motes			83	4	3
Benjamin Hollon, Greens			223	5	4
William R., Wright T, Ezekiel L., N.V.&M.Pennington, ills. Motes			19	14	5
James Osteen, do			70	5	2
George Tatum, illeg. Dowlings			76	1	4
WAYNE.					
Allen Rawls' orps. Staffords			26	4	4
WARREN.					
Isail Hight, insane, Latimers			200	16	2
Kinch. McKinneys ors. Kinseys			222	7	3
Midgally Conner, Jones			8	21	1
Keziah Williams, w. R. S. do			99	3	5
Thomas Peavy,jr. Hills			98	10	2
Moses Thompson, R. S. Adkins			172	15	1
Frances Hillman, wid. Sanders			240	23	2
Hinchy Johnson, Parhams			83	20	2
John Moody, Downs			59	25	1
Thomas J. Hammett, Adkins			57	12	5
Mary Armstrong, wid. Parhams			136	27	1
WASHINGTON.					
Samuel Shirly, Woods			140	8	1
William Johnson, Warthens			129	4	3
George Moye, Gilberts			215	3	1
Wm. M. Brantley orph. Jordans,			83	4	5
Nathaniel G. Holmes, Currys			64	18	2
Mathew Mills, Mannings			119	5	3
David Forchand, Tysons			55	2	4

Fortunate Drawers	Capts.	Dist.	No.	Dt.	Sec.
Counsel Jones, Jordans			116	8	4
Moses Cox, Avans			116	23	2
James Helton, Currys			66	24	1
Archibald McNeil, Floyds			244	19	1
WILKINSON.					
Patrick Willis, Fairchilds			114	3	1
Esther Lambert, widow, Shows			74	5	5
James Lawson, soldier, Currys			271	5	3
William Hearndon, Ragans			147	7	1
WILKES.					
Avry R. Hood, Reevec			323	1	4
Abm. B. Calloway, Woottens			181	6	5
Jane S. Lyon, wid. Washingtons			175	6	1
Samuel Thompson, Carters			129	19	1
Lucy Cosby wid. of soldier Lukers			6	17	2
Joseph M. Dent, Popes			168	9	2
Peter Curray, R.S. Richardsons			154	19	2

30th *DAY'S DRAWING*—April 10.

			No.	Dt.	Sec.
APPLING.					
David Carter's orphans, Stricklands			114	16	2
Elizabeth Aldredge, w.R.S., Mathis			251	6	1
BALDWIN.					
George S. Perdue, Thomas			193	30	1
Sarah Davis, widow, Ginns			190	5	4
William D. Amburn, Rowes			64	6	5
John Coley, Lingos			63	14	2
Wilson Gordy, Reddings battalion			141	7	5
Orphans of Henry Skinner, Pitts			108	33	1
BIBB.					
Stephen Garner, Bates			98	19	1
Rachel Cauly, hus. absent, landers			32	8	2
Joseph Shaw, Bates			103	2	2
J., J J,& P. Dunaway ,fa. ab., Beards			170	2	2
Michael Briggs, Lloyds			169	16	2
Eason Smith, Bates			163	5	2
Charles Ingram, Flanders			18	25	1
BRYAN.					
Orphans of William Manly, Stephens			96	9	5
BULLOCH.					
Elias Nichols, Lockharts			144	9	2
Ann Oneal's illegitimates, do			169	20	2
BURKE.					
Patrick McCann, Fountains			109	21	2
Irwin Hall, Corkers			76	9	3
E, A, S, M,E, & N. Ihly ills. Baileys			161	18	1
Mary & Devina Maund ors. Andersons			239	16	2
Zachariah Collins, Seegars			66	1	1
BUTTS.					
Charles Beacham, Masons			291	7	5
CAMDEN.					
Mary F. Bachlott, orphan, Wards			31	11	3
Peter Bernady, Millers			242	33	1
CHATHAM.					
William Belcher, Tenbrooks			31	11	3
Jas. G. John W. Eliza A.& Elizabeth J. Clifton, Haydens			115	19	1
Orphans of Alexander Irvine, do			13	21	1
George W. Coe, do			146	4	4
William Rose, do			231	2	1
CLARK.					
Richard Landers, Davenports			33	9	5
Sarah Gilbert, widow, McDonalds			237	19	2
William Murray, Humphreys			24	21	1
Thomas Gallaway, Andresons			325	23	3

Fortunate Drawers	Capts. Dist.	No.	Dt.	Sec.
Jonathan Gorley, Frosts		130	12	3
Charles C. Birch, Vinsons		78	2	2
Pernal Cook, Davenports		185	16	2
Reason Whitehead, soldier, Masters		17	5	1
Jack F. Cocke's orphans, ,Gahagans		214	7	5
Charles J. Winn, Herndons		86	10	3
Ferdinand Vickers, Wrights		229	1	2
Orps. of Thomas Gilbert, McDonalds		136	20	1
Isaac Mathews, R. S., Herndons		103	29	1
Eason Gee, Gahagans		2	1	3
Alfred Daniel, Echols		250	22	2

COLUMBIA.

Albert H. Collins, Coles		113	2	4
Rebecca Mills, orphan, Dranes		36	5	4

CRAWFORD.

George S. Kennedy, soldier, Lovetts		29	6	2
Hampton Ryan, Rhodes		137	17	2
Benjamin R. Market, Wilsons		15	9	5
John Adkins, Rhodes		167	18	1
Richard C. Ethridge, do		15	4	2
Nimrod B. Yarborough, do.		15	4	2
Jesse Mathews, do		16	6	5

DE KALB.

Lewis Thomas, Conns		245	2	4
Jeremiah Nesbit, R. S., Bakers		180	14	1
Brooker J. Jackson, Browns		120	17	2
Littleber Harbour, Spruces		184	22	2
John Reed, Bowlings		4	4	5
Martha Parker, illegitimate, Edwards		128	12	5
John Kisor, Howells		1	11	1
Tyrice Pearce, Edwards		191	2	3
Joshua Walston, Bowlings		180	23	1
George Waldrope, Conns		274	16	2
Nealy Goodwin, do		259	28	1
Jinsey Williamson, illegit., Bakers		164	32	1

EARLY.

Solomons Evers, Wilsons		144	6	1
Thomas Moy, do		87	14	1
Thomas Moy, do		3	4	2

EFFINGHAM.

Felix Hurst, Stricklands		88	15	5
Samuel Burkstiner, sol., Waldhaners		93	4	2

ELBERT.

John Maxwell, R. S., Hortons		181	21	2
Hannah Rhodes((widow, Dobbs		99	20	2
Elizabeth L. Akin, orphan, Harmonds		15	8	5
Ealum Hill, Carpenters		98	5	5
German Burton, Tates		147	1	2
George Cook, R. S., Boltons		196	21	1

EMANUEL.

Matthew Coleman, McGars		20	12	1
Easter Boiles, widow, do		203	7	5
Allen Lawrence, 49th		68	19	1
John R. Daniel, Fountains		246	3	2
Saladan Williams, illegitimate, 49th		185	17	2

FAYETTE.

Elizabeth Shelnut, widow, Wests		96	15	2
Champ Terry, Roziers		241	5	4
Gilbert Poe, Dodsons		4	2	3
William Roberts, Whartons		162	4	2
Wiley Roundtree, Dodsons		7	9	4
Isaiah Beck Seig, 9th		221	9	5
William Pegg, Whorters		223	6	3
James Stewart, R. S., Roziers		70	22	1

FRANKLIN.

Thomas J. Chappelear, Walters		52	6	2
Abner Sosebee, Andrews		172	9	2
James S. Fleming, Hudsons		144	6	5

Fortunate Drawers	Capts. Dist.	No.	Dt.	Sec.
Samuel T. Payne, Caudells		93	27	1
William W. Dickson, do		233	1	2

GREENE.

Warren G. Bickers, Dawsons		203	14	1
Douglas Watson's orphans, Newsoms		157	10	2
Orps. of Thos Greenwood, Dawsons		233	24	1
Harris Burks, Halls		9	31	1
Samuel Cessna, soldier, Rankins		154	11	3
Edward Broughton, Robinsons		164	10	3
Elizabeth Stringfellow, widow, do		134	9	5

GWINNETT.

Micajah Mayo, Finchers		153	21	1
Charles Walls, R. S., Robertsons		164	21	1
Robert Stanfield, Wallis		78	24	1
N., T., & B. Terry, orps. Woodroughs		3	31	1
Rice B. Green, soldier, Greens		131	16	1
Elizabeth McLelland,w.R.S., Evans		96	19	1
Alexander Stephenson, Caruthers		192	10	3
John Turner, sen. Hunicuts		44	27	1
Sarah Waits, widow, Bakers		141	2	4
Thomas Weems, Woodroughs		84	10	5
Thomas Cresswell, Whortons		102	31	1
Willis Bobo, illegitimate, Caruthers		268	10	2
William Mathis, jr. Woodroughs		80	16	2
Robert Mawhood, Caruthers		109	11	3
Isaac Brumeloo, Bakers		68	2	4
Alexander Miller, Greens		187	5	4

HABERSHAM.

William Kinney, Bryans		39	6	5
Nathaniel Wade, R. S., Jones		105	14	2
Asa Tate, Tates		52	3	1
William Wootten, Kenzies		18	2	2
Jemina Gilbert, widow, Suttons		102	12	3
Neeley Dobson, Bryans		105	13	5
Berry Turner, Bryans		220	11	2
Haywood English, Cross		3	4	3
William Ritchie, Martins		54	17	2
Hugh lPerce, R. S., angstons		119	14	1

HALL.

Nap.G.&John K Martin. ills. Smiths		1	12	1
Miner Cochran, Alreds		100	1	5
John Mullins, Wilsons		17	4	1
James Johnson, Garrards		166	14	2
Isham P. Pool, Roberts		198	5	4
Walker Mason, Hardages		199	1	2
Bartley Montgomery, sol, Yagers		4	1	2
Emeline Harp, illegit., Harrisons		120	26	1
Joseph W. Hamilton, Smiths		176	21	1

HANCOCK.

Reason Arnold, soldier, Brooks		6	6	2
John Rees, 111th		112	3	5
William Terrill, Adams		110	8	5
Samuel McWhorter, 114th		226	5	2
Etheldred Edwards, 108th		193	6	1
Zebulun Veazey, R S., 110th		32	7	4
James T. Gordon, 113th		51	4	4
Samuel W Ewing, 118th		182	4	6
William Osborn, Swints		212	7	5
Wyat Rervis do		306	6	1
Joseph B. Ponce, Densons		45	19	1

HENRY.

Richard Speak, Kites		240	8	5
James B. Piles, Bryants		58	20	2
John Lackey, Smiths		7	5	3
John Gayden, Grays		128	6	1
Archibald Skinner's orphans, Allens		199	17	1

(92)

Fortunate Drawers	Capts. Dist.	No.	Dt.	Sec.
Solomon Slisher, Shaws		99	4	1
Mary Payner, widow R. S., Allens		177	9	5
Fenton Starr, widow, do		155	8	5
John Taylor, Shaws		126	5	1
HOUSTON.				
William Girtman, soldier, Pitts		101	15	5
Jeremiah Walker, soldier, do		217	10	1
IRWIN.				
William Lancaster, Underwoods		203	23	2
JACKSON.				
Mary Street, widow, Stephens		214	5	1
John Story, soldier, Storys		256	20	2
John Camp, Landrums		78	15	2
Elias Greene, Venables		224	3	5
Henry Swann, soldier, Staplers		120	3	1
Isaac Boring, R. S., Landrums		278	14	1
Charles Ivy, Millers		141	7	3
Reuben Nash, Rogers		132	15	5
David Pierce, Venables		130	19	1
Elizabeth Cook, w. R. S., Lindseys		200	2	2
JASPER.				
Jefferson Clay, Holmes		195	26	1
William H. Prichett, sol., Comptons		136	8	1
John Compton, jr. Dardens		167	28	1
Nancy Heath, widow, Wilders		90	32	1
Vines Harwell, Prices		128	3	4
Willis Spier, Keys		41	6	1
Harrison V. Revill, Sparks		128	2	3
Willis M. Williamson, Holmes		162	24	1
Thomas W. Carroll, sol., Hollands		9	25	1
Darby Guinn's illegitimates, Sparks		142	7	4
Jeremiah Lumsden, R. S., Baynes		46	9	2
John Barnes, Farleys		80	1	2
John T. Boykin, Butts		203	2	5
Kinsman Knight, Keys		177	5	5
Sampson D. Harrison, do		207	11	1
James M. Williams, Barnes		58	5	2
Robert Williams, Reeves		86	12	3
Alfred Shorter, Holmes		246	2	4
William J. Smith, Keys		188	9	5
Wiseman Bridges, Shropshiers		13	32	1
JEFFERSON.				
Elizabeth Bowling, widow, Ross		160	13	2
James A. Caswell, Beatys		269	2	4
David Lanier, Waldens		219	27	1
Susan Vainright, widow, Elliotts		249	16	2
William Donaldson's orps. Causeys		224	20	1
JONES.				
Elias Jordan, Popes		31	27	1
Unity Jackson, widow, Lows		121	1	2
Jesse Smith's minors, Bowens		10	13	2
James Graves, Duncans		32	12	2
Mark Hicks, soldier, Bowens		50	6	2
Thomas McKinney, Lows		25	23	1
Archibald D. Jackson, Blounts		225	15	1
Frances M Moore, wid. Hendersons		189	3	2
Delina Farley, w R. S., do		99	11	3
Henry Pruett, Dosters		127	21	1
Amon McMillion, Newbys		78	1	5
Jemima Hasty, widow, Breedloves		16	9	2
George Ross, Blounts		129	15	1
Elizabeth Wall's minors, Stewarts		160	18	2
Hearndon Patterson, Hammocks		49	32	1
LAURENS.				
William Smith, Whiteheads		81	8	4
Eason Greene, Deans		10	20	2
Thomas P. Chairs, Barlows		190	7	3

Fortunate Drawers	Capts. Dist.	No.	Dt.	Sec.
Samuel Spark, orphans, Deans		216	23	2
Kean Sanford, Mizells		117	9	1
Sarah Duke's illegitimates, do		231	15	1
Reuben C. Martin, do		164	12	5
Samuel Faust, Spivy's		57	17	1
LINCOLN.				
James C. Henley, Hardys		223	11	5
Patty Sharp, w.R.S. Wiggintons		211	11	3
William Hawes, Graves		49	20	2
William Barnett, Lonorgans		279	12	3
Shelton Loflin, Gideons		147	32	1
MADISON.				
Garrott W. Parks, Adairs		143	9	2
Charles Finch, illegit. Bones		171	22	1
Betsey Cooper, w.R.S.Hancocks		106	2	5
MONROE.				
James Bryant, Browns		33	8	1
Joseph Godard, Johnsons		46	2	4
Benj. O. Conner, R. S. Douglass		98	12	5
——— Duncans orphs. Gammons		166	2	4
John S. Adams, Millers		114	4	5
George Martilner orph. do.		150	3	4
Gabriel McCoys orps. Houses		132	8	4
Nancy Oliver, h. ab. Woodwards		81	6	3
Mary Thornton, wid. Johnsons		229	4	1
Charles Roberts, sol. Knights		28	14	2
John Richardson, Greshams		14	11	1
John Riddle, R. S. Johnsons		7	13	1
MORGAN.				
Robert Watson, jr. Dawsons		25	14	2
James Parker, Christians		147	33	1
Lucy Clark, w. R. S. Canifaxs		76	16	1
William Anglin, Adairs		29	21	1
John C. Evans orps. Harwells		51	21	1
George Campbell, Gains		190	25	1
Harrison McClarin, Shearmans		58	27	1
Samuel C. Torbert, sol. Adairs		253	13	1
Benjamin F. Watts, Stokes		74	26	1
Jesse Reed, soldier, Christians		25	26	1
MONTGOMERY.				
William Bohanon, Pridgeons		285	14	1
Norman McRae, McMillons		333	7	5
NEWTON.				
Simeon W. Evans, illeg. Askews		168	18	1
Charles M. Berry, Pullins		97	6	2
William McGouirk, Snows		252	24	1
George Ruff, Hays		197	17	2
Isham Berry, R. S., Webbs		346	22	1
Richard McCartney,sol.Zachrys		136	15	2
Minford Wilhight, Webbs		198	2	4
John H. Burgess, Snows		152	12	2
Thomas H. Lane. Sommers		53	27	1
William Gober, R. S. Talleys		199	24	1
OGLETHORPE.				
Reuben S. West, Rhodes		105	14	2
John Gaulding, Holloways		147	5	2
Richard Thornton orphan, Seals		51	18	2
Martha Jourdan, wid. Arnolds		98	6	4
Lesley Carter, Holloways		5	2	5
John Richardson, sr. R. S. do		183	13	2
Britton Michael, Hills		235	13	2
Nelson Vaughan, Floyds		169	10	5

LAND LOTTERY REGISTER—No. 14.
[RECORDER OFFICE—PUBLISHED BY GRANTLAND & ORME—PRICE $3.]

NOTE—Section 1 is Lee County—2 Muscogee—3 Troup—4 Coweta—5 Carroll.

Fortunate Drawers Capts. Dist.	No.Dt.Sec.	Fortunate Drawers Capts. Dist.	No.Dt.Sec.
OGLETHORPE.		John Dobson, Bosticks	42 28 1
Thomas Neely, Holloways	4 2 2	**UPSON.**	
Larkin Smith, sr. do	204 5 4	James Lunsford, sol. Harralls	31 2 3
William Pittard, sol. Simmons	216 32 1	Agatha Patillo, wid. Paschalls	37 7 5
Thomas Davis, R. S. Rhodes	229 15 1	Vilinda McFarland, wid. Pettys	8 5 5
PIKE.		Jane Leveritt, widow, do	119 1 1
John G. Town's orphs. Suiters	52 11 5	George W. Smith, Saunders	97 11 5
PULASKI.		James W. Hamil, do	134 22 2
Robert N. Taylor, Kellams	87 1 5	**WALTON.**	
John Rozar, Powells	252 9 5	Thomas Jones, 249th	21 24 2
Thomas Allender, do	239 8 1	Derril Brazeal, 250th	36 12 5
Thomas J. Wheeler ill. Sparrows	69 11 3	Jeremiah P. Ransom, 503rd	318 22 1
Frances Harrell, Hurdleys	313 8 5	Willis Cobb, 559th	202 11 5
Daniel T. Clemmons, Thomas	107 8 1	William Guffin, soldier, 250th	47 2 3
PUTNAM.		Henry Greer, soldier, Pools	262 3 1
Henry Jones, Sawyers	22 3 3	**WAYNE.**	
Simeon Smith, Sparks	236 1 2	Ann J. Titchett, wid. Drawdys	170 3 4
Wigins Griffin, Allums	280 10 2	**WARREN.**	
Frances Hearn, soldier, Jones	220 13 2	Robert Black, jr., Kinseys	382 7 1
William Hurt, Marcus	205 29 1	Wormley Newman, Parhams	32 1 4
Joseph M. Sadler, Sparks	273 6 1	Robert Humphrey, Brinkleys	93 5 3
Orphs. of D. Anderson,Bledsoes	164 25 1	Andrew Danellys orphs. Jones	161 2 4
RABUN.		Sarah Reynolds,w.R.S. do	389 20 2
David Black, Mersers	29 1 2	Barbara Hutchinson, wid. Hales	323 20 2
Alexander Kell, Milligans	189 15 1	Anderson Walker illeg. Downs	124 8 1
Hannah Chastain, widow, do	111 9 2	John Gardner, Bulls	205 9 1
William Rich, do	210 5 5	William Kirk Baker, Hills	128 15 5
RICHMOND.		William Thompson, Adkins	225 11 5
Sarah Mayo, Wilcoxs	240 1 4	Bennet Yeats, Kinseys	251 28 1
T.&E.S.Ligon orps. Palmers	152 2 2	Thomas J. Grizzard orph. Jones	134 10 5
Keziah H. Russell, Huntingdons	67 10 3	Geo. W. Hardeway sol. Kinseys	234 33 1
Chieny Prouty, Augusta	169 1 2	Henry Champion, Saunders	37 22 1
Sarah Adams, widow, Blacks	129 4 2	**WASHINGTON.**	
Mitchell Nelson, do	43 8 3	Joseph S. Neely, sol. Woods	114 12 2
Greene James, Wilcoxs	217 2 4	John Conant, Floyds	121 2 5
William Duncan, Treadwells	138 30 1	Thomas Gilmores heirs, Avans	184 7 5
SCRIVEN.		Enoch Broughton, Jordans	168 2 5
Sarah Kemp, wid. Poytress	202 1 4	Wm. Kantons orps. Woods	189 1 1
Elizabeth Brounson, w.R.S.,do	137 15 1	James Cobb Peden, Whitfields	185 2 2
Benjamin Freemans orphans, do.	92 31 1	Daniel Coker, Floyds	150 27 1
Maryann & Gabriel McHenry,		Edmund Wiggins, Jordans	66 23 1
McClelands illegitimates, do	142 30 1	Elijah Powers, Woods	287 11 2
TATTNALL.		David Wimberly, sol. Wimberlys	68 13 2
David Mimms, Graces	38 5 5	Abraham Ayres, Avans	77 13 5
Frederick Mills, McCalls	88 10 2	George Veale, soldier, Oquins	123 23 1
William Tripler, R. S. Deloachs	128 23 1	George W. Massey, Floyds	12 25 1
TALIAFERRO.		John Dorch, Wimberlys	27 6 2
John L. Wingfield, Cobbs	8 9 5	James Horton, Oquins	167 9 2
Johnson Bosewell, Echols	161 10 2	Aylesbury Lord, Wimberlys	68 6 2
THOMAS.		N. Waller, for Wallers ors. Floyds	27 8 2
William Brumbley,	167 14 2	James Shirling, Wimberlys	75 10 1
TWIGGS.		Abram Elton, McLendons	122 14 1
John Faulk, Chamberlains	92 10 3	**WILKINSON.**	
Alex. Augelly, R. S. Streetmans	105 6 4	Elizabeth Bowen, wd. Fairchilds	199 4 1
Moses Duncan, Chamberlains	201 4 2	R.,L.&J.Weaver orps. Smiths	187 12 5
Joseph Graves, Graggs	79 33 1	Elizabeth Gaddy orph. Mathews	75 5 1
William Wimberly, do	226 16 2	James Willcoxs, Curreys	31 20 2
		Thomas Meadows, Halls	122 16 1

(94)

Fortunate Drawers Capts. Dist.	No.	Dt.	Sec.
Jesse Vaughn, R. S. Mathews	40	33	1

WILKES.

John Wells, sr.R.S. McDermots	46	12	5
David Plumb, sol. 164th	127	25	1
Mary Moncrieff, wd. Richersons	107	5	3
Sherod S. Little, Moors	253	33	1
Joseph Shepherd, Popes	162	7	1
Charles F. Sherburn, Charltons	203	16	1

31st DAY'S DRAWING—April 11.

APPLING.

Mary Mann, widow, Collins	36	5	2

BALDWIN.

Thomas Jones, Reddings	33	10	2
Samuel Flint, Perry's battalion	243	11	1
Henry H. Wheeler, Doles	218	21	2
Narcissa Tolbert, widow, Ginns	177	11	2

BIBB.

Mary Jernigan, widow, Carrs	79	2	5
Lewis B. Langford, Beards	84	2	1
Hardy Newson, soldier, Flanders	106	3	2
Stephen J. Garner, Carrs	259	12	3
Luke J. Morgan, soldier, Beards	175	3	4
David Patton, Carrs	138	1	1
Nimrod Jackson, Rutlands	253	15	1
Joseph Mosely, R S, Carrs	106	17	1

BRYAN.

Ann Hayman, widow R. S., Harveys	165	11	5
Asa Cox, do	184	9	5

BULLOCH.

Jesse Duke, Richardsons	49	4	5
Rowan Futch, do.	209	6	3
Abishai Turner, R S., Burnetts	266	2	3
James B. McCall, Richardsons	20	9	4
Elsey Beasley, Lockharts	239	25	1

BURKE.

Henry Turner, R. S., McKays	184	4	2
John Turner, do	118	6	3
Samuel Fickling, Dugas	183	5	4
John P Allen, Seegars	172	17	1
Edmund Grant, Wests	82	17	1
Nancy Haslip, wid. w., Lynchs	191	1	4
Robert Tarver, Fountains	275	16	2
Samuel Segar, Gordons	173	18	2
Jeremiah Atkinson, Wards	10	6	1
Thomas Floyd, Corkers	168	13	2
Andrew Hardwick, Baileys	92	11	3

BUTTS.

John Nance, Moores	141	23	1

CAMDEN.

Clementine Ganleer, hus ab. Wards	28	3	2

CHATHAM.

Lewis Ellerbee	81	17	1
Mary Putnam, widow, Baines	247	6	5
Hester Ann Shearman, widow, do	79	8	4
Adeline Stephens, orp Geredons	67	3	5
Robert Harvey, Reeds	93	5	5
Elinor Sanders, hus ab Garedons	92	22	2
Elizabeth Gionovoly wid Reeds	106	28	1

CLARK.

David Kimbell, R. S., Andersons	2	4	2
William H Puryear, do	186	7	3
Stephen Crow, R. S., Dickins	5	3	2
George Dent, Gahagans	152	13	1

COLUMBIA.

Ann E Harris, min.of Edw.,Carrolls	31	19	1

Fortunate Drawers Capts. Dist.	No.	Dt.	Sec.
James M. McDonald, Bealls	116	22	2
Lorenzo Willingham, Baileys	10	12	5
William Bardin, soldier,Tankersley,	128	1	5
Elias Mabry, R S, Adams	35	11	3
Sarah Eubanks, widow, Culbreaths	62	8	3
David Perryman, Dranes	245	4	3
Agnes Moffett,widow,Coles	233	3	3
Henry W. Cobb's orphans, Talberts	203	6	1
Araminta S. Musgrove, min. Adams	156	7	1
Thomas Dozier, sen Perrys	202	2	2
Ann Burnside, wid R S, Carrolls	175	15	2

CRAWFORD.

Joseph Jones, soldier, Rhodes	187	17	1
Dempsey Howell, soldier, Moors	32	8	3
James McGee's orphans, Tillers	49	7	1
Levi Peacock, Rhodes	248	24	1
William Pickard, soldier, Tillers	121	21	1

DECATUR.

David Strickland, Douglass	151	12	2
John Bryan, Hawthorne	13	11	2

DE KALB.

Reuben Carpenter, Bakers	155	1	1
Ephraim Stadifer, Stephens	253	2	4
Hasting Palmer, Conns	163	12	3
William R. Black, do.	59	9	3
Clemmons Mullins, Howells	101	31	1

DOOLY.

Charnick A. Tharp, Andersons	79	9	5

EARLY.

Willis Murphy, Wilsons	55	10	3
Daniel Roe, Grimsleys	80	10	3

EFFINGHAM.

Josiah Hawthorn, Elkins	94	10	3
Han. E. Fryermuth,wid.Waldhaners	315	15	1

ELBERT.

Thomas J. Heard, Boltons	271	5	1
Thomas Adams, sen. R S., Hortons	268	4	2
Washington Craft, Dunns	159	17	2
Joseph Allen, sen R S, Merritts	41	3	3
ames King, Deadwilders	125	9	2

EMANUEL.

Henry Douglass, idiot, Nabbs	243	6	1
Moses Jewil, Whiddons	68	16	2

FAYETTE.

Kinchen Bohannon, soldier, Browns	160	15	2
William Wodsworth, sol. Landrums	160	24	1
Sarah M. Wakefield, illegitimate,	102	5	4
John C. Lumpkins, 9th	165	19	1
Charles A. Dickson, Whortons	156	7	4
Joshua Cox, Craigs	256	18	2
Sarah Barrett, widow, do	199	5	5
Jacob Langley,	176	11	3

FRANKLIN.

Orps.ofT.D.Jordan,Blankinships	233	9	5
Charles Darby, sen. McDonalds	11	19	1
Cynthia C. Ashworth, ill. Boswells	23	28	1
Enoch Gaddess, Walters	236	10	2
Asa Bellamy, Stranges	98	1	4
Osban Russell, do	205	14	1
Lit. Cleveland, illegit., Stephens	32	6	3
Carlisle B. Crow, Corkers	238	26	1

GLYNN.

John Morrison, McLeods	86	1	5
William W. Hazzard, Dubignons	44	2	2

GREENE.

Eli Littlejohn, Bruces	67	28	1

(95)

Fortunate Drawers Capts. Dist.	No.	Dt.	Sec.
Nancy O'Conners. widow, Halls	179	5	4
Orps.ofJosephSingleton,Rankins	180	30	1
George G Floyd, Astins	252	4	2
Thomas A. Williams orph. Greens	40	14	2
John D. Carrill, Vincents	59	1	1
James Jenkins, R. S., Robinsons	305	15	1
Christian Thomas, il. Copelands	150	10	5
GWINNETT.			
Peggy Niblett, widow, Davis	131	23	1
James Callaway, Moores	118	3	4
James Bagley's orphans, do.	96	6	4
Thompson McGuire, sol. Davis	53	2	3
Roderick Mathews, Robertsons	198	7	1
Jesse Demsey, Caruthers	224	5	1
James Conner's orphans, Bakers	102	1	3
Wiley Bagley, Moors	126	23	1
Jesse Burrell, Caruthers	233	21	1
Charles Bradford, Whortons	161	22	2
John L. Hamilton, Bakers	140	3	1
Samuel L. Jones, Woodroughs	75	9	1
Silas M. Beavers orphan, Rollins	73	26	1
HANCOCK.			
Elizabeth Duckworth, wid. 117th	50	25	1
William Spence, 118th	136	9	5
Charles H. McClammy, 102d	152	9	5
Joseph R. Sasnett, 118th	87	2	1
Nancy Minton, widow, 113th	51	32	1
Elijah F. Lumsden, 104th	124	19	2
Seth Kennedy, R. S., 116th	251	8	5
Hamilton C Alford, Hillsmans	300	6	1
Benajah Killgore, 111th	15	6	1
Lewis H. Reese, 103d	114	1	5
Lewis Parker,jr. 101st	116	9	1
HENRY.			
William P. Long, Shaws	248	2	3
Reuben Edwards, Grays	150	11	1
John Harp, Allens	82	30	1
Sarah Dukes, widow, Shaws	156	3	4
Squire Lyons, Grays	140	2	1
Augustus Y. Adamson, Wards	166	3	4
Elisha Coker,sol.J.W.Harris's	149	25	1
HABERSHAM.			
Elisha Smith, Tates	130	14	1
Sarah Stone, widow, Kenzies	144	8	3
Frederick Corrups, Suttons	296	8	5
Thomas Blair, Langstons	216	14	2
David Quarles, Bryans	243	2	1
HALL.			
Isaac Lindsey, Wilsons	39	20	2
Eli Miller, Smiths	224	15	2
Joseph H. McCleskey, Floyds	186	33	1
Curtis Lard, Roberts	245	7	1
John Latta, Hardages	183	5	1
Thomas Montgomery, Hardens	32	33	1
Benj. Whorton, R. S., Garrards	110	27	1
HOUSTON.			
William W. Forehand, Batemans	72	29	1
Henry D. Moore, Yarboroughs	106	20	1
IRWIN.			
Elijah Folsom, Underwoods	255	8	5
Constant Underwood,widow, do	145	21	1
Hames H. Crum, Bradfords	108	8	1
John Tilman, 5th	192	12	1

JACKSON.			
Fortunate Drawers Capts. Dist.	No.	Dt.	Sec.
William H. Thomas, Storys	128	5	5
Moses H. Potts, Duprees	77	4	1
David Hunter, Georges	212	6	3
Bryant Dees, Bowdens	115	18	2
Joshua Whimberly, Millers	165	10	1
Oliver Strickland, Doss	222	21	2
Martha Gates, illegit., Watersons	178	19	1
Eliz. Yarbrough, wid. Bowens	230	6	3
Luke Pannell, Winns	258	33	1
Isaac Boring, R. S., Landrums	345	28	1
JASPER.			
Joseph Prince, Baynes	18	15	5
David Adams, R. S., Sparks	277	6	5
Ethel. Gardner's orps. Robersons	94	6	2
James Pinckard, Butts	97	1	2
Abraham Key, sol., Penningtons	221	8	3
Nancy Simmons, widow, Wilsons	124	25	1
Lucius N. Richardson, Clemmons	315	28	1
Thomas McDugle, Baynes	194	23	1
Andrew Lee, Wilsons	13	14	5
Washington Johnson, Trussells	215	7	1
Elender Turner, widow, Dardens	105	15	5
John Castelow's orps. Barnetts	212	24	1
Hugh McDonald, R.S.Farleys	199	12	2
John D. Mathis, Reeves	251	6	5
Joseph Crenshaw, Owens	196	5	2
David Alewine, Camerons	21	1	3
James Gibsons orphans, Butts	86	12	2
John Vandagrif, Hands	29	4	2
Pleasant Evans, Keys	188	1	1
John Maxey, Barnes	240	6	5
Rufus West, Parkers	104	19	2
Wm. Grimmer, R.S.Camerons	5	9	4
James Tinsleys orps. Wilders	86	20	1
Nicholas Johnson,sol.Comptons	126	14	5
Green Smith, Baynes	35	20	2
John Webb, R. S. Parkers	245	13	1
Benjamin Goolsby, Hines	104	12	5
JEFFERSON.			
Samuel T. Smith. Boyds	291	3	4
L.&T.Calhoun, ills. Waldens	20	20	2
Michael Musgrove, Beatys	207	11	5
Norvil Adams, Marshalls	240	19	1
John Ingram, Causeys	62	26	1
Simpson Chance, R. S. Jones	157	4	3
James A. Coleman, Elliotts	238	11	5
JONES.			
Josiah Calhouns minors,Bowens	111	20	2
Stephen Reaves, Davis	125	14	2
Ann Dunn, w. R. S. Blounts	56	22	1
Thomas J. West, Breedloves	120	30	1
Elijah W. Harrison, Hamocks	112	12	2
John Moor's minors, Blounts	63	4	2
Wm. Causey, Dosters	243	19	2
James Cadenhead, Mullins	88	2	3
Susannah Hansford,wid.Newbys	51	4	1
Jesse Ross, R. S. Mullins	234	23	1
Jane Gamble, wid. Bowens	334	7	5
Pharis Gore, soldier, Hills	92	19	2
Joseph Bradys orps. Lows	208	8	1
Wm. Atkins, Duncans	26	18	1

Fortunate Drawers Capts. Dist.	No.	Dt.	Sec.
Wm. Ford, Bowens	103	5	4
Syd. Chambless, wid. Robertsons	80	1	3
Jane Culbreath, w.R.S.Taylors	150	8	3
Mary McCulloch,h.a.Robertsons	6	5	1
LAURENS.			
John C. Culpepper, Plummers	335	3	4
Charles S. Guyton, Mizells	84	1	1
Mary Duncan, wid. Beachams	117	16	1
Rolin N. Yarborough, Deans	292	8	1
James Stewart, Hodges	214	20	1
LIBERTY.			
David Delk, R. S. 17th	104	6	1
John Shaw, soldier, 16th	197	8	1
William Jones, 14th	171	15	1
LINCOLN.			
Richard Morris' mins. Gideons	84	10	1
James Jaco, Graves	23	32	1
MADISON.			
Edward M. Ware, Hancocks	164	3	2
William T. Fowler, Christians	132	12	2
Delila Millican, widow, Hannas	141	8	5
McINTOSH			
Mary Ann Sallet, orp. Demeries	230	12	1
MONROE.			
William H. Parker, Greshams	264	16	2
J. H. Pickard, R. S. Woodwards	66	12	1
Seaborn Jacobs, Wrights	210	6	3
John Evans, Turners	204	9	2
William Miller, Johnsons	74	6	1
Davis Maddox, do.	72	3	4
Thomas Reynolds,R.S.Greshams	25	11	5
David Bryan, R. S. Douglass	99	13	5
Thomas M. Speer, Houses	10	11	2
Ellender Dennis, wid. Douglass	143	31	1
Robert Kelton, Greshams	32	31	1
MORGAN.			
Charles Loyd, soldier, Watsons	83	7	3
Green White, Christians	256	6	1
John Clinard, Butlers	246	11	3
Albert Few, Shermans	153	1	3
Willie Stocks, Whatleys	101	1	2
Elizabeth Evans, w. R. S. Adairs	87	6	5
Wm. R. Whatleys orps. Whatleys	40	1	4
Nathan Barnes' orphans, Adairs	53	18	2
George Thompsons ors. Boswells	89	1	5
John Applewhite, Canifaxs	71	25	1
MONTGOMERY.			
A. J. Haregroves, ill. McMillons	38	15	5
Israel Watson, soldier, Popes	56	4	5
James Brownings ors. Pridgeons	187	15	1
Needham R. Bryan, Ryals	176	33	1
NEWTON.			
William G. Bilbo, Dyers	132	4	3
William Osburn, Orrs	21	1	5
John McKendree, Webbs	146	6	2
Joseph Mize, sol. Penningtons	141	19	1
Eleanor Burgess, wid. Hays	112	27	1
Robert S. Leveritt, Pullins	36	4	5
Richard Stanfield, sol. Zachrys	297	28	1
George McCleland, Allreds	72	2	2
Jesse Wisdom, Talleys	12	26	1

Fortunate Drawers Capts. Dist.	No.	Dt.	Sec.
William Teal, Webbs	5	29	1
Cebron Duke, Newmans	87	1	1
William Hightower, Webbs	119	21	1
Larkin Brown, Clarks	40	22	2
George Norwood, Snows	178	16	2
William Gutrey, Clarks	55	10	5
James Wiggins, Hays	51	6	1
OGLETHORPE.			
Frances O. Tucker, Holloways	210	16	1
James Thomas, R. S., Hardmans	50	10	3
James Bradley, sr., Seals	51	7	3
Nancy Bridges, widow, do.	238	8	5
Booker W. Hubbard, Laceys	242	22	1
PIKE.			
Thomas R. Sherger, Hartsfields	71	12	2
PULASKI.			
Hardy Powers, soldier, Gilletts	67	19	2
Oliver G. Williford, Scarbroughs	220	21	1
PUTNAM.			
Lindsey Roberts, Choices	38	5	3
J., M. & M. Mayes mins. Brooks	29	13	5
Ainsworth D. Gatewood, Stinsons	21	2	4
Leroy Singleton, Wilks	380	3	4
Margaret Lynch, wid. Clarks	141	8	4
James Lloyd, Sawyers	84	8	3
John L. Dixon, Choices	32	1	3
John Colword, Blunts	23	11	3
Mary Blankinship, minor, Goods	156	23	1
Rebecca Hays, wid. Barnetts	296	22	1
RABUN.			
David Black, Mersers	260	4	1
Malinda Burrit illeg. Godfreys	92	1	5
Mary Harris, w. R. S., do.	226	2	2
RICHMOND.			
Willie Jones, Treadwells	215	29	1
William P. Bagley, do.	227	23	2
Mary Ellis, widow, 123rd	150	4	1
Nelson Carter, Ferris	59	5	2
Israel Gilbert, Augusta	239	7	5
Benajah S. Wilson, Ferris	345	7	1
William Eaton, Wilcoxs	45	3	1
William Wiggins, Kellys	239	2	3
Spencer Smith, Treadwells	174	23	1
SCRIVEN.			
John Faircloth, R. S. Kemps	174	31	1
Rolin Roberts, R. S., Kemps	134	25	1
Sarah Conyers, wid. Reaves	110	28	1
Orps. of Samuel Kemp, Poytress	147	20	2
TATTNALL.			
John Ruis, jr. Corseys	80	20	1
TELFAIR.			
James Drake, R. S., Wilkisons	232	7	5
TALIAFERRO.			
Maryann Watsons illegs. Towns	100	17	2
THOMAS.			
Isaac Duggar,	18	7	5
TWIGGS.			
Elijah Hammock, Graggs	227	3	4
Breton Smith, sol. Blackshears	250	30	1
William Walters, sol. Kellys	239	15	2
H. Thompson illeg. Wimberlys	165	12	3

(97)

Fortunate Drawers Capts. Dist.	No.	Dt.	Sec.	Fortunate Drawers Capts. Dist.	No.	Dt.	Sec.
Joseph Caudle, Blackshears	233	21	2	William Dossey, Rices	210	2	4
Thomas Chivers, Graggs	127	5	1	Job Huguley's orphans, Lukers	210	3	3
Willis Durham, Wimberlys	117	2	5	William Banks, R. S. Charltons	103	9	3
George Holman, R. S. Bosticks	91	30	1	Hiram McCormick, Hamocks	47	1	1
Orps. of McDaniel, Streetmans	97	11	1	David Updegraft, Popes	43	3	1
UPSON.				Wm. F. J.Flournoy,Washington	105	11	2
Silas Strickland, Harralds	43	11	1	TheophilusWarthen,sol.Amasons	216	5	4
Frederick Smith, Coopers	40	13	1	Robert Ware, Lukers	150	14	5
Richard Gibson, idiot,	167	15	1	Wade Wiggins, Hamocks	100	22	1
WALTON.				Jacob Bentley, Richardsons	222	20	1
Sugar J. Mathews, Rays	195	16	2				
Orphans of Simon Parker, 503rd	19	5	5	32d DAY'S DRAWING—April 12			
Nathan Whitley jr. Rays	100	30	1				
Cairy Reeder, 503rd	98	18	2	APPLING.			
Ann Anderson, w.R.S. 250th	240	3	3	Cela Philips, orphan, Mathis	208	19	2
Jacob Carpenter, Bexleys	227	3	3	John Sellers, Collins	122	5	5
Phillip Barnes, Davis	61	21	2	Elizabeth Nettles, orp. Stricklands	261	3	3
Marry Harris,wid.do.	255	31	1	BALDWIN.			
Oscar F. Perry, Rays	45	6	1	Orphans of Nicholas Pool, Wicks	137	2	3
Henry Terrell, do	123	26	1	George Searcy, R. S. Wheelers	244	5	5
WARE.				George S. Perdue, Wicks	32	12	3
John L. Stewart, Bryans	231	21	2	Robert Preswood, Rowes	16	1	5
L., N. & H. Douglass ills. Bryans	404	7	1	James K. Lewis, Pitts	39	14	5
John Lee, R. S. Motes	106	27	1	Wilson & Mary Hubbard, ills., Bivins	57	5	4
WAYNE.				John Goodwin, Thomas	199	3	3
Allen Robson, sol. McKinneys	69	13	2	BIBB.			
WARREN.				John D. Collins, Beards	173	11	2
William Wilder, Parhams	281	16	2	Robert S. Patton, Bates	2	4	5
Joshua Stanford,sr.R.S.Sanders	176	24	2	Sus. & Eliz. Combs, orps. Rutlands	88	6	4
Vinson R. Courcy, Jones	124	8	3	Daniel M. Wadkins, Carrs	239	3	4
Mar. Carroll, w. R. S. Parhams	208	10	2	William Waad, Bates	44	20	1
Jesse Magraw, Sanders	233	3	2	Thomas Lambert, do.	118	31	1
Martin Die, Downs	44	23	2	BULLOCH.			
Nathan Thigpen, R. S. do.	219	18	2	Rachel Grooms' illegits, Laniers	24	19	2
James Coxville, do.	109	21	1	Elizabeth Fletcher's ills., Lockharts	106	21	2
Mary Andrews, Brinkleys	120	18	1	James B. Miller, Deloachs	20	12	5
Sarah Hitchens' illegits. Downs	280	28	1	BURKE.			
WASHINGTON.				Sarah Skinner, w. R. S., Wests	238	6	1
R. Thompsons heirs, Rushings	218	15	2	Thomas Boyt, R. S., do.	253	21	2
William Phillips, McLendons	105	12	3	Rebecca Griffin, orphan, Dogass	99	7	4
Robert Fluker, Gilberts	123	19	1	Michael Wiggins' orphans, Baylels	107	7	4
Thomas Wright, Tysons	46	19	1	Moses Martin, Andersons	36	22	1
Martin Meek, do	192	5	2	Milly Stuart, widow, Brooms	123	30	1
Lemuel Allcocks orphans, do.	46	9	5	BUTTS.			
Frederick G. Horton, Woods	181	8	1	Matthew McMichael, sol. Robinsons	41	8	4
David Soloman, Floyds	102	28	1	Charles Heard, soldier, Kirksies	219	8	5
WILKINSON.				Thomas Payne, Hendrick	43	3	3
James Welch's orphan, Smiths	78	15	1	CAMDEN.			
Rebecca Wheeler, w. Mandersons	175	11	5	Mary O. Corb, orphan, Wards	11	2	4
Benjamin Cornelius, Smiths	18	9	4	CHATHAM.			
James Garrett, Currys	256	21	1	Watson Farnel w. s. sol. Baines	224	18	1
Elizabeth Jerkins' illegits. Halls	155	12	2	Hugh Archer, Geredons	104	21	1
William Brewner, Currys	228	1	2	Hiram Roberts, Reeds	300	28	1
John Ryle, Shows	20	11	2	Lydia Jordan, widow, do	187	10	5
Starling W. Axom, Fairchilds	97	15	5	Jonathan A. Johnson, Haydens	102	7	4
D. & Z. Thomas, orphans, Smiths	99	20	1	Becrof Penny, Nungazers	121	11	2
John Hall, Currys	185	3	4	Orphans of Robert Mackay, Baines	286	7	1
Isaac Hall, Mandersons	14	25	1	Susan A. McIntosh, w Geredons	179	17	2
WILKES.				Rebecca Town, widow, McDonnells	102	14	1
S. Psalmonds, w.R. S. Ragsdales	156	3	2	William Robertson, Baines	227	17	2
William Gresham, sol. Charltons	92	20	1	CLARKE.			
Sarah Stokes, wd. Richardsons	47	9	5	Suckey Nunnally, wid. Wrights	26	4	1
				Jeremiah Robertson, Herndons	220	28	1
				William Carmichael, sr. Lumpkins	32	23	2
				Ransom A. Whitehead, Herndons	46	2	5
				William H. Gardner, Ransoms	229	2	4
				Mary Coday, widow, McDonnells	13	29	1

(98)

Fortunate Drawers	Capts. Dist.	No.	Dt.	Sec.
James Pearman, Birchs		182	20	2
Stephen Beasley, Gahagans		33	5	4
Lucy Adams, widow, Birchs		17	4	5
Catharine Newton, widow, Gahagans		137	7	2
Alexander McRee, R. S. McCrees		145	2	5
Patrick Leonard, Lumpkins		59	19	1

COLUMBIA.

Fortunate Drawers	Capts. Dist.	No.	Dt.	Sec.
Bathsheba Liles, w. R. S., Carrolls		150	31	1
John Edwards, R. S., Coles		52	9	2
Mary White, widow, Culbreaths		136	6	1
John Hobbs, Dranes		140	32	1
Edy Stallings, w. R. S., Boltons		110	4	5
Edmund Wood, idiot, Stallings		9	5	2
Rachel Powell, w. R. S., Dranes		137	10	2
Benjamin Watkins, Talbots		46	13	2
Thomas Johnson, lunatic, Clarks		88	20	2
William L. Locklin, Carrolls		226	15	2
Orphans of George W. Dent, Stallings		292	10	2
William P. Carter, Clarks		45	15	2
Elijah Leshley, Carrolls		65	22	2

CRAWFORD.

Henry Simmons, Wilsons		88	3	1
Robert M. Ingram, Rhodes		48	2	5
Edmund Brown, Wilsons		204	9	5

DE KALB.

John Hammond, Howells		211	19	1
Benjamin Hampton, Conns		91	2	3
William W. Cowen, Merritts		155	3	5
William Hearston, Bowlings		85	3	5
John Davis, Browns		170	23	2
William Palmer, Conns		312	7	5
John Barnett, soldier, Smiths		172	16	2
William Avery, Scaifs		238	23	1
Elizabeth Dority, widow, Stephens		8	11	3
Allen Camron, R. S., Smiths		106	14	1
William Glenn, Bakers		54	31	1
Samuel Norwood, Stephens		154	24	1

DOOLY

Josiah Jones, R. S., Mannings		156	10	2
Samuel Barker, Andersons		89	14	2
Manning Shiver, Sarrs		221	20	1

EFFINGHAM.

Elizabeth Denmark, widow, Elkins		159	7	1
Nathaniel Zettler, Treutlins		20	1	4
William Black, sen. R. S., Hunters		156	3	3

ELBERT.

William O. Falkner, Deadwilders		181	1	4
Thomas W. Davis, soldier, Tuckers		14	10	1
Tolison Tinar, Carpenters		104	2	1
John Harper, Dunns		227	18	1
William D. Haynes, Merritts		87	9	2
Benajah Houston, Boltons		24	3	4
Jesse Hendrick, sr. R. S., do		173	3	2
Henry Duncan, Merritts		251	1	2
Evelina Adams, widow, Bells		255	25	1
Edward Herndon, jr. sol. Blackwells		105	9	3

EMANUEL.

William Parker, Chasons		121	12	2
Richard Edingfield, Nabbs		2	2	5
Samuel Maulden, Moores		225	21	1
Feraba Thompson's illegit., Arlines		169	9	3

FAYETTE.

Willis West, R. S., Whortons		92	5	2
John F. Sharp, Browns		26	8	3
Wilie Dunn, Craigs		24	21	2
John Cook, Browns		87	19	1
Elijah Falkner, Whartons		238	12	2

Fortunate Drawers	Capts. Dist.	No.	Dt.	Sec.
Jesse Austin, soldier, Whartons		229	7	1

FRANKLIN.

William King, Boswells		62	4	1
Littleberry Bagwell, soldier, do		249	4	2
Orphans of Abel Peeks, Walters		168	5	5
Edmund Rozee, R. S., do		297	15	1
Solomon Tate, D., Chandlers		111	4	3
Felix Vaughn, R. S., Caudells		191	28	1
John Sheridan, McDonalds		253	3	1
James Norwood, do		3	4	1
George W. Conally, Sanders		8	13	1
Garrett Gray, Stephens		160	16	1
Hannah Manley, idiot, Cokers		226	10	3

GLYNN.

William Piles, Burnetts		174	7	3

GREENE.

John S. Curry, soldier, Dawsons		125	23	2
Rachel Lawson, widow, Robins		246	31	1
John S. Barnett, Halls		126	21	2
Joseph Fitzpatrick, Winkfields		139	16	2
William H. Swinney, Webbs		6	5	3
George Hunt, jr., Southerlands		110	6	3
Winney Ward, wid. R. S., Knowles		220	18	1

GWINNETT.

John W. Medlock, Bakers		165	24	2
John Strayhorn, Whortons		92	13	5
David Watson, Caruthers		169	20	1
Charles C. Jackson, soldier, Moores		206	21	1
William Laughridge, Caruthers		32	10	1
David A. Landsdown, Moores		294	15	1
Samuel Harris, Finchers		61	6	3
Viennah Austin, illegit., Whortons		14	6	3
James Ford, Maddux		139	2	4
Eliz. Bonds, deaf & dumb, Mattox		14	6	5
Henry Easterling, Woodroughs		80	24	2
Alexander Pugh, Moores		123	6	1
Michael Burns, Hunicuts		177	9	3
Arbin Moore, Moores		134	10	2
John Anderson, Greens		41	4	4
Wm. P. Glover, Gholdston's battalion		283	7	1
John Mills, Rollins		129	3	1
William Bates, Hills		207	14	2
David Rutherford, soldier, Davis		67	17	1
Gideon Jerrel, sol. Gholdstons bat.		47	6	2
Joseph Edmondson, Hunicuts		272	22	2
John Eaton, R. S., Rollins		31	12	2

HANCOCK.

Gabriel Moss, jr., 103d		28	18	1
Daniel Mews, soldier, Brooks		29	6	4
Timothy W. Rosseter, R. S., 108th		249	13	1
John Davidson, 107th		21	15	2
Isaac Johnson, 113th		14	20	2
John Horton, soldier, Coxens		269	5	3
James M. Williams, 102d		94	24	2
Jesse Battle's orphans, Hunters		137	10	5
James Sasnett, 113th		74	6	5
Robert Carr, 104th		157	11	1
William P. Edwards, 101st		125	15	1

HENRY.

David Sanders, Allens		19	29	1
Nancy Smith, widow, T. Harris's		151	5	2
Ren Lewis, Grays		117	23	2
John Lovejoy, Wards		153	6	2
John W. Poyner, sol. T. Harirs's		242	7	1
George Boyd, Shaws		35	29	1

HABERSHAM.

George Wheeler, soldier, Bryans		204	5	1

(99)

Fortunate Drawers	Capts.	Dist.	No.	Dt.	Sec.
Obadiah Hooper,	Kenzies		64	7	2
Cobby Wheeler,	Cross		138	2	2
Francis D. Tate,	Tates		7	22	2
Joseph Prince,	do		106	5	1
Thomas Houston,	do.		223	5	1
Joel Bramblet,	Kenzies		269	20	2
D. Chitwood, g'dn for 1 min. ch.,	Tates		197	11	5
Sherwood Holcombe, R. S.,	Faines		53	4	3
James J. Johnson,	Tates		40	15	1
James Long's orphans,	Cross		157	27	1
Andrew Oneal,	Jones		332	28	1

HALL.

Ellis Buffington,	Hardages		101	17	1
John Byrd, jun.,	Walkers		209	21	2
William Smith,	Garrards		229	18	2
John Ingram, R. S.,	Roberts,		30	7	3
Harkilles Foster,	do.		228	4	1
John Casey, soldier,	Alreds		220	32	1
James Pugh,	Yagers		66	27	1

HOUSTON.

Isaac Royal's orphans,	Prices		123	18	2
Duncan Nickelson,	Moores		86	18	1
John E. Waters,	Becks		141	33	1

IRWIN.

James Brown,	McCalls		183	24	1
John Walker,	do,		264	3	1
Thomas J. Marsh,	do.		25	29	1

JACKSON.

James Cowen, R. S.,	Winns		35	12	5
Solomon, Strutton's orphans,	Millers		40	3	5
Francis Bell,	Venables		143	6	1
Uriah Damron,	Millers		137	15	5
Jackson Trout,	Allens		92	15	2
Gilderoy Thomasson,	Bowens		110	20	2
Bond Veal Brown, R. S.,	Doss		34	18	1
Mary Ellis, widow,	Millers		169	19	1
Overton Harrison,	Storys		87	23	1
Allen Millican,	do.		180	27	1
Moses Brian,	Allens		292	14	1
Kindred Blackstock,	Venables		92	9	1
William Wright's orphans,	Moone		341	8	1
Jonathan Baugh,	Bowens		170	6	3

JASPER.

Josiah C. Lewis,	Camerons		110	30	1
John Moore, orphan,	Butts		237	7	5
Nancy Peacock, widow,	Sparks		185	5	5
Robert Givings,	Keys		72	2	5
Mary Holloway, widow,	Baynes		97	4	2
Moses Perkins' orphans,	Shropshires		208	5	2
Josiah Flournoy's orphans,	Baynes		104	11	1
Francis McClendon's orps.	Owens		283	23	2
William Farley,	Reeves		59	6	5
Howell Cooper,	Hines		42	19	1
Job Atkinson,	Camerons		63	5	1
Suckey Edwards, hus. absent,	Keys		223	27	1
Ralph Jarrod,	Dardens		173	2	3

JEFFERSON.

Thomas Walker,	Elliotts		60	24	2
Eliza J. Holder, illegit.,	Marshalls		143	5	4
Orphans of Lloyd Belt,	Fords		59	11	1
Bartlett McDaniel,	Elliotts		109	12	3

JONES.

Demarquis D. F. Comer,	Spinks		191	19	2
Marion C. Smith, illegitimate,	Bowens		111	21	2
John P. McGraw,	Gibsons		95	2	4
John G. Ramsey's minors,	Bowens		229	4	2
Benjamin C. Smith,	Newbys		82	12	5

Fortunate Drawers	Capts.	Dist.	No.	Dt.	Sec.
Georgia C. Pickard, illegit,	Newbys		263	8	1
William Johnson,	Gibsons		230	15	2
Levi Kirk,	Bowens		148	33	1
Thomas Abner, soldier,	Blounts		181	21	1
Nancy Ruth, widow,	Borertsons		151	7	3

LAURENS.

Wayne Eilands,	Spivys		62	12	5
Joel M. Goodman, orp.	Plummers		104	25	1
Edward Shepherd,	Mizells		109	4	4
Washington A. Copper,	Barlows		189	1	1
Micajah Varsar,	Spivys		167	2	2
Williams Payne,	do.		157	7	1
John Burch,	Beachams		193	2	3
Uriah Johnson,	do.		202	30	1

LIBERTY.

E. W. Russell,	15th		243	24	1
Hetty McAuley, orphan,	15th		214	15	1

LINCOLN.

George Gaskins,	Graves		187	28	1
Equilla Gilmore, minor,	Parks		43	1	3
Francis Gatril,	Graves		135	31	1
Spencer Suddeth,	Parks		149	30	1

MADISON.

Isaac Bussey,	Bones		132	13	5
William Power, jr.	Hannahs		172	18	2
Eliz. Baxter, w. R. S.	Caldwells		118	5	4
James Thompson,sr.R.S.	Adairs		106	19	1
John B. Adair,	do.		220	12	3

McINTOSH

L.,M.&M.A.Pelcher.ors.	Terrells		156	6	5
Dexter Claflin,	do.		197	1	1
Jeremiah Johnson	do.		120	24	2
Berry Thomas,	do.		308	5	3

MONROE.

William McKenzie,	R.S.Houses		119	28	1
James W. Johnson,	Wrights		28	31	1
William B. Hill,	Pattersons		154	3	1
James F. Johnson,	Finchs		60	4	4
Minerva Thomas, ill.	Fergasons		235	3	5
George Watts,	Millers		25	12	3
D. B. Head,	Wrights		139	8	5
Ann Pye, wid.	Douglass		108	15	2
Moses D. White,	Greshams		227	10	1
James Wilder, J.	Millers		158	12	1
Isaac Downs,	Finchs		275	22	2
Elizabeth Russell, wid.	Johnsons		286	17	2
Allen Belchers orps.	Patterson	s	143	15	1
Joseph Cotton,	Woodwards		63	2	1
Samuel Drewry, sol.	Johnsons		55	14	1

MORGAN.

Edmund Eason,	Adairs		130	5	4
Martha Hill, hus. ab.	Ostians		121	5	4
Moses A. Hartsfield,	Dawsons		68	8	5
Archibald C. Taylor,	Boswells		136	2	2
Thomas Davis, soldier,	Baileys		202	1	1
George Brewer,	Dawsons		103	9	1
Edmund Browning, sol.	Adairs		214	16	2
Elizabeth Gainer, w.R.S.	Griggs		161	15	2
Mariah Gatlin, widow,	Boswells		63	6	3

NEWTON.

William Miller,	Orrs		197	8	5
Edward Dean,	Askews		106	8	4
William Hodnett,	Hays		32	5	3

(100)

Fortunate Drawers Capts. Dist.	No.	Dt.	Sec.
Joseph L. Lourance, Pullins	243	8	3
Samuel Wyatt, Summers	223	17	1
Amos Sawyear, Moss	135	10	5
Eldridge Holeyfield, Zachrys	67	17	2
William Hargrove, Snows	160	6	3
James L. Trimble, Hays	209	8	3
William Thompson, Orrs	83	9	3
Samuel Thompson, R. S. Moss	213	27	1
OGLETHORPE.			
Patience Varner, h. ab. Rhodes	152	23	2
Jacob Freeman, Rousseaus	92	21	1
Abram McCorkle, Bells	118	20	1
Jacob Eberhart, R. S. Floyds	271	8	1
Thomas Hale, Lacys	96	24	1
Humphrey Pittard, Burfords	235	29	1
Uel Martin, Floyds	274	8	1
George Crowders orps. Burfords	101	2	3
Rice Eason, Williamsons	99	3	1
Eliz. Simmons, wid. Hardmans	130	7	3
Fielding Dillards orps. Burfords	54	4	5
Hubbard Williams, Williamsons	44	3	2
Benj. Petuman, sol. Holloways	194	9	2
Rebecca Oaks, h. a. Williamsons	120	15	2
Joshua Luvrit, sol. Smiths	116	3	5
PIKE.			
Ginnethon Crawley, Suiters	8	12	1
Jehu Evans, do.	13	19	1
PULASKI.			
John Wilson, Thomas	240	11	5
William Haddocks ors. Sparrows	166	2	2
PUTNAM.			
Thos. Kendricks orps. Kendricks	22	10	2
John M. Weaver, idiot, Brooks	130	8	1
Edward Hays orps. Barnetts	120	15	1
Ascy Mitchell, Allums	210	12	1
Franklin C. Sandford, Bledsoes	200	6	2
Tatum Spruces orps. Wilks	50	3	5
Benj. Orrick, idiot, Kendricks	232	3	5
Henry Morton, Patricks	89	6	5
Samuel Belchers orps. Vinings	74	10	5
Madison G. Crockett, Brooks	268	3	1
Mathew Farley, sol. Slaughters	235	19	1
Orphs. of N. Coats, Kendricks	161	5	3
Nelly Sander's illegs. Clarks	211	6	3
RABUN.			
James Allen, jr. Milligans	34	33	1
Ervin Price, Godfreys	103	19	1
RICHMOND.			
Harrison Musgrove, sol. Raifords	134	27	1
William D. Abernathy, Augusta	86	21	1
Gideon Tompkins, Huntingtons	40	2	3
Louisa McMillan or. Treadwells	118	5	1
Thomas Roberts, soldier, Wilcoxs	16	17	1
Henry Johnson Smith, do.	112	6	3
William Cumming, sol. Mantzs	255	29	1
SCRIVEN.			
George Alderman, Humphreys	51	8	4
Edmund Roberts orph. Kemps	208	12	2
Stephen Blackburn, Stricklings	75	19	2
Tarlton Butler, Pollocks	21	6	1
Stephen Blackburn, Stricklings	3	26	1
Fortunate Drawers Capts. Dist.	No.	Dt.	Sec.
David Mimms, Graces	226	20	1
TELFAIR.			
Hugh Cook, Lampkins	204	3	5
Hiram Ryan, Wilkersons	268	6	5
Samuel Hargroves, do.	3	9	5
Benjamin Yarborough, do.	255	18	2
TALIAFERRO.			
Mahala Griffith, illegit. Echols	274	4	1
THOMAS.			
Silas E. Crawford	238	15	1
TWIGGS.			
John Eldridge, illegit. Pearsons	85	9	5
Wiley Jordan, do.	316	20	3
Orphs. of. A. Sapp, Blackshears	42	4	5
Elizabeth Fitzpatrick, w.R.S.do.	261	1	2
Smith Ham, Streetmans	117	27	1
UPSON.			
John Black, Harrells	168	5	3
Hannah Reeves illeg. Myricks	153	9	1
John Williams's orps. Hattoxs	213	29	1
WALTON			
Hipley Moate, 250th	149	3	4
William Wilkinson, sol. Hudsons	71	8	4
William H. Holder, Hudsons	19	19	2
William Richardson, solicit, do	126	1	4
James Linvingston, Pools	79	14	1
Luc. Moon, w.R.S. McQuertors	199	18	1
WARE.			
William L. Mobley, illeg. Lees	233	5	5
Isbin Gideons, Bryans	173	5	3
WAYNE.			
John U. Geigar, Staffords	192	27	1
WARREN.			
Claborn Huskeys orps. Parhams	97	21	1
Sarah Hodos illegits. Hales	145	11	1
Mary Jones, wid. Jones	202	8	3
Radford Johnson, Bulls	155	25	1
Tamblen G. Jones orps. Rogers	127	1	4
Elizabeth W. Cary, w.R.S. Hills	109	1	5
Jesse Harrod, Downs	129	7	1
Roberson, Logue, do.	40	16	1
Thomas W. Kent, R. S. do.	8	20	2
Missouri Pierson, illeg. Adkins	5	7	3
Seth Wilson, do.	38	1	1
Peyton Baker, Bulls	269	3	1
Elisha Hendrick, Hills	62	8	2
Caroline M. Wood, w.R.S. Jones	48	5	5
Osborne Lockett, Kinseys	282	15	1
Aaron Reece, Adkins	4	20	1
John Persons, sol. Latimers	172	24	1
WASHINGTON.			
James Kennedy, Woods	44	21	1
David Dortch, sol. Wimberlys	78	27	1
John Stokes' heirs, Floyds	27	6	5
Anderson Riddle, Whitfields	161	1	4
William R. Stansell, Oquins	121	7	2
James St. John, Whitfields	161	1	4
Savoy Cook, wid. McLendons	143	22	1
Elisha Bland, Avans	138	20	1
Ezekiel Watson, R. S. Tysons	105	3	3
George W. Horton, Woods	62	9	3

LAND LOTTERY REGISTER—No. 15
[RECORDER OFFICE—PUBLISHED BY GRANTLAND & OBME—PRICE $3.]

NOTE.—Section 1 is Lee County—2 Muscogee—3 Troup—4 Coweta—5 Carroll.

32d DAY'S DRAWING—Continued.

Fortunate Drawers Capts. Dist. No.Dt.Sec.

WILKINSON.

Name			
Meredith Statham, Halls	154	1	1
Morgan Sanders orphan, Mayos	141	8	1
Elizabeth Acock, widow, Shows	57	12	1
B. & D. Hearndon,lls.Mandersons	57	5	5
Charles Whitehurst, Shows	149	13	2
Martha A. Shoftner, wid. Mayos	175	4	1
Abigail Holmes, wid. Smiths	250	29	1
Mary Benson, wid. Fairchilds	276	12	3

WILKES.

Name			
Willis Hyde, Lukers	9	1	2
Barham Calloway, sol. Popes	212	5	4
Edwin Du'Bose, Lukers	86	7	2
Susannah Huff, sol's. wid. Popes	212	10	5
Edward Brown, soldier, Moors	36	10	1
Gideon Town, Popes	109	26	1
Stephen Bowen, Washingtons	210	24	1

33d DAY'S DRAWING—April 13

BALDWIN.

Name			
Jehu Callaway, Lingos	24	18	2
John Miles, sen., R. S., Wicks	216	5	7
G. T. Dortic, Buchanans	166	4	3
Martha Moore, widow, Thomas	40	21	1
Mary Bailey, widow, Buchanans	282	6	5
Jacob Bailey, do.	192	3	3
George L. McGehee, Reddings bat.	85	22	1

BIBB.

Name			
Benjamin Wade, Rutlands	227	9	2
Kennith Stewart, do.	109	15	1
John Harrell, Flanders	201	20	2
Richmond Bosworth, soldier, Lloyds	58	5	5
A.B., E. H., & W. H. Dane, ors. Bates	110	29	1
Edmund & Francis Usory, ills. Beards	96	9	3
Nathaniel Cornwell, Flanders	37	20	1

BRYAN

Name			
Moses Johnson, Harveys	96	12	2
Onesimus Futch, jun. do.	26	9	2

BURKE.

Name			
John Young, Dugas,	196	28	1
James Tindall, sen. R. S. Wards	110	3	1
Andrew Elton Wells, orphan, McKays	69	5	1
Hosea Rawls, Brooms	83	10	1
Avery Dye, R. S. Fountains	187	16	1
Hardy Gregory, sen. Seegars	208	9	5
Abraham Roberts, Wards	36	25	1
Lewis Bryant's orphans, Gordons	243	4	3
Alfred Inmon, Corkers	173	4	2
Hurins Leptrot, do.	184	14	1
Rachel Volloton, w. R. S. Fountains	70	8	3
James Stephens, R. S., Lynchs	55	32	1

BUTTS.

Name			
Britain Adams, Adams	221	13	1
Isaac W. Jackson, Kights	110	11	1
Arter Kilcrease, soldier, Hendricks	208	24	1

CAMDEN.

Name			
Jackson Whillin, orphan, Coxs	178	3	2
Langley Bryant, Beckwiths	219	4	3
Elizabeth Woodland, widow, do.	181	6	2

Fortunate Drawers Capts. Dist. No.Dt.Sec.

Name			
Mary S. Strobhart, widow, Geredons	89	17	1
Joseph R. Thompson, Haydens	125	5	2
Orphans of James Caruthers, do.	55	9	3
Orps. of Solomon Baisden, Nungazers	200	2	3
Jacob Waldburg	170	27	1
Catharine S. Patterson, wid. Baines	43	33	1
Jane McConkey, widow, Haydens	162	21	1
Charles H. Hayden, do.	163	3	1
James Folker, Bains	82	25	1
Margaret Ratry, widow, do.	308	3	4
Martha Hines, widow, McDonnells	349	3	4
Peres Graves, Baines	66	6	4
Gay Crawford, R. S., McDonnells	1	2	2
Mary Ansley, widow, Geredons	80	21	1
Francis Dickerson, Gaddys	160	2	2

CLARK.

Name			
Samuel Morgan, Birchs	43	4	1
James W. Cawley, Dickins	216	30	1
Edward Bowling, R. S., Ransoms	152	30	1
Reuben Hamilton, Davenports	44	13	1
Lewis Bradberry, R. S. Herndons	153	9	5
Wylie Bohannon, do.	63	10	3
George H. Connally, Ransoms	228	10	2
Jeremiah Matthews, Davis	95	23	2
M.T.Burt, alias Humphries, ill. Frosts	250	3	4
William Matthews, Davis	47	6	4

COLUMBIA..

Name			
Ors. of Seaborn P. Huchingson, Bealls	317	22	1
Absalom Garnett, Magruders	35	14	5
Melton McDonald, Bealls	154	10	1
William Baston, sen. Carrolls	131	11	5
Aug. W. & A. F. Clark, orps. Clarks	257	33	1
Robert Tucker, R. S., Adams	131	11	2

CRAWFORD.

Name			
John W. Rhodes, Rhodes	102	3	1
Jabez Johnson, soldier, do.	126	6	2

DE KALB.

Name			
William Ward, Spruces	158	31	1
William Little, Browns	93	19	1
Robert Smith, sen. Spruces	163	19	2
Mary Davis, widow, Browns	227	27	1
Charity Harris, wid. R. S. Smiths	20	7	5
John Tolison, Edwards	85	4	1
Robert J. Chandler, Howells	256	18	1
William A. McKay, Merritts	94	3	4
Hugh Brewster, R. S., Edwards	186	14	2
Mathew Henry, Smiths	46	5	2
Captain James Martin, Merritts	97	11	3

DOOLY.

Name			
Julia Calhoon's illegit. Sarvis's	111	5	2

EARLY.

Name			
John Hodges, Hairs	109	11	2
Jesse Morgan, Wilsons	55	21	1
Samuel Conuel Day, Speers	254	4	3
Reuben Wright, sen. Porters	248	15	2

EFFINGHAM.

Name			
Benjamin J. Metzger, Treutlins	3	7	4

ELBERT.

Name			
William Bond, Hammonds	92	14	5
William Kelly, Dobbs	99	4	2
Sarah Clark, widow R. S., Merritts	167	7	1
John Childs, Tuckers	29	8	1
Ann Banks, widow, Alstons	109	7	2

(102)

Fortunate Drawers	Capts. Dist.	No.	Dt.	Sec.
Henry P. Brawner, soldier, Boltons		70	19	1
Richard Ward's orphans, Blackwells		68	33	1
William H. Moon, Bells		28	16	5
Martha J. Shackelford, wid. Hortons		100	7	5
William D. McGuire, sol., Carpenters		61	6	5
Elijah L. Christian, Webbs		216	7	5
Martha Penn, wid. R. S., Hammonds		251	24	1
John McDonald's orphans, Dobbs		61	20	1
Daniel Thornton, Hortons		117	20	1
Benjamin Fortson's orphs. Blackwells		44	2	5
Simuel Brawner, Butlers		81	29	1
Hannah Burden, wid. R. S., Hortons		75	4	2
John M. White, R. S., Blackwells		85	21	1

EMANUEL.

George Mallard's orphans, McGars	101	20	2
Mary Bellomy's illegit. Daniels	120	17	1

FAYETTE.

Samuel Harcrow, soldier, Whartons	123	11	5
James McBride, jr. do	250	11	2
Wyatt Reeves's orpahns, Browns	192	8	5

FRANKLIN.

Rachel Ramsey, wid. R. S., Hudsons	135	12	5
John P. Carnes, Walters	211	9	3
Ottoway W. Vaughan, Blankinships	60	6	1
Elizabeth W. West, widow, Jones	193	24	1
John McFarland, Blankenships	82	14	1
Oliver H. Perry & Delilah T. Norwood, ills. Blankinships	151	3	4
Daniel Bryson, Stranges	135	19	2
Daniel Moseley, Tabors	218	12	1
John White, soldier, Boswelle	11	13	1

GLYNN.

Coothes R. Denison, Burnettes	27	27	1
John R. Sanders, do	209	11	5
John L. Dewit, do.	122	5	2

GREENE.

Sussannah Bridges, wid. R. S. Elys	135	10	1
John M. Calhoon, Knowles	370	3	4
Henry Daniel's orphans, Colcloughs	100	15	5
Josephus Echols, Robins	95	30	1
Nancy Hubbard, widow, Webbs	252	20	2
Eliza Ann Swann illegitimate, Elys	109	32	1

GWINNETT.

Charles Eastis, Evans	223	9	2
Rachel Bennett, deaf & d. Whortons	13	9	2
Mary Wing, widow, Hills	65	2	4
Edmund Bagley, Moors	201	17	1
Hannah Thomas, widow R. S., Bakers	159	14	5
Martin B. Carr, Davis	11	7	4
Nancy Bryan, widow, Maddux	86	7	3
William Bennett, Rollins	243	6	3
James Harrold, Caruthers	98	1	4
Robert Miller, Greens,	165	20	2
Elizabeth Bowman wid. Woodroughs	1	5	2
John W. Thompson, Moors	253	5	1
Littleton Hunt, R. S., Finchers	53	32	1
Robert Nash, Dunbars	8	9	4
Samuel M. Wardlow, Hunicuts	128	22	1
Simeon Conyer, Moors	119	20	1

HABERSHAM.

Christopher Vickery, sen., Bryans	241	7	1
Manoah Stephens, Suttons	131	8	3
John Blythe, soldier, Tates	136	11	3
Jacob Prayler, do.	294	1	2
James Z. Chandler, Bryans	10	7	1
Mordecai Brown, Jones	231	12	2

Fortunate Drawers	Capts. Dist.	No.	Dt.	Sec.
John Presly, Bryans		62	15	1
Jesse Linsey, Faines		161	97	1

HALL.

John Gresham, Smiths	185	21	1
Caleb Garrison, Hardens	300	1	4
John M. Nelson, Walkers	252	3	3
Peter Edwards, Dorseys	108	15	5
Robert Obar, sen. Hendricks	209	2	2
Jephthah Brown, Dorseys	245	11	5
Zimri Thomasson, Harrisons	262	6	5

HANCOCK.

Benjamin Jones, soldier, Hillsmans	93	21	1
Elijah Eubanks, 112th	90	17	2
Bennet, H. Ely, 106th	119	4	2
Catharine Cobb, widow, w. R. S. 113th	39	1	1
Elkins, Griggs, 109th	58	5	4
John Radney, 116th	241	3	3
William Silas, 107th	83	26	1
Joseph Cooper's orphans, 106th	224	1	2
Peyton Lundy's orphans, 108th	183	19	2
John Tarver, 117th	113	31	1

HENRY.

Samuel Moore, Millers	246	10	2
John Wyatt, R. S., do	105	22	1
James Howard, Grays	83	5	3
John McKinney, Millers	88	1	5
Parker Nowles, Grays	295	7	5
James Farmer, R. S., Wards	30	8	3
David P. Harris, Bryants	86	7	5
Clary Ann Ingram, illegit, Shaws	282	28	1

HOUSTON.

Thomas G. Barr, Hancocks	75	2	2
Susan & Betsey M. Mills, orps. Becks	147	9	2
Jane Edwards, illegit, Batemans	236	10	3
John Baldwin's orphans, Calhouns	16	28	1

JACKSON.

William Dodger, Allens	212	2	4
Levi Lowery, R. S. Millers	105	4	5
Thomas C. Barron, soldier, Rogers	19	9	2
Samuel J. Niblack, Allens	208	4	1
Thomas Finch, soldier, Paires	44	25	1
Sarah Honeycut, widow, Winns	10	8	4
Jonathan Kolb's orphans, Allens	148	26	1

JASPER.

Joel McLendon, Owens	170	4	5
James Wills, Shropshiers	231	4	1
Sally Thompson, illegit. Parkers	139	2	1
John H. Williams, Comptons	44	5	5
Bailey Freeman, Holmes	33	25	1
John Chafin, soldier, Hollands	168	21	2
Ieptha Clements, soldier, Erwins	129	6	5
Wiliam Trippe, Reeves	239	15	1
John H. Williams, Dardens	231	7	1
Henry White, Wilsons	225	5	1
Elizabeth Danielly, w R. S., Reeves	180	15	2
Kidar Vann, Camerons	111	14	1
Sarah Tucker, w. R. S., Baynes	31	6	1
James T. Hays, do.	171	10	5

JEFFERSON.

John Collins, Marshals	240	16	2
William Battey's orphans, Jones	243	6	5
William Wren's orphans, do	68	6	3
Robert Pyor's orphans, Ross	228	8	1
Simpson Chance, R. S., Jones	201	21	2
Laney Spann, w. R. S., Cunninghams	46	31	1
Mary Bass, illegitimate, do	48	4	5
Martha A. Kennedy, illegit, Boyds	214	1	2

Fortunate Drawers Capts. Dist.	No.	Dt.	Sec.
James Patterson, Beatys	77	1	2
Jonathan Ross, Ross	215	8	3
Morgan Rogers, Boyds	257	6	1
Alexander Gordon, Causeys	289	28	1
John Coleman, sen. R. S., Jones	154	30	1

JONES.

Jeremiah Lamar's orps., Breedloves	99	6	4
William Spinks, Spinks	126	2	1
John Wimberly, R. S., Robertsons	196	7	2
James Boothe, Popes	220	6	2
William Ruth's orphans, Robertsons	91	6	3
Jesse Braswell, jun., Popes	302	5	1
John Smith's minors, Bowens	107	10	2
Frances Gibson, widow, Woods	52	7	5
Irey T. Hobbs, Duncans	241	2	3
Anselm L. Evans, Spinks	77	5	5
Robert Baldwin's minors, Blounts	37	17	2
Jacob M. Guerry, Woods	17	3	3
James McBride, Sullivans	170	9	3
Ann Middlebrooks, widow, Dosters	227	21	1
John A. Prator, Mullins	82	6	1

LAURENS.

William Spell, Plummers	105	11	3
Frederick Askew, do.	43	26	1
John Leonard, Barlows	144	12	3
Richard Taylor, Plummers	232	2	4
James Marlow, R. S., Mizells	145	5	1

LIBERTY.

Burrell G. Whillington, jr. 17th	121	12	5
Nancy Townsend orphan, 16th	76	3	1

LINCOLN.

James Kinney, soldier, Hardys	336	7	1
Elijah Atha, Lonorgans	150	7	3
John H. Waltons mins. Prathers	236	9	1
Sackfill Walker, Frasers	52	3	3

LOWNDES.

Isben Gidden, soldier, 10th	248	13	1

MADISON.

Osborn Wiley, soldier, Bones	88	4	2
John Shadows, do.	190	17	2
P.S.&R.H.Hendrick ors.Caldwells	218	3	1
Samuel Vineyard, Hannas	117	3	1
William Brown, do.	23	13	2
James Sanders, R. S., Adairs	151	7	2
Ann Long, widow, Culbertsons	67	18	2

MONROE.

William Smiths orps. Turners	21	6	3
John Morris, Wrights	42	14	2
Richard Davis, Turners	166	23	1
Alexander Scott, Woodwards	139	1	5
Dsborn Rogers, (Rev.) Browns	31	30	1
Jeremiah Peddy, R. S. Turners	113	8	4
Rhoda Buffington, wid. Houses	109	8	5
William Orear, Woodwards	321	15	1
Laban Mathews, Browns	46	17	2
Chancey Corley, Johnsons	265	1	4
Mary King, w. R.S.,Woodwards	172	14	1
James Gilmore, Wrights	155	13	1
Harris Johnson, Finchs	195	3	4
William Tilly, R. S., Pattersons	65	1	2
William Casady, soldier, do.	103	3	2

MORGAN.

William Lane, sr. R. S., Adairs	158	8	3
William H. Brown's ors. Canifaxs	10	1	4

Fortunate Drawers Capts. Dist.	No.	Dt.	Sec.
Thomas Roberts, sol. Watsons	135	11	3
Peggy Hanson, w. R. S., Adairs	92	13	2
Martha Hackney, wid. Butlers	290	7	1
Mary Ware, widow, Harwells	7	15	2
Coleman Strange, Christians	140	29	1
William Lane, sr. R. S., Adairs	95	32	1
Obadiah B. Parrott, Beasleys	55	3	4
Bennett M. Ware, sol. Walkers	66	5	3

NEWTON.

Willis Williams, R. S., Clarks	7	4	3
William Watson, Newnans	251	18	1
Jesse Cockerel, Hays	74	19	2
William Wood, Graves	94	11	1
Jno.&Sus. Cornup, orps. Dyers	194	26	1
William B. Waters, Talleys	128	4	1

OGLETHORPE

James C. Johnson, Hardmans	250	3	3
John Teller, R. S., Floyds	10	7	1
William Huckaby, R. S., Bells	5	15	5
Mary Cooper, hus. ab. Hills	244	30	1

PIKE.

Charles Morris, Longs	79	1	2
Moses Joiner, Mays	312	6	1
William Gregory, Longs	150	8	1

PULASKI.

John Henley, Gilstraps	243	7	5
Bynum Syloy, widow, Sparrows	321	7	5
George Gilder, Kellams	103	1	3
IsomMcDonald,R.S.,Scarbrooughs	58	14	1
William F. Snelling, Bracewells	82	15	1

PUTNAM.

Isaiah Ansley, Allums	176	20	2
Zere Middlebrooks, Kendricks	264	22	1
Sarah Barnett, wid. Duprees	195	11	2
Elias James, Blacks	184	19	1
Benjamin Hearn, sol. Brooks	21	21	2
Daniel H. Zachrey, Duprees	35	12	1
Henry Alford, Kendricks	215	6	2
John Kings orphans, Allums	13	7	4
James McLendons ors. Sawyers	220	5	4
Toliver Stevens, Allums	71	17	1
Benjamin Linchs orps. Clarks	35	3	5
Lewis Herne, do.	188	10	5
William O. Love, Duprees	106	13	5
Civility Davis, h. ab. Kendricks	125	13	2
Joseph Whites orphans, Vinings	90	27	1

RABUN.

Mary Sanders, w. R. S., Becks	130	15	1
William Pell, Mercers	320	15	1
Curtis Pinson, Mercers	224	16	2
Elisha Coffee, Godfreys	10	1	2
Robert Rogers, Becks	183	11	2
Thomas Kelly, (Red.) Mercers	129	30	1
William Cobb, Godfreys	282	5	1

RICHMOND.

Joshua Jones, Kellys	5	1	2
John Hickle, Wilcoxs	244	3	2
John Pond, Blacks	9	2	3
Mary Anna Rone, orp. Treadwells	56	13	5
Jacob Greene, illegit. James	59	7	5
Daniel Howell, Keys	203	12	2

(104)

Fortunate Drawers	Capts.	Dist.	No.	Dt.	Sec.
Charles Hammond,	Wilcoxs		127	12	2
SCRIVEN.					
John M. Roberts,	Reaves		223	8	5
William Smith, orp.	Humphreys		69	27	1
John Morgan,	Hunters		271	7	5
TATTNALL.					
John Singleton,	Graces		137	7	4
Shadrack Sapp, jr.	Corseys		83	2	1
Michael M. Eason,	Conners		209	3	4
John T. Sharpe,	McCalls		66	13	1
TELFAIR.					
Willis Cook,	Barentines		162	7	3
TWIGGS.					
Jane Eldridge, w. R. S.,	Pearsons		125	10	1
John Denson, jr.	Holidays		329	20	2
Uriah Evans,	do.		45	8	2
Roderick Bush, ill.	Wimberlys		114	7	1
Silas Chance,	Holidays		93	16	2
N. McKenzie, w. R.S.,	Solomans		193	18	1
Ors. of W.McMullin,	Blackshears		209	3	3
Richard Brount,	Graggs		104	6	4
Elias Pearce,	Streetmans		19	30	1
Orps. of Jno. Whitehead,	Graggs		61	11	3
Orps. of Jas. Norman,	Bosticks		349	8	1
UPSON.					
Benjamin Tilman,	Hattoxs		2	10	5
Jonathan Richardson, sol.	Dukes		204	21	2
Chambers Cowan,	Ellis		107	6	5
WALTON.					
Lucy Odam's illegit.	Hudsons		119	8	1
Orphans of John West,	503rd		217	20	1
Senia Herndon, lunatic,	503rd		123	13	2
William Mirars, sol.	Hudsons		226	9	3
Reuben Weaver, sol.	Pools		45	30	1
WARE.					
Moses Prescutt,	Motes		5	8	5
Marian Wilkerson, illeg.	Dowlings		77	7	2
William Edmunds,	Motes		59	14	2
WAYNE.					
West Sheffield, R. S.,	Mannings		251	3	2
Moses Manning,	do.		167	9	1
Frances Harrison,	do.		104	24	1
Charles W. Chonaway,	do.		132	26	1
WARREN.					
A.,E.,M. & C. Spurlin, f.a.	Jones		15	14	5
John J. Johnson,	Brinkleys		172	11	5
Robert Gray,	Latimers		117	2	4

Fortunate Drawers	Capts.	Dist.	No.	Dt.	Sec.
James W. Carrell,	Hills		163	6	3
William Fowler,	Jones		36	11	1
Norrell Kelly,	Adkins		205	24	1
Allen Brainard,	Bulls		162	12	2
John Wilson,	Kinseys		4	10	2
Susannah Grizzard, wid.	Jones		124	23	2
Fanny McCrary, widow,	do.		18	9	3
James McNeal,	Downs		196	7	1
Mary Parker, widow,	Jones		226	20	2
John O. Laughlin,	Fords		264	21	2
Harrison Rees,	Kinseys		78	9	5
Persons Walker,	Bulls		134	24	2
Moses Rees,	Kinseys		118	11	5
William Kitchens,	Adkins		204	30	1
Elisha Allens orphans,	Rogers		155	2	4
WASHINGOTN.					
Josiah Fisks orps.	Floyds		186	15	2
David Carter, soldier,	Floyds		70	8	4
Enoch B. Smith,	Whitfields		236	3	5
John Blackburns orps.	Gilberts		84	7	5
Reuben Osborn,	Currys		212	1	2
Henry Bedgood, illeg.	Whitfields		103	7	2
Aaron Cox,	Woods		226	9	5
Joel P. Davis,	Oquins		175	5	4
William Casterlow,	Avans		62	7	4
Riley Barnes illegit.	McLendons		247	3	3
John Lee, R. S.,	Gilberts		95	28	1
Jessey Cherry,	Mannings		214	27	1
Mandafit Zalman, illegit.	Tysons		253	16	1
Benjamin Meeks,	Warthens		22	3	4
WILKINSON.					
Brice Ragan,	Halls		73	8	4
Samuel Nesbits orps.	Mayos		150	20	2
Sophia Heughs, wid.	Halls		194	2	5
Temperance Beck, h. ab.	do.		271	2	3
Charles Crafts orphans,	Curreys		226	19	1
Mary Purvis, wid.	Fairchilds		191	25	1
Sim. & Polly Adams orps.	Mayos		58	4	2
Jacob Curry,	Currys		185	15	2
Frederick Frenchs orps.	Shows		194	1	2
Sarah Proctor, widow,	do.		143	7	1
WILKES.					
Thomas W. Bolton, sol.	Lukers		115	17	2
Thomas Lesleys, minors,	Wests		23	14	1
Isabella Findley, widow,	Rices		237	15	1
Jacob Huguley,	Lukers		161	12	5
Charles Inge,	Greens		55	14	5
William Griggs,	Rices		93	1	3

☞ With the exception of 175 prizes drawn on Saturday last, which we cannot print on this sheet, the drawing is brought up to this day, Monday, 16th April. According to our estimate, about half the prizes have been drawn, and the whole will be finished by the 1st of June.

LAND LOTTERY REGISTER—No. 16
[RECORDER OFFICE—PUBLISHED BY GRANTLAND & OBME—PRICE $3.]

NOTE.—Section 1 is Lee County—2 Muscogee—3 Troup—4 Coweta—5 Carroll.
34th *DAY'S DRAWING*—April 14.

APPLING.
Fortunate Drawers	Capts. Dist.	No.Dt.Sec.
Bryant Hurst, Collins		69 4 5
William Cook, orphan, McDonalds		243 17 2

BALDWIN.
John Moore, Pitts		44 19 2
John Gill, Wheelers		34 6 1
Allen Watson, Buchannans		40 14 5

BIBB.
James Asby, Lloyds		14 9 1

BULLOCH.
Thomas Jones, Lockharts		161 9 2

BURKE.
Thomas Moore, illegitimate, Wests		67 15 1
John Murray, Thompsons		66 11 3
Jourden Leggett, Lynchs		227 32 1

CAMDEN.
Richard Gormon, Bailey		251 8 3

CHATHAM.
James Conner, Williams		158 13 2
Joseph Habersham, Haydens		126 18 1
Arthus Conery, McDonnells		88 1 4

CLARKE.
Jane Sibbald, widow, Gahagans		36 7 4
John P. Ball, Mastens		156 19 2
George Wilson, Davenports		213 9 3
George J. Strong, McCrees		66 2 5

COLUMBIA.
Catharine Jones, widow, Talbots		81 2 5
Orphan of John Pearre, Bealls		280 6 1
John L. Brooking, Clarks		114 10 2
Vinson Reese, Adams		210 5 1
James J. W. Burroughs, Livermans		12 3 1
Orphans of Wm. H. Boswell, Ramseys		71 4 2
Joseph Collier, Lukes		158 11 3

CRAWFORD.
Benjamin Weatherby, Rhodes		37 11 3
John H. Monk, do.		172 9 1

DECATUR.
Nathaniel H. Hicks, Hawthorns		20 4 3

DE KALB.
John Carter, Stephens		212 12 2
James Grisham, Merritts		25 27 1
Eli Thomas, for wife, Scaifs		177 14 1
Jacob Greethouse, R. S., Stevens		125 16 1

EFFINGHAM.
John Southwell, Stricklands		311 7 1

ELBERT.
William M. Almond, Webbs		158 6 3
Thomas Lyon, Alstons		236 33 1

EMANUEL.
James Scott, Swains		267 1 2

FAYETTE.
Thomas Pearce, insane, Browns		150 6 2
William Betterton, Morgans		254 23 2

FRANKLIN.
John A. D. Davis, T. Chandlers		189 3 1
Israel E. Crowell, Cokers		55 26 1

GREENE.
John T. Sankey's orps., Newsoms		24 12 2
John W. B. Snow, Knowles		55 24 1
Wilson Pope, soldier, Woodhams		13 23 1
Alfred P. King, Rankins		175 9 5
Orphans of John Love, Dawsons		358 3 4

GWINNETT.
Fortunate Drawers	Capts. Dist.	No.Dt.Sec.
John G. Park, Hunicuts,		204 10 3
John Pendley, sen., Moors		126 12 1
Barney Macken, Hunicuts		214 18 2
Berry Hill, for wife, Hills		33 11 3
Southard Segers, Finchers		220 11 6

HABERSHAM.
Levi Swain, Vickreys		172 30 1
Jisias Powell, do.		91 12 3
Amos Ladd, R. S.,		181 5 4

HALL.
Curtis Lard, Roberts		23 3 4
Joshua Bridges, Dorseys		124 6 3
William Land, Floyds		186 20 2
William Kelly, do.		96 4 3
James C. Watkins, R. S., Harrisons		203 19 2

HANCOCK.
Sterling Bartlett, 118th		32 9 3
John Simms, 107th		151 14 1
Enos Mershon's orphans, 113th		130 20 1
James Huckaby, 112th		129 2 5

HENRY.
Enoch Hill, soldier, T. W. Harris's		156 15 2
John Wood, soldier, Grays		6 1 5
Samuel Brady, soldier, Shaws		136 31 1
Thomas Warren, Grays		359 3 4

HOUSTON.
Benjamin A. Tharp, Farnals		116 6 3
John Adams, Batemans		2 22 2
Alexander Brannon, Pattens		121 19 1

IRWIN.
William Taylor, orphan, Dixons		20 16 1

JACKSON.
Charles B. Martin, sol., Watersons		47 13 5
Judith Shackelford, wid. Lindseys		389 7 1
M. Jarratt, w.hus. died in ser. Duprees		166 5 4

JASPER.
Jonathan Winchester, Hines		136 5 1
Matthew Pridgen, Wilsons		46 1 4
John Payne, Barnetts		125 15 2
John Cargile's orphans, Holmes		192 23 2
John Griggs, Butts		12 5 5

JEFFERSON.
Zachariah Tedder, Elliotts		159 5 3
Samuel Bowen, Jones		195 8 3

JONES.
Charles Connally, Gibsons		25 5 4
Loren S. McClendon, do.		270 20 2
Sarah Walden, widow, Robertsons		128 4 3
Thomas Reed, Taylors		45 5 1
Henry M. Buckner, Popes		54 4 2
Nancy Gorden, widow, Stewarts		146 11 5
Williams Williams, Davis		178 33 1
Christian Duckworth, w.R.S.,Bowens		172 19 1
Samnel Goldsmith Stewarts		258 2 4

LAURENS.
Hardy Smith, jr. Powers		84 1 3
Theophilus Brookins orps. Spiveys		17 21 1
James C. Moss, do.		143 3 5
Lewis Bell, Mizells		148 24 2
Archibald McDaniel, Spiveys		148 21 1
Thomas Darsey, Whiteheads		213 9 5
Micajah Vassar, Spiveys		230 2 2

LIBERTY.

Fortunate Drawers Capts. Dist.	No.	Dt.	Sec.
John Carter, orphan, 14th	52	20	2

LINCOLN.
William M. Sales, Wiggintons	174	12	5
Abner P. Manley, Parks	210	29	1

MADISON.
Doury Smith, sr., Caldwells	70	4	1

McINTOSH.
Anson Kimberly, Terrells	101	16	1

MONROE.
Joseph Dawson, sr. Greshams	159	12	2
Anthony Cozart, Wrights	143	6	3
Arthur Youngblood, or. Gammons	120	16	2
Elijah Currys orps. Pattersons	135	29	1

MORGAN.
Richard Carlton, Hitchcocks	233	7	5
Oliver Cosby, Adairs	162	5	1
John W. Evans, Canifaxs	50	1	5
O. H. Youngblood, Whatleys	7	11	3
Mark P. Jackson, Brooks	179	1	4
William Harris's orps. Sparks	246	3	4

MONTGOMERY.
Silas, Nancy, Mariah, Theoph. & E. Simmons ills. McMillons	10	12	2

NEWTON.
Elias, Hill, soldier, Zachrys	89	30	1
Campbell Powell, sol. Talleys	212	6	2
Isaac Perrys orphs. Newnans	82	22	1
Esther Hamby, widow. do.	228	6	1
Mary Pool, illegit. Summers	98	15	1
Laurence Easterwood, jr. Moss	26	15	2
John L. O'Neal, Webbs	78	8	4

OGLETHORPE.
Jacob Lawless, Burfords	231	10	1
Josiah Goolsby, Wilsons	127	20	2
George Jordan, Mays	28	19	1
Aaron Wilks, soldier, Smiths	165	3	2
John H. Phar, soldier, B. Hills	6	21	1

PULASKI.
John B. Greene, Bracewells	244	4	2
Robert H. Joiner, Hendleys	17	3	1
Seaborn Rainey, Hendleys	218	7	1
Spire Mills' orphans, Sparrows	246	20	2

PUTNAM.
Lewis Linch,	219	2	2
Silas Monk, R. S., Clarks	104	16	1
Jesse Little, Marcus	211	1	4

RICHMOND.
Elizabeth Sheffield, widow, do.	137	1	1
Parmily Walker, orph. Augusta	243	28	1
G. G. Holcombe, Hands	48	2	2
John Strickland, R. S. Kellys	35	4	4

SCRIVEN.
Jonathan Dickky, Kemps	220	33	1

TWIGGS.
Harmon Perryman, R. S., Bosticks	56	22	2
Joseph Graves, Graggs	196	3	4
Thomas J. Gates, Solomans	55	5	2

UPSON.
John Smallwood, Myricks	206	15	2
William McFarlin, Coupers	40	9	3

Fortunate Drawers Capts. Dist.	No.	Dt.	Sec.
James Meadows, orph. Harralds	134	8	3

WALTON.
Tilman S. Cole, 249th	228	29	1
James Gunter, R. S., Snow	129	5	1
M., H.&Jno. Scoggin. ills. 503rd	100	8	1
Aquilla Greer, soldier, Davis	167	23	1

WAYNE.
Wilie Robson, soldier, Mannings	90	2	4

WARREN.
Jeptha Newman, Bulls	121	22	2
Elizabeth Myrick, wid. Bulls	111	15	2
Samuel Camp, jr. Jones	55	1	5
Catharine, Dennis, wid. Parhams	75	6	5
Wm. & A. Cook, f. ab. Rogers	124	9	1
James Brooks, Downs	67	14	1

WASHINGTON.
Archibald Cone, R. S., Warthens	57	10	3
Silas Floyd, Floyds	156	20	2
Sarah Rogers, h. a. Whitfields	61	16	1
Reding D. Thigpen, McLendons	123	3	5
Eliz. Howard, w. R. S. Currys	218	17	1
Mathew Moore, Mannings	268	9	3
Francis B. Drake, Floyds	134	6	3
Ansel Sneeds orphans, do.	201	7	5
Michael Hansome, do.	72	11	1
Vashti Boyd, widow, Jordans	104	18	1
Wm. N. Hargroves heirs, Floyds	23	10	2
John S. Collins, Currys	16	33	1

WILKINSON.
Shir.&M. A. McCook, ills. Shows	89	13	2
Stephen Birds orps. Fairchilds	248	7	5
Isaiah Dykes, Shows	89	3	3
G. & A. Jamerson, ills. Matthew	210	9	3
John Wright, Fairchilds	211	7	5

WILKES.
Raphael Wheelers orps. Lukers	250	17	1
Thadeus Sappington, Reeves	132	2	1
John T. Graves' orps. Chunns	187	5	5
Henry Turner, sol. Richersons	17	7	4

35th DAY'S DRAWING—April 16.

APPLING.
David Williamson, Collins	18	27	1

BALDWIN.
William Searcy, Reddings	218	5	3
Mary Pryor, widow, Pitts	122	4	4
Fleming Grantland's orps. Buchanans	220	8	3
George Simpson, Lesters	130	23	1

BIBB.
Henry Johnston, Lloyds	13	14	1
Penelope Thompson, w. R. S., Beards	141	4	4
Thomas Howard, Carrs	187	1	4
William Johnston R. S., Rutlands	230	9	2

BRYAN.
David B. Wells, Harveys	135	2	1

BULLOCH.
James Aldermon, Lockharts	1	25	1
David Smell's orphans, Lockharts	212	21	2
Louis Greene, Barnetts	39	12	5
James F. Fagin, illegitimate, Turners	181	2	4
Frederick H. Miller Deloachs	152	21	1

BURKE.
John E. Oliver, illegitimate, Lewis	24	4	2
Henry Y. Utley, Gordons	202	2	1

Fortunate Drawers	Capts.	Dist.	No.	Dt.	Sec.
Benjamin Seegar	Seegars		59	8	5
Martha A. M. Beall, orp.	Baileys		158	6	2
Charles Allen,	Rogers		41	13	2
James Anderson,	Wards		16	22	2
James Martin's orphans,	do.		4	3	1
Celia Dillard, widow,	Fountains		60	20	1

BUTTS.

Henry Lee,	Kights		189	3	3
Samuel H. McLain,	Thaxtons		222	2	4
Delana Sturdivant, illegit.,	Adams		309	8	5

CAMDEN.

John Murphey,	Baileys		101	7	4
James Allain,	Wards		245	23	1
Abram Pratt,	Beckwiths		196	5	1

CHATHAM.

Henry Champion,	Geredons		34	13	1
Dr. John Berthelot,	do.		15	19	1
Charles Levistone,	McDonnells		105	3	1
Peter Wiltberger jr.			65	16	2
Thomas J. C. Rawls, orp.	McDonnells		37	2	4
Catharine Shick, widow,	do.		154	1	3
Solomon Shad, sen.,	Williams		290	5	1
J. Montmollen, or. of Jno.	McDonnells		198	15	1

CLARKE.

William S. Houge,	McDaniels		43	4	2
Joseph Bradswell,	Alreds		113	2	5
David Archer,	Gahagans		98	6	3
George Scott,	do.		135	33	1
Appleton Hagood,	Dickens		305	7	1
Wesley Nance,	Espys		132	4	2
James Beall,	Dickins		228	16	1
Henry Turner,	Wrights		232	32	1
Benjamin C. Franklin,	Gahagans		47	1	3
Bluford Fuller,	McDonalds		56	14	5
Christopher White,	Esps		104	24	2
Paul F. Eave,	Gahagans		23	6	3

COLUMBIA.

John Roberts,	Stallings		387	28	1
Mary Jemima Wood, widow,	do.		218	9	3
Wade Pryor,	Talberts		241	3	2
Thomas Shipp,	Dranes		194	14	2
John Gray, soldier,	Lukes		116	11	1
Stephen Phillips,	Clarks		21	19	1
Horatio Simes, soldier,	Ramseys		228	2	1
Morgan Mellown,	Bealls		3	12	2
Elizabeth Clark, illegit,	Stallings		222	22	2
Humphrey Evans,	Culbreaths		148	14	1

CRAWFORD.

Daniel Hicks,	Tillers		36	19	2
William Greene,	Hicks		199	26	1
John McCant's orphans,	Hamiltons		200	2	5
William P. Harris,	Tillers		110	21	1
John W. Ellis,	do.		243	13	2
William Griffin,	do.		116	19	2
Simeon Monk,	Rhodes		158	12	2

DECATUR.

William Esles,	Douglass		32	20	2
Thomas Fane, R. S.,	do.		17	9	4

DE KALB.

Zachariah Gordon, soldier,	Scaifs		23	3	3
Marget Leget, illegitimate,	Bollings		236	21	1
John B. Nelson's orphan,	Howells		70	15	1
Sarah Corley, widow,	Smiths		70	6	4
William F. Morris,	Stephens		57	1	1
Drewry H. Morris,	Browns		179	20	1

EFFINGHAM.

Cornelius Riesser,	Treutlins		2	15	1

Fortunate Drawers	Capts.	Dist.	No.	Dt.	Sec.
Elihu Wilson,	Stricklands		178	6	2
James Strickland,	Elkins		186	11	2

ELBERT.

Orphans of John Tate,	Tuckers		132	15	2
Theodosius Cook,	Bells		234	3	3
Barnet Jeter, R. S.,	Alstons		82	10	3
James Vickrey, soldier,	Dobbs		33	13	5
Thomas W. Oliver,	Boltons		18	2	1
John Wilkins,	Butlers		15	3	3
Charles Wright, jr.	do.		38	15	1
Henry Tyler, soldier,	Dobbs		193	9	1

EMANUEL.

Joseph Sumner, sr., R. S.,	Swains		181	10	3
Rebecca Harrell illegitimate,	do.		80	6	5
Henry Brown, jr.	McGars		178	5	4
Ann Snullpeace's illegit.,	Swains		250	2	3
Rhodam Pritchett, soldier,	57th		229	17	1

FAYETTE.

Stokely Evans, soldier,	Whortons		265	6	1
James Gibson,	9th		113	26	1
Thomas Parsons,	Dodsons		286	28	1
James Hubbard,	Whartons		32	9	5

FRANKLIN.

James Wilson, R. S.,	Cokers		231	18	1
Elizabeth Nixon, widow,	McDonalds		181	19	2
Orps. of Richard Rutherford,	Walters		276	22	2
Orphans of Daniel Manley,	Cokers		30	10	2
George W. Hudson,	Hudsons		81	3	1
Richard Wheeler,	Bennetts		138	12	3
Joel Maberry, sr., R. S.,	Andrews		159	4	5
Joel Rice, D.	Chandlers		148	12	3
Micajah Carter,	Walters		4	3	2
Maxfield Holmes,	Stephens		61	12	5
Ezekiel Holcomb,	Tailors		76	15	5
Thomas Hollingsworth,	Caudells		260	2	4
Samuel Burgess, sol. T.	Chandlers		239	30	1

GLYNN.

James Pendarvis,	Burnetts		209	12	3
Caroline Cole, orphan,	Dubignons		115	30	1
Christopher Burnett, soldier,	Burnetts		131	6	5

GREENE.

Joseph Winston,	Webbs		120	7	1
Willie C. Mason,	Dawsons		107	13	1

GWINNETT.

William J. Russell,	Hunicuts		248	4	3
Jonas McClung,	Cupps		156	9	5
Warner Cupp,	do.		207	27	1
Edward Stidham,	Hunicuts		169	15	2
Micajah & Perry Long, orps.	Rollins		12	31	1
Charles Randall,	Hills		138	12	2
William H. Fauster,	Moors		157	17	2
James Dillard,	Robertsons		171	11	5
Malone Cox, Gholdstons bat.			272	2	4
Benjamin Z. Williams, R. S., Elbars			34	15	5
Bauldy Melton,	Hills		306	5	3
Joseph Curbow,	Moors		97	3	4
William S. Harris,	Davis		83	21	2
George Paton, R. S., Gholdstons bat			208	10	1
Winn. Underwood, w. R. S.,	Bakers		227	19	2
Henry Curtis,	Greens		224	4	1
Allen Wilson,	Finchers		50	33	1

HANCOCK.

Brittain, Manning,	Densons		178	3	4
Joseph Lewis, R. S.,	114th		105	30	1
John Jones Sawyer, R. S.,	106th		186	6	1
Thomas Griffin, soldier,	Dicksons		45	4	3
Catharine Robinson, widow,	113th		198	4	2

Fortunate Drawers Capts. Dist.	No.Dt.Sec.
Edwin C. Thomas, orphan, 108th	246 3 1
John Buie, illegitimate, 113th	48 15 1
Elizabeth Seals, 114th	22 5 3
William Greene Brooks	210 1 2
Benjamin Wilkinsons, 113th	79 3 4

HENRY.

Charles Linder, Wards	134 32 1
Orsamus P. King, Harris	117 22 1
William Weldon, Risons	31 20 1
Joshua S. Mitchell, soldier, Grays	49 11 3
John Walker, sen. Smiths	198 5 1
George & Arch'd Waller, ills. Grays	223 10 1
Catharine Lawrence's ills, Morgans	119 16 1
Isaac R. Williams, Allens	13 17 1

HABERSHAM.

Iverson Carder, Kenzies	222 13 2
Lydia Sheffield, widow, do.	26 2 3
David Smith, soldier, Bryans	235 18 2
Isaac Hill, Tates	61 12 1
Malinda Coal, minor, Jones	74 9 5
Amon Austin's orphans, Bryans	196 11 2
Elnathan Davis, Suttons	159 5 4
Charles Crumbey, Fains	212 16 1

HALL.

Martin Pugh, Yagers	104 5 3
Henry Jones, Roberts	201 1 2
Hampton G. Maddox, ill., Hendricks	39 9 3
John West, Hardages	24 5 4
William Reis, Roberts	22 4 1
Elisha Henson, Hardages	39 3 5

HOUSTON.

John Nichols, Farnels	61 27 1
Martha Brannon, widow, Pattens	136 17 1
Nancy Jones, wid. R. S., Calhouns	232 18 1

JACKSON.

Rawley Crawford, Duprees	93 16 1
Nathaniel R. Hood, Rogers	35 5 3
Elisha Barson, Landrums	114 3 2
Samuel Buffington, Venables	40 5 2
Abraham Williams, sr. Rogers	262 20 2
Alfred Brooks, Storys	281 7 5
Stephen Benton's orps., Gathrights	131 33 1

JASPER.

John A. Zinn, Parkers	122 11 2
Abraham Holland, Baynes	244 18 1
Charles McDowell, Butts	236 5 5
Burrell Malone, Dardens	22 5 1
George Whaley, Camerons	20 30 1
James L. Nixon, Trussells	264 4 2
James A. Hascall, Holmes	216 17 1
John Richards, Parkers	235 10 2
William S. Douglass, Camerons	125 17 1
Margaret Newton, widow, Wilders	192 21 1
Albert Dunn, Sparks	120 16 1

JEFFERSON.

George Cotter, Boyds	129 21 1
James Spirey, Marshalls	37 24 1
Abraham Miller's orphans, Beatys	324 7 5
Sarah Fountain, w. R. S., Marshalls	143 16 1
D. Z. Jones, wounded man, Beatys	158 3 1
Laurie Causey, Causeys	79 4 1
John W. Manson, Causeys	72 15 5

JONES.

Willis Odum, Davis	41 2 4
Walter A. Rogers, Blounts	236 1 4
Alexander Y. Robinson, Davis	64 7 3
S. Helton, blind, Popes	90 4 5

Fortunate Drawers Capts. Dist.	No.Dt.Sec.
Ann Comer, widow, Taylors	48 1 3
Tristam E. Feagan, Hammacks	252 8 5
Levi Eckley, Woods	108 1 4
John Dickson, R. S., Duncans	122 16 2
Dave Dawson, Popes	202 22 1
George Gray, Mullins	169 28 1
Phillip B. Snead, R. S., Taylors	227 9 1
Robert D. Martin, soldier, Stewarts	67 21 1
W.Powell's ors.fa. d. in l.w. Duncans	129 6 3
Miles K. Harmon, Stewarts	28 26 1

LAURENS.

George Mimms, Powers	194 5 3
Wingfield Hightower, Plummers	170 8 3
Owin Carroll, R. S., Powers	55 11 2
Joshua Grant, Barlows	98 3 3
William Cooper, Whiteheads	60 15 5
Stephen Carter, Powers	55 11 2
John Wilcox, Barlows	100 5 4
Barrel Shiver, Coats	129 14 1
Benpamin Ramsey's orps. Spiveys	217 9 5
William Lock, Bohannons	203 2 2
Charles Roach, Whiteheads	174 29 1

LIBERTY.

Edward Booth, 17th	87 5 4
Mary Findly, orphan, 14th	49 7 5
John Saul's orphan, 17th	174 12 2
David Delk, R. S., 17th	321 1 4

LINCOLN.

Vincent Lockhart, Parks	183 3 4
Anthony Haynes, Levritts	137 3 5
George A. Winn, Graves	220 10 3
Pleasant Gresham, do.	78 16 2
Isaiah Willis, Wiggintons	174 3 5

MADISON.

Elijah Patton, Culbertsons	77 12 3
Isaac Bussey, Bones	154 2 5
John W. Groves, Phipps	186 10 1
Plunner Potter, Hannas	103 10 5
Francis P. Eberhart, do.	209 5 5

McINTOSH.

Jane Cribb, widow, Terrells	184 23 2

MONROE.

Stephen Bailey, R. S. Greshams	241 28 1
William Fail, Woodwards,	256 3 3
George Willis' orphs. Wrights	111 30 1
Thomas Durams orps. Douglas	92 1 1
George McKinney, Pattersons	209 22 2
John B. Turner, Woodwards	94 9 2
Enoch B. Hightower, Pattersons	261 3 4
Levi Fowler, Millers	244 6 1
Benjamin Bray, soldier, Rays	42 7 1
David Bivin, Greshams	200 7 1
Edward Bumbleton, Douglass	129 33 1

MORGAN.

William Williams' orps. Browns	28 4 2
James M. Morrow, Boswells	247 3 1
Gray Mabry, R. S., Dawsons	160 12 3
Simeon Sanders, Jennings	255 6 3
Robert H. Elliot, Whatleys	142 5 1
John Studthards, Watsons	58 24 2
Hiram Harralson, Christians	236 23 1
William Cox, do.	204 8 1

(109)

NEWTON.

Fortunate Drawers	Capts. Dist.	No.	Dt.	Sec.
John Tomlin,	Summers	182	11	5
John D. Kirkpatrick,	Hays	21	13	5
Jacob Awtry,	Talleys	225	9	1
Dudley Milum,	Smiths	55	7	1
Joseph Morris,	Talleys	112	30	1
Nancy & H. Lucas ills.	Pullens	252	19	2
Thomas Black,	do	117	3	2
Corzine McGraw,	Dyers	240	20	2
William Mann,	Moss	167	4	3
Laurence Easterwood, sr.	do.	167	31	1
James Savage,	Pullens	166	12	2
J. & T. Kennerly, mins.f.a.	Hays	164	1	2
Nimrod Smith, soldier,	Orrs	24	2	2
Chesley Kinney,	Moss	343	7	5
Samuel Thompson,	Pullens	78	20	2
Charles Williams, sr. R. S.,	do.	227	20	2
Archibald Miller,	Talleys	109	9	5

OGLETHORPE.

John Deverill,	Holloways	176	12	1
William L. Dodd,	Billups	67	23	2
William Smith,	Holloways	28	9	1
John Martin,	Hills	210	2	5
Nancy Andrews, w. R.S.,	Rhodes	62	5	4
Whitfield Landrum,	Rousseaus	100	28	1
Wiley S. Whithead,	Hardmans	3	17	1

PIKE.

John McDaniel, sol.	Pattersons	392	20	2

PULASKI

Amos Pipkins,	Scarbroughs	38	10	1
Martha E. Anderson, widow,	do.	51	10	3
Richard Gainys, orphs.	Thomas	8	3	3
Hiram Dykes,	Hendleys	274	12	3
Elizabeth Averett, wid.	Kellams	199	5	4

PUTNAM.

Moab Elam's orphans,	Vinings	26	10	1
William Hearn,	Sawyers	140	9	2
Abraham Carter,	Clarks	19	13	2
Nathaniel Black,	Blacks	41	18	2
Coleman Burges,	Clarks	147	2	5
Wiley Bryant,	Barnetts	363	8	1
Eli Harris' orphs.	Kendricks	232	24	1
Joseph Wilson, sol.	Wilkes	189	7	3
Sarah Jones, widow,	Vinings	75	10	3
Samuel Belchers orphs.	do.	58	1	3
Jas. Daves's chil.f.a.	Kendricks	283	9	5
M. & S. Hines orps.	Dismukes	138	7	5

RABUN.

John Green,	Godfreys	108	26	1

RICHMOND.

Henry Hatcher, R. S.,	Wilcoxs	57	1	2
James Harper,	Hands	66	4	1
Charles Sheriff,	Treadwells	128	7	5
Eliza Ross's orphans,	Raifords	131	12	3
Elijah Sturges,	Blacks	89	7	3
William H. Magee,	123rd	52	1	3
G. W. Huntington,	Huntingtons	131	2	4
Samuel H. Goldsmith,	do.	227	5	4

SCRIVEN.

David Conner,	Poytrees	151	6	1

TATTNALL.

Fortunate Drawers	Capts. Dist.	No.	Dt.	Sec.
Hardy Deloach,	Deloachs	216	19	2
Jeremiah McDonald,	Conners	21	7	3

TELFAIR.

Joshua Edenfield,	Wilsons	111	10	3
Alexander McRae, jr.	Robertsons	194	27	1

TWIGGS.

George Young, sol.	Blackshears	69	9	1
Garrison Cobb,	Bosticks	240	3	4
Thomas Jones,	Pearsons	39	4	4
William Mansfield,	Wimberlys	164	4	4
Joseph S. Willis,	Blackshears	214	2	1
Martha Greene, illeg.	Bosticks	70	27	1

UPSON.

James M. Hightower,	Myricks	66	10	3
David Taylor,	Coopers	306	20	2
James Smith,	Pettys	75	19	1
Absalom Cox,	Coopers	159	10	3
Wright Perkins, sol.	Dukes	245	22	1
Mary Ashburn, widow,	589th	100	9	1
John Tilman,	Dukes	122	2	2
William Van,	Harralds	148	4	3
John Kennedy, soldier,	Dukes	6	22	1
James B. Hooton,	589th	125	7	5
Wm. W. Walker, sol.	Pettys	110	18	2

WALTON.

Elizabeth Sturdivant, wid.	249th	169	15	1
James Shepard,	Snows	127	10	3
John Ramy, jr.	559th	74	11	3
Ford Butler,	Bexleys	78	5	5
Jesse Bentley, R. S.,	McQuertors	178	5	3
Joel Sims,	418th	254	21	2
Samuel Coleman, R. S.,	418th	66	15	2
Abraham Hetton,	Bexleys	34	5	1
Elizabeth Sextons orps.	Snows	100	32	1

WARE.

Mark Lotts orphans,	Motes	322	20	2
Elizabeth Stalby, hus. ab.	do.	46	4	5

WAYNE.

Moses Manning,	Mannings	130	9	3
M. & E. Harris, f.a.	McKinneys	124	4	1

WARREN.

John Morris' orphs.	Kinseys	60	3	4
John Boyds orphs.	Adkins	147	16	1
Roderick R. Moore,	Latimers	39	1	5
Washington Stewart, ill.	Stewarts	156	10	5
Presley Spinks, R. S.,	Brinkleys	311	5	3
George Henry,	Jones	128	6	3
James Kitchens,	Adkins	189	11	2
John Boyds, orphs.	do.	77	18	2
George Huff,	do.	150	28	1
Greene B. Johnson,	Parhams	112	29	1

WASHINGTON.

James Cato,	Warthens	38	2	1
Henry Cox,	Avans	27	22	1
Martin Swift,	Castelows	142	4	2
Frances Sheppard,	McLendons	224	12	3
Benjamin Hood,	Rushings	160	11	3
Lewis Cones orps.	Wimberlys	167	10	2
Simeon Sims' heirs,	Floyds	65	12	2
Sarah Wood, widow,	do.	51	17	2

(110)

Fortunate Drawers Capts. Dist.	No.Dt.Sec.
Wilie Rogers, Currys	144 23 1
Asa Deen, Gilberts	111 32 1
Isaac Johnson, McLendons	347 8 1

WILKINSON.

Isaac Stinson, Mayos	166 22 2
Moses Dykes, Shows	202 12 1
Wiley Hopsons orphs. Smiths	217 3 2
Alsa Barber, widow, do.	166 13 2
William Benton, sol. Williams	211 3 1
John Hughes, sol. Ragans	57 4 2
Jesse S. Marshal, Mandersons	135 10 3
Simon Johnsons orphs, Shows	250 12 3
Jos. & Riley King, illegs. Halls	202 9 1

WILKES.

Richard Flurry, Washingtons	228 7 5
George Willis, sr. R. S. Reeves	151 21 2
Mich'l L. Andrews, Richardsons	156 1 3
Hezekiah R. Elgin, Reeves	31 1 3
Willis Fullelove, Wootens	197 32 1
Rachael Sceales, widow, Moors.	110 23 1
Jonathan Douglass, McDermonts	209 13 1
Preslay Aydcock, Ragsdales	70 5 5
Elias Simons' minors, Reeves	150 18 2
Robert Cade, jr.'s ors. Richardsons	1 2 4
Isaac Calloways orphs. Reeves	156 11 1
John Kents orphans, do.	58 6 4
Isaac Eason, do.	12 3 3
Nancy Massey wid. Charltons	66 2 3
John Omeara, do.	176 5 4

36th DAY'S DRAWING—April 17.

BALDWIN.

Daniel McDonald, Wrights	230 25 1
Elizabeth Evans, w. R. S., Reddings	118 3 5
Nancy C. Worsham, w. R. S., Lesters	158 3 2
Josiah Doles, Buchanans	301 3 4
John Hoy, do.	248 30 1
Mary Brownlow, husband absent, do	92 9 3
James Thomas, R. S., Pitts	220 9 2
William Hand, R. S., Lesters	179 32 1

BIBB.

John Dies, Carrs	102 3 2
Jane Harrell, widow, Rutlands	30 3 1
Britain Braswell, Carrs	78 16 1
William Pace's orphans, do.	16 8 3
Hirne Hall, Beards	195 27 1
David S. Booth, soldier, do.	76 29 1
Serene H. Dwight, Pickards	66 13 2
Irvin Bulloch, Lloyds	21 12 5

BULLOCH.

Mary Cannon, Deloaches	129 22 2
Dilly Williams, w. R. S., Lockharts	251 5 2
Josiah&JamesDavis, orps. Deloachs	134 10 3

BURKE.

Powell Godbee, Dugas	49 23 1
Robert Kilpatrick, Gordons	91 11 5
James Grubbs, Corkers	76 19 1
Edward Rogers, soldier,	215 15 2

BUTTS.

Jesse Liddon, Kights	176 6 1
Alfred J. Magouirk, Hendricks	135 25 1
Ann K. Kinney, widow, Johnsons	74 4 5
Wiley S. Ferrell, Robisons	100 10 5

CAMDEN.

Fortunate Drawers Capts. Dist.	No.Dt.Sec.
James Bentham, Wards	122 15 2

CHATHAM.

Isaac Drigger's orphans, Reeds	126 1 2
Mary S. Raynes, widow, Gaddys	193 1 2
Thomas G. Miller,	242 16 2
Orphans of Barnett McKean, Haydens	241 23 2
Charles Richardson,	79 15 1
John D. Mongin, Baines	232 17 2
Orps. of Michael Long, McDonnells	48 26 1
Elethia J. Sark Stark, orphan, do.	252 2 1
S. Mitchell, orp. of Stephen, Geredons	8 15 5
John Boyd, McDonnells	216 9 2

CLARKE.

Joshua Stephens, jr. Vinsons	160 9 3
Orphans of Peter Puryear, Frosts	221 12 3
John Andrew, R. S. McCrees	2 5 4
James Barber, Dickins	56 27 1
John N. Birch, Birchs	217 10 3
Benjnin Elsberry, sr. R. S., Davis	117 14 1
John P. Dickinson, Herndon	223 8 3
Frances McRee, widow, McCrees	153 15 2
Susannah Hopkins, widow, Vinsons	345 20 2

COLUMBIA.

James Fleming, Baileys	123 21 1
Orps. of Wm. Eubanks, Culbreaths	237 4 1
John Wooding, Bealls	158 7 4
Samuel Blackwell, Stallings	121 26 1
Warren J. Ford, do.	132 23 1
Andrew Tierney, Bealls	260 5 3
Miles Murphy Baileys	155 4 1
Sarah W. Walker, widow, Carrolls	129 3 4
Isaac Winfrey's orphans, Boltons	7 5 4
Lewis Mallard, Clarks	214 23 2

CRAWFORD.

Elizabeth Hunter, w. R. S., Rhodes	26 11 1
Persilla Ellis, w. R. S., Ellis	198 2 1
Perry McGehee, Tillers	186 21 2

DECATUR.

Sarah Brooks, widow, Douglass	50 2 3

DE KALB.

Nancy Adams, hus. absent, Edwards	39 2 2
Reddick Massey, Howells	114 15 2
Elizabeth Bradford, widow, Browns	24 2 3
James Hooper, R. S., Conns	206 17 2
Green B. Histerly, for wife, Merritts	389 28 1
Samuel Henderson, Conns	119 11 1

EFFINGHAM.

Guilford Dudley, Treutlins	197 12 2
Christian E. Treutlin, do.	204 13 1
Gideon E. Zipperer, Waldhaners	189 24 1
Orps. of Jacob Schrodder, Treutlins	64 4 2
Elizabeth Jones, widow, do.	216 6 2

ELBERT.

Jesse C. Childers, Dobbs	245 17 1
Reuben Wanslow, Blackwells	239 17 2
William Nelmes, Merritts	42 1 4
Thomas Wheeler, sr. R. S., Blackwells	97 1 1
James S. Teasley, Hortons	161 23 2

EMANUEL.

Hiram M. Jackson, Swains	118 11 1
Orphans of Lewis Webb, Whiddons	7 1 1

FAYETTE.

James Stewart, R. S., Roziers	237 25 1
Jacob Mercer, R. S., Browns	183 32 1
John Lamberth, jr., Craigs	200 19 1
Joshua Townsend, Whartons	50 24 2

(111)

FRANKLIN.

Fortunate Drawers	Capts. Dist.	No.	Dt.	Sec.
Tandy D. King, soldier, do.		75	8	1
Copelin Hickman, Wests		171	33	1
Thomas Cox, Stephens		72	3	1
M. & W. W. Mays, illegits, Hudsons		11	5	1
Gillum E. Mills, Andrews		231	3	3
Jenjamin Allin, Stranges		233	5	4
William Gilmer, do.		34	10	2
John Allen, R. S., Boswells		169	17	2
Sam Wilson, (Tan. Downs,) Stephens		91	3	5
John Harris, Tabors		212	9	1
James Whitaker, Boswells		82	19	1
William C. White, D. Chandlers		193	19	1
Asa York, Stranges		53	3	2

GREENE.

John Shaw, R. S., Halls		64	8	1
Charles Burk, jr., Southerlands		51	11	1

GWINNETT.

James Hays, Woodroughs		56	11	3
Thompson T. Adams, do.		221	32	1
Martin Bawling, Finchers		6	5	2
David L. Warllow, Hunicuts		204	3	4
Samuel Maffett, Evans		107	12	2
Greenberry Waldrop, Caruthers		138	15	2
William Bruster, Hunicuts		190	10	2
Jesse Thrasher, Moors		241	11	2
William Beasley, Hills		60	18	2
William Vineyard, Finchers		21	3	5

HANCOCK.

Lloyd Kelly, R. S., 112th		200	8	1
Ezekiel Cothram, orphan, do.		185	8	3
Lewis Voicle, R. S., 114th		297	5	1
William Kilgore, soldier, Hunters		17	12	3
Zachariah Wilkinson, 113th		177	3	2
Samuel Turner, R. S., Adams		259	6	1
Charles V. Brooking, 118th		156	21	1
William Skinner's orphans, 111th		86	19	1
Mathias Brimberry, Calliers		182	15	2
Thomas Dickson, R. S., 114th		43	2	3
Jesse Warren, sr. R. S., 101st		100	8	5

HENRY.

Stephen Tredwell, Shaws		255	24	1
Sarah Street, widow, do.		117	6	5
David Sanders, soldier, Morgans		36	9	5
Josiah Askey, soldier, Shaws		253	10	3
Leonrad Keegle, Allens		70	10	1
Aaron Jarker, jr. Shaws		184	17	1

HABERSHAM

William Holcombe, Fains		51	1	2
Elisha Davidson, Langstons		2	13	1

HALL.

John & Mary Smith, illegits. Dorseys		110	1	3
James Oliver, jr. H. Floyds		68	26	1
John Dalrumple, Alreds		140	9	1
Charles Head, Roberts		155	3	3
Jesse D. Hardage, Hardages		210	30	1
Christopher Cox, illegit, Floyds		44	11	5
E., E. & N. Dunaway, ors. Harrisons		171	6	2
James Williams, Kerns		4	3	4

HOUSTON.

Cath. & J. P. D. Kelly, orps. Becks		218	20	2
Jeremiah McCormick, Yarboroughs		174	17	2

IRWIN.

John Gibbs, McCalls		96	8	1
Garry G. Foord, do.		77	19	1
Calvin Thigpen, Underwoods		199	10	3
Elijah Akins, Dixons		126	26	1

JACKSON.

Fortunate Drawers	Capts. Dist.	No.	Dt.	Sec.
Richard Wilson, Lindseys		193	1	4
John Minish, Rogers		40	6	5
Eldridge Nall's orphans, Millers		134	2	3
Absolem Wafford, R. S., Allens		1	11	2
John Venable, sen. Winns		155	6	4
William Walls, Venables		17	12	2

JASPER.

Samuel Howard, sol. Cummins		257	4	2
Thomas Dickson's orphans, Holmes		61	6	4
Thomas Maxey, Dardens		6	11	2
Thomas Hickson, Prices		231	11	3
Churchwell Rispiss' orphans, Hines		124	10	3
William Perry's orphans, Clemmons		247	12	2
Benjamin Hamrick, R. S., Wilders		46	22	2
Jonathan Griffith, Parkers		48	10	1
Joseph N. Carter, illegit, Owens		227	2	3
William Nichols, Dardens		22	7	3
John Spearman, sr. R. S., Butts		73	20	2
John Heard's orphans, Hines		235	12	1
Western Harvill, Keys		121	1	3
Jesse Wheatly, Wilsons		81	10	5
Baxter Estes, Holmes		53	5	1
Isom Hancock, Camerons		117	7	3
Francis Boykin's orphans, Butts		117	15	5

JEFFERSON.

Allen M. Irby, illegit, Cunninghams		19	22	2
Rebecca Neyland, orphan, Elliotts		115	1	4
John Beaty, insane, Causeys		39	32	1
Joel Luker, illegitimate, Ross		223	21	1
Sion Pennington's orphans, Jones,		23	4	2
Harris D. Austin, R. S., Ross		195	9	1
Kinchen Parker, do.		65	21	2

JONES.

Mary Smith, widow, Bowens		172	2	2
Anthony Lawson, Lows		126	11	5
William Shaw's orphans, Hammacks		272	21	2
Solomon Chapman, Blounts		221	3	5
Matthew Bolton, Popes		180	5	2
John Chamblish, Davis		174	6	3
Richard McManus, sol. Wellings		218	21	1
Robert S. Mangum, Mullins		46	6	4
Williams McMath, Stewart		74	1	1
Robert Greer, Lows		227	14	1
William Daniel, Popes		264	11	2
John B. Drinkard, Lows		38	16	2
George Scroggins, R. S. Mullins		243	5	3
Jesse A. Goodwin, Blounts		86	13	1
Joshua James, Popes		73	32	1
Benjamin L. Rainey, do.		195	4	2
James Rowe, R. S., Dosters		120	7	3
William Hasty, Breedloves		196	9	5

LAURENS.

Benjamin Yarborough's orps. Deans		194	33	1
Thomas Hart Powers		96	6	5

LIBERTY.

Patrick Denisons orphans, 17th		73	14	1
John Benton, 16th		7	10	3

LINCOLN

Thomas C. Carlisle, Parks		211	7	3
Joseph W. Glaze, Prathers		36	8	2
M. McVeal, for her mins. Gideons		57	2	3
Seaborn Mosely, Parks		274	14	1
John Moss, jr., Wiggintons		153	12	2
William Wethers, Levritts		49	4	1

MADISON.

Sarah Smith, w. R.S.,Culbertsons		63	30	1

(112)

Fortunate Drawers	Capts. Dist.	No.	Dt.	Sec.
William S. Hendricks, jr. Hannas		26	9	1
Reddick Mannen, Phipps		76	10	3
Robert McCurdy, Hannas		96	25	1
Dawson Williams, sol. Bones		282	7	5
McINTOSH				
John Hutson, Demeries		83	23	1
Mary Lasserra, wid. Terrells		14	1	4
MONROE.				
Allen Rigley, Finchs		81	14	5
David Aleson, Wrights		42	12	1
James Wadsworth, Pattersons		126	5	4
Philip J. Crask, Millers		184	1	2
Sarah Kitchings, w.R.S.,Douglass		227	21	2
Hez. Kendrick, R. S., Johnsons		243	19	1
John S. Fountain, Douglass		221	27	1
Lewis G. Hickman, Houses		140	4	5
Robert S. Duffee, Douglass		83	6	3
Catharine Collins, h. a. Finches		160	10	5
William Riley, Woodwards		89	4	2
Aaron Levingston, Turners		102	6	1
Cornelius Cohron, R. S. Browns		54	12	3
MORGAN.				
Seymour S. Beasley, Beasleys		248	16	2
Rachael Woodyard, widow, do		150	9	1
Jonathan Hightower, Browns		19	1	3
Nathan Formby, sr. Adairs		68	22	2
John Rooks, Shearmans		158	17	2
Wm. M. Roberts, Dawsons		197	2	5
William G. Rights orps.Canifaxs		191	6	3
MONTGOMERY.				
Ignatius Hall, R. S. Ryals		23	16	1
Alexander McKoy, Wynns		86	21	2
NEWTON.				
Wilson Daniel, Pullens		61	22	2
Stephen Cowart, Smiths		71	4	1
Samuel M. Akin, Talleys		236	11	5
Nathaniel L. Williams, Summers		132	21	2
John Stanton, R. S. Dyers		7	33	1
John W. Tommy, sol. Askews		7	8	4
James Dick, woun. sol. Newnans		51	6	4
Ephriam Mabrey, Penningtons		192	11	5
OGLETHORPE.				
Joseph Willingham, Bells		180	8	3
James Sorrow, Floyds		34	12	5
Thomas J. Fullelove, Hills		68	21	2
Andrew Pass, sol. Devenports		255	2	4
James Buchanan, Simmons		2	3	4
William Wright, Floyds		141	18	1
W. Christopher,R.S.,Williamsons		251	2	2
Redford Johnson, Hills		50	3	1
Isham Smith, Rousseaus		80	8	4
Pleasant Jones, Williamsons		162	6	5
PIKE.				
Josiah Pearson, Longs		230	31	1
PULASKI.				
Manuel W. Lovin, Sparrows		65	1	3
M.,D.A. & C.C.Snell ors. Kellams		99	1	3
Mur. McLeod, R. S. Bracewells		184	8	1
Elizabeth Pratt, wid. Sparrows		157	14	2
PUTNAM.				
Charles Bradleys orps. Sparks		168	7	3
Wilie Vinson, Sparks		149	2	1
Jesse Williams, Stinsons		204	20	1
William Robey, Sparks		148	28	1
Stephen Jones, R. S., Allums		265	22	1
Richmond Terrells orps. Blunts		225	30	1
Hez. Singletons orps. Chambers		84	3	1
John L. Nellums, Barnetts		25	1	4
Elias Landrum, Sparks		140	22	2
William Alexander, sol. Vinings		123	14	5
RABUN.				
Joseph Pinson, R. S., Mercers		232	19	1
Tilman Powell, Millicans		42	26	1
Rebekah Price, wid. Godfreys		227	23	1
James McClain, Millicans		38	12	2
Elkin Fosters orphans, do.		15	1	1
RICHMOND.				
Rhoda Ligon, wid. Palmers		242	2	2
Wm. M. Rowland, Huntingtons		57	3	2
W.,J. H. & J. Lang orps. Hands		185	5	3
Furnifold Greene, Blacks		186	2	1
J. W. Hunter, 119th,		89	3	5
Hugh M. Inglett, James		155	13	2
William B. Hammond, Wilcoxs		241	17	2
Jane McCoy, wid. Huntingtons		140	6	3
Charles Sturges, Treadwells		63	11	5
SCRIVEN.				
Richard W. Reaves, Reaves		241	10	3
Allen Waters, Humphreys		87	10	2
Samuel Griners orphans, do		216	13	1
Isaac Conyers, Reaves		175	18	2
TATTNALL.				
John Chesser, Conners		71	15	5
William Taylor, Deloachs		214	15	2
Philip F. Sapp, McDuffees		123	4	2
Martha Lord, w. R. S., Corseys		235	5	1
Major C. Grace, Graces		75	24	2
Eliz. Deloach, w. R. S., Deloachs		238	25	1
Mary C. Swobe, illeg. McCalls		159	10	2
James A. Tippins, Conners		57	9	2
Chesley A. Gess, McCalls		35	6	5
TELFAIR.				
Frances Butler, wid. Barentines		170	10	3
Jane Cook, wid. Lampkins		203	23	1
Adam Paramore, do.		23	30	1
TWIGGS.				
Mary Rouse, w. R. S., Holidays		173	16	2
Allen Rouse, do.		182	18	2
Hampton N. Dozier, do.		44	3	5
UPSON.				
James Jordin, Hattoxs		193	5	2
Mary Mitchells, illegs. Paschalls		183	1	4
John Hobbs, 589th		220	6	5
S.Helton,or.of P.Helton,Harrells		136	18	2
Joel T. Mock, Myricks		187	23	2
WALTON.				
Needham Benefield, Bexleys		67	16	1
Puckett Wood, McQuertors		110	15	2
Fielding Ellis, sol. Davis		163	16	1
James Huntons orps. do.		56	15	5
Sarey Gronad, widow, 418th		102	7	2
Ann Landers, w. R. S., 249th		168	11	2
John P. Winn, 249th		276	4	1
John Moate, Bexleys		112	4	5

LAND LOTTERY REGISTER—No. 17
[RECORDER OFFICE—PUBLISHED BY GRANTLAND & OBME—PRICE $3.]

NOTE.—Section 1 is Lee County—2 Muscogee—3 Troup—4 Coweta—5 Carroll.

36th DAY'S DRAWING—Continued

WARE.

Fortunate Drawers Capts. Dist.	No.Dt Sec.
Rachel Cradick, illegit. Bryans	45 6 3

WARREN.

James Ansley, jr. Sanders	34	22	1
Miles Joyner, Downs	253	19	1
Julian Greenes, illefits. Hales	84	2	5
John Land, Adkins	270	2	4
Culpeppers Orphans, Stewarts	186	9	1
Henry P. Pool, R. S., Kinseys	99	4	3

WASHINGTON.

William Beek, illeg. Tysons	129	8	5
Quinny Johnson, widow, do.	233	5	1
Jane Frizzle, wid. Rushings	215	7	3
William Avery, do.	129	31	1
Edwin Morris, Wimberlys	44	1	4
Samuel Renfroe, Floyds	79	29	1
Mitchell Watkins, Jr. Warthens	293	10	2
Mary King, wid. Whitfields	149	2	5
William M. Bennett, Currys	194	6	5
Edy Martin, widow, Gilberts	245	4	2
Ivey Lees orphans, Tysons	102	11	2
Alfred D. Moore, McLendons	64	23	2
John Covingtons orps. Tysons	129	1	2
Edmund R. Ballard, Jordans	46	33	1
James H. Cook, McLendons	51	24	2
Willey Massey, Floyds	79	9	2
Homer M. Laurence, Wimberlys	156	7	5
Lucy Short, widow, Floyds	234	17	1
Jesse Faust, Gilberts	174	20	2
David Greer, Avans	72	12	2
John Salter, Currys	169	12	5

WILKINSON.

Isaac Lindsey, Mathews	105	14	1
Simpsey Jones, Currys	203	8	1
Eli Wheeler, Mandersons	23	9	3
Needham Jones, orph. Fairchilds	79	8	2
Lewis P. Tessier, do.	249	3	3
James Loften, do.	22	18	1
Axom M. Mayos, Mayos	50	21	1
Nan. & Car. Mote, illegs. Shows	260	4	2
John Bowen, sr. R. S., Fairchilds	163	9	3
Dempsey Dillard, Mayos	23	10	3

WILKES.

Christopher Renders ors.Amasons	44	24	2
Ludowick M. Hill, do.	83	12	3
James Davant, sol. Charltons	179	14	2
Abi Bentlay, w. R. S., Chunns	163	20	1
Samuel Barnett, sol. Gardners	122	20	1
James Chambers' orphs. Lukers	23	18	2
Bennett Reeves, Ragsdales	221	2	5

37th DAY'S DRAWINGS—April 18.

APPLING.

John McIver, McDonalds	127	14	1
Dolcy Heren, widow, R. S., Collins	9	17	1

BALDWIN.

Elijah M. Callaway, Wicks	167	6	6

Fortunate Drawers Capts. Dist. No.Dt.Sec.

John Bulger, Buchanans	52	7	1
Henry Darnell, do.	54	12	5
Darkess Cone, widow, Wheelers	220	3	4
David Blakey, soldier, Pitts	168	6	3

BIBB.

Reuben Turner, Bates	58	22	1
Richard Mooney, do.	130	3	1
Nancy Irwin, widow R. S., Flanders	219	8	3
Thomas Howard, Carrs	125	6	1
John Bailey, soldier, Rutlands	209	22	1
Angus McKenzie, Bates	210	6	2
Henry Milburn, do.	58	11	1
Zach Williamson, sr. R. S., Beards	194	14	1

BRYAN.

Charles Bashlor, Harveys	82	13	6

BULLOCH.

Starling Parker, Richardsons	187	2	3
Uriah Rogers, Lockharts	3	1	2
Jacob Futch, Richardsons	87	20	2
Needham Lee, Standlands	114	21	1

BURKE.

Mary Dunn, widow, Bayleys	26	5	1
John Watkins, do.	111	23	1
John Nasworthy's orphans, Lynchs	140	10	2
Henry Robinson, Dukes	71	1	1
Archibald Bonnell, Dugas	119	6	4
Mary Brinson, widow, Wards	164	21	2
Nancy Sills, widow, Fountains	11	8	5
Jane Dunn, widow, R. S., Robinsons	254	9	5
M., V. & M. Royal, illegits, Lewis	11	12	2
Alfred A. Godbee, Dugas	15	20	2
Peter Mecaskel, Andersons	231	8	3

BUTTS.

John S. Gibson, R. S., Kirkseys	91	1	4

CAMDEN.

Wilson Brooks, Hopkins	8	1	3
John H. McIntosh, jr. Wards	218	12	3
Jane Spalding, orphan, Millers	250	21	1

CHATHAM.

Peter Dowell, Nungazers	67	4	4
Rowland Williams, orp. McDonnells	105	24	2
Eliza Ross, widow, Geredons	226	31	1

CLARK.

Hugh Nesbit, Frosts	162	6	2
Samuel Blakely, Alreds	147	3	2
Patsey Robertson, widow, Lumpkins	183	9	3
Samuel J. Cassels, Gahagans	58	3	2
Talton Sheets, soldier, Mastens	31	33	1
Susannah Hicks, wid. R. S., Wrights	9	6	1
Elijah Garner, Greens	146	3	1
Richard Richardson, Ransoms	66	2	4
Robert S. Gordon, Wrights	270	14	1
Williamson Ledbetter, Gahagans	104	9	3
Albert Y. Grisham, Dickens	266	28	1
James Turner, R. S., Alreds	39	13	1
M. & P. Angling, illegits, Cutchings	73	3	3
William Brassel, Espys	54	6	4
William Malone, R. S., Ransoms	142	10	3

COLUMBIA.

Orphans of James H. Smith, Ramseys	115	8	4
Willis Johnson, R. S., Dranes	190	5	5
Henry G. Hardin, Baileys	248	20	2
Jas., Jno., Wm., Sar. Nan. Matil. & P. Moy orps Livermans	70	26	1

(114)

Fortunate Drawers	Capts. Dist.	No.	Dt.	Sec.
Orp.of James C. Walker, Carrols		139	16	1
Betsey Petit, widow, R. S., Clarks		102	6	2
Judea Green's illegits, Talberts		56	9	1

CRAWFORD.

James McGehee's orphans, Tillers		41	19	2
Nathan B. Johnston, Ellis		302	8	1
Thomas Peebles, Tillers		39	12	3
William B. Simmons, soldier, Wilsons		198	9	2
Isaac Welch, do.		161	3	1
Joseph Grant's orphans, Rhodes		160	29	1

DECATUR.

Nathan Maples, Douglass		285	16	2
Joseph McGowen, do.		245	29	1
Asel Bell, Ferrells		71	3	3

DE KALB.

Dority's orphans, Stephens		189	13	2
William James, Smiths		362	7	1
Mason Chance, soldier, Andersons		26	8	4
Alfred Bankston, Bowlings		251	9	5
Thomas Duty, R. S., Howells		54	13	1
Daniel Harrison, Conns		220	12	1
Winney Rozier, widow, Howells		195	5	2
William Harris, do.		98	9	1

EARLY.

William Kelly's orphans, Grimsleys		117	4	4
Andrew Hobby, Porters		205	10	5

EFFINGHAM.

James Lanier, Edwards		135	19	1
Dennis Grady, Waldhaners		208	22	1
Mary Cath. Gnann, wid. Stricklands		72	16	2
John Waldhaner, sr. Waldhaners		193	27	1

ELBERT.

Madison Hudson, Bells		12	3	4
Charles Hudson's mins. f. a. Tuckers		80	24	1
Benjamin Brown, R. S., Blackwells		42	2	3
Orphans of Zimry Tate, Tates		52	2	5
William M. Brawner, Butlers		24	33	1
Elisha Ashworth, Hortons		95	17	2
Isaac Alexander, R. S., Dobbs		250	7	1

EMANUEL.

Abigail Stephens' illegits., Swains		188	20	2
Nancy Boatright, orphan, 57th		194	3	4
Jane Catharine Drew, illegit.,		89	11	3
Allen Gay, Moors		29	18	2
John Deal, do.		94	11	2

FAYETTE.

Miligan Smallwood, Craigs		246	14	1
John P. Dodson, Dodsons		189	1	4
William Dodson, do.		25	12	2
Reuben Yarborough, Wests		102	1	2
Sarah Dunn, orphan, Craigs		223	26	1

FRANKLIN.

John W. Payne, Caudells		175	10	2
Leonard Ramsey, soldier, Hudsons		125	22	
William Chatham, Boswells		216	10	2
Thomas Motes, Jones		29	3	2
Orphan of Richard Higgins, Cokers		227	13	1
Minors of John Parks, Hudsons		222	33	1
Pierce Bell, T. Chandlers		35	12	2
James Hatchcock, D. Chandlers		191	6	1

GLYNN.

James Smith, Burnetts		16	15	2
Thomas F. Harrison, McLeods		56	4	4
John Middleton, do.		196	6	5

GREENE.

Mofield Owins, Woodhams		202	12	2
Patience Johnson, hus. ab. Knowles		118	14	1

Fortunate Drawers	Capts. Dist.	No.	Dt.	Sec.
John H. Todd, Vincents		252	23	2
Isaac Callaway's orphans, Elys		49	6	3
Lowdy S. Calhoun, Knowles		45	5	2
Gilbert D. Johnson, soldier, Rankins		87	12	5
Dickerson D. Cosby, sol. Copelands		163	29	1

GWINNETTE.

Lewis Cooper, Hunicuts		192	15	2
William Cauley's orphans, Wallis		324	20	2
Kirkham McEwen, for wife, Maddux		12	13	1
Isham W. Born, Moors		148	27	1
William Griffin, Robertsons		79	23	1
Nicholas Rollins, Rollins		250	6	3
Kirham McEwen, Wallis		117	2	2
Lavinia M. Fraser, insane, Grens		112	4	2
Mary Reynolds, hus. absent, Davis		132	5	4
Nancy Crowell, wid. R. S., Bakers		109	4	3
Micajah Louge, Whortons		113	10	2
James Hays, Moors		51	23	2
Robert Jackson, Hunicuts		83	12	1
Anthony Bates, Whortons		159	7	4
Robert Kelly, do.		143	25	1
W. R. Laughbridge, dear&dumb,Davis		173	1	1
Archibald Thomas, Moors		56	9	3

HANCOCK.

Gabriel Moss, sen. 103d		178	24	2
Wimburn Dickerson, R. S., 110th		54	15	2
Thomas Little, soldier, Densons		240	21	1

HENRY.

Thomas W. Harris, Captain, Harris		119	12	3
Thomas Weems, Bryants		44	29	1
Drury Harrington, Allens		349	28	1
Joshua J. Evans, soldier, Breeds		100	6	1
Stephen Grice, Risons		97	5	2
James Brabbin, Shaws		176	25	1

HABERSHAM.

Colly Crane, Taits		77	7	3
Thomas Davis, soldier, Faines		242	11	3
John Potts, Bryans		369	7	1
Alford Edwards, Tates		200	5	5
Thomas Thomas, Cross		168	2	2
John Toweneson, idiot, Cannedys		116	11	3
Theophilus Taylor, R. S., Suttons		24	24	2
John Haynes, do.		19	4	5
Sherwood Holcombe, R. S., Faines		252	7	5
Watson Murdock,		177	15	5
William Sosebee, Tates		130	2	2
Isaac Bowen, Kenzies		220	15	1
Stephen Cobb, Tates		24	1	1
Abel Anderson, do.		199	29	1

HALL.

Peter Edwards, Walkers		167	13	1
Robert Cochrum, Alreds		140	3	5
Wilson M. Dickson, Wilsons		135	22	1
Thomas H. Johnson, Hardens		109	4	1
William Padget, do.		79	5	5
James Leathers, do.		295	20	2
Jehu Voyles, Floyds		69	11	5
Joseph Wilson, sen. Hardages		48	9	1

HOUSTON.

Elizabeth Johnson, wid. Yarboroughs		33	26	1
Abel Knight(illegitimate, Bozemans		223	6	1
William Brooks, Hancocks		167	7	5
Giles Mozingo, Calhouns		269	6	5
Enoch Norris, Pitts		9	27	1

IRWIN.

Joseph Tilman, 5th		203	13	1
Margaret McDermot, w. Underwoods		117	5	1
Samuel Knight, do.		132	31	1

(115)

Fortunate Drawers Capts. Dist.	No.Dt.Sec.
Elijah Hunter, Dixons	118 23 1
John R. Wetherington, 5th	157 28 1

JACKSON.

Jackson Trout, Allens	271 4 1
Ansey Fuch, widow, Georges	65 5 4
Jane Ware, widow, R. S., Rogers	180 3 4
William Smith, R. S., Doss	19 3 3
Edward Kent, Allens	12 8 3
James King, Millers	176 7 5
Mary Bradford, w. R. S., Lindseys	202 11 2
Sarah Ross, widow, Pairs	187 17 2
Wesley Hudson, Rogers	8 5 1

JASPER.

William Hames, Reeves	239 201
Abel F. Heath, Camerons	108 18 1
John A. Phelps, illegit, Sparks	213 9 1
Richard B. Hornbucke, Robersons	165 5 2
John Spurlin, Holmes,	85 9 2
William H. Traylor, Johnsons	78 14 5
William Stroud, Keys	200 8 3
James Wilson, Dardens	58 14 5
Daniel Freeman, R. S., Hines	77 11 1
Belinda Digby, widow, Parkers	173 30 1
James S. Hearn, Owens	64 3 1
Jonathan Hayes, Holmes	250 3 1
Jane Mathis, widow, R. S., Reeves	99 21 2

JEFFERSON.

Polly Blunt, orp. of Isaac, Marshalls	109 25 1
Robert Lowre, Causeys	89 2 5
Hugh McNeely, Boyds	19 6 5
John Bostick, Marshalls	61 23 1

JONES.

Jonathan Williams, Spinks	36 7 5
Jane Culbreath, widow, Taylors	238 5 4
Young G. Burke, Woods	24 8 3
Rachel Bowen, illegit, Spinks	14 14 1
William Simmons, R. S., Davis	57 9 1
Anderson Comer Taylors	64 1 5
Elizabeth Williams, illegit, Bowens	196 14 2
Benjamin Gachet, Breedloves	266 9 3
William Hogans, Woods	85 6 4
William B. Ousley, Mullins	95 9 3
Peyton Alford, Woods	206 25 1
John S. Brooks, Popes	84 30 1
Lucy Blount, widow, R. S., Blounts	140 23 1

LAURENS.

Elisha Evans, Whiteheads	72 1 2
Josiah D. Thomas, Mizells	32 11 3
Margaret Williamson, w. R. S., do	255 3 4
Benjamin Ramsey, Spiveys	72 8 4
Ann Grant's illegit children, Mizells	94 1 2

LIBERTY.

David Benton, 16th	14 8 1
Joseph Andrews, 15th	29 16 2
John Perry, 17th	194 1 4
John S. Law, 14th	182 10 2

LINCOLN.

Stern Simmons, jr. Lonorgans	158 10 2
Lemuel Winn, Graves	130 3 5
Thomas Lyon, Leveretts	39 23 1
Margaret Spires, Graves	99 25 1

MADISON.

Joseph McCune, Bones	264 9 5
David Lokey, illeg. Caldwells	120 6 2
William S. Sorrills, Adairs	109 12 1

M'INTOSH.

Fortunate Drawers Capts. Dist.	No.Dt.Sec.
Thos. Crawford, McCranies	107 4 3

MONROE.

John Wright, Wrights	174 6 5
Anness M. Lewis, orph. Knights	81 22 1
John Monk, R. S., Woodwards	230 28 1
James Herring, do.	75 15 5
Betsey Ann Walker, ill. Millers	242 3 1
Stephen Proctor, R. S., do.	143 5 5
John McBryde, Greshams	128 3 5
Archibald Smith, sol. Higgins	238 2 4
Benajah Boothe, Houses	367 7 1
Waitman Blackman, Johnsons	126 6 3
Flail Paine, do.	368 28 1

MORGAN.

John B. Watts, Butlers	202 3 1
Ann Harper, wid. Beasleys	62 2 4
Mary Starr, w. R. S. Gains	342 28 1
Eli Grier, Evans	257 20 2
William B. Glenn, Gains	27 8 1
David Deming, Youngs	198 10 3
Benjamin Hardison, Hitchcocks	188 12 5
Thomas Towson, Evans	174 5 5
Sarah D. Campbell, wid. Gains	164 11 2
John Morgan, sr. R. S., Harwells	252 29 1
Dawson Wiggins, Jennings	49 16 2

MONTGOMERY.

Steward Hamilton, R. S., Wynns	171 27 1
Murdock Gillis, do.	104 1 4
Daniel R. Browning, Pridgeons	68 22 1
Levi Sapp, R. S., Wynns	46 15 1

NEWTON.

Ann Bean, wid. Summers	198 11 2
Calvin J. Branham, Smiths	275 9 3
Martha, Jas., Irwin, Nan., Jar.	
M. & S. Stewart, mins. Moss	183 5 3
Andrew Pless, Talleys	42 7 4
Benjamin Jenkins, Hays	178 15 5
John D. Mann, Talleys	198 8 1

OGLETHORPE.

R.J.Christopher, sol.Williamsons	22E 8 3
John Massey, Rousseaus,	124 12 3
Thomas Thaxton, Williamsons	197 30 1
Leonard Bolton, sol. Billups	140 2 2
Let. Lawrence,w.R.S.Holloways	123 7 5
John N. McEwen, Hills	116 9 2
William S. Walker, Bells	6 11 3

PIKE.

James Daniel, sol. Bryans	161 11 1
Thomas Cook, Mays	45 10 1
James Dossett, Bryans	83 14 1
Stephen H. King, Orrs	108 23 1

PULASKI.

Isaac W. Mitchell, Bracewells	26 1 4
J. W. Bunn, orph. Kellams	220 12 2
James Parker, sr. Scarbroughs	218 26 1

PUTNAM.

W.R.Duett, well digger, Vinings	177 21 1
Johnson Bullocks orps. Bledsoes	195 11 1
Lewis Lynch,	118 24 2
George H. Young, Hailes	138 2 3

(116)

Fortunate Drawers Capts. Dist.	No.	Dt.	Sec.
William C. Wheler, Kendricks	176	11	5
Thomas L. Reed, Sawyers	190	15	2
Joab Pope, Allums	306	3	4
William Evans' orps. Chambers	107	1	2
Porter R. Vandaman, Brooks	237	3	2
Moses Welch, Stinsons	69	2	1
RABUN.			
Thomas J. Price, Godfreys	236	9	3
William Farris, R. S., do.	352	28	1
Mark Slewder, Mercers	116	10	3
Dread Massingale, sr. Mercers	231	1	2
RICHMOND.			
William Little, Wilcoxs	230	10	5
William Dunham, R. S., Blacks	40	20	1
Jacob McCullough, sr. Kellys	197	18	1
Albert G. Bogan, Hands	171	12	2
SCRIVEN.			
David Jones, Stricklings	64	4	1
TATTNALL.			
William Coward, Conners	18	12	3
Aaron Daniel, jr., Conners	161	32	1
TELFAIR.			
Archibald McRay, Wilsons	165	23	1
Peter Smith, Wilsons	79	7	3
Samuel Hargroves, Wilkinsons	2	4	3
Joshua A. Luke, Barentines	35	22	1
TWIGGS.			
John Young, jr. Pearsons	61	17	1
Jonathan Dickison, Graggs	296	1	2
James Spurlock, Solomons	29	10	3
Orph. of J. Broxton, Wimberlys	168	23	2
UPSON.			
James A. Greer, sol. Ezells	80	11	5
Samuel Moore, Hattoxs	262	4	2
Clayborn Jarrall, do	78	6	5
William Richardson, Dukes	173	7	2
James Hunts orps. Coupers	151	22	1
WALTON.			
Lewis Wayne, Pools	218	30	1
Drury Moate, 250th	16	20	1
Elizabeth Radford, widow, 250th	36	6	5
Long Shirey, Rays	14	10	3
James F. Norris, do	122	14	5
Eletha Dyer, R. S., 559th	247	20	1
WARE.			
Joel Lott, Motes	78	15	5
Lewis Davis, do.	203	29	1
WARREN.			
Edmond Murden, Stewarts	251	14	1
Lorenzo D. Hays, Sanders	66	10	1
Nancy Flewellen, wid. Brinkleys	116	9	5
John Willowby, illegit. Adkins	267	12	3
John Hardeways orphs. Kinseys	161	8	5
N. & W. A. Smith, ills. Stewarts	35	4	5
William Roland, Sanders	95	1	4
Hammond Purvis, Hills	135	1	4
Mary Gray, w. R. S., Parhams	212	32	1
Thomas Wynne, jr. Rogers	115	10	1
George Ray, orphan, Adkins	14	5	4
David Culpepper, sol. Fords	205	23	1
Frederick B. Heeth, Parhams	197	11	2

WASHINGTON.			
Fortunate Drawers Capts. Dist.	No.	Dt.	Sec.
Jessey Mills' heirs, Oquins	110	13	1
Grove Corbets orphans, Woods	139	14	5
Nathaniel Cains heirs, Avans	289	5	1
Elizabeth Ryland, wid. Castelows	28	12	5
Abraham Joiner, jr. Wimberlys	3	7	2
W.A.Tennelle, (dis.sol.) Mannings	56	7	3
James Ainsworth, Floyds	277	12	3
Jessey Croom, Oquins	211	18	1
WILKINSON.			
George A. Mock, Smiths	99	12	2
John Bellflowers, Fairchilds	59	8	2
William Brewner, Currys	68	20	2
James Hatfield, Halls	117	6	2
William Straham, R. S., do.	89	15	5
Hardy Steward, R. S., Mayos	240	1	2
WILKES.			
Dudley Stinsons orps. Chunns	229	11	1
S. Jenkins sr's. ors. McDermonts	50	4	2
Ebenezer Smith, Hamocks	34	3	4
Ed. W. McLaughlin, sol. Moors	203	12	3
John Ray, R. S. Chunns	43	13	1
John Moors orphans, Moors	228	20	1
Amos Stewart, R. S. Hanmocks	118	13	1

38th DAY'S DRAWINGS—April 19.

APPLING.			
Dicy Ogden, orphans, Stricklands	184	7	3
William Nettles, jun. McDonalds	47	8	3
BALDWIN.			
David Lovett, Buchanans	108	12	5
Henry Gee, Bivins	1	10	1
Francis V. Delaunay, Buchanans	64	3	2
BIBB.			
Hugh Morrison, Rutlands	35	3	2
Martin Johnson, soldier, Carrs	180	18	1
Mary & J. Woods, orps. Rutlands	207	16	2
BULLOCH.			
Thomas Rawls' orphans, Richardsons	35	15	5
McKeen Green McCall, McCalls	263	6	5
BURKE.			
James T. Gordy, illegitimate, Lynchs	279	9	5
Daniel Waltour, Forths	157	4	1
William Mitchell, sen. Brooms	271	2	1
S.,W.R.A.,I.& B. Sumner, ill. Gordons	181	3	2
Thomas S. Few, do.	74	33	1
Sabra Brinson, widow, R. S., Wards	176	12	5
Winney Hadley, wid. R. S., Gordons	106	7	1
Isham Jones, R. S.,	131	2	5
John Lewis, sen. Wards	94	17	2
BUTTS.			
William B. Shurling, Johnsons	113	6	1
CAMDEN.			
Benjamin Phillips, Coxs	208	16	1
John Omans, R. S., Hopkins	187	20	1
CHATHAM.			
James Harbock, Reeds	175	11	1
Ed. D. Courter's orps. McDonnells	124	4	2
Elizabeth Mulryne, widow, do	185	2	5
Sterry B. Fenner, do	217	6	2
Francis A. Coffin, Haydens	232	10	3
CLARK.			
Jesse White, Espys	65	14	1
Hiram Howard, Cutchins	31	8	1

(117)

Fortunate Drawers	Capts.	Dist.	No.	Dt.	Sec.
Gren Evans,	Lumpkins		136	3	4
Thomas Gallaway,	Andersons		153	17	1
Nathan Cook,	McDonalds		89	2	2
Talcott G. Smith,	Vinsons		194	17	1

COLUMBIA.

Fortunate Drawers	Capts.	Dist.	No.	Dt.	Sec.
Hugh Rees, R. S.,	Adams		21	2	5
Thomas Dooly,	Talbots		98	11	2
Beverly L. Culbreath,	Carrolls		165	13	2
Weathers Smith, R. S.,	Adams		108	7	1
Nancy H. Griffin, widow,	Ramseys		119	2	3
John Morris,	Stallings		92	18	2
Billington Blanchard,	Culbreaths		108	4	5
James Perry, soldier,	Lukes		6	4	3
Jehu Cliett,	Stallings		191	19	2
George Gray,	Bailys		98	12	1

CRAWFORD.

| Peter May, jr., | Wilsons | | 223 | 32 | 1 |
| Bartholomew Stovall, | Hamiltons | | 326 | 22 | 1 |

DE KALB.

| Benjamin Woodson, | Andersons | | 157 | 3 | 2 |
| Berry A. Fuller, | Bakers | | 26 | 13 | 1 |

DOOLY.

| Aaron Tison, | Mannings | | 90 | 18 | 2 |

EARLY.

| William Dixon, | Hairs | | 151 | 4 | 5 |

EFFINGHAM.

| Stephen Hester, jr., | Elkins | | 93 | 6 | 3 |

ELBERT.

William B. Key, R. S.,	Bells		166	24	2
Joseph Deadwilder, R. S.,	Deadwilders		54	24	1
Orphan of Usry Almand,	Butlers		37	3	1
Joseph Vickery, sen. R. S.,	Carpenters		172	11	3
Orphan of Joshua Cook,	Bells		32	11	2
Enos M. Tate,	Tates		109	20	1
Levi Hendrick,	Merritts		138	2	5
William Sittin,	Carpenters		216	3	2
Jas. Barger, orp. of G. B.,	Merritts		97	5	3
James R. Sadler,	Carpenters		167	12	3
John M. Christian,	Butlers		158	8	1
John Yoes,	Dunns		307	6	1

EMANUEL.

Howell McLemore,	Chasons		230	2	4
Orphans of Daniel Neel,	Whiddons		188	14	1
Orphans of William Holton,	Chasons		26	6	5
Cullen Cowart,	Daniels		151	23	1
Joseph Edingfield,	Nabbs		79	30	1

FAYETTE.

William Coffee,	Wests		59	12	5
Elijah Marshall,	Roziers		236	4	3
William Vickery,	Wests		213	19	2
David Dickson, R. S.,	Whartons		143	4	4
William Finch,	do.		180	21	1
Jacob Mercer, R. S.,	Browns		275	3	4
Fanning Brown,	rCaigs		85	32	1
James Lloyd, sr., R. S.,	do.		76	13	1

FRANKLIN.

Joel Weems,	Boswells		144	15	2
Nathan R. C. Williams,	Cokers		59	10	1
Pierce Kee, soldier,	Jones		94	7	5
John K. Landers, sol., D.	Chandlers		111	6	4
Nathaniel Glenn,	Stranges		23	9	2
Calvin Watson,	Cokers		60	28	1

GLYNN.

| Mary Raisden, widow, | Dubignons | | 96 | 28 | 1 |
| Sarah Hutson, widow, | Burnetts | | 344 | 8 | 1 |

GREENE.

| Littleberry Peak, | Woodhams | | 126 | 7 | 3 |

Fortunate Drawers	Capts.	Dist.	No.	Dt.	Sec.
Daniel K. Clifton,	Bruces		37	2	5
Albert Taylor,	Colcloughs		200	1	4
Joseph Bird,	Halls		62	4	5
Nancy Wood, widow, R. S.,	Robins		164	6	5
Alial B. Wood, orphan,	do.		69	7	5
Willie C. Mason,	Dawsons		210	10	1

GWINNETT.

George H. Glare,	Woodroughs		176	3	4
Isaac Steele,	Bakers		37	9	3
Nathan Bankston,	Rollins		27	3	4
Agnes McConnell, wid. R. S.,	Moors		221	3	2
James Holcombe,	Whortons		141	6	3
Christopher Baker, sen. R. S.,	Greens		36	6	1
Benjamin Evans' orps.	Caruthers		109	2	5
Russell Jones,	Evans		44	5	4
Thomas Meworn,	Wallis		252	10	2
William Still,	Woodroughs		192	24	1
Dennis Still, sen.	do.		173	4	1
Elizabeth Wallraven, wid.	Greens		193	8	1
Jesse Powell,	do.		213	32	1
Isaac Boring, jr.	Caruthers		230	20	2

HABERSHAM.

John Dickson,	Tates		48	1	1
Moses Anderson,	Kenzies		92	24	1
Andrew Wilson,	Bryans		97	2	3
Archibald Lindsey,	Fanes		84	1	5
Francis Self,	Vickreys		154	33	1
Isaac Hicks,	Suttons		41	6	4

HALL.

John Purdy,	Hardages		123	8	5
Charles Whitlock, soldier,	Harrisons		162	17	2
David Hyde, sen.	Alreds		129	8	3
James G. Davis,	Floyds		154	1	4
John W. Bramlet,	Roberts		130	5	1
Jesse Windsor, jun.,	Harrisons		178	8	1
John Miller,	Smiths		12	16	5
Job Brazilton,	Garrards		246	6	1

HANCOCK.

John Richardson, 118th			224	11	5
William C. Smith's orps.	Masons		135	17	2
John Latimer's orphans, 112th			45	8	1
Themus Norwood, 102d			223	2	5
Samuel R. Buffaloe, orphan,	Adams		22	8	2
Malcolm Johnson,	Hillsmans		176	7	2
Elizabeth R. Brown, orphans,	Calliers		24	13	2
Nicholas Andrews' mins. fa. ab. 111th			175	20	2

HENRY.

Samuel McClendon, R. S.,	Shaws		50	15	5
Robert B. Beard, soldier,	Wards		26	23	2
Yearly Denny,	Millers		183	23	2
George Ramsey, sol., T. W.	Harris		65	1	5
David McCalley,	Grays		153	7	1
Andrew M. Brown,	do.		126	4	2
William Scarborough,	do.		236	2	2

HOUSTON.

Jonathan Brooks,	Becks		191	24	1
William Norris,	Smiths		124	1	1
Robert Holt,	Farnells		197	13	2
Thomas & Espy Hall, orps.	Fudges		26	7	3
William Bird,	Farnalls		79	31	1

IRWIN.

| Elizabeth Wells, widow, | Dixons | | 193 | 15 | 2 |

JACKSON.

Elias McCullum,	Gathrights		151	1	1
Caroline A. Reeding, ill,	Staplers		39	7	4
Jane Bevers, widow, R. S.,	Allens		159	4	3
Nicholas Stiles, orphan,	Doss		100	27	1

(118)

Fortunate Drawers Capts. Dist.	No.	Dt.	Sec.
Nathaniel G. Henderson Moons	17	7	5
Jonathan W. Walker's orp. Rogers	191	23	1
Charles Bacon, Allens	104	7	1

JASPER.

Isaac W. Daniel, Reeves	193	7	3
David Watson's orphans, Camerons	119	19	2
Nancy Hallmark, illegit., Sparks	32	6	5
James Brown's orphans, Baynes	219	31	1
Susannah Parker, w. R. Sfl, Camerons	138	1	4
Richard S. Thomason, Parkers	25	28	1
Clement Diemer, Shropshires	181	26	1
Bennet Posey, R. S., Sparks	250	18	1
William Miller, s., R. S., Parkers	256	12	2
Martha Good, orphan Hincs	267	1	4
David Duck, soldier, Robinsons	239	27	1
Alexander's orphans, Hollands	63	16	2
Osborn Smart, Shropshires	31	11	5
James Stroud, Wilsons	189	4	5
David Allen's orphans, Camerons	25	4	5
David Patterson, Owens	190	11	5
Herod Pate, Camerons	70	10	5
Philip B. Richett, Prives	59	16	2
John Gwynn's orphans, Sparks	131	12	5

JEFFERSON.

Elijah Sutton, Cunninghams	75	10	1
James S. Turner, illegitimate, Ross	122	12	3
Sarah Thompson, w. R. S., Marshalls	232	30	1
Allen Futral, Elliotts	33	10	5
James Foreman, Waldens	198	18	1
Edward & Jordan, Kent, ills. Beatys	24	8	2

JONES.

William C. Osborn	76	2	5
Leving Moore, Popes	21	3	4
William B. Snellings, do.	173	33	1
Jesse Braswell, sen. do.	152	22	1
Willis Wilder, R. S., Robertsons	20	1	3
Sally Whitworth, widow, Hammacks	242	5	1
Thomas Owen's orphans, Davis	51	5	3
Nancy Marshborn's illegits. Newbys	214	10	3
Elijah W. Harrison, R. S., Hammacks	70	31	1
James Baty's orphans, Spinks	122	32	1
Letitia Calef, widow, Hammacks	49	30	1
Josiah Horn, Breedloves	9	4	2
Jacob McDaniel, R. S., Stewarts	142	5	2
Hannah Yawn's illegitimates, Davis	186	7	5

LAURENS.

Elizab. Searingin, w. R. S., Beachams	54	12	2
Davis Tucker, Hodges	203	7	5
Fleet Pope's orphans, Powers	297	3	4
Lunsford Griffin, Whiteheads	260	28	1
John Dent, Plummers	132	3	4

LIBERTY.

Thomas Baker, 15th	54	9	2
Moses Harrell, 17th	271	23	2

LINCOLN.

Archib'd McCorkle, R.S.Gideons	144	2	5
Thomas Trammell, Graves	231	5	2
Thomas C. Curry, jr. do.	152	4	4
Jacob Ammons, R. S., Frasers	232	14	1

LOWNDES.

Thomas Folsom, 1st	1	20	1

MADISON.

Isaac Moore, soldier, Bones	232	5	5
James C. Freeman, Caldwells	42	3	5
Benjamin Lokey, do.	219	33	1
Hubbard Hampton, Adairs	110	9	5

Fortunate Drawers Capts. Dist.	No.	Dt.	Sec.
John Simmons, Hannas	74	6	3
Coleman Pitts, Culbertsons	248	5	2
Jesse H. Cunningham, Hannas	155	11	2

McINTOSH.

Mary Dean, wid. Thorps	12	4	2

MONROE.

William Dyess, Douglass	160	1	4
John R. Jackson, Millers	164	2	5
Thomas Anderson, Wrights	183	7	2
John Crane, Millers	72	24	1
Hugh Hathorn, sol. Wrights	121	31	1
John Pinkard, Millers	198	22	2
John C. Goss, Johnsons	41	7	2
John Tollison, Greshams	92	18	1
Permelia Russell, illeg. Phillips	343	28	1

MORGAN.

Josiah Barrett, Sparks	219	2	4
Samuel C. Torbert, Adairs	201	18	1
Tabitha Hayne ,h.a. Christians	216	4	2
Archibald Crawford, Stokes	126	4	2
Zeno Fitzpatrick, Butlers	244	23	2
James Hewston, jr. Sparks	137	12	3
Elizabeth Beavers, wid. Stokes	114	3	4
Nathan Barnes' orps. Adairs	75	12	5
Benjamin A. Clark, Harwells	212	2	2
Elizabeth McSwain, Watsons	178	25	1
William Feagans, sr. Jennings	348	22	1
Simon Hughes, Watsons	200	3	3
Albert J. Peeples, orp. Whatleys	213	5	5
James C. Jones, Shermans	136	20	2
Dorcas Lanier, orph. Harwells	149	23	1

MONTGOMERY.

Archibald McColum, Pridgeons	50	32	1

NEWTON.

John Allen, Moss	148	24	1
James J. Piper, Snows	24	6	1
William Griffith, Bakers	280	7	5
William R. Martin, Graces	177	2	1
Allen Parker, Smiths	187	14	1
Lemuel Underwood, sol. Orrs	101	29	1
John E. Hodge, Pullens	163	18	2
John Rabb, Orrs	239	21	2
Willam Adison. Smiths	184	23	1

OGLETHORPE.

William Hartsfield, Holloways	253	1	2
Thomas McLain, R. S., Bells	122	10	5
Marg't Walker, or. Williamsons	142	14	1
Hollandberry Cooper,w.R.S.,Hills	229	3	4

PIKE.

S. Pernell, w.h. died in ser.Daniels	190	33	1
Elijah Robersons orps. Orrs	121	10	3
David Hambleton, sol. Weavers	180	6	2
Henry F. Embrey, Hartsfields	53	6	2
James H. Burt, Mays	362	20	2
William P. Sillmon, Shehees	10	8	5

PULASKI.

William Trull, Kellams	180	4	1
James M. Christians ors. Thomas	78	21	1
William Mayo, Kellams	48	29	1
Richard Doves ors. Scarbroughs	257	22	1
James Odams orps. Powells	255	11	5

(119)

Fortunate Drawers	Capts.	Dist.	No.	Dt.	Sec.
Owen Dillard,	Bracewells		26	25	1
Lewis Harrell,	Hendleys		117	29	1
PUTNAM.					
Alexander B. Harrison,	Blacks		215	2	2
James Ledbetters	orps. Sparks		97	7	1
Orps. of James Caswart,	Clark		316	7	5
Celia Orrick, w. R. S.	Kendricks		74	2	4
Nahor Marschall,	Stinsons		10	6	5
James Adair, sol.	Jenkins		193	21	1
Rebecca Worthington, w.	Marcus		94	15	1
Thomas Cheeves,	Vinings		177	30	1
Elias James, R. S.,	Blacks		9	15	5
Sarah Dickey w. R .S.	Slaughters		38	8	5
James Park,	Bledsoes		300	22	1
Martha A. Rogers, wid.	Goods		60	11	1
RABUN.					
Thomas Carver,	Becks		49	15	1
David Williams, sol.	Godfreys		65	18	2
John Palmour,	Becks		184	4	1
Amy Justice, widow,	do.		50	24	1
Alexander Strickland,	do.		238	7	3
Robert Brown,	do.		13	18	1
RICHMOND.					
Eliz. Cumming, h.a.	Treadwells		283	17	2
Sarah Crawley, widow,	Ferris		240	5	1
John Pond, sol.	Blacks		188	6	2
Lodoiska Strange, orp.	Kellys		158	18	1
Eugene F. Verdery,	123rd		182	12	5
SCRIVEN.					
Daniel Oglesby,	Poytress		162	12	5
John Hodges,	Hunters		242	10	3
Nancy Joiners illegs.	Poytress		180	9	5
TATTNALL.					
Eliz. Summerland, wid.	Corseys		44	30	1
William Tootle,	Dees		36	7	2
William Conner,	do.		174	2	4
Thomas Nemans ors.	McCalls		199	14	1
Mary McLeod, wid.	McDuffies		227	26	1
TALIAFERRO.					
Harmon Runnells,	Alfords		267	17	2
THOMAS.					
William G. Hopson,			82	2	1
TWIGGS.					
Thomas Hatcher, R. S.,	Bosticks		168	13	1
Daniel Stuckey,	Pearsons		75	13	2
Orps. of J.McCollum,Streetmans			252	20	2
James C. Dozier,	Holidays		66	23	2
Henry Crittendon,	Streetmans		166	3	2
Benjamin Minton,	do.		188	31	1
UPSON.					
Franklin Short,	Harrells		161	25	1
WALTON.					
Thomas Lindley,	418th		100	3	3
Benjamin Connel,	249th		212	3	4
John N. R. Garner,	559th		209	2	4
Joseph Sams,	Rays		3	19	2
Benjamin Few,	Davis		102	30	1
Robert F. White,	418th,		65	26	1
James Davis,	559th		199	6	3
John Butler,	Rays		222	7	1

Fortunate Drawers	Capts.	Dist.	No.	Dt.	Sec.
Triplett Cason, R. S.	Pools		217	9	1
Richard Moore, jr.	559th		34	21	2
Henry Beasley,	Snows		26	22	2
William Carmichael,	559th,		96	29	1
John Chafin,	418th		140	31	1
WARE.					
David A. Hendersons ors.	Bryans		154	6	4
WARREN.					
Silas Dye,	Downs		42	13	2
Robert E. Carroll,	Parhams		125	12	2
William R. Kent,	Downs		245	11	3
Mathew Cason,	Adkins		181	13	2
James McCurdy Casons,	do		166	19	1
Persons Walker,	Bulls		208	20	1
Joseph May,	Downs		223	9	3
James Coursey, sol.	Jones		23	17	1
John M. Sanford, illeg.	Hills		19	11	5
Daniel Dennis,	Parhams		134	22	1
John Todd,	Kinseys		236	19	1
Nathaniel Ward, R. S.	Parhams		117	25	1
Soloman Lockett, R. S.	Hills		177	20	2
WASHINGTON.					
John Harrel,	Woods		119	2	2
James Goodmans orps.	Tysons		11	9	5
William Carter,	Whitfields		250	10	5
Jesse Deen,	Gilberts		180	6	1
John Orr,	Currys		236	3	1
Benjamin Sparks, orphs.	Currys		28	1	2
John E. Gardner,	Mannings,		194	3	1
Lewis Cones orphs.	Wimberlys		172	2	1
Stephen Parker,	Mannings		152	12	5
Sarah Corbet, widow,	Woods		276	10	2
John Harrell;	do.		65	12	3
Jas. & Jam. Looper, ills.	Tysons		366	7	1
Seaborn A. H. ones,	McLendons		152	4	3
Edward McDaniel,	do.		27	25	1
Henry Townsend,	Tysons		47	18	2
Haney Maxwell, w.R.S.	Whitfields		85	31	1
John Morrison,	Mannings		130	6	4
WILKINSON.					
Morris Tribble, orp.	Mathews		269	10	2
Hansel Lasseter, R. S.	Currys		124	3	3
Doiley B. Jordan,	Mayos		211	8	3
William Davidson,	Smiths		223	7	3
Jesse Greer, lunatic,	Shows		246	3	3
Jesse Torbaville,	Mandersons		170	1	2
Needham Folk,	Smiths		83	8	2
Bryant Maridith, illeg.	Mathews		209	12	1
Wade Sanders,	Currys		140	33	1
Green Lewis,	Halls		258	4	1
Martha Sanders' ills.	Mathews		30	4	5
Daniel Miles,	Shows		137	12	2
Daniel Mayors,	do.		164	28	1
WILKES.					
Han. Reeves, w.R.S.	McDermonts		257	1	4
Dennis Paschall, sol.	Hopkins		288	6	1
Jesse Evans,	Washingtons		123	14	1
P. C. Edwards, w.R.S.	Hamocks		187	4	2
William Hancock, sr.	Reeves		18	3	4
Pleasant Perdue,	Rices		48	17	1
Micajah L. Jones,	Greens		244	33	1

39th DAY'S DRAWING—April. 20.

APPLING.

Fortunate Drawers Capts. Dist.	No.Dt.Sec.
Winney Moody, widow, Colliers	192 10 5

BALDWIN.

John Morris, R. S., Thomas	119 10 3
W. H. Crenshaw's orps., Buchanans	125 4 4
John Ellis Baker, Lesters	48 6 3
John Turk's orphans, do	11 27 1
Daniel Murphy's orphans, Ginns	234 30 1

BIBB.

Jesse Wright, Lloyds	142 13 1
Enoch Green, Pickards	107 11 3
James Hammock, soldier, do	58 29 1
David F. Wilson, Bates	19 31 1
Jesse Thrower, Carrs	153 32 1

BULLOCH.

William Woodcock, R. S., Deloachs	228 6 5
Thomas Causby, soldier, Standlands	156 5 2

BURKE.

Alexander Sanders, Corkers	140 9 3
Andrew Hardwick, Ballys	114 4 2
Elisha Bergeron, Thompsons	99 7 5
John Long, orphan, Lewis	74 9 3
John Young, Dugas	159 23 1
Henry Hilliard, Andersons	236 20 2
Francis Jenkins, R. S., Wards	205 31 1
Philip Sapp's orphans, Thompsons	177 19 1

CAMDEN.

Mary Gunby, widow, Wards	188 4 1

CHATHAM.

William Oglebay, Baines	265 8 5
Ebenezer L. Foster, Savannah	119 1 4
Uriah H. Bivins Baines	133 21 1
Silas Briggs,	106 13 1
Lucy Duraee, widow, Williams	79 10 1

CLARK.

Noah Prince, Frosts	111 9 5
Isaac Hightower, McDonalds	261 7 2
Levi Stewart, Deans	117 18 2
Samuel Hopkins, soldier, Echols	8 24 2
Archibald S. Jackson, McDonalds	10 9 5
George W. Shaw, Gahagans	167 19 1
Nathan W. Whitman, sol., Greers	249 7 5
William Whitton, jr. Andersons	111 1 4
Ulysses R. Lynch, Lumpkins	172 4 5

COLUMBIA.

James Rogers, Adams	34 3 1
Orps. of Benj. E. Winfrey, Ramseys	6 14 2
Overton Reynolds, Carrols	107 17 1
Washington W. Stone, Boltons	110 17 2
Daniel Vaughn, Perrys	205 5 4
Cordy B. Edwards, Clarks	233 8 3
Patrick J. Culbreath, Culbreaths	77 3 2
John Prather, Carrolls	214 16 1
Orps of Joseph Marshall, jr. Bailys	12 27 1
Lewis Powell, R. S., Ramsays	240 7 1
Wyche James, Dranes	104 15 1

DECATUR.

Mary Devereux, widow, Douglass	89 5 1
Nanly Lunn, do.	165 27 1
Mary Truluck, widow, Hawthorns	116 10 5

DE KALB.

Jonathan Gray, Conus	6 8 2
Sarah Stone, widow, Merritts	211 18 2
Sarah Hill, widow, Edwards	71 9 ¦
Thomas P. Wagnon, R. S., Howells	186 8 ¦
Francis Veal, Bollings	317 7 5

Fortunate Drawers Capts. Dist.	No.Dt.Sec.
Robert Kennady's orphans Stepens	23 16 5
John Brockman, Browns	136 22 2

DOOLY.

Thomas J. Levingston, Andersons	276 3 4

EFFINGHAM.

And. Williams, sr., R. S., Stricklands	169 2 2

ELBERT.

Archibald Magarety, Merritts	141 12 1
Charles Dean, soldier, Dobbs	90 22 2
Calvin P. Sanders, do.	115 13 2
Orphans of John C. Taylor, Bells	146 20 2
Nelson Burden, Hortons	115 7 1
Elijah Maxwell, soldier, Harmons	199 3 5
Thomas A. Banks, Blackwells	93 1 2
Joshua B. Nellums, Hortons	201 32 1
Orps. of Kindred Magarity, Merritts	34 8 1

EMANUEL.

Catharine Bell, widow, Fountains	233 16 2
Francis Miller, Moores	150 6 1

FAYETTE.

Laurence Smith, Craigs	256 7 5
Elijah Dodson, Dodsons	7 2 5
John Lawrence, Morgans	203 33 1

FRANKLIN.

Benjamin Harrison, Walters	155 6 3
John Bell, sen. Hudsons	61 5 3
Andrew Martin, Caudells	124 13 2
John Allen, R. S., Boswells	146 29 1
Julius Nichols, R. S., Hudsons	208 3 5
Julian Ayres, J. C., Walters	104 4 1
George Sheridan, Caudells	163 7 5
William C. Gober, Jones	13 7 3
John Stonecypher, R. S., Tabors	298 1 4
Frances Rose, hus. ab. D. Chandlers	156 32 1
James Vaughan, Blankinships	48 5 1

GLYNN.

Aaron Tyson, McLeods	48 3 1
Barny Gowen, orphan, do.	155 1 5
C. C. M. & C. Wallace, orps. do.	171 19 2
Robert Pritchard, Burnetts	145 11 2

GREENE.

Nathan Gooch, R. S., Winfields	9 9 3
Mehaly Wright, dumb, Rankins	19 12 1
Isaac A. Beddell, Greens	76 5 3
Elizabeth Lee, widow, Southerlands	25 15 2
Pleasant Baugh, Vincents	91 6 1
Mary Oneal, widow, Colcloughs	26 14 2
Henry Calton, Robinsons	110 23 2
Barbara Bethune, w. R. S., Greens	224 2 4
Charles Harris, Astins	102 18 2

GWINNETT.

Joseph Covey, R. S., Caruthers	170 12 5
Lorenzo D. Winn, Greens	242 10 1
Drewry Thompson, Hunicuts	5 5 4
Dennis Still, jun. Woodroughs	85 7 2
John B. Hainey, jr. do.	85 12 3
Jesse Rhodes, Greens	255 18 1
Job Smith, Finchers	69 9 2
Frederick Corly, Dunbars	127 30 1
George Moon, Robertsons	175 1 4
Benjamin Hazlerig, soldier, Mattox	264 21 1
James Red, Moors	226 12 1
William Hall, Davis	82 13 2
Letitia Williamson, widow, Rollins	142 6 5
William S. Harris, for wife, Davis	138 17 2
Meredith York, Wallis	109 22 1
David McWhorter, Hunicuts	172 22 1

LAND LOTTERY REGISTER—No. 18
[RECORDER OFFICE—PUBLISHED BY GRANTLAND & OBME—PRICE $3.]

NOTE.—Section 1 is Lee County—2 Muscogee—3 Troup—4 Coweta—5 Carroll.

39th DAY'S DRAWING—Continued

HANCOCK.

Fortunate Drawers Capts. Dist.	No.Dt.Sec.
William Tower, 102d	178 2 4
James McCook, 114th	257 2 3
Samuel Cook, 114th	85 2 4
John S. L. Acree, 108th	94 18 1
John Askew's orphans, 107th	9 11 5
Green Grant, 101st	200 20 2
Samuel Grantland, 117th	267 6 5
James H. Middlebrooks, 108th	50 22 2

HENRY.

James Fletcher, Bryants	299 5 1
John B. McElroy, McVicers	99 8 1
Elisha Crew, Harris	132 10 1
William Brock, Bryants	180 5 4
Aaron Dowdy, Allens	160 1 2
Joseph Henderson, Grays	215 6 3
William T. Burton, Kites	171 17 2
Moses Bay, R. S., Shaws	79 7 1
Shepherd K. Williams, Risons	171 20 2
Robert Johnson, soldier, Bryants	76 5 4
William Bonner, Wards	165 15 5
William Parker, Shaws	79 7 1
Elisha Brooks, soldier, T. Harris	200 14 1
John Penton, soldier, Smiths	157 14 1

HABERSHAM.

Hugh Pierce, R. S. Langstons	26 5 3
Everett Shuffield, Kenzies	224 12 2
Jeremiah McDaniel, R. S., Cross	199 10 5
John Smith's orphans, Kenzies	111 7 3
Callton Raguld, Suttons	276 9 3
William Smith, Langstons	259 3 3
William Cox, Bakers	169 32 1
Samuel Fain, Vickrys	124 30 1
David Caldwell, Jones	62 27 1

HALL.

William Sinyard, Harrisons	198 2 5
Mary Pennix, hus. absent, Wilsons	40 4 1
William Wood, Roberts	28 8 1
Henry Newton Dorseys	111 5 1
Charles Gravit, Yagers	48 4 2

HOUSTON.

Whitmore Price, Prices	169 1 4
William H. Jordan, Bozemans	141 3 1
McDaniel Page, Pattons	60 14 5
George T. Jameson, illegit. Duncans	266 2 1
Jesse Wall, Simpsons	274 7 1
Richard Johnson, Farnels	64 14 5

JACKSON.

John Todd's orphans, Venables	198 12 5
George Swain, Landrums	209 15 2
Allen Justus, Lindseys	215 25 1
James B. Bond, Bowens	216 3 1
Allen White, Storys	172 21 1
Elizabeth Palmer, w. R. S., Lindseys	106 8 5
Samuel Smith, sen. Winns	235 23 2
Elizabeth Lyle, wid. R. S., do.	121 6 2
Jane Hancock, widow, Venables	107 19 2
Jonathan Kolb's orphans, Allens	108 32 1

JASPER.

John H. Kenard Barnetts	239 6 1
Jacob Gordon, Baynes	151 11 1
Lucy Crenshaw, widow, Reeves	83 15 5

Fortunate Drawers Capts. Dist.	No.Dt.Sec.
Thomas Culbertson, Baynes	80 13 1
Ralph Jarrod, Dardens	190 12 2
Nancy Simmons, widow, Johnsons	118 1 3
James M. Godly's chil. fa.ab. Wilders	227 8 1
Nathan Warner, Holmes	213 11 5
James Buchanan, sr., R. S., Keys	171 18 1
Abner Smith, Sparks	1 7 4
Oliver Usher's orphans, Holmes	103 9 5
Richard Henderson, Parkers	226 7 1
Caty Sims, Reeves	183 2 2
Isaac Whaley, Robinsons	123 6 3
William Dewberry, Wilders	17 28 1
Isaiah Langley, Hines	24 6 5

JEFFERSON.

Aven Jordan, R. S., Cunninghams	44 3 1
Theophilus Powell's orps., Elliotts	216 9 5
Henry Darly, do.	91 7 4
John A. Parsons, Ross	161 30 1
Needham Purvis, do.	5 5 2
Mary Haddin, widow, R. S., Boyds	91 26 1

JONES.

Booker L. Russell, Stewards	171 1 4
William H. Lowe, Davis	23 33 1
Charles Dunning, Woods	249 33 1
Daniel Morgan's orphans, Popes	251 11 1
Robert S. Mangum, Mullins	71 7 4
William Sperlin, Robertsons	198 8 3
Asa Little, Dosters	186 16 1
Moses Smith's orphans, Hills	153 1 4
Thomas Hunt, Bowens	148 4 5
Payton Vinson, Gibsons	20 24 1
Henry B. Cone, Duncans	102 20 2
John Holiday, jr's orps. Hammacks	64 15 5
Thomas Moon, Dosters	161 5 4

LAURENS.

William Spell, Plummers	173 27 1
James Clemmons, Powers	252 7 1
Ann Locke, widow, Deans	271 3 4
Henry Hutto, R. S., do.	151 21 2
Elijah Coleman, Mizells	104 5 2
Benjamin Yarborough, R. S., Deans	43 4 4
Mary Mills, widow, Ballows	283 21 1
Bartholomew Ganey, R. S., Beachams	235 22 1

LIBERTY.

James A. Sandeford, 17th	203 8 3
Robert Hendry, R. S., 17th	229 2 1
Delilah Spinholster, wid., 17th	155 21 1

LINCOLN.

Susannah Wallace, wid. Levritts	174 2 3
Henry Thyess, do.	212 13 1

MADISON.

Cicero N. Jones, ill. Culbertsons	212 4 2
Sallathial M. Hailes, Caldwells	82 21 1
John Scott, jr. do.	208 16 2
Thomas Lawrence, Christians	141 5 4

McINTOSH.

Thomas A. Houston, sol. Thorps	201 19 1

MONROE.

Francis Power, Wrights	126 11 3
John Pinckard, Millers	102 8 3
Baldwin Davis, Browns	83 3 5
Thomas Warren, Johnstons	208 7 1

Fortunate Drawers Capts. Dist.	No.	Dt.	Sec.
Archibald Lary, Woodards	66	17	1
Spencer Moore, sol. Fergasons	73	11	5
Robert G. Turmon, sol. Houses	131	7	5
Thomas W. Banks, Pattersons	55	2	2
Smith Haynes, Turners	164	14	2
Benj. Humphrey, sol. Douglass	230	2	1
William Trice, Houses	87	27	1

MORGAN.

	No.	Dt.	Sec.
Alexander M. Brown, Jennings	258	12	3
Sion Hudson, Boswells	137	8	3
Rosan Myhand, w.R. S., Youngs	108	5	3
John Lucas, Beasleys	35	8	5
James Thomas sol. Christians	174	33	1
Richard Gray, sol. Hitchcocks	140	3	4
John Stapp, Watsons	259	14	1
John P. Wyatt, Stokes	263	20	2
Hannah Posey, wid. Harwells	234	26	1
Memory Fulgham, Adairs	143	27	1
Larkin W. Allen, Christians	147	3	1

MONTGOMERY.

	No.	Dt.	Sec.
Zachariah Hester, Wynns	274	9	5
Jamec J. Joyce, Popes	60	13	1
Mathias Adams, Wynns	30	1	5
James Faulkner, Pridgeons	250	10	2
Lovedam Curry, illeg. Wynns	170	21	2

NEWTON.

	No.	Dt.	Sec.
Nathan Chapman, R. S. Hays	293	7	1
Henry Mitchell, Dyers	41	18	1
William Legwin, Snows	103	7	3
Phillip Houseworth, Talleys	234	32	1

OGLETHORPE.

	No.	Dt.	Sec.
Gresham Vickers, sol. B. Hills	240	17	2
Asa J. Howard, Floyds	22	15	1
Miles W. Goolsby, Seals	208	17	1
Anderson Colley, sol. Mays	16	15	5
Lemuel Black, R. S. Floyds	42	8	4
Henry Rains, sol. Lacys	94	16	1
James S. Palmer, Rosseaus	46	6	3
William Landrum, sol. Smiths	178	6	1
Moses Jones, Holloways	14	7	3
Harrison, Birdsong, Rosseaus	179	7	3
Joel Tarpley, Hills	26	16	1
Ang. Culbreth, sol. Devenports	224	4	3
Randal Jones, sol. Mays	59	9	3
John A. Glenn, Floyds	230	1	1

PIKE.

	No.	Dt.	Sec.
Thos. Coventons orps. Mays	176	3	1
Asa Lanham, sol. Bryans	216	6	5
Samuel Weaver, Dannellys	179	23	1
Edwin Watts, Longs	115	5	4

PULASKI.

	No.	Dt.	Sec.
James Dillard, Powells	214	13	2
William Cunningham, Gilstraps	182	20	1
John Bryan, Scarbroughs	39	26	1

PUTNAM.

	No.	Dt.	Sec.
George Grier, Slaughters	92	12	1
Susanah Baugh, wid. Blacks	61	1	4
Reuben Ragland, Kendricks	116	4	5
Lewellyn W. Hudson, Bledsoes	259	6	5
John M. Smith, Sparks	287	28	1
Uriah Ward, Clarks	227	6	5

Fortunate Drawers Capts. Dist.	No.	Dt.	Sec.
William Wilmuntt, Allums	51	14	2
Eliz. C. Branham,w.R.S.,Bledsoes	190	20	2
Elizabeth Veal, widow, Goods	214	2	3

RABUN.

	No.	Dt.	Sec.
Delila Fox, widow, Mersers	96	15	5

RICHMOND.

	No.	Dt.	Sec.
George Goulds orphans, Blacks	23	31	1
John Ward, do.	105	8	2
Levi Florance, Huntingtons	83	16	1
Lewis Culbreath, sol. Wilcoxs	93	3	3
A. Fulchers orphans, Kellys	88	31	1
Richard Reid, Blacks	300	3	4
Lewis Culbreath, Ferris	9	23	2
Francis Clarke, Huntingtons	3	9	2
Joshua Pharoah, James	47	3	1
Emanuel Johnson, R. S., Kellys	238	12	1
Armand Harkins' orps. 119th	257	15	1

SCRIVEN.

	No.	Dt.	Sec.
Eliza Hendrick, ill. Humphreys	30	18	1
Fanny Little, w. R. S., Hunters	59	14	1
Nelley Freeman, minor, Roberts	24	16	1
Noah Strahorns minors. Hunters	134	12	3
James Moor, do.	120	21	1
J. Herrington, id.son of R.Roberts	64	5	2

TATTNALL.

	No.	Dt.	Sec.
Henry Hollon, R. S. Corseys	56	5	1
John McLendons orphs. Dees.	95	1	1
John Chesser, Conners	212	31	1

TELFAIR.

	No.	Dt.	Sec.
John Gants orphs. Wilkinsons	129	23	2
John Hagger, Barentines	236	23	2
Allen Ricketson, Wilkinsons	298	10	2

TALIAFERRO

	No.	Dt.	Sec.
Mary Stokes, illegit. Towns	123	6	2

THOMAS.

	No.	Dt.	Sec.
Benjamin McMillam,	26	33	1

TWIGGS.

	No.	Dt.	Sec.
James Green, Graggs	83	10	5
Orps. of A. Mitchell, Wimberlys	237	29	1
Richard Lindsey, Pearsons	56	6	1

UPSON.

	No.	Dt.	Sec.
Levi Spencer, Myricks	212	29	1
Hillary M. Crabb, Hattoxs	10	1	1
Richard Lyon, Paschalls	184	10	2
Joseph Thompson, Hattoxs	174	13	1

WALTON.

	No.	Dt.	Sec.
Josiah Camp, Hudsons	101	10	1

WAYNE.

	No.	Dt.	Sec.
Samuel Buroughs, Staffords	77	10	3
Richard W. Bryan, orphan, do	116	23	1

WARREN.

	No.	Dt.	Sec.
James Tensions orphs. Adkins	7	20	1
William Wilder, Parhams	207	25	1
Shadrack Potts, Adkins	235	6	1
Albert H. Story, illeg. Fords	92	5	1
Simon Hurst, Parhams	98	10	5
William Jordan, R. S., Jones	244	1	2
Fielding Hill, sr. Parhams	84	3	3
Charles Langham, Brinkleys	209	5	1
Hiram N. Walker, Downs	86	1	2
Barney Hart, Adkins	167	10	1
Thomas Martin, do	195	15	1

(123)

Fortunate Drawers Capts. Dist.	No.	Dt.	Sec.
Sarah Hodo's illegits, Hales	275	21	1
William Wiggins, R. S. Sanders	109	6	4
John Champion, R. S., Adkins	260	6	5
WASHINGTON.			
Patsey White, wid. Oquins	263	3	4
William Hodges, Warthens	17	14	1
Simeon Bland, Avans	194	4	1
John Spurlock, Warthens	49	9	2
John Hardin, sol. Floyds	70	14	5
John Williford, illegit. Woods	234	4	1
Richard Warthen, Warthens	92	2	1
Sampson Lee, R. S., Wimberlys	5	11	1
WILKINSON.			
William Lord, R. S., Mathews	14	14	2
John Thursbay, Mayos	136	8	3
Jesse Hooks, Halls	92	7	4
Ezekiel Boggs, R. S. Shows	217	13	2
Timothy Bloodworth, Mandersons	94	8	5
Green & J. Frederick, orps. Halls	170	5	2
W. & P. Parker, orps. Fairchilds	80	27	1
William G. Calloway, Shows	127	9	2
Robert Giles, Mayos	82	10	5
Allen Cannon, Fairchilds	325	8	1
WILKES.			
Eliz. J. Smith, w. Washingtons	127	29	1
Ors. of Nicholas Long, Charltons	223	6	5
Wylie Tomlinson, Reeves	126	20	2
Thomas D. Borom, Greens	80	3	4

40th DAY'S DRAWING—April 21.

APPLING.			
James Sapp, Morgans	142	7	1
James Boothe, do.	234	7	3
John Smith, Dedges	64	9	5
BALDWIN.			
Spencer Roberts, Buchanans	109	5	2
Edward Brown, R. S., Lingos	111	15	1
Thomas Glass' orpahns, Rowes	266	2	4
Mirabeau B. Lamar, Buchanans	37	14	2
William Harvey, Wheelers	171	7	5
Chil. of R. Reaves, fa. absent, Doles	143	7	1
Sarah Turner, orphan, Lingos	164	4	3
Abner Hammond, R. S., Bivins	33	18	1
Horatio N. Barkesdale, Wheelers	81	1	3
Catharine Dunlap, wid. Buchanans	147	22	2
Mildred S. Fleming, wid. do.	146	17	2
BIBB.			
David Flanders Flanders	134	21	2
James McDonald, R. S., Rutlands	163	10	5
Orphans of Henry Smith, Beards	262	22	2
George Jewett, Flanders	241	15	2
BRYAN.			
Elizabeth Harvey, widow, Harveys	31	31	1
Turner Jenkins, Stephens	51	4	5
BULLOCH.			
William Iler, Richardsons	118	5	2
Lucy Sheffield, widow, do.	129	5	4
BURKE.			
Silas Broxton's orphans, Dugas	308	1	2
Patsey Lodge, orpanh, Lynchs	96	4	5
Jesse White's orphans, Baxleys	256	19	1
John Skinner, Rogers	256	2	3
Stephen Cross, R. S., Lynchs	199	21	2
Parm. & R. Folds, illegits, Gordons	67	8	4

Fortunate Drawers Capts. Dist.	No.	Dt.	Sec.
Wright Williams, Dugas	36	3	4
William Young's orphans, do.	225	1	1
David Hall, Dugas	62	2	3
BUTTS.			
William Jones, Moores	4	22	1
Duke W. Jackson, Rights	146	2	5
CAMDEN.			
William B. North, Coxs	109	7	3
John Pearce, Baileys	135	2	4
CHATHAM.			
Charlotte S. Sawyer, orp. Haydens	186	22	1
Edw'd D. Courter's orps. McDonnels	144	20	1
Benjamin Briggs, do.	53	20	1
Sarah Parmenter, widow, Baines	211	4	1
John A. Smith, Reeds	297	5	3
Absalom Youmans, Gaddys	11	21	2
CLARK.			
James L. Jones, Davis	185	3	5
Josiah Cheatham, soldier, Deans	65	8	3
Larkin L. Baldwin, Herndons	201	5	4
Margaret Browning, w. R. S., do.	140	4	1
Madison R. Mitchell, Gahagans	179	3	3
COLUMBIA.			
Robert Bolton, Boltons	283	5	3
James H. Moore, Baldwins	146	9	1
Richard Scruggs, Baileys	42	22	1
Cass & Hezekiah Yon, ills., Dranes	252	25	1
Isiah W. Maddock, do.	292	7	1
Gideon Lantern, Coles	188	14	2
CRAWFORD.			
Hezekiah Jones, Wilsons	245	8	3
DECATUR.			
John Pollock, Manns	116	8	3
DE KALB.			
William Williams, Merritts	159	21	1
Elijah & Sar. Duke, illegits, Bakers	283	16	2
Isaac Reeves, Bowlings	7	7	2
Edward Howard, do.	84	6	5
DOOLY.			
Stephen Harward, Sarrs	166	10	5
Richard Coleman, Andersons	127	26	1
EARLY.			
William F. Carragan, Grimsleys	21	15	1
William Phillips, Speers	8	6	1
EFFINGHAM.			
William Wamack, R. S., Elkins	56	11	1
Benjamin Genobly, Waldhaners	170	11	8
ELBERT.			
James Dutton, Alstons	142	33	1
Simeon L. Pledger, Harmonds	177	8	1
David Cook, Dunns	249	2	4
William Parham, Webbs	109	30	1
EMANUEL.			
Furney Deal, 49th	199	2	4
FAYETTE.			
William Chamber, Browns	146	11	3
Thomas Hamack, Roziers	53	1	5
Mathew T. Bishop, Whartons	9	2	4
FRANKLIN.			
Thomas Mackie, R. S., Sanders	207	15	2
Benjamin Harrison, R. S., Walters	168	2	4
Amos W. Hammond, D. Chandlers	294	6	1
Hugh Crawford, Stephens	340	7	5
Orps. of Isaac J. Barrett, Walters	221	16	2
Orps. of Matthew Holden, Hudsons	190	22	1

Fortunate Drawers	Capts. Dist.	No.	Dt.	Sec.
GLYNN.				
John R. Sanders,		166	3	5
Jonathan Bowen, Dubignons		122	32	1
Martha Ratcliff, widow, McLeods		21	11	1
GREENE.				
John Conyers, Southerlands		138	7	1
Jane Flud, widow, R. S., Dawsons		62	15	5
Samuel Greene, soldier, do.		391	28	1
GWINNETT.				
Lucy Storer, widow, Caruthers		11	25	1
Maryann Phillips, widow, Davis		139	10	2
David Sparks, Evans		181	16	2
Ambrose Kirkland, Robertsons		188	3	5
John Headrick, Caruthers		4	1	3
Drury Lee, Woodroughs		96	10	5
Isaac ork, Hunicuts		27	2	5
Eli Thomas, Bowlings		342	8	1
Henry Sizemore, jr. Hills		107	16	2
HABERSHAM.				
John R. Waters, Jones		37	22	2
John W. Freeman, idiot, Vickreys		324	28	1
John Stanley, Faines		23	21	1
Elaxander J. Purkins, ill. Bryans		114	11	5
William G. Pitchford, do.		202	24	1
Henry B. Robertson, Tates		150	9	3
HALL.				
Arch'd. W. Whitehead, Hardens		14	5	3
Jesse Hulsey, R. S., Harrisons		197	5	3
William Pattersons, Hendricks		22	21	1
Daniel Pitmon, Walkers		192	11	3
John Martin, sen. Floyds		156	4	5
Elizabeth Lott, idiot, Garrards		196	5	3
Charles Hawkins, Yagers		143	11	3
HANCOCK.				
Robert Norris's orphans, 117th		127	1	1
Amey Newman, illegit, 112th		9	8	5
Mary Jernigan, widow, 106th		213	3	2
Eliza Tucker, orphan, 109th		118	27	1
HENRY.				
Mathew Wilkerson, Grays		34	9	5
Isaac H. Skinner, Risons		226	8	5
Silas Gordon, Shaws		160	2	4
Samuel Houston, R. S., Grays		189	11	1
Elias Gay, do.		8	19	1
William P. Newell, Bryants		27	3	5
John Camp, soldier, do.		210	3	2
James N. Wright, widow, Grays		71	8	3
Mary Young, widow, Grays		71	8	3
John Ellis, Allens		247	12	3
HOUSTON.				
Tilmon Dixon, Yarboroughs		76	22	1
Willis H. Bell, Moores		18	7	1
IRWIN.				
William Fussell, Dixons		147	24	1
Malcomb McInnis, do.		142	2	5
James Hayman, Bradfords		157	4	5
JACKSON.				
Daniel Baugh, Duprees		181	3	3
Joshua Goolsby's orps., Moons		155	1	2
John Thornton's orps. Rogers		106	26	1
Larkin Butler, soldier, do.		213	12	1
JASPER.				
Osborn Robinson, Trussells		155	14	2
James Keith, soldier, Farleys		80	23	2

Fortunate Drawers	Capts. Dist.	No.	Dt.	Sec.
Harrison Hamrick, Sparks		266	11	2
Washington Phelps's ors. Dardens		131	23	2
Reoney B. Watson, Johnsons		190	2	4
Lucas Powell, Doctor, Holmes		241	10	2
JEFFERSON.				
James B. Brown, Marshals		7	7	1
Thomas L. Irwin, Cunninghams		155	3	2
Wiliam J. Jordan, Beatys		183	20	1
Robert Lowry's orps., Causeys		222	10	5
JONES.				
James S. Newby, Newbys		297	10	2
Ambers Ward, illegit., Davis		147	21	2
Burrell Rabourn, soldier, do.		276	1	4
John Nash, Spinks		144	7	1
John Simmons's orps. Robertsons		16	25	1
George Clark, Simmons		157	29	1
Louisa Kirk's minors, Bowens		297	8	5
Anderson Wicks, Duncans		93	17	1
Alexander Sanders, Mullins		260	2	1
John Lockett, Newbys		81	9	2
Benjamin Dowing, Popes		77	11	3
LAURENS.				
Hardy Smith, R. S., Powers		98	4	4
Eli English, Barlows		141	15	1
Martha Moore's ill. child. Spiveys		148	6	2
Jnoa. Thigpen's mins., Beachams		70	1	3
LIBERTY.				
James Audley Maxwell, 14th		74	4	1
LINCOLN.				
Thomas Wallace, Leveretts		60	1	4
John Simmons, sol.l.w. Prathers		110	2	3
MADISON.				
John W. Streetman, Bones		186	26	1
McINTOSH.				
Peter Odend, sol. Terrells		296	1	4
Alexander McDonald, sol. Thorps		41	11	5
MONROE.				
James Johnson, Finchs		11	31	1
Jesse Aycock, Wrights		251	5	1
John Baxter, Houses		25	7	2
Malinda W. Booth, illegit. do		108	1	3
David Bryan, R. S. Douglass		121	4	3
Susannah Davis, wid. Millers		219	13	2
James Brewer, Pattersons		195	19	2
MORGAN.				
John McMurray, Jennings		191	11	3
Jesse Lee, R. S., Watsons		76	9	5
Martha Darnell, wid. Jennings		24	10	3
David Allen, Christians		152	20	2
John J. Boswell, Boswells		300	1	2
MONTGOMERY.				
John McEachens, orps. Wynns		29	7	2
Laban Barker, Ryals		206	5	1
NEWTON.				
Henry Teal, Webbs		104	1	2
Margaret Philips, wid. Hays		93	6	2
William Christopher, Newnans		114	5	3
Stephen Cowart, Smiths		201	14	1
James G. Rabb, Moss		37	3	2
James Taylor, Graces		51	5	4
Nathaniel Gary, Sumners		24	29	1
David F. Montgomery, Dyers		139	7	2

LAND LOTTERY REGISTER—No. 19
[RECORDER OFFICE—PUBLISHED BY GRANTLAND & OBME—PRICE $3.]

NOTE.—Section 1 is Lee County—2 Muscogee—3 Troup—4 Coweta—5 Carroll.

40th DAY'S DRAWING—Continued.

Fortunate Drawers Capts. Dist.	No.Dt.Sec.
OGLETHORPE.	
Martin Dowdy, Lacys	59 1 2
PIKE.	
Thomas G. Phillips, sol. Suitors	69 22 2
Zadock Blaylock, Longs	229 10 3
PULASKI.	
James Harrison, Scarbroughs	134 30 1
William Shipp, Gilstraps	268 16 2
PUTNAM.	
James Singletons orps. Blacks	59 7 1
Michael Dennis, Barnetts	26 3 5
Jones Rivers' orps. Sparks	69 2 2
Claborn Buckner, Kendricks	65 6 2
RABUN.	
Jesse Jones, Godfreys	14 6 4
Jonathan Critington, do.	199 10 1
RICHMOND.	
Furniford Greene, Blacks	96 6 3
Ezekiel Wood, Treadwells	156 13 1
Ezekiel Smith, jr. Wilcoxs	90 12 1
Mary Spain Strange, w. Kellys	234 8 3
Hamen M. Lear J. James & R.	
J. Marks orps. Huntingtons	215 5 3
Malakiah Fraser, Augusta	347 28 1
Ann Lartigue, widow, Hands	86 8 3
Redden Atwell, Kellys	70 9 5
Burril Byrd, Wilcoxs	214 13 1
Eliza Huges, wid. Treadwells	273 1 2
Alexander Gordon, Huntingtons	207 20 2
SCRIVEN.	
John Hiram Smith, Poytress	37 12 5
Ann Newton, w. R. S., Hunters	83 1 1
TATTNALL.	
John Fiveashs orps. Graces	238 2 2
William C. Stewart, McDuffies	75 11 3
TWIGGS.	
James Adams, Streetmans	233 6 1
William B. Shaw, Pearsons	73 21 2
Ruth Tharp, w. R. S., Bosticks	130 2 4
James Deshazo, Streetmans	90 4 2
UPSON.	
Othniel W. Tomme, 589th	100 15 2
William Williams, Paschalls	65 11 3
James Hattocks, Hattock's	16 4 5
WALTON.	
John Moate, Bexleys	62 1 1
Alexander Dyer, Rays	93 3 2
Puckett Wood, McQuertors	123 5 4
Joseph Camp, sol. 249th	164 18 2
Isaac Dial, 503rd	192 32 1
Susannah Beasleys ills. Snows	28 2 4
John Palmore, Hudsons	10 15 2
WAYNE.	
William Rawls, R. S., Staffords	190 16 1
WARREN.	
Ahisha Wood, Kinseys	371 28 1
John Mays, sr. do	220 3 2

Fortunate Drawers Capts. Dist.	No.Dt.Sec.
Soloman Newsom, jr. Adkins	110 31 1
Terry Oliver, sol. Stewarts	313 3 4
William Chalker, illeg. Adkins	104 1 1
Rhoda Walden, wid. Downs	225 5 2
Orps. of Mountain Hill, Lattimers	96 28 1
Ross O'Neal. R. S., Jones	178 20 1
WASHINGTON.	
Nathan Sabins, Gilberts	232 25 1
William Quicks, do.	140 9 5
John Dudley, Wimberlys	100 5 3
Thomas Johnson, Warthens	78 32 1
William Thigpen, Woods	147 11 2
Matilda Horton, wid. Oquins	97 2 4
John Acord, Avans	83 15 1
WILKINSON.	
Littleberry Mock, sol. Smiths	9 29 1
Martin S. Clance, Currys	89 27 1
William Burket, Shows	307 15 1
William Williams, do.	227 1 4
William Hickey, Halls	180 8 5
Andrew Nobles, Mandersons	107 10 1
Elizabeth Jenkins, illegs. Halls	43 16 2
WILKES.	
Ambrose Philips, Reeves	207 10 3
Christopher Briant, Chunns	47 13 2
Seaborn J. Fullelove, Wootens	133 12 3
George W. Lamar, Greshams	49 22 1
Elenor Corbett, Charltons	207 3 1
Felix Ramsey, Popes	36 5 1
Henry Curray, Richardsons	101 6 2

41st DAY'S DRAWING—April 23.

	No.Dt.Sec.
APPLING.	
Elizabeth Timmons, w. R.S., Collins	104 13 1
J., Z., H., D. N. & M. Man, do.	240 2 2
Abraham Eason, Morgans	195 17 2
Benjamin Timmons, illegitimate,	155 16 2
Permildia Turner. widow, Dodges	165 18 1
BALDWIN.	
George Searcy, Wheelers	226 2 3
Francis Asbury B. Wheeler, Doles	155 12 5
Sarah Anderson, blind, Wheelers	13 15 1
BIBB.	
J. W., S. & T. Y. Berry, ills. Rutlands	206 6 2
Jesse J. Duggan, Flanders	111 12 5
BULLOCH.	
David Lee, R. S., Laniers	15 5 1
BURKE.	
Seaborn Powell, Lewis	203 3 1
Lavina Lewis, orphan, Bayleys	124 9 2
Wade Brown, Gordons	144 11 2
Zilpha Parker, hus., absent, Roberts	14 19 2
James Jeffers' orphans, Wards	107 8 3
John Prior's orphans, Rogers	73 25 2
BUTTS.	
J. Willingham, w'd soldier, Hendricks	41 11 1
Eli Knight, illegitimate, Johnsons	166 19 2
Zeddack Hutson, soldier, Thaxtons	204 9 1
Silas Gilmore, Hendricks	129 2 3

CAMDEN.

Fortunate Drawers Capts. Dist.	No.	Dt.	Sec.
Orphans of Levy Johns, Coxs	344	7	5

CHATHAM.

Fortunate Drawers Capts. Dist.	No.	Dt.	Sec.
Matthew Hall McAlister, Haydens	226	12	3
Orphans of Gideon Rawson, Baines	248	5	1
John Gardiner, McDonnells	267	23	2
James Wall, Haydens	174	18	1
Patrick Reily, McDonnells	53	21	2
Andrew Brown, Savannah	159	27	1
Joseph M. Nungazer, Nungazers	36	8	1

CLARK.

Archibald S. Jackson, McDonalds	183	3	5
Lucretia Howard, w. R. S., Davis	61	15	2
Alford Daniel, Vinsons	288	5	1
John L. Oliver, Wrights	18	5	5
Mathew Yates, Gahagans	184	6	1
Catharine Newton, w. R. S., do.	203	9	1
Samuel Gallaher, Davis	251	13	1

COLUMBIA.

William Tindall, Carrolls	136	17	2
David Vincent, jr. Ramseys	28	7	3
Aquitla Flint, Talberts	156	11	5
Benjamin Fuller, soldier, Lukes	101	3	2
Dorson Cash, R. S., Dranes	34	29	1
Orphans of Ziba Hunt, Bealls	41	2	5
Elizabeth Lantern, w. R. S., Coles	10	21	2
Edward Prather's orphans, Dranes	19	33	1

DECATUR.

John H. Martin, Douglass	199	17	2

DE KALB.

Elisha Robinson, Lokeys	138	10	2
Hambleton Ware, Bowlings	194	8	3

EFFINGHAM.

Benjamin Genobly, Waldhaners	195	5	3
Levy Davis, jun. Elkins	38	6	2
William G. Porter, Treutlins	200	25	1

ELBERT.

Parke Blackwell, Blackwells	73	3	1
Elizabeth Seals, widow, Tuckers	133	24	1
Nathaniel Duncan, Meritts	334	7	1
John H. White, Butlers	10	19	1
Thomas J. Christian, Harmons	164	9	2
Sarah Blackwell, widow, Merritts	96	7	2
Samuel Kookogey, Boltons	21	7	2
William H. Sullivan, Dobbs	149	10	3
Abner Adams, Blackwells	95	8	2

EMANUEL.

Seaborn Rose, Chasons	139	10	5
Reuben Meek, Whiddons	87	23	2
Charles C. Jenkins, McGars	58	8	5

FAYETTE.

Nancy Hubbard, illegit., Whortons	216	18	2
John Yarbrough, Wests	27	12	1
John Lambert, Craigs	133	17	1
William Howell, soldier, Landrums	22	30	1
Ephriam West, Roziers	67	2	1
Silas Dunn, Craigs	228	28	1

FRANKLIN.

George Stovall, sr., R.S., Blankinships	133	4	5
Henry J. Mitchell do.	14	1	5
John K. Landers, D. Chandlers	54	14	1
John Bryan, R. S., Stephens	175	27	1
Henry Sewell, D. Chandlers	54	5	4
Gillam Westbrook, Jones	141	5	2
Green Sewell, Hudsons	231	34	1
James Marberry, Tabors	272	17	2

Fortunate Drawers Capts. Dist.	No.	Dt.	Sec.
Pike Beck, Dobignons	119	2	5
Lewrane Lord, orphan, Burnetts	88	21	1
John L. Dewit,	24	18	1

GREENE.

William Clifton, Bruces	86	22	2
Sterling Grimes, Dawsons	49	26	1
Robert Hackney, R. S., Webbs	168	1	4
Orphans of James Caldwell, Vincents	59	10	5
Sarah Robinnett, widow, Dawsons	4	10	5
Sarah Moore, widow, do.	25	10	2
Ephriam Price, R. S., Southerlands	180	29	1

GWINNETT.

James H. Say, Caruthers	30	7	1
Daniel Gray, Grens	117	10	5
Jesse George, R. S., Finchers	113	3	1
Thomas B. Turner, soldier, Caruthers	148	15	1
James Atwood, illegit., Hunicuts	165	3	5
Joshua Hill, soldier, Evans	213	5	4
John McDonald, jr. Bakers	171	31	1
Jackson Monroe, Maddux	165	6	3
Francis Adkins, fa. ab., Caruthers	144	3	4
Priscilla, Holdbrook, w. R. S., Greens	10	29	4
Buckner Harris, Hunicuts	112	10	1

HANCOCK.

John Rose, jr., Mahons	166	2	3
Charles V. Brooking, sol., Swints	275	7	5
Thomas J. Williams, 109th	180	7	3
Mourning Mews, widow, 116th	129	10	1

HENRY.

William Henly's orphans, Shaws	13	6	3
William Barkley, Kites	35	11	5
Mark McClusky's orphans, Harris	146	16	1
Samuel Oats's orphans, Millers	20	33	1
John Breed, Gosdens	84	26	1
Rachel Hand, w. R. S., Millers	146	23	2
James Gilbert, Shaws	27	12	3
William B. Mobley, Grays	214	20	2
John A. T. Upton, Wards	304	4	1
James Smith, Smiths	170	20	1
Thomas Owenby, Grays	195	17	1
Hiram Glazier, Kites	188	24	1
John Bailey, Wards	248	22	1

HABERSHAM.

James Cronan, R. S., Kenzies	120	11	3
Silas Bell, sen. Martins	96	21	2
Wiliam Smith, Langstons	226	6	3
Jonathan D. Chastain, Tates,	193	6	2
Jonathan McIntire, do.	42	31	1
James Forester, Jones	38	1	4
Andrew Sperlin, Tates	59	7	4
McK., L. & W. Scott, orps. Suttons	177	1	2
Philip Whitten, R. S., Tates	146	19	1
Fountain Tankersley. ones	140	23	2

HALL.

George Thompson, Yagers	263	2	4
Thomas Charles, Hardins	3	1	5
Nathaniel Harbin, Dorseys	253	28	1
Mary Garner, widow, do.	50	30	1
Absalom Thornton, orphan, Yagers	185	3	1

HOUSTON.

Ephriam Wilson, Moores	252	5	1
Henry Summerford, Becks	213	23	2
Meridith Mercer, Batemans	230	10	2

IRWIN.

Hardy Bryant, 5th	199	30	1
Dempsey Taylor, R. S., Dicksons	66	18	1

(127)

JACKSON.

Fortunate Drawers	Capts. Dist.	No.	Dt.	Sec.
Green R. Duke,	Allens	236	2	3
Nancy Thurmond, orp.	Duprees	19	15	5
Mary Street, wid. R. S.,	Staplers	205	33	1
George Shaw,	Allens	50	23	1
Samuel J. Hodge,	Staplers	71	11	1
Bardwell Billings,	Holmes	143	12	3
Thomas Ashcraft,	Winns	234	21	1
Thomas Moon,	Moons	164	27	1

JASPER.

Fortunate Drawers	Capts. Dist.	No.	Dt.	Sec.
Nancy Hill, widow,	Hines	128	20	2
John T. Rucker,	Shropshiers	184	9	3
Edward Wood,	Baynes	28	10	2
Benjamin F. Tuggle,	Wilders	77	2	2
Jeff. & Mad. Johnson, illegits.	Reeves	243	11	2
James Watson,	Camerons	183	28	1
Osborn G. Ogletree,	Bayners	91	6	5
Moses Morris,	Wilsons	154	4	1
William Norris,	Dardens	101	11	1
James Williams' orps.	Camerons	63	17	2
Barsheba Alread, widow.	Wilsons	285	22	1

JEFFERSON.

Fortunate Drawers	Capts. Dist.	No.	Dt.	Sec.
Owen Vining,	Cunninghams	60	17	2
Lexy Deal, orphan,	Marshalls	131	5	4
Thomas Mountain,	Ross	163	8	1
George McMullen,	Cunninghams	185	12	3
Nathan Brassell's orps.	Waldens	147	1	4
Druc. Glover, w. R. S.,	Cunninghams	272	14	1
Nathaniel Samples, R. S.,	do.	90	17	1
Norman McLeod,	Elliotts	239	33	1

JONES.

Fortunate Drawers	Capts. Dist.	No.	Dt.	Sec.
Gideon M. Courseys,	Newbys	121	6	1
Elizabeth Jones, wid.	Hammacks	158	2	4
Sarah Harris, widow,	Stewards	84	22	1
Jane Clark's illegits,	Hendersons	211	12	2
James Weeks' minors,	Stewarts	100	4	4
Anderson Comer's minors,	Toylors	142	15	5
Turner Chapman,	Blounts	76	4	5
James Feagin's orps.	Hammacks	78	30	1
Thomas Atkins,	Duncans	225	31	1
Reuben Burnett's orps.,	Robertsons	130	33	1
Martha Bivin, widow,	Duncans	255	1	2
John Jones,	Lows	17	8	3
Edmund Hammack, sol.	Willings	147	12	2

LAURENS.

Fortunate Drawers	Capts. Dist.	No.	Dt.	Sec.
Andrew A. Fuqua,	Mizells	146	24	2
Ann Harris	do.	232	2	1
David Young's orps.	Whiteheads	81	16	1
Ezekiel McLendon,	Powers	22	2	2
Henry Lewis,	Whiteheads	74	3	4
Richard Henderson,	Spiveys	64	11	5
Lewis Powell, R. S.,	Hodges	141	9	3
Thomas R. Harrison,	Mizells	154	26	1
James Knight, sen.	Whiteheads	201	21	1

LINCOLN.

Fortunate Drawers	Capts. Dist.	No.	Dt.	Sec.
Thomas Malone, jr.,	Gideons	105	7	4
John Lockhart,	Parks	127	21	2
Jonathan S. Prickett,	Wiggintons	227	5	1

MADISON.

Fortunate Drawers	Capts. Dist.	No.	Dt.	Sec.
John Moon, soldier,	Moons	236	9	5
William Edwards, R. S.,	Hannas	144	11	5
Samuel W. Connelly,	Christians	122	18	2
James Towns, R. S.,	Phipps	75	11	5
Patsey Welch, h. a.	Caldwells	215	6	1

McINTOSH.

Fortunate Drawers	Capts. Dist.	No.	Dt.	Sec.
Richard Horne,	Howards	74	2	5

MONROE.

Fortunate Drawers	Capts. Dist.	No.	Dt.	Sec.
William McKinney,	Pattersons	70	1	2
John B. Turner,	Woodwrads	130	9	2
Ezekiel Brumbelow,	Douglass	218	9	1
D. B. Head,	Wrights	145	15	2
Wm. Thorntons orps.	Pattersons	155	6	5
Sophia Harris, illegit.	Houses	228	10	2
Jonathan F. Bridges,	do.	217	13	1
James H. Carter,	Browns	143	10	1
William Jones,	Millers	163	6	1

MORGAN.

Fortunate Drawers	Capts. Dist.	No.	Dt.	Sec.
Martha Nutt, wid.	Gains	254	7	5
Juliana Radford, wid.	Shearmons	255	5	5
James Duke,	Sparks	2	6	3
Pleasant Moorman's orp.	Gains	37	31	1
Samuel Parker,	Canifaxs	210	27	1
Nancy Noel, h. a.	Adairs	196	10	1
Susan Hugh's illegits.	Griggs	54	6	1
Edmund Carlisle, R. S.,	Canifaxs	190	27	1
Dorcas Johnson, widow,	Ostians	46	2	2
Hobert Hall, sol.	Hitchcoks	175	6	3
Green Peavy,	Adairs	70	22	2
William Ware,	Harwells	100	11	5
Grief Linch,	do.	56	9	2
John Milligans orphs.	Boswells	252	17	2
William N. Roberts,	Youngs	139	9	5
George B. Whipple,	Griggs	170	7	1
David Gilston,	Canifaxs	52	16	1

MONTGOMERY.

Fortunate Drawers	Capts. Dist.	No.	Dt.	Sec.
Wm. W. Witherington,	Popes	14	19	1
Alexander McLennan,	do.	196	17	1

NEWTON.

Fortunate Drawers	Capts. Dist.	No.	Dt.	Sec.
Peter Davis Mann,	Talleys	215	26	1
Elisha Trimble,	Hays	56	13	2
Jesse Hill, illegit.	Bakers	99	8	2
Jesse M. Wilson,	Hays	169	8	3
William McCullers, sr.	Summers	46	5	4
Sarah Hughs, w. R. S.,	Hays	284	22	1
Thomas Grubbs,	Trammells	256	28	1
Laurene Baker,	Hays	40	2	5
Samuel Braswell, R. S.	Clarks	175	22	2
William Burk,	Snows	97	6	4
Gilam Scoggins,	Moss	179	17	1
William Keenum,	Snows	238	24	1
Peter H. Stanfield,	Zachrys	27	26	1
Henry Arrington,	Pullens	2	5	1

OGLETHORPE.

Fortunate Drawers	Capts. Dist.	No.	Dt.	Sec.
James Williams' orphans,	Dixs	209	10	1
Stephen D. Mosely,	Seals	258	2	3
Willey Carter,	Hardmans	22	11	5
Isaac Hardman,	Rousseaus	73	1	5
John McKee, R. S.,	Lacys	218	9	5
Gen. John Stewart, R. S.,	Dixs	8	4	4
John G. Holtzclaw,	do.	61	5	2
Winny Haynie, orph.	Devenports	1	4	3
John Bray,	Holloways	148	3	4
J. M. Thaxton, idiot,	Williamsons	149	11	2
Elizabeth Hancock, wid.	Holloways	15	5	2
Josah Crowley,	Rousseaus	114	18	2

PIKE.

Fortunate Drawers Capts. Dist.	No.	Dt.	Sec.
Adam Simmons, Daniels	93	8	4
Shadrack Perry, do.	112	15	2
Majors Harris, Mays	49	28	1
William Merrett, Daniels	16	18	1

PULASKI.

Daniel Harvel, Powells	144	33	1
Rewbin Bynum, Sparrows	269	5	1
David Millers orps. Bracewells	172	20	2
Zachariah Willis, Scarbroughs	9	4	1
Barny Williams, Hendlys	186	5	3
Josiah Wemburn, R. S., Thomas	241	8	1

PUTNAM.

William Goodson, Slaughters	388	28	1
Seaborn Williams, Goods	254	3	3
Jesse Bledsoe, Bledsoes	257	16	2
Albert Rogers, Blacks	59	6	2
Jesse Zachry, Clarks	8	8	2
John Jacksons orphans, Sawyers	207	2	5
Nicholas Langford, Marcus	221	6	3
Massa Thomas, R. S., Blacks	118	2	2
Benj. Joiner, Stinsons	237	9	1
John W. Hines, Blacks	79	6	3
Abagail Adams, w.R. S., Chambers	99	33	1
George Osborn, Clarks	98	31	1

RABUN.

James Suddeth, Godfreys	46	20	2
William Cobb, do.	82	3	4
Isham Edwards, Mercers	185	20	2

RICHMOND.

Sterling T. Combs, Huntingtons	176	20	1
Felix Labrosse, Ferris	197	24	1
Majers Watson, James	2	29	1
John M. Cooper, Treadwells	176	9	1
Samuel Dunwody, (Rev.) do.	189	24	2
James Higginbotham, Ferris	202	2	5
Larkin Berry, do.	107	4	2
Eliz. A. Byrd, wid. Huntingtons	367	20	2
Catharine Barry, wid. Mantzs	121	3	5
Ezekiel Nilms, Kellys	56	8	1
Mary Fraser, orph. Augusta	217	14	1

SCRIVEN.

Elbert Jeffers, Reaves	14	3	2
Susan Miller, wid. Lovetts	113	1	3
John Willson, Humphreys	183	30	1
William Burnes, sol. Branoms	115	16	1

TATTNALL.

Henry Magehees orps. Conners	136	21	1
Groves Sharpe, sr. Graces	237	2	3
Gadi Stricklin, Dees	203	5	5

TELFAIR.

James Hinson, Wilkinsons	229	24	1
Isaac Jones, R. S., Barentines	25	2	1

TWIGGS.

Josiah J. Evans, Wimberlys	33	1	2
Ichabud Ham, Streetmans	140	22	1
Benjamin Ray, R. S., Pearsons	30	4	1
Margaret Wiker, w. Streetmans	216	11	5
Arthur Davis, Holidays	133	7	4
Peter G. Thompson, Graggs	67	4	3
Ors. of J. McCollum, Streetmans	146	3	2
Richard Smith, Chamberlains	126	23	2
Alex W. Angelly, Streetmans	43	5	2

UPSON.

Fortunate Drawers Capts. Dist.	No.	Dt.	Sec.
Gilford Couper, Coopers	41	3	5
Lemuel Moore, Pettys	179	15	2
Eliz. Jenkins' illegits, Saunders	346	7	1
Franklin W. King, illeg. Pettys	158	22	1
Daniel Parker, jr. Myricks	169	4	2
Green Flournoy, Ellis	193	8	5
William Gordy, sol. Hattocks	12	9	5
Andrew Hood, Myricks	66	20	2

WALTON.

Elisha Lake, Snows	45	15	1
Sheriff Brustor, sr. McQuertors	97	12	3
James Robertsons orphs. 559th	115	7	2
James Tilmon, soldier, Snows	134	13	1

WAYNE.

Pliney Sheffield, McKinneys	88	5	2

WARREN.

William Mays, Kinseys	37	6	3
William Newsom, Adkins	69	1	2
Ezra Castleberry, Jones	135	11	2
Charles Mathews orphs. Kinseys	81	28	1
Henry Heeth, jr. Brinkleys	237	18	2
Elizabeth King, w. R. S., do.	4	29	1

WASHINGTON.

James Danielly, McLendons	103	13	1
George Wiggins, Wimberlys	276	28	1
Cath. 'Smiths, w.s.l.w. Warthens	136	30	1
Mitchell Lord, orph. Floyds	196	13	2
William Hall, Rushings	65	3	3
Tompkins C. Palmer, Rushings	228	3	4
Jethro Sumner, Woods	293	14	1
Sarah Irwin, orph. do.	212	19	1
Robert Williams, Gilberts	254	20	2
Church Harris's orps. Rushings	38	7	2
John Beeland, Woods	281	11	2
David Hattaway, Currys	134	8	4
Conrad Kettlar, Avans	37	14	5
William Sneed, Woods	220	23	1
Archibald Bolton, Floyds	232	27	1

WILKINSON.

Caro. & Henry Reed, ills. Halls	222	6	2
Jno. & Wm. Cole orps. Mathews	184	21	2
Stephen Low, orph. Fairchilds	91	4	3
Peter Buckles, R. S., do.	92	8	1
John Wooten, Shows	254	21	1

WILKES.

Catharine Lesley, widow, Wests	265	20	2
Thomas W. Butler, Carters	181	4	2
Morris Sutton, Ragsdales	280	9	5
Denatus McJenkins, sol. Reaves	21	6	4
William Smith, jr., Ragsdales	73	9	5
John Booker, jr. Greens	179	23	2
George Woolf, sol. Lukers	184	21	1
William Cousins, Carters	147	8	3
Samuel Thompson, do.	95	12	1
Purnal Truitt, Popes	176	16	1
George D. Taylors ors. Wootons	137	28	1

42d *DAY'S DRAWING*—April 24.

APPLING.

Hardy Hall, Dedges	50	4	3
Elisha Padgett, Morgans	184	18	1

(129)

Fortunate Drawers	Capts. Dist.	No.Dt.Sec.
Jesse Aldredge's orphans,	Mathis	101 2 5
Bauldy Britt,	Collins	217 20 2

BALDWIN.

Henry Lord,	Pitts	73 24 1
Andrew Du Bourg,	Buchanans	376 28 1
George L. Deming,	do.	10 28 1
George L. Deming,	do.	169 19 1
Charles Williamson,	do.	20 15 1
James Murry's orphans,	Bivins	244 24 1
Homer V. Howard,	do.	187 22 2
Orphans of Robert Wynn,	Reddings	101 8 4
John Covy,	Buchanans	241 3 4
Orphans of John Pitts,	Pitts	4 3 3
William Bird,	Buchanans	177 10 3
Armond Effry,	Ginns	190 4 5

BIBB.

James Patton,	Flanders	13 15 2
David Preston,	Pickards	142 31 1
Wiley Pope,	Swearingins	32 29 1
John Smith,	do.	168 7 2
Reddick, Garner, soldier,	Carrs	285 3 4
Simon Harrells's orps.	Rutlands	262 15 1
Lewis Foy,	Beards	60 6 1
Hockey L. Towns, soldier,	Bates	10 3 3
John Audulf,	Beards	34 4 5

BRYAN.

Aquilla Stephens,	Harveys	195 5 5
James Futch,	do.	44 20 2
Elizabeth Delegal, widow,	do.	70 12 5

BULLOCH.

Ancel Parish, orphan,	Burnetts	63 11 1
William Sheffield, orp.	Richardsons	239 19 1

BURKE.

Enoch Rogers,	Rogers	148 1 1
Seaborn Harrison,	Wards	184 11 5
Penelope Tipton, illegit.,	Lesters	185 19 1
George Folds,	Gordons	86 15 5
William Ballangy,	Corkers	10 2 1
Alfred Inmon,	do.	246 8 1
Elie Gordy,	do.	356 28 1

BUTTS.

John Kelly,	Chapmans	28 1 1
Alexander Harrin, R. S.,	Adams	165 22 1

CAMDEN.

John Pearce, R. S.,	Baileys	245 19 1
Henry Miller,	Coxs	182 11 3
Christopher T. F. Wilkey,	Millers	105 6 2
Susan Bond, orphan,	Wards	71 12 1

CHATHAM.

Thomas Palmer,	Bains	200 5 1
Thomas S. Wayne		230 3 4
John Johns,	Geredons	47 5 4
Hugh Archer,	do.	247 9 5
Henry D. Holland,	McDonnells	42 29 1
Orphans of Joseph T. Davis,	Gaddys	56 10 3

CLARK.

John Dean, soldier,	Deans	212 19 2
Joseph J. Griffin,	Frosts,	78 21 2
Aaron F. Nunnally,	Wrights	117 33 1
Aaron Hopkins,	Vinsons	232 23 2
Reuben Medders,	Coxs	128 9 2
William Love, soldier,	Wrights	240 23 1
William McRee, R. S.,	McCrees	215 11 3
James H. Blackshear,	Gahagans	137 9 5
Bedford Burnett,	Dickens	38 4 2
Richard E. Burke,	do.	125 13 5
Joseph Lee,	McDaniels	139 23 1

Fortunate Drawers	Capts. Dist.	No.Dt.Sec.
Thomas Jeffries,	Andersons	253 5 2
Elijah Humphries,	Gahagans	71 13 5

COLUMBIA.

Richard E. Doggett,	Baileys	214 18 1
Orps. of Dred Pace, jr.,	Culbreaths	31 9 1
James Bradberry,	Dranes	203 15 2
Benjamin Blanchard,	Culbreaths	63 8 4
Winneford Dunn, widow,	Baileys	144 22 1
George Cobb,	Dranes	263 22 1

CRAWFORD.

William Streetman,	Ellis	206 4 1

DECATUR.

Hannah Watson, widow,	Hawthorns	243 2 2

DE KALB.

James Wilson,	Bakers	282 11 2
William Burgess' orphan,	Conns	141 1 2
Washington Gilly,	do.	121 4 4
John Woodall, sen., R. S.,	do.	390 20 2

DOOLY.

Burrell Williams,	Sarrs	171 11 1

EARLY.

Samuel Currie's orphans,	Hairs	166 5 5
Wilkinson Doles,	Wilsons	159 21 2

EFFINGHAM.

David A. Strobhar,	Waldhaners	74 30 1

ELBERT.

Mitchell Glenn,	Butlers	169 12 3
Thomas Hilley, sen.	Hortons	59 13 1
Rebecca Harris, w. R. S.,	Blackwells	215 33 1
John Fain,	Dobbs	248 7 3
John Dennard,	Butlers	248 12 1
John Harris, sen., R. S.,	Dunns	65 5 5
Jesse White,	Dobbs	165 12 1
Lewis McGehee's orphans,	Merritts	206 8 5
A., J. W., & N. Roberts, ills.	Harmons	222 17 2

FAYETTE.

John Westermoreland, sol.	McClendons	16 8 4
Joseph T. Harkins,	Craigs	64 25 1
Isaih Beck, jun. 9th		37 10 1
William Vickrey,	Wests	155 20 2
Isaac Wilkinson,	Whartons	169 8 5
Wiley Davis, 9th		115 3 4
Andrew Smith,	Wests	40 1 3
James Davice, soldier, 9th		53 17 2

FRANKLIN.

Sampson Walls, R. S.,	Tabors	28 8 4
Joseph Edwards, R. S., T.	Chandlers	115 4 3
Orps. of John Bridgeman,	Stephens	181 10 1
Elizabeth Parks, hus. ab.	Hudsons	224 24 1
James Cash, R. S.,	Walters	35 7 5
Pleasant Holbrook, D.	Chandlers	227 3 5

GLYNN.

William W. Hazzard,	Dubignons	155 8 1
Sar. & Eliza Hendricks,	orps.Burnetts	207 4 2
Joseph Dubignon, sol.	Dubignons	90 10 5

GREENE.

Michael Lawrence,	Knowles	171 14 1
Erasmus McGibony,	Vincents	31 1 5
Wiley Roland,	Robins	228 2 2
Douglass Watson's orps.	Newsoms	105 24 1
Joseph Bledsoe,	Greers	11 6 4
Jane Bennett, wid.	Southerlands	181 30 1
Orps. of Charles Williams,	Robins	125 30 1
John Akers,	Woodhams	191 2 1

GWINNETT.

John Roper, R. S.,	Whartons	84 2 4
Thomas Pendley,	Moors	24 32 1

(130)

Fortunate Drawers	Capts. Dist.	No.	Dt.	Sec.
Jesse Compton, Moors		20	20	1
Hugh Bell, orphan, Greens		23	27	1
Alexnader Wright, Moors		186	25	1
Greenberry Holbrooks, Greens		136	10	2
Martha Smith, widow, Moors		187	6	3
Randolph Dalton, R. S., Shippys		17	11	3
John B. Cogswell, Cupps		11	2	2

HANCOCK.

Thomas B. Lawson, 109th		16	17	2
Julia Ann Peace, min. fa. ab., 113th		18	24	1
William G. Lary, illegitimate, 11th		300	7	5
Jeffry Goodwin's orphans, do.		57	2	2
James Wotten, 103d		120	3	3
Hannah Butler, d. & dumb. Hillsmans	306	8	1
John McWhorter, R. S., 114th		219	1	4
Jonathan Duck, soldier, Swints		83	29	1
Sidney Smith, Adams		136	7	5
Hiram Derackin's chil. fa. ab. 104th	261	1	4
Elbridge G. Williams, illegit., 112th		181	8	5
Miles G. Harris, 102d		90	14	2

HENRY.

Humphrey Posey, soldier, Shaws		1	19	1
Lewis Toller, R. S., Grays		120	32	1
Reps Osborn, Bryants		4	8	5

HABERSHAM.

Jeremiah Gaddy, Fains		80	5	5
Abraham Littlejohn, do.		76	21	2
Josias Powell, Vickreys		162	14	1
Francis J. Dover, R. S., Cross		247	2	3
E. C., D. & G. Parker, mins. Bryans	17	18	1
Drewry Robertson, Tates		16	1	4
Henry McAdams, do.		228	33	1
W. H. & O. Smith, illegits., Suttons		264	28	1
Thomas Bird, Bryans		89	19	1
Russell Duty, Fanes		235	5	5

HALL.

William Cochran, Yagers		79	4	5
Jesse Broadwell, Floyds		361	3	4
James Cockburn, soldier, Dorseys		243	10	5
William Dellafield, R. S., Garrards		33	12	5
Henry Pool, Roberts		239	10	3

HOUSTON.

Perry Wimberly, Wimberlys		87	16	1

IRWIN.

David Collins, Dixons		100	3	4
Enoch Hall, 5th		200	11	5
John H. Johnson, Underwoods		1	8	3

JACKSON.

Robert Allen, Allens		101	13	1
Joseph Heath, Duprees		55	8	3
Sarah Johnson, wid. R. S., Storys		202	16	2
Claiborn Dolton, Winns		64	11	3
Alexander McDonald, Landrums		248	17	2
George Hays, R. S., Millers		33	9	5
Benjamin W. Watkins, Doss		62	28	1
John McDaniel, soldier, Staplers		173	31	1
Thomas Morrison, Lindseys		70	9	3
Richard Morris, Landrums		149	1	1
Samuel McGuire, Doss		226	18	2
Fletcher Horton, Storys		265	21	2
Benjamin Wilson, Pairs		250	2	2
George Kellogg, Venables		171	4	2
James Wood, soldier, Staplers		62	11	2
Edward Alberson, Lindseys		163	14	2
Thomas Barnett, Gathwrights		239	7	1

JASPER.

John L. Barnett, Dardens		88	6	5

Fortunate Drawers	Capts. Dist.	No.	Dt.	Sec.
John Ray, Baynes		73	19	2
Sample Orr, Barnetts		141	6	1
John Johnson, Clemmons		204	22	2
Bennet Crawford, soldier, Dales		92	4	2
Jesse Evans, Baynes z		140	6	1
Edwin Ogletree, do.		102	23	1
James Belcher, Butts		101	30	1
Washington C. Cleveland, Holmes		59	10	3
Isham Hutson, Butts		46	11	3
George W. Keath, Owens		180	12	3
Joseph C. Post, Wilsons		201	2	2
John Bass, Owens		184	28	1
Charity McCray, widow, Baynes		60	3	1
M. & E. Coulson, mins. fa. ab. Hines		56	21	2
Elizabeth Porter, widow, Camerons		108	8	4
Isaac Hancock, Butts		20	9	2
Christopher W. Powell, Barnetts		195	5	4

JEFFERSON.

James Jackson, soldier, Elliotts		155	20	1
Nathaniel Samples, jr. Cunninghams		137	10	1
Jeremiah Burton, do.		53	8	1
Roberts Wadkins, Jones		197	4	1
Jonathan J. Mountain, Causeys		242	11	5
James Thompson, Marshalls		79	20	1
Nancy Marshall, widow, do.		27	2	1
Thomas Sandefer, Elliotts		24	15	2
Jame Brazil, Waldens		22	5	5
Norman McLeod, R. S., Elliotts		259	3	4

JONES.

Bird Diver's orphans, Mullins		173	2	2
Henderson Doster, Dosters		142	9	1
Henry Isham, Stewarts		196	14	1
John Smith, R. S., Dosters		232	3	4
Ann Dunn, widow, Blounts		11	21	1
Daniel Hunt, R. S., Hammacks		57	3	3
Willis S. Scott, soldier, Duncans		195	9	5
William Johnson, Davis		205	26	1
Alexander Redock, Gibsons		111	7	5
Easterling Ventress, Dusters		103	13	2
Amnsa B. Lipsey, Robertsons		170	15	2
Lewis H. Plant, soldier, Bowens		42	17	2

LAURENS.

Mastin G. Oneal, Spiveys		236	13	2
Frederick Cook's orphans, Deans		72	13	5
Nancy Spell, widow, R. S., Hodges		230	18	1
Joseph Livingston's orps. Plummers		70	3	4
James Archer, Beachams		11	19	2
Instant Hall, R. S. Hodges		76	8	5

LIBERTY.

Eliza G. Roberts, wid. 14th		37	29	1

LINCOLN.

John Hubbard, Wiggintons		223	3	2
Jefferson Winn, Graves		257	11	2
Stith Armstrong, do.		243	16	2
Micajah Henley, s.l.w. Hardys		105	18	2

MADISON.

James L. Griffith, Hannas		248	22	2
Sarah A. Littleton, illeg. Moons		101	32	1
Thomas Lumpkin, Bones		162	11	3
Peter Smiths orps., Caldwells		84	9	3

M'INTOSH.

William C. Cuthbert, Terrells		89	9	1
William Dunham, Thorps		39	30	1

MONROE.

Hugh Brown, Douglass		190	18	2
Hardy McGlawn, sol. Knights		47	3	5

(131)

Fortunate Drawers	Capts. Dist.	No.	Dt.	Sec.
Elizabeth Browning, ill.	Phillips	1	1	4
John B. Lovejoy,	Greshams	185	2	4
James Hilliard, illeg.	Douglass	116	12	2
Jesse Clower,	Wrights	68	1	4
William Lee,	Greshams	31	4	1
John Payne,	do.	66	5	1
Winnef'd Spratlen, w.R.S.	Houses	176	8	1

MORGAN.

Smith Wilkinson,	Harwells	196	12	5
Cooper R. Roberts,	Adairs	275	17	2
Agnes Harris, widow,	Sparks	106	6	5
Thomas J. Lucas,	Shearmans	163	30	1
Elizabeth Leavins, h. a.	Sparks	119	29	1
Alvah Wilson,	Youngs	252	21	2
Isaac Langston,	Whatleys	73	5	3
Samuel Beflah, R. S.	Adairs	186	6	3

MONTGOMERY.

James G. Conner,	Rials	127	2	2
William Alfred,	Wynns	107	30	1

NEWTON.

James Williams,	Graves	216	31	1
Walter Pool, R. S.	Summers	115	20	1
Robert Watson,	Snows	8	10	1
Joel L. Terrell,	Hays	51	27	1
Jacob McLendon,	Trammells	169	2	4
Nancy Hancock, widow,	Snows	45	8	3
Simeon Brooks,	Zachreys	141	2	5

OGLETHORPE.

William Atkinson,	Burfords	105	29	1
John M. Stephens, soldier,	Dixs	242	.4	2
Winn Johnson,	Lacys	132	4	1
Bushrod W. Bailey,	Rousseaus	252	5	4
Willis Eidson,	Rhodes	126	2	2
William Hatrsfield,	Holloways	221	6	5
Robert W. Lee,	do.	100	7	4
George Bone,	Floyds	145	10	1

PIKE.

Slaton Henly,	Daniels	123	8	1
Daniel Burnsides, sol.	Arlines	51	1	3

PULASKI.

Green H. Chairs,	Kellams	150	5	2
Wm. Andersons ors.	Scarbroughs	34	12	2

PUTNAM.

Hiram Read,	Blacks	21	4	5
Elizabeth Garard, w.	Kendricks	47	4	1
Reb. A. Kimbrough or.	Vinings	190	17	1
Samuel Smith, soldier,	Blacks	130	7	4
Levi H. Rood,	Marcus	15	1	4
William Parker,	Duprees	165	14	1
Noah Gordy,	Stinsons	17	4	2
James Bussey,	Mizes	116	5	2

RABUN.

Ralph Cobb,	Godfreys	10	12	1
David Elders,	do.	192	22	2
Hiram Gains,	Becks	258	1	4

RICHMOND.

Edward J. Harden,	Treadwells	197	3	4
Latham Hull,	Ellsworths	189	22	2
Caleb Hartfield,	Treadwells	381	20	2
Thomas S. Metcalf,	Ferris	228	7	5

Fortunate Drawers	Capts. Dist.	No.	Dt.	Sec.
Robert Raiford,	600th	64	6	3
Charity Maharrey, wid.	Bushs	219	19	1
John E. Shepard,	Augusta	174	8	5
Dabney Berry,	Blacks	232	5	4
Wilson, Eliza., Nath'l.	Isabella			
& Stephen Greene, ors.	Blacks	212	3	1
Joseph Sanderlin, orph.	Wilcoxs	17	8	1
R. D. Bridges,	Treadwells	170	28	1

SCRIVEN.

McClain McCleland, R. S.	Roberts	4	6	4
Sophy Thorn, w.R.S.	Stricklings	182	19	1

TATTNALL.

John Sikes,	Deloachs	168	19	2
John Joyce,	McCalls	104	15	5
Gabrieland Strickland,	Dees	286	10	2
William Taylor,	Deloachs	234	12	1

TELFAIR.

James Posey,	Barentines	196	11	5
Ellender Reid, h.a.	Wilsons	167	16	1
Duncan Graham, jr.	Lampkins	164	4	2

TALIAFERRO.

Edward McSwinnay,	Towns	204	4	1

TWIGGS.

John Pitman,	Holidays	131	3	3
Wm. Powell, (carp.)	Streetmans	168	22	1
McAllen Batts,	Solomons	204	23	1
Thomas Bryan,	Pearsons	149	4	2
Robert Collins,	do.	121	15	1
Sampson Bell,	Bosticks	8	18	1
James Smith,	Kellys	140	1	3

UPSON.

A. F. Edwards,	Coopers	184	15	1
Whittington Horn,	Myricks	164	3	5
Miles Ashburn,	589th	49	31	1
Henry Garlin,	Coopers	32	8	4
Thomas Belyen,	Harrells	58	5	1
William Rieves, sol.	Dukes	173	2	4
Reuben Holmes,	Hattocks	144	24	1

WALTON.

Philip Whitten,	503rd	195	1	2
Giles Lowrey,	Bixeys	227	11	1
Warren Dykes,	503rd	246	4	2
Ganaway Conner,	503rd	287	3	4
Henry W. Shelnutt,	Davis	224	29	1
Isaac Rosser,	McQuertors	130	11	2
Abel Crow,	Snows	149	10	5

WARE.

Lewis Davis,	Moats	168	24	1
Isbin Gideons,	Bryans	222	5	5

WARREN.

Allen Womble, jr.	Downes	229	10	1
John Torrence, R. S.	Hills	146	18	1
Asa Willowby, illegit.,	Adkins	181	2	5
Isaac Dyson,	do.	205	11	5

WASHINGTON.

William Thigpen,	Woods	229	1	4
Wm. Burgamy, R. S.	Warthens	157	5	1
Hannah Bray, wid.	Avans	107	27	1
Miles Rachels,	Warthens	63	11	2
Thomas Gilmores heirs,	Avans	63	6	2
William Watkins, R. S.,	Floyds	192	3	2

Fortunate Drawers Capts. Dist.	No.	Dt.	Sec.
Nancy Roades, wid. Avans	32	5	5
James Paramore, Gilberts	158	25	1
Sherod Sessions, Woods	82	32	1
Benjamin Thomas, Floyds	119	18	2
Nathan Mott, R. S. Warthens	266	7	5
Benjamin Rogers, Currys	61	1	4
Daniel McLeod, Wimberlys	34	6	5

WILKINSON.
James Mooring, sol. Currys	50	4	5
James Lewis, Mayos	174	14	1
Century Rowe, Smiths	187	19	2
Wiley Miller, Currys	251	21	1
James M. Hawthorn orp. Smiths	218	32	1
Bolin Radford, Mathews,	171	14	2
James Hall, Halls	82	22	2

WILKES.
John Billingslea, Rices	169	16	1
Joseph Shepherd, Popes	19	16	5
James Claxton, Moors	61	9	1
John Ray, R. S., Chunns	90	6	4
John Wood, R. S. Lukers	308	20	2
Bryan Tannang, Reeves	16	10	3

43d DAY'S DRAWING—April 25.

BALDWIN.
Orphan of John Crowder, Wicks	37	2	3
Pryor Wright, Buchanans	113	11	1
William Twilley, soldier, Pitts	144	8	4

BIBB.
Young Edwards, Lloyds	247	1	2
John Hudgins, Beards	68	23	2
Amos Horton's orphans, Rutlands	126	7	5
Augustus & Eliza Hatley, orp. Carrs	285	5	1
Ephriam Jones, soldier, Lloyds	16	13	2
Henry Land, Flanders	76	11	1
Jeffrey E. Thompson, Beards	122	21	1
Thomas Doles, Lloyds	250	11	3

BURKE.
J. Lewis's orphans, Rogers	24	3	5
Samuel Dowse, do.	118	3	1
Jemima Jones, wid. R. S., Brooms	229	21	2
Sarah Williamson, w. R. S., Dugas	109	3	5
Phenicy Sapp, widow, Thompsons	138	9	3
Charles Oliver, sr. idiot, Rogers	197	23	2

BUTTS.
James Cannon, illegit., Hendricks	230	3	1
Robert Williams, soldier, Moores	29	5	4
Samuel Horton, soldier, Kirksies	61	5	1
Simson R. Russell, Hendricks	27	32	1
Dolphin Lindsey, soldier, Thaxtons	218	33	1

CAMDEN.
Orphans of Joseph Paxton, Browns	69	6	1
Eliza Ann Couch, widow, Wards	2	11	1
Abram Bessent's orphans, do.	30	8	4
Richard A. Hill, do.	131	27	1
James M. Bates, Browns	9	19	1

CHATHAM.
Daniel Zettler, McDonnells	207	22	2
Thomas Douglass,	113	32	1
Mary Gugel, widow, Geredons	220	4	2
Joseph Averly Russell, Haydens	27	7	1
Anthony Oglesby, McDonnells	124	11	1
M. A. E. Donaldson, orp. of Ben., do	48	5	4

CLARK.
Fortunate Drawers Capts. Dist.	No.	Dt.	Sec.
William Hannah, Davenports	92	3	3
Lewis Bryant, Herndons	161	6	1
Orphans of John Holder, Dickins	203	2	5
Elizabeth C. Thomas, w. McDonalds	139	15	2
Samuel Brown, R. S., Espys	166	11	3
Samuel Kinney, Gahagans	186	27	1
Josiah Trible, Andersons	11	20	2
John Hunton, McCrees	66	12	3
John Matthews, McDonalds	457	19	1

COLUMBIA.
Robert Baley, Carrolls	75	2	5
James Z. Locklin, do.	84	7	3
William B. Beal, Ramseys	69	1	3
Dorothy Lassiter, w. R. S., Dranes	296	7	5
Henry P. Hampton, orp. Clarks	191	4	5
George W. Crawford, Ramseys	235	5	3
Rebecca Perryman, Talberts	134	3	3
Orphans of William Sullivan, Carrolls	189	6	5
Daniel D. Parker, Doctor, Ramseys	168	30	1
William W. Hardwick, Coles	192	16	1

CRAWFORD.
Josiah H. T. Abbott, sol., Lovetts	163	21	1
Cordelia Ann Calhoun, illegit, do.	10	23	2
John Logan, Tillers	9	2	1

DECATUR.
Samuel N. Bryant, Manns	99	32	1

DE KALB.
Jacob New, jr., Smiths	147	18	2
Anson Williams, Browns	178	3	5
James Donaldson, Conns	43	5	4
George Wolf Merritts	175	18	1
Daniel Harrison Conns	27	1	5
Allen Camron, R. S., Smiths	40	23	2
James Hicks, Howells	221	30	1

EARLY.
Nancy Henderson, widow, Speers	41	19	1

EFFINGHAM.
Edward Murry, fa.absent, Stricklands	180	3	1

ELBERT.
Charles N. B. Carter, orp. Blackwells	159	4	2
Lawrance M. Adams, Hortons	111	1	3
William Maxwell, Tuckers	97	7	4
Finney Moore, Tates	243	23	1
David B. Ramsey, Alstons	196	30	1
John H. Hudson, Tates	23	8	4
Samuel Smith, Dobbs	118	26	1
Jesse Hendrick, Merritts	131	24	2
Walker Hickman's oprs. Carpenters	195	4	1
L. H. & H. Bray, illegits., Hortons	187	9	1
Barnabas Pace, R. S., Merritts	68	2	3

EMANUEL.
Ephriam Webb, Chasons	96	14	5
Robert Green, 57th	59	11	3
Lewis Heath, Moores	202	29	1
Orphans of James Jowers, McGars	175	25	1

FAYETTE.
Andrew Shelnutt's orps. Wests	264	2	3
William Johnson, soldier, Whortons	110	22	1
Isaiah Smith, Dodsons	45	16	2

FRANKLIN.
Matilda Fowler, illegit., Jones	140	17	2
Lucy Holden, widow, Hudsons	90	13	5
Jeremiah Walls, illegitimate, Tabors	226	5	1
William H. Gober, jr., Hudsons	142	2	3
Clarissa Jones, widow, Boswells	134	2	5

LAND LOTTERY REGISTER—No. 20
[RECORDER OFFICE—PUBLISHHED BY GRANTLAND & ORME—PRICE $3.]

NOTE—Section 1 is Lee County—2 Muscogee—3 Troup—4 Coweta—5 Carroll.

43d DAY'S DRAWING—Continued

FRANKLIN.

Fortunate Drawers	Capts. Dist.	No.	Dt.	Sec.
James Lewis, Starnges		47	2	2
Absalom J. Baird, Blankinships		188	4	2
James C. Terrell, Boswells		5	30	1

GLYNN.

John A. Wylly, Dubignons	38	7	4
John Gorrie, McLeods	128	31	1

GREENE.

Ellis Low, Vincents	218	6	3
William S. Branch, R. S., Robinsons	167	19	2
Orps. of Newil Stoutamire, Robins	223	10	2
Myall Wall, R. S., Halls	163	15	1
Robert Ray, Newsoms	123	12	3
Elihu Hall, Robins	198	3	3
Orphans of William Lawson, do.	24	11	2

GWINNETT.

Rebecca Inlow, hus. ab. Dunbars	248	25	1
Lovick Pearce, Evans	245	18	2
Neil McPherson, Hunicuts	139	18	1
Michael Moore, Moores	46	9	1
Harman Davis, Hills	67	10	2
Richard Nolen, Davis	8	4	2
Absalom Martin, Caruthers	61	1	3
John Beauford, Davis	242	8	5
Thomas Creswell, Whartons	196	11	3
Bird Womack, soldier, Dunbars	278	10	2
Thomas Kircus, Davis	7	21	2
Stephen Harris, Greens	112	7	3
Margaret Smith, w. R. S., Moores	215	7	5
David Williams, Hunicuts	226	1	4
N., T. & B. Terry, ills., Woodroughs	81	10	1

HABERSHAM.

William Dodd, Suttons	154	7	5
Jeremiah Storer, jr. Kenzies	95	4	5
Clark Jackson, Bryans	29	31	1
Solomon Nichols's orgps. do.	86	5	3
Orps. of Nathaniel Wofford, Bakers	158	2	5
Ephraim McClain, Suttons	67	15	5
oseph Chaffin, Tatrs	116	13	2
John Franklin, Bryans	42	21	1
George Thrasher, R. S., Bakers	9	9	4
Larkin Ragsdale, Suttons	143	28	1

HALL.

Henry Dobson, Hendricks	169	21	1
John Thomas, Yagers	43	10	3
James Owen, Harrisons	243	20	2
Patrick O'Conner, Walkers	125	12	3
John A. Casey, Aireds	88	14	2
James B. Fulton, Dorseys	205	4	5
David Mills, Roberts	254	10	3

HANCOCK.

Abel Pew, 116th	289	7	1
Henry Harris, soldier, Adams	109	13	1
James McDaniel, illegit., Dicksons	121	15	5
James Swint, 118th	250	8	3
John Grant, idiot, 101st	212	21	1

HENRY.

John B. Smith, soldier, Wards	86	31	1
Peter Lewis, R. S., Grays	59	4	1
James Thurmond, sen. Kites	101	10	2
Thomas Haywood, Risons	152	6	1
Eli Lackey, Smiths	256	10	1

Fortunate Drawers	Capts. Dist.	No.	Dt.	Sec.
Absalum Hamby, Wards		383	7	1
Daniel Tingle, Harris		123	6	2
Elizab. & Harriss Lyons, ills. Grays		50	22	1

HOUSTON.

Jonathan Brooks, Becks	121	29	1
Lewis J. Jordan, Farnals	152	2	3
Moses F. Lewis, do.	190	23	1
Temperance Holly's illegits, Prices	67	13	5
M., E. & Jane Reid, orps. Farnals	208	15	2

IRWIN.

Murdock McDuffie's orps. Dixons	2	3	3
Dread Newsom, McCalls	55	3	1

JACKSON.

Bond Veal Brown, Doss	50	7	2
Elizabeth Gann's ill. chil. Watersons	304	8	5
Amanda M. Spurlock, ill. Staplers	257	9	5
John Randolph, Venables	9	5	1
Darcus Whitehead, hus. ab. Millers	141	10	5
John Tippin's orps. Venables	51	24	1
John B. Lowery, do.	240	22	1

JASPER.

Jane Hicks, widow, Owens	225	12	3
John Compton, jr., Dardens	259	7	5
Benjamin Dawson, Hands	138	7	2
Thomas R. Barker, Holmes	81	15	1
Robert Sanson, Hines	270	5	1
Tolbot Hatcher, Dardens	214	10	1
Elbert Moore, soldier, Comptons	134	12	5
Thomas N. Guffin, Dales	78	14	4
Thomas Berry, Trussells	133	5	3
H. W. & L. Colston, illegits. Hines	44	3	3
Caney Strickland, Camerons	132	27	1
Nathan Johnston, Owens	28	15	2
William Hay, soldier, Penningtons	97	2	5
William Johnson, Clemmons	150	7	1
Augustin J. Phelps, Sparks	25	3	2
John Fluker, R. S., Holmes	148	7	1

JEFFERSON.

Duncan Carmichael's orps. Waldens	113	1	2
Samuel Ford, soldier, Kings	340	20	2
Roger L. Gamble, soldier, Fords	231	22	1
William B. Pervis, Beatys	252	10	3
William Mathas's orphans, Ross	134	33	1
Mary Young, wid. Beatys	91	9	3
Alse Brewer, wid. Cunninghams	147	23	2
Susannah Jenkins, w. R. S., Causeys	8	12	5
John Murphy's orps. Cunninghams	160	27	1

JONES

Joshua Weeks, soldier, Popes	198	33	1
James Gordon, Mullins	184	12	2
John M. Hammack, Hammacks	93	8	5
Maulden Amos, R. S., Stewarts	98	25	1
Burton Paul, Newbys	137	4	5
Maxfield McCormack, Davis	54	32	1
William Perdue, do.	211	24	1
Jacob McDaniel, Jr., Stewarts	93	2	1
Lucy Ousley's illegits., Hendersons	154	27	1
Littleton C. Peerson, Newbys	43	11	2
Chesley P. Trice, Popes	228	10	1
Charles Dunning, Woods	36	19	1
John Powell, Gibsons	252	2	2
James H. George, Woods	33	19	1
Everlyn D. Nichols, do.	161	28	1

LAURENS.

Fortunate Drawers	Capts. Dist.	No.	Dt.	Sec.
Henry Domino, Deans		169	14	2
William Mills, Johannons		270	19	2
Henry Smith, Millers		277	3	4
John Oliver, orphan, Plummers		102	10	2
Edward St. George, Whiteheads		98	23	2
Elizabeth Murray, w. R. S., Plummers		168	4	3
Thomas Barlow, jr., Whiteheads		202	5	5

LIBERTY.

Josiah Law, 15th		79	21	2
Lawrence Anthony, orph. 17th		193	18	2

LINCOLN.

Moses Jones, Frasers		40	10	1
Isaac Gauntt, Lonorgans		193	13	2
Nancy Readbrux, wid. Gideons		304	8	1
Seaborn Florence, Lonogans		170	4	4
David Hammock, Graves		197	15	1

MADISON.

William Russill, Culbertsons		18	30	1
Wm. Howington, R.S. Christians		183	10	3
Noble Clements, Culbertsons		82	11	1

McINTOSH.

John, Paulet, Caroline, Edw'd & Emily Caldwell ors. Terrells		145	13	2
Norman & Wm. R. Gignilliat, do		112	7	1
Ann Ennis, wid. McCranies		131	2	3

MONROE.

James Bailey, Greshams		84	1	4
Robert Childs, Pattersons		201	29	1
William O. Hurt, Houses		107	8	4
John H. Milner, soldier, do.		109	3	1
Mary Willis, h. a. Greshams		114	3	3
John Finch, Finchs		178	16	1
William Nelson, Houses		118	17	2
Philip Cooper, Millers		64	10	5
Paul Wolf, do.		188	5	4
William Wilder, do.		3	21	1
Ths. L. Thomason, Woodwards		215	11	2

MORGAN.

Joel Phillips, Christians		205	20	2
William Lacy, do.		42	9	5
John W. Butler, Gains		17	1	5
Gilbert Wilson, Youngs		238	3	2
Winny Barfield, w. R. S., do.		311	6	1
Arthur L. Davis, sol. Boswells		8	5	3
Fanny Brown, wid. Stokes		3	3	4
George W. Fuller, Watsons		284	12	3

MONTGOMERY.

Burrell R. Calhoun, Wynns		73	10	5

NEWTON.

Isaac P. Gay, Trammells		92	17	2
David Jester, Graves		229	12	3
Seymoure Powell, R. S., Talleys		45	13	1
William Wallace, R. S., Graves		2	1	2
Thomas Williams, sol. Orrs		97	10	5
Golder Bushop, R. S., Moss		103	14	1
Joseph Morris, soldier, Talleys		109	22	2
Jonathan Cliatt, Trammells		108	18	2
Stasee Robertson, w. R. S., Graces		26	3	1
William Welch, Summers		159	11	5
Thomas Cockerell, sr. R. S., Hays		71	14	5
William Burk, Snows		111	22	1

Fortunate Drawers	Capts. Dist.	No.	Dt.	Sec.
Larkin Ragsdale, Talleys		235	7	5

OGLETHORPE.

Lesley G. Carter, Holloways		107	23	2
Samuel Brook, jr., Bells		163	8	3
Thomas Kent, Lacys		94	12	5
John W. Donohoe, Burfords		262	4	3
Mary Walton, wid. Rousseaus		92	10	2
Seabron Wilder, sol. Wilsons		278	7	5
Glenn Owen, senr. R. S., Rhodes		232	11	5
Willis Jones, jr. Mays		266	20	2
Morton Bledsoe, Arnolds		184	20	1
Elij. Cummings, sol. Williamsons		57	1	3
Samuel Davis, Arnolds		364	7	1
T. Fambrough, R. S., Wiliamsons		72	22	2
Michael E. Johnson, Burfords		36	4	3

PIKE.

David Hicks, R. S., Hicks		134	9	1
Thomas Hail, Longs		55	8	2

PULASKI.

M. C. Stegall, Sparrows		191	2	5
Reubin Bynums orphans, do.		38	16	1

PUTNAM.

John W. Hines, Blacks		274	21	1
Richard Burt, do.		15	7	2
Benjamin H. Ingram, Vinings		167	12	5
William Moore, Sawyers		208	3	3
John Bradbury, Blacks		2	13	5
Mary Ellis, insane, do.		110	12	3
Elender Richardson, (idi.) Clarks		173	11	5
Shepherd Mize, R. S. do.		227	11	5
James Allen, sr. Barnetts		155	7	3
Polly Millirons illegits. Clarks		46	14	2
Birdong Thornton, Allums		181	6	3

RABUN.

Humphrey Gains, Godfreys		76	11	2
Burrell Wall, Beck		209	9	5

RICHMOND.

M. Creswell, orp. Huntingtons		154	6	5
Elias B. Crane, Augusta		185	31	1
Moses Ogden, do.		271	19	2
James Mallory, 119th		184	9	2
James Pennells orphs. Wilcoxs		110	1	2
Thomas Hayes, Kellys		16	13	5
Littleberry Carenah, Wilcoxs		115	1	1

SCRIVEN.

William B. Mitchinor, Roberts		246	9	1

TATTNALL.

Redick Ganey, R. S., McDuffies		149	2	2
Thomas Bradley, Conners		3	2	3
Malcom Buie, McDuffies		264	7	5

TELFAIR.

Surinah Ricketsons ills. Wilkinsons		98	22	2
Cullen Bonney, Lamkins		267	20	2
Richard Wooton, Wilsons		230	1	4
William Matchet, Lamkins		154	14	1

THOMAS.

Francis Coker,		92	7	5

TWIGGS.

Orphs. of James Bales, Bosticks		94	2	5
Ors. of Wm. Harrell, Streetmans		102	11	5
William Summerlin, Solomons		34	9	2
Jno. Arnold, (drunk.) Wimberlys		129	7	5

(135)

Fortunate Drawers	Capts. Dist.	No.	Dt.	Sec.
Ezekiel Boggs, Blackshears		73	4	3
UPSON.				
Benjamin Mitchell, Pashalls		211	21	1
Richard Respess, R. S., 589th		319	7	1
WALTON.				
Orphans of John Freeman, 418th		99	7	3
Jeptha L. Smith, illegit. 418th		306	1	4
Henry Hardin, R. S. Rays		182	4	4
James F. Norris, do.		40	30	1
WARE.				
William Carver, sol. Motes		21	12	2
John Williams, Motes		220	3	5
WARREN.				
Fielding Hill, jr. Parhams		161	1	1
Hugh Montgomery, jr. Sanders		154	16	2
Isaac Johnson, Hales		50	4	4
Eddy Underwood, Jones		145	4	4
James Wynne, Rogers		142	11	2
Susannah Gibson, w. Brinkleys		105	9	2
Jesse Pate, do.		111	2	5
Richard Gunn, sr. R. S. Rogers		119	30	1
James Kelley, Adkins		110	5	3
Wiliam Shuffield, Seales		222	27	1
Gabriel Grimes, Kinseys		49	1	3
WASHINGTON.				
Mary Butcher, wid. Warthens		89	18	1
Elipah Powers, Woods		232	6	5
John Tharps, orphans, Tysons		231	19	1
George W. Collens, Currys		189	21	1
James Goodmans orps. Tysons		187	2	5
Agnes Bolton, widow, Woods		150	4	4
Samuel Pace, Avans		346	3	4
Wm. Burgamy, R. S. Warthens		165	11	3
Samuel Bedgood, Whitfields		216	7	1
WILKINSON.				
Anson Mims orphs. Halls		94	3	2
Hezek'h Bloodworth, orp.Shows		134	7	2
Julas Bales, Mandersons		198	23	2
Joel Meadows orphans, Shows		7	11	2
Jorial Bennet, Mayos		1	11	5
Joseph Mayo, Mandersons		3	15	5
Micajah Davenport, Smiths		84	15	2
Isaac Stephens, Currys		190	20	1
Job McLendon, Mayos		68	8	2
Richard Traile, sol. Shows		45	11	2
William A. Hall, Fairchilds		162	28	1
John Kent, do.		112	2	1
WILKES.				
Richard Flurry, Washingtons		93	23	1
Abraham Hammons, sol. Lukers		183	33	1
James Davis, Washingtons		281	7	5
John Hinton, Ragsdales		113	27	1
Joseph B. Johnson, R.S.Hopkins		278	22	2
Mary Reeves orphs. Amasons		42	33	1
Joseph M. Semmes orphs. Moors		33	8	3
Jeremiah Bentley, Chunns		179	6	1

44th *DAY'S DRAWING*—April 26.
APPLING.

Malcolm Morrison, Dedges		21	30	1

BALDWIN.

Fortunate Drawers	Capts. Dist.	No.	Dt.	Sec.
Bartlett Wicks, Esq. Wicks		76	7	1
Orphans of James Collins, do.		131	13	5
Solomon Dyre Belton, Ginns		139	15	1
Francis V. Delaunay, Buchanans		269	4	2
George Leaves, Lesters		82	23	1
Ann Wiley, widow, Buchanans		68	5	4
Amelia Reynolds, orphan, do.		167	25	1

BIBB.

Catharine H. Clark, orphan, Flanders		274	19	2
George Wright, Pickards		199	3	1
Alvis W. Harris, Beards		9	6	2
Alexander D. Brown, Carrs		85	9	2

BULLOCH.

Henry Goodman, soldier, Slaters		157	12	2
Rowland Thomas, Deloachs		28	5	5

BURKE.

Jane Marsh, orphan, Seegars		55	4	3
Holland Red, Brooms		193	4	1
Sarah Royal, wid. R. S., Dugas		116	21	2
John Haws, Andersons		122	11	1
Daniel Inmon, R .S., Corkers		95	4	3
Sabra Brinson, widow, Wards		203	6	3
Tarlton Lively, Dugas		102	33	1
William Mills, Thompsons		75	3	3
Matthew Floyd, Andersons		156	14	1

BUTTS.

Henry D. Knight, Johnson		287	5	1
Cely Lewis, illegitimate, Thaxtons		71	17	2
Royal Willard, soldier, Masons		27	3	3
John Ferrell, soldier, Robinsons		79	13	2
George D. McLain, Johnson		133	15	5

CAMDEN.

Sarah Garrett, widow, Coxs		234	10	1
J., E., W., & C. E .Reddock, Wards		276	22	1

CHATHAM.

Solomon Cohen, Haydens		94	16	2
Chs. Stewart, orp. of Chs. Nungazers		6	14	1
Mary Warner, widow, Geredons		28	7	1
Robert G. Wallace		75	4	3
Susannah C. King, wid. McDonalds		89	18	2
Isaac Scott, orphans, Haydens		37	8	3

CLARK.

Albert Y. Gresham, Dickins		45	18	1
Patrick Sawers, Alreds		95	9	2
Hinchy Winn, Herndons		230	5	4
John Knott, Wrights		119	11	5
Sophia Davenport, wid. Gahagans		102	21	2
David Treadwell, Davenports		144	30	1
Nancy Tignor, widow, Alreds		264	5	1
Wylie Bohannon, Herndons		113	11	3
Robert Knott, Davis		205	11	3
Charles B. Hunton, McCrees		229	23	1
James Doster, Herndons		63	6	4
Noah Prince, R. S., Frosts		85	20	1
Robert Stuart, Davenports		40	15	2

COLUMBIA.

W. G. Hughes, d. &d. Tankersleys		181	27	1
Wiliam Jenkins, Culbreaths		177	16	1
Alfred Johnson, Dranes		253	25	1
Augustus Crawford, Bealls		51	22	2
John Magruder's orphans, Talbots		76	24	2
Orphans of David Phillips, Carrolls		64	4	4
John Garnett, jr., Culbreaths		176	15	2
William Y. Barden, Bealls		110	3	2
Benjamin Carlisle, R. S., Coles		374	28	1
John Chrosbay, Dranes		42	14	6
Dossey Howard's orphans, Talbots		111	7	2

CRAWFORD.
Fortunate Drawers Capts. Dist. No.Dt.Sec.
Abraham Futrell, soldier, Wilsons   153 12 1
William Kelly, sen. Hicks   56 31 1
Abel Rooks, Wilsons   68 9 3

DECATUR.
James Dollerson, Douglass   94 30 1

DE KALB.
Sarah Ross, illegitimate, Merritts   225 4 1
Cyrus Harrington, Stephens   139 22 2
James Smith, Spruces   98 8 1
John Ivey, aHys   38 20 2
Daniel Stone, Browns   91 9 1

DOOLY.
William Hilliard, Bowens   208 2 3
Mathew R. Moore, Hogans   83 12 2

EFFINGHAM.
John Stevens, Treutlins   98 15 5
Ann Blitch, w. R. S., tricklands   164 15 1
Orphans of Robert Christie, Treutlins   87 12 1

ELBERT.
William Hudson, Bells   192 8 1
Nancy Cunningham, widow, Tates   66 14 5
John M. Good, Bells   221 21 2
James Kirbee, Boltons   78 29 1
Rebecca Martin, widow, Butlers   111 12 1
William Johnston, Tuckers   257 4 3
Thomas Eavanson, Blackwells   300 15 1
Isaac Almond, Deadwilders   209 32 1
Nathaniel M. Thornton, Boltons   77 13 2
Samuel Rembert, soldier, Tates   218 14 1
Marq. D. F. Therlkeld, Deadwilders   197 3 3

FRANKLIN.
Eli T. Wilmot, McDonalds   3 8 3
James Wheeler, Tabors   113 7 1
Michael Ragsdale, Caudells   71 10 5
Jeremiah B. Skelton, Walters   121 11 5
James Allen Barnes, Stephens   108 6 4
James H. Barton, T. Chandlers   242 2 4

FAYETTE.
Coalman Tucker, Whartons   194 2 2
Matthew Bates, McLendons   73 20 1
David Austin, 9th   115 24 1
John Barron, Browns   224 2 5

GREENE.
William Booles, Mercers   144 10 3
Charles Burk, jr. Southerlands   202 3 2
James Akins, sen. R. S., do.   251 16 1
Obadiah Thompson, illegitimate, do.   83 7 1
Martha Stanley, widow, Winkfields   96 9 1
Thomas Dawson, Dawsons   11 3 1
Robert & Thos. Totty, illegits, Astins   132 5 1
William Allen, Robinsons   286 11 2
James McMurray, soldier, Rankins   127 6 4

GWINNETT.
Edward Mathews, Woodroughs   158 5 4
John Strickland, jr. Hunicuts   58 33 1
Killet Sims, Bakers   168 10 5
Francis Shackelford, Cupps   33 2 4
James S. Wilder, Hunicuts   197 9 3
William McLain, do.   252 17 1
John Harbin, Robertsons   74 13 1
Colman Harrold, Caruthers   108 6 5
Elisha Jordan, Bakers   22 3 2
Renney Coleman, Hills   218 2 3
Henry Curtis, Greens   71 19 1
Reuben Benson, Moors   87 4 2
Rachel Minor, widow, Caruthers   248 2 1

CRAWFORD.
Fortunate Drawers Capts. Dist. No.Dt.Sec.
Thomas McEaver, Davis   149 24 2

HABERSHAM.
William S. Robertson, Tates   122 9 3
Matthew Arthur, R. S., Kenzies   108 27 1
Matthew Arthur, Bryans   103 2 4
John Chastain, Jones   161 11 3
Wiley Warwick, sr. Bryans   113 9 5
Benjamin Obanion, Langstons   93 10 1
Kitturah Cox, minor, Kenzies   240 18 2
Isham Caudell, Martins   20 8 2
Elizab. Nunalle, w. R. S., Bryans   130 23 2
John Mull, Kenzies   98 12 3
Absalom Pence, Cross   24 10 5

HALL.
William Mason, Hardages   315 8 1
John Mullins, sen. Hardens   142 4 3
Allen Stuart, lunatic, Walkers   31 6 5
Aaron Brown, do.   49 27 1
Fleming Parks, Roberts   165 1 2
C. Guthry, orp. f.d. in w.Walkers   31 3 2
Rebecca R. Jas. S. Eliz. K.
& Eph. B. Daniel, orps, Dorseys   50 15 1

HANCOCK.
Thomas S. Ransom, Lewis   106 10 2
Robert Norris, 118th   11 26 1
Nancy Capehart's illegit., 113th   212 11 5
Wiliams's orphans, 117th   82 14 5
Attala M. Smith, illegit., 114th   9 7 1
Trancina Maclellan, widow, 110th   87 32 1
Robert Mitchell, 102d   191 10 2
James Barnes, 102d   246 13 2
Nathan Youngblood, 117th   42 1 2
Alexander J. Harwell, Greens   237 5 5

HENRY.
Mary Lipham, widow, Shaws   193 21 1
W. S. & J. A. Collins, ills. Bryants   5 24 2
Henley Varner, soldier, Grays   68 3 4

HOUSTON.
R. Yarborough, w. Yarboroughs   294 6 5
Benjamin A. Tharp, Farnals   178 18 1
Thomas Page, Blanchards   156 1 5
Hiram Wadsworth, Calhouns   65 5 3
Wiliam Thompson, Pitts   90 6 5
Jeptha Henderson, Batemans   178 9 5

IRWIN.
James H. Mezell, Underwoods   45 28 1

JACKSON.
James Horton, Venables   50 11 1
S. A. & L. Jarratt, illegits. Moons   256 9 1
Charles M. Heard, Millers   131 14 2
John Hudson, Rogers   164 15 2
Henry Stoneham's orps. Duprees   219 15 1
Edward Kent, Allens   304 28 1
John Smith, R. S., Staplers   198 10 1
Isaac Young, Watersons   132 8 3
George Shaw, Allens   214 2 5

JASPER.
Thomas Key, soldier, Posts   186 12 1
William Trippe, Reeves   56 1 2
John Van Orden, Holmes   184 31 1
Jesse Crenshaw, Owens   158 28 1
John S. Murphy, Holmes   184 20 2

(137)

Fortunate Drawers	Capts.	Dist.	No.	Dt.	Sec.
F. S. & M. Smith, illegits.,	Hines	138	9	1
Israel Goree,	Robertsons	114	23	1
Bracket Owen,	Reeves	37	9	2
Umphry Baker,	Baynes	24	14	2
Peaty Maruda, illegits.,	Posts	147	4	3
James W. Crockett,	Keys	69	5	5
Washington Carlile, orp.	Parkers	83	24	2
Amanuel Findley,	do.	284	8	1
Ebenezer Whaley, sol.,	Farleys	115	1	3
E. G. Flemister, w. R.S.,	Parkers	205	6	1

JEFFERSON.

Rufus King,	Beatys	7	9	1
Woodson Bradshaw,	do.	88	30	1
Hartwell Watkins,	Elliots	88	29	1
Benjamin Elliott,	Ellitts	89	9	2
Thomas G. Cowart,	Marshalls	81	10	2
Reuben T. Burts,	do.	80	4	2
Agness Foreman, wid.	Waldens	197	8	3
Jane Bailey, widow,	Ross	246	10	1
Mitchell S. Duke,	Boyds	88	11	5
James Foreman,	Waldens	56	6	5

JONES.

William O'Lary,	Popes	109	12	2
Michael Burkhalter, R. S.,	Spinks	-32	19	2
Lou. Lucin. Em. Marg.
Matil.&J.Strength, ills.,	Blounts	116	21	1
Elias W. Jones,	Spinks	166	7	1
Rebecca Hamilton, widow,	do.	33	32	1
Susannah Oxford,w.R.S.	Taylors	177	9	1
Henry Smith, idiot,	Dosters	35	31	1
William M. Amos,	Stewarts	253	5	1
Littleton C. Peerson,	Newbys	147	10	3
Robert Moore,	Davis	196	3	2
Warren Parker,	Hammacks	18	12	2
Ebenezer Ormsby,	Popes	184	16	2
Rachel Griffin's ills.	Hendersons	40	6	4
John Alford,	Spinks	93	19	2

LAURENS.

Joshua Clarke,	Whiteheads	73	9	2
Robert Faircloth,	do.	108	4	1
Louis G. Linder,	Hodges	318	7	5
Synthia Dupree, widow,	Deans	90	11	2

LIBERTY.

| William Ward, 14th | | 90 | 10 | 3 |

LINCOLN.

William Glaze, s.l. w.	Ross	123	1	5
Eustus H. Rhodes,	Prathers	236	11	3
Isaiah Willis' mins.,	Wiggintons	250	7	3
Richard Sales, minor,	do.	170	7	3
Joshua Age,	Graves	229	10	2
Patty Sharp, wid.	Wiggintons	4	9	3

MADISON.

John Rhodes,	Hannas	144	10	1
Isaac Simmons, sr.,	do.	205	10	3
James Lee Adair,	Bones	104	12	1
James Coil, R. S.,	Christians	245	21	2
Mason Bryant,	Caldwells	29	19	2
Thomas Fayett,	Phipps	95	5	3
Joshua Stephens,	Caldwells	31	14	2

McINTOSH.

| Math. & S. Caulder, ors. | Terrells | 65 | 7 | 4 |

MONROE.

William Lawson,	Millers	273	15	1
Wiley Barron,	do.	64	0	3
Jesse Delay,	Millers	190	3	5
James Newberry,	Douglass	23	23	1
Isaac Morelands orps.	Turners	57	10	5
Green English, sol.	Johnsons	153	11	5
Ellender Dennis, wid.	Douglass	91	3	4
Britain Adams,	Wrights	123	15	5
Allen Chappell,	Gammons	25	6	3
Nelson F. Harris, ill.	Houses	236	6	5
Anguish McSwain,	Wrights	353	3	4
James P. Dozier, sol.	Stallings	120	6	4
Mary Hambleton, w.R.S.,	Browns	85	17	1
Richard H. Braddy,	Woodwards	214	5	3
Martha E. Maddox, orp.	Finchs	84	18	1
Benjamin Watson,	do.	62	19	1
William W. Hart,	Houses	58	17	1
William V. Collier,	Millers	52	1	1

MORGAN.

Alvan Myhand,	Gains	137	8	1
Jesse Morgan, sol.	Griggs	20	11	5
Benjamin Williams' ors.	Watsons	18	7	4
William Turner,	Jennings	70	13	5
Amos Brown,	Stokes	24	23	2
Benjamin W. Beard, sol.	Brooks	299	8	5
William Hubbard,	Baileys	235	14	1
Thomas Miles,	Jennings	107	29	1
Chandler A. Johnston,	Sparks	51	3	1
James Head, jr.	Gains	116	1	2
Richard C. Taylor, R.S.	Harwells	248	2	2
Paschal J. Watts,	Whatleys	282	16	2
Sally Rogers, Insane,	Christians	78	19	1

MONTGOMERY.

| John Calleham, | McMillons | 82 | 13 | 1 |

NEWTON.

Samuel Clark,	Hays	42	6	5
Letcher W. M. Smith, ill.	Zachreys	75	15	1
Stinson Hale,	Hays	146	15	1
Stanley Crews, sol.	Newnans	62	1	2
William Retherford,	Summers	237	3	1
William Barron,	Hays	3	1	4

OGLETHORPE.

Moses Smith, soldier,	Lacys	163	11	1
Joseph Stanfield,	Burfords	98	3	2
William Johnson,	Floyds	217	16	2
James Bradley, pr.	do.	292	23	2
Robert L. Gilham,	Rousseaus	182	12	2
Robert Trammell,	Smiths	37	16	5
James Bridges,	Wilsons	241	15	1
John Gresham, sr. R. S.	Dixs	10	17	1
Chester N. Case,	Rousseaus	70	10	3
Clement Floyd,	Burfords	90	12	5

PULASKI.

Mary Defnal, w.R.S.,	Sparrows	102	19	2
Jackson Hogan, illegit.	do.	255	8	3
Frederick Haudley,	Thomas	252	9	1

PUTNAM.

John Wallace, R. S.,	Blacks	99	14	1
Fountain S. Blackey,	Kendricks	253	10	2
Stephen Marchman, sol.	Goods	19	3	2

(138)

Fortunate Drawers Capts. Dist.	No.	Dt.	Sec.
Asa Rosser, Laamrs	152	8	3
John H. Walker, sol. Blacks	155	10	1
Beverly Slaughter, soldier,	196	18	1
William Arnold, Stinsons	32	5	2
John Hall, sol. Clarks	3	11	2
Geo. W. Gordon, orp. Bledsoes	214	12	2
Josiah Bowdin, Allums	177	12	3

RABUN.

Jesse Price, idiot, Godfreys	53	2	2

RICHMOND.

—— Lansdell, R. S., Hands	248	1	4
James Carey (Treadwells	77	24	2
Leist. & Field. Bell, orps. Kellys	183	21	1
Gilbert Cleland, Huntingtons	218	5	5
Armand R. Brux, Treadwells	191	3	1
Augustus V. Denham, Wilcoxs	4	4	1
George W. McCoy, Huntingtons	112	6	1
Stephen Kildredge, do.	135	18	2
Ephriam Rigdon, 123rd	152	17	1
Isaac Justice, sr. R. S., James	152	1	3
Obedience Bugg, deaf & dumb	212	7	3
William Mackie, Treadwells	95	5	2
Comfort Griffin, w. R.S. Blacks	32	19	2

SCRIVEN.

Richard W. Rieves, Reaves	181	2	2
James Lee, McCalls	174	10	5
Hezekiah Vickery, R. S., Poytress	86	2	4

TATTNALL.

James K. Archer, Conners	176	3	2
Nancy Salter, h. ab. Corseys	185	24	1
John Conner, Dees	68	13	5

TELFAIR.

Ivy Simmons, Wilkersons	204	5	2

TWIGGS.

Margaret Evans, wid. Bosticks	147	8	4
James James, sol. Streetmans	222	20	2
Mary Ann Lee, illeg. Solomons	43	30	1
James L. Dupree, Holidays	267	8	1
Ors. of G. Coffield, Blackshears	164	5	3
Celey Stephens, w. R. S. Kellys	126	7	2
Arthur Trulock, Wimberlys	121	1	4
Alfred Chance, Kellys	231	13	1
Orps. of M. Exum. Chamberlains	131	25	1

UPSON.

Robert Jackson, Hattoxs	213	7	3
John Black, soldier, Harralds	176	11	1
Deberry Chapman, sol. Dukes	15	12	3

WALTON.

Samuel Whatley, sol. 249th	218	10	3
Lem'l Dewren, sol. Hendersons	119	21	2
Goodwin Miller, sol. Snows	86	29	1
John H. Velvin, 250th	36	32	1

WAYNE.

Henry Russell, Mannings	58	4	5

WARREN.

Mary Hargrove, illeg. Downs	236	5	2
Wilbern Semore, orph. Hills	133	23	2
Thomas Redick, Latimers	85	23	1
Melmond M. Butt, Bulls	89	1	4
William Rivers, Adkins	155	9	2
Henry Wright, Hills	264	2	4

WASHINGTON.

Fortunate Drawers Capts. Dist.	No.	Dt.	Sec.
Grove Corbets orphs. Woods	215	5	4
James Smiths Worphs. oods	182	2	4
Daniel Smith, Whitfields	65	4	1
William Duke, Wimberlys	77	4	3
Orps. of Britton Jordan, Jordans	44	13	2
Littleton Mims, Gilberts	17	24	1
Charles West, sr. Wimberlys	124	2	2
A. Peacock, R. S., McLendons	210	7	1
Sarah Newman, wid. Woods	37	7	4
David Kennedy, Woods	221	4	2
Henry Townsend, Tysons	36	3	3
John Blackburns orps. Gilberts	325	7	5

WILKINSON.

John Kettles, jr. Currys	8	15	1
William Daniel, Halls	4	8	3
Jesse Mackey, Mathews	292	1	4
John F. Stuckey, f. ab. Curreys	46	2	1
William Statham, R. S., Halls	241	4	2

WILKES.

Benjamin Holtzclaw, Greshams	255	17	1
Elizabeth Norman, wid. Amasons	65	19	2
Jacob S. Bracell, Reeves	146	10	3
Eliz. Brown, wid. Washingtons	262	12	3
Mary King, wid. Reeves	186	4	4

45th DAY'S DRAWINGS—April 27.

APPLING.

Jesse Prescott, Collins	98	20	2

BALDWIN.

George Redfield, Weeks	132	13	2
James A. Perdue, soldier, Thomas	204	10	1
R. K. Hines, Buchanans	233	27	1
Rabun Collins, Pitts	242	11	2
Henry Meacham, sr. R. S., Doles	107	20	2

BIBB.

Joseph Shaw, Bates	240	30	1
Lavisa McKinney, wid. Rutlands	78	6	1
Simon Parker, Pickards	93	17	2
Sarah Darly, widow, Flanders	118	8	1
Jordan Ivy, soldier, Pickards	34	7	4
Zachariah Williamson, Beards	57	14	2
Samuel Owens, do.	243	18	2

BRYAN.

Henry Harn, Stephens	80	22	1

BULLOCH.

Lucrecy Rogers, widow, Lockharts	6	15	5
David Pridgen, R. S., Burnetts	2	21	1
Samuel Williams, jr., McCalls	12	32	1
Alexander Brannen, Lockharts	228	2	3

BURKE.

Sarah Preskitt, widow, Dugas	101	11	2
Eliza. J. Winn, illegitimate, Forths	183	27	1
Benjamin Tipton, Wards	158	18	2
Martin Herington, Thompsons	10	4	3
James H. T. Kilpatrick, Andersons	162	22	1
Britain Dawson, R. S., McKays	139	2	2
William Hust, Robinsons	212	26	1
Levie Sconiars, orphan, Lynchs	116	9	3
William R. Caldwell, Baleys	219	11	2
Berry Rodgers, do.	1	4	4
Sarah Atkinson, widow, Wards	144	21	1

(139)

Fortunate Drawers   Capts.   Dist.   No.Dt.Sec.
John R. Prescott, Corkers   122   6 1

BUTTS.
Hugh Hamail, soldier, Thaxtons   134 26 1
John M. Clure, Robinsons   237 11 2

CHATHAM.
William F. Leach, Baines   38 21 1
John Schenk, Haydens   250 15 1
Catharine Pettit, widow, do.   82   7 1
Ruxby M. Robins, widow, Geredons   152 19 1
William T. Scott, McDonnells   127 27 1
Orphans of John Stilwell, Baines   160   4 1
Col. John Shelman, R. S., Haydens   214   7 1
William S. Phillips, Nungazers   98   1 5
Ann M. White, widow, Baines   18   6 2

CLARK.
Charles Dougherty, Dickins   234   9 1
Ezekiel Akridge, R. S., Wrights   171   3 1
James Pike, Alreds   51 12 1
Tyre Harris, Andersons   210 10 5
Edward Bowling, Ransoms   59   1 4
Lucy Pinson, widow. Andersons   220 17 2
Tamer Dixon, widow, Gahagans   106 18 1
Joseph A. Hughey, Lumpkins   84   4 4
Margat Alred, widow, Alreds   144 20 2
John N. Birch, Birchs   197   3 2

COLUMBIA.
Liza Killingsworth, widow, Carrolls   149   3 2
Nimrod Jones R. S.   do.   256   5 5
James May, Adams   258 21 2
Arthur Perry, Boltons   46   3 3
Larkin Edwards, ill. child, Perrys   193   7 1
Mary Smith, widow, R. S. Dranes   256 31 1
Alexander McDonald, Carrolls   190   8 5
Elisha Bolton, orphan, Clarks   189   9 5
James Wright's orphans, do.   286   8 1
Benjamin Leigh, R. S. Dranes   234 24 1

CRAWFORD.
Matilda & Henry Howell, ills. Rhodes   67 13 1
Jacob Presnel, Wilsons   110 12 2
Hiram B. Rhodes, Rhodes   156 11 2
Silas Hoskins, soldier, Hicks   61 18 2
Abel Windham, Rhodes   55 22 2
Perlina Calhoun, father absent, Ellis   131 24 1
Mary A. Sanders' orphans, Rhodes   5   5 5

DE KALB.
Titas Starnes, soldier, Lokeys   69 23 2
Bennet Sorrel's orphans, do.   82   4 4
Meredith Brown, Bakers   102 11 3
Robert Harden's chil. fa. ab. Browns   48   8 3
William Norwood,   do.   2 17 1
John Criswell, Smiths   178 15 2

EARLY.
N., S. & Jackson Long, ills. Grimsleys   271   4 3

EFFINGHAM.
Elijah Blitch, Stricklands   125   2 5
Murry Reed,   do.   40   3 2
Thomas Mock, soldier, Treutlins   203 18 2

ELBERT.
Park Blackwell, Blackwells   6   3 2
Jesse Hendrick, soldier, Hortons   220   4 1
Stephen Edwards, Deadwhites   227 22 2
James Bell, Bells   72 13 2
Alexander Goldin's orphans, Butlers   191 10 3
Elbert G. Andrew, Hammonds   197   5 4
John Evans, Tates   151 15 1

EMANUEL.
Sarah Heard's illegits., Normans   119   2 1

FAYETTE.
Fortunate Drawers   Capts.   Dist.   No.Dt.Sec.
Martha Davis, widow, Wests   125   4 2
John Doss, soldier, Whartons   212   2 5
Arthur Denham, R. S., Craigs   100 10 3
Willis B. Nall soldier, McClendons   157   7 3
Elizabeth Smith, widow, Whartons   223 11 2

FRANKLIN.
Orps. of Alex Callerham, Stephens   52   8 2
Elizabeth Haney, w. R. S., Bennetts   15 26 1
David Vaughan, Blankenships   56 30 1
Sanford Guest, Andrews   159 20 1
Jedediah Garrison, R. S., Caudells   58   1 1
John H. Goodson, T. Chandlers   92   2 5
John Thomas,   do.   128 11 5
Edmund B. Taylor, Hudsons   198 19 2
Gabriel Smith, R. S., Stephens   157 11 2
Julius Nichols, R. S., Hudsons   201   2 4
Jesse Brown, T. Chandlers   66   5 5
Israel F. Crowell, Cokers   1   5 4
David Caudell, Caudells   223 19 1

GLYNN.
John Bigby, Burnetts   305   1 4

GREENE.
Joseph Tanner, Robins   85   7 4
Burgess Gentry, do.   146   2 1
Wilson Stallings, Woodhams   18   2 5
William Moore, Vincents   280   8 1
Margaret Stuart, widow, Rankins   97   2 2
William Credilla, sr., R. S., Bruces   22 11 2
Lauchlin Bethune's orps., Winkfields   47 12 1
Joseph Fitzpatrick   do.   74 18 2
Simeon Thackston, Newsoms   122 15 1
Orphs. of Micajah Webb, Woodhams   218 23 1
Emmor Bails, soldier, Dawsons   280 19 2
Edward Bartholomey, Bruces   168 12 1
Nancy Crawford, h. ab. Southerlands   42   4 4
Reubin Smith, R. S., Knowles   200   3 5

GWINNETT.
Thomas Boatwright's orps. Hills   108   9 1
Dickson Jordan, Bakers   73 15 5
Byrd Wisdom, Moors   84 21 1
James C. Reid, soldier, Greens   169 26 1
John Beauford Davis   92 29 1
Thomas Carter, Greens   66 22 2
Thomas L. Tanner, Woodroughs   173 12 1
John Johnson, Moors   107   7 3
Levi Cooper, Cupps   69 11 3
James Nolen, jr. Davis   146 30 1
James Thompson, Whartons   87   2 5
Job Red, Moors   20   3 4

HANCOCK.
Arthur Youngblood's orphans, 117th   58   1 2
Erasmus L. Acee, 107th   56 14 1
West Vinson, soldier, Dicksons   93   4 5
Nathan Culver, R. S., 111th   167   4 1
Daniel Higden R. S., 113th   231   8 1
J. S. & C. H. Griffin, illegits., Mapps 117 16 2
Thomas M. Brown, Masons   183 15 2
Robert Reynolds, fa. absent, Calliers   169 31 1
Benjamin Wade, 113th   187   7 1
Samuel M. Devereux, 116th   201 11 3
Daniel Hollomon, 114th   252 11 5

HENRY.
Weston Jenks, Risons   3   2 1
Isaiah Sanders, soldier, Wards   166 18 2
Lary Grice, Risons   39   3 4
Jesse M. Cook, Shaws   57 28 1
Willis Ellis, Harris   180 161

HABERSHAM.

Fortunate Drawers Capts. Dist.	No.	Dt.	Sec.
Martha Nicholes' minors, Bryans	136	22	1
James Roach, Tates	57	21	2
Benjamin Caudell, R. S., Jones	230	4	2
Jonathan Cox, Cross	43	9	5
Benjamin Wofford, R. S., Bakers	106	10	5
Thompson Collins, Vickrys	202	6	2
Levi C. Blair, minor, Langstons	225	14	1
James Helton, Bryans	225	4	2
Anslem R. Jarrard, do.	115	24	2
Mary Lewis, widow, Bakers	4	5	4
William N. Prince, Tates	232	7	3
A. B. Russell orp. of Wm., Langstons	246	19	1
Benjamin H. Thompson, Tates	148	2	5
David Rolston, Kenzies	2	12	3

HALL.

William W. Anderson, Hardages	256	1	4
Mary Whitmore, hus. absent, Wilsons	81	8	2
R., W. & J. Charles, orps. Hardens	111	2	3
Jesse Clayton, Walkers	123	2	3
Thomas Garner, Hendricks	244	6	5
Philip Chambers, Dorsey	102	5	5
Robert Cochrum, Alreds	8	25	1
William Mason, Hardages	70	7	4
Peter Faulkner, Harrisons	110	7	1
Washington Bond, Alreds	133	3	4
Neverson Cook, Hardages	87	8	5
David Craft, Alreds	101	15	5

JACKSON.

George McMillen, Winns	345	3	4
Mary Morgan, widow, Staplers	14	5	5
Stephen C. Durham, Duprees	198	10	2
William McDonald, Landrums	237	32	1
James Graham Storys	153	5	3
Martha E. Reidling, illegit., Staplers	14	9	4
Griffin Cheely, Millers	24	12	5
Samuel Pool, R. S., Storys	159	17	1

JASPER.

Benjamin Morris, Owens	163	11	2
Henry Boswell, Baynes	228	12	2
William Morgan, Hines	113	7	5
Isaac McClendon's orps. Holmes	213	15	2
Mason Harvell's orphans, Keys	270	6	1
Henry Crow, Shropshiers	69	19	1
John Truman's orphans, Reeves	2	8	5
John Irwin, Shropshiers	154	11	1

JEFFERSON.

Hugh Wilson, R. S., Ross	69	15	5
Needham Purvis, do.	140	10	1

JONES.

Alsey Hodges, ill, child. Stewarts	119	26	1
John L. Pogue, Newbys	247	8	1
Martha Gafford, widow, Duncans	2	7	1
Henry G. Lamar, Breedloves	94	1	1
Gillis Wright Taylors	78	4	3
Simon Stade, Breedloves	126	7	4
William Padgett, Stewarts	75	1	3
Michael J. Feagin, Hammacks	55	7	3
Peyton Ward, soldier, Taylors	164	5	2
Levi Manning, Hammacks	127	6	1
Pleasant Cox, Bowens	122	15	5

LAURENS.

Hugh Thomas's orphans, Deans	72	1	3
Moses Dean, Barlows	43	19	2
Alexander Peacock, do.	207	28	1
Eady Newsom's illegits. Plummers	127	9	3

LIBERTY.

Fortunate Drawers Capts. Dist.	No.	Dt.	Sec.
Orps. of Edward Mobly, 16th	245	12	3
Josiah Shephard, 15th	77	27	1
Richard F. Baker, 15th	43	5	1
Lairsa Rogers, wid. 16th	113	13	5

LINCOLN.

Noah Walton, Prathers	101	15	5
James Lockhart, Parks	224	1	4

MADISON.

Jeremiah Hall's orph. Hannas	103	18	2
Samuel Landers. do.	93	11	5
Bery Portwood, sol. do.	70	18	2

M'INTOSH.

Emaline, Edward W. Thomas & Henry Delegal ors. Thorps	82	6	5
Lydia Bennett. wid. McCranies	347	7	1

MONROE.

William Cannack, Browns	91	17	1
Jesse F. Chappell, sol. Woodwards	83	3	4
John Buffington, Johnsons	202	18	1
William Rays orphs. Douglass	97	16	2
Jesse Clower, sol. Wrights	272	22	1
Amos Jones, Browns	109	23	2
Allen Rowe, Houses	133	27	1
Reuben Stilwell, Millers	141	31	1
Thomas Buchanan, sol. Rays	21	1	1
Richard Parker, Johnsons	112	15	1

MORGAN.

James Calaway, Harwells	207	13	1
Robert Crawley, Canifaxs	23	8	1
Jane Wingfield|s ilegit. Griggs	34	24	1
William Evans, R. S., Adairs	58	24	1
Thomas Scates, sol. Watsons	244	12	2
Frances Franlin, wid. Canifaxs	174	11	1
Elijah Willard, Christians	244	7	3
Richard C. Taylor, R.S.Harwells	224	6	3
Francis Lawson, Dawsons	50	5	3
Benjamin G. Glover, Sparks	46	4	1
Holiday Howell, Beasleys	7	2	4
Richard R. Sims, Jennings	61	8	1

MONTGOMERY.

John & Lidey Curry, ills. Wynns	240	11	1

NEWTON.

Milly Higginbotham, wid. Snows	194	28	1
William Vickers' orps. Smiths	124	14	2
Ellet Wood, R. S. Talleys	80	3	4
William B. Hogde, orph. Hays	178	22	1
Archibald Baggott, Smiths	35	9	3
Willis Lyle, Graves	91	25	1
Charles Henderson, Graces	1	8	1
Christian Weaver, w.R.S. Moss	235	15	1
James Spears, Pullens	6	19	1
William Foster, Snows	118	25	1

OGLETHORPE.

Michael R. Griffith, Davenports	14	2	4
Valentine H. Merewether, Seals	62	4	3
Thomas Davis, R. S., Rhodes	40	7	1
James Sylvey, Williamsons	260	23	2
Wiliam Tiller, sol. Davenports	166	2	1
Coleman Mathews, Floyds	31	14	1
Eleanor Stansell, h. ab. Hills	139	29	1

LAND LOTTERY REGISTER—No. 21
[RECORDER OFFICE—PUBLISHHED BY GRANTLAND & ORME—PRICE $3.]

NOTE—Section 1 is Lee County—2 Muscogee—3 Troup—4 Coweta—5 Carroll.

45th DAY'S DRAWING—Continued

Fortunate Drawers Capts.	Dist.	No.Dt.Sec.

OGLETHORPE.

Fortunate Drawers Capts.	Dist.	No.	Dt.	Sec.
Lewis Brockman, R.S. Dixs		115	11	3

PIKE.

| Thomas S. Westrook, Longs | | 165 | 4 | 1 |
| William Akins, Daniels | | 7 | 6 | 3 |

PULASKI.

James Care, Powells		99	30	1
Shadrick Rozar, do.		158	9	2
William Smith, sol. Scarbroughs		108	17	1
J. Willoughby's mins. f.a.Thomas		21	4	3
James Care, Powells		22	16	2

PUTNAM.

Esra S. Howard, Chambers		136	3	2
Stephen Jones, R. S. Allums		179	7	1
Reubin Cross, Clarks		70	2	4
Thomas Black, Bledsoes		134	19	1
Rhoda Perdu, widow, do.		247	13	1
Elizabeth Sanders, w. Sawyers		167	1	4
Overall Waller, Barnetts		145	10	5
Tabitha Turman, w.R.S. Bledsoes		63	1	3
Hecter T. Goodwin, do.		30	5	3
Wiley Hopson, Dupress		243	10	3
Nathan'l Tomlinson,R.S.Allums		163	3	5
Wm. Slaughters orps. Chambers		153	30	1

RABUN.

John Dillard, Mercers		249	5	3
Andrew Miler, Mercers		99	6	5
William Jones, orp. Godfreys		211	5	2
William Faris, R. S., do.		78	1	4
Robert Rogers, R. S., Becks		103	9	2

RICHMOND.

William P. McKeen, Mantzs		99	24	1
John Denby, Kemps		152	13	2
Joshua Pharoah James		175	12	2

SCRIVEN.

Eliz. McKinney, wid. Poytres		90	21	2
Daniel Husk, Kemps		152	13	2
Mathew M. Potter, Poytress		235	18	1
Edmon Gross, do.		214	8	3
Noah Freman, Lovetts		79	32	1

TATTNALL.

| Jacob H. Stricklin, Dees | | 22 | 6 | 4 |
| John Fiveash's orps. Graces | | 133 | 8 | 1 |

TELFAIR.

| John Gant's orps. Wilkinsons | | 28 | 9 | 5 |
| Gilbert McLeod, Barentines | | 123 | 1 | 4 |

TWIGGS.

Theophilus Pearce, Streetmans		131	2	2
Darkis Johnson, wid. Pearsons		117	13	2
Orps. of Jesse Dobson, Bosticks		61	2	2
Peter, Mary, Euphama, Henry & W. Newberry. ills. Solomons		94	6	1
James Ennis, Graggs		230	15	1
John B. Mathews, R. S. Bosticks		397	7	1
Orps. of And. Wells, Pearsons		227	7	5
Lewis Ashwell, insane,Solomons		190	18	1

Fortunate Drawers Capts.	Dist.	No.Dt.Sec.
William Esom, Holidays		238 33 1
William D. Melton, Solomons		64 32 1

UPSON.

John J. Hightower, Hattoxs		211 15 2
Francis Nelson, Harrells		226 22 2
Daniel Blankinship, sol. Ezells		14 21 2

WALTON.

Wilson Adams, illegit. Snows		124 18 2
Mary Shepard, widow, Rays		169 23 2
William Potts, Davis		72 26 1
Solomon Davis, 503rd		384 28 1
Joshua Brantley, sol. 250th		100 13 5
Travis Hammock, sol. Davis		201 19 2
Isaac Baker, sol. 503rd		230 6 1
Wm. H. Ray, Rays		25 1 5
John Hutchins, Davis		19 8 1
James Johns, 503rd		153 18 1
William J. Cowan, 249th		246 10 3
William Mobly, 249th		267 4 2
Joel Brooks, Pools		1 27 1

WARE.

| Seaborn Goodwin, Greens | | 36 18 1 |

WAYNE.

William Clements, sol. Mannings		87 1 2
John Crews, McKinneys		52 23 2
Levi J. Knight, Mannings		223 23 1

WARREN.

Fielding Hill, sr., Parhams		233 3 1
Aaron Reece, Adkins z z		243 11 5
Binam Dickson, Downs		36 21 2
William Langham, R.S.Brinkleys		14 17 1
Mary Armstrong, w.R.S. Parhams		54 7 3
Richard Gunn, sr. Rogers		233 19 2

WASHINGTON.

Isaac Manning, Whitfields		39 18 1
Fanny Smith, wid. Tysons		167 24 1
Er'n Hichcock's heirs, Rushings		185 4 4
William A. Pierce, Whitfields		259 4 2
John Moody, Tysons		241 2 4
John Finnies' orps. Wimberlys		45 1 3
Abel Hodges, Avans		295 15 1

WILKINSON.

Mary King, wid. Shows		152 14 5
Phebe Gainor, wid. Smiths		288 1 4
John Polk's orphans, Halls		230 18 2
Nancy Adkerson, widow, Shows		9 17 2
Washington Butler, Halls		6 32 1

WILKES.

Anslem B. Leigh, sol., Hintons		49 3 3
Mackerness Goode, Charltons		222 32 1
Daniel Harvie, Wottens		60 7 2
Susan Whedbee, wid. Charltons		100 24 2
John Dyson, R. S. Lukers		276 5 7
John Dobbs, Reeves		4 10 1
John Jones, Amasons		35 1 4
Peter Lunceford, Washingtons		85 13 1
Daniel Owens, Moors		92 12 5
Samuel Terry, Reeves		156 24 1

(142)

46th DAY'S DRAWING—April 28.

BAKER.
Fortunate Drawers	Capts. Dist.	No.	Dt.	Sec.
Zilpha Harrol, orp.	Corquadalls	287	23	2

BALDWIN.
Henry Eberly,	Buchanans	211	10	1
Amelia B. Malcomb, wid.	do.	12	10	1
Elijah Moore's orphans,	Thomas	73	7	4
William Spurlock, R. S.,	Reddings	136	19	1
William W. Pool,	Wicks	237	5	3

BIBB.
Elijah Miller,	Beards	239	23	1
William Jackson,	Carrs	245	6	3
Samuel Nixon,	Pickards	27	10	1
Rolen Bivins,	Beards	251	12	2

BULLOCH.
Mary A. E. Reed, fa. in. Pen.,	Laniers	138	32	1
Elisha Garbett,	Richardsons	232	22	2

BURKE.
Jas. Navy, orp. of Wilson,	Gordons	75	33	1
James Spence,	Lynchs	59	24	2
Arnold Holley,	Gawfs	172	4	2
Lewis Whitfield, R. R.,	Gordons	219	28	1
Storing Wallace's orps.	Wards	194	8	3
Joel Futral,	Fountains	226	10	1

BUTTS.
Samuel Benton,	Robisons	248	5	4

CAMDEN.
John Cone,	Coxs	90	16	1
Thomas Clark,	Wards	111	16	2

CHATHAM.
John M. Jarvis,	Geredons	60	4	3
Orphans of John G. Young,	Baines	126	3	2
Patrick Pendergast,	Geredons	132	18	2
Maria Williams, widow,	Haydens	122	12	1
James Gallandet,	do.	186	28	1
Robert D. Papot,	Nungazers	155	26	1

CLARK.
Edward Huguenin,	Gahagans	221	14	2
William Dougherty,	do.	328	28	1
Britton Lasseter,	Wrights	14	9	3

COLUMBIA.
Moses Thompson, jr.,	Dranes	28	6	2
Marg. McCormack, h. ab.	Boltons	137	6	1
Elias A. Welbonr,	Baileys	31	14	5
William Hall,	Dranes	92	14	1
John Roberts,	Culbreaths	68	1	3
Conrad Wall's orphans,	Adams	290	5	3
William Hand,	Magruders	168	17	1
James F. Dozier,	Clarks	52	14	5

DE KALB.
James Dority,	Stephens	4	9	2
William York,	Bowlings	201	16	2
Greenberry McDonald,	do.	251	12	1
Sarah Garratt, w. R. S.	do.	103	12	3
Alfred Maner,	Bakers	185	16	1
Asa Thompson	Browns	215	8	1
Elijah Turner,	Spruces	234	19	2
Samuel Floyd,	Merritts	87	18	1

DOOLY.
George Hammack,	Andersons	21	11	2

EARLY.
William Dixon,	Hairs	255	19	2

EFFINGHAM.
Irwin Rahn,	Treutlin	123	15	1

ELBERT.
Moses CcCurley,	Carpenters	74	1	5

Fortunate Drawers	Capts. Dist.	No.	Dt.	Sec.
John Hendersons's orphans,	Alstons	67	13	2
Joshua Cook,	Bells	42	6	4
Eli Eavinson, R. S.,	Blackwells	83	8	5
George Upshaw,	Harmons	106	8	3
Joseph Allen, jr.,	Merritts	205	18	2
William Allen, R. S.,	Alstons	142	5	5
Henry Bramblet,	Hortons	63	1	1
John Highsmith,	Carpenters	73	20	2
Lemuel Banks,	Blackwells	76	25	1

EMANUEL.
Larence Folesome,	McGars	174	11	3
Charles Mercer,	Nabbs	54	23	1

FAYETTE.
Isaiah Durham,	Dodsons	127	10	5
Harrison Haisten, sol.,	McClendons	241	10	5
Herry H. Sharp's orphans,	Browns	206	2	4
James Champion, soldier,	9th	254	7	3
James Lloyd, jr.,	Craigs	143	2	4

FRANKLIN.
John Scull soldier,	Blankinships	77	20	2
James Caudell,	Caudells	167	21	1
James Chandler,	Hudsons	45	10	2
Jesse Rowell,	Stephens	11	6	1
Lewis Barton, T.	Chandlers	46	18	2

GLYNN.
Sarah Tison, widow,	McLeods	57	31	1

GREENE.
Aaron Springfield's orps,	Robinsons	180	2	5
Michael Manning,	Vincents	80	9	5
John Mallory,	Astins	238	3	1
John Hall, sen. R. S.,	Vincents	10	13	1

GWINNETT.
William Perry, sen.,	Evans	337	7	5
Frederick Thompson, jr.,	Maddux	58	7	3
Nathan Beachamp,	Finchers	394	20	2
Robert Cockrell,	Cupps	15	4	4
George Hopkins,	Shippys	28	17	1
James Chappell,	Evans	98	8	3
Wiliamson Turner,	Rollins	42	17	1
William Boyd,	Evans	45	18	2
Jason Bennett,	Rollins	178	31	1
Berry Hill,	Hills	221	31	1
William Hill, soldier,	Mattox	168	32	1

HANCOCK.
John Davies 112th		54	5	2
Jeremiah Jackson, 109th		75	7	2
Sarah Scott, widow,	Adams	231	5	1

HENRY.
John McBride,	Millers	148	2	4
Jeremiah Rhame,	Morgans	5	1	3
Jesse Jolly,	Kites	125	9	1
Claiborn Skinner,	Harris	200	6	5
Joseph McClendon, sol.	Morgans	209	9	3
Silas Barron, soldier,	do.	104	3	2
Elijah Strickland,	Smiths	210	25	1

HABERSHAM.
James Brock,	Bryans	209	24	1
Thomas Edwards, R. S.,	Tates	181	20	1
Robert Crumley,	Fains	245	20	1
Lewis Free,	Suttons	278	4	1
Francis Bird,	Vickreys	170	20	2
Hiram R. Skelton, sol.	Martins	216	25	1

HALL.
John B. Southard,	Yagers	142	6	2
Thomas Clark,	Harrisons	156	16	1
Jephthah Brown,	Dorseys	258	20	2
Sally McDow, illegitimate,	Alreds	88	24	1

(143)

Fortunate Drawers Capts. Dist.	No.	Dt.	Sec.
Robert A. Smith, orphan, Garrards	218	24	1
James J. McCleskey, Hardages	348	7	5
John McBrayer, Wilsons	153	3	4
John Smith, Smiths	224	13	2
James Hulsey, R. S., Hardens	172	8	5
Jeremiah Wisener, do.	15	22	2
Adam Garmon, Roberts	182	9	2
Wiley Harbin, Walkers	1	12	3
Charles Bagwell, Harrisons	169	5	4
John Hamilton, do.	13	5	5
C., C., H. & L. Payne, orps. Roberts	239	5	1
Frances Clements, w. R. S., Hendricks	149	20	1
Solomon Collom's, orps., Harrisons	41	16	1
Joseph Dunagan, soldier, Walkers	145	8	3
Benjamin Goss, sen. Roberts	133	3	2

HOUSTON.

Joshua Patesall, Hancocks	107	5	2
Elizabeth Also, widow, R. S., Smiths	192	12	5

JACKSON.

John Baugh, Duncans	231	10	5
Lawrence House, Landrums	241	6	1
John A. Bailey, Duprees	108	21	1
Thomas Graham, soldier, Rogers	247	33	1
Walton Harris, Duprees	55	11	3
Thomas Stapler, sr. R. S. do.	262	1	4
William Patton, R. S., Rogers	110	33	1

JASPER.

John B. Folds, Reeves	184	4	5
John White's orphans, Wilsons	35	24	2
James M. McCluer, Owens	32	4	5
Lorenzo D. King, Camerosn	4	11	3
Wesley Forbes, sen. Penningtons	314	5	3
Emeline J. Darden's ills., Johnstons	3	6	4
Thomas Morriss, Barnetts	54	19	1

JEFFERSON.

James H. Cook, Ross	124	7	3
Michael J. McCarty's orphans, do	11	4	5
Henry Ingram, orphan, Causeys	199	6	1
Dempsey Hall, jr., Marshalls	72	5	2
Nath'l Samples, R. S. Cunninghams	95	10	1

JONES.

Daniel Reynolds, R. S., Spinks	137	30	1
Lucy Benton, widow, Sullivans	302	20	2
James Welbourn, Dosters	52	26	1
Green Duke, Davis	58	30	1
Howell Alsabrooks, Stewarts	50	15	2
William W. Key, Taylors	224	2	3
Charity Simmons, illeg. Gibson	213	2	3
Lewis M. Lewis, Taylors	205	8	1
Thomas Thornton's orphans, Davis	65	10	5
John S. Zachery, Taylors	207	1	1
Elizabeth Smith, wid., R. S., Popes	163	21	2
Jordan Matthews, Davis	30	18	2

LAURENS.

Eason Allen, Spivys	36	16	2
Nancy Blanchet, wid., Beachams	229	5	3

LIBERTY.

Josph Andrws, 17th	177	4	3

LINCOLN.

John Ringo, Gidons	170	18	2
John McDowell, Prathers	331	28	1

MADISON.

Woodson H. Muckleroy, ill. Bones	43	22	2
Joshua Sorrow, Hannas	132	10	4

McINTOSH.

Francis Hopkins, Demeres	168	7	4

MONROE.

Fortunate Drawers Capts. Dist.	No.	Dt.	Sec.
William West, Turners	44	4	5
John Wooten, Finchs	180	2	1
Thos. C. McDowell, sol. Millers	32	2	3
J. S. Nash, Houses	44	11	3
Elizab'h Lipham, w.R.S., Browns	213	3	3
Pollard Payne, Greshams	264	23	2
Allen McNeal, Woodwards	145	4	3
John P. Riley, Douglass	1	14	1
Sinot Gilder, Phillips	24	9	1

MORGAN.

James Head, jr., Gaines	224	25	1
Brantley Hale, Jennings	59	4	2
M. & E. Connelll, ills. Christians	163	22	1
Sidney Duke, Canifavs	33	16	1
Alford Barnes, orph. Adairs	352	3	4

MONTGOMERY.

James C. Nash, Pridgeons	46	12	2
William D. Wall, do.	222	2	1
Asa Whitehurst, do.	125	12	5

NEWTON.

Thomas Kilpatrick, Bakers	198	8	5
Taletha Cammell, or. Trammells	242	15	2
John M. Sheppard, Askews	23	5	4
Mathew Smith, Newnans	241	7	3
Polly, William H. & Jesse H.			
Baily, orps. f. kil. in l. w. Hays	184	10	3
Hardy Richardson, Talleys	85	9	1

OGLETHORPE.

Mary Sorrow, widow, Floyds	169	11	5
Baxter S. Collins, sol. Billups	94	29	1
A. Wilingham, sol. Devenports	127	5	5
Porter D. Smith, illeg. Lacys	227	10	3
James Johnson, Seals	33	7	1
Moses Watkins, Lacys	235	4	3
Fanny Davis, w. R. S., Hills	73	15	2
Richard Bailey, Rousseus	180	11	2

PIKE.

Absalom Weldon, Longs	234	2	1
Winniford Pearson, w. R. S., do.	126	15	2

PULASKI.

Amos Wheeler, R. S. Sparrows	39	22	1
Archabal Odom, R. S., Powells	69	33	1

PUTNAM.

Nathan Dicksons' orps. Sawyers	27	14	2
Baldwin Norris, Brooks	142	2	1
Green B. Buckhanan, Blacks	8	6	5
Daniel Morrisson's orps. Allums	20	7	2
Pleasant Wright, sol. Goods	160	5	2
Daniel Baugh's orps. Blacks	18	15	1

RABUN.

Robert Brown, Becks	277	28	1
Asa Mercer, Mercers	90	2	1

RICHMOND.

E.J.&T.H.Harbuck ors. Murphys	248	3	1
John Martin, R. S., Blacks	157	3	3
John Williamson, Murphys	100	21	2
J. H. & T. P. Williams, f.a. James	21	33	1
William H. Bush, Treadwells	50	9	5
James Carey, do.	305	3	4
Absolem F. Murphy, Wilcoxs	44	2	8

(144)

Fortunate Drawers Capts. Dist.	No.	Dt.	Sec.
Joseph Dailey, Wilcoxs	16	6	1
SCRIVEN.			
William Eivy, Stricklings	140	2	5
Abraham Buford, sol. Roberts	14	29	1
Parnell Conner, Hunters	29	9	3
John Oliver, Lovetts	65	31	1
Jacob Welles, jr., Poytress	40	22	1
TATTNALL.			
Henry Flowers, R. S., Deloachs	116	5	1
Charles F. McCall, McDuffies	142	11	5
Richard Cooper, R. S., McCalls	222	5	1
TALIAFERRO.			
Jordan Taylor, Cobbs	173	1	2
TWIGGS.			
John G. Cooper, Chamberlains	31	9	3
Orps. of James Bales, Bosticks	170	5	3
WALTON.			
Hope H. Camp, 249th	63	15	5
John Sumeror, Bexleys	277	8	5
David M. Mozeloy, do.	257	12	3
WARREN.			
Sarah Beal, widow, Jones	142	7	5
Elipah Stanford, Sanders	201	13	1
Benjamin Bledsoe, R. S., Bulls	105	8	4
John N. Briges, illeg., Downs	61	9	3
WASHINGTON.			
Elizabeth Curry, wid. Currys	31	5	3
Benjamin Hood, Rushings	43	1	2
Harper Tcuker, Avans	119	6	5
James H. Veal, Oquins	128	5	4
William Horton, Gilberts	92	25	1
James Mallit, Rushings	88	8	4
Samuel Pace, Avans	220	16	2
WILKINSON.			
Jane Lawson, widow, Halls	140	13	1
John Riley, Mathews	199	19	1
R., L. & J. Weaver, orps. Smiths	55	8	1
James Scarborough, Currys	31	2	4
James Lindsey, Mathews	245	3	2
WILKES.			
William Dyer, Hopkins	236	17	2
S. Bowen, sr., R. S. Washingtons	53	1	1
Maryann Cratin, s.w. McDermans	72	11	2
John C. Leitner's ors. Charltons	195	22	2
William H. Mell, sol. Gardners	142	1	4
Benjamin Crabb, Charltons	152	4	1
William W. Prather, Lukers	100	3	2
William Poss, Hopkins	150	29	1

LAND LOTTERY REGISTER—No. 22

NOTE—Section 1 is Lee County—2 Muscogee—3 Troup—4 Coweta—5 Carroll.

[RECORDER OFFICE—PUBLISHHED BY GRANTLAND & ORME—PRICE $3.]

47th DAY'S DRAWING—April 30.

APPLING.

Fortunate Drawers Capts. Dist. No.Dt.Sec.

Joseph Powell, Collins	141	9 1

BAKER.
William Henderson, Porters	170	6 5

BALDWIN.
Theddeus Hubbard, Bivins	229	26 1
William C. Huson, Buchanans	24	3 5
William Bridges, Thomas	142	12 5
Benjamin Hall, Lingos	202	5 1
Orphans of Jonathan Bivins, Pitts	108	19 1

BIBB.
James Mosley, Pickards	234	25 1
Stephen J. Garner, Carrs	42	10 5
Mary Wilchar, idiot, Beards	230	16 1

BRYAN.
Benjamin C. Maxwell, Stephens	172	4 4
Onesimus Futch, R. S., Harveys	11	11 1

BULLOCH.
James Baker's orphans, Deloachs	41	16 2
William Collins's orphans, Burnetts	45	2 5

BURKE.
George W. Pearce, jr., Gordons	133	14 2
Fielding Stephens, Bayleys	23	5 1
Andrew B. Lawson, McKays	153	12 5
John McCullers, Robinsons	223	2 4
Rhesa McCroan, Rogers	72	4 4
Noah Griffin's orphans, Gordons	107	1 3
James Hurst, Thompsons	125	5 4

BUTTS.
Benj. Magouirk, sol. Hendricks	30	8 5
William P. Holificld, sol. Thaxtons	213	18 2

CAMDEN.
Whipple Aldrich, Wards	19	20 1
Joseph Cone, Coxs	173	3 5
John Bachlott, R. S., Wards	98	9 3

CHATHAM.
Orphans of Asa Loper, McDonnells	117	11 2
Louisa J. M. Schroder, wid. Geredons	14	3 5
Margaret McQueen, wid. Williams	126	2 4
William J. Clark, Gaddys	248	15 1
M. A. M. Powers, orp. of Pet., Baines	282	10 2
Dr. Lewis H. Furth, Geredons	258	8 5
Michael Densler, Williams	107	11 2
Mary M. Ker, orp. of Geo. Baines	260	11 2

CLARK.
Peleg Rogers' orps. Gahagans	165	17 1
James Beardin, McCrees	214	32 1
Abel Fleming, Wrights	206	3 5
J.J.M. A. & L. B. Hannah, ills. Mastins	11	16 1
Sally Lasseter, hus. absent, Wrights	72	21 2
Robert Sims, R. S. McDonalds	24	7 4
George R. Clayton, jr., Frosts	90	5 1
Orps. of Jabez Wilkins, Herndons	52	19 1

COLUMBIA.
Harris P. Spier, Carrolls	238	10 1
Lewis Kemp, Clarks	259	1 4
William Wiley, Boltons	240	2 2
Martha Ann Collins, idiot, Talbots	45	5 3
Noel W. Binion, Boltons	198	13 1
Elizabeth Flynn, w. R. S., Adams	39	5 5
David A. Perryman, Dranes	94	5 3
Mary Ann A. Fuller, ill. do.	267	4 3

Fortunate Drawers Capts. Dist. No.Dt.Sec.

Robert Mills, Adams	131	3 1

CRAWFORD.
Michael Welch, soldier, Lovetts	103	6 2
Wiley Wable, soldier, Tillers	370	28 1
John Sealey, Rhodes	234	29 1

DE KALB.
John Wade, soldier, Lokeys	100	31 1
Thomas C. Wilson, Scaifs	91	6 4
Osburn Mullins, Howells	126	10 2
Reubin Hollis, Bakers	68	29 1
Dillion Carsel, Howells	62	33 1
Reuben Holcombe, Bakers	246	25 1
Isaac L. Jordan, Browns	251	13 2
Jams Hughey, Conns	127	3 1
Robert Harden's chil. fa. ab. Browns	178	13 2

DOOLY.
Mary Posey's illegits, Andersons	15	12 1

EARLY.
Joseph Day, Porters	87	5 1
Silas Chambers, Wilsons	139	26 1

EFFINGHAM.
John Garnett, Waldhaners	34	20 1
Philip Ulmer, do.	117	11 1

ELBERT.
Robert P. Dickerson, Blackwells	270	7 5
Theadosius Cook, R. S., Bells	144	13 1
Thomas Smith, soldier, Boltons	65	20 2
Milton Christian, Harmonds	23	6 4
Michael Herndon, sol., Tuckers	185	4 1
John Taylor's orphans Dunns	37	19 1
Lauchlin McCurry, sen. Hortons	58	9 2
David Clark, R. S., Bells	301	1 4
Benjamin Brown, R. S., Blackwells	228	17 1
John S. Bramblet, Merritts	203	22 1

EMANUEL.
Moses Herrington, Chasons	222	19 2
Nathaniel Holton, McGars	26	20 2

FAYETTE.
William G. Faulker, Craigs	200	10 2
Jared Banister, Wests	141	3 5
Lewis Pritchett, Roziers	191	3 2
John Craven, Craigs	177	3 1
Wm. Gilliland, sen. R. S., Dodsons	69	29 1

FRANKLIN.
Matthew B. Hooper, jr., sol. Bennetts	1	6 1
Absalom Holbrook, do.	28	10 5
George Cockburn, R. S., do.	61	10 2
George Stovall, sr., R. S., Blankinships	42	22 2
Bryan Smith, idiot, Caudells	3	25 1
Matthew B. H. Cockerham, Bennetts	34	19 2

GLYNN.
Isaac Huston, Burnetts	237	4 3

GREENE.
B. M. Kicker, illegit., Rankins	229	3 1
Joseph W. Grimes, Dawsons	81	20 1
Martha Woods, Copelands	96	3 3
George Huff, soldier, Bruces	151	10 5
Ruth Garmon, widow, Woodhams	72	7 3
Leonard M. Bethune, Webbs	233	33 1
John S. Curry, Dawsons	229	7 3
Nancy Blanks, wid., R. S., Astins	24	28 1
Peyton Clements, Southerlands	285	10 2
William L. Tucker, Mercers	133	22 2

(146)

GWINNETT.

Fortunate Drawers Capts. Dist.	No.	Dt.	Sec.
Thomas Baity, jr., Hunicuts	218	22	1
Robert Jackson, do.	42	3	3
Thompson Hale, Woodroughs	72	11	5
Charles Walls, R. S., Robertsons	277	10	2
Reuben Bowling, do.	115	19	2
Charles Gates, jr., Bakers	89	10	5
Nathaniel Connally, Moors	92	2	2
Archibald Matthews, Woodroughs	214	33	1
John McGill, Evans	53	6	1

HANCOCK.

William Vickers' orphans, 118th	255	6	5
Allen Brown, 113th	41	9	3
Thomas G. Harwell, 103d	98	14	5
Rebecca Oliphant, widow, Hillsmans	6	7	1
James Brewer, 106th	131	3	2
John Thompson, 113th	144	3	5
Mary Pruett, widow, R. S., 112th	71	2	3
James Hall, sen., 116th	109	28	1
Hubbard H. Reynolds, 104th	142	7	2
Henry Burran, 117th	143	19	2

HENRY.

Lemuel Greene, Harris	216	2	4
Aaron Parker, R. S., Shaws	85	33	1
William McDuff, R. S., Kites	30	5	1
Ezegiel Cloud, R. S., Grays	253	8	1
Samuel Stevenson, Bryants	150	17	2
John Chambers, Risons	13	11	5

HOUSTON.

Joel B. Scott, Pattens	85	30	1
Abner Sanford, Becks	5	18	1
Cloah Edwards, hus. ab. Batemans	181	5	2
Edward Burch, R. S., Yarboroughs	71	5	1
John A. Johnson, minor, Batemans	117	3	4
Thomas Themby, R. S., Yarboroughs	58	21	2
Stephen C. Goddin, minor, Smiths	251	3	3
Edward Brooks, soldier, Pattons	277	7	1
John Giles, Prices	183	3	2

HABERSHAM.

John J. Chitwood, Tates	188	12	2
James Franklin, Kenzies	255	6	1
Jeremiah Cleveland, Langstons	7	19	1
William Hunt, Vickreys	18	20	2
Noel Zedford, do.	221	23	1
John Dickinson's orphans, Martins	22	8	4
Rachel Auston, widow, Bakers	268	4	1
John Greer, Jones	253	11	5
David Highfill, do.	1	12	5
John Tankersly, do.	179	5	5

HALL.

William Patterson, Hendricks	115	3	1
Mary Pierce, widow, Garrards	146	14	2
David Barton, Harrisons	250	19	1
Robert Black, Floyds	146	32	1
Rebec. R., Jas. S., Eliz. K. & Ephriam B. Daniel, orps. Dorsers	155	18	2
Darius Johnson, Garrards	115	5	2
John Brown, Roberts	228	25	1
J. D. & L. Hardage, illegits. Hardages	18	19	1
William Moore, Dorseys	45	9	3
James Collins, soldier, Garrards	254	3	4
Joseph McCutchen, R. S., Hardages	251	3	1
Frederick Conner, Dorseys	125	9	3
Ann Stricklin, widow, Alreds	161	24	1
S., E., M. & N. Reid, ils. Wilsons	153	4	4
Amos Brown, Hardens	27	9	5

JACKSON.

Frances Powell, widow, Winns	27	21	1

Fortunate Drawers Capts. Dist.	No.	Dt.	Sec.
Sarah Hinson, w. R. S., do.	166	9	3
Bennett D. Wood, Pairs	73	10	2

JASPER.

Moses Champion, Holmes	169	3	1
Joseph Moore, R. S., Dardens	285	5	3
Harrison Huff, soldier, Hollands	222	4	2
James Cameron, sr., R. S., Trussells	194	15	2
Simeon Dearin, Baynes	209	4	2
Jeremiah M. McClendon, Holmes	124	5	5
Riley Harwell, Keys	105	6	5
Agnes Brown, widow, Downies	34	4	1
Martha A. Darden's ills. Johnsons	119	22	2
Thomas R. Bishop, Reeves	100	2	5
John Carter, Camerons	151	9	3
Elizabeth Higginbotham, w. Baynes	34	23	2
Clement Diemer, Shropshiers	240	33	1
Riley Truitt's orphans, Trussels	91	18	1

JEFFERSON.

Winny M. Landon, illegit, Ross	183	2	1
Nathan Brassel, Waldens	112	19	1
Abel Moore, Jones	245	7	5
Hardy Medows, Boyds	152	28	1

JONES.

Joseph Bridges, Dosters	14	1	1
Henry Fagin, Gibsons	182	3	4
James Allen, Hendersons	134	5	1
Joseph Beard, Lows	162	32	1
James Thompson, Blounts	92	6	5
Milly Pool, husband absent, Davis	96	5	3
John Marsh, Stewarts	221	6	1
Warren Parker, Hammacks	57	13	2
William Douglass, sol., Sullivans	206	12	3
William Moughon, Taylors	105	25	1
Moses Smith's orphans, Hills	138	1	2

LAURENS.

Sarah Perkins' illegits., Mizells	65	15	5
Leonard Musselwhite, sr., Hodges	175	33	1
David Daniel, Newmons	8	12	2

LIBERTY.

Farwell Jones, 15th	35	16	2
John Bradley, 17th	205	12	2
Archibald Hodges, 17th	172	6	5
Benjamin Weathers, jr., 17th	300	4	1
Moses Westberry, 16th	235	21	1

LINCOLN.

Benjamin W. Syres, Parks	193	12	5
John Willingham, Graves	135	20	1
Andrew Lee, jr., Frasers	23	4	3
Stephen Brown, Hardys	138	6	1

MADISON.

William Meroney, sol. Sanders	83	11	1
Wilson Morgan, Christians	68	12	3
Alex. Thompson's min.f.a.Hannas	64	2	4
Loverd Moore, Culbertsons	169	6	2
George Butler, do.	41	5	1

M'INTOSH.

William Todd, Thorps	8	5	4
John C. James D. Charles H & Susan M. Pelot, orphs. Terrells	93	6	1
Barbara McIntosh, wid. Thorps	122	20	2

MONROE.

James G. Henly, illeg., Millers	30	6	1
Mary Furgason, w.R.S.,Greshams	167	6	1
Thomas U. Robertson, Fergasons	9	1	3
Norman Shaw, Millers	127	15	5
Joseph Rogers, Wrights	109	3	1

(147)

MORGAN.

Fortunate Drawers Capts.	Dist.	No.	Dt.	Sec.
Samuel Pattillo, Adairs	34	30	1	
Yearby Partee's orps. Christians	216	3	3	
Anderson Sims, Harwells	104	3	1	
Jeremiah Sparks, R. S. Sparks	198	3	1	
Wiley Ward, solder, Walkers	93	24	1	
Allen L. Bailey, Adairs	29	24	2	
George Barnett's orps. Christians	149	12	2	
Ruddy Bohannon, Adairs	172	3	3	
Jacob Williams, Walkers	242	17	1	
Joseph Smith's orps. Shearmans	92	3	1	
Peter W. Sharp, Griggs	155	7	2	
Samuel Fielding, Youngs	90	23	1	

MONTGOMERY.

Reubin Sapp, Wynns	159	19	2	
Thomas Darly, Wynns	66	11	1	
Henry C. Tucker, jr., Popes	12	30	1	
Alford Bryan, Ryals	240	16	1	
Jesse Browning, Nashs	327	7	1	

NEWTON.

Joseph Glenn, sol., Orrs	288	5	3	
John C. Gibson, Talleys	9	5	4	
Adam Kilpatrick, Summers	124	1	4	
Charles Coursey, Graves	124	1	4	
Elbert Wheeler, Pullens	131	4	4	
John W. Stansell, Snows	7	4	1	
Stephen Nolen, Smiths	72	2	1	

OGLETHORPE.

Joseph H. Berson, or. Williamsons	42	5	3	
Clark Taylor, sr., R. S., Lacys	175	14	1	
Stephen D. Mosely, Seals	239	9	2	
Dread Thornton, Lacys	104	10	5	
Thomas Neely, Holliways	33	11	2	
Jonathan Colquett, Lacys	236	13	1	
Samuel B. Brown, Bells	180	9	2	
Rolly Hopper, Lacys	104	6	2	
Josiah Jordan, sr's. ors. Arnolds	241	5	2	
J. Martin ill. of Nancy, Holliways	138	11	2	
W. Campbell, sr.R.S.Williamsons	338	28	1	
Asa J. Howard, Floyds	20	13	2	

PIKE.

George W. Darden, sol.Weavers	179	25	1	

PULASKI.

Malta Scarbrough, Scarbroughs	224	7	1	
Ica Atkinson, Thomas	41	4	5	
Isaac Johnson, Scarbroughs	33	16	2	
James Roach's orps. Gilstraps	260	21	2	

PUTNAM.

Benjamin Joyner, R. S. Stinsons	96	8	2	
John Gray, sol. Jenkins	220	5	1	
Noyal Goyne, Duprees	62	17	1	
Sary Brothers, illeg. Allums	132	24	2	
Birdong Thornton, do.	111	31	1	
Edward Dudley, Chambers	197	7	3	
—— Godwin's orps. Brooks	359	28	1	

RABUN.

Merick Johnson, Mercers	53	5	4	
Gideon Beck, Godfreys	8	1	4	
Juda Crain, widow, do.	8	27	1	
William Williams, Godfreys	56	4	1	

RICHMOND.

Fortunate Drawers Capts.	Dist.	No.	Dt.	Sec.
George Smith, R. S.,	238	2	5	
Richard Bush, Treadwells	248	6	1	
John Newman Philpot, Blacks	6	6	3	
James Holcombe, 119th	22	2	3	
Mary, Louisa, David, Helenna & Isaiah Bailey, orps. Hands	151	21	1	
John C. Tompkins, Kellys	333	8	1	
Robert Carter, orph. Ferris	56	3	2	

SCRIVEN.

Taton C. Ovington, Kemps	261	10	2	

TATTNALL.

John McDonald, Conners	22	31	1	

TELFAIR.

Martha Manning, h.a. Lampkins	368	7	1	
Noell Grantham, Wilsons	368	28	1	
Wm. Smith, Wilsons	90	6	1	

TALIAFERRO.

Anderson E. Hoor, Towns	108	5	1	

TWIGGS.

Allen Parker, Pearsons	81	31	1	
Harden Hughes, Wimberlys	133	6	5	
Orps. of Rbt. Reynolds, Pearsons	71	4	5	
W. M. McMurray, sol. Solomons	176	2	1	
Hardy H. Buck, Holidays	60	13	2	
Nicy Wadkins, illeg. Pearsons	45	11	3	
Thomas Bobbiit, jr. Bosticks	100	25	1	
Allen Liles, do.	30	22	2	
Laz. Soloman,R.S. Blackshears	105	5	3	

UPSON.

Green B. Moody, Ellis	253	10	1	
Daniel Blankinship, do.	217	4	2	
James S. McIntosh	86	2	3	
William Robertson, sol. Hattocks	51	9	3	

WALTON.

William Upshaw, Hendersons	314	7	5	
John P. Lucas, sol. Rays	143	4	3	
William Egan, McQuertors	61	8	5	
Nancy Mathews, w. R.S.,do.	151	14	2	
Margaret Robertson, wid. 559th	207	5	3	
Mary Smith's children, 249th	72	11	3	
Early Conner, 503rd	141	30	1	
George Price's orps. Pools	221	3	1	
Allen Roberts, McQuertors	105	5	5	
Harris Boman, 249th	112	21	2	
Charles Broach, 503rd	92	27	1	

WARE.

Lewis Green, sol. Lees	189	2	2	

WAYNE.

Richard Liverett, sr.R.S.,Staffords	60	12	5	
James Harper, sol., do.	155	22	2	

WARREN.

William Johnson, sr.R.S ,Kinseys	243	8	5	
Richard Smith, R. S. Brinkleys	114	6	2	
John W. Sherley, Jones	79	4	2	
Joel W. Perry, Parhams	211	14	1	
William Bridges, Downs	49	20	1	
Nathan Pate, Sanders	221	24	1	
Nancy Kesterson, h. ab. do.	209	14	1	
Wineford Heeth,w.R.S.,Brinkleys	214	31	1	
James Jackson, Rogers	245	20	1	

(148)

Fortunate Drawers Capts. Dist.	No.	Dt.	Sec.
Sivel Johnson, wid. Brinkleys	37	6	4
Richard Wiggins, R. S., Downs	29	4	5

WASHINGTON.

Alexander Houlton, Rushings	322	1	4
Abram Lamb, illeg. Gilberts	23	2	5
Joseph Edwards, Mannings	250	9	2
Wm. Mayo, sr. Currys	101	14	1
Sally, Louisa & Henry M. Tanner, illegitims. Wimberlys	64	20	1
Elisha Womble, Rushings	224	31	1
John Lord, sol. Wimberlys	105	22	1
John Herrington, Warthens	103	4	3
Jacob Chivers, Mannings	145	1	4
Grove A. Pease, Floyds	203	22	2
Allen Cain, Gilberts	155	5	3
Foreman Hodges, Avans	160	7	5
Jeremiah M. Tilley, Floyds	165	10	5
Catharine Smith, w. Warthens	379	7	1
Nancy Blair, w. R. S., do.	232	11	1
Uriah Peacock, McLendons	131	6	1

WILKINSON.

W.H.&E.H. Padgette,ills. Mayos	29	4	4
Tenneson Nobles, Smiths	23	3	2
William Jordan, do.	32	14	5
Lewis Thrower, Mandersons	190	3	4
Ann Heughs, widow, Halls	195	7	1
John Tynor, Mayos	248	9	1
Robert Ethridge, do.	74	11	1
Wilis Benson's orphs. Fairchilds	11	10	2
Rose Porter, widow, Halls	37	3	3

WILKES.

John B. Johns, Washingtons	95	24	2
Lang & P. Robuck ors. Hopkins	205	15	2
Nathaniel McCoy, sol. Carters	204	15	2
Taliaferro Jones, McDermonts	301	7	5
Mary Williamson, wid.Amasons	185	6	5
Obad. Wright's ors. Richardsons	103	2	1
Mary Anders, w. R. S. do.	63	13	1

48th *DAY'S DRAWING*—May 1.

APPLING.

Pheby McCleland, w. R. S. Collins	230	13	1

BALDWIN.

Mary Freeman, Rowers	102	32	1
Joseph Joiner, Lesters	81	15	5
Thomas Willis, Bivins	109	13	2
Orphans of Drury Jackson, Thomas	122	18	1
Samuel A. Plummer,	70	11	2

BIBB.

Joseph Willet, Flanders	222	23	1
Enoch James, sen. Lloyds	30	14	5
Daniel Monroe, Rutlands	14	6	1
Thomas Pickard, Pickards	12	7	4
James Dorman, Beards	97	24	1
Edmund Woods, Rutlands	86	9	2
M., S., M. & J. Ham, orps. Rutlands	253	20	1

BRYAN.

Moses Sugs, McCormicks	149	3	1

BULLOCH.

Jesse Moore, sen. Lockharts	287	16	2
David Beasley, do.	33	15	2

BURKE.

Fortunate Drawers Capts. Dist.	No.	Dt.	Sec.
Elijah Liptrot, Corkers	78	7	3
A. S. R. Milton, Bayleys	173	22	1
Tekill Folds, illegitimate, Gordons	271	22	1
Jonathan Baker, Andersons	15	8	2
Desire Stephens, w. R. S., Wests	18	5	1
John Lynch's orphans, Lynchs	303	3	4
John Lancaster's orps. Fountains	52	7	3
Simeon Lowry, R. S., Andersons	35	11	2

CAMDEN.

William G. Ponder, Browns	217	23	1
William A. Berrie, Halls	226	3	2
Labourn Tailor, Browns	65	1	4

CHATHAM.

Asa Wood, Savannah	125	5	3
Jas. T. Davis, orp. of T., McDonnells	1443	3	
James P. Screven, Haydens	125	6	3
Orphans of Noble W. Glen, do.	174	22	1
Ann Readick, widow, Williams	23	2	1
Michael Pendergast, Haydens	117	12	5
John B. Shaffer, Geredons	81	33	1
Orphans of Frederick Shaffer, do.	189	5	2
Henry Fisher, Nungazers	96	22	1

CLARK.

W. Broadnax's bins. fa. ab. Andersons	142	6	3
Jane W. Fulwood, w. R.S., Gahagans	231	32	1
Sarah Thompson, w. R. S., Andersons	186	1	4
David Kimbell, R. S., do.	67	9	2
Elijah Maner, Frosts	90	7	1
Betsey Ann Burke, widow, do.	114	33	1
George L. Earnest, Dickens	76	8	3
Sarah Glenn, widow, Wrights	316	8	1
Bluford Fuller, McDonalds	196	26	1

COLUMBIA.

Hervey Ball, Bealls	52	2	2
John Gibson's orphans, Clarks	98	29	1
Louisa M. Shields, illegit., Talbots	157	7	2
Matilda Tucker, w R. S. Magruders	6	12	2
John Roberts, Adams	62	14	5
Bud Philips, Carrolls	231	1	4
Levi Guy, illegitimate, Dranes	20	6	2
James Lovell, Culbreaths	170	2	5
Samuel Moor, Carrolls	28	4	4
William Porter, Boltons	169	7	2

CRAWFORD.

Thomas W. Glover, Tillers	277	9	5
English Brewer, Dukes	333	20	2
George Moore, soldier, Moores	129	11	5
Henry King, Rhodes	17	1	2

DE KALB.

William Maloney, sen. Bakers	231	30	1
John Collet, Lokeys	38	2	5
Isaac Chambers' children, Bakers	90	14	5
John Carpenter, Conns	229	14	1
John Dabbs, R. S., Hays	82	14	2
Andrew White, Scaifs	129	1	4
Lewis Williams, Browns	106	10	3
Josiah F. Melton, Smiths	141	5	3
Dice Pool, widow, do.	83	2	3

DOOLY.

Joab Tison's orphans, Mannings	249	25	1

EARLY.

Elijah Philman, Grimsleys	169	5	3

EFFINGHAM.

Elizabeth Merrill, widow, Elkins	75	17	2

ELBERT.

July Ferguson, illegit., Dobbs	176	18	1

(149)

Fortunate Drawers	Capts. Dist.	No.	Dt.	Sec.
William Ward's orps.	Blackwells	202	9	5
Orphan of John Roan,	Tates	334	20	2
William Bevill,	do.	83	4	4
Thomas Allen,	Alstons	9	9	1
Thomas Oglesby, R. S.,	Deadwilders	172	6	2
Orphans of Jesse Jones,	Bells	158	10	3

EMANUEL.

Amos Snell,	Whiddons	229	11	5
Abraham Maulden,	Moores	9	11	1

FAYETTE.

Sarah Vannoy, widow,	Hortons	15	32	1

FRANKLIN.

Robert McFarland, R. S.,	Bankinships	34	1	5
Richard Rowell,	Stephens	5	15	1
Penelope Cleveland, idiot,	do.	171	7	2
James Haley, D.	Chandlers	206	12	5
Robert R. Ash,	Hudsons	49	19	1
William Dobbs,	Boswells	223	24	1
James Dunlap,	Cokers	58	25	1

GLYNN.

James A. D. Lawrence,	Burnetts	212	2	3
Alexander Thomas,	McLeods	43	2	1
James Burney,	do.	268	4	3
Jefferson Graybill,	Burnetts	81	18	2
C.C.,M., M.& C. Wallace, ors.	M'Leods	137	9	2

GREENE.

Adiel Sherwood,	Webbs	149	16	1
Mathew Gastin,	Woodhams	50	20	2
William Meadows,	Colcloughs	229	22	2
Henry Peek,	Vincents	98	6	5
Allen Booles,	Greers	250	16	2
Isham Tooke,	Greenes	142	9	5
Israel Nunnely, R. S.,	Colcloughs	369	3	4
Thomas Crawford,	Webbs	246	1	4
Plottemy Janigan,	Vincents	383	28	1
Robert P. Johnson,	do.	146	8	5
William W. Lewis,	Astins	251	11	3
Lafayette Holland, orphan,	Elys	247	22	1

GWINNETT.

Mark Waits, soldier,	Gholdstons	233	31	1
John Farris	Woodroughs	27	10	5
P. L. W. Brooks,	Hunicuts	25	15	5
Elijah Welborn,	Moores	209	17	1
Philip Izely, R. S.,	Hunicuts	102	4	5
John McDonld, jr.,	Bakers	67	7	4
Geroge Buckanan,	Cupps	190	12	1
Frances Jones, hus. absent,	Rollins	96	5	1
William Head,	do.	192	3	5
Thomas Sizemore,	Hills	22	7	4
Drury Thompson,	Hunicuts	193	3	4
John Bankston, sr.	Rollins	39	14	1

HABERSHAM.

Jacob Holland,	Kenzies	18	26	1
Armisted Popham,	Tates	56	16	1
Daniel McDowell,	Suttons	313	7	5
David Lewis,	Fains	14	2	2
Robert Blythe, R. S.,	Tates	86	5	5
Jonathan McIntire,	do.	219	3	3

HALL.

James Lindsey, R. S.,	Harrisons	103	15	5
Elisha Henson,	Hardages	239	12	1
William Alred,	Alreds	139	4	1
Ephriam Cook,	Yagers	273	4	1
John Nicholson, sen.	Alreds	117	24	1
Robert Laurence,	Harrisons	100	3	1
Burwell Rives,	Hardens	95	5	4
Eli Dodgin,	Garrards	122	27	1

Fortunate Drawers	Capts. Dist.	No.	Dt.	Sec.
Benjamin Faulkner, sr.	Harrisons	185	9	3
Jesse Jay,	Hardens	41	2	1

HANCOCK.

John Dickson,	113th	229	31	1
Charles Abercrombie, sol.	Adams	201	9	2
Bartholomew Ingram, sen.	101st	65	13	2
Thomas Lumbley,	114th	21	4	1
Robert Mitchell, soldier,	Adams	110	6	5
Wilkinson Wilkins,	118th	91	13	1
Philip Forsyth,	117th	313	28	1

HENRY.

Lucretia A. Rogers, illegit.,	Grays	51	17	1
Robert Gwinnett,	Harris	128	3	3
Aggy Daverson, widow,	Millers	63	7	5
Benjamin Mosely, soldier,	Shaws	20	5	2
Eliza Tucker, illegitimate,	do	50	3	2
Thomas C. Russell,	Grays	62	5	3
Jefferson Kirkland,	Wards	70	6	2

HOUSTON.

Sarah Ammons' illegit.,	Wimberlys	152	18	1
Hugh Middleton, R. S.,	Batemans	89	5	5
David Bozeman,	Hancocks	251	9	2
James Hobby,	Becks	106	14	2

IRWIN.

Jonathan Smith,	McCalls	28	11	2
William Powell's orphans,	Jerigans	192	18	2

JACKSON.

Griffin Cheely,	Millers	146	12	5
Robert Wilson,	Duprees	115	22	1
Charles M. Warden,	Duncans	205	4	1
Isaac Rawls, R. S.,	Millers	63	8	1
John Johnson's orphans,	Lindseys	154	2	3
George W. Traylor,	Allens	53	10	2
Jonathan Farr,	Winns	185	20	1
George Sway, R. S.,	Venables	49	12	5
Noah Strickland,	Duprees	258	4	1
Henry H. Lay,	do.	19	1	2

JASPER.

George Cross's orphans,	Hines	72	9	2
Wesley Forbes,	Baynes	179	2	3
Benjamin Keys,	Wilders	199	9	2
Philip Stroud, R. S.,	Wilsons	123	13	1
Robert Andrews' orphans,	Reeves	95	15	5
William Penn, R. S.,	Holmes	69	25	1
William Mote,	Robersons	137	6	2
Isaac N. Morgan,	Hines	174	4	5
Robert Shearman,	do.	53	13	2
James Green,	Sparks	205	5	5
Wiley Phillips,	Robersons	1	24	2

JEFFERSON.

Rolin Reed,	Elliotts	238	8	1
James Sandefer,	do.	139	7	1
Isaac Willett,	Beatys	86	15	1
Henry Brassell,	Cunninghams	39	31	1
William J. Jordan,	Beatys	9	15	2

JONES.

Jesse Glasson, orphan,	Stewarts	120	14	5
Daniel Duffey,	Popes	50	13	5
Joel H. James,	do.	62	5	2
Edward E. Powers,	Woods	85	15	1
William Tooley's orps.	Popes	206	5	2
Henry Thompson's orps.	Bredloves	182	23	2
Right Causey,	Dosters	48	13	2
Nathan Benton's orphans,	Sullivans	217	12	2
James Conyer's orphans,	Blounts	33	24	2
John C. Duncan,	Davis	119	8	5
William M. Comer,	Spinks	15	6	3
Joel Reese's minors,	Bowers	212	5	3

(150)

Fortunate Drawers	Capts.	Dist.	No.	Dt.	Sec.
LAURENS.					
William Moreman, sr.	Hodges	249	22	2
Abraham Salom,	Spivys	225	8	5
Thomas Holmes, orphans,	Powers	88	19	1
James Coleman, sol. l. war,	Bohanons	45	7	4
Willis Drew's orphans,	Plummers	144	18	1
Norman B. Thompson,	Whiteheads	19	5	2
Murree Finney, Thomas		133	14	1
Ezekiel Smith, R. S.,	Mizels	99	14	5
LIBERTY.					
Charles Flowers,	16th	210	14	1
B. G. Whitington, sr. R. S.	17th	237	16	1
Hardy Deloach, R. S.	15th	122	19	2
Ann Winn, w. R. S.	14th	109	7	5
LINCOLN.					
Dennis Mahoney, sol.	Wiggintons	112	12	1
Mathews Collars, sr.R.S.	Frasers	281	5	1
Jonas Guices' mins.	Lonograms	11	3	2
MADISON.					
Patrick Scott,, R. S.	Caldwells	56	24	1
John Dickson,	do.	142	10	1
Cintha C. Lawless, illeg.	Adairs	76	1	1
Patrick Bohannon, sol.	Hancocks	30	21	2
Charity Ward, w. R. S.,	Adairs	151	2	4
McINTOSH.					
Martin Shaw, sr.	McCranies	254	15	2
Reubin King,	Terrells	112	1	3
H., Ann & D. Thomas orphs. do.	81	11	5
MONROE.					
John T. B. Turner,	Woodwards	249	10	3
Henry West,	Turners	252	12	1
John Brooks, sol.	Houses	102	2	5
John Woodward,	Stallings	244	12	1
Sarah W. Nixon, ill|.	Pattersons	190	19	1
John Bowden,	Finchs	54	14	5
Christopher Terrell,	Millers	165	12	5
William G. Quinn,	Douglass	206	2	3
Sarah Scott, orph.	Houses	245	6	5
Henry Smith, R. S.,	do.	291	5	1
James Wood,	Johnsons	161	10	1
Sol. Beckham, R. S.	Pattersons	249	21	1
MORGAN.					
William Barkley, R. S.	Jennings	279	23	2
Isaac N. Stallings,	Canifaxs	54	1	4
Thomas Gowdey,	Youngs	177	1	4
George W. Cotton,	Shearmans	237	3	4
Alford P. Ray,	Canifaxs	350	3	4
Catharine Langsford,w.	Beasleys	167	5	!2
David Gilston,	Canifaxs	69	15	2
Bannister Cochran, sol.	Osteens	211	29	1
Martha Nesbit, wid.	Evans	183	18	2
Hiram Rousseau,	Jennings	120	12	3
Margaret Head, w. R. S.	Gains	26	26	1
NEWTON.					
Jacob Autrey,	Talleys	190	6	5
Littleberry Branan,	Pullens	145	18	2
James Givens,	Trammells	33	33	1
Moses Trimble, sr. R. S.	Hays	99	10	1
Harrison Jones, sr. R. S.	Dyers	248	14	1
Thomas Wallace,	do.	69	16	2
Caroline, Weldon, Sparta &				
Proserp. Williams, ills.	Graves	19	8	3

Fortunate Drawers	Capts.	Dist.	No.	Dt.	Sec.
Jonathan S. Rook,	Hays	182	25	1
Ansel Hudgins, R. S.,	Graces	218	3	2
OGLETHORPE.					
Richard Dowdy, sol.	Simmons	230	28	1
Tolby May, Rhodes z z z	178	28	1
Frances O. Kelly,R.S.	Holliways	237	2	2
James Echols,	Lacys	79	22	2
Curecy McLeroy, h.a.	Hardmans	208	28	1
Stephen Allen,	Williamsons	11	18	1
PIKE.					
James C. Holmes, sol.	Weavers	225	11	2
Laudwell E. Melone, sol.	Suitors	143	2	2
Benjamin Bryant,	Orrs	117	5	5
James Scott,	Longs	126	5	5
Henry Lescare,	Daniellqs	155	8	3
PULASKI.					
Allen Wheeler,	Sparrows	133	7	1
Levi Bush, R. S.	Gilstraps	124	16	1
Rehum Readens ors.	Scarbroughs	68	4	3
Joney Savage, wid.	Powells	129	9	1
PUTNAM.					
Charles P. Gordon,	Bledsoes	167	7	3
Green Wiggins,	Duprees	92	23	1
Joel McLendon,	Sawyers	1	2	5
Reubin Ragland,	Slaughters	23	5	2
Briton Grant,	Allums	175	3	2
James R. Turner, Blacks z z	175	26	1
Pharrow Tomlin,	Vinings	142	17	1
Nathaniel Barksdale, sol.	Brooks	104	2	2
Smallwood P. Ellison,	Clarks	99	6	3
William Dennelly,	Goods	205	3	1
Sarah Williamson, orp.	Bledsoes	375	28	1
RABUN.					
Thomas Godfrey,	Godfreys	296	6	1
Joseph H. Jones,	do.	31	23	2
William Black, sr.	Mersers	109	12	5
RICHMOND.					
Gregory O. Green,	Ferris	286	5	3
Susan Luther, orph.	Wilcoxs	259	16	2
Honor Kale, wid.	Palmers	258	17	2
Morgan Daniel, illeg.	Augusta	149	28	1
H.B.,J. & T. Hickle, ors.	Wilcoxs	29	15	1
Caleb Hartfield,	Treadwells	133	7	5
James Moore, Esq.,	Mantzs	123	7	1
Elizabeth Haynie,w.R.S.	James	221	11	1
Rebecca Cock, widow,	Blacks	52	12	3
William A. Matheson,	Hands	99	28	1
Nicholas B. Williams,	Augusta	155	6	2
Francis Grace,	Huntingtons	13	12	1
Isaac Cliatt, sr. R. S.	Kelleys	117	9	2
SCRIVEN.					
Nancy Taylor, widow,	Poytress	186	10	5
John Buford, jr.	Robberts	6	7	4
Solo. Godwin's orps.	Humphreys	6	6	5
G. R. D. Patterson, sol.	Pollocks	117	6	4
TATTNALL.					
Hannah Smith, wid.	Deloachs	233	10	1
TALIAFERRO.					
Wiley Medows,	Gunns	109	1	2
Amos S. Harper,	Marshalls	79	6	1
Seaborn Dossey,	Cobbs	115	15	2

(151)

THOMAS.			
Fortunate Drawers Capts. Dist.	No.	Dt.	Sec.
Joseph Burch,	48	9	2

TWIGGS.			
Elijah E. Crocker, Graggs	146	19	2
William Wiley, Chamberlains	109	24	2
William Smith, R. S. Holidays	12	5	4
S. W. Wolton, Chamberlains	141	3	3

UPSON.			
John N. Brady, Hattoxs	30	16	1
William Sanders, Ellis	109	2	4

WALTON.			
William B. Gregory's orps. Pools	61	6	2
Simon Holt, 559th	287	4	1
Daniel Hagans, sol. Snows	71	21	1
Stephen Stanford, Hudsons	228	23	1
Alexander Dyer, Rays	165	4	3
Robert M. Echolds, McQuertors	288	14	1
James Nowel, Snows	47	23	2
Mitchell Wilkerson, do.	12	22	2

WARE.			
James Gillstrap, illeg. Motes	186	14	1
Dennis Dowling,	225	6	3

WAYNE.			
Mary Oneil, widow, Staffords	194	6	1

WARREN.			
George Underwood, Jones	144	4	5
Eliza Russell, widow, Bulls	70	11	5
William Jones, sr. Jones	167	3	1
Stephen Toller, Downs	5	17	1
Rhoda Newsom, w.R.S. Adkins	287	20	2
William McDaniel, do.	91	10	3
Dicy Newsom, widow, do.	84	12	5
Joseph Mathews, Sanders	22	27	1

WASHINGTON.			
Luke Nowell, Floyds	23	20	1
N. H. Harris, do.	93	14	1
Wm. Hardin, Woods	52	11	1
Wm. Musselwhite, Tysons	227	4	1
Mar. & Ed|H.Mayo ills. Jordans	293	5	3
Francis P. Miller, Tysons	3	1	1
Sabrina Oneal, do.	18	4	1
Evans Jenkins, do.	249	7	1
John Elie, Wimberlys	205	25	1
Charles West, do.	145	3	5
Ambrose Whittle, sol. McLendons	69	3	1
Soloman Long, Whitfields	244	5	1
McKeen Green, Floyds	128	8	5
George Messeck, sol. Gilberts	228	15	1
Isaac Vinson, Oquins	164	16	2

WILKINSON.			
John Edmundson, Mathews	205	8	3
John Mann, Halls	85	2	2
Jesse Devenport, Smiths	209	28	1
Louisa Dickson, widow, Shows	39	12	2
Betsey Mathews, widok, Currys	76	32	1

WILKES.			
Hezekiah Jones, Rices	58	12	5
John S. Jarrell, Reeves	195	2	1
Catharine Hay, wid. Charltons	64	1	2
George W. Lamar, Greshams	114	8	1
Elizabeth Roberts, wid. Lukers	210	1	4
John Dozier, Moors	178	14	1

Fortunate Drawers Capts. Dist.	No.	Dt.	Sec.
Benjamin D. Carter, Charltons	198	21	2
John C. Carter, Carters	102	22	2
Jonathan Gibson, Amasons	29	10	5
Levin Parkerson, R. S. Hopkins	247	24	1

49th DAY'S DRAWINGS—May 2.

APPLING.			
Mary & W. H. Coward, Morgans	187	31	1

BALDWIN.			
Charles R. Wynn, Wrights	155	10	2
Tomlinson F. Buchanan, Buchanans	204	2	2
Martin Russel, soldier, Pitts	214	26	1
Betsey Etheridge's ills. Perrys bat.	46	10	2
Basil Cone, Wheelers	174	9	1

BIBB.			
Thomas G. Bates, Bates	150	10	1
David Crocket, R. S., Pickards	55	1	1
Philo P. Atwell, Bates	73	22	1
Levin F. Chain, Rutlands	61	14	2
Rebecca L. Brooks, orphan, Carrs	205	16	2
John C. Pelot, Bates	147	15	2
John Dolton, R. S., Carrs	131	9	3
Simon Parker, Pickards	172	2	4
John W. Hamilton, Flanders	241	5	1

BRYAN.			
Henry W. Albritton, Harveys	225	7	5

BULLOCH.			
Thomas Mathis, Turners	11	4	1
Thomas Beasley, Lockharts	169	23	1
Benjamin Milton, Richardsons	47	12	2

BURKE.			
J. Lewis's orphans, Rogers	179	10	2
Hardy Perry, soldier, do.	172	12	1
Robert Allen, R. S., Robinsons	18	11	5
John Chance, Wards	200	8	1
Samuel Barber's orphans, Corkers	74	7	4
Elizabeth Barron, illegit., Gordons	154	22	2
Mary & Sarah M. Ballard, McKays	246	23	1
Jesse McClendon, Gordons	235	1	4
Alfred Eason, McKays	75	13	1
Alexander McMillon, orp. Dugas	29	2	5

CHATHAM.			
Ignatius Parsons, Bains	264	1	4
William Pitman, Gaddys	189	1	2
Tobias V. Gray, Bains	30	5	2
William Fox, McCormicks	248	19	1
Orps. of Anthony Trevoyer, Williams	133	4	3
Nathaniel Camfield, Geredons	13	25	1

CLARK.			
Robert Knott, Davis	278	8	1
Orps. of Jonathan Melton, Dickins	120	18	2
Arthur Cooper, soldier, Deans	140	14	5
Barton Hamilton, McDonalds	251	3	4
Rosalie D. Trobriend, alias Rosalie Gauvain, widow, Espys	139	6	1
Abraham M. Jackson, McDonalds	156	1	2
Orps. of Wm. Meriwether, Humphreys	93	9	3

COLUMBIA.			
Elom Fineh, Adams	295	23	2
Mitchell Carroll's orps. Dranes	157	6	5
Buckner Tankersly, Baileys	45	10	3
John Jenkins, Talbots	91	7	2
Major Liyon, Lukes	24	12	2

CRAWFORD.			
John Logan, Tillers	145	9	8
James Sanders, Rhodes	2	9	1

(152)

Fortunate Drawers	Capts. Dist.	No.	Dt.	Sec.
Joel Ethridge, R. S., Ellis		157	9	2
Elizabeth Evers, widow, Wilsons		125	13	1

DECATUR.

Susannah Gray, widow, Douglass		290	8	1

DE KALB.

Benjamin Harris, jr. Hays		73	19	1
Joseph Graham's orphans, Smiths		234	2	5
Elizabeth Donaldson's ills. Bakers		179	13	2
Edward Howard, Bollings		45	7	2
Richard Sturch, Harris		229	20	1
Charles Harris, Conns		213	22	2
J., H., E. & N. Beard, orps. Bollings		246	8	4
Ulysses M. C. Montgomery, Merritts		85	12	2
James A. Fuller, Bakers		126	2	3

DOOLY.

Eliza Yarborough's ills. Andersons		61	13	5
Caleb Faircloth, jr. Hogans		50	13	1

EARLY.

Henry Ball, soldier, Hairs		82	11	5
Othniel Weaver, Wilsons		93	9	1

EFFINGHAM.

David A. Strobhar, Waldhaners		242	4	1
Orps. of Jonathan Backly, Treutlins		151	2	4

ELBERT.

Jesse Edwards, soldier, Harmons		251	4	2
Samuel E. Self's orphans, Dobbs		62	18	1
Thomas Cook, R. S., Bells		212	23	2
Feburey Stephens, wid. Harmons		156	2	5
Orphans of Usry Almand, Butlers		6	1	1
James Cooker, illegit. Harmons		194	16	1
Thomas Morrison, soldeir, Bells		48	24	2
John Dickerson, Hortons		98	17	1
Margaret Jack, wid. R. S., Bells		64	27	1

EMANUEL.

Thomas Knight, McGars		81	2	3
Robert Dodd, Swains		161	5	2
Grace Wiggans widow, Moores		155	24	1

FRANKLIN.

Prudence Mosely, widow, Caudells		159	19	1
George Weems, Boswells		90	8	3
John Cockburn, Bennetts		114	2	5
Levi Hamby, do.		200	23	1
James Bentley, Blankinships		309	7	5

FAYETTE.

Henry Treadwell, Craigs		234	22	2
Charles Lyle, Wests		9	3	4
Mathew M. Penticost, sol. Landrums		87	31	1
Elisha Eastes, Whartons		143	7	2

GREENE.

John Barker, Newsoms		90	13	1
Benjamin Howard, Robinsons		66	9	2
Benjamin T. Parker, Knowles		130	17	1
William Forester's orps. Greenes		117	17	2
Mary Brooker, widow, Elys		114	29	1
David Ray, Halls		254	6	3
Silas Curry, Southerlands		202	7	5
Jane Hays, w.R.S., Winkfields		77	8	1
Randol Chapman, Bruce		15	20	1
Nathan Hobbs, Southerlands		196	32	1
George Hunt, R. S., Greenes		224	9	1

GWINNETT.

Curtis Caldwell, sen. Woodroughs		47	12	3
Thomas Hill's orphans, Hills		181	2	3
Washington Cupp, Rollins		89	8	5
William Sudderth, Moores		6	13	5
Daniel Clower, R. S., Caruthers		5	4	1
Ira Segers, Finchers		119	17	1

Fortunate Drawers	Capts. Dist.	No.	Dt.	Sec.
Thomas Gorden, Wallis		144	2	3
John Cates, Bakers		129	10	5
Thomas Grovett, Moores		37	14	1
Henry Kite, R. S., Greenes		69	11	2

HANCOCK.

William Seals, R. S., 114th		41	1	2
Archilaus Everitt, R. S., do.		10	14	5
Daniel Dennis's orphans, 112th		160	5	5
Emelus Jordan, 108th		137	4	2
George W. Cpyver, do.		223	8	1
Charlotte Morgan, w. R. S., 101st		143	2	1
Nelson S. Bedding, 108th		171	30	1
Philip Thurman, 104th		143	2	3
Henry Thompson, 118th		109	2	1
John Shy, 113th		927		1
Maria Christian Norris, illegit, 117th		256	25	1

HENRY.

Drewry J. Shell, Captain, Shaws		269	16	2
Luranda Powell, widow, Harris		190	12	5
Richard H. J. Holley, do.		219	5	3
Michael McKinney, Bryants		81	12	1
Benjamin Cagle, Shaws		165	3	4
Burrell Weldon, Risons		158	14	1
Zerah Lewis, Grays		128	25	1
George W. Adamson, Wards		92	19	1
William Burford, Harris		130	2	1
William Griffin, Morgans		249	20	1

HABERSHAM.

James Helton, Kenzies		36	7	3
Archibald Lindsey, Fanes		12	29	1
Charles Smith, Langstons		266	4	1
Benj. Hawkins, orp. of Mathew, Tates		187	21	2
Jane Ratley, widow, Kenzies		151	25	1
James Walker, Tates		168	6	5
Ezekiel McCrary, Kenzies		179	11	5
Thomas Dooly, R. S., Cross		39	33	1
John Clark, Kenzies		34	1	1
George Dodson, Vickreys		224	3	2
John Lovelady, Fanes		5	15	2
Sanders Glass, do.		256	16	2
Andrew G. Robison, Suttons		161	8	1
Hinton A. Hill, Tates		53	23	2

HALL.

Archibald Cockburn, Yagers		174	21	2
William M. McKutchin, Garrards		68	31	1
John Cox, R. S. Floyds		56	2	3
Sarah Waits, widow, Wilsons		190	9	5
Micajah Leech, Hardens		176	2	5
John Byrd, R. S., Dorseys		333	7	1
James Liles, Hardages		48	23	2
Rhody Payne, widow, Roberts		10	8	3

HOUSTON.

Alexander Smith, Batemans		222	8	3
Euphamy Simpson, w. R. S.,		4	7	3
Mary Howell, w. R. S., Yarboroughs		108	5	4

IRWIN.

Lewis Vicars, Underwoods		133	1	2

JACKSON.

Prudence Cowan, widow, Bowens		72	6	5
William Runnell's sen. R. S., Millers		49	13	5
John Calahan's orphans, Deprcs		86	13	2
Sylvanus Couch, Venables		209	26	1
John Tilery, Millers		270	7	1
Lewis Franklin, Landrums		253	17	2
Moses Wafford, Allens		67	7	2

JASPER.

Uriah A. Ransome, ill., Clemmons		58	16	1

LAND LOTTERY REGISTER—No. 23
[RECORDER OFFICE—PUBLISHHED BY GRANTLAND & ORME—PRICE $3.]

NOTE—Section 1 is Lee County—2 Muscogee—3 Troup—4 Coweta—5 Carroll.

49th *DAY'S DRAWING*—Continued.

JASPER.

Fortunate Drawers Capts. Dist.	No.	Dt.	Sec.
Robert Lawson, Barnetts	3	33	1
James L. Nixon, Trussells	9	3	1
William McDowell, Butts	128	12	2
Mary Owen, widow, Owens	202	2	4
John Sturdivant, R. S., Sparks	41	10	5
Landon Carter, Owens	49	4	2
Franklin Hervey, Holmes	176	6	3
Eli Strickland, Keys	222	5	2

JEFFERSON.

Mary Pryor, widow, R. S., Ross	298	5	1
Henry Fountain's orps. Cunninghams	115	10	5
Sherod H. Causey, Boyds	18	13	2
Garland Tarver, orphan, do.	136	29	1

JONES.

Allen Hinton, Spinks	107	14	1
John B. Messer, Blounts	64	4	5
Wiley Franks, Bowens	16	5	5
John E. Lewis, Taylors	191	12	5
Joseph Joley, Duncans	78	7	4
James P. Lowe, Davis	139	3	1
John Henderson, Gibsons	6	17	1
Thomas Hamilton, Woods	100	6	4
Mason Miller, Hammacks	182	8	1
Hartwell Porch's mins. fa. ab., Popes	112	7	5
Charles Davis, Spinks	101	4	2

LAURENS.

Richard Tucker, Powers	272	5	1
James Harpe, Whiteheads	17	8	5
Jane Davis, widow, Mizells	137	4	3

LIBERTY.

George Weather's orps. 17th	9	12	5
Mary E. Anderson, wid. 14th	151	6	2
George H. Laing, 17th	188	1	2
John Daniel, R. S., 17th	71	15	2
Archibald Barber, 17th	132	12	1

LINCOLN.

Guilford Pullin, sol. Wiggintons	7	4	2
Mathew Brunson, Levritts	76	9	2
Liddleton Hawes, Graves	206	1	1
Andrew Lee, jr. Frasers	71	2	2
Keziah Jenkin's minors, Parks	34	14	1
Jno. Colson's mins. f.a. Lonorgans	26	22	1
James Gray, jr., Levritts	200	5	4
Austin Moncreaf's mins. Gideons	250	13	2
Haywood Fraser, Frasers	97	1	5

LOWNDES.

Samuel Register, sol. 10th	80	11	3

MADISON.

A.McGrady, sol. Higginbothams	237	20	1
Henry Landers, Hannas	158	13	1
Joseph W. Walton, Osteans	231	2	4
Samuel Strickland, Bones,	117	10	3
James Sanders, jr. Adairs	94	20	2
N.A.&W.A.McCine, ills. Bones	90	1	4
W. Currington, w.R.S., Hannas	71	5	4
William Grimes, jr. do.	206	2	1

MONROE.

John Pepper, Houses	71	2	4

Fortunate Drawers Capts. Dist. No.Dt.Sec.

James McLendon & Mary Ann

Jenkins, illegits, Wrights	76	8	1
William B. Stewart, Millers	207	9	1
Isham Brooks, Houses	160	5	3
Edward Freman, Pattersons	50	20	1
Nelson Franklin's orps. Houses	125	29	1
Elizabeth Asberry, wid. Turners	173	1	4
Alexander McCain, Gammans	205	6	2

MORGAN.

John Combs, Youngs	121	3	2
John Rogers, sol. Walkers	154	13	1
Hail Talbot, Christians	142	10	2
Pleasant Farmer, Gains	174	5	4
James S. Corry, Youngs	2	31	1
John H. Shaw's orphan, do.	97	6	5
Jeremiah Sparks, R. S. Sparks	94	20	1
Kiah Rutledge, Watsons	104	11	2
Seth Ward, Boswells	27	11	2
Pechy Bledsoe, jr., Jennings	249	6	3
William S. Mathews, Youngs	3	8	1
Richard R. Sims, Jennings	215	10	2

MONTGOMERY.

Charles Boils, R. S., Pridgeons	239	5	3
Jesse Vaughan, do.	139	5	5
William Sullivan, illeg. Wynns	140	5	1
George Cooper, do.	7	21	1

NEWTON.

John Humphris, Smiths	237	24	1
Josiah Vickers, do.	291	1	4
John Farr, Hays	43	6	4
Henry Fullingin, col. Talleys	143	33	1
Jefferson C. Alman, ill. Graves	241	2	5
John C. Frashier, Summers	76	7	3
Jacob Baily, illegit, do.	182	4	3
Elijah W. Christian, Snows	156	6	1
Charles Williams, sr. Pullens	236	12	1
Frederick Vaughn, Summers	37	11	5
Samuel Johnson, Pullens	236	12	1

OGLETHORPE.

Whitfield Landrum, Rousseaux	320	15	2
Peggy Morris, wid. Burfords	255	10	1
Jno. Johnson,sr.R.S.Williamsons	88	18	1
James Story, sol. Williamsons	3	15	1
Arnold Stoker, Arnolds	208	7	5
Augustine Tarply, Dicks	219	2	5
William Guthrey, sol. Holloways	308	8	1
Daniel Kent, R. S., Rhodes	33	5	3
William Finch, R. S., Bells	188	33	1
Robert Smith, R. S. Holloways	75	5	2
Sherwood Wise, sol. Lacys	146	8	4
Mary Harrison, wid. Rhodes	181	17	1

PIKE.

Mary Brewer, w.R.S., Hicks	141	2	1
Harrison S. Wilkinson, Orrs	162	4	3
Nathan Edmunds, Mays	158	32	1
George Varner, sol. Suitors	81	26	1

PULASKI.

John Ricks, Kellams	57	6	2

(154)

Fortunate Drawers	Capts. Dist.	No.	Dt.	Sec.
Elizabeth Ballard, Powells		55	9	5
Ann Wilson, w. R. S. Thomas		226	15	1
Dugal C. McPhail, Kellams		109	24	1
Rasmus Gay, Powells		67	21	2
Penny Brown, illeg, Hendleys		73	22	2
PUTNAM.				
Mathew Williams, Hailes		242	9	1
John Mitchell, Slaughters		200	13	2
William Stubbs, Kendricks		6	29	1
Thomas Davis' orps. Marcus		174	15	2
Nathaniel Dent, soldier, Jones		197	6	3
Caleb Spivey, Sparks		52	9	3
Elizabeth Langford, w. Stinsons		218	10	2
Abram Peavy, Sparks		20	5	4
Orps. of H. A. Gindratt, Barnetts		72	16	1
Edward Daniel, Allums		37	25	1
John B. Ingram, Vinings		138	13	1
RABUN.				
Joseph Pinson, Mercers		139	5	3
William Jones, sr. Godfreys		208	21	1
RICHMOND.				
Wm. James Whitlock, or. Hands		167	11	1
S. E. Hamley, orp. Huntingtons		177	2	2
John Hickle, Wilcoxs		102	14	5
George Allen, Turknett, Blacks		165	2	3
John S. Coombs, Treadwells		147	14	1
SCRIVEN.				
Ransom Rogers, Humphreys		126	3	1
Joseph Spooner, do.		93	9	5
TATTNALL.				
James Wiggins, McCalls		165	15	2
TELFAIR.				
Jacob Matchet, Lamkins		23	1	2
TWIGGS.				
Needham Powell, Graggs		190	4	2
Peggy Sapp, wid. Blackshears		13	10	5
Jesse Parker, do.		43	23	1
Washington Nix, Wimberlys		217	12	3
Charles, Raily, R.S. Chamberlains		221	12	2
Jacob Harris, Holidays		211	20	1
UPSON.				
Isaiah A. Paschal, sol. Paschals		256	15	1
Allen J. Sims, Ellis		145	19	1
Mary Sinclair, w. R. S. Hattoxs		64	4	3
Elijah Reeves, soldier, Ezells		113	12	3
WALTON.				
James Mayo, 249th		12	2	2
Edward T. Chappel, Hudsons		111	5	5
Theophilus Killgore, 250th		147	15	1
Seaborn Jones, sol. McQuertors		207	22	1
Sunsberry Pepper, 249th		279	19	2
Joseph Brinn, Hudsons		104	8	3
Mathew Gilgrove, 559th		49	10	3
Marbil Stone's orphans, Rays		25	1	3
WARE.				
Ephriam E. Miller, Motes		226	11	2
Moses Turner, soldier, Bryans		237	20	2
Joab Ward, do.		248	28	1
WAYNE.				
Thomas Cribbs, sol. McKinneys		106	12	2
Josiah Robertson, sol. Staffords		302	6	1

Fortunate Drawers	Capts. Dist.	No.	Dt.	Sec.
J., N. & S. McNeal, ills. Downs		318	7	1
Abner Rogers, soldier, Hills		197	9	1
Wingfield Wright, do.		148	5	4
James Kitchins, sr. Adkins		254	30	1
WASHINGTON.				
Benjamin Meeks, Warthens		217	17	1
Sarah Gainer, orph. Whitfields		5	16	5
John Hardie, Manning		75	28	1
Abraham Joiner, R.S.Wimberlys		178	10	5
John Jordan, R. S. Jordans		139	10	3
Benjamin Tarbutton, Woods		1	3	2
Daniel Blount, do.		179	1	2
Henry Powell, sol. Gilberts		181	18	1
Reuben Kemp's orphs. do.		122	19	1
Abram Elton, R. S. McLendons		201	9	5
Elizabeth Hardiman, wid. Woods		1	19	2
WILKINSON.				
John Henderson, Currys		76	12	2
George Dykes, Shows		174	2	2
Sarah Napper, wid. Currys		165	16	1
Michael Pickle, do.		205	7	5
Abram Kingary, do.		40	2	1
Ann Welch, widow, Smiths		208	23	2
Isaac Keel, Fairchilds		318	20	2
Henry Askew's orphans, do.		49	2	3
Roderick Sutton, (J.P.) Currys		233	7	1
Alexander Nesbet, Mayos		66	32	1
WILKES.				
Eliza Ball, wid. Charltons		203	32	1
William M. Booker's ors. Carters		50	9	1
Elizabeth Bryan, wid. do.		186	4	2
William Thompson's ors. Moors		34	17	2
Felix Wellmaker, Lukers		16	11	2
John R. Talbart, Reeves		146	6	5
Jacob Lester, sol. do		221	5	4
William Richerson, Richersons		140	15	1
Walter B. Knapp, Charltons		151	22	2
Thomas L. Wooten, Wootens		88	11	1
Mary Anderson, w. R.S.Chumbs		168	33	1
John Dobbs, Reeves		134	20	1
Samuel Gray, Rices		138	18	1

50th DAY'S DRAWING—May 3.

APPLING.

Doley Herin, widow, Collins		298	8	5
Abraham Eason, Morgans		213	15	1

BALDWIN.

Cannon R. Rogers' orphans, Lesters		211	6	5
W. H. Crenshaw's orps. Buchanans		115	27	1
Hiram B. Troutman, Lesters		6	1	3
Ezekiel Sowell, Bivins		115	11	2

BIBB.

Elijah Miller, Beards		110	7	3
Nathan Parker, Lloyds		135	5	2
Clement Clements, sen. do.		95	10	5
Orps. of Henry Jemison, Beards		163	5	1

BRYAN.

Isham Vanedean, Stephens		126	16	1

BULLOCH.

John Edmonson, Burnetts		14	12	2
Joseph S. Burnett, do.		6	4	2
Stephen Moore, do.		22	3	5

(155)

BURKE.
Fortunate Drawers Capts.	Dist.	No.	Dt.	Sec.
Benjamin Grubbs, Corkers	87	21	1	
Striring B. Wallace, Wards	277	7	5	
Cader R. Powell, Dugas	364	28	1	
Homer V. Mulky, do.	130	24	1	
John Hadleigh, Gordons	14	8	5	
William Dilmon, do.	9	3	2	
John Naves, Dugas	242	22	2	
Brinson Fountain, Fountains	311	8	1	
Henry Hilliard, Andersons	281	3	4	
Stephen Cross, R. S., Lynchs	138	5	3	

BUTTS.
Francis Miller, soldier, Masons	5	12	1	
Martha Stephens, widow, Robinsons	219	10	1	

CAMDEN.
Randal Roberts, Baileys	138	4	2	
David Thompson, Mills	76	2	3	

CHATHAM.
E. S. C. Loper, or. of J. C.,McDonnells	195	23	1	
George R. Jessup, Baines	251	17	1	
Alexander McHardy, McDonnells	178	32	1	
Cath. Durkee, orp. of R. M., Williams	141	14	1	
George D. Cornwell,	24	13	5	
Jacob Waldburg,	42	13	5	

CLARK.
James Haile, jr. McCrees	218	11	1	
George W. Farrar, Deans	62	14	1	
David Meriwether, R. S., Alreds	250	21	2	
John J. Burrow, Vinsons	179	12	2	
Nicholas Ware's orphans, Davis	3	24	2	
Nathaniel Collins' orphans, Alreds	285	22	2	
Hugh B. Leeper, Espys	123	12	2	
James J. Crenshaw, Rimsons	105	10	3	
Francis Farrar, R. S., Wrights	110	10	5	
John Strong, Andersons	63	14	5	

COLUMBIA.
David Banks, Boltons	178	17	2	
Winefred Johnson, w. R. S., Clarks	140	8	4	

CRAWFORD.
George Trawick, Wilsons	2	10	3	
Israel Champion, Lovetts	305	6	1	

DECATUR.
Nathan Maples, Douglass	199	2	5	
John Johnson, do.	164	22	1	
Hardy Simpson, Hawthorns	33	5	5	
Caswell Emanuel, do.	175	5	5	

DE KALB.
William Bruce, R. S., Merritts	285	7	5	
Peter Windham, Browns	71	10	3	
Chapmon Powell, do.	168	3	3	
William Williams, Lockeys	248	10	1	
Samuel Powers, soldier, Bakers	91	8	3	
William Gresham, Andersons	227	2	1	
James Jones, Stephens	269	17	2	
Nathaniel Wade, do.	173	15	5	

DOOLY.
Jesse Fann, Andersons	126	6	4	
William Robertson's orphans, 582d	213	11	3	
Hilliard Powell, Hogans	11	33	1	
William Moore, Harris	180	21	2	

EFFINGHAM.
James A. Dasher, Waldhaners	219	12	1	
Orphans of James Shuman, Elkins	19	13	5	
Anderson Williams, jr. Stricklands	71	2	5	
John Christopher Cramer, Elkins	219	29	1	

ELBERT.
Luke White, jr. Hortons	48	20	2	

Fortunate Drawers Capts.	Dist.	No.	Dt.	Sec.
Rebecca Clark, w. R. S., Bells	247	11	5	
Lewis Wilhight, R. S., Boltons	207	4	3	
Benjamin Thornton, jr. Hortons	62	1	5	
Samuel Collins Tuckers	176	10	3	

EMANUEL.
Sarah Fortner's illegits, Swains	83	17	2	

FAYETTE.
Robert Mitchell, soldier, Whartons	130	26	1	
John Maddox, R. S., Roziers	41	26	1	
David Lay, Craigs	183	22	1	
John Vowell, do.	143	26	1	
Willis West, Whartons	332	20	2	
John Holloway, jr. Wests	47	15	1	

FRANKLIN.
John Bell, jr. Hudsons	203	12	5	
Henry Baxter, Jones	75	25	1	
Joel Burgess, T. Chandlers	158	4	2	
William Alman, Blankinships	122	2	4	
Susannah Arendell, w. R. S., Jones	20	5	1	
William Gilmer, Stranges	144	6	4	
Richard Pair, Walters	59	5	5	
Dennis Phillips, soldier, Cokers	205	15	1	
William A. McMillion, Boswells	197	7	5	
William Hammond, soldier, do.	246	33	1	
James W. Royster, Cokers	282	22	2	

GLYNN.
Henry Hornsby, Burnetts	1	8	2	
Lucy, Abigail&Charles Bills, orps. do.	162	15	5	

GREENE.
William Martin, Halls	9	8	3	
Albert W. Jones, Dawsons	68	2	5	
Henry Hodge, Winkfields	70	7	5	
John Copeland, Knowles	176	9	3	
William M. Brown, Bruces	71	14	2	
William Brooks, sr. R. S., Rankins	15	9	1	
Mary Brown, hus. absent, Robins	195	6	3	

GWINNETT.
John Fee, Davis	13	9	1	
William Coffey, Moors	119	6	1	
William J. Childress, Bakers	236	4	1	
Thomas Hill, Bennetts	53	14	1	
Dickson Naler, Greens	32	3	1	
Spencer Bobo, Caruthers	82	18	1	
William Humphrey, Moors	53	19	1	
Mary F. Collier, orphan, Hunicuts	114	16	2	
Philo P. Atwell, do.	176	22	1	
Mathew Cockram, Caruthers	242	7	5	
Samuel Rollins, Rollins	71	12	3	

HANCOCK.
Green Youngblood, 117th	152	26	1	
William Brown, 104th	150	18	1	
Thomas Kelly, 102nd	175	21	1	
Richard Parker, R. S., 110th	283	22	1	
Asa Simmerson, 111th	202	2	3	
Seaborn Johnson, 112th	171	21	1	
John Howell's orphans, do.	61	4	5	
William Terrill, Adams	191	13	2	
Arthur Slayton, Densons	211	22	1	

HENRY.
Mathew McMichael, Harris	64	7	5	
Ransom Tuggle, Grays	98	10	3	
James Gillees, R. S., Shaws	66	6	1	
Bedford Strickland, Risons	56	2	5	
Willie Heflin, sen. soldier, Breeds	69	1	5	

HABERSHAM.
Mary Whiten, widow, Suttons	40	6	2	
Simon Tate, Tates	187	7	3	

(156)

Fortunate Drawers Capts. Dist.	No.	Dt.	Sec.
William Ridley, Bakers	225	27	1
Elizabeth Dooly, w. R. S., Fains	95	7	4
David Oxford, Vickreys	2	12	5
John M. Brock, Bryans	5	2	1
James Stowers, Suttons	76	10	2

HALL.

Stephen Edwards, Dorseys	58	11	3
Jacob Crow, Wilsons	215	24	1
Louis Lamkins, Garrards	184	6	5
Patrick J. Murrey, Walkers	88	9	3
James McCoy, Dorseys	51	15	5
Eli Lofton, Walkers	85	11	1
Thomas W. Blaney, do.	143	13	1
Isaac Reid, Garrards	393	20	2
James Lindsey, Harrisons	291	15	1
Jeremiah Gibbs, Roberts	185	22	1
Isaac Henson, Harrisons	225	8	3
David Lay, Wilsons	75	6	3
James A. Whittinus, Wagnons	82	9	2
Jesse Clayton, Walkers	13	7	1
Berry Watkins, Alreds	185	9	5
James Oliver, jr. Floyds	79	18	1

HOUSTON.

Wiley Jones, soldier, Patteus	261	15	1
Benjamin Hunt's orphans, Hancocks	192	7	1
John M. Warren, Farnels	293	3	4
LarryMannen, Calhoons	80	30	1

IRWIN.

Farnal Drew, 5th	36	2	1
Elijah Grantham, Bradfords	174	27	1
James Martin, R. S., McCalls	12	10	2

JACKSON.

John A. Rhea, Allens	79	11	3
William Spurlock, Duprees	103	30	1
William J. Pate, Georges	62	6	5
Levi Akridge, sol. Watersons	159	13	2
Martha Harper's children, 248th	62	3	4
Bartley Martin, Winns	22	23	2
Joseph J. Singleton, Millers	81	21	2
Joseph Chapman, Venables	288	8	1
William L. Parr, Millers	194	8	5
William Blanks, Gathwrights	78	3	4
Micajah W. McCrary, Landrums	239	10	2
Robert Hemphill's orps. Storys	185	11	1
William Mainor, do.	76	14	1
Allen Millican, do.	2	5	3
Peter H. Strickland, Duprees	118	12	5
Samuel Harlin, Storys	245	9	1

JASPER.

G. & M. Lumpkin's ills. Wilders	150	2	3
Nath'l B. Hornbuckle, Dardens	191	12	2
Elizabeth Boykin, widow, Butts	188	27	1
Moses G. Greene, Sparks	119	2	4
William Lamb, Comptons	15	139	1
Francis Lawson, sol. Penningtons	186	24	1
Timoth Bradford, soldier, do	194	10	1
Bailey Barret's orps. Camerons	346	7	5
Isaac H. Webb, Shropshires	96	10	2
Byron Shell, soldier, Penningtons	37	12	1
Benjamin Wade's orps. Wilders	223	4	1
John W. Compton's orps. do.	265	11	2
Young S. Allen, Butts	115	6	5

JEFFERSON.

Ezekiel Arrington, Ross	293	8	5

Fortunate Drawers Capts. Dist.	No.	Dt.	Sec.
John Milton, Fords	29	16	5
Thomas Pierce, Elliotts	66	28	1
Thomas Barber, Marshalls	164	17	1
Priscilla Sandefer, wid. Elliotts	149	4	1
J. Murphy's orps. Cunninghams	30	15	2
Ponncy Cotheere, Boyds	115	12	3

JONES.

Ruben Roberts, R.S. Robertsons	230	11	5
James Mills, Popes	98	2	3
Thomas Stephen's orps. Dosters	48	27	1
Thos. A. Gordon's ors. Stewarts	217	22	1
Washington Gill, Mullins	151	6	5
William Barnes, sr.R.S. Taylors	218	1	4
Oliver H. Morton, jr. Hammocks	94	6	5
John Hamlin's minors, Bowens	290	15	1
Burton Pyland, Blounts	36	8	3
Joseph Beard's orps. Davis	79	21	1
Isham Sheat, do.	226	29	1
William Irwin, sol. Lewis	146	12	2
Edward M. Roberson, Dades	194	10	3
Mary Johnson, wid. Robertsons	123	31	1
Benjamin Steadham, Dosters	89	7	1
John E. Lewis, Taylors	52	21	2
Henry C. Harris, Stewarts	241	20	2
Samuel Moore, Hammocks	113	5	5

LAURENS.

Samuel Regan's oprhs. Deans	148	5	1
Mathew Smith, Plummers	231	11	1

LIBERTY.

James Audley Maxwell, 14th	251	5	3
John Mallard's orphan, 15th	279	22	2
Eliz. Quarterman, w. R. S., 14th	1	2	3

LINCOLN.

Shep'd Groce's mins.Wiggintons	98	14	1
Walter Nolly, Parks	17	5	3
Nancy H. Walton, wid. Prathers	254	5	3
John Lantern, Levritts	235	27	1
Wm. Walton's mins. Prathers	188	3	1
William Suddeth, s. l. w. do.	55	16	1

LOWNDES.

Lewis Blackshear, 12th	198	6	2

MADISON.

Lewis Millican, Caldwells	163	9	2
Jeptha V. Williford's orphs. do.	33	7	3
Allen Daniel, do.	199	29	2

McINTOSH.

Thomas E. Barber, Thorps	147	7	2
Charles Davis, McCranies	96	1	3

MONROE.

William Langley, jr. Douglass	254	9	1
Ezekiel Abbett, Wrights	2	6	1
—— Bethel's orps. Millers	59	21	1
Mathew F. Miller, Turners	147	28	1
Thomas Sadler, Pattersons	225	10	1
Gatew'd Richardson.sol.Higgins	180	24	1
Isaac Shaddix, Houses	162	2	5
Lot Gordy, Douglass	264	19	2

MORGAN.

Henry H. Bowls, Harwells	124	13	1
Unity Warren, widow, do.	168	5	2
Mary Peeples, widow, do.	137	17	2

(157)

Fortunate Drawers	Capts.	Dist.	No.	Dt.	Sec.
Joseph B. Stewart,	Browns		182	1	4
Redin Stocks,	Whatleys		167	5	3
Peter W. Lesley,	Stokes		163	18	1
MONTGOMERY.					
John Sullivan, illeg.	Wynns		75	3	1
Elizabeth Miller, wid.	Popes		230	30	1
Jacob Taylor, sol.	Ryals		45	3	3
Brinkley Gaudy,	Wynns		9	24	2
Wm. McLeod, do.			139	3	2
NEWTON.					
Solomon Williams,	Pullens		217	7	3
Thomas J. Peek,	Webbs		177	3	3
William A. Chislem,	Trammels		176	29	1
Elizabeth Clark, wid.	Bakers		141	2	2
Ezekiel H. Strickland,	Dyers		180	25	1
Thos. B. Garrotte,	Penningtons		189	20	2
George Sims, sol.	Allredds		225	3	3
Mark Thomerson,	Smiths		125	23	1
Henry Lane,	Hays		217	8	1
Mark M. Powell,	Allredds		206	27	1
Mathew Moss, sol.	Orrs		198	4	3
Sylvanus Pumphrey,	Orrs		134	18	2
Ziba Brown,	Pullens		237	16	2
OGLETHORPE.					
Elisha Tiller,	Floyds		73	6	5
Joel Hardeman,	Seals		29	19	1
John M. Coxe,	Hills		40	8	5
Obediah Smith,	Rousseaus		59	22	1
Shemei Mann's orphs.	Lacys		177	2	3
Jane Bradshaw, wid.	Hills		186	21	1
William W. Bird,	Dixs		269	22	2
PIKE.					
Barney Dunn, sol.	Weavers		9	2	2
John Hall's orphans,	Orrs		102	2	2
Jesse Walker,	Suiters		72	15	1
Alsey Mays,	Mays		130	12	2
PULASKI.					
Patsey Johnson, w.R.S.,	Gilstraps		117	5	3
James J. Vickers,	Thomas		189	11	5
Henry Sparrow,	Sparrows		275	20	2
Polly Ballard, illeg.	Gillstraps		65	7	2
Sessom Purkins, do.			194	14	2
William Mayo,	Kellams		173	19	2
Benjamin Loveless,	Scarbroughs		77	21	1
PUTNAM.					
Edmund Blunt's orps.	Blunts		317	7	1
Thos. Donnelly's mins. f.a.	Blacks		6	27	1
William Todd,	Stinsons		36	11	2
John W. Brown,	Clarks		287	17	2
Solomon D. West,	Blacks		163	10	1
John Wilson,	Chambers		200	12	3
Elias Bulloch,	Bledsoes		174	5	2
RABUN.					
James George,	Godfreys		226	28	1
RICHMOND.					
Littleberry Carenah,	Wilcoxs		138	3	5
William Bostwick,	Huntingtons		164	5	1
Leah Gresham's illegits.	Wilcoxs		90	11	5
Richard Walthall,	Augusta		146	11	2
John Woolfolk,	Treadwells		121	5	3
Oliver T. Boulevare, do.			157	19	2
SCRIVEN.					
Fortunate Drawers	Capts.	Dist.	No.	Dt.	Sec.
Asaiel Farmer,	Stricklings		42	1	1
Jacob Best, soldier,	Ushers		84	23	1
Sarah Coward, widow,	Kemps		208	2	5
TATTNALL.					
Wiliam Rogers, sr. R.S.	Conners		77	9	5
Peter Larimore,	Conners		150	15	1
TELFAIR.					
Peter Hatten,	Wilkinsons		153	8	3
Nathan Grantham, R.S.	Wilsons		287	22	2
George Hearcy,	Wilkinsons		219	8	1
TALIAFERRO.					
David Day,	Towns		77	1	3
Robert Porter,	Cobbs		39	7	1
THOMAS.					
John Slade,			64	12	3
TWIGGS.					
Orps. of J. Wheeler,	Streetmans		122	17	2
Mary Carter, widow,	Kelleys		48	7	1
David B. Rentfrow,	Graggs		130	7	1
Orps. of Wm. Beatty.	Solomons		207	24	1
Absolem L. Caudle,	Blackshears		191	23	2
John R. Grover,	Pearsons		298	7	1
UPSON.					
William Hardage,	Myricks		34	5	5
William B. Brooks,	Pettys		117	33	1
Lindsey Thornton, sol.	Hattoxs		154	32	1
Abner Carter, 589th			157	8	5
WALTON.					
Thomas Jones, 249th			18	1	4
Jesse Peters, R. S.	Bexleys		241	9	3
Geo. W. Adcock, 559th			29	1	5
Larkin Patrick, 249th			253	2	1
James Bexley,	Bexleys		174	13	2
Triplett Cason,	Pools		241	19	2
WAYNE.					
Thos. H. Armstrong,	Mannings		195	8	5
James Stewart's ors.	McKinneys		11	9	1
WARREN.					
Presley Spinks, R. S.	Brinkleys		106	3	5
Philip ones, do.			101	12	5
James, Mathew, Mary, & Eddy Newsom, illegits.	Adkins		12	8	4
Simon Harrel, R. S.	Brinkleys		131	12	2
Rees Johnson,	Kinseys		46	12	1
James McCallister's ors.	Downs		250	1	4
H. Hodgeins, for her ills.	Sanders		245	5	2
Hammond Purvis,	Hills		141	13	1
John Morris' orphs.	Kinseys		155	11	5
WASHINGTON.					
Jonathan G. Miller,	Avans		73	17	1
Anderson Riddle,	Whitfields		199	13	2
Reb'h. Bridges, w.R.S.	McLendons		12	12	3
WILKINSON.					
Enoch Garrett,	Currys		182	17	2
James B. Harper,	Mayos		38	18	2
Kindred Jones,	Halls		40	9	2
John M. Gressop, ill.	Williams		77	23	1
Garland Statham,	Halls		134	5	2
Meldridge Pace, w.R.S.	Currys		263	2	1
Martha Taylor,	Mathews		117	1	2

(158)

Fortunate Drawers Capts. Dist.	No.	Dt.	Sec.	Fortunate Drawers Capts. Dist.	No.	Dt.	Sec.
WILKES.				Elizabeth Goodwin, wid. Ransoms	186	4	3
				Sarah Smith, illegitimate, Davis	87	13	5
Garnet Andrew, Charltons	155	20	1	Charles S. Meriwether, Alreds	26	7	4
Zachariah Darden, sol. Moors	249	8	5	John C. Huddleston, Birchs	21	18	1
Mary Wynn, wid. Woottens	53	10	1	Cody Fowler, Gahagans	228	9	1
Humphrey Tomlinson, Reeves	201	15	1	Mary Moss, husband ab. McDonalds	335	20	2
John Ray, 164th	201	5	1	Garland W. Prince, Frosts	84	7	2
James Seay, Moors	74	13	2	Joseph Friddle, Davenports	134	7	5
Jacob N. L. Cain, Wooteens	195	2	4	John G. Mayne, Ransoms	102	3	5
Simp. McLendon, sol. Ragsdales	117	12	1	Joel Morton, Andersons	217	4	1
John O. Cosby, Carters	102	4	4	Harris House, McDonalds	131	20	1
John H. Norman, Amason	7	3	2	**COLUMBIA.**			
Fielding L. Hinton, Ragsdales	159	3	3	Martha J. Cleghorn, wid. Ramseys	20	921	1
Burnett Holcomb, Moors	240	10	2	Eliza W. Few, orphan, Talbots	271	11	2
Simeon Peteet, Washingtons	236	7	3	Hezekiah Boyd, do.	23	17	2
				Frederick Brown, R. S., Adams	118	7	5
				Jesse B. Bealle, Ramseys	31	3	3
				Nancy Bastin, widow, do.	83	11	2
				James Hogan, orphans, Dranes	40	14	1
51st DAY'S DRAWING—May 4.				**CRAWFORD.**			
APPLING.				Hughey Gilmore's orps. Dukes	217	5	4
Nancy Woods, widow, McDonals	72	5	4	Francis Williams, soldier, Lovetts	17	2	4
BALDWIN.				Hampton Ryan, Rhodes	167	4	1
Jeremiah Morris, Turners	100	3	5	**DECATUR.**			
Ledsey Smith, Lingos	7	5	2	Jesse Brock, Hawthorns	94	11	5
Robert Willis, Bivins	50	21	2	Thomas Freeman, Ferrells	212	4	3
Elizabeth Dismukes, widow, Wicks	93	7	2	**DE KALB.**			
Wiley Wicker, Lesters	47	17	1	John Jennings, Browns	171	1	2
Jane Howard, widow, R. S., Bivins	71	24	2	William Blake's orphans, Howells	50	7	1
Eliza M. Ethridge, idiot, Lesters	331	7	1	Robert Crenshaw, Lokeys	198	14	1
Adam Wilkinson Ginns	39	4	5	Josiah Cockburn, Browns	243	5	4
William W. Ware, Lesters	167	5	5	Joseph B. Gailbreath's orphans, do.	165	33	1
James F. Slater, Buchanans	272	1	4	Nimrod Argo, Bowlings	64	17	1
Richard J. Nichols, do.	223	13	1	Robert Smith, Howells	270	9	5
Micajah Beasly, orphan, Thomas	73	7	5	**EFFINGHAM.**			
BIBB.				William Womack, R. S., Elkins	20	27	1
Richard A. Benson, orphan, Beards	102	17	2	Godlip Snyder, R. S., Stricklands	148	1	4
George Stovall, Bates	75	11	1	**ELBERT.**			
Joel Wadsworth, Lloyds	30	4	2	Moses Haynes, R. S., Dobbs	169	4	4
James Wagnon, do.	132	16	2	William Arnold's orphans, Alstons	226	33	1
Benjamin Wade, Rutlands	142	12	2	John Karr, Merritts	178	9	1
Judith Wilkes, widow, Flanders	268	28	1	Silas Teasley, R. S., Carpenters	83	2	4
BULLOCH.				Richmond Skelton, do.	245	4	1
Esan Lee, Richardsons	215	5	5	Mary White, widow, Alstons	165	22	2
William Row, Deloachs	210	8	5	Early Cleveland, do.	38	19	1
Seleta Ann Driggars, illegitimate, do.	130	9	5	William Gaines, R. S., Blackwells	114	1	1
Brice Simmons' orphans, McCalls	215	3	4	**EMANUEL.**			
BURKE.				James Hancock, Fountains	24	11	5
Stephen W. Blount, Bailys	223	3	1	**FAYETTE.**			
Zachariah Huston, Dugas	232	6	1	Abraham Anderson, sol. Garrisons	22	12	5
Lucretia Nasworthy, widow, Lynchs	151	8	1	John Burke, Whartons	235	8	3
BUTTS.				Frankey Howell, w. R. S., Roziers	140	17	1
Spivey Cannon, soldier, Kirksies	77	8	5	**FRANKLIN.**			
Ira H. Maddox, Masons	235	20	1	William Alman, Blankinships	40	29	1
CAMDEN.				Lucius S. Thomas, D. Chandlers	59	6	4
Whipple Aldrich, Wards	11	17	1	John Westbrook, soldier, Jones	67	19	1
Daniel E. Martin, Coxs	61	7	3	Thomas Motes, do.	77	32	1
Orphans of Isaac Lang, Beckwiths	31	15	2	**GLYNN.**			
CHATHAM.				James Frewin, Dubignons	227	20	1
Ann Harper, widow, Geredons	122	8	5	Joseph Dubignon, do.	82	8	3
John C. Fitzpatrick, do.	55	11	1	**GREENE.**			
Edward Vernard, do.	217	3	3	Mathew Harris, R. S., Astins	41	5	4
Orps. of James O'Conner, do.	134	4	3	Ely Wood, Robins	78	2	1
Lucretia Spencer, widow, Baines	101	3	4	Edward Caldwell's orphans, Newsoms	131	19	1
Sarah Lillbridge, widow, Geredons	135	13	5	James Thompson, Colcloughs	121	6	4
Charles M. King, Haydens	236	4	3	Samuel C. Norris, Bruces	305	20	2
CLARK.				Elizabeth Holt's illegits., Woodhams	201	11	1
James Sansom, soldier, Wrights	241	12	1				
James A. Smith, Davenport	31	9	4				

(159)

Fortunate Drawers Capts. Dist.	No.	Dt.	Sec.
Orps. of Churchill Gatlin, Knowles	162	6	3
Jonathan Burges, Webbs	8	14	2

GWINNETT.

Zachariah Congo, Moores	141	14	2
Dennis B. Cook, Bakers	166	12	5
Ira Camp, Wallis	7	31	1
M., C. & M. C. Turner, orps. Dunbars	247	11	1
Mathew Winne, Evans	19	2	5
Bartholomew Jenkins, Greens	77	14	5
Richard Witherington, R. S., Bakers	171	9	2
James Yancey, Rollins	226	17	2
Thomas Gorden, R. S., Wallis	123	10	1
Amos Welborn, soldier, Moores	44	22	2
Jonathan Thornton, jr. sol. Dunbars	3	17	2
James M. Cooper, illegitimate, Cupps	68	25	1
Benjamin Congo, R. S., Moores	89	5	4

HANCOCK.

Horace Smith, 108th	23	6	5
Wiley Griggs' orphan 104th	3	13	5
Asaneth Alford, widow, 110th	68	32	1
Henry Porch, soldier, Masons	70	4	2
Burwell Cannon, 112th	196	12	3
Joshua B. Culver, 108th	14	8	3
John P. Given, 102d	83	3	1
John Griffis, sen. R. S., 112th	28	6	4
Ebenezer C. Vinson, Densons	48	19	1
Armstead Ransom, Hillsmans	159	22	2
Burges Blount's orphans, 113th	121	16	1
David Lewis's orphans, 101st	12	2	4

HENRY.

Mathew Bostian, Wards	88	2	1
Ephriam Stricklin, Millers	14	4	1
John Wyatt, R. S., do.	124	10	1
Tabitha Weems, widow, McVickers	164	26	1
Allen Gay R. S., Grays	74	15	1
James Hunt, Millers	95	6	5
Anny Bailey, widow, Wards	231	18	2
David Kuglar, do.	192	33	1
John M. Dobbins, Grays	191	10	5
Aaron Dowdy, Allens	7	13	5
Francis M. Greer, soldier, Grays	159	2	3
William Benton, Shaws	191	21	2

HABERSHAM.

George Bowers, Vickreys	230	21	1
Howard Cash, Bakers	224	7	5
Levi Center, Suttons	230	29	1
Daniel Bennett, Martins	58	5	3
Ezekal Fullar, Tates	92	24	2
Elijah Gaddes, Kenzies	243	10	2
James Purcel, Croos	22	12	2
Thomas Jenkins, soldier, Suttons	231	11	5
Burges Tilly, soldier, Worshams	46	10	3
George Vaughan, Bakers	185	6	2

HALL.

John Smith, soldier, Hendricks	68	12	5
William Cagle, Hardages	91	21	1
Thomas Whitworth, Yagers	137	2	1
Andrew Vickrey, Garrards	45	9	1
A. Duncan, hus. died, l. war, Dorseys	15	31	1
Ezekiel Putnam, Garrards	11	4	3
Benjamin Atkins, Harrisons	75	2	3
John Taylor, Hardages	206	21	2
E. & A. Hatley, orps. Harrisons	193	9	2
Philip Ageter's orphans, Yagers	58	3	1

HOUSTON.

Arthur Grady, R. S., Becks	97	12	5
Robert McManus's orps. Wimberlys	37	10	3
Luke Haddock's orphan, Batemans	29	5	5

Fortunate Drawers Capts. Dist.	No.	Dt.	Sec.
Albert Johnson, Farnals	18	33	1
Samuel High, Prices	47	20	1
Whitemore Price, do.	232	18	2

IRWIN.

Alexander McDaniel, Underwoods	233	9	5
Arnold McCrochen, rBadfords	79	24	1

JACKSON.

Whitehead Ryon, soldier, Staplers	172	9	5
Joseph Little, Allens	175	5	3
William McGinnis, Rogers	274	5	3
Joseph Murphy, Doss	174	5	1
John J. Scoggins, Bowens	95	2	5
James Morris, Moons	196	18	2
Samuel Smith, jr. Winns	271	1	4
Luke Parnell, do.	158	7	5
Thomas Nix, Lindseys	321	28	1

JASPER.

Jeremiah Askew, Hines	209	31	1
Peterson Thomas, Keys	62	7	2
William Lovejoy, soldier, Farleys	60	10	2
Alfred Cuthbert, Downies	86	9	1
James M. C. Hardy, Wilsons	8	10	5
Thomas K. Reaves, Dardens	33	3	3
Bardwell Billings, Holmes	119	23	1
Kittureh Godly, hus. absent, Wilders	213	10	5
Daniel Dodson, Trussells	11	16	5
Samuel Hughes, Camerons	95	1	2
James Horsley, Sparks	189	23	2
Mathew Hubbard, Robinsons	272	7	5

JEFFERSON.

Thomas Pierce, Boyds	37	18	1
John Gibson, fa. absent, Marshalls	107	6	4
John L. Rooks, Beatys	41	20	1
John E. P. Cowart, Elliotts	143	17	1
James M. Smith, illegitimate, Ross	79	28	1
Cath. Girtman, w. R. S., Marshalls	230	5	5

JONES.

Amos Nobles, Newbys	214	25	1
Richard Meader, Davis	280	16	2
Jeremiah Gaens, Newbys	149	9	5
Thomas Blanks, s. Taylors	45	12	1
John McCleroy, Davis	153	16	1
James Long, Spinks	58	12	1
John B. Harvey, Popes	91	7	5
Thomas A. Gorden, Stewarts	165	2	4
Henry Tarver, Gibsons	54	1	3
Micajah Blow, Popes	107	14	2
Zachariah Hester, R. S. Duncans	93	15	2
Sarah Rains, w. R. S., Hammocks	10	10	5
Carter B. Carlton, Robertsons	36	17	1
Charles Hollis, Sulivans	94	1	3

LAURENS.

James M. Yarborough, Deans	235	32	1
Amos Rowland, Spiveys	89	22	1

LIBERTY.

Leonard Dees, 17th	294	10	2
Huldah Harington, orph. 16th	25	6	5
Jane Farquharson, widow, 15th	141	6	5

LINCOLN.

Wm. H. Goocher, Wiggintons	147	6	2
John Mathews, Graves	66	22	1
Catharine Henderson, wid. Parks	78	24	2
Thomas Howard, jr. Graves	2	23	1

MADISON.

Thomas Millican, Christians	136	32	1

(160)

Fortunate Drawers	Capts. Dist.	No.	Dt.	Sec.
Sarah Fields, h. a. Bones		66	16	1
Rebecca Teaver, w.R.S. Hannas		194	21	1
M'INTOSH.				
Edward H. Bond, Terrells		200	5	2
Richard Green, R. S. McCranies		55	13	2
MONROE.				
Samuel Cowls, R. S., Turners		143	21	1
Robert Mitchell's orphs. Knights		93	28	1
Sarah Brown, w. R. S. Millers		213	21	2
John Couch, Phillips		128	14	1
James Hammett, sol. Millers		194	18	2
Augustus Crouch, orphan, do.		252	21	1
Lydia Chapman, w. R. S. do.		132	5	2
Elizab. Chewning, orp. Browns		186	5	4
Erastus W. Jones, J. Millers		66	12	5
Michael N. Clark, sol. Millers		163	17	1
Robert F. Sinclair, Pattersons		75	7	3
John Pratt, sr. Stallings		157	5	3
Thomas C. Gadds, sol. J. Millers		194	2	4
MORGAN.				
Margaret E. Cox, wid. Boswells		188	11	1
Alston H. Greene, sol. Walkers		21	9	1
Allacy A. White, ill. Shearmons		207	2	1
Thomas McCoy(jr. Dawsons		97	12	2
Stephen Moss' orps. Stokes		42	16	2
Mary G. Perry, wid. Shearmans		258	14	1
Greenberry Clay, Harwells		139	17	2
Samuel H. Watson, Watsons		213	17	2
Martin .Washington, do.		20	19	1
Susannah M. Wright, w.Canifaxs		213	20	1
John Howard, Stokes		157	15	2
Joel Gaar's orphs. Gains		159	33	1
MONTGOMERY.				
John Slaughter, Pridgeons		44	1	5
NEWTON.				
Rob Thompson, Orrs		105	3	5
Charles Cates, sol. do.		314	22	1
William H. Terry, Pullens		222	14	2
Martha Johnson, h.a. do.		245	5	4
William Kenum, Newnans		102	10	3
John Herridge, sol. Talleys		174	11	2
John Stroud, Graves		180	6	5
John King, Snows		145	12	1
OGLETHORPE.				
Thomas Wray, Bells		284	3	4
George Paschall, R.S. Rousseaus		150	13	2
John Swanson, sol. Dixs		120	19	2
Jonathan Colley, sol. Mays		210	10	3
Samuel Hales, Lacys		135	7	5
PULASKI.				
Hyram Pollard, Gilstraps		142	4	1
Moses Horn, do.		198	12	3
Richard Gainy's orphs. Thomas		77	6	2
Elizabeth Gregory, wid. do.		210	4	3
James Roach's orphs. Gilstraps		189	2	5
M., D.A.&C.C.Snell,ors Kellams		70	5	3
PUTNAM.				
Jeremiah Godwin, Vinings		97	9	5
Jethro N. Wood, Sparks		194	25	1
Jeremiah Cox, Allums		217	9	2
Sterling Dupree, Blounts		9	23	1

Fortunate Drawers	Capts. Dist.	No.	Dt.	Sec.
William Slaughter, Chambers		126	14	2
Jonathan Philips' orps. Sawyers		104	3	4
RABUN.				
William Jones, jr. Godfreys		21	31	1
RICHMOND.				
David Reid, Ferris		143	16	2
David Palmer, James		44	5	1
H.B.&S.Hauver,ors. Huntingtons		212	10	2
Samuel Hale, do.		273	14	1
Mitchell Nelson, Blacks		90	3	3
SCRIVEN.				
John Waters, Humphreys		88	25	1
John Mincy, do.		38	17	1
John B. Boykin, Stricklings		15	11	1
Mary Colson, wid. McCalls		357	8	1
TATTNALL.				
John Joyce, McCalls		17	27	1
Amos Fukeway, Graces		262	17	2
Joseph Dubberly, Dees		105	27	1
Seaborn Cason, do.		114	9	1
William Grace, Graces		231	3	2
TELFAIR.				
Norman McRae, Barentines		115	23	2
TALIAFERRO.				
Samuel Smith, sr. Alfords		179	28	1
Elvington H. Parker, ill. do.		223	5	2
Orps. of Thos. Swan, Marshalls		54	1	1
THOMAS.				
Amelia Donaldson, illegitimate		310	20	2
TWIGGS.				
Thomas McClaskey, Solomons		133	2	4
John Neal, sol. do.		242	7	3
John Sawyer, Graggs		167	4	5
Thaddeus G. Holt, sol. Solomons		149	5	1
Robert Knight Parker, Bosticks		160	10	1
Heymurick Mercer, Holidays		256	7	3
Robert Bedingfield, Graggs		30	6	5
Richard Stephens,R.S.Solomons		166	10	1
UPSON.				
Silvanus Moody, Hattoxs		103	7	4
Lecey Price, illeg. Paschalls		128	33	1
William Merritt, do.		147	30	1
Isaac Crow, Ellis		35	9	1
Henry Hooton, R. S. 589th		169	2	1
WALTON.				
William Brooks, Davis		61	17	2
Eliz. Paxton, wid. McQuertors		101	25	1
Nimrod Vinson, Bexleys		45	15	5
Appleton Wright, Snows		22	4	3
Thomas Smith, 503rd		48	1	4
WARREN.				
Elizabeth W. Cary, wid. Hills		239	18	2
Enoch Williams, Sanders		93	11	2
Washington Brown, Kinseys		54	7	5
Henry Wilson, jr. Sanders		209	10	5
Richard Powell, sol. Downs		200	12	5
Lev. Goulden orp. of Da. Kinseys		87	9	3
Amos Walden, Downs		136	2	4
M., W.A.&S.A. Bradock f.a. do.		13	6	2
Washington Glover, sol. Jones		79	2	2
WASHINGTON.				
Louis S. Avan, Avans		49	17	2

LAND LOTTERY REGISTER—No. 24
[RECORDER OFFICE—PUBLISHHED BY GRANTLAND & ORME—PRICE $3.]

NOTE—Section 1 is Lee County—2 Muscogee—3 Troup—4 Coweta—5 Carroll.

51st DAY'S DRAWING—Continued
WASHINGTON.
Fortunate Drawers Capts. Dist.	No.	Dt.	Sec.
John H. Duggan, Warthens	131	9	1
Edward Bartlet's orps. Woods	113	13	1
Nathan Renfroe, Rushings	100	21	1
Wm. F. Smith's orps. Jordans	242	2	3
Robert R. Williamson, Floyds	146	5	3
Thomas Bateman, Rushing	95	7	1
Cassina Manning, wid. Warthens	69	4	2
James Boatright, McLendons	71	18	1
Seth Hardison, Jordans	45	2	2
David Cox, Woods	254	4	1
Robert Tarver, sol. McLendons	51	33	1
Lydia Cain, wid. Avans	39	8	3
Robert White, Oquins	3	2	2
William L. B. Dermond, Avans	213	6	5

WILKINSON.
Margaret Wiliams, ill. Fairchilds	83	7	5
John Fountain, Currys	106	22	1
Elizabeth Russell, h. a. Halls	104	16	2
Lemuel Lavender, Currys	255	3	3
Elizabeth Benson, w. R. S. do.	188	5	3
Milley Lord, w. R. S. Mathews	147	3	4
Penny Eason's illegs. Fairchilds	217	11	5
Thomas Reeves' orps. Currys	47	15	2

WILKES.
Elizabeth Terrells, wid. Carters	257	4	1
Presley Aycock, sol. McDermonts	63	10	1
John P. Burdett, Lukers	62	10	2
Elizabeth Garrard,w.R.S. Moors	159	20	2
William W. Smyth, Chunns	279	6	5
William Huguley, Lukers	192	26	1
Bethamy Calloway, s.w. Amasons	36	9	1

52d DAY'S DRAWING—May 5
APPLING.
John Roberson, sol. Morgans	310	28	1
Hannah R. A. Rabb, orp. Collins	129	1	1

BAKER.
Daniel Dunivant, sol. Porters	157	6	3

BALDWIN.
Jacob Cobb, Reddings battalion	162	23	1
Michael Smith, Rowes	245	20	2

BIBB.
Reuben Williams, Lloyds	7	17	1
Levi Burnett, Bates	234	18	1

BRYAN.
John Vanbrackel, R. S., Harveys	34	4	5

BULLOCH.
Andrew Golden, R. S., Burnetts	154	22	2

BURKE.
John Folds, Gordons	141	10	1
Jeremiah Taylor, McKays	60	4	1
John Nasworthy's orps. Lynchs	42	8	2
Sarah Scarborough, w. Andersons	72	14	2
Hardy C. Maund, do.	39	13	5
Jesse Bass, soldier, Lynchs	152	10	1
James K. Turner, Forths	313	7	1

Fortunate Drawers Capts. Dist.	No.	Dt.	Sec.
George Madray, Roberts	203	12	1
Lucretia Greenway, w. Fountains	175	16	2

BUTTS.
Needham Lee, sol. Chapmans	295	4	1

CHATHAM.
Phila. Russell's orps. McDonnells	224	32	1
Charles Ulmer, soldier, Scotts	57	10	2
Daniel Carney, jr. Geredons	214	6	5

CLARK.
Thomas Epps, sol., Humphreys	179	8	3
Martin Bowles, Davis	146	3	4
Stephen C. Hester, Lumpkins	124	19	1
Garrett M. Grier, Herndons	82	23	1
Laurence Bryan, soldier, Mastins	195	23	2

COLUMBIA.
Bynum Rees, Talberts	101	7	5
Martha Mappen, wid. Clarks	303	7	1
Peter B. Short, Talbots	210	21	1
Richard Griffin, Boltons	34	7	5

CRAWFORD.
L. A. &M.J.McVeal, ills., Hicks	196	2	2
Young Man, do.	49	14	2

DE KALB.
John W. Davis, orphan, Scaifs	233	19	1
Littleberry Harris, Browns	300	20	2
John Daniel, Merrits	99	11	5
Nancy Ferguson, illegit, Scaifs	196	10	5
Moses D. Harris, Conns	9	12	1
Henry Mitchell, Bakers	104	12	3

EFFINGHAM.
Orps. of Edmund Canady, Elkins	213	4	2

ELBERT.
David Clark, R. S., Bells	304	1	4
Thomas Dutton, Carpenters	377	7	1
Peter Alexander, sol. Blackwells	222	31	1

FAYETTE.
Robert Beal, Whartons	139	23	2
Joshua Cox, Craigs	3	11	1
Charles Lyle, Wests	197	14	1
John Findley, R. S., Dodsons	123	24	1
John Coley, soldier, Whartons	43	1	1

FRANKLIN.
Martin Lovern, Stranges	139	4	5
Joel Sartin, do.	60	2	3
Isham Merritt, Walters	232	1	2
Orps. of W. Smith, D. Chandlers	178	23	1
Isham Lowery, Cokers	181	29	1
George Cockburn, Bennetts	146	27	1
Dennis Shay, Jones	349	20	2

GREENE.
John Penny, Robins	217	14	2
Sterling Grimes, Dawsons	219	21	1
William J. Barnett, Halls	80	12	2
Thomas A. Johnson, Dawsons	216	13	2
Mary Irwing, w. R. S., do.	153	5	5

GWINNETT.
William Hunney, Woodroughs	203	11	3
Polly Rigsby's illegits, Evans	242	30	1
H. Camp, (preacher) sol. do	185	22	2

(162)

Fortunate Drawers Capts. Dist.	No.	Dt.	Sec.
Enoch Benson, Finchers	133	3	1
Arch'd. McDaniel, Woddroughs	111	6	1
William Harrald, Caruthers	184	20	2
HANCOCK.			
Moses Wiley, soldier, Adams	363	7	1
HENRY.			
John McKnight, Shaws	264	3	4
Sampson Gray, Grays	128	20	1
William Allen, soldier, do.	42	19	2
William Junir, illegitimate, Millers	85	8	1
Simon Cardwell, Risons	197	5	5
Peter Harris, soldier, Morgans	221	29	1
David Mosely, Shaws	85	25	1
HABERSHAM.			
Tapley W. Bennett, min. Bakers	93	10	2
Sarah Smith, w.R.S., Worshams	167	15	2
Richard Cox, Cross	234	3	1
William Anderson, Tates	53	11	1
Moses Fagans, Bakers	61	3	2
Nathaniel Wade, Jones	154	8	1
Jonathan Haynes, Suttons	32	10	5
Margaret Wilks, widow, Jones	174	1	1
HALL.			
Isaac Sowel, Garrards	142	11	1
Linsey Payne, Yagers	86	2	2
Bartley Montgomery, Roberts	12	1	4
Edwin Pettigrew, Roberts	12	1	4
Milledge M. Ratliff, Alreds	112	17	2
William Miller, Roberts	163	3	2
Elisha Herring, Yagers	116	19	1
Francis Tolbert, Harrisons	287	5	3
Thomas Savage, sr. R.S., do.	154	4	2
HOUSTON.			
Thomas Doles, Moores	16	23	2
Henry W. Raley, Hancocks	191	18	1
George D. Dupree, do.	112	10	5
IRWIN.			
William Carlton, 5th	105	4	2
Geo. Foulsome's orps. McCalls	169	8	4
JACKSON.			
Littleberry Slaten, Winns	63	19	2
Travis Nixon, Pairs	275	14	1
Thomas Owens, 246th	21	9	3
Margaret Pendergrass, wid. Pairs	15	11	5
Robert Allen, Allens	133	8	4
William Moon, Lindseys	213	7	1
John A. Long, Storys	24	24	1
Sion Pritchett, Doss	159	5	2
Edward Dyer, Venables	139	6	5
JASPER.			
Buckner Eves, Wilsons	40	2	4
John B. Sisson, Baynes	288	7	5
Sally Broom, widow, Camerons	85	2	1
Anslem L. Early, Baynes	162	9	3
Amos Edmonds, Holmes	142	22	1
Madison Smith, illegit.Clemmons	115	5	4
Jacinth Shingleton, Butts	300	6	5
Levinia W. Cargile, wid. Holmes	168	16	2
Maradeth Adams, Roberson	93	4	5
James Ellis, soldier, Hands	33	1	5
Seaborn Jones, Sparks	7	8	5
JEFFERSON.			
James Cook, R. S., Elliotts	20	10	5

Fortunate Drawers Capts. Dist.	No.	Dt.	Sec.
Polly Powell, blind, Elliotts	263	21	1
David Clark, Cunninghams	94	8	2
Gordon Hadden, Jones	125	20	1
Jeremiah Howard, Beatys	247	15	2
Harris D. Austin, R. S., Ross	114	18	1
Eligh Hughs, Beatys	97	23	1
John Cox, do.	187	12	3
JONES.			
Thomas Moughon, Taylors	206	5	3
Joseph Franklin, Mullens	157	8	3
Charles Phillips, Gibsons	35	6	1
Edward Huff, S.T. Taylors	8	22	2
Jacob Fudge, Bowens	231	19	2
James Gates, jr. Gibsons	62	7	5
Philip B. Snead, Taylors	128	4	2
Leven Wright, Breadloves	240	5	4
Benjamin Braswell, Popes	141	7	4
Elizab'h Hinesly, w.R.S. Bowens	104	8	5
William Harris, do.	403	7	1
Joshua Burkhaltar, Spinks	55	25	1
LAURENS.			
Henry Hutto, R. S. Deans	191	15	2
LIBERTY.			
Palmer Goulding, R. S., 15th	21	4	4
Ann M. Kershaw, orphan; 15th	133	1	5
John B. Mallard, 15th	42	30	1
LINCOLN.			
John Suddeth, Gideons	161	4	3
Phil.Dill agent for LDill, Gideons	153	5	2
MADISON.			
John R. Streetman, Bones	99	2	4
Raney Fitspatrick, Higginbothams	61	23	2
McINTOSH.			
Christian, Jane, Barbara, Thos.			
A. & M. Caldwell, ors. Demeries	21	18	2
Jeremiah Lester, Terrells	237	1	2
MONROE.			
Absalom Gray, Wrights	79	19	1
George W. Rees, Pattersons	103	26	1
Robert Kelton, Greshams	124	6	2
William Slocumb, Millers	153	23	1
Terrah Richards, Douglass	215	28	1
David Waldrope, Wrights	293	5	1
Jesse Tollison, Greshams	193	10	5
William Malones orps. Turners	142	19	2
William Martin, R. S., do.	8	30	1
John L. Ponder, (dumb) Knights	187	24	1
Bird W. Tarver, Wrights	151	8	1
Judeth Cowls, w. R. S. Turners	119	11	3
MORGAN.			
Daniel Peavy, Adairs	193	3	2
Thomas Knight, Jennings	128	1	4
Miles Williams's orps. Whatleys	244	10	1
Jonathan Hightower, Browns	60	19	2
John D. Wade, Jennings	68	27	1
Benjamin R. Ray, Canifaxs	217	31	1
Andrew Hanna, Adairs	65	5	4
Lewis Bandy, R. S., do.	236	8	1
Richard Stewart's orps. Shermans	77	16	2
William Neal's orps. Boswells	31	4	2
George Spence, Watsons	99	4	5
MONTGOMERY.			
Henry Wood, illeg. Royals	80	26	1

NEWTON.

Fortunate Drawers	Capts.	Dist.	No.	Dt.	Sec.
Green B. Daniel,	Moss		61	11	5
Car., M. A., Eliz., Cath., Rebec.					
Sa'h. & Spot. Pierce, ors. Dyers			107	9	1
James Moor's orps. Pullens			150	24	2
David Henry, Smiths			31	7	4
John E. Hodge, Pullens			17	2	3

OGLETHORPE.

Francis O. Kelly, R.S., Holloways			302	1	4
Charles C. Ogden, Mays			29	11	5
Paschal Murphy's ors. Rousseaus			205	19	1

PULASKI.

David J. Walker, Heandelsy			76	26	1
M. J. Loper, orphan, Gilstraps			100	13	1
Jeremiah Forehand, do.			78	6	3
Rutha Beall, w. R. S., Thomas			65	3	2

PUTNAM.

Timothy Roby's orps. Mizes			84	29	1
John Bradford's orps. Bledsoes			17	16	1
Thomas Kimbrough, sol. Brooks			73	30	1

RABUN.

Rutha Carn's 4 illegs. Godfreys			161	14	5

RICHMOND.

James Higginbotham, Ferris			197	20	1
Eliza & W. Mastin, orps. 123rd			43	11	3
Adoniram Treadwell, sol. Bushs			32	7	5
Mary H. Johnson, or. Huntingtons			117	18	1
Robert Radford, soldier, Segos			172	2	5
John W. Hunter, 119th			1	18	1
Mary Davis, wid. Wilcoxs			87	7	5
Robert Dimon, Treadwells			33	21	1

SCRIVEN.

Susan Miller, illeg. Poytress			55	12	3

TATTNALL.

Amos Fukeway, Graces			237	22	1
Simon Smith, R. S. Conners			145	2	3
Joshua Fletcher, Dees			73	24	2
Corelius English, Corseys			112	11	5

TELFAIR.

Allen Powell, Wilsons			11	11	2

THOMAS.

William Sloan,			165	5	5

TWIGGS.

Mary Bedingfield, illeg. Graggs			341	20	2
William Pall, Streetmans			102	7	3
Abel Johnson, Blackshears			177	7	1
James H. Findley, Solomans			226	11	1
Joseph Collins, R. S. Bosticks			243	29	1

UPSON.

Samuel Jackson, orp. Ezells			74	9	2
Mary Trammell, wid. Harrells			392	28	1
Sarah Edward's illeg. Saunders			247	8	5
Urban C. Tignor, Dukes			19	3	5

WALTON.

Allen McQuertor, McQuertors			251	9	1
John Pace, 249th			242	17	2
Mary Mathews, wid. Bexleys			23	6	1
Leven M. Wallace, do.			108	10	2
Carter Parker, 503rd			129	6	4
Ransom Owen, Davis			159	9	5
Elizabeth Crow, wid. 559th			172	10	5
Thomas Ramsey, Bexleys			124	3	2

Fortunate Drawers	Capts.	Dist.	No.	Dt.	Sec.
George W. Walker, Pools			39	4	3
Elizabeth Weaver, h.a. Pools			215	3	2
Hampton Williams, 503rd			5	2	3
William Watson, Rays			216	9	2
Luc.,Em.&ElizHannah,ills.559th			173	5	2

WARE.

John McLain, Bryans			32	15	5
Jas., Candis, Rebecca, Michael & Lydia Catow, illegits. Moats			235	8	5

WAYNE.

James Ratliff, Mannings			107	9	3
Williby Mincy, Staffords			89	8	1

WARREN.

Edward T. Pinson, Sanders			63	1	5
William Hand, do.			1	4	5
William Downs, Downs			81	10	3
Henry Duberry, Hills			243	8	1
Margaret Lucky, wid. Adkins			289	15	1
Joseph E. Cobb, illeg. Downs			174	30	1

WASHINGTON.

William L. Gary's orps. Gilberts			235	28	1
Carleton Doles, orphan, Tysons			186	23	1
John Cordery, Wimberlys			116	16	1
Wiley W. Cullens, Floyds			160	3	4
John Shepherd, Wimberlys			56	5	2
Aaron Brantley, Jordans			61	16	2
Salathial Houlton, Rushings			235	9	5
Josiah R. Burney, Whitfields			3	8	2
Joseph Harrison, soldier, do.			146	9	2

WILKINSON.

Jane Nesbet, wid. Mayos			16	22	1
John Cros, Fairchilds			130	1	4
Thomas Williams, orph. Ragans			123	24	2
Joshua Hawkins, Mathews			177	22	2

WILKES.

Daniel Harky, Rices			154	21	1
Polly Wootten, wid. Popes			93	15	1
William W. Prather, Lukers			137	17	1
Joseph M. Murry, Gardners			11	1	5
John Bailey, Lukers			146	26	1
Lucinda Parish, illeg. Hopkins			229	9	1

53d DAY'S DRAWING—May 7.

APPLING.

Richard Strickland, McDonalds			203	9	5

BALDWIN.

John Cone, sen., Thomas			73	8	5
Edith Howard, w. R. S., Buchanans			130	21	1
Richard A. Batson, Lingos			314	28	1
James Williams, Wicks			94	21	1
Anderson Redding, R. S., Reddings			99	22	2

BIBB.

George Bland, Lloyds			233	21	1
M. A., E. & W. Durden, ors. Rutlands			247	2	2
Randal Stewart, do.			155	31	1
David Preston, Pickards			34	11	1
Littleton Williamson, Beards			12	6	4

BRYAN.

John Rogers, Harveys			12	1	5

BULLOCH.

Isaac Strain, McCalls			176	17	2
Frederick H. Miller, Deloachs			185	11	3
Alexander Knightknight, Richardsons			24	4	4

BURKE.

James Brown, Corkers			115	21	1

Fortunate Drawers Capts. Dist.	No.	Dt.	Sec.
William Pinrow, Seegars	230	8	5
Jeremiah Murray, Thompson	202	4	2
William Murphy, Gawfs	15	4	1
Littleton James Clark, illegit, Wests	41	5	5
Robert E. Broadnax, Bayleys	224	11	2
Joel Gay's orphans, Seegars	34	2	1
Hambleton Boyt, Gordons	163	4	3
Albert Godbee, Dugas	9	1	1
James Dunn, Robinsons	140	7	4
John Obanion, soldier, Gordons	55	2	5

CAMDEN.

Gilis McDonald, Beckwiths	202	20	1
George W. Thomas, do.	271	17	2
James Scott, do.	14	17	2
Silvester Bryant, do.	166	1	2

CHATHAM.

John Hance, Geredons	199	10	2
Orps. of Geo. B. Harris, McDonnells	274	22	2
Louisa A. Loper, orp. of Asa, Reeds	143	10	5
Henry Cook, Gaddys	151	32	1
Patrick Connelly, Geredons	168	27	1
Richard F. Williams, do.	113	11	5

CLARK.

Henry Janes, Davenports	99	9	5
William Melton, Dickins	177	22	2
Henry Turner, Wrights	47	21	2
Josiah Espy, idiot, Espys	158	5	1
Jesse Hightower, Herndons	81	7	3
Benjamin Lampley, McDonalds	137	3	2

COLUMBIA.

Leonard B. Smith, R. S., Ramseys	70	4	3
Britain Carroll, R. S., Dranes	35	7	2
James Wright's orphans, Perrys	54	2	4
Sarah Collins,w. R. S. Talbots	259	3	1
Thomas Tuder, Ramseys	93	2	5
Henry Wood, Stallings	34	3	2
Edmund Cartledge, Coles	57	24	2
Orps. of John McDonald, Carrolls	89	29	1
Adam Ivy, Adams	24	5	1
Joseph A. Smith, Bealls	72	7	2
Thomas H. Sergeant, Stallings	19	21	1

CRAWFORD.

Joshiah H. T. Abbott, Lovetts	21	22	2
M. & E. Renfroe, fa. absent, Tillers	137	6	3

DE KALB.

William T. Dabney, Edwards	23	23	2
John H. Goolsby, Browns	195	7	5
Cary Wolf, Merritts	108	12	3
Isaac S. Wood, Spruces	267	15	1
Randolph Arnold, Bowlings	159	18	1
William Henry, sen. Smiths	62	3	2
Larkin Simpson, soldier, Hayes	252	20	1
Thomas Harris, sen. Conns	74	24	2

EARLY.

George A. Wilson, Wilsons	78	22	2

EFFINGHAM.

Lewis Mallett, Stricklands	113	17	1

ELBERT.

Jane D. Martin, widow, Tuckers	244	8	1
Orphan of Thomas Dye, Bells	143	20	1
Orps. of Lauchlin McCurry, Hortons	257	21	2
Samuel J. McCay, fa. ab. Harmonds	208	1	1
William Alexander, Blackwells	256	12	1
William Haily, R. S., Dunns	190	8	1
Aaron Brown, Bells	118	4	3
Orphan of Joseph Bell, do.	138	24	1
Isaac M. Tate, Tates	164	31	1

FAYETTE.

Fortunate Drawers Capts. Dist.	No.	Dt.	Sec.
Sarah Barrett, w. R. S., Craigs	28	11	5
Benjamin McGehee, McClendons	228	14	2
Marlar Millinder, soldier,9th	132	2	4
Elisha Lambert, R. S., Craigs	137	14	2
Elizabeth Dukes, hus. absent, do	202	23	2
Jesse Styrons, Roziers	223	12	3
Thomas Brown, Craigs	107	23	1

FRANKLIN.

Adam Andrews, Hudsons	20	32	1
John Patterson, Caudells	195	3	1
John J. Patterson, Stephens	14	21	1
David Payne, soldier, Stranges	309	20	2
Adam Bell, T. Chandlers	126	31	1

GREENE.

Thomas C. Edwards, Elys	266	6	5
John L. Seymore, Southerlands	10	19	2
Samuel Hogg, R. S., do.	218	25	1
Wm. Moore, jr. son of Hugh, Vincents	36	5	5
Stephen Evans' orphans, Webbs	118	6	2
Francis McGowan, Halls	134	2	1
Nehemier Watson, soldier, Astins	209	20	1
George B. Mitchell, R. S., Halls	211	23	1

GWINNETT.

Joshua Baker, Greens	265	5	1
Ransbird Light, Rollins	164	12	2
Alexander Pugh, Moors	160	4	2
Joseph Turner, Caruthers	65	3	4
William Bennett, Rollins	133	30	1
Berry Atwood, Hunicuts	243	3	3
David P. Allen, Woodroughs	14	30	1
Dickson Naler, Greens	23	24	1
Nancy Bryan, w. R. S., Maddoxs	4	12	1
James Collins, Bakers	72	8	3
James M. Downy, Moores	31	16	2
Nathan Carter, Woodroughs	40	27	1

HABERSHAM.

Paraman W. Tate, Tates	310	6	1
James Russell, Bakers	273	28	1
Sarah Stephens, w. R. S., Bryant	184	32	1
Hannah Thomas, for mins., Suttons	231	13	2
Charloty Chaffin, illegitimate, Bryan	43	21	2
Francis Self, Vickreys	140	11	2
George O. Bruce, Suttons	206	11	1
Daniel Chitwood, Tates	239	8	5
Mathew Arthur, R. S., Kenzies	59	4	3
Abraham Pence, Cross	362	3	4
Archibald Grayham, jr., Fains	207	11	2
Charlotte Baker, widow, Langstons	67	6	3

HALL.

Alexander Castleberry, Hardens	132	4	5
Elisha Eubanks, Harrisons	234	13	1
Sary McAlister, wid. Roberts	252	18	1
Leving Irving, Floyds	219	13	1
Philip Wade, Dorseys	114	1	3
John Yourbrough, Hardens	232	5	2
Ruth Henderson, widow, Hardages	239	19	2
Sampson Pierce, Roberts	105	12	5
A. Duncan, w. hus. d. l. w. Dorseys	81	7	1
John Holcomb, Roberts	63	3	1
Benjamin Whorton, R. S., Garrards	10	2	5

HANCOCK.

William Watts, soldier, Mahons	135	6	3
Burch N. Roberts, 106th	3	6	1
John Lucas, R. S., 102d	215	9	2
G. Bledsoe's orphans, 106th	172	23	2
Franklin E. Ford, do.	102	6	4

(165)

Fortunate Drawers Capts. Dist.	No.	Dt.	Sec.
John Dennis' orphans 112th	28	17	2
Francis Foster, soldier, Lewis	112	22	1
Theophilus Thomas, 103d	70	7	3
Martin Eubank, 106th	272	4	1
Newman Richardson, 16th	74	8	1

HENRY.

Mary Boreland, widow, Grays	239	11	3
Sarah Dukes, widow, R. S. Shaws	6	2	5
Robert Luckey, Smiths	106	11	1
Wiley Strickling, soldier, Millers	219	11	5
Nathaniel Borum, soldier, T. Harris	55	2	1
Gabriel Bulls, Millers	233	20	2
Prucy Richerson wid. R. S., Gosdens	50	10	5
Joseph Kirk, soldier, T. Harris	57	8	2
Jacob Maddux, Grays	75	21	1
Joseph T. Greene, soldier, Shaws	192	14	1
Joseph Benton, R. S. Millers	219	7	5

HOUSTON.

Thomas Cato, Becks	134	11	5
John Howell, sr. Yarboroughs	179	6	2
John Laidler, soldier, Smiths	211	26	1

JACKSON.

James Allison's orphans, Millers	28	10	1
John Wall, sen. R. S., Venables	199	23	1
Thomas Doster, Allens	196	7	5
Middleton Cowen, Lindseys	100	5	1
Samuel Watson, Gathrights	207	18	1
John Camp, Landrums	131	29	1
William Moore, R. S., Duprees	225	24	1
Jane S. Jarratt, widow, Lindseys	95	14	2
John Thornton's orphans, Rogers	41	10	2

JASPER.

Booth Fitzpatrick, wounded, Hines	255	11	1
Aaron Miller, Holmes	110	7	5
William Kilby's orphans, Baynes	193	2	2
Robert O. Dale, Wilders	206	2	2
James Horsley, Sparks	30	10	1
Jefferson Harrison, Owens	90	11	3
James Lindsey's orphans, Keys	233	9	1
Meredith Thurmond, Hines	114	15	5
Mordecai Hill, R. S., Sparks	175	2	1
Drury Long's orphans, Keys	33	12	3
Joseph Deason, Robersons	49	6	4
Wiley Story, Keys	116	29	1
Samuel K. Croll, Robersons	357	28	1

JEFFERSON.

Rebecca Garvin, w. R. S., Boyds	162	12	1
William C. Powell, Ross	19	13	2
Sarah Reese, widow, Cunninghams	43	22	1
Ebenezer Bothwell, soldier, Fords	26	17	2
Samuel C. Boyd, Boyds	142	6	1
Jefferson Williams, Cunninghams	57	12	2
Felix Parker, Marshalls	159	11	1
William Barrow's orphans, Jones	94	14	5
Samuel Fowler, Marshalls	204	11	5

JONES.

John W. Taber, Davis	118	3	2
Sarah Hammock, wid. Spinks	139	5	1
Harriet C. Ticknor, wid. Popes	147	14	2
Benj. Richardson, sol. Sullevans	225	3	1
Robert Cruther's orp. Spinks	130	10	1
John Tickner, Breadloves	227	2	2
Harris Gresham's mins. Blounts	157	30	1
John Caldwell, Gibsons	170	4	2

LAURENS.

Nathan Joiner, Deans	208	8	5

Fortunate Drawers Capts. Dist.	No.	Dt.	Sec.
W. W. Whitehead, Whiteheads	211	13	2

LIBERTY.

Alexander Willis, -7th	13	13	5
John Bell, 17th	24	22	2

LINCOLN.

Thomas Curry, sr. Graves	255	23	2
Valentine Wethers, Levritts	1	15	5
William Quinn, sr. Gideons	112	8	4
Nathaniel Curry, Graves	115	10	2

LOWNDES.

John Kley, sol. 10th	37	21	2

MADISON.

Alexander Veal, Stephens	135	3	1
George Lumkin, Adairs	60	25	1
James Thompson, jr. do.	81	4	1
Charles Polk, sol. Higginbothams	235	5	2

McINTOSH.

Henry Gignilliat, Demeries	175	32	1
Richard W. Gould, Thorps	229	5	4

MONROE.

Samuel Barber, Millers	137	12	1
John Wooten, Finchs	308	7	5
Lewis G. Hickman, Houses	166	8	5
Joab Grub's orps. Browns	172	1	1
Thomas Caraway, Millers	116	8	1
Ezekiel Reese, Pattersons	12	8	5
William Rowe, jr. Houses	33	23	1
Samuel Holly, Pattersons	144	23	2
Jesse Willingham, Johnsons	90	8	5
James H. Miller, Browns	96	8	5
John Brooks, Houses	145	25	1
Mary Tredeway, w.R.S. Finchs	29	12	3
Eliz. Russell, w.R.S. Johnsons	67	5	2
Thomas Kent, Browns	49	16	1
John Miers, Millers	214	4	3

MORGAN.

Richard Jones, Christians	156	8	1
Ornon Whatley's orps. Jennings	50	19	2
James Leavins, Sparks	94	1	4
William Feagans, sr. Jennings	232	13	2
John P. Duke, Griggs	29	14	1
Joseph Few, Shearmans	23	7	3

NEWTON.

John Middlebrook, jr. Dyers	254	2	2
William Patrick, R. S., do.	12	17	1
Thomas Justiss, do.	170	3	1
Nancy Walker, h. a. Graces	161	3	2
Jane Darnell, wid. Hays	60	8	5
William Sears, Moss	53	21	1
John Harper, Graces	134	11	1
John Pickard, Moss	36	14	5

OGLETHORPE.

Daniel Foard, Hardmans	9	1	5
Lucy Williford, w.R.S. Holloways	32	27	1
Lucy Jackson, wid. Rhodes	83	21	1
Isaac Meadows, sol. Simmons	146	7	5
James Dodd, sr. R. S. Billups	37	7	1

PIKE.

William C. Jones, Mays	202	1	2
Daniel Bowling, Suiters	117	14	5

PULASKI.

Tabitha Arnold, wid. Gilstraps	20	7	4

(166)

Fortunate Drawers	Capts. Dist.	No.	Dt.	Sec.
James Oliver,	R. S. Hendleys	58	20	1
James T. Thomas'	ors. Thomas	172	17	2
Philip Troy,	Scarbroughs	149	22	1
Mary Thompson, wid.	do.	75	15	2

PUTNAM.

William Arnold,	Stinsons	169	9	5
Joel Walker,	Blacks	236	11	2
Evan Harvey's orps.	Kendricks	31	22	1
William Mason, sol.	Jenkins	90	12	3
Ainsworth D. Gatewood,	Marcus	238	11	2
Abraham Cutliff,R.S.	Kendricks	136	8	5
Allen Robertson,	Allums	62	4	4
Thomas King, sr.	R. S. do.	112	13	2
Uriah D. Cornett,	Vinings	201	17	2
Cherry Melton, (idiot)	Brooks	26	2	4
Lewis D. Veall,	Bledsoes	162	5	2
Abedna. Cramford's ors.	Allums	225	5	4
Thomas Dixon,	Mizes	147	6	5
Armstead Richardson,	Bledsoes	138	12	1
Henry W. Hall,	Blacks	239	1	4

RICHMOND.

E. B. Webster,	Augusta	95	13	1
Leon H. Hamilton,	Huntingtons	138	4	5
John Payne,	Bushs	89	6	4
Robert Radford,	Blacks	50	7	3
Hawkins Huff,	Huntingtons	149	15	5
Lewis B. Rhodes,	Kellys	78	2	5
Ann R. Bradley, orp.	Treadwells	62	11	5
Adna Rowe,	Augusta	4	11	2

SCRIVEN.

Humphrey Boyzemon,	Poytress	149	16	2
Wright Cole,	Kemps	13	10	1
Zoah Spooner,	Humpreys	105	31	1

TATTNALL.

Edmund Revels,	Conners	123	4	4
John Coward,	do.	203	14	2
Levin Clifton,	McDuffies	88	10	3
Daniel Camron,	do.	22	8	3

TELFAIR.

James Rowell,	Wootens	97	10	3

TALIAFERRO.

Nicholas Lion,	Hammacks	42	5	1

TWIGGS.

Solomon Eikner,	Blackshears	41	7	1
William Cook,	Solomons	80	5	1
John Sims,	Wimberlys	91	24	2
Sus. Bryan, w.R.S.	Chamberlains	56	17	1
Javers Harvey,	Wimberlys	105	6	3
Martha Hays, wid.	Blackshears	161	12	3
Isaiah Wheeler,	Holidays	206	1	4
Rhesa Street,	Streetmans	2	7	4
Samuel Mathews,	Bosticks	93	4	3
Ors. of Jn. Parks,	Chamberlains	159	26	1

UPSON.

Aaron Holdridge, sol.	Petties	52	6	3
William Arrant,	Coopers	3	7	1
Jones Person's, R. S.	Myricks	203	19	1
John Slaughter, sol.	Paschalls	125	24	1

WALTON.

John Davis, sol.	Davis	76	3	4
James Love,	250th	173	23	1

Fortunate Drawers	Capts. Dist.	No.	Dt.	Sec.
Stephen Hayes,	Berleys	290	7	5
Lorenzo D. Wood,	Rays	157	24	1
Orps. of Jesse Hitchcock,	418th	192	4	3
Thos. Weathernton,R.S.	Bexleys	220	2	5

WARE.

Jeremiah Underhill,	Dowlings	213	33	1

WAYNE.

Nicey Moore, wid.	McKinneys	78	13	1
Jacob Litsey, orph.	Staffords	112	16	2

WARREN.

Jeremiah Griffin,	Parhams	229	3	5
Mary Wood,	Kinseys	140	24	1
Jane Johnson's illegs.	Hales	190	2	1
John Coxville,	Downs	25	5	3
Willis Rhymes, R. S.	Brinkleys	68	11	1
Adam Jones, jr.,	Jones	16	26	1
George W. C. Shivers,	Brinkleys	145	22	1
Charles A. L. B. Oliver,	do.	32	4	2
Thomas Rivers, sol.	Adkins	110	14	2
William Wynne,	Rogers	134	4	5
Booker Davenport,	Adkins	234	5	5
Rhody Harris, wid.	do.	202	5	1
Lucy Morris, w. R. S.	Parhams	228	32	1

WASHINGTON.

Augustus Phelps,	Tysons	6	12	1
Foreman Hodges,	Avans	32	10	3
Joel Deen, sol.	Woods	268	22	1
Simeon Bland,	Avans	185	14	2
Silas Carter,	Tysons	252	6	3
Philemon Noble,	Gilberts	288	20	2
John Orr, sol.	do.	187	21	1
John W. Allen,	McLendons	217	31	1
Archibald Peacock,	R. S. do.	30	1	2

WILKINSON.

Edmund Culpepper,	Shows	238	22	1
William F. Shepherd,	Mathews	198	19	1
David Mann,	Smiths	63	32	1
Jonathan Rigby's ors.	Fairchilds	255	14	1
John Brazile,	Smiths	54	21	2
Sampson Dillard,	do.	49	6	5
Balden Gray,	Mayos	8	5	2
Robert Giles,	do.	132	11	2

WILKES.

Joshua Roach,	Chunns	330	7	1
Willis Whatley,	Greens	127	19	2
Walter Maddox, R. S.	Hamocks	30	10	5
Samuel T. Jack (	Greshams	132	9	3
Rhoda Rakesstraw, S. w.	Charltons	60	10	2
Mary Ludduth, wid.	Hopkins	63	14	1
Margaret Scott, wid.	Reeves	200	17	2
James Whites' orps.	Rice	288	22	2
James Crew orp.	Amasons	228	22	2
William L. Wilkerson,	Carters	6	24	2
William Murphey's orps.	Lukers	12	23	1
Simpson Fouch,	Chunns	33	9	3
Stephen Mallory, R.S.	Ragsdales	170	23	3

54th DAY'S DRAWING—May 8.
BALDWIN.

Jesse Humphries,	Doles	45	1	1
John M. Carter,	Buchanans	233	22	2
Ezekiel Sewell,	Bivins	60	14	1
John P. Miles,	Wicks	221	2	1

(167)

Fortunate Drawers. Capts. Dist.	No.Dt.Sec.
William Daniel, soldier, Wicks	78 8 2
James S. Calhoun, Buchanans	304 7 1
William M. Kraatz, do.	281 1 2

BIBB.

John Green, orphan, Rutlands	104 7 5
Thomas E. Rodgers, Beards	126 24 1
Samuel Williams, illegit, Rutlands	202 5 2
Christ. Chambless, R. S. Pickards	167 18 2
James Bridges, Beards	35 11 1

BRYAN.

Duncan Graham, Stephens	150 5 3
George C. Linder, do.	87 4 4

BULLOCH.

Jesse Lee, Burnetts	28 33 1
Benjamin Morris's orps. Richardsons	246 4 1
Covington Cribbs, Deloachs	41 2 3
Joshua H. H. Frier, do.	62 24 1
Benjamin Gidens, Burnetts	45 17 1
Jephthah Hagin, Laniers	208 20 2
Aaron Odum, Deloachs	193 5 3
Thomas Mills, McCalls	110 10 1

BURKE.

James Tedder, Wests	83 18
Watson Leggett, Corkers	334 3 4
Charles Wheeler, Roberts	80 25 1
Mary Ann Odum, idiot, Gordons	6 9 5
John J. Skinner, illegitimate, Wests	46 20 1

BUTTS.

Parham Linsey, soldier, Kirksies	20 10 5
Benjamin Stalnaker, sol. Thaxtons	121 2 3

CAMDEN.

Elihu Atwater, Halls	46 29 1
John Omans, Hopkins	151 3 2
Mary Neely, widow, Baileys	326 1 4

CHATHAM.

Thomas Fulton, Reeds	29 2 1
Orps. of Nathan Adams, Haydens	227 4 1
Jacob Waver, McDonnells	257 28 1
John D. Timmons, Baines	146 1 4
William Adams, Gaddys	29 1 4
Orps. of Jonathan Cline, McDonnells	223 22 2
Jacob Beazely, Nungazers	274 28 1
Charles Lowther, Haydens	128 16 2
James H. McLearan, Scotts	156 31 1
William O. Williams	262 22 1

CLARK.

William H. White, Birchs	45 3 5
Richard Dickin, R. S., Dickins	52 6 4
Edward Paine, do.	145 5 4
Anderson Fambrough's orps. Alreds	190 7 1
David H. Love, Wrights	233 28 1
Edwin Edwards, Herndons	9 21 2
Orps. of Robert Marrible, do.	246 12 1
Richard M. Wilson, Davenports	30 12 2
Francis J. Fagg, fa. absent, Echols	112 2 5

COLUMBIA.

Archibald Heggie, Bealls	57 33 1
Wiley Shields, Boltons	162 4 2
James D. Green, Bealls	93 2 2
Jared Pounds, do.	236 4 2

CRAWFORD.

John Wells, Wilsons	6 1 4
William Wright, R. S., do.	244 23 1
Jacob Lagrone, Rhodes	136 12 5
William Griffin, Tillers	129 22 1

DECATUR.

William Donalson, jr. Douglass	33 7 4

DE KALB.

Fortunate Drawers. Capts. Dist.	No.Dt.Sec.
Silas Baker, Browns	13 8 2
Thomas Akins, soldier, Andersons	127 17 2
William Dobbins, Merrits	197 6 1
Abraham Glover, Bowlings	276 14 1

DOOLY.

Rearaden A. Tharp, Andersons	34 2 3
Maley Joiner, illegitimate, do.	123 4 3
Marshall M. King, Sarrs	17 21 1

EFFINGHAM.

Jep Dykes, R. S., Elkins	192 5 4
Christ. E. Arnestorph, w. Waldhaners	163 9 1

ELBERT.

Margaret Webb, w. R. S., Deadwilders	240 20 1
Dredzel Pace, Merritts	7 22 1
Lewis Stowers, R. S., Carpenters	66 4 5
David Kerlin, soldier, Boltons	113 3 4
Thomas S. Hansard sol. Hortons	167 9 5
Charles Wright, Butlers	17 6 2
Orphans of John Harris, Dunns	168 3 1
Ann Underwood, widow, Hortons	129 25 1
Joseph Underwood, Dunns	99 6 1
Joseph Nix, soldier, Harmonds	32 3 2
Robert L. Edwards, Tuckers	147 11 5
Horatio C. Bowen, Butlers	225 9 3

EMANUEL.

John Brown, 49th	173 15 2

FAYETTE.

Mary Cleekler, widow, Whartons	35 4 2
John Garrett, Wests	181 5 1

FRANKLIN.

David Garrison, Caudells	245 25 1
Christ'r. Sewell, R. S., D. Chandlers	235 11 5
John N. Prickett, Hudsons	245 10 3
John W. Bennett, d.&d. Blankinships	196 23 1
Sarah Mitchell, idiot, T. Chandlers	142 21 1
Samuel Mosely, jr. Tabors	215 4 3
William W. Mitchell, Boswells	167 5 1
William Iley, Blankinships	115 11 1

GREENE.

Aphier F. B. Todd, orphan, Dawsons	181 3 1
Thomas Colquett, Robins	126 6 5
Edward H. Cogbill, Woodhams	106 33 1
William Correy, R. S., Dawsons	169 18 1
Lodwick, Alford, Webbs	210 17 2
Austin Bunch, Newsons	33 4 1
William L. Astin, Astins	267 5 3
Littleton Channell, do.	160 19 1

GWINNETT.

Richard Medlin, Hunicuts	23 5 3
William Horn, Davis	86 16 2
James McDill, Greens	139 8 3
Nancy Respiss, widow, Finchers	96 14 1
John M. Gardner, sol. Gholdstons	119 18 1
James W. Moore, Finchers	241 23 1
John Barry, sen. Hills	29 14 5
William Guthrie, R. S., Hunicuts	21 8 5
John Foster, Greens	340 8 1
Crenshaw Duke, Bakers	17 5 4
Alexander Moore, Greens	61 3 4
John N. Alexander, Hunicuts	109 15 2
Gadwell Pearce, soldier, Evans	30 2 1
Thomas Compton, Moors	192 1 1
Willis Moore, Finchers	167 22 1
Lewis Parham, Robertsons	137 8 5
Lewis Brown, Finchers	102 13 1

(168)

HANCOCK.

Fortunate Drawers. Capts. Dist.	No.	Dt.	Sec.
Sarah Huckaby, widow, 112th	95	6	3
Mary Smith, widow, Masons	61	8	4
E. & M. A. Wagnon, ills. Mahons	57	7	1
Jesse Cason, 112th	278	11	2
Burwell Bass's orphans, 101st	225	19	1

HENRY.

Stephen Grice, Risons	26	13	2
William C. Fincher, Gosdens	71	3	1
William Crew, Millers	119	12	5
Francis Lansing, McVickers	262	10	2
John Thaner, soldier, Grays	165	9	1
Jesse Goodwin, Harris	158	9	5
Hinche Mitchell, Wards	250	7	5
Philp Craney, Shaws	28	6	1

HABERSHAM.

John Warmack, Esq., Suttons	106	7	5
Benjamin Roberson, Tates	197	18	2
James Adams, Vickreys	197	29	1
David Welch, Bryans	105	8	5
John Gass, Fains	1304		5
John Robertson, Martins	199	8	3
James Q. Chandler, Bryans	13	1	5
Mathew Arthur, do.	123	17	2
David Allison, jr. do.	130	7	5
Moses Ayres, Bakers	217	9	3
Henry Tankersley, Jones	131	5	3
William Dedmon, Suttons	376	7	1
John Simmons, soldier, Fains	26	14	1

HALL.

William Thacker, Olreds	178	21	1
Volentine Nix, Hendricks	232	20	2
Lewis R. Powell, Hardens	1	22	2
Elijah Wade, Dorseys	191	33	1
Gillum Presslar, Alreds	48	6	4
Burton Mullins, Wilsons	231	16	2
Joseph M. Bond, Alreds	118	11	2
John Martin, sen. Floyds	341	7	5
Amos H. Chapman, Brooks bat.	304	7	5
Enoch R. Nelson, Hardens	140	1	2
Thomas Reynolds, orphan, Wilsons	253	24	1

HOUSTON.

Henry Smith, Smiths	30	6	2
Robert Weare, Moores	188	4	1
Robert Liscoe's orphans, Batemans	71	9	2
Stephen Brown, Farnels	71	10	2

IRWIN.

Jesse Townsend, Bradfords	241	8	5

JACKSON.

Mary Benton, w. R. S., Staplers	162	3	2
Francis Bell, Venables	109	15	5
Hardy Strickland, soldier, Bowens	141	1	4
Francis Ayres, R. S., Duncans	31	12	3
Tolbert Strickland Bowens	137	9	1
Joseph Ruckford sr., R. S., Allens	151	29	1
Jonathan Hemphill, R. S., Venables	256	14	1

JASPER.

Washington Potter, Reeves	71	8	1
Johnson Pate, Barnetts	192	20	1
Lucy Carrell's illegits, Johnsons	83	32	1
Green Culbertson, Baynes	193	32	1
Ludwell Foster, Keys	241	15	5
Freeman McClendon, Dardens	121	16	2
Edmond Jenkins, soldier, Clements	38	3	1
Edmond B. D. Compton, sol. Dales	78	7	5
James Cates, orphan, Robersons	177	10	5
William Riley, R. S., Trussells	111	3	5

Fortunate Drawers. Capts. Dist.	No.	Dt.	Sec.
William B. Stokes, Holmes	121	3	4
James Haiston, Johnsons	103	23	2
Peter Calaway, R. S., Keys	205	5	2
Iseal Gaston, Hines	142	21	2
Thomas Wood, Reeves	75	23	1
James M. Martin, Wilders	137	5	1
Franklin Macklemore, Butts	235	9	2

JEFFERSON.

Elijah Harrell's orphans, Boyds	38	13	1
James Pitman, Cunninghams	181	12	1
John Douglass, Waldens	42	2	4
John Batts, soldier, Marshalls	41	7	4
John R. Foster, Beatys	122	7	5
William Walker's orphans, Elliotts	302	28	1

JONES.

Thomas Bazemore, R.S., Gibsons	152	32	1
Daniel Reynolds, Spinks	149	4	4
John Dorsey, Gibsons	116	2	1
William Morrison, Newbys	33	9	2
Caswell D. Morris, Bowens	136	6	5
William Eubanks, do.	161	26	1
William Ussery, Mullins	181	24	2
Moses Davis, sol. Sullivans	130	31	1
James P. Hansford, Breadloves	97	13	2
Washington Burnett, Robertsons	100	12	2
Jesse S. Ellis, Newbys	274	20	2
Lewis Tull, Davis	180	3	5

LAURENS.

Edward Graham, Powers	362	9	5
David Kirkland, orp. Hodges	95	9	1
Thomas Miles, Whiteheads	147	15	5
William Champion, Deans	193	2	5
John Hodnal, Barlows	84	20	2
Calvin Williams, Powers	55	15	1

LIBERTY.

Cornelius Laying, 17th	181	28	1
Josiah Westberry, 17th	294	8	1
Asa Daniel, 17th	189	14	1
Rev. Noah Laney, 17th	247	23	2
James M. Fail's orphans, 17th	250	20	1

LINCOLN.

Charles Wallace, Levritts	302	7	5
Shadrack Gaither, Parks	65	16	1
John Clark, Frasers	116	12	3
Judeth Bussey, wid. Graves	157	23	2
Timothy C. Dunaway, Parks	166	20	1
Austin Moncreaf's mins. Gideons	129	14	5
Thompson Hardy, (G). Hardys	126	9	1
Simeon Brunson, Levritts	19	4	4

MADISON.

John Moore, Adairs	26	7	2
Sarah Floyd, w.R.S., Hannas	254	1	2

MONROE.

Mary Lavare, w.R.S., Pattersons	20	5	5
Jeremiah Johnson, Millers	244	17	1
Stephen Barkwell, Johnsons	305	22	1
Hamilton Goss, Wrights	27	18	1
Marshal Douglass, Douglass	192	72	1
John Cram, Millers	97	32	1
Jonathan Johnston, do.	70	29	1
Stephen H. Martin, Turners	253	3	4
Henry Nobles, do.	116	6	4

LAND LOTTERY REGISTER—No. 25
[RECORDER OFFICE—PUBLISHHED BY GRANTLAND & ORME—PRICE $3.]

NOTE—Section 1 is Lee County—2 Muscogee—3 Troup—4 Cow*e*ta—5 Carroll.
54th *DAY'S DRAWING*—Continued

MONROE.

Fortunate Drawers. Capts. Dist.	No.Dt.Sec.		
Thomas Johnston, Douglass	82	6	3
Rosina Farmer, illeg. Knights	272	2	1

MORGAN.

Francis Farrell, Shearmans	193	15	1
Lewis King's orphan, Youngs	98	4	3
John P. Herndon, Brooks	197	3	1
Jesse H. Smith, Christians	310	1	4
Abraham McAfee's ors. Youngs	141	24	1

NEWTON.

Abner F. Dearings, Webbs	214	11	3
John Roberson, R. S. Arrs	66	10	1
Thomas Allmon, Graves	171	5	2
James Roseberry, R. S. Webbs	95	7	5
Dempsey W. Clayton, Smiths	102	9	5
John Freeman, Summers	159	7	2
James W. Black, Pullins	7	6	1
Samuel Henry, Smiths	335	20	2
Eliz. Whatley, w.R.S.Webbs	238	21	2
Wiley Jones, Dyers	42	10	3
John McKendree, Webbs	237	11	3

OGLETHORPE.

Henry T. Dawson, Rousseaus	197	19	1
Elijah Dupree, do.	317	151	
Josiah Clarke, Burfords	255	22	1
Edmund Jourdan, R.S.Rousseaus	27	1	4
Clark Taylor, jr. Lacys	271	7	1
Shelton Eidson, R. S. Rhodes	96	2	4
Nancy Andrews, widow, do.	65	8	1
James Colley, sr. R.S. Arnolds	126	8	1

PIKE.

William Plant, sol. Daniellys	309	15	1
Esther McDonald, w.R.S.,Hicks	61	24	2
Robert Clayton, Mayos	200	9	1

PULASKI.

John McCre, Thomas	57	25	1
Richard Thomas, Scarbroughs	184	6	3
Bartlett Baker, Bracewells	93	11	3

PUTNAM.

Henry Griggs, sol. Kendricks	320	1	4
Isham Shurling, jr. Allums	286	14	1
David Walker, Vinings	129	13	2
Isom Shirling, sr.R.S.,Allums	40	21	2
John King, do.	82	23	2
John Lagron, Kendricks	254	5	3
James Veal, sol. Good's	71	30	1

RABUN.

Joel Coffee, jr. Milligans	254	6	5

RICHMOND.

John McDade, jr. Kellys	22	15	5
S.A.&M.N.Fox,ors.Huntingtons	65	5	2
David Vincent, Wilcoxs	141	10	2
Wm. B. Fox, Treadwells	274	8	5
Lott Williams, do.	227	24	1
Edward Thomas, Augusta	35	2	2
Mary Lark orp. Wilcoxs	57	13	1

Fortunate Drawers. Capts. Dist.	No.Dt.Sec.		
William, Elm, Michael, John &Catharine Barry, ors. Mantzs	268	8	5
Martha & Jas. Hall, ors. Kellys	171	24	1
Sarah Handley, wid. Blacks	299	4	1
Adam Hutchinson, Augusta	226	18	1
Eldridge Morgan, Wilcoxs	96	6	2

SCRIVEN.

Joseph Spooner, Humphreys	62	8	5
Orps. of Jesse Freeman, Reaves	227	9	5

TATTNALL.

Groves Sharpe, sr. Graces	202	10	1
George Johnson, Dees	149	12	5
Frederick Mills, McCalls	338	8	1
William Dampier, jr. Conners	250	9	1

TELFAIR.

Duncan McIntyre, Barentines	217	19	1
William Graham, Lampkins	136	26	1
James Geltin, Bryans	101	8	5
Daniel McRainie, Wilsons	182	22	2

TALIAFERRO.

Solomon Holmes, Echols	157	16	2
Daniel Lockett, Towns	2	21	2
Thomas Pitmon, Hammacks	128	9	1

TWIGGS.

John Nicks, Wimberlys	33	8	2
William McClendon, Holidays	381	28	1
James Evans, Graggs	242	28	1
Joseph Hasty, Kellys	37	28	1
Elizabeth Arnol. illegit. do	56	19	1

UPSON.

William C. Wilson, Myricks	25	2	3
William McFarland, sol. Hattoxs	133	33	1
Stephen Johnson, sol. Paschals	104	20	2
Daniel Chandler's orps. Myricks	162	20	1

WALTON.

Jourdan Edwards, Davis	38	22	2
Jesse Vandiford, Rays	219	2	1
Thomas Russell, 250th	161	16	1
Elizabeth Ramey, w.R.S.Snows	105	20	2
Fuller Millsap, sol. Hudsons	175	9	1
Elizabeth Bailey, 250th	230	26	1
William Wright, jr. Snows	214	6	1
Adaliza Watson, 250th	211	2	2
Samuel Agnew, 249th	10	20	1

WARE.

John Stalby, Motes	89	26	1
John Gatland, do.	229	19	1

WAYNE.

George Warren, R. S. Staffords	29	8	4

WARREN.

Elishama Worthen, Downs	159	9	3
Winney Williford, wid. do.	278	6	1
Selah Wade's illegs. Kinseys	145	14	2
Losson Cody, Sanders	1	7	3
Mary Hobbs, wid. Kinseys	227	3	1

WASHINGTON.

William J. Donaldson,sol.Tysons	62	9	2
Mary Daniel, wid. do.	61	1	1

Fortunate Drawers	Capts. Dist.	No.	Dt.	Sec.
Theophilus Bateman, Mannings		68	15	1
Anny Hardy, illeg. Gilberts		148	12	2
The. Bateman's heirs, Rushings		158	6	1
Anna J. Graddy, (blind) Tysons		29	9	5
Nancy Nobles, wid. Gilberts		153	25	1
Roan Oliver, do.		125	9	5
Elizabeth Albritton, wid. Woods		100	15	5
Isiah B. Avant, Avants		160	3	2
Reding D. Thigpen, McLendons		11	4	2
William Nobles, Gilberts		107	13	2
William Williams, Warthens		116	12	5

WILKINSON.

William Crumbly, Currys		47	10	5
Levy Johnson, do.		40	5	4
Frederick Dominy, jr. Fairchilds		239	21	1
Catharine C. Gibson, orp. Currys		16	1	1

WILKES.

Nathaniel McCoy, Carters		189	4	1
William Freeman, Rices		294	4	1
John Adams, Lesleys		121	23	1
John Russell, Hopkins		21	23	2
William McLeroy, do.		204	13	2
William Reed, Hamocks		45	27	1
Robert J. Sherman, Gardners		95	19	2
John C. Pope, Woottens		206	7	3

55th DAY'S DRAWING—May 9.

BALDWIN.

Alexander Irving, Reddings		340	22	1
James Obriant, Ginns		78	33	1
John Oler, Reddings		91	12	5
Augustus V. Smith, Lesters		109	17	1

BIBB.

William Pickard, Pickards		93	4	4
Lewis Bryant, orphan, Rutlands		69	24	1
Drury & Sarah Minor, illegits. Bates		167	8	5
Peter B. McCready, Lloyds		267	3	4
Alexander Bass, Swearingins		108	21	2

BURKE.

Charles McCann, Gaffs		88	6	1
Bales Barley, Dugas		127	10	1
Thomas Mehahan, Corkers		313	22	1
Hardy Wooten's orphans, do.		37	10	5
Catharine Castellow, illegit. Lesters		158	2	1
George W. Evans, Seegars		246	20	1
Zachariah Daniel, Dugas		237	33	1
Theophilus Gains, soldier, Forths		255	12	2
Zilpha Sapp, wid. R. S., Thompsons		97	31	1
Hardy C. Maund, Andersons		58	19	1
John Griffin's orphans, Dugas		131	11	1
Anthony W. Turner, McKays		57	2	4

BUTTS.

James R. Williams, Hendricks		146	5	1
Yelventon Thaxton, sol. Thaxtons		276	16	2
William A. McCune, Adams		53	3	4

CAMDEN.

Joseph Lockaler, Coxs		46	17	1
Jacob Miller, soldier, Wards		115	9	3

CHATHAM.

Alfred Batty, orp. of Geo., Haydens		15	7	5
John Smith, U. S., soldier, Baines		133	15	1
Thomas Kirk's orphans, Geredons		242	24	1
Marg. A. Chapman, w. McDonnells		181	23	1
Elizabeth Clerk., orp. of George, do.		198	1	4

Fortunate Drawers	Capts. Dist.	No.	Dt.	Sec.
George Houstoun, Nungazers		41	22	1
John Currin, Williams		132	14	2

CLARK.

Archibald Norris, soldier, Davis		25	21	1
William Tredwell, Davenport		127	7	2
Mary P. Smith, w. R. S., Gahagans		40	13	2
Artemas Hovater, do.		81	27	1
John Hodge's orphans, do.		164	15	5
Bryan Connally, do.		138	8	5
Thomas, J. Rogers, do.		1202		1
Susan Crawford, hus. ab. Ransoms		110	22	2
John W. Graves, Wright		214	10	5
William Williby, sr. R. S., Alreds		33	6	3

COLUMBIA.

Sarah Blanchard, w. R. S., Culbreaths		127	6	2
J., P. M. & C. Heron, ills. Dranes		249	5	5
Crawford Johnson, do.		10	15	1
William Sims, soldier, Ramseys		23	5	5
Orphan Adam Walker do.		182	19	2

CRAWFORD.

Andrew Luster, Tillers		225	2	2
Abraham Prince, Moores		193	3	5

DE KALB.

William Elum, Harris		166	3	3
Joseph Woodall, Howells		131	8	2
Royal Clay, jr. Stephens		155	3	1
James Langston, Howells		145	12	2

DOOLY.

William G. Love, Sarrs		299	7	1
Morning Bush's illegitimates, 582d		53	17	1

EARLY.

Benoni Keeton, Porters		139	33	1

EFFINGHAM.

Israel Weitman, Waldhaners		26	6	4
Jonathan Snyder, R. S., Stricklands		53	2	4
Christopher Baily, R. S., do.		76	14	5
Gottliel Seekinger, sol. Waldhaners		34	7	3
James Crane, do.		167	29	1

ELBERT.

Orphans of Isaac Mobley, Bells		43	12	1
Samuel N. Baily, sol. Blackwells		141	17	1
John Cook, R. S., Bells		167	6	3
Thomas Pledger, Harmons		138	7	3
Mid. W. Doct. H. & Jas. M. Hickmond, illegits, Carpenters		79	1	3
Isaac Jourdan, Dunns		180	11	3

EMANUEL.

Jacob Daughtry, R. S., Fountains		46	6	2

FAYETTE.

William Halsten, Roziers		134	12	2
James Waldrope, R. S., Whartons		12	3	5
John Robbards' orphans, do.		111	6	2
John Adcock, soldier, Browns		167	20	2
Elisha Glass, do.		46	23	2

FRANKLIN.

Orps. Rich. Higgins, sol. l. w., Cokers		11	8	1
John Walker, McDonalds		45	23	2
George Wiley, Stranges		113	15	2
Nimrod Andrews, soldier, Hudsons		116	15	1
Ambrose Millivee, Boswells		277	20	2
Henry Ware, Hudsons		130	1	2
Chesly Cawthon, T. Chandlers		233	3	4

GREENE.

Thomas Jipson, Dawsons		134	13	2
Stephen Gatlin, Ranklins		162	3	5
Thomas Grant, soldier, Dawsons		122	8	4
Noah Pippin, Mercers		84	13	2

(171)

Fortunate Drawers Capts. Dist.	No.	Dt.	Sec.
John T. Winston, Webbs	262	7	5
William Cone, Greens	38	3	3
Samuel Gentry, Dawsons	196	20	1
Joshua Cook, sen. Astins	19	7	4
Celey Rowland, widow, Woodhams	39	23	2

GWINNETT.

Mark Miller, Woodroughs	166	5	3
John Defoor, Greens	165	25	1
Arbin Moore, Moores	228	1	1
William Thompson, Davis	145	17	1
Richard Garrett, Finchers	83	18	2
George Dusen, Wallis	245	22	2
Martin P. Dye, Hunicuts	243	7	1
William F. Roper, Whartons	137	33	1
John Hainey, Greens	42	20	1
Henry Kite, R. S., do.	156	2	1
Joseph Brown's orphans, Davis	47	6	5
James Rice, sen. Wallis	134	19	2
John M. Anthony, Davis	209	10	3

HANCOCK.

David B. Mitchell, orphan, 102d	255	3	2
John L. Crawford, 114th	227	16	2
John Barnhart, soldier, Colquetts	107	15	5
John Richardson, orphan Brooks	65	11	1
Absalom Tarver, R. S., 117th	187	3	2
Sally Henderson, w. R. S., 106th	196	2	3
George Osburn, 118th	75	12	2
Lucy Evans, w. R. S., 111th	116	24	2

HENRY.

John A. Conger, T. W. Harris	269	23	2
William Campbell's orps. Grays	152	22	2
Overton Phelps' orphans, Harris	17	2	5
David Kuglar, Wards	37	15	2
William Bell, orphan, Bryants	174	1	2
Robert Curry, Kites	48	6	1
Pinckney Rieves, illegit, Bryants	128	17	1

HABERSHAM.

John Wilkinson, Bryants	240	5	5
James Gettins, do.	101	8	5
Major Ward, Jones	107	2	3
Robert Whisinhunt, Bryans	161	31	1
John Black, do.	238	4	2
William Black, do.	231	10	3
Thomas Crumbley, R. S., Suttons	50	6	3
William Fagan's minors, Jones	26	13	5
Robert Brown, Martins	278	15	1

HALL.

Moren Moore, soldier, Floyds	187	13	1
James Hutchins, Yagers	1	21	1
Jesse Dobbs, Hardens	53	424	2
Joseph Atkins, Harrisons	241	30	1
John L. Brooks, Yagers	183	12	2
Elijah Hulsey, jr. Harrisons	182	27	1
Thomas Burford, Yagers	208	13	1
George Tippin, Smiths	161	24	2
Benjamin West, Hardages	250	16	1
Thomas Williams, Smiths	117	31	1
William House, Yagers	51	6	3
Leonard Elington, Floyds	16	19	1

HOUSTON.

Elizabeth Mobly, orp. Yarboroughs	125	6	2
Abner Wimberly, Simpsons	273	8	1
Ezekiel Wright, Prices	96	18	2

IRWIN.

Daniel Henderson's orps. Bradfords	207	5	1
William Knight, jr. Underwoods	209	19	1

JACKSON.

Fortunate Drawers Capts. Dist.	No.	Dt.	Sec.
Elize Ann Rooks, illegit. Moons	170	11	1
Elizabeth Doster, wid. Gathrights	73	2	5
John L. Williamson, Lindseys	351	3	4
Samuel Robinson, Rogers	60	22	2
Jesse S. Shotwell, Moons	183	7	5
John Robison, R. S., Doss	150	21	1
John McGinnis, Rogers	111	6	3

JASPER.

Daniel Knowles, Camerons	205	21	2
Shadrack Kimbrough, jr. Parkers	54	2	4
Meshack Teal, Wilsons	124	1	2
James Duncan, soldier, Posts	169	22	1
Allen Edge, Shropshires	222	13	1
Aaron Miller, Holmes	29	26	1
Lidia Gardner, widow, Robinsons	359	8	1
Notley Mobley, Farleys	102	13	5
Mark McLeroy, Wilsons	246	8	3
Nancy Adams, w. R. S., Camerons	156	25	1
Griffin Scroggins, Sparks	67	22	1
Levin Turner's orphans, Dardens	91	29	1

JEFFERSON.

William Cowart, Elliotts	45	8	4
Mary Mock, widow, Beatys	111	9	1
James Cotter, R. S., Boyds	59	2	4
John McDougal's orps. Cunninghams	244	15	1
James Atwell, Elliotts	223	2	1
Marget McCarty, widow, Ross	120	20	2
Alexander Morrison's orps. Boyds	134	24	1
Ebenezer J. Cottle, Marshals	204	3	2
Ann Linsey, widow, do.	242	8	1
Daniel Wilkinson, Beatys	309	3	4

JONES.

Isaac Duncan, soldier, Lewis	242	16	1
Thomas Gildersleeve, Woods	107	15	2
Elizabeth Farmer, orp. Davis	116	2	5
William E. Kendall, Woods	118	10	2
Seaborn J. Martin, Stewarts	35	1	3
Silas Meacham, Woods	40	8	1
John Blow, jr. Popes	144	11	3
S. Chambless, w.R.S., Robertsons	148	3	3
Green Miller, Newbys	155	4	2
Elizabeth Wall's mins. Stewarts	205	11	2
Thomas Hamlin, Bowens	267	3	3
John Lamar, R. S., Breadloves	255	2	3
Jemeson A. Bayne, Spings	326	28	1
William Moore's orps. Popes	261	8	1
John Dorsey, Gibsons	150	13	1
Dilly Washam's illegs. Newbys	11	17	2
William Ruth's orps. Robertsons	63	23	1

LAURENS.

Samuel Jones, Plummers	209	2	3
Penelope Eason's illegs. Mizells	357	20	2
William J. Lofton, Spiveys	65	10	2
Frances Ronalson, widow, do.	216	10	5
John Fulwood, R. S. Mizells	43	8	2
Joshua Clarke, Whiteheads	60	5	1
William Moreman, jr. Hodges	47	2	5

LINCOLN.

Francis Gatril, Graves	17	10	1
Isaac Willingham, do.	136	5	2
William Fleming, Parks	194	21	1
Nancy Fraser, wid. Frasers	214	2	2

(172)

Fortunate Drawers	Capts.	Dist.	No.	Dt.	Sec.
MADISON.					
Francis Simmons,	Hannas		189	9	3
M'INTOSH.					
Lewis L. Sexton,	Terrells		205	12	1
MONROE.					
Peyton Baker, sol.	Millers		5	9	1
Emmonas. Lairdrum, ill.	Knights		111	8	4
Zachariah Rooks,	Douglass		81	6	4
James Smith,	Douglass		134	15	2
Joseph Dawson, sr.	Greshams		156	5	5
Westly Fowler,	Wrights		120	8	5
Samuel Kight,	Greshams		23	13	1
Gatewood Chisolm's or.	Wrights		408	20	2
Richard Thomas,R.S.	Pattersons		315	22	1
John J. Sweatman,sr.R.S.	Finchs		63	18	1
Benjamin Davis,	Houses		60	29	1
Joseph Griffin, R. S.,	do.		147	1	3
Daniel Talley,	Pattersons		185	8	5
Howell Ray,	Finchs		161	5	1
Jackey A. Parham,	Woodwards		63	26	1
MORGAN.					
Frances Knight, wid.	Watsons		73	13	1
George W. Beards,	Christians		11	7	1
Henry W. Sawls,	Beasleys		3	3	2
James Gilpin,	Browns		16	7	2
Samuel Harris, sol.	Shearmans		106	32	1
And. C. Middlebrooks,	Jennings		81	6	5
Rebeckah Ballard's illeg.	Adairs		246	18	1
Hendley J. Sammon,	Stokes		230	10	3
Timothy Veasey's orps.	Hills		57	8	3
Emily Duke, illeg.	Christians		212	11	3
Roderick Leonard,	Sparks		77	2	3
MONTGOMERY.					
John McIntosh,	Wynns		35	10	3
James G. Conner,	Rials		190	6	2
NEWTON.					
Stephen Floyd, orp. R. S.,	Pullens		165	10	3
David G. Liggin,	Dyers		290	4	1
Dennis Hills,	Pullens		59	3	3
John T. Swift,	Webbs		189	16	1
Claiborn Retherford,R.S.	Summers		18	21	1
McKendree Tucker,	Pullens		39	2	4
Car., Milly A., Eliz. Catharine, Reb., S. & S. Pierce, ors.	Dyers		38	12	3
Andrew Pless,	Talleys		216	27	1
Charles Banks,	Pullens		137	10	3
Sally Mills, w. R. S.,	Snows		53	8	3
Henry G. Holcomb,	Trammells		43	6	3
Marshal Smith,	Talleys		67	23	1
OGLETHORPE.					
Wilumson James, sol.	Dixs		179	3	2
Bird Parks,	Arnolds		104	4	4
James McHenry's orps.	Smiths		185	6	3
Nimrod Ray,	Rhodes		217	2	5
David T. Evans,	Williamsons		171	7	1
Charles L. Smith,	Holloways		187	5	2
Elisha Ray,	Dixs		209	6	5
PIKE.					
Nicholas Johnson,	Weavers		306	1	2
James Wilson, sol.	Shehees		77	7	4
Andrew McComb,	Mays		248	3	4
John Martin,	Bryans		98	8	2
PULASKI.					
John Powers,	Scarboroughs		97	1	3
James Yates,	Gilstraps		88	32	1
Emery Sermons,	Sparrows		221	5	5
Milly Cardin, w. R. S.,	do.		33	3	1
John J. Lanier,	Bracewels		50	28	1
Thomas Davis,	Gilstraps		99	5	5
Robert Savage,	Powells		18	8	5
Galsey Smith's illegitim.	do.		171	16	2
Abner Averett's orps.	Kellams		80	9	1
PUTNAM.					
Mathew Britt,	Kendricks		126	27	1
Isaac Thrash, sol.	Goods		291	4	1
Geo. Milliron's min. f.a.	Clarks		241	2	1
Elias James, R. S.,	Blacks		205	5	1
Joseph Kimball,	Clarks		260	15	1
Mary Stinson, wid.	Wilkes		95	1	3
Polly Skagg's orphan,	Vinings		168	17	2
Luus Tomlinson,	Allums		264	20	2
Eliza Johnson, widow,	Mizes		181	3	4
William Madux, sol.	Bledsoes		80	2	5
Sary Burnsides, illeg.	Wilkes		79	15	5
Josiah Bowdin,	Allums		242	29	1
Thomas J. Childers,	Sparks		198	23	1
Eliza D. Lane, orph.	Bledsoes		19	5	1
Buckner Cook,	Brooks		225	10	5
RABUN.					
John Shed,	Godfreys		224	8	1
John Palmour,	Becks		188	22	2
RICHMOND.					
Elliot W. Gregory,	Huntingtons		136	10	3
Ezekiel Smith,	Wilcoxs		35	14	2
Henry Hatcher, R. S.,	do.		6	8	1
James C. Philpot,	Mantzs		118	30	1
John Beach,	Augusta		48	3	5
Henry Harper,	Hands		361	20	2
J. W. Hunter, R. S.,	119th		190	10	1
SCRIVEN.					
Mary Godwin, wid.	Humphreys		177	12	5
TATTNALL.					
Elhannon McCall,	McCalls		2	15	2
William Mann, sr. R. S.	Graces		136	18	1
John Dias,	Deloachs		249	8	3
TELFAIR.					
Nathaniel Ashley,	Lampkins		78	1	2
Wright Ryals, R. S.	Barentines		191	29	1
TALIAFERRO.					
Francis O. Smith,	Alfords		82	3	2
TWIGGS.					
Wm. Stephens,sol.	Chamberlains		17	19	1
John Broxton,	Wimberlys		125	27	1
William Sanders,	Kellys		55	13	5
Henry Parker,	Blackshears		217	5	1
Orps. of Jno. Crawford,	Solomons		71	18	2
Mary Wadkins, h. a.	Graggs		198	10	5
William Solomon,	Solomons		63	8	5
WALTON.					
Thomas Patterson,	Bexleys		97	7	5
James Bell,	503rd		151	1	4
James Treadwell, sol.	Snows		16	12	5
James Beasley, sr.	559th		47	8	2

Fortunate Drawers Capts. Dist.	No.Dt.Sec.
Judith Whotely, w. R. S. 559th	186 1 1
Hugh L. Bell, 249th	235 3 2
David Patton, 418th	224 4 2
Jane Young, 250th	227 5 2
Hezekiah Gates, sr. R. S. Rays	106 4 3
Moses B. Hustis, Bexleys	34 5 4

WARE.
Thomas Newburn, Greens	190 9 3

WAYNE.
Susan Gipson, illeg. Staffords	153 29 1
John Rooks, R. S. McKinneys	205 6 3

WARREN.
John Wright's orps. Bulls	62 32 1
Aron W. Grier, sol. .Hills	236 6 3
John Gibson, Parhams	172 1 5
Nicholas Harbuck, R. S., Bulls	167 13 2
Stephen Toller, Downs	11 3 8
James Hall, Jones	159 6 2
Randolph Revil, Sanders	106 25 1

WASHINGTON.
John Jordan, R. S. Jordans	11 22 1
Laban Horton, Oquins	248 16 1
Hugh McLean, Mannings	206 10 2
Charles A. Ely, Floyds	87 8 3
Nancy Robinson, wid. Woods	269 9 5
Happy Cherry, wid. Mannings	95 3 3
James Brooks, orph. Floyds	137 26 1
John Bedgood, R. S. Wimberlys	137 21 1
Benjamin Cook, jr. Currys	8 7 4
James Singleton, Warthens	384 7 1
Roan Oliver, Tysons	128 10 1
Hillory Hooks, Warthens	18 13 1
John Pournell, sol. Floyds	65 27 1
Claudus Bynum, illeg. Currys	130 17 2
Sherod Hamelton, McLendons	230 13 2
Joseph Mott, Warthens	248 23 1
John Lawrence, R. S. Jordans	312 3 4

WILKINSON.
Shadrack Adams, Mayos	365 7 1
Thomas McCuller, R. S. Barrys	69 10 3
Alfred Stapleton, Mandersons	48 8 5
William Lindsey, sr. R. S. Halls	34 19 1
Samuel Montgomery, Shows	48 2 3
Silas Lesslie, soldier, do.	155 11 3
Hardy K. Etheredge, do.	122 1 4
Tenneson Nobles, Smiths	90 14 1

WILKES.
Zachariah Slaton, Washingtons	261 7 5
Widow of Fred. Akin, Reeves	127 5 4
Andrew Hammilton,R.S. Lukers	121 4 2
John Rorie's orps. Carters	247 5 2

56th DAY'S DRAWINGS—May 10

APPLING.
William Hurst, Collins	13 23 2

BALDWIN.
David Hill, Perry's battalion	7 12 1
William Searcy, soldier, Wrights	278 6 5
Joseph L. D. Phelps, Lingos	9 19 2
Abner Hammond, R. S., Bivins	55 9 2
Lavinia C. Brown, illegit. Buchanans	152 5 5

BIBB.
Fortunate Drawers Capts. Dist.	No.Dt.Sec.
Hardy Akridge, Pickards	143 8 5
Green J. & Drucilla Glaze, ills. Bates	209 8 1

BRYAN.
Moses Johnson, Harveys	62 2 2

BULLOCH.
Joseph Hodges, jr. Lockharts	37 27 1
John Strickland, Richardsons	303 20 2
George Roddenberry, R. S., do.	255 4 1
Lucy Wilkinson's illegit. Turners	208 26 1

BURKE.
Wade P. H. Hulen, illegit. Andersons	32 11 1
John McCarrell, Dugas	157 12 1
Moses Davis, Robinsons	174 2 1
Robert Allen, do.	213 9 2
Henry Wimberly, Dugas	61 11 2
Neil Kennada, soldier, Lynchs	11 2 1
David D. Travis, Rogers	96 10 1
Alfred R. Jarvis do.	131 31 1
Catharine Anderton, widow, Roberts	75 14 5
Mary Watkins, illegit. Robinsons	42 2 1
Matilda Hatcher, widow, Gordons	62 13 5

BUTTS.
Stephen G. Hure's orps. Hendricks	241 22 2
Hiram Bellah, illegitimate, Johnsons	120 23 1

CAMDEN.
Levin Gunby's orphans, Wards	74 2 2

CHATHAM.
William Roche, Haydens	172 10 3
John Phillips, Teubrooks	72 22 1
Priscilla Atkinson, widow, Baines	262 5 1
Thomas Jefferson Doston, Scotts	144 3 1
Elbert E. Craig, Maines	84 8 2
Charles McIntire, Haydens	207 17 2
John Guilmartin, McDonnells	51 15 1

CLARK.
Benjamin Parr, R. S., Davis	11 13 5
Thomas H. Tuck, do.	195 12 5
William P. Greene, Gahagans	230 8 1
Dicy Davenport, w. R. S., Davenports	136 1 5
Rachel M. Berry, orp. Gahagans	75 33 1

COLUMBIA.
Robert B. E. Burke, Carrolls	204 8 5
James Bently Price, Adams	84 14 5
William Anderson, Carrolls	168 5 4

CRAWFORD.
Slady Warren, Dukes	50 7 4
Charles Wilson, Wilsons	75 9 3
Peter Parton's orphans, Hicks	25 3 1
John Wittington, sen. sol. Moores	51 8 3

DECATUR.
Jacob Miller, Douglass	140 5 4

DE KALB.
Solomon Tingle, sol., Smiths	117 21 1
James Adams, Merritts	107 28 1
Albert G. Adams, illegiti Merritts	190 7 5
Littleton Daniel, jr. do.	250 5 3
Zachariah Holloway, Bowlings	263 4 3
Charles King, Conns	57 6 4
Benjamin Jourdan, Smiths	80 5 4
Laughlin Arendall, Conns	339 22 1
Benjamin Sims, soldier, Smiths	192 19 2
Polly Devenport, illegitimate, Browns	160 5 4
Robert Smith, blind, Howells	185 25 1
Thomas Duty, do.	140 24 2
Battle Tankersley, Conns	130 6 2

(174)

DOOLY.

Fortunate Drawers Capts. Dist.   No.Dt.Sec.
Alford Alsabrook, 582d   51 13 5

EFFINGHAM.

Samuel Dasher, soldier, Treutlins	55	17 1
Nathaniel Duggar, Elkins	22	9 3
Selena Smith, widow, do.	97	10 1
Orps. of W. J. Spencer, Waldhaners	212	3 2
Nathaniel B. H. McCall, Stricklands,	22	1 4
Geo. Armstorph, sr. R. S., Treutlins	115	4 1

ELBERT.

Thomas Molden, Hortons	34	10 3
Jedediah S. Miller, Tates	43	32 1
Josiah Dobbs' orphans, Dobbs	142	2 4
Elizabeth Skelton, widow, do.	257	7 1
P.Cunningham, hus.d.in army, Boltons	248	33 1
Jesse W. Taylor, Dunns	178	10 2
Thos. Threlkild's orps. Deadwilders	18	12 2
John Coker, Merritts	158	26 1
Tillitha White, husband absent, Dobbs	73	5 4
William Arnold, Tuckers	133	2 2
Lucy Howard, hus. absent, Alstons	147	17 1

EMANUEL.

Lewis Heath, Moores	54	2 5
Margaret Boatright, w. R. S., McGars	224	14 1
Elizabeth Lamb. widow, do.	129	1 3

FAYETTE.

Moses Stamps, Craigs	173	13 1
John D. Still, Browns	8	8 5

FRANKLIN.

Andrew Mauden, soldier, Sanders	120	15 5
John Simmons, McDonalds	47	4 5
William Bryan, jr. Stranges	108	10 5
John Perry, McDonalds	70	15 2
Mary Gaddess, w. R. S., Walters	221	13 2
John Langston, Hudsons	120	13 2
Calvin Ellis, T. Chandlers	96	11 1
Orps. James Hudlow, Cokers	37	16 1
David Caudell, R. S., Caudells	167	16 2
John Jeffers, Tabors	50	5 1
Elisha Lowery, Cokers	252	4 1

GREENE.

Cordelia Williams, ill. Copelands	115	18 1
Sarah Davis, w. R. S., Halls	28	20 2
James M.| Sayres, Robinsons	133	24 2
Orps. of Sterling Grimas, Dawsons	11	8 4
Eugenia J. Tally, widow, Robins	137	18 2
William L. Strain, Dawsons	160	11 2
James T. Allin, Vincents	153	2 4
John Colt, do.	246	5 5
William H. Price, Greers	28	5 1

GWINNETT.

Aaron Camp, Whartons	192	22 1
Elisha W. Chester, Hunicuts	214	28 1
Sarah Baker, w .R. S., Gholdstons	182	28 1
Hiram McClung, Woodroughs	193	16 2
Richard Bass, jr. Robertsons	37	13 5
James Heaton, Shippys	144	24 2
Tilman P. Cole, Woodroughs	101	27 1
Balaam J. Bridges, Robertsons	240	9 2
Robert Foster, do.	155	23 2
Ira Segers, Finchers	4	7 1
Thomas M. Connel, Greens	21	13 2
William Kenney, Moores	196	2 1
David Winburn, do.	243	3 4
Lucy Hicks' illegit. do.	62	10 5
Elias Davis, Davis	117	7 1

HANCOCK.

Fortunate Drawers Capts. Dist.   No.Dt.Sec.

Jesse Bellings, 118th	121	17 2
Martha Ransom, widow, 112th	29	1 3
Gabriel Moss, sen. 103d	6	15 1
Elizabeth Johnson, w. R. S., 11th	213	3 4
John Johnson, soldier, Hillsmas	294	28 1
James Waller's orphans, 108th	13	28 1
Epaphroditus Drake, R. S., 109th	201	31 1
Thomas H. Davis, 113th	103	19 2
Jepthy Harrison, Masons	58	6 2
Miles Rachels, 114th	251	15 2
John Tindle's orphans, 104th	36	3 2
James B. Reese, 103d	85	13 5
Daniel Henry, 106th	135	9 3
John W. Brown, 110th	35	20 1
John Bartlett, jr. 113th	206	18 1
Henry R. Stembridge, sol. Bullingtons	173	24 1

HENRY.

Sarah Causey, widow, Kites	6	20 1
William Parker, illegit., Morgans	228	18 1
Finch Farrow, orphan, Shaws	209	29 1
James Gilbert, do.	202	20 2
Sally Dowdy, wid. T. W. Harris's	246	11 5
Obadiah Hasty, Harris	132	11 1
Joseph McConnell, Wards	25	9 1
Robert Beard, R. S., do.	9	15 1

HABERSHAM.

John M. Brock, Bryans	291	8 1
Thomas Hall, Fains	271	20 2
James Carrell, Bakers	134	8 1
Robert Moat, minor, Bryans	130	6 1
James Cockerham, sr. Bakers	175	13 1
Jacob Whitehead, Langstons	113	6 4
Shepherd Jenkins, Worshams	13	4 3
Benjamin L. Weems, Bryans	254	15 1
John Haynes, Suttons	73	29 1
John Eaton, do.	124	12 2
Levi Male, R. S., Bryans	189	10 3

HALL.

William Ross, illegitimate, Garrards	8	16 1
Elijah Bratcher, Yagers	77	14 1
Archibald Harris, Dorseys	170	2 1
Jehu Voyles, Floyds	37	3 5
John Wilson, Hardages	218	11 2
George Trout, R. S., Hardens	200	22 2
William Mullins, soldier, Garrards	126	2 5
Amos H. Chapman, Brooks battalion	148	7 3
Adam Elrod, Hendricks,	134	1 1
Priscilla Shewbert, widow, Hardens	72	8 2
Henry H. Maddox, do.	133	15 2
Jesse Broadwell, Floyds	54	103
Samuel B. Landrum, Hardens	195	2 5

HOUSTON.

Robert McManus's orps. Wimberlys	210	23 2
Silas Lisenbea, do.	67	10 5
Samuel Hart's orphans, Pitts	156	18 1

JACKSON.

Hardeman Hooks, Landrums	161	11 5
Jonathan Walharins, Bowens	51	14 1
Simeon Lord, Duprees	151	20 2
Lorick Betts, Winns	92	25 1
Russell Jones, Duprees	207	2 2
Isaac Buchanan, Venables	47	1 4
Joshua Roberts, Allens	262	2 1

JASPER.

Thomas Cooper, Camerons	190	31 1
Robert Crockett, Holmes	52	13 5
Sterling Mize, Butts	99	15 1

Fortunate Drawers	Capts.	Dist.	No.	Dt.	Sec.
Sarah Reaves, w. R. S.,	Hines	119	5	2
Benjamin P. Robinson,	Shropshires	223	33	1
George W. Heard,	Robersons	13	3	1
George Crouch,	Parkers	259	23	2
James Farley,	Robersons	2	3	1
Molly O. Johnson, w. R. S.,	Barnetts	23	15	1
William Simonton,	Holmes	7	30	1
Sarah M. Foster, widow,	Baynes	233	32	1
Samuel Sharp, soldier,	Penningtons	246	19	2
Harmon Guynes,	Robersons	272	3	1
Mary House, widow,	Camerons	67	29	1

JEFFERSON.

Arthur P. Fort,	Elliotts	15	17	1
Wm. C. Smoker, R. S.,	Cunninghams	207	12	5
John Fleeting's orphans,	do.	56	4	2
Mitchell Davis,	Waldens	169	8	1
John Jordan,	Ross	128	24	1
James Patterson,	Beatys	189	7	5
Louisa Calhoun, illegit.	Waldens	79	17	2
Nathan Batts, soldier,	Elliotts	119	15	1
John W. Lafavor,	Ross	8	2	3
John Kennedy,	Boyds	211	11	5
Jonas Hyslip,	do.	148	12	1

JONES.

Elizabeth H. Clark, illeg.	Gibsons	66	3	2
Ruben Roberts,	Robertsons	98	7	4
Catharine Hamlin, wid.	Bowens	85	18	2
Reubin Williams,	Lows	12	19	2
Alphonzo D. Delauny,	Breadloves	39	31	1
Mary Benton, w. R. S.,	Bowens	282	1	4
Roger T. Huggins,	Newbys	90	17	1
James J. Harris,	Newbys	90	17	1
John Garland, jr.	Stewarts	12	10	3
Daniel McKay,	Gibsons	249	12	3
Isaac Pippin,	Dosters	72	30	1

LAURENS.

Washington Randal,	Whitebeads	223	13	2
Benjamin Varsy,	Mizells	121	6	5
William Hester, (idiot)	Powers	40	4	3
Haley Moreman,	Hodges	32	2	2
James Thomas,	Mizells	248	31	1
William Oneil's orps.	Spiveys	83	8	3
Miceal P. Capper,	Barlows	89	4	1

LIBERTY.

Benjamin Law, 14th		207	5	4
Shem Butler's orphans, 17th		335	8	1

LINCOLN.

David S. Murray, s. l.	Hardys	259	2	1
Children of Ag. Dolittle,	Leveretts	98	27	1
Benjamin Samuel, sr.	Gideons	42	11	2
Richard Hunter,	Lonorgans	64	5	4
Richard Haynes,	Leveretts	164	3	1
Joseph Lee,	Graves	205	5	3
Nathan Bussey's minors, do.		20	8	1

MADISON.

Willis S. Jurrell,	Hannas	84	24	1
William Baxter,	Bones	246	22	1
Bradley Mayness,	Phipps	18	13	5
John W. Streetman,	Bones	214	22	2
William Lokey, R. S.	Caldwells	351	7	1

McINTOSH.

Enoch Davis,	McCraines	145	12	3

MONROE.

Thomas Vaughan,	Millers	170	32	1

Fortunate Drawers	Capts.	Dist.	No.	Dt.	Sec.
William C. Robertson,	Pattersons	110	32	1
Thomas W. Banks,	do.	51	18	1
Augustus W. Foster,	Johnsons	14	7	5
Anne C. Gooden, orphan,	Browns	10	3	5
William Travis, f.a.	Millers	114	11	1
Pleasant White, sol.	Higgins	46	14	1
Joseph T. Robertson, J.	Millers	153	27	1

MORGAN.

Levi Lane's orphans,	Boswells	316	7	1
John Braddy,	Beasleys	8	4	3
Peter Campbell,	Canifaxs	137	12	5
Ann Nelson, w. R. S.	do.	212	13	2
William J. Davis,	Jennings	35	7	3
Nathan Formby, sr. R. S.	Adairs	150	24	1
Eleazer Lockwood,	Youngs	197	11	3
Joseph Smith,	Jennings	77	6	5
Joseph T. Camp,	Walkers	99	8	4
Eliz. Middlebrooks,w.R.S.	Sparks	192	11	1

MONTGOMERY.

James Calahan,	Pridgeons	163	4	1

NEWTON.

John Costly,	Summers	125	7	2
Ben. & Mary N. Goss, ors.	Hays	219	4	1
Susan K. Ponder, orph.	Webbs	178	*4	5
Jesse Harris, sol.	Bakers	131	4	2
Sarah Hughs, widow,	Hays	154	12	3

OGLETHORPE.

Joseph Dupree,	Burfords	106	15	1
Miller Bledsoe, sr.R.S.	Rousseaus	40	11	5
John Varner,	Williamsons	25	18	1
John Varner,	do.	52	9	1

PIKE.

Thomas Morris,	Mays	104	10	2
James B. Carter,	Hicks	22	14	5

PULASKI.

Jacob Parkerson,	Hendleys	205	2	2
Joseph Haskins,	Kellams	13	27	1
Jeffer. Armstrong, ill.	Scarbroughs	250	5	5

PUTNAM.

Samuel Jones, soldier,	Blacks	207	32	1
Charity Wheelus, wid.	Sparks	7	26	1
George R. C. Walton, or	Bledsoes	135	6	2
Elizabeth McLendon, wid.	Sawyers	29	8	3

RABUN.

Zachariah M. Chandler, ill.	Mesers	11	2	5
James Dillard,	do.	220	2	3
Eliza Cantrill, orph.	do.	47	10	3
John B. Price, (black)	Godfreys	112	32	1

RICHMOND.

Charles & Jos. Burch, ors.	Kellys	191	12	1
Isaac Whitlock,	Huntingtons	201	1	1
Charles J. Jenkins, jr.	James	185	32	1
John Millhouse,	Augusta	34	17	1
Elizabeth Dismeuk, w.R.S.	James	186	6	5
Dabney Berry,	Blacks	65	4	3
George W. Summers,	Huntingtons	86	2	5
Abigail Hall, wid.	Blacks	207	23	2
George Murrah,	Huntingtons	94	19	2
Alex. Cunningham, (M.D.)	Ferris	134	27	1

SCRIVEN.

John Hendrix, R. S.	Humphreys	189	9	1
James R. Roberts,	Roberts	152	10	5

(176)

TATTNALL.		
Fortunate Drawers Capts. Dist.	No.Dt.Sec.	
Thomas F. Wells, McDuffies	95	24 1
John Sikes, Deloachs	225	21 2
TELFAIR.		
James Posey, Barentines	174	9 5
William Howard, do.	271	4 2
TALIAFERRO.		
Sarah Johnson, wid. Echolds	255	7 5
TWIGGS.		
Thomas T. McCollum, Stretmans	162	5 3
Henry Lee, Solomons	114	22 2
Orps. of Richard Johnson, Graggs	58	8 1
Murria Little, Holidays	19	7 3
Freeman Finch, Solomons	147	1 1
Wilson Deshazo, Graggs	196	18 2
Thomas Fulton, R. S., Solomons	98	7 2
Charlotte Pearce, wid. Graggs	133	26 1
Anne Harrell, wid. Streetmans	213	8 3
Oliver Tison, Chamberlains	67	15 2
UPSON.		
James Hamel, jr. Ellis	171	19 1
Allen Stiwell, Paschals	386	28 1
Alexander Scogin, Hattoxs	61	28 1
James Jordin, Hattoxs	95	18 2
Elijah Luett, Harrells	81	7 4
WALTON.		
Samuel Coleman, 418th	46	7 3
James Carmichael, Bexleys	152	25 1
Thomas Landers, 249th	54	11 5
William Duke, 503rd	47	7 1
Zachariah Ellison, 250th	257	8 1
John F. Marlow, illeg. Davis	225	10 3
Israel Moore, Bexleys	224	8 3
James M. Ware, 559th	50	23 2
Henry Summerlin, Bexleys	177	23 1
WARE.		
Sampson Hall, Moats	107	2 1
WAYNE.		
Mathias Manning, Mannings	115	33 1
WARREN.		
Randolph Tharp, sol. Kinseys	109	14 2
Mariney Hardeway, h.a. Stewarts	24	5 5
Amos J. Persons, Bulls	200	9 2
Eli Brooks, Kinseys	114	9 3
William Akin's orp. Rogers	135	1 3
Joseph Beall's orps. Jones	21	3 2
Goulden Armstrong, Sanders	131	13 1
WASHINGTON.		
Sarah Mathews, w.R.S.Mannings	97	14 2
Felix Maxwell, Whitfields	213	24 1
Calvin King, do.	89	5 2
Riley Cherry, Mannings	208	27 1
Henry Johnson's orps. Gilberts	264	8 5
Job Smith, R. S. Lysons	8	7 1
Sarah Hicklin, wid. Oquins	357	7 1
Samuel Field's orphs. Gilberts	226	24 1
Nancy Brookins, w.R.S. Jordans	203	28 1
WILKINSON.		
Joel Meadow's orps. Shows	106	5 5
John Kinsawl, Fairchilds	214	8 5
Alexander Adams, Mandersons	48	1 2
Howell Whitehurst, Shows	253	5 5

Fortunate Drawers Capts. Dist.	No.Dt.Sec.	
John Nun, R. S. Mandersons	113	12 2
Mason Underwood, Shows	177	17 2
Isaac Howard, Halls	193	3 3
Augustus D. & F. Russell, fa.do	239	10 5
Edward R. Heath, Mayos	100	33 1
WILKES.		
Ann Sheerer, w.R.S., Hopkins	270	22 1
John T. Graves' orphs. Chunns	184	12 3
William Cousins, Carters	244	22 1
Nancy Nelms, w.R.S. Hamocks	117	1 5
William Lackey, Popes	113	21 1
57th DAY'S DRAWING—May 11.		
BALDWIN.		
Tomlinson Fort, Buchanans	242	1 4
Nancy Hogens, w. R. S., Thomas	231	17 2
Isaac Fuller, Lesters	183	16 2
Thomas Batson, Buchanans	196	2 5
John Oler, Reddings	206	30 1
John R. Roberston, Rowes	108	13 2
Fred'k. Sanford's orps. Buchanans	176	31 1
BIBB.		
Henry Williams, Bates	180	7 2
Cadwell W. Raines, Beards	24	4 5
Daniel Cotton, Lloyds	48	18 1
Clement Clements, R. S., do.	40	5 5
BULLOCH.		
Elenor Driggers, wid. Richardsons	204	33 1
John Duke's orphans, do.	236	3 4
Samuel Davis, R. S., do.	164	24 1
Sarah Tillman, widow, Burnetts	103	14 5
Thomas Beasley's orphans, Lockharts	149	8 5
John Hudler, R. S., Burnetts	328	1 4
Mary Tallant, widow Lockharts	223	4 3
BURKE.		
Charles Ward, Bayleys	242	11 1
Howell D. Burke, do.	218	7 5
Charles F. Seeger, soldier, Dukes	269	2 3
Peter Lequeux, Bayleys	132	6 5
Mary Sharp, hus. absent, McKays	94	9 5
James Jeffers' orphans, Wards	198	20 1
BUTTS.		
Thomas Benton, sol. Thaxtons	164	3 4
CAMDEN.		
Ezekiel Brown, Beckwiths	1	17 1
Vilet Woods, hus. absent, Baileys	318	15 1
CHATHAM.		
Elizabeth Bourke, lunatic, Baines	78	12 1
Augustus J. Delazies, Haydens	170	13 2
George A. Ash, Haydens	194	11 1
Shadrach Harper's orps. Tenbrooks	193	5 1
Ben. Brantley, shoe maker, Haydens	243	20 1
Eliza Bowler, widow, Geredons	155	10 5
Cyrus B. Carter,	45	10 5
Henry Pallett, McDonnells	256	17 1
William Conrad, do.	253	18 2
Mary Sparksman, husband ab. do.	138	11 3
CLARK.		
William Thomas, Wrights	217	19 2
William Wright, Andersons	137	1 3
Alexander McRee, R. S., McRees	108	3 5
James D. Hewell, sol. Humphreys	38	8 1
Maria Ward, hus. absent, Wrights	243	5 2
Benjamin T. Mosely, Gahagans	87	10 1
William Love, Wrights	51	9 1

LAND LOTTERY REGISTER—No. 26
[RECORDER OFFICE—PUBLISHHED BY GRANTLAND & ORME—PRICE $3.]

NOTE—Section 1 is Lee County—2 Muscogee—3 Troup—4 Coweta—5 Carroll.

57th DAY'S DRAWING—Continued

CLARK.
Fortunate Drawers	Capts. Dist.	No.	Dt.	Sec.
Richard J. Edwards, Vinsons		173	12	2
Amanda Beardin, illegit. Greers		233	6	3

COLUMBIA.
Seth Hunter, Coles		204	23	2
Ebenezer T. Williams, Bealls		105	6	1
William Smith, Coles		161	22	1
William Lambert's orphans, Clarks		152	8	5
George Gray, Baileys		247	19	1
John Carroll, Dranes		41	14	5

CRAWFORD.
Sherrod Whittington, Millers		360	8	1
John Walpole, soldier, Lovetts		27	23	2
Maryan Hoskins, w. R. S., do.		154	5	5
Samuel Harper, sr., R. S. Wilsons		184	5	1
Frederick Busby, Tillers		44	12	3
David Lagrone, Rhodes		217	2	3
Solomon Tingle minor, Dukes		229	8	5

DE KALB.
William Wallis, Merritts		86	27	1
Simpson Wingo, Conns		110	8	4
Lucretia Jones, illegitimate, Bakers		94	6	4
Solomon Ray's orphan, Stephens		110	11	3
Ephriam Carson, R. S., Howells		67	6	1

DOOLY.
Joseph Grayham's orphans, 582d		94	13	2

EFFINGHAM.
George Arnstorph, sen. Treutlins		207	12	3
Peter Fryermuth, Elkins		64	13	2
James Davis, Stricklands		5	8	3

ELBERT.
Berrien Oliver, Bell		71	20	2
Nelson B. Burton, Tates		44	23	1
Mary Johnson, w. R. S., Dunns		147	13	1
Hugh Haircrow, Hortons		282	5	3
Thomas Bevvill, Tates		43	10	1
Isaac N. Boltons, Boltons		152	7	3
John Nelms, Hortons		66	4	2
Archibald Burden, jr. Harmonds		255	13	1
Orps. of Minter Cunningham, Tates		45	8	5

EMANUEL.
Samuel P. Yowmans, Fountains		57	26	1

FAYETTE.
James Edmonson, Roziers		212	17	1
Cheadle Cochran, Craigs		222	30	1
William Pike, Roziers		266	17	2
Nancy Jones, w. R. S., Browns		209	33	1

FRANKLIN.
Lewis Williams, R. S., Tabors		148	14	2
Catharine Dodd, w. R. S., do.		206	32	1
Sarah Boswell, widow, Hudsons		39	11	5
John Sandidge, R. S., Cokers		154	11	5
Cornelius B. Fulgham, Bennetts		142	3	3
John Moss, Walters		29	17	2
Larkin Walters, do.		7	5	1

GREENE.
Lewis Mosely, Woodhams		316	28	1
Gracy Copeland, w. R. S., Bruces		262	3	3
Gray Credille, soldier, do.		158	10	1
Zachariah Johnes, jr. Astins		103	8	5
Thomas Lackey, Greers		33	18	2
Daniel Jott, R. S., Dawsons		248	1	2

CLARK (cont.)
Fortunate Drawers	Capts. Dist.	No.	Dt.	Sec.
William T. McHargue, Rankins		47	12	5
Daniel Clifton, soldier, Robins		86	11	5
John Riley, R. S., Rankins		211	28	1
Daniel Underwood, soldier do.		202	4	1
James Ballard, R. S., Vincents		76	23	2
Osbern Orear, Bruces		142	9	2
Anderson J. Pealor, Woodhams		54	9	3

GWINNETT.
Thos. Ballard, sr. R. S., Robertsons		206	5	4
Job Smith, Finchers		88	8	1
Jemison Ware, Bakers		148	9	5
Joseph Downey, Moors		113	5	2
William W. Downs, Hunicuts		224	10	2
Thomas Matthews, Woodroughs		103	21	2
William S. Heard, Bakers		103	12	5
Thomas Connelly, jr. Moors		57	14	1

HANCOCK.
Thomas C. Taylor, 104th		20	3	2
Thomas M. Hunt, 103d		101	24	1
James Pilcher, 114th		69	3	4
Jesse Lumley, do.		246	9	2
Nancy Harton, widow, 101st		261	6	1
Goldman Tapley, 117th		7	11	1
Solomon Patterson, 114th		182	21	1
Enoch Simpson's orphans, 117th		12	23	2

HENRY.
John Adair, Gosdens		79	6	4
Jane Elliott, orphan, Grays		33	2	5
John McKee, do.		47	7	5
George Peters, Bryants		13	11	1
Sarah Baley, deaf & dumb, Millers		249	8	3
William Butrell, sr. R. S., Harriss		70	17	1
Mathew Bostian, Wards		4	11	5

HABERSHAM.
Sar. & Hester, orps. of J. Bush, Suttons		86	25	1
John Taylor, Bakers		18	1	2
Margaret Lockroy, minor, Jones		185	12	2
John L. Richardson, Fanes		242	10	5
James M. W. Gortney, Langstons		116	10	2
Ezekiel Catlett, Jones		214	4	1
Nathaniel Wade, do.		111	10	1
Elijah Hulsey, Bryans		171	9	2
Robert Blythe, Tates		283	6	1
John Anderson, Kenzies		181	9	1

HALL.
John Villard, Hardens		254	9	2
Robert Hamilton, soldier, Harrisons		31	8	4
Joseph Tarbutton, R. S., Roberts		110	13	5
John E. Davis, Floyds		8	2	5
David Waits, do.		81	11	1
Thomas Lodon, Walkers		183	16	1
Magdalin Hill, husb. absent. Floyds		219	7	1
James Martin, Garrards		63	18	2
Benjamin Atkins, Harrisons		315	7	1
James Lard, Roberts		107	2	6

HOUSTON.
Joseph Mims, Byanchards		297	6	5
Nathaniel Cain, Wimberlys		246	2	2

IRWIN.
Nathan S. Paris, 5th		242	2	1

JACKSON.
Margaret Sway's illegit. Watersons		208	32	1
Lewis Hiner, R. S., Landrums		43	13	2
Jonathan W. Walker's orps. Rogers		203	3	2

(178)

Fortunate Drawers	Capts.	Dist.	No.	Dt.	Sec.
Ansel B. Wilson,	Doss		37	1	4
William Runnells, jr.	Millers		245	7	3
Joseph Thomas,	Rogers		48	16	1

JASPER.

Fortunate Drawers	Capts.	Dist.	No.	Dt.	Sec.
Abel P. Wilson,	Wilders		225	1	2
Joshua Kee,	do.		139	14	1
Robert Chaffin,	Trussells		316	22	1
Elizabeth Sansom, ill.,	Hands		209	8	5
Joseph McMichael,	Dardens		107	24	1
John Cooper,	Barnetts		125	22	1
Abraham Shepherd,	Robersons		129	11	3
John Freeman,	Hines		222	11	3
William Sparkman,	Parkers		38	13	5
John Heade,	Dardens		27	4	2
J. B. Roundtree,	Hines		151	31	1
John Marshall,	do.		109	14	1
Rachel Williams, hus. ab.	Barnetts		226	30	1

JEFFERSON.

Fortunate Drawers	Capts.	Dist.	No.	Dt.	Sec.
Sarah Fleming, w. R. S.,	Jones		272	3	4
Elizabeth Gaken, widow,	Ross		124	18	1
J.A.,M.A.&S.L.Cowart, orps.	Elliotts		52	12	5
Burrel Stephens, R. S.,	Cunninghams		41	31	1
Bryant Lane,	Boyds		288	15	1
Mary Tarver, widow	do.		141	1	1
Greene M. Turner, orphan,	Ross		91	2	5
Eliza Milton, widow,	Boyds		109	17	2
James Little,	Causeys		361	7	1
Jonas W. May	Marshalls		270	10	2
M.,R.J. & Wm. Young, ills.	Beatys		22	12	3

JONES.

Fortunate Drawers	Capts.	Dist.	No.	Dt.	Sec.
James Wilson,	Hammocks		64	22	1
Uriah Jones,	Bowens		39	3	3
Richmond Gorden,	Stewards		11	15	1
Rachel Simmons, h.a.	Popes		302	22	1
Edmund G. Sims' orps.	Woods		66	8	5
Benj. Downing, sol.	Sullivans		249	22	1
Robert Hart, R. S.	Hammocks		35	21	2
Levi Sattywhite, illeg.	Mullens		183	10	5
Levi Manning's ors.	Hammocks		223	21	2
Mary Hendrick, w. R. S.	do.		174	7	5
Mary H. White, wid.	Newbys		168	2	1
Weston A. Franks,	Woods		186	23	2

LAURENS.

Fortunate Drawers	Capts.	Dist.	No.	Dt.	Sec.
Simeon Vick,	Powers		170	11	5
Blake Lambert,	Deans		268	2	4
Noah Slaughter,	Hodges		143	8	3
Barrel McLendon,	Millers		205	11	1
Dennis McLendon,	Beachams		51	5	2

LIBERTY.

Fortunate Drawers	Capts.	Dist.	No.	Dt.	Sec.
Jonas Dregors 3rd jr. 16th			61	15	5

LINCOLN.

Fortunate Drawers	Capts.	Dist.	No.	Dt.	Sec.
E. Cason,ag't forW. Cason,	Parks		115	6	2
Thomas Jaco,	Gideons		160	17	1

MADISON.

Fortunate Drawers	Capts.	Dist.	No.	Dt.	Sec.
Robert Glover,	Christians		18	3	2
Abraham Whitaker,	Adairs		235	12	2
S. Higginbotham, sol.	Hancocks		187	15	2
Edmund Magnes,	Caldwells		184	11	2

McINTOSH.

Fortunate Drawers	Capts.	Dist.	No.	Dt.	Sec.
John D. Lindon, orph.	Terrells		87	6	4
John N. Mandechie,	Demeries		226	25	1
Evelina, Sarah, Mary, William & Louisa McIntosh,ors.	Thorpe		115	12	2

MONROE.

Fortunate Drawers	Capts.	Dist.	No.	Dt.	Sec.
Giles Dewberry,	Millers		252	3	1
William Norris, R. S.	Browns		248	9	2
Moses Jones,	Stallings		190	1	1
Franklin M. Mills, orp.	Millers		241	9	2
John Adams,	Finchs		203	1	4
Math. Raiford, (Rev.)	Woodwards		103	28	1
Wiley G. Higgins,	Greshams		179	3	4
John S. Fountain,	Douglass		132	28	1
H. D. Youngblood,	Woodwards		50	27	1
Zachariah Sulevant,	Douglass		138	28	1
John Keith,	Millers		324	8	1
W.,D.&E.Ingraham,ills.	Houses		142	8	4
Alfred Brooks,	Millers		223	25	1
Nathaniel G. Waller,	Browns		14	12	2
Thomas Tabb.	Millers		86	6	1

MORGAN.

Fortunate Drawers	Capts.	Dist.	No.	Dt.	Sec.
James Ware's orps.	Harwells		129	27	1
Levi Hadaway,	Christians		241	12	2
Rich'd M. Gilbert's ors.	Beasleys		173	7	3
John Sandafur,	Youngs		307	5	3
Dempsey Hughes			80	16	1
William Prince,	Christians		160	23	2
Mathew Cockrum,R.S.	Harwells		248	23	2

MONTGOMERY.

Fortunate Drawers	Capts.	Dist.	No.	Dt.	Sec.
John McQueen,	Popes		60	6	4

NEWTON.

Fortunate Drawers	Capts.	Dist.	No.	Dt.	Sec.
Willoughby Beardin,	Hays		120	19	1
Richard Q. Lane, sol.	Newnans		15	2	1
Abel Camp.	Pullens		8	3	1
Catherine Webb, wid.	Alredds		26	11	5
James Moss,	Graves		149	21	1
John S. Welch,	Moss		195	14	2
Solomon Phillips,	Hays		109	3	2
Mary Barkley, wid.	Summers		70	20	2

OGLETHORPE.

Fortunate Drawers	Capts.	Dist.	No.	Dt.	Sec.
Richard Goolsby, R. S.	Floyds		158	3	3
Robert B. Hammett,	Rhodes		171	12	3
T. Fambrough,R.S.	Williamsons		223	10	5
Val. Meriwether, sol.	Devenports		42	11	5
Hnry Jenkins, illeg.	Dicks		126	15	1
Burwell Appling,	Lacys		390	28	1
Littleberry Edward's orps.	Hills		10	10	1
Elizabeth Pryor's ills.	Devenports		20	7	3
James Sorrow,	Floyds		98	9	2
Alexander, McCaul,	Williamsons		50	6	5
Charles Barnett,	Hardmans		94	21	2
Rhoda Hancock's illegs.	Lacys		63	21	2
Henry P. Jones,	Holliways		56	26	1
Isaac Thornton,	Lacys		165	23	2

PIKE.

Fortunate Drawers	Capts.	Dist.	No.	Dt.	Sec.
Jehiel McDonald,	Hicks		284	5	1
Washington Davidson,	Longs		270	11	2

PULASKI.

Fortunate Drawers	Capts.	Dist.	No.	Dt.	Sec.
Wiley Kent,	Sparrows		146	24	1
Marin Johnson, h.a.	Kellams		161	8	4
John Smith, R. S.	Scarbroughs		25	32	1
Pernal Sermons,	Sparrows		99	2	3
William Haddock's orps.	do.		114	21	2

PUTNAM.

Fortunate Drawers	Capts.	Dist.	No.	Dt.	Sec.
Susan Sturges, wid.	Bledsoes		42	32	1

(179)

Fortunate Drawers Capts. Dist.	No.	Dt.	Sec.
Shadrach Crouch, sr.R.S.Blounts	197	10	3
William Bradley, Sparks	1	10	2
Barton S. Park, orph. Bledsoes	120	2	3
M. McKissack, Allums	298	6	5
Anna Clements, w.R.S. Barnetts	201	3	3
Wiley Bryant, sol. Vinings	175	4	3
Uriah Ward, Clarks	255	7	3
Sarah Rutledge, wid. Kendricks	26	31	1
A. D. Wooldridge's ors. Barnetts	86	23	1
John L. Jordan, Sawyers	201	14	2
Alexander Morrison, Allums	100	5	5
Winney Hardy, w.R.S. Vinings	99	5	2
Edmund Turner, Blacks	75	22	1
RABUN.			
Joseph Brown, Becks	296	6	5
James Strauthen, do.	242	3	4
RICHMOND.			
William Clayton, Blacks	172	7	1
John G. Polhill, do.	16	14	1
Orps. of R. Walker, Ferris	119	23	2
Philip Dossett, R. S. Wilcoxs	180	4	3
William H. Egan, Hands	263	7	5
Sarah Collier, wid. Mantzs	152	24	2
William Moody, 123rd	49	8	3
SCRIVEN.			
John G. McCall, McCalls	201	8	1
Nelly Swane, w. R. S. Roberts	236	31	1
TATTNALL.			
Martha McLeland, wid. Dees	175	5	2
TELFAIR.			
Lew. A. L. Lampkin, Barentines	243	13	1
William White, Lamkins	178	10	3
Joshua Edenfield, Wootens	125	10	3
TALIAFERRO.			
David Christopher, Cobbs	25	8	3
TWIGGS.			
Freeman Sauls, Holidays	94	15	2
Orphs. of Dennis McClendon, do	137	2	5
Horatio Folsom, Bosticks	57	14	5
Andrew Cunningham, R. S. do.	46	22	1
William McLendon, Holidays	110	10	2
John See, Pearsons	259	21	2
Isham Denkins, Graggs	45	24	2
Orps. of Jacob Clance, Bosticks	54	5	3
Anna Wall. wid. Solomons	18	8	1
Orps. of Steph. Stephens. Kellys	106	6	2
UPSON.			
Permelia Harp's illegs. Hattoxs	115	32	1
Martha Miller, wid. Myricks	354	28	1
John E. Ofil, sol. Petties	130	3	4
Mourning Joiner's illegs. Hattoxs	195	10	3
Daniel Bridges, do.	241	3	1
Beverley Cooper, sol. Harralds	143	7	4
Edmund Powers, Coupers	123	13	5
Zachariah Bins, sol. Paschals	150	12	1
John McHargue, Harrells	265	6	5
WALTON.			
William Blair, 250th	195	3	5
Thos. Weathernton,R.S.Bexleys	271	1	2
Priscilla Baker, wid. Hudsons	35	8	2

WAYNE.			
Fortunate Drawers Capts. Dist.	No.	Dt.	Sec.
John Johnson's orps. Staffords	53	8	5
John M. Geigar, do.	267	2	4
WARREN.			
Joshua Newsom Akins	201	1	4
Elizab'h Killebrew, w.R.S.Jones	311	28	1
Charles Mathew's ors. Kinseys	279	7	5
Nathan Mash, R. S. Adkins	188	6	1
John Torrence, R. S. Hills	88	12	5
WASHINGTON.			
William Parish, Oquinns	236	32	1
Langston Dubose, Witfields	57	6	3
William Williams, Gilberts	38	3	2
Henry Hodges, sr. Avans	202	10	2
Thomas Amosons, Warthens	201	18	2
A. B. Shehee, sol. Mannings	64	9	3
Lewis Walden, Whitfields	253	12	1
Victory S. Townsley, Floyds	280	5	1
William Ricks, illeg. Woods	41	11	3
James Cook, sol. Andrews	179	11	3
Newsom Taunton, Warthens	234	10	3
Josiah Ganey, Wimberlys	122	30	1
James Ray, Rushings	183	6	2
Moses Mott, Warthens	221	3	4
WILKINSON.			
Eliz| Bellflower, wid. Fairchilds	65	7	1
Henry Yearty, illeg. Curreys	98	17	2
Harriett Ward, illeg. Shows	190	2	5
John Hinton, Currys	44	17	1
Thomas Majors, Shows	91	15	2
Jesse Mackey, Mathews	9	7	2
Moses Sutton, Currys	21	2	2
Sea. & Thos. Crutchfield,ills.Halls	58	9	5
Riney, Arrelly, Wiley & Emeriah Cherry, orphans, Halls	148	15	5
WILKES.			
John Campbell, Moors	96	24	2
Jesse D. Ennis, Richardsons	171	8	4
William Evan's orphs. Rices	95	12	3
Rebecca Allison,sol.w. Charltons	233	10	5
Timothy, Carrington, Amasons	155	2	3
John Rorie's orphs. Carters	229	11	3
Thomas Cooper, Lukers	207	7	3
Joseph Burks, R. S. Ragsdales	2	7	2
Nathan Blackburn, R. S. Hopkins	54	5	5
John Dozier, Moors	121	4	1

58th DAY' SDRAWING—May 12.
BALDWIN.

Frederick J. Green, Doles	192	3	4
William Hand, Lesters	193	10	3
Thomas Humphries, Doles	139	22	1
William Martin, Thomas	128	4	4
John Fuller, R. S., Lesters	235	22	2
Horace R. Dinkins, Bivins	28	14	1
BIBB.			
James Buzbee, Rutlands	45	1	2
William Martin, Bates	169	5	2
Sarah Sommerell, widow, Carrs	5	10	2
Henry Carr, soldier, do.	90	1	1
Noah Golding, Pickards	164	30	1
Frederick Holmes, Beards	228	21	2

(180)

BULLOCH.

Fortunate Drawers	Capts.	Dist.	No.	Dt.	Sec.
Dilly Williams's illegit.	Lockharts		66	30	1
Nusom Corbett,	do.		17	1	3
Elisha Garbett,	Richardsons		238	18	1

BURKE.

Isaac Messex,	Rogers		310	7	5
Ezekiel Murray,	Thompsons		113	33	1
Ethel & C. Dunford, orps.	Andersons		63	4	3
Simeon Lowry, R. S.,	do.		354	20	2
Abraham Proctor,	Wards		31	13	2

CAMDEN.

Joseph Mizell,	Baileys		53	12	3
James C. Pearce,	do.		215	14	1

CHATHAM.

James Shipper,	McDonnells		223	16	1
James F. Wood,	Williams,		54	3	1
William S. Deveaux,	Haydens		10	4	1
Martin Roney,	McDonnells		67	30	1

CLARK.

Jesse M. Nix,	Gahagans		319	22	1
Lemuel B. Robertson,	Lumpkins		196	19	1
Francis Moore, R. S.,	Greers		73	23	1
Isma W. Wooldridge,	Andersons		181	18	2
Reuben Turner,	Wrights		216	6	1
John Berry,	Frosts		9	8	1
R. & W. T. Magby, illegits,	Greers		263	1	4
Joel H. Stubbs,	Espys		153	2	5
Peter Dudly,	Lumpkins		47	4	2
W. B. & C. O. Hawes, orps.	Wrights		59	7	2

COLUMBIA.

Lewis Kemp,	Clarks		241	9	1
John W. Wade, R. S.,	do.		63	10	5
Susan Pace, widow,	Stallings		128	1	3

CRAWFORD.

John G. Cowen,	Tillers		62	13	2
John W. Ellis,	do.		283	16	2

DE KALB.

William Gunnell, R. S.,	Smiths		76	2	2
William Carr, R. S.,	Browns		85	2	5
John W. Gilbert,	Stephens		410	7	1
Abel Matthews,	Conns		54	1	2
John Jones,	Bowlings		70	28	1
Ulysses Montgomery,	Browns		155	8	4

DOOLY.

Elisha Copeland,	Andersons		260	1	2
Alfred J. Lester,	do.		254	11	1

EFFINGHAM.

Orps. George G. Nowlan,	Waldhaners		55	7	2

ELBERT.

John Roan,	Tates		16	7	1
Sarah C. Floyd, illegit.	Harmons		73	11	3
Joseph Vickery, sen.	Carpenters		121	2	4
Thomas H. Highsmith,	do.		1	9	1
Thomas Thornton's orps.	Hortons		189	17	2
Thomas A. Banks,	Blackwells		90	5	2
James Lofton,	Alstons		192	5	5

FAYETTE.

John Davis,	Whartons		39	15	2

FRANKLIN.

John S. Clements,	McDonalds		29	24	1
Jane King, w. R. S.,	Boswells		67	2	4
John Graddy,	Blankinships		190	11	3
Eli Taylor,	Tabors		116	22	1
Thomas Sparks,	Stephens		55	12	5

GREENE.

Nath'l Hines, sen. R. S.,	Copelands		39	7	3
Orphans of Jordin Bruce,	Bruces		49	2	1

Fortunate Drawers	Capts.	Dist.	No.	Dt.	Sec.
George W. Sanders,	Astins		224	19	1
Joseph W. Grimes,	Dawsons		192	21	2
Mary Daniel, widow,	Vincents		258	16	2
Andrew J. Daniel, idiot,	Robinsons		77	4	2
William N. Morgan,	Dawsons		177	27	1
Jeremiah Sanford, sr. R. S.,	do.		38	30	1
James Hammest,	Elys		237	1	4

GWINNETT.

Ambrose Niles,	Madduxs		271	14	1
Jesse Thrasher,	Moors		37	23	1
Booker Jackson,	Davis		151	19	1
Robert Freeman,	Moors		115	29	1
William Owen,	Greens		139	28	1
James Brown,	Davis		293	23	2
Samuel Reid, R. S.,	Finchers		117	10	2

HANCOCK.

Michael Ely, soldier,	Hillsmans		154	17	2

HENRY.

Samuel Stegall, soldier,	Breeds		36	9	4
John W. Messer,	Millers		89	17	2

HABERSHAM.

E. Bryan, ag't for minor,	Worshams		79	12	1
Elizabeth O'Kelly, w. R. S.	Kenzies		130	22	1

HALL.

John Collins, R. S.,	Garrards		87	7	3
Willis Prince,	Roberts		26	6	1
Joseph W. Stephens,	Dorseys		134	17	1
Isaac Head,	Roberts		176	5	5
Alexander Goggans,	Hardens		119	19	1

HOUSTON.

Absalom Cartright,	Batemans		141	6	2
Abner Baty,	Farnals		222	18	1

JACKSON.

Robert Williams, insane,	Rogers		294	1	4
Richard Cain,	do.		98	22	1
John Pugh,	Doss		238	92	
Middleton Lowrey,	Venables		1	29	1

JASPER.

Robert Trippe,	Prices		193	8	3
Hannah Henderson, widow,	Holmes		147	7	3
John Boyd,	Trussells		21	5	4
William Y. Fannen's orps.	Owens		68	7	1
William Higgason,	Wilders		72	12	1
Leatha Pennington, wid.	Baynes		117	12	3
Fanny Diggler, widow,	do.		221	5	2
Edwin Zinn,	Parkers		217	1	2
Richard B. Hornbuckel,	Robertsons		248	5	5
Rebecca Gray, w. R. S.,	Farleys		29	12	5
Jacob Hovater,	Trussells		103	6	4
Hannah Dabney, w. R. S.,	Baynes		111	22	2
Samuel T. Rhodes,	Butts		7	23	2
James Irwin,	Owens		161	19	1
			144	7	3

JEFFERSON.

John McDowl,	Ross		124	4	3
Richard Palmer,	Boyds		169	4	1
Burrel Stephens, R. S.,	Cunninghams		201	25	1
Lydia Lowry, widow,	Causeys		68	5	5
Thomas Wren,	Beatys		93	3	1
Joseph Marshal,	do.		188	5	1
Isaac Chance,	Jones		254	12	2
Catharine Allen, w. R.S.,	Cunninghams		217	26	1

JONES.

William H. Watts, illeg.	Mullens		267	10	2
Richard Meader,	Davis		23	1	1
Rush Hudson,	Lows		35	26	1
James Graves,	Duncans		109	29	1

LAND LOTTERY REGISTER—No. 27
[RECORDER OFFICE—PUBLISHHED BY GRANTLAND & ORME—PRICE $3.]

NOTE—Section 1 is Lee County—2 Muscogee—3 Troup—4 Coweta—5 Carroll.
58th *DAY'S DRAWING*—Continued.

Fortunate Drawers	Capts. Dist.	No.	Dt.	Sec.
JONES.				
Milley McClendon, wid. Gibsons	273	16	2
John C. Smith, Popes	145	20	2
Samuel Patrick's mins. Blounts	251	22	1
David Marshall, sol. do.	123	8	4
LAURENS.				
John Russell, Barlows	37	15	1
Mary Taylor, wid. Plummers	45	6	2
Jehu Smith, Deans	157	9	1
Alexander Chisum, Spiveys	82	10	1
John Locke's orps. Deans	13	21	2
LIBERTY.				
Robert Q. Andrews, 15th	234	11	1
Samuel Jones, 15th	159	3	4
Baxter Smith, 16th	20	15	2
LINCOLN.				
Nathaniel Holiday, Gideons	122	14	2
MADISON.				
Richard W. Sorrells, Caldwels	87	8	1
John Colly, sol. Moons	44	2	1
Thomas J. Nash, sol. Sanders	95	5	1
Barnett Stephens, R.S. Hannas	222	19	1
John Gossett, sol. Sanders	3	19	1
McINTOSH.				
Richmond Peacock, Howards	222	12	1
MONROE.				
Orps. of Henry Pye, Douglass	204	27	1
Arg. Parham, w.R.S.Woodwards	396	7	1
Thomas B. Reese, Pattersons	96	33	1
Charles Thomas, do.	91	5	5
Tammerlin W. Rees, Finchs	245	1	4
John Redding, sol. Pattersons	194	6	2
Samuel Barron, Douglass	133	11	2
MORGAN.				
Jesse Straten, Youngs	94	9	3
John Lawnius, Adairs	131	13	2
Elizabeth Wiggen's illeg. Sparks	179	5	2
Isham Mosely, Jennings	59	29	1
Burrell Coggins, Shearmons	2T1	20	1
NEWTON.				
Mary M. Daniel, illegit. Orrs.	284	6	1
Lindsey Clark's orps. Bakers	287	7	5
Zilphy Baggott, wid. Smiths	203	24	1
Michael Smith, Pullens	79	22	1
George Hays, sr. Hays	101	4	5
Eldridge Holeyfield, Zachrys	138	3	2
Jesse Hays, Smiths	157	18	2
Moses Brown, R. S .Clarks	299	20	2
James B. Randall, Hays	150	14	1
OGLETHORPE.				
James R. Hart, Holloways	186	12	5
James Jewell, Hills	36	12	2
And. Hartsfield, sol. Holloways	150	22	2
Smithfield Martin, Bells	87	12	2
Edward for Wm. Jones, Burfords	27	8	4
William Callahan, Dixs	106	12	1

Fortunate Drawers	Capts. Dist.	No.	Dt.	Sec.
Elijah Bingham, Hartsfields	123	14	2
Wylie Clayton, Mays	243	15	2
Edward Moore, Meavers	237	13	1
Absalom Spradlin, Daniels	70	21	1
PULASKI.				
John Caruthers, Sparrows	37	4	2
Larkin Armstrong, or. Hendleys	206	15	1
PUTNAM.				
Honor McDaniel, Sparrows	37	4	2
William Todd, Stinsons	53	7	5
John Foster, sr. R. S. Blunts	240	5	3
Churchill Allen, Blacks	129	18	2
RABUN.				
Hubbard Qualls, Godfreys	109	23	1
RICHMOND.				
Eliza Meigs, wid. Murphys	253	29	1
Henry Wagner, Treadwells	68	7	2
John Fox, do.	251	21	2
John Hodges, Ferris	28	13	1
Sarah McKeen, wid. Mantzs	41	12	1
F. B. T. Brown, 600th	230	3	2
Mary Bugg, wid. Wilcoxs	211	3	3
William Rowe, soldier.	167	10	3
Hezekiel Salmon, R. S., Wilcoxs	175	12	1
SCRIVEN.				
Wm. Farmer's orps. Stricklings	118	11	3
Louisa Kittles, orph. Reaves	97	8	3
Joseph A. Mock, McCalls	139	7	5
TATTNALL.				
William Starling, R. S. Conners	131	1	3
James Stephens, sr. Deloachs	16	14	2
John E. Elliot's orps. Dees	204	22	1
Turby F. Thomas, McCalls	58	9	1
Jacob Taylor, Graces	80	10	2
Asa C. Tanner, Conners	33	3	4
Margaret Bowen, h.a. McDuffies	345	7	5
TELFAIR.				
Elias Hinson, Wilkinsons	1	8	4
TWIGGS.				
Orps. of Joseph Ragan, Holidays	192	2	4
Orps. of John Adams, Streetmans	70	33	1
Mathew Coleman, do.	65	3	1
Orps. of Eph. Chance, Pearsons	254	3	1
Nathaniel Eells do.	20	15	5
Ama Wall, w. R. S. Solomons	121	15	2
William Wall, Pearsons	156	3	1
Joseph S. Wills, Blackshears	182	5	1
William D. Melton, Solomons	188	28	1
UPSON.				
Nathan M. Watson, Saunders	129	8	1
Alford Gasaway, illeg. Ezells	170	18	1
Stephen Douglass, sol. Dukes	194	7	5
WALTON.				
William Wingett, Snows	19	12	2
John Dickinson, sol. Davis	41	15	5
Judith Harland, wid. Pools	25	18	2
Edward Wilkinson, sol Rays	83	5	4

(182)

Fortunate Drawers Capts. Dist.	No.	Dt.	Sec.
Amanda M. Hall, 250th	66	3	3
William Johns, 503rd	141	10	3
John Barrett, Bexleys	111	2	1
Reuben F. Foster, Snows	158	1	1

WARE.
James McDaniel, Greens	103	5	5
George Jennings, Bryans	8	23	1

WAYNE.
Roger Crews, orp. McKinneys	51	16	1

WARREN.
William R. Low, Jones	169	33	1
William Manning's ors. Brinkleys	91	15	5
Nancy Burson, w.R.S. Sanders	260	33	1
Absalom Corsey's orps. Jones	166	8	4
Benjamin Bledsoe, R. S. Bulls	11	9	4

WASHINGTON.
Gent. J. Smith, sol. McClendons	62	23	1
James Darbey, sol. Castelows	60	31	1
Rhoda Cook, wid. Warthens	163	11	5
Asa Peacock, McLendons	242	5	2
Nathan Amison, Warthens	216	2	3
The. G. Robinson, orph. Avans	152	7	1
Samuel Brown, sol. Tysons	188	24	2
William Avery, Rushings	231	10	2
Christian Tinsley, Gilberts	99	23	2
Rachel Conyers, wid. Castelows	124	33	1

WILKINSON.
Burrel Bass, Shows	131	1	4
James Waters, sol. Currys	79	3	5
Jane Lawson, w.R.S., Halls	157	2	1
Sarah Butler's illegs. Shows	92	1	4
Elizabeth Williams, widow, do.	165	4	4
John Nun, R. S. Mandersons	193	23	2
Jesse H. Marshall, do.	49	9	3
Allen Cannon, Fairchilds	186	3	1
Major C. Collins, sol. Ragans	171	23	1
Richard C. Pattishall,R.S.Shows	287	8	1

WILKES.
Sarah Stokes, w.R.S. Richersons	86	3	4
George Wilis, sr. R. S. Reeves	141	3	4
Sarah Holtsclaw, wid. Greshams	151	26	1
John Booker, sr. R. S. Greens	41	4	1

59th DAY'S DRAWING—May 14.

BALDWIN.
Ezra B. Jones, Buchanans	117	11	3
Benjamin J. Parham, Wheelers	232	8	3
Elizabeth Hoy, widow, Bivins	24	13	1
William McGinty, soldier, Pitts	179	22	2
David Lovett, Buchanans	108	20	1
Orphans of Joseph H. Grant, Wicks	234	10	5

BIBB.
James Wagnon, Lloyds	160	22	1
Clement Clements, jr. do.	122	17	1
Elijah Ethridge, Rutlands	187	1	1
Mary Stephens, w. R. S., Lloyds	135	12	3
Solomon Warner, Carrs	9	13	1
Joshua W. Shripshire, Bates	82	24	1
Volentine Rowell, Lloyds	154	8	5
William Bivins, soldier, Bates	66	8	3
Alexander E. Patton, Flanders	215	10	1

BULLOCH.
Fortunate Drawers Capts. Dist.	No.	Dt.	Sec.
Allen Rawls, Richardsons	181	10	2

BURKE.
Thomas S. Few, Gordons	44	33	1
Peter Lequeux, Bayleys	58	15	5
Meredith Carson, Rogers	56	3	4
Wiley R. Meadows, Lynchs	62	2	5
Elizer Lewis, R. S., Corkers	234	4	3
Charles Boatright, do.	105	2	5
Eli Johns, R. S., Roberts	125	25	1

BUTTS.
John E. Robinson, Johnsons	163	15	5
Walker Fitts, Kights	42	26	1

CHATHAM.
Orps. of George M. Herb, William	182	13	1
William K. Gurineau, Haydens	202	3	4
H. Fryermouth, orp. of Jno., Baines	213	11	2
Mary McKean, widow, Haydens	143	3	2

CLARK.
Elijah Hendon, soldier Deans	48	22	2
Malcolm McLeod, Davenports	71	22	1
Sus. McCommon, w. R. S., McCres	116	6	5

COLUMBIA.
Milton A. C. M. Brown, Ramseys	133	9	1
Harriet Price, illegitimate, Boltons	67	8	1
William Bell, Baileys	162	2	4
Nancy H. Tindall, widow, Ramseys	273	10	2
Mountain Hill, Adams	193	22	2

CRAWFORD.
Christopher Cochran, Ellis	66	11	2
Charles Pollard, Lovetts	20	21	2
Burwell Bulloch's orphans, Hicks	215	9	1

DECATUR.
Rolen Tate's orphans, Hawthorns	354	3	4

DE KALB.
William Harral, orphan, Andersons	24	8	1
George T. Anderson, Browns	53	23	1
George M. Wagnon, Howells	135	3	3
John Pendley, Browns	55	2	3
Leonard Randal, Browns	55	2	3
Joel Farmer, Edwards	226	6	1

DOOLY.
Baily Swearingin, Floyds	61	11	1
William B. Adams, Andersons	10	6	4

ELBERT.
Mial T. Riley's minors, Dunns	39	7	5
Mary Alexander, w. R. S., do.	113	9	3
Mary Allgood, widow, Bells	195	21	2
John W. Grenway, Dunns	219	24	1
Henry Bourne, Alstons	72	28	1
Isham Parham, soldier, Webbs	113	10	1
Nathaniel Prothro's orphans, Dobbs	211	2	5

EMANUEL.
Mary Stephen's illegitimate Swains	175	6	2
Zelpha Rich's illegitimates, do.	66	18	2
Seaston Spence, 57th	67	6	5

FAYETTE.
John Moon, Dodsons	138	29	1
William W. Chapman, sol., Browns	183	12	5
Stephen Johnson, Whartons	89	4	3
Robert R. Cox, soldier, do.	76	11	5
Wiliam Wood sen. Dodsons	17	1	1
John Meggs, Wests	156	5	5

FRANKLIN.
William Pair, idiot, Jones	43	25	1

(183)

Fortunate Drawers	Capts. Dist.	No.	Dt.	Sec.
Pleasant M. Chandler, T. Chandlers		299	8	1
William Ayres, Andrews		98	16	1
Maria Hudlow, widow, Cokers		105	2	1
Martha Tinsley's ills. Stephens		148	8	1
John Crider, illegitimate, Cokers		128	12	1
William Rudd's orps., T. Chandlers		103	27	1
James Hutcherson, R. S., Walters		48	8	1
Lucy Pearce, w. R. S., Blankinships		78	9	1

GREENE.

John N. Harris, soldier, Astins		318	3	4
Joseph C. Adkins, Dawsons		258	15	1
William Currey, soldier, Rankins		252	5	3
John Couch Southerlands		245	5	5
Arthur Kennedy, do.		108	2	1
William Terrell, Winkfields		175	22	1
Ruth Dawson, widow, Dawsons		36	17	2
Thomas Johnson, Rankins		289	4	1
William Cone, Greens		119	4	1

GWINNETT.

Edward Brown, Hunicuts		102	9	3
Abner Coleman, sr. R. S. Davis		195	15	2
Mahala Alhey, widow, Hunicuts		231	22	2
Mark Miller, Woodroughs		129	2	2
William Bass, Robertsons		141	9	5
Stephen T. Ellington, Wallis		137	11	2
William Field, jr. Moores		113	13	2
Fleming B. Nance, Caruthers		221	22	2
James Cochran, soldier, Woodroughs		21	7	5
Isahel R. Smith, Hunicuts		166	7	3
Elizabeth Ursery's illegit, Moores		38	13	2

HANCOCK.

Lemuel William's orphans, 116th		28	8	3
Susannah Holsey, w. R. S., 101st		240	17	1
Fanny D. Garland, orphan, 116th		252	23	1
Isaac Knowles, soldier, Grens		194	12	5
Polly Edwards, widow 101st		153	12	3

HENRY.

Jane Adair, widow, Gosdens		189	26	1
Thomas D. Weems, McVickers		210	15	1
David C. Edison, Morgans		199	9	1
Joseph Catchings, Shaws		224	3	4
John Vining's orphans, Bryants		156	26	1
Charles Wilder, Allens		13	2	5
Israel Parker, Risons		67	6	4
Alexander G. Murray, Smiths		92	3	4
Elisha Edwards, Kites		9	22	1
William Casey, R. S. Shaws		82	5	1

HABERSHAM.

Hannah Thomas, for mins. Suttons		68	10	5
Ebenezer Fain, jr. Fains		223	19	2
Leason Spiva, Bryans		75	20	1
Amos Chaffin, jr. do.		206	20	1
James McCroskey, Jones		66	19	2
Charles England, R. S., Fains		193	12	2
Lewis B. Wells, minor, Bakers		209	7	1
Jesse Monroe, Fains		35	19	2
Reuben Clark, Tates		39	16	1
Asa Reeves, Martins		76	12	3
Charles Baker, R. S., Bakers		3	13	2
John Lovern, Tates		211	10	5

HALL.

Thomas Bottoms, Hendricks		150	10	2
Wade Waits, Floyds		137	7	5
John McWhorter, Wilsons		74	1	2
Elizabeth Smith, w. R. S., Hendricks		43	24	1
Henry Barton, Roberts		17	13	5
John Barton, jr. Hardages		206	6	3

Fortunate Drawers	Capts. Dist.	No.	Dt.	Sec.
Barney Braden, Hardens		125	7	3
John Head, Hardages		185	3	3

HOUSTON.

Mark Kemp, Wimberlys		74	1	4
William Crabtree, R. S., Farnels		112	18	1
John Darnell, Moores		36	31	1
Thomas G. Barr, Hancocks		101	23	1

IRWIN.

Joseph Ball's orphans, McCalls		232	10	1

JACKSON.

James Buys, Venables		131	14	1
Micajah Walker, Moons		229	6	5
John Kirkland, Winns		110	9	1
Walter Timbs, Storys		237	11	1
Wade M. Hampton, Lindseys		191	1	2
Samuel G. Chapman, Venables		79	13	1
Micajah Miller, Storys		226	5	3
John Camron, Landrums		115	6	3

JASPER.

Isaiah Hill, Camerons		19	8	5
Joshua Patrick, do.		253	6	5
Josiah Hancock, Hines		15	2	5
Booker Esthers, orphan, Butts		63	12	3
Samuel Rowel,, do.		130	14	2
Chauncey H. Palmer, Holmes		203	3	4
Thomas Green, soldier, Hollands		5	22	2
George Mitchell, Baynes		199	12	1
David Huson's orphans, Camerons		65	11	2
Barsheba White, w.R.S., Wilsons		50	9	2
Charles Ross, Shropshires		324	22	1
William S. Williams, Parkers		4	13	5
Lucy Johnson, widow, Barnetts		174	17	1
Mary Lyon, orphan, Penningtons		119	31	1
Joseph Dawson, jr. Keys		3	12	1
Sally Ann Arrant, widow, do.		187	14	2
Martha Edmonson, widow, Baynes		199	12	3
William Whitfield, do.		89	16	2
James S. Brown, Wilsons		256	15	2
Brice C. Johnson, Barnetts		151	2	1

JEFFERSON.

Whitfield Stephens, Jones		282	6	1
Arthur Watkins, Marshalls		183	10	2
Robert Foyil's orphans, Jones		197	21	1
Daniel McDonald, Elliotts		175	23	1
Arthur Watkins, Marshalls		239	1	2
Elizab. Brown, wid. Cunninghams		147	9	3

JONES.

Elisha Brown, R. S. Spinks		201	3	5
Ebenezer Z. Duffie, sol. Sullivans		134	4	2
Thomas M. Parker, Hammacks		53	4	4
David Jones' orphs. do.		32	3	4
Elizabeth McBride, wid. Duncans		144	11	1
Abraham M. Lowe, Newbys		156	2	3
Joshua Hudson, Taylors		115	3	5
Wiley Williams, Woods		301	6	1
Silas Taylor, do.		30	12	5
John Martin, Davis		7	1	5
Thomas Phillips' orps. Gibsons		140	12	5
William Stanton, Duncans		123	11	2
Samuel Moore, sol. Sullivans		51	19	2
John M. Hansford, Dosters		226	23	2

LAURENS.

Elizabeth Hudson, wid. Mizells		17	20	2
Jesse Warren, Deans		21	17	1
Samuel Spurlock, jr. Hodges		104	31	1

(184)

Fortunate Drawers Capts. Dist.	No.	Dt.	Sec.
James McLauglan, Plummers	194	29	1
Peter Faust, Deans	239	2	5
James Forests' ors. Whiteheads	111	5	4
John Spicer, Mizells	271	9	3
William Shiver, Spiveys	110	19	1
Calip Hollinsworth, Barlows	226	9	2
John McBanes' orps. Mizells	63	13	2
James Spears, Thomas	191	9	3
LIBERTY.			
Mathew Jones, R. S. 16th	195	9	2
Keader Keaton's orphans, 16th	78	2	5
Mrs. Valley, wid. 15th	170	6	1
LINCOLN.			
Martha Lyon, minor, Gideons	170	4	3
MADISON.			
James Bones, sol. Sanders	149	5	3
Dennis Hopkins, orps. Hannas	166	12	1
Joshua Sorrow, do.	91	32	1
George Russell, R. S. Culbertsons	12	20	1
Jesse Willingham, R. S. do.	202	8	5
John Shadow, Bones	77	15	5
MONROE.			
Thomas McBurnett, Johnsons	147	5	5
James L. Wagoner, Turners	166	14	1
Charity M. Kay's 3 ills. Wrights	107	2	2
James Houzze, do.	141	4	2
Charles Stewart, R. S. Browns	27	5	3
Henry M. Buckner, Stallings	21	11	3
James Maddux, sol. Millers	223	10	3
Nathaniel W. Chamberlain, do.	134	5	5
Polly Freeman, wid. Johnsons	5	13	2
Mark Ray, R. S., do.	71	27	1
John Wright, Wright	148	10	1
David B. Gibson, Browns	144	10	5
MORGAN.			
Lawrence Smith, Hitchcocks	214	2	4
John Marable's orps. Evans	210	20	2
Joshua Phillips, Dawsons	219	3	5
Robert Bailey, Youngs	224	22	2
Edmund Carlisle, R. S. Canifaxs	137	1	5
Jonah Welborn, sol. Brooks	171	5	1
Richard Ogilby's orps. Walkers	379	3	4
Daniel Gainer, sol. Watsons	292	3	4
Nancy Farrars' ills. Hitchcocks	262	5	3
James Few's orps. Shearmans	126	10	1
MONTGOMERY.			
John G. Hambleton, ill. Wynns	115	14	5
Burrell R. Colhoun, Wynns	59	27	1
John R. French, sol. do.	48	7	5
Henry C. Tucker, sr. R. S. Popes	200	7	5
James Branch, Wynns	149	6	1
NEWTON.			
Freeman Godfrey, Pullens	219	9	2
Thomas W. Mize, Hays	221	18	1
John Middlebrooks, jr. Dyers	231	20	2
Nicholas Welch, jr. Summers	158	16	1
Thom., Wm., Joseph, Nancy, I. J., & Chs. Ewing, orps. do.	182	7	3
James Coggins, Bakers	379	28	1
William McCullers, jr. Summers	47	21	1
Benjamin Pierce, Dyers	22	11	1

OGLETHORPE.			
Fortunate Drawers Capts. Dist.	No.	Dt.	Sec.
James Butler, Rousseaus	177	5	1
Little Kinneybrew, sol. Rhodes	20	13	1
Sally Wright, wid. Williamsons	88	7	5
William Chaplain's orphs. Hills	3	15	2
Daniel Hall, Williamsons	275	19	2
PIKE.			
Druney S. Patsen, Daniels	2	30	1
Sinclear Lancaster, sol. Weavers	129	20	2
PULASKI.			
David Priel, Scarbroughs	50	7	5
John Leith, orph. Sparrows	330	7	5
James M. Taylor's orphs. do.	168	9	3
Peter Gilstrap, Gilstraps	88	12	1
Daniel Harrel, Powells	96	2	2
PUTNAM.			
William Hawthorn, R.S. Allums	155	7	1
Joseph S. Battley, Chambers	25	1	1
Elizabeth Bradley, wid. Sparks	50	11	5
Silas Wilkes, Allums	266	10	2
Rod. McDonald's orps. Vinings	131	21	2
Thomas Ferrell, Kendricks	173	26	1
William Smith's orps. Sawyers	28	9	4
Phebe M. Elam, wid. Vinings	25	18	2
William O. Smith, Jenkins	43	7	1
Lewis Jones, Vinings	158	5	5
Chloe Allen, w| R. S. Bledsoes	50	6	4
RABUN.			
William Godfrey, Godfreys	68	8	3
Samuel Teel, do.	123	3	1
RICHMOND.			
Leah McGar, widow, Wilcoxs	348	8	1
Jesse Johnson, soldier, Blacks	156	5	3
John & James Lewis, ors. Bushs	192	2	2
Joseph C. Eve, Hands	190	8	3
George Hill, Raifords	94	8	3
William Keener, Hands	35	1	2
Lewis Perkins, Kellys	215	2	3
TATTNALL.			
Joseph Rogers, Conners	162	1	4
Samuel Thornton, Deloachs	90	2	5
James Tootle, Dees	92	16	2
Elizabeth Gilmore, w.R.S.Graces	11	2	3
TELFAIR.			
John G. Barrow, Clements	53	12	2
Pleasant Statham, Barentines	258	5	1
TALIAFERRO.			
Jos. D. McFarland, Hammacks	10	13	5
THOMAS.			
Isaac Faircloth,	299	15	1
TWIGGS.			
Orps. of Wm. Pearce, Graggs	83	15	2
Mathew Albritton, Streetmans	90	1	3
John L. Saxon, Chamberlains	163	2	3
George Williams, Blackshears	57	16	2
Thomas Arrington, Solomons	161	21	1
Orps. of A. Mitchell, Wimberlys	185	28	1
William Culpeper, Bostwicks	188	17	2
Nancy Chance, wid. Pearsons	54	6	5
Penelope Wicker, ill. Streetmans	114	10	5
Orps.of D.Thompson, Wimberlys	113	9	1

Fortunate Drawers	Capts. Dist.	No.	Dt.	Sec.
UPSON.				
Franklin Brown, Ellis		199	11	1
Benjamin E. Davis, Coopers		123	11	1
Candassee Brown, widow, 589th		26	3	2
William Mitchell, Coopers		200	28	1
Harriet Malone's illeg. Hattoxs		243	16	1
WALTON.				
Larken Brooks, Davis		256	6	3
Samuel Mains, R. S. Hudsons		261	6	5
William Brand, R. S. do.		83	4	2
Peyton Mobly, 249th		45	13	2
WARE.				
John Guttery, Motes		160	33	1
Sampson Carver, do		238	19	2
WARREN.				
Nimrod B. Yarbrough, jr. Downs		208	2	2
James Howell, Downs		255	16	1
Job Hunter, do.		294	8	5
Reuben Griffin, Parhams		251	4	1
Martha Wilson, wid. Sanders		105	18	1
James G. Powers, Bulls		27	8	3
Tabitha Granage, illeg. Sanders		50	14	2
Francis Davis' orps. Kinseys		49	3	1
WASHINGTON.				
Joseph Debros' orphan, Avans		205	18	1
David Wood's heirs, Floyds		99	13	1
Frederick Horton, Gilberts		157	16	1
William Rawlings, sol. Floyds		136	4	5
William Jordan, Currys		106	29	1
Uriah Peacock, R.S.McLendons		237	17	2
William Hunt, Whitfields		325	15	1
Drewry Gilbert, jr. Gilberts		325	15	1
Cato Riddle, jr. Jordans		177	13	2
Nathan Dillard's heirs, Floyds		45	2	3
David Barron, Currys		149	1	4
William Burgamy, Oquins		67	32	1
WILKINSON.				
Isaiah Dykes, Shows		217	6	5
Calley Ethridge, wid. Halls		166	5	1
Daniel Miles, Shows		28	19	2
William Kemp, R. S. Currys		273	3	4
Seabourn Kingrey, do.		144	13	2
Richard T. Porter, Halls		14	23	1
James Lindsey, Mathews		86	13	5
Eleazer Brack, jr. Fairchilds		179	7	5
James Crumbley, Currys		73	12	3
Absalom Sutton, do.		134	9	2
WILKES.				
Frances Akin, idiot, Wottens		27	19	2
Berry D. Johnson, do.		163	26	1
James Pyrreen's orps. Amasons		14	12	5
Lewis Norman's orphs. Ragsdales		6	2	4
Joseph B. Johnson,R.S.Hopkins		178	11	2
James Lester, Reeves		9	18	1
William R. Lockett, jr. Moors		249	10	2
60th DAY'S DRAWING—May 15.				
BAKER.				
William Low, soldier, Corquadalls		113	12	5
Jonathan Vaughn, Porters		163	2	2
BALDWIN.				
Timothy Redding's orphans, Lesters		183	6	5
Henry Garey, Pitts		175	20	1

Fortunate Drawers	Capts. Dist.	No.	Dt.	Sec.
Henry Green, soldier, Wheelers		108	25	1
Henry Lord, Pitts		185	4	2
Jacob Barrow, Buchanans		13	6	4
John Casey, Wrights		69	20	1
BIBB.				
Alexander Smith's orps. Pickards		234	20	1
James W. Langford, Swearingins		103	10	1
Arianna Harrold, blind, Rutlands		56	1	5
John Murphy, merchant, Bates		72	18	1
Charles Crawford, Flanders		173	15	1
BRYAN.				
John V. Wells Stephens		241	13	1
BULLOCH.				
John Hobbs, Richardsons		173	11	1
BURKE.				
Susannah Thompson, widow, Wests		174	8	1
Marg. A. E. Royall, illegit. Gordons		84	12	3
Polly Massa, husband absent, Lesters		67	8	3
Alcy Kercy, w. R. S., Bayleys		11	23	1
William Gunn, Browns		44	16	1
Pamela Attaline Summer, ills.Gordons		140	10	5
BUTTS.				
John Hodge, soldier, Masons		186	29	1
CAMDEN.				
Winneford Hebbard, w. R. S., Wards		34	5	3
Isaac Newton Chappel, do.		234	15	1
Jacob Mickler, do.		218	13	1
William Stafford, Beckwiths		297	6	1
Elizabeth Mills, widow, Browns		166	7	5
Samuel Walker, Baileys		186	2	5
Silas Weeks, Beckwiths		244	5	3
CHATHAM.				
James Roberts, osl., McDonnells		246	7	5
Mariah Speakman, widow, Geredons		51	14	5
Josiah Davenport, Baines		267	6	1
Orphans of Louis Cooper, Geredons		27	7	2
William H. Burroughs		276	6	5
Sarah Thomas, or. Reeds		118	6	4
Sarah Ann Cruise, wid. McDonnalls		149	6	5
Margaret Ratrey, w. R. S., Baines		245	19	1
Philip Ulmer, Reeds		166	4	1
Augustus G. Hazzard, Geredons		71	11	2
Oliver Dunley, Reeds		260	17	2
CLARK.				
William M. Archer, Gahagans		63	22	1
Richard Thompson, sol. Andersons		39	12	1
Stephen Jackson, McDonalds		135	9	5
John Thrasher, sen. Lumpkins		49	2	4
Jeremiah Wyche, Gahagans		307	8	1
James Pike, Alreds		217	6	1
Peter G. Dodd, soldier, Frosts		191	6	2
COLUMBIA.				
Edmund Buggs' orphan, Beall		95	27	1
Elias Welborn, R. S., Baileys		282	17	2
John Roberts, Adams		26	12	1
John S. Heath, Bealls		88	18	2
Thomas Whittawer, Dranes		206	3	2
Thomas Roberts, orphan, Clarks		61	3	5
Orphans of John Lyon, Culbreaths		171	6	5
CRAWFORD.				
Isaac E. Hudson, Tillers		121	10	2
David Adams, Dukes		201	28	1
DECATUR.				
Brassel R. Bradford, Douglass		113	8	5
Alexander Goden, Hawthorns		63	22	2
DE KALB.				
William H. Morris, Bakers		94	12	2
Jacob New, R. S., Smiths		4	9	5

(186)

Fortunate Drawers Capts. Dist.	No.	Dt.	Sec.
Edward C. Harris, Merritts	150	2	2
Micajah Goodwin, Conns	251	3	1
Robert Gentry, Howells	29	22	2
John Biffle, R. S., Bollings	16	4	3
Thomas Walley, Howells	7	18	1
Thomas N. Spruce, Browns	17	11	1

DOOLY.

James Shiver, jun. Sarrs	72	6	4

EARLY.

Daniel E. Philips, R. S., Speers	235	25	1

EFFINGHAM.

Han. Elizab. Rahn, w. R. S., Treutlins	210	20	1
William G. Porter, do.	14	4	3

ELBERT.

Thomas J. Haynes, Merritts	26	8	1
Nehemiah V. Dillard, Butlers	121	9	2
Orphans of John Tate, Tuckers	57	16	1
John Coker, Merritts	173	22	2
Richard J. Seal, soldier, Hortons	46	5	5
Joseph Allen, sr. R. S., Merritts	52	24	2
Robert B. Underwood, Hortons	173	18	1
James Dillard, R. S., Butlers	47	28	1
Benjamin Thornton, jr. Hortons	42	12	5
Theodosius Cook, Bells	131	4	5
Lucy Hudson, hus. absent, Tuckers	250	24	1
Fanny Jones, w. R. S., do.	96	16	1

EMANUEL.

Wilson Drew, McGars	87	11	5
Willis Carter Chasons	246	11	2
Jesse Martin, Fountains	185	23	1
Edward J. Thornton, Moores	84	11	3

FAYETTE.

John M. Turner, Whartons	15	6	4
William Reeves, Browns	65	2	2
Henry Brock, Wests	229	11	2
Joshua Reaves, soldier, Landrums	167	17	1
Barnaba Wilkinson, Browns	74	32	1

FRANKLIN.

Mary Borum, widow, Caudells	112	8	5
James A. Reid, Blankinships	231	12	1
Word H. Walters, Walters	336	8	1
Levi Baker, Stranges	178	27	1
Jonathan J. Hays, R. S., Cokers	139	12	5
Alexander F. Ash, soldier, Hudsons	108	11	5

GREENE.

William C. Blythe, Bruces	149	26	1
John Groves, Dawsons	229	10	5
John Davis, Colcloughs	21	9	5
Mary Smith, widow, Dawsons	84	3	4
Augustin Stovall, Webbs	41	30	1
Hugh Hall, Robins	23	10	1
Henry Carr, Halls	150	2	5
Elizabeth Holt's illegits, Woodhams	118	1	4
Garrett Woodham, do.	47	8	1
Dangefield Bowden, soldier, Astins	135	22	2
Abner Baker, soldier, Bruces	241	13	2

GWINNETT.

William Norris R. S., Bakers	200	10	1
Joseph Blocker, Woodroughs	16	13	1
John Bagby, R. S., Moores	148	4	2
Auron Kemp, Hills	236	7	5
Mathias Turner, Rollins	63	2	5
Thomas Gorden, Wallis	126	7	1
Stephen C. Naler, Greens	296	4	1
Love Dempsey, Rollins	181	24	1
James Heaton, R. S., Shippys	39	10	3
Richmond Baker, do.	96	13	2

Fortunate Drawers Capts. Dist.	No.	Dt.	Sec.
Anselm Anthony, soldier, Whartons	114	14	2
Littleton Pearce, Evans	60	14	2

HANCOCK.

Robert N. Wright, soldier, Bishops	34	4	3
Iredell Murphy, 101st	61	2	1
Andrew Edwards, do.	120	3	5
Elizabeth Robertson, hush. ab. 108th	295	6	5
Robert Mitchell, 102d	167	2	1
Samuel Watts, 11th	49	12	2
Levin Ellis, R. S., Adams	39	8	4

HENRY.

Reps Osborn, R. S., Bryants	147	25	1
George W. Hill T. W. Harris's	233	10	3
James Gorer, Grays	244	8	3
William Rose, Bryants	145	7	2
John R. B. Williams, Allens	306	15	1
M. A. & E. C. Edwards, ills. Bryants	213	13	1
Charles Miller, sen. Millers	116	3	1
William McGledney, Grays	38	24	1
Martha & Susan Patrick, orps. Kites	51	30	1
William Shaw, Bryants	5	25	1

HABERSHAM.

Jonathan Allison, Vickreys	60	3	2
Loyd McRonney, Tates	115	2	5
Silvaster Rice, for minor, Bakers	130	19	2
Jarrett Turner, Vickreys	70	11	3
Benjamin Caudell, Cross	235	9	3
Charles Baker, R. S. Bakers	55	10	2
Elizabeth Williams's illegits. Suttons	129	6	1
Amos Ludd,	47	3	4
Abner Stark, Suttons	104	7	5
Robert Trammell, Fains	93	14	5
James Elard, jr. Bryans	97	14	5

HALL.

Bennet Pettigrew, Alreds	207	6	3
Benjamin Griffith, Roberts	163	8	5
Henry Newton, Dorseys	169	12	2
John Hamilton, R. S., Harrisons	200	6	3
Marvel Wood, Dorseys	42	2	2
John Williams, Roberts	176	5	1
Henry Gaines's orphans, Smiths	185	10	1
Buckner Ragen, R. S., Wilsons	159	8	5
William H. Bearden, Hendricks	53	8	4

HOUSTON.

Figers Taylor, Farnels	31	11	1
John W. Williams, Batemans	212	5	1

IRWIN.

Alexander Hobby, Jerigans	112	6	2

JACKSON.

Sexton Harper, Bowens	132	1	4
Daniel S. Watterson, Winns	170	2	3
Agnus Martin, do.	285	17	2
Travis Nixon, Pairs	118	3	3
Gideon Gunter, Doss	215	21	2
John M. Henderson, Lindseys	157	6	2
Hickman Newbern, Duprees	229	3	2
William Gideon's orphans, Venables	6	4	5
James McElhannon, Pairs	55	4	5

JASPER.

William Bryant, Sparks	163	25	1
George A. Hill, Wilders	247	4	3
Nancy Hays, w. R. S., Dardens	42	7	2
Elizabeth Akins, husb. absent, Butts	227	30	1
James Thornton, Reeves	82	5	4
Mary Ann & Malvina Ivy, ills, Homes	85	16	2
Thomas Davis's orphans, Parkers	150	11	3
Wiley F. McCendon's orps. Dardens	74	27	1
Charles P. Downey, Butts	184	11	1

(187)

Fortunate Drawers	Capts.	Dist.	No.	Dt.	Sec.
Polly Vickrey, widow,	Trussels		55	5	3
John Waits,	Hines		174	5	3
John Gilcoat,	Wilsons		207	9	2
JEFFERSON.					
Washington Nunn,	Causeys		179	21	1
John P. Harvey's orphans, ones			316	15	1
Elizabeth Hadden, w.	Cunninghams		28	18	2
Allen Jones,	Jones		120	12	5
Thomas McQuotty,	Cunninghams		41	4	2
Charles M. Fort,	Elliotts		2	24	2
William Ham,	Cunninghams		77	17	2
P., P. & B. Hollan, fa. ab.	Marshalls		82	12	2
JONES.					
Jacob McDonald's orp.	Stewarts		133	13	5
Turner Chapman,	Blounts		130	20	2
Willis Jones,	Duncans		302	3	4
Sarah Willis, widow,	Mullins		163	3	4
Wilson Pope,	Woods		233	8	5
John Pasmore, sr.	Newbys		150	33	1
Josephus Pasmore,	Bowens		233	12	1
Daniel Duncan,	Davis		94	27	1
Hezekiah M. Harmon,	Stewarts		161	15	5
Lewis J. Groce,	Davis		24	1	2
LAURENS.					
Daniel Ricks,	Powers		139	1	1
Thomas Hughes,	Barlows		197	2	1
Foster Glover,	Hodges		143	29	1
James McLauglan,	Plumers		52	5	2
Deadima Jeter, h.a.	Whiteheads		175	19	2
LINCOLN.					
Benjamin Samuel, sr.	Gideons		155	1	3
James Loftin,	do.		109	1	4
Thomas Fraser,	Frasers		152	11	3
Nicholas Guice,	R.S.Lonorgans		237	9	5
MADISON.					
Samuel Eberhart,	Culbertsons		40	4	5
John McLeroy,	Bones		195	12	1
Willis H. Strickland,	Hancocks		6	30	1
Hubbard Hampton,	Adairs		107	10	3
Samuel Patton,	Culbertsons		61	2	4
M'INTOSH.					
Liddy Ginkin's illeg.	Howards		59	1	3
MONROE.					
James Darby,	Douglass		39	21	1
James Carter,	Pattersons		26	5	4
John Peace, R. S.	Johnsons		153	7	4
John Towns, R. S.	Wrights		38	8	9
Ezekiel Atkin's orps.	Douglass		178	8	5
John Pratt,	Woodwards		250	4	3
George M. Gullett,	Wrights		91	11	3
Kenian Flanagan,	Fergasons		177	15	2
MORGAN.					
Richard S. Park,	Boswells		113	5	3
James M. Greene, sol.	Evans		12	1	2
Nathan Maxwell,	Sparks		218	17	2
David Coleman,	Harwells		239	2	1
John G. Heard, sr.R.S.	Watsons		147	10	2
John Elliott,	Whatleys		219	5	4
Warren Oneal's orps.	Butlers		102	10	5
Jonathan Holmes, w. R. S.	do.		125	19	1
Hollin Herring, w.R.S.,	do.		125	19	1
John C. Morgan,	Sparks		32	3	3
Ausborn Harris,	do.		142	11	5

Fortunate Drawers	Capts.	Dist.	No.	Dt.	Sec.
John M. Giles, R. S.	Jennings		127	1	3
MONTGOMERY.					
James Branch,	Wynns		204	2	1
NEWTON.					
Hillsman Boughan,	Webbs		16	9	3
William Kendrick, sol.	Orrs		227	1	1
Richard Mathews, sol.	Bakers		191	7	2
Elizabeth Young, h.a.	Allreds		41	1	5
Elizabeth Shell, w.R.S.	Graves		351	28	1
David Thrasher, sol.	Orrs		88	2	2
OGLETHORPE.					
Damaries Baldwin,wd.	Rosseaus		200	18	2
Charles H. Lee,	Holloways		167	21	2
William Embry, R. S.	Hardmans		106	1	3
John Reynolds,	Burfords		157	11	3
William P. Triplett,	Rousseaus		232	5	1
Thomas Thaxton,	Williamsons		194	21	2
Berry Arnold's orp.	Bells		78	6	4
Herbert C. Rainey,	Arnolds		118	2	3
John D. Milner,	Bells		26	7	1
Charles L. Gilmer,	Seals		26	7	1
Simeon Goolsby,	Floyds		39	10	5
Isham Rainey, sr.R.S.	Arnolds		54	18	1
Valentine H. Meriwether,	Seals		295	5	1
John Sims, sol.	Billups		171	15	2
PIKE.					
Joseph Rye, R. S.	Orrs		138	4	3
PUTNAM.					
Daniel Sturges' orps.	Bledsoes		77	11	2
Obedience Holliday, w.Kendricks			57	8	4
Seaborn J. Melton, sol.	Jones		9	10	2
Isaiah Mitchell,	Kendricks		140	13	2
Edy Hall, widow,	Blunts		133	12	5
James Kilpatrick,	do.		234	27	1
RABUN.					
Mabry Carns,	Godfreys		162	14	2
Jonathan Critington, R. S.	do.		238	4	3
Elijah Coffee,	do.		95	7	2
RICHMOND.					
Collin McCain,	Wilcoxs		202	11	1
N. H. Caffin,	Bushs		63	10	2
Jane Mahar, wid.	123rd		130	25	1
Thomas Lang,	Treadwells		86	12	1
John L. Merideth,	do.		56	32	1
Eliz. A. Mathews,w.	Huntingtons		222	10	3
SCRIVEN.					
John Willson,	Humphreys		258	3	1
Edward Mobbly's orps.	Hunters		23	9	1
TATTNALL.					
Tarlton Knight,	Dees		174	6	2
Mark Bowen,	Corseys		198	2	3
TELFAIR.					
Margaret Smith, wid.	Wilsons		236	25	1
Dorcas Powell, widow,	do.		23	11	5
James Mixon,	Barentines		226	5	5
John Clements,	Lampkins		7	14	1
TALIAFERRO.					
N. R. Lewis,	Moores		311	15	1
William T. Oneal, illeg.	do.		4	12	5
THOMAS.					
Simpson Strickland,			112	19	2

(188)

TWIGGS.

Fortunate Drawers	Capts. Dist.	No.	Dt.	Sec.
William Hughes, Streetmans		199	22	1
Alexander Angeily, R. S. do.		84	9	2
William N.L. Crocker, Solomons		115	7	5
Edward Vann, Bosticks		198	24	1
William Ham, jr. Streetmans		108	24	1

UPSON.

Reuben J. Crews, Harrells	154	12	1
William W. Creighton, Coopers	213	31	1
Jacob W. Pearce, sol. Petties	134	6	2

WALTON.

Samuel Holloway's orps. 249th	56	20	2
James Benifield, Bexelys	31	2	1
Elizabeth Giles, w R. S. 559th	18	9	1
James Thompson, sr. sol. Snows	197	9	5
James Robertson, sr. 418th	211	11	2
Richard Gywn, 250th	13	12	5
John Dorithy's orps. Snows	59	9	5
John M. Bently, Bexlys	274	7	5
James B. Chick, 503rd	212	2	1
George W. Robertson, 418th	135	11	1
Robert Coker, Snows	229	6	3

WARE.

Anney Wigins, w.R.S. Greens	25	16	2

WAYNE.

Mathias Manning, Mannings	152	2	1

WARREN.

William Pitcher, sol. Downs	68	10	1
Gustus Lockett, Hills	111	24	1
James H. McFarland,R.S.Rogers	54	27	1
Clement Wynne, do.	98	2	1
Elizabeth Mathews, wid. Kinseys	179	29	1
Nancy Redding, wid. Parhams	320	22	1
Harral Neal, sol. Jones	136	1	1
Benjamin H. Briges, illeg. child of Nancy Downs, Downs	119	24	2
Benj. Ricketson, R. S. Parhams	5	12	3
John Lin. Stewarts	103	33	1
Nancy Rhodes, widow, Downs	156	3	5
Hezekiah Cooksey, Hills 2	167	3	5
Elam T. Yarbrough, Downs	89	4	5
Drewry Bynum, R. S. do.	71	10	1
William B. Jones, Bulls	16	2	4
Francis Hill, w. R. S. do.	58	6	5
Eadiththa Holland, wid. Brinkleys	4	2	5

WASHINGTON.

Daniel Turner, Whitfields	159	6	3
William W. Curry, oprh. Currys	180	3	2
George R. Wood, sol. Woods	81	11	2
Cark Blandford, R. S. do.	98	5	2
Thomas Moy, Whitfields	36	15	2
Seaborn Whittle, Woods	241	16	2
Charles Rogers, sol. Floyds	152	18	2
William Winson, Whitfields	64	19	1
Aaron Tomlinson, R. S. Jordans	251	2	4
William Martin, Floyds	40	15	5
Bet. & Lou Ethridge,ors.Oquins	227	19	1
Tracy Harris, Rushings	129	24	1
Allen Davis, Whitfields	185	9	2
John Eastward, sr. Oquins	43	7	2

Fortunate Drawers	Capts. Dist.	No.	Dt.	Sec.
Josiah Hood, Rushings		9	4	4
John Renfroe, Oquins		228	24	1

WILKINSON.

John Wooten, Shows	6	6	1
Nathan E. Mayo, sol. Barrys	82	9	3
Thomas Underwood, sol.Branans	157	9	3

WILKES.

Thomas Trouton, Moors	23	3	5
James Brady's mins. f.a. Lukers	34	2	4
Andrew Wolf, sr. R. S. do.	178	5	1
Winston Evans, Rices	111	13	1
Cornelius O'Leary, Moors	141	11	2
Archibald Bryant, Chunns	53	13	5
Joseph B. Cofer, sol. Reeves	132	33	1
Phoebe Stinson, w. R. S. Chunns	24	2	1
Jesse Calloway, sol. do.	208	8	3
Ansyl Hudgins, Hopkins	209	3	2
Rebeckah Hood, w. R. S. 164th	4	19	2

61st DAY'S DRAWING—May 16.

APPLING.

Malachi Harper, Morgans	62	4	2
Ciler Framan, Collins	73	33	1
William Overstreet, McDonnells	199	11	2

BALDWIN.

Cannon R. Rogers' orps. Lesters	48	32	1
James Rousseau's orps. Buchanans	254	13	2
Nathaniel Knapp, do.	119	3	3
Milton N. Howard's orps. Bivins	30	9	5

BIBB.

M. A., S. W., & H. S. Riley, orps. Carrs	10	16	5
William Riley, soldier, Bates	127	7	1
Daniel Wadsworth, Lloyds	250	12	1
Jeremiah Welcher, Beards	120	29	1
Wiley Squires, Bates	350	7	1
Ann Hardin, widow, Flanders	33	6	1
Robert Thompson, Beards	265	7	5
John Scott, R S., Pickards	176	4	3

BRYAN.

E., L., M. & R. Hodges, Harveys	83	1	5

BULLOCH.

Benjamin Hodges' orphans. McCalls	99	13	2
William Miller R. S., Deloachs	178	1	2

BURKE.

Richard S. Brown, Corkers	20	14	5
Elizabeth Gordy, widow, Lynchs	104	3	3
Charles Roberts, orphan, Roberts	152	14	2
Sarah M. Marsh, illegit., Segars	137	29	1
Rigdon Heath, Wests	110	16	1
Lemon Dunn, Bayleys	51	7	5

BUTTS.

Sandrew Parker, Chapmans	193	9	3

CAMDEN.

Mary A. Hadderly, orphan, Wards	133	19	2

CHATHAM.

Robert Carr, McDonnells	199	6	2
John C. Gromet, Geredons	136	11	5
Thomas Bessinger, Haydens	222	8	5
Charles B. Jones, Williams	183	3	1
William Rose, Haydens	220	10	2
Zachariah M. Winkler, McDonnells	225	6	5
Edward Paddleford, Haydens	108	19	2
Orphans of George M. Herb, Williams	155	5	1
Stephen C. Greene,	69	14	5

LAND LOTTERY REGISTER—No. 28
[RECORDER OFFICE—PUBLISHHED BY GRANTLAND & ORME—PRICE $3.]

NOTE—Section 1 is Lee County—2 Muscogee—3 Troup—4 Coweta—5 Carroll.

61st DAY'S DRAWING—Continued

Fortunate Drawers	Capts.	Dist.	No.	Dt.	Sec.

CHATHAM.
Fortunate Drawers	Capts.	Dist.	No.	Dt.	Sec.
Martha Hines, w. R. S.,	McDonnell		87	20	1
Sarah H. Roberts, orphan,	Reeds		100	11	3
Ann Box, widow,	Baines		107	32	1
Jeremiah Sanders,	Haydens		26	1	2
Mary West, widow,	Geredons		126	17	1
Philip Young orphan,	Baines		173	12	3
William Henry Greene,	McDonnells		141	22	1

CLARK.
Bryon Shaw,	Echols		22	8	1
Clement Clifton,	McDonalds		151	20	1
John H. Smith, jr.	Gahagans		173	4	4
Zadock Sexton,	Lumpkins		36	2	5
Johnson Freeman,	Gahagans		105	3	3
Lewis Fields,	do.		185	5	2
Judith Adams, orphan,	Birchs		124	12	5
Edwin Edwards,	Herndons		27	9	3
William H. Dismuke,	McDonalds		195	18	1

COLUMBIA.
Elizabeth Sullivan, widow,	Carrolls		10	11	3

CRAWFORD.
Thomas Davis,	Lovetts		25	20	1
Merry A. Sanders' orphans,	Rhodes		120	8	3

DECATUR.
Isaac Philips,	Hawthorns		217	2	1
Dimsey Harrell,	Douglass		1	3	1

DE KALB.
William Maloney, sen.	Bakers		210	2	1
Alfred Maner,	do.		6	9	2
Thomas Dison,	Howells		61	22	2
Ingram Bass,	Smiths		11	30	1
William Beasley, R. S.,	Merritts		210	5	3
David Franklin, R. S.,	Stephens		212	9	2

EARLY.
Nancy Ellet,	Welsons		205	2	5
Willis Doles,	do.		163	1	4

EFFINGHAM.
Solomon Dasher, sol.	Waldhaners		218	8	3
Ephraim Driggers,	10th		89	28	1
Philip Horning,	Waldhaners		146	7	1
Joshua Lovett,	Treutlins		275	6	5
Maria P. Patterson, widow,	Elkins		167	30	1

ELBERT.
Neal Johnson,	Carpenters		187	29	1
James Johnson,	Tuckers		303	8	5
Thomas Akin, soldier,	Alstons		173	5	4
Violetty Turman, widow,	Harmons		29	33	1

EMANUEL.
Joshua Gay, sen. R. S.	Moores		54	13	2
Sarah Hampton widow,	Arlines		130	1	3
Miles Fields,	McGars		118	24	1

FAYETTE.
Frederick Sessions,	Browns		39	5	2
William Henderson, sol.,	Whartons		155	2	5
James Lollar,	Landrums		137	2	4
Chesley Burke, soldier,	Whartons		103	22	2
David Combs, blind & lame,	Wests		236	22	2

FRANKLIN.
Thos. H. Blankinship,	Blankinships		191	2	2
James Chandler, D.	Chandlers		167	3	2
Reuben Cox,	McDonalds		54	2	1
Hezekiah McFarland,	Blankinships		5	4	4

GREENE.
David Coker,	Walters		16	2	5
Robert Fleming, R. S.,	Sanders		45	2	5
John P. Hayes, soldier,	Cokers		188	2	5
Susannah Thrasher, illegit.	Walters		204	19	2
John Catlett,	Caudells		3	6	5
Richard W. Royston,	Boswells		147	5	4
William Lowe,	Newsoms		122	6	5
Peggy Bruce's illegitimate,	Bruces		127	23	1
Harrison H. Watts,	Newsoms		249	24	1
Allen B. Mallory,	Astins		67	20	2
Joshua Shropshire,	Halls		21	16	2
William Brooks, sen. R. S.	Rankins		236	5	3
James W. Godkin,	Dawsons		232	3	2
Josiah Cutwell,	Astins		101	33	1
Andrew Ray, R. S.,	Newsoms		44	4	2
Samuel Durham's orphans,	do.		4	19	1

GWINNETT.
James Cates,	Rollins		95	12	5
Henry Mathews,	Woodroughs		29	15	2
Timothy Swindle,	Whartons		254	33	1
William Owen,	Greens		130	15	2
Douglass Childers,	Finchers		9	9	2
Asa Reid,	do.		34	1	3
Francis Jones's mins. fa.ab.	Rollins		61	9	2
Wyatt Harris,	Moores		125	21	2
Mary Gordon, w. R. S.,	Madduxs		19	14	1
John Medlock, illegitimate,	Shippys		89	23	2
Mary Butler, widow,	Whartons		66	17	2

HANCOCK.
Matthias Dennis, R. S.,	103d		48	13	5
Jane Trawick, widow,	118th		161	33	1
Joseph Baldwin,	Greens		127	18	1
William G. Macon,	102d		255	9	2
John A. Evans,	111th		156	23	2
Lewis Parker, jr.	101st		4	15	2
Philip Gatewood,	108th		101	13	2
John B. Latimer,	112th		101	9	2
Richey Blair,	113th		8	6	2
Catharine Wilkins, widow,	118th		84	27	1

HENRY.
Marget Lang, widow,	Shaws		162	9	1
Thomas McClendon,	Gosdens		100	5	2
Zachariah Deason, R. S.,	Harriss		128	18	1
William Hand,	Bryants		59	15	2
Parker Nowles,	Grays		234	2	4

HABERSHAM.
Seaborn Holt, minor,	Langstons		4	6	1
William Ritchie,	Jones		272	23	2
Grenville Davis,	Fanes		254	3	2
Thomas Bird, R. S.,	Bryans		81	15	2
Benjamin L. Mahan, minor,	Jones		152	8	1
Thomas Jordan's orphans,	Martins		180	24	2
Elisha Dooly,	Kenzies		171	29	1

HALL.
Samuel Fowler,	Floyds		211	6	2
Nathaniel Harbin,	Dorseys		206	26	1
John Pugh,	Yagers		92	15	5
James Trout,	Smiths		70	23	1
Thomas Wade,	Dorseys		157	17	1
Meredith Castleberry,	Hardens		213	11	1
David Castleberry,	Roberts		161	13	2

HOUSTON.
Louis Wood, widow,	Calhouns		120	4	1

(190)

IRWIN.

Fortunate Drawers Capts. Dist.	No.	Dt.	Sec.
William Lastinger, Underwoods	178	2	3

JACKSON.

Jeptha Landrum, Landrums	251	8	1
William Kelly, Storys	75	23	2
Elisha Burson, Landrums	224	28	1
Charles H. Hardy, Millers	186	8	5
James Boyd's orphans, Venables	194	7	3
Thomas Benton, Duprees	57	11	2
John Rachford, Allens	26	18	2

JASPER.

John Bryant, Wilders	237	15	2
James Farrow, Holmes	133	13	1
John Doby, Wilsons	182	26	1
Mary Ann Weldon, illegit. Owens	195	11	3
Solomon Long, soldier, Farleys	276	1	2
Elias Sharp, Owens	237	4	2
Martha Burleson, widow, Wilders	123	7	4
Abimilek Youngblood, sol. Erwins	121	23	2
Mildred Freeman, w. R. S., Holmes	149	15	1
Bartlett Brown's orphans, Wilders	186	13	2
James Wilson, Dardens	37	12	2
Caleb W. Key, Wilsons	244	8	5
Elizabeth Waldup, lunatic, Barnetts	11	3	5
Martha M. Smith, illegitimate, Hines	118	4	1
Reuben Wilkinson, Baynes	83	7	2

JEFFERSON.

Nancy Wasden, orphan, Waldens	240	2	4
Emily Farmer, husband absent, Ross	131	21	1
Alfred S. Barr, orphan, do.	259	17	2
Rachel Gamble, widow Ross	85	8	5
Isaac Holmes, Boyds	213	7	5
Washington Marshall, ill. Marshalls	128	16	1
Isaac Lamb, R. S., Beatys	301	20	2
Simon Caldwell's orphans, Marshalls	145	12	5

JONES.

Noah Mercer, sr. Blounts	167	14	1
John S. Zachery, Taylors	35	2	4
Robert Pridgen, Hammacks	41	9	2
Hiram How, Hendersons	50	12	1
William Collin's orps. Newbys	109	19	2
John Oliver, Blounts	43	2	2
Cammel Busten, Bowens	42	23	2
Willis Winters, Robertsons	179	32	1
Edward Moreland, Gibsons	222	3	3
Noel Hasty, Popes	122	13	2
Elizabeth Carlton, w. Robersons	155	6	1
Thomas G. Duke, Davis	25	4	1

LAURENS.

Asa Watson, s.l.w. Bohannons	173	5	5
Jesse Forest, Whiteheads	81	5	3
John M. Ledlow, Mizells	90	3	2
William D. Wright, Plummers	85	10	5

LIBERTY.

James H. Smith, 16th	139	13	2
Bartley M. Shaw, 16th	135	5	3
Elizabeth Wallace, orph. 17th	53	10	3

LINCOLN.

William Jackson, s.l.w. Hardys	211	3	4
Susannah M. Bussey, w. Graves	126	8	3
Elizabeth Cason, minor, Parks	217	3	4
J. Hardy, ag't for M. Speights do.	141	20	2
Peyton W. Sale, Wiggintons	110	3	3

MADISON.

Fortunate Drawers Capts. Dist.	No.	Dt.	Sec.
David Cunningham, Hannas	80	13	2
Robert Woods, jr. Culbertsons	10	3	2
William Bragg, Caldwells	193	11	2
William Cochran, do.	203	30	1
Walter H. Bruce, Hannas	207	7	1

McINTOSH.

John Dyal, sol. Terrells	27	11	3
Eliza Fitzpatrick, widow, do	8	11	2
James Hogan, McCranys	11	10	5
Lachlan McIntosh, Demeries	51	3	4

MONROE.

Joel Bell, Fergasons,	207	26	1
James Pearson, Douglass	36	2	2
John Taylor, Finchs	142	8	5
Enoch Crabb's orps. do.	307	1	2
Samuel W. Langston, Turners	15	9	3
John Adams, Douglass	235	11	1
David Allison, sol. Wrights	139	2	5
Thomas Chapell, Woodwards	52	3	4
Alexander Russell, Phillips	17	29	1
William Mills, Houses	13	3	2
Robert Watson, Finches	102	5	3

MORGAN.

M. J. M. Bohannon, Adairs	212	8	3
Betsy Evans, wid. Harwells	221	15	1
Zachariah Fears, sol. Brooks	79	2	1
David Knight, Jennings	22	21	2
William Gilbert, R. S. Beaslys	214	21	1
James M. Greene, Whatleys	248	11	2
Francis J. Brown, Jennings	4	16	5
Elisha H. Stallings, Watsons	154	14	2

MONTGOMERY.

Henry C. Tucker, sr. R. S., Popes	179	26	1
Joseph Friday, R. S. do.	114	23	2
John Bohannon, Nashs	264	6	5

NEWTON.

Mad., Dicey, Eme., Jas. Hen. & M. A. Regolas, ills, Askews	129	23	1
Elijah Hearn, Pullins	67	7	5
Jesse Baker, Clarks	72	3	5
P., W., H. &J.H.Bailey, ors.Hays	246	15	2
Joseph Freeman, Summers	224	3	1
Thomas J. Day, Hays	219	15	2
Tolliver Hancock, Snows	155	23	1

OGLETHORPE.

Sarah Haynes, w. R. S. Dixs	211	8	5
Elizabeth Banks, wid. Lacys	84	13	5
Charles Jordan, Seals	69	4	4
Asa Pond, Rousseaus	29	5	2
James McIntire, Smiths	73	16	2
Zillah Hardman, w. R. S. Floyds	28	5	4
James Baley, soldier, Dixs	40	4	4
Joseph Stephens, sol. Devenoprts	5	2	4
Robert Smith, R. S. Holloways	254	8	1
William McWhorter, Dixs	171	26	1
Richard Hargrove, sol. Billps	177	17	1
Thomas Cason, Williamsons	34	9	3
George Bailey, Rousseaus	36	2	3
Carter Kidd, Holloways	56	21	1

(191)

PULASKI.

Fortunate Drawers Capts. Dist.	No.	Dt.	Sec.
James H. Warren, Kellams	250	3	2
John Buchan, Hendleys	145	7	2

PUTNAM.

William Veal, R. S. Duprees	202	19	1
Massa Thomas, R. S. Blacks	242	6	1
Robert Beall, Bledsoes	168	1	5
Jacob Miller, Stinsons	52	8	1
Mary H. Lane, widow, Lamars	149	18	2
Thomas W. Oneal, Sparks	15	13	2
Henry H. Gindrat's ors. Barnetts	112	2	4
Shadrack Ellis, Clarks	111	4	5
Cullen Reid, Blunts	284	23	2

RABUN.

Joseph H. Jones, Godfreys	258	1	2

RICHMOND.

E. Manton, Ferris	196	29	1
Richard Mooney, Mantzs	31	10	5
John Payne, Bushs	57	5	1
Peter Bethune, R. S. James	120	12	2
Joseph Zanity, Blacks	227	3	2
Etheldred Tarver, jr. James	191	16	1
James Toole, R. S., 119th	111	11	2
Charles Delaigle, Treadwells	283	12	3
Anselm Bugg, do.	137	11	1
Rich'd P. Spelman, Huntingtons	236	12	2
Benjamin F. Kenrick, do.	103	30	1
James Bones, Treadwells	73	4	3

SCRIVEN.

Benjamin Townson, Poytress	158	14	2
John F. Roberts, ill. Humphreys	221	9	1
John Brannan's orps. Reaves	97	20	1
William Usher, Hunters	39	6	2

TATTNALL.

Donald McLeod, orp. McDuffies	53	7	2
Elizabeth McCall, wid. McCalls	41	1	4

TALIAFERRO.

William Justiss, Hammacks	93	12	3

THOMAS.

John Sloan,	28	4	5

TWIGGS.

Eliz. Fitzpatrick, w. Blackshears	14	11	5
Benjamin Mathis, sol. Pearsons	78	12	5
Orps. of Jacob Clance, Bosticks	173	20	2
Ors. of T. Findley, Chamberlains	69	4	1
Norflett P. Parker, Bosticks	94	23	1
Ors. of N. Brady, Chamberlains	253	3	3
George Knight, do.	154	15	1
Elijah Bush, Wimberlys	310	8	5

UPSON.

Harrison Thomas, Ellis	2	20	2
Samuel Barron, Harrels	235	31	1
Comfort Scott's illeg. Paschalls	96	12	5
James W. Hamil, Saunders	59	6	1

WALTON.

Shadrack Jackson, Davis	17	2	2
Joshua Gilbert, Hudsons	266	6	1
John M. Dozier, 250th	218	16	2
Phebe Foster's illeg. Rays	26	30	1
Benjamin Thrower, 503rd	181	2	1
Shadrack Humphries' ors. Hudsons	3	4	2

WAYNE.

Fortunate Drawers Capts. Dist.	No.	Dt.	Sec.
Williby Mincy, Staffords	49	1	5

WARREN.

Philip Brantley's orps. Parhams	256	4	1
Wm. M. Butt, Bulls	180	13	1
John Springer, Bulls	112	20	2
Roister Heeth, R. S. Parhams	170	22	1
Miles Pate, Brinkleys	95	14	1
Benjamin S. Bledsoes, Hales	163	7	3
Mary Crawman, wid. Adkins	134	15	5
Clark Blandford, Bulls	378	7	1
Joel Mathews, R. S. Hills	17	14	2
Benjamin Denson, sol. Jones	172	7	2
Beuben Adams, Bulls	162	26	1
Lewis Braddy, R. S. Downs	159	15	2
Lav. R| Dabney, or. of James, do.	227	5	5
Michael Harbuck, Bulls	222	5	3
E. Bird & N. Weeks, ills. Stewarts	63	16	1

WASHINGTON.

William Warthen, R.S. Warthens	137	1	2
Daxid Cox, Woods	25	33	1
Peter Evans, Gilberts	251	23	1
Mary Tyson, illeg. Tysons	191	5	4
Erw. Hitchcock's heirs, Rushings	182	2	1
Leanda Lord, Wimberlys	95	11	1
Augustin Wilson, Floyds	220	22	1
Lewis H. Accord, Avans	59	19	2
Reney Dukes, orph. Rushings	210	1	1
William Cogbern, Warthens	81	4	3
Nathaniel Wicker's ors. Currys	215	1	2
Isaiah Johnson, Tysons	259	8	1

WILKINSON.

James Hall's orps. Mayos	46	5	3
Isham Underwood's orps. Shows	38	32	1
Sarah Howard, w.R.S. Halls	260	7	5
Isaac Smith, Mayos	78	18	1
John Gillet, Smiths	115	7	4
William Hatcher, R. S. Halls	149	4	5
Penny Eason's illegs. Fairchilds	239	22	2
William Williams' heirs, Shows	206	17	1
Wm. T. H. Stewart, sol. Barry's	45	14	1
S., P. & B. Summerford, ors. Halls	50	11	3
Frederick Beall, Mayos	217	5	2

WILKES.

Eliz| Psalmons, wid. Ragsdales	294	7	5
John Wells, jr. McDermonts	238	10	2
William Anderson, sr.R.S. Grens	209	3	1
James Walker, Lukers	151	4	2
James M. Hammock, Reeves	242	18	2
Wm. Snelson, sr. R. S. Popes	28	12	3
Purnal Truitt, do.	2	6	4
Drucilla Coats, sol. w. Charltons	14	20	1
Solon Porter, orp. Carters	160	16	2
Augusta A. Willis, wid. do.	139	17	1
William Kent, Woottens	19	7	1
L. J. S. & J.D.Hide.ills.Ragsdales	163	17	2

62nd DAY'S DRAWING—May 17.

APPLING.

David Mathis, Dodges	58	32	1
George Nettles, McDonalds	55	5	4

(192)

BALDWIN.

Fortunate Drawers Capts. Dist. No.Dt.Sec.
Arthur B. Davis, Buchanans 72 4 5
Benanuel Bower, Rowes 254 23 1
Ann Caroline Pryor, wid. Buchanans 15 19 2
Charles W. Butler, do. 165 2 1
Robert N. Parham, Doles 173 14 1
James Martin, Rowes 102 25 1

BIBB.

Elijah Neel, Pickards 90 7 3
Nancy Kenon, hus. absent, Rutlands 14 4 5
Robert McCrary, Bates 45 17 2
Burrel Wise, soldier, Carrs 3 27 1

BULLOCH.

Andrew Kicklighter, sen. Deloachs 210 21 2
John Grimes, Richardsons 53 14 2
John Crumpton, Lockharts 200 13 1
John Royalston, R. S., do. 205 10 1

BURKE.

Kiercy Wynn, widow, McKays 111 17 2
Henry Y. Utley, Gordons 119 7 3
Lewis Lancaster, Fountains 183 7 3
Sarah Scarborough, w.R.S., Andersons 134 6 5
Daniel Hutcheons, Lynchs 164 2 3
Geo., Jas. & M. Coburn, ills. Lesters 56 5 3
Elisha Watkins's orphans, Bayleys 235 33 1
Susannah Landstrip, wid. Brooms 15 33 1
Dawson Ponder, McKays 54 24 2
Stephen W. Blount, sen. Bayleys 207 6 5
Francis Floyd, Wards 7 12 5
Abraham I. H. Neyland, Bayleys 344 7 1

BUTTS.

Jemima Purgison, widow, Kirksies 141 11 5
Leonard Roan, soldier, Hendricks 118 18 2
David Ramsdill, R. S., Masons 35 13 2

CAMDEN.

Levin Gunby's orphans, Wards 31 9 2
William J. Bailey, do. 46 10 1

CHATHAM.

Patrick Norris, McDonnalls 135 2 5
John Chapman, do. 22 5 4
James Caruthers' orphans, Haydens 116 26 1
John Guilmartin, McDonnells 158 9 1
John B. Gilbert's orphans, Haydens 372 28 1
Charles Peroney Destra, do. 95 16 2
Frederick Rahfus, do. 35 10 2
Orps. of Frederick Shaffer, Geredons 25 11 1
Edward C. Batty, 98 12 2

CLARK.

Eli B. Tuck, Davis 127 9 3
Thomas Lambert, R. S., Alreds 119 25 1
John A. Bonduvant, Andersons 94 32 1
Thomas G. White, Frosts 297 22 1
Richard G. Henning, Espys 81 23 1
Jeremiah Maxey, soldier, Greens 147 24 2

COLUMBIA.

Leonard Maddox's orphans, Beals 263 3 1
John Jenkins, Talbots 55 18 1
John McDonnald's orps. Carrolls 171 11 2
John Pullin, Culbreaths 230 4 3
James Burrage, Dranes 65 24 1
Laurence Richardson, Adams 99 10 5
George Cleghorn's orps. Ramseys 245 15 1
Hartwell Filts, Clarks 154 25 1

CRAWFORD.

John F. T. Lowe's orphans, Wilsons 4 10 3
Edward Sherly, R. S., Ellis 135 5 4
John Evans, soldier, Tillers 89 3 1

DECATUR.

Fortunate Drawers Capts. Dist. No.Dt.Sec.
John Hazzard, Douglass 2 9 2

DE KALB.

William Strickland, Howells 178 7 2
Jonathan Gammon, Stephens 273 22 1
John Jones, do. 25 22 1

DOOLY.

Joel Joiner, Hogans 16 15 1

EARLY.

Bathena Kelly, Grimsleys 200 4 1

EFFINGHAM.

Abraham Blitch, sr. R. S., Stricklands 237 10 2

ELBERT.

James Hunt, R. S., Hortons 274 17 2
James S. Hinton, Dunns 33 13 2
James M. Faulknor, orp. Blackwells 181 3 5
Josiah Dobbs, Dobbs 309 6 1
Janet Hansard, w. R. S., Blackwells 27 14 1
Frederick C. Harmond, Harmonds 183 12 1
Oliver Threlkeld, Deadwilders 50 4 1
Elizabeth Evans, w. R. S., Tates 41 3 4
John Butler, Butlers 269 9 3
James O. Clark, Bells 209 7 3
James Cheeke, Boltons 187 32 1
Zachariah Rucker, Alstons 201 12 1

EMANUEL.

Warren Key, jr. Chasons 89 8 4
James Hargroves, illegitimate, 57th 143 4 2
Westley Snell, Snells 65 9 1
Charles C. Jenkins, McGars 31 6 4

FAYETTE.

Peter Greene, Browns 15 7 1
Sarah Wilkinson, w. R. S., Whartons 11 22 2
Solomon Whatley, soldier, Landrums 40 25 1
Elizabeth Spark, widow, Craigs 185 27 1

FRANKLIN.

Phiny Fleming, Sanders 160 15 1
William Bryan, sen. Stranges 225 2 4
Daniel Sanders, Sanders 78 17 1
Edmund B. Taylor, Hudsons 85 24 1
Willis Creek, Cokers 241 5 3
James Vaughter, Andrews 3 5 2
Oliver Russom, Hudsons 196 16 2

GREENE.

James Thackston, R. S., Newsoms 165 28 1
Samuel Gentry, Dawsons 77 3 1
Orps. of Joseph Simington, Rankins 199 5 2
William Bostick, Robbins 26 12 5
Orphans of William Winslet, Knowles 205 13 2
Isaac Goodwin, Hills 237 9 3

GWINNETT.

Polly Brooks, hus. absent. Moores 57 18 2
John Guttrie, Davis 169 3 2
Even Howell, Bakers 41 23 2
David Rowlins, Maddoxs 281 22 2
Elizabeth McClelland, widow, Evans 302 4 1
Joshua Bradford, Robertsons 81 5 4
Aaron Kemp, Hills 133 6 4
William McCearly, soldier, Gholdstons 139 19 1
William Burgess, Bennetts 106 11 5
Bedeuth Red, w. R. S., Moores 128 5 1
Samuel Kite, Greens 127 9 1
Daniel Price's orphans, Woodroughs 27 19 1
Richard Rollins, Rollins 101 24 1
Isaac Strickland, Moores 97 25 1
Elizabeth Lee, w. R. S., Whartons 70 8 1

(193)

HOUSTON.		
Fortunate Drawers Capts. Dist.	*No.*	*Dt.Sec.*
William Singleton, Simpsons	277	11 2

HANCOCK.		
Thomas Ingram, soldier, Bishops	132	1 5
Sarah Morris, widow, 111th	189	2 1
William Trawick, 118th	177	3 5
Simon T. Peak, Colquetts	5	9 3
James Macclellan, 110th	58	1 4
Joseph Vinson, 114th	280	15 1
James M. Flowers, Densons	114	14 5
Jacob P. Norton, 108th	101	5 1
Rhosana Rundle, w. R. S., Alfords	18	1 1
Richard Colwell, orphan, 112th	55	20 1

HENRY.		
Brigs Allum, Bryants	23	13 5
John Edwards, Kites	103	14 2
Charles Linder, Wards	43	28 1
George W. Reynolds, Risons	89	2 4
George Cagle, Shaws	230	3 3
Thomas L. Bentley, do.	40	10 5

HABERSHAM.		
Percila Hill, w. R. S., Langstons	85	27 1
Wm. Bruster, orp. of W. B., Suttons	121	8 4
Thomas Richardson, Fanes	22	2 1
Surry Davis, R. S., do.	266	22 1
Arthur Gilbert, Suttons	124	21 1
Martin Lance, Bryans	157	2 4
Hampton Holcomb, soldier, Suttons	9	5 5
Stephen Carrall, Fanes	23	25 1
Isaac Hickes, Suttons	133	7 2

HALL.		
Joab Martin, Garrards	229	6 1
Jesse Dodd, Harrisons	56	8 2
Wesley Maulden, Hardens	188	32 1
William Morris, sen. Alreds	231	4 2
Valentine Cain, Wilsons	4	7 4
Ezekiel Buffington, Hardages	189	28 1

IRWIN.		
Elijah Grantham, Bradfords	33	5 1
Lewis Martin, McCalls	85	20 2

JACKSON.		
William Wilson, Pairs	398	7 1
James Sailors, soldier, Rogers	4	7 2
Solomon Willbanks, do.	225	10 2
Meredith Kitchens, Allens	59	2 2
Elliott Hodge, soldier, Watersons	54	2 3

JASPER.		
Tyre Chaffin, Baynes	42	23 2
John C. Graves, Wilders	243	22 1
Thomas Ward, do.	233	23 1
Wiliam Porter, Camerons	1	1 3
Hugh Brannen, Dardens	74	3 3
Job C. Patterson, do.	42	4 3
James Griffin, soldier, Erwins	179	11 2
William Fears, R. S., Holmes	238	33 1
Josiah Reynolds, Reeves	48	21 1
George Clark, Sparks	88	11 3

JEFFERSON.		
John Stephenson, jr. Causeys	187	9 3
Edward Hunter's orphans, Jones	172	10 1
David Cox, Marshalls	73	1 4
Elizabeth Mathews, w. R. S., Ross	99	19 1
Charlotte Lockhart, widow, Jones	295	5 3

JONES.		
James W. Mitchell, Mullins	244	9 1
Richard T. Mastin, Dasters	309	28 1
Letisha Calif, w.R.S. Hammacks	88	2 4

Fortunate Drawers Capts. Dist.	*No.*	*Dt.Sec.*
Malichi Dawson, do.	41	13 5
John Massengale, Newbys	29	21 2
Arthur McPhiarson, Gibsons	57	19 2
Mary Martin, wid. Blounts	10	11 5
Lee Duncan, Duncans	249	11 2
Thomas J. Conner, Popes	229	29 1
Edmond Duncan, R. S. Davis	273	21 1
Ruth Freeman, h.a. Lows	63	7 1
Hillery Beggarly, Hendersons	114	30 1
Cyrus W. Stewart, Breadloves	249	15 1

LAURENS.		
James Thompson, Spiveys	157	5 2
Pleasant Slone, Whitheads	181	16 1
Permely Windham, w.R.S. Deans	81	4 2
Raleigh Hightower, Plummers	90	15 1
John Livingston, do.	7	16 5
Eliza Mimms, illeg. Hodges	14	8 4

LIBERTY.		
John Shaw, 16th	316	3 4

LINCOLN.		
William Eubanks' mins. Graves	99	27 1
Lewis Turner, s. l. w. Hardys	148	8 5
Alvin M. Grinage, Lonorgans	4	8 2
Killiss H. Roberts, Parks	54	18 2
Wm. Statham's mins. Prathers	245	18 1

MADISON.		
Nathaniel B. Gholsons, Hannas	185	2 1
Allen Vineyard, do.	325	28 1
John T. Mitchell, Stephens	71	21 2
H. Stephens, sol. Higginbothams	202	21 2
William Smith, Culbertsons	231	14 1
Nancy Hall, widow, Hannas	79	26 1
Ivey Thomas, do.	29	3 3
Patrick Scott, jr. Caldwells	145	15 1

McINTOSH.		
Mary Ann, Sarah Ann & Eveland Basset, orphs. McCranys	161	14 1
John Caulder, R. S. Demeries	91	3 4

MONROE.		
Jesse H. Dismukes, Woodwards	78	11 1
Thomas Hollis, Turners	168	4 1
M. B. Nash, Johnsons	95	11 5
Samuel McKenzie, R. S., Wrights	35	6 3
Henderson Buffington, Houses	185	18 2
Thomas S. Paley's ors. Douglass	231	2 3
Jeremiah Pearson, do.	315	3 4
Charles Stewart, Browns	94	25 1
Alexander Ponder, Finchs	117	6 3
Martha Hightower, wid. Turners	26	11 3

MORGAN.		
Joel Barnett, Christians	268	19 2
Josiah Moore, Gains	120	7 5
William G. Evans, Adairs	95	17 1
Allsey Beavers, Canifaxs	214	24 1
Azariah Bostwick's orps. Sparks	165	7 2
Tilman Gardiner, Whatleys	339	8 1
Alexander M. Brown, Jennings	233	15 1

MONTGOMERY.		
Catharine McGibbin, wid. Wynns	59	11 5

NEWTON.		
John L. Oneal, Webbs	298	6 1

Fortunate Drawers Capts. Dist.	No.	Dt.	Sec.
Bakel Graves, do.	260	5	1
Mitchell Beasley, Summers	92	10	1
Houston Aycock, do.	278	5	1
Jane Mann, wid. Penningtons	185	7	1
John Stamps, Clarks	253	12	2
Wilea Howell, Newnans	273	17	2
Benjamin Odom, Summers	190	3	3
Soloman Holliway, Snows	254	17	1

OGLETHORPE.

	No.	Dt.	Sec.
Josiah Crowley, Rousseaus	173	10	2
Milly Jordan, w. R. S., Arnolds	138	17	1
Anthony G. Smith, Holloways	156	4	3
Philip Ray, R. S. Bels	96	1	5
James R. Jennings, Rhodes	109	19	1
Charles Carter, sr.R.S.Holloways	251	15	2
Erasmus Swann, Rhodes	202	15	2
Hezekiah Martin, Seals	63	25	1
Augustus B. Paschal, Rousseaus	96	14	2

PIKE.

	No.	Dt.	Sec.
Margaret Trower, wid. Orrs.	31	7	2
Ethan Stroud, Hicks	51	10	1

PULASKI.

	No.	Dt.	Sec.
Levi E. Bush, Gilstraps	146	13	2
Isaac Burkhalter, sol. Sparrows	49	13	2
James O. Jelks, do.	154	22	1
Celia Kellum, wid. Gilstraps	101	8	3

PUTNAM.

	No.	Dt.	Sec.
Robert W. Walker, Blacks	173	9	3
John F. Bellamy, Allums	151	24	1
Daniel Buckner, sol. Kendricks	133	12	2
Thomas Gray, jr. Sparks	4	4	2
Elisha Greer, Allums	3	9	4
Frederick Conner, Duprees	14	10	5
Thomas King, sr. Allums	80	29	1

RABUN.

	No.	Dt.	Sec.
John Shed, sol. Godfreys	36	18	2
John Dillard, R. S., Mercers	83	4	1

RICHMOND.

	No.	Dt.	Sec.
Susan G. Neyland, wid. Wilcoxs	123	2	5
Isham Evans, Murphys	123	8	3
Joshua Whitaker, R. S. James	175	1	2
James P. Maguire, Treadwells	99	2	2
Mary Luther, wid. Wilcoxs	115	4	2
William H. C. Mills, Blacks	40	13	5
Thomas Ginn, Wilcoxs	12	24	2
Emanuel Johnson, R. S. Kellys	52	30	1
William Bones, Huntingtons	189	29	1
Elizabeth Churchill, Kellys	184	10	1
Nathaniel Brown, Treadwells	143	10	3

SCRIVEN.

	No.	Dt.	Sec.
James Conner, illeg. Ushers	113	20	2
Rob't Conghran's mins. Hunters	107	25	1
Joseph Humphrey's ors. McCalls	99	8	3
Abel McCardell, Humphreys	131	20	2

TATTNALL.

	No.	Dt.	Sec.
Mary Kite, wid. Dees	97	22	1
William Dubberly, Conners	135	7	1
Lorenzo D. Bowen, McDuffies	27	6	4
Nicholas Robinson, Dees	10	21	1
William Starling, R. S., Conners	97	27	1

TELFAIR.

Fortunate Drawers Capts. Dist.	No.	Dt.	Sec.
Peter K. Bailie, Lampkins	191	4	3
Jeremiah Davis, Williams	181	14	1
Daniel Laslie, Lampkins	27	3	2
Alexander B. McRae, Robertsons	225	12	1
Amos Anderson, Wilsons	145	15	5
Dan'l Finalson's ors. Robertsons	117	8	4
Catharine McRae, w. Barentines	63	15	2

TALIAFERRO.

	No.	Dt.	Sec.
Jehial Watson, Gunns	157	11	5

TWIGGS.

	No.	Dt.	Sec.
Orps. of S. Stirling, Stretmans	237	20	2
Mary Dawson, w. R. S., do.	146	5	4
John Waterer, Holidays	11	12	3
Charles Elms, Solomans	95	9	5
J. J. Dennard, sol. Chamberlains	151	13	2
Orps. of William Edwards, do.	230	27	1

UPSON.

	No.	Dt.	Sec.
James Smith, sol. Paschals	51	2	5
John F. Myrick, sol. Hattocks	220	2	2

WALTON.

	No.	Dt.	Sec.
James McCarty, McQuertors	97	24	2
Elizabeth Davis' orphan, do.	46	3	2
Hezekiah Gates, sr. Rays	331	7	5
John Osborn, Snows	133	18	2
Thomas Helton, 249th	11	7	3
William Moate, 250th	159	8	3
Redding C. Shipp, 418th	165	6	1
Eliz. Wornick, wid. Hudsons	229	1	1
Joseph Reede, do.	187	33	1
Nancy Haynes, illeg. 503rd	58	12	2
Sugar J. Mathews, Rays	308	15	1

WARE.

	No.	Dt.	Sec.
William G. Henderson, Bryans	27	12	5

WAYNE.

	No.	Dt.	Sec.
Sampson Altmon's orps. Staffords	82	3	5
Mary Walker, w. R. S. McKinneys	63	4	1

WARREN.

	No.	Dt.	Sec.
Thomas Lowe, sol. Stewarts	103	5	1
John Raley, Jones	65	29	1
Henry Shelton, Hales	187	19	1
Adam Granade, Sanders	244	3	3
James Ansley, for Oliv. Wall, do.	63	9	5
David Gibson, Brinkleys	268	7	5
Charles B. Jones, Jones	145	8	1
Sampson Wilder, jr. Hills	185	13	2
James Storey, jr. Sanders	7	8	3
Lewis Wright's orp. Bulls	2	16	1

WASHINGTON.

	No.	Dt.	Sec.
Molton Peacock, sol. McClendons	87	5	5
Sarah Hall, illegit. do.	1	5	5
William Slade, Floyds	241	8	3
Edwin Morris, Wimberlys	131	10	3
Lemuel Howard, Jordans	223	29	1
Daniel McLean, Mannings	206	4	3
Benjamin Brady's orps. Tysons	135	1	2
Daniel Eubank, Warthens	96	15	1
William Barwick, sol. Currys	127	2	3
William Musselwhite, Tysons	223	3	3
Charles Fisher, do.	245	16	2
Clarissa Avery, orph. Rushings	145	16	2

(195)

Fortunate Drawers	Capts. Dist.	No.	Dt.	Sec.
Archibald Cone, jr.	Warthens	62	21	2
Redding Hodges,	Avans	22	10	1
Chancy Johnson,	Tysons	110	13	2
Thomas Mills,	Rushings	249	9	1

WILKINSON.

Ranson Payne,	Fairchilds	147	20	1
Wade Nelson, sol.	Williams	214	29	1
Thomas Lewis,	Mayos	211	30	1
John Freeman, sr.	Currys	96	11	2
Richard Summerford,	Halls	97	22	1
William Lawson,	do.	157	7	4
Robert Goode,	Halls	282	7	1
Henry Easterling,	do.	243	15	1
Elizabeth Rogers, wid.	Smiths	193	33	1

WILKES.

James Flynt,	Carters	208	5	1
John Gibson, R. S.,	Moors	93	7	5
Alexander Edge,	do.	272	28	1
John B. Milner, sol.	Charltons	240	3	1
Sarah Boswell, wid.	Washingtons	91	1	2
Mary Philips, sol. wid.	Wootens	23	10	5
Thomas Pullin,	Richersons	182	3	5
Robert D. Knox,	Popes	153	16	2
L. McLendon's ors.	McDermonts	169	22	2
Bryan Fannang,	Reeves	44	9	2
Joel B. Sutton, sol.	Wootens	242	5	5
Samuel Whatley,	Greens	141	14	5
James D. Willis,	Reeves	155	5	4
Thomas Nash,	Washingtons	210	32	1

63d DAY'S DRAWING—May 18.

APPLING.

James Sapp, Morgans	15	21	1
Auston Smith, Dedges	222	6	3
John Hearn, McDaniels	116	1	5
Jonathan Crib. Dedges	123	5	1
Archibald Crafford, Morgans	177	9	2
David McCall, McDonalds	148	1	5
John Braswell, Morgans	132	6	4

BALDWIN.

Grief Hardaway, Doles	47	3	2
Hardy P. Humphrey, Rowes	174	19	2
Lott Loyd, Thomas	159	7	5
Hariet & Sar Goodwin, orps. Doles	152	7	4
Nancy F. Mitchell, hus. ab. Buchanans	91	13	5
James Montgomery, Lingos	201	16	1
Allen Box, illegitimate, Perrys	10	17	2
Charles Smith, Lesters	61	33	1

BIBB.

Joseph Wiggins, Lloyds	85	12	3
Malcolm Mathison, Beards	147	6	1
Malcolm Mathison, do.	4	33	1

BULLOCH.

Samuel Johnson, McCalls	78	3	5
Delia Burnside, widow, Richardsons	41	1	3
Joseph Hagan, sol. Standlands	85	2	3
Levy Buntin, Burnetts	139	3	5
John Hudler, R. S., do.	2	22	1

BURKE.

Theophilus Sapp, Thompsons	140	27	1
Pendleton Sapp, do.	277	15	1
Mary Godbee, w. R. S., Dugas	207	3	5
Elijah Kirsey's orphans, Bayleys	5	7	1
Samuel Barron, jr. do.	132	16	1

Fortunate Drawers.	Capts. Dist.	No.	Dt.	Sec.
Patience Daniel, fa. ab.	Corkers	201	6	3
John S. Grumbles, soldier,	Brooms	118	15	2
Elizabeth Hodges, widow,	Roberts	333	3	5
John Ward,	Brooms	145	1	3

BUTTS.

Jefferson A. J. Mason ill.	Masons	81	2	1

CAMDEN.

Edward Crews,	Coxs	182	13	2
Gustavus A. Cox,	do.	155	33	1
Kinchen Swearingin,	Baileys	186	17	1
John Le Pearce, illegitimate,	do	109	9	1
William Wilkerson, sen.	Coxs.	25	9	3
Elizabeth Andrews, widow,	Wards	82	10	2

CHATHAM.

Francis Champion,	Geredons	172	19	2
Margaret Bourquin, widow,	Gaddys	90	2	3
Joseph C. Whitney,		71	3	5
Jonathan Cooper,	Haydens	149	9	2
John Brantley, soldier,	Scotts	153	9	3
Richard Wayne,	Haydens	43	11	5
Sarah Courvoisie, wid.	McDonnells	79	4	3
Charles A. Higgins		279	4	1
John R. Grayson's orps.	Haydens	151	19	2
James Cleland,		299	3	4

CLARK.

Mercer Echols,	Vinsons	305	5	3
Nancy & Betsey Summers, fa. ab.,	do.	241	18	1
Orp. of Jeremiah Harris,	Frosts	115	13	1
Celia Harvell, widow,	Cutchins	5	10	3
William Bradshaw's orphans,	Vinsons	90	1	5
Marcus D. C. Johnson,	Davis	74	9	1
Patrick Jack,	Lumpkins	200	31	1

COLUMBIA.

John Nash, R. S.,	Adams	179	9	3
Martin B. Reynolds,	Carrolls	23	3	1
A., W. B. & M. J. Jenkins, ills.	Dranes	29	5	3
William Stallings	Bolton	326	8	1
Greaf Grammar Twoel,	Clarks	252	15	2
Leonard Sims, soldier,	Ramseys	177	24	2

CRAWFORD.

James B. Hamilton,	Hamiltons	60	10	1
Elizabeth Lagrone, widow,	Rhodes	104	2	5
Israel Champain,	ovetts	196	22	2

DE KALB.

William Grant,	Conns	65	10	1

DOOLY.

William Bush,	Sarrs	73	1	2
Arthur Rosseter,	Andersons	52	15	5

EARLY.

Elijah Philmon,	Grimsleys	252	10	1

EFFINGHAM.

Jeremiah Reiser,	Treutlins	14	7	1
John Martin Powledge,	do	166	6	2
Abraham Blitch, sen.	Stricklands	187	2	1

ELBERT.

Elium Evans, soldier,	Tates	92	4	3
Caleb Tinar,	Carpenters	6	2	1
Henry Faubs,	Dunns	50	18	1
James Lofton,	Alstons	124	7	5
Elizabeth Seals, w.R.S.,	Tuckers	212	20	2
Margaret Giffin, widow,	Boltons	265	2	1
William Rucker, R. S.,	Carpenters	201	6	1
Robert Hines's orphan	Alstons	75	30	1
Catharine Yoes, widow,	Dunns	123	12	5

FAYETTE.

Isiah Beck, jr. 9th		720	9	5
Joseph T. Harkins,	Craigs	115	5	5

(196)

Fortunate Drawers. Capts. Dist.	No.Dt.Sec.	Fortunate Drawers. Capts. Dist.	No.Dt.Sec.
John Moon, Dodsons	203 3 2	William Haynes, Suttons	69 20 2
Andrew J. Alsbury, illegit. Wests	166 21 2	John Popham, Tates	92 21 2
James Wright, Whartons	112 9 3	Nicholas Welch, R. S., Langstons	217 21 1

FRANKLIN.

HALL.

Hiram McCrackin, Tabors	1 3 4	John H. Bell, Hardages	195 31 1
Pleasant Hemphill, illegit. Caudells	114 6 5	Jeremiah Hill, Harrisons	74 19 1
Elisha Williams, sen. Stranges	30 9 1	James Loggins, sen. R. S., do.	47 9 3
Stephen Siddall, R. S., T. Chandlers	146 6 3	Hardy Griffin, Alreds	65 7 3
Sarah Boswell, wid. R. S., Hudsons	239 8 3	Gilford Light, Yagers	136 5 3
Thomas G. Dickson, Caudells	223 16 2	B.,R.W.,D.&J.S.Hill, fa. ab. Harrisons	81 21 1
Ransom Cain, Stephens	14 2 1	Noah Strong, Smiths	63 9 2
James Dailey, Jones	50 2 5	Robert Evens, Roberts	42 21 2
Isaac E. Cobb, T. Chandlers	134 17 2	William B. Box, Hardens	246 12 3
Zachariah Pruitt, Sanders	80 10 5		
Jesse Sewell, Hudsons	159 8 1	HOUSTON.	
Larkin Walters, Walters	205 28 1	John Wimberly, Batesman	293 4 1
		William Haddock, do.	153 17 2

GLYNN.

IRWIN.

John Victory, McLeods	249 13 2	James Griffin, R. S., Dixons	85 9 3

GREENE.

JACKSON.

Martha Cartright, widow, Rankins	58 13 1		
Adeline Harrison, orphan, Dawsons	41 3 2	Joseph Little, Allens	205 7 3
Orphans of Charles Miller, do.	134 3 2	John Camron, Landrums	91 1 1
William Forister, Greenes	113 7 3	William H. Claghorn, Storys	141 15 2
Jordin Bruce's orphans, Bruces	86 17 2	Amon Yarbbrough, Duncans	104 11 3
Leanner McColley, wid. Dawsons	145 2 4	James Buys, Venables	67 12 3
Amy Stringfellow, w. R. S., Robinsons	337 8 1	Mourning Wheeler, w. R. S., Millers	207 1 4
		Benjamin Stackton, Duncans	35 2 3
		John Evans, R. S., Bowens	99 7 2

GWINNETT.

		Wiliam Wafford's orphans, Ollens	153 23 2
James McDill, Greenes	250 33 1	Eldredge Nall's orphans, Millers	121 2 1
Bailey Curby, Moores	35 1 1	Joseph H. Murdock, Duncans	43 20 1
Thomas Taylor, Robertsons	103 33 1	James Kirkland, soldier, Watersons	146 2 2
Henry Jinnings, Caruthers	78 14 2	Charles Damron, R. S., Millers	10 9 2
Charles Yancy, orphan, Greenes	15 15 2	Wiley Franklin, illegitimate Moons	254 5 2
Samuel Day, Rollins	70 13 2		
Elisha Minchew's orphans, Caruthers	14 12 3	JASPER.	
Elizabeth Wigley's illegits. Davis	166 2 5		
William Findley, Woodroughs	21 5 2	Benjamin Hamrick, R. S., Wilders	160 14 2
Wilson Goss, Bakers	229 12 2	Thomas Gore, soldier, Erwins	130 11 2
John McDonald, Moores	38 21 2	Hiram Adams, illegitimate, Camerons	222 10 1
John Brown, Davis	19 7 2	Merrell Peacock, Johnsons	175 10 1
Thomas Wood, Bakers	319 7 5	Stephen E. Farley, Robersons	93 12 1
James B. Lion, do.	157 12 5	Jacob Hovarter, Trussells	41 8 5
		James Potts, R. S., do.	145 26 1

HANCOCK.

		Miles Stephens, Keys	181 17 2
Daniel C. Turner, 107th	363 28 1	Nancy Bryant, widow, Hands	229 23 2
Daniel M. Cook, 114th	107 12 3	D. Helderbran's chil. fa. ab. Holmes	69 14 2
Joseph Grant, R. S., 106th	69 12 1	John McMichael sr. R. S., do.	37 20 2
John Roe, sen. R. S., 101st	55 17 2	Timothy Landrum, R. S., Baynes	225 4 3
Daniel Green, Swints	151 11 2	John Shaw, do.	47 4 3
William Wyley, R. S., Adams	76 19 2	James R. White, Posts	47 5 3
Sarah Robinson, hus. absent, 114th	212 14 2	Mary King, w., R. S., Reeves	168 6 2
James Youngblood, sen. 117th	153 5 4	John Carrell, R. S., Barnetts	296 28 1
William Spence, 118th	36 22 2	Starling, Smith, Baynes	183 11 1

HENRY.

JEFFERSON.

		Ezekiel Causey, sen. Boyds	80 14 5
Thomas Gay, soldier, Bryants	72 15 2	Stephen Cotter, do.	54 21 1
John Williamson, R. S., Millers	169 12 1	Hugh McNeely, do.	74 24 1
William M. Greene, Shaws	34 10 5	Thomas Wren, Beatys	231 3 1
Isaac Williams, Allens	38 3 5	William Phipps, orphan, Jones	4 27 1
William McKnight, jun. Shaws	77 2 5	Charles M. Gamble, Ross	57 7 3
George Harrill, Gosdens	73 16 1	Robert Lowrie, Causeys	323 22 1
James Shearrar, Kites	240 12 2	William Barrow's orphans, Jones	118 10 5

HABERSHAM.

JONES.

Richard Chitwood, Bakers	137 6 5		
Thomas Robertson, Tates	226 7 3	Nahum Little, Dosters	228 30 1
Stephen Cobb, do.	179 4 5	William Hick's mins. f.a.Duncans	22 1 1
Nicholes Welch, Langstons	253 8 3	Elizabeth Terrell, wid. Stewarts	67 26 1
Allen Hancock, Bryans	108 8 5	Samuel C. Caulkings, Sullevans	84 8 1
James Eaton, Suttons	½9 2 5	Daniel Hunt, R. S., Hammacks	179 10 3
Garret Vandegrift, Fancs	13 2 4		

LAND LOTTERY REGISTER—No. 29
[RECORDER OFFICE—PUBLISHHED BY GRANTLAND & ORME—PRICE $3.]

NOTE—Section 1 is Lee County—2 Muscogee—3 Troup—4 Coweta—5 Carroll.
65rd DAY'S DRAWING—Continued

Fortunate Drawers.	Capts.	Dist.	No.	Dt.	Sec.
JONES.					
Frederick Wimberly,	Robertsons	298	3	4	
Jacob Rogers' minors,	Taylors	31	7	3	
William D. Ethridge,	do.	164	22	2	
Jordan S. Burk,	Breadloves	139	21	1	
Wm. McKisack,	Newbys	46	4	2	
Jimmy Clemmons,	w.R.S.Robertsons	2	8	1	
Ann Finney, wid.	Spinks	232	28	1	
Joseph Davie,	Duncans	115	10	3	
John Lamar, R. S.,	Breadloves	66	7	1	
Lary Lary, sol.	Popes	136	12	2	
William Vauzant,	Spinks	47	16	1	
LAURENS.					
Sarah Perkin's illegs.	Mizells	162	25	1	
Henry Shepherd's orps.	Barlows	153	18	2	
Mary Howard's illegs.	Spiveys	33	11	1	
John G. Coates,	do.	107	5	5	
Loozinsky Lambert,	Deans	239	4	3	
Robert Register,	Hodges	90	9	5	
D. Mathewson's ors.	Plumers	213	1	2	
Wm. J. Larkin's orps.	Barlows	85	3	2	
James Marlow,	Mizells	53	15	2	
Etheldred Thomas, R. S.	do.	31	4	4	
LIBERTY.					
Afanny Smith, w.R.S.	16th	150	23	1	
LINCOLN.					
Thomas A. J. Crawford,	Graves	225	13	2	
Britain Guice,	Frasers	244	31	1	
John Armstrong,	Graves	29	10	2	
William R. Statham,	Prathers	117	9	5	
Moses Jones, R. S.	Frasers	103	3	1	
MADISON.					
William Hayes, sol.	Hannas	228	14	1	
Wm. David's orps.	Culbertsons	143	13	2	
Oliver C. Powell,	Christians	99	11	1	
M'INTOSH.					
William Taylor,	Terrells	166	25	1	
MONROE.					
Susan McGlawn, wid.	Finchs	266	21	1	
James B. Smith,	Douglass	256	2	4	
Benjamin Bissup,	Gammons	83	9	2	
William T. Davis, illeg.	Rays	229	17	2	
John McGlawn,	Pattersons	182	32	1	
Samuel W. Langston,	Turners	17	6	5	
Jackson Thompson, illeg.	Houses	17	5	2	
John Richardson,	Greshams	189	20	1	
Wm. & Patsey Raley,	Wrights	320	8	1	
Elizabeth Parham, w.	Pattersons	257	3	4	
Elizabeth Lipham,	Browns	19	21	2	
Gabriel Howell's orp.	Finchs	15	17	2	
Frederick L. Crowder,	Millers	287	6	1	
Gabriel McCoy's oprs.	Houses	130	4	2	
John S. Duncan,	Woodwards	245	2	1	
John S. Beckham,	Stallings	25	30	1	
MORGAN.					
Jacob Williams,	Walkers	119	3	4	
Ruddy Bohannon,	Adairs	207	1	2	

Fortunate Drawers.	Capts.	Dist.	No.	Dt.	Sec.
William Anderson,	Hitchcocks	229	6	5	
Clayton, S. Woodley,	Browns	140	1	5	
Mary Phillips, wid.	Canifaxs	177	12	2	
George B. White,	Shearmans	2	14	1	
John Smith,	Hitchcocks	195	29	1	
MONTGOMERY.					
Brinkley Gandy,	Wynns	45	3	2	
NEWTON.					
Mitchell Beasley,	Summers	20	25	1	
Jordan Smith,	Clarks	127	8	3	
Elvina Delany, wid.	Hays	19	11	1	
John D. Mann,	Talleys	178	12	1	
Hugh L. White,	do.	30	12	1	
William N. Gibson,	Graves	97	8	1	
William Nolen,	Allredds	125	2	4	
John A. Craddock,	Askews	178	14	2	
Sampson Gibson,	Newnans	121	12	3	
Mathew Moss,	Moss'	59	31	1	
James Butrum,	Graces	157	13	1	
OGLETHORPE.					
John Holmes,	Smiths	19	6	4	
Eli R. Callaway's orps.	Hills	209	9	1	
John F. Richels,	Rousseaus	169	21	2	
David Wilkins,	Rhodes	156	6	3	
Elijah Butler's orps.	Hills	33	21	2	
Jacob Buzbin,	Burfords	62	10	3	
Elizabeth Davis, wid.	Hills	219	2	3	
Elizabeth H. Jones,	w.R.S.Lacys	93	25	1	
PIKE.					
James Howard, idiot,	Orrs	62	6	4	
PULASKI.					
Cynthia Crofford, wid.	Thomas	173	7	5	
William Bryan,	Scarbroughs	18	10	1	
Harrison Peacock,	do.	45	7	1	
PUTNAM.					
Overall Waller,	Barnetts	90	10	1	
Thomas Barrow,	Allums	229	18	1	
James M. Smedley,	Mizes	243	3	2	
Turner F. Pruitt,	Choices	74	5	2	
Sarah Philips,	w.R.S.Kendricks	226	2	4	
Samuel Linch,	Clarks	133	11	3	
Samuel Harwell,	Blacks	106	1	5	
Ralph Huff, sol.	Bledsoes	268	6	1	
Shadrack Rowe, R. S.	Clarks	101	11	3	
Lucy Argro, illeg.	Allums	190	1	4	
Thomas W. Cowen,	Sawyers	45	12	5	
William Flake, jr.	Bledsoes	115	22	1	
Samuel Bussey, (F.)	Blacks	67	7	1	
Sarah Sutton, w. R. S.	Vinings	249	10	1	
RABUN.					
P. & P. Lovelady, ors.	Godfreys	189	10	1	
Wm. Slewder,	Mercers	53	5	2	
RICHMOND.					
Richard Bush,	Treadwells	14	11	3	
Thomas Ginn,	Wilcoxs	134	21	1	
John Dillon,	Treadwells	132	14	1	
Abagail Stoy, wid.	Ferris	164	19	1	
Cath. B. Cormick,	w.Huntingtons	341	22	1	

(198)

Fortunate Drawers. Capts. Dist.	No.	Dt.	Sec.	Fortunate Drawers. Capts. Dist.	No.	Dt.	Sec.
Robert Tarver Knight, Kellys	127	23	1	Sherrard Sneed, Floyds	139	25	1
Mary Coghlan, widow,	177	15	1	**WILKINSON.**			
Comfort Griffin, wid. Blacks	115	8	1	Wm. Carswell, Halls	249	17	1
A. Cunningham, (M.D.) Ferris	111	24	2	James Castleberry, Shows	72	4	1
Wm. Smith, carpen. Treadwells	146	4	1	James Justice's orps. Fairchilds	325	20	2
John Forgason's orps. Wilcoxs	57	3	1	Milly Smith, wid. Mayos	188	3	3
SCRIVEN.				Mary Lindsey, widow, Halls	21	8	4
Thomas Nicholasson, Reaves	86	9	5	John Holder, Corrys	140	1	4
Alexander Welles, Roberts	45	31	1	Solomon Williams, Mandersons	157	5	4
TATTNALL.				**WILKES.**			
Josiah Collins, Corseys	148	7	2	Gideon Cooper, Popes	187	6	1
Sarah Conner, wid. Dees	49	8	4	David Mayo, Charltons	270	23	2
Solomon Mobley, sol. McCalls	130	10	2	A. H. Sneed, soldier	122	6	2
Elias Fiveash, R. S., Graces	93	23	2	Mary Brinton, wid. Carters	158	23	2
Zebulon Holingsworth, Corseys	42	1	3	Bar. Johnson, R.S., Washingtons	199	6	5
TELFAIR.				John Jones, Amasons	68	12	2
William New, Barentines	49	5	4	Elizabeth Wilson, wid. Rices	183	25	1
Nancy Hall, Robertsons	278	22	1	Solomon Pattern's orps. Wootens	77	15	1
David Fitzgerald, Barentines	391	20	2				
Stephen Boen, R. S. Wilsons	73	12	5	64th DAY'S DRAWING—May 19.			
TALIAFERRO.				**APPLING.**			
Robert H. Chapman, Towns	185	23	2	Major Hurst, Collins	206	14	1
THOMAS.				**BALDWIN.**			
Jacob Williams	262	16	2	Jacob Barrow, Buchanans	53	9	5
TWIGGS.				Thomas Ragland, Ginns	143	10	1
Orps. of T. Williams, Wimberlys	34	11	5	Lydia Kinney, widow, Lesters	149	17	2
James Davidson, sol. Pearsons	192	30	1	Bolling Hall, Lingos	83	9	5
Crumpton's orphs. Solomons	180	12	1	**BIBB.**			
John Henderson, illeg. Bosticks	30	8	1	Jacob Collins, orphans, Carrs	286	22	2
UPSON.				Henry Clemm, soldier, Pickards	223	11	1
Solomon Scrimshire, Paschals	201	2	5	**BRYAN.**			
Gibson Dawson, sol. Petties	114	3	5	C., J., S. R. & I. Sikes, Harveys	249	1	4
Shadrack Pugh, R. S.	225	33	1	**BURKE.**			
Jones Persons, R. S. Myricks	59	2	5	Henry S. Jones, Andersons	4	23	2
William McFarlin, Coupers	27	5	5	Alfred R. Jarvis, Rogers	247	2	2
George W. Hansford, Harrells	108	7	3	Joseph Spence, Lynchs	123	9	1
WALTON.				Sarah Broxton, widow, Dugas	179	3	5
John Bachus, soldier, 503rd	151	16	2	**BUTTS.**			
Thomas L. Winn, 249th	158	7	2	Bryant Hamil, Chapmans	174	4	1
Noah Nelson, 418th	10	2	3	Arch'd. McCurdy's orps.Robinsons	74	10	1
Thomas C. Stevens, sol. Hudsons	75	12	3	**CAMDEN.**			
John M. Booker, Snows	27	17	1	George W. Roberts, Baileys	126	1	1
WAYNE.				Cornelius B. Bessent, do.	50	12	5
Joseph Howell, Staffords	308	6	1	**CHATHAM.**			
WARREN.				Ors. of John R. Warner, Geredons	75	6	1
Wiley Harris, sr. sol. Fords	37	1	3	George R. Hendrickson, Haydens	211	20	2
Larkin Glover, sol. Downs	182	6	5	Hermon D. Grene, do.	6	8	5
Henry Wilson, Sanders	13	7	2	**CLARK.**			
Ruth Phillips, w. R. S. Downs	20	9	1	Richard M.D. Thompson, Birchs	113	28	1
William Bridges, do.	21	10	3	George B. Sims' orps. Wrights	103	11	5
Abner Huff's orps. Adkins	218	8	1	Benning B. Moore, Deans	94	24	1
WASHINGTON.				James Stephens' orphs. Wrights	126	10	5
James R. Brooks, Whitfields	215	5	4	**COLUMBIA.**			
Elisha Forshee, Oquins	177	8	3	Jane Snider, widow, Carrolls	135	16	1
C. & W. Veal, illegs. Mannings	169	6	5	Spsan Pullin, widow, Culbreaths	233	2	3
Larkin Griffin, Rushings	6	4	4	John Cole, Coles	93	3	4
John Dorch, Wimberlys	18	16	1	Willis Johnson, R. S. Dranes	214	11	5
Malachi Joiner, McLendons	225	16	2	**CRAWFORD.**			
Thomas Troutman, Woods	164	2	4	Samuel McBride, Tillers	57	15	1
Thos. Tanner's orps. Wimberlys	82	12	1	John S. B. Tarver, Wilsons	146	18	2
James Helton, Currys	48	11	3	Elisha Davis, do.	26	16	2
				Turner Persons, Hicks	65	6	4

(199)

Fortunate Drawers. Capts.	Dist.	No.	Dt.	Sec.
DE KALB.				
Thomas J. Adams, Merritts		278	12	3
John Bassett, soldier, Andersons		21	2	2
John Mitchel, soldier, Scaifs		207	13	2
James Hooper, jr.	Conns	177	10	2
Robert Atkinson, R. S., Howells		28	13	1
Joseph Strickland, Bakers		204	12	2
Richard Gragan,	Conns	78	5	3
Robert Ware,	Browns	60	33	1
EARLY.				
Jesse Williams, Wilsons		125	26	1
ELBERT.				
Transilvania Guin, W. Horton's		381	7	1
EMANUEL.				
Sarah Roberts, illegit. Swains		102	14	2
FAYETTE.				
Bird W. Linville, Roziers		44	10	1
Jeptha Yarbrough, Wests		225	26	1
FRANKLIN.				
Francis Durrett, Stephens		2	13	2
David Gortney, Blankinships		211	33	1
Temperance Manly, wid. Cokers		19	9	1
GRENE.				
James Daniel, Woodhams		108	3	1
Benjamin Copeland, R. S., Halls		373	28	1
Reuben H. Stewart, Vincents		47	7	2
Ezekiel Brown, Woodhams		19	10	1
GWINNETT.				
Samuel Hollis, Madduxs		122	22	2
Langston Bennett, Cupps		10	5	3
William M. Peters, sol. Mattoxs		105	15	1
Alssy Kemp, Moors		331	1	4
Fireliza Barker, widow, Moors		132	1	3
Samuel Bolt, Woodroughs		65	28	1
William Kemp, Hills		180	11	5
Eliz. Waldraven, w.R.S., Greenes		225	23	1
James Garner, Woodroughs		177	26	1
HANCOCK.				
Wotten Driskill's orphans, 108th		14	3	3
John L. Swinney, 113th		165	10	2
HENRY.				
Benjamin Fincher, jr. Gosdens		231	7	3
Moses Presley, R. S. Risons		199	33	1
David White, Bryants		127	12	5
Absolem Turner, Millers		151	23	2
Richard Curde, Wards		285	28	1
HABERSHAM.				
Mary Ann Herrin, w.R.S.,Jones		86	11	1
John Bryan, Tates		104	4	5
Enoch Davis, do.		177	8	5
Thomas Carder, Kenzies		4	5	3
James Crow, do.		178	10	1
John Reeves, Suttons		93	13	2
Joseph Berry, Tates		206	31	1
HALL.				
Joseph Dent, Dorseys		14	31	1
Amos Brown, Hardens		19	1	4
Aaron Adams, Harrisons		204	17	1
Jesse Thomas, Hardens		225	22	2
HOUSTON.				
Benjamin McKinney, Wimberlys		168	11	5
IRWIN.				

Fortunate Drawers. Capts.	Dist.	No.	Dt.	Sec.
James Magee, McCalls		143	22	2
JACKSON.				
Harvy A. Archer, Millers		133	20	2
Boley Wilson, Rogers		237	5	2
Richard Pentecost, sol. Georges		69	2	3
Samuel H. Barr, Rogers		75	7	4
Joseph Pinson, Lindseys		213	5	3
James Cain, Rogers		293	1	4
John Bradley, R. S. Landrums		322	28	1
JASPER.				
Thomas H. Smith,sol.Robinsons		275	7	1
Jeremiah Lumsden, R. S.,Baynes		186	19	1
James H. Estes, Dardens		169	24	1
JEFFERSON.				
Elenor McNeely, w. R.S. Boyds		100	6	2
Geo. Stanleton, sr. R.S., Beatys		39	2	3
Dicy Parsons, widow, Ross		62	11	1
JONES.				
Samuel Modesett, Duncans		223	9	1
Chares Philips, Gibsons		270	17	2
John Bently, Hammacks		237	12	1
Wiliam Allen, illeg. Hendersons		7	4	4
William Poe, Dosters		101	18	1
LAURENS.				
Isaac Kirksey's ors. Whiteheads		302	6	5
Edward Hearndon, Powers		75	1	5
Lewis McLendon, do.		87	5	2
Eason Allen, Spivys		199	8	5
Eliza Mimms, illeg. Hodges		14	8	4
LIBERTY.				
Wilburn Johnson, orp. 17th		263	21	2
Nelson Thomas, 15th		159	1	4
LINCOLN.				
Francis Strother's min. Gideons		158	11	1
Joseph Hammon, Lonorgans		204	31	1
Lewis Stovall's minors, do.		158	19	2
MADISON.				
Asa Hendrick, Hannas		145	7	5
MONROE.				
David Jones, Browns		223	6	5
James Wilder, sol. Jas. Millers		106	14	5
Drury Wheeles, Greshams		320	7	5
Jane E. Bell, wid. Pattersons		314	8	1
Hezek. Hendrick, R. S. Johnsons		245	13	2
Mary McCormack, wid. Wrights		229	5	5
Sally Hurt, orphan, Houses		98	33	1
MORGAN.				
Allen Jones, Christians		104	7	4
William Sanders, Jennings		231	3	4
Daniel Parker, R. S. Canifaxs		42	4	1
MONTGOMERY.				
John Slaughter, Pridgeons		257	3	3
NEWTON.				
Lewis Towers, sol. Tallys		120	9	3
Sarah Gordon, wid. Penningtons		118	8	4
Susanah Goss, wid. Hays		154	15	2
Charles McDonald, Tallys		5	14	1
John Edge, sol. Askews		130	21	2
Baley M. Freeman, Smiths		137	5	2
Jesse Willingham, Snows		25	3	4
Lewis Delany's orphs. Hays		211	10	2
John Carlisle, Snows		76	21	1
Jarratt B. Ellisson. Newnans		150	19	1

OGLETHORPE.
Fortunate Drawers. Capts. Dist. No.Dt.Sec.
Mary Young, widow, Bells	108	23 2
Jacob Busbin, sol. Billups	213	28 1

PIKE.
John Clayton, Mays	281	28 1
Joel Moultry, orphan, Hicks	63	23 2

PULASKI.
Abraham Wood, R. S. Thomas	24	17 1
Joseph Simmons, Sparrows	230	3 5
Mary Manning's illeg. Powells	114	13 5
James Little, Gilstraps	66	11 5

PUTNAM.
Thomas King, sr. R. S. Allums	149	17 1
Wiliam R. Heath, Chambers	198	31 1
John Hagan, Sawyers	246	30 1
William Scott, R. S. Vinings	151	24 2
Reuben Harrison, do.	230	7 3
Hicks Ellis, do.	55	7 5
John T. Langford, Marcus	121	18 1

RABUN.
William Wall, Becks	244	4 1
John Price, Godfreys	204	28 1
Ralph Cobb, do.	233	18 2

RICHMOND.
Larkin Brown, 119th	133	5 2
Eliza Ross' orps. Raifords	38	25 1
Hiram Mann, Huntingtons	98	8 5
Mathew Inglett, James	148	20 2
Charles Carter, Treadwells	38	7 3
James Palmer, James	295	7 1
Thomas G. Casey, Thomas	210	5 4

SCRIVEN.
Thomas Robbins, Poytress	205	3 4
Rebeckah Ponder, w. Stricklings	62	15 2
John L. Dowdy, do.	63	27 1
Benjamin Roberts, Roberts	149	1 3
Isaac Waters, Humphreys	70	2 5

TALIAFERRO.
William Justiss, Hammacks	110	26 1

TATTNALL.
Thomas Hilliard, Conners	233	1 4
Isham Stephens, Deloaches	162	24 2
Thomas Cudworth, McDuffies	157	3 4

TELFAIR.
Lughlim McLain, Robertsons	240	2 1
Joel Ricks, Wilkersons	74	4 2

TWIGGS.
Benj. Hoskin's orps. Bosticks	85	12 5

UPSON.
William Harrell, Harrells	69	26 1
Sarah Black's illegit. do.	159	14 2

Fortunate Drawers. Capts. Dist. No.Dt.Sec.
Cornelius Jeter, Coopers	355	7 1
Shadrack Ellis, sr. Ellis	156	8 5
Moses Duke, Myricks	207	8 5

WALTON.
William Clarke, jr. McQuirtors	169	17 1
Charles Sides, Hudsons	219	11 1
Allen McQuirtor, McQuirtors	84	5 5
Hiram Camp, 249th	187	16 2
William Kimbro, Bixleys	286	7 5

WARREN.
Benjamin Moreland's ors. Bulls	178	2 1
Julian A. Bray, wid. Hills	20	8 3
Orville Bull, Bulls	81	22 2
Joseph Williams, R. S. Adkins	215	6 5

WASHINGTON.
John Morell, sol. Jordans	25	7 1
Henry McKinnie, do.	61	24 1
William C. McLean, Mannings	57	27 1
James Gladdin, O'Quins	251	16 2
Joseph Barron, Currys	49	17 1
Levi Martin's orps. O'Quins	168	15 5
Zilphy Eccols, w. R. S. Tysons	113	1 4
C.&W.Griffins orps. Oquins	168	15 5

WILKES.
Elizabeth Dunn, orp. Greshams	42	8 1
Drury Callaway, Popes	336	28 1
Charles R. Green, Wottens	79	16 1
Raiphael Wheeler's orps. Lukers	64	12 5
William Hindsman, Washingtons	99	4 4
Robert McGinty's orps. Hamocks	215	19 1
Richard Fomby, Washingtons	64	6 4
Elizabeth Huling, w. R.S., do.	137	3 1
William Dyer, Hopkins	127	24 1

WILKINSON.
Hugh Ingram, Smiths	60	2 4
James Curry, Currys	189	2 3
Peter McArtha, Mayos	89	9 3
Lemuel Burket, Shows	13	1 4

☞ We shall take pleasure in furnishing the subscribers to our Lottery Register with any of the numbers that may have *miscarried*, for which we wish application to be made without delay. Notwithstanding the great care we have taken to send the sheets with *perfect regularity*, some mistakes have doubtless been made by us in the folding and directing of so large a number, and in the different Post Offices the errors of sending and delivering have been perhaps more numerous.

G. & O.

LAND LOTTERY REGISTER—No. 30
[RECORDER OFFICE—PUBLISHED BY GRANTLAND & ORME—PRICE $3.]

NOTE—Section 1 is Lee County—2 Muscogee—3 Troup—4 Cowèta—5 Carroll.

65th *DAY'S DRAWING*—May 21.

Fortunate Drawers. Capts. Dist. No.Dt.Sec.

APPLING.
Fortunate Drawers. Capts. Dist. No.Dt.Sec.
William Hammond, Morgans   131 15 2

BAKER.
Bryant Husk, soldier, Porters   124 5 3

BALDWIN.
David Cremer, Rowes   95 31 1
Thomas R. Huson, Ginns   79 23 2
Thomas Mounger, orp. Buchanans   238 13 2
John Murphy, Ginns   257 10 2
Newton Haws, soldier, Thomas   109 5 3
Benjamin Askew, Pitts   265 22 2

BIBB.
M. Mayo, hus. d. in serv. coun. Carrs   86 15 2
George Bland, Lloyds   164 5 5
Henry G. Orrick, Beards   99 3 4
Samuel Gillespie, Bates   183 18 1

BRYAN.
Josiah Douglass, Harveys   222 14 1

BULLOCH.
Harbert Corbett, Lockharts   27 13 1
George J. Walsh, do.   229 16 2

BURKE.
John Crozier, jr. Wests   297 1 4
Benjamin Greenway, Fountains   213 13 2
Henry & Wm. Caruthers, ills., Segars   13 2 2
William Poythress, R. S., Gordons   177 31 1
Christ & James Archy, orps. Corkers   67 31 1
Henry Bell, Bayleys   145 21 2

BUTTS.
John M. Parson, soldier, Kirksies   94 33 1

CAMDEN.
Victor Blanc, Wards   149 5 5

CHATHAM.
William Cannet, Baines   219 16 2
Louis Nicholas Maupas, Nungazers   159 4 1
Wiliam Williams, fireman, Haydens   177 20 1
Uriah Michell, McDonnells   96 3 4

CLARK.
Olive Johnson, hus. ab. Gahagans   8 1 1
John Berry, Frosts   171 5 5
Beaton Daniel, Vinsons   69 22 1
Isaac Jacks, Alreds   51 23 1
Sarah Durham, widow, Greers   30 26 1
Josiah C. Garrett, Davis   270 3 4
William H. Reynolds, Gahagans   120 10 1
William Etherington, do.   64 5 1
Isaac Coleman, McDonalds   221 23 2
John F. Foster, Lumpkins   188 18 2
Nelson Anderson, Andersons   107 9 2
John C. Pearson, Herndons   219 7 3

COLUMBIA.
Elisha Holliman's orps. Clarks   63 29 1
James S. W. Watson, Dranes   178 3 3
James Rowland, soldier, Magruders   151 7 1
Ann Crosbay, illegitimate, Dranes   55 11 5
Wiliam A. Fuller, Magruders   226 2 1

CRAWFORD.
Jameson Jordan, Lovetts   53 7 4
William Wright, R. S., Wilsons   150 12 5

DE KALB.
Thomas Oliver, Scaifs   62 22 1
Amos Hampton, Conns   137 19 2

Fortunate Drawers. Capts. Dist. No.Dt.Sec.
Isaiah Parker, soldier, Hayes   71 3 1
Jesse Curbe, for wife, Lokeys   154 7 4
John Cook, R. S., Conns   99 5 3
William Simmons, Stephens   145 23 2
George Heard, Browns   151 14 5

EFFINGHAM.
Thomas Wylly, R. S., Srticklands   186 11 3
William Pearson, Waldhaners   148 22 2

ELBERT.
Wells Smith, Tuckers   196 22 2
Binley Andrew, soldier, Webbs   179 24 1
Rachel Richards, wid. Harmonds   140 11 5
Sarah Moon, widow, Merritts   92 4 5
John L. Hinton, Dunns   209 11 2
Founten Jourden, Dunns   141 24 2
Patrick McMullens, sol. Carpenters   67 25 1
Gregory Grant, Tuckers   125 4 3
Betsey Ham, w. R. S., Harmonds   107 22 1
John M. Haynes, Hortons   296 8 1
Orphans of Brown Dye, Bells,   55 19 1
William King, R. S. Boltons   97 26 1
Vincent Hubbard, Bells   50 9 3
Jesse Maxwell, Hortons   267 9 3

EMANUEL.
William Hughbanks, Snells   9 26 1
Philip C. Club, Swains   45 11 5
Isaac Rowland, Whiddons   144 26 1

FAYETTE.
Jeremiah D. Mann, Whartons   139 10 1
Jemima Swann, widow, Wests   240 7 5
Samuel McLedon, sol. McLondons   145 23 1
Wiliam S. Maxwell, Whartons   74 4 3
Isham Brazil, soldier, McLendons   116 5 3
John Treadwell, Craigs   101 9 5
Elizabeth Smith, w.R.S., Whartons   160 14 1

FRANKLIN.
Charles Darby, jr. McDonalds   253 9 2
William Bryan, sen. Stranges   81 5 1
James Toney, Sanders   87 24 1
James Terrell, R. S., Boswells   36 29 1
Robert Malone, Hudsons   97 10 2
Thomas Graham, do.   219 10 2
Jesse Braughner, sr. Stranges   30 16 2
Alexander McMillion, R. S., Walters   165 4 5
William Abbott, sol. D. Chandlers   261 28 1
Sampson Meeler, Gaudells   118 10 3
John Selman, R. S. D. Chandlers   194 19 2
John M. Albritton, Blankinships   43 3 4

GREENE.
Robert Boggess, Southerlands   70 6 1
William Coleman's orphans, Halls   224 11 1
Robert Allison, soldier, Dawsons   4 14 1
William Davis, Akins   189 6 2
Reuben Allison, Dawsons   315 7 5
John H. Sims, Astins   106 3 4

GWINNETT.
Joseph Ratcliff, Hills   157 3 1
James Rice, sen. Wallis   46 7 1
Love Dempsey, Rollins   245 2 2
Joel Walker, Caruthers   145 22 2
Sally Moore, widow, Whortons   18 22 2
Elmina Jones, min. fa.ab. Moores   54 4 3
Timothy Swindle, Whartons   30 4 3
William Mires, Rollins   204 26 1

(202)

Fortunate Drawers. Capts. Dist.	No.Dt.Sec.
David Lowry, Greens	141 23 2
Zachariah Lee, Wallis	201 23 1
Darkis Beem, widow, Robertsons	186 11 5
Britton C. Harris, Davis	87 18 2
Charles Gates, jr. Bakers	185 3 2

HANCOCK.

William Johnson, 118th	94 17 1
Major Croom, do.	43 27 1
Sarah Dent, widow, 109th	118 9 2
Luke Elmore, 103d	144 17 1
Hardy C. Culver, Adams	49 29 1
Wright Martin, 103d	22 10 5
Philip Gatewood, 108th	98 21 1
Joseph R. Sarsnett, soldier, Swints	45 6 4
John Hancock, 112th	150 2 1
Irvin Reaves, soldier, Colquetts	247 5 5
Lewis L. Cheely, 111th	211 9 1

HENRY.

Jourdan Crafton, Grays	134 1 2
Daniel Smith, Smiths	155 2 1
Allen Hartsfield's orphans, Kites	134 14 1
James Lovelace, sol. T. Harris's	266 8 1
Brantly A. Rowlin, Gosdens	62 14 2

HABERSHAM.

William H. Steelman, Tates	121 20 2
John Vaughan, Kenzies	77 3 3
William Shipley, do.	15 18 1
James M. Kennedy, Worshams	154 18 1
William Dodd, Suttons	37 19 2
Amos Chaffin, sen. Bryans	123 7 3
Sarah Grooce, orp. of Jacob, Bakers	142 10 5
Amos Hollingsworth, Suttons	88 4 5
Kezia Russell, widow, Jones	233 29 1
Jeremiah Marton, Bryons	198 7 3
Jesse Berry, Tates	296 5 3
Jeremiah McMillion, do.	95 7 3
Alston Edwards, do.	89 10 2
Reuben G. Anderson, sol. Bryans	74 14 3

HALL.

John Sowell, Garrards	221 7 3
Isaac Sowell, do.	97 3 1
Stephen Garner, Dorseys	173 2 1
Benjamin Otwell's orphan, Yagers	259 2 4
John Carroll, Wilsons	176 3 5
Richard Y. Otwell, agers	13 4 4

HOUSTON.

Solomon Fudge, Fudges	20 1 1
Nancy Blackshear's ill. Batemans	35 3 1

IRWIN.

Newell Wells, Dixons	31 4 5
Joel Gornto, do.	46 3 4

JACKSON.

Margaret Jack, w.R.S., Staplers	39 11 2
James Wheeler, R. S., Bowens	134 5 4
Thomas Milsaps, Landrums	9 21 1
Henry Spellers' orphans, Bowens	327 8 1
Olleyman Dodgen, Allens	163 13 1
Thomas Ashcraft, Winns	68 6 4
Thomas Stapler, sr. R. Sfifi Duprees	182 9 3
Edmund Honeycut, Winns	68 6 4
Samuel D. Chapman, Venables	159 2 1
James McLester, Lindseys	8 22 1
Richard S. Thompson, Rogers	175 12 3
Mary Buckner, hus. absent, Storys	118 17 1

JASPER.

Josiah R. Brown, Butts	148 23 2
Grace Morris, widow, Wilsons	83 1 4

Fortunate Drawers. Capts. Dist.	No.Dt.Sec.
Allen Goolsby, Butts	131 11 3
Anna Parrott, widow, Shropshires	7 27 1
Thomas Thames, Reeves	45 1 4
Arvigini A. B. Lewis, ill. Camerons	187 10 3
John H. Brown, soldier, Posts	87 7 2
Abner Chapman, sr., R. S., Holmes	49 5 3
William Penn, R. S., do.	204 9 3
Charles Forbes, Penningtons	84 10 3
Jesse Parrott, Downies	151 11 3
James Carter, Keys	44 10 3
Jesse Gude, Owens	45 22 2
Malinda Humphrey, wid. Johnsons	171 12 1
Henry Hines, Robersons	171 8 3
John Jones, Camerons	150 10 3
James T. Barnett, Barnetts	154 5 4
John Saunders, Baines	287 1 4

JEFFERSON.

Gilford Ingram, Cunninghams	254 25 1
James Pool, Beatys	44 26 1
Flamuel Thompson, Ross	251 17 2
Mathew Marshall, do.	223 5 3
Robert Brady, jr. Cunninghams	310 5 3
John Peel, soldier, Kings	54 11 3
Catharine McBride, widow, Boyds	256 19 2
Seaborn Sammons, Waldens	18 14 2

JONES.

Henry Baggerly, Stewarts	1 32 1
Thomas Abner, Blounts	21 3 5
John S. Reaves, sol. Bowens	37 7 2
Amon McMillian, Newbys	131 22 2
Thomas Drawhorn, Gibsons	217 22 2
Gilbert D. Ansley, Stewarts	258 23 2
Jackson Hammack, Mullins	151 5 1
William Whitley, Duncans	395 7 1
Julius C. B. Mitchell, Popes	155 28 1
Willis Barron, Bowens	261 5 3
Samuel C. Lippitt, Woods	45 26 1
Ebenezer Calef, Davis	173 10 3
John Hamlin's minors, Bowens	73 8 2
William Johnson, sol. Gibsons	172 28 1
Nancy Letton's illegs. Spinks	141 1 3
John Hallam, Popes	76 7 5
John G. Ramsey's mins. Bowens	292 8 5
William Etrridge, sol. Duncans	177 12 1
Wilie Lowe, Spinks	142 20 1
James J. Harris, Newbys	31 5 1
Cadsman Pope, Bowens	37 24 2
Mathias Mount, Gibsons	142 24 1
William Wilder, R. S. Robertsons	52 10 5
George W. Cooke, Popes	162 5 5

LAURENS.

Benjamin Snelgrove's ors. Mizells	77 23 2
James T. McBain, Mizells	298 4 1
Williams Cross, Deans	100 4 5
Solomon W.G.Clark's ors.Mizells	200 18 1
Fleet Pope's orps. Powers	241 20 1
John Sauls, Mizells	246 24 1
James Johnson, Spiveys	137 24 2

LIBERTY.

John Shaw, 16th	67 22 2
John N. Way, 15th	143 3 3

LINCOLN.

Buck Jeter, Parks	259 4 3

McINTOSH.

George A. Smith, Terrells	91 2 4

(203)

Fortunate Drawers. Capts. Dist.	No.	Dt.	Sec.
Sarah Newson, wid. McCranies	241	25	1
Margaret Mannen's ills. Howards	167	6	2
MADISON.			
Jacob Strickland, Christians	183	7	1
Henry Ware's orps. Hancocks	45	4	5
Jesse L. Barnes, Higginbothams	141	27	1
George Clore, R. S. Phipps	14	1	3
Henry Williford, Hannas	32	20	2
MONROE.			
Temp. Woodall, idiot, Knights	238	22	2
William Holland, Millers	70	15	5
Sylvanus Kendrick, Johnsons	5	2	2
Dempsey Fountain, Douglass	130	11	5
Anguish McSwain, Wrights	90	11	1
Isaac W. Fuller, Woodwards	215	22	2
Emeline Johnson, illeg. Millers	133	5	1
MONTGOMERY.			
Clement Bryan, Ryals	58	10	3
MORGAN.			
John Huff, sol. Griggs	275	6	1
Seaborn Sanders, Shermans	29	16	1
Willie Register, Christians	143	8	4
Joel Anderson, Adairs	60	8	4
John C. Parkerson, Whatleys	38	7	1
Cullin Sims, Jennings	52	4	4
William Boman, Adairs	103	5	2
Samuel Wood's orps. Christians	136	15	1
John Wood, Beasleys	171	10	2
Jacob Jester's orps. Canifaxs	53	1	3
George Dean, Hills	217	5	3
David Parker, sol. Griggs	171	10	5
Elisha Jarvis, sr.R.S.,Jennings	169	15	5
Lawrence Smith, R. S. Hitchcocks	64	21	2
NEWTON.			
Samuel Henry, Smiths	116	3	3
Alexander Pless, Newnans	124	2	5
Watson P. Freeman, do.	254	10	1
John Strong, Graves	105	13	2
Abijah Brooks, sol. Zachrys	149	6	3
William Smith, R. S. Snows	3	23	1
James S. Morris, do.	53	26	1
Joseph Cates, Pullens	258	3	4
Fairnight Perry Tidwell, illegit.	199	7	1
OGLETHORPE.			
Elbert Hardman, s. Simmons	88	4	4
Reuben Glaze, R. S. Dixs	106	2	2
Hartsfield Hendon, Hardmans	198	17	2
John Birdsong, R. S. Rousseaus	57	19	1
Bailey Reed, Williamsons	109	6	3
PIKE.			
Joseph Davison, R.S.Hartsfields	254	29	1
Daniel Bowling, Suiters	8	6	4
Joseph Helton, sol. Pattersons	15	30	1
William Gray, Hartsfields	34	20	2
William Towles, Hicks	113	3	2
PULASKI.			
Tabitha Yearty, wid. Kellams	52	10	1
Abner Averett's orps. Kellams	235	17	1
Tyra Garrett, Sparrows	209	25	1
Mary Mills, wid. Sparrows	161	12	2
James Bynum, Gilstraps	177	7	3

PUTNAM.			
Fortunate Drawers. Capts. Dist.	No.	Dt.	Sec.
Thomas Pearce, Choices	175	31	1
William D. Cole, Bledsoes	14	12	1
William Hall's orps. Blacks	344	28	1
John Fetts, s. l. w. Lamars	72	23	2
Jane Ashfield, widow, Blacks	45	25	1
Oliver Davidson, Chambers	39	28	1
Richard Bonner, Marcus	220	9	1
John D. Stephens, Blacks	117	32	1
RABUN.			
Timothy Lee, Godfreys	197	13	1
RICHMOND.			
Bartholomew Kearns, Augusta	111	14	2
James Morgan, R. S. Mantzs	140	5	5
Richard A. Palmer, Augusta	27	2	3
Ephriam Rigdon, 123rd	158	27	1
SCRIVEN.			
Rachel Humphriss, w. McCalls	141	16	1
TATTNALL.			
John Dias, R. S. Deloaches	80	18	1
Mary Wright, wid. Conners	145	10	3
Daniel Gray's orps. Graces	219	10	5
Allen West, McCalls	329	3	4
Robert Larimore's orps. Conners	247	29	1
Salim Sapp, McDuffies	84	5	3
TELFAIR.			
James McLeod, Barrentines	122	33	1
Thomas H. Ashley, Wilsons	92	8	5
Mary McInnis, w. Lampkins	131	14	2
TWIGGS.			
Sarah L. Crabb, ill. Streetmans	199	2	3
Sarah Buchanan, wid., Bosticks	87	3	1
Thomas Jones, Pearsons	153	14	2
Benj. Durden's orps. do.	110	9	3
Julian Chitty, wid. Streetmans	301	6	5
UPSON.			
Charity Dickson's ills. Saunders	234	6	3
Gideon Macon, Harrells	153	28	1
Daniel Driggers, Pettys	29	15	1
WALTON.			
Leonidas Few, Snows	22	17	2
Edmund Smithwick, 250th	95	3	2
John J. Still, Bexleys	77	15	2
Thomas A. Gibbs, sol. 418th	242	20	1
Abraham Hilton, Bexleys	23	12	5
William M. Sandford, do.	5	22	1
Robert S. Scoggins, 418th	42	7	5
WARE.			
Theophilus Keen, Greens	148	25	1
Obadiah Osteen's orps. Motes	85	1	1
Anney Wigins, wid. Grens	243	17	1
Arthur Pitmaman, do.	817	3	4
WARREN.			
Merrell Monk, Bulls	108	5	2
Martha Rozier, h. ab. Adkins	255	10	3
Thomas Wynn, Parhams	123	1	1
Isaac Hubanks, Adkins	111	29	1
Susannah Johnson's illeg. Hales	30	11	3
A. Guthrie, wound, l.w.Kinseys	236	30	1
William Ingram, Adkins	159	16	1
Jesse Ricketson, sr. R.S. Bulls	86	8	4

Fortunate Drawers.	Capts. Dist.	No.	Dt.	Sec.
Andrew B. Stevens' orps.	Hills	131	8	4
Granville Moody, soldier,	do.	35	21	1

WASHINGTON.

Ambrose Powell, sol.	Gilberts	282	1	2
Mary & S. Parker, ills.	Whitfields	37	7	3
John Eastward, sr.	R.S. O'Quins	135	12	1
Henry Hodges, sr.	Avans	95	2	1
Ander. C. Long, lunat.	Whitfields	207	6	1
William Keaton's orps.	Woods	14	15	5
Sarah Thompson, wid.	Rushings	51	2	3
Elizabeth Blackly,	Avans	279	7	1
John Salter,	Currys	2	25	1

WAYNE.

Mary Gibson, wid.	Mannings	150	5	1
Samuel O. Bryan,	Staffords	217	8	5
William Oneil's orps.	do.	157	23	1

WILKES.

Zadock Sowell, R. S.	Greens	147	9	1
Daniel Owens,	Moors	118	23	2
Benj. S. Selby,	Charltons	69	31	1
John Orr,	Hopkins	50	8	3
Wm. J. W. Wellborn,	Charltons	332	3	4
Alexander Norris, R. S.	Greens	102	12	5
Tyre Johnson,	Popes	117	30	1

WILKINSON.

Needham Harvell's childr.	Shows	71	24	1
Nathaniel Spears,	do.	59	4	5
Josiah Hatcher,	Hals	165	6	5
John H. Wales,	Mandersons	69	6	3
James Curry,	Currys	223	20	2
Bentley Outler,	do.	208	18	1
John Ryle,	Shows	146	5	2
John Smith,	Smiths	235	23	1
M. & L. Johnsons, ors.	Mandersons	227	7	3

66th DAY'S DRAWING—May 22.

APPLING.

John Mixon,	Collins	328	8	1
John Peterson,	Dedges	206	9	3

BALDWIN.

Toliver Davis, R. S.,	Bivins	82	2	5
Robert Northcut's orphans,	Rowes	46	27	1
Henry Gee,	Bivins	43	9	2
Adam Wilkinson,	Ginns	33	22	2
William Scurlock, jr.	Reddings	161	22	2
Redding B. Musselwhite,	Ginns	261	4	1
Wm. Allen's orphans, Reddings bat.		78	4	*
Jane Miles, widow,	Wicks	22	16	5
Lucinda B. Worsham wid.	Lesters	218	4	3

BIBB.

Moses Tucker, soldier,	Swearingins	109	10	5
Mary Ann Dillard, orphan,	Flanders	174	6	1
Rufus K. Evans,	Bates	201	5	5
Sarah Summerell, w. R. S.,	Carrs	209	7	5

BULLOCH.

James Wilkinson,	Deloachs	260	8	1
Jane Futch, widow,	do.	1	15	2
Silas Corbin,	Richardsons	280	4	1

BURKE.

Sarah Bryan, orphan,	McKays	235	17	2
Henry Richards,	Lynchs	65	9	5
Benjamin Tipton,	Wards	332	7	1
Joseph Cross,	Lynchs	147	2	2

Fortunate Drawers.	Capts. Dist.	No.	Dt.	Sec.
Jonanna Lambert, illegitimate,	Lewis	234	2	3
Nathaniel Polhill,	Fountains	189	8	1
Graystock Roberts, R. S.	Roberts	11	6	5
Rebecca & Henry Gregory, ills.	Dukes	129	11	2
Sarah Collins, widow, R. S.,	Bayleys	85	1	3

BUTTS.

Wiliam Hamlett,	Chapmans	149	2	4
Calvin Rollins,	Masons	97	6	3

CAMDEN.

Lucy Spalding, widow,	Millers	201	2	1
Daniel Mickler, soldier,	Wards	193	12	1

CHATHAM.

Lee Lay,		16	7	4
James A. Sanderlin, sol.	McDonnells	155119		2
Ebenezer Jackson, sr. R. S.,		53	4	5
Maria Anna Peirce,	Baines	52	17	1
Dorcas Dow, widow,	do.	109	4	2
Nathaniel Camfield,	Geredons	191	22	2
Joseph Bird,	Gaddys	133	20	1
John R. Goldsmith,	McDonnells	81	5	2
Wiliam Dye, orphan,	Geredons	81	19	2
Richard Dowdy, R. S.,	McDonnells	87	4	3

CLARK.

William Matthews	McDonalds	25	4	2
Elizabeth Malone, widow,	Deans	45	9	1
John A. Hunt,	Coxs	242	18	1
James Hale, sen. R. S.,	McCrees	255	21	1
Wylie Glenn,	Gahagans	189	7	1
William Prichard,	Davenports	66	13	5
Eliza Moore, widow,	Espys	16	11	5
John Smith, R. S.,	McCrees	78	31	1
John Hunt,	Ransoms	166	22	1
Robert Dougherty orphan,	Gahagans	240	10	3

COLUMBIA.

William C. Avery,	Coles	122	6	4
James Whittaker,	Dranes	110	12	5
James H. Moore,	Boltons	205	10	2
Margaret Sims, widow,	Ramseys	204	4	3
Moses Wade's orphans,	Clark	212	9	5
James Gerald's orphans,	Talbots	53	16	2
William W. Young,	do.	334	8	1
Martha McGruder, widow,	Bealls	100	11	1
Tarlton F. Heath's orps.	ivermans	37	26	1
Elizabeth Crawford, wid.	Ramseys	250	5	2
Obedience D. Cobb, widow,	Talbots	214	6	3

CRAWFORD.

Arthur Stuckey's orphans,	Ellis	123	9	2
Samuel W. Hearn, soldier,	Wilsons	314	15	1
Sarah McCants, w. R. S.,	Hamiltons	261	19	2

DE KALB.

Thorrington Ward,	Stephens	14	13	1
William Gilbert,	Edwards	57	11	5
James Trimble,	Conns	210	26	1
Mary Black's illegitimates,	Lokeys	281	23	2
Charles Lively,	Edwards	17	33	1
James Martin,	Stephens	182	12	3

DOOLY.

Stephen M. Coleman,	Andersons	62	6	1

EFFINGHAM.

Jas. Todd, orp. of Wm.,	Waldhaners	103	15	1
Herman Elkins,	Elkins	65	6	5
Charles Bird,	Treutlins	175	21	2

ELBERT.

James F. Nunlee, R. S.,	Tuckers	62	25	1
Molly Hudson, widow,	Blackwells	222	12	2
Joshua Prothro,	Dobbs	173	8	5
Milly Murphy, widow,	Carpenters	62	28	1

(205)

Fortunate Drawers. Capts.	Dist.	No.	Dt.	Sec.
Frederick C. Harman, sol. Harmans		225	16	1

EMANUEL.

John O. Hatten, McGars		64	12	1
Elijah Padget's orphans, Chasons		158	5	2
Solomon Mercer's orphans, Nabbs		65	9	3
William Thornton, 49th		213	6	3

FAYETTE.

Benjamin Garrett, Dodsons		150	3	5
Allan Lambert, Craigs		157	4	2
Jesse C. Brown, Browns		162	20	2
Robert Boring, soldier, Landrums		313	15	1

FRANKLIN.

Samuel Dunlap's orphans, Cokers		23	20	2
Thomas G. Dickson, Caudells		365	28	1
Howard Cash, Walters		46	10	5
John Payne, sen. Strangers		101	16	2
Absalom Holbrook, Bennetts		134	12	1
William Aaron, soldier, Boswells		138	11	5
Allen Weems, do.		49	6	1
Adam Rogers, Bennetts		48	8	4
Clement Dollar, Boswells		207	29	1
Richard M. Manley, Cokers		207	8	1
Wiley D. Morgan, T. Chandlers		128	30	1

GLYNN.

John W. McLeod, McLeods		253	9	5
Bailly Forrester, Burnetts		176	21	2
John W. Turner, McLeods		55	21	1
John Brooker, Burnetts		215	18	2

GREENE.

John Colt, Vincents		142	25	1
Phebe Cogbill's illegits, Woodhams		159	1	2
Moses Jackson, R. S., Winkfields		232	4	1
Thomas Crawford, Webbs		215	21	1
Joshua Shropshire, Halls		63	33	1
Robert G. Stovall, Winkfields		185	18	1
Susannah Ricker, idiot, Rankins		7	19	2
Fanny Crompton, widow, Halls		97	19	2
Joseph Anderson, orphan, Robins		112	1	5
Archibald M. Jackson, do.		139	15	2
Richard Linsey, Newsoms		80	12	3
Alford Levingston, Rankins		70	2	3

GWINNETT.

David B. Driskill, Moores		17	3	2
James Waters' orphans, Hunicuts		7	6	5
John H. Hammond, do.		230	8	1
Robert Pritchett, Rollins		251	25	1
Thomas Stewart, Moores		37	13	2
Elizabeth Morris, w. R. S., Robertsons		151	10	3
William Bagwell, Woodroughs		237	10	3
James Williamson, Caruthers		310	7	1
Andrew Cain, Woodroughs		195	28	1
John Guttrie, R. S., Davis		87	15	5
Bethia Warren, widow, Moores		150	25	1
John Kite, orphan Bakers		214	17	1
John Pounds, soldier, Whartons		130	13	1
William Still, Woodroughs		186	15	1
William Liles, Hunicuts		69	8	2
Affanatious Massey, do.		81	24	2

HABERSHAM.

Wiley P. Warwick, jr. Bryans		50	2	1
John Holland, Suttons		165	7	1
James Blythe, Tates		22	8	5
Thomas Weems, Bryans		44	6	1
John Black, do.		119	9	5
Moses Brock, do.		103	25	1
James Forester, Jones		226	32	1
J., S., B. L., & S. Caps, orps. Tates		65	20	1

Fortunate Drawers. Capts.	Dist.	No.	Dt.	Sec.
Joel Wilbern's minors, Suttons		70	10	5
Elias Chaffin, Bryans		198	29	1
Merril Boling, Martins		320	7	1

HALL.

Elisha Herring, Yagers		266	21	2
Joseph Hipps, Hardages		52	7	4
Charles J. Lowry, Roberts		60	2	2
Thomas Carver, senr. Harrisons		109	2	3
Abner Patterson, Alreds		15	11	3

HANCOCK.

Joseph H. Green, 101st		247	7	3
John Berry's orphans, 102d		98	5	3
Barnabas M. Daggett, Adams		198	5	3
John Brownell, 118th		33	2	2
Mary Powell, widow, 113th		249	5	1
Robert R. Mathis's orphans, 17th		39	17	2
Penelope Trawick, w. R. S., 118th		193	25	1
William Askew, 104th		141	16	2
Francis Foster, 103rd		17	5	5
James Holsey's orphans, 101st		261	11	2
Moses Brown, 112th		219	12	3

HENRY.

James Jackson, Millers		38	9	3
Kugler's orphans, Grays		209	5	3
Sarah Collins, widow, Millers		66	29	1
Elisha Carroll, Grays		84	33	1
Marget McWalters, widow, do		25	12	5
James McCurdy, soldier, 7th		213	2	5
William Turner, Grays		235	6	1
William F. Stephenson, do.		380	7	1

HOUSTON.

Luke Bozeman, Hancocks		112	1	2
Jno., Wm. & S. Holton, orps. Farnels		153	14	1
Ollen, Joseph & Luke R. Ratliff, do.		251	10	3

IRWIN.

Elijah Akins, Dixons		27	11	1

JACKSON.

James Glenn, R. S., Duprees		33	12	1
Wiley Anthony, Rogers		30	19	1
Christopher Sailors, R. S., do.		79	1	1
James Huie, R. S., Winns		129	32	1
Catharine Reed, Widow, do.		209	6	2
John A. Bailey, Duprees		82	4	1
George W. Glenn, Storys		81	24	1
Benjamin Scoggins, R. S., Doss		217	18	2
John Venable, sen. Winns		74	3	5
Telemachus T. Montgomery, Storys		103	4	4

JASPER

Hartwell Ezell, R. S., Reeves		282	23	2
Nancy Heath, widow, Wilders		225	17	1
Theophilus Fowler, Keys		304	6	1
Thomas Hadley|s orphans, Wilders		266	22	2
Jonathan McLendon's orps. Owens		69	5	2
Green L. McMichael's orps. Barnetts		169	11	3
Wiseman Bridges, R. S., Shropshires		173	10	1
John C. Weldon, Sparks		132	17	2
Watson Shaw, Baynes		76	7	2
Eli Benson, Hines		151	10	2
William H. Lovejoy, Robersons		216	20	1
Lodowick Teal, R. S., Keys		7	9	3

JEFFERSON.

William E. Barrow, Jones		22	16	1
Temperance Donalson, wid. Causeys		222	8	1
John W. Whigham, Cunninghams		75	3	4

JONES.

William H. Robertson, Davis		67	12	5
Thomas Stewart, do.		156	12	2

(206)

Fortunate Drawers. Capts. Dist.	No.	Dt.	Sec.
Oliver Morse, Stewarts	227	15	2
Raleigh Spinks. Spinks	125	7	4
James D. Wilson, Bowens	174	3	4
Thomas Portch, Stewarts	230	12	2
Nahum Little, Dosters	157	10	1
Warren Massengale, Newbys	208	5	4
Hampton Dickson, Mullins	33	30	1
Wiliam F. Brown, Woods	169	19	2
Bailey Seaborn, Low's	237	22	2
Dickson Lumpkin, R.S.Mulins	109	7	4
Warren Massengale, Newbys	141	12	3
Martha Maulden, wid. Stewarts	84	19	1
William Cox, Sullivans	147	12	3
John Jones, orphan, Davis	147	7	5
David Hadaway, R. S. Dosters	86	1	1
Isaac Tickner, Breadloves	177	16	2
William Stewart, R. S. Popes	40	12	2
George Varner's mins. Taylors	25	11	2
LAURENS.			
Lucretia Daniel, wid. Mizells	170	7	5
Lewis Bush, Barlows	191	5	3
Wiliam J. Larkin's orps. do.	149	20	2
Thomas Pullin, sr. Hodges	81	30	1
Benjamin Mimms, jr., Hodges	331	30	1
Jas. Faircloth, idiot, Whiteheads	176	1	1
Jesse Snelgrove, Mizells	149	23	2
LIBERTY.			
John Way, jr. 13th	21	14	5
LINCOLN.			
Felix Crosson, Lonorgans	73	7	2
Sarah Turner, w. R. S. Frasers	256	3	4
John G. Strother, Gideons	46	9	3
James C. Henley, s.l.w. Hardys	239	5	5
Jesse Hardy, Parks	67	4	2
Hannah Groce, wid. Prathers	267	19	2
Singleton York, Leveretts	190	15	1
Adam Harnesberger, Frasers	131	19	2
MADISON.			
Alex. Human, R. S. Culbersons	97	19	1
John W. Gossett, Adairs	90	12	2
James Downs, Berrymans	55	3	2
John P. Vaughn, Phipps	223	2	3
McINTOSH.			
Robert A. Caldwell, Demeries	190	21	2
MONROE.			
Thomas Sadler, Pattersons	137	22	1
Drewry Allen's orps. Douglass	177	5	4
W. L. Q. C. D. Hunt, orph. do.	14	16	1
John Cooper, Houses	62	17	2
Margaret McSwain, h.a.Wrights	173	17	2
Amos Goree, do.	60	8	3
MORGAN.			
William Nelson, Stokes	91	22	2
Joseph T. Camp, Youngs	49	8	1
Warren Oneal's orps. Butlers	402	20	2
John Royston's orph. Gains	18	20	1
William Brown, Shearmans	76	12	1
Stephen Stovall, Christians	14	1	2
Rainey Duncan, Shearmans	88	23	1
John Malcom, Esq. Christians	5	7	2
James S. Evans, Ostians	306	7	5

Fortunate Drawers. Capts. Dist.	No.	Dt.	Sec.
Adam G. Saffold, sol. Walkers	258	23	2
Mathew H. Jones, Gains	54	22	2
Thos. Summerlin's orps.Jennings	143	12	2
NEWTON.			
Robert P. Ward, Penningtons	173	4	5
William Hoard, Hays	114	7	5
Betsy, Asa, Joshua B., Jordan J.			
& Sarena Harper, orps. Clarks	166	6	1
Elizabeth Niblett, widow do.	141	3	2
Robert Leak, sol. Askews	115	21	2
Hannah Cates, w. R. S. Pulling	265	10	2
John Webb, sol. Penningtons	75	17	1
Martin Kolb, Dyers	41	15	1
James Moss, Orrs	6	13	1
William Dowling, Smiths	111	19	1
OGLETHORPE.			
Jas. Johnson, son.of N.,Burfords	181	4	3
Edward Powell, Rousseaus	21	5	3
Alexander Jones, Rousseaus	37	6	5
Stephen Arnold, jr. Arnolds	43	10	2
James Johnson, Seals	104	33	1
John Billups, Rousseaus	272	6	1
William T. Gilham, do.	229	7	5
Polly Birdsong, wid. do.	64	16	1
Nathaniel H. Smith, sol. Smiths	71	4	4
John M. Andrews, Holloways	228	17	2
Robert Brooks, Williamsons	49	6	2
Elizabeth Jenkins, wd. Burfords	218	22	2
Andrew Thompson, R. S., do.	209	2	5
PIKE.			
Joseph Davidson, R. S. Longs	183	29	1
John P. Clegg, Hicks	105	4	4
PULASKI.			
James Bryan's orps. Kellams	183	6	5
PUTNAM.			
Christian Bruce, wid. Allums	100	2	1
Presley Prichard, R. S. Choices	251	2	3
John J. Ray, Clarks	162	4	4
John Mooneyham's orps. do.	125	10	2
George W. Hays, Dismukes	203	7	1
Zachariah House, Sawyers	43	13	5
RABUN.			
Chesley McKenzie, Godfreys	183	11	5
Absalom McKenzie, do.	101	6	5
Michael Fricks, Mercers	75	8	5
RICHMOND.			
Daniel S. Roman, Huntingtons	127	3	5
Susannah Johnson, Kellys	225	2	3
Benjamin Brantley, Huntingtons	101	15	2
Jeptha Daniel, R. S. James	86	8	1
Lucy M. Yarnold, wid. Wilcoxs	188	19	1
Elizabeth Howard, wid. Blacks	264	8	1
E. M., A. M. F., J. R., W. A. &			
P. C. Kain, orps. Treadwells	129	4	4
Polly Roe, wid. Murphys	149	18	1
SCRIVEN.			
Michael Janas, orph. Poytress	263	23	2
H. G., M. &J.E.Gill, ills. Roberts	163	27	1
Thomas G. Walker, Lovetts	80	7	3
TATTNALL.			
John Inman, Dees	149	7	1
John Wood's orps. Deloachs	201	8	3

(207)

TELFAIR.

Fortunate Drawers. Capts. Dist.	No.	Dt.	Sec.
Elijah Singletery, Barentines	214	5	5
Sarah Parker, h. ab. do.	229	2	2

TALIAFERRO.

	No.	Dt.	Sec.
Richard Anderson, Cobbs	216	8	1

TWIGGS.

	No.	Dt.	Sec.
Clary Stiles, widow, Bosticks	121	18	2
Torrence C. Conner, Wimberlys	253	21	1
John Linton, R. S. Bosticks	137	25	1

UPSON.

	No.	Dt.	Sec.
William Gresham, Paschalls	74	11	5
Zoroaster Robinson, Dupres	289	5	3
William Moates, 589th	179	11	1
Claborn Bishop, Hattoxs	86	19	2
Petter Draper, Duprees	75	29	1
James Perryman, sol. Dukes	48	17	2

WALTON.

	No.	Dt.	Sec.
Bird J. Delk, 503rd	325	1	4
Thomas Knight, R. S. 503rd	38	4	1
Alexander Johnson, 249th	87	13	1
William Waters, soldier, 418th	94	12	1
Elizabeth Sexton, wid. Snows	214	3	4
Henry Poss, sr. R. S. Bexleys	147	4	1
Hardy Harris, do.	207	18	2

WARREN.

	No.	Dt.	Sec.
Jona. Stanford, sr. sol. Sanders	33	20	1
Moses Y. Pruitt, Brinkleys	113	4	3
Archibald Justice, Seales	27	7	4
George W. C. Shivers, Hales	28	3	5
Jesse Burson's orphan, Adkins	193	3	1
Hugh Armstrong, Parhams	123	21	2
Henry Hannon, R. S. do.	162	11	1
Asa Chapman's orps. Hales	161	23	1
Elijah McMath, Kinseys	107	8	2
John Sims, sol. Downs	22	24	2

WASHINGTON.

	No.	Dt.	Sec.
Edward Bartlett's orps. Woods	42	9	2
Alex| Goodgain's orps. Jordans	392	7	1
Wright Mitts, Gilberts	67	18	1
Littleton Mathews, Mannings	158	4	1
Moses Wootan, Floyds	7	8	1
Abraham Joiner, sr. Wimberlys	81	3	2
John Ryland's heirs, Floyds	230	11	2
Mary Anderson, illeg. Warthens	79	16	2
Solomon Howard, R. S. Currys	209	19	2

WILKINSON.

	No.	Dt.	Sec.
Cane Stricklin, Fairchilds	117	5	2
Incil Spence, Halls	49	3	4
Micajah Polk, do.	180	5	1
Balas Carr, Smiths	213	8	1
Mathew Whittle, do.	54	6	2

WILKES.

	No.	Dt.	Sec.
Hillery Triplett, Greshams	11	12	5
James Mozley, Ragsdales	265	3	1
Fielding F. Ficklin, Moors	3	16	5
Mildred Carlton, wid. Hopkins	81	9	2
Mary Malessa Harris, illeg. do.	213	21	1
William Cole, Chunns	246	1	2
Mary Anderson, widow, do.	131	6	3
Winefred Calloway, wid. Popes	74	1	3
William Hampton, Woottens	181	12	3

67th DAY'S DRAWING—May 23.

APPLING.

Fortunate Drawers. Capts. Dist.	No.	Dt.	Sec.
Elizabeth Hall, widow, Colilns	91	4	2
Nathan Dean, Mathis	149	2	4

BALDWIN.

	No.	Dt.	Sec.
Thomas Whitwork, Thomas	5	3	3
Susannah Petigree, widow, Bivins	49	25	1
Redding B. Musselwhite, Ginns	221	17	1
Orphans of Drury Jackson, Thomas	327	7	5
Wiley McCrary, Lesters	131	1	1
Charles Willingham, soldier,	103	11	1
William Speights, Pitts	233	13	1
Basil Prichard, Wicks	309	5	3
Mary Ann Parsons, hus. ab. Lingos	101	13	5
Thomas Kemp, soldier, Wrights	86	6	3
Samuel Gammon, Wicks	217	7	5

BIBB.

	No.	Dt.	Sec.
James W. Howard, Beards	51	16	2
William Blanchard, Bates	12	7	1
A. W., M. E. & C. Etheridge, Rutlands	69	7	2
William Sanders, soldier, Beards	129	3	5
Samuel Armstrong, Bates	101	10	1
William B. Gamble do.	242	22	1

BRYAN.

	No.	Dt.	Sec.
Christiana Smith, widow, Harveys	77	17	1
John Vanbrackel, R. S., do.	61	14	5
Reuben English, do.	103	21	1

BULLOCH.

	No.	Dt.	Sec.
James Lastinger, Richardsons	1	14	5
Joshua Hodges, jr. McCalls	31	7	5
Elizabeth Jones, widow, Lockharts	207	10	5
Minza Rowe, Deloachs	33	23	2
Alexander Knignight, Richardsons	150	8	5

BURKE.

	No.	Dt.	Sec.
Delilah Davidson, widow, Roberts	237	21	2
William Umphres' orphans, Goodons	6	10	1
Samuel Rollins, R. S., Segars	209	16	1
James Cross, jr. Lynchs	182	2	3
John Rutledge, jr. Fountains	42	9	3

BUTTS.

	No.	Dt.	Sec.
Samuel Bruke's orphans, Robisons	101	2	1
Mark McLerroy, soldier, Kights	247	15	1
Martha Black, widow, Chapmans	42	10	1
Joseph Campbell, Johnsons	82	1	4
Richard Punds, Robisons	38	4	3

CAMDEN.

	No.	Dt.	Sec.
Enoch Mizell, Baileys	7	23	1

CHATHAM.

	No.	Dt.	Sec.
Elizab. Wamack, w.R.S.,McDonnells	153	13	2
Julian Sanderlin, widow, do.	91	7	1
John D. Timmons, Baines	142	3	5
Matthew Hall McAllister, Haydens	197	17	1
Orps. of John Naylor, McDonnells	152	6	2
James B. Allter, Baines	69	4	3

CLARK.

	No.	Dt.	Sec.
Sally Wilson, illegit. Davenports	154	17	1
Arthur Cheatham's orps. Gahagans	11	11	5
Benjamin F. McRee, McRees	295	3	4
John Yarbrough, Dickins	247	4	3
Hartwell M. Elder, Coss	46	3	5
James Hendon, soldier, Deans	120	11	1
Philip Allen, R. S., Herndons	279	8	1
Mahaley Edmonson wid. Lumpkins	132	1	1
John W. Smith, McCrees	235	2	1

COLUMBIA.

	No.	Dt.	Sec.
Matthew B. Fuller, Carrolls	2	8	3

(208)

Fortunate Drawers. Capts. Dist.	No.	Dt.	Sec.
Abraham W. Morris, minor, Bealls	171	21	2
Samuel Paul, Dranes	17	20	1
James M. Magruder, orp. Bells	149	7	4
Eleanor Tankersley, id. Livermans	51	21	2
Mary Bass, widow, Carrolls	178	21	2
James Wright's orphans, Perrys	10	6	3
Mary P. Pryor, widow, Adams	263	11	2
Elizabeth Freel, widow, R. S., Coles	235	3	3

CRAWFORD.

James H. Haff Dukes	189	4	3
Susannah Potter, widow, Tillers	143	21	2

DECATUR.

David Swicord, Douglass	78	10	1

DE KALB.

John Ward, sen. Edwards	285	8	1
Henry Grogan, Conns	214	8	1
James Eadis, Scaifs	138	25	1
Nancy Irwin, w. R. S., Stephens	163	23	1
Susannah Watson, widow, Conns	256	10	5
John W. Levell, Edwards	161	12	1
John W. W. Thompson, Howells	44	5	2
William McCurley, Merritts	146	1	2
William M. Hendon, Bowlings	130	5	5
Benjamin Paramore, Hays	204	7	1
William Eadis, Scaifs	19	8	4
Thomas Ray, soldier, Andersons	106	9	3
Martha Minchew, w. R. S., Smiths	272	5	3
Lothlin MćCurry's orps. Browns	93	10	3

DOOLY.

Mary Shiver, Floyds	126	22	2

EARLY.

Wm. Grantham, sr. R. S., Grimsleys	45	19	1
William Noyes, Speers	3	3	3

EFFINGHAM.

Charles Tondee, R. S., Elkins	17	3	4
Hermon Elkins, do.	254	4	2
Samuel Hist, do.	165	16	2

ELBERT.

Robert Pullum, sr. R. S. Hortons	182	7	2
John G. Higginbotham, Boltons	203	11	2
Enos Tate, Tuckers	159	1	1
Jephthah Rosser, Alstons	105	3	2
Amos Baker, soldier, Bells	221	15	2
Mary Ann Coulston, wid. Carpenters	47	16	2
Thomas Hinton, Blackwells	17	19	2
Mary Johnston, widow, Dunns	255	30	1
William Jourdan, Harmonds	44	13	5
John Duncan, sr. R. S., Merritts	194	11	5
Stephen W. Jordan, Hortons	120	23	2

EMANUEL.

John Phillips, Nabbs	269	1	4
Hester Williams, husb. ab. McGars	40	5	1
James Wales, jr. do.	114	10	1

FAYETTE.

George L. Roberts, Wests	141	25	1
James Gray, do.	121	9	1
James Horton, McLendons	38	2	4
Michael Austin, R. S., Wests	221	10	3

FRANKLIN.

Russell Blackwell, D. Chandlers	6	8	3
William Burroughs, Blankinships	60	1	3
Henry J. Brewing, Walters	306	7	1
William Harriss, sol. D. Chandlers	149	14	1
Tarlton Walker, McDonalds	183	6	3
Esther Johnson, widow, do.	254	19	1
Bithel Crump, Andrews	234	2	2
James H. Chambers, McDonalds	102	9	2

Fortunate Drawers. Capts. Dist.	No.	Dt.	Sec.
Annamas Tillison, T. Chandlers	103	2	5
James H. Barton, do.	189	10	5
Robert Mize, Cokers	154	21	2
John Moss, Walters	209	3	5
Dudley Jones' orphans, Boswells	43	7	5
Solomon D. Thomason, Bennetts	113	7	2
William Harriss, D. Chandlers	12	2	3
Nicholas Bellamy, Stranges	18	2	3
John Dunlap, Cokers	155	3	4
Michael Ragsdale, Caudells	105	7	5
Isaac Hancock's chil. fa. ab. Stephens	49	10	5
William J. Parks, Hudsons	35	5	2

GLYNN.

William Henston, R. S., Burnetts	151	5	5
Thomas Grant, soldier, do.	7	15	5
Mary Ann Brown, widow, McLeods	203	26	1
Mary Ann Blue, widow, do.	124	21	2

GREENE.

Eliz H. Perry, widow, Dawsons	77	14	2
James C. Hogg, Newsoms	10	14	2
Ezekiel Blanks, Robins	19	32	1
George Barnhart, R. S. Vincents	147	23	1
Leroy C. Edwards, Woodhams	216	20	2
Elizabeth Bunkley, widow, Rankins	82	7	3
Thomas Cunningham, sol. Dawsons,	127	12	3
John Malone's orphans, Robisons	109	5	1
Mary Hall, widow, R. S., do.	213	12	1
Martha Veasy, widow, Rankins	197	33	1
Austin Bunch, Newsoms	171	18	2
Elias Ivy, soldies, Artins	28	22	2
Joseph King, soldier, Rankins	142	9	3
Ruth Jarmon, w. R. S. Woodhams	37	4	1

GWINNETT.

Matthew Winne, Evans	157	20	2
James Sevton, Matoxs	214	14	1
Robert Miller, Greens	113	5	4
Samuel Paschal, Wallis	325	3	4
Benjamin Rhodes, sol. Gholdstons bat.	136	2	5
Jesse Campbell, Shippys	223	3	5
Siles King, Moores	270	8	1
Thomas Mullican, Rolins	88	2	5
Benjamin Z. Williams, R. S., Dunbars	185	8	1
Absalom Waits, Bakers	191	31	1
Samuel Melonee, do.	166	11	2
Asa Moore, Finchers	242	23	1
George Steen, Moores	187	6	2
Mary A. Fuller, hus. absent. Davis	229	19	2

HANCOCK.

Jane Ewing, widow, 118th	230	5	2
Sally Grace, widow, 108th	217	1	4
John S. Wilson, Coxens	245	9	2
James Thompson, 113th	38	19	2
Thomas M. Turner, orphan, Reaves	169	7	1
Reuben Ransom, 103d	169	4	5
Benjamin Bryant, 112th	123	18	1
John Wilkerson, soldier, Reaves	73	21	1
Thomas Mason, R. S., 112th	206	11	5
Charles Allen, 108th	79	5	2
Mary Miller widow, 118th	48	4	1
Lorenzo D. Beran, 103d	221	22	1
John C. Peck's orphans, 108th	33	2	3
Martha F. Freeman, blind, Lewis	146	4	3

HENRY.

Alexander Coldwell, soldier, Wards	111	10	5
William Lavender, Allens	233	5	2
Burton Whitaker, Grays	249	14	1
Jesse Goodwin, Harriss	100	7	2
William Bonner, Wards	173	9	2

LAND LOTTERY REGISTER—No. 31
[RECORDER OFFICE—PUBLISHED BY GRANTLAND & ORME—PRICE $3.]

NOTE—Section 1 is Lee County—2 Muscogee—3 Troup—4 Coweta—5 Carroll.
Conclusion of the 67th day's drawing, with the whole of the prizes drawn on the 68th' and 69th days, (May 24th and 25th) which completes our Lottery List.

APPLING.
Fortunate Drawers. Capts. Dist. No.Dt.Sec.
Silas Overstreet, McDonalds 29 9 2
William Yeates, Dedges 263 7 1

BALDWIN.
Grief H. Ferguson, Thomas 12 13 5
Philip Thurman, soldier, 129 9 2
Sarah Hand, w. R. S., Lesters 119 16 2
Gideon Flewellen, Wicks 137 21 2
Eliza Curry, illegitimate, Pitts 53 19 2
Samuel R. Gibson, Wicks 38 3 4
Rachel Trapp, widow, Bivins 59 2 3
Moses Night, Ginns 37 11 1
Josiah Mathews, soldier, Wheelers 140 6 2
Ezekiel Redding, soldier, do. 240 27 1
Martha Rogers, widow, Lesters 153 3 2
S., W., A. & C. Pendexter, ills. Bivins 10 8 1
Gabriel Wynn, Buchanans 294 5 3
Boswell Y. Evans, Doles 37 8 1
Elizabeth Babb, widow, do. 215 16 2
William Akridge, R. S. Ginns 249 31 1

BIBB.
Jeremiah Wilchar, Beards 305 32 1
Andrew Jeter, R. S., do. 33 27 1
Richard Bulloch, R. S., Pickards 65 2 5
Dempsey J. Justice, Beards 83 19 2
Joshua Jourdan soldier, Pickards 122 10 1
Samuel Gillespie, Bates 115 2 3

BRYAN.
Samuel Stiles, Stephens 24 23 1
T. K. McGilless, Harveys, 22 4 4

BULLOCH.
Noble W. B. Davis, Richardsons 65 12 5
Mary Driggers, widow, Deloachs 25 13 2
Casey Woodcock's illegitimates, do. 277 19 2
David Brown's orphans, Richardsons 99 1 4
Rachel Riggs, widow, Deloachs 283 22 2
William Moore, Lockharts 165 1 4
Nancy Dukes, widow, Richardsons 207 10 1

BURKE.
John Conner, soldier, Rogers 110 15 1
Barbary Johnson, widow, Brooms 51 8 5
Wiley Boddingfield, Robinsons 154 3 5
Hosa Berrien Hodge, illegit, Rogers 93 10 5
Matthew Brinson, Lesters 77 11 5
S., W. R.A.,I.&B.Summer, ills. Gordons 33 6 4
P. Bell, w. of T. Bell, R. S. Baileys 156 30 1
Gideon Harris soldier, Robinsons 33 6 4
Berry Hutchens, minor, Corkers 179 14 1
Benjamin D. Hill, Brooms 28 1 4
Benjamin Bell, R. S., Wests 249 3 4
William Greaves, R. S., Thompsons 71 5 2
Sarah Griffin, widow, Dugas 65 14 5
Nancy Owen, w. R. S., Fountains 275 4 1
Rolly Rollins, Segars 149 11 3
Susan Joiner, illegitimate, Lesters 113 16 1
Louisa Heath, w. R. S., Dugas 77 10 2
Leonard S. Acree, Andersons 73 13 2
John Pugsley's orphans, Robinsons 109 33 1
Alexander Young, soldier, Lewis 237 16 1
Mary Chance, w. R. S., Wards 137 16 1
Jesse McClendon Gordons 205 19 2
Elisha Horn, R. S., do. 105 9 5

BUTTS.
Stephen G. Hure's orphans, Kendricks 41 27 1
Elizabeth Parker, wid. Chapmans 84 4 2

CAMDEN.
Fortunate Drawers. Capts. Dist. No.Dt.Sec.
Silas & James Weeks, ills, Baileys 300 10 2
Susan Hawkins, hus. absent, Millers 59 5 3
Cornelius C. Bessent, Baileys 145 14 1

CHATHAM.
Orphans of Thomas Bourke, Geredons 17 9 3
Orphans of Nathan Adam, Haydens 65 6 1
Orphans of Joseph Brantley, Reeds 152 11 1
Samuel Wood, Baines 17 12 5
Oliver Dunley, Reeds 103 11 2
John Delberghe, Haydens 133 14 5
George Mingledorf, McDonnells 97 16 1
Anthony Segur, Haydens 82 7 4
John McIntire, McDonnells 66 8 1
William J. Harrison, do. 210 2 3
Edward C. Allinder, Haydens 193 4 3
Orps. of James McAnnally, Haydens 268 2 1
Alexander Pratt's orphans, do. 76 1 2
Jacob Lewis, McDonnells 137 2 2
Richard Gildon, Geredons 87 17 2
John Gill, McDonnells 149 5 2
John F. Berthelot, Geredons 177 3 4
Simon F. Davis 5 6 4
John C. Bell, Geredons 114 28 1
Leonidas Wylly, McDonnells 107 7 2

CLARK.
William Thomas, Herndons 14 9 2
Taply Hinson, Wrights 98 2 2
Barton Hamilton, McDonalds 166 5 2
Thomas B. Ward, do. 82 24 2
Simon Salter's orphans, Gahagans 148 9 1
Margaret Allred, w. R. S., Allreds 165 7 3
Benjamin Davis, sen. Davis 26 14 5
William Humphrey, Dickens 173 10 5
Rodmon Sisson, Gahagans 276 5 3
Henry Jackson, do. 219 1 2
Thomas Walsh, do. 174 11 5

COLUMBIA.
Aletha Flinn, orphan, Adams 95 15 2
M., W. R. & M. J. Jenkins, ills. Dranes 82 3 1
Elizabeth Sullivan's ills. Carrolls 127 33 1
Thomas Heggie, Bealls 12 6 1
Thomas Blanchard, Coles 74 3 1
Michael Smally, sr. R. S., Baileys 281 6 1
Dancey Adams, sr. R. S., Adams 173 25 1
James Fleming, Baileys 201 11 5
Mary Ann Clay, orphans, Coles 234 5 2
Sherwood Walton, Ramseys 171 9 1
Orphans of John Gray, Carrolls 72 14 5
Holt Clanton, R. S., Stallings 201 12 5
Yerby Roberts, Coles 157 3 1
Edward Wooding, Bealls 324 15 1
John T. Allen's orphans, Bealls 15 14 1
Elizabeth Howard, w. R. S., Talbots 201 12 3
John Harvill McGruders 225 8 1
Thomas J. Harris, Clarks 153 2 2

CRAWFORD.
Peter May, jr. Wilsons 125 18 1
William P. Harris, Tillers 390 7 1
Stephen Carter, Wilsons 288 11 2
Nathan Bridges, soldier, Rays 30 19 2
James A. Miller, Rhodes 139 32 1
Isaiah Culpeppers, Ellis 25 10 3
Thomas W. Glover, Tillers 254 20 1
William Edwerds, soldier, Lovetts 133 2 1

(210)

DECATUR.

Fortunate Drawers. Capts. Dist.	No.	Dt.	Sec.
Whitman H. Owens, Douglass	4	21	2
John Lunn, do.	193	9	5

DE KALB.

William Sims, Merritts	48	7	3
Elijah Bankston, R. S., Bowlings	218	21	
James B. Haerston, Stephens	239	11	5
Messer Spears, soldier, Scaifs	9	6	3
Cath. Harrington, w. R. S., Bakers	180	20	2
Thomas Duty, R. S. Howells	22	13	5
Edmund Reid, do.	8	7	2
William Turner, Stephens	241	10	1
William B. Sisson, Conns	337	22	1
Thomas Stovall's orphans, Howells	157	25	1
Hillsman Heard, Browns	46	12	3
John Pope, Scaifs	212	1	1
Aaron knight, R. S., do.	81	13	1
John Mariner, Merritts	63	2	3
John Woodall, sen. Conns	11	29	1
William Ezzard, Browns	175	7	2

DOOLY.

Simon Frasier's orphans, Mannings	250	23	2

EARLY.

Frederick Temples, sr. Grimsleys	91	15	1
James McKown, Grimsleys	173	6	3

EFFINGHAM.

John W. Exly, Stricklands	67	10	1
Solomon Arnstorph, Waldhaners	54	7	2
John J. Grovenstein's orps. Treutlins	97	33	1
Nathaniel Zettler, Treutlins	77	12	5

ELBERT.

James H. Ray, Carpenters	7777	10	5
Richard Ward's orphans, Blackwells	94	14	2
Elizabeth Heard, w. R. S., Alstons	55	6	4
John Banks, Tates	22	13	1
William Crawford, soldier, Dunns	54	17	1
Zachariah Rucker, soldier, Alstons	53	3	1
James Grissup, R. S., Dunns	29	3	1
William Whitman, soldier, Tuckers	303	4	1
John Cunningham, jr. Dunns	188	7	1
James L. Dudley, Merritts	15	10	1
Archibald Skinner's orphans, Boltons	25	4	3
Peter Allgood's orphans, Bells	37	11	2
Joseph Strickland, Dunns	125	3	4
Lawrence M. Adams, Hortons	203	10	2
Edward Weeks, Boltons	139	7	3
Thomas Anderson, Blackwells	247	13	2
Lucy Story, widow, Merritts	123	1	2
William Maxwell, soldier, Hortons	36	33	1
Thomas King, R. S. Dunns	351	20	2
Elisha Hamilton, Tates	61	13	2
William Whitman, Tuckers	245	11	2
William White, soldier, Alstons	145	14	5
Samuel Unice, Deadwilders	119	7	1

EMANUEL.

William Holton's orphans, Chasons	15	13	5
Benjamin Sherard, McGars	174	2	5
John S. Martin, 49th	125	17	2
Moses Jewell, Whiddons	1	92	
Elva Spivy's illegitimate, Arlines	175	24	2
Rocksey Ann Price, illeitimate, 57th	117	8	1
Robert Hall, McGars	31	10	3

FAYETTE.

Patrick Duvaine, Roziers	210	4	2
William Horgan, jr. do.	259	19	2
Sarah Wright, widow, Browns	39	1	4
John Watkins, illegitimate, do.	55	29	1
John Whatley, Whartons	98	1	3
John Angle, soldier, Garrisons	11	14	1
William Clayton, sol. McLendons	114	10	3
David Hanes, Dodsons	31	17	2
James Wilkins, Wests	185	1	4

Fortunate Drawers. Capts. Dist.	No.	Dt.	Sec.
Wilson R. Young, Dodsons	152	9	2
Edward Lattimore, Roziers	239	11	1
Larkin Millsaps, do.	319	1	4

FRANKLIN.

Cornelius K. Donehoo, Cokers	233	8	1
Richard F. Chappelear, Walters	320	28	1
William Stovall, T. Chandlers	131	5	5
Samuel Jackson, McDonalds	319	3	4
Berry King, soldier, Boswells	370	7	1
Henry W. Hardy, Walters	99	33	1
William Neal, Jones	121	33	1
Charlton Coker, Walter	158	20	1
Benjamin S. Pulliam, Blankinships	304	15	1
John Burton, R. S., Walters	53	4	1
Nathaniel White, Andrews	79	10	5
William Alexander, Stranges	77	5	2
John A. White, Bennetts	173	3	1
Abner Walters, Andrews	35	33	1
William Hughes, Hudsons	133	21	2
William Sewell, R. S., do.	143	18	1
Jesse Holbrook, R. S. D. Chandlers	291	5	3
Henry Cash, T. Chandlers	251	30	1
Charles M. Cawthon, Cokers	214	12	5

GLYNN.

John B. Flinn, McLeods	212	22	2
Joseph McLellan, do.	46	16	2
Robert Hazelhurst, Burnetts	41	8	3
James Pendarvis, do.	221	11	3
Frances Palmer, widow, McLeods	166	1	4

GREENE.

William Meadows, Colcloughs	97	20	2
Sarah Ann Martin, orp. Dawsons	39	18	2
Andrew Ray, Newsoms	102	15	2
Henry S. Beman, do.	69	28	1
William Hill, Dawsons	135	5	5
Joseph M. Baldwin, Astins	221	5	1
Clement Allen's orphans, Halls	245	5	3
Orphans of John Wallace, Astins	126	12	5
Mary Ann Chresmas, w. Southerlands	78	10	5
Mary Lawson, widow, Astins	69	8	4
William Hawkins, Elys	130	6	5
George Armstrong, Newsoms	22	5	2
Mark Jackson, Halls	219	14	1
John Wilson, Robins	42	8	3
Thomas Hicks, Elys	37	4	4
Mary Hightower, wid. Knowles	256	8	1
John Thompson, Souhterlands	97	5	4
Wooten Oneal's orphans, Colcloughs	89	19	2
Green B. Ellis, Knowles	9	14	2
Lauchlin Bethune's orps. Winkfields	233	10	2
Littleberry Sharrell, Greenes	195	11	5
James Daniel, Woodhams	197	1	2
Graves Swanson's orps. Southerlands	153	4	1
Wiliam Rowland, Dawsons	205	9	2
James Smith, Astins	33	28	1
Willis Dickin's orphans, Robinsons	179	16	1
Louisa, Wyly & Wiley, ills, Bruces	241	21	2
David Hogan, do.	189	13	1

GWINNETT.

Ephriam Ledbetter, Greens	87	7	4
Mahaney Sizemore, idiot, Moores	199	1	4
James Caldwell, Woodroughs	219	19	2
Job Red, R. S. Moores	311	20	2
James Hill, soldier, Evans	125	19	2
William Phillips, illegit. Madduxs	218	15	1
William Gordon, Hunicuts	149	4	3
Emeline Ferguson, ill. do.	127	11	5
Hezekiah Jones, Woodroughs	201	7	3
Heriah Davis, Caruthers	254	8	5
James Caldwell, Woodroughs	85	6	5
Allen Burch, soldier, do.	195	3	2
Caleb Higings, Hills	16	19	2
Elisha Vinson, Whartons	110	14	1

(211)

Fortunate Drawers. Capts. Dist.	No.	Dt.	Sec.
Sally Key, husband absent, Finchers	85	11	5
Jeremiah Craft, Rollins	58	8	3
Joseph Clark, orphan, Bakers	130	8	3
Henry Powell, Greens	113	10	3
William Abbott, Finchers	115	17	1
John Spence, Rollins	177	6	1
James Edmundson, jr. Moors	53	10	5
George W. Sylva, jr. Davis	97	6	1
Ephriam Barker, do.	182	1	2
William V. Griffith, Wallis	310	15	1
Stephen T. Ellington, do.	43	18	1
Mashack Red, Hills	93	13	5
Benjamin Z. Williams, Dunbars	157	22	2
Jane Jones, w. R. S., Robertsons	17	2	1
Benjamin Umpheris, Moors	174	4	3
William Fuqua, Greens	192	16	2
Sion Powell, soldier, Mattoxs	173	13	2
John Reed, orphan, Greens	229	13	2

HANCOCK.

Martha Whitehead, widow, 111th	213	1	4
Orphans of Hiram Deracan, 104th	157	8	1
Zachariah Perkins, Corseys	74	23	2
George M. Butts, Mahons	119	7	5
John Turner, 103d	271	6	5
George Giddens, 113th	137	13	2
Wiliam Dunn, 112th	183	12	3
Charles Everett, 118th	25	5	2
William Ray's orphans, 117th	144	1	4
Nancy Bass, lunatic, Bishops	135	5	1
Elizabeth Reid, widow, 108th	211	22	2
Martha Garland, widow, 116th	194	24	1
Leah Pope, widow, 112th	141	9	2
Henry T. Goodwin 104th	6	3	4
Charles Medlock, soldier, Masons	11	10	1
John Askew's orphans, 107th	145	2	2
Henry B. Mershon, 113th	112	11	2
Lovett Saunders, Reaves	113	23	2
William C. Mitchell, 101st	215	22	1
William Hitchcock, 118th	138	12	5

HENRY.

Abraham Haglar, Shaws	18	6	3
Jesse Griswold, Wards	224	27	1
Peter Z. Ward, do.	102	1	4
Johnson Powell, 7th	15	8	4
Elizabeth Garner, widow, Millers	49	7	3
Asa Henderson, illegit., Grays	46	11	5
Alsey H. Gunnells, illegit., Shaws	116	5	4
Henry Burks, Wards	37	9	1
Jacob Sikes, Grays	45	33	1
James Hutchison, Smiths	66	21	1
George Cagle, Shaws	153	22	1
John C. Simmons, Bryants	193	1	1
Elijah C. Hunter, Morgans	82	9	5
John Branan, Millers	281	9	5
John Connell, soldier, Breeds	66	3	1
Nancy Freeman's ills. Morgans	70	6	5
Elijah Callum, soldier, Shaws	30	32	1
Johnson Heflin, Gosdens	225	3	4
Reuben Nolen, Millers	197	9	2
E. Burnsides, w. hus. d. inl.w.Risons	267	16	2
John Downs, R. S., Shaws	169	13	1
Pleasant R. Weldon, Risons	113	21	2
George Cigo, illegitimate, Millers	141	22	2
Moses Cox, Harriss	85	6	1
Isaac J. Hartsfield, Shaws	209	23	2

HABERSHAM.

Thomas Dooly, Suttons	73	8	1
Samuel Hughes, do.	74	2	3
Jonas Denton, Tates	188	3	4
C. T. & S. A. Headrick, mins. Vickreys	1657	4	
James Kitchens, Bryans	94	4	2
Archibald Gaddes, Kenzies	247	16	1

Fortunate Drawers. Capts. Dist.	No.	Dt.	Sec.
William W. Smith, Fains	13	26	1
Robert Blythe, Tates	45	23	1
Mary Gasaway, for minor, Suttons	137	31	1
Howard Cash, R. S., Bakers	295	22	1
Josiah A. Bird, Worshams	206	8	1
William Taylor, soldier, do.	119	7	4
John Beardin, orp. of Arthur, Bakers	13	15	5
Margit Eaton, illegitimate, Suttons	25	8	1
Jonathan Sinyard, Kenzies	38	6	5
Jeremiah Gaddy, Fains	73	17	2
William C. Wyly, Suttons	170	5	4
Jeremiah Taylor, soldier, do.	119	7	4
Coalman Fergeson, Bryans	123	33	1
John McIntire, R. S. Tates	89	12	2
James Ward's orphans, Jones	125	11	2
Russel Davis, Bakers	74	8	4
Philip Martin, Martins	183	14	2
Micajah Turner, Vickreys	121	10	5
Elisha England, Bryans	153	31	1
Francis D. Tate, Tates	117	12	2
Edward Hawkins, Kenzies	94	7	4
Thomas Bryan, soldier, Bryans	214	17	2
Amos Hill, Suttons	85	7	3
Stephen Smith, Langstons	193	21	2
Frederick Corrups, Suttons	37	33	1

HALL.

Jemima Norris, w. R. S., Harrisons	38	12	1
William S. Rogers, Floyds	117	13	1
John Rogers, soldier, Hardages	245	1	2
James Oliver, sen. (F.) Floyds	241	18	2
Isaac N. Fleming, Roberts	124	10	5
Joab Martin, Garrards	129	26	1
Thomas Buffingtonfi Hardages	65	8	2
Mark Castleberry, sen. Hardens	194	6	3
Drury James, Smiths	247	10	3
John Doss, Yagers	43	7	3
Mary G. Brazil, orphan. Garrards	64	8	5
David McWyre, Wilsons	190	2	2
Jonas Bishop, Garrards	190	3	2
Lewis R. Powell, soldier, Hardens	61	7	2
Austin M. Garrett, Wilsons	10	4	5
Thomas Beardon, Harrisons	237	12	2
William Bennett, Wilsons	13	7	5
Elijah Johnson, Dorseys	126	1	5
Peter Wever, Hardens	18	4	2
Martin Thomas, Hardages	41	8	1
Benjamin Goss, jr. Roberts	65	23	1
Hiram Montgomery, do.	165	11	2
S. H., M. E. &J.C.Norris, ills. Alreds	153	7	2
Hiram Moat, Garrards	176	7	1
Edward Doss, Yagers	114	8	3
Warren Clayton, Wilsons	241	4	1
James Lard, Roberts	251	10	1
James Lard, jr. do.	234	8	5
James Stephens, do.	143	3	4
Jacob Reed, Alreds	201	13	2
Jehoiada Barnett, Harrisons	324	3	4
Peter Wood, Smiths	241	5	5
James Tippin, do.	32	18	1
William McDonald, Walkers	202	3	3
Hiram Liles, Hardens	87	3	2
George J. McCleskey, Hardages	245	12	1
Mark Bennett, Yagers	209	18	2

HOUSTON.

Wesley Williams, Calhouns	57	10	1
Neadom Smith, Batemans	103	2	3
Johnson Welborn, Moores	127	11	3
Simon Perry, Moores	198	3	5
Francis Fan's orphans, Hancocks	142	3	2
Elizabeth Burton, widow, do.	206	19	1

IRWIN.

Jacob Durham, R. S. McCalls	73	31	2

(212)

Fortunate Drawers.	Capts.	Dist.	No.	Dt.	Sec.
Stacy B. Hill, 5th			27	15	1
William Willis, Dixons			33	4	3

JACKSON.

Fortunate Drawers.	Capts.	Dist.	No.	Dt.	Sec.
John Vandeford, Duprees			179	16	2
Thomas Brack, Staplers			78	28	1
Thomas Slaten, Winns			218	28	1
Simeon Culpepper, Doss			265	16	2
James Cunningham, Storys			197	12	3
Alexander Reid, Venables			224	15	1
William Camron, Landrums			137	7	1
James McDonald, Pairs			153	6	1
Charles Bacon, Allens			230	16	2
James Smith, Millers			145	8	5
Alsey Right, w. R. S., Venables			161	11	2
Britten Braziel, R. S., Landrums			47	9	1
Rhoda Walker, widow, Millers			173	9	1
Sion Pritchett, Doss			13	13	1
Bennett Strickland, Duprees			211	31	1
James Hardin, Bowens			96	21	1
Francis Meriwether, Allens			263	5	3
Joseph Heath, Duprees			31	21	2
Andrew McLain, Watersons			21	24	1
Thomas M. Hampton, Bowens			266	9	5
Thomas B. Finch, Millers			332	1	4
James Cunningham, Storys			101	10	5
Thomas C. Barron, Rogers			136	5	5
Mary Johnson, widow, Allens			307	28	1
Charles H. Hardy, Millers			259	5	3
William Smith, Rogers			93	8	3
Jesse Harden, fa. ab. Landrums			205	17	1
James Wilson, sr. R. S., Duprees			103	28	1

JASPER.

Fortunate Drawers.	Capts.	Dist.	No.	Dt.	Sec.
Abraham Porter, Wilders			157	2	2
Russell J. Richeson, Clemmons			49	13	1
William L. Cannant, Camerons			46	23	1
Zachariah Kitchens, R. S., Keys			239	27	1
Henry Steel, R. S., Wilsons			196	16	1
Littleberry B. Phillips, Baynes			223	3	4
Samuel Turner, Keys			158	6	4
Jiles Dubary, soldier, Hands			191	26	1
William Belcher, Hines			224	10	5
William Glenn, soldier, Penningtons			92	9	5
Elizabeth Morgan, w. R. S., Hines			221	11	5
Willis Greene, Doctor, Holmes			355	16	2
Thomas Jackson's orps. Shropshires			76	1	3
Mary Adams, w. R. S., Sparks			23	16	2
Sarah Smith, w. R. S., Shropshires			76	1	3
Rosannah Bogan, deaf, Dales,			230	2	3
Elizabeth Cavender, illegit. Sparks			125	32	1
Hudson Kirk, Holmes			78	1	3
Thomas J. Dozier, Dardens			105	31	1
Sarah Fallin, widow, Wilsons			98	3	5
Sion Barnett, Barnetts			193	11	5
Zachariah B. Eagerton, Butts			206	15	1
James L. Martin. soldier, Cummins			151	18	2
Willis Johnson, Shropshires			260	19	2
Elijah Martin, soldier, Cummins			151	18	2
Thomas Rousseau, soldier, Clements			13	16	5
John Pryor, R. S., Dardens			142	4	5
Alsey Durham, do.			19	23	2
Abel Wilkerson Baynes			211	5	3
Allen Goolsby, Butts			12	5	3
Henry Parrott's orphans, Baynes			85	11	3
Joshua Callaway's orphans, Robersons			23	29	1
John Bean, soldier, Hands			77	4	5
Abel Wilkerson, Baynes			47	11	3
Lazarus Tillman, Shropshires			157	1	4
George Cross's orphans, Hines			74	3	2
William B. Whatley, Owens			127	12	1
Berry Welch, Barnetts			58	13	2
Lewis Dowdell, Reeses			17	7	1
John Stuart, R. S., Dardens			31	2	2
Catlett King, Baynes			176	1	2

Fortunate Drawers.	Capts.	Dist.	No.	Dt.	Sec.
Asa E. Stratton, Shropshires			172	18	1
William Norris, Dardens			105	23	2
Jus. M. Godby's chil. fa. ab. Wilders			44	9	3
Samuel Walker, sr, R. S., Sparks			210	12	5

JEFFERSON.

Fortunate Drawers.	Capts.	Dist.	No.	Dt.	Sec.
Stephen Durozeaux, R. S., Marshalls			51	2	2
Benjamin Elliott, Elliotts			209	1	4
John M. Glaze, Jones			24	31	1
Ezekiel Causey, sr. R. S., Boyds			336	7	5
Charles Cunningham, Cunninghams			161	6	5
James S. Calhoun, Marshalls			27	16	1
Isaac Chance, Jones			264	5	3
James Samples, Cunninghams			238	15	2
John Mills, Cunninghams			87	5	3
Thos., Jas. & Edward Fokes, Jones			134	7	3
Sarah Logue, illegitimate, Waldens			192	4	5
Littleton B. Fretwell, Cunninghams			9	3	5
Jesse Herring, soldier, do.			107	33	1
E.F.,M.I.,M.W. & J. T.Drake, ors.Jones			159	6	4
James Barfield's orps. Causeys			86	5	2
Joseph Marshall, Boyds			98	9	5
Aven Jordan, R. S., Cunninghams			89	10	1
Robert Fleming, sr. R. S. Jones			206	2	5
William Donaldson's orps. Causeys			133	1	4
Isaac W. Raiford, Jones			40	24	2
William W. Shepherd, Beatys			175	17	2
Elijah Walden, Waldens			74	7	2
Hugh Wilson, R. S., Ross			33	4	4
Elizabeth Pennington, wid. Jones			188	8	3
M.,S.A. & N. E. Brazil, ills. Waldens			125	1	1
Allen Rogers, Ross			101	8	1

JONES.

Fortunate Drawers.	Capts.	Dist.	No.	Dt.	Sec.
Joseph Slocumb, Davis			149	10	1
Lovick P. Jordan. Hammacks			181	5	3
Daniel Godard, Popes			171	17	1
John Dawkins, Taylors			139	12	2
Seaborn Huckly, Lows			2	2	1
Solomon Chapman, Blounts			164	10	5
Elizabeth Jones, wid. Davis			162	3	3
Isaac Moses, Lows			191	7	3
John Cawsey. Dosters			251	7	3
Abraham Bartee, do			95	19	1
Benjamin Reynolds' orp. Spinks			45	19	2
Appleton W. Melson, Taylors			149	22	2
Isham Phillips, R. S. Gibsons			214	22	1
Thomas Gay, Taylors			143	24	1
Titus Wimberley's orps. Woods			246	5	2
Isaac Johnston. Lows			1	6	5
Henry W. Walton, Bowens			56	17	2
Francis Maulden, Stewards			45	21	2
John C. Duncan, Davis			117	7	1
Orphs. of Daniel James, Lows			197	28	1
Hardy Morris, Bowens			229	15	2
Mary Dawkins, widow, Taylors			161	2	5
Wm. L. Chain's orps. Hammacks			92	5	5
James Lucas' orps. Gibsons			45	29	1
William Ussery, Mullins			94	8	4
John Gibson's orps. Woods			67	7	3
Malachi Murphy, Davis			13	8	3
Wm. F. Peebles mins. Blounts			20	11	3
Zachariah Harmon, Stewards			52	3	2
William McMath, do.			150	15	2
William Padget, do.			50	18	2
Henry Jones, Gibsons			138	33	1
Thomas Hudson. Davis			190	24	1
Jesse Smith's minors, Bowens			354	22	1
George H. Sims, Popes			72	7	5
William Braswell, Newbys			237	6	5
Lorenzo Hatchison, Spinks			193	6	5

(213)

Fortunate Drawers.	Capts.	Dist.	No.	Dt.	Sec.
Alfred Iverson,	Woods		121	5	1
Lory Alford, widow,	Mullins		97	15	1
Elizabeth Corder, h. a.	Gibsons		162	15	1
John Parrish,	Davis		266	8	5
Mathew Jones,	Duncans		45	4	2
Hosea Johnson,	Hendersons		118	21	2
Peter Northon, soldier,	Duncans		238	20	1
Abraham Johnston,	Lows		198	30	1
Jacob Lamb,	Mullins		213	12	5
Lewis Tull,	Davis		212	12	5

LAURENS.

William Fares, illeg.	Thomas		17	6	4
James Dean,	Barlows		29	6	5
William Bryan,	Whiteheads		181	22	1
Joseph Joiner, s. l. w.	Plummers		9	30	1
Willis Drew's orps.	do.		12	7	3
William Shiver,	Spiveys		108	13	1
Berry Forest,	Mizells		53	33	1
Osborn Beekham,	Plummers		246	2	1
Sarah Moss' illeg.	Spiveys		114	13	2
Edy Culpepper, wid.	Plummers		9	4	5
Gabriel Philips' orps.	Barlows		49	33	1
Robert Howell's orps.	Hodges		110	6	2
Jesse Snelgrove,	Mizells		59	28	1
Synthia Moore, w. R. S.	do.		28	21	2
Mary Culpepper's illegits.	Plummers		233	2	5
Vinson Watson,	Deans		113	6	3
Susannah Fountain's illegits,	Spiveys		38	4	5
Parker Bender,	Barlows		9	3	3
Harris Sea,	Hodges		224	5	3
Jane Shore's illegitimates,	Mizells		214	23	1
Jesse Joiner, R. S.	Whiteheads		70	3	2

LIBERTY.

Flem. & Bet. Terrell, orps.	17th		261	20	2
Wash. & &J. Whiddon, orps.	17th		69	7	1
Hiram & John Price, orps.	16th		185	10	3
Wm. B. Flemming,	15th		81	1	4
Noah Wesbery,	16th		160	5	1
Francis Lejels, soldier,	16th		123	3	2
James M. Smylie,	17th		15	18	1
Jehu Murray, soldier,	17th		157	10	5
Odingsale Hart,	14th		178	8	3
John Currie,	17th		174	10	1
Elizabeth Williams, orphan,	14th		174	23	2
James Brewer, soldier,	16th		109	16	1

LINCOLN.

Dennis Trammell,	Graves		246	6	5
Robert Fraser, sr.	Frasers		134	3	5
Edward Howard,	Graves		217	15	2
Jane Statham, widow,	Prathers		157	3	5
William Floyd,	Lonorgans		18	9	2
Nancy Vincent, wid.	Leveretts		193	17	1
Alexander Caraway,	Graves		60	15	1
Aaron Hardy,	Parks		55	6	3
Washington Russel,	Lonorgans		161	8	3
Mathew Stokes' minors,	Frasers		92	14	2
William Farrington,	do.		233	7	3
Theophilus Lantern,	Graves		72	10	3

MADISON.

Isaac David, R. S.	Culbertsons		32	5	1
Han. & Mor. Allen, illegs.	Bones		172	4	3
Nathan Meroney, R. S.	Adairs		68	21	1
Henry Ware's orps.	Hancocks		215	23	2
E. L. Christian's ors.	Higginbothams		110	2	5
Thomas C. Wilhight,	Phipps		251	11	5
William Luker,	Culbertsons		53	6	1
William David's orphans,	do.		25	19	1
Joseph Graham,	Hannas		68	11	5
John Landers,	Phipps		19	9	3

Fortunate Drawers.	Capts.	Dist.	No.	Dt.	Sec.
Thomas W. Freeman,	Caldwells		113	11	2
John Gholson,	Hannas		65	17	1
Nelson Thompson, illegit.	Berrymans		43	4	3
Gabriel L. Penn,	Phipps		175	6	5

M'INTOSH.

Shadrack Manning,	McCranys		149	7	2
William Taylor,	Terrells		4	23	1

MONROE.

Abraham Ledlow,	Woodwards		39	19	2
Samuel Mallet,	Johnsons		201	10	1
Josiah Hudgins, sol.	Stallings		177	13	1
William Swan,	Browns		79	6	2
W.D.&E.Ingraham, ills.	Houses		162	3	4
Wiley Barron, sol.	Millers		13	22	2
James Delay, J.	Millers		214	3	1
William Ferrell,	Trimbles		88	3	3
Melton Hann,	Millers		85	10	3
Jno. B. Thomaston,	Woodwards		150	1	5
Jeremiah Smith, sol.	Houses		171	3	2
Francis Power,	Wrights		280	22	2
Elget Driskel,	do.		204	11	3
Francis Miller, soldier,	Millers		103	6	1
William Davis,	Browns		169	2	5
Jesse Leavens, sol.	Sparks		236	5	1
David Russell, orph.	Turners		219	5	2
Peter Davis,	Douglass		59	22	2
P. Youngblood's ors.	Woodwards		60	9	5
Henry Gibson,	Turners		117	4	2
Wm. Langley, sr.	Fergasons		223	23	2
John Fergason,	Browns		277	17	2
Felix G. Cohron,	Phillips		222	11	1
Allen Rowe,	Houses		79	2	3
Nimrod Fergason,	Millers		39	15	1
James Stripling,	Houses		43	6	5
Henry Sturgess,	Millers		94	15	5
John Johnston,	Douglass		245	8	1
Alfred King,	Woodwards		75	27	1
James R. Smith,	Millers		153	19	2
Elizabeth Downs, dumb,	Gammons		197	21	2
Thomas Higginbotham, sol.	Millers		245	10	5
William Mills,	Houses		257	22	2
Harrison Lesueur,	Woodwards		225	11	3
John Murphey,	Pattersons		27	7	3
John Finch,	Finchs		238	28	1

MORGAN.

Michael A. Roberts,	Stokes		57	7	4
John H. Jones,	Harwells		31	8	3
Lewis King's orps.	Youngs		29	2	3
Samuel Parker,	Canifaxs		201	11	2
John Ashton,	Ostians		239	-8	1
Marcus Hemphill, sol.	Hills		153	24	1
Jesse Leavens, sol.	Sparks		236	5	1
Robert Howard,	Youngs		166	10	2
Samuel Paschall's orps.	Boswells		41	7	5
Littleton P. T. Harwell,	Ostians		51	11	5
Robert Esby,	Hitchcocks		46	15	2
Thomas Bandy,	Canifaxs		229	20	2
Rebec. Johnston, w.R.S.	Youngs		266	3	1
William Boman,	Adairs		239	3	2
James Mulkey's orps.	Brooks		155	1	4
William Gilbert, R. S.	Beasleys		45	3	4
Archey G. Garner,	Youngs		255	21	2
Susannah Bridges, w. R. S.,	Jennings		13	33	1
Josiah Barrett,	Dawsons		45	5	4
Josiah Lansford, soldier,	Hitchcocks		130	3	2
Samuel Patterson,	Whatleys		31	10	1
Eli W. Harrison,	Boswells		169	9	2
John H. R. Jestis,	Canifaxs		339	28	1

(214)

Fortunate Drawers. Capts.	Dist.	No.	Dt.	Sec.
James Henry, Harwells		52	27	1
William Willis, Stokes		5	33	1
Unity Warren, w. R. S., Harwells		5	3	1
John T. Peack's orphans, do.		174	3	2
Walter A. Partee, Christians		22	22	2
William Broughton, Stokes		66	10	5
Elbert Parter, Christians		45	4	1
Osborn Smith, Jennings		73	7	3
John R. Smith, Ostians		169	14	1
Mary Fogll, w. R. S., Jennings		217	28	1

MONTGOMERY.

	Dist.	No.	Dt.	Sec.
Thomas Clark, Ryals		116	27	1
William Alfred, Wynns		233	2	1
Hezekiah Hendrix, Popes		45	20	2
Farquhar McRae, Popes		89	7	4
William Browning, Pridgeons		124	8	5
David M:mms, soldier, Ryals		161	9	3
Loverd Bryan, do.		11	1	1
Charles Boils, R. S. Pridgeons		193	14	2

NEWTON.

	Dist.	No.	Dt.	Sec.
Archibald G. Gilbo's orps. Dyers		77	2	1
John Freeman, Summers		44	9	2
William D. Conyers, Pullens		160	3	1
Jesse Smith, sol. Penningtons		159	9	2
Willis R. Head, Allredds		174	20	1
Henry H. Talley, Summers		63	3	3
Fanny Prescott, w.R.S. Talleys		63	8	3
Joel Aycock, Summers		81	11	3
Andrew T. Hodge, Pullins		4	4	4
James Ivy Stewart, Snows		9	12	3
David Wright, Clarks		249	17	2
John D. Kirkpatrick, Hays		121	24	2
Joseph Willingham, Snows		113	18	2
Robert P. Ward, Penningtons		30	13	2
John F. Piper, sol. Newnans		62	3	3
Sarah Floyd, widow, Pullins		229	21	1
John Roberson, sr. Orrs		217	33	1
Elander Moss, widow, Graves		394	7	1
William Lummers, Allredds		1	10	5
Micajah Jones, Dyers		291	7	1
Iverson L. Graves, Hays		229	27	1
William D. Hughey, Moss		191	4	2
Charles Williams, sr. Pullens		78	7	2
William New, Talleys		337	28	1

OGLETHORPE.

	Dist.	No.	Dt.	Sec.
Nicholas Poss, Floyds		234	11	3
Clark Taylor, jr. Willsons		89	10	3
David Jinks, Floyds		240	7	3
Henry W. Gordon, B. Hills		36	5	3
Tali. L. Berry's orps. Holloways		177	18	2
Shelton Eidson, R. S. Rhodes		226	19	2
Wm. Simmons' orps. Hardmans		5	17	2
Baley Johns, Rousseaus		65	5	3
Parmenus English, R. S. Dixs		55	6	1
Betsey M. Jenkins, or.Rousseaus		264	5	1
James Tipper, sol. Devenports		102	7	1
James D. Johnson, Floyds		39	10	1
Magnus Carter, Billups		41	28	1
John McKee, R. S. Lacys		177	7	2
Peggy Wilson's illegs. Rousseaus		6	12	5
Delily McClain, illeg. Bells		283	11	2
James M. Thurman, Billups		284	16	2
Luke Smith, Hills		139	9	3
Henry Turner, Floyds		69	15	1
William Baldwin, sol. Smiths		57	12	3
James Duffill, Floyds		282	22	1
David Wilkins, Rhodes		195	5	1
James Buckhannon, Hardmans		107	3	4

Fortunate Drawers. Capts.	Dist.	No.	Dt.	Sec.
Isham Smith, Floyds		234	3	2
Elizabeth Sterling, w. Hardmans		66	6	5
John Hubbard, sr. R. S. Lacys		93	6	5
Joel Barnett, Burfords		9	6	4
Wm. N. Richardson, Williamsons		30	7	4
John B. Smith, Rousseaus		87	8	2
James S. Martin, Seals		109	11	5
Eve Beard, w. R. S. Lacys		181	8	3
Elizabeth Rowland, widow, Arnolds		205	22	2
Charles Barnett, Hardmans		50	13	2
Jacob W. Andrews, Holloways		113	12	1
Tilitha Gentery, deaf & dumb, Dixs		235	16	1
Wesley Shropshire, do.		270	4	3
Seaborn Wilder, Rousseaus		5	11	2
James Bailey, Dixs		188	21	1
Dorothy Freeman, wid. Williamsons		242	6	5

PIKE.

	Dist.	No.	Dt.	Sec.
Esther McDonald, wid. Hicks		185	12	1
John Howard, do.		125	3	3
Silas Moat, Orrs		166	29	1
George Holsey's orphans, Orrs		119	10	5
Clediah Storey, Hicks		97	1	4
John Irwin, Mays		245	10	2
John McDaniels, orphans, do.		219	6	2
James R. Gray, soldier, Daniellys		54	20	1

PULASKI.

	Dist.	No.	Dt.	Sec.
Catharine McGlothern, Hendleys		71	5	5
Shadrack Atkinson, Thomas		51	10	5
Charlotte Bailey, orphan, Hendleys		189	19	2
Baker Adams, Scarbroughs		153	1	2

PUTNAM.

	Dist.	No.	Dt.	Sec.
John Robertson, Bledsoes		28	15	5
Henry M. Tripp, Mizes		204	2	4
Peter Brown's orps. Sawyers		250	2	1
Amos Pilgrims, Clarks		39	27	1
Orps. of Andrew Park, Bledsoes		27	14	5
Sarah Hall, wife of H.H.ab.Blacks		37	8	5
Mathew Whitingbeall, Clarks		123	19	2
James Rosser, Barnetts		226	9	1
Nathaniel Black, Blacks		125	21	1
James Nicholson, Bledsoes		42	18	1
Bethina Burton, wid. Kindalls		8	8	1
James McLeary|s ors. Kendricks		123	6	5
Jesse W. Anderson, Bledsoes		35	10	1
Thomas B. Turner, Barnetts		189	32	1
Samuel Walker, Goods		130	13	2
Kinchin Taylor, Clarks		77	1	5
Samuel Cowles, Marcus		25	8	5
J. McGehee's ors. Kendricks		213	3	1
Green B. Buckhanon, Blacks		129	5	2
Thomas O. Lloyd, Sawyers		49	7	2
Martha Milton, wid. Vinings		138	3	3
William Cook, Bledsoes		117	14	2
Delilah Millirons, h.a. Clarks		214	17	1
Mason Tiller, Barnetts		20	6	4
Randal Dye's orphans, Chambers		126	13	2
Frederick Foster, Vinings		110	20	1
Thomas P. Bagley, Marcus		205	4	3
David Walker, Vinings		291	6	1
Alexander McDonald, Bledsoes		73	3	4
Hezekiah S. Dodwell, soldier, Brooks		240	22	2
William G. Flake, Stinsons		141	8	3
Joseph Stanford soldier, Slaughters		211	12	5

RABUN.

	Dist.	No.	Dt.	Sec.
Elizab'h McClain, wid. Godfreys		139	1	4
Nicholas Nix, Mercers		166	13	1
James Allen, Milligans		37	13	1
David Qualls, Godfreys		181	12	5
William Carnes, Godfreys		129	2	4

(215)

Fortunate Drawers.	Capts. Dist.	No.	Dt.	Sec.
David Fowler, sr.	Becks	197	7	2
John McClain's orphans,	Godfreys	282	8	1
Isham Nix,	Mercers	229	12	1

RICHMOND.

Fortunate Drawers.	Capts. Dist.	No.	Dt.	Sec.
Middleton Sego,	James	89	25	1
John A. Rozar, or.	Huntingtons	268	3	4
Wm. Erton Mealing,	Blacks	181	23	2
Thomas Richards,	Bushs	280	3	4
Elizabeth Winters, wid.	Kellys	125	8	3
Sarah, Kitty & Mary McMurphy, orphans of dec'd officer		213	2	1
John Stuckey's orps.	Kellys	28	2	3
Nathaniel Brown,	Treadwells	157	18	1
George A. B. Walker,	Augusta	145	31	1
J., E. & E. Stephens, orps.	Ferris	37	3	4
Robert Y. Blair,	Bushs	238	3	4
R.&F.A.M.Campbell'sors.	Huntingtons	174	9	2
Henry Mealing,	Treadwells	93	7	3
Henry Harper,	Raifords	56	2	2
Edmund Stuckey,	Kellys	237	6	3
Catharine Moore, wid.	Wilcoxs	189	9	2
William Thompson,	123rd	93	22	1
Eleanor Rich, hus. ab.	Segos	63	4	5
Peter D. Boutell, orphan,	Bushes	58	7	5
George Smith,		121	6	3
Raymond Ladeveze,	Ferris	125	14	1

SCRIVEN.

Fortunate Drawers.	Capts. Dist.	No.	Dt.	Sec.
Abigail McCleland, wid.	Roberts	109	9	2
Archibald Mills,	Poytress	163	13	2
Thomas Adkinson's ors.	Lovetts	1	13	2
Robert Bevill,	Stricklings	173	5	1
Allen Waters,	Humphreys	122	11	5
Thomas G. Walker,	Lovetts	39	14	2
William Windon,	Humphreys	231	23	1
Michael Doughtry	Kemps	225	20	1
James C. Dixon,	Humphreys	199	2	1
Thomas Mobly,	Roberts	138	5	4
Robert Bevill,	Stricklings	145	10	2
I. & T. F. Williams, illegits,	Poytress	13	8	4
Humphrey Bazemore,	do.	226	6	5
Orphans of Charles Strohaker,	Reaves	290	1	4

TATTNALL.

Fortunate Drawers.	Capts. Dist.	No.	Dt.	Sec.
Gabrieland Strickland,	Dees	41	32	1
Groves Sharpe, jr.	Graces	253	20	2
William Sapp, jr.	Dees	110	4	2
John Taylor, R. S.,	Deloachs	262	3	4

TELFAIR.

Fortunate Drawers.	Capts. Dist.	No.	Dt.	Sec.
Nancy B. McRae,		125	11	5
Hail Goldsmith,	Barentines	225	1	4
Cullen Bonney,	Lamkins	45	5	5
Reuben Dubose,	Wilkinsons	49	3	2
John Wilcox, jr.	do.	119	3	2

TALIAFERRO.

Fortunate Drawers.	Capts. Dist.	No.	Dt.	Sec.
Johnson Woodall,	Marshalls	122	4	3
James Swan,	Marshalls	73	13	5

THOMAS.

Fortunate Drawers.	Capts. Dist.	No.	Dt.	Sec.
Thomas Gill,		358	7	1

TWIGGS.

Fortunate Drawers.	Capts. Dist.	No.	Dt.	Sec.
Stephen Pitts,	Holidays	197	16	1
Etheldred Griffin, sol.	Graggs	298	22	1
Mary A. E. Miller, ill.	Holidays	97	18	1
Orp. of James Woodall,	Bosticks	113	9	2
John Higgs,	Pearsons	7	9	2
Eliz. Gilder, wid.	Chamberlains	30	11	1
Mary Jameson, w. R. S.	Bosticks	157	10	3
Orps. of Chs. Reynolds,	Pearsons	35	23	1
John Crittendon, R. S.	Stretmans	9	4	3
Clarky Dorman, wid.	Holidays	150	7	2

Fortunate Drawers.	Capts. Dist.	No.	Dt.	Sec.
William D. Bostick,	do.	27	18	2
Lear Lovit, wid.	Pearsons	104	14	5
Nancy McKenzie, wd.	Solomons	167	23	2
Wm. L. Richards,	Chamberlains	179	21	2
Council S. Bryan,	do.	111	19	2
Isaac Watts,	Bosticks	199	1	1
William Veal,	Graggs	82	8	1
Thomas Jones, R. S.	Solomons	49	23	2
Larkin Powell,	Blackshears	59	3	4
Thomas Pearce,	Streetmans	159	13	1

UPSON.

Fortunate Drawers.	Capts. Dist.	No.	Dt.	Sec.
William B. Scrimshire,	Paschalls	22	12	1
Thomas Wood,	Coopers	87	21	2
Allen Stillwell,	Paschalls	231	15	2
William Barron,	589th	190	4	3
Thomas S. Clark,	Paschalls	263	4	1
Sinclair McMullan,	Pettys	46	3	1
Miles G. Beach,	Ellis	314	3	4
Nathan Johnson,	Paschals	106	2	1
Thomas Sanders, R. S.	Ellis	32	6	4
John J. Lewis,	Hattoxs	105	1	2
Samuel W. Burton,	Pettys	184	22	1

WALTON.

Fortunate Drawers.	Capts. Dist.	No.	Dt.	Sec.
Willis D. Mathews,	McQuertors	162	2	2
Ann Hendrick, widow,	418th	25	17	2
Phillip Barnes,	Davis	117	1	1
Jesse M. Herring,	418th	70	1	4
Elijah Dye,	249th	117	7	5
Thomas Clack,	Rays	247	14	1
Elizabeth Aycock, wid.	559th	57	23	2
Gabriel Grice's orphans,	418th	115	3	3
John Dorithy's orps.	Snows	123	5	3
Boland Whitlow, sol.	Hudsons	74	17	1
Jesse Mitchell,	Rays	69	12	5
Thomas Inlow,	Hudsons	153	8	1
Jesse Jean,	Bexleys	58	2	2
David Edward, illeg.	do.	3	5	5
Jonathan Oaks,	559th	154	13	2
Uzzeil Baggett,	McQuertors	21	16	1
Joseph Dudley,	Hudsons	83	14	5
John Sentell,	250th	85	7	1
James Thompson,	250th	210	16	2
Thomas Bird,	559th	223	17	2
George W. Freeman's orphans,	Davis	110	11	5
John Cronick,	Hudsons	114	22	1
Thomas Brand,	do.	121	24	1
Henry Beasley, R. S.	Snows	270	4	1
Ferdinand Bankston,	McQuertors	284	15	1

WARE.

Fortunate Drawers.	Capts. Dist.	No.	Dt.	Sec.
Levi Lee, soldier,	Lees	249	4	1
Allen Osteen,	Bryans	261	4	1
Jeremiah Underhill,	Dowlings	286	21	1
Claton Jones,	Bryans	197	25	1
Samuel Gutery,	Motes	4	28	1

WAYNE.

Fortunate Drawers.	Capts. Dist.	No.	Dt.	Sec.
John Rooks, R. S.	McKinneys	102	9	1
Martin Manning,	Mannings	99	17	1

WARREN.

Fortunate Drawers.	Capts. Dist.	No.	Dt.	Sec.
James Norris, R. S.	Kinseys	6	19	2
Nancy Watson, wid.	Sanders	114	12	3
Isaiah Tucker's orps.	Parhams	215	13	1
Matthews White,	do.	55	33	1
Richmond Burnley, sol.	Seals	188	2	1
George H. Johnson, sol.	Latimers	242	9	2
John Kitching, illegit.	Adkins	242	5	3
Elizabeth Jones, h.ab.	Downs	13	3	4
Michael M. Botz,	Brinkleys	145	7	3

(216)

Fortunate Drawers. Capts. Dist.	No.	Dt.	Sec.
Alfred Mays, Kinseys	90	3	1
Mason S. Hardiway, do.	105	7	3
Asap R. Hill, Kinseys	29	30	1
Penelope Daniel, wid. Hils	19	27	1
Daniel Hamelton, Sanders	32	6	2
Stephen M. Myrick, Bulls	246	2	3
William Hilson, sol. Downs	79	1	4
Charles Riley, soldier, Jones	89	7	2
William Jones, sr. Jones	53	15	1
Catharine Harris, w.R.S. Hills	243	21	2
Asa Umphlet, R. S. Adkins	144	2	1
Larkin R. Gunn, Rogers	10	22	1
Wiley Grizzle, Brinkleys	213	14	2
Mary, Ju. & E. Robins, illegs. Downs	121	7	1
Elizabeth Moore's orphans, Bulls	121	10	1
Annanias Newsome, illegit. Adkins	41	13	1
John Griffin's orphans, Parhams	250	9	5
Freeman Allen, Rogers	197	10	5
Francis Beall's orphans, Jones	183	26	1
Sampson Wilder, soldier, Hills	99	9	1
Job Hunter, Downs	216	26	1
Reuben Rogers soldier, Hills	185	11	2
John V. Gordon, Fords	53	11	5
Robert McNair, Adkins	211	21	2
Robert Johnson's orphans, Stewarts	225	20	2
William Williford, Downs	233	16	1
Nancy Dozier, widow, Parhams	52	33	1
Dennis Lindsey, R. S. Jones	36	1	3
Warren H. Turner, Stewarts	43	5	5
Lewis Underwood, Jones	38	10	5
Elijah Waller, R. S. Sanders	127	3	2
Cynthy Spurlin, hus. ab. Jones	42	5	2

WASHINGTON.

Paul Williams, sol. McClendons	273	11	2
John Cocks, Avans	245	15	2
Sarah Hall's illegs. Wimberlys	6	13	2
Thomas W. Coker, Floyds	208	1	4
Solomon Long, Whitfields	126	20	1
Elizab'h Stanford, w.R. S.Jordans	2	3	2
Benago Phillips, Woods	139	1	2
William Hunt, Whitfields	272	19	2
Adam Calhoun, Tysons	97	4	3
Moses Cox, R. S. Avans	121	11	1
Jesse Dupre, do.	174	15	5
Josiah Ard, Tysons	125	2	3
John Ellis, Whitfields	127	4	3
Nathaniel Giles, Oquins	88	9	2
Jacob Stephen's heirs, do	260	14	1
Nauflight Howard's ors. Currys	115	9	5
John Mims, Gilberts	26	9	5
Thomas Brooking's ors. Jordans	243	4	1
Thomas Ragin, Woods	20	14	1
Henry Johnson's orps. Gilberts	106	9	5
Greene Andrews, Rushings	178	3	1
Germina Whitfield, w. Whitfields	149	9	1
Michael O'Conner, Currys	102	22	1
Moses Brown's orps. Woods	133	9	3
Quinney Pearson, illeg. do.	185	4	3
Jesse Amison, R. S. Warthens	113	30	1
Daniel Frasier, Mannings	273	20	2
Samuel Tompkins, soldier, Andrews	23	12	2
Joel Davis' heirs, Oquins	25	23	2
Joel Eccol's orphans, Tysons	253	23	2
Jacob Chester, illegitimate, do.	38	11	5
Louis S. Avan, Avans	347	22	1
James Page, Whitfields	133	3	1
John Mathis R. S. Jordans	123	27	1

Fortunate Drawers. Capts. Dist.	No.	Dt.	Sec.
Gabriel Stubbs, Currys	81	12	3
Isaac Moy, Whitfields	81	17	2
James C. Francis, do.	205	17	2
Nancy Johnson, widow, Warthens	48	15	5
Nathan W. Renfro, Currys	23	1	3
John Brantley, soldier, McClendons	273	5	3
Willis Johnson, jr. Warthens	124	5	1
Henry Washburn, McLendons	102	11	1

WILKINSON.

Robert Barnett, R. S. Mayos	132	11	5
Benjamin Aycock's ors. Shows	30	1	1
J. & S. Stapleton, ills. Branans	170	10	1
Alexander Adams, Mandersons	219	3	2
Amos Smith, Halls	309	1	4
Josiah Stephens, Shows	78	3	1
Joseph Brannon, do.	283	8	1
Amos Johnson, Mayos	163	24	1
Mitchell Pain, Fairchilds	31	32	1
Benjamin Aycock's orps. Shows	194	4	3
William Hatcher, Halls	207	9	3
Barney Tucker, Currys	57	3	4
Homer M. Bellflower, Fairchilds	95	22	1
W. & W. Taylor, ills. Mathews	221	14	1
Balas Carr, Smiths	10	18	1
Franklin J. T. Mitchell, Currys	20	18	1
Daniel McNeal, Mayos	48	3	4
Benjamin Winham, Fairchilds	157	1	5
William Morgan's orphans, do.	38	14	5
James Bloodworth, Mandersons	261	2	4
Nathan'l Cannon, R.S.Fairchilds	165	30	1
Anna McKinzey, or. Mandersons	122	3	2
Luke G. Weekes, Currys	30	24	1
Mary, Wm. & S. Nobles, f.a. Smiths	13	10	3
Mary Bye, w. R. S. Fairchilds	133	10	3
Spencer Douglass, R. S. Smiths	21	25	1
John & Sophia Arnold, orphs., Shows	147	13	2
Minerva Williams do.	241	6	3
Mary Salter, widow, Currys	205	1	4
William Minter, Mathews	114	2	3
Lewis Bend, Mandersons	74	2	1
Winlock C. Peason, Mathews	165	15	1
Richard Whitaker, soldier, Barrys	21	21	1
Burrel Mayo, Mayos	92	10	5

WILKES.

John H. Peters, Lukers	136	7	1
William Thornton, Hopkins	19	7	5
Henry Brooks, Amasons	149	11	5
William L. Smith, sol. Ragsdale	33	19	2
Emanuel Smith, Amasons	201	10	2
William H. Barnes, Wootens	6	10	3
Henry B. Gibson, R. S. Greens	50	16	1
Pernal Truitt,R.S. Washingtons	177	21	2
Robert Hammock, Rices	200	11	1
John Richeson, Greshams	151	15	2
Nicholas Miller, Washingtons	69	17	1
Joseph Victory, Moors	7	3	5
Winston Evans, Rices	5	8	1
John E. Nolen, Wootens	117	2	1
Mary Wellborn widow, Popes	29	6	1
William Richerson, Richersons	89	9	5
Coleman P. Owen, Reeves	57	2	5
Bailey Lunceford, sol., Washingtons	241	1	4
David Jackson do.	38	8	5
Nelson Roberts' orphans, Lukers	105	26	1
Drury B. Short, Washingtons	241	1	4
Johnson Wellborn's orphans, Popes	157	13	2
Peter C. Johnson, Washingtons	118	13	2
Yearby Philips, soldier, Amasons	217	21	2
Turner Bowls, Washingtons	3	5	3

INDEX FOR OFFICIAL LAND LOTTERY REGISTER

AARON, William 205
ABBETT, Ezekiel 156
ABBOTT, James, 34; John, 58; Josiah, 40, 132, 164; Seaborn, 9; William, 49, 201, 211.
ABERCROMBIE, Charles 149
ABERNATHEY, William 100
ABNER, Thomas 99, 202
ABSOLOM, Avery, 88; Owbry, 88.
ACANES, Killee 43
ACEE, Erasmus, 139; James, 137; John, 121.
ACKINS, William 75
ACOCK, Barden, 5; Reddick, 16.
ACCORD, John 125; Leonard, 209; Lewis, 191.
ACREE, Nathaniel 13, 39
ADAIR, James, 119; Jane, 183; John, 18, 99, 177.
ADAMS, Aaron, 53, 199; Abagail, 128; Abner, 126; Albert, 173; Alexander, 176, 216; Alfred, 83; Baker, 214; Brittern, 137; Britton, 101; Dancy, 209; David, 18, 20, 60, 95, 184; Evalina, 98; Fabian, 3; Hiram, 196; James, 8, 38, 125, 168; Jelotes, 59; Jesse, 11; John, 16, 72, 89, 92, 105; Joshua, 74; Judith, 160; Lawrence, 132, 210; Lewis, 191; Lucy, 98; Maradeth, 162; Mary, 212; Mathias, 121; Nancy, 17, 110, 171; Nathan, 209; Nicholas, (2), 20; Norville, 95; Polly, 104; Putnam, 2; Reuben, 17; Richard, 6, 63; Robert, 36; Sarah, 36; Shadrack, 175; Sun, 104; Thomas, 79, 94, 199; Thompson, 111; William, 4, 12, 53, 80, 167, 182; Wilson, 141.
ADAMSON, Augustus, 95; George, 132.
ADCOCK, Edmund, 59; George, 157; John, 170; William, 52.
ADISON, William 118
ADKERSON, Henry, 26, 78; Nancy, 140.
ADKINS, Francis, 126; John, 91; Joseph, 183; Samuel, 42; William, 38.
ADKINSON, Thomas, 215; William, 38.
AGE, Jushua 4, 137
AGEE, William 89
AGEES, Humphrey, 52
AGETER, Philip 159
AGNEW, Samuel 169
AIKEN, Fred 173
AIKINS, Sarah Ann 80
AINSWORTH, James 116
AJOHN, Eli 30
AKENS, John 24
AKERS, John, (2) 129

AKIN, Elijah, 34; Elizabeth, 91; Frances, 184; Fleming, 40; Jane, 62; John, 57; Samuel, 71, 112; Thomas, 189; William, 176.
AKINS, Elijah, 111, 205; Elizabeth, 186; James, 20, 136; John, 39; Milton, 80; Thomas, 167; William, 3, 79, 149; Winefred, 35.
AKONS, Daniel 24
AKRIDGE, Ezekiel, 139; Hardy, 173; Levi, 156; Virgil, 33; William, 209.
ALBERSON, Edward, 130; William, 89
ALBERT, Thomas 64
ALBRITTON, Amos, 78; Elizabeth, 170; H. 28; Henry, 131; Jesse, 46; Joel, 78; John, 53, 201; Lingear, 39! Mathew, 184.
ALBURY, Andrew 196
ALDERMAN, George 100
ALDRED, William 58
ALDREDGE, Elizabeth, 20; Henry, 85; Jesse, 7.
ALDRICH, Whipple 145, 158
ALDRIDGE, Elizabeth, 90; Jesse, 129.
ALDRUDGE, Thomas 77
ALESON, David 112
ALEWINE, David, 95; Elijah, 38.
ALEXANDER, Adam, 18; Isaac, 82, 114; James, 1; John, 167; Mary, 182; Orphan, 118; Peter, 161; William, 44, 112, 164, 210; Willis, 88; Wright, 36.
ALFORD, Asa, 9; Asanath, 159; Hamilton, 96; Henry, 41, 103; Isaac, 89; Isom, 31; John, 1, 137; Julius, 25; Lodowick, 167; Lory, 213; Peyton, William, 214.
ALFRED, William 131
ALHEY, Mahala 183
ALISON, Robert, 201
ALLAIN, James 107
ALLCOCK, Lemuel, 97; Sidney, 58.
ALLCORN, Jame, 20
ALLCUT, Thomas 78
ALLDAY, William 81
ALLEN, A., 54; Charles, 22, 24, 107, 208; Catherine, 180; Chloe, 184; Churchill, 181; Clement, 210; Clemmonthina, 35; David, 24, 39, 84, 118, 124, 164; Drewry, 74, 206; Eason, 143, 199, Edmund, 49; Edward, 39; Elisha, 104; Elizabeth, 40, 72; Freeman, 216; George, 12; Gray, 54; Han., 213; I., 54; James, 23, 65, 89, 100, 134, 146, 214; Jeremiah, 84; John, 38, 69, 89, 94, 111, 118, 120, 166, 209; Joseph, 18, 69, 94, 142, 186; Josiah, 66; Larkin, 122; Mar., 213; Mary, 82; Philip, 207; Reuben, 20; Robert, 130, 151, 162, 173; Samuel, 7; Stephen, 16,

59, 150; Stokes, 86; Washington, 40; William, 16, 64, 136, 162, 199, 204; Woodson, 29; Young, 156.
ALLENDER, Thomas 93
ALLGOOD, Mary, 182; Peter, 210; William, 75.
ALLINDER, Edward 209
ALLISON, Benjamin, 50; Chris., 44; David, 168, 190; Green, 19; James, 165; Jonathan, 186; Rebecca, 179; Robert, 86.
ALLRED, Aaron, 2; Margaret, 209.
ALLUM, Brigs 193
ALLUMS, Bryant 74
ALLMON, Thomas, 169; William, 155.
ALLMOND, Isaac, 136; Usry, 117, 152 William, 40, 69, 105.
ALMAN, Jefferson, 153; William, 158.
ALREAD, Barsheba 127
ALRED, Margaret, 139; William, 149.
ALSABROOKS, Alford, 174; Claborn, 43; Howell, 24, 145; Lewis, 6.
ALSLIN, David 34
ALSO, Elizabeth 143
ALTMAN, Sampson 194
AMBERSON, William 6
AMBPURN, William 90
AMBROSE, Hezekiah 49
AMISON, James, 29; Jesse, 45, 216; Josiah, 42; Nathan, 182.
AMMONS, Jacob, 57, 118; Jimia, 81; Nancy, 48; Sarah, 149.
AMOS, Elijah, 72; Leany, 85; Maulden, 132; William, 58, 137.
A..IOSON, Thomas 179
ANDERS, Mary 148
A..DERSON, Abel, 114; Abraham, 158 Amos, 124; Ann 8, 97; Athelson, 35; Brice, 32; D., 93; Edward, 45; Elizabeth 74; George, 182; Henry, 21, 75; Isaac, 81; Isham, 19; James, 7 52 21, 107; Jefferson, 79; Jesse, 2,1; John, 18, 98, 177; Joseph, 115, 205; Martha, 109; Mary, 61, 153, 154, (2) 207; Moses, 117; Neal, 10; Nelson, 201; Peggy, 50; Reuben, 23, 63, 202; Richard, 207; Samuel, 35, 57; Sarah, 45, 125; Sterling, 81; Thomas, 16, 118, 210; T. W., 4; V. P., 79; William, 33, 43, 50, 69, 75, 87, 131, 140, 163, 173, 191, 197
ANDERTON, Catherine 173
ANDLETON, John 39
ANDRESS, Jones 47
ANDREW, Binley, 201; Elbert, 139; Garnett, 158; John, 110; Nicholas, 117.
ANDREWS, Adam, 164; David, 11; D. M., 16; E. B., 16; Elbert P., 4; Elizabeth 196; Green, 216; Jacob,

214; John, 52, 67, 87, 206; Joseph, 143; Mary, 97; Micajah, 81; Nancy, 109, 169; Nimrod, 170; Michael, 110; Owen, 20, 53; Robert, 81, 149, 181.
ANGELLY, Alexander, 93, 128, 188.
ANGLE, John 210
ANGLIN, William 92
ANGLING, John, 24; M., 113; P., 113.
ANSLEY, Gilbert, 202; Isaiah, 103; James, 113, 194; John, 4; Mary, 101; Asa, 45.
ANTHONY, Anne, 21; Anselm, 186; John, 171; Lawrence, 134; Ruth, 60; Samuel, 60; William, 89; Wylie, 53, 205.
APPLETON, Samuel 4
APPLEWHITE, John . 13, 96
APPLING, Burwell, 178; David, 2.
ARNOLD, Bethany, 78; Charles, 81; John, 134; Reason, 91; Sanch, 44; Stephen, 13.
ARNAUD, John Petter 43
ARCHER, David, 107; Harvey, 41, 199; Hugh, 96, 129; James, 29, 130, 138; William, 184.
ARCHY, Orphan 201
ARD, Daniel, 4; John, 78; Josiah, 216; Neal, 75.
ARENDALL, Lawdwin 173
ARENT, John 18
ARGO, Lucy, 197; Nimrod, 158.
ARMOR, Andrew, 6; John, 11; Robert, 78.
ARMSTORPHE, George, 174, 177; Solomon, 210.
ARMSTRONG, George, 210; Goulden, 176; Hugh, 25, 207; Jeffer, 175; John, 197; Joseph, 43; Larkin, 181; Mary, 90, 141; Samuel, 207; Sary, 41; Stith, 130; Thomas, 157; Wiyliam, 32.
ARRANT, Sally Ann 183
ARRINGTON, Ezekiel, 156; Henry, 127.
ARTHUR, Mat., 136, 164, 168.
ASBERRY, Elizabeth 153
ASBY, David, 37; James, 105.
ASH, George, 176; Robert, 149; William, 5.
ASHBURN, Elisha, 27; Mary, 109; Miles, 131.
ASHCRAFT, Thomas 127.202
ASHLEY, John, 25, 29; Mary, 37; Nathaniel, 172; Thomas, 203; William, 78, 90.
ASHMORE, John 3
ASHORN, Reps 24
ASHTON, John 213

ASHWELL, Lewis —141
ASHE, Alexander — 186
ASHFIELD, Jane — 203
ASLIN, Susan — 16
ASKEW, Benjamin, 201; Frederick, 31, 103; Henry, 154; Jeremiah, 159; John, 121, 211; Mary, 36; S. W. A., 86; William, 205.
ASKEY, Jisiah — 111
ASTEEN, Sidney — 32
ASTIN, Robert, 49, 88; William, 40, 167.
ASWORTH, Cynthia, 94; Jeremiah, 40
ASHWORTH, Elisha — 114
ATCHISON, Winifred — 39
ATHA, Eliza — 103
ATKINS, Benjamin, 159, 177; Elizabeth, 187; Joseph, 171; Randol, 19; Thomas, 127; William, 95.
ATKINSON, Ica, 147; Jeremiah, 94; MARTHA, 43; Priscilla, 173; Robert, 199; Sarah, 138; Shadrack, 214; Silliccea, 14; Stephen, 16.
ATKISON, Job — 99
ATWATER, Elihu — 167
ATWOOD, Berry, 164; James, 126.
ATRIS, Peter, — 54, 74
ATTAWAY, Amos, 7; Parnal, 37.
ATTEWAY, Robert — 29, 78
AUDUFF, John — 129
AUDLEY, James — 156
AUSTIN, Amon, 108; David, 59, 136; Fielder, 78; Harris, 67, 111, 162; Jesse, 98; John, 27, 56, 64; Michael, 63, 208; Nathaniel, 56; Rachel, 146; Viennah, 98.
AUSBURN, Thomas — 66
AUTERY, Hannah — 65
AVAN, Lewis — 160, 216
AVANT, Isaiah — 170
AVARY, Isa — 63
AVERETT, Aaron, 48; Abner, 172, 203; Christopher, 74; Elizabeth, 109; Thomas, 89.
AVERIT, John — 58
AVERY, Clarissa, 194; William, 98, 113, 182, 204.
AWTRY, Jacob — 109, 150
AYCOCK, Benjamin, 216; Elizabeth, 101, 214; Houston, 194; Jesse, 124; Joel, 214; Milton, 15; Presley, 161.
AYDCOCK, Presley — 110
AYRES, Abraham, 93; Abram, 62; Baker, 11; Dor., 15; Francis, 168; Julian, 120; Moses, 168; Pinckney, 47; Sultana, 15; Thomas, 55; William, 183.
AXOM, Sterling — 97
BABB, Elizabeth — 32, 209
BACHELOR, Cornelius — 5
BACKLY, Jonathan — 152

BACKUS, William — 50
BACON, Charles, 118, 112; Henry, 31; Jonathan, 51; William, 27.
BACHELOTT, John, 145; Mary, 90.
BACHLOTT, Lewis — 20
BACHUS, John — 198
BADULY, John — 14
BAGBY, John — 186
BAGETT, Erwin — 66
BAGGERLY, Henry — 202
BAGGETT, Allen, 87; Bennett, 32; Uzziel, 215.
BAGGITT, Andrew — 8
BAGGOTT, Archibald, 140; Zilphy, 181.
BAGGS, Archibald — 11
BAGLEY, Edward, 102; Herman, 43; James, 95, 13; Thomas, 214; Wiley, 95; William, 96.
BAGWELL, Charles, 143; Littleberry, 98; William, 205.
BAILEY, Abraham, 81; Allen, 147; Anny, 159; Charles, 23; Charlotte, 214; David, 33; Edmond, 55; Elisha, 53; Isaac, 9; Jacob, 153; James, 214; John, 53, 65, 79, 83; Joseph, 54; Loyd, 41; Mary, 6; Orphans, 147; Pierce, 22; S., 69; Samuel, 27; Stephen, 108; Thomas, 19; William, 41, 81.
BAILIE, Peter — 194
BAILS, Emmor — 139
BAILY, William — 192
BAINES, Robert Scott — 8
BAIRFIELD, Thaddeus — 19
BAIRD, Absalom, 133; James, 42, 13
BAISDEN, Mary, 117; Solomon, 101.
BAITES, James — 31
BAITS, Robert — 64
BAITY, Thomas — 146
BAKER, Abner, 186; Anderson, 25; Ann, 78; Beal, 80; Benjamin, 12; Blake, 71; Charles, 186; Dempsey, 86; John, 66; Jonathan, 148; Levi, 186; Pleasant, 70; Priscilla, 58, 179; Richard, 12; Richmond, 186; Sarah, 174; Silas, 66; Wiley, 27; William, 3, 54, 93.
BALDWIN, Charles, 27; Damaries, 187; John, 102; Joseph, 17, 189, 210; Laomi, 36; Larkin, 123; Robert, 31, 103; William, 214.
BALES, James, 134, 143; John, 39; Julas, 135; William, 71.
BALEY, Robert, 132; Thomas, 193.
BALL, Eliza 154; Henry, 30, 152; Hervey, 148; James, 27, 71; John, 105; Joseph, 183; William, 20, 40.
BALLARD, Elizabeth, 153; James, 78; Rebecca, 172.
BALLARD, David, 6; Edmond, 113;

Frederick, 20; George, 102; James, 177; Mary, 151; Polly, 157; Sarah, 151; Thomas, 12, 177.
BALLENGER, John 17
BALLENGY, William 129
BALY, Thomas 51
BANDY, Lewis, 162; Luke, 30; Thomas, 213.
BANKER, Edward 4
BANKS, Ann, 101; Charles, 172; David, 155; Drury, 55; Elizabeth, 190; Henry, 59; John, 210; Joseph, 24; Lemuel, 142; Mildred, 88; Thomas, 120, 122, 175, 180; William, 97.
BANKSTON, Alfred, 114; Elijah, 210; Ferdinand, 215; John, 148; Joseph, 2; Nathan, 117; William, 74, 79.
BANYON, William 80
BARBER, Alsey, 110; Archibald, 54, 152; George, 54; James, 110; Mary, 22; Reese, 75; Rhoda, 89; Samuel, 151, 165; Thomas, 57, 156; William, 6.
BARDEN, James, 18; William, 135.
BARDIN, William 94
BAREFIELD, Winney, 134; Winnie, 71
BARFIELD, Orphan, 212; Larkin, 78; Sampson, 70.
BARGANER, Manusra 54
BARBARON, Elizabeth 78
BARGER, James 117
BARGERON, Abi 5
BARHAM, Jane 54
BARKER, Bartlett, 6; Eldridge, 31; Ephriam, 210; Fiveash, 199; Hubbard, 27; John, 45, 71, 72, 89, 152; Joseph, 64, 88; Laban, 124; Nathaniel, 87; Samuel, 98; Thomas, 133
BARKLEY, Mary, 178; William 150.
BARKLY, Robert, 51; William, 126.
BARKSDALE, Horatio, 123, 42; F., 9; Nathaniel, 150.
BARKWELL, Stephen 168
BARLEY, Bales 170
BARLOW, Thomas, 134; Willie, 18.
BARNARD, John, 34; Lucy, 47.
BARNES, Alford, 143; Elizabeth, 60; George, 53; James, 136; Jesse, 203; John, 92; Pulian, 66; Littleton, 51; Mar., 57; Nathan, 96, 118; Philip, 97, 215; Ransom, 63; William, 45, 156, 216.
BARNETT, Anna, 90; Caroline, 39; Charles, 178, 214; Francis, 89; George, 147; James, 202; Jehoida, 211; Joel, 193, 214; John, 50, 60, 98, 130; Nathaniel, 35; Robert, 216; Samuel, 113; Sarah, 103; Solomon, 59; Thomas, 88, 130; William, 17, 27, 72, 66, 74, 92.
BARNHART, George, 208; John, 171;

Mahala, 81.
BARNWELL, William, ...50
BARR, Alfred, 190; Robert, 23; Samuel, 41, 199; Thomas, 102, 183.
BARRENTINE, David, 52; Martha Ann 21.
BARRETT, Bailey, 156; Isaac, 123; John, 182; Josiah, 118, 213; Sarah, 94, 164; Sion, 212; W. C. W., 83.
BARRON, Elizabeth, 151; Fanny, 39; Henry, 9, 54; John, 136; Joseph, 70; Samuel, 181; Smith, 80; Thomas, 212.
BARROW, Josiah, 10; Thomas, 6; Wiley, 63.
BARRY, Catherine, 128; John, 187; Orphan, 89, 169.
BARSON, Elisha, ...108
BARSTOW, Jedediah 49
BARTEE, Abraham 212
BARTHOLOMEW, Edward 2
BARTLETT, Austin, 90; Edward, 161 207.
BARTLEY, John 174
BARTON, David, 146; Henry, 183; James, 136, 208; John, 29, 91, 183; Josiah, 55; Lewis, 142; Robert, 55.
BARWICK, Samuel, 35; William, 194.
BASHLOR, Charles 113
BASKIN, John 43
BASS, Alexander, 170; Burrell, 182; Burwell, 168; Edward, 46; Elizabeth, 64; Ingram, 189; Jesse, 161; John, 130; Mary, 102, 208; Nancy, 211; Richard, 27, 174; William, 69, 183.
BASSETT, Abner, 72; John, 199; Orphan, 193; Richard, 38.
BASTIN, Nancy 158
BASTON, William 101
BATEMAN, Benjamin, 15; Claiborn, 7; David, 62; Elimina, 62; Jerh., 4; John, 21; Theophilus, 170; Thomas, 161.
BATES, Anthony, 114; Issachar, 28; James, 80, 132; John, 49, 53; Mathew, 136; Thomas, 151; William, 98.
BATHUM, William 60
BATLY, Alfred, 170; William, 102.
BATTEY, Edward, 192; Joseph, 184.
BATTLE, Jesse, 98; Joseph, 80; William, 62, 79.
BATSON, David, 55; Richard, 16, 163; Thomas, 176.
BATTS, John, 168; McAllen, 131; Nathan, 175.
BATTY, Susan 54

BATY. Abner, 180; James, 118; Thomas, 17.
BAUGH, Daniel, 124, 143; John, 143; Jonathan, 99; Pleasant, 120; Susannah, 122.
BAWLING, Martin, 111; Reuben, 146.
BAXTER, Elizabeth, 99; Henry, 155; J., 34; John, 47, 124; William, 175
BAY, Moses ------121
BAYNE, Charles, 81, 86; Elizabeth, 67; Jemison, 171.
BAZEMORE, Humphrey, 215; John, 168; Nathaniel, 87; Riley, 85.
BEACH, Abiel, 22; John, 172; Miles, 215.
BEACHAM, Charles, 90; Henry, 57.
BEAIRD, William ------79
BEAL, Robert, 61, 161; Sarah, 2; William, 132.
BEALIE, Reason ------51
BEALL, Amanda, 32; Egbert, 25; Elizabeth, 58; Feraby, 45; Francis, 216; Frederick, 191; Harrison, 35; Hugh, 130; James, 33, 107; John, 44; Joseph, 176; Martha, 107; Mathew, 67; Mayfield, 70; Robert, 23, 62, 191; Rutha, 162; Sampson, 131; William, 89.
BEALLE, Jesse ------158
BEAN, Ann, 115; John, 212.
BEARD, Alexander, 67; Benjamin, 137; Eve, 214; George, 172; Joseph, 146, 156; Moses, 66; Robert, 117, 174; Thomas, 4; Orphans, 152.
BEARDEN, Amanda, 177; William, 186.
BEARDIN, James, 145; John, 211.
BEARDING, Elisha, ------6
BEARDON, Thomas, 7; Willoughby, 178.
BEARFIELD, Jesse, 59; M. A., 83.
BEASLEY, Allen, 65; David, 148; Elijah, 23; Elsy, 94; Henry, 119, 215; James, 172; John, 11, 67, 89; Joshua 1, Micajah, 158; Mitchell, 194, 197; Robert, 61; Seymore, 112; Stephen, 98; Susannah, 125; Thomas, 151, 176; William, 26, 38, 111, 189.
BEATY, David, 6, 31; Hugh, 34; Robert, 56.
BEATTY, John, 111; William, 157.
BEAUCHAMP, Nathan ------142
BEAUFORD, John ------133, 139
BEAULINEAU, George ------32
BEAVERS, Allsey, 193; Elizabeth, 77, 118; Robert, 41; Silas, 95.
BEAZELEY, Jacob ------167
BECHHAM, Osborn ------77
BECK, Gideon, 147; Isaiah, 91, 129, 195; Pike, 126; Sarah, 8; Solomon,

45; Temperance, 104; Thomas, 42; Willis, 78.
BECKHAM, James, 70; John, 197; Osborn, 213; Samuel, 32; Solomon, 9, 150.
BECKWORTH, Hansell, 10; Israel, 31.
BEDDELL, Isaac, ------120
BEDGOOD, Henry, 104; John, 29; Samuel, 39.
BEDDINGFIELD, John, 86; Mary, 163; Robert, 160; Wiley, 209.
BEEBEE, Justin ------52
BEEK, William ------113
BEELAND, John ------128
BEEM, Darkis ------202
BEGGARLY, Hilary ------193
BELCHER, Allen, 99; Daniel, 87; Henry, 99; James, 130; John, 71; Mary, 62; Samuel, 99, 109; William, 36, 67, 90, 212.
BELDING, Nelson ------152
BELK, John ------62
BELL, Adam, 164; Aser, 114; Benjamin, 209; Catherine, 120; David, 88; Elias, 39; Eliza, 75; Fielding, 138; Francis, 99, 168; Henry, 201; Hugh, 173; James, 16, 139, 172; Jane, 199; Jesse, 10; Joel, 190; John, 8, 120, 155, 165, 196, 209; Joseph, 164; Leister, 138; Lewis, 57, 105; Mathew, 38; P., 209; Pierce, 114; Russell, 4; Rutha, 29; Sarah, 57; Seaborn, 1; Silas, 126; Simeon, 23; Spencer, 61; Thomas, 65, 67; William, 10, 171, 182; Willis, 124.
BELLAH, Hiram, 173; Nathaniel, 31; Samuel, 131.
BELLAMY, Asa, 94; John, 194; Mary, 79, 88, 102; Nicholas, 59, 208.
BELLFLOWER, Elizabeth, 179; George 116; Homer, 216.
BELLINGER, Marg. ------69
BELLINGSLEY, Jesse ------174
BELOTE, Alfred ------70
BELT, Loyd ------99
BELTON, Solomon ------135
BELYEN, Thomas ------131
BEMAN, Carlile, 19; Henry, 210.
BEMEN, Laveing ------88
BENDER, Parker ------213
BENEFIELD, James, 188; John, 6, 42; Needham, 112.
BENHAM, Elias ------41
BENNETT, Aaron, 42; Almira, 20; Amasa, 5; Benjamin, 47; Daniel, 70, 159; Dixon, 67; Elizabeth, 3; Fannie, 17; George, 34; Jane, 129; Jason, 142; John, 47, 67, 75, 167; Jurial, 135; Langston, 199; Lydia, 140; Mark, 211; Rachel, 102, 211; Richard, 7; Robert, 47; Tapley, 162;

William, 102, 113, 164, 211.
BENSON, Eli, 205; Elizabeth, 65, 161; Enoch, 11, 162; John, 4, 33, 58; Mary, 101; Rachel, 41; Reuben, 136; Richard, 158; Willis, 148.
BENTHAM, James
BENTLEY, Abi, 113; Jacob, 97; James, 16, 152; Jeremiah, 135; Jesse, 109; John, 34, 188, 100; Thomas, 193.
BENTON, David, 115; James, 63; John, 11, 111; Jonathan, 31; Joseph, 165; Lucy, 143; Mary, 168, 175; Nancy, 30; Nathan, 149; Samuel, 142; Stephen, 108; Thomas, 176, 190; William, 110, 159.
BERAN, Lorenzo ___208
BERGERON, Elisha ___120
BERNADY, Peter ___90
BERNARD, John ___59
BERRIEN, William ___57
BERRIE, William ___148
BERRY, Cendy, 87; Charles, 92; Dabney, 131, 175; Isaac, 63; Isom, 92; Jesse, 202; John, 66, 180, 201, 205; Joseph, 199; Larkin, 128; Orphan, 125; Rachael, 173; Richard, 2; Simon, 27; Talley, 214; Thomas, 47, 133; William, 67.
BERRYHILL, John ___9
BERSON, Joseph ___147
BERTHELOT, John ___107, 209
BERTRAM, Alexander ___45
BESSEM, Cornelius ___209
BESSENT, Abram ___132
BESSINGER, Thomas ___188
BESSINGTON, Cornelius ___198
BEST, Henry, 77; Jacob, 157; William, 61.
BETHEL, Orphan ___156
BETHUNE, Barbara, 120; Lauchlin, 139, 210; Leonard, 145; Peter, 191; William, 8.
BETOOT, Edmond ___67
BETTERTON, Joshua, 63; Levi, 17; William, 105.
BETTS, Lorick ___174
BEVERS, Jane ___117
BEVIL, Delia ___84
BEVILL, Robert, 215; Thomas, 177; William, 149; Zachariah, 71.
BEVINS, William ___62
BEXLEY, James, 157, William, 41.
BICKERS, Warren ___91
BICKHAM, Young ___106
BIFFLE, Ann, 80; John, 186; Lav., 80; Min., 80.
BIGBY, John ___139
BIGGS, Joseph ___84
BILBO, William ___96
BILBRO, Archibald ___214

BILL, William ___37, 63
BILLIARD, John ___39
BILLINGS, Bardwell ___127
BILLINGSLEA, John ___132
BILLS, Orphans ___155
BILLUPS, John, 206; Robert, 47.
BING, Edward ___53
BINGHAM, Elijah, 61, 181; John, 65
BINION, Noel, 145; R. B., 2.
BINNS, Burwell, 44; Christopher, 27; Zachariah, 179.
BIRCH, Charles, 91; John, 110, 139.
BIRD, Charles, 204; Elizabeth, 8! Francis, 142; Ivey, 8! Joseph, 117, 204; Josiah, 211; Penelope, 52; Stephen, 106; Thomas, 129, 189; 215; Wiley, 33; William, 117, 129, 157; Wilson, 70.
BIRDEN, Jane ___30
BIRDSONG, Harrison, 122; James, 71; John, 16, 203; Jolly, 206.
BISHOP, Claiborn, 207; James, 58; Jonas, 211; Mathew, 123; Seth, 19; Thomas, 146.
BISSUP, Benjamin ___197
BIVENS, William ___75
BIVIN, David, 108; Martha, 127.
BIVINS, Appleton, 62; David, 72; James, 26; Jonathan, 145; Rolen, 142; Shadrack, 1; Stephen, 57! Uriah 120; William, 182.
BLACK, Allen, 82; David, 93, 96; James, 169; Jesse, 32; John, 58, 100, 138, 171, 205; Lemuel, 74, 122; Martha, 207; Mary, 204; Nathaniel, 109, 214; Ryle, 12; Robert, 93, 146; Samuel, 42; Sarah, 200; Thomas, 16, 66, 109, 141; William, 21, 23, 94, 98, 150, 171.
BLACKBORN, John ___70
BLACKBURN, John, 104; Stephen, 100
BLACKEY, David, 113; Fountain, 137
BLACKHURN, Jesse, 29; John, 19, 138; Nathan, 179.
BLACKEY, Elizabeth ___204
BLACKMAN, Amos, 54; Waitman, 115.
BLACKSHEAR, James, 45, 129; Lwis, 156; Nancy, 202.
BLACKSTOCK, William ___90
BLACKSTONE, James ___1
BLACKWELL, James, 4; Park, 126; Russell, 208; Samuel, 110; Sarah, 126.
BLACKWOOD, Jane ___12
BLAILOCK, Charles ___1
BLAIR, Horace, 72; Hugh, 85; James, 16; Levi, 140; Middleton, 26; Nancy, 148; Rachey, 189; Robert, 74, 215; Thomas, 95; William, 81, 179.

BLAKE, Elizabeth, 71; Meredith, 21; William, 18, 158.
BLAKELY, Samuel ———————113
BLALACH, Hardin ———————40
BLALOCK, John, 32;Jonathan,32.
BLANC, Victor ——————— 201
BLANCHARD, Benjamin, 129; Billington, 117; Sarah, 170; Thomas, 209; William, 207.
BLANCHETT, Nancy ——————143
BLAND, Elisha, 100; George, 163, 201; John, 25; Simeon, 123, 166.
BLANDFORD, Clark ———————188, 191
BLANEY, Thomas ——————156
BLANKENSHIP, Daniel, 141, 147; Mary, 96; Thomas, 189.
BLANKS, Ezekiel, 208; James, 34; Nancy, 145; Thomas, 159; William, 150.
BLANTON, David, 42; James, 144.
BLARE, George ——————————23
BLASSINGAME, Wyatt ——————56
BLAYLOCK, Zadock ____ __ 125
BLEDSOE, Benjamin, 19, 144, 182, 191; G., 11, 164; Jesse, 128; John, 173; Joseph, 129; Marg., 13; Miller, 175; Morton, 144; Pechy, 153.
BLITCH, Abraham, 192, 195; Ann, 136; Elijah, 139; Moore, 26.
BLOCKER, Joseph, 186, Redding, 43.
BLOME, Cesaire ————————19, 58
BLOODWORTH, Hezekiah, 135; James 216; Tim, 52; Timothy, 123.
BLOUNT, Burgess, 159; Council, 89; Daniel, 154; Joseph, 7; Lucy, 9, 115; Mary Ann, 56; Peter, 77; Stephen, 78, 158, 192; Thomas, 8, 11; William, 6.
BLOW, John, 171; Micajah, 159.
BLUE, Mary Ann ————————208
BLUNT, Edmond, 157; Polly, 115.
BLUSTER, Dulcina ——————53
BLYTHE, Charles, 2; James, 46, 205; John, 12, 102; Jonathan, 31; Robert, 149, 177, 211; William, 186.
BOATRIGHT, Charles, 182; James, 161; Margaret, 174; Nancy, 114; Rolly, 62.
BOATWRIGHT, Thomas ————139
BOBBITT, Thomas ——————147
BOBO, Spencer, 155; Willis, 91.
BOEN, Stephen ————————198
BOGAN, Albert, 116; Eliza, 61; James, 35; Rosannah, 212.
BOGGESS, Robert ——————201
BOGGS, Ezekiel, 123, 135; James, 78
BOHAM, Joseph ——————58, 83
BOHANON, Duncan, 81; Wiley, 101; William, 92.
BOHANNON, Buddy, 147, 196; John,

190; Joseph, 38, 57; Kinchen, 94; Orphans, 190; Patrick, 150; William, 3; Wylie, 135.
BOLIES, Easter —————————91
BOLINGS, John ————————14
BOILS, Charles ——————153, 214
BOLEN, Subel ————————70
BOLING, Merrill, 205; William, 12.
BOLLER, John ————————31
BOLLING, Daniel ———————203
BOLT, Benjamin, 36; Samuel, 199.
BOLTON, Agnes, 135; Archibald, 128; Chris., 26; Elisha, 139! Isaac, 177; Leonard, 115; Mathew, 111; Robert, 123; Thomas, 104.
BOMAN, Elizabeth, 102; Harris, 147; William, 203, 213.
BOMANS, Bennett ——————77, 81
BOMER, James, 64; Richard, 203.
BOND, Charles, 59; Christopher, 58; Edward, 160; Elizabeth, 98; James, 121; Joseph, 168; Lewis, 216; Richard, 42; Robert, 85; Samuel, 30, 79; Susan, 129; Washington, 140; William, 101.
BONDS, Riley ————————104
BONDURANT, John ——————192
BONE, A. S., 49; George, 131; W. J., 49.
BONES, James, 184, 191; John, 71; William, 194.
BONNELL, Archibald —————16, 113
BONNER, James, 13, 21, 64; Richard, 203; William, 121, 208.
BONNEY, Cullen ———————134, 215
BOOG, John ————————17
BOOKER, John, 128, 182, 198; William, 75, 154.
BOOLES, Allen, 149; Jesse, 33; William, 136.
BOON, Jesse, 49; Lewis, 40; Martin, 52.
BOOTH, Benejah, 115; David, 110; Edward, 108; James, 87, 89; Melinda, 124; Tapley, 54.
BOOTHE, James ————64, 103, 123
BORDERS, Isaac, 67; John, 11.
BORELAND, Mary ———————165
BORING, Isaac, 92, 95, 117; Robert, 205.
BORN, Isham —————————114
BORNS, M. A. B. ————————72
BORUM, Edmond, 22; George, 11; James, 22; Mary, 186; Nathaniel, 165; Thomas, 123.
BOSEWELL, Johnson ——————93
BOSTIAN, Mathew ———————159
BOSTIC, William ———————192
BOSTICK, Garland, 12; John, 60, 80, 115; Matilda, 14; William, 215.

BOSTONIAN, Mathew 177
BOSTRUM, Gabriel 66
BOSTWICK, Azariah, 193; Charles, 64; William, 157.
BOSWELL, Henry, 140; John, 124; Josias, 19; Sarah, 177, 195, 196; William, 105.
BOSWORTH, Jacob, 1; Richmond, 101
BOSWORTHY, Josiah 53
BOTHWELL, Tbenezer 166
BOTTOMS, Thomas 183
BOTTS, John 3
BOTZ, Michael 215
BOUGHAN, Hillsman 187
BOULWARE, Oliver 156
BOURDEN, Redden 15
BOURQUIN, Benedict, 12; Margaret, 195.
BOURKE, Thomas 209
BOUTELL, Peter 215
BOW, Samuel 45
BOWDEN, Anna, 50; Dangerfield, 186; John, 150.
BOWDON, Mary 10
BOWDIN, Daniel 89
BOWEN, Christopher, 81; Durham, 49; Edwin, 54; Elizabeth, 93; Herod, 29; Horatio, 167; Isaac, 114; John, 54, 58, 113; Lorenzo Dow, 194; Margaret; 181; Mark, 187; Mary, 71; Penelope, 33; Rachael, 115; S., 144; Samuel, 105; Stephen, 101; Thomas, 31; Uriah, 44.
BOWER, Benannuel 192
BOWERS, Fielding, 66; George, 159; Job, 30; Jonathan, 124; Lawson, 50
BOWLDING, Edward 101
BOWLER, Eliza 176
BOWLES, David, 81; Henry, 86, 156; Martin, 161; Turner, 216.
BOWLING, Daniel, 165; Edward, 75, 139; Elizabeth, 92; John, 17; Martin, 70; Orphans, 6.
BOWN, Edward 24
BOX, Allen, 195; Ann, 189; William, 196.
BOYANTON, Stewart 44
BOYCE, Joseph 18
BOYD, Alexander, 18 ; Andrew, 23; Bruce, 66; George, 98; Henry, 10; Hezekiah, 158; James, 2, 190; John, 69, 74, 80, 109, 110, 180; Mary, 17; Samuel, 165; Sarah, 40; S. K., 42; Vashti, 105; William, 142.
BOYET, Elizabeth 63
BOYETT, John 42
BOYKIN, Byuns, 89; Elizabeth, 156; Francis, 41; John, 92, 160.
BOYT, Hamilton, 164; Thomas, 97; William, 65.
BOYZEMAN, Humphrey 166

BOZEMAN, David, 149; Luke, 205.
BRAAMLET, John, ... 117
BRABIN, James 114
BRACEWELL, Jacob 138
BRACK, Eleazer, 22, 42, 185; James, 57; Thomas, 212.
BRACKIN, Mary 24
BRADBERRY, Eli, 40; James, 129; Lewis, 72, 101; William, 19.
BRADBURY, John 134
BRADDY, John, 175; Lewis, 191 Richard, 137; Thomas, 41.
BRADEN, Barney 183
BRADFORD, Brassel, 185; Charles, 79, 95; Elizabeth, 110; Isaiah, 57; James, 34, 57; John, 163; Joshua, 192; Mary, 114; Nathaniel, 21; Robert, 23; Sarah, 86; Timothy, 156; Wiley, 12.
BRADLEY, Anne, 166; Chauncy, 10; 61; Charles, 112; Elizabeth, 184; Ire, 44; James, 96; 137; John, 89, 199; Newman, 12; Thomas, 134 William, 179.
BRADLY, John, 146; Thomas, 86.
BRADOCK, Orphan, ... 160
BRADSHAW, Jane, 157; Jordan, 1 William, 195; Woodson, 137.
BRADSWELL, Joseph, ... 107
BRADY, Benjamin, 194; Cullen, 35; James, 188; John, 151; Joseph, 95; Louisa, 89; Martha Ann, 45; N., 191; Robert, 202; Samuel, 105; Thomas, 83.
BRAGAN, Richard, ... 41
BRAGG, Mary, 6; Samuel, 7; William, 38, 190.
BRAINARD, Allen, ... 104
BRAMBLETT, Henry, 82, 142; James, 56; Joel, 99; John, 145.
BRAMELOO, Isaac 90
BRAMLET, Henry 30
BRANAN, Edwin, 28; John, 211.
BRANCH, Hester, 64; James, 184, 187; Piercy, 10; William, 16, 37, 56, 133
BRAND, Malachi, 58; Thomas, 215; William, 184.
BRANHAM, , Benjamin, 14; Calvin, 155; Elizabeth, 30, 122; John, 19.
BRANNAN, John, ... 53
BRANNEN, Alexander, 138; Hugh, 193; John, 4.
BRANNON, Alexander, 105; James, 18; Joseph, 216; Littleberry, 150; Martha, 108.
BRANTLEY, Aaron, 163; Benjamin, 176, 206; Edwin, 58; E. D. M., 10; Harris, 22; James, 19, 56; John, 52, 195, 216; Joseph, 8, 72, 209; Joshua 141; Philip, 191; Simeon, 3; Spen-

cer, 35, 81; William, 90; Zachariah, 12.
BRASCH, Henry, 1
BRASEL, Sarah, 54
BRASS, Brittain, 3
BRASSEL, Nathan, 146; William, 113.
BRASSELL, Brittain, 86; Elias, 6; Henry, 149; Jesse, 118; Nathan, 127.
BRASWELL, Benjamin, 162; Brittain, 110; Jacob, 42; James, 9; Jesse, 86, 103; John, 195; Lurana, 42; Samuel, 127; William, 66, 212.
BRATCHER, Elijah, 174
BRATHER, Richard, 28, 38
BRAUGHNER, Jesse, 56, 201
BRAUGHTON, Belethia, 40
BRAWN, James, 1
BRAWNER, Henry, 102; Simuel, 102; William, 114.
BRAWNIN, William, 57
BRAY, Benjamin, 108; Hannah, 131; H., 132; John, 127; Julian, 200; L. H., 132.
BRAZEAL, Darrill, 93
BRAZIEL, Britten, 212; Elizabeth, 21; Patsy, 63.
BRAZELL, Anson, 29; Robert, 55.
BRAZIL, Bud, 56; Isham, 201; James, 129; Mary, 211; Orphans, 212.
BRAZILE, John, 166
BRAZILTON, Job, 117
BRAZWELL, Jacob, 42
BREED, John, 126
BREEDLOVE, John, 43
BREWEN, Horatio, 1
BREWER, Alford, 71; Alse, 133; Elizabeth, 20, 72; Elizabether, 148; George, 99; James, 124, 213; Jesse, 50; Mary, 153; William, 116.
BREWING, Henry, 208
BREWSTER, Hugh, 101
BRIAN, Moses, 99
BRIANT, Christopher, 125
BRIARS, William, 3
BRIDEWELL, Henry, 86
BRIDGEMAN, John, 129
BRIDGER, Bartlett, 32
BRIDGES, Balaam, 37, 174; Benjamin, 188; Daniel, 179; James, 51, 137, 167; Jeremiah, 59; John, 144; Jonathan, 127; Joseph, 65, 146; Joshua, 88, 105, 213; Nancy, 96; Nathan, 209; R. D., 131; Rebecca, 157; Ritter, 71; Seaborn, 48; Susannah, 102; Warren, 32; William, 145, 147, 198; Wiseman, 92, 205.
BRIDEWELL, Moses, 57
BRIGGS, Benjamin, 123; George, 46; Michael, 90; Silas, 120.
BRIGHT, Levi, 22
BRIMBERRY, John, 18; Mathias, 111

BRINN, Joseph, 154
BRINNER, William, 63
BRINKLEY, Elizabeth, 74
BRINSON, Jeremiah, 41; Mary, 52, 113; Mathew, 211; Moses, 86; Sabra, 116, 135; Unity, 51.
BRINTON, Mary, 198
BRITT, Bauldy, 129; Mathew, 172.
BRITTAIN, John, 36
BRITTON, Sanford, 24
BRITTS, Agnes, 24
BROACH, Charles, 147; Littleberry, 15
BROADNAX, John, 24; Robert, 164; William, 148.
BROADWELL, Jesse, 130, 174
BROCK, Henry, 186; James, 142; Jesse, 158; John, 156, 174; Moses, 205; William, 121.
BROCKINGTON, Lemuel, 42
BROCKMAN, Bledsoe, 42; James, 28; John, 120; Lewis, 141.
BROCKSTON, John, 172
BROMLEY, James, 88
BRONNSON, Elizabeth ___
BROOK, Jesse, 51
BROOKER, John, 205; Mary, 152.
BROOKIN, Nancy, 176
BROOKING, Charles, 111, 126; Edward, 88; John, 105.
BROOKINGS, Thomas, 216
BROOKINS, Theophilus, 105
BROOKS, Abijah, 203; Alfred, 80, 108, 178; Allen, 51; Berm, 74; Edward, 146; Eli, 176; Elisha, 121; Henry, 216; Isac, 152; James, 31, 51, 84, 106; Joel, 141; John, 115, 150, 165, 171; Jonathan, 117, 133; Julius, 65; Larken, 185; Mary, 59, 62, 87; Micajah, 34; Nathan, 71; Oliver, 45; Peter, 88; P. L. W., 149; Polly, 192; Rachael, 46; Rebecca, 151; Robert, 9, 11, 206; Samuel, 134; Sarah, 41, 110; Silas, 19; Simeon, 131; Terrell, 86; Thomas, 32; Wiliam, 6, 49, 50, 53, 114, 151, 155, 160, 189; Wilson, 113.
BROOM, Miles, 29; Patrick, 14; Sally, 162.
BROOTON, Nathan, 32; William, 64. 64.
BROTHERS, Sarey, 147
BROUGHTON, Edward, 91; Elijah, 26; James, 69; John, 21; Rachael, 56; William, 214.
BROUNT, William, 104
BROWER, James, 146
BROWN, Aaron, 136, 164; Agnes, 146; Alexander, 122, 135, 193; Alford, 54; Allen, 146; Ambrose, 54; Amos, 54, 137, 146, 169; Andrew, 117, 126; Ann, 29; Augustine, 87; Bara, 47; Bartlett, 190; Benjamin,

28, 114, 145; Bond, 99, 133; Burwell, 8; Candassee, 185; David, 82, 209; Dempsey, 10; Drucilla, 26; E., 32; Edmond, 98; Edward, 17, 69, 101, 123; Elisha, 183; Eliza, 59, 183; Elizabeth, 10, 18, 88, 117, 138; Ezekiel, 176, 199; Fanny, 117, 134; F. B. T., 32, 182; Fielding, 59; Francis, 190; Franklin, 185; Frederick, 32, 75, 158; George, 5; Harriet, 59; Henry, 39, 67, 107; Hugh, 130; James, 20, 21, 40, 62, 65, 89, 99, 118, 124, 163, 180, 183; Jesse, 139; John, 6, 39, 50, 55, 146, 157, 167, 196, 202; J., 32; Jane, 17; Jeptha, 142; Jepthah, 102; Jesse, 205; Joseph, 47, 171, 179; Josiah, 202; Larkin, 31, 42, 96, 200; Lavina, 173; Lemuel, 26; Lewis, 167; Loam, 15; Mary, 30, 155, 208; Meredith, 69, 139; Milton, 182; Mordecai, 102; Moses, 71, 181, 205, 216; Nancy, 11, 14; Nathaniel, 77, 194, 215; Patrick, 30; Penny, 153; Peter, 7; Richard, 188; Richmond, 3; Robert, 119, 143, 171; Roland, 27; Samuel, 53, 132, 147, 182; Sarah, 160; Shelldrake, 24; Spencer, 83; Stephen, 146; Thomas, 18, 139, 164; Uriah, 26; Wade, 125; Washington, 160! Whitfield, 79; William, 5, 7, 49, 53, 54, 62, 77, 103, 155; Zachariah, 22; Ziba, 157.

BROXTON, J., 116; Sarah, 198.

BRUCE, Aziel, 2; Christian, 206; Daniel, 12; Elizabeth, 4; George, 164; Jane, 79; Jordin, 180, 196; Peggy, 189; Robert, 23; Walter, 190.

BRUKE, Samuel, _____26, 207
BRUMBALO, Susannah, _____79
BRUMBELOW, Ezekiel, _____127
BRUMBLY, William, _____93
BRUNER, Thomas, _____85
BRUNSON, Mathew, 153; Simeon, 168; William, 63.
BRUSTER, William, _____110, 193
BRUSTOR, Sheriff, _____128
BRUX, Armabd, 138; Leon, 16.

BRYAN, Anna, 7; Clement, 203; Hardy, 88; J. A., 29; Langley, 39; Laurence, 161; Mary, 22; Miles, 19; Nancy, 102, 164; Needham, 96; Richard, 122; Sarah, 204; Thomas, 131, 211; William, 174, 192, 197, 201, 213.

BRYAN, 147; Anna, 7; Clement, 203; Council, 215; David, 96, 124; Dorcas, 41; E., 180; Edward, 56; Elizabeth, 154; Hardy, 88; J. A., 29; James, 206; John, 22, 62, 94, 122, 126, 199; Joseph, 58; Langley, 39; Laurence, 161; Loverd, 83; Mary, 22; Miles, 19; Nancy, 102, 164; Needham, 96; Richard, 122; Samuel, ·204; Sarah, 204; Sus., 166; Thomas, 131, 211; William, 174, 192, 197, 201, 213.

BRYANT, Archibald, 1, 188; Benjamin, 150, 208; Hardy, 126; James, 4, 92; Jesse, 53; John 10, 190; Langley, 101; Lewis, 16, 59, 101, 132, 170; Loverd, 214; Meson, 137; Nancy, 196; Nathan, 34; Samuel, 132; Silvester, 163; Thomas, 70; William, 186; Wylly, 109.

BRYSON, Daniel, _____23, 103
BUCHANAN, Benjamin, 12; George, 41; Henry, 6; Isaac, 174; James, 112, 121; John, 24, 191; Micajah, 63; Tomlinson, 151.

BUCK, Hardy, _____147
BUCKALEW, Martin, _____43
BUCKANA, George, 149; Thomas, 140
BUCKHANNAN, Sarah, _____203
BUCKHANON, Greene, 143, 214; James, 214.
BUCKHOLTS, Peter, _____36
BUCKINGTON, Ezekiel, _____193
BUCKLES, Peter, _____128
BUCKNER, Benjamin, 25; Claborn, 125; Daniel, 194; Freland, 58; Henry, 105, 184; Mary, 27, 202; Parham, 41; Singleton, 24.
BUFFALOE, Samuel, _____117
BUFFINGTON, Alfred, 83; Ellis, 99; Henderson, 193; John, 140; Osborn, 18; Rhoda, 103; Samuel, 108; Thomas, 85, 211.
BURFORD, Abraham, 144; William, 152.
BUGG, Anselm, 191; Edmond, 185; Eliza. M. L., 54; Martha, 72; Mary, 181; Obedience, 58, 138; R. W., 54.
BUIAS, Caswell, _____54
BUIE, John, 108; Malcom, 134.
BULGER, Ann, 32; John, 113.
BULL, Elizabeth, 81; Orville, 200.
BULLARD, Mahala, 82; Robert, 25; Wiley, 34; William, 56.
BULLOCH, Burwell, 182; Elias, 157 Hawkins, 67; Irvin, 110; Noble, 75 Richard, 59, 209; William, 49.
BULLOCK, Johnson, _____115
BULLS, Gabriel, _____165
BUMBLETON, Edward, _____108
BUNCH, Austin, 167, 208; David, 45.
BUNKLEY, Elizabeth, _____208
BUNN, J. W., _____115
BUNTIN, Levy, _____195
BURCH, Allen, 210; Charles, 32, 175; Edward, 47, 146; John, 99; Joseph, 151, 175; Louisall, Morton, 34.
BURCKHALTER, Isaac, _____194

BURDETT, James, 82; John, 32.
BURDETTE, John, ...161
BURDEN, Hannah, 102; Nelson, 120.
BURDIN, Absalom, ...79
BURDON, Archibald, ...177
BURFORD, Samuel, 49; Thomas, 171; William, 11.
BURFOR, Mathew, ...51
BURGAMY, William, 131, 135, 185.
BURGER, Levin, ...86
BURGESS, Coleman, 109; Eleanor, 96; Joel, 4, 155; John, 61, 92; Jonathan, 159; Samuel, 107; William, 83, 129, 192.
BURGISS, Robert, ...64
BURK, Charles, 111, 136; Edward, 71; Howell, 82; James, 51; Jordan, 197; William, 61, 127, 134, 191; Young, 115.
BURKE, Betsy Ann, 148; Howell, 176; Jeremiah, 1; John, 72, 158; Richard, 139; Robert, 173; Thomas, 69; Willie, 80.
BURKES, William, ...49
BURKETT, Lemuel, 45, 200; William, 125.
BURKHALTER, Jacob, 48; Joshua, 162; Michael, 137.
BURKS, Chesley, 189 ;Harris, 91; Henry, 86, 211; John, 4; Joseph, 179.
BURKSTEINER, Samuel, ...91
BURLESON, Martha, ...190
BURNAP, John, ...62
BURNE, Thomas, ...71
BURNES, George, 3; William, 18, 128
BURNETT, Bedford, 129; Christopher, 107; Isma, 69; Jeremiah, 62; Levi, 161; Reuben, 127; Samuel, 49.
BURNEY, David, 4; Elizabeth, 39; James, 15, 148; Josiah, 163; William, 47.
BURNLEY, Henry, 26; Richmond, 215
BURNS, James, 7; Leonard, 6; Michael, 98.
BURNSIDE, Ann, 94; Daniel, 131; Delia, 195; E., 211; Sarah, 172; Thomas, 20, 30.
BUROUGHS, Samuel, ...122
BURRAGE, James, ...192
BURRAN, Henry, ...146
BURREL, Jesse, ...46
BURRELL, Jesse, ...95
BURNETT, Joseph, ...154
BURRIT, Malinda, ...96
BURROUGH, Benjamin, 40; Joseph, 14; James, 49.
BURROUGHS, James, 105; William, 185, 208.
BURROW, John, ...155

BURT, Henry, 85; James, 118; Malinda, 37; M. T., 101; Nancy, 28; Richard, 134; William, 2.
BURSON, Elisha, 190; Isaac, 9, 45; Nancy, 183.
BURTON, Elizabeth, 211; German, 91; Henry, 60; James, 90; Jeremiah.
BURTON, Bethina, 214; Elizabeth, 211; German, 91; Henry, 60; Isaac, 14; James 90; Jeremiah, 130; John, 210; Leroy, 56; Mary, 8; Nelson, 177; Rachael, 83; Reuben, 16; Samuel, 215; Thomas, 33; William, 121.
BURTS, Reuben, ...137
BURTZ, Reuben, ...89
BURWELL, Hardy, ...70
BBUSBEE, James, ...179
BUSBY, Frederick, ...177
BUSBIN, Jacob, 200; Sarah, 41.
BUSE, Thomas, ...32
BUSH, Elisha, 191; Hezekiah, 23; J., 177; John, 66; Levi, 150, 194; Lewis, 20; Mourning, 170; Richard, 147, 197; Roderick, 103; Samuel, 46; Thomas, 5; Wilie, 32; William, 143, 195.
BUSHOP, Golder, ...134
BUSSEY, Dempsy, 86; Francis, 9; Isaac, 99, 108; James, 131; Jane, 57; Judith, 168; Nathan, 24, 175; Samuel, 197; Susannah, 190.
BUSTER, Cammell, ...190
BUTCHER, Mary, ...135
BUTLER, Benjamin, 44; Charles, 192; Curry, 66; Dempsy, 41; Elijah, 41, 199; Ford, 109; Francis, 112; George 146; Greene, 38; Hannah, 130; Henry, 53; James, 184; John, 1, 26, 40, 44, 66, 75, 119, 134, 192; Joshua, 28; Larkin, 124; Malachi, 10; Mary, 15, 189; Phineas, 35, 61; Robert, 78; Sarah, 183; Shem, 175; Harlton, 100, Thomas, 128; Washington, 141; Wiley, 33; William, 45.
BUTT, John, 7, 56; Melmond, 138; Simmons, 37; Zachariah, 3.
BUTTE, James, ...71
BUTTRAM, James, ...197
BUTTRELL, William, ...177
BUTTS, George, 211; James, 11, 24, 70.
BUYS, James, ...183, 196
BUZBEE, Allen, ...62
BUZBIN, Jacob, ...197
BYNUM, Claudus, 173; Drewry, 188; James, 203; John, 9; Rewbin, 128; Ruben, 74, 134; Silvey, 41.
BYRD, Burrill, 125; Elizabeth, 128; Ezekiel, 11; John, 12, 99, 152..
BYRON, Josiah, ...40
CABINESS, Elizabeth, ...38

CABOS, John, ...3333
CADE, Robert, ...88, 110
CADENHEAD, James, ...95
CAESAR, Sarah, ...43
CAFIS, Robert, ...36
CAGLE, Benjamin, 152; George, 193, 211; Malinda, 79; William, 159.
CAID, Diannah, ...72
CAIN, Allen, 148; Andrew, 205; Jacob, 158; James, 199; Lydia, 161; Nathaniel, 116, 177; Ransom, 196; Richard, 180; Valentine, 193; William, 87.
CALAWAY, Peter, ...168
CALDWELL, Alexander, 208; Bienford, 33; Caroline, 86; Curtis, 151; David, 121; Edward, 158; Fanny, 50; J., 165; James, 69, 126; Orphans, 133, 162; Robert, 206; Samuel, 50; Simon, 3, 190; William, 138.
CALEF, Ebenezer, 202; Letitia, 118, 193.
CALHOON, Adam, 218; John, 21; Julia, 101.
CALHOUN, Burrell, 134; Delia, 132; Elbert, 16; James, 167, 212; J. N. T., 95; Joseph, 24; Josiah, 95; Louisa, 175; Lowdy, 114; Martha, 3; Perlina, 138; Samuel, 26, 37.
CALLAGHAN, John, ...39
CALLAHAN, Elijah, 27, 29; James, 175; John, 152; Sterling, 53; William, 181.
CALLAWAY, Abraham, 90; Eli, 57; Elijah, 32, 113; Isaac, 110, 114; James, 140; Jehu, 101; Joshua, 212; Mary, 83; William, 71.
CALLAR, William, ...34
CALLEHAM, John, ...137
CALLERHAN, Alexander, ...139
CALLOWAY, Barham, 101; Bethany, 161; Drewry, 200; Eli, 197; Jesse, 188; J. M., 36; William, 42, 123; Winifred, 207.
CALLUM, Elijah, ...211
CALTON, Henry, ...120
CALVERT, John, ...63
CAMERON, James, ...146
CAMFIELD, Edward, 83; Nathaniel, 151, 204.
CAMMELL, Talletha, ...143
CAMP, Aaron, 174; Abel, 178; Arthur, 51; Burrell, 83; Clary, 53; Daniel, 2, 46; Edmund, 39; Edward, 59; H., 161; Harrison, 87; Hiram, 200; Hope, 144; John, 92, 124, 165; Joseph, 125, 175, 206; Josiah, 122; Lewis, 40; Littleberry, 86; Samuel, 106; Tapley, 50.
CAMPBELL, Amanda, 46; Anderson, 82; Daniel, 62; Dorcas, 9; Eliza, 21; George, 92; Howell, 85; Isaac, 48; James, 52; Jesse, 208; John, 18, 44, 179; Joseph, 207; Neill, 64; Orphans, 215; Peter, 175; Sarah, 115; William, 1, 36, 171; W. S., 147.
CAMRON, Allen, 98, 132; Daniel, 166; John, 39, 193, 196; Robert, 79; William, 212.
CANADA, Nathan, ...61
CANADY, Edwin, ...161
CANANT, William, ...89, 212
CANAWAY, Mourning, ...36
CANDLER, John, ...49
CANE, Joseph, 12; William, 48.
CANNACK, Daniel, ...59
CANNET, William, ...201
CANNON, Allen, 123, 182; Burwell, 159; Charles, 23! Dempsy, 30; James 132; John, 57, 66; L. S., 36; Mary, 110; Nathaniel, 216; Spivey, 158; Wiley, 35; William, 49.
CANTER, Joshua, ...6
CANTRELL, Jesse, ...11
CAPEHART, Nancy, ...136
CAPPER, Michael, ...175
CAPPS, Eli, ...6
CAPS, Orphans, ...205
CARAWAY, Alexander, 213; Benjamin, 58; Thomas, 165.
CARDEN, Dicey, 27; Milly, 172.
CARDER, Iverson, 108; Thomas, 199.
CARDWELL, John, 43; Simon, 37, 162
CARE, James, ...141
CARENA, Littleberry, ...157
CARENAH, Littleberry, ...134
CAREY, James, 138, 143; Mary, 86.
CARGILE, John, 18, 67, 105; Lavinia, 112.
CARLEY, James, ...30
CARLILE, Jane, 72; John, 57; Washington, 137.
CARLISLE, Benjamin, 135; Edmund, 127, 184; John, 77, 199; Thomas, 111; Willis, 29.
CARLTON, Archibald, 37; Carter, 149; Elizabeth, 190; Henry, 1; Mildred, 207; Richard, 106; William, 162.
CARMICHAEL, Duncan, 135; James, 176; William, 97, 119.
CARNES, Isoh, 87; John, 80, 101; Mabry, 7; William, 214.
CARNEY, Daniel, ...161
CARNES, Mabry, 187; Rutha, 35, 163.
CAROL, Douglas, ...69
CARPENTER, Hamilton, 61; Jacob, 10, 97; John, 148; Reuben, 94.
CARR, Balas, 207, 216; Henry, 179, 186; Hugh, 50; James, 83; Martin, 102; Richard, 41; Robert, 98, 188; William, 74, 180.
CARRAGAN, William, ...123

CARRAL, Stephen, 193
CARREL, James, 174
CARRELL, James, 104; John, 196; Lucy, 168; Maydeline, 62; Thomas, 66.
CARRILL, John, 95
CARRINGTON, Timothy, 179
CARRIOL, Thomas, 83
CARROLL, Anne, 18; Brittain, 164; Elisha, 205; John, 33, 202; Mar., 97; Mitchell, 151; Orphan, 177; Owin, 108; Robert, 119; Thomas, 92; Welcome, 9.
CARSEL, Dilion, 145
CARSEY, David, 23; Jesse, 87.
CARSON, Andrew, 59; Ephriam, 17, 177; Meredith, 182; Sarah, 85; William, 11.
CARSWELL, William, 198
CARTER, Abner, 157; Abraham, 50, 109; Armstead, 28; Augustine, 59; Benjamin, 151; Charles, 132, 194, 200; Cyrus, 176; David, 90, 104; Edmond, 75; Edward, 58; Elander, 22; Elizabeth, 58, 60, 79; Gardner, 17, 79; George, 62; Henry, 79; James 3, 30, 46, 89, 127, 175, 187; Job, 60; John, 8, 10, 21, 32, 105, 106, 146, 151, 166; Joseph, 111; Landon, 153; Lesly, 92, 134; Magnus, 214; Mary, 157; Mathews, 185; Micajah, 107; Mitalda, 88; Montford, 89; Nathan, 164; Nelson, 96; Robert, 17, 147; Shadrack, 78; Silas, 166; Stephen, 108, 209; Thomas, 49, 78, 139; Willey, 127; William, 46, 71, 98, 119; Willis, 186.
CARTLEDGE, Edmond, 75, 164; Thomas, 59.
CARTS, Joseph, 54
CARTWRIGHT, Absalom, 180; Martha, 196.
CARUTHERS, Henry, 201; James, 5, 101, 190; John, 16, 64, 181; Nancy, 11, 15; William, 28, 201.
CARVER, Richard, 55; Sampson, 185; Thomas, 51, 119, 205; William, 135.
CARY, Elizabeth, 160; John, 100; Miles, 4.
CASE, Chester, 137
CASEY, John, 99, 133, 185; Lettis, 75; Thomas, 200; Uriah, 66; William, 183.
CASH, Dorian, 126; Henry, 210; Howard, 159, 211, 205; James, 128; John, 24.
CASHAW, Lodowick, 3
CASHIN, Orphan, 61
CASON, Abner, 50; E., 178; Elizabeth, 190; Jesse, 168; John, 51, 67; Seaborn, 160; Thomas, 190; William, 25, 43, 119; Willis, 11.
CASPAR, George, 37
CASSELL, Samuel, 113
CASSELLWY, John, 175
CASSIDY, Hugh, 20; William, 103.
CASTELLOW, Catherine, 170; John, 95; William, 104.
CASTLEBERRY, Alexander, 164; David, 189; Ezra, 128; James, 198; Louisa, 28; Mark, 211; Mary, 29; Meredith, 189; Peter, 75; William, 64.
CASTLES, Absalom, 57
CASWART, James, 118
CASWELL, Isham, 29; James, 92; John, 59.
CATHENS, Ransom, 18
CATCHINGS, Joseph, 183; Philip, 34.
CATES, Charles, 160; Hannah, 206; James, 168, 189; John, 60, 152; Joseph, 203; William, 46.
CATLETT, Ezekiel, 177; John, 189; Laban, 46, 53; William, 66.
CATO, James, 109; Thomas, 165.
CATOW, Orphans, 163
CAUDELL, Benjamin, 186; David, 174 Isham, 136; James, 142; Jesse, 79.
CAUDLE, Absalom, 157
CAUDLER, John, 18, 193; Nathan, 137; S., 137.
CAUDWELL, James, 210
CAULEY, Rachael, 90; William, 114.
CAULKINS, Samuel, 196
CAUSEY, Elizabeth, 89; Ezekiel, 24, 196, 212; Laurie, 108; Sarah, 174; Sherrord, 153; William, 95.
CAVENAH, Catherine, 49
CAVENDER, Elizabeth, 212; Martha, 46.
CAVER, John, 38
CAWDER, Charles, 34; Joseph, 97.
CAWLEY, James, 101; Thomas, 82.
CAWSEY, Absalom, 3; John, 212; Right, 149.
CAWTHON, Chelsey, 170
CAWTHORN, Charles, 210
CENTER, Abner, 34, 85; John, 5, 61; Levi, 159; William, 47.
CESSNA, Samuel, 91
CHAFIN, Joel, 58; John, 102, 119; N. H., 187.
CHAFFIN, Amos, 183, 202; Charloty, 164; Elias, 205; Joseph, 133; Robert, 34, 178; Tyre, 41, 193.
CHAIN, John, 1; Levin, 5, 151; William, 212.
CHAIRS, Greene, 131; Thomas, 92.
CHALKER, William, 125
CHALMERS, Andrew, 9

CHAMBERLAIN, Nathan, _____184
CHAMBERS, Isaac, 148; James, 113, 208; John, 146; Philip, 140; Silas, 145; William, 123.
CHAMBLESS, Christ., 167; S., 171; Sid., 96; Zach, 28.
CHAMBLISH, John, _____116
CHAMPAIN, Israel, _____195
CHAMPION, Frances, 195; Henry, 107; Israel, 155; James, 142; Jesse, 6; John, 24, 123; Moses, 146; William, 168.
CHANALER, John, _____2
CHANCE, Alfred, 138; Cannon, 63; Eph., 181; Isaac, 180, 212; Jacob, 179; John, 151; Mary, 209; Mason, 114; Silas, 104; Simpson, 95, 102; Stephen, 52.
CHANCY, Asa, _____55
CHANDLER, Ambrose, 15; Daniel, 169; Edward, 2; Gray, 25; James, 21, 102, 142, 168, 189; Jemsy, 87; Joel, 53; John, 46, 62; Pleasant, 183; Robert, 101; William, 50; Zachariah, 175.
CHANNELL, Littleton, _____167
CHAPLAIN, William, _____184
CHAPLING, Elizabeth, _____88
CHAPMAN, Abner, 202; Amos, 168, 174; Asa, 207; Benjamin, 11; Deberry, 138; Henry, 42; John, 36, 192; Joseph, 156; Laban, 60; Lydia, 160; Marj. 170; Nathan, 122; Randol, 152; Robert, 198; Samuel, 41, 183, 202; Solomon, 111, 212; Turner, 127, 187; William, 182.
CHAPPELL, Allen, 137; Benjamin, 37; Edward, 154; James, 142; Jesse, 140; John, 18, 77; Samuel, 45; Thommas, 2, 190; William, 38; Wilson, 8.
CHAPPLEAR, Ann, 15; Richard, 210; Thomas, 91.
CHARLES, Orphan, 140; Thomas, 126.
CHASTAIN, Hannah, 93; Jeremiah, 31; John, 82, 136; Jonathan, 126; Rainey, 17.
CHATFIELD, John, _____83
CHATHAM, George, 41; Sarah, 88; William, 114.
CHAWKER, Samuel, _____25
CHEATHAM, Arthur, 207; Isham, 79; Josiah, 123.
CHEEK, John, 49; Roland, 11; Rowland, 63; William, 79; Willis, 192.
CHEEKES, James, _____192
CHEELY, Griffin, 140, 149; Lewis, 202.
CHEEVES, Thomas, _____119
CHERRY, Happy, 173; Howell, 28; Jessey, 104; Orphans, 179; Polly, 62; Riley, 176; Samuel, 1; Wiley, 142.
CHERRYTREE, Jacob, _____48
CHESSEH, John, _____112, 122
CHESHIRE, Richard, _____38
CHESTER, Elisha, 174; Jacob, 216.
CHEWNING, Elizabeth, _____160
CHICHESTER, Alfred, _____41
CHICK, James, _____188
CHILDERS, Douglas, 189; Jesse, 110; Mastin, 84; Richard, 7, 52; Thomas, 35, 172.
CHILDRESS, William, _____155
CHILDS, Nimrod, 43; Robert, 134; William, 89.
CHISLER, Mary, _____59
CHISLEM, William, _____157
CHISLM, Gatewood, _____172
CHISLOM, William, _____51
CHISLUMNS, Andrew, _____1
CHISUM, Alexander, _____181
CHISSON, John, _____47
CHITTY, Julian, _____203
CHITWOOD, Daniel, 164; John, 146; Richard, 196.
CHIVERS, Jacob, 148; James, 79; Thomas, 97.
CHRESMAS, Mary, _____210
CHRISMAS, Richard, 63; Samuel, 80.
CHRISTIAN, Charles, 72; E. L., 74, 213; Elijah, 86, 102, 153; James, 118; John, 117; Milton, 145; Sally, 38; Thomas, 126; William, 14.
CHRISTINE, Robert, 136; Victor, 33.
CHRISTOPHER, David, 179; Eliz., 53; R. J., 115; W., 112, 124; William, 6, 25.
CHRISWELL, John, _____139
CHRISTWOOD, Cory, 65; D., 99; James, 66.
CHOICE, Cyrus, _____26
CHONOWAY, Charles, _____104
CHROSBAY, Ann, 201; Elizabeth, 69; John, 135.
CHUNOWAY, Charles, _____71
CHURCHILL, Elizabeth, _____194
CIGO, George, _____211
CLACK, Thomas, _____215
CLAFLIN, Dexter, _____99
CLAGHORN, William, _____196
CLAIBORNE, William, _____77
CLANCE, Jacob, 191; Martin, 125.
CLANDELL, Benjamin, 140; David, 139.
CLANTON, Holt, _____29
CLARDY, Abraham, 88; Elliott, 21.
CLARK, Asa, 5; August, 101; Benjamin, 83, 118; Catherine, 135; Cenus, 48; David, 27, 145, 161, 162; Edward, 37; Elizabeth, 107, 157, 170, 175; Francis, 5, 23; George, 124,

193; Isabella, 30; James, 1, 192; Jane, 127; Jeremiah, 89; J. M., 71; John, 152, 168; Joseph, 211; osiah, 169; Littleton, 164; Lindsey, 181; Lucy, 92; Michael, 160; Needham, 88; Rebecca, 155; Reuben, 183; Robert, 89; Samuel, 10, 54, 137; S. B., 16; Silas, 78; Solomon, 202; Thomas, 5, 34, 44, 63, 142, 214, 215; William, 30, 80, 101, 145.
CLARKE, Calphrey, 41; Francis, 122; George, 12; John, 35; Joshua, 131, 171; Samuel, 35; William, 75, 79, 200.
CLARY, John, _____75
CLAXTON, James, _____132
CLAY, Augustus, 5; Greenberry, 160; Jefferson, 92; Mary, 209; Mastin, 54; Royal, 170.
CLAYTON, Dempsy, 169; George, 145; Henrietta, 17; Jesse, 140, 156; John, 200; Robert, 169; Warren, 211; William, 210; Wylie, 181, 179.
CLEAKLER, Jesse, 140; Mary, 167.
CLEAVELAND, Absalom, 79; Benjamin, 33; Jeremiah, 15.
CLEGG, Elizabeth, 30; John, 206.
CLEGHORN, George, 192; James, 5; Martha, 158; Robert, 26.
CLELAND, Gilbert, 138; James, 195.
CLEMENS, John, 180, 187; Sarah, 61.
CLEMENTS, Amanda, 50; Andrew, 50; Anna, 179; Austin, 21; Bishop, 7; Clement, 10, 78, 154, 176, 182; Francis, 143; Jeptha, 102; John 14, 32, 60; Noble, 31, 134; Peyton, 145; William, 17, 141.
CLEMM, Henry, _____198
CLEMMONS, Daniel, 93; James, 121; Wiley, 71.
CLEMONS, Jinny, _____197
CLEVELAND, Early, 158; Jeremiah, 146; Lit, 94; Penelope, 149; Washington, 130.
CLIATE, Thomas, _____66
CLIATT, Isaac, 150; Jonathan, 134.
CLIETT, Jehu, _____116
CLIFTON, Clement, 189; Daniel, 117, 177; George, 66; Levin, 166; Orphans, 90; William, 46, 126.
CLINARD, John, _____96
CLINCH, Elizabeth, _____21
CLINE, Jonathan, _____39, 167
CLOFTON, Smith, _____9
CLORE, George, _____203
CLORIE, George, _____54
CLOUD, Ezekiel, _____146
CLOWER, Daniel, 12, 152; Jesse, 131; Simeon, 28.
CLUB, Philip, _____201
CLURE, John, _____139

COAL, Malinda, _____108
COATS, Drucilla, 191; John, 197; Morgan, 3; N., 100.
COBB, Benjamin, 78; Catherine, 102; Christian, 29; Garrison, 109; George, 128; Henry, 94, 83; Isaac, 196; Jacob, 39, 51, 75, 161; Joseph, 163; Mark, 39; Nancy, 22; Obedience, 204; Ralph, 35, 130, 200; Stephen, 114, 196, Thomas, 36; William, 103, 128.
COBURN, Orphans, _____192
COCHRAN, James, _____183
COCHRAN, Alexander, 31; Banister, 151; Cheadle, 171; Christopher, 182; Hen., 21; Jacob, 9; Leslie, 50; Mat., 53; Thomas, 53.
COCHREN, William, _____66
COCHRUM, Charles, 27; Miner, 91.
COCK, Rebecca, _____150
COCHBORN, George, _____145
COCKBURN, Archibald, 152; George, 161; James, 130; John, 152; Joshiah 158.
COCKE, Jack, _____62, 91
COCKER, Thomas, _____216
COCKERALL, Jesse, _____103
COCKERAM, ames, 174; Mary, 155.
COCKERELL, Thomas, _____6, 134
COCKERHAM, Mathew, 145; Richard, 63.
COCKERHL, Thomas, _____28
COCKRELL, Robert, 142; William, 20
COCKRUN, Mathew, 178; Robert, 114; 140.
CODAY, Mary, _____97
CODY, Lawson, _____169
COE, George, 90; William, 39.
COFER, oseph, _____188
COFFEE, Cleveland, 67; Edward, 41; Elijah, 67, 103, 187; Elisha, 51; Joel, 169; Nancy, 38; Winneford, 54.
COFFEY, William, _____155
COFFIELD, G., 138; S., 13.
COFFIN, Francis, 116; Simeon, 34.
COGAN, Dennys, _____1
COGBERN, William, _____191
COGBILL, Edward, 167; P., 27; Phebe, 205.
COGGAN, James, _____8
COGGIN, Burrell, _____89
COGGINS, Burrell, 181; James, 184.
COGLAND, Mary, _____198
COGSWELL, John, _____130
COHEN, Solomon, _____135
COHOON, Felix, _____213
COHRON, Cornelius, _____112
COIL, Elizabeth, 33; Gideon, 33; James, 37.
COKER, Charlton, 210; Daniel, 93; David, 189; Elisha, 93; John, 174,

186; Jonathan, 77; Rober, 188; Sylvia, 52; William, 65.
COLE, Caroline, 107; John, 83, 128, 198; Tillman, 174; William, 128, 203, 207; Wright, 166.
COLEMAN, Abner, 183; Benney, 136; Clar., 87; Clarissa, 41; David, 77, 187; Elijah, 123; Isaac, 201; James, 55, 95, 150; John, 70, 193; Mathew, 91, 181; Plazetta, 66; Pleasant, 2; Richard, 25; Samuel, 109, 176; Stephen, 204; Thomas, 30; Tillman, 106; William, 201.
COLESON, William, ———————————45
COLEY, John, 90, 161; William, 33.
COLHOUN, Burrell, ———————184
COLLARS, Mathews, ———————154
COLLENS, George, ———————135
COLLETT, John, ————————148
COLLEY, Anderson, 122; James, 32; 176; Jonathan, 160; Samuel, 49, 85; Sarah, 14; William, 21.
COLLIER, Anthorette, 28; Joseph, 105; Mary, 155; Meredith, 79; Miles, 54; Sarah, 179; William, 64, 137.
COLLINS, Albert, 91; Baxter, 143; Benjamin, 53; Brdg. 17; Catherine, 112; David, 130; Diannah, 59; George, 55; Hardy, 79; J. A., 135; Jacob, 198; James, 135, 146. 165; Jesse, 63; John, 54, 69, 97, 102, 106, 180; Joseph 16, 163; Josiah, 16; Major, 182; Mary, 145; Mials, 38; Nathaniel, 155; Rabun, 138; Robert, 131; Samuel, 14, 155; Sarah, 11, 78, 164, 204, 205; Thompson, 140; William, 190, 195; Zachariah, 90.
COLLON, Henry, 50; Solomon, 143;
COLLY, John, ——————————181
COLQUETT, James, 25; Jonathan, 147.
COLQUIT, Thomas, ———————167
COLSON, John, 153; Mary, 163; Paul, 22, 58.
COLSTON, Orphans, ———————133
COLT, John, ————————174, 205
COLTER, Bradford, ————————36
COLWELL, Hiram, 7; Richard, 193.
COLWORD, John ——————————96
COLYER, William, ——————————15
COMBS, David, 189; Elizabeth, 97; James, 83; John, 62, 153; Sterling, 128; Sus., 197.
COMER, Anderson, 115, 127; Ann, 50, 108; DeMarquis, 99; William, 149.
COMES, John, ——————————61
COMPTON, Hzeekiah, 79; Jesse, 130; John, 92, 133, 156; Thomas, 167.
CONANT, John, —————————193
CONE, Abel, 58; Archibald, 39, 106,

195; Arnold, 78; Bachlott, 145; Basil, 151; Darkess, 113; Henry, 121; John, 20, 39, 142, 163; Lewis, 109, 119; Margaret, 62; Peter, 7; Samuel, 1, 8; William, 171, 183.
CONER, James, ——————————75
CONERY, Arthur, ————————105
CONGER, John, —————————171
CONGHRAN, Robert, ——————194
CONGLETON, Allen, ——————77
CONGO, Benjamin, 159; Zachariah, 159
CONISON, Barbara, ———————86
CONNAL, James, ————————— 74
CONNALLEY, Bryan, 170; Lucy, 62.
CONNALLY, Charles, 87, 105; George, 98; Nathaniel, 146.
CONNELL, Benjamin, 119; Daniel, 6; E, 143; John, 211; M., 143; Thomas, 174.
CONNELLY, Charles, 53; George, 101; Gin., 37; John, 59; Lurany, 46; Patrick, 164; Samuel, 127; Thomas, 177.
CONNER, Benjamin, 92; David, 109; Early, 147; Frederick, 143, 194; Ganaway, 131; James, 95, 131, 172, 194; John, 55, 74, 82, 138, 209; Midgally, 90; Parnell, 144; Peter, 8; Sarah, 79, 198; Thomas, 193; Torrence, 207; William, 119.
CONNERAT, Catherine, ——————5
CONNERS, William, ———————61
CONNOR, William, ————————14
CONRAD, William, ———————176
CONYER, Simeno, ——— ——— 102
CONYERS, Isaac, 112; James, 149; John, 124; Rachell, 182; Sarah, 96; William, 214.
COODY, A. L., ——————————65
COOK, Archibald, 20; Benjamin, 173; Buckner, 172; C. T., 39; Daniel, 196; David, 130; Dennis, 159; Elizabeth, 39, 92; Ephriam, 149; Frederick, 130; George, 60, 91; Henry, 164; Hugh, 100; James, 39, 40, 69, 143, 160, 179; Jane, 113; Jeremiah, 86; Jesse, 139; J. M., 39; Joel, 11, 79; John, 14, 20, 98, 170, 171, 201; ohnson, 20; Joshua, 117, 142; Lewis; Mariah; Nathan; Neverson; Orphans, 39; Pernal, 26, 91; R. E., 39; Rhoda, 182; Roland, 79; Roswell, 10; Savoy, 100; Susannah, 29; Theodisius, 107, 145, 186; Thomas, 115, 152; Valentine, 35; William, 14, 80, 105, 166, 215.
COOKE, George W., ———————202
COOKER, James, ————————152
COOKSEY, Hezekiah, 188; Thomas, 65.
COOKSY, Hannah, ————————38
COOMBS, John, —————————154

COOPER, Ann, 36; Arthur, 151; Betsy, 92; Beverly, 179; Edmond, 37; Eliza, 84; George, 153; Gideon, 198; Henry, 4, 38; Hollonberry, 118; Howell, 99; Isa, 90; James, 86, 159; Jeremiah, 83; John, 3, 54, 84, 138, 144, 178, 206; Jonathan, 195; Joseph, 102; Levi, 139; Lawis, 114; Louis, 185; Mary, 103; Philip, 134; Richard, 144; Samuel, 13; Thomas, 82, 174, 179; William, 108.
COOPPER, William, _____ _____59
COPE, Rosetta, _____16
COPELAN, John, _____,155
COPELAND, Benjamin, 53, 199; Elisha, 180; Gracy, 177; Obediah, 56.
COPPER, Washington, 99; William, 70
CORB, Mary, _____97
CORBET, Grove, 116; Sarah, 119.
CORBETT, Elenor, 135; Grove, 138; Harbert, 210; Isham, 46; Nusham, 180.
CORBIN, Richard, 17; Silas, 23, 204.
CORBIT, Jesse, _____56
CORDER, Elizabeth, _____213
CORDERY, John, _____163
CORLEY, Chaney, 103; Frederick, 120; Sarah, 107.
CORMICK, Catherine, _____197
CORNELIUS, James, _____97
CORNETT, Uriah, _____166
CORNUP, John, 103; Sus., 103.
CORNWELL, Elijah, 63, 86, 88; George, 155; Nathaniel, 101.
CORREY, William, _____167
CORRINGTON, Eemeline, _____34
CORRUPS, Frederick, _____95, 211
CORUM, Ann, _____48
CORRUTH, James, _____62
CORRY, James, _____153
CORSEY, Absolom, 182; William, 22.
CORSON, Thomas, _____ _____ 52, 55
COSBY, Dickerson, 114; John, 158; Lucy, 90; Wingfield, 16, 55.
COSTLEY, Mary, 80; Orphans, 35.
COSWERT, Thomas, _____71
COTHEREE, Pouncy, _____56
COTHERN, William, _____4
COTHRAN, Ezekiel, _____111
COTTEN, Cary, _____78
COTNEY, Francis, 25; James, 171; Stephen, 196.
COTTER, Goegre, 108; James, 171; Stephen, 196.
COTTLE, Ebenezer, _____9, 171
COTTON, Daniel, 176; George, 150; James, 77; Joseph, 99; William, 87.
COTTRELL, Hetty
COTTINCAN, Lucy, _____52
COUCH, Eliza, 132; John, 183, 160; Joseph, 30; Sarah, 30; Silvanus, 152.

COULSON, E., 130; M., 130.
COULSTON, Mary Ann, _____208
COUNT, Ira, _____159
COUPER, Gilford, 74; Guifford, 128; James, 69.
COURCY, Vincent, _____197
COURSEL, Charles, 147; James, 53, 119; Nathaniel, 127.
COURSON, John, _____138
COURTER, Ed., 116; Edward, 123.
COURVOISIE, Sarah, _____195
COUSINS, Adams, 69; Greene, 45; William, 127, 176.
COUTRIL, Eliza, _____175
COVENTON, Thomas, _____122
COVEY, Andrew, 53; Joseph, 120.
COVINGTON, Cloe, 52; John, 113.
COVY, John, _____128
COWAN, Chambers, 61, 104; George, 80; James, 17; Prudence, 152.
COWAR, M., _____24
COWARD, John, 84, 166; Mary, 151; Sarah, 157; W. H., 151; William, 116.
COWART, Augustus, 56; Cullen, 117; John, 159; Orphans, 178; Penny, 83; Stephen, 112, 124; Thomas, 137; William, 171; Zachariah, 75.
COWEN, James, 99; John, 180; Middleton, 165; Thomas, 197; William, 7, 98, 141.
COWLES, Judith, 162; Samuel, 160, 214.
COX, Aaron, 104; Absalom, 109; Asa, 94; Charles, 72; Christopher, 111; David, 161, 191, 193; Delaney, 52; George, 1; Gustavus, 195; Henry, 109; James, 3, 28; Jeremiah, 160; John, 152, 162, 216; Jonathan, 140; Joshua, 94, 160; Kitturah, 136; Malone, 107; Margaret, 160; Mathew, 71; Moses, 90, 211, 216; Penelope, 33; Pleasant, 140; Reuben, 189; Richard, 63, 162; Robert, 182; Samuel, 78; Thomas, 15, 33, 111; Vincent, 85; William, 27, 40, 43, 108, 121, 206.
COXE, John, _____157
COXVELL, James, 97; John, 166.
COY, Wilson, _____6
COZART, Anthony, _____106
COZEN, Charles, _____86
CRABB, Asa, 47; Benjamin, 144; Enoch, 190; Hilary, 122; Rebecca, 28; Sarah, 203.
CRABBS, Enoch, _____80
CRABTREE, Tillman, _____183
CRADDICK, Rachel, _____113
CRADDOCK, John, 197; Robert, 38.
CRAFFORD, Archibald, _____195
CRAFT, Archibald, 43; David, 44, 140; Jeremiah, 211; John, 75;

Washington, 64, 94.
CRAFTON, John, 10; Jourdan, 202.
CRAFTS, Charles, ----------------------104
CRAIG, A. K., 79; Edward, 22; Elbert, 173; Lewis, 69.
CRAIN, Judah, -------------------41, 147
CRAM, John, ------------------------168
CRAMER, John, ----------------------155
CRAMFORD, Abedna, 6; Elizabeth, 41
CRANE, Colley, 114; Elias, 134; James, 170; John, 60, 118; Sarah, 52; Stephen, 12.
CRANEY, Philip, ---------------------168
CRARY, Lewis, -------------------------3
CRASK, Philip, ----------------------112
CRATIN, Mary Ann,-------------------144
CRAUSBY, Thomas, -------------------120
CRAVEN, John, ----------------------145
CRAW, Carlisle, ---------------------- 94
CRAWFORD, Archibald, 118; Augustus, 135; Bennet, 130; Catherine, 74; Charles, 185; David, 80; Edward, 33; Elizabeth, 204; George, 132; Hugh, 123; J., 49, 71; J. E., 49; James, 22; John, 171, 172; Lemuel, 23; Nancy, 139; Rawley, 108; Riley, 74; Robert, 58; Sarah, 85; Silas, 100; Susan, 170; Thomas, 115, 149, 197; Vict., 53; William, 210.
CRAWLEY, Geimethan, 77, 100; Robert, 140; Sarah, 119; Turner, 71.
CRAWMAN, Mary, ------------------191
CREDILLA, William, ----------------139
CREDILLE, Gray, --------------------177
CREIGHTON, Samuel, 63; William, 188.
CREMER, David, 201; Francis, 50.
CRENSHAW, H. H., 120; James, 155; Jesse, 136; Joseph, 34, 95; Lucy, 121; Micajah, 29; Robert, 158; S. M., 22; W. H., 120.
CRESWELL, M., 134; Thomas, 91, 133.
CREW, Carter, 63; Elisha, 121; Jane, 166; William 168.
CREWS, Edward, 46, 195; John, 141; Martin, 3; Reuben, 188; Stanley, 137.
CRIBB, Jane, 108; Jonathan, 195.
CRIBBS, Covington, -------------69, 167
CRIDER, John, -----------------------183
CRIPS, John, -------------------------11
CRISWELL, Whitmel, -----------------36
CRITTENDEN, Henry, ---------------119
CRITTENDON, J., 61; Lee. 57; Ro., 26.
CRITTENTON, John, -----------------215
CRITTINGTON, Jonathan, -----125, 187
CROCKER, Elijah, 151; William, 188.
CROCKETT, David, 151; James, 137;

Madison, 100; Robert, 174.
CROFFORD, Cinthia, 197; Thomas, 8; William, 19.
CROFTON, Archibald, ----------------47
CROLL, Samuel, --------------------165
CROMPTON, Fanny, ----------------205
CRONAN, James, ---------------21, 126
CRONICK, John, --------------------215
CROOM, Jesse, 14, 116; Major, 202.
CROSBY, Calvin, --------------------42
CROSS, George, 149, 212; Isaac, 42, 69; James, 207; John, 42, 63, 163; Joseph, 204; Reuben, 141; Stephen, 123, 155; William, 62, 203.
CROSSOM, Felix, -------------------206
CROSSON, John, --------------------86
CROUCH, Augustus, 160; George, 28; 176; Shadrack, 179.
CROW, Abel, 131; Elisha, 50; Elizabeth, 163; Henry, 140; Isaac, 69, 160; Jacob, 156; James, 37, 199; Martin, 1, 87; Samuel, 5, 59; William, 27, 66.
CROWDER, Frederick, 197; George, 64, 100; John, 132; Nancy, 32.
CROWELL, Israel, 105, 139; Nancy, 114.
CROWLEY, Abraham, 83, 86; Josiah, 194; Joseph, 127; Martin, 38.
CROXTON, James, -------------------46
CROZIER, John, --------------------201
CRUISE, Sarah, --------------------185
CRUM, Harmon, 9; James, 46.
CRUMBIE, James, -------------------34
CRUMBLEY, Anthony, 311 Charles, 108; James, 185.
CRUMBLY, John, 45; William, 170.
CRUMLEY, Benjamin, 12; Henry, 60, 63; Robert, 142.
CRUMLY, Thomas, ------------------171
CRUMP, Bethel, --------------------208
CRUMPTON, 16; John, 192; Orphan, 198.
CRUMS, Hames, --------------------95
CRUTCHFIELD, Francis, 86; Orphan, 179.
CRUTHER, Robert, -----------------165
CUDWORTH, Thomas, --------------200
CULBERSON, Elizabeth, ------------53
CULBERTSON, Greene, 12, 168; Madison, 34; Robert, 54; Thomas, 121.
CULBREATH, Archibald, 2; Aug., 122; Beverly, 117; James, 23, 40; Jane, 96, 115; Lawis, 122; Patrick, 120; William, 58.
CULLENS, Alec, 175; Andrew, 179; Miles, 78; Wiley, 163.
CULPEPER, David, 29; Edmund, 45; ohn, 96; Malechia, 19; Martha, 17;

William, 184.
CULPEPPER, David, 116; Edward, 166; Ely, 213; Isaiah, 209; ohn, 70; Mary, 213; Orphans, 116; Simeon, 212.
CULVER, George, 152; Hardy, 202; Isaac, 88; James, 78; Joshua, 159; Nathan, 139; Seaborn, 34.
CULWELL, Littleton, ...63
CUMING, F., ...27
CUMMINS, Benjamin, ...27
CUMMINGS, Elizabeth, 119, 134; William, 100.
CUNNINGHAM, A. 199; Charles, 212; David, 190; Drury, 65; James, 212; Jesse, 118; John, 27, 210; Joseph, 21, 79; Minter, 177; Nancy, 136; P., 174; Su., 8; Thomas, 64, 208; William, 86, 122.
CUPPS, Henry, 40; John, 69; Warner, 107; Washington, 152.
CURBE, Jesse, ...201
CURBY, Bailey, ...196
CURD, Richard, ...199
CURETON, Highly, 8; Martha, 40; William, 37.
CURINGTON, W., ...153
CURL, Norfleet, ...49
CURLEE, James, ...5
CURLEY, James, ...14
CURRAY, Henry, 125; James, 84; Peter, 9.
CURRIE, John, 213; Samuel, 128.
CURRIN, John, ...170
CURRY, David, 35; Elijah, 54, 106; Eliz 209; Elizabeth, 144; Jacob, 104; James, 82, 200, 204; John, 78, 98, 140, 145; Liddy, 140; Lovedam, 122; Nathaniel, 165; Robert, 171; Silas, 152; Thomas, 28, 118, 165; William, 32, 89, 183, 188.
CURTIS, Henry, ...107, 136
CUSTARD, Jesse, ...10
CUTHBERT, Alfred, 159; William, 130.
CUTLIFF, Abraham, 166; Lucinda, 25.
CUUTS, Joseph, ...34
CUTWELL, Josiah, ...189
DABBS, John, ...8, 40, 148
DABNEY, Anderson, 24; Hannah, 180; Lav., 191; William, 164.
DAGGETT, Barnabas, ...205
DAILEY, James, 196; Joseph, 87.
DAILY, B., 40; J., 40; James, 40; Joseph, 144; Moses, 40.
DALAUNY, James, ...80
DALE, Robert, ...165
DALEY, William, ...79
DALLAS, George, ...64
DALMEYDA, David, ...25
DALRUMPLE, John, ...111

DALTON, Bailey, 47; Randoph, 130.
GAL 14 ....
DAME, John, ...18, 80
DAMPIER, Mary, 10; William, 169.
DAMRON, Charles, 60, 196; Uriah, 99
DANE, Orphan, ...101
DANELLY, Andrew, ...53
DANELLY, Andrew, ...93
DANFORTH, Samuel, 73; Thomas, 62
DANIEL, James, 1, 58, 115, 199, 210; Jepthah, 206; John, 91, 153, 161; Jonas, 74; Joshua, 44; Littleton, 70, 173; Lucretia, 206; Major, 61; Mary, 180, 181; Moses, 24; Obediah, 63; Orphans., 136, 146; Patience, 195; Penelope, 216; Solomon, 75; Susan, 1; Thomas, 62, 85, 111, 138, 167; Wilson, 112; Zachariah, 170.
DANIEL, Aaron, 116; Abel, 8; Alford, 126; Allen, 156; Andrew, 180; Asa, 168; Beaton, 201; Cordele, 60; David, 24, 78, 146; Edward, 154; Green, 163; Henry, 79, 102; Isaac, 118.
DANIELLY, Elizabeth, 102; James 128.
DANELLY, Rhody, 32; William, 150.
DANSBY, John, ...21
DARBY, Charles, 94, 201; James, 182, 187; John, 4; William, 58.
DARDEN, Emeline, 142; George, 147; Martha, 146; Samuel, 87; Warren, 81; Zachariah, 158.
DARDIN, Jonathan, ...51
DARLEY, Henry, 121; Sarah, 138.
DARLY, Thomas, ...147
DARSEY, Thomas, ...105
DARSY, Thomas, ...50
DART, Ubanus, ...20
DASHER, James, 155; Joshua, 81, 35; Samuel, 174; Solomon, 189.
DAUCHY, Luther, ...66
DAUGHTRY, Berrien, 2; Jacob, 170; Joseph, 38; Susannah, 73.
DAUSY, Joseph, ...54
DAVANT, James, ...113
DAVENPORT, Booker, 166; Dicey, 173; Josiah, 185; Micajah, 135; Sophia, 135.
DAVES, James, ...109
DAVICE, James, ...139
DAVID, Berry, 38; Isaac, 47, 213; William, 197, 213.
DAVIDSON, Delilah, 207; Elijah, 82; Elisha, 111; Green, 21; James, 198; John, 41, 98; Joseph, 206; Oliver, 203; Washington, 178; William, 3, 119.
DAVIE, Joseph, ...57, 197
DAVIES, Daniel, 64; John, 142; Sarah 46.
DAVIS, Abigail, 44; Abraham, 90; Allen, 188; Ann, 42; Archibald, 3;

Arthur, 45, 134, 128, 192; Ashborn, 42; Ashburn, 33; Baldwin, 121; Benjamin, 172, 185; Betsy, 59; Charles, 41, 156; Civility, 103; Clement, 67; D., 34; David, 85; Delilah, 1; Dolphin, 10; Eanos, 10; Edward, 1; Eldridge; Elias, 174; Elisha, 198; Elizabeth, 7, 35, 194, 197; Elnathan, 108; Enoch, 175, 199; Esther, 66; Fannie, 143; Fanny, 38; Francis, 185; George, 37, 61; Grenville, 189; Harmon, 133; Henry, 56; Heriah, 210; Hugh, 53; Israel, 69; James, 19, 23, 37, 61, 110, 117, 119, 148, 177; Jane, 17, 153; Jeremiah, 19, 194; Jesse, 78; Joel, 104, 216; John, 25, 27, 52, 85, 79, 105, 161, 186, 166, 177, 180; Josiah, 110; Joseph, 33, 129; Levy, 126; Lewis, 116, 131, Mahala, 18; Martha, 139; Mary, 67, 84, 101, 163; Mitchell, 175; Moses, 168, 173; Noble, 209; Peter, 213; Robin, 1; Russell, 211; Samuel, 48, 134, 176; Sarah, 90, 174; Simon, 209; Solomon, 141; Surry, 193; Susannah, 124; Thomas, 6, 8, 11, 41, 48, 56, 79, 78, 89, 93, 98, 99, 114, 140, 154, 172, 174, 186, 189; Toliver, 204; Wilie, 17, 75, 129; William, 32, 80, 85, 87, 175, 197, 201, 213; Zion, 4.

DAVISON, Aggy, 149; Joseph, 203; William, 54.
DAWDY, Aaron, _____40
DAWKINS, James, 2; John, 21, 212; Mary, 212.
DAWSEY, Joseph, _____87
DAWSON, A., 19; Benjamin, 133; Britain, 138; Burwell, 19; Davis, 108; George, 15; Gibson, 197; Henry, 33, 169; John, 75, 78; Joseph, 106, 172, 183; Malichi, 193; Mary, 194; R., 36; Robert, 84; Ruth, 183; Thomas, 87, 136.
DAY, Alonza, 49; Connell, 101; David, 167; Joseph, 145, Nathaniel, 25; Robert, 40; Samuel, 196; Thomas, 190; William, 38, 85.
DEADWILDER, Joseph, 117; Lindsey, 18.
DEADWYLDER, Joseph, _____59
DEAL, Furney, 123; John, 114; Lexy, 127; William, 56.
DEAN, Charles, 40, 120; Edward, 99; George, 203; Harmon, 32; James, 213; John, 129; Mary, 118; Morning, 36; Moses, 140; Nathan, 207.
DEARING, Abner, 169; Reuben, 43; Simeon, 146.
DEASON, Zachariah, _____18, 189
DEAVENPORT, John, _____59

DEBROS, Joseph, _____185
DEDMON, William, _____168
DEEL, Meshach, _____61
DEEN, Asa, 110; Jesse, 119; Joel, 78, 166.
DEES, Bryant, 95; Cynthia, 28; Leonard, 159; Mark, 87; Moses, 58; Orphan, 28; Sarah, 31.
DEESON, Joseph, _____165
DEFNAL, David, 29; Mary, 137.
DEFOOR, John, _____171
DEGRAFFENREID, John, _____24
DELAFIELD, William, _____130
DELAIGLE, Charles, _____191
DELAMOTTA, Jacob, _____69
DELANEY, Daniel, 74; William, 80; Lewis, 199.
DeLANY, Elvina, _____197
DELAUNAY, Frances, 116, 135; James, 49, 50.
DELAUNY, Alphonzo, _____175
DELAWARE, Robert, _____89
DELAY, James, 213; Jesse, 137.
DELAZIE, Augustus, _____176
DELBERGHE, John, _____209
DELEGAL, David, 4; Edward, 4; Elizabeth, 129; Emeline, 4; Henry, 4; Jane, 4; Orphans, 140; Thomas, 4; William, 4.
DELK, Bird, 207; David, 96, 108; Jacob, 23; Stephen, 91.
DELOACH, Elizabeth, 112; Ephriam, 4; Gen., 64; Hardy, 70, 109, 150.
DELPHY, Samuel, _____35
DEMERE, Mary, 30; Raymond, 42.
DEMING, David, 115; George, 129.
DEMPSEY, Henderson, 30; Love, 186; 201.
DEMPSY, Levi, _____59
DEMSEY, Jesse, _____95
DEMSY, Barnett, _____37, 56
DENBY, John, _____141
DENHAM, Arthur, 139! Augustus, 138.
DENISON, Coothes, _____102
DENKINS, Isham, _____179
DENMAN, William, _____46
DENMARK, Elizabeth, _____98
DENNARD, Green, 26; John, 129.
DENNIS, Catherine, 87, 106; Daniel, 74, 119, 152, Ellender, 96, 137; Gren, 37; John, 165; Mathias, 189; Michael, 125.
DENNISON, Cootheer, 85; Patrick, 111.
DENNY, Elrood, 25; Yearly, 117.
DENSLER, Dr., 79; Henry, 22; Michael, 145.
DENSLOW, Allen, _____20
DENSON, Benjamin, 191; John, 104.
DENT, Frances, 26; George, 94, 98;

John, 118; Joseph, 90, 199; Nathaniel, 154; Sarah, 202; Thomas, 38.
DENTON, John, 8; Jones, 211.
DEPOISTER, Lewis, ...48
DEREKIN, Hiram, ...211
DERMOND, William, ...161
DESHAZO, James, 125; Wilson, 90, 176.
DESON, Joseph, ...86
DESSANBLEAUX, L. P., ...45
DESTRA, Charles, ...40
DEVAMPERT, Thomas, ...58
DEVANE, Francis, ...85
DEVEAUV, Major Peter, ...79
DEVENPORT, Elizabeth, 39; John, 151; Orphans, 39; Polly, 173; Stephen, 49.
DEVEREAUX, Major, 8; Mary, 120; Samuel, 43, 139; William, 180.
DEVERIL, John, ...109
DEWBERRY, Jesse, 70; Jiles, 178; Martha, 90; William, 121.
DEWITT, Ann, 30; John, 102, 126.
DEWREN, Lemuel, ...138
DIAL, Henry, 41; Isaac, 135.
DIAS, John, ...172, 203
DIBBLE, Caleb, ...18
DICK, James, ...112
DICKEN, John, ...7
DICKENS, James, 81; Nimrod, 40; Robert, 81.
DICKERSON, Francis, 101; George, 23; John, 152; Nathan, 143; Robert, 145; William, 59; Winburn, 114; Zazhariah, 85.
DICKEY, Sarah, ...119
DICKIN, John, ...28
DICKINS, Willis, ...210
DICKINSON, D. F., 61; John, 110, 146.
DICKISON, John, 181; Jonathan, 116.
DICKKY, Jonathan, ...106
DICKLIN, Richard, ...167
DICKSON, Binam, 141; Charity, 203; Charles, 94; David, 59, 117; Elvy, 45; George, 10; Hampton, 206; James, 26, 60; John, 108, 117, 149, 150; Thomas, 27, 111, 196, 205; William, 32, 91; Willis, 111.
DIE, Martin, ...97
DIEMER, Clement, ...118, 146
DIES, John, ...110
DIGBY, Bilinda, ...115
DILL, Catherine, 62; Phil., 162.
DILLARD, Celia, 107; Dempsy, 113; Edmund, 28; Fielding, 100; James, 107, 122, 175, 186; John, 141, 194; Mary, 204; Nathan, 185 Nehemiah, 186; Owen, 119; Sampson, 116.

DILLON, John, 197; Michael, 79; Thomas, 72.
DILLY, William, ...180
DILMON, William, ...59, 155
DILWORTH, James, ...65
DIMON, Robert, ...162
DINGLER, Fanny, 180; Nancy, 57.
DINGLEY, Joseph, ...73
DINKINS, John, ...179
DISMUKES, Elizabeth, 10; Jesse, 193.
DISON, Thomas, 189; William, 59.
DIVERS, Bird, ...130
DIXON, Ann, 61; Daniel, 72; James, 35, 215; John, 12, 87, 96; Joseph, 6; Luiza, 151; Martha, 29; Nathen, 69; Tamar, 139; Thomas, 52, 186; T illmon, 124; William, 117, 142.
DOBBINS, John, 159; William, 167.
DOBBS, Jesse, 171; John, 141, 154; Josiah, 174, 192; William, 149.
DOBSON, Henry, 133; Jesse, 141; John, 93; Neely, 47, 91.
DOBY, John, ...190
DODD, Catherine, 177; George, 81; James, 163; Jesse, 193; Peter, 185; Robert, 152; William, 109, 133, 202
DODGEN, Otleman, 202; Eli, 149.
DODGER, William, ...130
DODSON, Daniel, 1, 159; Elijah, 119; George, 152; John, 114; Samuel, 79.
DODWELL, Hezekiah, ...214
DOGGETT, Richard, ...129
DOKE, Alexander, ...81
DOLES, Carlton, 163; Josiah, 110; Thomas, 132, 162; Wilkinson, 129; Willis, 189; Zachariah, 49.
DOLLAR, Clement, 205; Cynthia, 65.
DOLTON, Claiborn, 130; John, 151.
DOMINGO, Frederick, ...170
DOMINO, Henry, 134; John, 7.
DONALD, Elizabeth, ...81
DONALDSON, Amelia, 160; Elizabeth, 152; James, 132; M. A. E., 132; Temperance, 205; Thomas, 26; William, 30, 60, 92, 167, 169.
DONAN, Han., ...4
DONCHO, Barnet, 66; James, 134.
DONEHOO, Cornelius, ...210
DONNELLY, Thomas, ...157
DOOLEY, Eli; Jesse.
DOOLITTLE, Abraham, 5; Ag., 175.
DOOLY, Elisha, 189; Elizabeth, 156; John, 85; Thomas, 47. 79, 117, 152, 211; William, 21.
DORENTON, C. E. M., ...82
DORITHY, James, 25, 78; John, 188, 215; Robert, 204.
DORITY, Elizabeth, 98; James, 142; Orphan, 114.
DORMAN, Alfred, 36; Clarky, 215; James, 16, 148; Sanford, 61.

DORSEY, John, 171, 168; William, 38.
DORTCH, David, 100; John, 93, 198; Russell, 52.
DOSS, Edward, 211; Green, 63; John, 139.
DOSSETT, Philip, _____ 179
DOSSEY, Seaborn, 150; William, 97.
DOSTER, Elizabeth, 171; Henderson, 130; James, 135; Thomas, 43.
DOSTON, Thomas, _____ 173
DOTIC, D. C., _____ 101
DOTSON, Asap., 4; David, 85.
DOUGHERTY, Charles, 139; Samuel, 83; William, 142.
DOUGHTRY, John, 45; Michael, 81, 215.
DOUGLAS, H., 97; James, 83; Jane, 82; John, 51, 168; L. N., 97; Spencer, 216; William, 83, 146.
DOUGLASS, Henry, 94; Jane, 79; M. A., 60; Marshall, 168; Josiah, 101; Stephen, 181; Thomas, 132; William, 108.
DOVER, Anderson, 43; Francis, 63, 130; Lawson, 70.
DOVES, Richard, _____ 118
DOW, Dorcas, _____ 204
DOWDELL, James, 61; Lawis, 24, 212.
DOWDY, Aaron, 159; Sally, 174.
DOWELL, Peter, _____ 113
DOWING, Benjamin, _____ 124
DOWLING, Dennis, 151; Jabey, 6; 206.
DOWNEY, Charles, 186; Joseph, 177.
DOWNING, Benjamin, 178; Edward, 42; Mathew, 63.
DOWNS, Ambrose, 39; Elias, 38; Elizabeth, 213; George, 64; Isaac, 99; James, 206; John, 8, 15, 212; Nancy, 188; Rachel, 4; Richard, 20; William, 163, 177.
DOWNY, James, 164, Josejh, 2, 30.
DOWSE, Samuel, _____ 132
DRACE, Frank, _____ 38
DRAKE, Epaphroditus, 174; Francis, 107; James, 73, 96; Mary, 35; Meredith, 21; Orphan, 212.
DRANE, Stephen, _____ 75
DRAPER, Peter, _____ 207
DRAWDY, James, _____ 39
DRAWHORN, Thomas, _____ 202
DREGORS, James, _____ 178
DRENT, Farnol, _____ 156
DREW, Jane, 114; Willis, 150, 213; Wilson, 186.
DREWRY, Samuel, _____ 99
DRIGGERS, Daniel, 203; Elenor, 176;

Ephriam, 189; Isaac, 110; Seleta, 158.
DRINKARD, John, *_____ 111
DRINKWATER, D., _____ 85
DRISKELL, Elget, _____ 213
DRISKILL, David, 205; Wotten, 199.
DRIVER, Julius, _____ 44
DRUMMOND, Mar., _____ 23
DRYDEN, John, _____ 39
DUBARY, Jiles, _____ 212
DUBBERLY, John, 29; Josejh, 39, 160; William, 194.
DUBERRY, Henry, _____ 163
DUBIGNON, Joseph, ___ 63, 129, 158
DUBOIS, John, _____ 18
DUBOSE, David, 52; Edwin, 101; Langston, 179; Peter, *35; Reuben, 215.
DUBOURG, Andrew, _____ 30, 129
DUCK, Divid, 15, 118; Jonathan, 120.
DUCKETT, Jacob, _____ 63, 70
DUCKWORTH, Christian, 105; Elizabeth, 95.
DUDLEY, Edward, 147; Edmond, 74; George, 45; Guilford, 110; James, 30, 210; John, 23, 125; Joseph, 35, 215; Peter, 180; Sarah, 58; William, 26, 55, 74.
DUETT, W. R., _____ 115
DUFFEE, Robert, _____ 112
DUFFEY, Daniel, _____ 149
DUFFIE, Ebenezer, _____ 183
DUFFILL, James, _____ 214
DUGGAN, Archibald, 7; Jesse, 125; John, 161.
DUGGAR, Isaac, 96; Nathaniel, 174.
DUKE, Beverly, 82; Cebron, 96; Coleman, 51; Crenshaw, 167; Elijah, 123, 127; Emily, 172; Green, 143; James, 81, 127; Jesse, 94; John, 165, 176; Mitchell, 137; Moses, 200; Robert, 25; Sarah, 92, 123; Sidney, 143; Stephen, 72; Thomas, 15, 190; William, 46, 138, 176.
DUKES, Elizabeth, 164; Frederick, 3; Hamilton, 38; J., 38; Nancy, 209; Rachel, 38; Reney, 191; Sarah, 95, 165.
DUMAS, John, _____ 64
DUNAGON, Joseph, _____ 143
DUNAWAY, James, 28; Johnson, 70; Orphans, 69, 90; William, 47.
DUNBAR, George, _____ 45
DUNCAN, A., 159, 164; Absalom, 46; Daniel, 187; Edmond, 193; Henry, 198; Hinton, 37; Isaac, 171; James, 25, 31, 171; Jesse, 44; John, 43, 50, 149, 197, 208, 212; Lee, 193; Nancy, 96; Moses, 36, 93; Nathaniel, 126; Orphans, 92; Pearson, 40, 57; Rainey, 206; William, 31, 52, 93.

DUNFORD, Orphan, ...180
DUNHAM, Timothy, 82; William, 116, 130.
DUNLAP, James, 75, 149; John, 208; Patrick, 27, 82; Samuel, 205.
DUNLEY, Oliver, ...185, 208
DUNN, Albert, 108; Anne, 95, 130; Barney, 157; David, 51; Elizabeth, 200; Gatewood, 22; James, 164; Jane, 113; John, 10, 16, 17, 23; Lemon, 188; Mary, 113; Sarah, 114; Silas, 126; Willie, 99; William, 211; Winiford, 129.
DUNNEWAY, Aug., ...32
DUNNING, Charles, ...121, 133
DUNRE, Wineford, ...26
DUNSTON, William, ...9
DUNWOODY, Samuel, ...128
DUPREE, Drury, 38; Elijah, 169; James, 138; Jesse, 215; Josejh, 175; Martha, 45; Orbin, 16; Sterling, 160; Synthia, 137; William, 41, 86.
DURAM, Thomas, ...108
DURBIN, Sarah, ...37
DUREAUZEAUX, Stephen, ...67, 212
DURDAN, John, ...75
DURDEN, Orphans, ...163
DURDIN, Benjamin, 203; Joseph, 58.
DURHAM, Abraham, 52; Alsey, 212; Isabel, 36; Isaiah, 142; Jacob, 211; James, 53; Jeptha, 71; Joshua, 1; Samuel, 69, 189; Sarah, 201; Silas, 2; Stephen, 140; Willis, 97.
DURKEE, Cath., 155; Lucy, 120.
DURRENCE, Jane, 64; William, 19, 71
DURRETT, Francis, ...199
DURRITT, Rice, ...33
DUSEN, George, ...171
DUTCH, Jeremiah, ...26
DUTTON, James, 123; Thomas, 161.
DUTY, Russell, 130; Thomas, 174, 210, 114.
DUVAINE, Patrick, ...17, 210
DWIGHT, Serene, ...110
DYAL, John, ...190
DYALL, John, ...74
DYE, Avery, 101; Brown, 201; Elijah, 215; Martin, 171; Randall, 214; Silas, 119; Stephen, 2; Thomas, 164; William, 204.
DYER, Alexander, 19, 125, 150; Edward, 162; Eletha, 116; Elisha, 34; Washington, 44; William, 144, 200.
DYESS, Thomas, 86; William, 118.
DYKES, George, 154; Hiram, 109; Isaiah, 106, 185; Jep., 167; Moses, 110; Shadrack, 68; Warren, 131; Zaddock, 39.
DYRE, Edmund, ...69
DYSON, Isaac, 131; John, 141.
EADIS, Joseph, 208; William, 208.

EADS, William, ...59
EADY, John, ...75, 36
EAGAN, John, ...4
EAGERTON, Zachariah, ...212
EARNEST, George, ...148, 5
EASON, Abraham, 125, 154; Edmund, 99; Iredell, 7; Isaac, 110; Michael, 104; Penelope, 171; Penny, 161, 191; Rice, 100; Whitmell, 60.
EAST, Benjamin, ...27
EASTCO, George, ...34
EASTEN, Josejh, ...74
EASTERLING, Henry, ...42, 98, 195
EASTERS, Jiles 24
EASTES, Elisha, ...152
EASTIS, Charles, ...102
EASTWARD, John, ...204
EASTERWOOD, John, 21; Lawrence, 106, 109.
EASTWOOD, John, ...10, 188
EATON, George, 1; John, 98, 178, 196; Marget, 211; William, 96.
EAVANS, Jane, ...61
EAVE, Paul, ...107
EAVINSON, Eli, ...142
EAVENSON, Thomas, ...26
EAVES, Lewis, 44; Thomas, 57.
EBERLY, Henry, ...142
EBERHARDT, Jacob, ...100
EBERHART, Francis, 108; Joseph, 100; Samuel, 187.
ECCOLS, Joll, 216; Philip, 77; Zilphy, 200.
ECHOLDS, Robert, ...151
ECHOLS, James, ...150
ECHOLS, Elizabeth, 46; Josephus, 102; Mercer, 195; Obediah, 2, 21; Samuel, 51.
ECKELS, Joel, ...29
ECKLEY, Levi, ...108
ECTOR, Eleanor, ...28
EDDINS, William, ...59
EDENFIELD, David, 81; James, 61; Joshua, 109.
EDGAR, Hugh, 4; John, 16.
EDGE, Alexander, 195; Allen, 171; John, 199.
EDDINGFIELD, Josejh, 114; Joshua, 179; Richard, 98.
EDMONDS, Amos, ...162
EDMONDSON, Benjamin, 34; Eli, 20, 27; James, 177, 211; John, 46, 154; Joseph, 98; Mahaly, 207; Martha, 183; Peter, 40; Samuel, 60; Wily, 62.
EDMUND, B. D., ...168
EDMUNDS, Amos, 83; James, 60; Joel, 65; Nathan, 153; William, 104.
EDMUNDSON, John, 150; Nancy, 87.
EDSON, Calvin, ...84
EDWARD, David, 215; Sarah, 165.
EDWARDS, Alford, 114; Alfred, 49,

30; Alston, 202; Ambrose, 89; Andrew, 186; Anna, 31; A. T., 131; Cloah, 146; Cordy, 120; Cynthia, 51; E. C., 186; E. C., 186; Edwin, 167, 189; Elisha, 183; Ethelred, 91, 70; Isaac, 89; Isam, 128; Isham, 74; James, 78, 59, 9; Jane, 102; Jesse, 152; John, 64, 2, 98, 193; Jordan, 169; Josejh, 148, 5, 129; Larkin, 139; Leron, 208; Littleberry, 178; M. A., 186; P. C., 119; Permelia, 22; Peter, 102, 114; Phebe, 56; Pilot, 80; Polly, 180; Reuben, 88, 95; Richard, 177; Robert, 167, 180; Stephen, 139, 156; Sucky, 99; T. L., 2; T. W., 8; Thomas, 142. 47, 6, 30, 164; William, 20, 98, 127, 184, 209; Willim, 3; Wyatt, 70; Young, 132.

EELLS, Nathaniel, ... 181
EFFRY, Armand, ... 129
ELAM, Hodijah, 86; Moab, 109; Phebe, 184.
ELARD, James, ... 186
ELDER, David, 131; Edward, 44; Harrison, 62; Hartwell, 207; Howell, 30; Littleberry, 29; Thomas, 87.
ELDERS, David, ... 47
ELDRIDGE, Jane, 29, 104! John, 100 (2).
ELGIN, Hezekiah, ... 110
ELIE, John, ... 151
ELKINS, Herman, ... 208, 204
ELLARD, James, ... 34
ELLERBEE, Lewis, ... 94
ELLET, John, 15; Nancy, 189.
ELLETT, James, ... 38
ELLINGTON, Mrs., 64; Stephen, 183, 211; William, 171.
ELLIOTT, Benjamin, 137; James, 82; Robert, 108.
ELLIOTT, Benjamin, 212; Jane, 177; John, 181, 187.
ELLIS, Calvin, 174; Fielding, 112; Green, 210; Henry, 80; Hicks, 200; James, 162; Jane, 40; Jesse, 168; John, 81, 124, 106, 180, 216; Jonathan, 81; Levin, 186; Polly, 62, 42; Porsilla, 110; Shadrack, 19, 191, 200; Willis, 139.
ELLISON, George, 49; Henry, 69; Jarratt, 199; Robert, 29; Smallwood, 150; Zach, 176.
ELLISTON, George, ... 62
ELLSWORTH, John, ... 22
ELMORE, Luke, 202; Mark, 40.
ELMS, Charles, ... 194
ELRIDGE, Daniel, ... 58
ELROD, Adam, ... 21, 174
ELSBERRY, Benjamin, ...8, 110, 209
ELTON, Abram, ... 93, 10, 154

ELUM, William, ... 170
ELY, Berrnett, 102; Charles, 173; Michael, 180.
EMANUEL, Asia, 88; Caswell, 155.
EMBRY, Henry, 118; Hiram, 79; Joseph, 6; William, 187.
EMMON, Alfred, ... 127
ENDSLEY, John, ... 19
ENGLAND, Charles, 183; Elisha, 211.
ENGLISH, Cornelius, 163; Eli, 124; George, 58; Green, 137; Haywood, 91; Josejh, 74; Parmenus, (2) 214; Reuben, 207.
ENLOW, Rebecca. 133
ENNIS, Ann, 134; James, 141, Jesse, 179; Mary, 18; Nathaniel, 7.
ENOCHS, Floyd, ... 2
EPPES, Thomas, ... 79
EPPS, Thomas, ... 161
ERWIN, Eleans, 64; James, 85; Richard, 65.
ESBY, Robert, ... 213
ESOM, William, ... 141
ESPY, James, 53; John, 40; Josiah, 164
ESSOM, Alfred, ... 151
ESTES, Abraham, 67; Baxter, 112; James, 199, 81; William, 106; Zephaniah, 60.
ESTERS, Booker, ... 183
ESTIS, William, ... 33
ETHEREDGE, Hardy, 173; John, 36; William, 197.
ETHERIDGE, Bet, 188; Betsy, 151; Calley, 185; Eliza 158; Joel, 152; Lon, 188; Orphans, 207; Peason, 18; Richard, 20, 91; Robert, 148; William, 202, 39.
ETHERINGTON, William, ... 201
EUBANK, Martin, ... 165
EUBANKS, Daniel, 194; Elizha, 164; 102; George, 15; Sarah, 94; William, 193, 168, 110.
EVANS, Anslem, 103; Augustin, 35; Barwell, 23; Benjamin, 117; Betsy, 190; Boswell, 209; David, 172, 78; D. J., 5; Elihu, 195; Elisha, 115; Elizabeth, 192, 110, 96, 39; George, 160; Green, 117, 40; Henry, 87; Humphrey, 106.
EVERINGHAM, John, ... 82
FAGAN, James, 106; William, 170.
FAGANS, Momes, ... 162
FAGIN, Henry, ... 146
FAGLES, William, ... 35
FAIL, William, ... 28, 108
FAILS, James, 168; John, 34.
FAIN, David, 63; Ebenezer, 183; John, 129; Lovett, 80; Mercer, 37; Samuel, 121; Thomas, 107.
FAIR, Rachel, ... 82
FAIRCLOTH, Allen, 22; Caleb, 152; Isaac, 185; James, 206; John, 96,

54; Mathew, 71; Robert, 137.
FALKNER, Elijah, 98; Isaac, 21; William, 98.
FALLAN, Fleet, ...59
FALLIN, Jesse, 57; Sarah, 212.
FAMBROUGH, Anderson, 36; T., 134, 178.
FANN, Jesse, ...155
FANNARY, Bryan, ...195
FANNIN, A. B., 72; Isham, 54; William, 80.
FARES, William, ...213
FARIS, William, ...141
FARLEY, Dalina, 92; James, 175; Jane, 28; Martha, 53; Mathew, 100; Stephen, 47, 196; William, 99.
FARLIE, Farlie, ...18
FARMER, Asiel, 157; Elizabeth, 170; Emily, 190; Henry, 64; James, 101; Joel, 182; Pleasant, 153; Rosina, 169; Sarah, 81; Thomas, 54; William, 86, 19, 180, 181.
FARNEL, Watson, ...97
FARQUHARSON, Jane, ...159
FARR, Francis, 211; Jesse, 4; John, 153, 6; Jonathan, 149.
FARRAR, Francis, 155, 30; George, 155; Nancy, 184.
FARRELL, Charles, 56; Francis, 169; Henry, 10.
FARRINGTON, William, ...213
FARRIS, John, 149; William, 116.
FARROW, Dorothy, 64; Finch, 174; James, 190; Thomas, 69.
FAUBS, Henry, ...195
FAUGHTENBERRY, Jas., ...10
FAULK., John, ...93
FAULKNER, Benjamin, 149; James, 122, 192; Job, 46; Joel, 89, 9; John, 63, 50; Peter, 140; Vincent, 8; William, 145.
FAUST, Jesse, 113; Peter, 184; Samuel, 92.
FAUSTER, William, ...108
FAYETT, Thomas, ...137
FAVER, Moses, ...18
FEAGAN, James, 127; Michael, 140; Feistram, 108; William, 31.
FEAGANS, William, ...118
FEAGINS, William, ...165
FEARS, Aug., 9; William, 9, 193; Zachariah, 190.
FEATHERSTONE, Jane, ...41
FEDRICKS, John, ...18
FEE, John, ...155
FELLS, Cary, ...70
FELTON, William, ...47
FELTS, Hartwell, ...72
FENNEL, David, 38; William, 36.

FENNER, Sterry, ...166
FERGASON, Caroline, 17; Daniel, 75; John, 17, 213; Marshall, 17; Nancy, 17; Nimrod, 2L3; Wiley, 17.
FERGESON, Coleman, ...211
FERGISON, Grief, ...209
FERGUSON, Benjamin, 7; Daniel, 40; Isaac, 80; July, 147; Uancy, 161.
FERRELL, Cuthbert, 78; John, 135; Thomas, 19, 184; Wiley, 110; William, 21, 213.
FERRILL, John, 19; Micajah, 47.
FERRIS, Robert, ...64
FETTS, Jenny, 72; John, 203.
FEW, Albert, 96, 31; Benjamin, 119; Elize, 158, 182; James, 184; Joseph, 165; Leonidas, 203; Thomas, 116.
FICKLING, Fielding, 207; Samuel, 94.
FIELD, William, ...183
FIELDING, Samuel, ...147
FIELDIS, Richard, ...77
FIELDS, Lewis, 189; Miles, 189; Samuel, 176; Sarah, 160; William, 84.
FILGHMAN, Nan, ...2
FILLINGBAST, T. S., ...72
FINCH, Charles, 92; Elizabeth, 56, 29; Elom, 151; Freeman, 176; John, 134; Thomas, 102, 212.
FINCHER, Benjamin, 199; John, 64; Jonathan, 9; William, 168.
FINDLAY, Isabella, 104; T., 191.
FINDLEY, William, ...196
FINK, John, ...213
FINLEY, Catherine, 80; Emanuel, 137; James, 163; Jane, 69; John, 83; Mary, 108; William, 77.
FINNEY, Anne, 197; Arthur, 80; Morrel, 150; Simeon, 72; Wiley, 24.
FINNIES, John, ...141
FISH, Calvin, ...53
FISHER, Charles, 194; Elizabeth, 34; Henry, 148.
FISKE, Josiah, ...104
FITCHETT, Eliza, ...33
FITTS, John, 82; Walker, 182.
FITZ, Hartwell, ...192
FITZGERALD, David, ...198
FITZPATRICK, Booth, 165; Elizabeth, 100, 191; Henley, 38; John, 158; Joseph, 98, 53, 139; Ranny, 162; S., 21; Thornton, 38; Zeno, 118.
FIVEASH, Elias, 89, 29, 198; John, 29, 141, 125.
FLAKE, William, ...70, 197, 214
FLANAGAN, Alex, 80; Isaac, 63; John, 71.
FLANDERS, David, ...123
FLANNAGAN, Kenian, ...187
FLANORIGAN, William, ...8
FLEETWOOD, Reloy, ...73

FLEMING, Abel, 82; Arel, 145; Isaac, 15, 211; James, 91, 110; John, 209, 175; Mary, 24; Mildred, 123; Phinny, 192; Robert, 79, 189, 212; Sarah, 6, 178; William, 80, 9, 28, 170.
FLEMISTER, E. G., 137; John, 88.
FLEMNING, William, ———————213
FLETCHET, Christopher, 4; Elizabeth, 97; Joshua, 162; William, 19.
FLEWELLEN, Gideon, 32, 209; Nancy, 116.
FLINN, Aletha, 209; Charles, 69; Elizabeth, 145; George, 1.
FLINT, Aquilla, 126; James, 194; Samuel, 94.
FLORANCE, Levi, ———————122
FLORENCE, Seaborn, 134; Th., 9.
FLOURNOY, Green, 128; John, 81; Josiah, 99; W. F. J., 97.
FLOUERS, Charles, 150; William, 89.
FLOWERS, Elizabeth, 54; Henry, 144; James, 193; Samuel, 142; William, 47, 25.
FLOYD, Clement, 137; David, 71; Elizabeth, 30; Francis; George, 95; John, 206; Joseph, 52; Margaret, 25, Mathew, 135; Sarah, 28, 180, 168, 214; Silas, 108; Stephen, 172; Thomas, 94; William, 213.
FLUD, Jane, ———————124
FLUKER, John, 133; Robert, 97.
FLURRY, Richard, ———————135, 110
FLUTCHER, James, ———————122
FLYNN, Elizabeth, 52; John, 210.
FOARD, Daniel, 165; Wyatt, 87.
FOGIL, Mary, ———————214
FOKES, Calvin, 24; Orph., 212.
FOLDS, George, 129; John, 143, 161; Par, 123; R., 123; Tekill, 148.
FOLESOME, Lawrence, ———————142
FOLK, Needham, ———————119
FOLKER, James, ———————101
FOLKNER, Willis, ———————71
FOLSOME, Elijah, ———————95
FOLSOM, Horatia, 179; Thomas, 118.
FOMBY, Aaron, 47; Nancy, 22; Pleasant, 18; Richard, 200; Thomas, 73.
FONTAINE, Frederick, 80; Henry, 80; L., 80.
FOORD, Garry, ———————110
FOOTMAN, Edward, ———————82
FORBES, Charles, 202; Wesley, 143, 149.
FORCE, John, ———————77
FORD, Franklin, 164; James, 98; Joel, 79; Samuel, 133; Thomas, 23; Warren, 110.
FOREMAN, John, ———————118
FOREHAND, David, 90; William, 29; Win., 95.
FOREMAN, Agnes, 137; Isaac, 17; James, 137.
FOREST, Shuger, ———————37
FOREST, Berry, 213; James, 184; Jesse 190.
FORESTER, Benjamin, 31; James, 126; Jane, 205; William, 153.
FORGASON, Emeline, 210; John, 198.
FORMBY, Nathan, ———————176, 112
FORRESTER, Bailley, ———————205
FORRISTER, William, ———————196
FORRIST, William, ———————3
FORROW, John, ———————74
FORSHEE, Elisha, ———————198
FORSYTH, Philip, ———————149
FOR8, Arthur, 177; Charles, 187; Elizabeth, 15; John, 82; Tomlinson, 177
FORTNER, Sahar, ———————155
FORTSON, Benjamin, ———————102
FOSTER, Abigail, 86; Arthur, 30; Augustus, 175; Ebenezer, 120; Elijah, 63; Elkin, 112; Francis, 165, 205; Frederick, 214; Harkilles, 50, 99; James, 8; John, 167, 168, 182, 201; Levi, 108; Ludwell, 9, 168; Nathaniel, 40; Newett, 3; Phebe, 191; Reuben, 182; Robert, 23, 35, 174; Samuel, 80; Sarah, 175; Stephen, 57; William, 28, 80, 140.
FOUCH, Simpson, ———————166
FOULSOME, George, ———————162
FOUNTAIN, Brinson, 155; Dempsey, 203; Green, 33; Henry, 153; John, 161, 178, 112; Susannah, 213; William, 58.
FOWLER, Anthony, 4, 67; Cody, 157; David, 215, 38; John, 23, 61; Matilda, 129; Samuel, 165, 189; Sarah, 22; Theophilus, 204; Thompson, 71; Westley, 172; William, 104, 62, 96.
FOWLES, Maryann, ———————87
FOX, Delilah, 122; John, 58, 181; Mary, 10; Orph., 169; William, 169, 151.
FOY, Lewis, ———————129
FOYE, Robert, ———————183
FRAMAN, Ciler, ———————188
FRAMBROUGH, Anderson, ———————167
FRANCIS, James, ———————216
FRANKLIN, Benjamin, 107; David, 23; Dove, 189; Francis, 140; Henry, 79; James, 146; Jesse, 18; John, 133; Josejh, 122; Lewis, 152; Nathan, 23; Nelson, 153; Wiley, 196.
FRANKS, Marion, 27; Weston, 178; Wiley, 153.
FRASER, Allen, 9; Andrew, 15; Lavinia, 114; Nancy, 170; Robert, 213; Simon, 67.
FRASERS, Samuel, ———————18
FRASHIER, John, ———————153
FRASIER, Daniel, ———————216
FRASURE, Thomas, ———————7

FRAZER, Elizabeth, 41; Malakiah, 125; Polly, 74.
FRAZIER, Haywood, 153; Mary, 128; Simon, 210.
FREDERICKS, Green, 123; J., 123.
FREE, Lewis, ----142
FREEL, Elizabeth, ----208
FREELAND, Isaac, ----63
FREEMAN, Bailey, 199, 102; Benjamin, 21, 88, 93; Cavan, 2; D., 45; Daniel, 115; Dorothy, 214; Edward, 77, 153; Fred, 15; Garrett, 88; George, 215; Hartwell, 30; Isham, 43; Jacob, 100; James, 118; Jeptha, 88; Jesse, 170; John, 48, 124, 135, 169; 178, 195, 214; Johnson, 189; Joseph, 190; Josiah, 15, 31; M., 45; Mary, 148; Martha, 208; Mildred, 190; Nancy, 211; Nelly, 122; Noah, 141; Polly, 184; Robert, 66, 180; Ruth, 193; Thomas, 9, 158, 213; Watson, 203; William, 81, 170.
FRENCH, Elizabeth, 62; Frederick, 104; 84; John, 184.
FRETWELL, Littleton, ----212
FREWIN, James, ----158
FRICK, Michael, ----206
FRICKS, Henry, ----47
FRIDDLE, Joseph, ----158
FRIER, H. H., 167; Joshua, 167.
FRITH, Christopher, ----31
FRIZZLE, Jane, ----113
FRUIN, James, ----88
FRYDAY, Josejh, ----190
FRYERMONTH, Han 94; H., 182; John, 43; Peter, 177, 62.
FUCH, Ansey, ----118
FUDGE, Jacob, 162; Solomon, 202.
FULCHER, Ann, 29; James, 61; A., 122.
FULGHAM, Cornelius, 177; Memory, 122.
FULLAR, Ezekal, 159; Thomas, 56.
FULLELOVE, Seaborn, 125; Thomas, 112; Willis, 110.
FULLER, Amos, 83; Benjamin, 44, 126; Berry, 117; Bluford, 107, 148; Eldridge, 24, 27; George, 41, 134; Isaac, 176, 203; James, 152; John, (2) 8, 178; Mary, 22, 145, 208; Matthew, 207; William, 75, 88, 201.
FULLINGIN, Henry, ----153
FULLINGTON, Caleb, ----27
FULSOM, Orphons, ----79
FULTON, James, 133; Silas, 77! Thomas, 176, 167.
FULWOOD, Jane, 148; John, 170.
FUNDERBURK, Isaac, 88; John, 89; William, 9.
FUQUA, Amos, 163; Andrew, 127; William, 211.

FURCROW, Cornelius, ----35
FURGUSON, Mary, ----146
FURLOW, Martin, 44; Osborn, 82.
FURTH, Lewis, Dr., ----145
FUSSEL, William, ----124
FUTCH, Jacob, 113; James, 129; Jane, 204; John, 30; Onesimus, 101, 145; Rowan, 94.
FUTRAL, Allen, 118, 57; Joel, 142.
FUTRELL, Abraham, 136; John, 62 Micajah, 79.
GAAR, Joel, ----160
GACHET, Benjamin, ----12, 15
GADDES, Archibald, 211; Elijah, 159; James, 37; Mary, 174.
GADDESS, Alexander, 23; Enoch, 94; Randall, 43.
GADDS, Thomas, ----160
GADDY, Elizabeth, 93; Jeremiah, 130, 211.
GAENS, Jeremiah, ----159
GAFFORD, Martha, ----140
GAHAGAN, Matheas, ----29
GAILER, James, ----46
GAINS, Humphrey, 16; James, 22; Frances, 11.
GAINEY, Richard, ----160
GAINOR, Phebe, 141; Phoebe, 81.
GAINY, Richard, ----109
GAILEY, Mary, ----6
GAILY, James, ----43
GAINER, Daniel, 184; Elizabeth, 99; Richard, 61; Sarah, 154; Susannah, 75.
GAINES, Allen, 54; George, 66; Henry, 186; Hiram, 131; Humphrey, 134; Theophilus, 170.
GAITHER, Eli, 4; Shadrack, 168.
GAKEN, Elizabeth, ----178
GALAWAY, James, ----5
GALE, Jennet, ----49
GALLAHER, Samuel, ----126
GALLANDET, James, ----142
GALLOWAY, Thomas, ----90, 117
GAMAGE, Solomon, ----26, 62
GAMBLE, Charles, 196; James, 39; Jane, 95; Rachel, 90; Roger, 133; William, 207.
GAMMELL, Aairs, ----61
GAMMON, Joel, 24; Jonathan, 192; Samuel, 207.
GANDY, Brinkley, 157, 197; Griffin, 29.
GANEY, Bartholomew, 121; Josiah, 178; Mathew, 36; Redick, 134.
GANLEER, Clementine, 94; Genevieve, 43.
GANN, Elizabeth, ----133
GANOBLY, Benjamin, ----126
GANT, John, 122, 141; Mary, 55.
GARARD, Elizabeth, ----131

GARBETT, Elisha, _____142, 180
GARDNER, Cinthia, 71; Ethel, 95; Jason, 34; John, 93, 119, 126, 167; Lydia, 117; Nancy, 66; Reddick, 129; Samuel, 20; Tillman, 193.
GARNEY, Henry, _____185
GARLINGTON, Nancy, _____61
GARLAND, Fanny, 183; Martha, 211; John, 9, 24, 175.
GARLICK, Edward, _____39
GARLIN, Henry, _____131
GARMON, Adam, 143; Ruth, 145.
GARNER, Archie, 213; Charles, 26, 36; Elijah, 113; Elizabeth, 211; James, 199; John, 66, 119; Mary, 126; Stephen, 32, 90, 94, 145, 202; Sturdy, 23; Thomas, 140; William, 53.
GARNET, Elizabeth, _____69
GARNETT, Absalom, 101; Iabez, 44; John, 145; Major, 59.
GARRARD, Elizabeth, 25, 161; James, 88.
GARRAT, James, _____4
GARRATT, Sarah, _____142
GARAY, Henry, _____185
GARRELL, Stinson, _____26
GARRET, Charney, _____69
GARRETT, Austin, 211; Benjamin, 88, 205; Daniel, 8; Enoch, 16, 157; James, 48, 97; John, 88, 135, 167; Jonathan, 41, 56; Josiah, 201; Lyra, 203; Richard, 26, 171; Riley, 12; Sarah, 135; Thomas, 11; William, 87.
GARRISON, Calet, 53, 102; David, 167; Jedediah, 37, 139; Levi, 43; Morris, 43.
GARROTT, James, _____35
GARROTTE, Samuel, 35; Thomas, 157.
GARTHIN, Levi, _____13
GARTNEY, James, _____177
GARTRELL, Joseph, 84; William, 62.
GARTWELL, Joseph, 84; William, 62.
GARVIN, Rebecca, 165; Sarah, 87.
GARY, Nathaniel, 124; Nicholas, 87; William, 162.
GASKIN, George, _____99
GASS, John, _____168
GASSAWAY, Alford, 181; Mary, 211.
GASTIN, Iseal, 148; Matthew, 49.
GATES, Charles, 146, 202; Hezekiah, 173, 194; James, 162; Martha.
GATEWOOD, Ainsworth; 96, 166; Philip, 189, 202.
GATHRIGHT, James, 74; Miles, 50.
GATLAND, John, 71; Sarah, 169.
GATLIN, Churchhill, 157; Edward, 6; Lemuel, 49; Mariah, 99; Stephen, 170.
GATRIL _____

GAULDING, John, 92; Jesse, 32, 35.
GAUNTT, Isaac, _____134
GAUSE, Martha, _____58
GAUTIER, Peter, _____9
GAUVAIN, Rosalie, _____151
GAY, Allen, 114, 159; Craaford, 101; Elias, 124; Elizabeth, 30; Gilbert, 11, 134; James, 5; Joel, 57, 164; Jordan, 17; Joshua, 11, 189; Rasmas, 154; Thomas, 196, 212; William, 4, 27.
GAYDEN, John, _____21, 91
GEE, Eason, 91; Henry, 115, 204.
GEIGAR, John, 100, 178cm_; 1 (etao
GEIGAR, John, _____100, 178
GELTIN, James, _____169
GENOBLY, Benjamin, _____123
GENOND, Vni. _____7
GENTERY, Letitha, _____214
GENTRY, Burges, 139; D., 64; Elisha, 27; Robert, 186; Samuel, 171, 192.
GEORGE, Arthur, 38; Isaac, 54; James 15, 133, 157; Jesse, 126; Joseph, 3; Mary, 50, 89.
GERROLD, Benjamin, 46; James, 204.
GERRARD, Jacob, _____22
GESS, Shesley, _____112
GETLINS, Thomas, _____171
GIBBS, Claiborn, 41; Jeremiah, 156; John, 111; Thomas, 203.
GIBSON, Catherine, 170; Churchwell, 7; David, 184, 194; Frances, 103; Henry, 4, 67, 213, 216; James, 95, 107; John, 51, 84, 113, 14, 147, 148, 159, 173, 195, 212; Jonathan, 151; Mary, 204; Nancy, 29; R. T., 26; Richard, 97; Sampson, 197; Samuel, 209; Sarah, 88; Susannah, 135; William, 197.
GIDDEN, Isben, _____103
GIDDENS, Benjamin, 167; George, 211.
GIDEON, Elizabeth, 63; Hozea, 63; Isben, 100; William, 186.
GIDEONS, Benjamin, 39; Isben, 131.
GIEL, Charles, 88; John, 105, 209; Orphans, 206; Thomas, 215; Washington, 156.
GILLIAMS, William, _____23
GILLEES, James, _____155
GILLET, David, 29; John, 191.
GILLELAND, William, _____145
GIGNILLIAT, John, 83; Henry, 165.
GIGNILLIATT, Nor, 134; William, 134.
GIGOR, Sarah, _____87
GIHAM, • Ezekiel, _____4
GILBERT, Allen, 32; Arthur, 193; Drury, 185; Isael, 185; James, 126; 174; Jemima, 91; John, 16, 26,

180, 192; Joshua, 191; Lucinda, 32; Nathan, 52; Richard, 178; Sarah, 90; Thomas, 32; William, 11, 190, 204, 213.
GILBRETH, Joseph, ...158
GILCOAT, John, ...67, 187
GILDER, Elizabeth, 215; George, 103; Sinert, 143.
GILDERSLEEVE, Thomas, ...86, 171
GILDON, Richard, ...209
GILES, Elizabeth, 188; John, 56, 146, 187; Nathaniel, 216; Robert, 123, 166.
GILHAM, Robert, 137; William, 206.
GILKEYSON, Margaret, ...43
GILFORD, John, ...38, 89
GILL, Charles, 88; John, 105, 209; Orphan, 206; Thomas, 215; Washington, 156.
GILLAMS, William, ...23
GILLEES, James, ...155
GILLELAND, William, ...145
GILLESPIE, George, 59; James, 69; Samuel, 201; William, ...33, 64....
GILLET, David, 29; John, 191.
GILLEY, John, ...17, 85
GILLIS, Murdock, ...115
GILLY, Washington, ...129
GILMER, Charles, 187; William, 71, 111, 155.
GILMOR, William, ...56
GILMORE, Elizabeth, 184; Equvilla, 99; Hughey, 1, 158; James, 44, 103; Samuel, 72; S. H., 86; Silas, 125; Thomas, 39, 93, 131.
GILPIN, James, ...172
GILSTON, David, ...127, 150
GAILSTRAP, James, 151; Lewis, 86; Peter, 184.
GINDRATT, H. A., 154; Henry, 191.
GINKIN, Liddy, ...187
GINN, Jesse, 88; Thomas, 194, 197.
GIONOVOLY, Elizabeth, ...94
GIPSON, Susan, ...173
GIRTMAN, Catherine, 159; William, 92.
GITTENS, John, ...20
GIVEN, John, ...159
GIVENS, James, ...150
GIVINGS, Robert, ...99
GLADDEN, James, ...200
GLADDING, Jonathan, ...66
GLARE, George, ...117
GLASGOW, Abediah, ...2
GLASS, Elisha, 170; Levi, 28; Sanders, 152; Sarah, 46; Thomas, 39, 123.
GLASSON, Jesse, ...150
GLAZE, Joseph, 11; John, 212; Orjhan, 173; Reuben, 203; Thomas, 77; William, 137.

GLAZIER, Hiram, ...127
GLEASON, Joel, ...67
GLEDNEY, Samuel, ...70
GLEN, Nobel, 148; Sarah, 148.
GLENN, George, 205; James, 205; John, 122; Joseph, 147; Mathew, 21; Mitchell, 129; Nathaniel, 117; Wiley, 85, 204; William, 62, 115, 98; 212.
GLISSON, Evan, 78; James, 62; Riley, 45.
GLOVER, Abraham, 167; Barzilla, 41; Benjamin, 140; Druc., 127; Frosier, 187; Kelly, 22; Larkin, 198; Robert, 178; Richard, 70; Sarah, 44; Thomas, 42, 148, 209; Washington, 160; William, 7, 23, 49, 79, 85, 98; Wylie, 31.
GLOVERS, Richard, ...28
GNANN, Mary, ...114
GOBER, John, 17; William, 92, 129, 132.
GIDARD, Daniel, 212; Joseph, 92.
GODBEE, Alberd, 113; Albert, 163; Howell, 110; Moses, 87; William, 87.
GODBY, James, 212; Mary, 195.
GODEN, Alexandef, ...185
GODREY, ...
GODFREY, Freeman, 184; Littleton, 21; Thomas, 150; William, 184.
GODKIN, James, ...189
GODLY, James, 121; Kitturah, 159.
GODWIN, Jeremiah, 19, 160; Martha, 23; Mary, 172; Solo, 150.
GOGGINS, Alexander, ...180
GOLDEN, Alexander, 139; Andrew, 49, 161; Gilley, 32.
GOLDIN, Thomas, ...25
GOLDING, Noah, 178; J. W., 22.
GOLDSMITH, Hale, 215; John, 90, 204; Samuel, 44, 105, 109.
GOLDSTEINE, David, ...58
GOOCH, James, 49; Nathan, 120.
GOOCHER, William, ...159
GOOD, John, 136; Martha, 117.
GOODDOWN, Jacob, ...53
GOODE, Macheness, 141; Robert, 81, 195.
GOODEN, Arm, ...175
GOODGAIN, Alexander, ...207
GOODGAME, Alexander, ...55
GOODIN, Josiah, ...11
GOODMAN, James, 119, 135; Joel, 99; Henry, 135.
GOODSON, Alexander, 3; John, 139; William, 128.
GOODWIN, Elizabeth, 158; Hecter, 141; Henry, 211; Isaac, 192; James, 36; Jeffery, 130; Jesse, 57, 111, 168, 208; John, 44, 97; Micaja, 186; Nealy, 91; Orphon, 148, 195; Richard, 71; Robert, 10; Seaborn, 141;

Shadrack, 31.
GOOLESBY, Wade, ...27
GOOLSBY, Allen, 202, 212; Benpamin, 95; Catty, 60; Elizabeth, 63; James, 67; Jesse, 78; John, 164; Joshua, 124; Josiah, 11, 106; Micajah, 47; Miles, 122; Miless, 61; Peter, 22, 77; Richard, 178; Simeon, 187; Tandy, 58.
GORDEN, James, 118; John, 216; Nancy, 105; Thomas, 152, 159, 186.
GORDON, Alexander, 103; Charles, 150; George, 37, 80, 138; Henry, 199; Jacob, 121; James, 91, 133; John, 41; Josejh, 23; Larkin, 47; Mary, 52, 189; Richmond, 178; Robert, 113; Sarah, 199; Thomas, 156; William, 210; Zachariah, 107.
GORDY, Eli, 128; Elizabeth, 188; James, 116; Lott, 156; Noah, 131; Wilson, 90.
GORE, Pharis, 95; Rachel, 34; Richmond, 71; Thomas, 196.
GOREE, Amos, 70, 206; Israel, 136.
GORER, John, ...186
GORLEY, James, 25; Jonathan, 91.
GORMAN, John, 17; William, 26; Richard, 105.
GORORTO, David, 21; Joel, 202.
GORRIE, John, ...133
GORTNEY, David, ...199
GOSDIN, Elizabeth, ...70
GOSS, Benjamin, 143, 211; Hamilton, 168; John, 118; Matthew, 33; Orphon, 175; Susannah, 199; Wilson, 70, 199.
GOSSETT, John, ...181, 206
GOULD, George, 122; Richard, 165; William, 77.
GOULDEN, Lev., ...160
GOULDING, Palmer, ...162
GOWAN, John, ...23
GOWEN, Barney, 120; James, 11.
GOWDY, Thomas, ...150
GOYALE, Nancy, 39; Noyal, 147.
GRACE, Cannon, 70; Frances, 150; Hez., 29; John, 42, 69; Major, 112; Sally, 208; Thomas, 20, 64; William, 160.
GRADDY, Anna, 170; John, 180.
GRADY, Dennis, ...114
GRAGAN, Richard, ...199
GRAHAM, Daniel, 86; Duncan, 131, 166; Edward, 168; James, 40, 140; Josejh, 152, 177, 213; Sarah, 42; Thomas, 143, 201; William, 33, 169.
GRAMMAR, Gread, ...195
GRANAD, Sarcy, ...112
GRANADE, Adam, 194; Solomon, 51.
GRANAGE, Tabitha, ...185

GRANT, Ann, 115; Britton, 150; Charles, 20; Edmond, 90; Elizabeth, 5; Green, 212; Gregory, 201; Jesse, 11, 64; John, 133, 175; Jonathan, 120; Josejh, 18, 114, 182, 196; Josua, 108; Ketuma, 62; Nancy, 5; Priscilla, 42; Thomas, 5, 38, 170, 208; William, 5, 62, 195.
GRANTHAM, Elijah, 157, 193; Elizabeth, 156; Nathan, 11, 157; William, 208.
GRANTLAND, Elizabeth, 156; Flemming, 106; Nathan, 4, 151; Noel, 147; Samuel, 121; Seaton, 10; William, 208.
GRAVES, Bakel, 194, George, 177; Iverson, 214; James, 92; John, 33, 106, 170, 175, 193; Josua, 106; Joseph, 93, 106; Peres, 101; Richard, 62; William, 64.
GRAY, 9nn, 62; Annia, 1; Annis, 62; Absolom, 17, 162; Balden, 166; Buchner, 87; Daniel, 126, 203; David, 126, 69; Garrett, 98; George, 33, 108; Gregneris, 33, 201; Isaac, 30, 114; James, 27, 70, 153, 208, 214; John, 1, 26, 147, 209; Joshua, 1; Jonathan, 120; Mary, 116; Matilda, 55; Rebecca, 27, 41, 180; Richard, 122; Robert, 104; Sampson, 162; Samuel, 154; Seborn, 52; Stephen, 55; Susannah, 152; Thomas, 107, 194; Tobias, 151; William, 58, 203.
GRAYBILL, Jefferson, ...149
GRAYHAM, Archibald, 164; Duncan, 7, 8, 131; Joseph, 213; Thomas, 143, 200.
GRAYSON, John, ...195
GRAVIT, Charles, ...121
GREATHOUSE, William, ...105
GREAVES, Bakel, 194; Iverson, 214; James, 93; John, 33, 106, 170, 175, 193; Joseph, 93, 106; Peres, 101; Richard, 62; William, 64.
GREEN, Alston, 160; Burwell, 44; Charity, 45; Charles, 200; Esson, 92; Elias; Elizabeth, 50, 59; Enoch, 120; Frederick, 39, 173, 178; Frances, 159; Funderford, 113, 125; Garrett, 98; Gregorry, 81, 150; Henry, 185; Isaac, 37; Jacob, 103; James, 106, 116, 122, 149, 167, 187, 190; John, 2, 16, 106, 109, 167; Joseph, 205; Juden, 114; Julian, 113; Lemuel, 17, 146; Lewis, 147; Louisa, 52; Louise, 106; Martha, 66, 108; Mary, 27; McKeen, 16, 151; Michael, 140; Myles, 59; Moses, 156; Orphan, 131; Richard, 160; Robert, 32, 104, 132; Samuel, 124; Stephen, 188; Transylvania, 199; Thomas, 3, 107, 183;

William, 20, 36, 37, 46, 55, 107, 108, 173, 188, 190; Willis, 20, 212; Villet, 9.
GREENWWOD, John, 8, 40, 88; Thomas, 15, 91.
GREER, Acquilla, 106; Carlton, 55; David, 84, 113; Elisha, 187; Elizabeth, 83; Frances, 159; Garrett, 161; Gilbert, 88; Henry, 93; James, 26, 116; Jesse, 119; John, 31, 146; Josua, 19; Lititia, 69; Robert, 11; Thomas, 79, 88.
GREGORY, Elizabeth, 160; Elliot, 172; Hardy, 101; Henry, 204; John, 74; Joseph, 51; Rebecca, 204; Reuben, 19; William, 103, 151.
GRENADE, Carlton, _____ 55
GRESHAM, Albert, 135; Ferdinand, 28; Harris, 165; James, 72; John, 102, 137; Leah, 87, 157; Little, 21; Pleasant, 108; William, 58, 97, 155, 207.
GRESSOP, John, _____157
GRICE, Gabriel, 215; Jesse, 40; Lary, 139.
GRIER, Aaron, 173; Eli, 115; Elisha, 16; Garrett, 161; George, 122; John, 59.
GRIFFACE, Charles, _____ 55
GRIFFESS, Jacob, _____ 13
GRIFFETH, Jacob, _____ 14
GRIFFICE, Juniper, _____ 19
GRIFFEITH, Benjamin, 186; David, 20; James, 130; John, 2; Jonathan, 111; Mahala, 100; Robert, 57; William, 51, 118, 211.
GRIFFIN, Asa, 84; Blany, 77; C., 200; Comfort, 138, 198; D. J., 4; Ethelred, 215; Hardy, 70, 196; Henry, 59; James, 27, 56, 196; Jeremiah, 166; Job, 62; John, 5, 22, 72, 116, 170; Joseph, 8, 9, 12, 79, 177; J. S., 27; Larkin, 48, 198; Margaret, 195; Mary, 78; Michael, 40; Nancy, 57, 117; Noah, 145; Orphans, 139; Rachel, 137; Rebecca, 97; Reuben, 185; Richard, 161; Robert, 11; Sarah, 209; Thomas, 107; W., 114, 200; Wiggins, 93; William, 25, 53, 107, 152, 167.
GRIFFIS, John, _____ 59, 75, 159
GRIGGS, Asherry, 35; Brian, 2; Elias, 102; Henry, 169; James, 81; John, 105; Malissa, 18; Wiley, 159; William, 104.
GRIMAGES, Josh, _____ 28
GRIMER, Joseph, _____180
GRIMES, Elisha, 37; Gabriel, 44, 51, 119; James, 40; John, 192; Josejh, 145; Josiah, 50; Sterling, 126, 161, 174; Thomas, 31; William, 153.
GRIMNER, William, _____ 95

GRINDALL, John, _____ 63
GRINAGE, Alvin, _____193
GRINER, Samuel, _____112
GRINSTED, Robert, _____ 28
GRISHAM, Albert, 113; James, 105; Josiah, 21.
GRISSUP, James, _____210
GRISWOLD, Jesse, _____211
GRIZALL, Adali, _____ 85
GRIZZARD, Susannah, 104; Thomas, 93.
GRIZZLE, Joseph, 19; Thomas, 16; Wylie, 216.
GROCE, Hannah, 206; Lewis, 187; Shepard, 157.
GROGAN, Henry, 208; Williford, 23.
GROOCE, Sarah, _____202
GROMET, ohn, _____188
GROOMS, Conniel, 22; Rachel, 97; Robert, 85.
GROOVER, Jacob, _____ 79
GROVENSTEIN, John, 210; Joseph, 36.
GROVER, James, 85; John, 39, 157.
GROVES, John, _____108
GROSS, Edmon, 141; Ellison, 61; John, 38; Mary, 23; Solomon, 18; William, 60.
GROVER, John, _____ 11
GROVETT, Thomas, _____152
GRUB, Joah, _____165
GRUBBS, Benjamin, 155; James, 110; Thomas, 127.
GRUMBLES, John, 195; Robert, 33.
GUDDIN, Stephen, _____146
GUDE, Jesse, _____202
GUERRY, Jacob, _____103
GUEST, Sanford, _____139
GUFFIN, Gorge, 31; Thomas, 133; William, 93.
GUGEL, Mary, _____132
GUICE, Brattain, 197; Louis, 77; Nicholas, 187.
GUILMARTIN, John, _____173, 192
GUINN, Darby, 92; Luke, 87; Martha, 82; Transilvania, 199.
GULLETT, George, _____187
GUNBY, Levin, 183, 192, Mary, 120.
GUNN, Elizabeth, 32; Gabriel, 31; James, 44, 89; Larkin, 90, 216; William, 73, 185; Richard, 135, 141.
GUNNELL, William, _____180
GUNNELLS, Alsie, 211; M., 32; Stephen, 41.
GUNTER, Gideon, 186; James, 106.
GURINEAU, William, _____182
GUTHREY, Frances, 24; William, 153.
GUTHRIE, A., 203; Robert, 77; William, 167.
GUTHRY, C., _____136
GUTRIE, John, 88; William, 96.

GUTTERIE, Samuel, 215
GUTTERY, John, 185
GUTTRIE, John, 205, 192; Morgan, 40.
GUY, Ennis, 59; Levi, 148.
GUYNES, Harmon, 175
GUYTON, Charles, 95
GWINNETT, Robert, 149
GWYN, John, 118; Richard, 188.
HABERSHAM, Josejh, 105
HACKNEY, Martha, 103; Mary, 42; Robert, 126.
HADDERLY, Mary, 188
HADAWAY, David, 205; Levi, 178.
HADDAWAY, Levi, 71
HADDEN, Elizabeth, 187; Gordon, 162
HADDIN, Mary, 121; William, 63.
HADDOCK, Elizabeth, 77; Luke, 159; William, 18, 100, 178, 196.
HADEN, Anson, 46; Charles, 101.
HADLEY, Thomas, 205; Winnie, 116.
HADLEIGH, John, 155
HADMARK, George, 70
HAERSTON, James, 210
HAGAN, Daniel, 151; Francis, 36; John, 200; Joseph, 195.
HAGAN, Jeptha, 166
HAGGER, John, 122
HAGWOOD, James, 87
HAGGNEWOOD, Wiley, 42
HAILE, James, 155
HAILES, Salathiel, 121
HAILY, William, 164
HAIN, Eugenia, 25
HAINES, Irwin, 5; Richard, 175; Sarah, 190; William, 196.
HAINEY, John, 120, 171
HAIRCROW, Hugh, 177
HAIRSTON, James, 168; Peter, 50.
HAISTEN, Harrison, 142; William, 170.
HAISTON, John, 49
HAKINS, Benjamin, 151
HALE, Brantley, 143; Drucilla, 78; James, 204; Sameul, 160; Thomas, 100; Thompson, 146; William, 36, 87.
HALES, James, 57; Samuel, 160; Stinson, 137.
HALEY, James, 149
HALEYFIELD, Eldrige, 181
HALF, Pool, 52
HALIFIELD, Willis, 3
HALL, Abigail, 175; Alexander, 54; Amanda, 182; Armager, 82; Benjamin, 13, 145; Bolling, 198; Daniel, 38, 184; David, 123; Dempsey, 41, 143; Edy, 187; Elijah, 132; Elizabeth, 14, 207; Enoch, 14, 130; Erwin, 90; Espy, 117; Hardy, 128; Henry, 45, 166; Hirn, 110; Hugh, 186; Ignatius, 112; Instant, 130; Isaac, 97; James, 89, 132, 146, 169, 173, 191; Jeremiah, 140; John, 24, 44, 60, 67, 74, 75, 97, 138, 142, 157; Kindred, 33; L. M., 22; Martha, 169; Mary, 208; Nancy, 51, 61, 193, 198; Permelia, 55; Philo, 27; Robert, 26, 27, 127, 210; Ruthy, 45. Sampson, 176; Sarah, 23, 194, 214, 216; Seaborn, Standley, 8, 46; Stanley, 46; Thomas, 8, 117, 134, 174; William, 8, 65, 75, 120, 128, 135, 142, 203; Zachariah, 54.
HALLAM, John, 202
HALLIDAY, Nathaniel, 181; Samuel, 21.
HALLMARK, Nancy, 118
HALLOWAY, Norvelle, 71
HAM, Betsy, 201; Elenor, 51; Ichabud, 128; Orphan, 33; Stephen, 19; Smith, 100; William, 187, 188.
HAMACK, Thomas, 123
HAMIAL, Hugh, 139
HAMBETON, Mary, 137
HAMBY, Absalom, 133; Daniel, 54; Esther, 106; Isaac, 13; John, 49; Levi, 152; Nancy, 80; Orphan, 70; William, 44.
HAMBLET, Richard, 36
HAMBLETON, Claricy, 36; Cogbill, 64; David, 118; John, 184.
HAMBEICK, George, 142; Hannah, 47; Hiram, 25; John, 24, 34.
HAMEIL, George, 90
HAMEL, James, 176
HAMELTON, Sherord, 173
HAMES, William, 115
HAMIL, Bryant, 198; James, 93, 191; Simeon, 36.
HAMILTON, Abigail, 30; Andrew, 173; Barton, 151, 201; Bartow, 66; Daniel, 216; David, 70; Elisha, 210; Everard, 90; George, 78; James, 195; John, 95, 143, 151, 186; Josejh, 40, 91; Leon, 166; Rebecca, 136; Reuben, 101; Robert, 177; Simpson, 83; Steward, 115; Thomas, 153.
HAMLETT, William, 36, 204
HAMLEY, Rebecca, 64; S. E., 154.
HAMLIN, Catherine, 174; John, 156, 202; Thomas, 171.
HAMMACK, E., 39; Edmund, 127; Hope, 64; Jackson, 202; John, 28, 50; Johnson, 49; Littleton, 54; Mansell, 24; Nancell, 64; Willoughby, 63.
HAMMEL, John, 7
HAMMETT, James, 60; Robert, 178; Thomas, 90.
HAMMOCK, Daniel, 77; David, 34; Elijah, 96; James, 120, 191; John,

134; Robert, 216; Sarah, 165; Travis, 141; William, 66.
HAMMON, Josejh, ...199
HAMMOND, Abner, 70, 123, 173; Amos, 123; Charles, 104; John, 70, 98, 205; Susannah, 53; William, 113, 155.
HAMMONS, Abra., ...135
HAMNER, Mathew, ...58
HAMMERS, Mathew, ...83
HAMPHILL, Jonathan, ...168
HAMPTON, Amos, 201; Benjamin, 98; Henry, 132; Hubbard, 118, 187; Jacob, 11; John, 24; Sarah, 189; Thomas, 212; Wade, 183; William, 207.
HAMRICK, Benjamin, 111, 196; Harrison, 124; John, 26; William, 50.
HANCE, John, ...164
HANCOCK, Allen, 196; Elizabeth, 127; Isaac, 67, 130, 205; Isom, 111; James, 155; Jane, 121; Jeremiah, 59; Joel, 44; John 65, 202; Josiah, 183; Mary, 46; Nancy, 131; P. G., 35; Rhoda, 178; Richardson, 44; Robert, 9; Taliaferre, 190; William, 71, 119.
HAND, Bayard, 4; Daniel, 38; Henry, 49; ohn, 21; Josejh, 19, 38; Rachel, 126; Sarah, 209; William, 20, 55, 59, 110, 142, 163, 179, 189.
HANDLEY, Frederick, 137; Sarah, 169.
HANES, David, ...210
HANEY, Elizabeth, 139; Jem, 28.
HANN, Melton, ...213
HANNA, Andrew, ...162
HANNAH, Alexander, 22; Orphan, 145, 163; William, 132.
HANNIGAN, James, ...6
HANNON, Henry, ...206
HANSARD, Janet, 192; Joseph, 8; Thomas, 167.
HANSFORD, George, 198; John, 183; Susan, 95.
HANSOME, Michal, ...58, 106
HANSON, James, 13; John, 6; Peggy, 103; Richard, 38; Thomas, 44.
HARAL, William, ...162, 182
HARALDSON, Bradly, ...44
HARALSON, Jesse, ...80
HARB, Wiley, ...143
HARBIN, John, 136; Nathaniel, 20, 126.
HARBOUR, Littleberry, ...91
HARBROOK, John, ...89
HARBUCK, Henry, 58; James, 16; Michael, 191; Nicholas, 22, 173; Orphans, 143; William, 81.
HARCROW, Samuel, ...102
HARDAGE, Adam, 10; Jesse, 111; Orphans, 146; William.

HARDAGREE, Elenor, ...40
HARDEMAN, Elizabeth, ...154
HARDAWAY, Grief, 195; James, 33; John, 116.
HARDEMAN, Benjamin, 28; Joel, 157; Thomas, 48.
HARDEN, Edward, 38, 131; Henry, 113; James, 71; John, 38; Patrick, 54; Sandlin, 19; Robert, 139, 145; William, 64.
HARDEWAY, George, 93; Marging, 176.
HARDIE, John, ... 81, 154
HARDIN, Adam, 64; Ann, 188; Henry, 134; James, 67, 212; Jesse, 212; John, 123; William, 151.
HARDING, Hudson, 53; Thomas, 35.
HARDISON, Benjamin, 115; Seth, 161.
HARDIWAY, Mason, ...216
HARDMAN, Andrew, 94, 120; David, 35; Judd, 3; William, 132.
HARDWICK, Andrew, 94, 120; David, 35; Judd, 3; William, 132.
HARDY, Aaron, 213; Anny, 170; Charles, 30, 190, 212; Henry, 210; J., 190; James, 160; Jesse, 206; Thompson, 165; Winny, 179.
HARE, Joel, ...70
HAREGROVES, A. J., ...96
HARGIS, Philip, ...70
HARGROVE, Charles, 89; Isaac, 22; James, 191; John, 36; Mary, 138; Richard, 190; Robert, 61; Samuel, 100, 116; William, 19, 100, 106.
HARKINS, Armand, 122; Josejh, 129, 195.
HARKNESS, Robert, ...23, 50, 53
HARKEY, Daniel, ...163
HARLAND, Judith, 181; Zachariah, 71.
HARLEY, Joseph, ...33
HARLIN, Samuel, ...156
HARMON, Frederick, *; Hazekiah, 187; Miles, 108; Zachariah, 212.
HARN, Henry, 137; William, 57.
HARNAGE, George, ...11
HARNELL, Victor, ...33
HARNESBURG, Adam, 206; Mary, 44
HARON, Daniel, ...141
HARP, Emaline, 91; John, 24, 95; Maunin, 18; Permelia, 179; Raleigh, 2.
HARPE, James, ...31, 153
HARPER, Ann, 115, 158; Amos, 150; Bedford, 69; Edmond, 63; Henry, 172, 215; Joaines, 109, 147, 157; John, 95, 165; Joseph, 53; Malachi, 188; Martha, 156; Mary, 34; Nathaniel, 16; Orphans, 206; Shadrack, 176; Samuel, 177; Sexton, 186; Shad., 46; Shadrack, 176; Solomon, 55; William, 25, 31, 75.

HARRALL, Hardy, 18; Morgan, 2; Orphan, 85.
HARRALSON, Hiram, 108; J., 56; Joseph, 71; Vincent, 61.
HARREL, Daniel, 184; John, 84.
HARRELL, Ann, 176; Demsy, 189; Elijah, 168; Francis, 93; H. H., 87; James, 102; Jane, 110; John, 101, 119; Lewis, 119; Moses, 118; Rebecca, 107.
HARRIS, Agness, 131; Alcy, 23, 43; Alexander, 65; Alvis, 135; Ann, 94, 127; Archibald, 174; Ann, 94, 127; Ausborn, 187; B., 36; Benjamin, 26, 152; Britton, 202; Buckner, 126; Camilla, 78; Catherina, 216; Charity, 101; Charles, 120, 152; Church, 128; Clara, 45; Cob. W., 38; Daniel, 19; David, 9, 102, 21; Edward, 6, 40, 69, 186; Eli, 109; Elizabeth, 36, 79; George, 164; Gideon, 209; Graves, 77; Hardy, 45, 207; Henry, 133, 156; Inverson, 22; Jacob, 154; Jarnes, 33, 43, 175, 202; Jeremiah, 195; Jesse, 8, 175; John, 11, 20, 35, 74, 111, 129, 167, 183; Josejh, 89; Joshua, 86; Lewis, 3; Little, 41; Littleberry, 161; Majors, 54, 128; Mary, 96, 97; Mary, Melissa, 207; Mathew, 158; Miles, 130; Moses, 161; N. H., 151; Nathan, 75; Nelson, 137; Orphans, 109; Peter, 162; Polly, 80.
HARRISON, Aacline, 196; Alexander, 119; Benjamin, 120, 123; Charity, 80; Daniel, 114, 132; Edward, 21; Eli, 54, 213; Elijah, 95, 118; Elizabeth, 75; Francis, 104; George, 45, 67; Henry, 88; James, 125; Jefferson, 165; Jeftha, 174; Jesse, 74, 89; John, 40, 75; Jonathan, 30; Joseph, 48, 163; Mariah, 53; Martha, 40; Mary, 6, 153; Overtow, 99; Reuben, 83, 200; Robert, 18; Sampson, 92; Seaborn, 17, 129; Thomas, 114, 127; Tilman, 60; Vinson, 2; William, 209.
HARRELSON, Simon, 129, 157; Solomon, 35; William, 134, 200.
HARRELSON, Elenor, 47; William, 71
HARROLD, James, _____43
HARRILL, George, _____196
HARRIN, Alexander, _____129
HARRINGTON, Catherine, 210; Drewry, 114; Huldah, 159; Silas, 136.
HARROD, Jesse, _____100
HARROL, Cohnan, 136; Zilpha, 142.
HARROLD, Arianna, _____185
HATCHCOCK, James, _____114
HATCHER, Henry, 109, 172; Isham, 58; James, 65; John, 16, 36; Joseph, 65.

HART, Boncy, 122; Elizabeth, 61; James, 181; Moses, 33; Oginsdale, 213; Robert, 175; Samuel, 174; Thomas, 26, 111; William, 137.
HARTFIELD, Caleb, _____131, 150
HARTLEY, Fere., _____78
HARTON, Nancy, _____177
HARTFIELD, A., 83; Allen, 202; Andrew, 181; Berry, 28; Isaac, 211; Mary, 24; Moses, 99; Richard, 74, 86; William, 41, 118, 131.
HARVEY, Daniel, _____128
HARVELL, Celia, 195; Mason, 140.
HARVEY, Benjamin, 46; Betsy, 55; Edmund, 37; Elizabeth, 123; Evan, 29, 166; Javers, 166; John, 74, 158, 187; Nathaniel, 189; Polly, 34; Robert, 33, 94; Stephen, 42; William, 123.
HARVIL, Elliss, _____42
HARVILL, John, 209; Weston, 111.
HARWARD, Stephen, _____123
HARWELL, Alexandre, 136; Anderson, 54; James, 38; Littleton, 213; Needham, 204; Riley, 146; Samuel, 197; Thomas, 146; Vines, 92.
HASCELL, James, _____108
HASKIN, Joseph, 175; Maryann, 177.
HASLET, M. A., _____10
HASLIP, Nancy, _____94
HASTY, Jemima, 3, 9, 92; Joseph, 169; Noel, 190; Obediah, 174; William, 111; Willis, 52.
HASWELL, John, _____7
HATCHER, Josiah, 1, 55, 204; Matilda, 73; Sarah, 42; Thomas, 119; Torbet, 133; William, 19, 191, 216.
HATCHETT, William, _____51
HATFIELD, Jane, 116; Washington, 26.
HATHHORN, James, 49; Thomas, 3, 18; William, 63.
HATHORN, Hugh, _____118
HATLEY, Orphan, _____132, 159
HATTAWAY, David, _____138
HATTEN, John, 205; Peter, 157.
HATTOCK, Elijah, 39; James, 125.
HATTON, William, _____39
HANVER, Orphans, _____160
HAWES, Liddleton, 153; Orphans, 180; William, 92.
HAWKINS, Allen, 64; Aug., 3; Bessium, 209; Charles, 124; Edward, 211; William, 79, 210.
HAWL, William, _____32
HAWORD, James, _____11, 70
HAWPE, George, _____40
HAWS, John, 135; Newton, 201; Hawthorn; James, 132; John, 48; Josiah, 94; William, 184.
HAY, Catherine, 151; Gideon, 2; Isaac,

87; James, 9; John, 110; Joseph, 8; William, 133.
HAYDEN, Anson, ...65
HAYGOOD, Appleton, ...157
HAYLES, Elizabeth, 66; Jane, 15.
HAYMAN, Ann, 94; James, 124; Stouten, 10, 42.
HAYMON, Jere, ...82
HAYNES, Anthony, 108; Jasper, 83; Jonathan, 162; John, 114, 174, 201; Martha, 61; Moses, 1, 25, 158; Nancy, 94; Smith, 122; Thomas, 186; William, 98.
HAYNEY, Elizabeth, ...150
HAYNIE, Elizabeth, 127; James, 1; Tabitha, 118.
HAYNES, Jesse, 181; John, 29.
HAYS, David, 97; Ed., 78; Edw., 5; Edward, 100; Eliza, 60; George, 206; Gilbert, 45; James, 27, 111, 114; Jane,, 152; Lorenzo, 116; Martha, 45, 166; Nancy, 186; Rebecca, 96; Thomas, 88.
HAYWOOD, Thomas, ...133
HAZARD, John, ...133
HAZELHURST, Robert, ...23, 210
HAZELRIG, Benjamin, ...120
HAZZARD, Augusta, 185; Thomas, 37; William, 94, 129.
HEAD, Charles, 111; D. B., 99, 127; HUBBER, 81; Isaac, 180; James, 137, 143; John, 43, 56, 183; Margaret, 44, 150; Thomas, 8; William, 149; Willis, 214.
HEADE, John, ...178
HEADRICK, C. T. & A., 211; George, 79; John, 124.
HEARCY, George, ...157
HEARD, Charles, 50, 97, 136; Daniel, 40; Eliza, 18; Elizabeth, 210; Frederick, 25; George, 61, 175, 201; Hilsman, 210; John, 111, 187; Sarah, 139; Susan, 85; Thomas, 94; William, 49, 177.
HEARDON, Jeremiah, ...58
HEARN, Benjamin, 103; Elijah, 190; Elizabeth, 50; Frances, 93; James, 115; John, 28, 195; Samuel, 204; William, 109.
HEARNDEN, James, ...34
HEARSTON, William, ...98
HEATH, Abel, 115; Cicero, 83; Edward, 176; Isaac, 17; James, 34; John, 185; Josejh, 130, 212; Jordan, 49; Lewis, 132, 174; Louisa, 209; Moses, 47; Nancy, 92, 205; Rigdon, 188; Samuel, 52; Tarleton, 204; William, 33, 200.
HEATON, David, 47; James, 176, 186.
HEBBARD, Wirmeford, ...185

HEETH, Abraham, 35; Frederick, 116; Henry, 128; Kozster, 191; Winifred, 35.
HEFLIN, John, 211; Sarah, 32; Wiat, 40; Wilie, 155.
HEFNER, John, ...17, 49
HEGGIE, Archibald, 167; Thomas, 209
HEIDERPRAN, D., ...196
HEITH, F. B., ...39
HELMS, John, ...62
HELTON, Abraham, 109; Ezekiel, 74; James, 90, 140, 152, 198; Joseph, 203; S., 108, 112; Thomas, 17, 193.
HEMPHILL, John, 156; Marcus, 213; Pleasant, 196; Robert, 60, 89; Tilman, 61; Henden; T. H., 55.
HENDERSON, Alexander, 80; Andrew, 51; Asa, 211; Catherine, 159; Charles, 140; Daniel, 171; David, 119; E., 85; George, 23; Greenville, 61; Hannah, 180; Henry, 52; Hilary, 83; James, 11; Jeptha, 136; John, 64, 142, 153, 154, 186, 198; Joseph, 121; Martha, 24; Mary, 6; Michael, 82; Nancy, 132; Nathaniel, 118; Richard, 45, 121, 127; Ruth, 164; Sally, 171; Samuel, 110; Simeon, 75; William, 87, 145, 189, 194; Winnie, 5; Zadock, 67.
HENDON, Andrew, 69; Elias, 1; Elijah, 182; Hartsfield, 203; Henry, 1; James, 207, 208; Robin, 61; Thomas, 46.
HENDRICK, Ann, 215; Asa, 199; Elisha, 100; Eliza, 122; Hezekiah, 83, 199; Jesse, 98, 132, 139; Levi, 117; Mary, 178; Orphans, 103; Siah, 90; Whitehead, 82; Zack, 45.
HENDRICKS, Elizabeth, 129; James, 72; Sarah, 129; William, 112.
HENDRICKSON, George, ...198
HENDRIX, John, ...175
HENDRY, Robert, ...121
HENLEY, James, 92; John, 103; Micajah, 130; Sarah, 15.
HENLY, James, 146, 206; Slaton, 131; William, 126.
HENMAN, Frederick, ...33
HENNIGAN, Darby, ...82
HENRING, Richard, ...191
HENRY, Benjamin, 85; Daniel, 174; David, 163; George, 109; James, 214; John, 36; Mathew, 101; Nancy, 19; Samuel, 33, 169, 203; Sarah, 33; William, 52, 57, 164.
HENSON, Elias, 108; Elisha, 149; Isaac, 156; Joseph, 88.
HERB, George, 182, 188; William, 49.
HERBERT, Hardy, ...37
HEREN, Dolcy, ...113
HERIN, Dolsy, ...154

HERNDON, B., 101; Benjamin, 15; Cornelius, 84; D., 101; Edward, 56, 98; John, 169; Joseph, 51; Michael, 145; Sena, 104; Walker, 3; William, 90.
HERNE, Lewis, ...103
HERON, Orphans, ...170
HERRON, James, 22; William, 29.
HERRIAGE, Ruben, ...
HERRIDGE, John, ...160
HERRIN, Elijah, 27; Mary, Ann, 199; Warren, 18; William, 27.
HERRING, Elisha, 162, 205; George, 62; Hollen, 187; James, 28, 115; Jesse, 212, 215.
HERRINGTON, Eph., 49; J., 122; John, 148; Martin, 138; Moses, 145.
HERVIE, Franklin, ...153
HESTER, David, 39; Elizabeth, 5; Stephen, 46, 117, 161; Thomas, 52; William, 77, 175; Zachariah, 52, 122, 159.
HEUGHS, Ann, ...148
HEUSTON, William, ...208
HEWELL, James, 176; Love, 85.
HEWSTON, James, ...118
HICK, William, ...196
HICKEL, Orphan, ...150
HICKES, Isaac, ...193
HICKEY, Benjamin, 19; James, 20; Stephen, 46; William, 125.
HICKLE, John, ...103, 134
HICKLIN, Sarah, ...176
HICKMAN, Capelin, 111; Lewis, 112, 165; Martha, 88; Mary, 85; Walter, 132.
HICKMOND, Orphan, ...170
HICKS, Daniel, 107; David, 134; Eliza, 38; Gillam, 85; Irwin, 38; Isaac, 117; Jane, 132, 133; Lewis, 60; Lucy, 174; Mark, 92; Nathaniel, 105; Susannah, 113; Thomas, 17, 46, 210.
HICKSON, Thomas, ...111
HIDE, Austin; J. D., 29; Noel, 83; Orphan, 29, 191.
HIGDEN, Daniel, ...139
HIGDON, Charles, ...28
HIGGASON, William, ...180
HIGGINBOTHAM, Alexander, 8; B., 30; Elizabeth, 146; James, 128; 163, John, 208; Milly, 140; Robert, 21; S., 178; Thomas, 213.
HIGGINS, Caleb, 210; Charles, 195; Reuben, 50; Rich, 170; Richard, 114; Roger, 175; Wiley, 178.
HIGGS, John, ...215
HIGH, Samuel, ...159
HIGHFILL, David, 146; John, 40.
HIGHSMITH, David, 24, 87; Jacob,
45; James, 42; John, 40, 142; Thomas, 180.
HIGHT, Ishmall, 90; Wylie, 16.
HIGHTOWER, Charnell, 61; Elizabeth, 71; Enoch, 108; Isaac, 1, 120; James, 38, 109; Jesse, 59, 164; John, 141; Jonathan, 112, 162; Martha, 193; Mary, 210; Math, 2; Raleigh, 193; William, 96; Wingfield, 108.
HILL, Abner, 62, 83; Alfred, 25; Ambrash, 56; Amos, 211; Anderson, 46; Asap, 215; Benjamin, 61, 88, 209; Berry, 105, 142; B. K., 38; Burwell, 72; Catherine, 2; David, 52, 173; Ealium, 91; Elias, 106; Enoch, 105; Fielding, 122, 135, 141; Frances, 188; Frederick, 39; George, 34, 184, 186; Henry, 45, 75; Hilton, 132; Isaac, 20, 108; Isaiah, 183; James, 1, 18, 64, 72, 84, 210; Jeremiah, 196; Jesse, 127; Joseph, 53; Joshua, 126; Ludowick, 113; Magdeline, 177, Martha, 99; Martin, 52; Mordecai, 80, 165; Mountain, 125, 182; Nancy, 129; Orphan, 47, 74, 75, 193; Persilla, 193; Richard, 132; Richard, 132; Sarah, 88, 120; Stacy, 212; Thomas, 2, 36, 152, 155; Walten, 25; Wil., 4; Will'by, 48; William, 86, 99, 132, 142, 210.
HILLES, William, ...49
HILLIARD, Dennis, 31; Henry, 120, 155; James, 131; J. M., 1; Seaborn, 64; William, 136.
HILLS, Dennis, ...172
HIIL, Francis, 82; Thomas, 129.
HILSMAN, Francis, 90; James, 15.
HILSON, William, ...65
HILTON, Abraham, ...203
HINDSMAN, William, ...200
HINER, Lewis, ...177
HINES, Elizabeth, 60; Henry, 202; H. H., 23; James, 7, 37, 69; Jesse, 38; John, 128, 134; Lamach, 94; Martha, 101, 189; Nathaniel, 180; Orphan, 109; R. K., 138; Robert, 38, 195.
HINESLY, Elizabeth, 162; Thomas, 28
HINGSON, John, ...59
HINSON, Elias, 181; James, 30; Jesse, 30; John, 128; Sarah, 146; Tapley, 209.
HINTON, Allen, 153; Fielding, 158; James, 192; John, 1, 72, 135, 179, 201; Thomas, 208.
HIPPS, Joseph, ...205
HISSKEY, Washington, ...65
HIST, James, ...208
HISTERLEY, Green, ...110
HITCHCOCK, Er'n, 141; E. R. W., 191; Jesse, 166; John, 2; Ranford, 22; William, 74, 211.

HITCHENS, Sarah, ...90
HITE, Gabriel, ...70
HIXON, Elizabeth, ...82
HOARD, William, ...206
HOBBS, Henry, 72; Irey, 103; John, 23, 37, 98, 112, 185; Joseph, 70; Mary, 169; Nathan, 152; Orphan, 61; Robert, 42; Solomon, 77.
HOBB, Alexander, 786; Andrew, 114; James, 40, 149; William, 32.
HOBSON, John, 60; Joseph, 46.
HODGE, Andrew, 214; Elliott, 193; Henry, 155; Hosa, 209; John, 1, 118, 163, 185; Samuel, 127; Tolleston, 40; William, 54.
HODGEINS, H., ...157
HODGES, Abel, 141; Alfred, 5; Alsy, 140; Archibald, 146; Benjamin, 188; Elias, 80; Elijaha, 47; Elizabeth, 195; Foreman, 148, 166; Hardy, 25; Haris, 8; Henry, 179, 104; John, 64, 101, 119, 170, 181; Joseph, 42, 74, 173; Joshua, 207; Orphan, 188; Redding, 195; Sherwood, 71; William, 123.
HODNAL, John, ...168
HODNETT, William, ...99
HODO, Sarrah, ...100
HOFF, James, ...208
HOGAN, David, 210; Francis, 35; James, 158, 190; Thomas, 29.
HOGANS, William, ...115
HODGE, William, ...139
HOGEN, Nancy, ...176
HOGG, Aggy, 44; James, 208; Lucy, 16; Samuel, 164.
HOGUN, Jackson, ...137
HOLLBROOK, Absalom, 145, 205; Greenberry, 130; Jesse, 210; Pleasant, 129; Thomas, 63.
HOLCOMB, Burnett, 158; Ezekial, 107; Hampton, 193; Henry, 172; James, 41, 147; Reuben, 145; Sherwood, 99; Solomon, 63.
HOLCOMB, Alford, 43; G. H., 106; James, 51, 64, 117; Reuben, 17; Sherwood, 114; William, 111.
HOLDEN, Lucy, 132; Thomas, 55.
HOLDBROOK, Christopher, 36; Priscilla, 126.
HOLDEN, Mathew, ...123
HOLDER, Elizabeth, 99; John, 44, 63, 132, 198; Samuel, 46; William, 100.
HOLEFIELD, Eldridge, ...100
HOLIDAY, James, ...34
HOLDRIDGE, Aaron, ...166
HOLIFIELD, William, ...145
HOLLAN, Orphans, ...187
HOLLAND, Abraham, 108; Edith, 188; Elisha, 74; Elizabeth, 34; Green, 19; Henry, 129; Isaac, 9;

Jacob, 10, 149; James, 71; John, 78, 205; LaFayette, 149; Thomas, 5, 30; William, 203.
HOLLEMAN, David, 25, 45; Frederick, 192.
HOLLEY, Arnold, 142; Benjamin, 31; James, 85; Presley, 50; Richard, 152; William, 35, 43, 62.
HOLLIDAY, Henry, 55; John, 121; Obedience, 187; Priscilla, 16.
HOLIFIELD, Orphans, ...57
HOLLINGSWORTH, Isaac, 51; Jacob, 83; Thomas, 107; Zilphy, 64.
HOLLINSWORTH, Amos, 15, 202; Calip, 28, 184; John, 45; Thomas, 17; Zebulon, 198.
HOLLIS, Charles, 159; Elizabeth, 37; Reuben, 145; Samuel, 199; Thomas, 41, 54, 193.
HOLLIWAY, Benjamin, ...194
HOLLOMAN, Daniel, 139; Elisha, 201; John, 15; Leis, 7.
HOLLOMON, William, ...27
HOLLON, Brinkley, 34; Benjamin, 90; Henry, 122.
HOLLOWAY, James, 41; John, 155; Mary, 99; Samuel, 188; Zachariah, 173.
HOLLY, Pleasant, 53; Samuel, 86, 165; Temperance, 133; William, 20.
HOLMAN, George, 97; Jacob, 61.
HOLMES, Abigail, 101; Edwin, 21; Frederick, 179; Garnet, 30; Isaac, 190; Isaiah, 75; James, 150; John, 197; Jonathan, 187; Keziah, 62; Maxfield, 107; Nathan, 90; Reuben, 131; Solomon, 169; Thomas, 150.
HOLMS, Solomon, ...56
HOLOWAY, Asa, ...42
HOLSEY, George, 28, 214; James, 205, Susannah, 183.
HOLT, Cicero, 20; Elbert, 47; Elizabeth, 158, 186; James, 70; Richard, 43, 70; Robert, 117; Samuel, 20; Seaborn, 189; Simon, 151; Thaddeus, 160; Thomas, 55.
HOLTON, James, 205; Nathaniel, 52, 145; William, 117, 210.
HOLTZCLAW, Benjamin, 138; Hosea, 75; John, 127; Sarah, 182.
HONEYCUT, Edmond, ...202
HOOD, Alfred, 51; Andrew, 128; Avery, 90; Benjamin, 109, 144; Elisha, 22, 84; Green, 22, 62; John, 78; Josiah, 188; Nathaniel, 108 Rebeckah, 188; Sion, 42; William, 48.
HOOF, Sylvester, ...1
HOOK, Thomas, ...86
HOOKS, Hillary, 87, 173; Jesse, 123.

HOOPER, Enoch, 62; James, 110, 199; Mathew, 145; Obediah, 99; William, 5, 66.
HOOTON, Henry, 160; James, 109.
HOOVER, John, _____49
HOPKINS, Aaron, 129; Dennis, 184; Elisha, 69; Francis, 143; George, 17, '142; James, 34; Josiah, 54; Margaret, 3; Samuel, 120; Susannah, 110; William, 4, 67.
HOPPER, Jonathan, 89; Rolly, 147; Thomas, 71.
HOPSON, Hardy, 10, 22; Martin, 4; Wiley, 36, 110, 141; William, 119.
HORGAN, William, _____210
HORN, David, 63; Elisha, 209; Isaac, 55; John, 6, 10; Josiah, 118; Mary, 28; Moses, 160; Sarah, 22; Whittington, 131; William, 4, 167.
HORNBUCH, Richard, _____115
HORNBUCKLE, Nath'l, 156; Richard, 180.
HORNE, Richard, _____127
HORNING, Philip, _____189
HORNSBY, Henry, 155; P. J. E., 33.
HORSELEY, Greene, 9; James, 159, 165; Val., 15.
HORSELY, John, _____61
HORTON, Amos, 132; Fletcher, 130; Frederick, 97, 185; George, 100; Hubbard, 48; James, 82, 93, 136; John, 9; Joshua, 2; Laban, 88, 173; Matilda, 125; Samuel, 132; William, 56, 64, 144.
HOSCH, Mathew, _____19
HOSKINS, Benjamin, 200; John, 28; Silas, 139; Silvanis, 22; William, 28, 54.
HOSLEY, Eliz., _____44
HOUGE, William, _____107
HOUGHTON, Alexander, 57; John, 29, William, 88.
HOULTON, Alexander, 148; Salathiel, 163.
HOUSE, Harris, 158; Lawrence, 143; Mary, 175; William, 57, 67, 75, 171; Zachariah, 45, 206.
HOUSTON, Benajah, 98; James, 56; John, 24, 44; Samuel, 124; Thomas, 16, 99, 124.
HOUSTOUN, George, _____171
HOUZE, Auderson, _____31, 60
HOUZZE, James, _____184
HOVATEL, Artemas, _____170
HOVARTER, Jacob, _____180, 196
HOW, Hiram, _____190
HOWALL, Thomas, _____38
HOWARD, Abraham; Alexander, 131; Sas, 122, 147; Benjamin, 152; Dossey, 135; Edith, 163; Edward, 77, 87, 123, 152, 213; Elizabeth, 25,

40, 106, 206, 209; Esra, 141; Groves, 33; Harmon, 33; Hiram, 116; Homer, 129; Isaac, 176; James, 102, 197, 207; Jane, 158; Jermiah, 162; John, 9, 160, 214; Lemuel, 194; Lucretia, 126; Lucy, 174; Mary, 17, 197; Martha, 80; Milton, 188; Norflight, 216; Robert, 213; Samuel, 111; Sarah, 88, 191; Solomon, 207; Thomas, 69, 106, 113, 159; William, 42, 77, 176; Willis, 80.
HOWEL, Richard, _____70
HOWELL, Abraham, 60; Alexander, 69; Daniel, 103; Dempsey, 94; Even, 192; Frankey, 158; Gabriel, 197; Henry, 38, 139; Holliday, 140; Isaac, 8; James, 185; John, 27, 53, 155, 165; Joseph, 5, 46, 198; Joshua, 25; Levina, 33; Mary, 152; Matilda, 139; Mayberry, 71; Michael, 52; Robert, 213; Sarah, 4; Wilea, 194; William, 126.
HOY, Elizabeth, _____182
HOUSEWORTH, Michal, 71; Philip, 122.
HOYAT, John, _____27
HUBANKS, Isaac, _____203
HUBBARD, Bennett, 41; Booker, 96; Elijah, 71; James, 107; John, 130, 214; Joseph, 49; Mary, 97; Mathew, 159; Nancy, 102, 136; Orphans, 82; Samuel, 15; Thaddeus, 145; Timothy, 77; Vincent, 201; William, 137; Wilson, 97.
HUBBELL, T. M., _____38
HUBERT, Moses, _____22
HUCKABY, Abby, 83; David, 89; James, 105; Sarah, 168; William, 103.
HUCKLEY, Seaborn, _____212
HUDDLESTON, John, 158; William, 44, 61.
HUDGENS, Reuben, _____42
HUDGINS, Ansel, 150, 188; John, 132; Josiah, 29, 87, 83, 213; Reuben, 65.
HUDLER, John, _____176, 195
HUDNO, James, _____174
HUDLOW, Maria, _____183
HUDSON, Charles, 114; David, 31, 66; Eli, 67; Elijah, 33, 183; Elizabeth, 5, 33, 183; George, 107; Isaac, 185; John, 132, 136; Joshua, 63, 183; Llewellyn, 122; Lucy, 186; Madison, 114; Molly, 204; Rush, 180; Sion, 122; Thomas, 212; Wesley, 115; William, 75, 136.
HUDSPETH, Mark, 69; Thomas, 88; William, 2, 72.
HUEY, James, _____21
HUFF, Abner, 198; Edward, 162;

George, 109, 146; Harrison, 146; Hawkins, 166; John, 203; Presley, 58; Ralph, 197; Ransom, 6; Susannah, 10; William, 69.
HUGES, Eliza, 125
UHGHBANKS, William, 201
HUGES, Dempsey, 178; George, 20; Harden, 147; Jane, 49; John, 110; Samuel, 70, 159, 211; Simon, 118; Sophia, 104; Thomas, 187; W. G., 135; William, 36, 82, 188, 210.
HUGHEY, Joseph, 139; William, 214.
HUGHEY, James, 145
HUGHS, Eligh, 162; John, 27; Sarah, 127, 175; Susan, 127.
HUGINS, Dolly, 88
HUGUENIN, Edward, 142
HUGULEY, Charles, 6; Jacob, 104; Job, 97; William, 161.
HUIE, James, 205
HULEN, Wade, 173
HULING, Elizabeth, 200
HULL, Latham, 131
HULSEY, Elijah, 177, 171; Hardin, 34; James, 143; Jemmins, 86; Jesse, 124.
HULSY, Asa, 59
HUMAN, Alexander, 206
HUMBER, Robert, 86
HUMPHRIES, Elijah, 129; George, 33; James, 69, 90; Jesse, 166; Joseph, 28; M. T., 101; Rachel, 203; Robert, 93; Shadrack, 191; Thomas, 179.
HUMPHREY, Benjamin, 122; Hardy, 195; Joseph, 194; Malinda, 202; Mathew, 18.
HUMPHRIS, John, 153
HUNLEY, William, 25
HUNNEY, William, 161
HUNNICUT, Sarah, 102
HUNT, Benjamin, 156; Daniel, 130, 196; Elijah, 66; Elizabeth, 66; George, 98, 152; Isaac, 66; James, 159, 192; John, 26, 27, 116, 204; Littleton, 102; Matilda, 66; Orphans, 33, 206; Sarah, 66; Thomas, 44, 121, 177; Turner, 37; William, 2, 26, 66, 72, 146, 185, 216.
HUNTER, Abraham, 22; Bryabt, 53; David, 95; Edward, 193; Elijah, 115, 211; Elizabeth, 110; Hardy, 82; Henry, 25; Job, 185, 216; John, 163; J. W., 25, 112, 172; Martha, 41; Mary, 54; Richard, 175; Robert, 66; Seth, 177.
HUNTINGTON, G. W., 109
HUNTON, Charles, 135; James, 112; John, 132.
HURE, Stephen, 173,, 209
HURST, Bryant, 105; Felix, 30, 91; John, 145, 88; Major, 20, 198; Simon, 122; William, 173.
HURT, Benjamin, 29; Sally, 199; William, 43, 93, 134. •
HUSK, Bryant, 201; Danuel, 47, 141; Jacob, 58.
HUSKY, Claiborn, 100; John, 75.
HUSON, David, 183; Judith, 37; Thomas, 201; William, 145.
HUST, William, 138
HUSTES, Moses, 173
HUSTON, Isaac, 145; John, 6, 57; Zachariah, 158.
HUTCHENS, Berry, 209; Mary, 29.
HUTCHEONS, Daniel, 192
HUTCHERSON, James, 183
HUTCHESON, Henry, 26
HUTCHINGS, Seaborn, 101
HUTCHINS, James, 171; John, 141; Rigdon, 21.
HUTCHINSON, Adam, 169; Barbara, 93; David, 85; Jane, 211; John, 89; Seaborn, 49.
HUTCHISON, Lorenzo, 221
HUTSON, Anna, 33; Isham, 130; John, 111; Sally, 52; William, 117; Zaddack, 125.
HUTTO, Henry, 121, 162
HYDE, David, 117; Willis, 19, 101.
HYDRICK, Powell, 48
HYSLER, Daniel, 23
HYSLIP, James, 175; Winney, 9; Zerubabel, 89.
ICKNER, Michaiel, 73
IHLY, Orphan, 90; Samuel, 55.
INGLET, Hezekich, 27; Hugh, 25, 112; John, 10; Matthew, 210; William, 13.
INGRAHAM, David, 40; E., 213; George, 70; Orphan, 178; N. D., 213
INGRAM, Bartholomew, 149; Benjammin, 134; Burwell, 53; Charles, 90; Clary, 102; Consel, 36; Gilford, 202; Henry, 143; Hugh, 200; John, 18, 86, 89, 95, 99, 154; Robert, 98; Thomas, 37, 186; William, 203.
INLOW, Thomas, 42, 215
INMAN, Alfred, 101
INMON, Daniel, 135
IRBY, Allen, 111; Henry, 86.
IRVINE, Alexander, 85, 90, 170; Leving, 164.
IRWIN, David, 44, 89; Hannah, 22; James, 180; John, 140, 214; Nancy, 113, 208; Sarah, 128ffi Thomas, 124; William, 156.
IRWING, Mary, 161
ISAIN, Henry, 130
ISLER, John, 32
IVERSON, Alfred, 213
IZLY, Philip, 149

IVEY, Ephriam, 62; Henry, 12, 15; John, 136.
IVINS, Rebecca, _____16
IVY, Adam, 164; Calvin, 87; Charles, 92; Elias, 208; Henry, 44; John, 89; Jordan, 138; Orphan, 186.
JACK, James, 29; Margaret, 152; Patrick, 195; Samuel, 166.
JACKS, Isaac, _____26
JACO, James, 96; Thomas, 178.
JACOBS, Seaborn, 96; Mordecai, 64; Benjamin, 65.
JACKSON, Aaron, 10; Abraham, 151; Amos, 23; Archibaol, 92, 120, 126, 205; Benjamin, 63; Booker, 180; Brooker, 91; Celia, 34; Charles, 98; Clark, 85, 133; Cornelius, 31; Daniel, 88, 216, 20; Drury, 148, 207; Duke, 123; Ebenezer, 204; Edward, 53; Henry, 209; Hiram, 110; Isaac, 101, 24; Ivy, 42; James, 42, 72, 130, 147; Jeremiah, 27, 82, 142; John, 41, 42, 42, 118, 127; Lewis, 81; Low, 57; Lucy, 165; Luisone, 7; Nimrod, 94; M., 30; Mark, 106, 210; Mary, 70; Milly, 30; Moody, 27; Moses, 5, 205; Peyton, 32; Priscilla, 81, 45; Robert, 48, 114, 138, 146; Samuel, 163, 210; Shadrack, 48, 191; Solomon, 48; Stephen, 185; Thomas, 212; Unity, 92; Whilen, 101; William, 23, 29, 33, 44, 57, 88, 142, 190.
JAMES, Daniel, 111; David, 72; Drury, 211; Elias, 172, 119, 103; Elizabeth, 81; Enoch, 148; George, 17; Green, 93; Henry, 164; James, 138; Joel, 149; John, 66, 27; Jordan, 42; Joseph, 25, 74; Josiah, 5; Joshua, 212; Mary, 43; Stephens, 101; William, 114; Williamson, 172; Wyche, 120.
JAMERSON, Edy, 5; Jena, 106; Mary, 215.
JAMESON, George, _____58, 121
JANAS, Michael, _____206
JANIGAN, Plottemy, _____149
JARMON, Ruth, _____208
JARRAL, Claiborn, _____116
JARRALD, Gideon, _____50
JARRAT, M., 105; Patterson, 75; S. A. & L., 136.
JARRATT, James, _____165
JARRED, Anslem, _____140
JARREL, John, 150; Willis, 175.
JARROD, Ralph, _____121, 99
JAROC, John, _____33
JARVIS, Alfred, 173, 198; Elisha, 203, 3; George, 3; ohn, 142.
JAY, Jesse, 149; William, 49.
JARIDSON, James, _____8

JEAN, Jesse, _____215
JEFFERS, Elbert, 128; James, 125, 176; John, 174.
JEFFERSON, John, _____89
JEFFRIES, Thomas, _____129
JELKS, James, _____194
JEMISON, Henry, _____154
JENCKS, William, _____86
JENKINS, Ashford, 36; Augustus, 72; Azaties, 75; Bartholomew, 38, 159; Benjamin, 115; Bethsheba, 16; Betsy, 214; Celah, 79; Charles, 53, 126, 175; Christine, 75; Daniel, 89; Edward, 168; Elizabeth, 97, 125, 206; Evans, 151; Francis, 120; Henry, 178; James, 95; John, 151, 191; Keziah, 153; Mary, Ann, 153; Orphan, 195, 209; S., 116; Shepherd, 74; Susannah, 133; Thomas, 15, 159; Turner, 123.
JENKS, Willis, 81; Weston, 139.
JENNING, David, _____74
JENNINGS, Creed, 21, 31; George, 182; James, 194; John, 158.
JERNIGAN, Elias, 85; James, 45, 47; Mary, 94, 124.
JERREL, Gideon, _____98
JESTER, Nathan, 79; David, 134, 41; Jacob, 203.
JESTIS, John, _____213
JESSUP, George, _____155
JETER, Andrew, 209; Barnett, 107; Buck, 202; Cornelius, 51, 71, 200; Dedima, 186; James, 32; Nathan, 37.
JETT, Daniel, 177; Ferdinand, 36; John, 62.
JEWEL, James, _____181
JEWELL, Moses, _____210
JEWETT, George, _____123
JEWIL, ames, 181; Moses, 93.
JINKS, David, 214; Isaac, 47; John, 53.
JINKINS, Owen, 54; William, 135.
JINNINGS, Henry, _____196
JIPSON, Thomas, _____170
JOCEY, Henry, _____2
JOHNAKINS, Jesse, _____32
JOHNES, Zachariah, _____177
JOHNS, Bailey, 214; Eli, 182; James, 7, 34, 39, 141; John, 129, 148; Robert, 36, 40; William, 182.
JOHNSON, Abel, 163; Amos, 3, 26, 44, 216; Albert, 59; Alexander, 207; Alford, 135; Annie, 57; Augus, 77; 71; Berry, 185; Brice, 183; Chaney, Bar, 198; Barberry, 209; Benjamin, 195; Crover, 170; Cornelius, 93; Darcus, 127; Darius, 146; Darkis, 141; Dempsy, 43; Eliza, 172; Elizabeth, 114, 174, 211; Emanuel, 122, 194; Emeline, 203; Enoch, 85; Fannie, 36; Freeman, 58; George, 169,

215; Gilbert, 114; Green, 88, 109; Harris, 103; Henry, 23, 70, 176, 216; Hinchy, 90; Hosea, 213; Isaac, 75, 98, 110, 135, 147, 212; Isaiah, 191; Jabez, 101; Jack, 86; Jacob, 1, 34, 56, 72; James, 4, 24, 28, 41, 99, 103, 124, 143, 189, 202, 214; Jane, 166; Jeff, 127; Jeremiah, 71, 99, 168; Jesse, 4, 6, 42, 184; Joel, 24; John, 6, 104, 130, 139, 146, 149, 153, 155, 174, 179, 214; Jonathan, 97, 168; Jones, 206; Joseph, 86, 135, 185; L., 204; Levi, 170; Lucy, 183; M., 204; Mad, 127; Malcom, 117; Marcus, 195; Marm, 178; Martha, 80, 116; Mary, 157, 163, 177, 208, 212; Merrick, 147; Michael, 134; Molly, 70, 175; Morris, 173; Moses, 101; Nancy, 216; Nathan, 215; Neil, 189; Nicholas, 95, 172; Olive, 201; Otis, 39; Quinney, 113; Patsy, 157; Peter, 216; Penance, 114; Philip, 25, 40; Ratford, 100; Redford, 112; Rees, 157; Richard, 16, 121, 176; Robert, 81, 121, 148, 216; Samuel, 153, 195; Sarah, 6, 87, 130, 176; Seaborn, 34, 255; Sid, 71; Simon, 110; Sivel, 58, 148; Solomon, 33, 37, 49; Stephen, 169, 182; Susannah, 203, 206; Thomas, 31, 37, 71, 98, 114, 125, 161, 183; Tyre, 204; Uriah, 99; Washington, 95; Wilburn, 199; William, 2, 19, 22, 28, 30, 38, 41, 61, 78, 90, 99, 130, 132, 133, 137, 147, 202; Willis, 113, 198, 212, 216; Winifred, 155; Winn, 130.

JOICE, John, ...3
JOINER, Abraham, 154; Absalom, 42, 116; Benjamin, 128; Bennett, 80; Henry, 33; Jesse *; James, 122; Joel, 191; John, 3, 64, 85, 131, 160; Joseph, 167; Malichi, 75, 198; Moses 103; Mourning, 179; Nancy, 119; Nathan, 165; Robert, 105; Susan, 209.
JOLEY, Joseph, ...153
JOLLY, Jesse, 142; Joseph, 50.
JOHNSTON, Abrahen, 213; Chandler, 157; Charles, 64; Darcus, 64; Ellerander, 61; Eli, 43; Ephriam, 20; Esther, 208; Henry, 106; John, 213; Launcelot, 80; Littleton, 84, 85; Nathan, 18, 114, 133; Rebecca, 213; Samuel, 53; Thomas, 38, 169; William, 46, 57, 86, 106, 136.
JONES, Adam, 87, 166; Albert, 155; Alexander, 86, 206; Allen, 187, 199; Amos, 6, 140; Armstrong, 51; Benjamin, 72, 102; Burwell, 55; Charles, 188; Cicero, 121; Clarissa, 132; Clayton, 215; Cora, 8; Counsel, 90;

David, 44, 54, 116, 183, 199; Dinah, 8; Dudley, 208; D. Z., 86, 108; Edmund, 85; E., 35; Elias, 137; Elizabeth, 21, 37, 86, 110, 127, 197, 207, 212, 215; Elmina, 201; Ephriam, 132; Erastus, 54, 160; Ezra, 10, 182; Fanny, 186; Farnwell, 146; Frances, 149; Francis, 189; Green, 51; Hardy, 25; Harrison, 150; Hartwell, 44; Henry, 30, 46, 50, 81, 93, 103, 178, 212; Isham, 116; Isaac, 5, 128; James, 34, 72, 81, 119, 123, 155; J. A., 8; Jane, 216; Jemima, 132; Jesse, 55, 125, 149; John, 18, 31, 39, 40, 58, 72, 86, 127, 141, 180, 191, 198, 202, 206; Jones, 88; Joseph, 94, 150, 198; Josiah, 45; Katherine, 105; Kindred, 39, 157; Levi, 126; Lewis, 81, 184; Lucretia, 177; Mathew, 87, 184, 206, 213; Margaret, 21; Mary, 100; Micajah, 83, 119; Michael, 214; Miles, 82; Moses, 122, 134, 178, 197; Moson, 38; Nathan, 74; Nancy, 108, 177; Needham, 113; Nimrod, 139; Orin, 18; Philip, 157; Pleasant, 112; Randal, 122; Reuben, 1, 9, 51, 63, 165; Robert, 7, 19, 87; Russell, 88; 116, 174; Samuel, 77, 95, 171, 175, 181; Sarah, 19, 23, 109; Seaborn, 119, 154, 162; S. and E. S., 89; Silas, 45; Simeon, 56; Simpsy, 113; Stephen, * Taliaferro, 147; Tambling, 100; Thomas, 45, 61, 71, 84, 93, 94, 105, 109, 157, 203, 215; Uriah, 178; Wiley, 23, 32, 33, 156, 169; William, 18, 22, 30, 34, 49, 51, 56, 72, 80, 96, 123, 127, 141, 151, 154, 160, 165, 181, 188, 216; Willis, 134, 187; Zachariah, 59.

JORDAN, August, 4; Avon, 121; Avew, 121; Benjamin, 4, 30; Britton, 138; Burrell, 3; Burwell, 47; Charles, 190; Dempsey, 46; Dioley, 119; Dixon, 139; Elias, 92; Elisha, 136; Emelus, 157; George, 80, 106; Isaac, 50, 145, 170; Jacob, 83; James 34, 112; Jameson, 201; John, 17, 22, 154, 173, 175, 179; Josiah, 41, 147; Joshua, 208; Lewis, 133; Lovick, 15, 212; Lydia, 97; Mathew, 50; Milly, 194; Stephen, 208; T., 27; Thomas, 189; T. D., 94; Wiley, 100; William, 8, 24, 121, 122, 124, 148, 149, 185.
JORDIN, Jane, ...176
JOSEPH, Lester, ...9
JOSHUA, Jones, ...103
JOURDAN, Bastan, 28; Benjamin, 173; Edward, 169; Founten, 23, 75, 201; Martha, 92; Mathew, 82; William, 208.
JOWELL, Rispy, ...10

JOWERS, James, 32
JOY, Elizabeth, 24
JOYCE, James, 122; .ohn, 64, 131, 160.
JOYNER, Abraham, 207; Miles, 58, 113; William, 10.
JUDAH, William, 75
JUDD, Daniel, 7
JUNIR, William, 162
JURRELL, Willis, 175
JUSTICE, Aaron, 40, 70; Allen, 21; Amy, 119; Archibald, 207; Blake, 42; Daniel, 89; Dimpsey, 209; Isaac, Sr., 138; James, 198; ·John, 31; Thomas, 165; William, 191, 200.

KAIN, Orphans, 206
KALE, Honom, 150
KARR, John, 158
KAY, Charity, 184
KEADLE, John, 74
KEARNS, Bartholomew, 203
KEATON, Keador, 184; William, 93, 204.
KEE, Joshua, 178; Pierce, 117.
KEEBLER, John, 36
KEEGLE, Leonard, 111
KEEL, Isaac, 154; Levin, 8; Martin, 54.
KEEN, Theophilus, 103
KEENAN, Michael, 129
KEENER, Lawson, 15; William, 184.
KEENUM, William, 127
KEENY, Ebenezer, 33
KEETON, Benoni, 170
KEISTER, Jacob, 1
KEITH, George, 130; James, 124; John, 178; Maky, 40.
KEEL, Alexander, 83; James, 22.
KELLARD, James, 28
KELLER, Elias, 8
KELLEY, Bethina, 192; Cath, 111; Elijah, 33; Francis, 150; James, 84, 135; John, 15, 59, 75, 129; J. P., 111; Loyd, 111; Mary, 57; Moses, 57; Norrell, 104; Reuben, 18; Thomas, 155; William, 23, 54, 101, 136.
KELLOGG, George, 129
KELLUM, Celia, 194; Seth, 50.
KELLY, Ann, 52; Elijah, 1; Jarrett, 86; James, 54, 41; John, 62; J. J. W., 54; Lydia, 7; Patrick, 61; Robert, 114; Reuben, 72; R., 54; Thomas, 103; William, 10, 31, 33, 47, 105, 114, 161, 190.
KELTON, Robert, 90, 168
KEMBELL, William, 5
KEMP, Aaron, 186, 192; Alsy, 199; Charles, 90; Harvin, 77; James, 80, 36; Lewis, 180; Reuben, 154; Samuel, 96, 207; Sarah, 93; Stephen, 17; Thomas, 62; William, 185, 199.
KENARD, John, 121

KENDALL, Elizabeth, 171
KENDRICK, Abel, 6; Benjamin, 191; Hez, 112; John, 81, 30; Sylvanus, 203; Thomas, 100.
KENEDA, Neil, 173
KENLY, John, 18
KENNEDY, Arthur, 183; David, 138; George, 91; James, 45, 101, 202; John, 109, 175; Josiah, 44; Robert, 120; Samuel, 45; Seth, 46, 72, 95; Thomas, 72; William, 2.
KENNEMUR, Obadiah, 63
KENNERLY, J., 109; T. 109.
KENNON, Charles, 18; E., 42; James, 56; M., 42.
KENNY, John, 70; Michael, 36; William, 174.
KENON, Nancy, 192
KENT, Daniel, 1, 153; Edward, 115, 118, 136; Elizabeth, 36; John, 16, 110, 135; Jordan, 118; Levi, 45; Mark, 183; Sampson, 89; Stephen, 47; Thomas, 134, 165; Wiley, 178; William, 20, 119, 191.
KENUM, William, 160
KER, Mary, 145
KERCY, Alcy, 185
KERLIN, David, 167
KERNS, Hubbard, 29
KERSHAW, Ann, 162
KESTERSON, Nancy, 147; Thomas, 56
KETTLER, Conrad, 128
KEY, Abraham, 95; Burwell, 27; Caleb, 190; George, 56; Salley, 211; Thomas, 136; Warren, 192; William, 28, 111, 145.
KEYS, Benjamin, 149
KIBBE, William, 45
KICKER, B. M., 143
KICKLIGHTER, Andrew, 192
KIDD, Robert, 22
KIGHT, Samuel, 172
KILBY, William, 165
KILCREASE, Arter, 101; Robert, 43; ·Willis, 56.
KILDREDGE, Stephen, 138
KILGORE, Benajah, 95; William, 17.
KILGROVE, Mathew, 154
KILLGORE, Theophilus, 154; William, 111.
KILLEBREW, Elizabeth, 179
KILLINGSWORTH, Liza, 139
KILPATRICK, Adair, 147; James, 138, 187; Martha, 89; Robert, 110; Thomas, 143; William, 56.
KIMBALL, Joseph, 16, 172; Mary, 69.
KIMBELL, David, 24, 148
KIMBERLY, Ansel, 106
KIMBLE, John, 86
KIMBROUGH, Reb., 131; Shadrack, 171; Thomas, 163; William, 200.
KINDLE, Henry, 57

KING, Alfred, 105, 213; Berry, 210; Calvin, 176; Catlett, 212; Charles, 119, 158, 173; Drewey, 53; Elcy, 46; Elizabeth, 128; Franklin, 128; Henry, 148, 17; James, 5, 94, 115; Jane, 180; John, 103, 6, 43, 160, 169; Joseph, 110, 208; Lewis, 169, 213; Lorenzo, 143; Marshall, 167; Margaret, 62; Mary, 103, 113, 138, 140; Misora, 22; Nathan, 35; Ralph, 23; Renben, 150; Riley, 110; Rufus, 44, 137; S., 75; Silas, 208; Stephen, 6, 115; Susannah, 135; Tandy, 111; Th., 5; Thomas, 37, 166, 194, 200, 210; William, 75, 98, 201; Willis, 9; Winifred, 23; W. 5.
KINGARY, Abraham, ---------------154
KINGERY, Benjamin, ---------------185
KINGLEY, Joseph, ------------------17
KINLEY, S. A., --------------------22
KINGSLEY, Loucresy, ---------------69
KINGSMORE, John, ------------------85
KINNEY, Anne, 110; Chesley, 109; James, 103; Lydia, 198; Orsamus, 108; Thomas, 85; William, 91.
KINNEYBREW, Little, ---------------184
KINSALL, John, --------------------42
KINSAME, John, --------------------176
KINSEY, Absalom, 49; Daniel, 84.
KINT, Henry, ----------------------35
KIRBEE, James, --------------------136
KIRBO, Joseph, --------------------106
KIRK, Elijah, 83; Hudson, 212; John, 8; Joseph, 165; Levi, 99; Louisa, 124; Thomas, 170; Wiley, 53.
KIRKLAND, Ambrose, 36, 53, 124; Daniel, 42; David, 168; James, 196; Jefferson, 149; John, 183.
KIRKPATRICK, Jane, 39; John, 109, 214.
KIRSEY, Aley, 26; Elijah, 195.
KISOR, John, ----------------------91
KITCHEN, James, 109; John, 32.
KITCHENS, Meredith; James, 154, 211; Sophronia, 6; Zachariah, 212.
KITCHINGS, Sarah, -----------------112
KITCHING, John, -------------------215
KITE, Henry, 152, 171; M. & D., 43; John, 205; Joseph, 194; Samuel, 20, 192.
KITTLES, Louisa, ------------------181
KLEY, John, -----------------------165
KNAPP, Hanford, 55; Nathaniel, 188; Walter, 154.
KINNEY, Samuel, -------------------132
KNIGHT, Aaron, 210; Abel, 114; David, 190; Dencilla, 3; Eli, 125; Enoch, 50; Francis, 172; George, 191; Henry, 135; James, 24, 127; John, 78; Kinsman, 92; Levi, 141; Matthew, 74; Nealy, 25; Richard, 53; Robert, 198; Samuel, 114; Tarlton, 187; Thomas, 152, 162, 207; Walton, 16; William, 1, 86, 171; Woody 47.
KNIGHTNIGHT, Alexander, --------163
KNIGHTKNIGHT, Alexander, -------207
KNOLE, Washington, ----------------39
KNOP, Frederick, ------------------63
KNOTT, Benjamin, 73; John, 135; Robert, 135, 151.
KNOWHMAN, A., --------------------54
KNOWLES, Daniel, 171; James, 2; Isaac, 183.
KNOX, Hugh, 49; Robert, 195; Samuel, 37.
KOLD, Martin, 206; Jonathan, 102, 121; Joshua, 6; Peter, 41.
KOLLOCK, Mehetabel, ---------------52
KOOKOGY, Samuel, -----------------126
KOPMAN, Morris, -------------------50
KRAATZ, William, -----------------167
KUGLAR, David, 159, 171; Orp., 205.
KYTLE, Zachariah, -----------------34
LABROSSE, --------------------Felix,128
LABUZAN, Charles ------------------35
L'ACEE, John, ---------------------18
LACEY, Philenion, -----------------28
LACKEY, Eli, 133; John, 91; Samuel, 81; Thomas, 177; William, 176.
LACY, Noah, 47! Pleasant, 47; Randolph, 78; William, 57, 134.
LADD, Amos, --------------------17, 105
LADEZVEZE, Raymond, -------------215
LAFVOR, John, --------------------175
LAGRON, John, --------------------169
LAGRONE, David, ------------------177
LAIDLER, John, -------------------165
LAING, Simeon, -------------------21
LAING, George, ------------------153
LAKE, Daniel; Elisha, 127.
LAMAR, Basil, 25; Bennington, 54; George, 125, 151; Henry, 140; Jeremiah, 103; John, 171, 197; Mirebeau, 123; Philip, 37.
LAMB, Abraham, 77; Abrams, 148; Elizabeth, 174; Isaac, 190; Green, 47; Jacob 24, 213; James, 2; John, 31; Sarah, 73.
LAMBERT, Allan, 205; Blake, 178; Elisha, 164; Esther, 90; George, 10; James, 20, 61; Joanna, 204; John, 63, 163; Luzunsky, 197; Thomas, 97, 192; Washington, 27; William, 37, 177.
LAMBERT, John, ------------------110
LAMPE, Christian, -----------------62
LAMPKIN, Arme, 72; George, 70; Lew, 179; Lewis, 156; William, 36.
LAMPIN, John, 56; Sampson, 11.
LAMPLEY, Benjamin, ---------------164
LANCASTER, John, 148; Lewis, 192; Mahala, 46; Sinclair, 184; William,

92.
LANCE, Martin, ...193
LAND, Henry, 30, 132; Hiram, 47; John, 113; Sarah, 45; William, 105.
LANDERS, Ann, 112; Densly, 47; Henry, 153; John, 117, 126, 213; Richard, 90; Samuel, 140; Taprell, 23; Thomas, 176.
LANDON, Winny, ...146
LANDON, Daniel, ...80
LANDRETH, Thomas, ...53
LANDRUM, Elias, 112; Epsy, 50; George, 5; Jepthah, 190; Micajah, 12; Orphaus, 172; Samuel, 174; Timothy, 196; Whitfield, 153, 109; William, 122.
LANDSTRIT, Susanah, ...192
LANE, Alexander, 59; Benjamin, 4, 84, Bryant, 178; Eliza, 172; Henry, 157; John, 13; Levi, 31, 175; Mary, 191; Micajah, 14; Richard, 178; Samuel, 51; Wiley, 29; William, 113.
LANEY, Noah, ...168
LANG, Isaac, 158; John, 56, 59; Margaret; Orphan, 112; Thomas, 187.
LANGFORD, Lewis, 94; James, 185; Elizabeth, 13, 154; Nicholas, 128; William, 57.
LANGHAM, Benjamin, 19; Charles, 122; James, 87; Robert, 30; William, 141.
LANGLEY, Catherine, 69; Isaiah, 121; Jacob, 94; John, 85; William, 156, 213; James, 45.
LANGSTON, Edith, 23; Elizabeth, 20; Elvy, 1; Esaac, 131; James, 17, 170; John, 26, 40, 174; Nancy, 1.
LANGSFORD, Catherine, ...150
LANHAM, Asa, ...122
LANIER, Dorcas, 21, 118; James, 114, John, 172; Sterling, 15.
LANKFORD, Stephen, ...32
LANSDELL, ...38
LANSFORD, Josiah, ...213
LANSING, Francis, ...168
LANSING, Francis, ...168
LANTERN, Elizabeth, 126; Giedon, 123; Joseph, 1; Theophilus, 213.
LANTON, John, ...156
LARANCE, John, 53; William, 49.
LARAMORE, Peter, ...157
LARD, Curtis, 95, 105; James, 177, 211.
LARENCE, John, ...63
LARISCY, William, ...74
LARK, Mary, ...169
LARKIN, Joseph, ...85
LARKIN, William, ...197, 206
LAROCHE, E. L. M., ...61

LARRY, William, ...130
LARTIGNE, Anne, ...125
LARY, Lary, ...197
LARY, Archibald, ...122
LASETER, Abram, ...29
LASHLEY, Edmond, ...59
LASLIE, Daniel, ...4, 194
LASSERA, Mary, ...112
LASSERA, Lewis, ...82
LASSETER, Abram, 75; Benjamin, 86; Brittain, 142; Dorothy, 132; Gray, 55; Hansell, 62, 119; Joel, 55; John, 57; Sally, 145.
LASTINGER, James, 207; Gerborn, 20; William, 190.
LATHAM, Amos, ...17
LATHRANTS, James, ...77
LATIGNE, Orphans, ...25
LATIMER, John, ...117, 188
LATIMORE, Edward, ...210
LATTA, David, 63; John, 93.
LAUGHLIN, John, ...104
LAUGHRIDGE, John, 82; Robert, 17; W. H., 114; William, 98.
LAULER, David, ...92
LAURENCE, Robert, ...149
LAURENS, George, 40; Joseph, 173.
LAVARE, Mary, ...168
LAVENDER, George, 62; Lemuel, 161, William, 87, 208.
LAVENSWORTH, M. C., ...39
LAW, Benjamin, 175; John, 115; Josiah, 134.
LAWCHE, Orphan, ...84
LAWLESS, Cyntha, 150; Jacob, 86, 106; John, 35; William, 89.
LAWRENCE, Allen, 91; Bent, 4; Catherine, 108; Michael, 129; Homer, 113; James, 149; John, 78, 35, 120, 181; Laborn, 77; Let., 115; Robert, 83; Thomas, 15, 121; Wesley, 79.
LAWSON, Andrew, 82, 145; Anthony, 111; David, 53; Francis, 156, 140; Irwin, 70; James, 90, 86; Jane, 144, 182; Martha, 35; Mary, 210; Rachel, 98; Robert, 153; Roger, 61; Thomas, 130, 74; William, 137, 133, 195.
LAY, David, 155, 156; Henry, 149; Lee, 204.
LAYING, Cornelius, ...168
LEACH, Mathew, 80; William, 139.
LEAK, Robert, 206; Wesley, 3.
LEALMAN, Thomas, ...
LEAVINS, Elizabeth, 121; Jacob, 9; James, 165, 213.
LEDBETTER, Henry, 3; James, 32, 119; Sarah, 8; William, 113.
LEDLOW, Abraham, 213; Adam, 89; Epriam, 210; John, M., 100, 190.
LEECH, Micajah, 152; Lee, 143, 146, 153; Andrew, 34, 89, 96; Anslem,

141; Charles, 14, 189; David, 33, 124; Drury, 124, 163; Elizabeth, 120, 192; Esan, 158; Henry, 107, 176; Ivey, 113; James, 51, 138; Jesse, 124, 167; John, 97, 103; Joseph, 129, 175; Joshua, 25, 33, 36; Levi, 215; Lucinda, 64; Mary, Ann, 138; Needham, 113, 161; Rachel, 51; Ransom, 35; Robert, 86, 131; Sampson, 123; Timothy, 77, 203; William, 15, 131; Zachariah, 202.
LEFTNITCH, Mary, _____82
LEGET, M. M., 73; Margaret, 107.
LEGGETT, Watson, 167; Jeremiah, 64, Jourden, 105; Lewis, 64.
LEGRONE, Jacob, 167; Elizabeth, 195, Micajah, 152.
LEGWIN, William, _____122
LEIGH, Benjamine, 139; Isaam, 77.
LEITCH, Archibald, _____79
LEITH, Charles, 75; John, 184; Mary, 19.
LEITNER, John, C., _____144
LEJELS, Francis, _____213
LEMON, Jincy, 89; Wallace, 57.
LEONARD, Isaac, 63; James, 49; Joseph, 62; Patrick, 98; Roderick, 172; William, 49.
LEOPARD, John, _____8, 103
LEPCY, Ann, 62 (?); Annie, 62.
LEPER, Hugh, _____155
LEPTRA, Hurinis, _____101
LEG EUR, Peter, _____176
LEQUEUX, Peter, _____182
LESCARE, Henry, _____150
LESSET, Claudi, _____11
LESHLY, Edward, 50; Elijah, 98.
LESLEY, Peter, 157; Thomas, 104.
LESLIE, Silas, _____173
LESSURER, Charles, _____73
LESURER, Joseph, 14; Harrison, 213.
LESTER, Alfred, 180; Edward, 59; Henry, 15; acob, 74, 133, 155; James 41; Jeremiah, 162; John, 185; Joseph, 18; Nixon, 14; William.
LETTON, Nancy, _____202
LEVERELL, John, _____208
LEVERETT, H. J., 84; Robert, 96; William, 23.
LEVERITT, Jane, _____93
LEVINGSTON, Aaron, 112; Alford, 205; Altama, 58; James, 100; John, 59; Thomas, 120.
LEVISTON, Charles, _____107
LEVY, Lewis, _____84
LEWIS, Peter, 133; Ren, 98.
LEWELLEN, William, _____10
LAZENBY, Henry, _____5
LEWIS, Aley, 84; Annese, 115; Archibald, 20; Arvigini, 202; Benjamin, 43; Cely, 135; Charles, 42; David, 149, 158; David, 31; Eliza, 55; Elizer, 182; Fanny, 16; Felix, 31; Fielding, 20; George, 45; Green, 119; Henry, 127; J., 132, 157; Jacob, 78, 208, 184; James, 5, 97, 133; John, 46, 116, 153, 156, 184, 215; Jones, 132; Joseph, 107; Josiah, 99; Lavinia, 175; Lewis, 125; Mary, 140; Mary Ann, 78; Michael, 66; Moses, 133; N. R., 187; Peter, 133; Ren, 98; Sterling, 8; Thomas, 195; William, 149; Zera; 152.
LIDDON, Jesse, _____110
LIGGETT, Jeremiah, _____40
LIGGIN, David, _____172
LIGGON, John, _____13
LIGHT, Emanuel, 53; Gilford, 196; Ransford, 164; William, 75.
LIGHTFOOT, Benjamin, 5; John, 88.
LIGHTNOR, Samuel, _____79
LIGON, E. S., 93; G., 93; Marshall, 1; Mary, 86; Rhoda, 111; Tomitha, 83.
LILES, Allen, 147; Bathsheba, 98; Hiram, 211; James, 152; Philip, 6; William, 205.
LILLIBRIDGE, Sarah, _____158
LIN, John, _____188
LINCH, Benjamin, 103; Grief, 127; Lewis, 106; Samuel, 197.
LINDER, Charles, 108, 193; George, 167; Louis, 137.
LINDLEY, Thomas, _____119
LINDON, John, _____178
LINDSAY, Archibald, 117, 152; Humphrey, 12; Isaac, 113; James, 156, 165, 185; Mary, 36; Parham, 167.
LINDSEY, Dennis, 32, 216; Dolphin, 132; Henry, 15; Isaac, 95; James, 144, 149; Mary, 198; Richard, 122; Thomas, 62; William, 173.
LINDSY, Dennis, 55; Mary, 5.
LINN, Lucy, _____30
LINSEY, Ann, 171; Green, 73; Jesse, 102; Reason, 6; Richard, 205; William, 73.
LINTON, John, _____207
LINVILLE, Bird, 199; John, 40.
LINZY, Ambrose, _____7
LION, James, 196; Nicholas, 166.
LIONS, Redmond, _____28
LIPHAM, Elizabeth, 143, 197; George, 72; Mary, 24.
LIPMON, Mary, _____136
LIPPITT, Charles, 54; Samuel, 202.
LIPSEY, Amasa, _____130
LIPTROT, Elijah, 148; James, 73.
LISENBEA, Silas, _____174
LISCOE, Robert, _____168
LITTLE, Asa, 121; Fanny, 122; James, 81, 178, 200; Jesse, 87, 106; Joseph, 159, 196; Murrit, 176; Nahum, 196, 206; Robert, 4, 34; Sherod,

94; Thomas, 20, 34, 114; William, 106, 116.
LITTLEJOHN Abraham, 79; Eli, 94.
LITTLETON, E. A., 70; Sarah, 130; Southey, 34.
LITSY, Jacob, 166
LIVELY, Charles, 203; Ruben, 75; Torleton, 135.
LIVERETT, Richard. 147
LIVERMAN, Con, 87
LIVINGSTON, James, 100; John, 193; Joseph, 21, 130.
LIYON, Major, 151
LIZENBY, Hawley, 81
LLOYD, Edmund, 3; Jones, 96; Thomas, 3.
LOANE, Henry, 74
LOCHALER, Joseph, 170
LOCHLIN, William, 98
LOCKALER, Joseph, 20
LOCKE, Ann, 121; John, 181.
LOCKETT, Cullen, 12; Gustus, 188; Hugh, 13; Osborn, 100; William, 185.
LOCK, William, 105, 108
LOCKETT, John, 124; Solomon, 118, 169.
LOCKHART, Charles, 11; Charlotte, 193; Henry, 93; Isaac, 18; James, 140; John, 127; Polly, 78, 10.
LOCKLIN, James, 132
LOCKROY, Margaret, 177
LOCKWOOD, Eleazer, 175
LODGE, Patsy, 123
LODON, Thomas, 53, 177
LOFLIN, James, 9; Shelton, 92.
LOFTEN, James, 113, 187
LOFTIN, James, 46, 195; Jane, 1.
LOFTON, Eli, 156; James, 180; William, 42, 171.
LOGAN, John, 132, 151; Philip, 39.
LOGGINS, James, 196
LOGNE, Roberson, 100
LOGUE, Sarah, 212
LOKEY, Benjamin, 118; Davis, 115; John, 175.
LOLLAR, James, 188
LONDON, John, 26
LONG, Ander, 204; Arm, 9, 103; Drury, 63, 165; Henry, 85; Jackson, 139; James, 99, 159; John, 15, 51, 120, 162; Micajah, 107; Michael, 110; M. S., 139; Orphans, 20; Perry, 107; Richard, 77; Sarah, 69; Solomon, 151, 190, 216; Thomas, 13; William, 95.
LOOPER, David, 55; James, 119; John, 119.
LOOSER, John, 86
LUCKETT, Thomas, 10

LUCKEY, Reuben, 47; Robert, 165.
LUCKY, Margaret, 163
LUD, Amos, 186
LUDDUTH, Mary, 166
LUETT, Elijah, 176
LUINLEY, Jesse, 177
LUKE, Daniel, 84; John, 49; Joshua, 116.
LUKER, James, 7; Joel, 111; Valentine, 38; William, 213.
LUMBLEY, Thomas, 149
LUMKIN, George, 165
LUMMERS, William, 214, 21
LUMPKIN, Dickson, 206; Elizabeth, 77; G., 156; George, 70; John, 28, 94; M., 156; Thomas, 130; William, 8.
LUMSDEN, Elijah, 95; Jeremiah, 92, 199.
LUNN, John, 48; Nanly, 120.
LUNDAY, Peyton, 102
LUNDY, Jane, 22; Thomas, 78.
LUNSFORD, Bailey, 216; James, 93, 30, 78; Peter, 141.
LUPO, Moreland, 80
LUSAS, George, 44; James, 212, 63; John, 147, 164, 122; Nancy, 109; Samuel, 75; Thomas, 131.
LUSTER, Andrew, 170
LUTHER, Mary, 194; Susan, 150.
MACON, Giddon, 203; William, 189.
MADDOCK, Isaih, 123
MADDON, William, 57
MADDOX, Aaron, 24; Davis, 96; Fulden, 30; Hampson, 108; Henry, 174; Ira, 158; Jacob, 165; John, 155; Leonard, 192; Marebon, 137; Walter, 166; William, 75.
MADDUX, Andrew, 29; Chapman, 55; James, 63, 184; John, 9.
MADROY, George, 161
MADUX, William, 172
MAFFETT, Samuel, 111
MAGARITY, Kindred, 120
MAGEE, James, 18, 199; Joseph, 31; William, 109.
MAGEEHEE, Michol, 79
MAGBY, Orphan, 180
MAGNES, Edmund, 178
MAGNIRE, Hester, 61
MAGOUIRK, Alfred, 110; Benjamin, 145; William, 89.
MAGRAW, Jessie, 97; John, 99.
MAGRUDER, James, 208; John, 135; Martha, 204; Sarah, 36; Zodock, 26.
MAGUIRE, James, 194
MAHAN, Benjamin, 189
MAHAR, Jane, 189
MAHARREY, Charity, 131
MAHON, William, 52
MAHONEY, Dennis, 83, 150

MAIMS, Anson, 135
MAJORS, Thomas, 179; William, 90.
MALCOM, John, 205
MALCOMB, Amelia, 142
MALL, Levi. 174
MALLARD, George, 102; Lewis, 110; John, 156, 162.
MALLERY, John, 2
MALLETT, Lewis, 164; Samuel, 213.
MALLORY, Allan, 189; Horace, 64; James, 134; John, 73, 142; Stephen, 166; William, 20.
MALOINS, Sarah, 6
MALONE, Burrell, 108; Charles, 36, 55; Christopher, 43; Elizabeth, 204; Francis, 44; Harriet, 185; Henry, 49; John, 208; Nancy, 33; Robert, 46, 201; Thomas, 127; William, 113, 162.
MALONEY, Samuel, 75; William, 148, 189.
MALTON, Nathan, 75
MAN, Ephriam, 125
MANES, Alfred, 142
MANGHAM, Robert, 121; Thomas, 58, 71; William, 146.
MANING, Mary, 200
MANLY, Abner, 106; Daniel, 107; Hannah, 98; Phillis, 52; Temperance, 199; Tempy, 79; William, 90.
MANLEY, Daniel, 35; Richard, 205.
MANN, Abner, 109; Alexander, 45; David, 166, 52; Hiriam, 200; Jane, 194; Jerimiah, 40, 201; John, 115, 151, 197; Joel, 77; Mary, 94; Peter, 127; Shemei, 157; William, 87, 61, Young, 161.
MANNING, Aexander, 9; Benjamin, 39; Britton, 107; Cas, 87; Cassina, 161; Isaac, 141; Jane, 9; Job, 35; John, 78; Levi, 24, 64, 140, 178; Martha, 147; Martin, 215; Mathias, 176, 188; Michael, 142; Moses, 104, 109; Shadrack, 213; William, 182.
MANNEN, Lewis, 70; Margaret, 203; Redrick, 112.
MANNIN, Larry, 156
MANOR, Alfred, 189; Elijah, 148; William, 156.
MANSFIELD, William, 109
MANSUN, John, 108
MANTON, E., 191
MANUS, Richard, 83
MAPLES, Nathan, 155
MAPP, Jeremiah, 44; John, 44.
MAPPEN, Martha, 161
MAQUOIRK, David, 19
MARABLE, John, 184
MARADITH, Bryant, 119
MARBERY, James, 126; Joel, 46.

MARCH, George, 27
MARCHMAN, Albert, 86; Asa, 5; Henry, 21; Stephen, 137.
MARGARY, Archibald, 120
MARIDITH, Wilie, 52
MARIDLEY, Robert, 167
MARINER, John, 210
MARKET, Benjamin, 91
MARLEY, James, 25
MARLOW, James, 103, 197; John, 176; Patrick, 73.
MARKS, Orphan, 125
MAROODER, Petit, 137
MARPLES, Nathan, 114
MARSH, Jane, 135; John, 146; Martha, 55; Mathews, 202; Sarah, 188; Thomas, 99.
MARSHALL, David, 181; Elijah, 69, 117; Green, 16; Jessie, 116, 182; John, 3, 70, 178; Joseph, 120, 180; Nohor, 119; Nancy, 130; Samuel, 8; Washington, 190; William, 16.
MARSHBURN, Nancy, 118
MARTILNER, George, 92
MARTIN, Aaron, 55; Absolum, 133; Andrew, 56, 120; Agnus, 186; Bartley, 156; Charles, 105; Daniel, 158; David, 78; Eddy, 72; Edy, 113; Elijah, 212; Francis, 78; George, 29; Hezekiah, 194; Jane, 164, 172; James, 10, 70, 72, 79, 101, 107, 156, 168, 177, 192, 204, 214; Jessie, 6, 21, 186; John, 19, 24, 42, 61, 109, 124, 126, 143, 168, 172, 183, 210; Joab, 193, 211; Joshua, 32, Lewis, 193; Levi. 200; Martha, 31; Moses, 97; Nancy, 77, 147; Orphan, 91; Polly, 15; Rebecca, 136; Robert, 108; Sarah, 77, 210; Susana, 30; Smithfield, 181; Stephen, 168; Thomas, 16, 122, 211; Uel, 100; William, 44, 155, 188; Wright, 46, 202.
MASEY, Thomas, 31
MASHBURN, Jefferson, 9
MASON, Jefferson, 195; John, 40; Joseph, 35; Lurania, 19; Thomas, 83, 208; Walker, 91; Wilie, 107, 117; William, 140, 166.
MASSA, Polly, 185; William, 24.
MASSENGALE, Dread, 4; John, 193; Warren, 206.
MASSEY, Affanatius, 205; Bacharas, 39, 78; Elijah, 79; George, 93; John 115; Nancy, 110; Reddick, 110 Wyley, 113.
MASSINGALE, Dred, 116
MASTIN, Eliza, 163; Richard, 47, 193.
MASTERS, Bartholomew, 26
MATCHET, Holden, 19, 73; Jacob, 154; William, 42, 134.
MATHA, William, 133

MATHER, Benel, ...6
MATHEWS, Abel, 180; Alexander, 51; Abel, 180; Alexander, 51; Archibald, 146; Benjamin, 10; Bettsey, 151; Charles, 128, 179; Colemon, 140; Diey, 78; Elizabeth, 51, 187, 188, 193; Enoch, 31; Francis, 91; Henry, 189; Isaac, 91; Jermiah, 101; Jessie, 91; John, 18, 39, 40, 42, 74, 86, 159; Joll, 3, 39, 191; Jordon, 143; Joseph, 151; Josiah, 55, 209; Laban, 103; Littleton, 207; Mary, 19, 163; Mary Ann, 51; Mancy, 73, 147; Richard, 187; Roderick, 95; Samuel, 15, 155; Sarah, 176; Sugar, 97, 194; Thomas, 177; William, 51, 101, 153, 204; Willis, 215.
MATHEWSON, D., 197; Malcom, 195 William, 150.
MATHIS, Benjamin, 191; David, 191; Jane, 53, 115; James, 73; John, 29, 95, 216; Penelope, 71; Peter, 7; Robert, 205; Thomas, 151; William, 91.
MATHISON, Daniel, ...46
MATTELT, James, ...144
MATTINS, Josiah, ...56
MATTOCKS, George, ...26
MATTOX, Charles, 26; John, 57; Richard, 82.
MAUDCHIE, John, ...178
MAUGUM, Robert, ...111
MAULDEN, Abraham, 149; Elias, 39; Frances, 212; Jessie, 82; Martha, 206; Samuel, 89; Wesley, 193.
MAUND, Hardy, 161; 170; Mary, 90.
MAWHOOD, Robert, ...91
MAWPAS, Lewis, ...201
MAXWELL, Benjamin, 145; Elijah, 120; Henry, 117; James, 124; Jessie, 201; John, 89, 91; Nathan, 187; Reuben, 52; William, 36, 75, 201, 132.
MAXIE, Russell, ...80
MAXEY, Jerimah, 192; John, 95; Thomas, 111.
MAY, Henry, 25; James, 139; Johnas, 178; Jessie, 40; Joseph, 119; Peter, 117, 209; Thomas, 188; Tolby, 150.
MAYBERRY, Joel, ...107
MAYES, J. M., ...96
MAYFIELD, Jacob, 63; James, 2.
MAYN, James, ...73
MAYNARD, Rebecca, ...37
MAYNE, John, ...158
MAYNES, Samuel, ...185
MAYNESS, Bradley, ...175
MAYO, Axom, 113; Burrell, 216; David, 198; Ed., 180; James, 154; Joseph, 135; M., 201; Margaret, 151; Nathan, 188; Sally, 24; Sarah, 93; Susan, 22; William, 118, 148, 157.
MAYORS, Daniel, ...119
MAYS, Allan, 85; Alfred, 216; Alsy, 157; John, 125; Orphans, 111; William, 35; 128.
McADAMS, Henry, ...130
McAFREE, Abraham, ...169
McALHONY, Ann, ...88
McALLISTER, Mathew, 207; M. H., 126; James, 157; Sarah, 164.
McANNALLY, James, ...209
McAULEY, Petty, ...99
McAUTHOR, John, 55; Peter, 200.
McBANE, John, ...184
McBOIN, James, ...202
McBRAIN, John, ...143
McBRIDE, Elizabeth, 183; James, 102, 103; John, 142, 115; Kathryn, 202; Samuel, 50, 198.
McBURNETT, Hester, 38; Thomas, 184.
McCAIN, Alexander, 15; Callum, 187; William, 32, 45.
McCALL, Alexander, 178; Charles, 47; David, 85, 195; Elizabeth, 191; Elhanon, 172; James, 94; John, 42, 179; Nathaniel, 174.
McCALLEY, David, ...117
McCANN, Charles, 170; Mariah, 30; Martin, 63; Patrick, 90.
McCANNE, Hugh, ...22
McCANT, John, ...107
McCANTS, Sarah, ...11
McCARD, Em, 78; Len, 78; Nancy, 90.
McCARDELL, Able, 194; James, 26.
McCARKLE, Abram, 100; Samuel, 100
McCARLES, Samuel, ...19
McCARMACK, Hirum, 97; Jerimiah, 111; John, 73; Margaret, 142.
McCARNACH, John, 37; Mary, 199.
McCARNELL, Agnes, 117; Joseph, 174.
McCORNICH, Henry, ...32
McCARRELL, John, ...62, 175
McCARTNEY, William, ...92
McCARTER, Eveline, ...63
McCARTY, Daniel, 40; James, 78; Margaret, 171; Mary, 19; Michiel, 171.
McCAY, Gabreal, '199, 92; Nathaniel, 170, 7; Robert, 7; William, 6.
McCEARLY, William, ...92
McCLAIN, Deliah, 244; Elizabeth, 214; Ephriam, 112; James, 112; John, 215; Sethil, 83.
McCLAINY, S., ...82
McCLANE, Ephiam, ...28
McCLARIN, Harrison, ...92
McCLASKEY, Thomas, ...160

McCLAUNNY, Charles, ...95
McCLEELAND, M., 93; George, 96; McClain, 131.
McCLELLAND, John, 42; Joseph, 210; Phoebe, 148.
McCLELAND, Abagale, ...215
McCLELLON, Marker, 179; Phoebe, 1.
McCLENDON, Denis, 179; Frances, 99; Joseph, 142; Thomas, 189; William, 179.
McCLEROY, John, ...159
McCLESKIE, James, ...143
McCLUER, John, ...143
McCLUM, Hirum, ...174
McCLUNG, Jonas, ...107
McCLUSKY, George, 211; Hirum, 12; Joseph, 95; Mark, 126.
McCOME, Andrew, ...172
McCOMMON, Sus, ...182
McCONKY, Jane, ...101
McCONNELL, Agnes, ...23
McCOOK, Jamica, 121; Shir, 106.
McCOLLEY, Lanier, ...196
McCOLLUM, Thomas, 176; J., 119, 128.
McCOLUM, Archibald, ...118
McCORDY, Dar, ...42
McCORKLE, Archibald, ...118
McCORLLEY, Joseph, ...50
McCORQUODALE, John, ...43
McCOURLY, William, ...2
McCOWAN, David, 9; Duncan, 18; John, 3.
McCOY, Conellius, 41; George, 138; Henry, 19; Jane, 42; James, 156; Nathanel, 148; Samuel, 164; Thomas, 25, 160.
McCRANE, Jones, ...78
McCRANEY, Daniel, ...55
McCRARY, Aser, 78; Ezekiel, 152; Fannie, 10; Isabelle, 51; Peg, 4; Peggy, 55; Robert, 192; McCajah, 156.
McCRAY, Charity, ...130
McCRAW, John, ...3
McCRACKIN, Arnold, 159; Hirum, 196; Robert, 83; William, 51.
McCRE, John, ...169
McCREDY, Peter, ...170
McCROSKEY, James, ...183
McCUIN, Allbrittian, ...55
McCULLEN, Eelias, 117; William, 127
McCULLENS, Charles, 31; Hardy, 49; William, 184.
McCULLER, John, 145; Thomas, 173.
McCULLOUGH, Mary, ...96
McCULOH, Jacob, 116, 29; J., 27; Samuel, 31.
McCUME, Joseph, 115; William, 170.
McCUNE, Orphan, ...153
McCURDY, Archibald, 198; Elias, 43;

James, 205, 119; John, 43, 64; Moses, 5; Robert, 31, 112.
McCURLEY, Moses, 142; William, 208.
McCURLLY, William, ...72
McCURRY, Daniel, 31; Louchlin, 164, 145; Lothlin, 208.
McCUTCHEON, Joseph, ...146
McDADE, John, ...169
McDANIEL, Andrew, 80; Alexander, 159; Danuel, 36; Davis, 86; Elizabeth, 72; Jacob, 127, 137; James, 133; Jeremiah, 2; John, 84, 214; Homer, 181; Mary, 80; Winn, 151.
McDERMONT, Margaret, ...
McDILL, James, ...167, 196
McDONALD, Alexander, 139, 214; Archibald, 105; Charles, 199; Daniel, 110, 130, 183; Ester, 169, 214; Giles, 104; Greenberry, 142; Hugh, 95; Isiam, 103; J. S.; Jacob, 187; James, 212, 123, 94; Jehiel, 178; Jeneniah, 109; John, 26, 43, 51, 89, 96, 102, 124, 126, 149, 164, 192, 196; Mar, 23; Martha, 28; Melton, 101; Orphan, 19, 22; Rad, 184; William, 20, 211.
McDOWELL, Charles, 108; Daniel, 149 Elizabeth, 4; ohn, 143, 180; Robert, 57; Seth, 6; Susanna, 4; Thomas, 143; William, 153.
McDUFF, William, ...146
McDUFFIE, Merdoff, ...133
McDUCAL, John, ...171
McEACHEN, John, ...124
McELHAMAN, James, ...186
McELROY, Anderson, 19; John, 121; Thomas, 37; Christion, 86.
McEVA, Thomas, 136.
McEWEN, John, 115; Kirkman, 114.
McFARLIN, Robert, 149! William, 106
McFARLAND, Hazekiah, 189; James, 188; John, 102; Joseph, 184; Vilanda, 93; William, 169.
McFARLIN, C., 37; John, 53.
McGAR, Len, ...184
McGARITY, Wilson, ...46
McCAUCHY, William, ...29
McGEE, Ephern, 58; James, 94, 214; Ruben, 51.
McGEHEE, Ansel, 49; George, 101; James, 114; Jerry, 110; Lewis, 72, 129; Nathan, 29.
McGENNIS, Daniel, 171; Phelix, 38; William, 154.
McGHEE, Benjamin, ...164
McGIBBEN, Kathryn, ...193
McGIBONEY, Eranus, ...129
McGILL, John, ...70, 142
McGILLIS, Hanna, 20; T. K., 209.
McGLAMERY, John, ...29

McGLAUN, Hardy, 130; James, 187.
McGLAWN, John, 197; Susian, 177.
McGLEDNEY, William, 186
McGLOGAN, Kathryn, 214
McGOUIRK, William, 92
McGOWEN, Frances, 164; Joseph, 114; Zack, 32.
McGRADY, A., 153
McGRAW, Corzene, 109
McGREGON, Charles, 75
McGRIFF, Thomas, 45
McGUINTY, Robert, 200; William, 182.
McGUIRE, Fredrick, 21; Samual, 130; Thompson, 95.
McGUIRE, Fredrick, 37; William, 101.
McHARDY, Alexander, 155
McHARGUE, John, 179; William, 177.
McHENLEY, James, 172
McINNIS, Mary, 203; Newcome, 124.
McINNIS, Mary, 203; Newcome, 124.
McINNISH, John, 5
McINVALE, James, 79
McIVER, John, 113
McINTIRE, Charles, 173; Duncan, 168; Hugh, 7; James, 190; John, 209, 211; Jonathan, 126, 149; Philip, 50.
McINTOSH, Orphan, 178; Barbarer, 146; James, 147; John, 113, 172; Locklan, 190; Mary, Ann, 10; Susan, 97.
McJENKINS, Denatus, 128
McJONES, James, 12
McKAY, Danial, 175; William, 14, 101
McKEAN, Barnett, 110; Mary, 182.
McKEE, John, 127, 177, 214; Frances, 14.
McKEEN, Vt., 21; Sarah, 181; William, 141.
McKENDREE, John, 96, 169
McKENNEY, George, 108; James, 105; John, 189; Kinch, 90; Mary, 47; Michael, 152; Thomas, 92.
McKENNIN, Elizabeth, 141; Lovison, 138; William, 127.
McKENZIE, A., 21; Absolem, 206; Anguis, 113; Chestly, 206; Hanna, 16; Hardy, 3; N., 104; Nancy, 215; Samuel, 193; William, 41, 99.
McKIDDEN, Alexander, 34
McKINNY, Abraham, 20; Benjamin, 199; Charles, 9; Elizabeth, 141; Henry, 200; M., 21, 200; Sineon, 34.
McKESSACK, M., 179; William, 197.
McKLEROY, A., 38; Zakais, 38.
McKAY, Alexandrie, 112
McKNIGHT, John, 21
McKARKLE, Robert, 23
McKUTCHEN, William, 152

McLAIN, Andrew, 212; Daniel, 194; George, 136; Hugh, 45; John, 35, 86, 163; Lughlin, 200; Samuel, 107; Thomas, 118; William, 200, 136.
McLANE, John, 6
McLAUGLIN, Ed, 161; James, 184.
McLAURAN, Archibald, 3
McLEALAND, Joseph, 51
McLEAN, Hugh, 173
McLEARY, James, 214
McLEE, Henry, 47
McLEOD, Alexander, 9; Daniel, 132; Lonaldfi 191; Duncan, 13; Gilbert, 141; Hugh, 82; James, 203; John, 49, 205; Malcom, 102; Mary, 119; Mur, 112; Norman, 29, 130.
McLELAND, Elizabeth, 91, 192
McLEMORE, Howell, 49, 117; Freeman, 168.
McLERAN, Mary, 167; Elizabeth, 38.
McLEROY, Cursey, 150; Mar., 207, 171; Sarah, 28; Charles, 28; John, 54, 187; William, 170.
McLESTER, James, 202
McLUNGE, Reuben, 70
McMAHAN, Susannah, 51
McMANUS, Richard, 111; Robert, 154, 714.
McMASTER, William, 89
McMATH, A., 207; Hackeliah, 35; William, 111, 212.
McMICHAEL, Charity, 8; Green, 205; John, 196; Joseph, 31, 178; Mathew, 97, 155; Seaborn, 53.
McMICKENS, M., 62
McMILLAN, Alexander, 201; Allen, 202; Amon, 92; G., 151; George, 146; Jeremiah, 202; John, 15, 122; Louisa, 100; William, 155.
McMINN, Charles, 61
McMULLIN, Fielding, 6, 57; George, 127; Henry, 55; Patrick, 201; Sinclair, 215; William, 104.
McMURRAN, David, 21
McMURRAY, Eliza, 90; James, 136; John, 124.
McNAIR, James, 48; Robert, 58, 71, 216.
McNEAL, Andrew, 50; Margaret, 28; William, 28.
McNULY, Allen, 143; Eleanor, 41, 199; Hugh, 115, 196.
McNEESE, Daniel, 9
McNEIL, Archibald, 90; David, 216; James, 104; J. N., 154.
McPHELL, Charles, 144; Dugal, 154.
McPHERSON, Arthur, 193; Neil, 133.
McQUIRTOR, Allen, 200; David, 120; John, 183.
McQUEEN, John, 178; Margaret, 145.

McQUERTER, Allen, 163
McRAE, Alexander, 31, 109; Christopher, 38; Farquahard, 15, 214; Neal, 13; Norman, 160.
McRAY, Nancy, 215; Norman, 92.
McRAINER, Danial, 169
McREE, Alexander, 98, 176; Benjamin, 207; Frances, 110; William, 129.
McRONNEY, William, 186
McSWAIN, Anguish, 203; Anquish, 137; Asia, 15; Elizabeth, 118; Margaret, 206.
McSWINEY, Edward, 131
McTYRE, Mary, 32
McVAY, Margaret, 83
McVEAL, L. A., 161; M., 111; M. J., 161.
McWALTERS, Hugh, 51
McWHORTER, Margaret, 31; Walter, 205.
McWHORTERS, John, 33, 130; Samuel, 91.
McWYER, Daniel, 211
MEACHAN, Henry, 138; Lyaman, 31; Silas, 171.
MEADER, Richard, 180
MEADOR, Jason, 64, 83; Richard, 159
MEADOWS, Christopher, 68; Isiac, 163; Jacob, 38, 64; James, 106; Joel, 135, 175; Thomas, 16, 93; Venson, 23; Wiley, 150; William, 149, 210; Wylie, 182.
MEALING, Earton, 215; Hinton, 168.
MEANS, John, 13
MEARNOEY, Nathan, 213
MECASKEL, Peter, 113
MEDCOCK, John, 98
MEDDER, Reuben, 129
MEDDOWS, Hardy, 146; William, 54.
MEDLOCK, Charles, 211; John, 184.
MEEHEHAN, Thomas, 170
MEEKS, Benjamin, 104, 154; Brittian, 50; Martin, 97; Noah, 4; Reban, 136; William, 12.
MEELER, Sampson, 201
MEGAHEE, Susan, 17
MEGEE, Thomas, 31
MEGGS, John,
MEHODO, Ann, 82
MEIGS, Daniel, 19; Elisia, 181.
MELL, William, 144
MELON, Morgan, 107
MELONE, Codwell, 150
MELTON, Eleel, 14
MELONEE, Samuel, 208
MELORE, John, 16
MELSON, William, 15
MELTON, Appleton, 212; Bauldy, 107; Cherry, 166; Denson, 4; Jonathan, 151; Josiah, 148; Richard, 167; Seaborn, 187; William, 141, 163, 181.

MENEFIE, William, 70
MERCER, Asa, 143; Charles, 142; Dennis, 40; Dicey, 4; Garner, 22; Henry, 110, 117; Hymnrich, 160; John, 19; Levy, 71; Meridith, 126; Noah, 190; Riley, 26; Solomon, 205; William, 214.
MERCHANT, Christian, 88; Isaac, 9.
MERIDITH, Nathan, 73; William, 29, 48.
MERKASON, Daniel, 86
MERONY, William, 156
MERREL, Elizabeth, 148
MERRIDA, Clarissa, 31
MERRIDITH, John, 187
MERRIDY, Wyatt, 252
MERRIT, Isam, 56, 161; Joseph, 26; William, 128.
MERRIWETHER, Charles, 158; David, 26, 155; Frances, 212; James, 20; Joseph, 59; Richard, 8, 33; Valentine, 140, 178, 187; William, 62, 151.
MERSHON, Enos, 105; Jemina, 40; John, 211.
MESELLE, James, 136
MESSER, John, 153, 180
MESSEX, Isaic, 180
MESICK, George, 151
METCALF, Martha, 5, 131
METZGER, Benjamin, 101
MEWBORN, Thomas, 117
MEWS, Daniel, 47, 98; Moren, 126.
MICHAEL, Brittiam, 92
MICHAL, Rebecca, 26
MICKEL, Jerimiah, 89
MICKLER, Daniel, 204
MIDDLEBROOKS, Andrew, 172; Anderson, 103; James, 121; Jerry, 103; James, 121; John, 71, 165, 185; Thomas, 50.
MIDDLETON, Hugh, 149; James, 31; John, 10, 114.
MIERS, John, 165; Wm., 201.
MIKELL, General, 14
MILAM, Benjamin, 44; Dudley, 109.
MILBURN, Henry, 113
MILES, Abraham, 75; Daniel, 119, 185; Jane, 204; John, 101, 165; Josiah, 88; Thomas, 52, 72, 137, 168.
MILHOUSE, John, 175
MILLIFORD, Winnie, 169
MILIRONS, Isiaac, 172
MILK, William, 174
MILLARD, Mason, 153
MILLENDER, Marla, 164
MILLER, Aaron, 165, 171; Abraeram, 108; Alexander, 27, 91; Archibold, 108; Charles, 16, 186, 196; Cynthia, 3; David, 128; Elizabeth, 157; Elizah, 95, 142, 154; Eperraim, 154;

Frances, 4, 120, 151, 155, 215; Frederick, 106, 163; George, 54; Goodwin, 138; Green, 171; Henry, 129; Jacob, 71, 170, 173, 191; James, 9, 43, 97, 165, 209; Jedicaah, 174; Jonathan, 157; Jididaer, 59; Makaga, 183; Mark, 171, 183; Martha, 69, 84, 179; Mary, 41, 201, 215; Mathew, 156; Nancy, 58; Pott, 208; Richard, 37; Robert, 102; Shadrack, 55; Susan, 128, 163; Wiley, 19, 132; William, 96, 99, 188.
MILLICAN, Allen, 99, 156; Charles, 50; Delita, 96; John, 80; Levi, 21; Louis, 156; Thomas, 59.
MILLIGAN, John, ...127
MILLIRONS, Delila, 214; Polly, 134.
MILLIVEE, Ambrose, ...170
MILLS, Archibald, 215; Asaph, 32; Chesley, 37; Eliz., 149; Elizabeth, 185; Franklin, 178; Frederick, 16, 169; James, 156; Jessie, 74, 116; John, 6, 98, 212; Mary, 121, 203; Mathew, 90; Orphans, 102; Rebecca, 91; Richard, 32; Robert, 145; Sally, 172; Sarah, 28, 47; Spine, 106; Stephen, 38; Thomas, 167, 195; William, 190, 213.
MILNER, John, 134, 187, 195; Pitt, 44.
MILSAPS, Larkin, 69, 210; Thomas, 202; William, 169.
MILTON, Asa, 148; A., S. R., 11; Benjamin, 151; Eliza, 178; John, 156, 18; Martha, 214; Peter, 87.
MIMMS, Benjamin, 206, David, 214, 93, 100; Eliza, 199; George, 108.
MIMS, Elizabeth, 193, 73; Gidden, 20; John, 216; Littleton, 138.
MINCE, James, ...2
MINCHEN, Elisha, 196; Joseph, 75; Martha, 208.
MINCY, Williby, 163; Willonghby, 191.
MINGELDORF, George, ...209
MINISH, John, ...111
MIMICH, John, ...8
MINOR, Racheal, 136; Samuel, 11; V. A., 82; S. M., 82; Will, 36.
MINSEY, John, ...160
MINSHEW, Nathan, ...87
MINSHON, Calvin, ...39
MINTER, Benjamin, 119; Calvin, 39; Jessie, 2; John, 39; Nancy, 95; William, 216.
MIRAR, William, ...104
MITCHAM, Randolph, 87; Silas, 54.
MITCHELL, A., 122, 184; Alsy, 100; Buttey, 13; Benjimin, 135; David, 171; Elizabeth, 50; Franklin, 216; George, 164, 183; Hartwell, 15;

Henry, 24, 31, 33, 82, 122, 126, 161; Hinche, 168; Isaac, 115; Isaih, 187; James, 49, 193; Jesse, 35, 215; John, 154, 193, 199; Jonathan, 53; Josiah, 32, 108; J. T., 34; Julian, 74; Julius, 202; Madison, 123; Mary 112; Math, 80; Nancy, 195; Peter, 23; Polly, 70; Robert, 44, 136, 155; 160, 186; S., 110; Sally, 81; Sarah, 167; Stith, 39; Thomas, 57; Uriah, 207; Wiley, 5; William, 30, 73, 116, 185, 187, 211.
MITCHINOR, William, ...134
MITTS, Wright, ...207
MIXON, James, 187; John, 204, 69; William, 13.
MIZE, Joseph, 96; Robert, 208; Shepard, 134; Sterling, 174; Thomas, 184.
MIZEL, Agsa, 12; David, 16, 7, 75; Ena, 207; Joseph, 180.
MOAT, Robert, ...174
MOATE, Drury, 116; Hiram, 211; John, 112, 125; Riley, 35, 100; Silas, 214; William, 194.
MOATES, William, ...207
MOBLEY, Elizabeth, 171; Edward, 157; George, 44; Isaac, 171; James, 38; Nathan, 71; Payton, 185; William, 100, 126, 141.
MOCK, George, 116; Granville, 89; Joel, 112; Joseph, 181; Littleberry, 125; Mary, 3, 171; Thomas, 139.
MODESET, Isabel, 86; Samuel, 199.
MODESETT, John, ...31
MOFFETT, Agnes, ...94
MOLDEN, Thomas, ...174
MOLLESON, John, ...94
MOLLET, Rebecca
MOLLOY, Elizabeth, ...74
MOLLESEN, John, ...94
MONCREAF, Austen, ...153, 168
MONCRIEF, Mary, ...94
MONK, John, 105; Larray, 203; Robert, 39; Silas, 106; Simon, 107; William, 58.
MONROE, David, 148; Jackson, 40; Jesse, 183.
MONTFORD, Elizabeth, 3, 64; Fort, 37.
MONTMONLEN, John, ...107
MONTGOMERY, Bartley, 91, 162; Benjamin, 80; David, 124; Hiram, 211; Hugh, 135; James, 195; Mar, 22; Samuel, 173; Telemachus, 205; Thomas, 95; Ulysses, 152, 180.
MOON, Archibald, 44; George, 120; James, 14; John, 59, 127, 182, 196; Luc., 100; Sarah, 201; William, 162.
MOODY, Elizabeth, 29; Green, 147; John, 12, 16, 94, 141; Simeon, 57;

Silvaners, 160; Sylvanus, 8; William, 13, 179; Winnie, 120.
MOONEY, Richard, 191
MOONY, Richard, 113
MOONYHAM, John, 206
MOORE, Abel, 146; Alexander, 167; Alfred, 113; Ammosa, 21; Anderson, 59, 73, 147; Arbin, 98, 171; Asa, 208; Benning, 198; Burell, 25; Deward, 181; Elbert, 133; Elija, 142; Eliza, 204; Elizabeth, 216; Ethelard, 41; Evaline, 89; Fimey, 132; Francis, 180; George, 12, 59, 148; Henry, 95; Hugh, 27; Irvin, 89; Isaac, 118; Esarel, 176; James, 4, 7, 21, 63, 122, 123, 150, 163, 167, 204; esse, 147; oel, 42; oem, 3, 81, 83, 95, 105, 116, 168; Joseph, 146; Josiah, 193; Lemenl, 128; Loverd, 46; Leving, 118; Martha, 15, 101, 124; Mathen, 106, 136; Michal, 133; Moren, 171; Moses, 64; Nancy, 2; Nicey, 166; Richard, 119; Robert, 69, 137; Roderick, 109; Sally, 201; Samuel, 25, 102, 116, 148, 156, 183; Sarah, 40, 59, 63, 81, 126; Spencer, 122; Stephen, 69, 154; Synthia, 213; Tillman, 86; Thomas, 8, 105; Warren, 74; Whithington, 87; William, 146, 155, 209, 134, 139; Willis, 167.
MOORING, James, 132
MOORMAN, Pleasant, 127
MOPHIT, Mary Ann, 54
MOREE, Tamar, 56
MORELAND, Ben, 32, 200; Edmond, 190; Isaac, 137; Robert, 24; William, 4.
MORELL, John, 52, 200; William, 52.
MOREMAN, Haley, 175; William, 150.
MORERAN, Jesse, 5
MORGAN, Charlott, 152; D. & W., 54; Daniel, 121; Eldridge, 169; Elizabeth, 212; Frederick, 81; Griffin, 12; Henry, 56; Hiram, 17; Isaac, 149; James, 12, 28, 203, Jesse, 5, 88, 101, 137, 110; John, 17, 104, 115, 187; Josiah, 13; Luke, 94; Mary, 3, 140; Samuel, 101; Sarah, 81; Thomas, 56; Wiley, 205; William, 53, 57, 140, 180, 216; Wilson, 146.
MORLAND, Francis, 6; William, 14.
MORMAN, William, 171
MORRIS, Abraham, 208; Alonzo, 83; Benjamin, 140, 167; Burrel, 34; Caswell, 168; Charles, 103; Drury, 107; Edwin, 113, 194; Elanza, 15; Elizabeth, 205; George, 43; Grace, 102; Hammah, 62; Hardy, 212; Isham, 81; James, 37, 159, 203; Jeremiah, 158; Jesse, 11; John, 103, 109, 117,

120, 157; Joseph, 109, 133; Littleton, 54; Lucy, 166; Moses, 127; Murrell, 50; Nancy, 50; Nathaniel, 28; Obediah, 79; Osteen, 79; Peggy, 153; Richard, 96, 130; Samuel, 41; Sarah, 193; Thomas, 66, 175; Warren, 18; William, 23, 35, 43, 63, 107, 185, 193.
MORRISON, Alexander, 171, 179; Anguish, 25; Daniel, 143; Hugh, 20, 116; John, 119; Malcom, 135; Thomas, 130, 152; William, 32, 168.
MORROS, Thomas, 75
MORROW, Ann, 74; Eving, 83; Nancy, 44; Elizabeth, 27; James, 108; Joseph, 18.
MORSE, Oliver, 206
MORTON, Joel, 158; Oliver, 156; John, 16; Henry, 100.
MOSES, Isaac, 212; Stephen, 160.
MOSELEY, Benjamin, 149, 176; Daniel, 102; David, 162, 144; Isham, 181; Lewis, 177; Mathew, 44; Nancy, 47; Prudence, 152; Samuel, 145, 43, 167; Sarah, 71; Seaborn, 110; Stephen, 147, 127; Thomas, 35; William, 29.
MOTE, Car, 113; Nan, 113; Silas, 11; William, 62, 149.
MOTES, Mary, 158! Thomas, 114; John, 53.
MOTT, Nathan, 42
MOUGHON, Thomas, 167; William, 44.
MOULTRIE, Joseph, 10
MOULTRY, Joel, 200; Patience, 71.
MUCKLEROY, Woodson, 143
MUKEY, James, 213
MULKEY, Homer, 155; James, 3; Moses, 63.
MULL, John, 136
MULLOY, Stephen, 32
MULLEY, William, 53
MULLICAN, Thomas, 208
MULLIKIN, Tandy, 33
MULLIN, Clarissa, 94
MULLINS, Burton, 168; B. W., 31; James, 7; John, 91; Malone, 53; Osborne, 145; William, 174.
MULRINE, Elizabeth, 116
MUNFORT, Robert, 74
MUNROE, Orphans, 52
MURDEN, Edmund, 116; Levinia, 43.
MURDOCK, Joseph, 196; Watson, 114
MURPHY, Absolom, 143; Benjamin, 22; Cherry, 44; Daniel, 88, 120; Edmund, 13; Iredell, 186; J. 156; John, 103, 133, 136, 201, 213; Joseph, 159; Malachi, 212; Milly, 204; Myers, 110; Nancy, 82; Paschal, 163,

Randolph, 4; Thomas, 64; William, 87, 94, 164.
MURPHREY, Henry, 35; William, 166.
MURRAH, George, 7, 175; James, 82. Jehu, 183.
MURRAY, Jeremiah, 164; John, 105; Elizabeth, 133; Ezekiel, 180; Daniel, 175; Alexander, 183; William, 90.
MURRIN, Mary, _____4
MURRY, Ed., 132; Margaret, 4; Joseph, 163; John, 52; Nancy, 11; James, 129; Patrick, 156.
MUSGROVE, Sampson, 63; Harrison, 100; Araminta, 94; Michael, 95; Musselwhite; Redding, 204, 207; William, 151, 207; 194.
MUSTIN, Ely, _____51
MYERS, David, 63; Elizabeth, 29; Lucinda, 54.
MYHAND, Alvin, 6, 137; Rosan, 122.
MYRICK, Elizabeth, 106; Evans, 70; John, 13, 87, 194; Richard, 58; Stephen, 216.
NABB, William B., _____36, 79
NAIL, Burrell, 24; Richard, 36.
MAILOR, Dixon, 164; Stephen, 186.
NAISH, Frances, 40; Jeremiah, 63.
NALER, Dixon, 155; Joseph, 33.
NALL, Eldridge, 111; Thomas, J., 40; William, E., 57.
NALLS, Sarah, _____57
NANCE, Fleming B., 183; John, 94; Wesley, 107.
NAPIER, Thomas, _____64
NAPPER, Sarah, _____154
NASH, James C., 143; J. B., 143; John, 124, 195; Reuben, 92; Robert, 102; Thomas, 181, 195; Thomas J., 47; W. B., 193.
NASWORTHY, Lucretia, 158; John, 113, 161.
NATION, Catherine, _____53
NAVES, John, _____155
NAVY, James, _____142
NAYLOR, John, _____207
NEAL, Lindsey, 46; Harral, 188; William, 210; John, 160; William, 162.
NEALY, Mary, _____167
NEASMITH, Charles, 72, 49; Eleander, 20.
NEEL, Daniel, 117; Elijah, 192; William, 21.
NEELY, John, 39; Joseph, 93; Thomas, 93, 147; Wm. A., 5.
NELMS, Daniel, 45; John, 177; Nancy, 176; Nathaniel, 82; William, 110
NELLUMS, John, 112; Joshua, 120.
NELSON, Ann, 175; Alexander, 31;

Exum, 55; Enoch R., 168; Charles, 8th, 36; Francis, 141; James M., 28; James H., 28; John, 102; John B., 107; Noah, 198, 45; Mitchell, 93; Mitchell, 160; Perry, 53; Wade, 195; William, 206, 44, 134.
NESBIT, Hugh, 113; Jane, 163; Jeremiah, 91; Samuel, 104.
NESBITT, Alexander, 154; Hugh, 61; John, 36; Martha, 150; Samuel, 72; William, 15.
NETTLES, Elizabeth, 97; George, 191; William, 116; Isaac, 77.
NEVELL, William, _____124
NEVIL, Abraham, _____71
NEVILLE, Peter, 26; James, 64.
NEVITT, John, _____69
NEW, Benjamin, 51; Daniel, 19; Jacob, Jr., 132; William, 214, 198.
NEWBERN, Bitha, _____51
NEWBERRY, Ephamma, 74; Henry, 74; James, 137; Mary, 74; Orphan, 141; Peter, 74.
NEWBORN, Luke, _____63
NEWBURN, Dread, 29; Hickman, 186; Thomas, 173.
NEWBY, James, _____124
NEWLEY, James S., _____57
NEWELL, William P., _____56
NEWMAN, Amey, 124; Charles, 77; Hilary,, 84, 45; Jepthah, 106; John, 147; Thomas, 119; William, 19, 20, 52; Wormley, 93.
NEWSOM, Ananis, 216; Dicey, 151; Dread, 133; Eady, 54; Edy, 140; Elizabeth, 71; Frederick, 81; G. & Mar., 35; Gideon, 45; Hardy, 94; Joel, 37; John, 42, 48; Joshua, 179, 22.
NEWSOME, Lucy, _____75
NEWSOM, Orphean, 157; Roderick, 151; Sarah, 203; Silas, 43; Solomon, 125; William, 128.
NEWTON, Catherine, 98, 126; Clary, 72; David B., 35; Henry, 121, 186; Isaac, 185; John, 18; Levi, 83; Margaret, 108.
NEYLAND, Abraham I. H., 192; Henry, 20; Rebecca, 211; Susan, 194.
NIBLACK, Samuel, 102; William, 36.
NIBLETT, Elizabeth, 206; Peggy, 95.
NICHOLES, Martha, _____140
NICHOLS, Abraham, 29; Evelyn, D., 133; Elias, 90; Henry, 50; Julius, 120; John, 33, 108, 139; Simon W., 50; Solemn, 133; William, 111, 16; Richard J., 158.
NICHOLSON, Elizabeth, 16; James, 214; John, 149, 80.
NICHOLAR, Vincent, _____72
NICHOLASSEN, Thomas, _____198

NICKELSON, Duncan, _____99
NICKILSON, Duncan, _____21
NICKSON, Travis, 186; William, 27.
NIGHT, Moses, _____209
NILES, Ambrose, 180; Henry, 40.
NILMNS, Egekeel, _____128
NIX, Isom, 215; James, 83; Jesse, 180; John, 78, 169; Joseph, 167; Liddy, 29; Nicholas, 214; Thomas, 158.
NIXON, Travis, _____162
NIX, Valentine, 168; Washington, 154
NIXON, Elizabeth, 107; James L., 153; James, 75, 108; Samuel, 142; Sarah, 150.
NOBLE, Hamilton, 64; John, 89; Philemon, 166.
NOBLES, Andrew, 58, 125; Anna, 170; Amos, 158; Henry, 168; James, 42; James Jackson, 50; Levy, 47; Mary, 10; Orphan, 216; Teneson, 173; Tennison, 148; Wallis, 39; William, 55, 35, 170.
NOEL, Nancy, _____127
NOLAN, James, _____55
NOLEN, John E., 216; Richard, 133.
NOLENS, James, 139; Stephen, 147.
NOLES, Zachariah, _____9
NOLL, Eldridge, _____196
NOLLY, Walter, _____156
NOLEN, Rubin, 211; William, 197.
NORELL, James, 151; Willis B., 139.
NORMAN, Benjamin, 19; Carolin, 2; Elizabeth, 138; Gideon, 75; Isaac M., 33; James, 104; John H., 158; Lewis, 185.
NORRELL, Ann, _____54
NORRIS, Alexander, 204; Archibald, 170; Baldwin, 143; Enoch, 114; James, 215, 77, 116, 135, 215; Jennins, 212; Maria C., 152; Mourning, 77; Orphan, 211; Patrick, 192; Robert, 124, 136; Samuel, 158; Sanford, 24; William, 212, 127, 186, 56, 178, 117, 80.
NORTH, William, _____123
NORTHCUTT, Robert, _____204
NORTON, Jacob P., 193; Jonathan, 47; Lewis, 73; Nehemiah, 2; William, 59, 87.
NORSWORTH, James, _____61
NORTHINGTON, Wm., _____7
WORWOOD, Delilah, 102; George, 96; James, 98; Samuel, 98, 88; Themus, 117; Thomas, 5; William, 139.
NORTHINGTON, William, _____81
NOWELL, Isham, 22, 78; James, 90; Luke, 151.
NOWLAN, George, 180; Nathaniel, 17.
NOWLES, Parker, _____102, 189
NOYES, William, _____208
NUN, John, 176, 182; Washington, 187.

NUNELLY, Israel, _____63
NUNGAZER, Joseph, _____126
NUNLES, James, _____
NUNN, James, F., _____53
NUNNOLLY, Aaron F., 129; H. A. B., 53; Suckey, 97; Elizabeth, 136.
NUNNELY, Israel, _____149
NUTT, Martha, _____127
OAKS, Rebecca, 100; Jonathan, 215.
OATS, Samuel, _____16, 126
OBANION, Benjamin, 136; Green, 82, 63; John, 164.
OBAR, Robert, _____102
OBRIANT, James, _____170
OCONNER, James, 158; Michael, 216; Nancy, 95; Patrick, 133.
OCONNOUR, Francis, _____35
ODOM, Archibald, 143; Dempsey, 51.
ODEN, Mills, _____29
ODENA, Peter, _____124
ODOM, Aaron, 167; Benjamin, 194; ODOM, Elizabeth _____14
Brian, 42; Dildatha, 75; James, 74; John, 84; Mary, 167; Robert, 30.
ODUM, Willis, _____108
OFIL, John, _____179
OGDEN, Charles, 38, 163; Dicey, 116; James, 118; Lucy, 104; Moses, 134.
OGILBY, Richard, _____184
OBLEBAY, William, _____120
OGLESBY, Benjamin, 48, 74; Tatum, 154.
OGLESBY, Anthony, 132; Daniel, 119; Urb, 4.
OGLETREE, Edward, 130; Osborne, OGLETREE, David, 14; William, 13. 127; William, 80, 57.
OKELLY, Elizabeth, 63, 180; Francis, 163.
O'LARRY, William, _____137
O'LEERY, Cornelius, _____188
OLDERSHAW, John, _____33
OLER, John, _____170, 176
OLIVER, A. L. B., 166; Berrieu, 177, Charles, 132; James, 59, 78, 79, 111, 156, 166, 211; John, 4, 49, 106, 126, 134, 144, 190; Martin, 25; Nancy, 92; Ordin, 25; Peter, 52; Roney, 170, 172; Terry, 125; Thomas, 107, 201; William, 38.
OLIVER, John, _____14
OLLIVER, Walleton, _____12
OLSON, Charles, _____173
OMANS, John, _____87, 116, 167
OMEARA, John, _____110
O'NAIL, George _____14
O'NEAL, Andrew, 99; Ann, 90; Harrison, 87; John, 106, 193; Mary, 120; Mastin, 130; Philip, 27; Ross, 125; Sabrina, 151; Thomas, 191; Warren, 21, 206; William, 50, 175,

180; Wootten, 23, 210.
O'NEEL, James, ...85
O'NEIL, Mary, ...ː...............151
O'NEILL, William, ...204
OQUIN, Silas, ...87
ORDON, John, ...136
OREAR, Osborn, 177; William, 103.
ORMESBY, Daniel, ...137
ORR, Christopher, ...13
ORR, Daniel, 44; John, 119, 166, 204; Sample, 130; William, 27.
ORRICK, Benjamin, 100; Celia, 119; Henry, 201.
OSBORN, John, ...194
OSBORNE, James 12
OSBORNE, George, 128, 171; James, 31; John, 81; Reps., 130, 186; William, 91, 96, 118.
OSBURN, Britton, 134; L. & J., 48; Nelson, 46; Reuben, 58, 104; Washington, 56; William, 7.
OSTEEN, Allen, 215; James, 32, 55, 90; Obediah, 203; Wiley, 7.
OTWELL, Benjamin, 202; Rich, 27; Richard, 202.
OUSLY, William, ...115
OUTLAW, Frederick, ...16
OUTLER, Bentley, ...204
OVERBY, Peter, ...35
OVERSTREET, George, 55; Silas, 209; William, 5, 188.
OVERTON, Aaron, 18; Gilcrest, 56.
OWEN, William 14
OWEN, Bracket, 137; Bricy, 40; Coleman, 216; Glenn, 134; Hardiman, 21, 50; James, 133; John, 53, 88; Mary, 153; Nancy, 209; Ransom, 163; Samuel, 138; Thomas, 118, 162; William, 180, 189.
OWENBY, Thomas, ...126
OWENS, Barsheba, 8; Daniel, 204; Isaac, 45; John, 55; Whitman, 210.
OWINS, Myfield, ...114
OWSLY, Lucy, ...133
OXFORD, David, 156; Susannah, 137.
PACE, Banabas, 132, 40; Dredgel, 167, 129; Dredsel, 82; Dredziel, 50; John, 163; Kendred, 29; Mildred, 157; dridge, 36; Polly Edenton, 35; Stephen, 31; Samuel, 135; Susan, 180; Samuel, 144; William, 78, 110.
PACKARD, George, ...99
PADDLEFORD, Edward, ...79
PADGET, Abraham, 56; Elisha, 128; Elyah, 205; William, 113, 140, 212; Orphan, 148.
PAGE, David, 64; Joseph, S., 34; James, 216; John, 26; McDaniel, 121; Mary, 42; Thomas, 136; William, 34.

PAINE, Edward, 167; Flail, 115; John, 191, 82; Thomas, 62.
PAIR, Richard, 155; William, 182.
PALEMORE, John, ...80, 2
PALMER, Balaam, 89; Chauncey, 173; David, 160; Elizabeth, 121; Francis, 210; George M., 23; James, 122, 200; Orphan, 46; Hastings, 94; Richard, 180, 203; Tompkins, 128; Thomas, 129.
PALL, Burton, 133; William, 163.
PALLET, Henry, ...72
PALMOUR, John, ...119
PANNELL, Luke, 95; William, 50.
PANTON, Jas. W., 38; Orphan, 32.
PAPOT, Robert, ...142
PALMORE, Elijah, 85; John, 125, 172; Nancy, 63; William, 90.
PALMORES, Elisha, ...41
PAR, Bridges, ...20
PARAMORE, Adam, 112; Benjamin, 209; James, 83, 132; Noah, 22; Stephen, 89.
PARDY, Samuel, ...42
PARHAM, Arg., 18; Benjamin, 182; Elias, 19; Elijah, 36; Elizabeth, 197; Isham, 182; Jackey, 172; John, 32; Lewis, 167; Ransom, 61; Robert, 192; Sion, 43; William, 123.
PARIS, Isaac, 32; Rhoda.
PARISh, Jas., ...52
PARKER, Aaron, ...146
PARK, Barton, 179; John, G., 105; Richards, 187.
PARKER, Aaron, 111; Allen, 118, 147; Benjamin, 152; Caroline, 81; Carter, 163; Christopher, 77; Cuyler, 34; Daniel, 128, 132, 199; David, 203; Elenor, 72; Elizabeth, 209; Elvington, 159; Felix, 165; Gabriel, 30; George P., 17, 34; Ika, 188; Isaiah, 2, 201; Israel, 183; James, 16, 80, 92, 115; John, 72; Jesse, 154; Joshua, 25; Kinchin, 111; Lemuel P., 13; Lewis, 30, 189, 95; Martha, 90; Mary, 104, 208; Maxey, 10; Mathan, 59, 154; Norfleet, 191; Orphans, 123, 130; Richard, 45, 140, 155; Robert K., 160; S., 204; Samuel, 3, 127, 214; Sandrew, 188; Sarah, 207; Simon, 72, 97, 138, 151; Susannah, 34, 118; Starling, 113; Stephen, 119; Thomas, 183; Warren, 137, 146; William, 21, 63, 82, 96, 98, 121, 131, 172, 174; Zilpha, 125.
PARKERSON, Jacob, 175; John, 203; Levin, 151.
PARKMAN, Jesse, ...47
PARMENTER, Sarah, ...123
PARKS, Bird, 83; Birds, 172; Elizabeth, 129; Fleming, 136; Garratt, 92; James, 119; John, 114, 166; Joseph,

33, 34, 80; Nancy, 39; Thomas, 77; Welcome, 80; William J., 46; William, 208, 74.
PARMER, John, ...26
PARNELL, Luke, 139; S. & M., 61.
PARNIDORE, Benjamin, 173; W. L., 15.
PARRIS, Allen, 22; Elizabeth, 22; Henry, 86; Margaret, 177.
PARRISH, Amel, 129; John, 213, 49; Lucinda, 163; William, 79, 77.
PARROTT, Adeline, 72; Anna, 202; Henry, 212; Jesse, 31, 202; Obediah, 102; Tyre, 75.
PARSON, John, 201; Joseph, 30.
PARSONS, Dicy, 199; Mary, 207; Samuel, 2; Thomas, 107.
PARTEE, Walter, 214; Yearby, 44, 147.
PARTIN, John, ...28
PARTON, Peter, ...173
PARVIS, John, ...121
PASCHAL, Augustus, 194; George, 159 Isaiah A., 154; Samuel, 208, 213.
PASCHALL, Dennis, 119; Samuel, 84.
PASS, Andrew, 112; Edmunds, 35; Thomas, 38; William, 21; Willis, 71.
PASSMORE, John, 55, 187; Joseph, 187.
PATSALL, Benjamin, ...143
PATE, Aaron, 6, 56; Drury, 4; Herod, 118; Jesse, 133; Joel, 61; Johnson, 168; Jourdan, 12; Miles, 191; Nathan, 147; Rebeccah, 119; Sterling, 16; Thomas, 83; W. J., 156.
PATESON, Dreiney, 184; Jno., 75.
PATEY, John, ...75
PATILLO, Agatha, ...93
PATMAN, James, ...13
PATON, David, 173; George, 107; Howard, 5; William, 57.
PATRICH, Henry, 11; Joshua, 57, 183
PATRICK, Larkin, 15; Orphan, 186; Paul, 64; Robert, 16; Samuel, 181; William, 165, 3.
PATTERSON, Abner, 205; Catherine, 100; Charles, 53; Daniel, 55; David, 17, 118; G. R. D., 150; Herndon, 92; James, 75, 103, 175; Jeremiah, 56; Job C., 193; John, 63, 72, 164; Robert, 14; Samuel, 213; Solomon, 177; Thomas, 172; William, 146, 124.
PATTILLO, John, 2; Leroy, 51; Samuel, 147.
PATTERN, Solomon, ...198
PATTISHALL, Richard, ...182
PATTON, Alexander, 182; David, 94; Elijah, 108; Jacob, 86; James, 129,

20; Robert, 97; Samuel, 187; William, 143.
PAULLETT, Richard, 87; Paul, 2; Robert, 47; Samuel, 208.
PAVERFORD, Edward, ...188
PAWL, Price, ...5
PAXTON, Elizabeth, 160; James, 43; Joseph, 132.
PAYNER, Mayner, ...92
PAYNE, Calvin, 88; David, 164; George, 34; Isham, 26; John W., 2, 114; John, 205, 105, 166, 131; Lott, 88; Linsey, 162; Mitchell, 1, 216; Orphan, 143; Pollard, 143; Ransome, 195; Rhody, 152; Samuel, 91; Thomas, 97; William, 99, 9; John, 131.
PAYNES, Charles, ...88
PEACE, John, 187; Julia Ann, 130.
PEACK, John, ...214
PEACOCK, A., 138; Alex, 140; Archibald, 166; Asa, 182; Harrison, 197; Isham, 94; Merell, 196; Moulton, 194; Nancy, 99; Richmond, 181; Wriah, 148, 185.
PEAK, Simon T., ...193
PEALOR, Anderson, ...177
PEARCE, Charlotte, 176; Daniel S., 29; Elias, 104; Gadwell, 167; George W., 144; Jacob W., 188; John, 123; 129, 195; James, 180; Lovick, 133; Levy, 64; Littleton, 186; Lewis, 183; Lucy, 88; Theophelus, 141; Thomas, 215; Thomas, 203, 105; Tyrice, 52, 91; William, 184.
PEAMAN, James, 98; Robert, 18.
PEARRE, John, 105; Levi, 43; Mary, 75.
PEARSON, A. & L., 71; Hiram, 5; James, 190; Jeremiah, 193; John, 201; Jones, 166; Josiah, 112; Permidia, 1; Quinney, 216; William, 201; Winiford, 143; Winlock C., 216.
PEASE, Grove, ...43
PEAVY, Abraham, 154; Daniel, 162; Green, 127; James A., 138; Shadrick, 35; Thomas, 90; William H., 59.
PEDDY, Jeremiah, ...103
PEEBLES, Albert, 118; Isham, 11; Mary, 156; Thomas, 59, 111; William, 212.
PEGG, William, ...
PEEK, Henry, 149; John, 208; John C., 86; James R., 78; Littleberry, 117.
PEEKS, Abel, 98; John, 24.
PEEL, Asa, ...77
PEELER, Jacob, ...88
PEERSON, ...Littleton C., 133, 137
PERRY, Arthur, 139; William, 34.

PEET, Thomas, 157
PETTY, Lazarus, 26
PEIRCE, Maryann, 204
PELCHER, Orphan, 99
PELFROY, Joseph, 59
PELL, William, 103
PELOT, Orphan, 146; John C., 157.
PENCE, Abraham, 167! Absaloun, 136; Melin & Susan, 47.
PENDARVIS, George, 37; James, 106, 210.
PENDERGAST, Michael, Patrick, 142.
PENDERGRASS, Margaret,
PENDEXTER, S. W. A. C., 209
PENDLEY, John, 182; Thomas, 128; John, 40.
PENDLY, John, 105
PENN, Gabriel, 213; Martha, 100; William, 202, 149.
PENNELL, James, 134; Jonathan, 56.
PENNINGTON, Elizabeth, 212; Henry, 19; Leatha, 180; Orphan, 90; Sion, 111; Thaddeus, 88; William J., 19.
PENNIX, Mary, 121
PENTON, John, 121
PENNY, Becrof, 97; Ed, 35; John, 161
PENTECOST, Mathew, 152; Richard, 199.
PEPPER, John, 153; Sunsberry, 154.
PERCE, William, 27
PERDUE, David, 18; George, 90, 97; Jesse, 138; Pleasant, 119; Rhoda, 141; Sarah, 81; William, 133.
PERKERSON, Isaac W., 43
PERKINS, Brinson, 20; David, 33; James, 84; Lewis, 184; Moses, 99, 3; Robert, 5; Sarah, 146, 50, 197; Stephens, 25; Wright, 109; Zazhariah, 211.
PERMENTER, H. F., 30; Nathaniel, 39.
PERONEY, Charles, 192
PERNELL, S., 118
PERRITT, Rebecca, 25
PERRYMEN, David, 94, 7; Harmon, 106; Jones, 207; David A., 145; Rebecca, 112.
PERSONS, Amos, 176; George W., 60; Jones, 198; John, 100, 86; Rachael, 81; Turner, 197.
PERVIS, Edward, 80; Jesse, 111.
PERRY, Alfred, 13; Alfred G., 6; Doctor, 62; Docton, 85; Elizabeth, 48; Edward W., 48; Eliza, 208; Hardy, 151; James, 117; Joel W., 147; John 115, 147; Mary G., 160; Oliver H., 102; Oscar F., 99; Peter, 18; Prudence, 77; Richard, 88; Shadrack, 128; Simon, 211; Isaac, 106; Wiley, 44; William, 142, 110.
PETEET, Simeon, 158

PETERMAN, Benjamin, 100
PETEN, Edmund, 74
PETERS, George, 177; Jesse, 157, 19; John H., 216; Thomas, 78; William, 78; William M., 199.
PETERSON, John, 10, 64, 204.
PETIT, Betsy, 114; Catherine, 139.
PETIGREE, Susannah, 207
PETTIGREW, Bennett, 186; Edwin; James, 30.
PETTIJOHN, James, 27
PETTIS, Moses, 14; William, 15.
PETTIT, Millmond, 85
PETERMAN, Benjamin, 100
PEW, Abel, 133
PHAR, Jacob, 50
PHAROAH, Joshua, 13, 121, 141
PHARR, John H., 106; Sarah, 3.
PHELPS, Augustin J., 133; Elizabeth, 12; Joseph, 173; Joseph L. D., 59; Overton, 171; Thomas, 57.
PHILIPS, Ruth, 198; Sarah, 197; Stephen, 107.
PHILLIPS, Abner, 12, 23; Ambrose, 125; Benjamin, 116, 39; Cela, 97; David, 135; Dennis, 155; Elias, 81; Elijah, 86; Francis, 87 Harrington, 78; Issac, 189; James, 56; Joel, 134, John, 14, 115, 173; Joseph, 3; Jonathan, 160; Margaret, 124; Mary Ann 124; Miles, 79; Sarah, 197.
PHILPOT, Jas. C., 22; James, 172.
PHILPS, Augustus, 166; Benago, 216; Benjamin, 60; Bud, 148; Charles, 162, 199; Daniel, 2, 186; David, 26; Elizabeth, 24; Gabriel, 148; Isom, 212; James, 22, 28; John, 14, 115, 208; Joshua, 184; Littleberry, 212; Lleyellyn, 44; Mary, 195, 197; Miles, 43; Solomon, 178; Thomas, 183, 125; Wilder, 26; Wiley, 149; William, 21, 43, 53, 210; Yearby, 216.
PHILMON, Elijah, 148, 195.
PHINISEE, John, 18
PHIPP, Elbert, 18
PHIPPS, Joseph, 18; Thomas, 24.
PICKARD, J. H., 96; John, 165; Thomas, 36, 148; William, 193, 170.
PICKEL, Michael, 154
PICKETT, Betsy, 52; Elizabeth, Eli., 7
PICKINS, Elijah, 2
PIERCE, Benjamin, 184; David, 92; Green, 31; Hugh, 31, 91, 121; James 57; James C., 26; Jesse F., 56; John, 85; Mary, 146; Orphan, 172, 163; Sampson, 164; Seth, 41; Thomas, 156, 159; Warten, 3; William, 63, 83; William A., 141.
PIERSON, Missouri, 100
PIKE, Ezekiel, 10; James, 185, 139; Jacob, 5; William, 177.
PILCHER, James, 177; William, 35,

39.
PILE, Abraham, 86; Mary, 42.
PILES, James B., 91; Peter, 83; William, 98.
PILGRIM, Amos, ...214
PINCKARD, James, 95; John, 121; Sarah, 47.
PINDER, William, ...17
PINKARD, John, ...118
PINKSTON, Jas., ...62
PINROW, William, ...164
PINSON, Curtis, 103; Elijah, 2; Edward, 163; Edward T., 163; Elizameth, 42; Joseph, 32, 112, 154, 83, 199; Lucy, 139.
PIPER, James, 118; John F., 214.
PIPKINS, Amos, ...109
PIPPIN, Isaac, ...175, 89
PITCHER, John, 43; William, 188.
PITCHFORD, William, ...124
PITMAN, Arthur, 203; Elijah, 64; John, 7, 131.
PITMON, Daniel, 124; Linza, 84.
PITTARD, Humphey, 100; William, 93.
PITTMAN, Barnes, 12; Ethelred, 88; James, 168; Jeffrey, 5; John, 26, 30, 78; Philip, 40; William, 151; Wimrod, 58.
PITTMON, Henry, 14; Thomas, 169.
PITT, Thomas, ...20
PITTS, Aaron, 63; Coleman, 118; Daniel, 53; Elihi, 28; Isaac, 63; John, 35, 129; Samuel, 87; Stephen, 55, 215.
PLANT, Lewis H., 130; William, 169.
PLASTER, Benjamin, ...33
PLEDGER, Simeon, 123; Thomas; Wesley, 59.
PLESS, Alexander, 203; Andrew, 115, 172.
PLUCKIT, Joseph, ...88
PLUCKETT, Richard, ...88
PLUMB, David, ...94
PLUIMMER, Joseph E., ...34
PLUMMER, Joseph, 64; Samuel, 148.
POACHER, Henry H., ...43
POE, Gilbert, 91; Jonathan, 18, 54; Stephen, 37; William, 15, 199.
POGUE, John L., ...140
POLHILL, John, 179; John G., 29; Nathaniel.
POLK, Anna F., 54; Charles, 165; John, 141; Micajah, 207.
POLLARD, Charles; Hyram, 160; John 44; Joseph, 12; William, 12.
POLLOCK, John, ...123
POLLY, Robert, ...64
PONCE, Joseph B., ...91
POND, Alexander, 193; Dawson, 192; John, 116, 162; John H., 18; Rebecca, 200; Susian, 175; William G., 148.
PONNEY, Juicy, ...33
POOL, Hardy, 70; Henry, 130; Isham, 21, 91; James, 202; Matthew, 77; Nicholas, 97; Samuel, 34, 41; William, 34; Walter, 131.
POOLE, Dice, 147; Dudley, 39; Henry, 113; Mary, 106; Milley, 146; Samuel, 140; William W., 142.
POOR, Robert, ...102
POPE, Brittain, 5; Cadsman, 202; Daniel, 42; David, 8; Fleet, 202, 118; Hardy, 88; Henry, 62; Jacob, 77; John, 210, 170; Joab, 116; Leach, 211; Nathaniel, 75; Uriah, 64; Wiley, 129; Wilson, 187, 105.
POPHAM, Armstead, 149; John, 196.
POPWELL, James, ...54
PORCH, Hartmell, 153; Henry, 159; Mary Ann, 47.
PORKS, John, ...16
PORTCH, Thomas, ...206
PORTER, Abraham, 212; Anthony, 39 Elizabeth, 130; Elbert, 214; James, 20; John, 1, 3, 15; John S., 43; Richard, 47; Richard H., 185, 7; Samuel, 148; Solon, 191; Thomas D. 43; William, 193, 25, 3, 70 ,186, 126.
PORTEVENT, James, ...35
PORTWOOD, B., 24; Bevy, 140.
PORYON, Ann Carolina, 196; Elizabeth, 6; John, 212; Mary, 106; Wade, 107; William, 26, 57.
POSEY, Benjamin, 5; Bennet, 118; Hannah, 122; Humphrey, 23, 130; James, 131, 176; Mary, 59, 145; Uriah, 47, 40.
POSS, Frances, 51; Henry, 35; Nicholas, 214; William, 144.
POST, Joseph C., 130.
POTTER, Augustin L., 21; Matthew M., 141; Plumma, 108; Susannah, 208; Washington, 168.
POTTS, Francis, 12; James, 47, 196; John, 113; Moses, 95; Shadrach, 58, 122; William, 42, 141.
POULSON, Jonathan, ...31
POUNDS, Jared, 167; John, 205.
POUND, Isham, 52; John B., 7.
POWEL, John, ...173
POWELL, Ambrose, 204, 59; Allen, 163; Alexander, 7; Anne, 9; Benjamin, 16, 33, 44; Barnett, 183; Cader R., 155; Chapmon, 155; Campbell, 106; Christopher, 130; Dorcas, 187; Edward, 206; Francis, 46, 52, 64; Hardy, 20; Henry, 211, 154; Hilliard, 155; James, 8; James L., 31; Jesse, 117; John, 133; John-

son, 211; Joseph, 145; Larkin, 215; Lewis, 211, 120; Lucas, 124; Luranda, 152; Mark. M., 157; Mary, 205; Martha, 51; Nat. W., 9; Nancy M., 36; Needham, 154; Nelson, 42; Neson, 26; Oliver C., 197; Presley, 170; Polly, 162; Richard, 160; Rachel, 98; Samuel H., 20; Sarah, 17; Seaborn, 125; Seymore, 134; Sion, 211; Tillman, 112; Theophilus, 121; William C., 165; William, 24, 25, 131; W., 108; William R., 30.
POWER, Ann, 81; Francis, 121, 213; John, 64, 172; Lewis R., 168; William, 85, 99.
POWERS, Edmund, 83, 179; Edward, 149; Elijah, 93, 135; Hardy, 96; James G., 71, 185; Nicholas, 35; Orphan, 145; Samuel, 155; Thomas, 21; William, 149; Zara, 62.
POWLEDGE, John Martin, ...195
POYNER, John, ...98
POYTHRESS, William, ...201
PRATER, John, ...103
PRATERS, Edward, ...25
PRATHER, Edward, 126, 62; John, 120; William, 144, 163.
PRATT, Abram, 107; Alexander, 209; Elizabeth, 112; John, 160, 187.
PRAY, Jonathan, ...78
PRAYLER, Jacob, ...102
PRECHARD, William, ... 63
PRENDERGAST, John, ...33
PRESCITT, Sarah, ...138
PRESCOAT, Jesse, ...138
PRESCOTT, John, 139; Moses, 90; Tommy, 214.
PRESCUTT, Moses, ...104
PRESLER, Peter, ...47
PRESLEY, Elizabeth, 6; John, 63, 102; Jonathan, 15; Moses, 199.
PRESNAL, Jacob, ...39
PRESNELL, Jacob, ...79, 139
PRESSLER, Gillam, 168; Peter, 53.
PRESSLY, William, ...18
PRESTON, David, 129, 163; William, 25.
PRESWOOD, Robert, ...97
PRICE, Clem, 29; Daniel, 192; Ephriam, 126; Erwin, 100; George, 147; Hiram, 182, 213; James, 173; Jesse, 18, 138; John, 175, 200, 213; Leoy, 160; Lucus, 75; Margaret, 72; Matilda, 39; M. A., 17; N. C., 17; Rebeccak, 112; Robert, 31; Rocksy Ann, 210; Thomas, 116; Whitmore, 121, 159; William, 4, 174.
PRICKARD, Presley, 206; Rhodam, 106
PRICHARD, William, ...204
PRICHETT, Sion, ...162
PRIDGEN, Luke, 85; Mathew, 105; Robert, 190.

PRINCE, Abraham, 170; Daniel, 38; Garland, 158; Joseph, 95, 99; M., 24; Noah, 17, 55, 120, 135; William, 178; Willis, 180.
PRITCHARD, Isaac, ...8
PRITCHETT, Nicholas, 85; Rhodam, 106; Sion, 212; Thomas, 43.
PRICHET, John, ...41
PRICKETT, John, 167; Jonathan, 127, Lewis, 145; Robert, 205; Sarah, 138; William, 92.
PRIDDY, Judith, 28; Robert, 49.
PRIDGET, David, 138; Edwin C., 10; Elizabeth, 20.
PRIEL, David, ...64
PRIOR, John, ...125
PRITCHARD, Robert, ...120
PROCTOR, Abraham, 180; Clarky, 36, Francis, 82; John, 88; Moses, 62; Sarah, 103; Stephen, 115; William, 36.
PRONTY, Chieny, ...93
PROSSER, Oter, ...35
PROTHRO, Joshua, 204; Nathaniel, 182.
PROUDFOOT, Hugh, ...83
PRUETT, David, 6; Henry, 93; Itta, 23; Mary, 146; Moses Y., 207; Samuel, 37; Turner, 197; Zachariah, 196, Zalia, 79.
PSALMON, John, 78; S., 97.
PUCKETT, John, ...30
PUGH, Alex., 68, 98, 164; Francis, 25; James, 99, 180; John, 189; Martha, 53, 108; Sampson, 44; Shadrack, 22, 198.
PUGSLEY, John, ...209
PULASHI, John, ...4
PULLEY, Benjamin, ...36
PULLMAN, Benjamin, 210; James, 5; Jane, 5; Robert, 208; Thomas, 43; William, 5, 79.
PULLIN, Gilford, 153; John, 192; Othiel, 21; Peter, 47; Robert, 27; Samuel, 36; Susan, 198; Telitha, 34; Thomas, 12, 15, 44, 153, 195, 206.
PUMPHRY, Gilvamis, ...157
PUNDS, Richard, ...207
PURCEL, James, 159; John, 63.
PURCILL, Ann, ...17
PURICEL, James, ...27
PURDUE, Elizabeth, 45; Juely, 37
PURDY, John, ...117
PURGESON, Bev., 49; Jermina, 192.
PURIFOY, M. Cawell, ...89
PURNELL, Richard, ...29
PURVIS, Hammond, 116, 157; Mary, 104; Needham, 14, 110; Silpha, 1; William, 14, 157.
PURYEAR, Jermina, 17; Peter, 49,

110; William, 94.
PURKINS, Alexander, 124; Samuel, 12 Sessum, 157.
PUTNAM, Ezekiel, 27, 159; Mary, 94; Simeon, 12.
PYLAN, Burton, ...156
PYE, Allen, 77; Anne, 99; Beneer, 25; Henry, 180; James, 64.
PYREEN, James, ...185
QUIN, William, ...165
QUINEY, Hurson, ...37
QUARTERMAN, Elijah; William, 44.
QUALES, David, ...95
QUALLS, David, 214; Hubbard, 181.
QUICKS, William 125
QUINN, William, 10, 150; Mathew, 136.
RABB, Hannah, 161; James, 124; John, 118.
RABOURN, Burrell, ...124
RABUN, John W., ...58
RACHELS, Joseph, 19; Miles, 131, 174
RACKLEY, Frankey, ...11
RADDEN, James, ...41
RADEN, Thomas, ...74
RADFORD, Albert, 163; Bohn, 132, Bolen, 73; Elizabeth, 116; Frederick, 26; Juliana, 127; Patsey, 28; Robert, 163, 166.
RADNEY, John, 37, 102; Polley, 57.
RAGAN, Brice, 58; Joseph, 181; Thomas, 216, 198; William M., 5.
RAGLAND, Abner, 61; Callton, 121; John S., 50; Reuben, 122, 150.
RAGSDALE, Ira, 37; Larkin, 64, 132; Lawrence, 134; Leonard, 182; Michael, 136, 208.
RAGSDALL, Charlton, ...61
RAHFESS, Frederick, ...192
RAHN, Erwin, 142; Hannah, Eloz., 40, 42; Manuel, 49.
RAIFORD, Isaac, 212; John, 69; Matthew, 178; Patience, 20; Robert, 5, 130.
RAILEY, Charles, ...10
RAILY, Charles, ...154
RAINEY, Benjamin, 111; Daniel, 4; Elizabeth, 19; Frederick, 29; Herbert, 187; Mary, 110; Seaborn, 106; William, 61, 87, 89.
RAINS, Henry, 122; Sarah, 159.
RAINWATER, Salmon, ...42, 72
RAKESTRAW, Rhode, ...166
RALEY, Charles, 10, 55; Henry, 10, 162; John, 194; Patsey, 189; Ruth, 89.
RALHEY, Margaret, ...185
RALL, Isaac M., ...33
RALLS, Isaac, ...149
RAM, Ann, Elizabeth, ...1
RAMES, Caldwell, ...175

RAMEY, Nathaniel,, ...183
RAMSTY, David, ...192
RAMSDELL, Absolom, 31; Elbert R., 23; John, 202.
RAMSEY, Alexander, 49; Benjamin, 108, 115; David, 132; Felix, 125; George, 117; James, 6; John, 99; Rachel, 102; Samuel, 30, 114; Thomas, 163; William, 85.
RAMY, John, ...109
RANDAL, Washington, ...175
RANDALL, James, ...181
RANDOLPH, Edwin J., 42; John, 133, Robert, 26.
RANEY, Elizabeth, 169; Isaac, 183.
RANKINS, Robert C., ...57
RANSOM, Armstead, 159; Jeremiah, 93; Martha, 174; Reuben, 17, 208; Thomas, 136.
RANSOME, Uriah A., ...152
RASBERRY, Polly, ...13
RATCHFORD, John, ...190
RATCLIFF, Allen, Jos., & Lukie, 205; James, 163; Joseph, 201; Martha, 124.
RATFORD, Joseph, ...168
RATTEIF, Benjamin, ...78
RATTEY, Jane, ...152
RATTIFF, Milledge, ...162
RAWBERSON, Mimrod, ...19
RAWINS, Richard, ...81
RAWLES, Allen, 90; Hosea, 101; Isaac M., 33; Joseph, 28; Moses, 2; Nancy, 43; Sarah, 52; Thomas, 107, 116; William, 125.
RAWLINGS, William, ...185
RAWSON, Gideon, 126; Jesse, 54.
RAY: Alford P., 150; Andrew, 189, 210; Benjamin, 128, 162; Caleman L., 46; David, 152; Elisha, 172; Gabriel, 74; George, 116; Howell, 172; Isaac, 8; James, 8, 54, 177; John, 8, 23, 73, 116, 130, 132, 158, 206; Mark, 6, 184; Nimrod, 172; Philip, 194; Robert, 63, 65, 133; Solomon, 177; Thomas, 87, 208; Tollison, 40; William, 140, 141, 211
RAYS, Mark, ...61
READ, Asa, 4; Joseph E., 54.
READBURX, Nancy, ...134
READIN, John, ...81
READINS, Rheum, ...150
REAVES, Frederick, 5; Irvin, 202; Lovick, 64; John,. 202; R., 123; Richard, 112; Sarah, 175; Thomas, 159.
RED, Bedutha, 192; David, 39, 70; James, 120; Job, 210; Meshack, 211; Thomas, 52.
REDCOCK, Alexander, ...130
REDD, Holland, 135; Job, 139.
REDDIN, Arch, 6; James, 41.
REDDING, Alexander, 163; Ezekiel,

42, 209; John, 181; Nancy, 188; Timothy, 185; William, 39; William S., 30.
REDFIELD, George, 138
REDICK, Amos, 148; Jacob, 1; Thomas, 4, 138.
REDOCK, J. E. W. Q C., 135
REGAN, Martha, 29; Samuel, 156.
REECE, Aaron, 141; Peter, 40.
REED, Caro & Henry, 128; Catherine, 205; Elender, 131; Ezekiel, 13, Hiram, 131; Jacob, 111; James A., 186; James, 22; James C., 139; Jesse, 92; ohn, 211, 91, 58; Josiah, 51; Martha, 38; Mary Ann, 142; Murry, 139; Orphan, 146; Robin, 149; Railey, 203; Thomas, 105, 116; Wililam, 170, 3.
REEDER, Cairy, 97
REEDLING, Caroline, 117
REEDY, Caroline, 83; William, 80.
REEKS, John, 44
REES, Bynum, 161; Elenor, 22; George 162; Hugh, 117; John, 9; Thomas, 1.
REESE, Aaron, 100; Daniel, 62; Elizabeth, 30; Ezekiel, 165; Harrison, 104; James B., 174; Joel, 149; Lewis, 95; Mose, 104; Rose, 2; Sarah, 165; Tamerlin, 181; Thomas, 181; Vincent, 105.
REEVES, Allen, 37; Asa, 183; Bennett, 52, 113; Edwin, 20; Frederick, 71; Han, 119; Hannah, 100; Isaac, James, 62; John, 199; Josiah, 28; Mary, 135; Micajah, 154; Ransom, 47, 16; Simon, 18; Thomas, 22, 161; Thompson, 35; William, 186; William M., 25; Wyatt, 102.
REGAN, Martha, 29; Samuel, 156.
REGISTER, David, 24; Nancy, 71; Robert, 197; Samuel, 153; Willie, 203.
REGOLAS, Orphan, 190
REICKER, Zachariah, 210
REID ,Alexander, 212; Asa, 189; Brice, 75; Cullen, 191; Edmond, 210; Elizabeth, 211; John, 13, 14, 26; Isaac, 156; James, 54; Joseph D., 23; Mary, 26; Orphan, 33, 50; Richard, 122; Samuel, 180.
REIDLING, Martha, 140
REILY, Patrick, 39, 126
REIS, William, 105
REISER, Jeremiah, 195
REID, William A., 9
REMBERD, Samuel, 136
REMSHART, Elizabeth, 33
REMSON, Benjamin, 57
RENDER, Christopher, 113
RENFRO, John, 188; Nathan, 216, 161; Orphans, 164.

RENFROE, Alfred, 10; Samuel, 58, 113.
RENTFRO, David B., 157
RERVIS, Wyat, 91
RESPASS, Richard, 135; Nancy, 1*7
RETHERFORD, Claiborn, 172; Willaim, 137.
REVEL, Randolph, 173
REVELL, Nancy, 29
REVELS, Edmonds, 166; Jeremiah, 32, 64.
REVERE, Pichard, 56
REVIER, John, 71
REVILLS, Harrison, 92
REYNE, Robert, 19
REYNOLDS, Amelia, 135; Benjamin, 2, 11, 12, 44, 80; Charles, 215; Daniel, 168; Elzy., 55; George, 193; Hubbard, 146; John, 38, 69, 187; Joseph P., 26; Josiah, 193.
REYNOLDS, Laskin, 70, 59; Martin, 114; Mary, 195; Overton, 120; Peter, 6; Robert, 22, 139, 147; Sarah, 93; Susannah, 37; Thomas, 96, 168; William, 201.
RHAME, Jeremiah, 142
RHAN, Hannach, 186
RHEA, John, 156
RHEAGAN, Buckner, 186
RHODER, Samuel, 180
RHODES, Benjamin, 208; Dicey, 8; Eustens H., 137; Hannah, 91; Hiram, 139; Jesse, 120; John, 19, 137; John W., 101; Joseph, 45; Joseph, P., 14; Lewis B., 166; Nancy, 132, 187; Rich, 81; Richard, 51; Sally, 64; Thomas, 52; William, 25; Willis, 25.
RHYMES, Willis, 10, 166
RIALS, Mariah, 26
RICE, James, 2, 171, 201; Joel, 107; Leonard, 59; Moses, 56; Silvester, 85; Sylvester, 186; Thomas, 8, 11.
RICH, Eleanor, 215; John, 59, 72, 80; Richmond, 17; William, 93; Zelpha, 93.
RICHARD, Reuben, 59
RICHARDS, Ansil, 62; Henry, 204; Jediah, 102; John, 108; Liddy, 30; Rachel, 201; Terrah, 162; Thomas, 215; William B., 32; William L., 215
RICHARDSON, Armsted, 166; Benjamin, 165; C., 24; Charles, 110; Cos. P., 15; Caniel, 38; Daniel, 8, 40; Elender, 133; Gatewood, 156; James V., 43; James, 69; John, 6, 92, 117, 143, 197, 178, 171; John G., 26; John L., 11; Jonathan, 104; Lawrence, 192; Newman, 7; Peter T., 7; Prucy, 7; Richard, 113; Rosan, 23; Thomas, 193; Trimiken, 83; William, 214, 216, 116, 74, 99, 6.

RICHER, Edward, 59; Susannah, 205.
RICHERSON, William, 154; Russell, 212.
RICHETSON, Surinah, ...134
RINCHOUR, Benjamin, ...1
RICHETT, Philip, ...118
RICKER, James, 87; Louisa, ...87
RICKETSON, Allen, 122; Benjamin, 187, 188; Jesse, 203.
RICKS, Daniel, 187; John, 153; Richard P., 12; William, 179.
RIDDLE, Anderson, 157; Ann, 22; Anthony, 100; Cato., 185: John. 92; P., 22.
RIDLEY, Charles L., 21; Jonathan, 26; William, 156.
RIDON, Elizabeth Ann, ...21
RIECHELS, John, F., ...197
REIDLING, John, ...57
RIEVES, Pickany, 171; Richard, 138; William, 131.
RIESSER, Cornelius, ...107
RIGBY, Jonathan, ...166
RIGDON, Ephriam, ...138, 203
RIGGELL, Joel, ...34
RIGGINS, Ebenezer, ...87
RIGGS, Rachel, ...209
RIGHT, Alsey, 212; Amos G., 47; Armond, 47; Moses, 4; Thos. R., 25.
RIGHTS, William, ...112
RIGLEY, Allen, ...112
RIGSLEY, Polly, ...160
RILEY, Charles, 216; John P., 143; John, 144, 177; Joseph, 5; Leut. 44; M. C., 87; Mial, 182; Orphan, 188; William, 54, 112, 167, 188.
RINGO, John, ...143
RION, Philip, ...57
RIPLEY, Lewis, ...81
RISPISS, Church, 3; Churchwell, 111.
RITCHERSON, Zarah, ...38
RITCHIE, David, 21; William, 91, 189
RIVERS, Joel, 87; John E., 18; Jones, 74, 125; Joseph, 71; Mayr Ann, 29; Thomas, 166; Vincent E., 39; William, 138.
RIVION, John, ...88
RIX, Patience, ...87
ROACH, Charles, 108; James, 140, 147, 160; Joshua, 166.
ROAN, John, 149, 180; Leonard, 192.
ROBBINS, Thomas, ...200
ROBERSON, Allen, 19; Andrew G., 152; Benjamin, 168; Davis, 57; Edward, 156; Elijah, 118; Emelia, 83; John, 214, 175, 35, 62, 169, 13, 161; Martha, 62; P. M., 83; Passyuas, 24; Pendleton J., 51; Sarah, 62; Stacee, 134; William, 62.

FOBERTS, A. S. W. and N., 128; Aaron, 88; Abraham, 55, 101; Allen, 147, 212; B. M. & K., 55; Benjamin, 200; Burch N., 164; C. L. C., 1; Charles, 92; Chartes, 188; Cooper, 131; Easter, 32; Edward, 100; Elisha, 55; Eliza G., 130; Elizabeth, 151; George, 198, 208; Graystock, 204; H. J. J., 58; Hiram, 97; James, 7, 35, 175, 185; Jesse, 88; John, 104, 107, 142, 148, 185; John F., 191; Jonathan, 71; Joshua, 174; Killis, 193; Lindsey, 96; Mary, 22; Michael, 213; Mitchell, 63; Nelson, 216; Owen, 50; Randall, 155; Reuben, 156, 175; Rolin, 96; Rurby, 139; Sarah, 189, 199; Spencer, 123; Tabitha, 73; Thomas, 100, 103, 185, Tharp, 49; Wiley, 7; William, 1, 12, 59, 91, 112, 127; Yearby, 209.
ROBERTSON, Charles, 54; Drury, 128; Elizabeth, 186; Faver, 82; Frier, 85; George W., 54, 188; Henry, 58, 124; James, 42, 128, 188; Jeremiah, 97; Josh, 175; Josh, 175; Joseph, 77; Joshiah, 154; ohn, 17, 32, 168, 214; Lemuel, 180; Margaret, 147; Mary Ann, 52; Mary M., 49; Patsy, 113; Richard, 37; Theo, 55; Thomas, 196; Thomas U., 146; William, 26, 97, 136, 147, 155; William C. 175; William H. 205.
ROBEY, William, ...111
ROBY, Timothy, ...163
ROBINETT, Sarah, ...126
ROBINSON, Alex., 63, 108; Benjamin, 175; Catherine, 107; Claiborn, 43, 49; Elisha, 126; Henry, 113; John, 182; John R., 47; Lunice, 47; Nancy, 173; Nicholas, 194; Orphans, 216; Osborn, 124; Richard, B., 23; Samuel, 45, 171; Sarah, 196; Tempe, 59; Terrell, 4; Thte. G., 182; Thomas G., 26; William, 88; Zachariah, 21; Zaraster, 207.
ROBINS, Thomas, ...61
ROBISON, Benjamin, 31; Beverly, 64; James, 77; Joshua, 52; Moses, 35.
ROBSON, Allen, 97; Wylie, 106.
ROBUCK, James, ...54
ROCHE, William, ...173
ROCKWELL, Charles, 73; Riely, 22; Stoddard, 58.
RODENBERRY, George, ...173
ROE, Daniel, 94; John, 18; John, Sr., 196; Polly, 206.
ROEBUCK, Lang, ...148
ROGERS, Abner, 154; Adam, 205; Benjamin, 132; Britian, 9; Cannon, 154; Cannon R., 188; Charles, 188; Curran, 10; Edward, 110; Elizabeth, 195; Enoch; Harvey, 145; Henry, 54; Isham, 11; Jacob, 44; Jacobb,

197; James, 51, 78, 81, 120; John, 77, 153, 163, 211; Joseph, 146, 184; Lairsa, 140; Lucresy, 38; Lucretia, 20, 149; Martha, 119, 209; Mary, 70; McNiece, 80; Morgan, 103; Osborn, 103; Peleg, 145; Ransome, 154; Reuben, 216; Robert, 38, 89, 103, 141, 61; Sally, 106, Simon, 39; Thomas E., 167; Uriah, 113; Walter, 108; William, 29, 86, 157, 211; Willie, 110; Winifred, 52.
ROGERSON, James, ...5
ROI, John, ...173
ROGNEMORE, William B., ...6
ROLAND, William, ...116
ROLLINS, Calvin, 204; James W., 7; Nicholas, 114; Richard, 192; Rolly, 209; Samuel, 207, 155.
ROLLO, William, ...9
ROLSTON, David, ...140
ROMAN, David, ...206
ROMONDON, Peter, ...73
RONALDSON, Frances, ...171
RONE, Marianna, ...103
RONIE, Joseph, ...88
RONEY, Martin, ...180
ROOKS, Abel, 14, 136; Hardaman, 174; John, 173, 215, 112, 215; John L., 159; Orphan, 171; Vardeman, 54; Zachariah, 177.
ROOD, Levi H., ...131
ROOK, Jonathan S., ...150
ROPER, John, 128, 85; William M., 171.
RORIE, John, ...179
ROSAR, Shadrack, ...141
ROSE, Frances, 120; Henry D., 86; John, 126; Michael, 26; Seaborn, 126; William, 37, 70, 90, 188.
ROSEBERRY, Thomas, ...169
ROSS, Eliza., 109, 113, 200; Charles, 183; George, 92, 28; James, 24; Jesse, 95; Jonathan, 103; John, 41; John B., 1; Larkin, 24; Sarah, 115, 59, 136; William, 174.
ROZIER, Winnery, ...114
ROSSEAU, Hiram, ...150
ROSSER, Asa, 138; Isaac, 131; James, 214; Jeptha, 208; Thomas, 55.
ROSSITER, Arthur, 195; Timothy, 98.
ROUGHTON, Enoch, ...93
ROUNDTREE, Wiley, 91; George R., 29; J. D., 178; Louiza, 22; William, 18.
ROUNSEAVILLE, R. L., ...5
ROUSE, Allen, 112; Mary, 112.
ROUSSEAU, John, ...51
ROW, William, ...158
ROWE, Allen, 140; Century, 132; Edna, 166; James, 111; Joshua, 19;

Martin, 28; Minza, 207; Shadrack, 35, 197; William, 181; William, Jr., 165.
ROWEL, Samuel, ...183
ROWELL, Elijah, 59; James, 166; Jesse, 142; Valentine, 182; Richard, 149.
ROWLAND, Amos, 159; Elizabeth, 214 George, 90; Isaac, 201; James, 201; Seely, 171; Wiley, 128; William, 112, 210.
ROWLIN, Brantley, ...202
ROWLING, Sherwood, ...58
ROWLINS, David, 191; Thomas, 37.
ROWSAN, Thomas, ...211
ROWZAY, Forster, ...88
ROY, James, 210; John, 8.
ROYAL, Arthur, 7; Isaac, 99; M. V. M., 113; Margaret, 185; Sarah, 135; Sarah Ann, 11; Stephen, 88.
ROYALSTON, John, ...16, 192
ROYSTER, James, ...155
ROYSTON, John, 206; Richard, 189.
ROYSTER, James, ...155
ROZAR, John, 93; John A., 215.
ROZIER, Elias, 37; Edmund, 98; Martha, 203.
RUCKS, Ann D., 20; E. W., 20; James, 81.
RUCKER, Barden, 88; Feiling, 55; John, 127; Milly, 56; William, 8, 195; Zachariah, 88, 192.
RUDD, William, ...183
RUDE, William, ...62
RUDOLPH, Zebulon, ...43
RUFF, Gerorge, ...92
RUIS, John, ...29, 96
RUMSEY, Fields, 5; Rich P., 11.
RUMMALS, Ephriam, ...40
RUNNELS, David, 35; Harmon, 119; James, 25; William, 52, 152.
RUNNYMORE, Michael, ...3
RUSHING, John, ...73
RUSK, John, ...16
RUSS, James, ...33
RUSSEAN, James, ...188
RUSSELL, A. B., 140; Alexander, 190 Augustus, 175; Booker, 121; Dovid, 213; E. W., 99; Elizabeth, 99, 161, 165; Elizabeth, 62, 151; Ethel, 89; George, 184; Henry, 138; Ignacius, James, 18, 164; Jane M., 39; John, 170, 181; John M., 80; Joseph Averly, 132; Keziah, 93, 202; Osban, 94; Permelia, 118; Phila, 160, Simpson R., 132; Thomas, 167; Thomas C., 149; Washington, 213; William, 178; William J., 107.
RUSSIL, William, ...134
RUSSOW, Oliver, ...192
RUTH, Mary, 99; Nancy, 57; William, 103, 171; Rutherford, David, 97;

Henry, 78; Hiram, 89; James, P., 12, 24; John G., 19; Richard, 107; Robert, 84; William, 78.
RUTLAND, B. B., 8; Roderick, 77.
RUTHLEDGE, Ann, 82; John, 23, 207; Kiah, 153; Richard, 30; Sarah, 179.
RY, William, ...9
RYAL, Abel, 70; Wright, 172.
RYALLS, John, ...61
RYALS, Henry, ...64
RYAN, Francis, 78; Hampton, 91; Humpton, 158; Lewis, 4.
RYE, Joseph, 187; Mary, 216.
RYLAND, Elizabeth, 116; John, 207.
RYLE, Anna P., 14; John, 97, 204.
RYLANDER, James, ...10
RYON, Whitehead, 159; Philips, 86.
SABINS, Nathan, ...125
SACRAL, Thomas, ...36
SACICUS, Solomon, ...55
SADLER, James, 9, 117; Joseph, 59, 93; Thomas, 206.
SADDLER, Thomas, 156; William, 11.
SAFFOLD, Aaron, 206; Sarah, 62.
SAILORS, Christopher, 83, 205; David, 18.
SAILS, James, 193; Richard, 137.
SALE, Peyton W., ...190
SALFNER, Dorothy, ...1
SALLET, Mary Ann, ...96
SALLIS, James, ...74
SALLY, Jacob, ...80
SALLEY, William, ...86
SALOM, Abraham, ...149
SALMON, Hezekiel, ...181
SALTER, John, 113, 204; Nancy, 138; Sarah, 75; Simon, 209; Tabitha, 79.
SAMMONS, Henry, 172; Seaborn, 202.
SAMPLES, James, 212; Nathaniel, 127, 130, 143; William, 15.
SAMS, Joseph, 119; Reuben, 23.
SAMUELS, Benjamin, 175, 187; Harris, 34.
SANDERS, Alexander, 27, 72, 120, 124; Am., 58; Benj., 84; Calvin, 120; Daniel, 192; David, 98, 111; Ellender, 51, Ellinor, 94; Elizabeth, 141, 25; George, 180; George W., 69; Hensley, 20, 72; Isiah, 139; James, 6, 54, 151, 153; Jeremiah, 189; John, 45, 79, 102, 124; Julius, 34; Lovett, 211; Luke, 72; Manyard, 82; Mary, 55, 41, 103; Martha, 119; Merry, 189; Morgan, 101; Nellie, 71, 100;Reuben, 40; Samuel R., 30; Seaborn, 203; Simeon, 108; Stephen, 70, 46; Thomas, 215; Washington, 69; William, 3, 151, 172, 199, 207; Wright, 4, 73; Wade, 119.

SANDAFUR, John, ...178
SANDEFER, James, 149; Thomas, 130.
SANDEFORD, James, 121; Jonathan, 77.
SANDERLIN, James, 204; Joseph, 131; Julian, 207.
SAPP, A., 100; Charles, 14; Homer, 74; James, 123, 195; Levi, 115; Peggy, 154; Pendleton, 195; Phenice, 132; Philip, 120, 112; Reubein, 147, Salim, 203; Shadrack, 104, 25; Theophilus, 194; William, 215; Zilpha, 170.
SAPPINGTON, Thaddeus, ...106
SARSNETT, Joseph, ...202
SARTIN, Joel, ...161
SARTAIN, Elijah, ...47
SASNETT, James, 50; Joseph, 95.
SASSNETT, James, ...98
SATTERWHITE, John, ...50
SATTYWHITE, Levy, ...178
SAUCER, John, ...84
SAUL, John, ...108
SAULS, Charles; Elizah, 46; Elizabeth, 46; Frances, 32; Freeman, 179; H. & E., 46; John, 202.
SAULTER, Lucrecy, ...41
SAUNDERS, Burwell, 81; John, 202; Miles, 78; Silas, 77.
SAUSING, Charles, ...56
SAVAGE, James, 38; John, 18; Joney, 150; Robert, 172; Thomas, 34, 162, William, 41.
SAWLS, Samuel, ...172
SAWYERS, Amos, 100; Charlotte, 123; John J., 107, 160; Patrick, 135.
SAWYER, John, ...49
SANFORD, John, 45; Littlebery, 42; William, 203.
SANDIDAGE, John, ...177
SANDIFER, Priscilla, ...
SANDIFORD, Nathaniel, ...61
SANDING, Benjamin, ...15
SANFER, Samuel, ...70
SANFORD, Abner, 146; Allen, 72; Franklin, 100; Frederick, 176; Henry, 17; Jeremiah, 180; John, 119; Kean, 92; Mel., Em., 2.
SANGES, John, ...54
SANKEY, John, ...105
SANSOM, Elizabeth, 178; Franklin, 55; James, 158; Robert, 15; William, 33; Robert, 31, 133.
SCALES, Thomas, ...20
SCARBORO, Sarah, ...161
SCARBROUGH, Aaron, 74; James, 144; Lewis, 47; Metta, 147; S. L. D., 72; Sarah, 192; William, 117.
SCARLET, Francis, ...69
SCATES, Thomas, ...140
SCAY, Jane, ...158
SCEALES, Rachel, ...110

SCHENK, John, 139
SCHROCLER, Louisa J. M., 145
SCHRODDER, Jacob, 110
SCOGGIN, Gilliam, 127; John J., 9; Philip, 38; Thomas.
SCOGGINS, Alexander, 176; Benjamin, 205; Green B., 43; James, 75; John, 159; Robert, 203; Orphons, 106.
SCOTT, Alex C., 27
SCROGGIN, George, 111, 83; Griffin, 171.
SCONNIERS, Levic, 138
SCREVEN, James P., 148
SCRIVEN, John, 11
SCRIMPSHIRE, William, 215
SCRUGGS, Josiah T., 4; Richard, 123.
SCUGGS, John G., 42
SEA, Harris, 213
SEABORN, Bailey, 206
SEABROVE, John, 86
SEAL, Richard, 186
SEALE, David, 59; Elizabeth, 108, 126, 195.
SEALS, Joel, 85; Lewis, 36; William, 152; Williams, 19; Willis, 56.
SEALY, John, 5
SEARINGIN, Elizabeth, 118
SEARS, Albert, 75; Marcus, 85; William, 165.
SEARSBROOK, William H., 28
SEARCY, George, 97, 125; Orphan, 87; William, 106, 173.
SEC, John, 179
SCOTT, Adam, 72; Alex, 78; Alexander, 103; Andrew, 9; Aquilla, 80; Comford, 191; George, 107; Isaac, 135; James, 80, 105, 150, 164; Jane, 9; John, 65, 121, 188; John B., 146; Joseph, 89, 200; Josiah, 90; Margaret, 166; M. K. L. W., 126; Patrick, 149, 193; Samuel, 50; Sarah, 141, 150; Thomas, 61; William, 86; Willis, 130; William, T., 139.
SEEGAR, Benjamin, 107
SEEKINGER, Gotteil, 170
SEELEY, John, 145
SELF, Frances, 164
SEGAR, Charles, 176; Samuel, 94; Ira, 152; Segard, 105.
SEGERS, John; Ira, 174.
SEGO, Joshua, 71
SEGO, Middleton, 215
SEGUR, Anthony, 209
SELBY, Benjamin, 204; Christian, 75.
SELF, Frances, 117; Isaac, 61; Samuel, 152.
SELLERS, John, 97
SELMAN, Benjamin, 50; John, 20.
SEMMES, Joseph, 135
SEMORE, Wilburn, 138
SENTELL, Martin, 19, 74; John, 215.

SERGENT, Thomas, 164
SERMONS, Emory, 172; Pernall, 178.
SERVOY, Lawrence, 33
SESSIONS, Frederick, 87, 189; herod, 132.
SESSON, Hannah, 79
ETTLES, William, 44
SEWELL, Christopher, 75, 167; Ezekiel, 166; Henry, 126; Green, 126; Jesse, 196; William, 210.
SEXTON, Elizabeth, 207; James, 208; John, 29; Lewis L., 172; Zodock, 189.
SEYMORE, John L., 164
SHACKLEFORD, Judith, 105; James, 14; Francis, 136; Loyd, 80; Martha, 102, 40.
SHAD, Solomon, 107
SHADDICKS, Isaac, 156
SHADDIX, Robert, 47
SHADOW, John, 103, 184
SHADRACK, Samuel, 61
SHADWICK, Nancy, 29
SHAFFER, Frederick, 148, 192; James, 38; John, 3, 148.
SHAFTNER, Martha, 101
SHARBUTT, Warner, 35
SHARRELL, Littlebery, 210
SHARP, Elias, 190; Henry, 37; James, 12, 63; John, 98, 104; Joshua, 42; Mary, 176; Nancy, 53; Paddy, 137; Peter, 147; Patty, 92.
SHARPE, Groves, 64, 128, 169, 215; Henry, 142; John, 13, 19; Samuel, 175.
SHARTLES, Luanzie, 10
SHAW, Archibald, 65; Bartley, 190; Bryan, 189; George, 120, 127, 136; Henry, 51; Hiram, 40; Horace, 2, 54; James, 82; John, 53, 80, 80, 96, 111, 153, 196, 202; Joseph, 90, 138; Margaret, 41; Martin, 149; Mary, 10; Norman, 146; Peter, 161; Shaw, 77; Watson, 205; William, 111, 125, 186; Dennis, 37, 161.
SHEARER, Jane, 81
SHEARLY, William, 5, 55
SHEARMAN, Hester, 94; Robert, 149
SHEARRER, James, 196
SHEAT, Isham, 156
SHED, John, 172, 194
SHEETS, Talton, 113
SHEFTALL, Sheftall, 36
SHIFLET, James, 49
SHEFFIELD, Eliz., 106; James, 14; Lucy, 122; Lydia, 108; Lydia, 108; West, 104; Phiney, 128; William, 129.
SHEHEE, A. B., 179
SHELL, Byron, 156; Drury, 152; Elizabeth, 187.
SHELLMAN, John, 139

SHELMAN, Augustus, 50 ;John, 20.
SHELNUT, Elizabeth, ...91
SHELNUTT, Andrew, 132; Henry, 131
SHELTON, Henry, ...194
SHENK, John, ...65
SHEPHERD, Abraham, 178; David, 80; Elijah, 34; Edward, 99; Henry, 197; John, 163, 131, 24; Josiph, 94, 132; Lorenzo, 88; Samuel, 52; S., 73; Thomas, 57; William, 166; 212.
SHEPARD, James, 81, 109; Mary, 141; Mown, 51.
SHEPHARD, Josiah, ...140
SHEPPARD, Frances, 109; John, 143.
SHEPPERSON, Jincy, ...42
SHERBORN, Charles, ...72, 74
SHERGER, Thomas, ...96
SHERIDAN, Abner, 33; George, 120; John, 98.
SHERIFF, Charles, ...109
SHERMAN, John, 45; Robert, 170.
SHERRAH, Ann, ...176
SHERRARD, Benjamin, ...210
SHEWHERT, Pricilla, ...74
SHERWOOD, Adiel, ...149
SHI, Seaborn, ...88
SHICK, Catherine, ...107
SHIELDS, John, 50; Louisa, 148; Robert, 59; Wiley, 167.
SHIERLING, Isham, ...169
SHINES, William, ...86
SHINGLETON, Jacinth, ...162
SHINN, Mary Ann, 74; Orphans.
SHIPLEY, William, ...202
SHIPP, Mark, 80; Redding, 194; Thomas, 107; William, 61, 125.
SHIPPER, James, ...180
SHIREY, Elizabeth, 19; Long, 116.
SHIRLEY, John, 147; Samuel, 90.
SHIRLING, James, 93; Isom, 169.
SHIVER, Barrel, 108; Daniel, 28; James, 186; Manning, 98; Mary, 208; William, 184, 213.
SHIVERS, George, ...166, 207
SHLY, Susannah, ...30
SHOCKLEY, Gabriel, 85; Patsy, 46.
SHOEMAKER, John, ...24
SHOFNER, Eliz., ...36
SHOFTNER, Sereno, ...58
SHOLAR, John, ...34
SHOLLER, John, ...87
SHOPSHUR, Wesley, ...32
SHORE, Jane, ...213
SHORES, Isaac, 36; Riley, 54.
SHORT, Drury, 216; Franklin, 119; John, 30, 77; Lucy, 113.
SHORTER, Alfred, 92; James, 10.
SHORTS, William, ...59
SHORTWELL, Jesse, ...171
SHOULDER, Randel, ...63

SHROPSHIRE, Joshua, 182, 189, 205, Wesley, 214.
SHUFFIELD, Everett, 121; George, 49; Isom, 27; John, 11, 72; William, 45, 135.
SHURMAN, James, ...155
SHUMATH, Elizabeth, ...9
SHURLEY, Nathaniel, 40; William, 116.
SHURMAN, Eli, ...55
SHY, John, ...152
SIMES, Horatio, ...107
SIMINGTON, Joseph, ...192
SIMMERSON, Asa; Betsy, 31.
SIMMON, Arthur, 24; Francis, 172.
SIMMONS, Adam, 61, 128; Adair, 4; Brice, 158; Charity, 143; David, 32; Greenville, 12; Henry, 98; Isaac, 13, 137; Ivy, 138; J., 64; Jesse, 45; John, 19, 34, 118, 124, 168, 174, 211; Joseph, 33, 200; Leonard, 194; M., 59; M. T. & E. 57; Mary Ann, 57; Moses, 3; Nancy, 95, 121; Reuben, 9, 70; Richard, 21; S. N., 57; Seaborn, 37; Silas, 106 Solomon, 41; Sterns, 115; Valentine, 7; William, 32, 57, 80, 114, 115, 201, 214.
SIMMS, Tbner, 19; Allen, 154; Benjamin, 173; Charles, 19; Cullen, 203; David, 16; Elizabeth, 72; George, 157, 212; Jacob, 52; John, 105, 166, 187, 201, 207; Killet, 136; Mary, 52; Richard, 140, 153; Robert, 18, 145; William, 4, 170, 210.
SIMONS, Elias, ...110
SIMONTON, Samuel, 30; William, 175
SIMPSON, Arthur, 83; Enoch, 177; Euphony, 152; George, 106; Hardy, 40, 155; John, 10, 56; Larkin, 164; Thomas, 50; William, 3, 26; Wilson, 58.
SIMS, Anderson, 147; Annie, 2; Clayborn, 61; Coty, 121; George, 198ffi Jemmy, 35; Joel, 109; John, 201; Lewis, 37; Margaret, 204; Marion, 56; Simeon, 109; William, 25.
SINCLAIR, Mary, 154; Robert, 160.
SINGLDFIELD, Moses, ...55
SINGLETERY, William, ...58, 193
SINGLETERRY, Arthur, 74; Elijah, 207; Thos., 58.
SINGLETON, Hez., 112; James, 78, 125, 173; Jones, 13; Joseph, 95, 156; Leroy, 96; Thomas, 61; William, 53, 193.
SINGLITON, John, ...104
SINYARD, Jonathan, 211; William, 121.
SIRMON, Josiah, ...-..............78
SISSON, John, 162; Obadiah, 14; Rod-

mon, 75, 209; William, 40, 210.
SITIAN, William, ...5
SITTIN, William, ...117
SIZEMORE, Henry, 88, 124; Mahaney, 210; Thomas, 199.
SKAGGS, Polly, 172; Tabitha, 40.
SKELTON, Elizabeth, 174; Hiram, 142; Jeremiah, 136; Richmond, 158.
SKINNER, Archibald, 91, 210; Catherine, 8; Claiborne, 142; Henry, 73, 90; Isaac, 124; John, 7, 123; Jones, P., 14; Sarah, 6, 97; William, 111.
SKIPPER, Benjamin, ...54
SKRIMES, Benjamin, ...78
SKRINE, William A., ...25
SKURLING, Orphan, ...104
SLACK, John, ...62
SLADE, John, 157; Simon, 140; William, 14, 194.
SLAIN, Mathew, ...78
SLANTER, Beverly, ...138
SLAPPY, William, ...72
SLATEN, Thomas, 212; William, 73.
SLATER, James, ...158
SLATON, Arthur, 155; Cornelius, 82; Elisha, 57; Zachariah, 173.
SLATTER, John, 12; Lamuel, 52; Nancy, 52.
SLATTON, Charles, ...63
SLAUGHTER, Henry, 71; John, 160, 166, 199; Martin, 50; Noah, 178; Richard, 34; William, 141, 160; Wilson, 6.
SLEDGE, Alexander, 54; Charles, 30; Collins, 55; Green, 51; Zelpha, 51.
SLEWDER, Mark, 116; William, 22, 197.
SLISHER, Solomon, ...92
SLOAN, John, 191; William, 163.
SLOCUM, Fitzgrald, ...44
SLOCUMB, Jesse, 83; John, 70; Joseph, 212; William, 162.
SLOWERS, Lewis, ...167
SMALLEY, Michael, ...209
SMALLWOOD, James, 80; John, 106 Milligen, 114.
SMARTT, Orphan, ...89
SMEAD, Patrick H., ...25
SMEDLEY, James, ...197
SMELL, David, ...106
SMELTER, Gabriel, ...33
SMILEY, James, 213; Archibald, 26; Edmond, 27; Edward, 25; Elizabeth, 14; James, 27; Jehu, 12, 14; Kern, 27; Mary, 25; Peter, 13; Newet L., 27; Robin, 27; Robert, 11; William, 25, 28.
SMART, Osborn, ...118
SMITHWICK, Edwin, 203; Eliz, 58; Robert, 88.
SMYTHWICK, John, ...44

SMOKER, William, ...175
SMYTH, William, ...161
SMITH, Abner, 37, 121; Afany, 197; Alexander, 37, 121, 152; Amos, 216, Anderson, 50; Andrew, 88, 129; Ann, 15, 42; Anthony, 194; Augusta, 170; Austin, 194; Archibald, 115; Attaler, 136; Baxter, 37, 181; Benager, 10; Benjamin, 2, 57, 73, 99; Betsy, 19; Breton, 96; Bryan, 145; Caleb, 65; Cath, 128; Catherine, 148; Charles, 152, 172, 195; Christiana, 207; Daniel, 138, 202; David, 10, 23, 30, 88, 108; Drury, 106; Eason, 90; Ebenezer, 116; Elihu, 87; Elijah, 50; Eliza, 20, 77; Elizabeth, 34, 69, 123, 143, 139, 183, 201; Elisha, 95; Enoch, 104; Emamel, 216; Ezekiel, 41, 44, 125, 149; Falcott, 75; Francis, 84, 172; Franklin, 82; Frederick, 97; Babriel, 139; Galses, 172; Gent J., 182; George, 70, 93, 147, 202, 215; Greene, 95; Hannah, 150; Hardy, 12, 105; Henry, 46, 55, 86, 100, 123, 137, 150, 168; Horace, 159; Hugh Black, 49; Isaac, 88, 191; Isahel 183; Isaiah, 34, 132; Isham, 112; Isom, 214; J., 19; James, 4, 10, 29, 32, 53, 70, 85, 109, 113, 114, 126, 131, 136, 138, 158, 159, 172, 190, 194, 96, 210, 212, 213; Jehu, 181; Jeptha, 135; Jeremiah, 135; Jessie, 56, 92, 169, 212, 214; Jiney, 19; Job, 14, 120; Jobe, 177; John, 5, 19, 21, 22, 29, 31, 46, 49, 50, 51, 55, 55, 59, 61, 70, 72, 81, 88, 103, 111, 121, 122, 123, 123, 129, 130, 133, 136, 143, 159, 159, 170, 178, 181, 189, 196, 204, 207, 214; John, Hiram, 125; Jolie, 176; Jonath, 149; Jordan, 197; Joseph, 24, 72, 77, 147, 164, 175; Judah, 90; Katherine, 128; L., 15; Larkin, 93; Lawrence, 120, 184, 203; Leavin, 18; Ledsey, 158; Leonard, 164; Letcher, 137; Lindsey, 79; Lovet, 38; Lucretia, 84, 214; M. A., 19; Maddison, 162; Margaret, 22, 133, 187; Marion, 99; Marshal, 172; Martha, 33, 130, 190; Mary, 3, 34, 111, 139, 147, 168, 170, 186; Mathew, 143, 156; Michael, 161; Michal, 181; Milly, 198; Moses, 121, 137, 146; Nancy, 98; Nathaniel, 206; Meadom, 211; Nicholas, 6; Nimrod, 109; Obediah, 157; Orange, 46; Orphans, 44, 75, 116, 130, 137; Osborn, 214; P. & P., 44; Patience, 78; Peter, 116, 130, 13; Porter, 143; R. S., 15; Rachael, 39; Ralph, 42; Rebecca, 45; Reuben, 47, 139; Richard, 42, 128, 147; Robert, 11, 36,

64, 75, 101, 143, 153, 158, 190; Samuel, 95, 121, 131, 132, 159, 160; Sarah, 18, 20, 30, 111, 158, 162, 212; Selena, 174; Sidney, 130; Simeon, 7, 93, 35; Simon, 163; Spencer, 96; Starting, 196; Stephen, 211; Talcott, 117; Thomas, 17, 35, 51, 145, 160, 173, 198; Weathers, 117; Wells, 201; William, 10, 17, 23, 30, 31, 33, 38, 50, 48, 55, 59, 64, 74, 80, 89, 92, 99, 103, 104, 109, 115, 117, 121, 126, 128, 141, 147, 151, 177, 193, 198, 203, 211, 212.
SNEED, Sarah, 87; Sherrard, 198; William, 128; A. H., 198; Leaston, 33, 82.
SNEAD, Ansel, 106, Philip, 107, 162.
SNELGROVE, Benjamin, 202; Catherine, 54; Edward, 21; esse, 206.
SNELL, Amos, 149; David, 16; Orphan, 112, 160; Wesley, 192.
SNELLING, Hannah, 93; William F., 103.
SNELLGROVE, Mark, ...2
SNELLINGS, Robert, 37; Samuel, 46; William, 118.
SNELSON, John, 10; William, 191.
SNIDER, Jane, ...198
SNOE, Eli, ...63
SNOW, Edmunds, 19; Isaac, 80; John, 105.
SNOWDEN, William, ...34
SNULLPEACE, Ann, ...107
SNYDER, Catherine, 79; Godlip, 56; John, 81; Jonathan, 170.
SOLIEY, William, ...64
SOLOMON, Davis, 97; Laz., 32, 147; William, 172.
SORRELL, Bennett, 139; James W., 18
SORRELLS, Mildred, 21; Richard, 181
SORRILLS, William, ...115
SORROW, James, 4, 178; Jesse M., 24; Joseph, 112; Joshua, 143, 184; Mary P., 13, 143.
SOSSBY, William, ...114
SOSEBEE, Abner, ...91
SOUTHARD, John B., ...142
SOUTHWELL, Edward, 49; William, 58.
SOUTHWILL, John, ...105
SOWELL, Ezekiel, 154; James, 45; John, 22, 202; Zadock, 204.
SPAIN, John, 54; Rcahel, 73.
SPALDING, Jane, 112; Lucy, 204.
SPANN, Henry, 9; Laney, 102.
SPARKS, Benjamin, 119; David, 124; Henry, 34; Henry St. J., 83; Jeremiah, 153, 147; Levin, 6; Samuel, 92; Thomas, 180; William, 34.
SPARKSMAN, Mary, ...176
SPARKMAN, William, ...178

SPARROW, Henry, ...157
SPEAK, Richard, ...91
SPEAKMAN, Mariah, ...185
SPEAKS, Marg. Y., ...20
SPEARMAN, Edmund, 27; John, 111; Robert, 41.
SPEARS, James, 11, 184; Joshua J., 49; Nathaniel, 204.
SPEED, Wade, ...52
SPEER, Thomas, ...96
SPEERS, James, 140; Messer, 210.
SPEIGHTS, M., 190; William, 207.
SPELL, Navy, 130; Reason, 77; William, 103, 121.
SPELLER, Menry, ...202
SPELLMAN, Richard, ...191
SPELMAN, Richard, ...83
SPENCE, George, 162; Incil, 207; James, 142; Jeremiah, 33; John, 211; Joseph, 198; Leaston, 182; William, 95, 196.
SPENCER, Grenville, 1; Levi, 122; Lucretia, 158; William J., 43, 52, 173.
SPERLIN, Andrew, ...34, 126
SPERLING, William, ...121
SPICER, John, ...184
SPIER, Harris P., 145; Willis, 92.
SPIRES, Margaret, ...115
SPIKES, Daniel, 3; Jonathan, 87.
SPINKS, Presley, 109, 157; Raleigh, 105.
SPINHOLSTER, Delilah, ...121
31, 206; William, 103.
SPIVA, Leason, ...183
SPIVEY, Caleb, 154; Edva, 210; Jones P., 11, 82.
SPIREY, James, ...107
SPRADLIN, Absalone, 181; David, 41; William, 38.
SPRATTIN, Winifred, ...131
SPRATTING, William, ...10
SPRIGHT, Elizabeth, ...54
SPRINGER, John, ...191
SPRINGFIELD, Aaron, ...142
SPRUCE, Tatum, 100; Thomas, 186.
SPULLOCK, James, ...116
SPURLIN, Cinthy, 216; John, 115; James, 58.
SPURLOCK, Amanda, 133; John, 123; Samuel, 183; William, 156, 142.
SQUIRES, Wiley, ...188
STAAR, Mary, ...2, 115
STAFFORD, William, ...87, 185
STAHNS, Titus, ...139
STATBY, Elizabeth, ...109
STALBY, John, ...169
STALKNER, Benjamin, ...167
STALLINGS, Edy, 95; Elisha, 190; Harbar, 61; Isaac, 33, 150; James, 9, 57; Malachier, 77; Sally, 56; William, 80, 195; Wilson, 139.
STAMP, John, ...194
STAMPER, Martin, ...87

STAMPS, Henry, 81; Moses, 174.
STANDIFER, Ephriam, 94; Joshua, 40.
STANDLAND, R. T., ...6
STANFIELD, Jehu, 42; John, 35; Joseph, 86, 137; Peter, 10, 127; Richard, 96; Robert, 91.
STANLEY, Ezekiel, 15; Ira, 15; John, 124; Martha, 136; Samuel, 50.
STANSEL, William, ...100
STANSELL, Bennett, 15; Eleanor, 140; John, 147.
STANTON, John, 57, 112; William, 183.
STAPIER, Thomas, ...80
STAPLER, Elizabeth, 1; John, 43; Thomas, 202.
STAPLETON, Alfred, 72, 173; George 199.
STAPP, John, ...34, 122
STARE, Joshua, ...75
STARK, Abner, 186; Alethia, 72; Elethia, 110.
STARKIE, William 65
STARKS, William, ...5
STARLING, Levy, 59; Thomas, 16; William, 87, 181, 194.
STARNES, Daniel, ...37
STARR, Fenton, 92; John, 50.
STARKEY, Jesse, ...44
STATHAM, Garland, 157; Jane, 213; Richard, 55; William, 116, 138, 193.
STATLER, Thomas, ...143
STAUDIFER, Young, ...126
STEDMAN, Edward, 107; Benjam., 156; William, 6.
STEED, Jesse, 30; Philip, 88.
STEELE, Henry, 212; Isaac, 117.
STEELMAN, William H., ...202
STEEN, George, ...208
STEGALL, Benjamin, 79; M. C., 134; Samuel, 180.
STEMBRIDGE, Henry R., ...174
STEPHEN, John, 17; Stephen B., 18.
STEPHENS, Abigail, 114; Aquilla, 129; Adeline, 94; Alex., 79; Andrew, 58; Barnett, 181; Burrell, 180; Cely, 138; Desire, 148; Elijah, 80; Fielding, 145; Hampton, 22; H., 193; Isaac, 135; Isham, 200; J. F., 2; Jacob, 6, 55, 216; James, 38, 39, 181, 198, 211; Jane, 41; John, 51, 70, 32, 174, 131, 136, 203; John P., 11; Jonas, 70; Joseph, 70, 180, 190; Joshua, 216; Manoah, 102; Margaret, 89; Martha, 155; Mary, 182; Miles, 196; Orp., 215; Pherelby, 152; Priscy, 55; Reuben, 52; Richard, 100; Sarah, 62, 164; Shadrack, 21; Stephen, 179, 24; Thomas J., 10, 156; Taliver, 103; Whitfield, 183; William, 23, 172; Willis, 77.
STEPHENSON, Alexander, 91; James, 41; John, 56, 193; Samuel, 146; Stephens, 83; William, 205.
STEPHENTON, Alexander, ...72
STEPTOE, John, ...2, 31
STERLING, Elizabeth, 214; Orj., 194.
STERRETT, Ruth, ...64
STEVENS, Andrew, 207; Burrell, 178; Isaac, 32; Milledge, 32; Thomas C., 198; Wilkins, 61.
STEWARD, Ann & Mary, 61; David, 62; Hardy, 55, 116; John, 39; John, 13, 51; John W., 18; Sarah, 71; W. H., 39.
STEWART, Agnes P., 13; Alexander, 83; Allen, 28; Ames, 116; Ann & Isaac, 48; Ayres, 193; Charles, 56, 135, 184, 193; Eliabeth, 79; Frederick, 37; Gresham, 47; Isaac, 56; James, 34, 79, 91, 96, 110; John, 97, 127; Joseph, 157; Judith, 9; Kenneth, 101; Levi, 120; Mims, 115; Nancy, 45; Randall, 163; Reuben, 199; Richard, 162; Robert, 58, 74; Thomas, 25, 205; Washington, 109; William, 10, 15, 50, 153, 191, 206.
ST. GEORGE, Edward, ...134
STIGLER, William, ...3
STILES, Claiborn, 85; Clary, 207; Nicholas, 117; Samuel, 209.
STILWELL, John, 139; Reuben, 140; Still, Dennis, 117, 120; John, 85, 174, 203; Robert, 27; William, 117, 205.
STIIWELL, Allen, ...175, 205
STINSON, Dudley, 10, 116; Isaac, 110 Mary, 172; Rhebe, 188.
STIROUS, Jesse, ...164
ST. John, James, ...100
STOCKS, Hillary P., 13; Willie, 96.
STOKES, John, 100; Reddin, 157; Sarah, 97; William, 168.
STOCKTON, Benjamin, 196; Joseph B., 47.
STODGILL, Durrett, ...40
STODGHILL, Joel, ...20
STOKER, Arnold, ...153
STOKES, Cordy D., 54; Mary, 122; Mathew, 213; Sarah, 182.
STONE, Daniel, 136; Hillary, 8; James K., 74; John R., 78; Marbil, 154; Osborn, 87; Pleasant, 193; Sarah, 95, 120; Thomas, 83; Washington, 120; William, 61.
STONECYPHER, John, ...120
STONEHAM, Henry, ...136
STOUTAMIRE, Jane, 79; Nuil, 133.
STOVALL, Augustin, 186; Bartholonum, 117; George, 82, 126, 145,

158; John, 18; Lewis, 199; Robert, 205; Stephen, 206; Thomas, 210; William, 210.
STOVER, Jacob, 56; Jeremiah, 133.
STOVEY, Wiley, ----------------165
STOWER, Elizabeth, 8; R., 8.
STOWERS, James, 156; Jesse, 18.
STOY, Abigail, ----------------197
STORY, James, 153; James, Jr., 194; John, 92; Kediah, 214; Lucy, 210; Pierce, 10; William, 51.
STOKES, Mary, ----------------50
STRHAM, Samuel, 11; William, 79.
STRAHN, Neill, ----------------23
STRAHOMS, Noah, ----------------122
STRAIN, Isaac, 163; William L., 174.
STRANGE, Benjamin P., 13; Cleman, 103; ohn, 43; Lodoesky, 119; Mary Spain, 125.
STRANTHEN, James, ----------------179
STRATEN, Jesse, ----------------181
STRATHAM, William R., ----------------197
STRATON, Asa, ----------------80
STRATTON, Asa, ----------------212
STRAUTHER, James, ----------------58
STRAYHORN, John, ----------------98
STREET, James, 51; Jord. D., 75;
STRAWN, Absalom, 40; Littleton, 57. Mary, 92, 127; Phesa, 166; Sarah, 111.
STREETMAN, J., 61; John R., 44, 124, 162, 175; Samuel P., 13; William, 129.
STRENGTH, Orp., ----------------137
STRICKLAND, Alexander, 38, 119; Bedford, 155; Bennet, 21; Caney, 133; Carlos, 85; David, 94; Eli, 153, Elijah, 142; Ephriam, 18; Ezekiel, 157; Gabrieland, 131, 215; Gadi, 128; Hardy, 168; Henry, 37, 40; Isaac, 192; James, 107, 213; Jacob, 203; John, 33, 40, 106, 136, 173; Joseph, 62, 199, 210; Noah, 149; Oliver, 95; Peter, 21, 87, 156; Richard, 163; Samuel, 153; Sarah, 6; Silas, 97; Simpson, 187; Wiley, 6; Willis, 24, 38, 187; William, 192.
STRICKLIN, Ann, 146; Cain, 207; Eli, 165; Ephriam, 159; Jacob, 141.
STRINBRIDGE, Anderson, ----------------5
STRINGFELLOW, Amy, 196; Elizabeth, 91; Robert, 40.
STRIPLIN, Moses, ----------------80
STRIPLING, David, 44; James, 31, 213; Thomas, 31.
STROHAKER, Charles, ----------------215
STROBAR, David, ----------------152
STROBARD, David, ----------------129
STROBBERT, Mary S., ----------------101
STRONE, Gabriel B., ----------------10
STRONG, Charles, 19; Christopher B.,

1; Elizabeth, 87; John J., 105, 155, 203; Martha, 75; Montford, 33; ;Moah, 31, 196; Sherwood, 59; William, 30, 89.
STROTHER, Aaron, 2; Francis, 199; John, 206.
STROUD, Ethan, 194; James, 118; John, 160; Philip, 149; William, 115.
STRUTTON, Solomon, ----------------99
STRAUD, James, Ivey, ----------------214
STUART, Allen, 136; James, 157; John, 6, 212; Margaret, 139; Milly, 97; Richard, 83; Robert, 87, 135; William, 33.
STUBBS, Gabriel, 216; Joel, 180; John, 4, 25, 113; Rowland, 55; Thomas P., 13; William, 154.
STUCKEY, Arthur, 204; Daniel, 78, 119; Edmund, 77; Edwood, 215; John, 35, 138, 215; Lewis, 3.
STUDDARD, Margaret, ----------------48
STUDIVANT, Caroline, ----------------89
STUDTHARDS, John, ----------------108
STUNALAND, Dempsy, ----------------33
STURD, Richard, ----------------151
STURDIFANT, William, ----------------55
STURDIVANT, Abner, 73; Delana, 107; Elizabeth, 109; James, 74; John, 20, 40, 153.
STURGEN, Susan, ----------------178
STURGES, Charles, 112; Elijah, 109; John, 10.
STURGESS, Daniel, 187; Henry, 213.
STURGIS, B. H., ----------------42
STURMAN, William, ----------------43
STUVAIL, William, ----------------3
SUDDETH, James, 128; John, 162; Spencer, 99; William, 70.
SUDDITH, James, 35; William, 156.
SUDDOTH, John, ----------------3
SUDDUTH, Lawrence, 24; William, 152.
SUEGNE, William Eaton, ----------------53
SUGS, Moses, ----------------148
SULEVANT, Zach, ----------------178
SULLIVAN, Elizabeth, 189, 209; John, 157; William, 126, 132, 153.
SULTON, Absalom, 185; Benjamin, 45; Elijah, 44.
SUMIROR, Henry, ----------------25
SUMMER, Aderline, 185; Orphan, 209
SUMMERELL, Sarah, ----------------179, 204
SUMMERFORD, Henry, 88, 126; Orphan, 191; Richard, 195.
SUMMERLAND, Elizabeth, ----------------119
SUMMERLIN, Henry, 176; Thomas, 206; William, 134, 79, 42.
SUMMERS, George W., 175; Nancy, 195.

SUMNER, Jethro, 128; Joseph, 107; S. W. R., 116.
SUMOROR, John, ...144
SURRENCY, Inney P., 12; Jacob, 90; John P., 12.
SUTTEY, James. 69
SUTTON, David, 5; Dozier, 17; Elijah, 118; Joel, 195; John, 34; Morris, 128; Moses, 179; Peter, 19; Roderick, 154; Sarah, 197.
SUTTONFIELD, William, ...72
SUTTY, James, ...43
SWAIN, George, 121; Levi, 105; Mary 83; Stratling, 72.
SWAM, Eliza. Ann, 102; Thomas, 160
SWAN, Erasmu, 194; John, 215; Thomas, 45; William, 23, 51, 54, 213.
SWANE, Nellie, ...178
SWANN, Henry, 92; Jemima, 201; William, 213.
SWANSON, Graves, 210; John, 160.
SWAY, George, 149; Margaret, 177.
SWEARENGIN, Kichen, ...195
SWEARINGIN, Baily, ...182
SWEATINAS, John, ...172
SWEET, Nathan, ...36
SWICORD, David, ...208
SWIFT, John, 172; Martin, 109; Thomas, 41.
SWIGHOPPER, Abiel, ...52
SWIM, Enoch, ...2
SWINDEL, Timothy, ...189
SWINDLE, Timothy, ...201
SWINNER, William, ...98
SWINNEY, John P., 14; John, 199; Hiram, 42.
SWINT, James, ...133
SWOBE, Mary, ...112
SKYES, Jean, 20; John, 121, 175; John M., 49.
SYLOY, Bymun, ...103
SYLVA, George, ...211
SYRES, Benjamin W., ...146
TABER, John, 165; Frances, 17; Kezekiah, 51.
TABB, John, 72; Thomas, 178.
TAFF, George, 46; William, 46.
TAILOR, Thomas, ...196
TALANT, Mary, ...176
TALBORT, John, 1, 154; Elihu, 45; Hail, 153; John, 59.
TALLANT, John, ...2
TALLEY, Daniel, 172; Elisha, 35; Eugenia, 174; Henry, 214; Orphan, 148; William, 27.
TALLY, Nathan, 79; Racel, 77.
TAMPLIN, Mary, ...34
TANKERLAY, Carter, ...34
TANKERSLEY, Buckner, 151; Eleanor,

208; Fountain, 126; Henry, 168; John, 70, 146; Rolen, 27; Battle, 173.
TANTON, Charles, 9; Nathan, 9; Bryan, 132.
TANNER, Asa, 181; Gideon, 24; John, 33, 70; Joseph, 34, 139; Thos., 5; Thos. L., 56, 139, 198.
TAPLEY, Adam, 14; Goldman, 177.
TABPTTON, Benjamin, 154; Humphrey, 63; Jos. 27.
TARPLEY, Augustine, 153; Coleman, 4; Joel, 122.
TARVER, Absalom, 37, 171; Bird, 162; Ethelrod, 191; Garland, 153; Henry, 159; John, 102, 198; Mary, 178; Robert, 94, 161; R. R., 89; Seth, 33; William, 36; 37.
TATE, Asa, 43, 91; Abraham, 12; Enos, 117, 208; Francis, 211; Isaac, 164; Jesse, 79; John, 40, 84, 107, 186; Paramon, 164; Rolon, 164; Simon, 155; Solomon, 98; William, 23; Zinny, 75, 114.
TATES, Thos., ...23
TATNALL, Elizabeth, 19; Joaiah, 26; George, 90.
TAUNT, Erwin, 64; James, 5; Thomas, 74; Vincent, 85.
TAUNTON, Henry, 26; Newsom, 40; Sally, 22.
TAZHERY, Sarah, ...16
TAYLOR, Abner, 28; Albert, 117; Clark, 169; Clark, Jr., 214; Clark, Sr., 147; Daniel, 15, 109; Dempsey, 126; Edward, 19; Eli, 180; Edmond, 192; Figgers, 186; George, 128; Henry, 42; Isaac, 52; Jacob, 47, 181; James, 33, 44, 124, 184; Jeremiah, 161, 211; Jeptha, 2; Jesse, 174 ;Jordan, 144; John, 6, 20, 31, 56, 71, 92, 120, 145, 159, 177, 190, 215; Kitchen, 214; Labonirn, 11, 148; Levi, 30; Lewis, 47, 57; Lida, 53; Martha, 157; Mary, 181; M. & W. 215; Moses, 22; Nancy, 131; Northford, 58; Paschel, 10; Richard, 103, 137, 140; Robert, 45, 92; Silas, 183; Simon, 43; S. M., 29; T., 29; Tekal, 12; Theophilus, 50, 114; Taliaferro, 84; Thomas, 37, 44, 177; T. S. & M., 4; William, 4, 17, 80, 112, 105, 112, 131, 197, 211, 213.
TEAL, Emanuel, 77; Henry, 124; Jesse, 31; Lodawick, 205; Shadrack, 171; Thomas, 86; William, 96.
TEAKLE, John, ...31
TEASLEY, Beverly, A., 36; James, 110; John, 75; Silas, 158; Thomas, 23.

TEAT, Henry, ...21
TEAVER, James, 38; Rebecca, 160.
TECHSTONE, Thomas, ...70
TEDDER, James, ...167
TEDLEY, William, ...57
TELLER, John, ...103
TEMILLE, W. A., ...116
TEMPLES, Frederick, ...210
TEMPLETON, Green, 44; Zephaniah, 41.
TENDALE, Samuel, ...13
TENERSON, John P., ...11
TENSIONS, James, ...122
TENSION, Linney, ...74
TEPTON, Reuben, ...1
TERNOR, Thomas, ...69
TERRILL, Christopher, 150; Elizabeth, 196; Flem., Bet., 213; Henry, 97; James, 201, 2; James C., 133; Richmond, 112; William, 16, 47, 91, 183.
TERRELLS, Eliz., ...16
TERRY, Champ. A., 1; John, 45; Nathan, 74; N. T. B., 91; Orphan, 133; Priscilla, 3; Samuel, 141; William H., 150; William, 86.
TESSIER, Lewis, ...113
TERRILL, William, ...155
THACKER, William, ...168
THACKSTON, James, 192; Seamon, 40
THAMES, Thomas, ...202
THAPSON, James, ...64
THARP, Charnick, 94; Ruth, 125; Vinson, 19; William, 52.
THARPE, Benjamin, 105, 136; John, 135; Randolph, 176; Rearaden, 167; Wyatt, 73.
THAXTON, J. M., 127; Simeon, 139; Thomas, 115, 187; Yelverton, 170.
THEMBY, Thomas, ...146
THERILL, Sarah, ...1
THERLKILD, John, 59; Willis, 20.
THIGPEN, Calvin, 111; J. H. M., 45; William, 125, 131; Nathan, 97; Reading, 106; Reding, 170.
THIRLDEL., Marquis, ...136
THIRLKILD, Willis, ...59
THOMAS, Archibald, 70, 114; Alex., 149; Allen, 32; Benjamin, 84, 132; Christina, 43, 95; Charles, 181; Caleb, 29; Drury, 36; David, 28; D. & Z, 97; Ethelred, 197; Elizabeth, 132, Eli., 105, 124; Edwin, 207; E. C., 72; Furly, 181; Feraba, 98; Gill, 56; George, 164; Hugh, 140; Henry, 19; Harrison, 191; Hannah, 79, 102, 164, 183; Isaac, 47; Ivey, 193; Josiah, 115; Joseph, 43, 178; Jonathan, 20, 78; John, 6, 9, 27, 70, 87, 133, 139; Joel, 27; Jesse, 88; James, 81, 166, 96, 110, 122, 175; Lydia, 1; Lucius, 158; Lewis, 91;

Michael, 82; Mossa, 128, 191; Martin, 49; Mary, 74; Nelson, 199; Navey, 48; Queen, 24; Opp, 150; Peterson, 159; Rowland, 135; Rolly, 72; Richard, 169, 172; Samuel, 14, 86; Stewart, 5, 8; Sarah, 185; Thomas, 35, 79, 114; T. A., 35; Theophilus, 165; William, 12, 14, 44, 53, 52, 79, 95, 176.
THOMASSON, Solomon, 208; Zimri, 102.
THOMASTON, John, 213; Thomas, 134.
TOMPKINS, John, 146; Samuel, 216.
THOMPSON, A., 77; Alex, 146; Andrew, 216; Ann, 75; Asa, 142; Benjamin, 140; D., 184; David, 28, 155 Dorothy, 61; Drewey, 120, 149; Edmond, 20; Elamuel, 202; Eliz., 54; Eph., 56, 79; Francis, 31; Frederick, 27, 142; George, 96, 126; Gideon, 34; Granville, 21; H., 96; Henry, 70, 149, 152; Isabella, 41; James, 10, 130, 139, 146, 158, 193, 188, 215; John, 8, 15, 20, 21, 41, 49, 69, 51, 79, 102, 146, 208; Jer., 6; Jerem, 50, 54; Jesse, 1, 120; Jeffrey, 132; Joseph, 24, 101, 122; Leighton, 78; M., 22; M. A., 9; Mark, 21; Martha, 23; Mary, 166; Moses, 90, 142, 141, Normond, 150; Nelson, 213; Obediah, 136; Peter, 128; Polly, 11; R., 97; Ro., 9; Rob., 160; Robert, 2, 188; Richard, 25, 118, 185, 198, 202; Sally, 102; Samuel, 41, 90, 100, 109, 128; Sarah, 118, 148, 204; Susannah, 185; Vinson, 77; Wells, 20; William, 24, 37, 40, 74; 93, 100, 136, 171, 215.
THOMSON, James, ...165
THONER, John, ...168
THORN, Middleton, 20; Seaborn, 5, 79; Saphy, 131.
THORNTON, Absolom, 126; Benjamin, 155, 186; Virdong, 134, 146; Daniel, 102; Dred, 146; Edward, 17, 186; George, 2; Isaac, 178; James, 186; John, 124, 165; Jonathan, 26; Jor., 61; Lindsay, 157; Mary, 92; Nathaniel, 136; Richard, 92; Samuel, 184; Thomas, 143, 180; William, 127, 205, 216; Yancy, 3.
THORP, Randolph, 32; Vinson, 19.
THRASH, Isaac, 172; Susan, 79.
THRASHER, David, 187; John, 185; Jesse, 111, 180; George, 133; Susannah, 189.
THRELKELD, Oliver, 192; Thomas, 174.
THRIBRAND, P. C., ...8
THROWER, Benj., 191; Lewis, 148;

. Jesse, 120; John, 82.
THURMON, James, 133, 214; Fielding, 88; Meredith, 165; Nancy, 127. Philip, 152, 209; Susan, 24.
THURSBAY, John, ...123
THWEATT, James, ...28
THYESS, Henry, ...121
TODD, Adams, 47; Aphier, 167; Benjamin, 24; James, 204; John, 12, 114, 119, 121, Keziah, 10; Lewis, 4; Manderson, 7; Martha, 7; William, 61, 146, 157, 181.
TOLBUT, Frances, 162; Narcisse, 94; William, 75.
TOLER, William, ...511, 73
TOLES, John, ...3
TALKER, Joseph, ...20
TOLLER, Demsey, 50; Lewis, 130; Stephen, 151, 173.
TOMBINSON, Leroy P., ...13
TOMERSON, Joanna, 56; Mark, 157.
TOMLINSON, Aaron, 188; Elizabeth, 41; John, 78, 118; Humphrey, 158; L., 32; Orp., 172; Wylie, 123.
TOMKINS, John, ...61
TOMLIN, John, ...106
TOMBIN, Pharrow, ...150
TOMLINSON, Nathaniel 141
TOMME, Octniel, ...125
TOMMEY, Joseph, ...24
TOMMY, John, ...112
TOMPKINS, Gideon, 100; John, 62; William G., 17.
TONDEE, Charles, ...208
TONEY, James, ...201
TOOKE, Isham, 17, 63; Mary, 86; William L., 32.
TOOKES, Arther, ...64
TOOLE, James, ...191
TOOLEY, William, ...149
TOOTLE, James, 184; William, 119.
TOOTON, Rigdon, ...2
TORBAVILLE, Jesse, ...119
TORBUT, Samuel, ...92, 118
TORNSON, Obadiah, ...77
TORPY, Patrick, ...46
TORRANCE, Esther, ...1
TORRENCE, John, ...131, 179
TOTTY, Robert, ...136
TOUCHSTONE, Henry, 31; Robert, 78
TOWER, William, ...121
TOWERS, Lewis, ...199
TOWLE, Fred, ...29
TOWLES, William, ...203
TOWN, Rebecca, 97; Gideon, 101.
TOWNESON, John, ...114
TOUNS, James, ...127
TOWNS, Hockey, 129; John, 93, 56, 187.
TOWNSLEY, Victory, ...179
TOWSON, Thomas, ...115

TOWNSEND, Henry, 119, 138; Joshua, 49, 110; Jesse, 72, 168;J ohn, 191; Nancy, 103; Thomas, 40; Stephen, 56.
TRAEL, William, ...36
TRAILE, Richard, ...135
TRAINUM, William, ...51
TRALL, William, ...36
TRAMMELL, Dennis, 213; Mary, 163 Nancy, 80; Robert, 137, 186; Thomas, 118.
TRAVIS, David, 75, 173; William, 175
TRAWICK, George, 155; James, 44; Jane, 189; Jossey, 52; Moses, 15; Penelope, 205; William, 193.
TRAYLER, Lucy, ...10
TRAYLOR, Dunstan, 6; George, W., 149; John, 32; Pashal, 10; William, 115.
TREADWAY, Mary, ...50
TREADERWAY, Mary, ...165
TREADWELL, David, 135; Henry, 152; James, 172; John, 6, 8, 201; Joshua, 72.
TREBLEFIELD, Abel, ...35
TREDWELL, Adoniram, 163; Stephen, 111; William, 169.
TREUTTEN, Christian, ...110
TREVAYER, Anthony, ...151
TREZEVANT, Orphan, ...89
TRIBBLE, Joel, 86; Josiah, 132; Morris, 119.
TRICE, Benjamin, 72; Chesely, 133; James, 28; William, 122.
TRIGGS, John, ...7
TRIMBLE, Elisha, 127; James, 100, 204; John, 33, 79, 89; Moses, Sr., 150.
TRIPLET, William, ...93, 187
TRIPLETT, Hilary, 206; William, 16, 22, 55.
TRIPP, William, ...136
TRIPPE, Henry, 214; John, 45; Robert, 180; William, 102.
TROBRIEVD, Rosalee, ...15
TRONLON, Thomas, ...188
TROUT, George, 174; ackson; ames, 189; Rachel, 209; Sarah, 80.
TROUTMAN, Hiram, 154; Thomas, 198.
TROWER, Margaret, ...194
TROY, Philip, ...166
TRUETT, John, 35; Pernal, 128; Purnal, 191; Purnell, 216.
TRUITT, John, 31; Pernell, 64; Riley, 146; William, 83.
TRULL, William, ...118
TRULUCK, Arthur, 138; Mary, 119, 120.
TRUMAN, John 140

TUCK, Eli, 192; Thomas, 172.
TUCKER, Abraham, 80; Barney, 216; Coleman, 136; Daniel, 26; Davis, 118; Eliza, 124, 149; Frances, 96; Harper, 143; Henry, 147, 184, 191; Isaiah, 78; John, 12; Jasiah, 215; Matilda, 148; McKendree, 172; Moses 204; Orphans, 55; Lewis, 8; Richard, 153; Robert, 101; William, 43.
TUDER, Thomas, _____164
TUFT, Gardner, _____30
TUGGLE, Benjamin, 127; Ransom, 155.
TULL, Lewis, 168, 213; Mary, 1.
TULLY, Hiram, _____56
TUMBLINSON, James, _____45
TUNNILL, Patrick, _____9
TUBERVILLE, Nath, 9; Peter, 64.
TURK, John, 120; Theodosius, 72.
TURKNETT, Catherine, George, 19, 154
TURMAN, Robert, 122; Viletta, 189; Thomas, 43; Tabitha, 141.
TURNER, Abishai, 94; Absolom, 85, 199; Anthony, 170; Berry, 91; Daniel, 196; David, 188; Edmund, 179; Elijah, 141; Ellender, 95; Green, 56, 178; Henry, 16, 79, 94, 106, 107, 164, 214; James, 6, 113, 118, 150, 161; Jarratt, 186; Jarril, 56; John, 46, 47, 53, 70, 91, 94, 108, 127, 205, 211; Jonas, 48; Joseph, 164; Josiah, 43; Larkin, 19; Levin, 171; Lewis, 193; Mathew G., 58; Mathias, 186; Micajah, 211; Miles G., 74; Moses, 154; Orphans, 159; Permelia, 125; Pleasant, 9; Reuben, 19, 113, 180; Richard, 37; Robert, 2; Samuel, 111, 212; Sarah, 123, 206; T. B., 150; Thomas, 8, 43, 126, 208, 214; Wade, 24; Warren, 216; William, 137; Williamson, 142.
TWEEDWELL, William, _____2
TWIGG, Ruth, _____42
TWILLY, Elijah, 48; William, 10, 132.
TWILLEY, Joseph, _____88
TYLER, Henry, _____107
TYNER, John, _____46, 56
TYSON, Aaron, 120; Eason, 9; Martha, 80; Mary, 191; William, 55.
ULMER, Charles, 161; Philip, 145, 185 William, 23.
UMPHRIES, Benjamin, _____211
UMPHLETT, Asa, _____216
UMPHREY, Jesse, 70; Robert, 28.
UMPHRES, William, _____207
UMPHRY, Jesse, _____70
UMPHREY, Robert, _____28
UNDERHILL, Jeremiah, _____166, 215
UNDERWOOD, Adolphus, 7; Ann, 167 Constance, 95; Daniel, 177; Eddy, 135; George, 157; Isham, 191; Joseph, 167; Lemuel, 118; Lewis, 216; Mason, 176; Thomas, 188; William, 49, 107; Winiford, 59.
UNIS, Samuel, _____210
UPCHURCH, Charity, _____63
UPDERGRAFF, David, _____39, 97
UNDERGROVE, Mary, _____4
UPSHAW, George, 11, 142; William, 147.
UPSON, Stephen, _____38
UPTON, John, _____126
URQUAHART, Neill, _____38
URSERY, Elizabeth, 183; John, 39, 74; William, 168, 212.
USHER, Abel, 44; Henry, 64; Oliver, 121; Thomas, 71; William, 191.
USORY, Edward, 101; Francis, 101.
USSERY, John, _____74, 81
UTTEY, John, 106; Henry, 192.
VAINRIGHT, Susan, _____92
VALLATON, Rachel, _____59
VALLEY, Mrs., _____184
VAMGHAN, Jonathan, _____185
VAN, William, 109; Joseph, 25.
VANBRACKEL, John, 207; Moses, 161; W. H., 52.
VANCE, George, 18; Levin, 21.
VANDAMAN, Porter, _____116
VANDEFORD, John, _____50
VANDEGRIF, John, _____95
VANDEGRIFF, Garrett, _____196
VANDIFER, John, _____212
VANDIFORD, Jesse, _____169
VANEDEAU, E. Isham, _____154
VANN, David, 82; Edward, 188; Edwerd, 43; Kidar, 102.
VANNOY, Sarah, _____149
VAN ZANDT, William, _____73, 197
VARNADOE, Nancy, _____24
VARNER, George, 206, 10, 153; Henley, 136; John, 175; Patience, 100.
VARSAR, Micajah, _____12, 99, 105
VARSY, Benjamin, _____175
VAUGH, John, 2; Thomas, 175.
VAUGHN, Daniel, 120; David, 43, 139 Felix, 98; Frederick, 153; George, 159; Jesse, 94, 153; John, 34, 202, 206; Martha, 17; Nelson, 92; Ottaway, 102; William, 35, 40.
VAUGHTER, James, 192; Tabitah, 82.
VAYLES, John, _____174
VEAL, Alexander, 165; Elizabeth, 122; Grancis, 120; Gerrard, 89; James, 169, 140; Lewis, 166; Nathan, 71; Orphans, 198; Waiters, 30; William, 140, 191.
VEALE, George, _____93
VEASEY, Elijah, 44; Timothy, 172.
VEASY, John, 30; Martha, 208.
VEAYLES, Jehn, _____114

WAGNON, Daniel, 11; E. N., M. A., 168; George, 182; James, 158; Thomas, 72.
WAGNOR, John, 70
WAGON, William, 16
WAGONER, James, 184; Thomas, 120, William, 73.
WAILY, Ebenezer, 137
WAINRIGHT, James, 51
WAITS, Absalon, 208; David, 177; John, 187; Philip, 55.
WAKEFIELD, Charles, 43; Sarah, 94.
WAKEMAN, Mark, 20
WALBURG, Jacob, 101
WALBOLT, William, 15
WALBERY, Jacob, 155
WALDANER, John, 114
WALDEN, Amos, 160; Elijah, 212; John, 40; Lewis, 179; Rhoda, 125; W. G., 86.
WALDER, Frances, 84
WALDOUR, Charles, 26
WALDROPE, David, 162; George, 91; Greenberry, 111; Major, 75.
WALL, Anna, 179, 181; Burrell, 134; Dred, 7; Elizabeth, 92, 171; Ezekiel, 13; Henry, 32; James, 126; Jesse, 121; John, 165; Maddox, 18; Myall, 133; Oliver, 194; Sampson, 129; William, 181, 200; William D., 143.
WALLACE, Adam, 39; Benjamin, 70; Charles, 168; Elizabeth, 190; Epps, 64; Fereby, 52; Filding, 53; James, 50; John, 52; Josiah, 34; Levin, 163; Norman, 65; Orphans, 135; Robert, 135; Storing, 142; Stririn, 155; Susannah, 121; Thomas, 124; William, 4, 85, 177.
WALLDEN, Martin, 22
WALLDRIEFEE, John, 70
WALLER, Archibald, 108; Edward, 62, Elijah, 216; George, 108; Hiram, 58; James, 174; John, 85; Jno., 61; N., 93; Nathaniel, 178; Newbell, 34; Overall, 141, 197.
WALLEY, Thomas, 17
WALLIS, Albert, 10; James, 88; John, 89; Thomas, 20; William, 34.
WALLMAKERS, John, 72
WALLRAVEN, Elizabeth, 117
WALLS, Charles, 91, 146; Conrad, 142 Jeremiah, 132; Sampson, 23; William, 111.
WALLY, Thomas, 186
WALPOL, John, 177
WALSH, George, 201
WALSTON, Henry, 18; Joshua, 88; Sarah, 105.
WALTERS, Daniel, 116; William, 96.
WALTON, Benton, 38; Edward A., 3; George, 175; George R. C., 29; Hen-

VEAZEY, Alanson, 12; Stephen, 3.
VEAZEY, Zebulon, 93, 89
VELVIN, John, 138
VENABLE, John, 27, 63, 111, 205
VENTRISS, Easterling, 130
VERDERY, Amanda, 71; John, 119.
VERNERY, Edward, 158
VESTAL, David, 4
VIAL, Elizabeth, 41
VICK, Simeon, 178
VICKERS, Josiah, 153; Lewis, 152; James, 157; Gresham, 122; Martin, 30; Sarah, 12; William, 146, 140; Stephen, 40.
VICKERY, Andrew, 159; Christopher, 102; Hezekiah, 138; James, 23, 107; Joseph, 117, 180; Marnaduke, 79; Polly, 187; William, 117, 129.
VICTORY, Joseph, 52; John, 196; Joseph, 216.
VIGAL, Marian, 51
VILLARD, John, 27, 177
VINCEN, Alcy, 16
VINCENT, David, 126; Davis, 169; Henry, 72; Isaac, 52; Payton, 86.
VINDEFORD, Jesse, 25
VINES, William, 21
VINEYARD, Allen, 193; Samuel, 103; William, 53, 111.
VINNINGS, Cosby, 31; John, 183; Owen, 127.
VINSON, Attis, 9, 159; Ebenezer, 159; Elisha, 21, 63, 210; Isaac, 6, 151; Jeremiah, 26; Joseph, 193; Nancy, 213; Nimrod, 160; Peyton, 34, 121; Pleasant, 39; Willie, 112.
VOCELLES, Jacques, 52
VOICLE, Lewis, 111
VOLLOTIN, Rachel, 101
VOSS, Pimkney, 86
VOWEL., John, 157, 27
WABBLE, Wiley, 145
WADDEL, William, 11
WADE, Benjamin, 101, 139, 156, 158. Celah, 169; Charles, 182; David, 82; Elijah, 168; Hampton, 23; James, P., 53; Jereusha, 75; John, 145, 180; John D., 162; Nathaniel, 64, 91, 155, 162, 177; Philip, 164; Samuel, 85; Thomas, 65, 189.
WADKINS, Benjamin, 59; Daniel, 97; Mary, 172; Nicy, 147; Robert, 130.
WADSWORTH, David, 188; Hiram, 136; Isaac, 44; James, 112; Joel, 158, William, 63, 94.
WAFFORD, Absalom, 111; Benjamin, 140; Isaiah, 18; Moses, 15; William, 196.
WAGNER, Henry, 181; Louis, 80.
WAGGNON, James, 182

ry, 212; John, 71, 103; Joseph, 153, Mary, 134; Nancy H., 156; Noah, 140; Robert, 86; Robert A., 25; S. W., 151; Seth G., 80; Sherwood, 209.
WAMCAK, William, 123, 156; Elizabeth, 207.
WAMBLE, Elisha, 148; Henry, 28.
WANSTON, John, ...36
WANSLOW, Reuben, ...110
WARD, Ambers, 124; Charles, 53, 176, David, 20; Francis, 33; Harriet, 179; James, 211; Jeremiah, 47; Joah, 154, John, 30, 61, 122, 195, 208; Major, 171; Mariah, 176; Nathan, 85, Nathaniel, 119; Peter Z., 211; Peyton 21, 140; Richard, 210; .Robert, P., 206; 214; Samuel, 57; Seth, 153, Thomas, 193; Thorrington, 204; Uriah, 122, 179; Wiley, 147; William, 97, 101, 137, 209; Winney, 98.
WARDLAW, Absolom, 82; David, 111, James, 17; Samuel, 102.
WARE, Bennett, 83, 103; Burrell, 17; Edward M., 96; Edwin R., 8; Hambleton, 126; Henry, 170, 203, 213; James, 9, 176, 178; Jane, 31, 115; Jemison, 177; John, 74; Johnson, 56; Mary, 103; Michalos, 165; Robert, 97, 199; William, 127; William W., 158.
WARMACK, John, ...168
WARNER, Elijah, 89; Mary, 135; Nathan, 121; Solomon, 182.
WARNOCK, Eli, 75; John, 39.
WARREN, Bettna, 205; Chesley, 70; Enity, 214; George, 169; James H., 191; Jesse, 7, 5, 44, 111, 183; John M., 156; Joseph, 41; Josiah, 34; Slany, 173; Thomas, 105, 121; Unity, 156.
WARTHEN, Elisha, 169; John, 10; Rebecca, 62; Richard, 123; Theophelus, 97; William, 81, 191.
WARWICK, Wiley, ...21, 136, 205
WASDEN, Nancy, ...190
WASH, Thomas, ...209
WASHAM, Anderson, 46; Dilly, 171; Polly W., 85; Harry, 216.
WANSLOW, Reubens, ...72
WASHINGTON, G. H., 52; Martin, 160; Robert B., 23.
WATERER, John, ...194
WATERS, Allen, 112, 215; Charles, 16.
WALDROP, James, 170; Magor, 41.
WALDSON, Benjamin, ...30
WALDRAVEN, Elizabeth, ...199
WALDRUP, Elizabeth, ...190
WALES, James, 208; John, 204 .
WALHARINS, Jonathan, ...174

WALKER, Adam, 170; Anderson, 93; Betsy Ann, 115; Charles, 71; Chesley, 73; Daniel, 4, 13, 45; David, J., 163, 169, 214; Elijah, 51, 58, 722; Etathan D., 44;. George, 57, 163; Hiram, 122; J. A., 29; J. S., 57; James, 36, 53, 114, 152, 191; Jane, 56; Jeremiah, 92; Jeese, 157; Joel, 166, 201; John, 2, 21, 47, 99, 108, 138, 170, 206; John B., 41; Jonathan, 118, 118, 177; Lee, 10; Lewis, 88; Linsey, 39; M., 29; M. & C., 64; Margaert, 118; Mary, 29, 194; Memory, 9, 27; Micajah, 183; Nancy, 165; Nathaniel, 9, 35; Parmalee, 106; Persons, 104; R., 179; Rebecca; Rhoda, 212; Robert, 194; Riley, 4; Sachfill, 103; Samuel, 185, 212, 214; Sarah, 110; Tarleton, 8, 208; Thomas, G., 215; William, 109, 168; Willis, 12.
WATERS, Isaac, 200; James, 205; John, 13, 79, 99, 115, 124, 160; John E., 56; William B., 103; William, 207.
WATKINS, Arthur, 183; Benjamin, 98, 130; Berry, 15, 156; Hartwell, 137; Jacob, 42; James, 105; Jesse, 65; John, 113, 210; Mills, 6; Moses, 143; William, 58, 131.
WATSON, Adlai, 169; Allen, 105; Asa, 190; Benjamin, 137; Calvin, 117; Cassandra, 20; Catherine, 9; David, 65, 98, 118; Douglas, 91, 129; Elias, 28; Elijah, 22; Elisha, 51; Ezekiel, 100; Hannah, 129; Henry, 57; Israel, 96; ames, 11, 127, 201; Jason, 52; Jechiel, 22; Jehiel, 194; Jese, 3; John H., 65; Jonathan, 7; Joshua, 34; Leroy, 39; Magers, 58; Majers, 7; Majors, 128; Maryan, 96; Michael, 86; Mithael, 63; Moses, 86; Nancy, 215; Nathan, 181; Nehemier, 164; Renoy, 124; Robert, 92, 131. 190; Robert A., 27; Samuel, 160, 165; Sarah, 61; Seth G., 6; Susannah, 208; Thomas, 1, 53, 70; Thos., 27; Vinson, 213; William, 22, 55, 59, 163; Winifred, 15.
WATTERSON, Daniel, ...186
WATERS, Joseph, 35; Larkins, 196.
WATTHALL, Richard, ...157
WATTS, Benjamin, 92; Edwin, 122; George, 99; Harrison, 189; Henry, 2, 53; Isaac, 215; James M., 70; John, 75; Paschal, 137; Richard, 70; Samuel, 186; Thomas B., 6; William, 164, 180.
WAVER, Jacob, ...167, 59
WAY, John, 38, 202, 206; Thomas, William, 20.

WAYNE, George, 31; Lewis, 116; Richard, 195; Thomas, 129.
WEATHERS, Benjamin, r., 146; George 153; J. D., 18; Stephen, 44.
WEATHERTON, Thomas, ...179
WEATHERBY, Benjamin, ...105
WEAVER, Christion, 140; Elizabeth, 163; Hannah, 84; Isham, 32; John, 100; Julius, 79; Othniel, 152; R. L. & J., 93; Reuben, 104; Samuel, 122; Travis, 65; Wiley G., 39.
WEBB, Catherine, 178; Claiborn, 53; Ephraiun, 132; Ewell, 37; Isaac H., 50, 156; James, 57; John, 95, 206, 18, 78; Lewis, 110; Margaret, 167; Micajah, 139; Thomas, 53.
WEBBER, Dorcas, ...43
WEBSTER, Ann, 50; E. B., 166; Richard, 42.
WEEB, John Gilbert, ...37
WEED, Henry D., ...36
WEEKS, Charles, 77; Edwards, 210; James, 127, 209; Joseph, 50; Joshua, 133; Luke G., 216; Orphan, 191; Silas, 185; 209.
WEEMS, Alen, 205; Benjamin L., 174; George, 152; Joel, 117; Tabitha, 159; Thomas, 91, 114, 183, 205.
WEITMAN, Israel, ...170
WELCH, Ann, 154; Berry, 212; David, 168; Isaac, 114; James, 97; John, 187; Michael, 145; Moses, 116; Nancy, 49; Nicholas, 10, 184, 196; Patsy, 127; William, 134.
WELBORN, Amos, 159; Elias, 142, 185; Elijah, 149; Johnson, 138, 211; Jonah, 184.
WELBOURN, James, ...143
WELDEN, Pleasant, ...211
WELCHER, Elizabeth, 48; Jeremiah, 188; John E., 216.
WELDON, Absalom, 143; Burrell, 152, John, 205; Mary Ann, 190; William, 108.
WEEKS, Theophilus, ...11
WEELBORN, John G., 29; Johnson, 216; Mary, 52; William, J. W., 204.
WELLESS, Jacob, ...144
WELLMAKER, Felix, ...154
WELLBORN, Thomas, ...13
WELLS, Abna, 46; Abner, 19, 50; Alexander, 198.
WELLS, Anderson, 141; David B., 52, 106; Elizabeth, 117; Elton Andrew, 101; ames, 8, 15; John, 8, 15, 56, 99, 191; John V., 167; Lewis, 183; Newell, 202; Thomas F., 176.
WELSH, Caleb, ...3
WELSHER, Jeremiah, ...50
WEMBURN, Josiah, ...128

WESBERRY, Noah, ...213
WEST, Alford, 17; Allen, 203; Benjamin, 53, 171; Charles, 138; Elizabeth, 102; Ephriam, 126; John, 29, 202, 206, 104, 108; Major, 22; Margaret, 189; Nancy, 63; Reuben, 92; Rufus, 95; Solomon D., 157; Thomas, 39; William, 2, 53, 74, 82, 143, 155; Willis, 98.
WESTBERRY, Josiah, 168; Moses, 146.
WESTBROOK, John, 158; Gillum, 126; T., 78; Thomas, 141; 16.
WESTER, John R., ...77
WESTMORELAND, John, 129; William, 8.
WESTON, Sarah, ...81
WETHERBY, John, ...4
WETHERS, Valentine, 165; William, 34, 111.
WETHERSBY, Gideon A., ...51
WETHERTON, Thomas, ...166
WEVER, Peter, ...211
WHALEY, George, 108; Isaac, 121.
WHARTON, Benjamin, ...164
WHATLEY, Elizabeth, 13, 54, 169; Fanny, 24; Ornom, 165.
WHATTEY, Elizabeth, 169; Greenes, 59.; John, 210; Jadith, 173; Michall, 78; Samuel, 138, 195; Solomon, 192; Thomas J., 41; William, 212, 96; Willis, 63, 84, 166.
WHEATTEY, Jesse, ...111
WHEDBE, Susan, ...141
WHEELIS, Lewis, 13; Lydia, 89.
WHEELUS, Charity, ...75
WHEELESS, Drury, ...199
WHEELER, Allen, 89, 150; Al. & P., 71; Amos, 143; Charles, 167; Cobby, 99; Elbert, 147; Eli, 113; Francis A., 125; George, 98, 108; George G., 7; Henry, 94, 28; Ishah, 166; J., 157; James, 202; James F., 32; John, 27; oseph, 44, 89;Mourning; Richard, 107; Rebecca, 97; Raphael, 200, 106; Susan, 39; Sinthia, 39; Thomas, 93, 110; W., 56; Wash. 45; William, 7; William C., 116.
WHIDDEN, Wash & J. 213
WHIDDON, Mary, ...30
WHILEHEAD, William, ...165
WHILEHURST, Asa, ...21
WHILLINGTON, Burrill, ...103
WHIMBERLY, James, 53; Josuah, 95.
WHINGHAM, John, ...205
WHIPPLE, George, ...127
WHITAKER, Abraham, 77; Benjamin, 44; Burtin, 208; Daniel, 6; James, 111; Joshua, 194; Richard, 216; Samuel, 16; Thomas, 185.
WHITEACHER, Isham, ...18

WHITEHEAD, A. A., 46; Archibald, 124; Darcus, 133; Jacob, 174; Jas., 46; Martha, 211; Mary, 46; Nancy, 46; Ransom, 70, 91; Sophia, 46; Thomas, 56; Wells, 46; Willey, 109; Willis, 63.
WHITE, Alacy, 160; Allen, 17, 25, 121; Anne, 139; Andrew, 148; Bartey, 53; Barsheba, 183; Charity, 16; Christopher, 107; Christian, 71; David, 199; Hugh, 197; Henry, 102; James, 4, 56, 166, 196; John, 17, 40, 46, 78, 126, 102; 143, 210; Joseph, 86, 103; Jesse, 116, 127; Mary, 98, 158, 178; Mathews, 215; Moses, 99; Nathanial, 210; Nelson, 18; Patsy, 123; Pleasant, 175; Robert, 16, 119, 161; Steele, 7; Steele, Col., 33; Thomas, 192; Tibither, 174; Vincent, 24; William, 62, 65, 80, 83, 111, 167, 179, 210.
WHITES, James, _____166
WHITTAKER, Abraham, 178; James, 204; John, 8; Thomas, 9; George, 49.
WHITTEN, Philip, 126, 131; Robert, 48.
WHITTEY, William, _____202
WHITTINGTON, B. G., 150; Irving, 70; Sherrod, 177.
WHITTOCK, Charles, 56; Jordan, 1; Kersey, 1.
WHITTON, Milleson, 1; Sophia, 1; William, 120.
WHITTLE, Ambrose, 5, 151; Mathew, 207; Seaborn, 188.
WHITEWORK, Thomas, _____207
WHITWORTH, Sally, 118; Thomas, 159; William, 46.
WHLEY, William, _____196
WHLY, William, 151; William C., 211
WHLLEY, Thomas, _____201
WHLLY, John, 133; Leonidas, 209.
WHORTON, Benjamin, 95; John, 23, 70; Thomas, 30.
WHITFIELD, Bryant, 39; Gernima, 216; John, 18; John, 21; Lewis, 142; Robert, 39; S. & M., 72; William, 18, 183.
WHITLEY, Nathan, 97; Nathan, 74.
WHITENUS, James, _____156
WHITLAW, Boland, _____215
WHITEHURST, Asa., 143; Souell, 176.
WHITEN, Mary, _____155
WHITENHURST, Charles, _____101
WHITESIDE, John, _____89
WHITMAN, Nathan, 120; William, 210.

WHITNEY, Joseph C., 195; Josiah, 23; Willard, 27.
WHITINGBEALL, Mathew, _____214
WHUTACK, Charles, _____
WHITLOCK, Elizabeth, 43; Grace, 175
WICKER, Julus A., 10; Mathew, 81; Nathaniel, 191; Penelope, 184; Robert E., 55; Wiley, 158.
WICKS, Anderson, 124; Bartley, 135.
WIDNER, Moses, _____3
WIGGANS, Alfred, 74; Grace, 152.
WIGGEN, Elizabeth, _____181
WIGGINS, Anney, 188; Dawson, 115; Edmund, 93; George, 128; Green, 77, 150; James, 54, 96, 154; Joseph, 195; Lewis, 2; Michael, 97; Orrin, 74; Richard, 148; Wade, 97; William, 96, 123.
WIGLEY, Elizabeth, _____196
WIKER, Margaret, _____128
WILBANKS, Gillam, 4; Gillan, 30; Marshall, 2; Solomon, 24, 193.
WILBERN, Joel, _____205
WILBORN, Samuel, _____32
WILCHER, Fred, 48; Mary, 145; Mason, 48; Oliver, 48.
WILCOX, John, _____108, 215
WILD, Jarard, _____39
WILDER, Charles, 183; Francis M., 46; James, 99, 136, 199; John, 21; Jonathan, 36; Milton, 19; William, 97, 122, 134, 202; Willis, 118; Sampson, 62, 194, 216; Seaborn, 134, 214.
WILHAR, Jeremiah, _____209
WILEY, Absalom, 52; Ann, 135; George, 170; James, 75; Leroy, 62; Louisa, 210; Moses, 162; Osborn, 103; Sarah, 63; William, 145.
WILHIGHT, John, 92; Minford, 92; Rix, 25; Thomas, 213.
WILHITE, Lewis, _____155
WILKER, Margaret, _____128
WILKERSON, Abel, 212; Ester, 32; Joseph, 58; Malcom G., 36; Marian, 104; Mathew, 124; Smith, 131; William, 89, 166, 195.
WILKES, Aaron, 106; Jesse, 59; Judith, 158; Margaret, 162; Reuben, 39; Silas, 184.
WILKIE, Christopher, _____129
WILKINS, Samuel, _____12
WILKINGS, Jabez, _____145
WILKINSON, Adam, 158, 204; Baruaba, 186; Benjamin, 108; Betsy, 22.
WILKISON, Edward, _____181
WILL, Joseph, _____16
WILLARD, Elijah, 140; Royal, 140.
WILLBANKS, Richard, _____27
WILLCOX, James, _____93
WILLEFORD, Elizabeth, 47; John, 47;

Mary Ann, 47; Wilson, 47.
WILLES, ames, ---1
WILLER, John, ---71
WILLET, Isaac, 149; Joseph, 78.
WILLETT, Joseph, ---148
WILLIAMS, Abraham, 12, 188; Adaline, 77; Allen, 57; Amons, 51; And. 120; Anderson, 65, 155; Anthony, 170; Anson, 132; Avington, 75; Barney, 128; Benj., 26, 107; Benjamin, 9, 85, 139, 208, 211; Berryan, 33; Burrell, 129; Calvin, 168; Charley, 214; Charles, 109, 127, 153; Chloe, 19; Clarke, 89; Cordelia, 174; Cornelius B., 44; Daniel, 32, 45; David, 119, 133; Dawson, 112; Dennis, 3; Dilly, 110; Dred, 58; Ebenezer, 177; Eldridge, 130; Elias, 30; Elisha, 196; Elizabeth, 115, 186, 213; Enoch, 15, 160; F., 25; Frances, 158; Frances E., 184; J. G., 26; Hampton, 163; Henry, 48, 58, 176; Hester, 208; Hezekiah, 29; Holstow, 87; Hubbard, 28, 100; Isaac, 108, 196; Jacob, 147, 197, 198; James, 10, 75, 92, 98, 111, 127, 131, 163; James K., 59; Jefferson, 18, 165; Jesse, 2, 46, 112, 199; Joel, 79; John M., 24, 33; John, 17, 4, 9, 58, 74, 82, 100, 134, 186, 46, 52, 72, 35; John H., 102, 147; John W., 1, 186; Jonathan, 115; Joseph, 28, 81, 200; Keziah, 90; Lucy, 34; Lemuel, 183; Letitia, 120; Littleton, 163; Levicy, 21; Lewis, 148, 177; Margaret, 115, 161; Mariah, 33, 142; Mark, 48; Mathew, 154; Martin, 49; Matilda, 86; Miles, 162; Minerva, 216; Moses, 73; Nancy, 44; Nathan, 117; Nathaniel, 112; Nichols, 150; Orphan, 136, 215; Orphans, 150; Paul, 216; R., 23; Rach., 81; Rachel, 178; Reuben, 65, 161; Richard F., 164; Robert, 70, 92, 128, 132, 180; Robert W., 41; Rowland, 113; Ruben, 175; Stephen, 83; Saladan, 91; Samuel, 138, 167; Sarah, 147; Seaborn, 128; Shephard, 121; Soloman, 55, 157, 198; T., 198; Temple C., 45; Thomas, 43, 95, 126 134, 163, 171; Tott, 169; W. H., 26; Watson, 103; Wesley, 211; Wiley, 183; William, 6, 8, 55, 75, 88, 105, 108, 123, 124, 155, 167, 170, 179, 183, 191, 201; Willis, 103; Wriah, 2; Wyat, 85; Wright, 123.
WILLIAMSON, Charles, 129; David, 106; E. C., 62; James, 205; Jinsy, 91; John, 13, 47, 196, 143, 42, 171; Joseph, 6; Nathan C., 12; Robert R., 161; Sorah, 21, 50, 150, 132; Walker, 59; William, 5, 64, 100, 92; Zach, 113; Zachary, 138.

WILMOT, Eli, ---136
WILMOTH, William, ---85
WILMOUTH, Nancy, ---57
WILMUTT, William, ---122
WILSON, Aliel, 178; Allen, 107; Alva, 131; Andrew, 117; Ann, 154; Ansel, 178; Augustin, 191; Baley, 199; Banajah, 96; Benjamin, 46, 130; David, 120, 65, 72; Elihu, 107; Elija, 61; Elizabeth, 198; Ephrian, 126; Francis, 42; Gilbert, 134; George, 88, 105, 164; Henry, 160, 198; Hugh, 140, 212; James, 190, 32, 34, 51, 107, 129, 172, 178, 190, 206, 212, 115; Jesse, 127; John, 157, 27, 29, 46, 47, 81, 85, 100, 104, 174.
WILSON, Jesse, 127; John, 157, 27, 29, 46, 47, 81, 85, 100, 104, 174, 187, 208, 210; Margaret, 43; Martha 185; Mathew, 2; Peggy, 214; Randal P., 41; Richard, 111, 167; Robert, 15, 149; Sally, 207; Samuel, 21, 50, 111; Sarah, 38; Sette, 100; Tabitha, 82; Thomas, 63, 145; William 13, 51, 52, 63, 64, 169, 193; Young, 63.
WILLIBY, Soloman, 98; William, 170.
WILLIFORD, E., 24; Hardy, 19; Henry, 203; J., 24; Jeptha; John, 80, 89, 123; Levin, 78; Lucy, 165; M., 24; Olive, 96; W., 24; William, 216.
WILLINGHAM, A., 143; Charles, 207; Isaac, 34, 171; J., 125; Jesse, 165, 199; John, 146; Joseph, 112; Lorenza, 94; William, 74.
WILLIS, Alexander, 165; Augusta A., 191; Fielding, 11; George, 77, 108, 110, 182; Isaiah, 137, 108; James D., 195; James L., 82; John W., 7, 75, Nahum, 28; Patrick; Robert, 158; Sarah, 41, 187; Thomas, 147; William, 212, 214; Zachariah, 128.
WILLOUGHBY, Asa, 131; J., 141; Jessie, 75; John, 105.
WILLS, Edward, 17; James, 102; Joseph, 109, 181; Mary, 134; William, 34.
WILLSON, John, ---128
WILLY, Leonidas, ---8
WILTBURGER, Peter, ---107
WIMBERLEY, Perry, ---130
WIMBERLY, Abner, 171; David, 93; Frederick, 3, 197; Henry, 173; John, 44, 103, 196; Josua, 21; Perry, 80; Titus, 212; Wiley, 30; William, 93; Zachariah, 85.
WINBURN, Josiah, 22, 128; Sarah, 85; David, 174.
WINCHEL, Albert, ---77
WINCHESTER, David, 41; Jonathan, 105.

WINDHAM, Abel, 139; Benjamin, 216; Permely, 193; Peter, 165.
WINDON, William, ...215
WINDSOR, Jeese, ...117
WINFREY, Benjamin, 120; Isaac, 110; Samuel, 3; Sarah, 62; William, 22.
WING, Edward, 70; Mary, 102.
WINGETT, William, ...181
WINGFIELD, Charles, 58; John, 93.
WINGFRY, John, ...51
WINGO, Simpson, 177; William, 24.
WINHAR, Allen, ...55
WINKLE, John, ...90
WINN, Ann, 150; Charles, 91; Elizabeth J., 138; George, 108; Hinchey, 135; Jacob, 50; James, 135; Jefferson, 130; John, 112; Kirttery, 192; Lietleton, 64; Lemuel, 115; Lovenzo, 120; Mary, 158; Robert, 129; Thomas, 198; William, 166; Gahiel, 209; Mathew, 159, 208; Hinchey, 11.
WINSETT, Mahala, ...41
WINSHITT, Samuel, ...83
WINSLETT, Samuel, ...56
WINSLETT, William, ...192
WINSOM, Williams, ...42
WINSTON, ohn, 171; Joseph, 107.
WINTERS, Elizabeth, 215; Moses, 31; Willis, 190.
WISDOM, Bird, 139; Jesse, 61, 96.
WISE, Augustus, 53; Burrell, 192; John, 86; John U., 20; Nancy, 7; Riely, 9; Sherwood, 81, 153; Zachary, 12.
WISENER, Jeremiah, ...143
WITHERINGTON, George, 127; Richard, 159.
WITTICH, Earnest, 3; Lucus L., 28.
WITTINGTON, Charles, ...173
WOFFARD, James, 16, 49; John, 3; Nathaniel, 133.
WOLF, Andrew, 188; Cary, 164; George, 132, 128; Paul, 133.
WOMACK, A., 41; Bird, 133; William, 10, 80, 158.
WOMBLE, Allen, 131; N., 7.
WOOD, Abisha, 125; Abraham, 200; Alial, 117; Asa, 148; Bennett, 146; Caroline, 100; David, 185; Dempey, 78; Edmond, 98; Eli, 158; Elisha, 16; Ellett, 140; Ezekiel, 125; George A., 188; Green, 62; Harris, 51; Henry, 162, 164; Isaac S., 164; James, 23, 180, 58, 130; Jethro; John, 47, 57, 105, 132, 202, 206; Lazarus, 80; Leonard, 16; Lerenzo D., 166; Louisa, 189; Mary, 166; Mary Jemima, 107; Nancy, 33, 117; Niarvel, 186; Peter, 211; Polly, 64; Puckett, 112, 125; Samuel, 203; Sarah, 109;

Thomas, 79, 215, 96, 168, 59; Thomas W., 8; Violet, 176; Wiley, 19; William, 57, 123, 121, 103; William A., 52; Willis, 53.
WOODALL, James, 215; John, 43, 49, 129, 210; Johnson, 215; Joseph, 170, 38; Philip, 17; Temp., 203; William, 79, 15.
WOODHAM, Garret, ...186
WOODCOCK, Casey, 209; William, 120.
WOODFIRD, Moses, ...86
WOODHARD, Jesse, 21; Racheal, 112.
WOODING, Edward, 209; John, 110.
WOODLAND, Elizabeth, ...101
WOODLEY, Clayton, ...197
WOODLY, Milly, ...50
WOODRUFF, Lueretin, ...56
WOODRUM, John, ...72
WOOD, Reading, ...13
WOODS, Edmonds, 148; Edward, 127; Johua, 62; Martha, 145; Mary & J., 116; Nancy, 158; Robert, 19, 190; Samuel, 209.
WOODSON, Benjamin, 117; Rachael, 35; Williams, ...48
WOODWARD, George Lee, 20; John, 150.
WOODY, Henry, 34; Samuel, 43.
WOOLDRIDGE, A. D., 179; Isma, 180; Thomas, 82.
WOOLFOLK, John, ...157
WOOTAN, James, 71; Moses, 207; Willis, 35.
WOOTERS, Judy, ...85
WOOTEN, H., 11; Hardy, 67; John, 63, 79, 128, 143, 165, 188, 52; Mourning, 39; Polly, 163; Sarah, 8; Spencer, 4; Thomas L., 11, 154; William, 44, 91.
WOOTTON, Richard, ...134
WORD, Sally, ...51
WORLAND, John, ...82
WORLEY, Obadiah, ...2
WORRELL, William, ...80
WORSHAM, Archer, 87; Archie, 72; D. B., 47; John G., 28, 47; Lucinder, 204; Nancy, 110; William C., 59; William T., 74.
WORTHY, Ellison, ...15
WORTKINS, Elisha, ...192
WOTTON, James, ...130
WRAY, Adeline, 45; Elizabeth, 45; Sidney, 45.
WREN, Thomas, ...180, 196
WRENN, William, ...102
WRINGFIELD, Jone, ...140
WRINKLER, Zachariah, ...188
WRY, Margaret, ...89
WRING, Daniel, 15; Elizabeth U., 15.
WRIGHT, Alexander, 130; Alfred, 85;

Appleton, 160; Avy, 19; Charles, 6, 107, 167; Danial, 74; David, 214; Ezekial, 24, 171; Elizabeth, 53; George, 26, 135; Gillis, 40; Henry, 138; Isaac, 79; James, 3, 47, 82, 124, 139, 164, 196, 208; Jesse, 120; John, 40, 74, 106, 115, 173, 184; Leven, 162; Little 8, 20; Lewis, 194; Luke, 155; Mary, 80, 203; Martha Ann, 80; Mehaly, 120; Michael, 15; Moses, 6, 7; Nancy, 31; Obediah, 28; Pleasant, 143; Pryor, 132; Ruben, 30, 88, 101; R. W., 5; Robert, 186; Solomon, 87; Sally, 10, 184; Sara, 10; Samuel, 23; Susana, 160; Thomas, 26, 52; Wingfield, 154; William, 28, 99, 112, 167, 169, 176, 190, 201.

WYATT, John, 102, 122, 159; J. L. J., 81; Lamira, 21; Samuel, 8, 100.

WYCHE, Elizabeth, 43; Jeremiah, 185.

WYNN, Amelia, 78; Charles, 151; Henry, 49; John, 31; Robert B., 3; Thomas, 203.

WYNNE, Clement, 188; John, 4; Terrell, 35; Thomas, 116.

YANCEY, Charles, 196; James, 159, 53; Lewis, 57; William, 33.

YARBORO, Amos, 196; Elizabeth, 152; James, 159.

YARBOROUGH, S., 4; Thomas, 21.

YARBRO, Elam, _____188

YARBROUGH, Amen, 34; Benjamin, 110, 111, 121; Elizabeth, 95; Isaac, 37; Jeptha, 199; John, 164; Jno., 126, 207; Joseph, 6; L., 54; Margaret, 44; Minhod, 91, 185; Nancy, 49; R., 136; Reuben, 114; Roland, 96.

YARNOLD, Lucy, _____206

YATES, Dannell, 78; James, 172; Mathew, 126; Sarah, 50; William, 57.

YAWN, David, 52; Elizabeth, 67; Hannah, 118.

YEARBY, Henry, _____83

YEARTY, Henry, 179; Tabitha, 203; Vincent, 47.

YEATS, Bennet, 93; James, 172.

YEATES, William, _____209

YERTY, Jacob, _____81

YOES, Catherine, 195; John, 117.

YON, Chas., 123; Hez., 123.

YORK, Asa, 111; Calvin, 44, 54; David, 57; Isaac, 73, 124; John, 12; Meredith, 120, 129; Singleton, 206; Thomas, 43; William, 142.

YOUNG, Alexander, 209; Benedict, 69; David, 19, 127; Elijah, 24; Elizabeth, 187; George, 109, 115; Henry, 2, 61, 89; Isaac, 136; Jacob, 86; James, 52, 81, 85; Jane, 173; John, 74, 101, 116, 120, 142; Mary, 124; 133, 200; Orphan, 178; Philip, 189; Rhoda, 33; Sophia, 62; Sus, 15; Susannah, 57; Thomas, 15, 18, 24, 70; William, 72, 123, 204; Wilson, 209, 210.

YOUNGBLOOD, Abimeleck, 190; Arthur, 139, 106; H. D., 178; James, 196; O. H., 106; Peter, 41; P., 90, 213.

YOURBERRY, Henry, _____54

YOURBROUGH, John, _____164

YOWMAN, Samuel, _____177

YOUMANS, Absalom, 123; Samuel, 82.

ZACHARY, Benjamin, 17; Daniel, 103. Jesse, 128; John, 143, 190.

ZALMAN, Mandefit, _____

ZAMITY, Joseph, _____191

ZEDFORD, Noel, _____146

ZEIGLER, Israel, _____43

ZETLER, Daniel, 132; Nathaniel, 98, 210.

ZILLNER, Andrew, _____57

ZINN, Edmin, 180; John, 208.

ZIPPERER, Gideon, 110; Jonathan, 63.

ZORN, Daniel, _____25

ZUBER, Robert, _____28

www.ingramcontent.com/pod-product-compliance
Lightning Source LLC
Chambersburg PA
CBHW071233230426
43668CB00011B/1415